新现代汉英词典

The New Modern Chinese-English Dictionary

总顾问：杨宪益
主　编：谢振清

中国国际广播出版社

责任编辑:郭广
封面设计:唐宇

图书在版编目(CIP)数据

新现代汉英词典/谢振清主编. —北京:中国国际广播出版社,
1997.4

Ⅰ.新… Ⅱ.谢… Ⅲ.汉英-词典 Ⅳ. H316

中国版本图书馆 CIP 数据核字(97)第 01695 号

新现代汉英词典
THE NEW MODERN CHINESE-ENGLISH DICTIONARY
谢振清 主编
中国国际广播出版社出版
(北京复兴门外广播电影电视部内 邮编:100866)
新华书店经销
北京外文印刷厂印刷

787×1092 32 开本 41 印张 1500 千字
印数:1～20000 册
1997 年 4 月第 1 版 1997 年 4 月第 1 次印刷
ISBN 7-5078-1472-6/H·102
定价:82.00 元

《新现代汉英词典》编委会

目 录

前　言

这是一本适合中等文化程度以上读者使用的语言工具书。它为汉语读者学习英语提供了便利，也兼顾了英语读者学习汉语的需求。

本词典共收单字与多字条目近4万余条。选取单字的原则是：主要选收组词力强、使用频率高的字；同时，也选收了一些专业性较强的通用字。多字条目中，既有一般常用词汇，又有时代感强、近年出现并流行的新词语，如："斗富"、"发烧友"、"下海"、"跳槽"等等；同时还选取了一些常见的经济和法律词汇，如："股份制公司"、"合资经营企业"、"起诉书"、"按揭"等。因篇幅有限，有些条目作为例句出现在主词条目中，如"计划"条目中有：～调拨；～生育；～市场。本词典为有些条目提供了多种释义和译文，供读者选用。

本词典在编纂过程中，参考了国内外各种类型的词书，并注意到同类词典的长处，尽力做到取其精华。在本词典出版之际，首先感谢中国国际广播出版社总编辑吴绪彬先生以及王先豫老师和中国国际广播电台译审陈德浓先生给予本书的大力支持和热情指导。

限于出版时间仓促，编者水平有限，谬误之处，望广大读者不吝指正，以便再版时修订。

编者

1997年2月

用法说明

一、条 目

1. 本词典所收条目分单字条目与多字条目。
2. 单字条目按汉语拼音字母顺序排列。同音异调的汉字按声调顺序排列。同音同调的汉字，按笔划多少排列。形同而音或调不同的，如好（hǎo）和好（hào），分立条目，并在字后注时“另见……”
3. 多字条目分列于单字条目之下。同一单字条目下有多个多字条目时，按第二个字的汉语拼音字母顺序排列；第二字相同时，按第三字排列，依此类推。

二、注音

1. 单字条目和多字条目均用汉语拼音字母注音。声调一般只注原调，不注变调，轻声字注音不标调号。
2. 儿化音只在基本形式后面加“r”，不标语音的实际变化。如：昨儿 zuór。
3. 多字条目的注音采取连写法。并列结构的多字条目与条目中并列词的注音用“-”连接并列部分。如：“言简意赅” yánjiǎn-yìgāi
4. 多字条目的注音中音节界限有可能混淆时，用隔音号“’”隔开。如割爱 gē’ài

三、释义

1. 单字条目一般均标明词类，注在〈 〉内；[ ] 内的文字代表该字所属的学科和使用范围。单字条目有多种用法而词类又相同时，则词类注在圈码前，如：〈动〉①…②…③…；用法多种而词类不同时，则分别注在圈码后面，如：①〈名〉… ②〈形〉… ③〈动〉… 以此类推。
2. 单字或多字条目有不同用法时，用圈码① ② ③…分别释义。
3. 释义一般用对应的英语词语。同一义项下有两个以上释义时，释义之间用分号隔开。一个释义有两个以上例句时，例句之间用 . 隔开。需进一步阐明的释义则放在（）括号内。

四、检字法

本词典备有汉语拼音音节索引，以供检索。

略语表

1. 专门用语

[地] 地理学
[电] 电学
[动] 动物学
[法] 法律
[纺] 纺织
[佛] 佛教
[化] 化学
[计] 计算机
[机] 机械
[建] 建筑
[交] 交通
[教] 教育
[金] 金融
[经] 经济
[剧] 戏剧
[军] 军事
[历] 历史
[林] 林业
[逻] 逻辑
[美] 美术
[农] 农业
[气] 气象学
[商] 商业
[摄] 摄影
[生] 生物
[生化] 生物化学
[生理] 生理学
[数] 数学
[体] 体育
[天] 天文学
[外] 外交
[无] 无线电
[物] 物理学
[心] 心理学
[畜] 畜牧业
[药] 药物学
[医] 医学
[印] 印刷
[语] 语言
[乐] 音乐
[哲] 哲学
[政] 政治
[植] 植物
[宗] 宗教

2. 词类略语

〈代〉　代词
〈动〉　动词
〈副〉　副词
〈介〉　介语
〈敬〉　敬辞
〈谦〉　谦辞
〈旧〉　旧时用法
〈口〉　口语
〈连〉　连语
〈量〉　量词
〈名〉　名词
〈数〉　数词
〈书〉　书面语
〈叹〉　叹词
〈套〉　套语
〈象〉　象声词
〈助动〉　助动词

汉语拼音检字表

white

皑皑 ái'ái (of snow, frost, etc.) pure white：～的雪山 a snow-capped mountain

癌 ái [医] cancer; carcinoma：肺～ cancer of lung

癌扩散 áikuòsàn metastasis (proliferation) of cancer

癌症 áizhèng cancer

呆 ái 〈动〉 stagnate
另见 dāi

呆板 áibǎn rigid; stiff; dull; inflexible; stereotyped：动作～ stiff and awkward movements

ǎi

嗳 ǎi 〈叹〉[表示不同意或否定]：～，别客气了。Come on. Don't stand on ceremony
另见 āi; ài

嗳气 ǎiqì belch; eructation

嗳酸 ǎisuān rising up of acid from the stomach (a symptom of hyperacidity of the gastric juice)

矮 ǎi 〈形〉[身材短] ① short ② [高低的] low ③ [级别、地位低] ～一级 a grade lower than others

矮半截 ǎibànjié inferior to others; be a grade lower than sb.

矮凳 ǎidèng low stool

矮墩墩 ǎidūndūn dumpy; pudgy

矮杆稻 ǎigǎndào short stalk rice

矮杆品种 ǎigǎn pǐnzhǒng short-stalked variety; short-straw variety; short-stem crop

矮个儿 ǎigèr low-built person; short person

矮胖 ǎipàng short and stout; squat; dumpy; roly-poly

矮人 ǎirén ① short person; dwarf ② Pigmy (Pygmy)

矮小 ǎixiǎo short and small; low and small; undersized：身材～ short and slight in figure

矮子里拔将军 ǎizi lǐ bá jiāngjūn choose a general from among the dwarfs; pick the best person available

蔼 ǎi 〈形〉 ① amiable; friendly; gentle ② 〈书〉 luxuriant

蔼蔼 ǎi'ǎi ① lush; luxuriant ② dim; dark

蔼然 ǎirán friendly; amiable; kind; gentle; affable

霭 ǎi 〈书〉[云、气] haze：暮～ evening haze ② [薄雾、轻雾] mist：烟～ mist and clouds

ài

艾 ài 〈名〉① [植] Chinese mugwort; wormwood ② end; stop：方兴未～ in the ascendant; be just unfolding; rising ③ 〈形〉 pretty, beautiful, handsome
另见 yì

艾窝窝 àiwōwo steamed cake made of glutinous rice with sweet filling

艾滋病 àizībìng [医] AIDS (acquired immune deficiency syndrome 的首字母综合)

砹 ài [化] astatine (At)

唉 ài〈叹〉[表示伤感或惋惜] oh; ah; well: ～,我的计划恐怕不能实现了。Well, I'm afraid my plan won't be fulfilled.

爱 ài〈动〉① love: ～祖国 love one's country. ～我中华,修我长城 Love the Chinese nation, repair the Great Wall ② like; be fond of; be keen on: ～看电视 like watching TV ③ treasure, cherish; take good care of; hold dear: ～集体荣誉 cherish the good name of a collective ④ be in the habit of; be apt to: ～发脾气 be apt to lose one's temper; be short-tempered. 食物在夏天～变质。Food is apt to deteriorate in summer.

爱不释手 àibùshìshǒu like (love) sth. so much that one cannot bear to part with it; be fond of and unwilling to part with; fondle admiringly

爱财如命 àicái-rúmìng love money as one loves one's life; love money as much as life itself; be greedy for money; be a money-grubber

爱称 àichēng pet (affectionate) name; diminutive; term of endearment

爱搭不理 àidā-bùlǐ get (give) the cold shoulder; turn a cold shoulder

爱戴 àidài love and esteem; love (respect) and support; revere: 受到…的～ enjoy the love and esteem of …

爱尔兰 ài'ěrlán Ireland: ～人 the Irish; Irishman. ～语 Irish

爱抚 àifǔ fondle; pet; caress; show tender care for

爱管闲事 àiguǎn-xiánshì like to poke one's nose into other people's business; love meddling in other people's affairs; officious

爱国 àiguó love one's country; be patriotic: ～公约 patriotic pledge. ～华侨 patriotic oversea Chinese. ～同胞 patriotic fellow-countryman. ～心 patriotic feeling; patriotism. ～一家。All patriots come together like one family. ～者导弹 patriot missile. ～主义教育 education in patriotism. ～卫生运动 patriotic public health campaign. ～志士 ardent patriot

爱好 àihào ① like; be fond of; be keen on; have a passion for; love: ～京剧 be keen on Beijing Opera. ～自由 love freedom; be freedom-loving ② interest; fancy; hobby; one's liking; appetite: 读书是我的～。Reading is my hobby.

爱好者 àihàozhě hobbyist; enthusiast; amateur; lover (of sports, art, etc); those who are addicted to: 体育～ sports enthusiast; sports fan. 音乐～ music-lover

爱护 àihù care; treasure; cherish; take good care of; show genuine affection for: ～备至 give every attention to. ～动物者 zoophile. ～国家财产 take

安枕无忧 ānzhěn-wúyōu rest assured without anxiety; sleep at peace

安之若素 ānzhī-ruòsù regard sth. with equanimity; bear (hardship) with equanimity; be imperturbable

安置 ānzhì arrange for; place; find a place for; settle; set; help settle down: ~办公室 placement office

安装 ānzhuāng fix; fit; assemble; erect; mount; install: ~电话 install a telephone; have a telephone installed. ~费 installation fee; mounting cost

桉 ān [植] eucalyptus[总称]

桉树 ānshù eucalyptus; eucalypt

氨 ān [化] ammonia: 合成~ synthetic ammonia

庵 ān 〈名〉① hut ② nunnery; Buddhist convent: 尼姑~ nunnery

谙 ān 〈动〉〈书〉 know well

谙记 ānjì learn by heart

谙练 ānliàn 〈书〉 skilled; conversant; proficient

谙熟 ānshú be proficient in; be conservant with: ~英语 be well versed in the English language

鹌 ān quail: ~蛋 quail's egg

鞍 ān〈名〉 saddle

鞍鼻 ānbí saddle nose

鞍部 ānbù saddle (of a hill or mountain); upper bend

鞍马 ānmǎ [体] pommelled horse; side horse; vaulting horse ② saddle and horse; life on horse-back

鞍马画 ānmǎhuà painting of horses

鞍马劳顿 ānmǎ-láodùn tired because of long travel on horseback; fatigued by a long journey

鞍子 ānzi saddle: 给马装上~ saddle up

ǎn

俺 ǎn 〈方〉① [我们,我们的,不包括听话的人] we: ~村 our village ② [我,我的] I or my: ~娘 my mother

铵 ǎn [化] ammonium

àn

岸 àn 〈名〉[河、湖的] bank; shore: 上~ go ashore. [海的] coast; seashore: 波浪拍打海~。The waves washed the seashore.

岸然 ànrán in a solemn manner; gravely; solemnly: 道貌~ look sanctimonious; assume the appearance of a man of integrity; be sanctimonious; look dignified

岸上 ànshàng bank; shore: ~存仓 storage ashore. ~交货 tallying ashore

按 àn 〈动〉 ① press; push down: ~电钮 push (press) a

button ② leave aside; shelve ③ restrain; control: ～不住心头怒火 be unable to restrain (control) one's anger ④ keep one's hand on; keep a tight grip on: ～剑 put hand on a sword ⑤〈介〉according to; in; accordance with; by; per; in the light of ; on the basis of: ～年代计算 per annum

按比例 àn bǐlì in proportion; at the ratio; pro rata; proportionate: ～发展 develop in proportion

按兵不动 ànbīng-bùdòng take no action; keep (remain) quiet; halt the troop and wait; hold the troop in readiness for combat; bide one's time

按部就班 ànbù-jiùbān keep rules; follow the prescribed order; keep to conventional ways of doing things; step by step

按成 ànchéng according to percentage; proportionately: ～分配红利 distribute the bonuses proportionately

按次 àncì in due order; in sequence: ～发言 speak in due order

按工计酬 àngōng-jìchóu pay according to work

按股分红 àngǔ-fēnhóng sharing profits according to contributions

按揭 ànjiē mortgage; charge: ～贷款 mortgage loans

按劳分配 ànláo-fēnpèi distribution according to work; to each according to his work

按劳力包 àn láolì bāo allotting responsibility according to labour power

按理 ànlǐ according to principle or reason; in the ordinary course of events; normally: ～不应当这么办。Logically, it shouldn't be done this way.

按脉 ànmài feel (take) the pulse

按摩 ànmó [医] massage

按捺不住 àn'nàbùzhù cannot control (contain) oneself: ～心中的仇恨 be unable to suppress any longer the bitterness in one's heart

按钮 ànniǔ push button: ～控制 push-button control

按期 ànqī on time; according to schedule

按时 ànshí on time; on schedule; regularly: ～完成 fulfil on time

按需分配 ànxū-fēnpèi distribution according to need; to each according to his need

按语 ànyǔ note; remarks; comment

按照 ànzhào according to; in accordance with; in the light of; on the basis of; as

按质论价 ànzhì-lùnjià fix the price of a product according to its quality; base price on quality

案 àn〈名〉① long table; table; desk ② legal case, law case; case: 破～ clear up (solve) a criminal case ③ file; record: 有～可查 be on file (record) ④ proposal; a plan submitted for consideration: 提～ motion;

proposal. 方～ programme

案板 ànbǎn kneading or chopping board (usu. rectangular)

案犯 ànfàn case criminal

案牍 àndú official correspondence (documents)

案件 ànjiàn legal case; law case; case:～发案率 crime rate. 刑事～ criminal case

案卷 ànjuàn records; files; archives:～材料 materials in the case file

案例 ànlì case; example of case; established case:～研究 case study

案情 ànqíng facts of a case; details of a case; case:了解～ investigate the details of a case; make a thorough investigation of the case

案头 àntóu on one's desk:～日历 desk calendar. ～剧 closet drama

案验 ànyàn investigate the evidence of a case

案由 ànyóu [法] subject matter of a case

案子 ànzi ① long table; counter ②〈口〉law case; case

暗 àn〈形〉① dark; dim; dull:灯光很～。The light is rather dim. ② secret; hidden; covert:明人不做～事。A person who is aboveboard does nothing underhand. ③ unclear vague; hazy:对情况若明若～ have only a vague idea of the situation; The situtation is a little murky.

暗暗 àn'àn secretly; inwardly; to oneself:她～吃了一惊。She was startled but didn't show it.

暗堡 ànbǎo [军] bunker

暗藏 àncáng ① hide; conceal ② hidden; covert:～的破坏分子 covert wreckers

暗娼 ànchāng disguised prostitute; unlicensed (unregistered) prostitute

暗淡 àndàn dim; gloomy; obscure; dismal; bleak:～的画图 dismal picture

暗地里 àndìli in secret; on the sly; stealthily; secretly; covertly:～进行的阴谋 secretly underhand intrigues

暗斗 àndòu secret strife; veiled strife

暗渡陈仓 àndù-chéncāng do a thing in secret; steal a march on; advance secretly along an unknown path

暗害 ànhài ① kill secretly; murder; assassinate; do secret injury to ② stab sb. in the back

暗含 ànhán imply:她的回答～着对我们工作的批评。Her reply implied a criticism of our work.

暗号 ànhào secret sign (signal)

暗盒式录音机 ànhéshì lùyīnjī cassette recorder

暗记儿 ànjìr secret mark

暗箭 ànjiàn an arrow shot from hiding—an attack by a hidden enemy; a stab in the back

暗箭伤人 ànjiàn-shāngrén stab sb. in the back; injure sb. by underhand means

暗礁 ànjiāo submerged rocks; hidden reef

暗捞 ànlāo covert gain

暗流 ànliú undercurrent
暗色 ànsè dark colours
暗杀 ànshā assassinate
暗伤 ànshāng ① internal (invisible) injury ② indiscernible damage
暗事 ànshì clandestine or illicit action
暗示 ànshì hint; insinuate; drop a hint; give sb. an inkling: 他只是～有可能。He merely hinted at the possibility.
暗送秋波 ànsòng-qiūbō make eyes at; make secret overtures to; stealthily give sb. the glad eye
暗算 ànsuàn secret plot; plot against; plot in secret: 遭人～ fall a prey to a plot
暗探 àntàn secret agent; spy; detective
暗无天日 ànwútiānrì complete darkness; total absence of justice; an abyss of darkness; dark days
暗喜 ànxǐ feel pleased but not show it: 不由得心中～ cannot help feeling secretly pleased
暗笑 ànxiào laugh (smile) in one's sleeve; snicker; snigger
暗影 ànyǐng ① shadow ② [天文] umbra
暗喻 ànyù metaphor
暗指 ànzhǐ imply; allude to
暗中 ànzhōng in the dark; by stealth; in secret; on the sly: ～摸索 grope (feel, fumble) in the dark
暗自 ànzì inwardly; to oneself; secretly: ～落泪 cry to oneself; shed a tear in secret. ～庆幸 congratulate oneself; consider oneself lucky

黯 àn 〈形〉 dim; gloomy
黯淡 àndàn dismal; dim; dull; gloomy
黯然 ànrán ① faint; dim ② downcast; dejected; low-spirited; gloomy
黯然神伤 ànrán-shénshāng feel dejected (depressed)
黯然失色 ànrán-shīsè be cast into the shade; appear very dull or poor in comparison; be overshadowed; be eclipsed; pale into insignificance

āng

肮 āng
肮脏 āngzāng dirty; filthy; foul; sordid; squalid: ～的目的 foul (shady) purposes

áng

昂 áng ①〈动〉 hold (one's head) high; raise: ～首挺胸 go with head high and chest out; raise one's head proudly ②〈形〉high; soaring: 群情激～。Popular feeling ran high.
昂昂 áng'áng high-spirited; brave-looking
昂藏 ángcáng tall and imposing: ～七尺之躯 a tall strapping man; a manly man
昂贵 ángguì dear; costly; expen-

sive

昂然 ángrán upright and unafraid; proud and bold

昂首 ángshǒu hold one's head high: ～阔步 stride forward proudly; march forward with one's head high

昂扬 ángyáng high-spirited: 斗志～ have high morale; be strong in morale; be full of militancy; be full of fight

àng

盎 àng ①〈名〉an ancient vessel with a big belly and small mouth ②〈形〉vigorous; full of life

盎然 àngrán alive; exuberant; abundant; full; overflowing

盎司 àngsī ounce [英制重量单位],又作"盎斯"

āo

凹 āo ①〈形〉concave; dented; hollow; sunken: ～凸不平 rugged; full of bumps and holes; uneven ②〈动〉dent; sink; cave in: 路～下去了。The road caved in.

凹版 āobǎn intaglio; gravure: ～印刷 gravure (intaglio) printing

凹地 āodì concave ground; hollow; delve; pit

凹面镜 āomiànjìng concave mirror

凹透镜 āotòujìng concave lens

凹凸印刷 āotūyìnshuā embossing; die stamping

凹陷 āoxiàn sunken; hollow; depressed; pit; swaying: 双颊～ hollow (sunken) cheeks

凹眼 āoyǎn ① sunken eyes ② celophthalmia

熬 āo 〈动〉boil; stew; cook in water: ～白菜 stewed cabbage
另见 áo

áo

遨 áo 〈动〉go on a pleasure tour; stroll; saunter

遨游 áoyóu roam; travel through; wander: ～四海 roam about the various parts of the world

嗷 áo

嗷嗷 áo'áo [表示动物或人的叫声] 吓得～叫 scream with fright

嗷嗷待哺 áo'áo-dàibǔ cry piteously for food; crying with hunger; waiting to be fed with cries of hunger

熬 áo 〈动〉① boil; stew; decoct: ～浓糖浆 boil down syrup ② endure; hold out; go through; bear; stand: ～过苦役 endure the hard labour
另见 āo

熬出头 áochūtóu have gone through all sorts of ordeal: 这苦日子啥时候才能～。I wondered when these bitter days would come to an end.

熬煎 áojiān suffering; torture

熬苦 áokǔ suffer privations; endure hardships

熬夜 áoyè sit up all night; stay up late (all night); burn the midnight oil

翱 áo〈动〉〈书〉take wind; soar

翱翔 áoxiáng fly about; soar; hover:苍鹰在空中～。The eagle hovered in the sky.

鳌 áo〈名〉a huge legendary turtle

鳌头独占 áotóu-dúzhàn perch alone on the whale's head; come out first (top, at the top); be the champion; head the list of successful candidates

鏖 áo〈动〉〈书〉engage in fierce battle

鏖兵 áobīng〈书〉fight hard; bloody battle

鏖战 áozhàn〈书〉engage in fierce battle; fight hard; fight a bloody battle

ǎo

拗 ǎo〈方〉bend so hard to break
另见 ào; niù

袄 ǎo〈名〉a short Chinese-style coat or jacket:皮～ fur coat; fur garment

媪 ǎo〈名〉〈书〉old woman

ào

坳 ào〈名〉a depression in a mountain range; col:山～ col

拗 ào
另见 ǎo, niù

拗口 àokǒu hard to pronounce; awkward-sounding; twist the tongue:～令 tongue twister

拗体诗 àotǐshī poems that do not conform to the rule of conventional versification

傲 ào〈形〉① proud; haughty; arrogant:孤～ proud and aloof ② brave; refuse to yield to; defy

傲岸 ào'àn haughty; proud:～的青松 a proud and towering pine

傲骨 àogǔ lofty and unyielding character; self-esteem; spirit of loftiness

傲慢 àomàn haughty; overbearing; insolent; arrogant:态度～ be arrogant in manner; put on airs; arrogant attitude

傲气 àoqì air of arrogance; haughtiness:助长某人～ feed sb.'s arrogance

傲气凌人 àoqì-língrén humiliate others with one's haughty temper (airs)

傲然 àorán proud; lofty; loftily; unyieldingly; proudly

傲视 àoshì look down on (upon); despise; contempt for; turn up one's nose at; scorn; treat with disdain; show disdain for

傲性 àoxìng proud temperament

奥 ào 〈形〉 abstruse; hard to understand; profound: 深～ profound; abstruse

奥林匹克运动会(奥运会) Àolínpǐkè Yùndònghuì (Àoyùnhuì) the Olympic Games; the Olympics; the Olympiad

奥博 àobó ① extensive and profound in meaning ② (of a person) widely read

奥秘 àomì secret; profound; mystery: 自然的～ mysteries (secrets) of nature

奥妙 àomiào mystic; profound; marvellous; subtle; what's behind it: ～无穷 extremely subtle

奥义 àoyì profound meaning

澳 ào 〈名〉an inlet of the sea; bay (often used in place names: 三都～ Sandu Bay

澳大利亚 Àodàlìyà Australia: ～人 Australian

澳门 Àomén Aomen (Macao)

澳洲 Àozhōu Australia (the continent)

懊 ào 〈动〉① repent; regret 〈形〉② annoyed; vexed ③ remorseful; regretful

懊悔 àohuǐ feel remorse; repent; be regretful; regret: 他～做错了事情。He repented of his wrong doing.

懊恼 àonǎo feel vexed (annoyed); be chagrined (upset); feel remorseful and angry

懊丧 àosàng low in spirits; depressed; crestfallen; dejected; despondent

鏊 ào 〈名〉a flat iron plate for making cakes

鏊子 àozi griddle

B b

bā

八 bā 〈数〉 eight

八拜之交 bābàizhījiāo become sworn brothers (sisters); sworn brotherhood; the relationship between sworn brothers (sisters)

八辈子 bābèizi eight lifetimes—a long time: 这简直是倒了～霉了。What interminable rotten luck!

八成 bāchéng eighty per cent: ～新 eighty per cent new; practically new. 事情有了～啦。We stand a fair chance of success.; It's almost as good as settled. ② most probably; most likely: ～她不来了。Most probably she isn't coming.

八方 bāfāng the eight points of the compass; all directions: ～呼应 responses from every direction; cooperation from all

八股文 bāgǔwén eight-part essay (a literary composition prescribed for the imperial civil service examinations, known for its rigidity of form and poverty of ideas); stereotyped writing; the "eight-legged essay"; stereotyped eight-section essay; jargon

八卦 bāguà eight trigrams (eight combinations of three whole or broken lines formerly used in divination); eight diagrams

八级工 bājígōng eighth-grade worker; top-grade worker

八级工资制 bājí gōngzīzhì eight-grade wage scale

八九不离十 bā-jiǔ bùlí shí about right; pretty close; very near: 猜个～ make a very close guess

八路军 Bālùjūn the Eighth Route Army (led by the Chinese Communist Party during the War of Resistance Against Japan)

八面玲珑 bāmiàn-línglóng be all things to all men; be smooth and slick (in establishing social relations); be a perfect mixer in any company; capable of dealing with all men; try to please everybody or offend nobody

八七扶贫攻坚计划 bāqī fúpín gōngjiān jìhuà plan to assist 80 million people in having sufficient food and clothing within seven years

八仙过海，各显神通 bāxiān'guòhǎi, gèxiǎnshéntōng like the Eight Immortals crossing the sea, each one showing his (her) special prowess; like the Eight Immortals soaring over the ocean, each of you show your true worth; vie with each other

八仙桌 bāxiānzhuō Eight Immortals table—an old fashioned square table for eight people

八小时工作制 bāxiǎoshí gōngzuòzhì eight-hour day; eight working-hour

八一建军节 Bā-Yī Jiànjūnjié Army Day (August 1, anniversay of the founding of the Chinese People's Liberation Army)

八月 bāyuè ① August ② the eighth month of the lunar year; the eighth moon:～节 the Mid-Autumn Festival (15th day of the 8th lunar month)

八字 [旧时用天干、地支表示人出生的年、月、日，合起来是八个字，用于推算一个人命运的好坏] bāzì Eight Characters (in four parts, including the year, month, day and hour of a person's birth, each pair consisting of one Heavenly Stem and one Earthly Branch, formerly used in fortune-telling)

八字没一撇 bāzì méi yīpiě Not even the first stroke of the character "八" is in sight — there's not the slightest sign of anything happening yet; Nothing has been done so far.; Nothing tangible is in sight yet.

八字帖(儿)[旧俗订婚时先交换八字贴，又叫"庚贴"] bāzìtiěr a written marriage proposal on which are stated the hour, day, month, year of one's birth

巴

bā 〈动〉① wait anxiously; hope eagerly:～望 look forward to ② stick to; cling to:爬山虎～在墙上。The ivy clings to the wall. ③〈方〉be next to; be close to

巴不得 bābude hope eagerly; eagerly look forward to; be only too glad (to do sth.); earnestly wish; make up to:我们～他马上能来。We wish he could come at once.

巴结 bājie curry favour with; fawn on; flatter; try hard to please sb.

巴黎公社 Bālí gōngshè the Paris Commune (the world's first dictatorship of the proletariat, established by the French working class after smashing the old state machine, 1871)

巴掌 bāzhang ①〈名〉palm; hand ②〈动〉slap (in the face); box (on the ear):打他一～ slap him in the face; give him a slap (a box on the ear)

扒

bā 〈动〉① dig up; rake; pull down:～树根 dig up the root of a tree ② hold on to; cling to:～窗台 hold on to the window sill ③ push aside:～开草丛 push aside a thick growth of grass ④ take off; strip off:～狗皮 skin a dog

另见 pá

扒车 bāchē climb onto a slow-going train, etc.

扒拉 bāla push lightly; touch lightly:把钟摆～一下 give the pendulum a light push; set the pendulum swinging

另见 pá

芭 bā

芭蕉 bājiāo plantain; banana:～扇 palm-leaf fan

芭蕾舞 bālěiwǔ ballet:～演员 ballet dancer

吧 bā

① 〈象〉 crackling:～～两声枪响。Crack! Crack! Two shots rang out. ② 〈动〉〈口〉 pull at (draw on) one's pipe

吧嗒 bāda ① smack one's lips (in surprise, alarm, etc.):她～了一下嘴,一声也不言语。She smacked her lips but did not utter a word. ② pull at (a pipe, etc):他～着叶子烟打主意。He puffed at his pipe as he wondered what to do.

吧唧 bājī ① 〈象〉:他光着脚～～地在泥里走。He squelched barefoot through the mud. ② smack one's lips ③ pull at (a pipe, etc.)

疤 bā

scar

疤痕 bāhén scar; sore

疤瘌 bāla scar

疤瘌眼儿 bālayǎnr ① an eye with a scar on the eyelid ② a person who has such an eye

捌 bā

〈数〉 eight (used for the numeral 八 on cheques, etc. to avoid mistakes or alterations)

笆 bā

〈名〉 basketry

笆斗 bādǒu round-bottomed basket

笆篱 bālí bamboo or twig fence

笆篱子 bālízi prison; jail

粑 bā

〈名〉 cake

粑粑 bāba cake:玉米～ corn cake

bá

拔 bá

〈动〉 ① pull (out, up); pluck; winkle out:～草 weed; pull up weeds ② draw; suck out ③ select, choose; pick; promote:提～ promote. 选～ select from candidates ④ surpass; stand out among:出类～萃 be distinguished from one's kind; stand out among one's fellows ⑤ capture; seize:～据点 capture enemy's stronghold

拔白 bábái dawn

拔除 báchú uproot; remove; wipe out; pull out:～敌军哨所 wipe out an enemy sentry post

拔萃 bácuì stand out from one's fellows; be out of the common run:～出群 stand head and shoulders above others; be outstanding

拔地 bádì rise sheer (steeply) from level ground; tower:～而起的高楼 a towering building

拔钉子 bádīngzi pull out nails (a metaphor for eliminating obstacle or persons impeding the progress of works)

拔河 báhé tug-of-war

拔尖 bájiān first-class; outstanding; top-notch; tiptop:他在厂里工作是～的。He is a tiptop worker at the factory.

拔锚 bámáo weigh anchor

拔苗助长 bámiáo-zhùzhǎng try to help the shoots grow by pulling them upward; spoil things by

schools and revering only Confucianism
罢工bàgōng strike; go on strike; walk out; (lay) down tools
罢官 bàguān be dismissed (removed) from office
罢教 bàjiào teachers' strike
罢课 bàkè students' strike
罢了bàle 〈助〉[用在陈述句的末尾,有"仅此而已"的意思,常跟"不过、无非、只是"]:你就是不想去～。You just don't want to go, that's all.
罢了bàliǎo 〈助〉[表示"容忍、算了"的意思]:她不愿来也就～。Well, if she doesn't want to come, it can't be helped.
罢免bàmiǎn dimiss; remove; recall:～权 right of recall; recall
罢民 bàmín erring men; vagrants
罢市 bàshì shopkeepers' strike; close up shop; merchants' strike; cease trade
罢手 bàshǒu give up:不试验成功,我决不～。I will never stop until the experiment succeeds.
罢休bàxiū stop; cease; give up; let the matter drop:不达目的,决不～。We will never give up till we attain our goal.
罢职 bàzhí remove from office; dismiss

霸 bà 〈名〉① chief of feudal princes; overlord ② tyrant; despot; bully:恶～ local tyrant (despot) ③ hegemony; hegemonist power; hegemonism ④〈动〉dominate; tyrannize over, lord it over:各～一方 dominate a region respectively
霸道bàdào ① (feudal) rule by force of dictators ② tyranny; overbearing; domineering; high-handed; violent in action; the tyrant's way ③[形容酒或药等的烈性]strong; potent
霸权bàquán hegemony; supremacy:～主义 hegemonism
霸头 bàtóu ① labour contractor; gangmaster ② overlord; hegemon
霸王bàwáng ① [秦汉之间楚王项羽的称号]Xiang Yu, the Conqueror (232 — 202 B. C.) ②[比喻极端蛮横的人] despot; overlord
霸业 bàyè accomplishments of obtaining the dominant position
霸占 bàzhàn occupy (seize) by force; grab; usurp; forcibly occupy:～某人财产 forcibly occupy sb.'s property
霸政bàzhèng hegemonism or rule by force; oligarchy
霸主bàzhǔ ① [封建社会诸侯的首领] a powerful chief of the princes of the Spring and Autumn Period (770—476 B. C.) ② [称霸的人或集团]overlord of the state; hegemon:～地位 overlordship; hegemony; domineering position

ba

吧 ba〈助〉①[用在句末表示商量、请求、提议、命令等]帮帮他～! Help him! 你来～! Come, if you will! ② [用在句末表示同意或认可]好～ all right ③

[在句末表示揣测、疑问]她会来～？ She'll come, won't she? ④[在句中表示停顿，带假设的语气]走～，不好；不走～，也不好。It's no good whether leaving or not.
另见 bā，bà

bāi

掰 bāi 〈动〉① break off with hands (the fingers and thumb)：～腕子 hand wrestling ② sever; break off：～交情 break off relationships

bái

白 bái〈形〉① white ② blank; plain; clear; pure; unmixed：～开水 plain boiled water ③ free (of charge); gratis：～吃 eat without pay ④〈副〉in vain; for nothing; to no end; without results; waste efforts：～费力气 labour without results〈名〉⑤ White (as a symbol of reaction)：～色恐怖 White terror ⑥ wrongly written or mispronounced：写～字 wrongly write a character ⑦ spoken part in opera, etc.：道～ spoken part in opera ⑧〈动〉explain, state, clear up; present：自～ explain oneself; confessions

白皑皑 bái'ái'ái (of snow, frost, etc.) pure white：～的雪铺满田野。The fields were all covered with pure white snow.

白白 báibái ① free (of charge); gratis; without pay ② in vain; of no avail; to no end (purpose); for nothing：～跑了一趟 go for nothing; make a trip to no end

白班儿 báibānr day shift

白板[哲] báibǎn tabula rasa (mind as a blank board); clean slate

白报纸 báibàozhǐ newsprint

白璧微瑕 báibì-wēixiá a flaw in a white jade—a slight blemish; a flaw in a gem; small faults (defects)

白璧无瑕 báibì-wúxiá flawless white jade; man's flawless character; impeccable moral integrity

白菜 báicài Chinese cabbage

白痴 báichī ① idiot; ament ② idiocy

白搭 báidā〈口〉no good; no use

白饭 báifàn plain cooked rice; rice with nothing to go with it

白费 báifèi in vain; waste：～力气 waste one's efforts; draw water with a sieve; plough the sands; labour lost

白宫 Báigōng the White House[美国]

白骨精 báigǔjīng White Bone Demon

白圭微瑕 báiguī-wēixiá a flaw (stain, slight blemish) in a precious stone

白圭有玷 báiguī-yǒudiàn a flaw in a jade baton; spot on a white jade; There are lees to every wine.

白话 báihuà spoken Chinese; colloquial Chinese; vernacular (language): ～文 vernacular style of writing; writings in the vernacular. ～文学 vernacular literature

白晃晃 báihuānghuāng shining and bright; gleaming; glaring

白金汉宫 [英国] Báijīnhàngōng Buckingham Palace

白酒(干) báijiǔ (gān) *gaoliang* wine; white spirit

白卷 báijuàn blank examination paper: 交～ hand in a blank examination paper; hand in an examination paper unanswered

白脸 báiliǎn white face, face painting in Beijing opera etc, traditionally for the villain: 唱～ play the villain; pretend to be harsh and severe

白领工人 báilǐng gōngrén white-collar worker

白茫茫 báimángmáng (of mist, snow, floodwater, etc.) a vast expanse of whiteness: 下了一场大雪,田野上～一片。After the heavy snow, the fields were a vast expanse of whiteness.

白蒙蒙 báimēngmēng (of smoke, fog, steam, etc.) hazy; misty: 城市笼罩在一片～的晨雾中。A haze of morning mist veiled the city.

白米 báimǐ (polished) rice: ～饭 (cooked) rice

白面 báimiàn wheat flour; flour

白面书生 báimiànshūshēng a fair-complexioned scholar; an inexperienced youth (young scholar)

白描 báimiáo ①[美]line drawing in traditional ink and brush style ② simple, straightforward style of writing

白沫 báimò frothy saliva; foam: 口吐～ foam at the mouth

白内障 báinèizhàng [医] cataract: ～摘除术 cataract extraction

白嫩 báinèn (of skin) fair and clear; delicate

白皮书 báipíshū white book; white paper

白票 báipiào white paper

白旗 báiqí white flag; a flag used in battle to signal surrender

白热 báirè white heat; white glow; incandescence: ～化 turn (become) white-hot; bring…to the boiling point; intense; sharpen

白人 báirén white man or woman

白刃 báirèn naked blade; naked sword: ～战 hand-to-hand combat; bayonet charge

白日做梦 báirìzuòmèng dream daydreams; cherish a pipe (fond) dream; day-dreaming

白色 báisè ① white (colour) ② White (as a symbol of reaction): ～据点 White stronghold; stronghold of reaction

白色人种 báisèrénzhǒng Europoid; white race; European

白手起家 báishǒu-qǐjiā start from scratch; start empty-handed; build up from nothing; raise a house with empty hands; pull oneself up by one's own bootstraps

白条 báitiáo white slip, an informal note without an official seal affixed; a promissory note with little binding force

白头 báitóu ① hoary head; old age ② unsigned; anonymous

白头偕老 báitóu-xiélǎo reach old age together—said of a couple; live to a ripe old age in conjugal bliss; remain a devoted couple to the end of their lives

白皙 báixī (of skin) fair and clear:皮肤～ have a fair complexion; be fair-complexioned

白眼 báiyǎn supercilious look:遭人～ be treated with disdain

白杨 báiyáng [植] white poplar

白衣战士 báiyī zhànshì warrior in white; medical worker

白玉无瑕 báiyù-wúxiá flawless white jade; perfect

白纸黑字 báizhǐ-hēizì put it down in black and white; written in black ink on white paper; black characters (letters) on white paper; unchangeably

白昼 báizhòu daytime; day

白(别)字 bái (bié) zì wrongly written or mispronounced; malapropism; wrong word:读～ mispronounce a Chinese character

白族 Báizú Bai nationality (living in Yunnan Province)

bǎi

百 bǎi ①〈数〉hundred:～花盛开 flowers bloom luxuriantly; a hundred flowers in bloom ②〈形〉all; all kinds of; various; numerous:～业 all professions ③〈副〉very; always:精神～倍 with high spirit; full of energy

百般 bǎibān in every possible way; in a hundred and one way; by all manner of means; by every means:～劝说 try to persuade sb. in every possible way. ～奉承 tirelessly fawn upon; flatter sedulously. ～刁难 create all sorts of obstacles; create obstructions of every description

百倍 bǎibèi a hundred times; a hundred-fold:信心～ be full of confidence; with full confidence

百弊 bǎibì ① all kinds of maladies or evils ② many drawbacks or disadvantages

百步穿杨 báibù-chuānyáng shoot an arrow through a willow leaf at a hundred paces; split a willow wand at a hundred paces; shoot with great precision

百尺竿头,更进一步 bǎi chǐ gāntóu,gèng jìn yī bù make still further progress; continue to do better; forge further ahead

百出 bǎichū [贬义] numerous; full of; plenty of:矛盾～ full of contradictions

百川归海 bǎichuān-guīhǎi All rivers flow to the sea.; All things tend in one direction.

百读不厌 bǎidú-bùyàn be worth reading a hundred times; can be read a hundred times with delight

百发百中 bǎifā-bǎizhòng fire at the target a hundred times without a single miss; shoot with extreme accuracy; Every shot tells.; a hundred shots, a hundred bull's-eyes

百废俱兴 bǎifèi-jùxīng put a hundred broken things right at the same time; get all neglected projects started at once

百分比(～～率) bǎifēnbǐ(～～lǜ) percentage

百分点 bǎifēndiǎn one percentage point:增加两个～ an increase of two percentage points

百分号 bǎifēnhào percentage symbol (%)

百分率 bǎifēnlǜ percentage; per cent

百分数 bǎifēnshù percentage; per cent

百分之百 bǎifēnzhībǎi hundred-per-cent; thorough-going; out and out:～的谎言 an out-and-out lie

百分制 bǎifēnzhì hundred-mark system

百感交集 bǎigǎnjiāojí have mixed feelings; All sorts of feelings well up in one's heart.; run (capture) the gamut of emotions

百工 bǎigōng craftsmen

百花奖 bǎihuājiǎng Hundred-Flower Prize

百花齐放,百家争鸣 bǎihuā qífàng, bǎijiā zhēngmíng Let a hundred flowers blossom and a hundred schools of thought contend.

百花齐放,推陈出新 bǎihuā qífàng, tuīchén chūxīn Let a hundred flowers blossom; weed through the old to bring forth the new

百花争艳 bǎihuā-zhēngyàn a hundred flowers contend in beauty; the flowers are a riot of colour

百货 bǎihuò general merchandise: 日用～ articles of daily use. ～商店 general store; department store

百科全书 bǎikē quánshū encyclopaedia

百孔千疮 bǎikǒng-qiānchuāng riddled with gaping wounds; full of ills and troubles; afflicted with all ills; be seriously damaged

百里挑一 bǎilǐ-tiāoyī one in a hundred; one in a thousand; cream of the crop:～的人品 He's one in a thousand.

百炼成钢 bǎiliàn-chénggāng be tempered in repeated struggles; be tempered into steel; be tempered into a person of iron will

百年不遇 bǎinián-bùyù not seen once in a hundred years:～的水灾 the biggest flood in a century

百年大计 bǎinián-dàjì a project of vital and lasting importance; a fundamental task crucial for generations to come

百年纪念 bǎinián jìniàn centenary; centennial

百年树人 bǎinián-shùrén it takes

a hundred years to educate the people：十年树木，～。It takes ten years to grow trees，but a hundred to rear people.

百年之后 bǎinián-zhīhòu when sb. has passed away；after sb.'s death

百色齐全 bǎisè-qíquán a complete range of colours

百十 bǎishí a hundred or so：～户人家 about a hundred households

百思不解 bǎisī-bùjiě remain puzzled after pondering over sth. a hundred times；remain perplexed despite much thought；cannot understand after repeated thinking

百索不得 bǎisuǒ-bùdé make an extensive search in vain

百万 bǎiwàn million

百闻不如一见 bǎi wén bùrú yī jiàn To see sth. once is better than hearing about it a hundred times.；There is nothing like seeing for yourself.；Seeing is believing.

百无禁忌 bǎiwújìnjì all taboos in abeyance（a magic formula credited with the power of neutralizing offences against taboos）

百无聊赖 bǎiwúliáolài bored stiff；bored to death；idle away time aimlessly；overcome with boredom

百无一失 bǎiwúyīshī no danger of anything going wrong；no risk at all；perfectly safe；surefire

百姓 bǎixìng common people

百业凋敝 bǎiyèdiāobì all business declining

百依百顺 bǎiyī-bǎishùn be ready to comply with all requests；be all compliance

百战百胜 bǎizhàn-bǎishèng fight a hundred battles，win a hundred victories；emerge victorious in every battle；be ever-victorious；be invincible

百折不挠 bǎizhé-bùnáo be undaunted by repeated setbacks；be unswerving；be indomitable

百足之虫，死而不僵 bǎi zú zhī chóng，sǐ ér bù jiāng The centipede goes on wriggling when he's already dead；A centipede does not topple over even when dead；A centipede even when dead won't fall to the ground；A centipede dies but never falls down.

佰 bǎi〈数〉hundred（used for the numeral 百 on cheques，etc. to avoid mistakes or alterations）

柏 bǎi〈名〉cypress

柏树 bǎishù cypress

柏油 bǎiyóu tar；pitch；asphalt：～路 asphalt road（pavement）；tar-paved road

摆 bǎi〈动〉① put；place；set… in order；arrange：把东西～好 set the things in order ② put on；assume；show off：～出一副官架子 assume the airs of an official ③ sway；wag；wave：～

尾巴 wag tail ④ state clearly; lay bare; talk about:～家常 engage in small talk; talk about domestic trivial ⑤〈名〉pendulum

摆布 bǎibù be ordered about; [常用被动式]dictate to; manipulate:任人～ be dictated to; allow oneself to be ordered about; be at the mercy of others

摆荡 bǎidàng swing; sway

摆动 bǎidòng swing; sway:柳条迎风～。The willows swayed in the breeze.

摆渡 bǎidù ① cross a river by boat; ferry ② ferryboat; ferry

摆放 bǎifàng put; place; lay

摆格 bǎigé〈方〉stand on one's dignity

摆架子 bǎijiàzi make a great show; put on airs; assume great airs; make a display

摆开阵势 bǎikāi zhènshì put (place) in battle array; draw up troops for battle; deploy troops in battle formation

摆空架子 bǎi kōngjiàzi make an empty show; put on a showy air; put up airs

摆阔 bǎikuò flaunt (parade) one's wealth; be given to display; show off:他爱～。He is fond of showing off. ～性消费 conspicuous consumption

摆龙门阵 bǎi lóngménzhèn〈方〉chat; gossip; spin a yarn

摆门面 bǎi ménmiàn keep up appearances; put up an impressive front

摆迷魂阵 bǎi míhúnzhèn set a trap; lay out a scheme to bewitch sb.

摆弄 bǎinòng ① move back and forth; fiddle with:你别来回～那儿盆花了。Don't move those flower pots back and forth. ② order about; manipulate

摆平 bǎipíng be fair to; be impartial to:～关系 be impartial in dealings with people

摆谱儿 bǎipǔr〈方〉try to appear rich and elegant; try to impress

摆设 bǎishè ① decorate and furnish a room ② ornament; decorations:小～ knickknack

摆事实,讲道理 bǎishìshí,jiǎng dàolǐ set forth the facts and discuss them rationally; present the facts and reason things out; set forth facts and reason things out

摆手 bǎishǒu ① shake one's hand in admonition or disapproval ② beckon; wave:他向我摆了摆手,要我跟着他。He beckoned me to follow him.

摆摊子 bǎitānzi ① set up a stall ② maintain a large staff or organization

摆脱 bǎituō cast off; abandon; throw off; dispense; rid; free oneself from; break away from:～困境 extricate oneself from a predicament. ～贫困 get rid of (eliminate, shake off) poverty; put an end to poverty

摆样子 bǎiyàngzi be just for show; just show off; do sth. for show

摆针 bǎizhēn pointer (on a meter, scales, etc.)
摆钟 bǎizhōng pendulum clock

bài

败 bài 〈动〉① defeat; beat:打~对手 beat the opponent ② fail:不计成~ not consider success or failure ③ spoil; ruin ~事有余 spoil everything. 伤风~俗 corrupt public morals. 战~国 a defeated state ④〈形〉bad; decayed; withered:开不~的花朵 never faded flowers
败北 bàiběi suffer defeat; lose a battle
败笔 bàibǐ ①[用于书画] a faulty stroke in calligraphy or painting; a faulty part in a piece of painting ②[用于诗文] a faulty expression in writing
败兵 bàibīng a defeated army; an army in flight; defeated troops
败坏 bàihuài spoil; ruin; debase; undermine; deteriorate:~人心 corrupt people's minds; deprave; perversion of one's mind
败家子 bàijiāzǐ prodigal son squandering the family fortune; profligate; spendthrift; wastrel; black sheep
败局 bàijú lost game; losing battle:~已定。The game is as good as lost.
败类 bàilèi degenerate; riffraff; dregs of society; scum of a community:民族~ scum of a nation
败露 bàilù (of a plot, etc.) become known; be brought to light; fall through and stand exposed; be uncovered
败落 bàiluò decline (in wealth and position):一个封建家庭的~ the decline of a feudal family
败(害)群之马 bài(hài)qúnzhīmǎ a horse that spoils the whole herd; a black sheep; one who brings disgrace on his group
败诉 bàisù [法] lose a case (lawsuit); be cast in a suit:~案件 defeat suit
败退 bàituì fall back; retreat in defeat
败谢 bàixiè wither and fall
败兴 bàixìng be disappointing; kill joy:~而归 get back disappointed; return crestfallen; return in low spirits
败仗 bàizhàng lost battle; defeat:打~ suffer a defeat; be defeated
败者为贼,成者为王 bàizhě wéi zéi,chéngzhě wéi wáng Failure makes a rebel, success a prince
败子回头金不换 bàizǐ huítóu jīn bú huàn A repentant prodigal is better than gold.

拜 bài 〈动〉① make a courtesy call:回~ pay a return visit ② do obeisance; worship; prostrate oneself: ~佛 worship Buddha at a temple ③ call on; pay a visit:~访街坊 call on neighbours ④ formally establish or swear relationships:~她为师 formally acknowledge her as one's teacher or master ⑤〈敬〉[用于人事往来]~谢

humbly thank; express one's thanks:你的新书我已～读了。I have read your new book.

拜把子 bàibǎzi become sworn brothers; blood brother

拜别 bàibié take leave of

拜倒 bàidǎo prostrate oneself; fall on one's knees; bow before sb.

拜读 bàidú 〈敬〉 have the honour to read:～大作 have the pleasure of persuing your work

拜访 bàifǎng call on; pay (make) a visit; visit; be on a visit; drop in (on sb.)

拜候 bàihòu call to pay one's respects; call on

拜会 bàihuì pay an official call; make an official visit

拜见 bàijiàn ① pay a formal visit; call to pay respects ② meet one's senior or superior

拜金主义 bàijīnzhǔyì money worship; mammonism; plutolatry

拜年 bàinián pay (make) a New Year call; make a ceremonial call on New Year; wish sb. a Happy New Year

拜师 bàishī formally become a pupil to a master

拜寿 bàishòu congratulate an elderly person on his birthday; offer birthday felicitations

拜堂(天地) bàitáng(tiāndì) (of bride and groom) make ceremonial obeisances—perform the marriage ceremony

拜托 bàituō〈敬〉 ask a favour of sb.; request sb. to do sth.; entrust:～你捎个口信给他。May I ask a favour of you to take a (an oral) message to him?

拜物教 bàiwùjiào festishism

拜谒 bàiyè 〈书〉 ① pay a formal visit; call to pay respects ② pay homage (at a monument, mausoleum, etc.)

稗 bài 〈名〉 ① tares; weeds; panic (grass) ② unofficial; folk

稗记 bàijì books of anecdotes

稗史 bàishǐ historical romance; books containing anecdotes; unofficial history

稗子 bàizi barnyard grass; barnyard millet

bān

扳 bān 〈动〉 pull; turn:～闸 pull switch. ～过来 pull it over

扳道工 bāndàogōng switch tender; switchman; pointsman

扳机 bānjī trigger

扳手 bānshou ① spanner; wrench ② lever (on a machine)

扳子 bānzi spanner; wrench

班 bān 〈名〉 ① class; group; team:高级～ advanced class. 作业～ work team ② squad; section ③ company (of actors):戏～儿 theatrical troupe ④ shift; duty:轮～ on duty by turn ⑤ 〈形〉regular; scheduled:头～火车 first train. 搭下一～飞机去 leave by next plane

班车 bānchē regular (regularly-run) bus; scheduled bus

班次 bāncì ① order of classes or grades at school：在学校时，他～比我高。At school he was in a higher class than me. ② number of runs or flights：增加客车～ increase the number of runs of passenger trains

班房 bānfáng jail：坐～ be (put) in jail

班机 bānjī regular air service; (regular) flight; airliner

班级 bānjí classes and grades in school：我们在中学是同一个～。We used to be in the same class when at high school.

班轮 bānlún regular passenger (cargo) ship; regular steamship service; liner ship; liner：～运输 liner trade

班门弄斧 bānmén-nòngfǔ wield an axe at the door of the master Lu Ban; display one's slight skill before an expert; show off one's scanty knowledge in the presence of an expert; teach one's grandmother to suck eggs

班期 bānqī schedule (for flights, voyages, etc.)：～表 a table of scheduled flights, voyages, etc.; timetable

班师 bānshī withdraw troops from the front; return after victory

班长 bānzhǎng ① class monitor ②〈军〉squad leader ③ (work) team leader

班主任 bānzhǔrèn teacher in charge of a class; [小学的] form teacher; form master (mistress)：～津贴 allowances for teachers in charge of classes

班子 bānzi ① group; team; setup：生产～ a team in charge of production ② company (of actors); (theatrical) troupe

班组 bānzǔ team; group：～计件制 group piece work system; gang piece work system

般

般 bān ①〈名〉type; sort; kind; way：百～ by all means; in a hundred ways ②〈助〉like; as; alike in：一～模样 look alike ③〈动〉同"搬"(bān)

另见 bo，pán

般配 bānpèi suit; be well matched; match each other

颁

颁 bān〈动〉① promulgate; issue; proclaim ② distribute; award

颁布 bānbù promulgate; proclaim; publish; issue：～命令 issue an order; promulgate a decree

颁发 bānfā ① promulgate ② award; confer; distribute：向某人～奖章 award sb. a medal

颁行 bānxíng issue for enforcement

斑

斑 bān〈名〉spot; speck; speckle; stain：窥见一～ see segment of a whole

斑白 bānbái grey; grizzled：头发～ with grizzled hair; grey-haired

斑斑 bānbān full of stains or spots：血迹～ bloodstained

斑驳 bānbó mottled; motley

斑驳陆离 bānbó-lùlí mixed

colours (tints); variegated; motley and chopped in appearance

斑点 bāndiǎn spot; stain; speckle

斑痕 bānhén mark; trace

斑斓 bānlán bright-coloured; gorgeous; multicoloured; varicoloured; [动物] brindled: 五彩～ multicoloured

斑马 bānmǎ zebra: ～线(人行横道线) zebra crossing

斑纹 bānwén streak; stripe; markings

斑竹 bānzhú mottled bamboo

搬 bān 〈动〉① remove; move; take away: 把书桌～走 take the desk away ② move: ～往新居 move to a new house ③ copy mechanically; apply indiscriminately: 死～教条 slavishly follow dogma

搬兵 bānbīng call in reinforcement; ask for help

搬家 bānjiā ① move (house): 他们下星期～。They are moving next week. ② remove; move: 把这张桌子搬搬家,别挡路。Please move the table out of the way.

搬弄 bānnòng ① move sth. about; fiddle with: 别～枪栓。Don't fiddle with the rifle bolt. ② show off; display: ～学问 show off one's erudition

搬弄是非 bānnòng-shìfēi tell (carry) tales; stir up enmity; sow dissension (discord); make mischief

搬起石头打自己的脚 bānqǐ shítóu dǎ zìjǐ de jiǎo lift a rock only to drop it on one's own feet; lift a rock only to have one's toes squashed

搬迁 bānqiān relocate; remove; move out: ～户 relocated households

搬上舞台 bānshàng wǔtái be presented on the stage; stage

搬演 bānyǎn perform; act

搬移 bānyí move; remove; shift

搬用 bānyòng copy mechanically; apply indiscriminately; apply mechanically; use indiscriminately

搬运 bānyùn carry; convey; transport: ～工人 transport worker; porter; carrier; [码头上的] stevedore; docker

瘢 bān 〈名〉 scar

瘢痕 bānhén scar

癍 bān 〈名〉 rash on skin; flecks; abnormal pigmentary deposits on the skin

bǎn

板 bǎn 〈名〉① board; plank; [金属的] plate ② [中国打击乐器] ban clappers ③ [乐] time; an accented beat in traditional Chinese music; pressure ④ 〈形〉 rigid; stiff

板板六十四 bǎnbǎnliùshísì rigid; unaccommodating; stick to rules strictly

板擦儿 bǎncār blackboard eraser

板锉 bǎncuò flat file

板凳 bǎndèng wooden bench or

stool

板斧 bǎnfǔ broad axe

板钢 bǎngāng slab

板鼓 bǎngǔ small drum for marking time

板胡 bǎnhú *banhu* fiddle; a bowed stringed instrument with a thin wooden soundboard

板结 bǎnjié harden: ～的土壤 hardened and impervious soil

板块 bǎnkuài plate: ～边界 plate boundary. ～碰撞 plate collision

板上钉钉 bǎnshàng dìngdīng that clinches it; that's final; no two ways about it

板上画 bǎnshànghuà panel painting

板式 bǎnshì modes in Chinese operatic music

板书 bǎnshū writing on the blackboard; blackboard-writing

板刷 bǎnshuā scrubbing brush

板条箱 bǎntiáoxiāng crate

板鸭 bǎnyā pressed (dried) salted duck

板眼 bǎnyǎn ① orderliness: 她说话有板有眼 Whatever she says is well presented. ② measure in traditional Chinese music

板执不通 bǎnzhíbùtōng be a stickler for rules; adhere stubbornly to one's own opinions; admit of no alternative

板纸 bǎnzhǐ paperboard; board: 牛皮～ kraft board

板子 bǎnzi ① board; plank ② bamboo or birch for corporal punishment

版 bǎn 〈名〉① printing plate (block): 排～ composing. 制～ plate making ② edition: 修订～ revised edition ③ page (of a newspaper): 头～ frontpage

版本 bǎnběn edition: ～目录 catalogues of the edition. ～图书馆 depository library

版次 bǎncì the order in which editions are printed

版画 bǎnhuà traditional Chinese print; print; engraving; block print

版刻 bǎnkè carving; engraving

版面 bǎnmiàn ①[报纸、杂志每页的整面] space of a whole page ②[版面编排] layout (makeup) of a printed sheet: ～设计 layout

版权 bǎnquán copyright; literary property: ～所有 All rights reserved. ～法 copyright law

版权页 bǎnquányè copyright page; colophon

版式 bǎnshì [版面格式] format: ～精美 recherché format

版税 bǎnshuì royalty (on books); [按一定百分数付给作者的稿酬] copyright royalty; copymoney

版图 bǎntú territory; domain

bàn

办 bàn 〈动〉① do; manage; tackle; attend to; handle: ～事公道 be fair and square in handling affairs ② run; establish; set up: ～报 run a newspaper ③ buy; purchase; get sth. ready: 筹～展览会 prepare an exhibition ④ punish; bring to justice:首恶必～ must punish the chief culprits

办案 bàn'àn handle a case; take charge of a case

办报 bànbào run a newspaper

办差 bànchāi take charge of missions

办到 bàndào get sth. done; accomplish:他们能～的事情，我们也能办得到。Whatever they can accomplish, we can too.

办法 bànfǎ way; means; measure 她这个人～多。She is resourceful. 借钱不是个～。Borrowing money is no way out.

办公 bàngōng attend to business; handle official business work (in the office):～室自动化 office automation (OA)

办货 bànhuò make purchases for an organization or enterprise; purchase

办结 bànjié handle and wind up a legal case

办理 bànlǐ handle; manage; conduct; transact; deal with:～贷款手续 handle procedures for a loan

办实事 bànshíshì handle concrete affairs in a down-to-earth manner

办事 bànshì manage business; handle affairs:～公开 making public the work; open work system. ～事机构 administrative organ; working body; agency

办学 bànxué run schools; carry on education:～模式 type of education

办置 bànzhì buy (durables); purchase

办罪 bànzuì punish (by law)

半 bàn〈形〉① half; semi:～个月 half a month ② halfway; in the middle:～山腰 half way up a hill ③ very little; the least bit:一星～点 very little; a wee bit ④ about half; partly:～新的 half-new. ～开玩笑地说 say sth. half jokingly

半百 bànbǎi fifty (years of age):年近～ getting on for fifty; approaching fifty

半辈子 bànbèizi half a lifetime:她活了～了，还不知道这个吗? How can a person of her age be ignorant of such a thing?

半边天 bànbiāntiān ① half of the sky ② hold up the sky (① a metaphor for the tremendous role played by China's women in the socialist revolution and construction ② a general term for women of New China):妇女～ women shoulder half of heaven

半场 bànchǎng [体] half (of a game, contest)

半成品 bànchéngpǐn semifinished products (articles); semimanufactured goods

半大 bàndà medium-sized; biggish:～桌子 a table of medium size

半导体 bàndǎotǐ semiconductor:～集成电路 semiconductor integrated circuit

半点 bàndiǎn the least bit：没有～慌张 not the lease bit flurried

半吊子 bàndiàozi ① dabbler；smatterer ② tactless and impulsive person

半封建 bànfēngjiàn semifeudal

半公开 bàngōngkāi semiovert；more or less open

半工半读 bàngōng-bàndú part-work and part-study

半官方 bànguānfāng semiofficial：据～人士称 according to semiofficial sources

半机械化 bànjīxièhuà semimechanization

半价 bànjià half price：～出售 sell at half price

半截 bānjié half (a section)：话只说了～儿 finish only half of what one has to say

半斤八两 bànjīn-bāliǎng six of one and half a dozen of the other；not much to choose between the two；much of a muchness；the pot calling the kettle back；well matched

半径 bànjìng radius

半开化 bànkāihuà semicivilization

半劳动力 bànláodònglì auxiliary manpower；semiablebodied or part-time (farm) worker

半老徐娘 bànlǎoxúniáng an attractive middle-aged woman

半路出家 bànlùchūjiā become a monk or nun late in life—switch to a job one was not trained for；switch to a new profession (a new field of study late in life)

半票 bànpiào half-price ticket；half fare

半瓶醋 bànpíngcù one who only has a superficial knowledge of；one who has just a little learning；dabbler；smatterer

半旗 bànqí flag at half-mast；half-mast：下～ hang (fly) a flag at half-mast

半球 bànqiú hemisphere：东(西)～ the Eastern (Western) Hemisphere

半晌 bànshǎng〈方〉① half of the day：前～ morning；forenoon ② a long time；quite a while：我想了～才想起来。It took me a long time to recall it. 他们去了～，不见回。They've been away quite a while，and haven't returned yet.

半身不遂 bànshēn-bùsuí paralysis of one side of the body；[医]hemiplegia

半生 bànshēng half a lifetime：～戎马 led a soldier's life for many years

半生不熟 bànshēng-bùshú half cooked；underdone

半失业 bànshīyè semiemployed；partly employed；underemployed

半熟练工人 bànshúliàn gōngrén semiskilled worker

半数 bànshù half the number；half：～以上 more than half；majority

半死 bànsǐ half-dead：气得～ be half-dead from anger；nearly faint with rage

半天 bàntiān ① half of the day ②

a long time; quite a while:他～说不出话来。He remained tongue-tied for a long time.

半途 bàntú halfway; midway:～而废 give up sth. halfway; leave sth. half-done (unfinished); abandon halfway

半推半就 bàntuī-bànjiù yield with a show of reluctance; give way after making a show of declining:说了几句客气话,她也就～地把礼物收下了。She accepted the gift after making a polite show of declining.

半吞半吐 bàntūn-bàntǔ mince one's words

半脱产 bàntuōchǎn a partial sabbatical from work; partly released from productive labour; partly released from one's regular work

半微观世界 bànwēiguān shìjiè semimicroscopic world

半文盲 bànwénmáng semiliterate

半新不旧 bànxīn-bùjiù no longer new; showing signs of wear.

半心半意 bànxīn-bànyì half-hearted; not with all one's heart

半信半疑 bànxìn-bànyí half believe and half doubt; dubious; half convinced

半休 bànxiū half-day rest

半夜三更 bànyè-sāngēng in the depth of night; late at night

半月刊 bànyuèkān semimonthly (a periodical); fortnightly

半真半假 bànzhēn-bànjiǎ ① half-genuine, half-sham; partly true, partly false ② half in jest, half in earnest

半制品 bànzhìpǐn semimanufactured goods; semifinished products

半中间 bànzhōngjiān middle; halfway

半自动 bànzìdòng semiautomatic:～化 semiautomation

半自给经济 bànzìjǐ jīngjì substantially self-sufficient economy

扮 bàn〈动〉① play the part of; disguise oneself as; be dressed up as:他在戏里～一位渔民 In the opera he plays the part of a fisherman. ② put on an expression:～鬼脸 make faces; make grimaces

扮戏 bànxì ① (of actors) make up ②[旧][演戏] perform on stage; play a role in a play; play the part of

扮相 bànxiàng the appearance of an actor or actress in constume and makeup; the makeup of an actor or actress

扮演 bànyǎn act; play (perform) the part of; personate; have a role (in a play, etc.)

扮装 bànzhuāng (of an actor, etc.) put on makeup; disguise

伴 bàn ①〈动〉accompany; attend:～奏 accompany with musical instruments ②〈名〉companion; partner:舞～ dancing partner. 作～ keep sb. company

伴唱 bànchàng ① vocal accompaniment ② accompany (a singer)

伴读 bàndú reader-companion

伴君如伴虎 bànjūn rú bànhǔ To be in the king's company is tantamount to living with a tiger.; being close to the emperor is like being close to a tiger

伴郎 bànláng groomsman; best man

伴侣 bànlǚ companion; partner; mate:终身～ lifelong companion (mate)

伴娘 bànniáng bridesmaid

伴送 bànsòng see sb. off; accompany:他们～我到火车站。They saw me off at the railway station.

伴随 bànsuí accompany; follow; attend:～…而来 in the wake of …

伴舞 bànwǔ ① accompanying dancer ② (hired) dancing girl; escort

伴音 bànyīn ① accompanying sound; sound accompaniment; aural ②［戏剧、电影等的］background music

伴奏 bànzòu accompany (with musical instruments):钢琴～ piano accompaniment

拌 bàn〈动〉mix; stir:搅～ stir; mix; agitate

拌和 bànhé mix and stir; blend

拌面 bànmiàn noodles served with soy sauce, sesame butter, etc.

拌种 bànzhǒng dress seeds; seed dressing

拌嘴 bànzuǐ quarrel; bicker; wrangle:与人～ bicker with sb. (about sth.)

绊 bàn ①〈名〉fetters; trammels ②〈动〉cause to trip; be a hindrance; cause to stumble:～了一跤 trip over sth.

绊倒 bàndǎo trip over; stumble over

绊脚石 bànjiǎoshí stumbling block; obstacle

绊手绊脚 bànshǒu-bànjiǎo encumber the free movement of one's limbs (as heavy clothing, etc.); be in the way

瓣 bàn〈名〉① petal ② valve ③ piece; fragment:把梨切成四～ cut the pear in four

bāng

邦 bāng〈名〉state; nation; country:联～ federation; confedreation; union

邦本 bāngběn (the poeple are the) pillars of the state

邦国 bāngguó nation; state; country

邦交 bāngjiāo diplomatic relations; relations between two countries

邦联 bānglián confederation

梆 bāng〈名〉［打更用的］～子 watchman's clapper

梆子 bāngzi［打击乐器］wooden clappers with bars of unequal length

梆子腔 bāngziqiāng［中国戏曲声腔之一］clapper opera

帮 bāng〈动〉① help; assist;

aid:互～ help each other ② [指从事雇佣劳动] work:～短工 work as a casual labourer ③ 〈名〉clique; gang; band:四人～ the Gang of Four ④ 〈量〉[指人的群伙] a group of; a band of; a gang of:一～学生 a group of students

帮办 bāngbàn ① [旧] assist in managing:～军务 assist in handling military affairs ② deputy:副国务卿～ Deputy Undersecretary (of the U. S. Department of State)

帮厨 bāngchú help in the mess kitchen

帮倒忙 bāngdàománg be more of a hindrance than a help; do a disservice to

帮工 bānggōng hired man (hand); lend a hand with farmwork

帮会 bānghuì underworld gang; secret society

帮伙 bānghuǒ gang; clique; band

帮口 bāngkǒu clans; clique;～行会 clans and guild

帮困助耕 bāngkùn-zhùgēng help those with hardship to farm

帮忙 bāngmáng help; give (lend) a hand; do a favour; do a good turn:我要请他们～。I'll ask them to help. 她来找人～。She came for help.

帮派 bāngpài faction:～体系 factionalist setup

帮派体系 bāngpàitǐxì factional organization (setup)

帮腔 bāngqiāng ① [乐]vocal accompaniment in some traditional Chinese operas ② chime in with sb.; take up sb.'s refrain; echo sb.

帮手 bāngshou helper; assistant

帮闲 bāngxián ① hang on to and serve the rich and powerful by literary hack work, etc. ② literary hack

帮凶 bāngxiōng accomplice; accessary

帮助 bāngzhù assist; help; aid

浜 bāng 〈名〉creek; small river

bǎng

绑 bǎng 〈动〉bind; tie up; bind sb.'s hands behind him

绑带 bǎngdài ① bandage ② puttee

绑匪 bǎngfěi kidnapper

绑赴刑场 bǎngfù xíngchǎng be tied and taken to the place of execution; be taken to the execution ground

绑架 bǎngjià ① kidnap; carry away by force:～犯 kidnapper ② [农] staking

绑票 bǎngpiào kidnap (for ransom); kidnap sb. and hold him to ransom

绑扎 bǎngzā ① wrap up; bind up:～伤口 bind up (dress) a wound ② tie up; bundle up; pack:～行李 tie up baggage

榜 bǎng 〈名〉① list of names posted up:发～ announce (publish) the list of successful candidates ② notice; announcement

榜上有名 bǎngshàng yǒumíng one's name is on the list of successful candidates

榜首 bǎngshǒu the first place on a list of successful candidates; the first place in a contest, etc.: 位居～ rank first; come first

榜样 bǎngyàng model; pattern; example: 树立～ set an example (to or for sb.)

膀 bǎng 〈名〉① arm; upper arm ② wing (of a bird) ③ shoulder

膀臂 bǎngbì ① upper arm; arm ② capable assistant; reliable helper; right-hand man

膀阔腰圆 bǎngkuò-yāoyuán broad-shouldered and solidly-built; hefty; husky

膀子 bǎngzi ① upper arm; arm: 光着～ be stripped to the waist ② wing (of a bird): 鸡～ chicken wings

bàng

蚌 bàng 〈名〉 freshwater mussel; clam; mother-of-pearl: 鹬～相争。The crane and the mother-of-pearl fight to death.

棒 bàng ①〈名〉 stick; club; staff ②〈形〉strong; good; fine; excellent: 功课～ excellent in study

棒冰 bàngbīng ice-lolly; popsicle; ice-sucker; frozen sucker

棒槌 bàngchui wooden club (used to beat clothes in washing)

棒喝 bànghè a blow and shout to waken one from error: 当头～ direct sharp warning

棒球 bàngqiú baseball; ～场 baseball field

棒术 bàngshù cane fencing

棒子面 bàngzimiàn cornmeal; corn flour: ～粥 cornmeal porridge (mush)

傍 bàng ①〈介〉 near; beside; [时间] at; toward(s): ～晌 at noon 〈动〉② draw near; be close to ③ depend on: ～人门户 depend (be dependent) on sb. else

傍壁篱人 bàngbì-lírén rely (depend) on others for maintenance; dependent

傍大款 bàngdàkuǎn 〈方〉 A young man or woman who depends on (goes around or cohabits with) the nouveau riche

傍近 bàngjìn be close to; near: ～晌午 about noon

傍晚 bàngwǎn toward evening; at nightfall; at dusk

傍午 bàngwǔ about noon

谤 bàng 〈动〉slander; vilify; smear; defame

磅 bàng ①〈量〉pound [与数词连写时] lb. ②〈名〉scales: 放在～上 put it on the scales ③〈动〉weigh (in the scales)
另见 páng

磅秤 bàngchèng platform scale (balance)

镑 bàng 〈名〉 pound (a currency): 英～ pound sterling

bāo

包 bāo ①〈名〉bundle; parcel; packet;package: 邮～ postal parcel (packet) ②〈量〉[用于成包的东西] box; bale; pack, packet; sack:一～毛巾 a package of towels〈动〉③ pack up; wrap:～书皮 put a jacket (cover) on a book ④ undertake the whole thing ⑤ assure; guarantee ⑥ hire; charter:～一辆公共汽车 charter a bus

包办 bāobàn take everything on oneself; monopolize everything:～代替 take the affairs of other people into one's own hands

包庇 bāobì harbour; shield; hide up:～坏人 hide up an evildoer

包藏 bāocáng contain; harbour; conceal:～祸心 harbour evil intentions

包产到户 bāochǎn dàohù [农]fix farm output quotas for each household

包场 bāochǎng book a whole theatre or cinema; make a block booking

包抄 bāochāo outflank; envelop

包车 bāochē ① charter a bus, etc. ② [旧] a vehicle (esp. a rickshaw) hired for one's exclusive use

包饭 bāofàn ① get or supply meals at a fixed rate; board:在附近的饭馆里～ board at a nearby restaurant ② meals thus arranged

包袱 bāofu ① cloth-wrapper ② a bundle wrapped in cloth ③ millstone round one's neck; load; weight; burden:思想～ a load (weight) on one's mind

包工 bāogōng contract for a job; undertake to perform; work within a time limit and according to a specifications; work by contract

包工头 bāogōngtóu labour contractor

包购包销 bāogòu bāoxiāo exclusive right to purchase and sell

包管 bāoguǎn assure; guarantee: 这件活 5 天完成,～没问题。We'll finish this job in five days without fail. ～退换。Merchandise will be exchanged if found unsatisfactory.

包裹 bāoguǒ ① wrap up; bind up:用布把伤口～起来。Bandage up the wound. ② bundle; package; parcel: ～单 parcel form

包含 bāohán contain; include; imply; involve; embody: ～阴险用心 harbour the sinister of

包涵 bāohan excuse; forgive; bear with:我唱得不好,请多多～。Excuse (me for) my poor singing.

包户扶贫 bāohùfúpín responsibility to households and aid to the poor

包机 bāojī ① charter a plane ② a chartered plane

包括 bāokuò include; consist of; comprise; incorporate:房租每月 100 元,水电费～在内。The rent is 100 yuan a month, including water and electricity.

包揽 bāolǎn undertake the whole thing; take on everything

包罗 bāoluó include; cover; embrace:民间艺术～甚广。Folk art covers a wide range.

包罗万象 bāoluówànxiàng all-embracing; all-inclusive; panoramic; comprehensive:～的长篇小说 a panoramic novel

包容 bāoróng ① pardon; forgive ② contain; hold

包税 bāoshuì tax-farming

包台子 bāotáizi renting counters

包围 bāowéi surround; encircle:房子被松林～着。The houses are surrounded by a pine forest.

包厢 bāoxiāng boxes (stalls) in a theatre; stage box

包销 bāoxiāo have exclusive selling rights; be the sole agent for a production unit or a firm; exclusive sales; underwrite［用于有价证券］:～合同 exclusive sales contract

包修、包换、包赔 bāoxiū, bāohuàn, bāopéi three guartantees for repair, replacement or compensation of faulty products

包圆儿 bāoyuánr ① buy the whole lot:你少算一点的话,这些我～了。If you give me a reduction, I'll buy the whole lot. ② finish up (off):剩下的活儿我们～了。We'll finish off what's left of the work.

包月 bāoyuè ① make monthly payment ②［旧］hire (as a rickshaw) by the month:拉～ have a monthly job as a rickshaw boy

包扎 bāozā wrap up; bind up; pack:～伤口 bind up (dress) a wound

包装 bāozhuāng ① pack; packing; package; wrap up:设计～ design a package ② package:～歌手 package a singer

包租 bāozū ①［为了转租而租进］rent land or a house for subletting ②［在一段时期内专由某方面租用］charter:～合同 charter contract

剥 bāo〈动〉strip; shell; peel; skin

另见 bō

剥得精光 bāo dé jīngguāng strip bare; strip to the skin

剥去 bāoqù［衣服］strip; take off;［水果等的皮］peel; pare;［壳］husk; shell;［动物的皮］skin; flay:～画皮 rip off the mask

煲 bāo〈名〉① a kind of deep pot:电饭～ eletric rice cooker ② use this kind of pot for cooking

褒 bāo〈动〉praise; commend; extol; honour

褒贬 bāobiǎn ① pass judgement on; appraise; comment:人们对她～不一 People pass different judgements on her. ② bāobian cry down; speak ill of; criticize:背地里～人 speak ill of sb. behind his (her) back

褒奖 bāojiǎng commend and award;praise and houour
褒善贬恶 bāoshàn-biǎn'è glorify virtue and censure vice
褒义 bāoyì commendatory (complimentary) sense

báo

雹 báo 〈名〉hail
雹暴 báobào hailstorm
雹害 báohài damage by hail
雹灾 báozāi disaster caused by hail
薄 báo 〈形〉① flimsy; thin ② [感情冷淡] cold; indifferent; lacking in warmth:待他的情分不～ treat him quite well (generously) ③[味道] weak ④ [不肥沃] poor; barren
另见 bó;bò
薄板 báobǎn sheet metal; sheet:不锈钢～ stainless sheet steel
薄饼 báobǐng thin pancake
薄脆 báocuì thin and brittle biscuit; crisp fritter
薄地 báodì poor (barren) land

bǎo

饱 bǎo ①〈形〉full; plump ②〈副〉fully; to the full〈动〉③ having eaten one's fill; be full ④ satisfy:一～眼福 feast one's eyes on sth.; enjoy to the full watching (a show, scene, etc.)
饱餐 bǎocān eat to one's heart's content:～一顿 eat and drink one's fill
饱尝辛酸 bǎocháng-xīnsuān go (have been, pass) through the mill; put through the mill; taste to the full the bitterness of life
饱汉不知饿汉饥 bǎohàn bùzhī èhàn jī The well-fed don't know how the starving suffer.; One who is in comfortable circumstances doesn't know the bitterness of misfortune
饱和 bǎohé saturation:～的市场 saturated market
饱经沧桑 bǎojīng-cāngsāng have experienced many vicissitudes of life:他一生～。He has experienced the vicissitudes of life.
饱经风霜 bǎojīng-fēngshuāng have experienced great hardships; have gone through thick and thin; have weathered many storms; weather-beaten
饱满 bǎomǎn full; plump:颗粒～的小麦 plump-eared wheat. 精神～ full of vigour (vitality); energetic
饱暖 bǎonuǎn being well-fed and well-clad—easy circumstances
饱暖思淫欲 bǎonuǎn sī yínyù When one is fed and warmed, one's sexual desires will come up.; Luxury leads to sex; Material comforts lead to sexual desire.
饱食终日 bǎoshí-zhōngrì three square meals a day; loaf around all day long; be sated with food; eat one's fill all day long
饱受 bǎoshòu suffer enough

from; have one's fill of:～虐待 be subjected to every kind of maltreatment

饱私囊 bǎosīnáng line one's pocket; swell personal fortunes

饱眼福 bǎoyǎnfú feast one's eyes on sth.; enjoy to the full (watching a scene, show, etc.)

宝 bǎo ①〈名〉treasure; treasured object:国～ national treasure ②〈形〉precious; treasured:～珠 precious pearl ③〈敬〉[旧时用于称别人的家眷、铺子等]:～号 your shop

宝贝 bǎobèi ① treasure ② darling; deary; dearie ③[嘲弄语] a good-for-nothing; queer character:真是个～! What a good-for-nothing!; What a fellow!

宝刀不老 bǎodāo-bùlǎo A good sword remains always sharp (never gets dull).; old but still vigorous in mind and body; (you will find his) good sword sharp enough

宝贵 bǎoguì valuable; precious:～意见 valuable advice (suggestion)

宝卷 bǎojuàn precious book; precious scrolls

宝库 bǎokù treasure-house; treasury:知识～ gold mine of knowledge

宝石 bǎoshí precious stone; gem

宝物 bǎowù treasure

宝藏 bǎozàng hidden treasure; treasury; precious (mineral) deposits; mine; treasure-trove

宝座 bǎozuò throne; seat of power

保 bǎo〈动〉① protect; safeguard; defend:～乌纱帽 protect official post ② keep; preserve; maintain:～持劳动人民的本色 maintain the distinctive character of the working people ③ guarantee; ensure:～一方平安 ensure the safety of all those living under one's jurisdiction ④〈名〉guarantor:找～人 find a guarantor

保安 bǎo'ān ① ensure public security:～人员 security personnel ② ensure safety (for workers engaged in production):～措施 security measures. ～规程 safety regulations. ～装置 protective device

保安族 Bǎo'ānzú Bo'an (Pao'an) nationality (living in Gansu Province)

保本保值 bǎoběn bǎozhí (deposits) with principal and interest safeguarded against price increases

保膘 bǎobiāo keep domestic animals fat

保镖 bǎobiāo bodyguard

保不住 bǎobuzhù most likely; more likely than not; may well:这天儿～会下雪。Most likely it's going to snow.

保藏 bǎocáng keep in store; preserve:食品～ food preservation

保持 bǎochí keep; retain; maintain; preserve:～警惕 maintain vigilance against; keep constantly on the alert

保存 bǎocún preserve; conserve; keep:这批文物～得很完好。

These cultural relics are well preserved.

保单 bǎodān guarantee slip; guaranty; warranty

保底金 bǎodǐjīn *baodijin*, counter business leasing, a special term for a system of renting counters in state-owned stores, by which the renter guarantees his monthy business turnover from the counter, and on this basis of the sales amount the store that lets out the counter also receives a fixed proportion of income

保管 bǎoguǎn ① take care of:负责～工具 be responsible for the care of tools ② warehouseman; storeman; storekeeper ③ certainly; surely

保户 bǎohù the insured; policy holder

保护 bǎohù protect; defend; safeguard:～文物 protect cultural relics

保价信 bǎojiàxìn insured letter

保健 bǎojiàn health maintenance; health care (protection):～品 health food; protective foods. ～操 health (setting-up) exercises. ～箱 health valise; medical kit

保教 bǎojiào child care and education

保洁 bǎojié keep a public place clean; do sanitation work

保举 bǎojǔ recommend sb. for office with personal guarantee; guaranteed recommendation

保龄球 bǎolíngqiú ① tenpin bowling; tenpins; bowling ② bowling ball

保留 bǎoliú reserve; retain; keep (hold) back:～工资 retained salaries. ～名额 seats reserved for future nominations

保密 bǎomì maintain secrecy; keep sth. secret:这事绝对～。This must be kept absolutely secret.; This is strictly confidential.

保姆 bǎomǔ ① housemaid; housekeeper ② (children's) nurse

保全 bǎoquán save from damage; guard; protect; preserve; keep sth. intact:～面子 save one's face (honour); keep up appearances

保释 bǎoshì [法]release on bail; bail

保守 bǎoshǒu ① keep; guard ② conservative:～主义 conservatism

保税区 bǎoshuìqū bonded area; free zone

保送 bǎosòng recommend sb. for admission (to school, etc.) on merits

保外就医 bǎowài-jiùyī [法] remain out of custody and obtain medical treatment

保卫 bǎowèi defend; safeguard:～祖国 defend one's country. ～部门 public security bodies

保鲜 bǎoxiān keep vegetables, fruit, etc. fresh; preserve freshness:～纸 handi-wrap

保险 bǎoxiǎn ① insurance:～单 insurance policy. ～费 premium. ～公司 insurance company ②safe; secure:～成功 be sure to succeed. ～箱 safe; strong box

保养 bǎoyǎng ① take care of one's health ② preserve; maintain; keep in good repair; uptake:～工 maintenance worker. ～费 maintenance cost

保佑 bǎoyòu bless and protect:老天～ blessings from heaven

保幼人员 bǎoyòu rényuán daycare workers

保育 bǎoyù child care; child welfare:～员 child-care worker; nurse. ～院 nursery school

保育率 bǎoyùlǜ [畜] survival of grown animal

保障 bǎozhàng ensure; guarantee; safeguard:～人民言论自由 guarantee freedom of speech for the people

保证 bǎozhèng guarantee; warrant; ensure; pledge:～金 cash deposit; earnest money; security. ～有限公司 company limited by guarantee

保值 bǎozhí keep the value:～储蓄 value guaranteed deposit

保职停薪 bǎozhí tíngxīn retain the job but suspend the salary

保质保量 bǎozhì bǎoliàng guarantee both quality and quantity

保重 bǎozhòng take good care of oneself; look after oneself

保住 bǎozhù keep; retain; hold on to:那村子一定要～。That village must be held at all costs. ～不败的记录 keep a perfect record

堡 bǎo 〈名〉 fort; bulwark

堡垒 bǎolěi fort; fortress; bulwark; stronghold; blockhouse; citadel

bào

报 bào〈动〉① report; declare; announce; inform (of):～主管部门备案 shall be filed with the department in charge ② reply; reciprocate; respond:～之一笑 respond with a smile. ～答某人的好意 reciprocate sb.'s good wishes ③ repay; show gratitude to; recompense:～养育之恩 make oneself worthy of sb.'s care and upbringing ④ show vengeance to:～私仇 revenge for private grudge ⑤〈名〉 newspaper:光明日～ Guangming Daily

报案 bào'àn submit official report on case; report a case to the security authorities; register complaints at court

报表 bàobiǎo forms for reporting statistics, etc.; report forms

报酬 bàochou reward; remuneration; pay:不计～ not concerned about pay; irrespective of remuneration

报仇 bàochóu have (take) one's revenge (on sb. for sth.); avenge oneself (on sb. for sth.); wreak one's vengeance; breathe revenge (vengeance)

报答 bàodá repay; requite:我怎么也～不了您们的恩情。How

can I ever repay you for your kindness?

报单 bàodān taxation form; declaration form

报到 bàodào report (oneself) (to); report for duty; check in; register: 向大会～ register at the congress

报道 bàodào report; press release; coverage: 据～ It is reported (that …)

报恩 bào'ēn pay a debt of gratitude

报废 bàofèi ① report sth. as worthless ② discard as useless; reject; scrap

报复 bàofù retaliate; make reprisal(s); take vengeance on; revenge; avenge: ～关税 retaliatory duties (tariff)

报告 bàogào ① report; make known: ～上级机关 report to the superior organs in charge ② make a speech on; report; talk; lecture: ～书 written report. ～文学 reportage

报关 bàoguān declare sth. at customs; apply to the customs; declaration at the customs: 有东西要～吗? Anything to declare? ～单 bill of entry; customs declaration. ～行 agent for clearing customs; customs broker

报馆 bàoguǎn newspaper office

报国 bàoguó dedicate oneself to the service of one's country: 以身～ lay down one's life for one's country

报户口 bàohùkǒu apply for a residence permit: 给新生婴儿～ register the birth of a child

报价 bàojià quote; offer; [开价] quoted price: ～单 quotation of prices

报警 bàojǐng ① report (an incident) to the police: 报火警 report a fire ② give an alarm: 鸣钟～ sound the alarm bell

报考 bàokǎo apply for an (entrance) examination; sign up for examinations

报名 bàomíng apply for admission (to); enter one's name; sign up (for): ～入学 apply for admission to school

报幕 bàomù announce the items on a (theatrical) programme: ～员 announcer

报批 bàopī report (submit) sth. to the higher authorities for approval

报社 bàoshè general office of a newspaper; newspaper office

报审 bàoshěn report (submit) sth. to the higher authorities for examination

报失 bàoshī report the loss of sth. to the authorities concerned

报税 bàoshuì make a statement of dutiable goods; declare dutiable goods: ～单 duty declaration form; taxation form

报摊 bàotān news-stand; news stall

报销 bàoxiāo submit an expense account; apply for reimbursement; claim a refund; give a statement on one's expenses

(for trip on business)

报喜 bàoxǐ report good (happy) news:～不报忧 report only the good news and not the bad

报信 bàoxìn inform (of); notify: 通风～ tip off information

刨 bào ①〈动〉plane sth. down; plane ②〈名〉plane; planer; planing machine

另见 páo

刨冰 bàobīng water ice (powdered or in shavings)

刨床 bàochuáng planer; planing machine

刨刀 bàodāo ① planer tool ② plane iron

刨工 bàogōng ① planing ② planing machine operator; planer

抱 bào〈动〉① carry (hold) in one's arm(s); embrace; hug:～小孩儿 take a baby in one's arms ②[希望等] foster; nourish; harbour; entertain; cherish; [态度] assume ③ have one's first child or grandchild ④〈量〉armful:一～柴 an armful of firewood

抱病 bàobìng be ill; be in bad health:～工作 go on working in spite of ill health

抱不平 bàobùpíng be outraged (indignant) at an injustice (done to another person):打～ come to the defence of sb. against an injustice; take up the cudgels against the injustice done to sb.

抱残守缺 bàocán-shǒuquē cherish the outmoded and preserve the outworn to be conservative; retain what is old and outworn

抱粗腿 bàocūtuǐ be hanger-on of the rich and powerful; latch on to the rich and powerful

抱佛脚 bàofójiǎo clasp Buddha's feet — profess devotion only when in trouble; do nothing until the last minute

抱负 bàofù aspiration; ambition: 很有～ have high aspirations; cherish high ambitions

抱恨终天 bàohèn-zhōngtiān feel bitter regret to the end of one's days; have an aching void in one's heart

抱歉 bàoqiàn be sorry; feel apologetic; regret:叫你久等了,很～。Very sorry to have kept you waiting.

抱头鼠窜 bàotóu-shǔcuàn cover the head and scurry away like a rat to its hole; flee helter-skelter; run wildly like cornered rats

抱头痛哭 bàotóu-tòngkū weep in each other's arms; cry on each other's shoulders

抱养 bàoyǎng adopt (a child)

抱冤 bàoyuān feel wronged; nurse a grievance

抱怨 bàoyuàn complain (of); grumble (at); blame:她～他没本事。She complained of his inability.

豹 bào〈名〉leopard; panther

暴 bào〈形〉① sudden and violent; sharp:～风骤雨 mighty storm; storm ② cruel; harsh and tyrannical; brutal; savage: 凶～ fierce and brutal ③ irritable; short-tempered; hot-tempered:～脾气 hot temper; irascible temper ④〈副〉suddenly and fiercely:～食～饮 drink and eat too much at one meal 〈动〉⑤ bulge; stand out; stick out:青筋直～。The blue veins stand out (on one's temples). ⑥ expose; broadcast:～尸街头 expose corpse in the street (open)

暴病 bàobìng sudden attack of a serious illness:得～ be suddenly seized with a severe illness. ～而死 die of a sudden illness

暴跌 bàodiē sharp drop (in prices); slump

暴动 bàodòng insurrection; rebellion; riot:举行～ raise an insurrection; stage a riot

暴发 bàofā ① break out:山洪～。Torrents of water rushed down the mountain. ② suddenly become rich or important; get rich quick:～户 upstart; parvenu; nouveau riche

暴发户 bàofāhù upstart; parvenu; nouveau riche

暴风雨 bàofēngyǔ rainstorm; storm; tempest:遇上～ be caught in a storm

暴君 bàojūn tyrant; despot

暴力 bàolì violence; (brutal) force:～犯罪 violent crimes. ～机器 instruments of violence; violent machinery

暴利 bàolì fabulous (huge, exorbitant) profit:牟取～ seek exorbitant profits

暴露 bàolù expose; bring to light; bring … into the open; make … public; disclose; lay bare:～文学 literature of exposure; exposé literature. ～思想 expose thoughts. ～真面目 show oneself in one's true colours; reveal one's true features

暴露无遗 bàolù-wúyí be thoroughly exposed

暴乱 bàoluàn riot; rebellion; revolt:平定反革命～ suppress (put down, quell) a counterrevolutionary rebellion

暴虐 bàonüè tyrannical; barbarous; despotic; cruel; brutal

暴跳如雷 bàotiào-rúléi fly into a rage; become infuriated; stamp with rage; have a fit; go (fly) into a tantrum

暴徒 bàotú ruffian; thug

暴行 bàoxíng savage act; outrage; atrocity

暴躁 bàozào irritable; irascible; short-(hot-)tempered; unruly

暴涨 bàozhàng [物价] rise sharply (suddenly); soar; [河水] be in spate

暴政 bàozhèng tyranny; despotic rule

暴卒 bàozú die a sudden death; die suddenly

曝 bào

另见 pù

曝光 bàoguāng ① [照相] exposure:多次～ multiple exposure. ～表 exposure meter ② expose; make (sth. bad) public

爆 bào〈动〉burst; blast; explode:火～的市场 exploding market

爆出冷门 bàochū-lěngmén produce an unexpected winner (a dark horse); come the sleeper

爆发 bàofā burst out; erupt; explode:他们的劳动热情～了起来。Their labour enthusiasm blossomed forth.

爆满 bàomǎn ① be filled to capacity② have a full house:演出场场～ The show had a full house of every performance

爆棚 bàopéng (of a cinema, theatre, etc.) have a full house; house full

爆炸 bàozhà blow up; explode; detonate; blast:～性消息 explosive news; shocking news

爆竹 bàozhú firecracker; cracker; squib:～迎新 Firecrackers are being let off to welcome in the New Year.

bēi

杯 bēi〈名〉cup; [玻璃的] glass; [有柄的] mug; [高脚的] goblet

杯弓蛇影 bēigōng-shéyǐng mistaking the reflection of a bow in a cup for a snake — extremely suspicious; self-created suspiction; imaginary fears

杯盘狼藉 bēipán-lángjí Cups and trays are scattered around in disorder.; Soiled dishes (and cups) were piled up at random.

杯赛 bēisài cup (a competition):去年他们参加了那次～。They played in the cup last year.

杯水车薪 bēishuǐ-chēxīn trying to put out a burning cartload of faggots with a cup of water—an utterly inadequate measure; make an utterly inadequate effort to save a grave situation; a drop in the bucket; make a useless attempt

杯中物 bēizhōngwù the contents of the cup—wine

卑 bēi〈形〉① low; mean; vile ② modest; humble

卑鄙 bēibì mean; vile; base; despicable:～无耻 mean and vulgar

卑鄙龌龊 bēibǐ-wòchuò sordid; foul; base; mean

卑躬屈膝 bēigōng-qūxī be servile (to); be submissive; cringe (to); lick sb.'s shoes (boots); make a great show of obedience and courtesy

卑劣 bēiliè mean; base; sordid; despicable

卑视 bēishì look down upon; despise; scorn

卑微 bēiwēi petty and low

卑以自牧 bēiyǐ-zìmù keep modest so as to cultivate one's character

卑职 bēizhí (used by subordinate officials in addressing superiors) your humble subordinate; I

背 bēi〈动〉① carry on the back:～一捆草 carry a bundle

of straw on the back ② bear; shoulder:～得起这样的责任 shoulder such a responsibility
另见 bèi

背包 bēibāo ① knapsack; rucksack; infantry (field) pack; backpack ② [军]blanket roll

背包袱 bēi bāofu carry a bundle on one's back, a metaphor for an ideological burden that affects one's work, study and progress

背带 bēidài ① braces; suspenders ② sling (for a rifle); straps (for a knapsack)

背负 bēifù bear; carry on the back; have on one's shoulder:～着人民的希望 with people's expectations always on one's mind

背黑锅 bēi hēiguō bear a black pot, a metaphor for suffering over the faults of others of being unjustly wronged; take the blame for others

背篓 bēilǒu a basket carried on the back:～商店 back-basket store; packbasket-shop

背债 bēizhài be in debt; be saddled with debts:背了一屁股债 be heavily in debt; be up to one's eyes in debt

悲 bēi 〈形〉① sorrowful; sad; melancholy ② compassionate ③〈动〉grieve; mourn; lament ④〈名〉grief; sorrow; feeling of sadness

悲哀 bēi'āi grieved; sorrowful

悲惨 bēicǎn miserable; wretched; tragic:～的局势 tragic situation

悲楚 bēichǔ grief; sorrow

悲愤 bēifèn grief and indignation:～填膺 be filled with grief and indignation

悲歌 bēigē ① sad melody; stirring strains ② [乐] elegy; dirge; threnody ③ sing with solemn fervour

悲观 bēiguān pessimistic:～心理 pessimistic frame of mind. ～厌世 pessimism and world weariness

悲欢离合 bēihuān-líhé grief at separation and joy in union; suffer and rejoice, separate and meet again; sorrows and joys of human life, separations and encounters

悲剧 bēijù tragedy

悲凉 bēiliáng sad and dreary; forlorn; desolate

悲鸣 bēimíng utter sad calls; lament

悲切 bēiqiè mournful; grieved

悲伤 bēishāng sad; grieved; sorrowful

悲酸 bēisuān grieved; sad; bitter

悲天悯人 bēitiān-mǐnrén bemoan the state of the universe and pity the people; lament the state of the universe and pity the fate of mankind

悲痛 bēitòng grievous; woeful; sorrowful:化～为力量 turn grief into strength. 令人～的 sad; sorrowful; grievous

悲喜交集 bēixǐ-jiāojí with mingled feelings of joy and sorrow; feel grief and joy intermingled

悲喜剧 bēixǐjù tragicomedy

悲壮 bēizhuàng tragic and touching(moving); solemn and stirring; stirring song

碑 bēi 〈名〉 monumental stone; (stone) tablet; stele

碑记 bēijì a record of events inscribed on a tablet

碑碣 bēijié an upright stone tablet; stele

碑林 bēilín [汉至近代] Forest of Steles

碑铭 bēimíng an inscription on a tablet

碑帖 bēitiè ① rubbing from a stone inscription ② model for calligraphy made from rubbings

碑文 bēiwén inscription (on a tablet); stele inscription

běi

北 běi 〈名,形〉 north

北半球 běibànqiú the Northern Hemisphere

北冰洋 Běibīngyáng the Arctic (Ocean)

北大荒 běidàhuāng the Great Northern Wilderness (in northeast China)

北大西洋公约组织 Běidàxīyáng Gōngyuē Zǔzhī the North Atlantic Treaty Organization (NATO)

北伐战争 běifá zhànzhēng (1926—1927) the Northern Expedition; the Northern Expeditionary War

北方 běifāng ① north ② the northern part of the country, esp. the area north of the Huanghe River; the North: ～话 northern dialect

北风 běifēng north wind

北极 běijí ① the North Pole; the Arctic Pole ② the north magnetic pole

北京人 Běijīngrén [考] Peking Man (Sinanthropus Pekinensis)

北美洲 Běiměizhōu North America

北南对话 běi-nán duìhuà North-South dialogue

北欧 Běi'ōu Northern Europe (including Denmark, Norway, Sweden, Finland and Iceland)

北纬 běiwěi north (northern) latitude

北温带 běiwēndài the north temperate zone

bèi

贝 bèi 〈名〉 ① shellfish ② cowrie ③ [姓氏] (Bèi) a surname

贝雕 bèidiāo shell carving: ～画 shell picture; shell mosaic

贝壳 bèiké shell (of shellfish)

备 bèi 〈动〉 ① have; be equipped with: 德才兼～ have both ability with political integrity ② be ready for; prepare: ～有现货 in stock ③ provide (prepare) against; take precautions against ④ 〈名〉 equipment ⑤ 〈副〉 fully; in every possible way

备案 bèi'àn be filed with; put on

file (record); for the record; keep on record
备不住 bèibuzhù 〈方〉 perhaps; possibly:～他们一会儿来。Perhaps they'll come in a little while.
备查 bèichá (keep) for reference; for future reference
备件 bèijiàn spare parts
备考 bèikǎo note for reference
备课 bèikè (of a teacher) prepare lessons
备料 bèiliào ① get the materials ready ② prepare feed (for livestock)
备忘录 bèiwànglù aide-mémoire; memo; memorandum
备用 bèiyòng reserve; alternate; spare; standby:～款项 reserve funds. ～设备 reserve equipment; spare equipment; standby equipment; standby facility
备注 bèizhù remarks:～栏 remarks column

背 bèi〈名〉① the back of the body ② back side of an object 〈动〉③ with the back facing [towards]; turn away ④ abandon, leave ⑤ recite (from memory); earn by heart:～课文 recite the text ⑥ break; violate; betray:～盟弃信 violate a treaty
另见 bēi
背城借一 bèichéng-jièyī a fight with the back to the city — a death struggle; fight to the last ditch
背道而驰 bèidào'érchí run counter to; act in direct contravention to; go (diametrically) against
背地里 bèidìli behind sb.'s back; privately; on the sly:她当着面恭维你,～净使坏。She flatters you to your face while playing dirty tricks behind your back.
背对背信用证 bèiduìbèi xìnyòng-zhèng back-to-back letter of credit
背风 bèifēng out of the wind; on the lee side; leeward
背光 bèiguāng be in a poor light; do sth. with one's back to the light; stand in one's own light
背后 bèihòu ① behind; at the back; in the rear:门～ behind the door ② behind sb.'s back:～捣鬼 plot (scheme) behind the scenes; play underhand tricks
背景 bèijǐng background; backdrop:历史～ historical background (setting) 这事肯定有～。Someone must be behind this.
背井离乡 bèijǐng-líxiāng leave one's native place (esp. against one's will); be away from home
背靠背 bèikàobèi ① back to back:～坐着 sit back to back ② criticize or expose sb. without his knowledge
背离 bèilí depart from; deviate from:价格～价值。Prices differ from value.
背面 bèimiàn the back; the reverse side; the wrong side:信封的～ the back of an envelope
背叛 bèipàn betray; forsake

背弃 bèiqì cast aside; desert; renounce; betray; violate; go back on

背书 bèishū ① recite a lesson; repeat a lesson ② [支票上的] endorsement (on a check); endorse

背水一战 bèishuǐ-yīzhàn fight with one's back to the river—fight to win or die

背诵 bèisòng recite; repeat from memory

背心 bèixīn a sleeveless garment: 毛～ sleeveless woollen sweater

背信弃义 bèixìn-qìyì be perfidious; be faithless; treachery; act in bad faith; be guilt of perfidy

背影 bèiyǐng a view of sb.'s back; a figure viewed from behind: 凝望着她逐渐消失的～ gazing at her receding figure

背约 bèiyuē break (violate) an agreement; fail to keep one's promise; go back on one's word

倍 bèi ①〈形〉twice as much; double: 信心～增 with redoubled confidence ②〈名〉times: 六～ six times

倍儿 bèir〈方〉awfully; terribly: ～棒。It's awfully good. or Great!; ～新 brandnew; up-to-the-minute

倍加 bèijiā double; extra; duplex; extraordinary: ～爱护 take extra care of; redouble one's loving care of

倍数 bèishù multiple

倍数效应 bèishù xiàoyīng [经] multiplier effect

倍增 bèizēng double; redouble; multiplication: 产量～。The output has doubled.

悖 bèi〈书〉①〈动〉go against; go counter to; contrary to: ～情 against human nature ②〈形〉erroneous; perverse; offensive

悖理 bèilǐ irrational; contrary to reason

悖论 bèilùn paradox; dilemma

悖谬 bèimiù absurd; preposterous

悖逆 bèinì disloyal; treasonable; rebellious

被 bèi ①〈名〉quilt ②〈助〉[用在动词前构成被动词组]～骗 be deceived ③〈介〉[用在句子中表示主语是动作的承受者]帽子～风刮掉了。The cap was blown off.

被保险人 bèibǎoxiǎnrén the insured; insurant; the assured

被保险物 bèibǎoxiǎnwù subject of insurance

被袋 bèidài bedding bag

被单 bèidān (bed) sheet: ～布 sheeting

被动 bèidòng passive; unactive: 陷于～ be thrown into passivity; find oneself in a most unenviable position

被服 bèifú bedding and clothing (esp. for army use): ～厂 clothing factory

被俘 bèifú be captured; be taken prisoner

被告 bèigào defendant; [刑事的] the accused: ～席 [法庭的] dock

被害人 bèihàirén the victim; the

injured party
被里 bèilǐ the underneath side of a quilt
被面 bèimiàn the facing of a quilt：绣花～ an embroidered quilt cover
被迫 bèipò be compelled；be forced；be under duress (compulsion)
被褥 bèirù bedding；bedclothes
被上诉人 bèishàngsùrén appellee
被套 bèitào ① bedding bag ② (bag-shaped) quilt cover；slipcover for a quilt ③ cotton wadding for a quilt
被通缉犯 bèitōngjífàn wanted criminal
被选举权 bèixuǎnjǔquán the right to stand for election；the right to be elected
被选举人 bèixuǎnjǔrén the person to be elected；candidate of an election
被"宰" bèizǎi［购物］be ripped-off；be done for
被罩 bèizhào (bag-shaped) quilt cover；slipcover for a quilt
辈 bèi〈名〉① generation in family：晚～ the younger generation ② life；lifetime：一～子 for life
辈出 bèichū emerge (come forth) in large numbers；appear，one after another：人才～ people of talent emerging in large numbers；man of talents come out in succession
辈分 bèifen order of seniority in the family or clan；position in the family hierarchy：她的～比我大。She ranks as my senior in the clan.
辈数儿 bèishùr order of seniority in the family or clan；position in the family hierarchy：我岁数小，～大。I am young in years but ranks high in family seniority.
惫 bèi〈形〉exhausted；fatigued
惫乏 bèifá tired；weary
惫懒 bèilǎn tired out；exhausted
惫色 bèisè tired look：面带～ look tired

bēn

奔 bēn〈动〉① run quickly；gallop：狂～ run wildly ② rush about；rush to；hurry：～来～去 rushing about ③ flee；run away：～窜 flee about
另见 **bèn**
奔波 bēnbō rush about；be busy running about：两地～ shuttle back and forth between two places
奔驰 bēnchí move along quickly；speed；［马等］gallop
奔放 bēnfàng bold (expressive) and unstrained；untrammelled；licence［文艺］：～的感情 unrestrained feeling. ～不羁的野马 an unbridled steed
奔赴 bēnfù hurry to (a place)；rush to
奔流 bēnliú ① flow swiftly；pour out ② swift torrent；racing current
奔忙 bēnmáng be busy rushing

about; bustle about:农民们一天到晚～着。Farmers are busy working day and night.

奔命 bēnmìng rush about on errands; be kept on the run

奔丧 bēnsāng hasten home for the funeral of a parent or grandparent; hasten home unpon the death of one's parent

奔逃 bēntáo flee; run away; [动物等] scamper away

奔腾 bēnténg ① gallop:犹如万马～ like ten thousand horses galloping ahead ② surge forward; roll on in waves:河流～而过。The river rushes pass.

奔泻 bēnxiè (of torrents) rush down; pour down

奔走 bēnzǒu run; be busy running about:～相告 run about to spread the news; rush about telling the news (message). ～呼号 go around campaigning for a cause

běn

本 běn〈名〉① root or stem of plants:草～ grass family ② origin; basis; foundation:胜利之～ the foundation of victory ③ capital; principal:～利 pincipal and interest ④ copy:剧～ script ⑤〈形〉original; one's own; native:～来面目 in one's true colours. ～厂产品 the product of our factory ⑥〈量〉book; volume:两～参考书 two books of reference ⑦〈副〉originally:～属于 originally belong to ⑧〈动〉follow; base on; according to:～着这一原则 base on the principle ⑨〈代〉this, current, present:～月 this month

本部 běnbù headquarter:校～ main campus

本埠 běnbù this town or city (where one is)

本地 běndì this locality:～风光 local colour. ～货 local (native) goods

本分 běnfèn one's duty; bounden duty; one's part; one's role:尽～ do one's duty

本国 běnguó one's own country:～资源 national resources:～语 native language; mother tongue

本行 běnháng in one's line (occupation, profession):他的～是学医。His line is medicine.

本籍 běnjí one's original domicile; one's permanent home address

本届 běnjiè current; this year's:～毕业生 this year's graduates

本金 běnjīn ① [存款等] principal ② [资本] capital

本科 běnkē regular college course; undergraduate course:～学生 undergraduate

本来 běnlái original:～面目 one's true features (colours). 就～的意义 in the proper sense

本利 běnlì principal and interest

本领 běnlǐng skill; ability; capability

本命年 běnmìngnián one's year of birth considered in relation to the Twelve Terrestrial Branches

本末 běnmò ① the whole course of an event; ins and outs ② essential and non-essential:～倒置 put the cart before the horse; reverse (confuse) cause and effect; turn sth. upside down

本能 běnnéng instinct:出于～ by instinct

本年度 běnniándù this year; the current year:～计划 this year's plan. ～国家预算 the national budget for this fiscal year

本票 běnpiào cashier's cheque (check); promissory note

本钱 běnqián ① capital ② what is capitalized on; sth. used to one's own advantage

本色 běnsè ① true (inherent) qualities; distinctive character: 工人阶级的～ the true qualities of the working class ② běnshǎi natural colour

本事 běnshi ① ability; talent; skill ② [故事情节] original story; source material

本土 běntǔ ① one's native country (land) ② metropolitan territory

本位 běnwèi standard:～币 standard money

本文 běnwén ① this text, article, etc. ② the original text; the original

本息 běnxī principal (capital) and interest

本小利微 běnxiǎo-lìwēi small capital and little gian—a small business; have tiny funds and small earnings; earn profits with small capital

本性 běnxìng nature; natural disposition:～难移。The leopard can't change his spots

本义 běnyì original meaning; literal sense

本意 běnyì original idea; real intention

本着 běnzhe according to; in line with; in conformity with:～政策办事 act according to the policy

本职 běnzhí one's own job (work); one's duty:～业务 one's own field of endeavour

本质 běnzhì essence; nature; intrinsic quality; innate character

本子 běnzi ① book; notebook:改～ go over students' written exercises; correct papers ② edition:这两个～都是明本。Both of these are Ming Dynasty block-printed editions.

本族语 běnzúyǔ native language; mother tongue

苯 běn [化] benzol; benzene

苯胺 běn'àn aniline

bèn

奔 bèn ①〈动〉go ahead; go straight towards:～50岁了 be getting on fifty ②〈介〉towards ～东走去 walk towards east
另见 bēn

奔命 bènmìng be in a desperate hurry

奔头儿 bèntóur bright prospect;

sth. to strive for：大有～ have a bright prospect

笨 bèn〈形〉① dull；stupid；foolish：愚～ stupid ② clumsy；unskilful；awkard：嘴～ clumsy of speech

笨蛋 bèndàn fool；idiot

笨口拙舌 bènkǒu-zhuōshé awkward in speech；slow of speech；inarticulate

笨鸟先飞 bènniǎo-xiānfēi Clumsy birds have to start flying early —the slow need to start early.；A slow sparrow should make an early start.

笨手笨脚 bènshǒu-bènjiǎo clumsy；heavy-handed：他做事～。His fingers are all thumbs.

笨头笨脑 bèntóu-bènnǎo muddleheaded；with a wooden head

笨重 bènzhòng heavy；cumbersome；unwieldy：～的家具 heavy (cumbersome) furniture

笨拙 bènzhuō clumsy；stupid；awkward；slow-witted：动作～ awkward (clumsy) in movement

bēng

崩 bēng〈动〉① collapse ②［帝王］die；pass away：驾～（of emperor）die

崩解 bēngjiě disintegrate；collapse；crumble

崩溃 bēngkuì collapse；breakdown；crash；crumble；fall apart；disintegrate：精神～ a nervous breakdown

崩裂 bēngliè burst (break) apart；crack

崩龙族 Bēnglóngzú the Benglong (Penglung) nationality (living in Yunnan Province)

崩塌 bēngtā collapse；crumble

崩陷 bēngxiàn fall in；cave in

绷 bēng〈动〉① stretch (draw) tight：把绳子～直 stretch the rope straight ② tighten：紧紧～在身上 tighten the body ③ spring；bounce：～回 spring back

绷带 bēngdài bandage

绷子 bēngzi embroidery frame；tambour；hoop

béng

甭 béng〈方〉needn't；don't；do not have to：～着急 don't hurry

běng

绷 běng〈口〉〈动〉① show a long face：～着脸 pull a grim (long) face；look displeased ② strain oneself；stifle temper：～住劲 strain one's muscle

另见 bēng

bèng

泵 bèng〈名〉pump：高扬程～ high lift pump

泵房 bèngfáng pump house

迸 bèng ①〈动〉burst forth；

burst out; gush; spurt; spout: ～起浪花 spray spindrift

迸发 bèngfā burst forth; burst out 房间里～出一阵笑声。There was an outburst of laughter in the room.

迸裂 bèngliè burst; burst open; split

迸流 bèngliú gush; pour; spurt

蹦 bèng〈动〉skip; leap; hop; bounce; jump: 欢～乱跳 dancing and skipping with joy

蹦蹦跳跳 bèngbèng-tiàotiào bouncing and vivacious: 孩子们～地进了电影院。The children bounced into the cinema.

bī

逼 bī〈动〉① force; compel; drive; threaten: ～于无奈 be compelled against one's will ② extort; press for; exert pressure for: ～债 press for payment of debts (loans) ③ press on towards; press up to; drive near: 兵～城下。The troops drove near the outskirts of the town. ④〈形〉close: ～邻 very close neighbour

逼供信 bī-gòng-xìn obtain confessions by compulsion and give them credence; force a confession and give credence to it

逼和 bīhé (in chess, etc.) force a draw; end in a draw

逼婚 bīhūn force into marriage

逼近 bījìn press on towards; close in on; approach; draw near: ～敌主力 close in on the main force of the enemy

逼人 bīrén pressing; threatening: ～太甚 press (push) people too hard

逼上梁山 bīshàng-liángshān be driven to join the Liangshan Mountain rebels; driven to drastic alternatives; driven to revolt; be forced to do something desperate

逼视 bīshì look at from close-up; watch intently

逼问 bīwèn ① force sb. to answer ② question closely

逼债 bīzhài press for payment of debts; dun

逼真 bīzhēn true to life (nature); lifelike

bí

鼻 bí〈名〉nose: ～子底下的事 things under one's nose

鼻尖 bíjiān tip of the nose

鼻孔 bíkǒng nostril

鼻青脸肿 bíqīng-liǎnzhǒng a bloody nose and a swollen face; badly battered: 被打得～ have one's face bashed in; be beaten black and blue

鼻涕 bíti nasal mucus; snivel: 流～ have a running nose

鼻形指数 bíxíng-zhǐshù nasal index

鼻烟 bíyān snuff: ～盒 snuffbox. ～壶 snuff bottle

鼻炎 bíyán rhinitis

鼻音 bíyīn nasal sound: 说话带～ speak with a twang

鼻子 bízi nose:高～ high-bridged nose;high nose

鼻祖 bízǔ father; founder; originator; the earliest ancestor

bǐ

匕 bǐ〈名〉an ancient type of spoon

匕首 bǐshǒu dagger

比 bǐ〈动〉① compare, match; compete; contrast; emulate:～干劲 compete with each other in drive ② draw an analogy; compare to; liken to:可～作 may be compared to ③ gesticulate; gesture ④ copy; model after ⑤〈名〉ratio; proportion:成正～ direct ratio (proportion)〈介〉⑥ [用来比较性质、状态和程度的差别]than:她比我强。She is better than I. ⑦ [双方得分的对比] to (in a score):以二～一获胜 win the match by a score of two to one ⑧〈形〉next to

比方 bǐfang ① analogy; instance:打～ draw an analogy ② suppose

比分 bǐfēn [体] score:场上～是四比二。The score is 4 to 2.

比附 bǐfù make a farfetched comparison

比葫芦画瓢 bǐ húlù huà piáo draw a ladle by the gour; copy mechanically

比画 bǐhua gesture; gesticulate:她～着讲。She made herself understood with the help of gestures.

比价 bǐjià price parity; price ratio; rate of exchange; price relations:～剪刀差 pirce parity scissors

比肩接踵 bǐjiān-jiēzhǒng overcrowed with people; follow closely one after another; one follows on the heels of another

比较 bǐjiào ① compare (with); contrast; parallel (with); comparison ② fairly comparatively; relatively:～完整的工业体系 fairly comprehensive industrial system. 比较文学 comparative literature

比例 bǐlì ① proportion; ratio:～包干 [金]policy of "proportionate sharing of the revenue" (the sharing of the revenue of the locality with the central authorities in proportions determined by the ratio of the locality's expenditure to its revenue) ② scale:按～绘制 be drawn to scale

比量 bǐliang ① take rough measurements (with the hand, a stick, string, etc.) ② make gestures

比邻 bǐlín ① neighbour; next-door neighbour ② near; next to:跟车站～的那家百货商场 the department store next to the railway station

比率 bǐlǜ ratio; rate

比美 bǐměi compare favourably with:rival

比拟 bǐnǐ compare (to); parallel; draw a parallel; liken (to):无

可～的 incomparable; beyond compare; matchless

比配 bǐpèi be equally matched; match well

比如 bǐrú for example; for instance; such as

比赛 bǐsài match; competition: 足球～ football match. 自行车～ bicycle race

比上不足,比下有余 bǐ shàng bùzú, bǐ xià yǒuyú not up to those above, but above those below—middling; passable; tolerable

比试 bǐshi ① have a competition: 不信咱俩～～。If you don't believe me, let's have a competition and see. ② make gestures: 两个演员拿长枪一～,就开始对打起来。With a flourish of their spears, the two performers started sparring with each other.

比手画脚 bǐshǒu-huàjiǎo (make oneself understood) with the help of gestures

比武 bǐwǔ demonstration of and competition in military skills

比物此志 bǐwùcǐzhì place one's intentions on things

比翼双飞 bǐyì-shuāngfēi fly wing to wing—happy couple; flying side by side; pair off wing to wing

比喻 bǐyù ① compare (one thing to another) ② analogy; metaphor

比照 bǐzhào ① according to; in the light of ② contrast

比值 bǐzhí specific value; ratio

比重 bǐzhòng ① proportion; percentage ② [物] specific gravity

彼

彼 bǐ〈代〉① that; the other: 此起～伏 as one falls, another rises ② he; she; the other party

彼岸 bǐ'àn ① the other shore ② [佛]Faramita; the Beyond; the other world

彼岸性 bǐ'ànxìng [哲] other-sidedness; Jenseitigkeit

彼此 bǐcǐ each other; one another; both parties: ～适应 mutual adjustment. ～世界 the hereafter (Jenseits)

彼一时,此一时 bǐyīshí, cǐyīshí That was one situation and this is another — times have changed.; Circumstances alter cases.; Different times call for different actions.

笔

笔 bǐ ①〈名〉pen; writing brush ② technique of writing; calligraphy or drawing: 文～ style of writing. ～情墨趣 flavour of the brush and ink ③〈量、名〉sum (of money): 一～款子 a sum of money. 能画几～ can draw pictures ④〈动〉write: 代～ write down for sb.

笔触 bǐchù brush stroke in Chinese painting and calligraphy; brushwork; touch; style of drawing or writing: ～轻巧。The touch is light.

笔答 bǐdá answer questions in writing

笔底下 bǐdǐxia ability to write: ～来得快 write with ease

(facility)

笔调 bǐdiào tone; style: ～优美的小说 elegant novel

笔端 bǐduān tip of the brush—style of writing or painting

笔法 bǐfǎ ① technique of writing, calligraphy or drawing; style of writing: ～雄浑 bold handwriting ② pencraft

笔锋 bǐfēng the tip of a writing brush; vigour of style in writing; sharpness of style: ～指处 at the point of one's pen

笔供 bǐgòng written confession

笔画 bǐhuà strokes of a Chinese character

笔会 bǐhuì ① correspondence forum; in the form of a discussion by correspondence ② Pen Association

笔记 bǐjì ① take down (in writing) ② notes: 记～ take notes ③ pen jottings (a type of literature consisting mainly of short sketches)

笔迹 bǐjì a person's handwriting; hand: ～潦草难以辨认 an illegible scribble

笔尖 bǐjiān ① nib; pen point ② the tip of a writing brush or pencil

笔力 bǐlì vigour of strokes in calligraphy or drawing; vigour of style in literary composition

笔录 bǐlù ① notes; record; transcript ② write down; take down

笔帽 bǐmào the cap of a pen, pencil or writing brush

笔名 bǐmíng pen name; pseudonym

笔墨 bǐmò pen and ink; words; writing: 他们激动的心情难以用～来形容。Words can hardly describe how excited they were.

笔墨官司 bǐmò-guānsi paper arguments; paper polemics; written polemics

笔试 bǐshì written examination; pen-and-paper test

笔算 bǐsuàn ① do a sum in writing ② written calculation

笔谈 bǐtán written discussion about; discussions in written form

笔套 bǐtào ① the cap of a pen, pencil or writing brush ② the sheath of a pen (made of cloth, silk or thread)

笔体学 bǐtǐxué graphology

笔筒 bǐtǒng pen container; brush pot

笔误 bǐwù slip of the pen; clerical error; graphical error

笔下留情 bǐxià-liúqíng be merciful in writing; spare sb. in making critical attacks

笔形 bǐxíng the form of a stroke or a combination of strokes (in Chinese characters)

笔译 bǐyì written translation

笔友 bǐyǒu pen friend; pen pal

笔战 bǐzhàn paper warfare; written polemics

笔直 bǐzhí perfectly straight; straight as a ramrod; bolt upright: 身子挺得～ stand straight as a ramrod; draw oneself up to one's full height

鄙 bǐ ①〈形〉low; mean; vulgar; base; despicable ②〈动〉despise: 可～ despicable; disdain; look down

鄙薄 bǐbó despise; scorn; belittle

鄙夫 bǐfū ① a mean person; an ignorant person ② your humble servant; I

鄙见 bǐjiàn my humble opinion; my idea

鄙贱 bǐjiàn ① lowly; humble ② despise; disdain

鄙吝 bǐlìn stingy; miserly; parsimonious; mean

鄙陋 bǐlòu shallow; superficial: ～无知 shallow and ignorant; illiterate; superficial and ill-formed

鄙弃 bǐqì disdain; loathe

鄙人 bǐrén your humble servant; I

鄙视 bǐshì despise; look down upon; disdain; hold in contempt; take a scorn attitude towards

鄙俗 bǐsú vulgar; philistine

鄙意 bǐyì my humble opinion

bì

币 bì〈名〉money; currency; [硬币] coin

币值 bìzhí currency value: ～坚挺。Currency value is firm.

币制 bìzhì currency (monetary) system: ～改革 currency reform; monetary reform

必 bì ①〈副〉certainly; surely; necessarily: 战则～胜 surely win the battle if fighting ②〈动〉have to; be bound to; must: ～有缘故 must have some reasons

必备 bìbèi essential; prerequisite: ～知识 prerequisite knowledge

必不可少 bìbùkěshǎo absolutely necessary; indispensable; essential

必得 bìděi must; have to: 我～去一趟。I simply must go.

必定 bìdìng ① must; have to: 她～知道。She must have known it. ② be bound to; be sure to: 明天我～把图纸送到。I'll be sure to send you the blueprints tomorrow.

必然 bìrán inevitable; necessary: ～王国 realm of necessity. ～的认识 recognition of necessity

必修课 bìxiūkè required (obligatory) course; requirement

必须 bìxū must; have to: ～厉行节约。It is imperative to practise economy.

必需 bìxū necessary; indispensable; essential: ～生产资料 necessary means of production; required means of production

必需品 bìxūpǐn necessities; necessaries

必要 bìyào necessary; indispensable; essential: ～生活资料 necessary means of livelihood. ～学分[美国,教育] requirements

必由之路 bìyóu-zhīlù inevitable course; necessary way; the only road to; the road one must take (follow) for …

毕 bì ①〈动〉finish; complete;

accomplish; conclude:事已完～ sth. is completed (done) ②〈副〉 all; altogether; fully; completely:真相～露 reveal (show) one's true colours

毕竟 bìjìng after all; all in all; in the final analysis; in the long run:个人的力量～是有限的。After all, individual strength is limited.

毕其功于一役 bìqígōngyúyí' yì accomplish the whole task at one stroke

毕生 bìshēng all one's life; lifetime:～事业 lifework; work of a lifetime

毕业 bìyè finish school; graduate:～答辩会 graduation oral examination. ～分配 job assignment on graduation. ～生就业制度 system for employing graduates. ～论文 graduates' dissertation (thesis). ～设计 diploma-winning design; graduation project

闭 bì〈动〉① shut; close ② obstruct; block up; stop up

闭关锁国 bìguān-suǒguó seclusion; lock one's doors against the world

闭关自守 bìguān-zìshǒu cut oneself off from the outside world; closing the door to the outside world; policy of "closed-door"; national seclusion; wall our country off from international exchange; self-seclusion

闭会 bìhuì close (end, adjourn) a meeting:委员会～期间 when the committee is not in session

闭口不谈 bìkǒu-bùtán refuse to say anything about; avoid mentioning

闭路 bìlù closed circuit; closed-loop circuit:～电视 closed-circuit televison

闭门羹 bìméngēng cold shoulder treatment; slam the door in one's face; rebuff; find the door slammed; be met with a door banged shut

闭门思过 bìmén-sīguò shut one's door and reflect one's misdeeds; meditate on one's own faults behind closed door; shut oneself up and ponder over one's mistakes

闭门谢客 bìmén-xièkè close the door to visitors; stop receiving visitors

闭门造车 bìmén-zàochē shut oneself up in a room making a cart; work blindly behind closed doors; work at (on) a project without reference to what the world requires

闭目塞听 bìmù-sètīng shut one's eyes and stop one's ears—cut oneself off from reality

闭幕 bìmù ① the curtain falls; lower the curtain: ② close; conclude:大会已胜利～。The congress has come to a successful close.

闭幕词 bìmùcí closing address (speech)

闭幕式 bìmùshì closing ceremony

闭塞 bìsè ① stop up; close up:鼻孔～ with one's nose stuffed up ② hard to get to; out-of-the-way; inaccessible ③ unenlightened:消息～ ill-informed ④ [电] blocking

庇 bì〈动〉shelter; shield; protect

庇护 bìhù shelter; protect; shield; take under one's wing: ～权 right of asylum. ～所 sanctuary; asylum

庇匿奸宄 bìnì-jiānguǐ shelter a criminal

庇荫 bìyìn ① (of a tree, etc.) give shade ② shield

敝 bì〈形〉① old; shabby; tattered; worn-out ② my; our:～公司 our firm

敝旧 bìjiù ragged; worn-out; shabby

敝俗 bìsú corrupt customs; bad habits

敝帚自珍(～～千金) bìzhǒu-zìzhēn (～～ qiānjīn) value one's own old broom — one loves what is his own; cherish something of little value simply because it is one's own; Everything is nice in one's own garden.

裨 bì〈动〉benefit; advantage 另见 pí

裨补 bìbǔ ① make up; remedy ② benefit; advantage; profit

裨益 bìyì benefit; advantage; profit:大有～ be of great benefit

辟 bì ①〈名〉〈书〉monarch; sovereign ②〈动〉ward off; fight off; keep away

辟邪 bìxié exorcise evil spirits

辟邪归正 bìxié-guīzhèng repudiate heresy and restore orthodox religion

碧 bì ①〈形〉(sky-) blue; bluish green ②〈书〉green jade

碧草如茵 bìcǎo-rúyīn carpet of green grass

碧蓝 bìlán dark blue:～的海洋 the blue sea

碧绿 bìlǜ dark green

碧血 bìxuè blood shed in a just cause

碧玉 bìyù jade; jasper:小家～ pretty daughter of simple family

蔽 bì〈动〉cover; hide; block; shelter:受蒙～ be kept in ignorance

蔽匿 bìnì hide; conceal

蔽上蒙下 bìshàng-mēngxià deceive superiors and hoodwink subordinates

蔽障 bìzhàng keep in obscurity; obstacle to faith or clear vision

弊 bì〈名〉① evil; vice; abuse; corrupt practice; malpractice; fraud:作～ cheat ② harm; disadvantage; shortcomings:利与～ advantages and disadvantages

弊病 bìbìng ① evil; malpractice; malady:社会～ social evils ② drawback; disadvantage

弊端 bìduān corrupt practice; evil; abuse; malpractice; defects:～丛生 all kinds of corrupt practices prevailing

弊多利少 bìduō-lìshǎo The disadvantages outweigh the advantages.; more disadvantages than advantages

弊绝风清 bìjué-fēngqīng Abuses swept away and the air cleared.; All the malpractices have been abolished and the social habits are good.

弊政 bìzhèng political abuses; bad policies; misgovernment

壁 bì ①〈名〉wall (of house, etc.) ② cliffside; perpendicular ③ barrier; rampart; breastwork: 坚～清野 strengthen the defences and clear the fields

壁报 bìbào wall newspaper: 办～ put up a regular wall newspaper

壁橱 bìchú built-in wardrobe or cupboard; closet

壁灯 bìdēng wall lamp; bracket light

壁挂 bìguà [工美] (wall) hanging

壁虎 bìhǔ gecko; house lizard

壁画 bìhuà mural (painting); wall painting; fresco: 敦煌～ the Dunhuang frescoes

壁垒 bìlěi defence; barrier; rampart: ～分明 two sharply opposed sides. 关税～ tariff wall

壁垒森严 bìlěisēnyán ① closely guarded; strongly fortified ② sharply divided; rival camps confronting each other

壁炉 bìlú fireplace

壁上观 bìshàngguān watch a fight without helping either party; detached view; uninvolved

避 bì〈动〉① avoid; dodge; evade: 不～艰险 defy hardships and dangers ② prevent; repel; keep away: ～弹 repel bullet (bomb)

避风 bìfēng ① take shelter from the wind; haven; harbour; ② stay away from trouble: ～港 harbour (a metaphor for a place or work unit untouched by political movements)

避讳 bìhuì ① taboo on using the names of emperors; name avoidance ② a word or phrase to be avoided as a taboo; evade; dodge

避雷针 bìléizhēn lightning rod

避免 bìmiǎn avoid; refrain from; avert: 设法～了一场事故 succeed in averting an accident

避难 bìnàn take (seek) refuge; seek asylum: ～所 asylum; refuge; sanctuary; haven

避实击虚 bìshí-jīxū staying clear of the enemy's main force while striking at his weak points

避暑 bìshǔ ① be away for the summer holidays; spend a holiday at a summer resort ② prevent sunstroke

避嫌 bìxián avoid doing anything that may arouse suspicion; avoid arousing suspicion

避邪去妖 bìxié-qùyāo avoding evil spirits and banishing devils and demons

避孕 bìyùn avoid conception; contraception: ～失败 contraceptive failure

避重就轻 bìzhòng-jiùqīng evade

serious matters and take up trifles;take up the minor issue to evade the major one;avoid the important and dwell on the trivial; keep silent about major charges while admitting minor ones

臂 bì〈名〉① arm ② upper arm

臂膀 bìbǎng arm

臂章 bìzhāng ① armband; armlet ② ［军］ shoulder emblem (patch)

臂肘 bìzhǒu elbow

biān

边 biān 〈名〉① side; edge; rim; margin; verge: 田～地头 edges of fields ② border; frontier; boundary: 拓～ expand frontiers ③ bound; limit: 无～ boundlessness ④〈副〉边…边… along; while: ～学～干 learn on the job; learn while working; learning while doing. ～调整～改革。Reform should be proceeded along with the readjustment. ⑤〈介〉over: 我们～喝茶～闲谈。We had a chat over a cup of tea.

边城 biānchéng border (frontier) town

边陲 biānchuí border area; frontier

边地 biāndì border district; borderland

边防 biānfáng frontier (border) defence: ～部队 frontier guards. ～检查 frontier inspection. ～站 frontier inspection station

边锋 biānfēng (in football, etc.) wing; wing forward

边关 biānguān frontier pass: 镇守～ guard a frontier pass; hold a frontier command

边际 biānjì bound; limit; boundary: 不着～ not to the point; wide of the mark; irrelevant: ～收入 marginal revenue

边疆 biānjiāng border area; borderland; frontier; frontier region: 保卫～ guard the frontier

边界 biānjiè border; boundary: ～的走向 the alignment of the boundary line. ～线的划法 delineations of the boundary line

边境 biānjìng border; frontier: ～兑换 exchange of frontier. ～贸易 frontier trade; border trade

边卡 biānqiǎ border checkpoint

边塞 biānsài frontier fortress

边缘 biānyuán edge; verge; border; fringe; brink; margin: ～科学 borderline science; fringe science; frontier science

边远 biānyuǎn outlying; remote: ～省份 remote border provinces

边寨 biānzhài borderland village

编 biān〈动〉① weave; plait; braid: ～草帽 weave straw hat ② form; organize; arrange in a list: ～组 arrange in groups ③ edit; compile: ～教材 compile teaching materials ④ write; compose: ～歌曲 compose songs ⑤ invent, fabricate; make up; cook up: ～瞎话 make up a lie

编次 biāncì order of arrangement
编凑 biāncòu fabricate; invent; make up; cook up: 他可真会瞎～! He's quite good at making up stories!
编导 biāndǎo ① write and direct (a film, play, etc.) ② [剧] playwright-director ③ [舞剧] choreographer-director ④ [影视] director; scenarist-director
编订 biāndìng compile and edit
编队 biānduì ① form into columns; organize into teams ② formation (of ships or aircraft)
编发 biānfā edit and send (a manuscript)
编号 biānhào ① number: 给树苗～ number the saplings ② serial number
编后 biānhòu editorial afterword
编后语 biānhòuyǔ post-editorial remarks
编辑 biānjí ① edit; compile ② editor; compiler: ～部 editorial office (department). 总～ editor-in-chief; chief (general) editor
编剧 biānjù ① write a play; [影视] write a scenario ② playwright; [影视] scenarist; (screen-)writer
编码 biānmǎ coding
编目 biānmù ① make a catalogue; catalogue ② catalogue; list
编内 biānnèi in-staff: ～人员 in-staff personnel
编排 biānpái arrange; lay out: 文字和图片的～ the layout of pictures and articles
编审 biānshěn [职称] ① senior editor: 副～ associate senior editor ② read and edit; copy editor
编外 biānwài (of personnel) not on the permanent staff; not on the regular payroll; off-staff: ～人员 personnel not on the permanent staff; personnel not on the regular payroll; off-staff personnel
编写 biānxiě ① compile: ～教科书 compile a textbook ② write; compose: ～剧本 write a play
编选 biānxuǎn select and edit; compile
编印 biānyìn compile and print; publish
编造 biānzào ① work out; draw up; compile: ～预算 draw up a budget ② invent; fabricate; concoct
编者 biānzhě editor; compiler: ～按 editor's note; editorial note
编制 biānzhì ① weave; knit; braid ② make; draw up; work out: ～生产计划 work out a production plan. ～程序 programme composition ③ organization; establishment; authorized strength; footing: ～人员 establishment strength
编著 biānzhù compile; write
编撰 biānzhuàn compile; write
编纂 biānzuǎn compile: ～词典 compile a dictionary

鞭 biān 〈名〉① whip; lash: 马～ horsewhip ② sth. resembling a whip: 教～ pointer; rod ③ a string of small firecrackers ④〈动〉lash; flog; whip:～马 whip a horse

鞭策 biāncè spur on; urge on; give an impetus to; encourage; prompt:这对我们是个～。It is an impetus (encouragement) to us.

鞭长莫及 biāncháng-mòjí too far away for one to be able to help; beyond one's control (grasp); beyond the reach of one's authority (power)

鞭打 biāndǎ whip; lash; flog; thrash

鞭炮 biānpào ① firecrackers ② a string of small firecrackers

鞭辟入里 biānpì-rùlǐ trenchant; incisive; penetrating; in-depth

鞭挞 biāntà lash; castigate:无情地～吃人的旧社会 mercilessly castigate the cannibalistic old society

biǎn

贬 biǎn ①〈动〉degrade; relegate; demote:～黜 demote ②〈动〉reduce; devalue:～价 lower (reduce) prices ③〈动〉depreciate; censure:褒～ appreciate or depreciate; praise or blame

贬斥 biǎnchì ①[降低官职] demote ②[贬低并排斥] denounce

贬黜 biǎnchù demote

贬低 biǎndī belittle; play down; disparage; diminish:～…价值 diminish its importance

贬毁 biǎnhuǐ disparage and defame

贬价 biǎnjià reduce the price; mark down:～出售 sell at a reduced price

贬义 biǎnyì derogatory sense:～词 derogatory term

贬谪 biǎnzhé banish from the court; relegate; demotion; transfer

贬值 biǎnzhí ① devaluate; devaluation [指政府规定的贬值] ② depreciate; depreciation [指货币自然的贬值]:通货～ currency depreciation

扁 biǎn〈形〉flat

扁担 biǎndān carrying pole; shoulder pole:～精神 spirit of shoulder pole

扁豆 biǎndòu hyacinth bean

扁体字 biǎntǐzì squat-shaped handwriting

匾 biǎn〈名〉horizontal inscribed board or embroidered silk banner:横～(～额) a horizontal inscribed board

biàn

变 biàn〈动〉① change; turn; become different:改～ change ② become; change into:他已～为优秀学生。He has become an excellent student. ③ alter; change; transform:～农业国为工业国 turn an agricultural country into an industrial country ④〈名〉an unexpected turn of event：兵～ mutiny；revolt

变本加厉 biànběn-jiālì become aggravated；be further intensified；go from bad to worse；(act) in an intensified manner；intensify one's efforts；redouble one's efforts to

变产 biànchǎn sell off one's property

变成 biànchéng change into；turn into；become；transform into

变动 biàndòng ① alteration；change：文字上作一些～ make some changes (alterations) in the wording ② change

变法 biànfǎ political reform；constitutional reform：～而治 rule through reform：～维新 Constitutional Reform and Modernization (1898)

变革 biàngé change；reform；transform；alter：～经济关系 alter the economic relations

变故 biàngù misfortune；accident；mishap；unforeseen event；contingency：发生了～。Something quite unforeseen has happened.

变卦 biànguà change one's mind；change one's tune；go back on one's word；back out：他说好来的，可是～了。He agreed to come，but backed out.

变化 biànhuà change；vary：气温的～ variations (fluctuations) of temperature

变化无常 biànhuà-wúcháng constantly changing；changeable；capricious：高山天气～。In high mountains the weather is changeable.

变换 biànhuàn vary；alternate：～手法 vary one's tactics

变幻 biànhuàn change irregularly；fluctuate

变幻莫测 biànhuàn-mòcè change unpredictably；changeable；erratic；capricious：～的天气 erratic weather

变幻无常 biànhuàn-wúcháng constantly changing；unsettled；changing all the time；hop from one thing to another；changeful

变价 biànjià appraise at the current rate：～出售 sell at the current price (going rate). 固定资产～收入 income derived from the increased prices of the fixed assets

变节 biànjié make a political recantation；turn one's coat

变卖 biànmài sell off (one's property)：～产业 sell off one's estate

变迁 biànqiān changes；vicissitudes：张家庄的～ changes in Zhang Village. 时代～ the changes of the times

变色 biànsè ① change colour；discolour ② change countenance；become angry

变态 biàntài ①［生］metamorphosis ② abnormal；anomalous：～反应 allergy. ～心理 abnormal psychology

变通 biàntōng be flexible；adapt sth. to circumstances；accommodate sth. to circumstances：～办法 flexible measures；adaptation；accommodation

变戏法 biànxìfǎ juggle；conjure；

play magic; perform conjuring tricks

变相 biànxiàng in disguised form; in another form:～涨价 a rise in prices in another form; disguised price increases; camouflaged price hikes

变心 biànxīn cease to be faithful; change loyalties; break faith

变形 biànxíng ① transform; transfigure; be out of shape; become deformed:商品价值的～ transformation of commodity value ② distortion; deformation

变样 biànyàng change in shape or appearance:几年没见,她还没～。She hasn't changed any since I saw her last.

变质 biànzhì go bad; deteriorate; turn:牛奶～了。The milk has turned.

变种 biànzhǒng variety; variation; variant

变奏 biànzòu variation:～曲 variations (on a theme)

便 biàn 〈形〉① convenient; handy ② informal; ordinary 〈名〉③ convenience; ease:随～ do what you like ④ shit or piss; excrement or urine:小～ piss ⑤ 〈副〉 simply; just; then; in that case:那～不同 then it is different

便当 biàndang convenient; handy; easy

便道 biàndào ① shortcut:抄～走 take a shortcut ② pavement; sidewalk:行人走～。Pedestrians walk on the pavement. ③ makeshift road

便饭 biànfàn an ordinary meal; a simple meal; potluck:跟我一块儿吃顿～吧。Come along and take potluck with me.

便服 biànfú ① everyday clothes; informal dress ② civilian clothes

便函 biànhán informal letter sent by an organization

便捷 biànjié ① convenient ② quick; nimble

便利 biànlì ① convenient; easy:到火车站去的～旅馆 hotel convenient to the railway station ② for the convenience of; facilitate:拖拉机使耕地～。Tractors facilitate farming.

便民 biànmín for the convenience of the people

便民措施 biànmín-cuòshī make things convenient for people; convenience-for-people measures

便所 biànsuǒ lavatory; toilet; W.C.

便条 biàntiáo (informal) note

便席 biànxí informal dinner

便宴 biànyàn informal dinner:设～饯行 give a farewell dinner for sb.

便衣 biànyī plain clothes; civilian clothes:～公安人员 plain-clothes public security personnel

便宜 biànyí convenient; advantageous

便于 biànyú easy to; convenient for:～携带 easy to carry

便中 biànzhōng at one's conve-

nience; when it is convenient
便酌 biànzhuó informal dinner

遍 biàn ①〈名〉time in repetition ②〈介、副〉all over; throughout; all around; everywhere
遍布 biànbù spread all over; be found everywhere:～全国 all over the country
遍地 biàndì all around; everywhere:～开花 bloom all over the place; flourish everywhere
遍及 biànjí extend (spread) all over
遍体鳞伤 biàntǐ-línshāng be beaten black and blue; The body is all covered with wounds.; be black and blue all over

辨 biàn〈动〉distinguish; discriminate; discern; differentiate:明～是非 clearly distinguish right from wrong
辨别 biànbié distinguish; discriminate; discern:～力 ability to see things in one's true light; power of discrimination. ～是非 distinguish between right and wrong; make distinction between right and wrong; tell right from wrong
辨明 biànmíng make a clear distinction; distinguish
辨认 biànrèn identify; make out; recognize: 不能～ beyond recognition
辨析 biànxī differentiate and analyse; discriminate:同义词～ synonym discrimination
辨正 biànzhèng critically study; identify and correct (errors):忠实的～ differentiation and correction of historical facts

辩 biàn〈动〉argue; debate; dispute:争～ argue
辩白 biànbái make explanations; try to justify oneself (for)
辩驳 biànbó refute; dispute against:无可～ beyond all dispute
辩辞 biàncí explanation; argument
辩护 biànhù ①［法］defend; plead:～律师 defence lawyer (counsel). ～人 defender ② justify; defend; come out (speak) in defence of; argue in favour of:不要为自己的缺点～。Don't try to justify your mistakes.
辩护权 biànhùquán right to defence
辩解 biànjiě ① explain away; provide an explanation; try to defend oneself; argue that…; justify ②［法］exculpation
辩说 biànshuō argue; debate
辩证 biànzhèng dialectical:～法 dialectics. ～唯物主义 dialectical materialism

辫 biàn〈名〉① plait; braid; queue ②［把柄］a mistake or shortcoming that may be exploited by an opponent; handle:揪～子 seize on sb.'s mistake or shortcoming; capitalize on sb.'s vulnerable point; take it as a handle againist sb.

biāo

标 biāo 〈名〉① mark; sign; label:商～ trade mark ② tender; bid; public commercial bidding:招～ invite public tender (bidding) ③ award; prize:锦～ prize; title; trophy ④ 〈动〉 mark; quote; label:～上号码 put a number on

标榜 biāobǎng ① advertise; parade; brag about; flaunt:～沽名 advertise oneself to seek fame ② boost; excessive praise:互相～ boost each other; exchange excessive praise

标本 biāoběn ① specimen; sample ② the root cause and symptoms of a disease:～同治 treat a disease by looking into both its root cause and symptoms

标兵 biāobīng pacesetter; pacemaker; model; example:被树为～ be cited as a pacesetter

标尺 biāochǐ ① surveyor's rod; staff ②［水利］staff gauge

标底 biāodǐ (to go) above the reserve; base number of a tender

标点 biāodiǎn ① punctuation:～符号 punctuation mark ② punctuate

标号 biāohào grade:水泥～ grade of cement

标记 biāojì sign; mark; symbol

标价 biāojià ①［标出货价］mark a pirce ②［所标明的价钱］marked price; posted price

标卖 biāomài sell at marked price; sell by tender

标明 biāomíng mark; indicate:箱子上～"小心轻放"。The crate is marked "Handle with care".

标签 biāoqiān label; tag:贴～ attach (put, stick on) a label to; label

标示 biāoshì mark; indicate

标题 biāotí heading; headline; title:小～ subheading. ～音乐 programme music

标新立异 biāoxīnlìyì create sth. new and original; create what is new and original; do sth. unconventional or unorthodox; try to be deliberately unconventional;［贬义］strain after originality

标语 biāoyǔ slogan; poster; 张贴～ put up slogans (posters):～牌 placard

标致 biāozhi (usu. of women) beautiful; handsome

标志 biāozhì ① mark; signify; indicate; designate ② sign; symbol; mark; hallmark

标准 biāozhǔn standard; criterion:～产量计酬 paying remuneration according to standard output

彪 biāo 〈名〉a young tiger

彪悍 biāohàn intrepid; doughty; valiant

彪形大汉 biāoxíng dàhàn burly chap; husky fellow; hefty fellow

彪壮 biāozhuàng tall and husky; hefty:～的小伙子 a hefty young man

膘 biāo 〈名〉 fat (of a domestic

animal)：牲口～肥体壮。The animals are plump and sturdy.

镖 biāo〈名〉a dartlike weapon (used in former times)

镖师 biāoshī (in former times) armed escort (of travellers or merchants' caravans)

biǎo

表 biǎo〈名〉① watch：手～(wrist) watch ② meter; gauge：电～power meter ③ table; form; list：一览～general chart ④ surface; outside：徒有虚～only have a handsome look ⑤〈动〉express; show; manifest：略～寸心 just to show one's gratitude

表白 biǎobái express or state clearly; explain; clarify; explain oneself：～诚意 assert one's sincerity

表报 biǎobào statistical tables and reports

表册 biǎocè statistical forms; book of tables or forms：公文报告～documents, written reports and statistical forms

表尺 biǎochǐ rear sight

表达 biǎodá express; show; convey; deliver; voice：～能力 ability of expression. 无法～beyond expression. 非语言所能～can't be conveyed by words

表弟 biǎodì the son of one's father's sister or of one's mother's brother or sister, who is younger than oneself; younger male cousin; cousin

表哥 biǎogē the son of one's father's sister or of one's mother's brother or sister, who is older than oneself; older male cousin; cousin

表格 biǎogé form; table：填～fill up (in, out) a form

表功 biǎogōng claim merit for oneself; boast of one's bit of contribution

表姐 biǎojiě the daughter of one's father's sister or of one's mother's brother or sister, who is older than oneself; older female cousin; cousin

表决 biǎojué vote; take a vote on (a question)：举手～vote by show of hands

表里 biǎolǐ inside and outside：～不一 think in one way and act in another. ～如一 think and act in the same way; be what one professes to be; make one's appearance tally with one's inner mind

表露 biǎolù show; reveal：她很着急，但并没有～出来。She was very worried, but didn't show it.

表妹 biǎomèi the daughter of one's father's sister or of one's mother's brother or sister, who is younger than oneself; younger female cousin; cousin

表面 biǎomiàn surface; superfices; face; appearance; outside：～文章 surface formality; specious writing; lip service：～

消费 apparent consumption

表亲 biǎoqīn ① cousin ② cousinship

表情 biǎoqíng ① express one's feelings ② expression:～不自然 look awkward; wear an unnatural expression

表示 biǎoshì ① show; express; indicate:～关切 show concern ② expression; indication:友好的～ an expression of friendship; a friendly gesture

表述 biǎoshù define; exposition; formulation

表态 biǎotài take a stand; clarify one's position; declare one's stance

表现 biǎoxiàn show; display; express; acquit oneself:～(不)好 acquit oneself well (ill); give a good (bad) account of oneself. ～手法 technique of expression

表演 biǎoyǎn perform; play; act:～理论 stage theory; theory of acting. ～唱 sing with action; an item combining singing, dancing and acting

表扬 biǎoyáng praise; publicly commend:～好人好事 commend good people and good deeds

表彰 biǎozhāng cite; commend; honour:～劳动模范和先进工作者大会 national conference to commend models and advanced workers

婊 biǎo

婊子 biǎozi prostitute; whore:～还想立牌坊 It is like a woman of easy virtue who, while selling herself, believes she must have a monument erected to her chastity.

裱 biǎo 〈动〉① mount (a picture, a painting, etc.) ② paste up:～糊 paste paper on

裱褙 biǎobèi mounting(a picture)

裱糊 biǎohú paper (a wall, ceiling, etc.)

裱画 biǎohuà picture-mounting

裱装 biǎozhuāng mount (a picture, etc.)

biē

憋 biē ① shut up; hold back; suppress:～着一肚子火 seething with anger; be filled with pent-up anger ② suffocate; smother:～得人透不过气来 one could not hardly breathe

憋气 biēqì ① feel suffocated (oppressed) ② choke with resentment; feel injured and resentful:憋着一肚子气 have pent-up grievances

瘪 biē ～三 a wretched-looking tramp who lives by begging or stealing
另见 biě

bié

别 bié 〈动〉① leave; take departure; part:久～故乡 leave one's native place for years ② differentiate; distinguish ③ [用别针等] pin; clip ④〈副〉[不

要] don't ⑤〈名〉distinction: 男女有～ distinction between sexes ⑥〈代〉another; other: ～处 another place

另见 biè

别材 biécái unusual ability or talent

别称 biéchēng another name; alternative name

别出心裁 biéchū-xīncái have an unconventional idea; an out-of-the-ordinary idea; adopt an original approach; try to be different

别集 biéjí authologies of individual authors' works

别具匠心 biéjù-jiàngxīn show ingenuity; have originality

别具一格 biéjù-yīgé have a style of one's own; have a unique (distinctive) style

别开生面 biékāi-shēngmiàn open up a fresh outlook; create a new form; break fresh ground; in a novel way

别来无恙 biélái-wúyàng You have been well, I trust, since we parted?

别离 biélí take leave of; leave

别论 biélùn another or a different matter: 又当～ should be regarded as a different matter

别人 biérén ① someone else: 家里只有父亲和我,没有～。There are only my father and I in our family—nobody else. ② biéren other people; others; people

别墅 biéshù villa

别树一帜 biéshù-yīzhì set up a new banner; found a new school of thought; have a style of one's own; raise another standard; start a new school

别说 biéshuō to say nothing of; not to mention; let alone: ～在下雪,你现在出去也太晚了。It's far too late for you to go out, not to mention the fact that it's snowing.

别提 biétí no need to mention; you can well imagine: 她那个高兴劲儿啊,就～了。You can well imagine how happy she was.

别有风味 biéyǒu-fēngwèi have a distinctive flavour

别有天地 biéyǒu-tiāndì an altogether different world; a place of unique beauty; Here is quite a different sort of life. ; scenery of exceptional charm

别有用心 biéyǒu-yòngxīn with ulterior motives (purpose); have something up one's sleeve; have an axe to grind; have an ulterior object in view

别传 biézhuàn unofficial (separate) biography

别致 biézhì distinctive; novel; unique; new and unusual

别字 biézì wrongly written or mispronounced character: 读～ mispronounce a character

蹩 bié ①〈动〉[手腕等] sprain (one's wrist): ～痛了脚 hardly sprain one's ankle ②〈形〉lame

蹩脚 biéjiǎo poor; shoddy; incompetent; low-grade; bungling; clumsy; inferior in quality or skill: ～货 inferior (poor) stuff

biě

瘪 biě 〈形〉 sunken; shrivelled; wizened; flat
另见 biē

biè

别 biè
另见 bié

别扭 bièniu ① difficult to deal with; hard to get along with: 闹～ be at odds (with) ② can not see eye to eye ③ not smooth; awkward: 这个句子读起来怪～的。This sentence reads rather awkward.

bīn

宾 bīn 〈名〉 guest

宾格 bīngé ［语］ the objective case

宾客 bīnkè guests; visitors

宾朋满座 bīnpéng-mǎnzuò Guests and visitors fill up the seats.; The house is full of guests.

宾语 bīnyǔ ［语］ object

宾至如归 bīnzhì-rúguī Guests feel at home.; Guests come here as if they were returning home.; make sb. free at one's home; a home (away) from home

宾主 bīnzhǔ host and guest: ～频频举杯。Host and guests proposed repeated toasts.

彬 bīn

彬彬有礼 bīnbīn-yǒulǐ refined and courteous; urbane: 我扣上上衣的扣子，～地走上一步。I buttoned up my jacket and moved forward with ceremonious deference.

傧 bīn

傧相 bīnxiàng attendant of the bride or bridegroom at a wedding

滨 bīn ① 〈名〉 bank; brink; shore ② 〈动〉 be close to (the sea, a river, etc.); border on: ～海城市 a city bordering on the sea

缤 bīn

缤纷 bīnfēn in riotous profusion: 五彩～ colourful; blazing with colour

濒 bīn ① 〈动〉 be close to (a river, the sea, etc.): ～湖 border on the lake ② be on the brink (verge) of; be on the point of: ～死 on the verge (brink) of death; dying; on the point of death

濒近 bīnjìn close to; close on

濒临 bīnlín be close to; border on; be on the verge of: 河北省～渤海。Hebei Province is on the Bohai Sea.

濒行 bīnxíng be about to start on a journey

濒于 bīnyú be on the verge (eve, edge, point, brink) of: ～破产 be on the verge of bankruptcy; verge on bankruptcy

bìn

摈 bìn〈动〉discard; abandon; get rid of: ～诸门外 shut (lock) sb. out

摈斥 bìnchì dismiss; reject: ～原则 exclusion principle

摈除 bìnchú discard; get rid of; dispense with: ～繁文缛节 dispense with all unnecessary formalities

摈弃 bìnqì discard; cast away; abandon: ～社会渣滓 discard the dregs of society

殡 bìn〈动〉① lay a coffin in a memorial hall ② carry a coffin to the burial place

殡车 bìnchē hearse

殡殓 bìnliàn encoffin a corpse and carry it to the grave

殡仪馆 bìnyíguǎn the undertaker's; funeral parlour (home)

殡葬 bìnzàng funeral and interment

鬓 bìn〈名〉temples; hair on the temples

鬓发 bìnfà hair on the temples: temples

鬓角 bìnjiǎo temples; hair on the temples

bīng

冰 bīng ①〈名〉ice〈动〉② ice; put ice around; put on the ice: 把汽水～上 ice the bottle of soft drink ③ feel cold

冰雹 bīngbáo hail; hailstone: 下～了。It's hailing.

冰场 bīngchǎng skating (ice) rink; ice stadium; ice arena

冰雕 bīngdiāo ice sculpture; ice engraving: ～艺术 art of ice engraving

冰冻 bīngdòng frozen; iced: ～三尺,非一日之寒 It takes more than one cold day for the river to freeze three feet deep — the trouble has been brewing for quite some time

冰窖 bīngjiào icehouse

冰冷 bīnglěng ice-cold

冰凉 bīngliáng ice-cold: 我两手冻得～。My hands were freezing.

冰球 bīngqiú ①［体］ice hockey: ～运动员 puckster ②［冰球运动使用的球］puck

冰上表演 bīngshàng biǎoyǎn ice show. ～舞蹈 ice dancing

冰上运动 bīngshàng yùndòng ice-sports: ～会 ice-sports meet

冰霜 bīngshuāng ① ice and frost ② moral integrity ③ austerity

冰箱 bīngxiāng icebox; refrigerator; fridge; freezer

冰消瓦解 bīngxiāo-wǎjiě melt like ice and break like tiles; vanish from the scene; be thoroughly removed; dissolve; disintegrate

冰鞋 bīngxié skating boots; skates

冰镇 bīngzhèn iced ～汽水 iced soda water

兵 bīng〈名〉① soldier: 当～ be a soldier; serve (enlist) in the armed forces ② weapons; arms: 秣马厉～ feed the horses and sharpen the weapons ③ army;troops ④ rank-and-file soldier, private ⑤ military strategy

兵变 bīngbiàn mutiny

兵不血刃 bīngbùxuěrèn (win a battle) without bloodshed; gain victory with unstained swords; the edges of the swords not being stained with blood— win a victory without firing a shot

兵不厌诈 bīngbùyànzhà There can never be too much deception in war.; Nothing is too deceitful in war.; All is fair in war.

兵多将广 bīngduō-jiàngguǎng a very large army with many able generals—very powerful military forces

兵工 bīnggōng war industry:～厂 munitions (ordnance) factory; arsenal

兵工企业 bīnggōngqǐyè arms enterprise; arsenal

兵贵精不贵多 bīng guì jīng bú guìduō Troops are valued for quality rather than for number.

兵荒马乱 bīnghuāng-mǎluàn turmoil and chaos of war:在～的年代 in chaotic war years

兵家 bīngjiā ① military strategist in ancient China ② military commander; soldier:～必争之地 a place contested by all strategists; strategic point

兵舰 bīngjiàn warship

兵力 bīnglì military strength; forces; troops: ～部署 troop disposition; deploy the forces. ～对比 relative military strength.

兵临城下 bīnglínchéngxià The attacking army has reached the city gates.; the city is under siege

兵马 bīngmǎ troops and horses; military forces

兵马俑 bīngmǎyǒng [考] wood or clay figures of warriors and horses buried with the dead; terra-cotta warriors and horses in battle array; soldiers and horses figures

兵痞 bīngpǐ army riffraff; army ruffian; soldier of fortune

兵器 bīngqì weaponry; weapons; arms:～博物馆 armoury museum

兵权 bīngquán military power; military leadership

兵戎 bīngróng arms; weapons

兵戎相见 bīngróng-xiāngjiàn resort to arms and fight for his one' own domination; cross swords with …; meet on the battle ground

兵书 bīngshū a book on the art of war

兵团 bīngtuán army; formation; corps:～农场 army farms. 生产建设～ production and construction corps

兵险 bīngxiǎn war risks:～包括在内 including war risks

兵饷 bīngxiǎng soldier's pay and provisions

兵械 bīngxiè ordnance; armament

兵役 bīngyì military service:服～ serve in the army; perform military service：～法 military service law

兵员 bīngyuán soldiers；troops：三十万～ 300,000 troops；an army of 300,000 strong

兵源 bīngyuán manpower resources（for military service）；sources of troops

兵种 bīngzhǒng arm of the services

bǐng

丙 bǐng ①〈名〉the third of the ten Heavenly Stems（天干）②〈数〉third：～等 the third grade；grade C

丙纶 bǐnglún polypropylene fibre

丙酮 bǐngtóng［化］acetone

秉 bǐng〈动〉① hold；grasp：～笔 hold a pen ② control；take charge of；preside over：～权 be in power

秉承 bǐngchéng take（orders）；receive（commands）；act on（sb.'s advice or instruction）

秉持 bǐngchí adhere to（principles，etc.）；hold onto

秉赋 bǐngfù ① possess；be endowed with ② natural endowment；gift

秉公 bǐnggōng impartially；justly：～无私 handle affairs impartially（justly）；handle affairs according to the law

秉性 bǐngxìng nature；disposition；natural distinct

秉直 bǐngzhí honest；upright

柄 bǐng〈名〉① handle；shaft ② stem：叶～ leaf stalk；petiole ③ handle；target：笑～ butt of jokes

柄臣 bǐngchén powerful minister（of a monarchy）

柄权 bǐngquán be in power；exercise control

饼 bǐng〈名〉① cake：月～ moon cake ② sth. shaped like a cake

饼肥 bǐngféi cake（fertilizer）

饼干 bǐnggān biscuit；cracker

饼子 bǐngzi（maize or millet）pancake

屏 bǐng〈动〉① get rid of；reject；put（cast）aside ② hold（one's breath）：～着气 catch（hold）one's breath

另见 píng

屏弃 bǐngqì throw away；discard；abandon；reject

屏息 bǐngxī hold one's breath：～静听 listen with bated breath

禀 bǐng〈动〉① report（to one's superior for instructions）；petition ② be endowed with；receive（order）

禀报 bǐngbào report（to one's superior or senior）

禀呈 bǐngchéng present or submit（to one's superior or senior）

禀（秉）承旨意 bǐngchéng-zhǐyì take orders from；on the instructions of；take one's cue from

禀赋 bǐngfù gift；natural endowment：极有～的人 a man of great natural endowments

禀复 bǐngfù report back（to one's

superior or senior)

禀告 bǐnggào report (to one's superior or senior)

禀气 bǐngqì innate vital force

禀帖 bǐngtiē a report or petition to government authorities

禀性 bǐngxìng natural disposition; natural instincts: ～刚愎 be perverse in temper; have a perverse temper

bìng

并 bìng 〈动〉① merge; combine; incorporate ② parallel: 肩～肩站着 stand shoulder to shoulder ③〈副〉side by side; simultaneously; equally: 齐头～进 go forward together ④〈连〉and

并处 bìngchǔ [法] in addition sentence to…

并存 bìngcún exist side by side: 多种经济成分～。Multiple sectors of the economy exist side by side.

并蒂莲 bìngdìlián ① twin lotus flowers on one stalk ② a devoted married couple

并发 bìngfā be complicated by; erupt simultaneously; concur: ～效应 simultaneous effect

并驾齐驱 bìngjià-qíqū advance hand in hand with; run neck and neck; keep abreast of (keep pace with, be on a par with) one another

并肩 bìngjiān shoulder to shoulder; side by side; abreast: 三人～而行。The three of them walked abreast. ～作战 fight side by side; fight shoulder to shoulder

并举 bìngjǔ simultaneous development; develop simultaneously

并列 bìngliè stand (place) side by side; be juxtaposed; put sth. on a par with: ～第一 tie for first place; be both winners

并排 bìngpái side by side; abreast: 不要～骑车。Don't all cycle abreast.

并且 bìngqiě and; besides; moreover; furthermore: 工作艰巨，～时间紧迫。The job is difficult and, moreover, time is pressing.

并入 bìngrù merge into; incorporate into

并入帐内 bìngrù-zhàngnèi pass to the account of; place to the account of

并吞 bìngtūn swallow up; annex; absorb: ～中小企业 swallow up medium and small enterprises

并网发电 bìngwǎng-fādiàn combining electricity systems in generating electricity

并行 bìngxíng ① walk abreast; run side by side ② carry on (two things) at the same time

并用 bìngyòng use two things simultaneously: 手脚～ use both hands and feet

并喻文化 bìngyù-wénhuà co-figurative culture

并峙 bìngzhì (several powerful states) rival with each other

并重 bìngzhòng lay equal stress on; pay equal attention to

病 bìng〈名〉① illness; sickness;disease ② troubles; corrupt practices:通～ common trouble ③ defect; weakness; fault ④〈动〉fall ill:她～了三天。She was ill for three days.

病残患者 bìngcánhuànzhě the disabled (deformed)

病虫害 bìng-chónghài plant diseases and insect pests

病床 bìngchuáng ① hospital bed:这所医院有 500 百张～。The hospital has 500 beds. ② sickbed:我在她～旁边守了好几夜。I watched beside her sickbed for several nights.

病从口入 bìngcóngkǒurù Diseases come in at the mouth.; Diseases enters by mouth.

病倒 bìngdǎo be down with an illness; be laid up

病毒 bìngdú virus:～病 virosis

病房 bìngfáng sickroom; ward (of a hospital):内科～ medical ward

病根 bìnggēn ① an incompletely cured illness; an old complaint ② the root cause of trouble:他犯错误的～在于个人主义。His error stems from individualism.

病故 bìnggù die of an illness

病号 bìnghào sick personnel; person on the sick list; patient:老～ one who is always ill; chronic invalid

病急乱投医 bìngjí luàn tóuyī One is so dangerously ill that he indiscriminately consults a wrong doctor.;turn to any doctor one can find when critically ill—try anything when in a desperate situation

病假 bìngjià sick leave:～工资 sick pay; sick benefits. 请～ ask for sick leave

病苦 bìngkǔ suffering caused by illness

病况 bìngkuàng state of an illness; patient's condition

病历 bìnglì medical record; case history:～卡 health record

病例bìnglì diagnosing case; case

病魔 bìngmó the demon of disease—serious illness:～缠身 be possessed by the demon of disease—be afflicted with a lingering disease

病情 bìngqíng condition of a patient:～公报 medical bulletin

病人 bìngrén patient:～角色 patient role. 门诊～ outpatient. 住院～ inpatient

病入膏肓 bìngrùgāohuāng The disease has attacked the vitals — beyond cure.; incurable; mortally sick; fatal

病史 bìngshǐ medical history; case history

病逝 bìngshì die of illness

病死 bìngsǐ die of illness

病榻 bìngtà sickbed

病态 bìngtài morbid (abnormal) state; morbid condition:～经济 sick economy. ～心理 morbid mentality (psychology); morbidity. ～社会 diseased society

病退 bìngtuì withdrawal due to illness: ① employees retiring due to illness ② urban youths who fell ill or were unfit to work in the countryside were allowed to return to the cities

病愈 bìngyù recover (from an illness)

病员 bìngyuán sick personnel; person on the sick list; patient

病院 bìngyuàn a specialized hospital: 传染～ isolation hospital; infectious deseases hospital

病在危笃 bìngzàiwēidǔ be ill and failing fast

病征 bìngzhēng symptom (of a disease)

病重 bìngzhòng be seriously ill

病状 bìngzhuàng symptom (of a disease)

摒 bìng 〈动〉 brush aside; get rid of; dismiss

摒绝 bìngjué dismiss; get rid of

摒弃 bìngqì abandon; exclude; discard; get rid of

bō

拨 bō〈动〉① turn; move (stir) with hand; adjust with slight finger movement: ～算盘 tick off beads on abacus ② set aside; allocate; appropriate: ～粮 allocate provisions ③ [钟表] set ④ [电话号码] dial ⑤ 〈量〉 group; batch: 轮～儿作业 work by turns

拨付 bōfù appropriate (a sum of money); pay

拨款 bōkuǎn allocate (appropriate) funds: 军事～ military appropriations

拨乱反正 bōluàn-fǎnzhèng setting things right; bringing order out of chaos; set to right things which have been thrown into disorder; set things to right in all spheres

拨弄 bōnòng ① play (fiddle) with; move to and fro; twiddle: ～铅笔 fiddle about with a pencil ② stir up; incite; provoke: ～是非 stir up trouble; make trouble; stir thing up ③ manipulate; order about

拨冗 bōróng find time in the midst of pressing affairs; set aside time for a special purpose out of a tight schedule

拨弦乐器 bōxián-yuèqì plucked string (stringed) instrument; plucked instrument

拨正 bōzhèng set right; correct: ～航向 correct the course

波 bō 〈名〉 ① wave: 短～ short wave ② an unexpected turn of events; unexpected changes: 风～ disturbance; storm; scene

波长 bōcháng wavelength

波荡 bōdàng heave; surge: 海水～。The sea surges.

波动 bōdòng rise and fall; surge; undulate; fluctuate: ～汇率 fluctuating exchange rate

波段 bōduàn wave band: ～开关 band switch; waver

波及 bōjí involve; spread to; affect: ～范围很广 extensively affect

波澜 bōlán great waves; billows

波澜起伏 bōlán-qǐfú (of a piece of writing) with one climax following another

波澜壮阔 bōlán-zhuàngkuò ① surge forward with great momentum; sweep ahead magnificently; unfolding on a magnificent scale; ② torrential

波浪 bōlàng wave:～式的起伏 in a wave-like manner; the form of an undulating movement; expand in a series of waves

波涛 bōtāo great waves; billows: ～滚滚 waves rolling ～汹涌 waves surging turbulently; waves running high

波音 bōyīn ①［乐］mordent ② Boeing:～747 Boeing 747

波折 bōzhé twists and turns; setback; turns:发生～ meet with setbacks

玻 bō

玻璃 bōlí glass

玻璃板 bōlibǎn glass plate; glass top (of a desk)

玻璃厂 bōlichǎng glassworks

玻璃钢 bōligāng glass fibre reinforced plastic

玻璃纤维 bōli xiānwéi glass fibre

玻璃纸 bōlizhǐ cellophane; glassine

钵 bō〈名〉① earthen bowl ② alms bowl (of a Buddhist monk)

钵盂 bōyú alms bowl (of a Buddhist monk)

剥 bō〈动〉peel; skin; shell:～豆 shell beans. ～光……外衣 strip one of one's mantle. ～开画皮 expose … for what it is

剥夺 bōduó deprive (of); divest (of); expropriate:～某人权利 deprive sb. of one's rights; take away one's rights. ～资格 disqualify

剥离 bōlí (of tissue, skin, covering, etc.) come off; peel off: be stripped:表土～ topsoil stripping

剥落 bōluò come off; peel off:墙上涂料已～了。The paint on the wall has peeled off.

剥脱 bōtuō ① strip off ② come off; peel off

剥削 bōxuē exploit; flee:～收入 income from exploitation. ～心态 exploitative mentality

菠 bō

菠菜 bōcài spinach

菠萝 bōluó pineapple

播 bō〈动〉① seed; sow:春～ spring sowing ② broadcast:～出乐曲 broadcast the music

播报 bōbào broadcast reports

播发 bōfā broadcast: ～新闻 broadcast news

播放 bōfàng ① broadcast ② broadcast a T.V. programme

播讲 bōjiǎng talk over the radio: ～园艺知识 give a radio talk on gardening

播弄 bōnòng ① order sb. about ② stir up

播弄是非 bōnòng-shìfēi stir things up; stir up trouble; sow dissension; spread rumours and cause trouble

播送 bōsòng transmit; broadcast; beam:～音乐 broadcast music. 扬声器在～中国乐曲。The loudspeaker was playing Chinese music.

播音 bōyīn broadcast; transmit: ～室 broadcasting studio; broadcast studio; studio

播映 bōyìng ① film broadcast ② broadcast on television

播种 bōzhòng sowing; seeding: ～面积 sown area; seeded area. ～期 sowing (seeding) time

bó

伯 bó〈名〉① father's elder brother; uncle ②［爵位］earl; count

伯父 bófù ① father's elder brother; uncle ② a term of address for a man of one's father's generation who is older than one's father; uncle

伯爵 bójué earl; count: ～夫人 countess

伯母 bómǔ wife of father's elder brother; aunt

驳 bó〈动〉① refute; rebut; argue: 反～ refute; retort ② transport by lighter: 起～ set sail

驳岸 bó'àn a low stone wall built along the water's edge to protect an embankment; revetment

驳斥 bóchì refute; rebut; denounce; disprove

驳船 bóchuán barge; lighter

驳倒 bódǎo refute; demolish sb.'s argument; overcome (sb.) by argument; succeed in refuting

驳回 bóhuí turn down; reject; overrule: ～上诉 reject an appeal

驳价 bójià (of a buyer) haggle over prices

驳面子 bómiànzi not spare sb.'s sensibilities; not show due respect for sb.'s feelings

驳运 bóyùn transport by lighter; ligher: ～费 lighterage

帛 bó〈名〉silks: 玉～ jades and silks

帛画 bóhuà painting on silk

帛书 bóshū a book copied on silk

泊 bó〈动〉moor; berth: ～船 moor a boat
另见 pō

泊位 bówèi berth: 深水～ deep water berth

泊位费 bówèifèi berthage

勃 bó ①〈形〉vigorous; thriving; exuberant: 蓬～ vigorous; flourishing ②〈副〉suddenly

勃勃 bóbó thriving; vigorous; exuberant: 生气～的创造力 vigorous creative power

勃发 bófā ① thrive; prosper: 游兴～ be seized with a desire to travel ② break out: 战争～。War broke out.

勃然 bórán ① suddenly; excitedly; agitatedly: ～变色 agitatedly change colour ② vigorously; prosperously (in a vigorous and flourishing state)

勃然大怒 bórán-dànù fly into a rage; fly (flare) up; burst into a fit of temper

勃兴 bóxīng rise suddenly; grow

vigorously; surge forward; burst forth

舶 bó〈名〉oceangoing ship:巨～ a huge ship

舶来品 bōláipǐn imports

脖 bó〈名〉① neck ② sth. shaped like a neck:～儿长的瓶子 a bottle with a long neck

脖颈儿 bógěngr back of the neck; nape

博 bó〈形〉① abundant; rich; plentiful ② learned ③〈动〉win; gain:～得美名 win a good reputation

博爱 bó'ài universal love; universal fraternity (brotherhood); love for humanity

博采众长 bócǎi-zhòngcháng learn widely from others' strong points:～,独树己见 examine the theories of others and then develop one of his own

博大 bódà broad; extensive

博大精深 bódà-jīngshēn broad and profound; extensive and profound:～的知识 sweeping knowledge

博得 bódé win; gain:～全场喝采 draw loud applause from the audience; bring the house down

博古通今 bógǔ-tōngjīn possess a wide knowledge of things ancient and modern—erudite and informed; be conversant with things past and present—erudite and informed; be versed in both ancient and modern knowledge; have both ancient and modern learning

博览 bólǎn read extensively (widely):～群书 be well-read

博取 bóqǔ try to gain; court:～欢心 curry favour

博士 bóshì doctor:～学位 doctor's degree; doctorate

博士后 bóshìhòu ① postdoctoral student or researcher ② postdoctoral study or research ③ postdoctoral; postdoctorate:～科研人员 postdoctoral researchers

博闻强记 bówén-qiángjì wide learning and a powerful memory; have wide learning and a retentive (poweful) memory; have encyclopedic knowledge

博物 bówù general name for zoology, botany, mineralogy, physiology, etc.

博物馆 bówùguǎn museum:中国革命～ the Museum of the Chinese Revolution

博物院 bówùyuàn museum

博学 bóxué learned; well-read; erudite:～多才 be well-read and versatile; have a wealth of knowledge; be a brilliant man of wide learning; be of great learning and great ability

博弈 bóyì have a game of chess; play chess:～理论 game theory

搏 bó〈动〉① wrestle; combat; fight ② beat; throb

搏动 bódòng (of the heart, the blood, or the pulse) beat rhythmically; throb; pulsate

搏斗 bódòu wrestle with; struggle; fight

搏杀 bóshā ① fight with a weapon ② (in chess games) be locked in a fierce contest

膊 bó〈名〉arm

薄 bó〈形〉① slight; scanty; small:～薪 small salary ② unkind; stingy; mean; ungenerous:待遇不～ a fair remuneration ③〈动〉despise; belittle; look down; slight:厚今～古 stress the present rather than the past ④〈副〉slightly ⑤〈介〉toward(s); near

另见 báo, bò

薄产 bóchǎn small property

薄地 bódì unfertile land

薄礼 bólǐ small (unworthy) gift

薄利 bólì small profits:～多销 small profits but quick turnover; larger sales at a small profit; small profit, large sale volume

薄命 bómìng [多指妇女] born under an unlucky star; born unlucky; ill-fated:～女子负心汉 an unfortunate girl and a heartless man

薄情 bóqíng inconstant (unfaithful) in love; ungrateful; fickle:～郎 an unfaithful husband; a heartless lover

薄弱 bóruò weak; frail; vulnerable:技术力量～ lack qualified technical personnel

bǒ

跛 bǒ〈形〉be lame:～了一只脚 lame in one leg

跛脚(腿) bǒjiǎo (tuǐ) lame

跛行 bǒxíng limp; limping; walk lame:～本位制 [经] lame standard

跛子 bǒzi lame person; cripple

簸 bǒ〈动〉winnow with a fan; fan

另见 bò

簸动 bǒdòng ① jolt; bump; toss ② strike (a gong)

簸箩 bǒluo shallow basket

bò

薄 bò

另见 báo; bó

薄荷 bòhe field mint; peppermint

薄荷醇 bòhechún menthol; peppermint camphor

薄荷糖 bòhetáng peppermint drops

簸 bò

另见 bǒ

簸箕 bòji ① dustpan ② winnowing fan ③ loop (of a fingerprint)

bǔ

卜 bǔ〈动〉① divine:～卦 divine by the Eight Diagrams ② foretell; predict ③ select; choose; ～宅 choose house ④〈名〉divination

卜辞 bǔcí oracle inscriptions of the Shang Dynasty (c. 16-11th century B. C.) on tortoise shells or animal bones; oracle-bone inscriptions

卜筮 bǔshì divination

卜疑 bǔyí allaying doubts through divination

补 bǔ 〈动〉① repair; mend; patch:修桥～路 build bridges and repair roads ② make up; supply; fill:弥～赤字 meet (make up) a deficit ③ nourish:～元气 help restore vitality ④ 〈名〉help; benefit; use:无～于事 do not help matters; won't help

补报 bǔbào ① make a report after the event; make a supplementary report:调查结果以后～。Findings will be reported later. ② repay a kindness

补差 bǔchā [退休工人] make up a deficiency:他又搞～去了。He is again working to "make up a deficiency".

补偿 bǔcháng make up; compensate; reimburse:～贸易 compensatory trade

补充 bǔchōng ① supplement; replenish; complement ② supplementary:～读物 supplementary reading material. ～侦查 supplementary investigation

补发 bǔfā supply again (sth. lost, etc.); reissue; pay retroactively:～增加的工资 pay increased wages retroactively

补过 bǔguò make amends for one's faults

补给 bǔjǐ [军] supply:～点 supply point. ～品 supplies. ～线 supply line

补救 bǔjiù remedy:无可～ be past (beyond) remedy; irremediable; irreparable

补考 bǔkǎo make-up (examination):～英语 make up an examination in English

补课 bǔkè ① make up (missed) lessons ② [教师] give remedial lessons

补票 bǔpiào buy one's ticket after the normal time

补品(药) bǔpǐn(yào) tonic

补缺 bǔquē fill (up) a vacancy; supply a deficiency:～配套 make sure that complete sets of equipment are available

补税 bǔshuì ① pay the taxes one has evaded ② pay an overdue tax

补台 bǔtái repair a "platform" (to support leaders or colleagues in their work by seeking to repair the deleterious effects or damage created through their faulty work)

补贴 bǔtiē subsidy; allowance:生活～ living allowance

补习 bǔxí take supplementary lessons (after school or work):～学校 continuation school

补休 bǔxiū make-up vacation days (for people who keep working during holidays and official days of rest); take deferred holidays

补选 bǔxuǎn ① by-election ② hold a by-election (for)

补养 bǔyǎng take a tonic or nourishing food to build up one's health

补益 bǔyì ① benefit; help:有所～be of some help (benefit) ② be of help (benefit)

补助 bǔzhù subsidize:～金 subsidy; grant-in-aid; grant

补足 bǔzú make up a deficiency; bring up to full strength; fill up; supplement:～挤占的流动资金 make up the working capital which has been squeezed out

捕 bǔ 〈动〉① catch; seize; ② arrest:搜～逃犯 track down and arrest the escaped criminal

捕风捉影 bǔfēng-zhuōyǐng catch at shadows; speak or act on hearsay evidence; beat the air; make groundless charges

捕俘 bǔfú [军] capture enemy personnel (for intelligence purposes)

捕获 bǔhuò catch; capture:～法[法] law of prize

捕捞 bǔlāo fish for (aquatic animals and plants); catch:～能力 fishing capacity

捕拿 bǔná arrest; apprehend; capture; catch

捕杀 bǔshā catch and kill

捕捉 bǔzhuō catch; seize;～镜头 seize the right moment to get a good shot. ～逃犯 capture an escape

哺 bǔ ①〈动〉feed (a baby); nurse ②〈名〉food of chewing; the food in one's mouth:吐～ disgorge food

哺乳 bǔrǔ feed a baby at the breast; nurse; suckle:～室 nursing room

哺喂 bǔwèi feed

哺养 bǔyǎng feed; rear

哺育 bǔyù ① feed ② nurture; foster; develop; bring up

bù

不 bù 〈副〉①[用在动词、形容词和其他副词前表示否定]can not; no:～多 not much. ～愿意 not willing; reluctant ②[单用,否定对方的话]:她知道吧?—～,她不知道。She knows, doesn't she? — No, she doesn't. 她～知道吧?—～,她知道。She doesn't know, does she? —Yes, she does. ③〈方〉[用在句末表示疑问]你身体好～? How are you? ④[“不”字前后叠用相同的词,前面常加“什么”,表示不在乎或不相干]:什么远～远的,我去定了。No matter how far it is, I'll go there anyhow. ⑤[跟“就”搭用,表示选择]:晚上她～是看电视,就是看书。She either watches TV or reads books in the evening.

不安 bù'ān ① unsettled; unstable; unrest ② ill at ease; uneasy; perturbed:～本分 be discontented with one's lot

不白之冤 bùbáizhīyuān a wrong that has not been righted; unrighted wrong; unredressed injustice; gross injustice

不测 bùcè accident; eventuality; contingency; mishap; misfortune:以防～ provide against eventualities (any contingency)

不成大器 bùchéngdàqì (someone) will never amount to much

不成敬意 bùchéngjìngyì just a little token to show my respect to you

不出所料 bùchū-suǒliào as (was) expected; as might have been expected; not surprising

不打自招 bùdǎ-zìzhāo make a confession under no coercion; confess without being pressed; unsought confession

不得不 bùde bù can't but (do); have no choice but (to do); have to (do)

不得了 bùdéliǎo ① terrible; horrible; serious: 没有什么～。Nothing serious. ② very; extremely: 她遇到我们高兴得～。She was extremely pleased to meet us.

不得已 bùdéyǐ against one's will; not of one's own volition: ～而为之 act against one's will. ～而求其次 have to take the second best; have to be content with the second best

不等价交换 bùděngjià jiāohuàn exchange of unequal values; unequal exchange

不动产 bùdòngchǎn real estate (property); immovables

不对 bùduì ① incorrect; wrong: 这样做～。It's wrong to act like that. ② [单用,表示否定对方的话] no: ～,我没有那么说。No, I didn't say that. ③ amiss; abnormal; queer: 这机器声音～。The machine makes a queer noise. ④ be in disagreement; be at odds

不对路产品 bùduìlù chǎnpǐn unmarketable goods; goods which are inadaptable to actual needs

不二法门 bù'èrfǎmén the one and only way; the only proper course to take

不二价 bù'èrjià fixed prices; uniform prices

不乏 bùfá there is no lack of: ～其人 such people are not rare; there is no lack of such people

不法 bùfǎ lawless; illegal; unlawful: ～行为 unlawful practice; an illegal act. ～之徒 a lawless person

不凡 bùfán out of the common run; extraordinary: 自命～ have an unduly high opinion of oneself; consider oneself a person of no ordinary talent

不妨 bùfáng it would be well if …; there is no harm in; might as well: 你～试一试。You might as well have a try.

不费吹灰之力 bùfèichuīhuīzhīlì as easy as blowing off dust; as easy as falling off a log

不分 bùfēn make no distinction (difference) (between): ～青红皂白 indiscriminately. ～胜负[体] end in a draw; tie; a dead heat. ～是非 make no distinction between right and wrong; fail to distinguish right from wrong

不分彼此 bùfēn-bǐcǐ make no distinction between one's own and sb. else's; share everything; be on very intimate terms

不服 bùfú refuse to obey (comply); refuse to accept as final; remain unconvinced by; not give in to: ～裁判 refuse to accept the referee's ruling

不服水土 bùfú-shuǐtǔ be not acclimatized; not accustomed to the climate (of a new place)

不符 bùfú not agree (tally, square) with; not conform to; be inconsistent with: 言行～ deeds not matching words. 她说话前后～。What she said was self-contradictory.; What she said didn't hang together.

不甘 bùgān be unwilling; be not resigned (to): ～人后 be unwilling to lag behind. ～示弱 not to be outdone; refuse to admit being inferior; reluctant to show weakness

不甘心 bùgānxīn not reconciled to; not resigned to

不共戴天 bùgòngdàitiān will not live under the same sky (with one's enemy)—absolutely irreconcilable: ～的敌人 a sworn enemy; a mortal foe. ～之仇 inveterate hatred

不够 bùgòu not enough; insufficient; inadequate: 我们做得很～。We haven't done nearly enough.

不顾 bùgù in spite of; regardless of: ～后果 regardless of the consequences

不关痛痒 bùguān-tòngyǎng of no consequence; immaterial

不管 bùguǎn ① not care; disregard ② no matter (how, what, etc.); however: ～三七二十一 recklessly; regardless of consequences; come what may. ～怎样 anyhow

不轨 bùguǐ against the law or discipline: 行为～ act (conduct) against the law

不过 bùguò ①〔用在形容词性的词组后面,表示程度最高〕: 那就再好～了! It couldn't be better!; That would be superb! ② only; merely; no more than: 他参军的时候～16 岁。He was only sixteen when he joined the army. ③ but; however; only: 她精神还不错,～胃口不大好。She feels pretty well, but she hasn't much of an appetite.

不过如此 bùguò-rúcǐ only just so-so

不含糊 bù hánhu ① unambiguous; unequivocal; explicit ② not ordinary; really good: 她那手乒乓球可～。She is a very good table-tennis player. 他这活儿做得真～。He's really made a good job of it. ③ not be afraid of: ～他们。I am not afraid of them.

不寒而栗 bùhán'érlì shiver all over though not cold—tremble with fear; shudder

不好惹 bù hǎorě not to be trifled with; not to be pushed around; stand no nonsense: 他这个人可是～的。He's not a man to be trifled with.

不好意思 bù hǎoyìsi be ashamed (to do); feel embarrassed

(bashful); be ill at ease; find it embarrassing (to do sth.)

不合 bùhé disagree with; be unsuited; be out of keeping with; not conform to:～客观情况 out of accord with the objective conditions

不和 bùhé ① be at odds (with); be on bad terms; be not on good terms (with) ② discord

不怀好意 bùhuái-hǎoyì harbour evil designs; not with the best of intentions

不欢而散 bùhuān'érsàn part on bad terms:会议～。The conference broke up in discord.

不慌不忙 bùhuāng-bùmáng unhurried; calm; leisurely

不会 bùhuì ① be unlikely; will not (act, happen, etc.):他～不知道。It's not likely that he doesn't know. ② have not learned to; be unable to:她～游泳。She doesn't know how to swim. ③ [表示责备语气]:你就～打个电话问一问? Couldn't you have phoned up and asked? 她不能来,你～早点儿告诉我吗? You might have told me earlier she couldn't come.

不及 bùjí ① not as good as; inferior to:我学习～你刻苦。I don't study as hard as you do. ② find it too late:躲避～ too late to dodge. 后悔～ too late for regrets

不即不离 bùjí-bùlí be neither familiar nor distant; keep sb. at arm's length

不计其数 bùjì-qíshù countless; innumerable:每日过往旅客～。There are countless passengers coming and going every day.

不记名投票 bùjìmíng tóupiào secret ballot

不济 bùjì not good; of no use:他眼力～了。His eyesight is failing.

不假(加)思索 bùjiǎ (jiā)-sīsuǒ (act, respond, etc.) without thinking; without hesitation; readily; offhand

不简单 bù jiǎndān ① not simple; rather complicated ② remarkable; marvellous:他们有这么大的进步真～。It's remarkable they've made such good progress.

不见得 bùjiànde not necessarily; not likely:～对 not necessarily correct

不见棺材不掉泪 bù jiàn guāncaibù diàolèi not to shed tears until one sees his own coffin; refused to be convinced until one is faced with grim reality

不骄不躁 bùjiāo-bùzào not conceited or rash; free from arrogance and rashness

不结盟 bùjiéméng nonalignment:～国家 nonaligned countries. 奉行～政策 pursue a policy of nonalignment

不解之缘 bùjiězhīyuán an indissoluble bond; an irrevocable commitment:他早年就和绘画结下了～。Early in his life he was irrevocably committed to painting.

不禁 bùjīn can't help (doing

sth.); can't refrain from:看她那滑稽的样子,我~笑了起来。She looked so funny that I couldn't help laughing.

不仅 bùjǐn not the only one:这~是我一个人的看法。I'm not the only one who holds this view.

不进则退 bùjìnzétuì move forward, or you'll fall behind

不近人情 bùjìn-rénqíng out of keeping with common feelings; unreasonable

不经一事,不长一智 bù jīng yī shì, bù zhǎng yī zhì you can't gain knowledge without practice; wisdom comes from experience

不景气 bùjǐngqì [经]depression; slump; recession

不胫而走 bùjìng'érzǒu get round fast; spread like wildfire:这本词典一经问世,~。As soon as it was published, the dictionary had a big circulation.

不久 bùjiǔ ① soon; before long ② not long after; soon after:插完秧~就下了一场雨。It rained soon after we had transplanted the rice seedlings.

不咎既往 bùjiù-jìwǎng Let bygones be bygones.; forgive sb.'s past misdeeds; irrespective of sb.'s past

不拘 bùjū ① not stick to; not confine oneself to:字数~。No limit is set on the length (for an article). ② no matter (what, who, etc.); whatever:~什么工作,只要对国家有益的,我们都愿意接受。We're ready to accept any job whatever, so long as it is in the interest of the country.

不拘形式 bùjū-xíngshì not particular about form; informal

不拘一格 bùjū-yīgē not to stick to one pattern; follow no set form (pattern):~挑选人材 recruit able people without overstressing qualifications

不倦 bùjuàn tireless; untiring; indefatigable

不堪 bùkān can't bear; can't stand; unbearable:~回首 can't bear to look back; find it unbearable to recall:~设想 inconceivable; be dreadful (unbearable) to contemplate; unimaginable. ~一击 crumble at the first blow; cannot withstand (even) a single blow

不看僧面看佛面 bù kàn sēngmiànkàn fómiàn not for the monk's sake, but for the Buddha's—(do sth. for a person) out of deference to sb. else

不可 bùkě ① cannot; should not; must not:~一概而论 must not make sweeping generalizations ②[用在非…~]:非你去~。It won't do unless you go.

不可分割 bùkě-fēngē inseparable

不可告人 bùkě-gàorén not to be divulged; hidden:~的动机 motives that cannot bear the light of day; ulterior motives. ~的勾当 a sinister trick

不可估量 bùkě-gūliàng inestimable; incalculable; immeasurable; beyond measure:～的损失 an immeasurable loss

不可救药 bùkē-jiùyào incurable; hopeless; incorrigible; beyond cure; beyond help or remedy

不可开交 bùkě-kāijiāo [只做"得"后面的补语]:忙得～ be up to one's eyes in work; be awfully (terribly) busy

不可磨灭 bùkě-mómiè indelible: ～的功绩 ineffaceable merit; unforgettable meritorious deeds

不可胜数 bùkě-shèngshǔ countless; innumerable

不可收拾 bùkě-shōushi irremediable; hopeless; unmanageable; out of hand:～的局面。The situation would get out of hand.

不可思议 bùkě-sīyì inconceivable; unimaginable; unthinkable

不可同日而语 bùkě tóngrì ér yǔ can not be mentioned in the same breath

不可一世 bùkě-yīshì hold one's head high; consider oneself unexcelled (second to none) in the world; overbearing; swashbuckling

不可逾越 bùkě-yúyuè impassable; insurmountable; insuperable: ～的鸿沟 an impassable chasm; an unbridgeable gulf

不可捉摸 bùkě-zhuōmō unpredictable; difficult to ascertain: ～的哲理文章 intangible philosophical essays

不客气 bù kèqi ① impolite; rude; blunt:说句～的话 to put it bluntly ② you're welcome; don't mention it; not at all ③ please don't bother; I'll help myself

不愧 bùkuì be worthy of; deserve to be called; prove oneself to be:他～是律师的儿子。He was not the son of an attorney for nothing.

不劳而获 bùláo'érhuò reap without sowing; profit by or reap the fruits of other people's toil

不理 bùlǐ refuse to acknowledge; pay no attention to; take no notice of; ignore:见了人～ cut sb. dead

不利 bùlì ① unfavourable; disadvantageous; harmful; detrimental ② unsuccessful:首战～ lose the first battle

不良 bùliáng bad; harmful; unhealthy: ～影响 harmful (adverse) effects

不了了之 bùliǎo-liǎozhī settle a matter by leaving it unsettled; end up with nothing definite; end up without any tangible results

不料 bùliào unexpectedly; to one's surprise:早上天气还好好的,～下午竟下起雨来了。It was so fine this morning. Who would have thought it would rain in the afternoon!

不吝 bùlìn [用于征求意见] not stint; not grudge; be generous with: ～指教 not be stinting with comments or criticism

不灵 bùlíng not work; be ineffective:这机器～了。The machine doesn't work.

不论 bùlùn no matter (how, what, who, etc.); whether... or...; regardless of: ～性别年龄 regardless of age or sex

不买帐 bùmǎizhàng not go for it; not care; be unwilling to accept sb.'s authority over oneself; give no heed to: 对于官僚主义，群众是～的。The masses won't go for bureaucracy.

不满 bùmǎn resentful; discontented; dissatisfied: 心怀～ nurse a grievance

不忙 bùmáng there's no hurry; take one's time.

不免 bùmiǎn unavoidable; inevitable; would naturally: ～失望 would naturally be disappointed

不妙 bùmiào (of a turn of events) not too encouraging; far from good; anything but reassuring: 情况～。Things are none too encouraging.

不明 bùmíng ① not clear; unknown: ～飞行物 unidentified flying object (UFO). ～国籍的飞机 a plane of unidentified nationality; an unidentified aircraft ② fail to understand: ～是非 confuse right and wrong

不鸣则已，一鸣惊人 bùmíngzéyǐ, yīmíngjīngrén one doesn't speak unless one can say something sensational

不谋而合 bùmóu'érhé happen to hold the same view; happen to coincide with

不睦 bùmù not get along well; be on bad terms; be at odds

不能 bùnéng cannot; must not; should not

不能不 bùnéng bù have to; cannot but: ～表示惋惜 cannot but express regret

不怕不识货，就怕货比货 bùpà bùshí huò, jiù pà huò bǐ huò don't worry about not knowing much about the goods; just compare them and you will see which is better

不偏不倚 bùpiān-bùyǐ without bias and without favour; avoid leaning to either side; impartial; impartiality and justice; even-handed

不平 bùpíng ① injustice; unfairness; wrong; grievance ② indignant; resentful: 消除心中的～ allay one's resentment

不平衡 bùpínghéng disequilibrium: 工农业发展～ the disequilibrium between the development of industry and agriculture

不起眼 bùqǐyǎn not attract attention; not be noticeable; not be attractive.

不巧 bùqiǎo unfortunately; as luck would have it: 我到那儿，～他们刚走。As luck would have it, they had just left when I arrived.

不求甚解 bùqiú-shènjiě not seek deep understanding; be content with a superficial understanding; not seek to understand things thoroughly

不屈不挠 bùqū-bùnáo unyielding; indomitable; dauntless:

～，前仆后继 dauntlessly step into the breach as others fall

不然 bùrán ① not so：其实～。Actually this is not so. ②[用在句子开头，表示否定对方的话] no：～，事情没有那样简单。No，it's not as simple as that. ③ or else；otherwise；if not：你得早点去，～就赶不上火车了。You've got to leave a bit early，otherwise you'll miss the train. 要去就别迟到，～，就甭去了。Either be there on time，or don't go at all.

不仁 bùrén ① not benevolent；heartless ② numb

不忍 bùrěn cannot bear to：我们～看到老年人生活穷困，无人照料。We cannot bear to see old people living in poverty and neglect.

不容 bùróng not tolerate；not allow；not brook：～侵犯 brook no violation

不如 bùrú ① not equal to；not as good as；inferior to：论手巧，一般人都～你。Few can equal (compare with) you in manual dexterity. ② it would be better to：要是这样我还～呆在家里。In that case I might as well stay at home.

不入虎穴，焉得虎子 bù rù hǔxué，yān dé hǔzǐ How can you catch tiger cubs without entering the tiger's lair?；If you do not venture into a tiger's den，how can you get the tiger's cub?；No pains，no gains；Nothing is achieved without effort.；Nothing venture，nothing have.

不三不四 bùsān-bùsì ① neither one thing nor the other；neither fish nor fowl；nondescript：～的词句 nondescript expressions ② suspicious (characters)；dubious；shady；with no character：他常常和一些～的人鬼混。He often hangs around with some dubious characters.

不善 bùshàn ① bad；ill：来意～ come with ill intent ② not good at：～管理 not good at managing things ③ not to be pooh-poohed；quite impressive：别看我身体不强，干起活来可～。I do not look strong，but I do all right in work.

不声不响 bùshēng-bùxiǎng quiet；silent：她～地走进屋来。She slipped into the room without a word.

不胜 bùshèng ① cannot bear (stand)；be unequal to：体力～ be physically unequal to (a task)；be physically incapable of coping with (a job) ②[表示不能做或做不完]：看～看 find it difficult to read so many books，etc. ③[用于情感方面] very；extremely：～感激 be very much obliged；be deeply grateful

不胜枚举 bùshèng-méijǔ be too numerous to mention；defy enumeration

不失时机 bùshī-shíjī lose no time；not miss the opportune time；seize the opportune moment

不失体面 bùshī-tǐmiàn not lose face; maintain one's dignity

不失为 bùshīwéi can yet be regarded as; may after all be accepted as: 这～一个办法。This, after all, is one way of doing it.

不识大体 bùshí-dàtǐ fail to see the larger issues; ignore the general interest

不识好歹 bùshí-hǎodǎi not to know chalk from cheese; cannot tell good from bad; not to know what is good for one

不识庐山真面目 bùshí lúshān zhēn miànmù fail to see what Lushan Mountain really looks like—fail to see the truth about a person or a matter

不识时务 bùshí-shíwù ignorant of the present state of affairs (of the trend); show ignorance of the times; have no proper understanding of how things stand; show no understanding of the times

不识抬举 bùshí-táijǔ not know how to appreciate one's favours; fail to appreciate one's kindness

不受理 bùshòulǐ ① [法] reject a complaint ② [外] refuse to entertain (a proposal)

不死心 bùsǐxīn unwilling to give up; unresigned: 失败了还～ not be reconciled to one's failure

不速之客 bùsùzhīkè uninvited (unexpected) guest; gatecrasher

不通 bùtōng ① be obstructed; be blocked up; be impassable: 电话～。The line's dead. ② not make sense; be illogical; be ungrammatical: 文章写得～。The article is badly written.

不同 bùtóng not alike; different; distinct: 在～的程度上 to varying degrees

不同凡响 bùtóng-fánxiǎng extraordinary; out of (the) common run; out of the ordinary

不痛不痒 bùtòng-bùyǎng scratching the surface; superficial; perfunctory: ～的批评 superficial criticism

不妥 bùtuǒ not proper; inappropriate: 这样处理，恐怕～。I'm afraid this isn't the proper way to handle the case.

不外 bùwài not beyond the scope of; nothing more than: ～两种可能。There are only two possibilities.

不闻不问 bùwén-bùwèn take no notice of; shut one's eyes to; be indifferent to; turn a blind eye to

不问 bùwèn ① pay no attention to; disregard; ignore: ～性别 irrespective of sex ② let go unpunished; let off: 胁从～。Those who acted under duress shall go unpunished.

不务正业 bùwù-zhèngyè ① not do honest work; not live by honest labour ② ignore one's proper occupation; not attend to one's duties

不惜 bùxī not stint; not spare; stint no effort: ～工本 spare neither labour nor money; at all costs; spare no expense; spare no cost; at any cost

不下于 bùxiàyú ① as many as; no less than:展出的新产品～100 种。There are as many as 100 new products on show. ② not inferior to; as good as; on a par with

不相干 bù xiānggān be irrelevant; have nothing to do with:～的话 irrelevant remarks

不相容 bù xiāngróng incompatible

不相上下 bùxiāngshàngxià be on even terms (with); be roughly the same (as); match; balanced; without much difference

不详 bùxiáng ① not well known; not quite clear:言之～ be stated too briefly; not be given in detail ② [书信中用语]: no need to go into details; let me spare you the details

不祥 bùxiáng ominous; inauspicious:～之兆 an ill (evil) omen

不像话 bù xiànghuà ① unreasonable; ridiculous ② shocking; outrageous; bad beyond description:这种行为真～。Such behaviour is really shocking.

不像样 bùxiàngyàng ① in poor shape; unpresentable; in no shape to be seen:～的批评 The criticisms are not up to the mark. ② [用在"得"后作补语，表示无法形容] beyond recognition:破得～ worn to shreds

不孝 bùxiào be an unfilial son or daughter; act contrary to filial piety

不屑 bùxiè disdain to do sth.; think sth. not worth doing; feel it beneath one's dignity to do sth.:～置答 disdain to reply

不懈 bùxiè untiring; unremitting; indefatigable:作～的努力 make unremitting efforts; make a sustained effort

不信任案 bùxìnrèn'àn no-confidence motion

不信任投票 bùxìnrèn tóupiào vote of no-confidence

不兴 bùxīng ① out of fashion; outmoded ② impermissible; not allowed:～这样做。That's not allowed.

不行 bùxíng ① not be allowed; won't do; be impossible: 我们没你～。We can't do without you. ② be no good; won't work: 她教书不大行。She's not much good as a teacher. ③ not be good; be poor:料子不错，手工～。The material is fine, but the workmanship is poor. ④ [用在"得"字后面做补语]: awfully; extremely:她困得～了。She's terribly sleepy.

不幸 bùxìng ① misfortune; adversity:遭～ meet with a misfortune ② unfortunate; sad:③ unfortunately:她～以身殉职。To our great sorrow she died at her post.

不许 bùxǔ ① not allow; must not:～说谎。You mustn't tell lies. ② [用于反问句] can't:何必非等我，你就～自己去吗? Why wait for me? Can't you go yourself?

不学无术 bùxué-wúshù ignorant and incompetent; have neither learning nor skill; be lacking in both learning and practical ability; not to study and know nothing

不逊 bùxùn rude; impertinent:出言～ speak insolently

不言而喻 bùyán'éryù self-evident; self-explanatory; It goes without saying that...; taken for granted; it stands to reason

不要紧 bùyàojǐn ① it's not serious; it doesn't matter; never mind:路远也～,我可以骑车去。It doesn't matter how far it is; I can go by bike. ② it looks all right, but:你这一嚷～,把大家都吵醒了。You may think it's all right for you to shout, but you've woken everbody up.

不要脸 bùyàoliǎn shameless; have no sense of shame; brazen-faced; lose all sense of shame

不依 bùyī ① not comply; not go along with:我劝她休息,她怎么也～。I advised her to have a rest, but she simply wouldn't hear of it. ② not let off easily; not let sb. get away with it:你要是再这样,我可～你。If you do this again, I won't let you off so easily.

不宜 bùyí not suitable; inadvisable

不遗余力 bùyí-yúlì spare no effort; make every endeavour; do one's utmost; leave no stone unturned; spare no pains

不已 bùyǐ endlessly; incessantly:赞叹～ praise again and again

不以为然 bùyǐwéirán object to; take exception to; not approve of:她父母对她抽烟颇～。Her parents strongly disapprove of her smoking.

不义之财 bùyìzhīcái ill-gotten wealth (gain); money obtained by dubious means; filthy lucre

不翼而飞 bùyì'érfēi disappear mysteriously; vanish; melt into thin air;[钱等] take wings to itself

不由得 bùyóude can't help; cannot but:他说得这么透彻,～你不信服。He spoke so cogently that you couldn't help being convinced.

不由自主 bùyóu-zìzhǔ can't help; involuntarily:～地流下了眼泪 cannot help shedding tears; be unable to hold back one's tears; shed tears in spite of oneself

不虞之备 bùyúzhībèi have a second string to one's bow

不予 bùyǔ not grant; not give:～考虑 refuse to take into consideration; will not consider

不远千里 bùyuǎn-qiānlǐ make light of travelling a thousand *li*; go to (take) the trouble of travelling a long distance; make light of travelling from afar

不约而同 bùyuē'értóng do or think the same without prior consultation; happen to coincide:我们～地大笑起来。Simultaneously, we burst out laughing.

不在话下 bùzài-huàxià ① be nothing difficult; not amount to much; be a cinch; to say nothing of; not to mention ② beyond question; without question

不在其位，不谋其政 bùzài qíwèi, bùmóu qízhèng He who holds no rank in a state does not discuss its policies.; unwilling to comment on sth. which is not one's own concern; If it's not your job, you don't worry about it.

不在意 bù zàiyì ① pay no attention to; take no notice of; not mind. ② negligent; careless: 我一点也～。I don't mind at all.

不择手段 bùzé-shǒuduàn use all kinds of methods; by hook or by crook; unscrupulously; stop at nothing; have no scruples about; by fair means or foul; use every means in one's power to

不怎么 bùzěnme not very; not particularly: 我～想去。I'm not particularly keen on going.

不战则已，战则必胜 bùzhàn zéyǐ, zhàn zé bì shèng Fight no battle unless we can win it.

不折不扣 bùzhé-bùkòu out and out; pure and simple; without any reservation; without the slightest discount; in full sense; in every sense; one hundred per cent; to the letter

不争气 bù zhēngqì be disappointing; fail to live up to expectations: 他这个人真～。This chap has let us down.

不正之风 bùzhèngzhīfēng unhealthy practices; evil winds; unwholesome tendency: 纠正行业～ correcting unhealthy practices in trade and professions

不知好歹 bùzhī-hǎodǎi can't tell good from bad; not know what's good for one

不知所措 bùzhī-suǒcuò not know what to do; be at a loss (to do, for); be at one's wits' end

不知所云 bùzhī-suǒyún can't make out what is meant; not know what one is talking about or what one has said

不知天高地厚 bùzhī tiāngāo dìhòu not know the height of the heavens or the depth of the earth—have an exaggerated opinion of one's abilities; not understand things

不值 bùzhí not worth: ～一提 not worth mentioning

不止 bùzhǐ ① incessant; without end: 大笑～ roar with laughter ② more than; not limited to: 她恐怕～60岁了。She is probably over sixty.

不只 bùzhǐ not only; not merely

不至于 bùzhìyú cannot go so far; be unlikely: 他们～连这一点道理也不明白。They must have more sense than that.

不置可否 bùzhì-kěfǒu not to say yes or no; decline to comment; not say anything definite; make no comment; not to give a definite answer

不中用 bù zhōngyòng useless; no good for use; good for nothing; without any talent or ability

不抓辫子 bù zhuā biànzi not pulling the pigtail; not seizing upon sb.'s mistakes as a handle

不准 bùzhǔn not allow; prohibit; forbid:～动手［揭示语］Hands Off. ～乱扔杂物［揭示语］No Littering. ～照相［揭示语］No Camera. ～随地吐痰［揭示语］No Spitting.

不着边际 bùzhuó-biānjì not to the point; wide of the mark; neither here nor there; irrelevant:她越讲越～。The more she talked, the further she strayed from the point.

不自量 bùzìliàng not take a proper measure of oneself; overrate one's own abilities:～力 not have a proper measure of oneself; overrate one's own abilities; overreach oneself

不足 bùzú ① not enough; insufficient:信心～ lack confidence ② not worth:～称道 not worth commending ③ cannot; should not

不足道 bùzúdào not worth mentioning; inconsiderable; of no consequence

不足挂齿 bùzú-guàchǐ not worth mentioning; nothing to speak of

不足为训 bùzú-wéixùn not fit to serve as a model; not to be taken as an example; not an example to be followed; not to be taken as authoritative

布

布 bù ①〈名〉cloth; textile:棉～ cotton cloth〈动〉② publish; proclaim; declare; announce:公～ publish ③ spread; disseminate:散～谣言 spread gossips ④ arrange; deploy; dispose:～阵 deploy troops

布帛 bùbó cloth and silk; cotton and silk textiles

布达拉宫 Bùdálāgōng the Potala Palace (the former palace of the Dalai Lamas, in Lhasa, Tibet)

布点 bùdiǎn location distribution; layout

布店 bùdiàn cloth store; draper's; piece-goods store

布告 bùgào (public) notice; announcement; bulletin; proclamation

布景 bùjǐng ①［剧］setting; scene ② composition (of a painting)

布局 bùjú overall arrangement; layout; geographical distribution; distribution

布朗族 Bùlǎngzú the Blang (Pulang) nationality, or the Blangs, inhabiting Yunnan

布匹 bùpǐ cloth; piece goods

布头 bùtóu ① leftover of a bolt of cloth ② odd bits of cloth

布纹纸 bùwénzhǐ wove paper

布鞋 bùxié cloth shoes

布依族 Bùyīzú the Bouyei (Puyi) nationality (living in Guizhou Province)

布置 bùzhì ① arrange; fix up; dispose; decorate:～就绪 complete the disposition of ② assign;make arrangements for

步 bù〈名〉① step; pace ② stage; step:撤军工作分两～。The troops will be pulled out in two stages. ③ condition; state; situation:落到这一～ come to such a state〈动〉④ go on foot; walk:～下山坡 walk down the slope ⑤ tread:亦～亦趋 follow slavishly

步兵 bùbīng ① infantry; foot ② infantryman; foot soldier

步步登高 bùbù-dēnggāo ascend step by step; rise steadily in one's career

步步为营 bùbù-wéiyíng advance gradually and entrench itself at every step; make a stand (consolidate) at every step

步调 bùdiào step; pace:～一致 keep (in) step (with); march in step; act in unison

步伐 bùfá step; pace:加速建设的～ quicken the pace of construction. 跟上时代的～ keep pace with the times

步履 bùlǚ walk:～蹒跚 walk haltingly; hobble along. ～维艰 have difficulty in walking; walk with difficulty

步枪 bùqiāng rifle

步人后尘 bùrénhòuchén follow in sb.'s footsteps; tread in other people's (foot) steps; follow in the wake of others; tread in sb.'s (foot) steps

步行 bùxíng go on foot; walk

步骤 bùzhòu step; move; measure; procedure:有计划有～地进行工作 carry on the work step by step in a planned way

怖 bù〈动〉be afraid of; fear

部 bù〈名〉① section, part; division:局～ part ② ministry; department; unit:～定标准 standard set by a ministry. 门市～ retail department ③ headquarters:师～ division headquarters ④ troops; forces ⑤ 三～字典 three dictionaries ⑥〈动〉command:所～甚众 command many troops

部队 bùduì ① army; armed forces ② troops; force; unit:通讯兵～ signal troops. 野战～ a field army unit

部分 bùfen part; section; share

部件 bùjiàn parts; components

部类 bùlèi category; division

部落 bùluò tribe:～社会 tribal society

部门 bùmén department; branch:政府各～ various government departments

部首 bùshǒu radicals by which characters are arranged in traditional Chinese dictionaries:[汉字的]简化～ simplified radicals

部署 bùshǔ ① disposition; arrangement; deployment:战役～ disposition (of troops) for a campaign ② arrange; map out; dispose:～重点工程 arrange for the construction of key projects

部属 bùshǔ ① subordinate; troops under one's command ② affiliated to a ministry:～机构 organizations affiliated to the

ministry
部委 bùwěi ministries and commissions
部下 bùxià ① troops under one's command ② subordinate
部长 bùzhǎng minister; head of a department (under the Party Central Committee): 对外贸易经济合作部～ Minister of Foreign Trade and Economic Cooperation. ～级会议 conference at ministerial level. ～助理 assistant minister. 省委宣传部～ Director of the Propaganda Department of a Provincial Party Committee

埠 bù〈名〉① wharf; pier ② port

簿 bù〈名〉notebook; book
簿册 bùcè books for taking notes or keeping accounts
簿记 bùjì bookkeeping
簿子 bùzi notebook; book

C c

cā

拆 cā
另见 chāi

拆烂污 cālànwū〈方〉do sloppy (slovenly) work; mess things up; leave things in a mess; make a mess of

擦 cā〈动〉① run:摩拳～掌 rubbing one's hands together ② scrub; wipe; clean:～枪 clean a gun ③［药］put on; spread on; apply:在脸上～香脂 put some cream on the face ④ brush; pass lightly over or touch lightly against ⑤ scrape (into shreds)

擦背 cābèi rub one's back with a towel while bathing

擦边球 cābiānqiú［体］edge ball; touch

擦亮 cāliàng polish; rub; shine: ～眼睛 sharpen one's eyes (vigilance); highten one's vigilance

擦伤 cāshāng bruise; rub the skin off; chafe; scratch

擦网球 cāwǎngqiú［体］net ball

擦洗 cāxǐ clean (with water or alcohol):这个手表该～了。This watch needs cleaning.

擦油 cāyóu rub oil (on, over); oil; grease

cāi

猜 cāi〈动〉① guess; speculate ② suspect

猜测 cāicè guess; surmise; conjecture; speculate:没有根据的～ a baseless conjecture

猜忌 cāijì be suspicious and jealous of; be suspicious and resentful

猜谜 cāimí ① guess a riddle ② guess:快说吧,别让我～了。Now out with it. Don't keep me guessing.

猜破 cāipò guess right:她的意思我早就～了。I guessed what she meant long ago.

猜拳行令 cāiquán-xínglìng play the finger game; play the finger-guessing game at a wine party

猜透 cāitòu guess right:我猜不透她的心事。I can't figure out what's on her mind.

猜想 cāixiǎng suppose; guess; suspect

猜中 cāizhòng guess right; guess; solve (a riddle):我～了。I was right in my guess (conjecture).

cái

才 cái ①〈名〉ability; gift; talent:多～多艺 be gifted in may ways② 〈副〉[表示事情发生不久]:节目～开始。The performance has just started. ③ [表示事情发生或结束得晚]你怎么～来? Why are you so late? ④ [表示只有在某种条件下然后怎么样,前面常有"只有、必须、因为、由于"等配合]:只有肯努力,～能得到好的学习成绩。Only you study hard, can you get good results. ⑤ [对比起来数量小、能力差等]:当时她～5岁。She was only five years old then.

才干 cáigàn (practical) ability; capability; competence

才华 cáihuá intellect; brilliance: ～出众 of uncommon brilliance

才华(气)横溢 cáihuá(qì)-héngyì brim with talent; have superb talent

才略 cáilüè ability and sagacity (in political and military affairs)

才貌 cáimào talent and appearance:～出众 of exceptional talent and distinguished appearance. ～双全 be endowed with both beauty and talent

才能 cáinéng ability; talent; faculty:～差别 diversity of talents

才识 cáishí ability and insight:～过人 be gifted with talent and insight far beyond the average person

才疏学浅 cáishū-xuéqiǎn have little talent and less learning; wanting ability and shallow in knowledge; be an indifferent scholar

才思 cáisī imaginative power and creativeness (in writing)

才思敏锐 cáisī-mǐnruì acuity of wit

才学 cáixué talent and learning; knowledge; scholarship:～人品 scholastic ability and attainments and personal character

才智 cáizhì ability and intelligence

才子 cáizǐ gifted scholar; man of parts; talented man: ～佳人 talents (scholars) and beauties

材

cái〈名〉① timber:木～ timber; lumber; wood ② material; stuff:药～ medicinal materials ③ capable talent ④ ability; talent; aptitude: 因～施教 teach students in accordance with their aptitude ⑤ coffin

材料 cáiliào ① material; stuff; data;原～ raw material ② [记载个人经历的] dossier

材料学 cáiliàoxué materials science; hylology

财

cái〈名〉 wealth; property; valuables: ～经工作 financial and economic work

财宝 cáibǎo money and valuables

财产 cáichǎn property; estate; means; assets; substance:～继承 property inheritance; succession to property

财阀 cáifá financial magnate; plutocrat; tycoon

财富 cáifù wealth; riches:自然～ natural wealth. 物质～ material wealth

财经 cáijīng finance and economics：～纪律 financial discipline

财会 cáikuài finance and accounting：～人员 accountants

财力 cáilì financial resources；financial capacity：～负担限度 limits of financial capacity

财贸 cáimào finance and trade

财迷 cáimí money-grubber：～心窍 be blinded by the love of money；be absorbed in the pursuit of wealth；have one's head turned by greed

财权 cáiquán ① property ownership；right of property ② economic rights；power over financial affairs

财神 cáishén the god of wealth

财团 cáituán financial group：国际～consortium

财务 cáiwù financial affairs：～包干 system of fixed quotas for revenues and expenditures. ～大检查 general check-up on the financial work

财物 cáiwù article of property；property；belongings

财源 cáiyuán financial resources；coffers；［国家的］source of revenue

财政 cáizhèng （public） finance：～包干 fiscal responsibility system. ～赤字 financial deficits. ～公开 make public the administration of finance. ～结余 surplus in the budget；financial surplus. ～收支平衡 balance of revenue and expenditure；Revenue and expenditure are in balance. ～性货币发行 issuance of money for financial purpose

裁

裁 cái 〈动〉① cut；cut into parts：用剪刀～纸 cut paper with scissors ② cut down；reduce；dismiss：～减人员 cut down （reduce） the staff ③ decide；judge；discern：～夺 consider and decide 〈名〉④ sanction；check：经济制～ economic sanction ⑤ form：文学体～ types or forms of literature

裁处 cáichǔ consider and solve；decide and take action：这件事由你～。This matter will be left in your hands.

裁定 cáidìng order；ruling；adjudication：～书 written order

裁缝 cáiféng tailor：［做女服或童装的］dressmaker

裁剪 cáijiǎn cut out （a garment）

裁减 cáijiǎn reduce；cut down：～机关工作人员 reduce （cut down） the staff of organizations

裁决 cáijué make a ruling；judge；decide；rule；ruling；adjudication；decision

裁军 cáijūn reduce armaments：～谈判 disarmament talks

裁判 cáipàn ① judge；decide ② ［体］ act as referee：～员 referee；judge；umpire

裁员 cáiyuán cut down the number of persons employed；reduce the staff：这家饭店已～30人。The hotel has dismissed 30 people from its staff.

cǎi

采 cǎi〈动〉① pick; pluck ② gather; collect: ～桑 gather mulberry leaves ③ take; adopt; accept: ～取一系列措施 adopt a series of measures ④ extract; mine: ～储比例 ratio between exploitation and reserves. ～区 mining area

采办 cǎibàn select and purchase on a considerable scale (esp. for a special occasion): ～年货 make special purchases for the Spring Festival

采伐 cǎifá chop; fell: ～工业 felling industry

采访 cǎifǎng (of a reporter) collect news; gather material; have an interview with; reporting; news coverage; cover: ～开会情况 cover a conference

采风 cǎifēng collect folk songs

采购 cǎigòu purchase; procure: ～员 purchaser. ～站 purchasing station

采光 cǎiguāng (natural) lighting; daylighting

采集 cǎijí gather; collect: ～经济 gathering economy

采掘 cǎijué excavate: ～设备 equipment for excavation

采矿 cǎikuàng mining: ～工程 mining engineering

采买 cǎimǎi ① select and purchase ② purchasing agent: 她可以当～。She can handle the purchasing job.; She can do all the purchasing for the occasion.

采煤 cǎiméi coal mining; coal extraction; coal cutting: ～工作面 coal face. ～回收率 coal recovery

采纳 cǎinà accept; take; adopt: ～某人意见 take sb.'s advice

采暖 cǎinuǎn heating: ～设备 heating equipment (facilities)

采取 cǎiqǔ adopt; assume or take: ～步骤 take steps

采写 cǎixiě (of a journalist) interview and write about

采用 cǎiyòng use; adopt; employ: ～良种 introduction of better strains of seeds

采油 cǎiyóu oil extraction; oil recovery

采摘 cǎizhāi pick (fruit, flowers, leaves, etc.); pluck: ～棉花 pick cotton

采制 cǎizhì gather and process: ～中草药 gather medicinal herbs and prepare them for use

彩 cǎi〈名〉① colour: ～色影片 colour film ② coloured silk; colour festoons: 剪～ cut the ribbon ③ cheer; applause: 喝～ acclaim; cheer ④ variety; splendour ⑤ lottery prize: 中～ win a prize (in a lottery, etc.)

彩笔 cǎibǐ colour pencil; crayon

彩车 cǎichē decorated vehicles; floats (in a parade)

彩绸 cǎichóu coloured silk

彩灯 cǎidēng coloured lights

彩电 cǎidiàn ① colour television (broadcasting) ② colour television set; colour TV

彩虹 cǎihóng rainbow

彩绘 cǎihuì coloured drawing or pattern:～陶 pottery with coloured drawings. ～俑 painted figurines

彩扩 cǎikuò enlargement of colour photographs

彩礼 cǎilǐ betrothal gifts (from the bridegroom to the bride's family); bride price

彩练 cǎiliàn coloured ribbon

彩墨画 cǎimòhuà painting in ink and colour

彩排 cǎipái dress rehearsal

彩票 cǎipiào lottery tickets

彩旗 cǎiqí coloured banner; bunting

彩券 cǎiquàn lottery ticket

彩色 cǎisè colour:～电视 colour television. ～照片 colour photographs

彩塑 cǎisù painted sculpture:～泥人 a painted clay figurine

彩陶 cǎitáo painted pottery (of a Neolithic culture)

睬 cǎi〈动〉pay attention to; take notice of:不要～他。Take no notice of him.; Ignore him.

踩 cǎi〈动〉step on; stamp; tread; trample:把火～灭 stamp out (tread down) the fire

踩水 cǎishuǐ[体] tread water

踩着别人肩膀往上爬 cǎizhebié rénjiānbǎng wàngshàng pá be intent on personal advancement at the expense of others

cài

菜 cài〈名〉① vegetable; greens:青～ green vegetables ② food:上街买～ go to the market to buy food ③ dish, item or course in menu:粤～ Guangdong dishes

菜板 càibǎn chopping board

菜帮 càibāng outer leaves (of a cabbage, etc.)

菜场 càichǎng food market; vegetable market; market

菜单 càidān menu; bill of fare; carte:～成本论 theory of menu costs

菜地 càidì vegetable plot

菜篮子 càilánzi ① basket for carrying vegetables and food items ② non-staple food:～工程 "shopping basket" project—a project for increasing food production; "market-basket" project; "vegetable basket" project

菜类作物 càilèi zuòwù green crops; cole crops

菜农 càinóng vegetable grower

菜圃 càipǔ vegetable garden; vegetable farm

菜谱 càipǔ menu; cookbook; recipe

菜市 càishì food market

菜蔬 càishū ① vegetables or greens ② (vegetable and meat) dishes prepared for a meal or a feast

菜摊儿 càitānr vegetable stall; booth for vegetable

菜肴 càiyáo cooked dishes (usu. meat dishes)

菜园 càiyuán vegetable garden; kitchen garden; vegetable farm

菜籽 càizǐ ① vegetable seeds ②

rapeseed

cān

参 cān〈动〉① join; take part in:～加生产 take part in production ② refer; consult:～照原文 refer to the text ③ call to pay one's respect:～谒烈士陵园 pay homage at the mausoleum of the martyred heroes

参拜 cānbài pay a courtesy call; pay respects to; make a formal visit to

参半 cānbàn half; half-and-half:疑信～ half believing, half doubting

参股 cāngǔ purchase of shares in enterprises

参观 cānguān visit; have a look around:～学校 visit a school. ～名胜古迹 go on sightseeing trips to scenic spots and historical monuments. ～游览 visit places of interest; go sightseeing

参加 cānjiā ① join (a group, organization, etc.); take part in (an activity):～会议 attend a meeting ② give (advice, suggestion, etc.):这件事你也来～点儿意见吧? Come and give us your view on the matter, won't you?

参见 cānjiàn ①[用于书或文章的注解] see:～第十章。See Chapter 10. ② pay one's respects to (a superior, etc.)

参看 cānkàn ① see [用于书或文章的注解]:～下面注解。See note below. ② read sth. for reference; consult:～有关书刊 consult relevant books and periodicals

参考 cānkǎo refer to; consult; for reference:～性计划 plan serves suggestions; production targets as reference

参谋 cānmóu ① staff officer:～长 chief of staff ② give advice

参赛 cānsài participate in a match or contest:～选手 contestant

参数 cānshù [数] parameter

参议 cānyì counsel; advise:～员 senator. ～院 senate

参与 cānyǔ take part in; partake in; participate in:～放款 participation loan

参阅 cānyuè refer to; confer (cf.)

参赞 cānzàn ① counsellor:商务～ commercial counsellor ② participate in planning; serve as an adviser:～军务 participate in military planning

参战 cānzhàn enter a war; take part in a battle:～国 belligerent state

参照 cānzhào refer to; consult; with reference to:～标准(依据) point of reference

参政 cānzhèng participate in government and political affairs. ～议政 participate in the administration and discussion of state affairs

餐 cān ①〈动〉eat; take a meal:饱～ eat one's fill ②〈名〉meal; food:便～ light meal

餐车 cānchē restaurant car; dining car; diner:列车上有一节～。There is a dining car on the train.

餐风宿露 cānfēng-sùlù eat in the winds and sleep in the dews—hardships of travel or a hard life in the open country

餐巾 cānjīn napkin:～纸 napkin paper

餐具 cānjù dinner set; tableware

餐馆 cānguǎn restaurant

餐厅 cāntīng ① dining room; dining hall ② restaurant

餐饮业 cānyǐnyè food and beverage trade

餐桌 cānzhuō dining table

cán

残 cán 〈形〉① cruel; ferocious savage:凶～ cruel ② remnant; remaining:～兵 remnants of routed troops ③ incomplete; broken; deficient:～品 substandard goods ④ crippled; maimed

残暴 cānbào cruel and ferocious; brutal; savage

残兵败将 cánbīng-bàijiàng remnants of a routed army.

残存 cáncún remnant; surviving; remaining:～的古动物 surviving ancient animals

残废 cánfèi disabled; crippled; handicapped:～军人 disabled (crippled) armyman

残羹剩饭 cángēng-shèngfàn remains of a meal; leftovers; crumbs from the table.

残骸 cánhái [被毁物的] wreckage

残害 cánhài cruelly injure or kill

残货 cánhuò damaged or substandard goods; shopworn goods

残疾 cánji physical disability; deformity:～人 handicapped people; the handicapped; disabled persons:～院 sanitarium

残迹 cánjì remaining trace, sign, etc.; vestiges

残酷 cánkù cruel; brutal; relentless:～竞争 cutthroat competition

残留 cánliú remain; be left over

残品 cánpǐn damaged articles; defective goods

残缺 cánquē incomplete; with parts missing:～不全 incomplete; fragmentary

残忍 cánrěn cruel; ruthless

残杀 cánshā murder; massacre; slaughter; kill savagely; butcher

残生 cánshēng one's remaining years

残余 cányú remnants; remains; survivals; vestiges:～势力 remaining (surviving) forces

残渣 cánzhā grounds; dregs; remnants; residue; slag:～余孽 dregs of the old society; dregs and leftover evils; dross and remnant evils

蚕 cán〈名〉silkworm

蚕豆 cándòu broad bean (the plant, the pod or the seed)

蚕茧 cánjiǎn silkworm cocoon

蚕农 cánnóng silkworm breeder; sericulturist

蚕桑 cánsāng silkworm breeding

and mulberry growing (as an industry)

蚕食 cánshí nibble at; encroach upon:～鲸吞 gnaw as a silkworm or swallow as a whale; seize another country's territory by piecemeal encroachment or wholesale annexation; encroach in various ways upon the territory of another country

蚕室 cánshì ① silkworm nursery ② castration chamber

蚕丝 cánsī natural silk; silk

惭 cán〈动〉feel ashamed:～愧 be ashamed of; feel abashed

cǎn

惨 cǎn〈形〉① miserable; pitiful; tragic:～遭杀害 be massacred in cold blood ② savage; cruel:～无人道 inhuman; brutal; brutal and callous ③〈副〉to a serious degree; disastrously

惨案 cǎn'àn tragedy; bloody incident; horrors; [政治性的] massacre; [凶杀] murder case; tragic case

惨白 cǎnbái deathly pale: 脸色～ look deathly pale

惨败 cǎnbài be crushingly (disastrously) defeated: 入侵之敌～而退。The invaders retreated after suffering a disastrous defeat.

惨不忍睹 cǎnbùrěndǔ too horrible (ghastly) to look at

惨淡 cǎndàn dismal; gloomy; bleak:～人生 bleak life

惨淡经营 cǎndàn-jīngyíng keep… going by painstaking effort; take great pains to carry on one's work under difficult circumstances; do something with painstaking efforts

惨祸 cǎnhuò horrible disaster; frightful calamity

惨境 cǎnjìng extremely miserable condition; dire straits

惨剧 cǎnjù dreadful, fatal event; tragic event; calamity; disaster

惨绝人寰 cǎnjuérénhuán tragic beyond compare in this human world; extremely tragic (brutal):～的暴行 an atrocity of unparalleled savagery

惨痛 cǎntòng deeply grieved; bitter; painful:～的经验 bitter experience

惨无人道 cǎnwúréndào inhuman; brutal: 遭受～的迫害 be subjected to inhuman persecution

惨遭不幸 cǎnzāobùxìng die a tragic death; meet a sad end

惨重 cǎnzhòng heavy; disastrous; grievous: 损失～ suffer heavy (grievous) losses:～的灾难 grievous calamity

惨状 cǎnzhuàng miserable condition; pitiful or horrible sight

càn

灿 càn〈形〉bright; illuminating

灿烂 cànlàn bright; splendid; brilliant; magnificent; glorious:～的前景 bright prospects

cāng

仓 cāng〈名〉 warehouse; storehouse:谷～ barn; granary

仓储 cāngchǔ keep… in a storehouse; warehousing:～式商店 cut-price (reduced-price) supermarket; warehouse-type supermarket [英国][场地大,顾客须购买一定数量的商品]

仓促(猝) cāngcù hurried; hurriedly; in a hurry; hasty; hastily:～行事 act in haste

仓单 cāngdān warehouse receipt; godown warrant; dock warrant

仓房 cāngfáng warehouse; storehouse

仓皇 cānghuáng in panic; in a flurry; hurry-skurry(-scurry):～失措 scared out of one's wits

仓库 cāngkù warehouse; storehouse; godown:～交货 ex godown; ex warehouse; ex store

仓租 cāngzū warehouse storage charges

苍 cāng〈形〉① dark green:～松 green pines ② blue:～天 the blue sky ③ grey; pale; ashy: 脸色～白 look pale

苍白 cāngbái ① pale; pallid; wan:脸色～ look pale ② lifeless; flat:这篇文章～无力。This article is flat writing.

苍劲 cāngjìn ① old and strong:～挺拔的青松 hardy, old pines ② vigorous and bold:他的书法～有力。His calligraphy is vigorous and forceful.

苍老 cānglǎo ① old (in appearance); hoary; (of an old man's voice) hoarse:他显得～多了。He looks much older than before. ② (of calligraphy or painting) vigorous; forceful

苍凉 cāngliáng desolate; bleak: 过去这一带满目～,现在已经完全变了样。The once desolate area has changed entirely.

苍茫 cāngmáng ① vast; boundless ② indistinct:暮色～ deepening shades of dusk; gathering dusk

苍穹 cāngqióng the vault of heaven; the firmament

苍生 cāngshēng the common people:～涂炭。The people were plunged into an abyss of misery.

苍天 cāngtiān blue sky; Heaven

苍蝇 cāngying fly; housefly:～拍 flyswatter

沧 cāng〈形〉(of the sea) dark blue

沧海 cānghǎi the deep blue sea; the sea

沧海桑田 cānghǎi-sāngtián Seas change into mulberry fields and mulberry fields into seas—time brings great changes to the world.; evanescence of worldly affairs

沧海一粟 cānghǎi-yīsù one grain afloat on a vast ocean; a drop in the ocean

沧桑 cāngsāng [见"沧海桑田"] many vicissitudes of life:～变化 interchange of sea and land

舱 cāng〈名〉cabin:客～(passenger) cabin. 装～ stow the hold

舱单 cāngdān shipping bill

舱口 cāngkǒu hatchway; hatch

舱面 cāngmiàn deck; on deck:～货物 goods carried on deck; on deck goods

舱内货 cāngnèihuò underdeck cargo

舱室 cāngshì cabin

舱位 cāngwèi ① cabin seat or berth ② shipping space:～包租 berth charter

cáng

藏 cáng〈动〉① hide; store; conceal:他～在树后。He concealed himself behind the trees. ② store; keep; lay by

藏垢纳污 cánggòu-nàwū shelter evil people and countenance evil practice; give shelter to all evil:～之地 a sink of iniquity; cesspool

藏龙卧虎 cánglóng-wòhǔ hidden dragons and crouching tigers—talented men still remained in concealment

藏匿 cángnì conceal; hide; go into hiding.

藏身 cāngshēn hide oneself; go into hiding:无处～ have no place to hide

藏书 cángshū ① collect books; keep books ② a collection of books; library:～家 book collector

藏拙 cángzhuō keep one's weakness unexposed; hide one's inadequacy by keeping quiet

cāo

操 cāo〈动〉① hold; grasp:～刀 hold a sword in one's hand ② act; do; operate:～之过急 act with undue haste; be too hasty ③[语言] speak:～着一口流利的德语 speak fluent Geman〈名〉④ drill; exercise:体～ gymnastics; exercises ⑤ conduct

操办 cāobàn manage affairs; make preparations or arrangements for:～婚事 make preparations for a wedding

操场 cāochǎng playground; sports ground; drill ground

操持 cāochí manage; handle:这件事由你～。I'll leave the matter in your hands.

操典 cāodiǎn drill book (manual); drill regulations

操法 cāofǎ methods and rules for military drill or physical exercise

操课 cāokè [军] military drill; lecture as part of military training:～时间 time for military drill or lecture

操劳 cāoláo work hard (at, for); be preoccupied with:～过度 overwork oneself

操练 cāoliàn drill; train

操神 cāoshén take trouble:让您～受累了。Sorry to have put you to so much trouble.

操守 cāoshǒu discretion in conduct;personal integrity; self-discipline and restraint

操心 cāoxīn worry about; take trouble; take pains:这件事,你不必~了。You needn't worry about it. 不少父母为子女操碎了心。Many parents go to a lot of trouble for their children.

操之过急 cāozhī-guòjí act with undue haste: 不宜~。It's no good being overhasty (overzealous).

操纵 cāozòng ① operate; manage; control:~机器 operate machines ② manipulate; rig; govern:~市场 manipulate the market; rig the market

操作 cāozuò operate; manipulate; handle:~规程 rules of operation

糙 cāo〈形〉coarse; rough; rude:~纸 rough paper

糙米 cāomǐ brown rice; unpolished rice

cáo

曹 cáo〈名〉① people of the same kind ② (Cáo) a surname

嘈 cáo

嘈杂 cáozá noisy:人声~ a hubbub of voices

漕 cáo〈名〉water transport (esp. of grain)

漕粮 cáoliáng grain transported to the capital by water in former times

漕运 cáoyùn the transport of grain by water to the capital in former times

槽 cáo〈名〉① trough:水~ water trough ② groove; notch

槽床 cáochuáng troughstand

槽钢 cáogāng channel iron

cǎo

草 cǎo ①〈名〉straw; grass; hay; ②〈形〉careless; rough ③〈动〉draft:起~文件 draft a document

草案 cǎo'àn draft (of a law, a plan, etc.)

草包 cǎobāo ① straw bag; straw sack ② a bungling oaf; good-for-nothing

草本植物 cǎoběn zhíwù herbs

草编 cǎobiān straw-woven ware; straw knitting; straw weaving

草草 cǎocǎo carelessly; perfunctorily; cursorily:~了事 do sth. carelessly; get through with sth. any old way

草测 cǎocè make a preliminary survey

草场 cǎochǎng meadow; pasture; grassland

草创 cǎochuàng start (an enterprise, etc.):~时期 initial (pioneering) stage

草丛 cǎocóng a thick growth of grass

草地 cǎodì ① grassland; meadow; pasture ② lawn

草稿 cǎogǎo (rough) draft; rough (foul) copy

cradle; seedbed; source; hotbed

cēn

参 cēn
另见 cān

参差不齐 cēncī-bùqí uneven; jagged; be different; be irregular; be varied; [水平、程度等] not level: 学生英语水平～。The students are not level in English.

céng

层 céng 〈名〉① storey; tier; stratum: 六～大楼 a six-storey building ② layer: 一～薄冰 a thin layer (sheet) of ice ③ 〈副〉 layer upon layer: ～～包围 surround ring upon ring

层层 céngcéng layer upon layer; ring upon ring: ～把关 check at each level

层出不穷 céngchū-bùqióng emerge in an endless stream; appear one after another; come thick and fast; be continuing without end

层次 céngcì ① gradation; levels: 行政～ administrative levels ② order; arrangement (of ideas, colour, etc.): ～分明 [文章等] well arranged; coherent structure

层递 céngdì [剧] (即高潮) climax

层叠 céngdié one on top of another: 层层叠叠的雪峰 range upon range of snow-capped mountains

层峦 céngluán range upon range of hills: ～起伏 range upon range of undulating hills

层面 céngmiàn level; facet: 审美活动的～ facet of aesthetic activity

层序 céngxù hierarchy: 技术～ skill hierarchy. 阶级～ class hierarchy.

曾 céng 〈副〉 formerly; once; sometime ago: 她～教过我法语。She once taught me French. 我未～去过英国。I haven't been to Britain.
另见 zēng

曾几何时 céngjǐhéshí It was not long before …; only a short while ago; not long after

曾经 céngjīng once; formerly: 我以前～见过她。I have seen her before.

曾经沧海 céngjīng-cānghǎi have seen much of the world; have experienced great changes; have sailed the seven seas; have experienced the vicissitudes of life

cèng

蹭 cèng 〈动〉① rub; scrape; scratch: 他的手～破了皮。He grazed his hand. ② rub against sth. and get stained ③ move slowly: 快干吧！别～时间了。Get on with your work. Don't dawdle. ④〈方〉cadge; scrounge:他常～吃～喝。He's always cadging meals and drinks.

chā

叉 chā〈名〉① fork:钢～ steel fork ② cross:在拼错的词上打一个～ mark the wrongly spelled word with a cross ③〈动〉work with a fork; fork:～草上垛 fork hay onto a stack
另见 chá,chǎ

杈 chā〈名〉wooden fork; hayfork; pitchfork
另见 chà

差 chā〈名〉① difference; dissimilarity; discrepancy:时～ time difference ② mistake:偏～ deviation ③ balance
另见 chà,chāi

差别 chābié difference; distinction; disparity:城乡～ disparity (difference) between town and country. ～出生率 differential birth rate

差别关税 chābié guānshuì differential rates of duty; differential duties

差错 chācuò ① mistake; error; slip ② mishap; accident:万一这女孩子出了～怎么办? What if anything should happen to the girl?

差额 chā'é difference; margin; balance:～调节税 regulatory taxes on differential incomes. ～选举 competitive election; selective election

差价 chājià price differences; price disparities between; price differentials

差距 chājù gap:找～ find out where one lags behind; find where the gap lies; find out shortcomings

差强人意 chāqiáng-rényì barely satisfactory; just passable; not too disappointing

差异 chāyì difference; divergency; discrepancy

差之毫厘,谬以千里 chā zhī háolí,miùyǐ qiānlǐ A small discrepancy leads to a great error.; The discrepancy of a single hair will lead an error of a thousand *li*.; A miss is as good as a mile.

插 chā〈动〉① insert; thrust; stick in:把门～上 blot the door ② interpose; insert:～入几句话 put in a few additional words. ～入广告 insertion

插班 chābān join a class in the middle of the course

插队 chāduì[不按次序排队] jump the queue; cut in on a queue

插花 chāhuā arrangement of flowers; flower arrangement

插曲 chāqǔ ① interlude; song in a film or play ② episode

插手 chāshǒu ① meddle in; poke (push) one's nose into; get one's finger into the pie ② join in; take part in

插图 chātú illustration; plate:丰

富的～课本 well-illustrated textbook

插嘴 chāzuǐ put (throw) in a word; chop (chip) in; interrupt; chime in

chá

叉 chá 〈动〉 block up; jam

茬 chá 〈名〉 ① stubble:麦～ wheat stubble ② crop; batch:换～ change crops

茬口 chákǒu ① crops for rotation ② soil on which a crop has been planted and harvested ③ chance; opportunity

茬子 cházi stubble:刨～ dig up the stubble

茶 chá 〈名〉 ① tea:沏～ make tea. 头泡～ the first infusion of tea ② tea plant

茶杯 chábēi teacup

茶匙 cháchí teaspoon

茶道 chádào [日本] tea cult; tea ceremony

茶点 chádiǎn tea served with pastries; tea and pastries; refreshments

茶房 cháfáng waiter (who serves tea and does odd jobs in a hotel, teahouse, theatre or train)

茶馆 cháguǎn teahouse:开～ run a teahouse

茶话会 cháhuàhuì tea party; tea forum

茶镜 chájìng glasses with citrine or brown-coloured lenses; sunglasses

茶具 chájù tea set; tea-things; tea service

茶楼 chálóu teahouse with two or more storeys

茶盘 chápán tea tray; teaboard

茶水 cháshuǐ tea or plain boiled water (supplied to walkers, etc.)

茶叶 cháyè tea leaves; tea

茶余饭后 cháyú-fànhòu over a cup of tea after a meal — at one's leisure; (to become the subject of) teahouse and wineshop gossip

茶园 cháyuán ① tea plantation ② a place where tea and soft drinks are served; tea garden

茶盅 cházhōng handleless teacup

茶砖 cházhuān compressed tea; brick tea

茶座 cházuò ① teahouse; tea-stall with seats; saloon:音乐～ music saloon ② seats in a teahouse or tea garden:这家茶馆有 40 多个～儿。There are over 40 seats in this teahouse.

查 chá 〈动〉 ① check; examine:～某人的身分 check up on sb. ② investigate; inquire into; look into:～一～事故的原因 find out the cause of an accident ③ look up; consult:～档案 look into the archives

查案 chá'àn investigate into a case

查办 chábàn investigate and deal with accordingly:撤职～ dismiss sb. and have him prosecuted; dismiss a person from office and prosecute him

查抄 cháchāo make an inventory of a criminal's possessions and confiscate them; confiscate

查处 cháchù investigate and prosecute(deal with)

查点 chádiǎn check the number or amount of; make an inventory of: ～出席人数 check the number of people present; check the attendance. ～存货 make an inventory of the goods in stock; take stock

查对 cháduì check and verify: ～原文 check against the original (text, manuscript, etc.)

查访 cháfǎng go around and make inquiries; investigate: ～案情 investigate the details of a crime

查封 cháfēng confiscate and seal up; seal up; close down

查号台 cháhàotái (at a telephone exchange) directory inquiries; information

查户口 cháhùkǒu check residence cards; check on household occupants

查获 cháhuò ferret out; hunt down and seize; track down; apprehend: ～罪犯 track down (ferrect out) a criminal. 当场～脏物 seize the spoils on the spot

查禁 chájìn ban; prohibit; suppress: 依法～淫秽书刊 have pornographic literature banned according to law

查究 chájiū investigate and ascertain(cause, responsibility, etc.): ～责任 find out who should be held responsible

查勘 chákān survey; prospect: ～地界 survey the boundaries of a piece of land

查看 chákàn look over; examine: ～帐目 examine the accounts

查明 chámíng find out; discover; ascertain; investigation has now revealed that...: ～真相 find out the truth; ascertain the facts

查票 chápiào check tickets: ～员 ticket-inspector

查讫 cháqì checked

查清 cháqīng make a thorough investigation of; check up on: ～一件事情的来龙去脉 find out how sth. started and developed

查实 cháshí verify

查税 cháshuì make a tax inspection

查无实据 cháwúshíjù investigations show (reveal) no evidence against

查询 cháxún inquire about: ～地址 inquire about sb.'s address

查验 cháyàn check; examine: ～护照 examine a passport. 接受口岸检查机关的～ submit to inspection by the inspection office at the port

查阅 cháyuè look up; consult: ～字典 consult a dictionary; look up a word in the dictionary

查帐 cházhàng examine (check, audit) accounts; audit: ～员 auditor

查证 cházhèng investigate and verify; check: ～属实 be checked and found to be true;

be verified

搽 chá〈动〉put (powder, ointment, etc.) on the skin; apply:～雪花膏 put on vanishing cream

碴 chá〈方〉be cut (by broken glass, china, etc.)

碴儿 chár ① broken pieces; fragments:玻璃～ fragments of glass ② sharp edge of broken glass, china, etc. ③ feeling of animosity; grudge; the cause of a quarrel ④ sth. said or mentioned:接不上～ cannot take the cue; cannot take the hint

察 chá〈动〉examine; look into; inspect; scrutinize; observe:～其言,观其行 check what he says against what he does; examine his words and watch his deeds.

察办 chábàn investigate a case and determine how to handle it

察访 cháfǎng make firsthand observations and inquiries; make calls and investigate

察觉 chájué be conscious of; become aware of; perceive:开始我没有～到她有病。At first I wasn't aware that she was ill.

察勘 chákān survey

察看 chákàn examine carefully; inspect; survey:～风向 watch which way the wind is blowing

察其言,观其行 cháqíyán, guānqíxíng check a person's words and watch his deeds; check what a person says against what he does

察言观色 cháyán-guānsè examine a man's language and observe his countenance; carefully weigh up sb.'s words and watch the expression on his face; watch a person's every mood

chǎ

叉 chǎ〈动〉part so as to form a fork; fork:～着腿站着 stand with one's legs apart

衩 chǎ 见"裤～"
另见 chà

chà

汊 chà〈名〉a branch of a river

汊口 chàkǒu mouth of a tributary

杈 chà〈名〉(tree) branch
另见 chā

杈子 chàzi (tree) branch

岔 chà ①〈名,动〉fork ②〈名〉accident; trouble:你放心吧,出不了～。Don't worry, everything will be all right.

岔开 chàkāi ① branch off; diverge ② diverge to (another topic); change the subject (of conversation) ③ stagger:把休假日～ stagger the days off

岔口 chàkǒu fork (in a road)

岔路 chàlù branch road; byroad; side road

岔子 chàzi ① trouble; accident:

发动机出了什么～? What's wrong with the engine? ② mistake; error; fault:找～ find (pick) fault

刹 chà〈名〉Buddhist temple:古～ ancient temple
另见 shā

刹那 chànà in the twinkle of an eye; in an instant (flash); in a twinkling

衩 chà〈名〉vent or slit in the sides of a garment
另见 chǎ

诧 chà〈动〉be surprised:～异 be surprised; be astonished (amazed)

差 chà〈动〉① differ from; fall short of:～得远 a far cry ② wanting; short of:～5个人 five people short〈形〉③ wrong:这你可说～了。You're wrong here. ④ poor; inferior; not up to standard:这台收音机质量～。This radio is poor in quality.
另见 chāi

差不点儿 chàbudiǎnr almost; very nearly; practically:她委屈得～要哭出来。She felt so hurt that she could hardly keep back her tears.

差不多 chàbuduō ① almost; nearly; about:～六点了。It is nearly six o'clock. ② about the same; similar:他们俩高矮～。They two are about the same in height.

差得多 chàdéduō far from …

差点儿 chàdiǎnr ① almost; nearly; all but:我～摔了一跤。I all but stumbled. ② not quite enough; not quite up to the mark:她的技术还～。Her technique is not quite up to the mark.

差劲儿 chàjìnr no good; disappointing

姹 chà〈形〉beautiful

姹紫嫣红 chàzǐ-yānhóng brilliant purples and reds — beautiful flowers; deep purples and bright reds; a riot of brilliant purple and tender crimson

chāi

拆 chāi〈动〉① take open; take apart:～信 open a letter ② disassemble; dismantle; unknit:～除军事基地 dismantle military bases

拆除 chāichú dismantle; tear down; demolish:～破房子 pull down a dilapidated old house. ～障碍物 dismantle (remove) obstacles

拆穿 chāichuān expose; reveal; unmask; lay bare:拆穿…的面目 expose someone in his true colours as …; show someone up for

拆东墙补西墙 chāi dōngqiáng bǔ xīqiáng tear down the east wall to repair the west wall—resort to makeshift solution; reinforce one place at the expense of another

拆毁 chāihuǐ demolish; pull down; tear down

拆借 chāijiè a short-term loan made at a daily interest

拆开 chāikāi take apart; open; separate:把机器～disassemble a machine

拆款 chāikuǎn day-to-day loan; call money

拆卖 chāimài sell by the piece (things usu. sold by the set):这套家具～。This set of furniture can be sold by the piece.

拆迁 chāiqiān dismantle and move; have one's house pulled down (dismantled) and its occupants move elsewhere

拆散 chāisàn disjoin; [家庭、合伙] break up:～鸳鸯 separate lovers; break up a married couple

拆台 chāitái let sb. down; pull away a prop from behind; cut the ground (pull the rug) from under the feet of; undermine:不要拆我的台。Don't let me down.

拆息 chāixī a daily interest rate on private loans or deposits; short-term interest

拆洗 chāixǐ wash after removing the padding or lining; take apart and clean:～机器 take apart and clean machines

拆卸 chāixiè disassemble; dismantle; dismount; tear down

拆帐 chāizhàng payment by a share of the takings

钗 chāi〈名〉hairpin (formerly worn by women for adornment):金～ a gold hairpin

差 chāi ①〈动〉send on an errand; dispatch:～她去办件事。Send (dispatch) her on an errand. ②〈名〉errand; job:兼～ moonlight

另见 chā,chà

差旅费 chāilǚfèi allowances for a business trip

差遣 chāiqiǎn send sb. on errand (mission); assign; dispatch

差使 chāishǐ ① send; dispatch; assign ② chāishi official post; billet; commission; job:他一点也不喜欢他这新～。He doesn't like this new job of his at all.

差事 chāishi errand; assignment:给你们一件～。Here's a job for you.

差役 chāiyì ① corvée; requisitioned service; duties ② bailiff (runner) in a feudal *yamen*

chái

柴 chái〈名〉firewood; wood:打～ cut firewood

柴火 cháihuo firewood; faggot

柴米油盐 chái-mǐ-yóu-yán fuel, rice, oil and salt — chief daily necessities; bread and butter:～的人生 "bread and butter" details of life

柴窑 cháiyáo chai kiln

柴油 cháiyóu diesel oil:～机 diesel engine

豺 chái〈名〉jackal

豺狼 cháiláng jackals and wolves;

[指人] wolf:～成性 rapacious and ruthless; wolfish-hearted; wolfish
豺狼当道 cháiláng-dāngdào jackals and wolves hold sway—the cruel and the wicked are in power

chān

掺 chān〈动〉见"搀"
搀 chān〈动〉① help sb. by the arm; support sb. with one's hand ② mix; adulterate:用水～酒 mix wine with water
搀兑 chānduì mingle; mix
搀扶 chānfú support sb. with one's arm; assist sb. to walk: ～某人起来 assist sb. to his feet
搀混 chānhùn mix up:两种药给～在一起了。The two drugs have been mixed up.
搀和 chānhuo ① mix:粗粮细粮～着吃 have a mixed diet of fine and coarse grain ② meddle; disturb; cause trouble:你别在这儿瞎～。Don't hang around interfering.
搀假 chānjiǎ adulterate:～的酒 adulterated wine. ～货 adulterant
搀杂 chānzá mix; mingle; blend; [酒等] sophisticate:～使假 mix in the inferior or fake

chán

谗 chán〈名〉slander; backbite
谗害 chánhài calumniate or slander sb. in order to have him persecuted; frame sb. up:捏造事实～某人 frame the case against sb.
谗言 chányán slanderous talk; false charge; calumny:～可畏。Slanderous talk (Calumny) is dreadful.
婵 chán
婵娟 chánjuān ① lovely (used in ancient writings to describe women) ② the moon
馋 chán〈形〉greedy; gluttonous:嘴～ fond of good food; greedy
馋涎欲滴 chánxiányùdī mouth drooling with greed; lick one's chops; mouth watering:使我～ make my mouth water
馋嘴 chánzuǐ ① gluttonous ② glutton; a greedy eater
禅 chán〈名〉① prolonged and intense contemplation; deep meditation:～坐 sit in meditation ② Buddhist
禅房 chánfáng ① Buddhist monks' living quarters ② Buddhist temple
禅让 chánràng peaceful shift in rule; abdication; abdicate and hand over the crown to another person
禅师 chánshī Chan Master; Meditation Master; meditators; an honourable title for a Buddhist monk
禅堂 chántáng a room or hall in a

Buddhist monastery set apart for meditation; meditation room or hall

禅宗 chánzōng Chan Buddhism; Chan sect; Zen

缠 chán〈动〉① wind; twine ② tangle; tie up:我整天都被工作～着。I am tied to my work all day.

缠绵 chánmián ① lingering:～病榻 be bedridden with a lingering disease ② touching; sentimental:～悱恻 full of sentimentality; touching

缠磨 chánmo pester; bother:这件事一直～着我。This problem has long been bothering me.

缠绕 chánrào ① wind round; twine (about):藤～在树干上。The vine twines about a tree trunk. ② worry; harass

缠手 chánshǒu (of a matter) be troublesome; be hard to deal with; (of an illness) be hard to cure:这件事有些～。That's a rather troublesome matter.

蝉 chán〈名〉cicada

蝉联 chánlián continue to hold a post (title); stay on a position for another term:～冠军 win the championship in succession

蝉蜕 chántuì ① cicada slough (used as a Chinese medicine) ② free (extricate) oneself

潺 chán

潺潺 chánchán murmur; purl; babble:～流水 murmuring stream

蟾 chán

蟾蜍 chánchú ① toad ② the fabled three-legged toad in the moon ③ the moon

蟾宫 chángōng Toad Palace—the moon

chǎn

产 chǎn ①〈动〉produce; yield:～粮区 grain-producing area ② give birth to:她昨晚～下一女孩。She gave birth to a girl last night.〈名〉③ product:矿～ mineral product ④ property; estate:房地～ real estate (property)

产次 chǎncì[计生] parity

产地 chǎndì place of production (origin)

产地证明书 chǎndì zhèngmíngshū certificate of origin

产儿 chǎn'ér ① newborn baby ② result; product

产房 chǎnfáng delivery room

产妇 chǎnfù lying-in woman; woman in childbirth; puerpera

产羔率 chǎngāolǜ sheep reproduction rate; lambing rate

产供销 chǎngòngxiāo production, procurement of the means of production and marketing; production, supply and marketing of products

产假 chǎnjià maternity leave

产科 chǎnkē ① obstetrical department; maternity department ② obstetrics

产量 chǎnliàng output; yield

产品 chǎnpǐn product;[农] produce:~范围 range of products. ~分成合同 product-sharing contract. ~升级换代 upgrading and updating of product

产前产后 chǎnqián chǎnhòu before and after production

产权 chǎnquán property right

产生 chǎnshēng produce; bring forth; engender; yield; give rise to:~结果 produce result

产物 chǎnwù product; result; outcome:集体智慧的~ result of collective wisdom

产销 chǎnxiāo production and marketing:~平衡 balance of production and marketing

产业 chǎnyè ① property; estate ② industry:~结构 industrial structure. 第三~ tertiary industry

产值 chǎnzhí output value:总~ total output value

谄 chǎn〈动〉flatter; curry favour with; toady to; fawn on; curry favour with

谄媚 chǎnmèi fawn on; flatter; toady; curry favour with:~逢迎 fawn on sb.; flatter for favour. ~奉承 stoop to flattery. ~文学 obsequious literature

谄上欺下 chǎnshàng-qīxià be servile to one's superiors and tyrannical to one's subordinates

谄谀 chǎnyú flatter servilely

铲 chǎn ①〈名〉shovel; ②〈动〉move (lift) with a shovel; shovel

铲车 chǎnchē forklift truck

铲除 chǎnchú wipe out; root out; uproot; eradicate:~战争的根源 root out the causes of war

铲子 chǎnzi shovel; spade

阐 chǎn〈动〉make clear; explain

阐发 chǎnfā elucidate

阐明 chǎnmíng explicate; expound; elucidate; exposition; give an explanation; clarify

阐释 chǎnshì explain; expound; interpret

阐述 chǎnshù set forth; expound; elaborate:~意见 set forth one's views

chàn

忏 chàn〈动〉repent

忏悔 chànhuǐ repent; show penitence for; confession:对自己罪行表示~ show penitence for one's misdeeds

颤 chàn〈动〉quiver; vibrate:~动 vibrate; quiver
另见 zhàn

颤动 chàndòng vibrate; quiver:树叶在微风中~。The leaves quivered (trembled) in the breeze.

颤抖 chàndǒu shake; tremble; quiver; shiver:吓得两腿~ shake in one's shoes

颤声 chànshēng tremolo

颤巍巍 chànwēiwēi (usu. of aged people) tottering; faltering:老太太~地走出屋来。The old lady came tottering out of her room.

颤音 chànyīn shake; trill

chāng

伥 chāng〈名〉the ghost of one devoured by a tiger, who helps the tiger to devour others

昌 chāng〈形〉prosperous; flourishing

昌明 chàngmíng flourishing; well-developed; advanced: ～盛世 time of prosperity

猖 chāng

猖獗 chāngjué unbridled; rampancy; run wild; be rampant

猖獗一时 chāngjué-yīshí be rampant for a while; run wild for a time

猖狂 chāngkuáng on the rampage; frantic; blatant; unbridled; furious; savage; reckless

娼 chāng

娼妇 chāngfù bitch; whore

娼妓 chāngjì prostitute

cháng

长 cháng ①〈形〉long: 这条河很长。This is a long river.〈名〉② length: 那座桥有 100 米～。The length of the bridge is 100 metres. ③ strong point; forte ④〈动〉be good at; be strong in: 他～于绘画。He is good at painting.

长波 chángbō long-wave

长城 Chángchéng the Great Wall

长处 chángchù strong (good) point; merit; good qualities

长辞 chángcí leave forever—die; pass away: 与世长辞 depart from the world forever

长此以往 chángcǐyǐwǎng if things go on like this; if things continue this way

长存 chángcún live forever

长凳 chángdèng backless bench

长度 chángdù length: 测量长江的～ survey the length of the Yangtze River

长短 chángduǎn ① length ② strong and weak point; merits and demrits; gossip: 议论别人～ gossip about others

长吨 chángdūn long ton

长河 chánghé long river—endless flow: 绝对真理的～ the endless flow of absolute truth

长话短说 chánghuà-duǎnshuō to make a long story short

长江 chángjiāng Changjiang (Yangtze) River: ～三峡工程 Three Gorges Project on the Yangtze River

长久 chángjiǔ long; permanent; long-term; lasting: ～之计 a long-term policy; a permanent planning; lasting solution

长空 chángkōng the vast sky: 万里～ the vast expanse of the sky

长廊 chángláng ① a covered corridor or walk; gallery ② the Long Corridor (of the Summer Palace in Beijing)

长年 chángnián all the year round
长年累月 chángnián-lěiyuè year in year out; over the years
长跑 chángpǎo long-distance running; long-distance race: 我们每天～。We go long-distance running every day. 这次运动会,我参加了一万米～。I ran the 10,000-metre race at the sports meet.
长篇大论 chángpiān-dàlùn a lengthy speech or article
长篇小说 chángpiān xiǎoshuō full-length novel; novel
长期 chángqī long-term; of long duration: ～病号 patient with chronic disease. ～存款 long-term deposits. ～共存 long-term coexistence
长期共存,互相监督 chángqī gòngcún, hùxiāng jiāndū long-term coexistence and mutual supervision (a principle upheld by the Chinese Communist Party in its relations with China's other democratic parties)
长驱直入 chángqū-zhírù drive straight in; drive deep into
长寿 chángshòu long life; longevity: 祝你～! Wish you a long life!
长途 chángtú long distance: ～电话 long-distance (trunk) call
长途跋涉 chángtú-báshè make a long, arduous journey; trudge a long distance; trek a long way
长线产品 chángxiàn chǎnpǐn oversupplied products; goods in excess supply; slow-selling products
长效 chángxiào enduring effect
长吁短叹 chángxū-duǎntàn utter sighs and groans; moan and groan
长远 chángyuǎn long-term; long-range: ～打算 long-term plan
长征 chángzhēng ① expedition ② the Long March
长治久安 chángzhì-jiǔ'ān lasting political stability; maintain long-term social stability
长足 chángzú by leaps and bounds; rapid; speedy: ～的进步 rapid progress; great strides forward

场 cháng 〈名〉 ① level open space: ～院 threshing ground ② country fair, market: 赶～ go to market
另见 chǎng

肠 cháng 〈名〉 ① intestines; bowels ② heart: 愁～ pent-up feelings of sadness. 好心～ kindhearted
肠鸣 chángmíng [医] borborygmus
肠胃 chángwèi intestines and stomach; stomach; belly: ～不好 suffer from stomach trouble
肠炎 chángyán [医] enteritis

尝 cháng〈动〉 ① taste; try the flavour of: ～酒 taste wine ② experience; come to know ③ 〈副〉 ever; once
尝试 chángshì try; have a try (at); attempt
尝受 chángshòu have a personal experience of (hardship, mis-

ery, etc.); taste (the bitterness of life, etc.)

尝味 chángwèi try the flavour; taste; savour:这是一道名菜,你一定要~。Do have a taste of this well-known dish.

尝鲜 chángxiān have a taste of a delicacy; have a taste of what is just in season

尝新 chángxīn taste something just in season

常 cháng ①〈形〉common; ordinary; usual:习以为~ be used (accustomed) to sth. ②〈副〉frequently; often; usually:他~来吗? Does he often come here?

常备不懈 chángbèi-bùxiè always be on the alert; be ever prepared against; all-time preparedness against

常备军 chángbèijūn standing army

常常 chángcháng frequently; often; many a time; more often than not:我俩~通信。The two of us frequently write to each other.

常规 chángguī convention; routine; common practice:~包装 conventional method of packing. ~能源 conventional energy sources

常会 chánghuì regular meeting; regular session

常见 chángjiàn be common:这儿的春天,风沙是~的。Duststorms are common here in spring.

常见病 chángjiànbìng common ailment; common disease; common encountered disease

常居地 chángjūdì habitual residence

常礼 chánglǐ common courtesy; etiquette (in everyday life)

常理 chánglǐ general rule; what is normal:按~ normally

常例 chánglì common practice

常年 chángnián all the year round; year in year out:~法律顾问 permanent legal adviser

常情 chángqíng reason; sense:按照~,他们会提出这个问题同我们讨论的。It stands to reason that they will take up the matter with us.

常任 chángrèn permanent; standing:安理会~理事国 permanent member of the Security Council. ~制的国家公务员 public servants whose tenure in office is permanent

常设 chángshè established for long-term; standing; permanent:~机构 standing body; permanent organization

常识 chángshí ① general knowledge; elementary knowledge:科学~ general knowledge of science ② common sense

常事 chángshì common happening; routine

常务 chángwù day-to-day business; routine:~董事 managing (executive) director

常用 chángyòng in common use; common:~字 Chinese characters in common use

常用词语 chángyòng cíyǔ everyday expressions

常住人口 chángzhù rénkǒu resident population; regular residents

常驻 chángzhù resident; permanent: ～记者 resident correspondent. ～人员 permanent personnel

偿 cháng 〈动〉 ① compensate for; pay back; repay ② fulfil; meet

偿付 chángfù pay; pay back: ～期限 term of payment

偿还 chánghuán pay back; repay; refund; repay

偿命 chángmìng pay with one's life (for a murder); a life for a life

偿清 chángqīng pay off; clear off: ～债务 clear off a debt

偿债 chángzhài pay a debt: ～能力 debt-paying ability; liquidity

chǎng

厂 chǎng 〈名〉 factory; works; plant; mill

厂房 chǎngfáng ① factory building ② factory workshop

厂风 chǎngfēng factory atmosphere

厂家 chǎngjiā factory; mill: 有些～濒临破产。Some of the factories are verging on bankruptcy.

厂矿企业 chǎngkuàng qǐyè factories and mining enterprises

厂礼拜(～休日) chǎnglǐbài (～xiūrì) factory rest day

厂商 chǎngshāng factory owner; firm: ～投资判断 investment decision of firms

厂史 chǎngshǐ factory history

厂务会议 chǎngwùhuìyì factory-level meeting

厂校挂钩 chǎng-xiào guàgōu link up factories with schools

厂长 chǎngzhǎng director of a factory: ～负责制 system of a factory director's responsibility

厂址 chǎngzhǐ the site (location) of a factory: 选择～ choose a site for building a factory

厂主 chǎngzhǔ factory owner; millowner

场 chǎng 〈名〉 ① a place where people gather; ground: 操～ playground; drill (sports) ground ② 〈名〉 farm: 国营农～ state farm ③ 〈名〉 site; spot: 当～抓住 caught on the spot ④ [剧] stage: 上～ come on the stage ⑤ scene ⑥ [用于文娱体育活动] 一～球赛 a ball game 另见 cháng

场次 chǎngcì the number of showings of a film, play, etc.

场地 chǎngdì space; place; site; field: ～使用权 right to the use of a site. ～心理学 field psychology

场合 chǎnghé occasion; situation: 外交～ a diplomatic occasion

场面 chǎngmiàn ① scene (of fiction, drama, etc.); spectacle ② occasion; scene: 友好的～ a scene of friendship ③ appearance; show; front: 摆～ keep up appearances

场所 chǎngsuǒ place; location;

arena：公共～ public place

敞 chǎng ①〈动〉open：～着门 leave the door open ②〈形〉spacious；open

敞地制 chǎngdìzhì open field system

敞怀 chǎnghuái have one's shirt unbuttoned：bare one's chest

敞开 chǎngkāi ① be wide open：～思想 speak one's mind；open up one's thought；say what's on (in) one's mind ②［货物等］unlimited；unrestricted：～供应 sufficient supply；unlimited supply；be supplied without any restriction

敞口 chǎngkǒu open：～花钱 reckless spending

敞亮 chǎngliàng ① light and spacious：这间屋子很～。This room is light and spacious. ②(of one's thinking) clear

敞篷车 chǎngpéngchē open car

氅 chǎng〈名〉cloak

chàng

怅 chàng〈形〉depressed；disappointed；sad：～然 disappointed；upset

怅然 chàngrán disappointed；upset

怅惘 chàngwǎng depressed；dispirited；disconsolate；melancholy：感到～ feel depressed

畅 chàng〈形〉① unimpeded；smooth：～行无阻 advance unimpeded；go about unimpeded ② uninhibited；free：～饮 drink one's fill

畅怀 chànghuái to one's heart's content：～痛饮 drink to one's heart's content

畅快 chàngkuài free from inhibitions and happy；carefree：心情～ have ease of mind；be carefree and happy

畅抒 chàngshū freely express：～己见 air one's own views freely

畅所欲言 chàngsuǒyùyán speak out one's mind freely；express one's opinions freely；speak without any inhibitions

畅谈(叙) chàngtán (xù) talk to one's heart's content；have an animated talk (with)

畅通 chàngtōng unimpeded；unblocked：这里过去是穷乡僻壤，现在铁路公路都～了。This formerly inaccessible place can now be easily reached by road and rail.

畅想 chàngxiǎng give full play to one's imagination

畅销 chàngxiāo be in great demand；sell like hot cakes；sell well；have a ready market for：～书 best seller. ～小说 popular novel

畅叙 chàngxù chat cheerfully (usu. about old times)：～友情 recall old friendship heartily；relive an old friendship

畅游 chàngyóu ① enjoy a trip (to)；have a pleasant tour；enjoy a sightseeing tour：～名胜古迹 enjoy a trip to places of historic interest ② enjoy a good swim

倡 chàng 〈动〉 advocate initiate

倡导 chàngdǎo promote; take the initiative

倡始 chàngshǐ initiate; start; found

倡始人 chàngshǐrén initiator; founder

倡议 chàngyì propose; initiate; sponsor: ～书 initial written proposal; proposal

倡议权 chàngyìquán [外] initiative

唱 chàng〈动〉 ① sing: 齐～ sing in unison ② call; cry: 鸡～三遍 The cock has crowed for the third time. ③〈名〉a song or a singing part of a Chinese opera

唱白脸 chàngbáiliǎn wear the white makeup of the stage villain; play the villain; pretend to be harsh and severe

唱本 chàngběn the libretto or script of a ballad-singer

唱词 chàngcí libretto; words of a ballad; song lyrics

唱段 chàngduàn [剧] aria

唱对台戏 chàng duìtáixì put on a rival show; set oneself up against; set up a rival stage in opposition to; stage rival dramas in competition with; enter into rivalry

唱反调 chàng fǎndiào sing a different tune; harp on a discordant tune; strike up a tune that runs counter to: ～的人 devil's advocate

唱高调 chàng gāodiào use high-flown words; affect a high moral tone; chant bombastic words

唱歌 chànggē sing (a song): 他很会～。He is a good singer.

唱功 chànggōng art of singing; singing: ～戏 dramas which are built around singing skills

唱红脸 chàng hóngliǎn wear the red make-up of the hero; play the hero; pretend to be generous and kind

唱机 chàngjī phonograph; record player; gramophone

唱名 chàngmíng roll call: ～表决 a vote by roll call

唱盘 chàngpán turntable (of a record player)

唱片 chàngpiàn phonograph (gramophone) record; disc; disk: ～录制 disk recording. ～制造商 recordmaker. 放～ play a phonograph record. 灌～ cut a disc

唱腔 chàngqiāng [剧] music for voices in a Chinese opera

唱双簧 chàng shuānghuáng ① give a two-man comic show (with one speaking or singing while hiding behind the other who gesticulates) ② collaborate with each other

唱颂歌 chàng sònggē psalm-singing

唱挽歌 chàng wǎngē sing the elegy for…

唱戏 chàngxì sing and act in an opera

唱针 chàngzhēn gramophone needle; stylus

唱做念打 chàngzuòniàndǎ ［剧］ singing, acting, recitation and acrobatics; singing, gesticulating, elocution and acrobatics

chāo

抄 chāo〈动〉① copy; transcribe: 请把稿件～一下。Please make a fair copy of the manuscript. ② plagiarize; lift

抄本 chāoběn hand-copied book; transcript; book in manuscript

抄道 chāodào ① take a shortcut ② shortcut: 走～去要近5公里路。If you take the shortcut, it will be 5 kilometres closer.

抄获 chāohuò search and seize; ferret out

抄件 chāojiàn duplicate; copy

抄录 chāolù make a handwritten copy of; copy

抄袭 chāoxí ① copy (from); crib (from); lift; plagiarize: ～行为 act of plagiarism ② ［军］ launch a surprise attack on the enemy by making a detour

抄写 chāoxiě copy; transcribe: ～卷子 manuscript rolls

钞 chāo〈名〉banknote

钞票 chāopiào banknote; paper money; bill: ～挂帅 money in command

超 chāo〈动〉① surpass; overtake: ～世界先进水平 surpass advanced world levels ② go beyond; transcend: ～尘脱俗 transcend world affairs ③〈形〉 super; ultra; extra: ～音速 supersonic speed

超编 chāobiān exceed personnel quotas; overstaff

超标 chāobiāo exceed standard

超常 chāocháng surpass the normal or the ordinary

超产 chāochǎn overfulfil a production quota (target): ～奖励 receive extra payment for overfulfilment of work quotas. ～粮 grain output in excess of a production target; surplus grain. ～百分之十五 exceed the production quota by 15%

超车 chāochē overtake another car: 不准～［揭示语］No Overtaking

超出 chāochū go beyond; overstep; exceed: ～预算 go beyond the budget

超储 chāochǔ surplus stock piles

超导技术 chāodǎo jìshù ［物］ superconductor technology

超度 chāodù ［宗］ expiation of the sins of the dead; salvation; release souls from purgatory

超额 chāo'é above plan (quota): ～保险 overinsurance. ～利润分成 retain varying portions of the profit over and above the assigned profit norms

超凡 chāofán ① transcend the worldly ② out of the ordinary; extraordinary; uncommon

超凡脱俗 chāofán-tuōsú detach from the world; beyond worldly affairs

超负荷 chāofùhè excess load; overload

超高频 chāogāopín ultra-high frequency(uhf):～变压器 ultrahigh-frequency transformer
超耗 chāohào excess consumption
超功利主义 chāogōnglìzhǔyì transcendental utilitarianism
超过 chāoguò exceed;excel; surpass; outstrip
超级 chāojí ① superb; of superior quality ② super:～商场(市场)supermarket
超计划利润留成 chāojìhuà lìrùn liúchéng share the amount earned over and above the planned profit
超龄 chāolíng overage:～团员 overage Youth League member. ～学生 pupils who are overage
超期服役 chāoqīfúyì [军] extended active duty; extended service in the army
超前 chāoqián leading:～精神 a surpassing spirit. ～消费 overconsuming for a period of time
超群 chāoqún head and shoulders above all others; distinguished; transcendent; sublime; preeminent
超脱 chāotuō ① unconventional; original ② be detached; stand (hold, keep) aloof:～现实 detach oneself from reality
超现实主义 chāoxiànshízhǔyì surrealism
超音速 chāoyīnsù supersonic speed:～喷气机 superjet
超越 chāoyuè surpass;transcend; go beyond:～法律 go beyond the law
超载 chāozài [交] overload:～能力 overload capacity
超支 chāozhī overexpenditure; overspending:～户 excess expenditure household
超重 chāozhòng overweight:～行李 excess luggage. ～信 overweight letter

cháo

巢 cháo 〈名〉 nest:鸟～ bird's nest
巢居 cháojū dwell in trees
巢穴 cháoxuè den; nest; lair; hideout
朝 cháo ①〈动〉face; look:这房子～南。The house looks to the south. ②〈名〉dynasty:宋～ the Song Dynasty ③〈介〉towards; to:～北走 go northward
朝拜 cháobài pay religious homage to; worship; pay respects to (a sovereign)
朝臣 cháochén courtier
朝代 cháodài dynasty; reign:～变换的频率 quick succession of dynasties
朝奉 cháofèng a term of address for a rich man or a pawnshop assistant
朝贡 cháogòng pay tribute to; offer tribute to; present tribute
朝觐 cháojìn ① have an audience with a sovereign ② go on a pilgrimage to a shrine or a sacred place
朝圣 cháoshèng [宗]pilgrimage;

hadj; look to … as one's Mecca:～团 hadj group

朝廷 cháotíng imperial (royal) court

朝向 cháoxiàng turn towards; face

朝野 cháoyě the court and the commonalty; the government and the public:～各方人士 people of various circles either in or out of government

朝政 cháozhèng court affairs; governmental activities; imperial rule

朝中有人好做官 cháozhōng yǒu rén hǎo zuòguān One may be recommended and put in an important position if his relatives or friends have status and power.

嘲 cháo〈动〉jeer at; sneer at; ridicule

嘲讽 cháofěng sneer at; taunt:他带着～的神情斜了她一眼。He gave her a sideway glance with a sneering look on his face.

嘲弄 cháonòng make fun of; scoff (at); mock (at); poke fun at; ridicule

嘲笑 cháoxiào jeer at; laugh at; ridicule; deride

潮 cháo〈名〉① tide:落～ ebb tide ② current; upsurge; tide:怒～ raging tide ③〈形〉damp; moist:火柴受～了。The matches have got damp.

潮呼呼 cháohūhū damp; dank; clammy:下了几天雨,屋子里什么都是～的。After several days' rain, everything in the house became damp and clammy.

潮流 cháoliú ① tide; tidal current; ② trend:时代～ trend of the times

潮气 cháoqì moisture in the air; humidity

潮湿 cháoshī moist; damp

潮水 cháoshuǐ tidewater; tide:～上涨了。The tide is coming in.

潮位 cháowèi the level of the tidal current at its flow or ebb; tidemark

潮汐 cháoxī ebb and flow of the tide; morning and evening tides:～电站 tidal power station

chǎo

吵 chǎo〈动〉① make a noise; disturb ② quarrel; wrangle; squabble:～翻了天 kick up a terrific row ③〈形〉noisy:～得很 terribly noisy

吵架 chǎojià quarrel; have a row; wrangle:我跟他～了。I had quarrel with him.

吵闹 chǎonào make a noise; brawl; wrangle; kick up a row

吵嚷 chǎorǎng make a racket; shout in confusion; clamour

吵嘴 chǎozuǐ quarrel; bicker:从来不跟别人～ never quarrel with anybody

炒 chǎo〈动〉fry; stir-fry

炒菜 chǎocài ① make dishes ② a stir-fried dish:我要了两个～一

个汤。I ordered two dishes and a soup.

炒货 chǎohuò roasted seeds and nuts

炒冷饭 chǎolěngfàn ① stir-fry cold rice ② do the same old thing; tell the same old story

炒买炒卖 chǎomǎi-chǎomài "stir-fry" in buying and selling: ～外汇 stir-fry in buying and selling foreign exchange

炒鱿鱼 chǎoyóuyú stir-fry squid — dismiss sb. from office; fire sb.; give sb. the sack: 被～ get the sack. 这个厂长在企业竞争中大胆使用"炒鱿鱼"的做法。Under the circumstances of competition among enterprises, this factory director daringly used the method of "stir-frying squid."

chē

车 chē 〈名〉① vehicle; car: 用～运货 carry goods in a vehicle ② machine: 开～ set the machine going ③ [象棋] chariot ④ 〈动〉 lathe; turn: ～光 smooth sth. on a lathe

车船使用牌照费 chēchuán shǐyòng páizhàofèi driving licence tax on vehicles and boats

车次 chēcì ① train number ② coach number (indicating order of departure)

车到山前必有路 chē dào shānqián bì yǒulù The cart will find its way round the hill when it gets there — things will eventually sort themselves out.

车队 chēduì motorcade

车匪路霸 chēfěilùbà road banditry

车费 chēfèi (passenger's) fare: 到颐和园～多少? What's the fare to the Summer Palace?

车祸 chēhuò traffic (road) accident

车间 chējiān workshop; shop: ～经济核算 workshop economic accounting

车库 chēkù garage

车辆 chēliàng vehicles: 来往～ traffic

车马费 chēmǎfèi travel allowance

车马坑 chēmǎkēng [考] chariot pit

车牌 chēpái license plate

车皮 chēpí railway wagon or carriage; flatcar or freight car: 3～货物 three freight cars of goods

车票 chēpiào train or bus ticket; ticket

车水马龙 chēshuǐ-mǎlóng incessant (endless) stream of horses and carriages — heavy traffics (on the street); a flow of traffic; be crowded with people and vehicles

车速 chēsù speed of a motorcar

车胎 chētāi tyre

车厢 chēxiāng (railway) carriage; coach

车载斗量 chēzài-dǒuliáng load with carts and measure with pecks; immense quantities; plentiful

车站 chēzhàn [火车的] (railway) station; [公共汽车的] (bus)

stop; depot

车照 chēzhào driving license

chě

扯 chě〈动〉① tear:～下假面具 tear off (down) the mask ② pull:～后腿 hold sb. back (from action); pull one back; be a drag on sb. ③ gossip; chat:咱俩好好～一～。Let's have a good chat. ④ buy (cloth; thread, etc.)

扯淡 chědàn talk nonsense; talk the rubbish all the way; nonsense

扯后腿 chě hòutuǐ hold sb. back (from action); be a drag on sb.; be a hindrance to sb.

扯谎 chěhuǎng tell a lie or fib; lie:他对我扯了个谎,我真信了。He told me a fib, and I swallowed it whole.

扯家常 chě jiācháng talk about everyday matters; engage in small talk; chitchat

扯皮 chěpí dispute over trifles; argue back and forth; bicker:政府机构不应互相～。Government organizations should not pass the buck to each other. 互相～ wrangle endlessly with each other over (about) sth.

扯碎 chěsuì tear to pieces; tear up

扯腿 chětuǐ ① drag sb.'s feet ② (usu. used in) ～就跑 immediately take to one's heels

chè

彻 chè〈形〉thorough

彻查 chèchá make a thorough investigation (of a case)

彻底 chèdǐ thorough; complete; thoroughgoing:～调查 make a thorough investigation. ～的唯物主义者 consistent materialists; thoroughgoing materialists. ～改革 all-out reform

彻头彻尾 chètóu-chèwěi out-and-out; from beginning to end; to the bone (marrow); out-right; blatant; downright:～的骗局 a blatant fraud

彻悟 chèwù thoroughgoing enlightenment

彻夜 chèyè all night; all through the night; from dusk to dawn: ～不眠 lie awake all night; sit up all night. 工地上灯火～通明。The lights were ablaze at the worksite all through the night.

掣 chè〈动〉① pull; tug ② draw ③ flash past:电～雷鸣。Lightning flashed and thunder rolled.

撤 chè〈动〉① remove; take away; dismiss:～除军事基地 dismantle military installations ② withdraw; evacuate

撤兵 chèbīng withdraw troops

撤除 chèchú remove; dismantle: ～军事设施 dismantle military installations

撤防 chèfáng withdraw a garrison; withdraw from a defended position
撤换 chèhuàn dismiss and replace; supersede
撤回 chèhuí withdraw; recall; repeal:～起诉 withdraw an accusation; revoke a court action
撤诉 chèsù (of the plaintiff) withdraw an accusation; drop a lawsuit
撤退 chètuì withdraw; retreat; draw off; pull out
撤销 chèxiāo cancel; repeal; rescind; revoke:～定货单 recall an order. ～合同 cancel a contract
撤职 chèzhí dismiss sb. from his post; remove sb. from office; discharge sb. from his post:(被)～查办 be dismissed (discharged) from one's post and prosecuted. ～处分 punishment by dismissal
撤走 chèzǒu withdraw; leave:～使馆人员家属 withdraw the families of the embassy staff

澈 chè〈形〉(of water) clear; limpid
澈底 chèdǐ thoroughgoing; thorough

chēn

琛 chēn〈名〉treasure
嗔 chēn〈动〉① be angry; be displeased ② be annoyed (with sb.)
嗔怪 chēnguài blame; rebuke
嗔色 chēnsè an angry or sullen look:微露～ look somewhat displeased

chén

臣 chén〈名〉official under a feudal ruler; vassal; subject; minister:君～ the monarch and his subjects
臣服 chénfú submit oneself to the rule of; pay homage to; yielding one's allegiance to; pledge fealty
臣僚 chénliáo civil and military officials in feudal times
臣民 chénmín subjects of a feudal ruler; liege subjects; liegeman
臣属 chénshǔ inferior; vassal:～国 tributary state

尘 chén〈名〉① dust; dirt:一～不染 not stained with a particle of dust; spotless ② this world; this human world:～俗 this mortal world
尘埃 chén'āi dust
尘凡 chénfán the present world; the mortal world
尘世 chénshì this world; this mortal life
尘土 chéntǔ dust:满身～ be covered all over with dust
尘嚣 chénxiāo hubbub; uproar
尘烟 chényān ① a cloud of dust:～滚滚 clouds of dust churning ② smoke and dust

辰 chén〈名〉① celestial body;

日月星～ the sun, the moon and the stars ② time; day; occasion:良～美景 beautiful scene on a bright day

辰时 chénshí the period of the day from 7 a.m. to 9 a.m.

辰星 chénxīng the Chronographic Star

沉 chén 〈动〉① sink:船～了。The boat has sunk. ② keep down; lower:把脸一～ put on a grave expression ③ concentrate; be calm 〈形〉④ heavy:这箱子太～了。This box is too heavy. ⑤ deep; profound:睡得很～ be in a deep sleep; be fast asleep; be sound asleep

沉甸甸 chéndiāndiān heavy:～的谷穗 heavy ears of millet

沉淀 chéndiàn settle; sendiment; precipitate:显意识的～ precipitate down from the conscious

沉浮 chénfú ① sink and rise; bob on water ② ups and downs of fortune; vicissitudes:宦海～ vicissitudes of an official career

沉寂 chénjì ① quiet; still ② no news:消息～。There has been no news whatsoever.

沉浸 chénjìn be immersed in; be permeated with; be plunged in:全城～在节日气氛中。The whole city was permeated with a festival atmosphere.

沉静 chénjìng ① quiet; calm ② calm; serene; placid:心情～ be in a placid mood

沉沦 chénlún sink into vice; degrade

沉闷 chénmèn ①［天气等］oppressive; dreary ②［作品等］dull; tedious ③［心情不舒畅］depressed; in low spirits

沉迷 chénmí indulge (in); wallow (in):～于奢侈生活 wallow in luxury

沉湎 chénmiǎn be given to; wallow in:～酒色 wallow in voluptuousness

沉没 chénmò sink; founder:渔船于暴风雨中～。The fishing boat foundered in a hurricane.

沉默 chénmò silent; reticent; uncommunicative:～寡言 sparing of words; taciturn; uncommunicative

沉溺 chénnì engross oneself in; be intoxicated with; be addicted to; be infatuated with; wallow in:～于酒色 wallow in sensual pleasures

沉思 chénsī ponder; meditate; brood (on, over); muse (on); contemplate; think deeply

沉痛 chéntòng ① extremely painful; deep feeling of grief; remorse; grievous ② bitter; serious:～教训 bitter lesson

沉陷 chénxiàn ① sink; cave in:地震后路基～了。The earthquake made the roadbed cave in. ②［建］settlement

沉冤 chényuān gross injustice; unrighted wrong; grievous wrongs:她的10年～终于得到昭雪。After being a victim of gross injustice for ten long years, she was finally rehabilitated.

沉重 chénzhòng ① heavy ② serious; critical:心情～ with a heavy heart

沉住气 chénzhuqì keep calm; deep cool; be steady

沉着 chénzhuó calm; cool-headed; composed, steady; placid: ～应战 accept the challenge calmly

沉醉 chénzuì get drunk; be intoxicated

忱 chén〈名〉sincere feeling; true sentiment:谢～ thankfulness

陈 chén ①〈形〉old; stale;～年老酒 old wine〈动〉② lay out; put on display ③ explain; state

陈兵 chénbīng deploy troops; station troops; mass troops

陈仓暗渡 chéncāng-àndù do one thing under cover of another; adultery by mutual consent; secret relations with one's sweetheart

陈词 chéncí ① present one's views:～恳切 set forth one's opinions in an earnest tone ② stale words; hackneyed words: ～滥调 hackneyed and stereotyped expressions; clichés

陈放 chénfàng lay out; set out; display

陈腐 chénfǔ old and decayed; stale; outworn

陈规陋习 chénguī-lòuxí outdated conventions and bad customs; outworn customs and bad habits; outmoded conventions and bad customs; bad customs and habits

陈货 chénhuò old stock; shop-worn goods

陈旧 chénjiù out-of-date; time-worn; outmoded; obsolete; old-fashioned:～设备 obsolete equipment

陈列 chénliè show; exhibit; display:～品 exhibits. ～室(馆) exhibition room (hall)

陈年 chénnián of long standing; preserved for a long time:～老酒 old vintage wine

陈腔(词)滥调 chénqiāng(cí)-làndiào worn-out lingoes; often-repeated trash; old stuff; clichés; hackneyed and stereotyped expressions

陈设 chénshè ① furnish; set out: 这房间～简单。The room is simply furnished. ② furnishings:～瓷 ornamental porcelain

陈述 chénshù relate; state; explain; dwell on:～自己的意见 state one's views

陈诉 chénsù state; recount:～委屈 state one's grievances

陈帐 chénzhàng old debts; long-standing debts

晨 chén〈名〉morning:清～ early morning; dawn

晨操 chéncāo morning exercises

晨光 chénguāng the light of the early morning sun; dawn

晨光熹微 chénguāng-xīwēi first rays of the morning sun; the dim light of dawn

晨曦 chénxī the first rays of the morning sun

晨星 chénxīng ① stars at dawn ② morning star

chèn

衬 chèn〈动〉① line; place sth. underneath② set off: 反～ set off by contrast

衬布 chènbù lining cloth

衬裤 chénkù underpants; pants

衬领 chènlǐng detachable collar (affixed to the inside of the collar of a Chinese tunic)

衬裙 chènqún underskirt; slip; petticoat

衬衫 chènshān shirt

衬托 chèntuō set off; make … stand out in high relief; serve as a foil to: ～音乐［戏剧电影等］background music

衬衣 chènyī ① shirt ② undergarments; underclothes

衬纸 chènzhǐ slip sheet; interleaving paper

称 chèn〈动〉fit; match; suit 另见 chēng

称身 chènshēn (of a garment) fit: 这件外套我穿了挺～的。This coat fits me perfectly.

称心 chènxīn after one's heart; to one's liking: ～满意 be fully satisfied

称心如意 chènxīn-rúyì after one's own heart; very gratifying and satisfactory: ～的工作 a most satisfying job

称愿 chènyuàn be gratified (esp. at the misfortune of a rival)

称职 chènzhí be fit for the post; be up to one's work; be competent for one's job; fill a post with credit

趁 chèn ①〈动〉avail oneself of; take advantage of ②〈介〉while: 这面～热吃吧。Eat the noodles while they are hot. ③〈方〉be rich in; be possessed of: ～钱 have lots of money

趁便 chènbiàn when it is convenient; at one's convenience: 他回来的路上～去书店看了看。He stopped at the bookstore on his way home.

趁火打劫 chènhuǒ-dǎjié fish in troubled waters; plunder a burning house; stir up trouble to serve one's own ends; loot a burning house; take advantage of sb. 's misfortune to do him harm; take advantage of a troubled situation

趁机 chènjī take advantage of the opportunity; seize the chance

趁空 chènkòng use one's spare time; avail oneself of leisure time: 我们～去看了看老李。We went to see Lao Li when we happened to have a few minutes to spare.

趁热打铁 chènrè-dǎtiě strike while the iron is hot; make hay while the sun shines; seize (take) time by the forelock

趁势 chènshì take advantage of a favourable situation

趁手 chènshǒu conveniently; without extra trouble: 请你～把门带上。Please shut the door after you.

趁早 chènzǎo as early as possible; before it is too late

谶 chèn 〈名〉 augury; foreboding; prophecy

chēng

称 chēng 〈动〉 ① weigh: 给我～一公斤苹果。I'd like one kilogram of apples, please. ② call ③ say; state: 拍手～快 clap one's hands with satisfaction ④ commend; praise: 见～于世 be well spoken of; well-known ⑤ 〈名〉 name: 别～ another name 另见 chèn

称霸 chēngbà lord it over others; dominate

称便 chēngbiàn find sth. a great convenience

称兵 chēngbīng start military operations

称臣 chēngchén declare oneself a vassal or subject; acknowledge one's allegiance to a ruler

称道 chēngdào speak approvingly of; praise; acclaim: 值得～ be praiseworthy

称得起 chēngdeqǐ deserve to be called; be worthy of the name of

称帝 chēngdì proclaim oneself emperor

称号 chēnghào name; title; designation

称呼 chēnghū ① call; address ② form of address

称快 chēngkuài express one's gratification; express joy and jubilation

称王 chēngwáng proclaim oneself king: ～称霸 act like an overlord; lord it over; domineer

称王称霸 chēngwáng-chēngbà lord it over others; rule supreme; act like an overlord; domineer; play the tyrant

称谓 chēngwèi term; terminology; appellation

称羡 chēngxiàn express one's admiration or envy

称谢 chēngxiè express one's thanks; thank: ～不止 thank sb. again and again

称兄道弟 chēngxiōng-dàodì treat (address) each other as brothers; call ··· brothers; call cousins with; fraternize with; be on intimate terms

称雄 chēngxióng rule the roost; hold sway over a region; swagger like a conquering hero

称许 chēngxǔ praise; commendation

称誉 chēngyù sing the praises of; praise; acclaim

称赞 chēngzàn praise; commend; speak highly of: 值得～的 commendable; praiseworthy

撑 chēng 〈动〉 ① prop up; support ② [船] push or move with a pole: ～船 pole a boat ③ maintain; keep up ④ fill to the point of bursting: 我肚子有点～。I'm rather full.

撑场(门)面 chēngchǎng (mén) miàn keep up appearances; maintain the appearance

撑杆 chēnggān vaulting pole: ～跳高 pole vault; pole jump

撑腰 chēngyāo back up; bolster

up; support

瞠 chēng 〈动〉 stare

瞠目 chēngmù stare (in alarm, embarrassment, confusion, etc.): ～相视 stare fixedly in each other's face

瞠目结舌 chēngmù-jiéshé be struck dumb; stare tongue-tied; stare dumbfounded

chéng

成 chéng 〈动〉 ① succeed; accomplish: 大功告～。The great task has been completed. ② become; turn into ③ help complete: ～人之美 help others to completion of a worthy goal ④ 〈名〉 achievement; result: 坐享其～ sit idle and enjoy the fruits of others 〈形〉⑤ capable; able ⑥ fully developed; fully grown: ～人 adult ⑦ ready-made; established: 现～服装 ready-made clothes ⑧ in considerable numbers or amounts: ～年累月 for many months and years ⑨ 〈量〉 one tenth: 增产一～ a 10% increase in output

成案 chéng'àn ① precedent ② legal case

成败 chéngbài success or failure: ～在此一举。Success or failure hinges on this one action.

成比例 chéngbǐlì be in proportion to; be proportionate to

成本 chéngběn cost: 生产～ production cost

成材 chéngcái ① grow into useful timber: 这棵树已经～了。This tree has grown to full size. ② become a useful person: 她长大了一定能～。She'll grow up to be somebody.

成分 chéngfèn ① composition; component (part) ② (class) status

成风 chéngfēng become a common practice; become the order of the day: 旅游～。Tourism has become very popular.

成功 chénggōng succeed; be a success

成规 chéngguī established practice; set rule; groove; etiquette; convention

成果 chéngguǒ result; fruit; outcome: ～管理 management by result

成婚 chénghūn get married

成活率 chénghuólǜ survival rate

成绩 chéngjì result (of work or study); achievement; success: 在比赛中取得良好的～ get good results in a tournament

成家 chéngjiā ① (of a man) get married: 他还没有～。He's not married yet. ② become a specialist or expert

成见 chéngjiàn preconceived idea; prejudice: ～很深 be deeply prejudiced. 我对他们毫无～。I have no prejudice against them at all.

成交 chéngjiāo close (conclude) a bargain; strike (clinch) a deal: ～额 volume of business; volume of transaction

成立 chénglì ① found; establish;

set up ② be tenable; hold water:这个论点能～。This argument is tenable (holds water).

成龙配套 chénglóng-pèitào fill in the gaps to complete a chain (of equipment, construction projects, etc.); link up the parts to form a whole; serialize

成名 chéngmíng become well-known; come to fame:～成家 become a well-known specialist; achieve personal fame and career; become famous and expert

成年 chéngnián ① grow up; come of age:～人 grown-ups; adults ② all year:～在外 be away from home all year

成批 chéngpī group by group; in batches

成品 chéngpǐn finished product (goods):～粮 grain end-product. 半～ semi-finished product

成器 chéngqì grow up to be a useful person

成千上万 chéngqiān-shàngwàn thousands and tens of thousands; thousands upon thousands:～的人 tens of thousands of people

成亲 chéngqīn get married:她已成亲了。She has got married.

成全 chéngquán help sb. to attain his end:这件事我们一定要～你。We'll certainly help you to get what you want.

成群 chéngqún in groups; in great numbers:～的鸟 flocks of birds. ～的蜜蜂 swarms of bees

成群结队 chéngqún-jiéduì in crowds:学生～地到海滩上玩儿去了。Groups of students went to the beach to play.

成人 chéngrén ① grow up; become full-grown:长大～ be grown into manhood ② adult; grown-up:～教育 adult education

成人之美 chéngrénzhīměi help sb. achieve success; aid in carrying out the good designs of others; help sb. to fulfil his wish

成色 chéngsè ① the percentage of gold or silver in a coin, etc.; the relative purity of gold or silver ② quality

成事 chéngshì ① accomplish sth.; succeed:他这样做成不了事,只会误事。If he goes at it this way he'll never succeed. Instead he'll make a mess of things. ② a thing that is past or finished

成事不足,败事有余 chéng shì bùzú, bài shì yǒuyú unable to accomplish anything but liable to spoil everything; never able to achieve, always able to ruin; never make, but always mar

成熟 chéngshú ripe; mature:梨子快～了。The pears will soon be ripe. 她到十六岁发育～。She had reached maturity by the time she was sixteen.

成套 chéngtào ① form a whole set ② complete set:～设备 a complete set of equipment

成文法 chéngwénfǎ written laws;

statute law; statutory law

成问题 chéng wèntí be a problem; be open to question (doubt, objection):雪再不停,明天的比赛就要～了。If the snow doesn't stop, I doubt if we can have the game tomorrow. 我们完成生产指标不～。We will fulfil the quota without fail.

成效 chéngxiào effect; result:～显著 produce a marked effect; achieve remarkable success

成心 chéngxīn intentionally; on purpose; with deliberate intent:别生气,她不是～的。Don't be angry. She didn't mean it.

成行 chéngxíng embark on a (planned) journey:未能～ didn't leave as planned

成形 chéngxíng ① take shape:我们的计划开始～了。Our plan is beginning to take shape. ② shaping; forming

成型 chéngxíng (of workpieces or products) be in finished form

成药 chéngyào ready-made medicine; patent medicine

成因 chéngyīn contributing factor; cause of formation

成语 chéngyǔ set phrase (usu. composed of four characters); idiom

成员 chéngyuán member (of a group or family):正式～ a full member

成长 chéngzhǎng grow up; grow to maturity:年轻一代的健康～ the healthy growth of the younger generation

成(胜)者为王,败者为寇 chéng (shèng) zhě wéi wáng, bàizhě wéikòu Whether one will become a king or an outlaw depends on whether he is successful or not.; Legitimacy belongs to the victor.

丞 chéng 〈名〉 an assistant to an official (in ancient China):县～ county magistrate's assistant

丞相 chéngxiàng prime minister (in ancient China); chief minister

呈 chéng 〈动〉 ① present; offer ② assume (form, colour, etc.); show:～现出笑容 show a smiling face ③〈名〉 document submitted to a superior; petition:辞～ (written) resignation

呈报 chéngbào submit a report; report:向上级～ report (sth.) to the higher authorities

呈递 chéngdì present; submit:～国书 present credentials (letters of credence)

呈核 chénghé submit for consideration (approval)

呈览 chénglǎn submit sth. to a higher authority for perusal

呈请 chéngqǐng submit an application (for); apply (for)

呈文 chéngwén petition

呈现 chéngxiàn present; display; appear; emerge; show:～一片繁荣景象 present a picture of prosperity

呈献 chéngxiàn respectfully present：～花圈 lay a wreath with due formality

诚 chéng ①〈形〉honest；sincere ②〈名〉sincerity；earnestness：开～布公 sincerity and without reserve ③〈副〉really；indeed

诚服 chéngfú submit oneself willingly（to sb.）：心悦～ feel a heartfelt admiration

诚惶诚恐 chénghuáng-chéngkǒng with reverence and awe；in fear and trepidation

诚恳 chéngkěn sincere；cordial；wholehearted

诚然 chéngrán ① truly；really：他喜爱他的小狗，那小狗也～可爱。He loves his puppy，and the puppy is really lovable. ②［与"但是"连用］no doubt；to be sure；it is true：水灾～是严重的，但是它吓不倒我们。True，the flood is serious，but it can't scare us.

诚实 chéngshí honest；upright：～可靠 honest and reliable

诚心 chéngxīn sincere；sincerity；cordiality：～诚意 with one's whole heart；from the bottom of one's heart；wholeheartedly

诚意 chéngyì good faith；sincerity：缺乏～ lack good faith

诚挚 chéngzhì sincere；cordial：～的接待 a cordial reception

承 chéng〈动〉① bear；carry；hold：冰薄～不住卡车重量。The thin ice cannot bear truckloads. ② undertake；contract (to do a job)；accept：～包国外建筑 contracting for buildings overseas ③ be grateful to sb. (for)；be indebted (to sb. for a kindness)：～您过奖。You flatter me. ④ carry on；continue：继～ carry on；inherit

承办 chéngbàn ① undertake；contract (for)：～案件数［法庭等的］case load ② organize：～单位 organizer

承包 chéngbāo contract (for)：～责任制 contract responsibility system. 农民的～经济 contracted economic undertakings of peasants. ～山 contracted hills. ～商 contractor

承保 chéngbǎo undertake to provide insurance；accept insurance；cover：指定的～风险 risks designated for cover. ～人 insurer

承担 chéngdān undertake；take；assume：～经济责任 bear financial responsibility

承兑 chéngduì accept；honour：～人 accepter. ～信用证 acceptance letter of credit

承建 chéngjiàn accept a commission for a construction project

承接 chéngjiē ① hold out a vessel to have a liquid poured into it ② continue；carry on：～上文 continued from the preceding paragraph ③ undertake the task of；contract to accept：～来料加工 accept customers' materials for processing；undertake the processing of supplied materials

承揽 chénglǎn contract to do a whole job；undertake an entire project：～合同 contract of work. ～物资运输业务 undertake the transportation of materials

承蒙 chéngméng be grateful (indebted) to sb. (for); be granted a favour

承诺 chéngnuò promise to undertake; undertake to do sth.

承前启后 chéngqián-qǐhòu serve as a link between past and future; take over from the past and set a new course for the future

承认 chéngrèn recognize; acknowledge; admit：～错误 admit one's mistake; acknowledge one's fault

承上启下 chéngshàng-qǐxià form a connecting link between the preceding and the following

承受 chéngshòu bear; stand; withstand; endure; sustain：～力 sustaining ability

承销 chéngxiāo act as sales agent

承销品 chéngxiāopǐn consigned goods

承运 chéngyùn (of transportation companies, etc.) undertake the transportation of (goods)

承运人 chéngyùnrén carrier

承载 chéngzài bear the weight of：～能力 bearing (carrying) capacity; load-bearing capacity

承制 chéngzhì undertake to manufacture for others：～配套器材 accept orders for manufacturing necessary accessories

承做 chéngzuò undertake to make for others：我店～西式服装。We accept orders for Western-style clothes.

城 chéng〈名〉① city wall; wall：长～ the Great Wall ② city; town：～市居民委员会 urban neighbourhood committees

城邦 chéngbāng city-state

城池 chéngchí city wall and moat; city

城防 chéngfáng city defence：～巩固。The city is closely guarded. ～部队 city garrison. ～工事 defence works of a city

城关 chéngguān the area just outside a city gate

城建 chéngjiàn urban construction; city building：～规划 city planning; construction programme for a city

城建部门 chéngjiàn bùmén urban development departments

城郊 chéngjiāo outskirts (of a town); suburbs：在北京～ in the suburbs (on the outskirts) of Beijing

城楼 chénglóu tower over a city gate; gate tower：在天安门～上 on the rostrum of Tian An Men

城墙 chéngqiáng city wall

城区 chéngqū the city proper

城市 chéngshì city; town：～规划 city planning. ～合作银行 urban cooperative banks

城下之盟 chéngxiàzhīméng a treaty concluded with the enemy who have reached the city wall; terms accepted under duress; a treaty signed under coercion

城乡 chéngxiāng city and countryside; town and country: ～差别 difference between town and country. ～分割 urban-rural split. ～结合部 urban-rural continuum

城镇 chéngzhèn cities and towns: ～基本养老保险 basic old-age insurance in cities and towns

乘 chéng〈动〉① ride; take: ～公共汽车 ride in a bus; go by bus ② take advantage of; avail oneself of 无隙可～ no crack to get in by; no loophole to exploit ③ multiply: 5～2 等于 10。Five times two is ten.

乘敌之隙 chéngdízhīxì exploit the openings the enemy leaves us; take advantage of a crack on the enemy side; exploit the enemy's blunder

乘法 chéngfǎ [数] multiplication

乘风破浪 chéngfēng-pòlàng ride the wind and cleave the waves; brave the wind and the waves

乘火打劫 chénghuǒ-dǎjié take advantage of sb.'s misfortune to do him harm

乘机 chéngjī avail oneself of the opportunity; take occasion (to do); seize the chance; exploit the opportunity

乘警 chéngjǐng vehicular police

乘客 chéngkè passenger

乘凉 chéngliáng enjoy the cool; relax in a cool place

乘龙快婿 chénglóng-kuàixù an excellent or ideal son-in-law (usu. of high social or official position)

乘人之危 chéngrénzhīwēi take advantage of sb.'s precarious position; take advantage of sb.'s misfortune (others' difficulties, precarious position, trouble)

乘胜前进 chéngshèng-qiánjìn march forward in triumph; continue the triumphant advance; advance from victory to victory

乘务员 chéngwùyuán attendant (on a train); trainman or trainwoman; vehicular attendants

乘隙 chéngxì take advantage of a loophole; turn sb.'s mistake to one's own account: ～突围 seize an opportunity to break through the encirclement (siege)

乘兴 chéngxìng while one is in high spirits: ～而来 arrive in high spirits; set out cheerfully. ～作了一首诗 improvise a poem while in a joyful mood

乘虚而入 chéngxū'érrù get a chance to step in; sneak in; take advantage of a weak point; break through at a weak point

盛 chéng〈动〉① fill; ladle: ～汤 ladle out soup ② serve ③ hold; contain: 这个礼堂能～800人。This hall is enough for a eight hundred people.
另见 shèng

盛器 chéngqì container; vessel

程 chéng〈名〉① rule; regulation: 规～ rules ② procedure; order ③ journey; stage of a journey: 送她一～ accompany her part of the way ④ distance; 行～ distance of travel

程度 chéngdù level; degree; extent:文化～ level of education

程控 chéngkòng programme control:～电话 programme-controlled telephone

程式 chéngshì form; pattern:formula:～化 stylize. 公文～ forms and formulas of official documents

程序 chéngxù order; course; procedure; programme〈计〉:～设计 programming

程序控制 chéngxù-kòngzhì [自动化] pre-programmed automatic control

惩 chéng〈动〉punish; penalize: 依法～办贪污分子 punish embezzlers according to law

惩办 chéngbàn punish:依法～ punish according to law

惩处 chéngchǔ punish; penalize: ～罪犯 punish criminals; inflict punishments on criminals

惩罚 chéngfá punish; impose (inflict) a penalty on; penalize:～价格 penalty prices. ～税率 penalty rate

惩戒 chéngjiè punish sb. to teach him a lesson; discipline sb. as a warning:～法 penal law

惩前毖后、治病救人 chéngqián-bìhòu,zhìbìng-jiùrén learn from past mistakes to avoid future ones and cure the sickness to save the patient; take warning from the past in order to be more careful in the future, treat the illness in order to save the patient

惩一儆百 chéngyī-jǐngbǎi punish one to warn a hundred; make an example of sb; punish sb. as a warning to the rest.

惩治 chéngzhì crack down on; mete out punishment to; combat:～腐败 combat corruption

澄 chéng ①〈形〉clear; limpid ②〈动〉purify; clarify:～其思虑 purify one's thoughts
另见 dèng

澄碧 chéngbì clear blue:湖水～。The lake water is a clear blue.

澄彻 chéngchè transparently clear; crystally clear:江水～见底。The river is so clear that you can see to the bottom.

澄清 chéngqīng ① clear; limpid; transparent ② clear up; clarify:～事实 clarify some facts

橙 chéng〈名〉① orange (the tree and the fruit):甜～ sweet orange ② orange colour

橙黄 chénghuáng orange colour

橙子 chéngzi orange (the fruit)

chěng

逞 chěng〈动〉① show off; flaunt; make a display of:～强 flaunt one's superiority; display sham courage ② indulge; give free rein to ③ carry out (an evil design); succeed (in a scheme):得～ succeed in one's schemes

逞能 chěngnéng make a display of

one's ability; parade one's ability

逞强 chěngqiáng flaunt one's superiority: ～好胜 parade one's superiority and strive to outshine others

逞威风 chěng wēifēng show off one's strength or power; swagger about; lord it over

逞性子 chěng xìngzi self-willed; wilful; wayward; headstrong

逞凶 chěngxiōng resort to violence

逞英雄 chěng yīngxióng play the hero; do something out of bravado

骋 chěng〈动〉① gallop: 驰～ dash about; gallop about ② give free rein to

骋怀 chěnghuái give free rein to one's thoughts and feelings

chèng

秤 chèng〈名〉balance; [杆秤] steelyard

秤锤 chèngchuí the sliding weight of a steelyard

秤杆 chènggǎn the arm (beam) of a steelyard

秤钩 chènggōu steelyard hook

秤盘 chèngpán ① the pan or dish of a steelyard ② either of the pans or dishes of a balance; scale

秤砣 chèngtuó the sliding weight of a steelyard

秤星 chèngxīng gradations marked on the beam of a steelyard

chī

吃 chī〈动〉① eat; take; have: ～药 take medicine ② eat at; have one's meals ③ live on (off): 靠山～山。Mountaineers rely on the mountains. ④ annihilate; wipe out: ～掉敌人一个团。annihilate an enemy regiment. ⑤ exhaust; be a strain ⑥ suffer; incur: ～批评 be criticized ⑦〈介〉by

吃饱了撑的 chībǎole chēngde restless from overeating (said of sb. doing sth. silly or senseless)

吃不饱 chībubǎo ① not have enough to eat ② (of factories, etc.) cannot operate at full capacity; operate under capacity: 由于原料缺乏，他们厂长期处于～状态。Owing to a constant shortage of raw materials, their factory has not been running at full capacity.

吃不得 chībudé ① cannot eat; cannot be eaten: 她胃不好，～油腻的东西。She has stomach trouble and cannot eat oily food. ② cannot bear; cannot suffer: ～苦 cannot stand any hardships

吃不开 chībukāi be unpopular; won't work: 他这种工作作风到哪儿都～。Such a work style as his isn't popular anywhee.

吃不了兜着走 chībuliǎo dōuzhezǒu get more than one bargained for; bear all consequences; find (land) oneself in serious trouble

吃不上 chībushàng ① be unable to get something to eat:～一顿饱饭 be unable to get a square meal ② miss a meal

吃不下 chībuxià not feel like eating; be unable to eat any more:我不太舒服,～饭。I'm not very well and don't feel like eating.

吃不消 chībuxiāo be too much for one; can't bear any longer

吃不住 chībuzhù be unable to bear or support:电视太重,这个架子～。The stand is not strong enough for this heavy TV set.

吃穿 chīchuān food and clothing:他们很讲究～。They're fastidious about their food and clothing.

吃醋 chīcù be jealous (usu. of a rival in love)

吃大锅饭 chī dàguōfàn everybody "eating out the same big pot"; everybody "sharing food from the same big pot"; everybody "eating the rice cooked in one big pan"

吃得开 chīdekāi be popular; be much sought after; get along all right

吃得来 chīdelái be able to eat; not mind eating

吃得上 chīdeshàng ① be able to get sth. to eat; can afford to eat ② be in time for a meal; be able to get a meal:十一点半以前赶回去还～饭。If we get back before eleven thirty, we won't be too late for lunch.

吃得下 chīdexià be able to eat:她已经好多了,饭也～了。She's much better; she's got an appetite now.

吃得消 chīdexiāo be able to stand (exertion, fatigue, etc.); can bear

吃耳光 chī'ěrguāng get a slap in the face

吃饭 chīfàn ① eat; have a meal ② keep alive; make a living:靠打鱼～ make a living by fishing

吃官司 chī guānsi get into trouble with the law; serve a jail term

吃馆子 chī guǎnzi eat in a restaurant; dine out:他们要请我～。They're going to invite me out to dinner. 她难得～。She seldom dines out.

吃喝风 chīhēfēng common practice of feasting; live a sybaritic life; be a sybarite; like wining and dining

吃喝嫖赌 chīhē-piáodǔ go dining, wining, whoring and gambling—lead a dissipated life

吃喝玩乐 chīhē-wánlè have a good time, wining and drinking; idle away one's time in pleasure-seeking; eat, drink and be merry; gluttony and pleasure-seeking

吃后悔药 chī hòuhuǐyào feel remorse; regret:你要先考虑好再去,免得～。Think it over before you go so that you won't regret it later.

吃回扣 chī huíkòu get commission

吃荤 chīhūn eat meat

吃劲 chījìn entail much effort; be a strain: 她挑一百斤也不～。She can carry 100 jin on a pole without straining herself.

吃惊 chījīng be startled; be shocked; be amazed; be taken aback: 大吃一惊 be flabbergasted

吃苦 chīkǔ bear hardships: 我小时候吃了不少苦。I suffered a great deal in my childhood.

吃苦耐劳 chīkǔ-nàiláo bear hardships and stand hard work; work hard and endure hardships

吃苦头 chī kǔtóu suffer; have a rough time

吃亏 chīkuī ① incur losses; stand to lose; get the worst of it; come to grief; suffer: 有的人～就在于不老实。Some people come to grief on account of their dishonesty. ② be at a disadvantage: ～在不懂外语 be at a disadvantage in knowing no foreign language

吃里扒外 chīlǐ-páwài live off one person while secretly helping another

吃力 chīlì ① entail strenuous effort; be a strain: 她身体好，干这点儿活不算～。She's strong; this bit of work won't be too much for her. ② tired; fatigued

吃偏饭 chī piānfàn enjoy favoured treatment

吃请 chīqǐng accept an invitation to dinner (extended as a bribe); eat on invitation

吃软不吃硬 chīruǎn bù chīyìng can be persuaded by reason but not be cowed by force; yielding to soft approach but rejecting force; be open to persuasion, but not to coercion

吃水 chīshuǐ ① drinking water: 过去这里～很困难。It used to be difficult to get drinking water here. ② absorb water: 这块地不～。This plot of land absorbs little water. 这种大米～。You need a lot of water in cooking this kind of rice. ③ [航运] have a draught (draft) of: 这船～2米。The ship has a draught of 2 metres. 空载～ light draught. ～线 waterline

吃素 chīsù abstain from eating meat; be a vegetarian

吃透 chītòu have a thorough grasp (understanding) of: ～文件精神 understand a document thoroughly

吃闲饭 chī xiánfàn lead an idle life; live in idleness; be a loafer or sponger

吃现成饭 chī xiànchéngfàn eat what is already prepared—enjoy the fruits of others' work

吃香 chīxiāng be very popular; be much sought after; be most welcome; [货物等] be in great demand

吃香的喝辣的 chīxiāngde hēlàde have tasty food and strong drinks—eat well

吃小灶 chī xiǎozào eat from a private stove (The term referred to being treated to the highest collective dining standard.)

吃一堑,长一智 chī yī qiàn,zhǎng yī zhì A fall into the pit, a gain in your wit.

吃硬不吃软 chīyìng bù chīruǎn yielding to force but rejecting a soft approach

吃斋 chīzhāi practise abstinence from meat; be a vegetarian for religious reasons

吃着碗里,瞧着锅里 chīzhe wǎnlǐ, qiáozhe guōlǐ eat at the bowl and look at the pot—feel no satisfied with what has already been obtained, and be still insatisably avaricous to get more

吃重 chīzhòng ①arduous; strenuous ② carrying (loading) capacity:这辆卡车～多少? What's the carrying capacity of this truck?

吃准 chīzhǔn be sure; be certain; be positive:她～小张过三两天就会回来。 She is quite sure Xiao Zhang will be back in a couple of days.

吃罪 chīzuì bear (take) the blame:～不起 cannot take the blame

哧 chī〈象〉:～～地笑 titter

笞 chī〈动〉 beat with a stick, cane, etc.

笞刑 chīxíng flogging as a punishment

嗤 chī〈动〉 laugh at

嗤嗤 chīchī the sound of ripping, tittering, frying, burning, etc.:两个姑娘交头接耳～笑着。The two girls tittered and whispered in each other's ears.

嗤笑 chīxiào laugh at; sneer at:报之以～ respond with a sneer

嗤之以鼻 chīzhīyǐbí sniff at; snort with contempt at

痴 chī 〈形〉① silly; stupid; foolish; idiotic:白～ idiot ② crazy about

痴呆 chīdāi ① dull-witted; stupid ②[医] dementia

痴迷 chīmí infatuated; obsessed; crazy

痴情 chīqíng ① unreasoning passion; infatuation ② be infatuated

痴心 chīxīn infatuation:一片～ sheer infatuation

痴心妄想 chīxīn-wàngxiǎng hope vainly for; have a wishful thinking; daydreaming; fond dream

痴子 chīzi ① idiot ② a mad person

chí

池 chí〈名〉 pool; pond:养鱼～ fishpond

池塘 chítáng pond; pool

池鱼之殃 chíyúzhīyāng a disaster for the fish in the moat—trouble not of one's own making

池浴 chíyù bathing in a common bathing pool

弛 chí〈动〉 relax; slacken

弛缓 chíhuǎn relax; calm down: 局势渐趋～。Things are easing up.

弛禁 chíjìn annul a prohibition; lift a ban

弛懈 chíxiè slack; lax

驰 chí〈动〉① gallop; speed: 奔～ run quickly; speed ② spread: 名～天下 be known all over the world ③ turn eagerly towards

驰骋 chíchěng ① gallop ② be very active: ～文坛 be very popular in the literary world; play an outstanding role in the literary world

驰名 chímíng famous; become well-known: ～中外 be well-known at home and abroad; have won fame both at home and abroad

驰行 chíxíng (of vehicles) go at full speed; speed: 火车向北～。The train was speeding north.

驰援 chíyuán rush to the rescue

迟 chí〈形〉① late; delayed: 对不起,我来～了。I'm sorry I'm late. ② slow; tardy ③ slow; obtuse

迟迟 chíchí slow; tardy: ～不表态 not state one's position even after stalling for a long time. 他们为什么～不来? Why are they taking so long to come?

迟钝 chídùn dull; obtuse; blunt; slow-witted

迟缓 chíhuǎn slow; tardy: 进展～ make a tardy progress

迟误 chíwù delay: 请注意不要～。Mind you don't delay.

迟延 chíyán delay; postpone

迟疑 chíyí hesitate; waver: 毫不～地同意了 agree without hesitation

迟疑不决 chíyí-bùjué hesitate to make a decision; be irresolute; be undecided

迟早 chízǎo sooner or later; early or late

持 chí〈动〉① hold; grasp: ～枪 hold a gun ② keep; hold ③ support; maintain: 支～ support; maintain ④ manage; run: 操～ manage; handle

持币抢购 chíbì qiǎnggòu rushing to buy with cash in hand

持币选购 chíbì xuǎngòu buy selectively with cash in hand

持家 chíjiā run one's home; keep house: ～有方 be good at running one's home

持久 chíjiǔ lasting; durable; protracted: ～战 protracted warfare

持平 chípíng ① hold the line: 第一季度的蔬菜上市量与去年同期～。The quantity of vegetables on the market in the first quarter has maintained the same level as the same period last year. ② fair; unbiased

持球 chíqiú [体] holding

持续 chíxù last; continue; sustain: 生产的～发展 sustained growth of production

持有 chíyǒu hold: ～护照 hold a passport

持之以恒 chízhīyǐhéng do sth. perseveringly; persevere

持重 chízhòng prudent; cautious;

chóng

虫 chóng〈名〉insect; worm:~害insect pest

虫情 chóngqíng pest situation:~测报 pest forecasting

虫灾 chóngzāi plague of insects

重 chóng ①〈副〉again; once more; anew:久别~逢 meet again after a long separation ②〈动〉repeat; duplicate:这两个例子~了。These two examples duplicate each other. ③〈名〉layer:万~山 ranges of hills; countless mountains

重版 chóngbǎn ①(of books, periodicals, etc.) be republished ② republication

重播 chóngbō ① rebroadcast a programme (from the same station) ② resow (the same field)

重操旧业 chóngcāo-jiùyè return to one's former career; go back to one's profession; take up one's old job

重重 chóngchóng ① full of:顾虑~ be full of misgivings. ~困难 endless difficulties ② circle:~包围 be encircled ring upon ring; heavily be sieged; be besieged circle upon circle

重打锣鼓另开张 chóngdǎ luó gǔ lìng kāizhāng reopen a business to the beating of gongs and drums; start all over again

重蹈覆辙 chóngdǎo-fùzhé follow the same disastrous road; repeat the same mistake; follow the same old road to ruin

重叠 chóngdié pile up; overlap:精简~机构 simplify overlapping organs

重读 chóngdú [教] repetition of the year's work:~生 pupils who repeat the year's work

重犯 chóngfàn repeat (an error or offence):吸取教训,避免~错误 draw a lesson from past errors so as to prevent their recurrence

重逢 chóngféng meet again; have a reunion:久别~ meet again after a long separation. 旧友~ reunion of old friends

重复 chóngfù duplicate; repeat:~生产 duplication (repetition) in production; overlapping production

重婚(罪) chónghūn(zuì) bigamy

重建 chóngjiàn rebuild; reconstruct; reestablish

重申 chóngshēn reiterate; reaffirm; restate; reassert; recapitulate

重施故技 chóngshī-gùjì play the same old trick; repeat a stock trick

重温旧梦 chóngwēn-jiùmèng again indulge in one's pipedreams; renew one's old dream; revive an old dream

重现 chóngxiàn reappear:当年的战斗场面又~在他们眼前。The battle scenes of those years reappeared in their mind's eye.

重新 chóngxīn again; anew; afresh:~考虑 reconsider. ~做人 start one's life afresh; turn over a new leaf

重行 chóngxíng begin doing sth. again; take up sth. again:～审查 reexamine

重演 chóngyǎn ① react ② repeat:故伎～ repeat the same (stock) trick

重阳 chóngyáng the Double Ninth Festival (the 9th day of the 9th lunar month)

重印 chóngyìn reprint:～本 reprint

重整旗鼓 chóngzhěng-qígǔ regroup for battle; pull one's forces together and start afresh; rally one's forces (after a defeat)

崇 chóng ①〈形〉high; lofty ②〈动〉esteem; respect; worship:尊～ revere; worship

崇拜 chóngbài worship; adore; venerate; [贬义]make a fetish of

崇高 chónggāo lofty; noble; sublime; high:～的气节 lofty moral integrity

崇古非今 chónggǔfēijīn prize (exalt) the past and despise (disparage) the present

崇敬 chóngjìng esteem; respect; revere:他很～这位老教授。He has great respect for the old professor.

崇山峻岭 chóngshānjùnlǐng lofty ridges and towering mountains

崇尚 chóngshàng advocate; uphold:～勤俭 advocate industry and thrift

崇洋媚外 chóngyángmèiwài worship things foreign and fawn on foreigners; worship and toady to things foreign

chǒng

宠 chǒng〈动〉love; favour; dote on:别把孩子～坏了。Don't spoil the child.

宠爱 chǒng'ài favour; make a pet of sb.; love ardently

宠儿 chǒng'ér favourite; pet; minion; pampered favourite

宠惯 chǒngguàn pamper (a child); indulge

宠物 chǒngwù pet animal; pet

宠信 chǒngxìn be specially fond of and trust unduly (a subordinate)

chòng

冲 chòng〈形〉① strong; vigorous:这药味很～。This medicine has a strong smell. ② powerful; with plenty of dash〈动〉③ face:窗户～北开。The window faces north. ④ punch ⑤〈介〉facing; towards:～南走 go south

另见 chōng

冲床 chòngchuáng punch (press); punching machine

冲劲儿 chòngjìnr ① vim and vigour; dash ② strength (of liquor); kick:这酒～大。This wine has a lot of kick in it.

chōu

抽 chōu〈动〉① draw; pull; takeaway: ～水 drawing water from (the well; etc.) ② take out (from in between): 从文件夹里～出一份报告 take a report out of the file ③ sprout; bud; put forth: 高粱～穗了。The sorghum is coming into ear. ④ shrink ⑤ whip; lash; thrash: ～牲口 lash a draught animal ⑥ levy: ～税 levy a tax

抽查 chōuchá make a spot check (test); selective examination

抽搐 chōuchù ① twitch ②［机］tic

抽打 chōudǎ ① lash; whip; thrash ② chōuda beat (a carpet, blanket, etc.): 毯子得好好～一下。The blanket needs a good beating.

抽调 chōudiào transfer;［军队等］detach; move: ～劳动力 transfer of manpower

抽多补少 chōuduō-bǔshǎo take from those who have a surplus and give to those who have a shortage

抽肥补瘦 chōuféi-bǔshòu draw from the fat to subsidize the lean; take from those who have better and give to those who have the worse; taking things from the better-off collectives and giving them to the poorer ones

抽风 chōufēng ①［机］convulsions ② go crazy; lose one's senses: 别～了! Don't be crazy! ③ pump air

抽筋 chōujīn ① pull out a tendon ② cramp: 腿～ have a cramp in the leg

抽空 chōukòng manage to find time (to do)

抽签 chōuqiān draw (cast) lots

抽取 chōuqǔ ① draw; collect: ～版税 receive a royalty ～百分之二佣金 charge a commission of 2%

抽缫 chōusāo reeling of wild silk

抽纱 chōushā drawnwork

抽身 chōushēn leave (one's work); absent oneself: ～引退 retire from active public life; withdraw from one's post

抽水马桶 chōushuǐ mǎtǒng flush toilet; water closet

抽税 chōushuì levy a tax

抽逃资金 chōutáo zījīn spirit one's money away

抽象 chōuxiàng abstract: ～概念 abstract concept. ～地谈问题 speak in abstract terms

抽芽 chōuyá put forth buds; sprout bud

抽样 chōuyàng take a sample; sampling: ～调查 sampling investigation; sample survey

chóu

仇 chóu〈名〉① enemy; foe: 嫉恶如～ hate evil like an enemy ② enmity; hatred: 结～ become enemies; start a feud

仇雠 chóuchóu enemy; foe: ～敌战之国 hostile (warring) countries

仇敌 chóudí foe; enemy

仇恨 chóuhèn hatred; enmity; vengeance; hostility

仇人相见，分外眼红 chóurén xiāngjiàn, fēnwài yǎnhōng When two foes meet, their eyes flash fire.; Enemies see red the moment they meet.

仇杀 chóushā revengeful murder; kill in revenge

仇视 chóushì be hostile to; have animosity against (towards); look upon with hatred

惆 chóu〈形〉sad; disappointed

惆怅 chóuchàng sad; sorry; depressed; melancholy; disconsolate

绸 chóu〈名〉silk; woven silks

绸缎 chóuduàn silks and satins; silk fabrics

绸缪 chóumóu sentimentally attached; affectionate: 情意～ be head over heels in love

畴 chóu〈名〉① kind; division: 范～ category ② farmland ③ domain

酬 chóu〈动〉①〈敬〉propose a toast; toast ② pay; repay ③ friendly exchange: 应～ have social intercourse with ④ fulfil; realize ⑤〈名〉reward; payment: 稿～ payment for an article or book written

酬报 chóubào remuneration; reward; recompense; requite

酬宾 chóubīn bargain sales

酬答 chóudá ① thank sb. with a gift ② respond with a poem or speech

酬金 chóujīn monetary reward; emolument; remuneration

酬劳 chóuláo ① reward; remunerate ② thank sb. with a gift

酬谢 chóuxiè thank sb. with a gift; present sb. with a gift as a reward or as a token of one's appreciation

稠 chóu〈形〉dense; thick: 人烟～密 densely populated; populous

稠密 chóumì dense: 人口～ densely populated; populous. 交通网～ a dense communications network

愁 chóu ①〈动〉bother about; worry about: 她会～出病来的。She'll worry herself into illness. ②〈形〉sad; worried; heavy-hearted; sorrowful: ～思 feeling of sadness; melancholy

愁肠百结 chóucháng-bǎijié suffer great agonies of the mind; downcast; broken-hearted; overwhelmed with sorrow and longing

愁苦 chóukǔ anxiety; distress

愁眉苦脸 chóuméi-kǔliǎn knit one's brows; pull a long face; look worried and miserable; have a worried look

愁闷 chóumèn feel gloomy; be in low spirits; be depressed: 她工作不顺利，心里十分～。She was very cast down by setbacks in her work.

愁容 chóuróng worried look; sad

look; anxious expression

愁绪 chóuxù gloomy mood:小儿子的欢笑使她～全消。Her little son's bright smiles dispelled all her gloom.

愁云 chóuyún gloomy clouds — gloom; melancholy:喜讯传来,人们脸上的～消散了。The gloomy expressions on their faces disappeared at the good news.

筹 chóu ①〈动〉prepare; plan:统～ overall planning. ～款 raise funds (money) ②〈名〉chip; tally; counter

筹办 chóubàn prepare for; make arrangements for:～军需 make arrangements to meet the military requirements

筹备 chóubèi prepare; arrange:～展览会 make preparations for an exhibition. ～委员会 preparatory committee

筹措 chóucuò raise (money):～经费 raise funds

筹划 chóuhuà plan to do sth.; plan and prepare; make plans for

筹集 chóují raise (money):～资金 pool funds; raise money (funds); funding; collect money for

筹建 chóujiàn prepare to build:～费 expenses for preparatory work

筹借 chóujiè try to get a loan:～款项 try to borrow money

筹码 chóumǎ chip; counter; tally

筹谋 chóumóu lay plans; devise strategies

筹募 chóumù collect (funds):～福利基金 collect welfare funds

筹算 chóusuàn ① calculate with chips (in ancient times) ② calculate; reckon

筹议 chóuyì draft proposals on

筹资 chóuzī financing; prepare funds

踌 chóu

踌躇 chóuchú hesitate; waver; falter; shilly-shally; be undecided:～满志 highly self-satisfied with one's success; complacent; enormously proud of one's success; exceedingly gratified

踌躇不决 chóuchú-bùjué hesitating; irresolute

chǒu

丑 chǒu〈形〉① ugly:～小鸭 ugly duckling ② disgraceful; abominable; disgusting; scandalous:出～ make a fool of oneself ③〈名〉clown in Beijing opera, etc.

丑恶 chǒu'è ugly; foul; hideous; infamous:～现象 ugly (evil) phenomena

丑化 chǒuhuà uglify; distort; denigrate; vilify; discredit; defame

丑话 chǒuhuà ① vulgar language; abusive words ② blunt words

丑剧 chǒujù farce; foul performance

丑陋 chǒulòu ugly

丑事 chǒushì abominable affair;

scandal; disgraceful performance

丑态 chǒutài disgusting manner; unseemly manner; ugly (ludicrous) performance:～百出 cut a ridiculous figure; make a spectacle of oneself; utterly ridiculous

丑闻 chǒuwén scandal; obscene tales

丑行 chǒuxíng disgraceful conduct; shameful (scandalous) behaviour

瞅 chǒu〈动〉look at:让我～～。Let me have a look. 他～了我一眼。He took a look (glance) at me.

chòu

臭 chòu〈形〉① smelly; malodorous; stinking; foul:～鸡蛋 a rotten egg② disgusting; odious; detestable; notorious:～钱 filthy money (lurce)

另见 xiù

臭不可闻 chòubùkěwén malodorous; evil-smelling; a stench in everyone's nostrils

臭骂 chòumà strongly abuse; pour forth abuses on; curse angrily

臭美 chòuměi show off shamelessly; be disgustingly smug:你看她打扮得花里胡哨的,真～! Look how gaudily she is dressed, what a shameless display!

臭名远扬 chòumíng-yuǎnyáng notorious

臭名昭著 chòumíng-zhāozhù notorious; infamous; of ill repute

臭气 chòuqì bad smell; stink:～熏天 foul up the air with stink; give off a very offensive smell; stink to the skies

臭钱 chòuqián stinking money; filthy money

臭味相投 chòuwèi-xiāngtóu like drawn to like; share the same rotten tastes (habits); be two of a kind

chū

出 chū〈动〉① go (come) out:～国 go abroad ② issue; put forth:～布告 put up a notice; post an announcement ③ produce; turn out:～人才 turn out talents ④ exceed; go beyond:～格 go beyond the limit ⑤ take place; arise; happen; occur:这事～在四十年前。It happened forty years ago. ⑥ vent:～气 vent one's spleen ⑦ publish ⑧ pay out; expend:量入为～ keep expenditures within the limits of income ⑨〈名〉a dramatic piece:一～戏 a play; an opera

出版 chūbǎn publish; come off the press:～商 publisher. ～社 press; publishing house. ～物 publication. ～自由 freedom of the press

出操 chūcāo go out for drill or a workout

出差 chūchāi make a business

trip; go away on a mission; be on a business trip; go on a working tour: ~费 allowances for a business trip

出产 chūchǎn ① yield or manufacture; produce ② product; produce

出厂 chūchǎng (of products) leave the factory: ~价 ex-factory price; producer price

出场 chūchǎng ① [演员] appear on the stage; come on the stage ② [剧本] enter ③ [体] enter the arena: ~运动员名单 list of players for the match

出超 chūchāo export surplus; favourable balance of trade; excess of exports

出车 chūchē ① dispatch a vehicle: 公共汽车早 5 点~。Bus service starts at 5 a. m. ② be out driving a vehicle: 老张~去了。Lao Zhang is out with the car.

出丑 chūchǒu make a fool of sb. or oneself

出处 chūchù source (of a quotation or allusion): 注明 ~ indicate the source; give references. 我不知道这个典故的~. I don't know the original source of this allusion.

出错 chūcuò make a mistake: 她管帐很少~。She seldom makes a mistake in the accounts.

出点子 chū diǎnzi offer advice; make suggestions

出动 chūdòng ① set out; start off: 待命 ~ await orders to set out (go into action) ② send out; dispatch: ~飞机 30 架次 fly 30 sorties. 反动当局~军队镇压罢工。The reactionary authorities called out troops to put down the strike.

出尔反尔 chū'ěrfǎn'ěr go back on one's (own) word; act in bad faith; contradict oneself; be inconsistent

出发 chūfā ① set out; start off: 小分队于拂晓前~。The detachment set out before dawn. ② take... as a starting point in consideration; proceed from: 从国家利益 ~ proceed from the considerations of national interests

出发点 chūfādiǎn ① the starting point of a journey ② starting point (in discussion, argument, etc.); point of departure

出访 chūfǎng go abroad on an official visit: ~亚洲 5 国 go on an official visit to five Asian countries

出风头 chū fēngtóu show off; seek (be in) the limelight; cut a smart figure

出格 chūgé ① be out of the ordinary; be outstanding ② overstep the bounds; exceed what is proper: 她这样做太 ~ 了。What she's doing is most improper.

出工 chūgōng show up for work; go to work.

出国 chūguó go abroad: ~ 留学 go abroad to study. 他们出过两次国。They have been abroad twice.

出乎意料 chūhū-yìliào contrary to one's expectations; out of one's reckoning; unexpectedly

出活 chuhuó yield results in work; get a lot done.

出嫁 chūjià (of a woman) get married; marry

出价 chūjià offer a price

出境 chūjìng leave the country:～签证 exit visa. 驱逐～ deport

出口 chūkǒu ① speak ② exit; outlet ③ export:～加工区 export processing zones. ～商品结构 mix of export goods. ～退税制度 export refund system

出来 chūlái ① come out:太阳～了。The sun has come out. ② emerge; arise; appear:要是～新问题怎么办? What should we do if a new problem crops up? ③ [用在动词后,表示动作由里向外朝着说话的人]:从大厅里走出一个人来。Someone came out of the hall. ④ [用在动词后,表示动作完成或实现]:工人们终于把这种优质钢炼～了。The workers finally succeeded in making the high-grade steel. ⑤ [用在动词后,表示由隐蔽到显露]:我一眼就认出他们来了。I recognized them the moment I saw them.

出栏 chūlán sold from the farm of animals stock

出类拔萃 chūlèi-bácuì distinguished; preeminent; outstanding; towering above the rest

出力 chūlì put forth one's strength; exert oneself:他们为我们省的医疗卫生工作出过不少力。They have done quite a lot of the medical and health work of our province.

出路 chūlù way out; outlet:剩余劳动力的～ outlet for surplus labour power; employment of the surplus labour force

出乱子 chū luànzi go wrong; get into trouble

出落 chūluo (of a young person, esp. a young girl) grow (prettier, etc.):二年不见,这姑娘～得更漂亮了。The girl has grown prettier than ever since I last saw her two years ago.

出马 chūmǎ go into action; take the field:亲自～ take up the matter oneself; attend to the matter personally; take personal charge of the matter

出卖 chūmài ① sell; put on sale; offer for sale ② betray

出毛病 chū máobìng go wrong; be out of order:汽车～了。The car is out of order.; Something has gone wrong with the car.

出门 chūmén ① go out:她刚～,一会儿就回来。She's just gone out, she'll be back soon. ② leave home; go on a journey:～在外,要多加小心。Look after yourself when you're away from home. ③〈方〉(of a woman) get married; marry

出面 chūmiàn appear personally; act in one's own capacity or on behalf of sb.:他愿出力,不愿～。He's willing to help out but not to act on anyone's behalf.

出名 chūmíng become well-known

(famous); be noted (famed) for

出没 chūmò appear and disappear; haunt

出没无常 chūmò-wúcháng appear and disappear unexpectedly; come and go unpredictably

出谋划策 chūmóu-huàcè give counsel; mastermind:躲在背后～ mastermind a scheme from behind the scenes

出纳 chūnà ① receive and pay out (money) ② cashier

出品 chūpǐn ① produce; manufacture; make ② product

出其不意 chūqíbùyì take sb. by surprise; catch sb. unawares: ～地捕获 catch by surprise

出奇制胜 chūqí-zhìshèng win by a surprise attack; achieve success with original ideas; defeat one's opponent by a surprise move

出勤 chūqín attendance at work: ～率 rate of attendance

出清存货 chū qīngcúnhuò clearing stock

出人头地 chūréntóudì come to the fore; stand head and shoulders above others; stand out among one's fellows; rise head and shoulders above others

出人意料 chūrényìliào exceeding all expectations; beyond all expectations

出任 chūrèn take up the post of: ～省长 take up the post of provincial governor

出入 chūrù ① come in and go out ② discrepancy; divergence: 她说的和事实有～。What she says does not square with the facts. ～证 pass (identifying a staff member, etc.)

出色 chūsè outstanding; remarkable; splendid: 干得很～ do a remarkable job; acquit oneself splendidly

出山 chūshān come out from the mountains; come out to assume leadership: 这厂只有请他～才有可能救活。The only way to rejuvenate this factory is to ask him to come out to assume leadership.

出身 chūshēn (class) origin; parentage; family background

出神 chūshén be spellbound; be in a trance; be lost in thought: 青年钢琴家的演奏使我们听得出了神。We were held spellbound by the performance of the young pianist. 她坐在那里～。She sat there, lost in thought.

出生 chūshēng be born: ～地 birthplace. ～率 birth rate

出生入死 chūshēng-rùsǐ go through fire and water; brave untold dangers; at the risk of life and limb: 革命战争中～的英雄 heroes who risked death in the revolutionary wars

出世 chūshì ① come into the world; be born; come into being: 她～才一个月，她妈妈就去世了。Her mother died a month after she was born. ② renounce the world; keep aloof from worldly affairs ③ rise high above the world

出事 chūshì meet with an accident; have an accident: ～地点 scene (of an accident); trouble spot (area)

出手不凡 chūshǒu-bùfán make skilful (masterly) opening moves (in chess, etc.)

出售 chūshòu offer for sale; sell

出台 chūtái emerge on stage: 正式方案不久将～。The formal plan will soon be unveiled. ～价格 the disclosed price

出庭 chūtíng appear in court

出头 chūtóu ① lift one's head; be freed from misery (persecution, etc.); ② appear in public; come forward: ～露面 appear in public; show oneself; be in the limelight

出徒 chūtú complete one's apprenticeship

出土 chūtǔ be unearthed: ～文物 unearthed relics; archaeological objects; antiquities unearthed

出污泥而不染 chū wūní ér bùrǎn emerge unstained from the filth

出席 chūxí be present (at a meeting, social gathering, etc.); attend: ～会议 attend a meeting. ～人数 number of persons present; attendance

出息 chūxi promise; prospects: 有～ promising. 没～ good-for-nothing

出线 chūxiàn [体] go through to the finals; qualify for the finals; qualify for the next round of competitions; attain eligibility: 获得～权 win the qualifying round

出现 chūxiàn appear; take shape; occur; emerge; [问题] crop up: 处理新～的问题 deal with problems that have recently cropped up

出言不逊 chūyán-bùxùn make impertinent remarks; speak insolently

出演 chūyǎn ① show; perform ② play the part of; act

出洋相 chū yángxiàng make a show (fool) of oneself; cut a miserable figure

出于 chūyú start from; proceed from; stem from: ～对同志的关怀 out of concern for one's comrades

出于无奈 chūyú-wúnài as it cannot be helped; there being no alternative

出院 chūyuàn be discharged from hospital; leave hospital: ～证明 hospital discharge certificate

出月子 chū yuèzi (of a woman after childbirth) complete her month of confinement

出诊 chūzhěn (of a doctor) pay a home visit (to the patient); make a house call; out-call

出征 chūzhēng go on an expedition; go out to battle: ～的战士 soldiers sent on an expedition

出众 chūzhòng be out of the ordinary; be outstanding: 成绩～ get outstanding results in study or work

出租 chūzū hire; let; rent out; [土地] lease: ～汽车 taxi

(cab). ～汽车司机 cabbie

初 chū ①〈名〉beginning; in the early part of: 九月～ early in September〈形〉② first (in order): ～雪 first snow ③ junior; elementary; rudimentary: ～中 junior middle school ④ original: 和好如～ become reconciled ⑤〈副〉for the first time: ～具规模 begin to take shape

初版 chūbǎn ① first edition ② be first published: 这部词典于1990年～。This dictionary was first published in 1990.

初保额 chūbǎo'é [投资担保] initial amount of guarantee

初步 chūbù initial; primary; preliminary; tentative: ～繁荣 initial prosperity; beginnings of prosperity. ～加工 initial processing

初出茅庐 chūchū-máolú ① just come out of one's thatched cottage—at the beginning of one's career; be young and inexperienced ②〈形,名〉fledgeling: 他是～的剧作家。He is a fledgeling dramatist.

初创 chūchuàng newly established: ～的企业 a newly-established enterprise

初次 chūcì for the first time: 国民收入～分配 primary distribution of the national income. ～演出 première; [演员的]début

初等 chūděng primary; elementary: ～教育 primary education.

初犯 chūfàn ① first offender ② first offence

初稿 chūgǎo first draft

初婚 chūhūn ① first marriage ② newly married

初级 chūjí elementary; primary: ～产品 primary products. ～学位 first degree. 社会主义～阶段 primary stage of socialism

初交 chūjiāo new acquaintance

初校 chūjiào [印] first revisal

初恋 chūliàn ① first love: 他仍然忠于他的～。He remained true to his first love. ② the first stage of falling in love

初露锋芒 chūlù-fēngmáng display one's talent for the first time

初露头角 chūlù-tóujiǎo begin to show ability or talent: ～的新诗人 budding poets

初年 chūnián ① the first years of a historical period: 清朝～ in the first years of the Qing Dynasty ② first spring month (i.e. the first month of the lunar year)

初期 chūqī initial stage; early days: 战争～ in the early days of the war

初赛 chūsài preliminary contest; preliminary

初审 chūshěn trial of first instance; first trial: ～案件 case of first instance. ～法庭 court of first instance

初生牛犊不怕虎 chūshēng niúdú bùpà hǔ A new-born calf is not afraid of tigers—young people are fearless.; A new-born calf makes little of tigers.

初始 chūshǐ initial; first; primary

初试 chūshì ① first try (attempt): 他～云雨情 he having his first taste of love ② preliminary examination

初探 chūtàn preliminary study of; tentative study of; tentative probe into; initial probe into; tentative inquiry into

初选 chūxuǎn primary election

初学 chūxué begin to learn; be a beginner:我是～,还不会拉曲子。I'm just a beginner; I can't play a tune yet.

初旬 chūxún the first ten days of a month

初叶 chūyè early years (of a century):19世纪～ early in the nineteenth century

初愿 chūyuàn one's original intention

初中 chūzhōng junior middle school:～后、高中后的分流 regulate the flow of graduates of junior and senior middle schools

初衷 chūzhōng one's original intention:不改～ will not change one's original intention

chú

刍 chú 〈动〉 hay; fodder:反～ chew the cud

刍言 chúyán (my) superficial remarks; (my) humble opinion

刍议 chúyì my humble opinion; tentative proposal; modest proposal; rustic opinion

除 chú 〈动〉① do away with; get rid of; eliminate; exterminate:兴利～弊 promote what is beneficial and abolish what is harmful ② divide:10除以2得5。10 divided by 2 is 5. ③〈介〉except; besides:～他以外,我们都去。We all went except him.

除暴 chúbào eliminate despots

除尘器 chúchénqì dust remover

除非 chúfēi ①[表示唯一条件] only when (if):～你去请她,不然她是不会来的。Only when you go and ask her personally will she come. ②[表示不计算在内] unless:～我打电话给你,否则你不要来。Don't come unless I ring you up.

除根 chúgēn root out; uproot:斩草～ pull up weeds by the roots

除害灭病 chúhài-mièbìng rid scourges and eradicate diseases

除旧布新 chújiù-bùxīn eliminate (get rid of) the old to make way for the new; do away with the old and set up the new

除了 chúle ① except:～老罗,我都通知到了。I've notified everyone except Lao Luo. ②[与"还"、"也"等连用] besides; in addition to:懂法语的,～我还有两个人。There are two others besides me who know French. ③[跟"就是"连用] if not... (then...); either ... (or ...):这几天～刮风,就是下雪。Recently we've been having either windy or snowy days.

除名 chúmíng expel; [教] exclusion

除外 chúwài except; be excepted; not including:他每天去办公,星期六和星期天～。He goes to office every day except Saturday and Sunday (on Saturday and Sunday).

除夕 chúxī New Year's Eve

厨 chú〈名〉kitchen

厨房 chúfáng kitchen:～用具 kitchen utensils; kitchen ware

厨房有人好进餐,朝里有人好做官 chúfáng yǒurén hǎo jìncān, cháolǐ yǒurén hǎo zuòguān The influence of friends in the right place can make a man's lot much easier.

厨师 chúshī cook; chef

锄 chú ①〈名〉hoe〈动〉② hoe; work with a hoe:～草 hoe up weeds; weed with a hoe ③ eliminate; uproot

锄地 chúdì hoe the fields; do hoeing:锄玉米地 hoe the cornfields

锄耕农业 chúgēng nóngyè tillage with mattocks; hoe agriculture; hoe ploughing in agriculture

锄奸 chújiān anti-espionage; eliminate traitors; ferret out spies; remove a bunch of hidden traitors from

锄头 chútou ① pickaxe ②〈方〉hoe

雏 chú ①〈名〉chick; nestling ②〈形〉young (bird); little:～鸭 duckling

雏儿 chúr ① a young bird; nestling:鸭～ duckling ② a young, inexperienced person; fledgling

雏鸡 chújī chick; chicken

雏形 chúxíng ① embryonic form; embryo; premature form ② miniature:新社会的～ a prototype of a new society

橱 chú〈名〉cabinet; wardrobe

橱窗 chúchuāng show (display) window; shopwindow; showcase:布置商店～ dress a shopwindow. ～陈列品 a window array

橱柜 chúguì cupboard ② a cupboard that also serves as a table; sideboard

chǔ

处 chǔ〈动〉① live; dwell:穴居野～ live in wilds and dwell in caves ② get along with:我们相～得很好。We get along quite well. ③ be in (a place, etc.); exist:～在一个伟大的历史时代 live in a great historical era ④ handle; manage; handle affairs; manage affairs ⑤ punish; sentence:～以三年徒刑 sentence sb. to three years' imprisonment

另见 chù

处罚 chǔfá punish; penalize

处分 chǔfèn be disciplined; take disciplinary action against:组织～ organizational penalties. ～职工 imposition of sanctions against staff and workers

处境 chǔjìng ① situation:～动态评价 dynamic assessment of the situation ②[不利的] predicament; plight:～困窘 be in a sorry plight; be in a tight spot

处决 chǔjué ① put to death; execute:依法 ～ put to death in accordance with the law ② handle and decide; manage and make decisions

处理 chǔlǐ handle; deal with; tackle; dispose of:～价格 reduced price. ～品 clearance goods; items for disposal

处女 chǔnǚ virgin; maid:～作 maiden work (effort); first effort

处事 chǔshì ①handle affairs; deal with matters:她～严肃,态度却十分和蔼。She handles affairs in a businesslike yet friendly way.

处世 chǔshì conduct oneself in society:～哲学 philosophy of life; code of conduct

处死 chǔsǐ put to death; execute

处心积虑 chǔxīn-jīlǜ have all along nurtured schemes to; set one's mind on; deliberately scheme (plan); ceaselessly intrigue; rack one's brains

处刑 chǔxíng condemn; sentence; submit to punishment; mete out penalty

处于 chǔyú be in a certain state (condition):(使…)～水深火热之中 plunge… into an abyss of suffering; plunge … into dire misery; live in the abyss of suffering

处之泰然 chǔzhītàirán remain composed; be calm and composed; take things calmly; take it easy

处置 chǔzhì ① handle; deal with; manage; dispose of:～失当 mismanage; mishandle ② punish

杵 chǔ 〈名〉① pestle:～臼 mortar and pestle ② a wooden club used to beat clothes in washing ③ poke:把纸 ～ 个窟窿 poke a hole in the paper

础 chǔ 〈名〉plinth

础石 chǔshí stone base of a column; plinth

储 chǔ ①〈动〉store up; save; keep (have) in reserve:冬～白菜 cabbages stored for the winter ②〈名〉heir:王～ crown prince

储备 chǔbèi store; reserve; lay up:外汇～ foreign exchange reserve. 人才～ personnel reserve

储币待购 chǔbì-dàigòu save up money for purchases

储藏 chǔcáng keep; store; preserve and save; lay by:～图书馆 depository library

储存 chǔcún lay in; lay up; store; stockpile; deposit:把钱～在银行里 deposit the money in a bank

储放 chǔfàng store; leave in sb.'s care:把行李 ～ 在寄存处 check one's luggage at the checkroom

储户 chǔhù depositor

储量 chǔliàng reserves:探明 ～ proved reserves

储蓄 chǔxù ① save; deposit ② savings:定期(活期)～ fixed

(current) deposit. ～存款折 saving deposits passbook
储油 chǔyóu oil storage
储运 chǔyùn storage and transportation: ～作业 distribution activities
楚 chǔ ①〈形〉clear; neat: 一清二～ perfectly clear ②〈名〉suffering; pain: 凄～ miserable
楚材楚用 chǔcái-chǔyòng use local talents
楚材晋用 chǔcái-jìnyòng great person given important post by another country
楚楚 chǔchǔ bright and clear; tidy; neat: ～动人 delicate and attractive; lovingly pathetic. 衣冠～ immaculately dressed
楚辞 chǔcí ballads of Chu; elegies of Chu; Songs of Chu; *Chu ci*-style works
楚剧 chǔjù Chu opera (popular in Hubei and part of Jiangxi)

chù

处 chù〈名〉① place: 敝～ my place. 停车～ parking lot ② point; part: 长～ strong point ③ office; department: 人事～ personnel department
另见 chǔ
处处 chùchù everywhere; here and there; in all aspects
处所 chùsuǒ place; location
处长 chùzhǎng head of a department (office, etc.)
怵 chù〈动〉fear: ～惕 feel apprehensive
怵然 chùrán apprehensive; frightened
绌 chù〈形〉inadequate; insufficient
畜 chù〈名〉livestock; domestic animal
另见 xù
畜肥 chùféi animal manure
畜类 chùlèi domestic animals
畜力 chùlì animal power: ～农具 animal-drawn farm implements
畜生 chùsheng ① domestic animal; livestock ②［骂人语］beast; dirty swine
畜疫 chùyì epidemic disease of domestic animals
搐 chù〈动〉jerk; twitch
搐动 chùdòng (of muscles, etc.) twitch; jerk
触 chù〈动〉① touch; contact: 请勿～摸陈列品。Don't touch the exhibits, please. ～到痛处 touch a sore spot ② move: 他们苦难的经历深深地～动了我们。The story of their sufferings moved us deeply.
触电 chùdiàn be struck by electric current; get an electric shock; electrocute: ～身亡 be killed by electric current
触动 chùdòng ① touch sth., moving it slightly: 她在暗中摸索着，忽然～了什么东西。Groping in the dark, she suddenly touched something. ② move sb.; stir up sb.'s feelings; shake: 这句话～了她的心

事。That remark reminded her of something she'd had on her mind for a long time.

触犯 chùfàn offend; [法] violate (break) the law

触及 chùjí touch: ～ 事物的本质 get to the essence of a matter

触礁 chùjiāo strike a rock (reef); run on rocks

触景生情 chùjǐng-shēngqíng be moved by what one sees; recall old memories at familiar sights; The sight strikes a chord in one's heart.

触觉 chùjué sense of touch; touch

触类旁通 chùlèi-pángtōng draw parallels from inference; comprehend by analogy; appreciation

触霉头 chùméitóu come to grief

触摸 chùmō touch; feel: 请勿 ～ 展品。Please don't touch the exhibits.

触目 chùmù meet the eye; conspicuous: ～ 惊心的 shocking; startling; horrid

触怒 chùnù enrage; irritate; exasperate

触痛 chùtòng ① touch a tender (sore) spot; touch sb. to the quick ② [医] tenderness

触网 chùwǎng [体] touch net

黜 chù 〈动〉 remove sb. from office; dismiss

黜免 chùmiǎn dismiss (a government official); remove (sb. from office)

矗 chù 〈书〉 stand tall and upright

矗立 chùlì tower over; stand erect

chuāi

揣 chuāi 〈动〉 tuck (into); thrust (into); keep sth. in one's clothes: ～在怀里 tuck into the bosom
另见 chuǎi

chuǎi

揣 chuǎi 〈动〉 ① reckon; calculate ② guess; imagine; conjecture: 不～冒昧 take the liberty
另见 chuāi

揣测 chuǎicè give a guess; conjecture; try to find

揣度 chuǎidù conjecture; reckon; estimate

揣摩 chuǎimó try to figure out; try to fathom

chuài

踹 chuài 〈动〉 kick; tread; stamp: ～ 开门 kick the door open

chuān

川 chuān 〈名〉 ① river; stream: 百～归海。All rivers flow into the sea. ② plain: 米粮～ rich rice-producing area

川菜 chuāncài Sichuan food; Sichuan cuisine

chuáng

床 chuáng〈名〉bed：两～铺盖 two sets of bedding
床单 chuángdān sheet：～布 sheeting
床垫 chuángdiàn mattress
床铺 chuángpù bed
床上用品 chuángshàng yòngpǐn bedding；bed clothes
床榻 chuángtà bed；couch
床头 chuángtóu the head of a bed；bedside：～灯 bedside lamp；bedlamp. ～柜 bedside cupboard
床位 chuángwèi bed；[船、车等] berth：～占用率 bed occupancy rate
床罩 chuángzhào bedspread；counterpane
幢 chuáng〈名〉① a pennant or streamer used in ancient China ② a stone pillar inscribed with Buddha's name or Buddhist scripture
另见 zhuàng

chuǎng

闯 chuǎng〈动〉① dash；rush；charge：横冲直～ charge about furiously ② temper oneself (by battling through difficulties and dangers)：～过关 come triumphantly through the ordeal. ～物价关 getting over the price reform hurdle
闯祸 chuǎnghuò have an accident；get into trouble；cause disaster
闯江湖 chuǎngjiānghú make a living wandering from place to place (as a fortune-teller, acrobat, quack doctor, etc.)
闯劲 chuǎngjìn spirit of a pathbreaker；pioneering spirit；heroic effort
闯南走北 chuǎngnán-zǒuběi travel widely；journey north and south

chuàng

创 chuàng ①〈动〉start；create；establish；initiate：～优质产品 create fine-quality products. ～记录 set a record ②〈形〉new；first；initial
另见 chuāng
创办 chuàngbàn set up；found；establish：～人 founder. ～资本投资 initial capital investment
创导者 chuàngdǎozhě prime mover
创汇 chuànghuì earn foreign exchange (income)
创建 chuàngjiàn establish；found；set up：～工作 preliminary groundwork
创见 chuàngjiàn original (new) idea；originality
创举 chuàngjǔ pioneering undertaking；pioneering efforts；pioneering action (work)；great beginning
创刊 chuàngkān start publication：～号 first number；initial issue
创立 chuànglì found；originate：

～新学派 found a new academic school

创设 chuàngshè ① found; create; set up ② create (conditions, etc.): 为他们的学习～有利的条件 create favourable conditions for their studies

创始 chuàngshǐ initiate; originate; start: 世界贸易组织的～国 founding nations of World Trade Organization

创世 chuàngshì creation: ～神话 myths of creation

创收 chuàngshōu create income: ～提成 obtain additional income from a percentage of the gains

创新 chuàngxīn create sth. new; break new ground; blaze new trails; innovation: 要有～精神。We must have the break-new-ground spirit.

创业 chuàngyè start an undertaking; do pioneering work: ～精神 spirit of a pathbreaker; enterprising spirit

创议 chuàngyì ① propose ② proposal

创意 chuàngyì create (advertising) concepts; creative ideas (for advertisement): ～部门 creative department

创优 chuàngyōu create excellence: 争先～ strive to be advanced and create excellence. ～活动 the activity of creating excellence

创造 chuàngzào create; produce; bring about: ～历史 make history

创作 chuàngzuò create; produce; creation: 文艺～ literary and artistic creation. ～思想 ideas guiding literary or artistic creation

chuī

吹 chuī 〈动〉 ① blow; exhale; puff: ～一口气 give a puff; breathe out ② play (wind instruments): ～长笛 play the flute ③ boast; brag: 自～自擂 blow one's own trumpet ④ flatter; laud to the skies ⑤ break up; fall through; break off: 他们俩～了。That couple have broken up.

吹吹打打 chuīchuī-dǎdǎ beating drums and blowing trumpets; piping and drumming

吹吹拍拍 chuīchuī-pāipāi boasting and toadying

吹打乐 chuīdǎyuè an ensemble of Chinese wind and percussion instruments

吹得天花乱坠 chuīdé tiānhuāluànzhuì laud (sb. or sth.) to the skies; make a great deal of hullabaloo (ballyhoo)

吹风 chuīfēng ① dry one's hair (with a blower): ～机［理发用］hair drier; blower ② deliberately let out inside information in an informal way: ～会 briefing

吹胡子瞪眼 chuīhúzi-dèngyǎn froth at the mouth and glare with rage; foam with anger.

吹灰之力 chuīhuīzhīlì with the

least effort; as easy as to blow away the dust; just a small effort

吹毛求疵 chuīmáo-qiúcī find fault (with); split hairs; nit-pick; carp (at); be very fastidious

吹牛 chuīniú brag; talk big; draw the long bow:～拍马 boast and flatter

吹捧 chuīpěng flatter; sing praises of; extol:对某人大肆～ extol sb. to the skies

吹嘘 chuīxū lavish praises on oneself or others; blow one's own trumpet; brag (of, about)

吹奏 chuīzòu play (wind instruments):～乐 wind music. ～乐器 wind instrument

炊 chuī〈动〉cook:～事 cooking; kitchen work

炊具 chuījù cooking utensils

炊事 chuīshì cooking; kitchen work: ～用具 kitchen (cooking) utensils

炊烟 chuīyān smoke from kitchen chimneys

炊帚 chuīzhǒu pot-scouring brush; brush for cleaning pots and pans

chuí

垂 chuí〈动〉① droop; hang down; hang; bend down:～柳 drooping willow ② drop; shed:～泪 shed tears ③〈敬〉condescend:～询 condescend to inquire ④〈书〉approaching; nearing:～老 approaching old age; getting on in years

垂爱 chuí'ài〈套〉[多用于书信] have gracious concern for (me)

垂成 chuíchéng be approaching success or completion

垂钓 chuídiào fish with a hook and line; go angling

垂暮 chuímù towards evening:～之年 in one's declining years; in old age

垂青 chuíqīng show appreciation for sb.; look upon sb. with special favour

垂手 chuíshǒu with one's hands at one's sides:～侍立 stand respectfully in attendance

垂首 chuíshǒu hang (bow) one's head:～默哀 bow one's head in silent mourning

垂死 chuísǐ dying; moribund:～挣扎 deathbed struggle; give dying kicks; last-ditch struggle; in one's death throes

垂头丧气 chuítóu-sàngqì downcast; downhearted; crestfallen

垂危 chuíwēi be critically ill; be in danger; at one's last gasp

垂涎 chuíxián drool; slaver; hanker after; covet:～欲滴 make one's mouth water copiously—be unable to hide one's greed; keep a covetous eye on

垂询 chuíxún〈套〉deign (condescend) to inquire into sth.

捶 chuí〈动〉beat (with a stick or fist); pound

捶打 chuídǎ ① beat; pound; thump; ～衣服 beat clothes (when washing them) ② beat with quick, light blows：他用拳头～酸痛的腿。He beat on his aching leg with his fist. ③ temper; steel; toughen

捶胸拍案 chuíxiōng-pāi'àn beat the breast and pound the table

槌 chuí〈名〉beetle; mallet

锤 chuí〈名〉① weight ② iron hammer ③〈动〉strike with a hammer

锤炼 chuíliàn ① forge; steel and temper ②［词句］polish; refine：～词句 refine upon the wording

锤子 chuízi hammer

chūn

春 chūn〈名〉① spring：大地回～。Spring returns to the world. ② life; vitality：妙手回～。Expert medical knowledge brings the dying back to life.; (of physician) bring back life to a patient ③ love; lust

春播 chūnbō spring sowing：～作物 spring-sown crops

春潮 chūncháo spring tide

春风 chūnfēng spring wind; vernal breezes：～满面 (one's face) shine with happiness; beam with satisfaction; radiant with happiness

春耕 chūngēng spring ploughing：～大忙季节 busy spring ploughing season

春光 chūnguāng sights and sounds of spring; spring scenery：～明媚 a sunlit and enchanting scene of spring

春旱 chūnhàn a long dry spell in spring; spring drought

春画 chūnhuà pornographic pictures

春假 chūnjià spring holidays

春节 chūnjié the Spring Festival

春卷 chūnjuǎn spring roll (a thin sheet of dough, rolled, stuffed and fried)

春联 chūnlián Spring Festival couplets (pasted on gateposts or door panels); New Year scrolls

春秋 chūnqiū ① spring and autumn; year：几度～ several years ② age：～已高 be advanced in years ③ history; annals ④ the Spring and Autumn Period (770-476 B.C.)

春色 chūnsè ① spring's colours; spring scenery：～满园。Spring's colours fill the garden. ② joyful look; wine-flushed face

春天 chūntiān spring; springtime

春汛 chūnxùn ①［渔业］spring (fishing) season ②［水利］spring flood (freshet)

春意 chūnyì ① spring in the air; the beginning (awakening) of spring：～盎然。Spring is in the air. ② thoughts of love

春游 chūnyóu spring outing

春种 chūnzhòng spring sowing

春装 chūnzhuāng spring clothing; spring costume

椿 chūn〈名〉① Chinese toon ② tree of heaven

chún

纯 chún〈形〉① pure; unmixed: ～金 pure gold ② pure and simple; simple ③ skilful; well versed; accomplished: 功夫不～ not skilful enough; The skill is far from accomplished.

纯粹 chúncuì pure and simple; pure; unadulterated

纯度 chúndù degree of purity

纯洁 chúnjié pure; unselfish and honest: ～性 purity

纯净 chúnjìng pure; clean: ～的水是透明的。Pure water is transparent.

纯利 chúnlì net profit

纯朴 chúnpǔ honest; simple; unsophisticated: ～敦厚 simple and honest. 文风～ simplicity of style

纯收入 chúnshōurù net income (receipt)

纯熟 chúnshú skilful; proficient; well versed

纯贞 chúnzhēn pure and faithful: ～的爱情 pure and faithful love

纯真 chúnzhēn pure; sincere: ～无邪 pure and innocent

纯正 chúnzhèng pure; honest: 动机～ with a pure motive

纯挚 chúnzhì pure and sincere: ～的友情 pure and sincere friendship

唇 chún〈名〉lip

唇齿相依 chúnchǐ-xiāngyī be closely related to each other like lips and teeth; interdependent as lips and teeth

唇膏 chúngāo lipstick

唇枪舌剑 chúnqiāng-shéjiàn argue heatedly; cross verbal swords

唇舌 chúnshé argument; words

唇亡齿寒 chúnwáng-chǐhán when the lips are gone the teeth will be exposed to the cold; be so closely related that they share a common lot

淳 chún〈形〉pure; honest

淳厚 chúnhòu simple and honest; simple and kind; devoted

淳朴 chúnpǔ simple-hearted and honest; unsophisticated; honest

醇 chún ①〈名〉mellow wine; good wine ②〈形〉pure; unmixed ③ [化] alcohol

醇和 chúnhé (of quality, taste, etc.) mellow; pure

醇厚 chúnhòu mellow; rich: 酒味～。The wine is (tastes) mellow.

醇酒 chúnjiǔ good wine

醇美 chúnměi pure and sweet; mellow: ～的嗓音 a pure and sweet voice

chǔn

蠢 chǔn〈形〉① foolish; stupid; silly ② clumsy ③〈动〉wriggle

蠢笨 chǔnbèn awkward; stupid; clumsy

蠢蠢欲动 chǔnchǔn-yùdòng be ready for action; start to make

trouble; itch for action; eager for action

蠢动 chǔndòng ① wriggle; squirm; ② create disturbances; stir up trouble; insidious move (on the part of the enemy or bad elements)

蠢货 chǔnhuò［骂人话］blockhead; dunce; idiot

蠢人 chǔnrén fool; blockhead

蠢事 chǔnshì folly:干～ commit a folly; play the fool

chuō

戳 chuō ①〈动〉stab; prick; poke:在纸上～了一个洞 poke a hole in the paper ②〈名〉stamp; seal

戳穿 chuōchuān ① pierce through; puncture ② lay bare; expose:～…的神话 explode the myth of…

戳记 chuōjì stamp; seal

戳破 chuōpò ① puncture ② expose; lay bare

戳子 chuōzi〈口〉stamp; seal:在文件上盖个～ put a seal (stamp) on a document

chuò

绰 chuò〈形〉ample; spacious

绰绰有余 chuòchuò-yǒuyú more than sufficient; enough and to spare; more than enough

绰号 chuòhào nickname; sobriquet

绰约多姿 chuòyuēduōzī (of a girl) graceful

辍 chuò〈动〉cease; stop

辍笔 chuòbǐ stop in the middle of writing or painting

辍学 chuòxué discontinue one's studies; leave off one's study; drop-out

cī

刺 cī〈象〉swish; wham:～的一声,她滑了一个跟头。Swish! She slipped and fell.

另见 cì

刺啦 cīlā the sound of ripping, tearing, or scratching:～一声,他划着了火柴。Scratch! He struck a match.

疵 cī〈名〉flaw; defect; blemish:无～ flawless; impeccable

疵点 cīdiǎn flaw; fault; defect

疵品 cīpǐn defective goods

疵瑕 cīxiá flaw; blemish

cí

词 cí〈名〉① word; term:技术～ technical term ② speech; statement; lines of play:闭幕～ closing speech ③ *ci* is a lyric with lines of irregular length set to a certain melody

词不达意 cíbùdáyì the words fail to convey the idea

词典 cídiǎn dictionary

词锋 cífēng vigour (pungency) of style

词汇 cíhuì vocabulary:～学 lexicology

词集 cíjí *ci* works published in anthologies
词句 cíjù ① terms and phrases; expressions ② sentences
词律 cílǜ prosody of ci poems
词牌 cípái *ci* melody names
词谱 cípǔ collection of tunes of ci poems
词人 círén lyricists; *ci* poets; *ci* poem writers; *ci* writers
词义 cíyì sense of a word; lexical meaning:～学 semantics
词语 cíyǔ words and expressions; terms
词源 cíyuán origin of a word:～学 etymology
词藻 cízǎo flowery language; rhetoric
词组 cízǔ phrase; word group; expression

茨
cí ①〈名〉thatch (a roof) ②［植］puncture vine

祠
cí〈名〉temple
祠产 cíchǎn property of the ancestral hall
祠规 cíguī ancestral hall regulations
祠堂 cítáng family temple; ancestral temple

瓷
cí〈名〉porcelain; china:青～ blue china; celadon
瓷雕 cídiāo porcelain carving
瓷饭碗 cífànwǎn "ceramic rice bowl" refers to the practice by which municipal or district authorities take responsibility for the profits and losses of collectively-owned enterprises
瓷刻 cíkè porcelain carving
瓷瓶 cípíng china vase
瓷器 cíqì porcelain; china:细～ fine china
瓷实 císhi〈方〉solid; firm; substantial:她身体很～。She is solidly built.
瓷窑 cíyáo porcelain kiln; china kiln
瓷砖 cízhuān decorative tile; glazed tile

辞
cí〈名〉① diction; phraseology ② a type of classical Chinese literature:《楚～》The Songs of Chu ③ speech〈动〉④ refuse; decline:固～ firmly decline ⑤ resign ⑥ dismiss; fire; sack; discharge:～退职工 dismiss (discharge) workers ⑦ take leave:告～ take one's leave
辞别 cíbié say good-bye (to); bid farewell (to); take leave (of)
辞格 cígé figures of speech
辞工跳槽 cígōng-tiàocáo leave one's work and go to another
辞岁 císuì bid farewell to the outgoing year; celebrate the lunar New Year's Eve
辞谢 cíxiè decline (with thanks)
辞行 cíxíng say goodbye (to sb.) before going on a journey; take one's leave
辞职 cízhí resign; quit office; hand in one's resignation

慈
cí ①〈形〉kind; loving:心～ kindhearted; tenderhearted ②〈名〉mother:～命 mother's command

慈爱 cí'ài affection; loving-kindness

慈悲 cíbēi merciful; benevolent: ～为怀 be kindhearted

慈母 címǔ loving mother; mother

慈善 císhàn charitable; benevolent; philanthropic: ～机关 charitable (philanthropic) institution (organization)

慈祥 cíxiáng kindly: ～的笑容 kindly smile

慈颜 cíyán kindly face (of one's parents or elders)

磁 cí〈名〉① magnetism: 起～ magnetization ② procelain; china

磁场 cíchǎng magnetic field

磁带 cídài recording tape: ～录音机 tape recorder

磁化 cíhuà magnetize

磁疗 cíliáo magnetotherapy

磁盘 cípán [计] magnetic disk: ～操作系统 disk operating system (DOS). ～存储器 magnetic disk memory

磁铁 cítiě magnet

磁头 cítóu magnetic head (of a recorder)

磁性 cíxìng [物]magnetism

磁针 cízhēn magnetic needle

雌 cí〈形〉female

雌性 cíxìng female; femina

雌雄 cíxióng ① male and female ② victory and defeat: 决一～ have a showdown; fight (battle) it out

糍 cí

糍粑 cíbā cooked glutinous rice pounded into paste; glutinous rice cake

Cǐ

此 cǐ〈代〉this: ～处 this place; here

此岸 cǐ'àn [佛] this shore; temporality

此地 cǐdì this place; here: ～人 local people

此地无银三百两 cǐdì wú yín sānbǎi liǎng A thief posts a marker saying: "The missing treasure is not buried here."; "There is no silver buried here," put up by the man in the legend over the place where he hid his money

此后 cǐhòu after this; hereafter; henceforth: 他1956年到农村去,～一直在那儿工作。He went to the countryside in 1956 and has worked there ever since.

此呼彼应 cǐhū-bǐyìng as one calls out, another responds; echo and reecho

此举 cǐjǔ this measure, action or step

此路不通 cǐlù-bùtōng [揭示语] No Thoroughfare; Road Closed

此起彼伏 cǐqǐ-bǐfú rising here and subsiding there; ebb and flow; rise one after another

此外 cǐwài besides; in addition; moreover: 她一生就写过这三部书,～没有别的著作了。Besides these three books, she didn't produce any other work during her lifetime.

此性 cǐxìng［哲］thisness; this sidedness

此一时,彼一时 cǐyīshí, bǐyīshí This is one situation and that was another.; Things are now different from what they were.; Times have changed.

此致 cǐzhì greetings written at the end of a letter to somebody by name:～敬礼［书信用语］with best (kindest) wishes; with high respect; respectfully

cì

次 cì ①〈名〉order; sequence: 车～ train number〈形〉② next; second:～子 second son ③ inferior; second-rate:～棉 poor quality cotton ④〈量〉time:四～ four times

次等 cìděng second-class; second-rate:～货 second-rate (goods); seconds

次第 cìdì ① order ② one after another

次货 cìhuò inferior goods; substandard goods

次级 cìjí secondary:～文化 secondary culture. ～系统 subsystems

次品 cìpǐn shoddy goods; inferior goods; substandard products

次数 cìshù number of times; frequency:～不多 not very often

次序 cìxù order; sequence

次要 cìyào less important; minor; secondary:～情节 subplots. ～矛盾 secondary contradiction

次之 cìzhī take second place:该区矿藏,以锡最多,铁～。Among the mineral deposits of the region tin occupies first place; iron comes second.

伺 cì

另见 sì

伺候 cìhou wait upon; serve:难～ fastidious; hard to please

刺 cì ①〈名〉thorn; splinter; prickle〈动〉② prick; pierce; stab:～伤 stab and wound ③ assassinate:被～ be assassinated ④ detect; spy ⑤ criticize; irriate:～伤痛处 touch one to the quick

另见 cī

刺刺不休 cìcì-bùxiū gabble on and on; wag one's jaws (tongue)

刺刀 cìdāo bayonet

刺耳 cì'ěr grating on the ear; jarring; ear-piercing; harsh:～的话 harsh words; sarcastic remarks

刺痕 cìhén scarification

刺骨 cìgǔ piercing (cold):寒风～。The wind is piercing (stabbing).

刺激 cìjī stimulate; irritate:～生产 stimulate production. 物质～ material incentives. ～性［电影、小说］thrill

刺客 cìkè assassin

刺杀 cìshā ① stab;［暗杀］assassinate ② bayonet charge

刺探 cìtàn spy out; pry into; detect

刺绣 cìxiù ① embroider ② embroidery

刺眼(目) cìyǎn(mù) ① offend the eye ② dazzling：亮得～ dazzlingly bright

赐 cì 〈动〉 grant; confer; favour; bestow：恩～ bestow (favours, charity, etc.)

赐复 cìfù kindly favour me with a reply; please favour me with a reply

赐教 cìjiào grant instruction; condenscend to teach

赐予 cìyǔ bestow (on); grant：～指教 be so kind as to give me your advice

cōng

匆 cōng 〈副〉 hurriedly; in haste; hastily

匆匆 cōngcōng in a hurry; hurriedly：～来去的过客 fleeting transients

匆促 cōngcù hastily; in a hurry：时间～ be pressed for time

匆忙 cōngmáng hurriedly; hastily; in haste

葱 cōng ①〈名〉onion; leek：大～ green Chinese onion ②〈形〉green：～翠 fresh green; luxuriantly green

葱白 cōngbái very light blue

葱翠 cōngcuì fresh green; luxuriantly green：～的竹林 a green bamboo grove

葱黄 cōnghuáng light yellow; greenish yellow

葱茂 cōngmào (of vegetation) verdant and luxuriant

葱青(绿) cōngqīng(lǜ)［瓷器釉］onion green; green of onion sprouts; bright green

葱郁 cōngyù verdant; luxuriantly green：～的松树林 a verdant pine wood

聪 cōng ①〈名〉faculty of hearing ②〈形〉quick at hearing; acute hearing

聪慧 cōnghuì bright; intelligent

聪明 cōngming clever; wise; bright; intelligent; resourcefulness：～才智 one's ability and cleverness; one's wisdom and talents

聪明反被聪明误 cōngming fǎn bèi cōngming wù Cleverness may overreach itself.; A wise man can be ruined by his own wisdom.

聪明一世，糊涂一时 cōngming yīshì, hútù yīshí clever all one's life, but stupid this once; a usually wise man may occasionally act foolishly

聪颖 cōngyǐng intelligent; bright; clever：～过人 far surpass others in intelligence; be exceptionally bright

cóng

从 cóng ①〈介〉from; through; pass by：～长远看 from a long-term point of view ②〈副〉ever：～不迟到 be never late〈动〉③ follow：～师 be an appren-

tice ④ comply with; obey:～命 obey an order; comply with sb.'s wish ⑤ join:～军 join the army; enlist ⑥〈名〉follower; attendant ⑦〈形〉accessary; secondary:主～ the primary and the secondary
另见 cōng

从长计议 cóngcháng-jìyì give the matter further thought and discussion; take one's time in reaching a decision

从此 cóngcǐ from this time on; from now on; from then on; henceforth; thereupon

从…到… cóng…dào from … to …:从无到有,从小到大 grow out of nothing and expand from a small to a large force

从而 cóng'ér thus; thereby; consequently

从犯 cóngfàn [法] accessary; accomplice

从价税 cóngjiàshuì ad valorem duties

从宽 cóngkuān leniently:处理～ handle leniently

从来 cónglái from the past till the present; always; at all times; all along:我～没有见过她。I've never seen her before.

从量税 cóngliàngshuì specific duty; specific tariff

从略 cónglüè be omitted; be left out

从命 cóngmìng do sb.'s bidding; comply with sb.'s wish; obey an order:欣然～ gladly comply with sb.'s wish

从前 cóngqián formerly; before; [故事开头] once upon a time; once

从容 cóngróng unhurried; leisurely; calm; deliberate:～不迫 calmly; take it leisurely and unoppressively; take one's time in doing

从容就义 cóngróng-jiùyì go to one's death unflinchingly; meet one's death like a hero

从师 cóngshī follow a teacher or a master:～学艺 follow a master and learn his craft

从事 cóngshì go in for; engage in:～科研工作 be engaged in scientific research

从属 cóngshǔ subordinate (to):～地位 subordinate status. ～关系的法律 law of sub-ordination. ～文化 subculture; dependent culture

从速 cóngsù as soon as possible; without delay:～处理 deal with the matter as soon as possible; settle the matter quickly

从头 cóngtóu ① from the beginning:～做起 start from the very beginning ② anew; once again:～再来 start afresh; start all over again

从小 cóngxiǎo from childhood

从刑 cóngxíng accessary punishment

从严 cóngyán strictly; severely:批判～ criticize strictly

从业 cóngyè take up an occupation; get a job:～年限 entire period of actual operation

从优 cóngyōu with preferential treatment:价格～ at special or bargain prices. 条件～ offer most favourable terms

从中 cóngzhōng from among; out of; therefrom: ～吸取教训 draw a lesson from it. ～渔利 play both ends against the middle. ～作梗 place obstacles in the way; hinder sb. from carrying out a plan

丛 cóng〈名〉① clump; thicket; bush: 树～ a clump of trees ② crowd; collection: 人～ a crowd of people ③〈动〉gather; crowd together: ～生 grow thickly (profusely)

丛集 cóngjí gather together; crowd together

丛林 cónglín woods; forest; jungle

丛生 cóngshēng ① (of plants) grow thickly: 荆棘～ be overgrown with brambles ② (of diseases, evils, etc.) break out

丛书 cóngshū a collection of books; series; library: 自学～ self-study series

淙 cóng

淙淙 cóngcóng gurgling: 流水～～ a gurgling stream

còu

凑 còu〈动〉① gather (put) together; pool: ～情况 pool information ② happen by chance; take advantage of: ～空 try to find time (to do sth.)

凑份子 còufènzi club together (to present a gift to sb.)

凑合 còuhe ① gather together; assemble ② make do: 有什么就～着用什么吧。Let's make do with what we have. ③ not too bad; passable: 她的德语还～。Her German is not too bad.

凑集 còují [金钱等] scratch up; scrape together; raise; pool: ～钱 raise funds

凑近 còujìn get closer; get nearer: 我～他的耳根小声说了几句。I whispered something in his ear.

凑钱 còuqián pool money

凑巧 còuqiǎo ① luckily; as luck would have it; by chance ② happen: 她～在家。She happened to be at home.

凑热闹 còurènao ① join in the fun ② add trouble to: 我够忙的，别再来～了。I'm busy enough as it is, don't give me more trouble.

凑数 còushù ① make up the number (amount) ② serve as a stopgap

凑整儿 còuzhěngr make up a round number: 我这儿有96元，你给我4元，凑个整儿吧。I've got 96 yuan with me. Please give me 4 yuan to make up a round hundred.

cū

粗 cū〈形〉① thick: ～竿 a thick rod ② coarse; gross; rough: ～布 coarse cloth ③ gruff; husky: ～声大气 a deep, gruff voice ④ careless; negligent:～枝大叶 crude and careless; in a perfunctory way ⑤ rude; unrefined; vulgar:说话很～ speak rudely; use coarse language ⑥〈副〉slightly; roughly:～通文字 can read and write a little

粗暴 cūbào rude; rough; harsh; brutal; violent:～的态度 a rude attitude

粗笨 cūbèn clumsy; unwieldy:动作～ clumsy. ～的家具 unwieldy furniture

粗鄙 cūbǐ vulgar; coarse:言语～ vulgar in speech

粗糙 cūcāo coarse; rough:～的描写 general description. 做工～ crudely made; of poor workmanship

粗茶淡饭 cūchá-dànfàn coarse tea and plain fare; homely meal

粗大 cūdà ① thick; bulky:～的手 big strong hands ② loud:～的嗓门 a loud voice

粗放经营 cūfàng jīngyíng extensive management

粗犷 cūguǎng ① rough; rude; boorish ② straightforward and uninhibited; bold and unconstrained; rugged

粗活 cūhuó heavy manual labour; rough work; unskilled labour

粗加工 cūjiāgōng rough machining; roughly process; roughing

粗粮 cūliáng coarse food grain (e. g. maize, sorghum, millet, etc. as distinct from wheat flour and rice)

粗鲁 cūlǔ rough; rude; boorish

粗略 cūlüè sketchy; rough:作～估计 make a rough estimate

粗浅 cūqiǎn superficial; shallow; simple:～的体会 a superficial understanding

粗疏 cūshū careless; raw; inattentive; crudity:～豪放 barbaric simplicity

粗俗 cūsú vulgar; coarse; unrefined:～行为 gross behaviour

粗陶 cūtáo crockery; rough pottery

粗通 cūtōng have a rough idea; know a little

粗细 cūxì ①(degree of) thickness:碗口～的钢管 steel tubes as big as the mouth of a bowl ② crudeness or fineness; degree of finish; quality of work

粗线条 cūxiàntiáo ① thick lines; rough outline:～描写 a rough sketch ②[作风粗率] rough-and-ready; straight forward; slapdash

粗心 cūxīn careless; thoughtless; negligent:～大意 careless; negligent; inadvertent

粗养 cūyǎng unpunctilious animal husbandry

粗野 cūyě rough; uncouth; boorish; rude; gross:举止～ behave boorishly

粗枝大叶 cūzhī-dàyè crude and careless; sloppy; slapdash:～的工作作风 a crude and careless style of work

粗制滥造 cūzhì-lànzào ① be roughly made ② roughcast; roughwrought; turn out rough and slipshod work

粗中有细 cūzhōng-yǒuxì

have something refined in his rough ways

粗重 cūzhòng ①（of voice，etc.）loud and jarring：～的喘息声 loud breathing ② big and heavy；bulky：③ thick and heavy：眉毛浓黑～ bushy black eyebrows ④ strenuous；heavy

粗壮 cūzhuàng ① sturdy；thickset；brawny：～的胳臂 brawny arms ② thick and strong ③ deep and resonant：声音～ have a deep，resonant voice

cù

促 cù ①〈动〉urge；promote；spur：敦～ press；urge ②〈形〉（of time）short；hurried；urgent：短～ of very short duration

促成 cùchéng help to bring about；facilitate；help to realize：～目标 enabling objectives. ～其事 help to bring about a success

促进 cùjìn promote；encourage；further；hasten；heighten；accelerate：～健康行为 health-enhancing behaviour. ～因素 promotive factor

促使 cùshǐ impel；urge；spur：改革开放～许多人学习外语。The reforms and the policy of opening the country to the outside world spur many people on to study foreign languages.

促膝谈心 cùxī-tánxīn have a heart-to-heart talk（with）；have a tête-a-tête（with）；sit side by side and talk intimately

猝 cù〈形〉sudden；abrupt；unexpected

猝不及防 cùbùjífáng be taken unawares；be caught off guard

猝而 cù'ér suddenly；unexpectedly：～夭逝 die a sudden early death

猝然 cùrán suddenly；abruptly；unexpectedly

猝死 cùsǐ［医］sudden death

醋 cù〈名〉① vinegar ② jealously（as in loving affairs）：～意（feeling of）jealousy. 吃～ feel jealous

醋罐子 cùguànzi a jealous woman

醋劲儿 cùjìnr jealousy：～大发 be seized with a fit of jealousy

醋精 cùjīng［食品］vinegar concentrate

醋意 cùyì jealousy（in love）

簇 cù ①〈量〉cluster；bunch：一～鲜花 a bunch of flowers ②〈名〉cluster；pile；bouquet ③〈动〉crowd together；form a cluster；pile up：花团锦～ bouquets of flowers and piles of brocades

簇居 cùjū live in a community

簇聚 cùjù gather in clusters；cluster

簇新 cùxīn brand-new；span-new

簇拥 cùyōng gather round；cluster round

cuān

汆 cuān〈动〉quick-boil：～丸子

quick-boiled meat balls with soup

蹿 cuān 〈动〉① leap up ② spurt; spray

蹿上跳下 cuānshàng-tiàoxià bounce up and down

cuán

攒 cuán 〈动〉collect together; assemble：自己～一辆自行车 assemble a bicycle oneself
另见 zǎn

cuàn

窜 cuàn〈动〉① scurry; flee：抱头鼠～ cover the head and scurry away like a rat ② change; correct：点～ make some alternations (in wording) ③ banish

窜犯 cuànfàn raid; overrun

窜(篡)改 cuàn(～)gǎi tamper with; alter; falsify; revise：～文稿 mutilate a manuscript. ～帐目 manipulate an account

窜扰 cuànrǎo harass：～边境 harass the border area

窜逃 cuàntáo flee in disorder; escape; [动物等] scamper off

篡 cuàn〈动〉usurp; seize：～夺领导权 usurp leadership

篡夺 cuànduó usurp; seize：～政权 usurp state power

篡改 cuàngǎi distort; tamper with; misrepresent

篡位 cuànwèi usurp the throne

cuī

崔 Cuī a surname

崔巍 cuīwēi lofty; towering：山势～。The mountains stand tall and imposing.

催 cuī〈动〉① urge; hurry; press ② speed up; hasten; expedite：春风～绿。The spring wind speeds the greening of the plants.

催办 cuībàn press sb. to do sth.; press sb. to expedite some business matter

催逼 cuībī press (for payment of debt, etc.)

催促 cuīcù urge; hasten; press：不要～我。Don't rush me.

催眠 cuīmián lull (to sleep); hypnotize; mesmerize：～曲 lullaby; cradlesong

催命 cuīmìng persistently urge or press sb.

催讨 cuītǎo press for payment of a debt or return of sth. borrowed

催债 cuīzhài press for payment of debt; dun sb. for payment of debt

催租 cuīzū press a tenant to pay rent; press for payment of rent

摧 cuī〈动〉break; destroy; demolish：坚不可～ be so strongly built as to be unbreakable

摧残 cuīcán ① destroy; devastate; ravage; disrupt; lay waste by ② [对女性] abuse

摧毁 cuīhuǐ destroy; ruin; demolish; shatter; smash; pull down; tear down: ～廓清 defeat and completely wipe out; wipe (mop) the floor with sb.

摧枯拉朽 cuīkū-lāxiǔ crushing dry weeds and smashing rotten wood; easily overcome; all-powerful; sweep away all obstacles in the way

cuǐ

璀 cuǐ

璀璨 cuǐcàn〈形〉bright; resplendent: ～夺目 dazzling

cuì

脆 cuì〈形〉① brittle; crisp; fragile: 香～可口 crisp, fragrant and pleasant to taste ② clear; crisp; ringing: 嗓音～ a crisp voice

脆嫩 cuìnèn tender and crisp

脆弱 cuìruò weak; frail; flimsy; weak; slimsy: 长得～ be of a frail constitution

脆爽 cuìshuǎng ① (of food) crisp and refreshing ② (of sound or voice) clear and sharp

萃 cuì ①〈名〉a gathering of people or a collection of things: 出类拔～ be far above the average; outstanding ②〈动〉assemble; come together; 荟～ assemble

萃集 cuìjí gather; assemble: 港口船舶～ ships gathering in harbour

萃聚 cuìjù gather; assemble: 群英～ heroes of our time getting together

啐 cuì〈动〉spit; expectorate: ～一口唾沫 throw out some spittle

淬 cuì〈动〉temper (a metal workpiece) by dipping in water, oil, etc.; quench

淬火 cuìhuǒ quench: ～硬化 quench hardening

悴 cuì 见“憔悴”

瘁 cuì〈形〉overworked; tired

粹 cuì ①〈形〉pure ②〈名〉essence; the best: 国～ the quintessence of Chineseculture

翠 cuì〈形〉deep green; emerald

翠绿(青) cuìlǜ(qīng)[瓷器釉] blue-green; kingfisher blue; turquoise

翠生生 cuìshēngshēng fresh and green: ～的秧苗 fresh and green rice seedlings

cūn

村 cūn ①〈名〉village: 渔～ a fishing village ②〈形〉rustic; boorish

村落 cūnluò village; hamlet

村民议事制度 cūnmínyìshìzhìdù system under which villagers discuss their issues

村舍 cūnshè cottage

村寨 cūnzhài stockaded village; village

村长 cūnzhǎng village head

村镇 cūnzhèn villages and small townships

皴 cūn〈动〉(of skin) be chapped from the cold: 他的手~了。His hands were chapped from the cold.

皴裂 cūnliè (of skin) be chapped from the cold: 手足~。Both one's hands and feet were chapped from the cold.

cún

存 cún〈动〉① live; exist; survive: 残~ surviving ② keep; store; preserve: ~粮 store up grain ③ accumulate; collect ④ deposit: 把钱~在银行里 put money in a bank ⑤ check; leave with: 把箱子~在服务台 check one's suitcases in at the desk ⑥ harbour; cherish: ~着很大希望 cherish high hopes

存案 cún'àn register with the proper authorities

存车处 cúnchēchù [自行车] bike shed; bike parking lot; cycle-stand

存单 cúndān deposit receipt; certificate of deposit

存档 cúndàng keep in the archives; place on file; file

存放 cúnfàng ① leave with; leave in sb.'s care: 他把箱子~在朋友那里了。He has left his suitcase with a friend of his. ② deposit (money): 把钱~在银行里 put money in a bank

存户 cúnhù depositor

存货 cúnhuò goods in stock; stock; inventory: 减价出清~ a clearance sale. ~周转率 inventory turnover ratio

存据 cúnjù written statement (e.g. a certificate, receipt, etc.) kept as evidence or as a record

存款 cúnkuǎn money on deposit; deposit: ~单 deposit slip. 定期~ fixed deposit. 活期~ current deposit

存栏数 cúnlánshù the number in a pen

存量 cúnliàng stock: ~流量分析 stock-flow analysis

存亡 cúnwáng live or die; survive or perish

存息 cúnxī interest on a deposit

存心 cúnxīn ① intention; purpose: ~不良 have evil intentions ② intentionally; on purpose; deliberately

存在 cúnzài exist; existence; being: ~主义 existentialism

存折 cúnzhé bankbook; deposit book; passbook: ~保管证 passbook custodian certificate

cǔn

忖 cǔn〈动〉turn over in one's mind; ponder; speculate

忖量 cǔnliàng ① think over; turn over in one's mind: 我~了半天,还拿不定主意。I turned the matter over in my mind for a long while but still could not come to a decision. ② conjecture; guess

cùn

寸 cùn ①〈量〉*cun*, a unit of length (=1/3 decimetre) ②〈形〉very short; very little; small

寸步 cùnbù a single step; a tiny step: ～不让 not to yield a (single) step; fight every inch of the way. ～不离 follow sb. closely; keep close to. ～难行 be difficult for sb. to move a single step—can't do anything

寸草不留 cùncǎobùliú leave not even a blade of grass; be devastated

寸金难买寸光阴 cùnjīn nán mǎi cùnguāngyīn An inch of gold will not buy an inch of time.; Money can't buy time

寸头 cùntóu crew cut: 我要理个～。I want my hair cropped short.

寸土 cùntǔ an inch of land—a very small piece of land: ～寸金。An inch of land is an inch of gold.

寸心 cùnxīn feelings: 聊表～ just to show my appreciation; as a small token of my feelings

cuō

搓 cuō〈动〉① rub with the hands; twist: ～线 twist thread ② [面粉等] knead

搓板 cuōbǎn washboard

搓澡 cuōzǎo give or get a rub-down with a damp towel

搓弄 cuōnòng rub, knead, or twist idly: 她手里～着手绢。She was twiddling her handkerchief

搓揉 cuōróu rub; knead; twist: 我把那封信～成一团,扔进了字纸篓。I crumpled the letter into a ball and threw it into the wastepaper basket.

搓绳 cuōshéng twist a rope: ～缚飓风 twist a rope to bind a typhoon; with inadequate means

磋 cuō〈动〉consult

磋切 cuōqiē learn from each other by exchanging views

磋商 cuōshāng consult (with); confer (with); negotiate (with): 与某人～某事 consult with sb. about sth.

撮 cuō〈动〉① bring together; scoop up: ～走一簸箕土 scoop up a dust pan of dirt ② pick; take up with the fingers; ～一点盐 take a pinch of salt ③〈名〉pinch; a handful of: 一～盐 a pinch of salt

撮合 cuōhe make a match; bring together; act as go-between

撮弄 cuōnòng ① make fun of; play a trick on; make a fool of; tease ② abet; instigate; incite

撮要 cuōyào ① make an abstract; outline essential points ② extracts; abstract; synopsis

蹉 cuō

蹉跎 cuōtuó waste time; idle away:～岁月 idle away one's time; let years and months slip by — waste one's time; spend one's life in fruitless efforts

cuò

挫 cuò〈动〉① subdue; lower:～敌人的锐气 deflate the enemy's arrogance ② defeat; frustrate:受～ suffer a setback

挫败 cuòbài frustrate; foil; thwart; defeat; baffle; override

挫伤 cuòshāng ①［医］contusion; bruise ② dampen; discourage:～积极性 dampen (deflate, blunt) sb.'s enthusiasm; throw cold water on sb.'s enthusiasm

挫折 cuòzhé setback; rebuff; adversity; frustration:遇到～ meet with a setback; suffer a rebuff (setback)

措 cuò〈动〉① arrange; manage; handle:不知所～ be at a loss what to do; be at one's wits' end ② make plans:筹～款项 raise funds

措词(辞) cuòcí wording; diction:～刻薄 harsh terms (language); incisive phraseology

措施 cuòshī measure; step:采取重大～ adopt an important measure

措手不及 cuòshǒu-bùjí be caught unawares (unprepared); make a surprise attack on; attack them before they know what's happening

措置 cuòzhì handle; manage; arrange:～失当 be improperly handled; be mishandled

锉 cuò ①〈名〉file ②〈动〉make smooth with a file; file

锉刀 cuòdāo file; grater

错 cuò〈形〉① wrong; erroneous; mistaken:他的看法～了。His opinions were wrong. ② interlocked and jagged; complex:盘根～节 with twisted roots and gnarled branches〈动〉③ alternate; stagger:～缝接合 alternate joint ④ rub; grind:～牙 grind one's teeth (in one's sleep) ⑤〈名〉mistake; fault; demerit:出～ make mistakes

错爱 cuò'ài undeserved kindness; misplace affections

错案 cuò'àn misjudged case

错别字 cuòbiézì erroneous characters

错处 cuòchu fault; demerit

错待 cuòdài treat unfairly; treat badly:他们不会～你的,你放心好了。You can rest assured that you'll be treated well.

错怪 cuòguài blame sb. wrongly

错过 cuòguò miss; let slip:～机会 miss an opportunity

错觉 cuòjué illusion; misconception; false notion; wrong (false) impression

错开 cuòkāi stagger:时间～的合同制度 staggered contract system

错乱 cuòluàn in disorder; in confusion; deranged

错位 cuòwèi [医] dislocation: 肘关节～ dislocation of the elbow

错误 cuòwù ① mistake; error: ～百出 full of mistakes; riddled with mistakes ② wrong; mistaken; erroneous: ～估计 miscalculation

错字 cuòzì ① wrongly written character ② misprint

错综复杂 cuòzōng-fùzá intricate; complex; complicated and confused; complex and mixed; intricate and complex

D d

dā

耷 dā〈名〉big-eared

耷拉 dāla droop; hang down:～着脑袋 hang one's head

搭 dā〈动〉① put up; build:～浮桥 put up a pontoon bridge ② put over; hang over ③ join; come into contact:前言不～后语 speak incoherently ④ throw in more; add ⑤ carry:请你把这台收音机～回家吧。Please help carry this radio home (in your car). ⑥ take (a plane, ship, etc.):～飞机 go by plane

搭班子 dā bānzi constitute a group:厂领导正在重新～。The factory leadership is in the midst of structuring the work force.

搭伴 dābàn join company (with sb.):～旅行 travel in company

搭档 dādàng cooperate (with); team up (with):老～ old partner

搭钩 dāgōu establish contact or connection with

搭话 dāhuà ① make (enter into a) conversation; get a word in ② send word

搭伙 dāhuǒ ① join as partner:他们明天去参观长城,我也想～去。They're going to visit the Great Wall tomorrow and I'd like to join them. ② eat regularly in (a mess, etc.):他们都在厂里食堂～。They all eat in the factory cafeteria.

搭架子 dā jiàzi ① build a framework; get (an undertaking, etc.) roughly into shape ② put on airs; assume great airs

搭界 dājiè ① have a common boundary:两县～的地方 the place where the two counties meet ②［多用于否定］have some contact with; have sth. to do with:我们跟这件事不～。This has nothing to do with us.

搭救 dājiù rescue; go to one's rescue

搭配 dāpèi ① put together (with); go together (with) ② tie-in:～售货办法 a tie-in sale ③［语］collocation

搭腔 dāqiāng ① respond; answer:她问了两遍,没人～。She repeated her question, but nobody answered. ② talk to each other

搭桥 dāqiáo build a bridge; span a bridge ② act as go-between:由于你给我们～,这笔买卖算做成了。This business deal has come off thanks to you for acting as go-between for us. ～铺路［指关系］bridge relations between. ～牵线 build bridge and pull line

搭讪 dāshàn strike up a conversation with sb.; say sth. to smooth over an embarrassing situation:她很尴尬,～着走开了。Feeling embarrassed, she muttered a few words and walked off.

搭手 dāshǒu give a hand; help:她赶紧跑来～。She hurried over to give me a hand.

搭售 dāshòu sell along with something else

搭载 dāzài (of trucks, freighters, etc.) pick up extra passengers or freight

答 dā

另见 dá

答理 dāli acknowledge (sb.'s greeting, etc.); answer; respond:我跟她打招呼,她没～我。I greeted her but she didn't respond.

答腔 dāqiāng ① answer; respond ② talk to each other

答应 dāying ① reply; answer:我敲了几下门,但没有人～。I knocked at the door several times, but there was no answer. ② promise; agree:他～帮助我们。He promised to help us.

dá

达 dá〈动〉

① reach; arrive at; attain:不～目的,决不罢休。Refuse to give up before the aim is achieved. ② extend:公路四通八～。Highways radiate in all directions. ③ express; convey; communicate:词不～意。The words fail to convey the idea. ④ understand thoroughly:通情～理 be understanding and reasonable; be sensible ⑤〈形〉eminent; distinguished:～官 ranking official; powerful official

达标 dábiāo [达到国家规定的体育锻炼标准] reach the mark (reach the standards for athletic training stipulated by the state); up to the standard

达成 dáchéng reach; arrive at; conclude:～协议 reach an agreement

达到 dádào achieve; reach; attain:～目的 attain the aim

达尔文主义 Dá'ěrwénzhǔyì Darwinism

达观 dáguān take things philosophically; have broad perspective:～者 philosopher

达赖喇嘛 Dálài Lǎma the Dalai Lama

达斡尔族 Dáwò'ěrzú the Daur (Tahur) nationality, or the Daurs (Tahurs), distributed over Heilongjiang Province, the Inner Mongolia Autonomous Region, and the Xinjiang Uygur Autonomous Region

达意 dáyì express one's idea; convey one's idea

打 dá〈量〉

dozen:论～出售 sell by the dozen

另见 dǎ

答 dá〈动〉① answer; reply:对～如流 answer fluently ② return; repay:报～ repay; requite
另见 dā

答案 dá'àn answer; solution; key:练习的～ key to an exercise

答辩 dábiàn ① answer; reply (to a charge, argument, etc.); defend ② [毕业时的] oral defence (of a graduation thesis)

答词 dácí thank-you speech; answering speech; reply

答访 dáfǎng pay a return visit (call)

答复 dáfù reply; answer; respond:～问题 reply (respond) to a question

答卷 dájuàn answer sheets:她以实际行动交了一份令人赞叹的人生～。By her concrete actions, she turned in a laudable answer sheet on life.

答数 dáshù answer (to an arithmetic problem)

答谢 dáxiè express appreciation (for sb.'s kindness or hospitality); acknowledge; return thanks to:～宴会 return (reciprocal) banquet

靼 dá

靼靼 Dádá Tartar

dǎ

打 dǎ〈动〉① beat; strike; hit; know:～钟 ring the bell ② break; smash:碗～了。The bowl is broken. ③ fight; attack:～成一团 fight together ④ negotiate; make representations:～官司 go to law (against sb.) ⑤ play:～篮球 play basketball ⑥ forge; make (in a smithy):～一把刀 forge a knife ⑦ paint; draw:～手印 put one's finger print on a document ⑧ raise; hoist ⑨ calculate; estimate; reckon:～草稿 work out a draft
另见 dá

打败 dǎbài ① beat; defeat ② suffer a defeat; be defeated

打扮 dǎbàn dress up; make up; deck oneself out; doll oneself up; make oneself out to be

打包 dǎbāo ① bale; pack:～费 packing charges ② unpack

打抱不平 dǎbàobùpíng take up the cudgels for a person against the injustice done to him; champion the cause of justice; defend sb. against an injustice; interfere on behalf of the injured party

打笔墨官司 dǎ bǐmò guānsī engage in a (paper) polemic with sb.

打不住 dǎbuzhù ① be more than ② not be enough:这么多准备工作,2天时间是～的。Two days aren't enough for so much preparatory work.

打草惊蛇 dǎcǎo-jīngshé beat the grass to frighten away the snake — act rashly and alert the enemy

打岔 dǎchà ① interrupt (a conversation); cut in ② interfere with; disturb

打成一片 dǎchéng-yīpiàn become one with; identify oneself with; merge with: 和群众～ be (become) one with the masses

打打闹闹 dǎdǎ-nàonào have boisterous fun; horseplay

打倒 dǎdǎo ① strike down; knock down ② overthrow; [口号] Down with

打得火热 dǎdéhuǒrè hobnob with; fraternize with; be on terms of intimacy; carry on intimately with; ardent flirtation with; Their dealings have become thicker.; join in a love feast; cheek by jowl; be very thick with each other

打的 dǎdī 〈方〉 go by taxi; take a taxi

打底 dǎdǐ ① eat sth. before having a drink ② feel secure 心里不～ feel insecure ③ 见"打底子" ④ [纺] bottoming

打底子 dǎdǐzi ① sketch a plan, picture, etc.: 这篇文章我先打个底子。I'll make a draft of the essay. ② lay a foundation

打点 dǎdian ① get (luggage, etc.) ready: ～行李,准备出发。Pack the luggage and make ready to depart. ② bribe sb.

打点滴 dǎ diǎndī [医] inject intravenously; drip: 病人正在～。The patient is on a drip.

打赌 dǎdǔ bet; stake: 与某人为某事～ bet sb. on sth.

打断 dǎduàn ① break: ～脊梁骨 break the backbone ② cut short; interrupt: 别～她的话。Don't interrupt her.

打盹儿 dǎdǔnr take a nap; doze off

打发 dǎfa ① send; dispatch ② dismiss: 挥手～某人 dismiss sb. with a wave of the hand

打翻身仗 dǎ fānshēnzhàng fight in order to turn over: 化肥厂去年亏损,今年大～,年终盈利30万元。The chemical fertlizer plant took a loss last year. This year it fought to turn over, and by the end of the year, it had a profit of 300,000 yuan.

打非 dǎfēi crack down on illegal publications

打工仔(妹) dǎgōngzǎi (mèi) migrant (itinerant) labourer (worker) (specifically young man or girl, generally rural who travels to another part of the country, usually to city, to find work)

打官腔 dǎ guānqiāng speak in a bureaucratic tone; talk like a bureaucrat; stall with official jargon

打官司 dǎ guānsi go to law against; file suit; carry on lawsuit; litigate; engage in a lawsuit

打棍子 dǎ gùnzi use the big stick on; come down with the big stick upon; bludgeon

打哈哈 dǎhāha make fun; crack a joke: 别拿我们～。Don't make fun of us.

打哈欠 dǎhāqian yawn

打鼾 dǎhān snore

打击 dǎjī hit; blow; attack; crack down on:～经济领域的严重犯罪活动 crack down on serious criminal activities in the economic field. ～乐器 percussion instrument; [爵士乐的] traps

打假 dǎjiǎ crack down on sham and shoddy commodities

打交道 dǎ jiāodào deal with; have dealings with:不要同那个人～。Don't have any dealings with that fellow.

打搅 dǎjiǎo disturb; trouble:对不起,～您了! Sorry to have bothered you.

打开 dǎkāi open; unfold:～眼界 widen (broaden) one's horizon. ～思路 thought-provoking

打开天窗说亮话 dǎkāi tiān chuāng shuō liànghuà frankly speaking; let's not mince matters; let's be frank and put our cards on the table

打瞌睡 dǎ kēshuì doze off; nod

打量 dǎliang ① measure with the eye; look sb. up and down; size up ② think; suppose; reckon

打猎 dǎliè go hunting

打乱 dǎluàn confound; upset; muddle; mess up:～计划 upset a scheme

打闷棍 dǎ mēngùn ① (of a robber) give sb. a staggering blow with a cudgel ② give sb. a stunning blow

打牌 dǎpái play mahjong (cards)

打屁股 dǎ pìgu ① beat on the buttocks; spank ② take sb. to task

打破 dǎpò break; smash:～行政隶属关系 break away from administrative webs of affiliation. ～砂锅问到底 insist on getting to the bottom of the matter; searching for brass tacks

打气 dǎqì ① pump up; inflate (a tyre) ② pep up; boost (bolster up) the morale

打前站 dǎqiánzhàn act as an advance party; set out in advance to make arrangements

打情骂俏 dǎqíng-màqiào fool around and banter in flirtation

打趣 dǎqù banter; tease; make fun of

打入十八层地狱 dǎrù shíbā céng dìyù banish to (sink … in) the lowest depths of hell—condemn to eternal damnation

打扫 dǎsǎo sweep; clean:～房间 clean a room

打手 dǎshou hired roughneck (thug); hatchet man

打算 dǎsuàn intend; plan; mean: 不～放弃 have no intention to give up

打算盘 dǎ suànpan calculate on an abacus; use (work) an abacus:打小算盘 be petty and scheming; be calculating

打碎 dǎsuì break into pieces; smash; destroy:玻璃杯～。The glass is smashed to pieces. ～旧的国家机器 smash (destroy) the old state machinery

打胎 dǎtāi have an (induced) abortion

打太极拳 dǎ tàijíquán ① practise (do) *taijiquan*; do *taijiquan* exercises (calisthenics) ② dodge and shirk

打天下 dǎ tiānxià ① seize state power ② win success in a big enterprise; start an enterprise

打听 dǎtīng inquire about; pry into: ～消息 inquire about the news

打通 dǎtōng ① open up; dig through: ～关节 open the channel to the top authorities concerned ② [电话] get through (on the telephone): 电话打不通。I can't get the call through. ～思想 straighten out one's thinking; talk sb. round

打退 dǎtuì beat back (off); repulse: ～敌人的进攻 repulse an enemy attack

打退堂鼓 dǎ tuìtánggǔ beat a retreat; draw from; give up; back out; draw in one's horns

打响 dǎxiǎng ① start shooting; begin to exchange fire ② win initial success: ～了秋耕第一炮。The autumn ploughing got off to a good start.

打消 dǎxiāo give up; dispel; cancel; withdraw: ～念头 give up the idea

打小报告 dǎ xiǎobàogào inform secretly on a colleague (sb.)

打掩护 dǎ yǎnhù provide cover for; shield: 为主力部队～ provide cover for the main force

打烊 dǎyàng (of shops) put up the shutters; close for the night

打印 dǎyìn ① put a seal on; stamp ② cut a stencil and mimeograph; mimeograph

打圆场 dǎ yuánchǎng mediate a dispute; smooth things over

打招呼 dǎ zhāohu ① greet sb.; say hello ② notify; let sb. know: 你什么时候去广州,给我打个招呼。When you go to Guangzhou, please let me know. ③ warn; remind: 事先已跟你们打过招呼了。I've already warned you.

打折扣 dǎ zhékòu ① sell at a discount; discount in: ～商店 cut-rate store ② fall short of a requirement or promise

打着灯笼没处找 dǎzhe dēnglong méichù zhǎo not to be found even with a lantern—hard to come by; rare

打着…招牌 dǎzhe…zhāopái put up the signboard of; under the signboard of…; parade a signboard as…

打肿脸充胖子 dǎzhǒng liǎn chōng pàngzi slap one's face until it's swollen in an effort to look imposing — puff oneself up to one's own cost; an impudent attempt to represent the defeat as a victory; pose as a fat man by slapping the face until it is swollen

打中 dǎzhòng hit (the mark): ～要害 The thrust goes home.; deal a blow at the heart; strike where it hurts; hit squarely on the chin; hit on the vital spot; hit where it really hurts

打主意 dǎ zhǔyi ① think of a

plan; evolve an idea:打定主意 make up one's mind ② try to obtain; seek; plan:另～ seek another way

打转 dǎzhuàn spin; rotate; revolve

打嘴巴 dǎzuǐba slap sb.'s face

打坐 dǎzuò quiet-sitting; sit in meditation

dà

大 dà〈形〉① large; big:～城市 a big city ② great; important:～人物 important person ③ strong; heavy:～雨 heavy rain ④ loud:声音太～ too loud ⑤ age; eldest:他比我～两岁。He is two years senior to me. ～哥 eldest brother ⑥ main; major; general ～路 main road ⑦ size:他穿多～的鞋? What size shoes does he wear?〈副〉⑧ greatly; fully:～笑 laugh heartily ⑨ [用在时令或节日前表示强调]:～清早 early in the morning ⑩ [用在"不"后,表示程度浅或次数少]:不大清楚 not too clear

大案 dà'àn major cases; great case

大伯子 dàbǎizi husband's elder brother; brother-in-law

大半 dàbàn ① more than half; most; ② in all probability; very likely:他～会比我们早回来。In all probability he will get back before us.

大包大揽 dàbāo-dàlǎn take on in a big way

大包干 dàbāogān all-round contract system; the "big" responsibility system

大笔 dàbǐ ① pen:～一挥 with one stroke of the pen ② your writing; your handwriting:这是令尊的～。This is your father's handwriting.

大便 dàbiàn ① defecate; have a bowel movement; shit:～不通 (suffer from) constipation ② stool; human excrement; shit; faeces:去化验～ have one's stool examined

大辩论 dàbiànlùn great (mass) debate

大伯 dàbó ① father's elder brother; uncle ② uncle (a polite form of address for an elderly man)

大不了 dàbuliǎo ① at the worst; if the worst comes to the worst:～我走着回去。If the worst comes to the worst, I'll walk back. ② [多用于否定] alarming; serious:划破点皮,没有什么～的。It's nothing serious, just a scratch.

大材小用 dàcái-xiǎoyòng put fine timber to petty use; use talented people for trivial tasks; waste one's talent on a petty job; great talent employed in small capacity; great genius in little employment; waste or misuse of materials or talents; employ a steam-engine to crack a nut

大操大办 dàcāo-dàbàn make arrangements in a big way

大彻大悟 dàchè-dàwù grand realization of;[佛] bodhi

大臣 dàchén minister (of a monarchy)

大吃大喝 dàchī-dàhē indulge in extravagant eating and drinking; eat and drink to one's heart's content; eat and drink one's fill

大吃一惊 dàchī-yījīng be taken aback; be filled with amazement; be greatly shocked (at); dumbfounded

大处着眼,小处着手 dàchù zhuóyǎn,xiǎochù zhuóshǒu keep the general goal in sight while taking hold of the daily tasks in hand

大吹大擂 dàchuī-dàléi make a big (great) fanfare; trumpet loudly about; beat the drum; talk big

大慈大悲 dàcí-dàbēi infinitely compassionate and merciful

大葱 dàcōng green Chinese onion

大打出手 dàdǎ-chūshǒu come to blows; get into a fight

大胆 dàdǎn bold; daring; audacious:～尝试 make a bold trial

大刀阔斧 dàdāo-kuòfǔ ① make bold (snap) decisions; take drastic measures ② slashing; sweeping; drastic

大道理 dàdàolǐ great (major) principles; great truth

大敌 dàdí formidable enemy; arch enemy:～当前 a formidable enemy stands before one; be faced with a formidable foe

大抵 dàdǐ generally speaking; in the main; on the whole

大地 dàdì earth; mother earth:走遍祖国～ travel all over the land

大典 dàdiǎn ① grand ceremony:开国～ founding ceremony (of a state) ② a body of classical writings; canon:《永乐～》 Yongle Canon

大度包容 dàdù-bāoróng regard with kindly tolerance; be magnanimous and tolerant; be magnanimous

大而全 dà'érquán all large and all inclusive; big and all-embracing; big and complete

大发横财 dàfā-hèngcái amass unprecedented riches; make piles of money; reap huge profits

大发雷霆 dàfā-léitíng fly into a passion; fly into a violent rage; flare up

大法 dàfǎ fundamental laws and principles (of a state); constitution

大方 dàfāng ① generous; liberal ② natural and poised; unaffected; decent; seemly; in good taste:衣着～ be dressed in good taste; be decently dressed

大风大浪 dàfēng-dàlàng violent storms and waves; wind and waves; great storms:人类社会是从～中发展起来的。It is amid great storms that human society progresses.

大概 dàgài ① general idea; broad outline:我跟你～说说。I told you briefly. ② general; rough; approximate:～的估计 a rough estimate ③ probably; most likely; presumably: ～将有 800 人出席。There will be approximately 800 people present.

大改 dàgǎi major reform

大哥大 dàgēdà [即移动电话] mobile phone; cellular telephone

大公无私 dàgōng-wúsī ① selfless; unselfish ② perfectly impartial

大功 dàgōng great merit; extraordinary service; distinction: ～告成 be crowned with success; come to a successful conclusion

大鼓 dàgǔ ①〈乐〉bass drum ② *dagu*, versified story sung to the accompaniment of a small drum and other instruments

大观 dàguān grand sight: 洋洋～ spectacular; grandiose; imposing

大规模 dàguīmó large-scale; extensive; massive; mass: ～生产 large-scale production

大锅饭 dàguōfàn big communal pot: 吃～ everybody eating from the same big pot; get equal pay regardless of the work done

大喊大叫 dàhǎn-dàjiào ① shout at the top of one's voice ② conduct vigorous propaganda

大汉族主义 dàhànzúzhǔyì Han chauvinism

大好河山 dàhǎo-héshān beautiful rivers and mountains (of a country); one's beloved country

大合唱 dàhéchàng cantata; chorus:《黄河～》The Yellow River Cantata

大后天 dàhòutiān three days from now

大话 dàhuà big words; tall talk; big talk; exaggeration: 说～ talk big; exaggerate

大茴香 dàhuíxiāng anise; star anise

大会 dàhuì ① plenary session; congress; general membership meeting ② mass meeting; mass rally: 庆祝～ a celebration meeting

大祸临头 dàhuò-líntóu disaster is imminent; disaster is hanging over one

大机器工业 dàjīqì gōngyè large-scale machine industry; modern industry

大吉 dàjí ① very lucky; highly auspicious: ～大利 good luck and great prosperity (an expression of good wishes) ② [用在动词或动词结构后,表示诙谐的说法]: 关门～ close down (up) for good

大计 dàjì a major programme of lasting importance; a matter of fundamental importance: 共商～ discuss matters of vital importance

大家 dàjiā ① great master; authority: 书法～ a great master of calligraphy; a noted calligrapher ② an old and well-known family; a distinguished (prominent) family: ～闺秀 a girl from a good family; a well-bred girl ③ all; everybody: ～的事～管。

Everybody's business should be everybody's responsibility.

大家庭 dàjiātíng big family; community:贾家是个～,有三代人。The Jias are a big family with three generations.

大减价 dà jiǎnjià price cutting; grand sale; great reduction in price; opening sales; radical reduction

大检修 dà jiǎnxiū overhaul; general overhaul; major overhaul

大街 dàjiē main street; street:～小巷 streets and lanes. 逛～ go window-shopping; stroll around the streets

大节 dàjié political integrity (lit. "major integrity"):一个人不但～要好,小节也应该好。One should have not only political integrity, but also integrity in personal life.

大捷 dàjié great victory

大惊失色 dàjīng-shīsè turn pale with fright

大惊小怪 dàjīng-xiǎoguài fuss (about); get alarmed for nothing

大局 dàjú general situation; overall public interest:顾全～ take the interests of the whole into account

大举 dàjǔ carry out (a military operation) on a large scale:～进攻 mount a large-scale offensive; attack in force

大考 dàkǎo final examination

大课 dàkè a lecture given to a large number of students; enlarged class

大客车 dàkèchē bus; coach

大快人心 dàkuài-rénxīn (usu. of the punishment of an evil-doer) affording general satisfaction; most gratifying to the people; to the immense satisfaction of the people

大款 dàkuǎn wealthy (rich) businessman; nouveau riche

大老粗 dàlǎocū uncouth fellow

大力 dàlì strongly; vigorously; energetically:～支援 give energetic support to

大量 dàliàng ① a large number; a great quantity:积累～资金 accumulate large funds ② generous; magnanimous:宽宏～ large-minded

大龄青年 dàlíng-qīngnián "old" unmarried youths

大龄未婚青年 dàlíng wèihūn qīngnián a single man or woman of around thirty who is in want of a spouse

大楼 dàlóu multistoried building:居民～ apartment house; block of flats

大陆 dàlù continent; mainland:中国～ the mainland of China

大路 dàlù main road; highway

大路货 dàlùhuò popular commodities; run-of-the-mill goods; articles of average quality

大略 dàlüè ① sketch; outline ② generally; roughly

大妈 dàmā ① father's elder brother's wife; aunt ② aunt (an affectionate or respectful form of address for an elderly woman)

dài

戴 dài〈动〉① wear; put on:～帽子 put on one's hat ② respect; honour:拥～ support (sb. as leader)

戴绿帽子 dài lǜmàozi[比喻妻子有外遇] be a cuckold; be cuckolded

戴帽子 dài màozi pin the label of … on sb.; stick a label on; clamp the label on sb.

戴孝 dàixiào wear mourning (for sb.)

戴罪立功 dàizuì-lìgōng atone for one's crimes by doing good deeds; redeem oneself by good service

带 dài〈名〉① belt; gridle; tape; string:丝～ silk ribbon ② tyre ③ zone, area:寒～ frigid zone〈动〉④ carry; bring; take:你随身～了什么? What did you bring with you? ⑤ do sth. incidentally:上街时给～点茶叶来。When you go out, get me some tea. ⑥ bear; have:面～笑容 wear a smile ⑦ lead; head ⑧ bring along; lead:～兵 be in command of troops ⑨ look after; raise; bring up:～孩子 look after children

带病 dàibìng in spite of illness:～工作 go on working in spite of illness; carry on work while sick

带电作业 dàidiànzuòyè live-wire work

带动 dàidòng ① drive; put (set) in motion ② bring along; lead; spur on:～全局 promote the work as a whole

带劲 dàijìn ①energetic; forceful; enthusiastic ② interesting; exciting; entertaining

带利息 dàilìxī cum interest

带领 dàilǐng ① lead; guide ② take round:～某人参观工厂 take sb. round the factory

带路 dàilù lead the way; act as a guide

带头 dàitóu take the lead; take the initiative; set an example:～作用 leading (forward) role; role of an initiator (vanguard; pace-setter). ～羊 the lead sheep; ringleader

带徒弟 dài túdi train (take on) an apprentice

带孝 dàixiào wear mourning for a parent, relative, etc.; be in mourning:给父亲～ wear mourning for one's father

带信 dàixìn send a letter; send word

带职 dàizhí in service; on the job:～学习 on-the-job training

殆 dài ①〈形〉dangerous; perilous ②〈副〉nearly; almost:敌人伤亡～尽。The enemy were practically wiped out.

大 dài
另见 dà

大夫 dàifu doctor; physician

大王 dàiwang great king (a term of address for a king or a bandit

chief, used in traditional operas and novels)
另见 dàwáng

代 dài ①〈动〉replace; take the place of; act for:他～我去。He'll go in my stead. ②〈形〉acting:～理部长 acting minister〈名〉③ times; period; era:唐～ the Tang Dynasty ④ generation:成长中的一～ the growing generation

代办 dàibàn ① do sth. for sb.; act on behalf of sb. ②[外] chargé d'affaires

代笔 dàibǐ write (a letter, etc.) for sb.; be a ghost writer

代表 dàibiǎo ① representative; delegate:～制 representation. ～资格 qualifications of representatives ② represent; stand for:～时代精神 embody the spirit of the era. ～作 representative works; masterpiece ③ on behalf of

代词 dàicí [语] pronoun

代耕 dàigēng farming for others

代沟 dàigōu generation gap

代购 dàigòu purchasing done by an agent; act as a purchasing agent:～代销点 purchasing and marketing agency; supply and marketing centre

代号 dàihào code name

代际 dàijì inter-generation:～关系 inter-generational relationship

代价 dàijià price; cost

代课 dàikè take over a class for an absent teacher:～教师[英国]supply teacher;[美国] substitute teacher

代劳 dàiláo do sth. for sb.; take trouble on sb.'s behalf:这事请你老罗～吧。Will you do this for us, Lao Luo?

代理 dàilǐ ① act for ② acting:～处 agency. ～人 agent; deputy; proxy

代人受过 dàirén-shòuguò suffer for the faults of another; bear the blame for sb. else; be made a scapegoat

代售 dàishòu sell on commission; be commissioned to sell sth. (usu. as a sideline):此处～邮票。Stamps sold here.

代替 dàitì take the place of; replace; substitute for:以甲～乙 substitute A for B

代销 dàixiāo be commissioned to sell sth.; sales on a commission basis

代写 dàixiě ghostwrite:～信 ghostwrite a letter

代谢 dàixiè ① supersession:新旧事物的～ the supersession of the old by the new ②[生] metabolize

代行 dàixíng act on sb.'s behalf:～职权 function in an acting capacity

代言人 dàiyánrén spokesman; prolocutor; mouthpiece

代议制 dàiyìzhì representation; representative system (of government):～政府 representational government

代用 dàiyòng substitute:～品 substitute

袋 dài〈名〉bag; sack;[口袋]

pocket;［钱袋］purse:购物～ shopping bag

袋泡茶 dàipàochá teabag

袋鼠 dàishǔ kangaroo

袋装 dàizhuāng in bags:～奶粉 milk powder in bags

贷 dài〈动〉① lend or borrow:向银行～款 get a bank loan ② shift (responsibility); shirk:责无旁～ be one's unshirkable responsibility ③ forgive; pardon:严惩不～ punish without any mercy ④〈名〉loan:农～ agricultural loan

贷方 dàifāng［簿记］credit side; credit

贷款 dàikuǎn ① give (grant) a loan; provide a loan; extend credit to ② loan; credit:～抵押品 security for a loan. ～利率 price of loan; lending rate. ～审查 ascertainment of loan

贷学金 dàixuéjīn student loans

待 dài〈动〉① treat; deal with:～人热情友好 treat people hospitably and kindly ② wait (for); await:有～改进 remain to be improved; have yet to be improved ③ need; ④ going to; about to:～说不说 swallow what one was about to say

待机 dàijī await an opportunity; bid one's time

待价而沽 dàijià'érgū wait for the right price to sell; wait for the highest bid

待考 dàikǎo need checking; remain to be verified:此说是否正确～。Whether or not this is true remains to be verified.

待命 dàimìng wait orders; pending further orders:～出发 be ready for orders to start out

待人处世 dàirén-chǔshì the way one treats people and conducts oneself in society

待人接物 dàirén-jiēwù the way one gets along with people

待续 dàixù to be continued

待业 dàiyè waiting for (awaiting) job assignments; awaiting (waiting for) employment

待遇 dàiyù ① treatment ② pay; wages; salary; remunerations; pay and conditions; terms of employment:～优厚 liberal wages and benefits; excellent pay and conditions

怠 dài〈形〉idle; neglect; indolent; slack

怠惰 dàiduò idle; lazy; indolent

怠工 dàigōng (hold a)slowdown; slacking at work; go slow; sabotage:～者 saboteur

怠慢 dàimàn treat with neglect; cold-shoulder; slight

逮 dài〈动〉① reach:力有未～ beyond one's reach (power) ② arrest

另见 dǎi

逮捕 dàibǔ arrest; take into custody:～证 arrest warrant

黛 dài〈名〉a black pigment used by women in ancient times to paint their eyebrows

黛绿 dàilǜ dark green

dān

单 dān〈形〉① single; one:～对配偶家庭 single pair family. ～行道 single tract ② odd:～号 odd number ③ thin; weak:～薄 thin and weak ④ simple ⑤〈副〉singly; alone; only:不要～凭热情去工作。Don't work by enthusiasm only 〈名〉⑥ sheet:床～ bed sheet ⑦ bill; list:提货～ bill of lading

单帮 dānbāng a travelling trader working on his own:跑～ travel around trading on one's own

单本位制 dānběnwèizhì monometallic standard

单边 dānbiān unilateral:～贸易 unilateral trade

单兵教练 dānbīng jiàoliàn single soldier training

单薄 dānbó ①(of clothing) thin:穿得～ be thinly clad ② thin and weak; frail:身体～ have a poor physique ③ insubstantial; flimsy; thin:论据～ a feeble argument

单产 dānchǎn per-unit yield; per unit area yield; unit production

单程 dānchéng one way; one path:～车票 single ticket; one-way ticket. ～出境签证护照 single exist visa in one's passport. ～贸易 one-way trade

单纯 dānchún ① simple; pure ② merely; alone:～技术观点 conclusive concern about technique; putting technique above everything else. ～升学教育 overemphasis on university-oriented education. ～任务观点 single-minded duty mentality

单打 dāndǎ singles:男子(女子)～ men's (women's) singles

单单 dāndān only; alone:别人都来了,～她没来。She's the only one absent.; Everybody else is here.; Everybody has come except her.

单刀直入 dāndāo-zhírù come directly to the point; talk straight

单调 dāndiào dull; flat; monotonous:～劳动操作 monotomous work

单独 dāndú alone; single-handed:～完成工作 finish the work single-handedly. 外国～投资 sole foreign investment

单方面 dānfāngmiàn unilateral; one-sided:～的积累 unilateral accumulation

单杠 dāngàng [体] ① horizontal bar ② horizontal bar gymnastics

单挂号 dānguàhào ordinary registered mail (which does not require a receipt for the sender)

单号 dānhào odd numbers (of tickets, seats, etc.)

单价 dānjià unit price

单据 dānjù bill; document

单利 dānlì simple interest

单枪匹马 dānqiāngpǐmǎ all by oneself; single-handed; alone

单亲家庭 dānqīn jiātíng single-parent family; one parent family

单日 dānrì odd-numbered days (of the month)

sb. 's presence; to sb. 's face:他～着我的面撒谎。He is telling me lies to my very face.
另见 dàng

当班 dāngbān be on a shift

当兵 dāngbīng be a soldier; serve in the army

当场 dāngchǎng on the spot:～逮住 be caught red-handed; catch in the act

当初 dāngchū originally; at the outset; in the first place; at that time:～他就不该这么做。He should never have acted the way he did in the first place.

当代 dāngdài contemporary; present-day; of our time

当地 dāngdì local; in the locality:～法律 law of the land; lex loci; local law:～诉讼 local action

当机立断 dāngjī-lìduàn make a prompt decision; prompt decision at the right moment; make a quick decision

当家 dāngjiā keep house; manage the house:～作主 be the master of one's own affairs (fate, destiny); be masters of the house

当局 dāngjú the authorities:政府～ the government authorities

当局者迷,旁观者清 dāngjúzhě mí, pángguānzhě qīng The spectators see the chess game better than the palyers.; One who is in the game is blind, while a bystander sees through everything.

当面 dāngmiàn to sb. 's face; in sb. 's presence:～弄清楚 straighten things out face to face

当面锣对面鼓 dāngmiàn luó duìmiàn gǔ direct confrontation and face-to-face argument

当面一套,背后一套 dāngmiàn yī tào, bèihòu yī tào act one way to your face and another behind your back

当年 dāngnián ①[指过去] in those years; in former times ② the prime of life:她正～。She is in her prime.
另见 dàngnián

当权 dāngquán hold power; be in power:～政党 ruling political party

当前 dāngqián ① before one; facing one:一事～,应该先想到人民的利益。Whenever something crops up, one should first think of the interests of the people. ② present; current:～的中心任务 the central task at present

当然 dāngrán ① without doubt; certainly; of course; to be sure ② natural:我们取得成功是～的。It is quite natural that we should succeed. ③ ex officio:～成员 an ex officio member (of a committee, etc.)

当仁不让 dāngrén-bùràng take something as one's obligation; take it as one's obligation to assume such authority; not pass on to others what one is called upon to do; not decline to shoulder a responsibility

当时 dāngshí[指过去] at that

time; then
另见 dàngshí

当事 dāngshì ① be in charge; be in control ② concerned; involved: ～国 the state directly involved; the country concerned ③ the authorities or the parties concerned

当事人 dāngshìrén person (party) concerned; interested party; [律师的] client: 诉讼～ litigant

当头 dāngtóu ① right overhead; right on sb.'s head; head on ② facing (confronting) one; imminent: 国难～。The country was in imminent danger.

当务之急 dāngwùzhījí a burning issue of the moment; top priority; the (most) pressing demand of the day; urgent task on hand; pressing business (affair) before one

当心 dāngxīn ① take care; be careful; look out: ～! 汽车来了。Look out! There's a car coming.; Mind that car. ② the centre of the chest; centre

当选 dāngxuǎn be elected: ～总统 president-elect. ～人 the elected

当政 dāngzhèng be in power; be in office

当之无愧 dāngzhīwúkuì deserve; be worthy of; merit (deserve) the reward; fully deserve a title

当中 dāngzhōng ① (in the) middle; (in the) centre ② among; [在两者之间] between

当众 dāngzhòng in the presence of all; in public: ～出丑 make a show of oneself

dǎng

挡 dǎng 〈动〉 ① block; keep off; prevent: ～雨 keep off the rain; shelter one from the rain ② cover; block; get in the way of: ～亮 cover the light 〈名〉 ③ blind; fender ④ gear: 前进～ forward gear

挡车 dǎngchē be in charge of looms and check the quality and quantity of the products

挡驾 dǎngjià turn away a visitor with some excuse; decline to receive a call (visit); decline to receive a guest

挡箭牌 dǎngjiànpái ① shield ② excuse; pretext

挡泥板 dǎngníbǎn mudguard (of a car); fender

挡住 dǎngzhù ① stop; halt ② shield; screen ③ block: ～…潮流 stem the tide of (against)

党 dǎng 〈名〉 ① (political) party ② [中国共产党] Party: ～的建设 Party-building

党八股 dǎngbāgǔ stereotyped Party writing; Party jargon

党报 dǎngbào ① party newspaper (organ) ② the organ of the Chinese Communist Party; the Party organ

党代表制 dǎngdàibiǎozhì system of Party representatives

党的集中领导 dǎng de jízhōng lǐngdǎo centralized leadership

of the Party
党的纪律检查委员会 dǎng de jìlǜ jiǎnchá wěiyuánhuì Party discipline inspection committee
党费 dǎngfèi Party membership dues
党风 dǎngfēng Party style of work
党籍 dǎngjí Party membership：开除～ expel from the Party
党纪 dǎngjì Party discipline：～国法 Party discipline and the law of the land
党课 dǎngkè Party class；Party lecture：听（讲）～ attend（give）a Party lecture
党龄 dǎnglíng age qualification of a Party member；Party standing；Party age
党内 dǎngnèi inner-Party；inside the Party；within the Party：～政治生活准则 guiding principles of inner-Party political life
党派 dǎngpài political parties and groups；party groupings：～关系 party affiliation
党派斗争 dǎngpài dòuzhēng factional strifes（struggle）
党徒 dǎngtú［贬］① member of a clique or a reactionary political party ② henchman
党团 dǎngtuán ① political parties and other organizations ② the Chinese Communist Party and the Chinese Communist Youth League；the Party and the League：～员 Party and League members ③ parliamentary group of a political party
党外 dǎngwài outside the Party：～人士 non-Party personages
党委 dǎngwěi Party committee：～领导下的厂长负责制 director of a factory takes responsibility for production under the leadership of the Party committee
党务 dǎngwù Party activities；Party matters；Party work；Party affairs
党校 dǎngxiào Party school：～工作者 active workers in the Party schools
党性 dǎngxìng Party spirit；Party character
党羽 dǎngyǔ［贬］members of a clique；adherents；henchmen
党员 dǎngyuán Party member：～大会 general membership meeting of a Party organization；meeting of all Party members
党政分工 dǎngzhèng fēngōng division of labour between Party and government organizations
党政机关 dǎngzhèng jīguān Party and government organs
党支部 dǎngzhībù Party branch
党中央 dǎngzhōngyāng Central Committee of the Party
党总支 dǎngzǒngzhī general Party branch
党组 dǎngzǔ leading Party members' group（in the government's departments and people's organizations）

dàng

当 dàng ①〈形〉proper；right：安排得～ be properly arranged

〈动〉② treat as; regard as; take for: 一分钱要～两分用 make good use of every penny ③ equal to; match: 他一个人能～两个人。He can do the work of two persons. ④ think: 我～是她呢。I thought it was her. ⑤ pawn: ～衣服 pawn one's clothes; put one's clothes in pawn

另见 dāng

当耳边风 dàng ěrbiānfēng turn a deaf ear to; in one ear and out the other

当家子 dàngjiāzi a member of the same clan; a distant relative with the same family name

当年 dàngnián the same year; the current year: ～价格 the current year's prices; price for the indicated year

另见 dāngnián

当票 dàngpiào pawn ticket

当铺 dàngpù pawnshop: ～老板 pawnbroker

当日 dàngrì the same day; that very day: ～有效 good for the date of issue only

当时 dàngshí at once; right away

另见 dāngshí

当事 dàngshì ① treat sth. as a serious matter; take sth. seriously: 她根本不拿工作当回事儿。She doesn't take the job seriously at all. ② be important; count: 我说话不～。What I say doesn't count.

当月 dàngyuè the same month; the current month: ～交货 current month delivery

当真 dàngzhēn ① take seriously ② really true ③ really; sure enough

当做 dàngzuò take for; treat as; regard as: 别把我～外人。Don't treat me like an outsider.

档 dàng〈名〉① archives ② [商品等的] grade: 高～商品 high-grade goods

档案 dàng'àn archives; records; files: ～管理员 archist. ～资料来源 documentary sources; documentary sources of information

档次 dàngcì grade: ～较高的消费品 high-grade (better quality) consumer goods

荡 dàng〈动〉① swing; sway: ～秋千 play on a swing ② wash; rinse: 涤～ cleanse; wash away ③ wipe off; clear away: 倾家～产 lose a family fortune ④ wander; roam; loaf: 游～ loaf about ⑤〈形〉loose (in morals); dissolute: 放～ dissipated; dissolute ⑥〈名〉marsh; shallow lake

荡涤 dàngdí cleanse; clean up; wash away

荡平 dàngpíng mop up; wipe out

荡然无存 dàngrán-wúcún all gone; nothing left: 大火之后，过去那些雄伟建筑～。After the fire, nothing remained of the once magnificent buildings.

荡漾 dàngyàng move in ripples; undulate

dāo

刀 dāo ①〈名〉knife; sword:～出鞘 off with sword sheath ②〈量〉[纸] one hundred sheets (of paper)

刀把子 dāobàzi ① the handle of a knife ② (sword) hilt ③military power; power ④ sth. that may be used against one; a handle

刀兵 dāobīng ① weapons; arms ② fighting; war:～再起 the renewal of armed conflict

刀耕火种 dāogēng-huǒzhòng slash-and-burn cultivation; "slash and burn" in farming

刀功 dāogōng (in preparing food) cutting and slicing skill

刀光剑影 dāoguāng-jiànyǐng the glint and flash of daggers and swords

刀具 dāojù cutter; cutting (knife) tool

刀片 dāopiàn ① razor blade ② (tool) bit; blade

刀枪 dāoqiāng sword and spear; weapons:～不入，飞檐走壁 immunity to bullets and power to fly

刀山火海 dāoshān-huǒhǎi a mountain of swords and a sea of flames; most severe trials; fire and water

叨 dāo
另见 dáo，tāo

叨叨 dāodao talk on and on; chatter away

叨唠 dāolao talk on and on; chatter away:她～了半天，人都不爱听。She chattered for a long time and bored everybody.

dáo

叨 dáo
另见 dāo，tāo

叨咕 dáogu grumble; mutter

dǎo

祷 dǎo〈动〉pray:做～告 say (give) one's prayers

祷告 dǎogào pray; say one's prayers

祷念 dǎoniàn say a prayer

祷文 dǎowén prayer

蹈 dǎo〈动〉① tread; step:赴汤～火 go through fire and water ② skip; trip:手舞足～ dance and stamp

蹈火 dǎohuǒ fire walking

蹈袭 dǎoxí follow slavishly:～…覆辙 follow the same old disastrous road

倒 dǎo〈动〉① fall; topple:摔～fall over ② collapse; close down; be overthrown:那家工厂～闭了。That factory has gone bankrupt. ③ change; exchange:～班 work in shifts ④ down with:～阁 down with the cabinet

倒把 dǎobǎ engage in profiteering; speculate:投机～ engage in speculation and profiteering

倒班 dǎobān change shifts; work in shifts; work by turns: 昼夜～work in shifts round the clock

倒闭 dǎobì close down; go bankrupt: 小企业的～率 mortality rate of small businesses

倒车 dǎochē [中途换车] change buses (trains, etc.)
另见 dàochē

倒戈 dǎogē change (turn) one's coat; transfer one's allegiance

倒阁 dǎogé force the government to resign; bring down a cabinet

倒买倒卖 dǎomǎi-dǎomài profiteer by buying and selling

倒霉 dǎoméi be unlucky; get into trouble; have bad luck; ill-fated; rotten luck

倒手 dǎoshǒu (of merchandise, etc.) change hands

倒台子 dǎotáizi rerent the rented counters to other traders

倒胃口 dǎowèikou spoil one's appetite: 这样的戏剧真叫人～。I've no stomach for such dramas.

倒休 dǎoxiū change one's shift to get leave later

倒爷 dǎoyé profiteering reseller; change-hands profiteer; profiteer

倒帐 dǎozhàng bad debt

岛 dǎo〈名〉island; isle: ～国 island state

岛屿 dǎoyǔ islands and islets; islands

捣 dǎo〈动〉① beat; strike; pound with a pestle, etc.; smash: ～药 pound medicine ② disturb; trouble

捣蛋 dǎodàn make trouble: ～鬼 trouble-maker; trickster

捣鬼 dǎoguǐ do mischief; play a dirty trick (on)

捣毁 dǎohuǐ smash up; demolish; destroy: ～敌军据点 destroy enemy strongpoints

捣乱 dǎoluàn make trouble; create disturbances

捣碎 dǎosuì pound to pieces

导 dǎo〈动〉① lead; guide; divert: ～淮入海 channel the Huai River into the sea ② instruct; teach; give guidance to: 教～ instruct; teach ③ transmit; conduct

导弹 dǎodàn guided missile

导电 dǎodiàn transmit electric current; conduct electricity

导航 dǎoháng navigation; pilot; guide: ～卫星 piloting satellite

导火线 dǎohuǒxiàn fuse; primer; spark-plug: 战争的～ incident that triggers off a war

导论 dǎolùn introduction (to a thesis, etc.); introductory remarks

导生 dǎoshēng [教] monitor: ～制 monitorial system

导师 dǎoshī tutor; teacher

导向 dǎoxiàng guide; guidance: 坚持广播电影、电视的～ persist in correct guidance through radio, film and television

导言 dǎoyán [书等的]introduction

导演 dǎoyǎn ① direct (a film, etc.) ② director

导游 dǎoyóu ① guide (conduct) a

sightseeing trip; guide tours ② tour guide; guide: ～图 tourist map

导致 dǎozhì lead to; cause; bring about; result in: ～战争 lead to war

dào

盗 dào ①〈动〉rob; steal: 监守自～ steal what is entrusted to one's care ②〈名〉robber; thief

盗案 dào'àn a theft case; a case of larceny

盗版 dàobǎn pirating; piratical edition

盗匪 dàofěi bandits; robbers: 肃清～ exterminate banditry

盗卖 dàomài illegally sell (public property)

盗名欺世,混淆视听 dàomíng qī shì, hǔnxiáo shì tīng hoodwink world public opinion by calling black white

盗窃 dàoqiè theft; steal: ～犯 thief; burglar. ～保险 burglary and robbery insurance

盗取 dàoqǔ steal; embezzle

盗用 dàoyòng embezzle; peculate; misappropriate: ～公款 embezzle public funds; peculation of state revenue. ～…名义 illegally use (usurp, pirate; appropriate) the name of …

盗贼 dàozéi robbers; bandits

悼 dào〈动〉mourn; lament: 哀～死者 mourn for the deceased

悼词 dàocí memorial speech: 致～ make a memorial speech; deliver a funeral oration

悼念 dàoniàn mourn for (over); grieve over; lament for

道 dào〈名〉① road; way; path ② way; method: 养生之～ the way to keep fit ③ morals; morality: ～义 morality and justice ④ doctrine; principle ⑤ Taoism; Taoist: 老～ Taoist priest〈动〉⑥ say; speak: 常言～ as the saying goes ⑦ think; suppose: 我～是老张呢,原来是你。So it's you, I thought it was Lao Zhang.〈量〉⑧[用于某些长条形的东西]: 一～烟 a stream of smoke ⑨[用于门、墙等]: 两～门 two successive doors ⑩[用于命令、题目等]: 出10～题 set ten questions (for an examination) ⑪[表示"次"数]: 上5～菜 serve five courses

道德 dàodé morality; morals; ethics: ～法庭 court of ethics. ～修养 ethical cultivation. 有～的人 man of moral integrity

道别 dàobié bid farewell; say goodbye

道高一尺,魔高一丈 dào gāo yīchǐ, mó gāo yīzhàng The evil is strong, but the good is ten times stronger.

道教 dàojiào Taoism

道具 dàojù stage property; properties; props

道理 dàolǐ ① truth; principle ② reason; argument; sense; hows and whys: 我们要讲～。We must be reasonable.

道路 dàolù road; way; path: ～泥

泞。The road is muddy.

道貌岸然 dàomào'ànrán assume the appearance of a man of integrity; put on a show of perfect honesty and deep seriousness; put on the front of a man of integrity

道破 dàopò point out frankly; lay bare; reveal:一语～ lay bare the truth with one penetrating remark

道歉 dàoqiàn apologize; make an apology:我把她的生日给忘了,应该向她～。I should apologize to her for forgetting her birthday. 她得向你～。She owes you an apology.

道听途说 dàotīng-túshuō pick up hearsay knowledge; get by hearsay; rumour; gossip; hearsay

道徒 dàotú a follower of Taoism

道喜 dàoxǐ congratulate (on, upon); offer one's congratulations (on, upon)

道学 dàoxué Neo-Confucianism

道义 dàoyì moral principles; morality and justice; right principles:～上的支持 moral support

到 dào〈动〉① reach; arrive at (in):春天～了。Spring has come. ② go to; leave for:～广州去 go to Guangzhou ③［用做动词的补语,表示动作达到目的或有了结果］:办得～ can be done ④〈形〉thoughtful; considerate:不～之处请原谅。Please excuse me if I have been inconsiderate in any way. ⑤〈介〉up to, up until:从星期二～星期五 from Tuesday to Friday ⑥［点名时答语］Here! (Present!)

到岸价格 dào'àn jiàgé cost, insurance and freight

到场 dàochǎng be present; attend; show up; turn up

到处 dàochù everywhere; all over the place; at (in) all places

到达 dàodá arrive; get to; reach:～港 port of arrival. ～站 destination. 代表团于今晨～北京。The delegation arrived in Beijing this morning.

到底 dàodǐ ① at last; finally; in the end:可她～还是没去。But she still didn't go in the end. ② to the end:坚持～ persist to the end ③ after all ④［加强语气,用在 what, who, when 等疑问词之后］:这～是怎么回事? What on earth is the matter?

到点 dàodiǎn it's time to do sth.; time is up:～了,该下班了。It's time to knock off.

到货验收 dàohuò yànshōu inspection of merchandise received

到家 dàojiā reach a very high level; be perfect; be excellent:我这笔字写得还不～。My calligraphy is far from perfect.

到来 dàolái arrival; advent

到期 dàoqī fall (become) due; mature:这张票据下月～。This bill will mature next month.

到手 dàoshǒu be received; come to hand; in one's hands (possession)

到头 dàotóu to the end; at an

end:～来 after all; finally; in the end

到…为止 dào…wéizhǐ till; until; up to:到现在为止 up to now; so far

到职 dàozhí take office; arrive at one's post

倒 dào〈动〉① pour; tip:把炉灰～入垃圾箱 tip cinders into a dustbin ② reverse ③ turn upside down; move backward:～车 back a car〈副〉④ but; on the contrary:春天来了,～下起了雪。It's spring, yet it is snowing. ⑤[表示事情不是那样]indicating that sth. is not what one thinks;[表示让步或转折] used to denote a transition or concession:东西～不坏,就是价钱太贵了。It is not bad, only it is a bit too dear. ⑥[表示催促或追问]:你～快点走啊! Can't you be quicker!

倒背如流 dàobèirúliú can recite sth. backwards —know sth. by heart

倒车 dàochē back a car:我倒着车开进车库。I backed my car into the garage.

倒打一耙 dàodǎ-yīpá make false charges; make unfounded counter-charges; put the blame on one's victim; recriminate

倒挂 dàoguà ① hanging upside down (it is a metaphor for the inverted position of a matter.) ② reversal of the natural order of things; drop away from:购销价格～ purchasing prices higher than selling prices; the selling prices drop away from the state purchasing prices

倒果为因 dàoguǒwéiyīn take effect for cause

倒流 dàoliú flow backwards:商品运输上的～ transporting goods back to their place of origin

倒赔 dàopéi lose money instead of making money

倒数 dàoshǔ ① count from bottom to top or from rear to front; count backwards:～计时 countdown. ～第二行 the second line from the bottom. 他住在这条胡同里～第二家。He lives in the last house but one in this lane. ②〈数〉reciprocal

倒贴 dàotiē ① pay instead of getting paid ② (of a woman) pay for the upkeep of her paramour; keep a gigolo

倒退 dàotuì go backwards; step (slip) back; recede

倒行逆施 dàoxíng-nìshī go against the tide of history; set back the clock; turn back the wheel of history; try to put the clock back; perverted action

倒因为果 dàoyīnwéiguǒ take cause for effect

倒置 dàozhì put upside down; reverse:轻重～ reverse the order of importance

倒转 dàozhuǎn turn the other way round; turn back; reverse:～乾坤 turn back the course of events

稻 dào〈名〉rice; paddy:～草人 straw man

稻谷 dàogǔ paddy

稻糠 dàokāng rice chaff
稻壳 dàoké rice husk (hull)
稻田 dàotián (rice) paddy; rice field; paddy field
稻秧 dàoyāng rice seedlings; rice shoots
稻子 dàozi rice; paddy

de

地 de [用在状语的后面]:天渐渐~冷了。The weather is getting cold.
另见 dì

的 de〈助动〉① [用在定语后面]:她~母亲 her mother. 别开我~玩笑。Don't make fun of me. ② [用来造成没有中心词的"的"字结构]:他说他~,我干我~。Let him say what he likes; I'll just get on with my work. ③[用在谓语动词后面,强调动作的施事者、时间、地点等]:谁买~? Who bought it?. 他们是昨天进~城。They went to town yesterday. ④[用在陈述句末尾,表示肯定的语气]:你这两天真够辛苦~。You've really been working hard the past few days.
另见 dí,dì

得 de〈助动〉① [用在动词后面,表示能够或可以]:吃~ eatable. 他去~,我为什么去不~? If he can go, why can't I? ② [用在动词和补语中间,表示可能]:他拿~动。He can carry it. ③ [用在动词或形容词后面,连接表示程度或结果的补语]:笑~肚子痛 laugh till one's sides split
另见 dé; děi

dé

得 dé〈动〉① get; gain; obtain; win:取~经验 gain experience ② take; catch:~病 be taken ill; fall ill ③ (of a calculation) result in:3 加 3~6。Three plus three is six. ④〈口〉be finished; ready:饭~了。Dinner is ready.〈形〉⑤ fit; proper:~用 fit for use ⑥ elated complacent ⑦〈叹〉~,又搞错了。Look! I've got it wrong again.
另见 de, děi
得标 débiāo have one's tender accepted
得不偿失 débùchángshī one loses more than one gains; more loss, less gain; more loss than gain; pay too dear for one's whistle; not worth the outlay; not worth powder and shot; gain not equal to loss; the loss outweighs the gain; the game is not worth the candle
得逞 déchěng [贬义] have (get) one's way; succeed (in doing evil); accomplish (an evil purpose)
得宠 déchǒng be in favour with sb.; find favour with sb.
得寸进尺 décùn-jìnchǐ give him an inch and he will take a mile; make ever greater demands; be insatiable

得当 dédàng apt; appropriate; proper; suitable: 措词～ aptly worded; appropriate wording

得道 dédào ① attain the Way ② support a just cause: ～多助,失道寡助。A just cause enjoys abundant support while an unjust cause finds little.; A just cause gains great support while an unjust one gains little.

得法 défǎ do sth. in the proper way; get the knack: 管理～ be properly managed

得分 défēn score: 客队的 3 号～最多。Player No. 3 of the visiting team scored the most points.

得过且过 déguò-qiěguò muddle on (along); drift along

得劲 déjìn ① feel well ② fit for use; handy: 这把锹我用起来很～。This spade is just right for me.

得力 délì ① helpful; capable; competent: ～助手 capable assistant ② benefit (from)

得人心 dérénxīn have the support of the people; be popular: 他们做那件事很～。That was a very popular move on their part.

得失 déshī ① gain and loss; success and failure: 个人～ personal gain or loss ② advantages and disadvantages; merits and demerits: 两种办法各有～。Each of the two methods has its advantages and disadvantages.

得势 déshì come into power; hold sway

得手 déshǒu go smoothly; come off; do fine; succeed

得体 détǐ appropriately; properly: 措词～ be appropriately worded

得天独厚 détiān-dúhòu be richly endowed by nature; abound in gifts of nature; enjoy exceptional advantages

得心应手 déxīn-yìngshǒu act in an expert way; do sth. with high proficiency; handle with ease

得意 déyì elated; exalted; complacent: ～忘形 be beside oneself with joy (glee); forget oneself in one's excitement. ～扬扬 with an elated look; with evident pride; have one's nose in the air; cock-a-hoop

得益 déyì benefit; profit: 读者的意见使我～不少。I benefit considerably from the readers' comments.

得志 dézhì fulfil one's wish; attain one's ambition; achieve one's object: 不～ fail to attain one's ambition: 少年～ have a successful career at an early age

得罪 dézuì incur the displeasure of sb.; offend

德 dé 〈名〉① morals; virtue; morality: 美～ moral excellence ② heart; mind: 同心同～ be of one heart and one mind ③ kindness; favour: 感恩戴～ bear a debt of gratitude for past kindness

德昂族 Dé'ángzú the De'ang nationality, or the De'angs, inhabiting Yunnan Province

德才兼备 décái-jiānbèi have both ability and political integrity; equipped with both ethics and talent

德高望重 dégāo-wàngzhòng of high morality and great reputation

德行 déxíng ① moral integrity; moral conduct; virtue ② déxing shameful; disgusting

德性 déxìng moral character; moral integrity

德育 déyù moral education; education in ethics

德智体全面发展 dé-zhì-tǐ quánmiàn fāzhǎn educating students morally, intellectually and physically

děi

得 děi 〈动〉① need:这个工程～一年才能完成。This project will take a year to complete. ② be sure to; will:要不快走,我们就～迟到。We'll be late if we don't hurry. ③〈助动〉must; should; ought to; have to:你～认真考虑一下。You must think it over seriously.
另见 de,dé

dēng

灯 dēng〈名〉lamp; lantern; light

灯彩 dēngcǎi ① coloured-lantern making ② coloured lanterns (formerly used on the stage)

灯光 dēngguāng lamplight:～艺术家 luminist

灯红酒绿 dēnghóng-jiǔlǜ red lanterns and green wine — scene of debauchery; feasting and revelry:～,纸醉金迷 lead a gay life; go (be) on a racket

灯火 dēnghuǒ lights:～管制 black out. ～辉煌 be ablaze with lights; brilliantly illuminated

灯节 dēngjié Festival of Lanterns; the Lantern Festival

灯笼 dēnglong lantern:挂～ hang a lantern

灯谜 dēngmí riddles written on lanterns; lantern riddles:猜～ guess a lantern riddle

灯市 dēngshì lantern fair (on the 15th day of the first lunar month)

灯烛 dēngzhú lamps and candles — lights:～辉煌 ablaze with lights; brilliantly illuminated

灯座 dēngzuò lampstand

登 dēng〈动〉① climb; scale; mount; ascend:～岸 go ashore; land ② record; register; publish; enter:～新书广告 announce a new edition. ～帐 enter an item in an account book; charge to an account

登岸 dēng'àn go ashore; land

登场 dēngchǎng [剧] appear on the stage; go up on the stage; enter

登峰造极 dēngfēng-zàojí be at the zenith (of); come to a climax; the peak of perfection

登高 dēnggāo ① ascend a height:

～远眺 ascend a height to enjoy a distant view ② climb hills or mountains on the Double Ninth Festival

登基(极) dēngjī(jí) ascend the throne; enthronement; accession to the throne; be enthroned; take the throne

登记 dēngjì enter; record; register; check in: ～股东 shareholder (stockholder) of record

登陆 dēnglù land; disembark: 台风将于明晨～。The typhoon will land tomorrow morning.

登门 dēngmén call at sb.'s house: ～拜访 pay sb. a visit

登山 dēngshān mountain-climbing; mountaineering: ～队 mountaineering party (expedition). ～运动 mountaineering. ～运动员 mountaineer

登台 dēngtái come on the stage; appear on the platform

登载 dēngzǎi publish in the newspaper; carry

děng

等 děng ①〈名〉grade; class; rank: 头～品 first rate goods; top quality goods ②〈形〉equal: 大小不～ unequal in size ③〈动〉wait; await ④〈助动〉[用在人称代词或名词后面,表示复数]老张～三人 Lao Zhang and two others〈助动〉⑤ [表示列举未尽] and so on; etc. ⑥ [用于列举后结尾] 北京、上海、天津、广州、等四大城市: big cities such as Beijing, Shanghai, Tianjin and Guangzhou.

等别地位 děngbié dìwèi scalar status

等次 děngcì place in a series; grade: 产品按质量划分～。The products are graded according to quality.

等待 děngdài wait (for); await: ～时机 wait for one's chance; bide one's time

等到 děngdào by the time; when: ～敌军赶到,游击队已经转移了。By the time the enemy troops arrived, the guerrilla force had already disappeared.

等第 děngdì ① grade in an imperial examination ② place in a competition

等级 děngjí ① grade; rank; class: 划分～ grade; classify ② order and degree; social stratum: ～的差别 distinction of rank. ～观念 the concept of (social) status. ～评定 ranking; rating

等价交换 děngjià jiāohuàn equal value exchange; exchange at equal value

等量齐观 děngliàng-qíguān equate one with another; put on a par

等同 děngtóng equate (with); be equal (to); treat as equivalent

等外 děngwài substandard: ～品 substandard goods

等闲 děngxián ① ordinary; unimportant: ～之辈 ordinary people ② aimlessly; thoughtlessly: 大好时光,不可～度过。Don't fritter away your precious time.

等闲视之 děngxián-shìzhī take sth. lightly (casually); make nothing of

等于 děngyú be equal to; amount to; be equivalent to; be tantamount to

dèng

澄 dèng〈动〉[液体] (of liquid) be clear; settle
另见 chéng

澄清 dèngqīng [液体] become clear; settle

瞪 dèng〈动〉open one's eyes wide; gaze at; stare at

凳 dèng〈名〉stool; bench

dī

滴 dī ①〈动〉drip (by drops): ~眼药 put drops in one's eyes ②〈名〉drop: 一~水 a drop of water

滴答 dīda [钟表声] tick; tick-tack

滴灌 dīguàn trickle irrigation; drip irrigation

滴水不漏 dīshuǐ-bùlòu ① tightly packed or completely enclosed ② watertight (fig.)

滴水穿石 dīshuǐ-chuānshí Constant drops hollow a stone.; Constant dripping wears away the stone.

滴水之恩,当涌泉相报 dīshuǐzhī'ēn, dāng yǒngquán xiāngbào A small favour is worth great reward.

堤 dī〈名〉dyke; dam; embankment: ~坝 dyke and dam

堤岸 dī'àn embankment: ~权[法] riparian right

堤坝 dībà dykes and dams

堤防 dīfáng dyke; embankment: ~工程 dyke building; embankment project

提 dī
另见 tí

提防 dīfáng guard against; beware of; take precautions against

低 dī ①〈形〉low: ~水平 low level ②〈动〉bend; droop: 害羞地~下头 lower one's head coyly

低产 dīchǎn low yield; low productivity: ~作物 low-yielding crop

低潮 dīcháo low tide (water); ebb

低档 dīdǎng low-class; low-grade: ~商品 low-grade goods

低调 dīdiào ① low-key ② low tone

低估 dīgū underestimate; undervalue; underrate

低耗 dīhào low consumption

低级 dījí ① low-grade; elementary ② vulgar: ~趣味 low taste; vulgar interests; philistine taste

低龄化 dīlínghuà become lower in age: 目前各国都面临着犯罪~的趋势。At present, every nation faces the tendency of crimes being committed by younger people.

低能 dīnéng imbecile; feeble-minded; mental deficiency:～儿 feeble-minded child; imbecile

低贱 dījiàn low and degrading; humble

低廉 dīlián cheap; low:价格～。Prices are low.

低劣 dīliè inferior; low-grade:质量～ of inferior quality

低落 dīluò low; downcast:情绪～ be low-spirited

低人一等 dīrényīděng inferior to other people

低三下四 dīsān-xiàsì servile; abject; lowly; humble; mean

低声 dīshēng in a low voice:～下气地 humbly; obsequiously; submissively

低头 dītóu ① lower (bow, hang) one's head:～认罪 hang one's head and admit one's guilt; plead guilty ② yield; submit:决不向困难～ never bow to difficulties

低息 dīxī low interest:～贷款 a low-interest loan

低消耗 dīxiāohào low consumption (of raw materials, fuel, etc.):保持高产、优质、～ maintain a record of high production, good quality and low consumption

低血糖 dīxuètáng [医] hypoglycemia

dí

迪 dí〈动〉enlighten; guide

迪斯科 dísīkē disco:～舞厅 discotheque

荻 dí〈名〉a kind of reed

涤 dí〈动〉wash; cleanse

涤除 díchú wash away; do away with; eliminate:～旧习 do away with old customs

涤荡 dídàng clean up; wipe out

嘀 dí

嘀咕 dígu ① talk in whispers ② grumble (about); murmur (against):不要为那件事～。Don't grumble about that.

嫡 dí〈形〉① legitimate ② of direct descent; of lineal descent; closely related; [兄弟等] full; whole

嫡传 díchuán handed down in direct descent (from)

嫡亲 díqīn blood relations:～兄弟 full (whole) brothers; blood brothers. ～长辈 close relation of one's from the previous generation

嫡系 díxì ① direct line of descent:～后代 direct descendants ② disciples taught by the master himself

嫡子 dízǐ legitimate son

笛 dí〈名〉① bamboo flute ② whistle:汽～ air siren

笛子 dízi bamboo flute:吹～ play the flute

敌 dí ①〈名〉enemy; foe:化～为友 turn an enemy into an ally ②〈动,名〉match; equal:势均

力～ match each other in strength ③〈动〉oppose; fight; resist:以寡～众 fight against heavy odds

敌对 díduì hostile; antagonistic; opposing:～行为 hostile act; hostility

敌国 díguó enemy state

敌情 díqíng information concerning the enemy; enemy's situation:～观念 awareness of enemy presence

敌人 dírén enemy; foe

敌视 díshì be hostile (antagonistic) to; adopt a hostile attitude towards

敌手 díshǒu rival; match; opponent

敌探 dítàn enemy spy

敌我矛盾 díwǒ-máodùn contradictions between the enemy and ourselves

敌意 díyì enmity; animosity; hostility:怀有～ have enmity (hostility) against sb.

的 dí〈形〉exact; real; true:～确 really; truly; indeed

dǐ

诋 dǐ〈动〉slander; defame:丑～ use bad language against; revile

诋毁 dǐhuǐ slander; vilify; calumniate; defame

底 dǐ〈名〉① bottom; base:桶～ the buttom of a bucket ② the hearts of a matter; ins and outs:交～ give someone the bottomline ③ rough draft ④ end:年～ the end of a year ⑤ background; ground:黑～白点的布 cloth with white spots on a black background

底版 dǐbǎn photographic plate; negative

底册 dǐcè a bound copy of a document kept on flle

底层 dǐcéng ① ground floor [英国]; first floor [美国] ② bottom; the lowest rung:旧中国劳动人民被压在社会的最～。In old China the working people were kept at the bottom of society.

底肥 dǐféi base fertilizer (applied before planting)

底稿 dǐgǎo rough (foul) copy; draft; manuscript

底价 dǐjià base price

底片 dǐpiàn photographic plate; negative

底数 dǐshù ① the truth or root of a matter; how a matter actually stands:心中有～ know how the matter stands ② [数] base number

底细 dǐxì details; ins and outs; exact details

底下 dǐxia ① under; below; beneath:树～ under the tree ② next; later; afterwards:他～说的话我就听不清了。I didn't catch what he said next.

底限 dǐxiàn the lowest limit; minimum

底子 dǐzi foundation; base; grounding:英语～好 have a

good grounding in English. ～薄 poor economic foundation

抵 dǐ〈动〉① support; sustain; prop: 用手～着下巴颏儿 prop one's chin in one's hands ② resist; withstand: ～住暴风雨 withstand the storm ③ compensate for; make good ④ mortgage: 用房屋作～押 mortgage a house ⑤ reach; arrive at (in): ～达上海 arrive in Shanghai

抵补 dǐbǔ make up for; compensate

抵偿 dǐcháng ① compensate for; make good; give sth. by way of; payment for: ～损失 make good a loss ② atone for

抵触 dǐchù ① be in conflict (with); collide (with) ② contravene: 不同宪法～ must not contravene the constitution

抵达 dǐdá arrive; reach

抵抗 dǐkàng resist; stand against; fight back: ～诱惑 wrestle (be proof) against temptation

抵赖 dǐlài deny; refuse to admit

抵命 dǐmìng pay (atone) with one's life

抵数 dǐshù make up the number; serve as a stopgap

抵消 dǐxiāo set off; offset; counteract

抵押 dǐyā mortgage; phypothecate; impawn; hold in pledge: ～品 security; pledge

抵御 dǐyù resist; withstand

抵债 dǐzhài pay a debt in kind

抵制 dǐzhì combat (reject); counteract; boycott; resist

dì

帝 dì〈名〉① the Supreme Being: 上～ God ② emperor: 称～ proclaim oneself emperor ③ (short for) imperialism

帝冠 dìguān imperial crown

帝国 dìguó empire: ～政府 imperial administration

帝号 dìhào imperial title

帝王 dìwáng emperor; monarch: ～的称号 emperor's title

帝位 dìwèi throne: ～的更替 changes in the throne

帝制 dìzhì monarchy; monarchical system

缔 dì〈动〉conclude; contract

缔交 dìjiāo ① establish diplomatic relations ② form (contract) a friendship

缔结 dìjié conclude; establish: ～条约 conclude a treaty

缔约 dìyuē conclude (sign) a treaty: ～国 signatory states; signatories. ～双方 both contracting parties

缔造 dìzào found; create; build: ～者 architect; creator

弟 dì〈名〉younger brother

弟弟 dìdi younger brother; brother

弟妹 dìmèi ① younger brother and sister ② younger brother's wife; sister-in-law

弟兄 dìxiong brothers: 亲～ blood brothers

弟子 dìzǐ disciple; pupil; follower:～破师 the disciples' betrayal of the masters

递 dì ①〈动〉hand over; give; pass; deliver:～辞呈 give in one's resignation〈副〉② in turn ③ in the proper order; successively:～升 promote to the next rank

递补 dìbǔ fill vacancies in the proper order

递加(增) dìjiā (zēng) increase progressively; increase by degrees

递减 dìjiǎn decrease (reduce) progressively; decrease by degrees

递交 dìjiāo present; send (in); deliver:～国书 present credentials

递解 dìjiè escort (a criminal) from one place to another:～回籍 send (a convict, etc.) to his native place under escort

递升 dìshēng promote to the next rank

递增 dìzēng increase progressively; increase by degrees:产量平均每年～百分之十。The output increased at an average rate of 10 per cent a year.; The output showed a yearly average increase of 10 per cent.

的 dì〈名〉target; bull's-eye
另见 de,dí

地 dì〈名〉① earth ② land; soil:高～ highland ③ field:下～干活 go and work in the fields ④ floor; ground:水泥～ cement floor ⑤ locality; place:～处山区 be located in a mountain ⑥ position; situation:立于不败之～ be in an invincible position ⑦ background ⑧ distance:30 里～ a distance of 30 *li*
另见 de

地板 dìbǎn ① floor board ② floor:水泥～ cement floor

地步 dìbù ①condition; situation; plight ② extent:你不可把困难夸大到这样的～。You must not exaggerate the difficulties to such an extent.

地产 dìchǎn landed property; real estate; landed estate

地大物博 dìdà-wùbó vast territory and rich resources; a big country abounding in natural wealth

地带 dìdài district; region; zone; belt:森林～ a forest region

地道 dìdao ① pure; real; genuine ② good; fine:法语说得～ speak good French

地地道道 dìdi-dàodào out-and-out; outright; hundred-percent

地点 dìdiǎn place; site; locale:故事发生的～ the locale (scene) of a story

地段 dìduàn a section (sector) of a town; district; area:～医院 community hospital

地方 dìfāng ① place; region ② local:～财政 local finance. ～民族主义 local nationalism. ～统筹基建拨款 appropriations for capital construction projects undertaken by the local governments. ～戏 local operas. ～主义 sectionalism.

地广人稀 dìguǎng-rénxī a vast but thinly populated area; a vast territory with a sparse population

地基 dìjī ① ground ② foundation

地窖 dìjiào cellar

地尽其力 dìjìnqílì maximizing land power

地雷 dìléi (land) mine：埋～ plant (lay) mines

地理 dìlǐ geography：～环境 geographical environment. ～经济学 geoeconomics

地膜覆盖 dìmó fùgài covering with ground sheet

地利 dìlì ① favourable geographical position; topographical advantages：～人和 favourable terrain and friendly people ② land productivity

地灵人杰 dìlíng-rénjié a remarkable place produces outstanding people

地貌 dìmào general configuration of the earth's surface; landforms

地面 dìmiàn ① the earth's surface; ground：高出～3米 three metres above ground level ②［建］ground; floor：水磨石～ terrazzo floor ③ region; area; territory

地盘 dìpán territory under one's control; domain：军阀互相争夺～。The warlords competed for spheres of influence.

地皮 dìpí ① land for building ② ground：雨停了，～还没有干。The ground is still wet after the rain.

地痞 dìpǐ local ruffian; ruffian：～流氓 riffraff; hoodlum; rowdy

地气 dìqì vital breath (*qi*) of earth

地契 dìqì title deed for land

地勤 dìqín［航空］ground service：～人员 ground crew; ground personnel

地球 dìqiú the earth; the globe：～同步卫星 geostationary satellite; synchronous satellite

地区 dìqū region; area; locality; district：～差价 differences in regional price levels; price gaps between different localities

地势 dìshì features (of a place); lie of the land; topography; terrain：～险要。The terrain is strategically important.

地税 dìshuì land tax

地摊 dìtān street vendor's stand or stall (with goods spread out on the ground for sale)

地毯 dìtǎn carpet; rug

地铁 dìtiě subway; tube; underground

地图 dìtú map

地委 dìwěi prefectural Party committee：～书记 secretary of the prefectural Party committee

地位 dìwèi position; rank; status：国际～ international standing. 经济～ economic status

地下 dìxià underground; subterranean：～包工队 underground contract teams. ～工厂 underground factories. ～刊物 illegal

publications; underground publications
地形 dìxíng topography; terrain: ～险阻 inaccessibility of terrain
地域 dìyù region; district: ～分工 geographic division of labour. ～人种 local race
地震 dìzhèn earthquake; seism: 这次～为里氏 7 级。The shock was 7 magnitude on the Richter scale.
地址 dìzhǐ address: 回信～ return address
地质 dìzhì geology: ～调查 geological survey
地主 dìzhǔ ① landowner; landlord ② host: 尽～之谊 perform the duties of the host
地租 dìzū (land) rent: 级差～ differential rent

第 dì ① [用在数词前表示次序] ～三世界 the Third World ② 〈名〉 house; mansion: 府～ mansion
第二 dì-èr second: ～产业 secondary industry. ～梯队 second echelon. ～类物资 second category of material goods; supplies under Category Ⅱ. ～文化 second culture
第三 dì-sān third: ～产业 tertiary industry; service industry. ～类物资 supplies under Category Ⅲ. ～者插足 the involvement of a third party (a love triangle)
第一 dì-yī first: ～把手 those who are in primary responsibility. ～产业 primary industry. ～流 first-class; first-rate. ～生产力 primary productive forces. ～线 front line; forefront. 生活的～需要 life's prime want
第一性 dì-yī xìng primary; primacy: 经济和政治关系中的～ primacy in the relations between economics and politics

谛 dì ① 〈副〉 carefully; attentively: ～听 listen attentively ② 〈名〉meaning; significance

diǎ

嗲 diǎ〈形〉①flirtatious: 说话～声～气 speak in a coquettish voice ② good; nice

diān

滇 Diān short for 云南
颠 diān〈动〉① turn over; fall: ～覆 overturn; subvert; upset ② bump; jolt ③〈名〉top; summit: 塔～ the top of a pagoda
颠簸 diānbǒ bump; toss; jolt: 浪打得船～不停。The waves continuously tossed the boat.
颠倒 diāndǎo turn upside down; reverse; invert: ～历史 turn history upside down. ～黑白 call white black and black white; stand truth on its head; confuse right and wrong; turn black into white; transpose black and white; confound black and white

颠倒是非 diāndǎo-shìfēi confound right and wrong; reverse right and wrong; turn things upside down; reversal of right and wrong; reversal of the truth and falsehood; turn right into wrong

颠覆 diānfù overturn; subvert:～活动 subversive activities; subversion

颠来倒去 diānlái-dǎoqù over and over

颠沛流离 diānpèi-liúlí wander about homeless; drift from place to place

颠扑不破 diānpū-bùpò irrefutable; indisputable; incontrovertible:～的真理 irrefutable truth

颠三倒四 diānsān-dǎosì ① turn things topsy-turvy ② confused; incoherent; disorganized

巅 diān〈名〉 mountain peak; summit

巅峰 diānfēng summit; peak; pinnacle:这些运动员正处于～状态。The athletes are in top form.

癫 diān〈形〉 mentally deranged; insane

掂 diān〈动〉 weigh in the hand

掂量 diānliàng ① weigh up; think over ② weigh in the hand

掂算 diānsuàn estimate; calculate; weigh

diǎn

点 diǎn〈名〉① point; place:沸～ boiling point. 居民～ residential area ② drop:雨～ raindrops ③ dot; spot 墨～ ink spots ④〈量〉tiny amount; a little; a bit:吃一～东西 have (get) something to eat ⑤ [时间单位] o'clock:上午八～钟 eight o'clock in the morning〈动〉⑥ put a dot:～一个逗号 make a comma ⑦ touch lightly as with finger; brush or rod; skim:蜻蜓～水 dragonflies skimming (over) the water ⑧ drip ⑨ check one by one:～货 check over goods ⑩ select; choose:～菜 order dishes (in a restaurant) ⑪ light; kindle; burn:～火 kindle the flames; set fire to

点播 diǎnbō ① [农] dibble seeding; dibbling ② request a programme from a radio station:听众～的节目 a programme by request; (listeners') request. 听众～的流行歌曲 pop songs for the asking

点播节目 diǎnbō jiémù request programme; requested item:听众～ a request programme for listeners

点菜 diǎncài choose dishes from a menu; order dishes (in a restaurant)

点唱 diǎnchàng (of an audience) request a number (a song, an aria from a traditional opera, etc.)

点滴 diǎndī ① a bit ②［医］intravenous drip：打葡萄糖～ have an intravenous glucose drip

点交 diǎnjiāo hand over item by item

点校本 diǎnjiàoběn collated and punctuated edition

点面结合,以点带面 diǎnmiànjiéhé, yǐdiǎn-dàimiàn combine work on key points with work in other areas; promote work in all areas by drawing upon experience gained in the work on key points; link work at selected spots with that in entire areas

点明 diǎnmíng mention clearly; point out

点名 diǎnmíng ① call the roll：～册 roll (book) ② mention sb. by name

点破 diǎnpò expose; lay bare; show up sth. in a few words

点球 diǎnqiú［足球］penalty kick

点燃 diǎnrán light; kindle; ignite：～火把 light a torch

点收 diǎnshōu take over according to the list

点数 diǎnshù check the number (of pieces, etc.); count：找你的钱别忘了点点数。Don't forget to count your change.

点题 diǎntí bring out the theme

点头 diǎntóu nod (one's head)：～哈腰 bow unctuously. ～之交 (have a) nodding acquaintance (with)

点心 diǎnxīn desert; light refreshments; pastry

点验 diǎnyàn examine item by item

点缀 diǎnzhuì ① embellish; ornament; adorn ② use sth. merely for show：贴几张画～～ put up some pictures for more atmosphere

点子 diǎnzi ① drop ② key point ③ suggestion; idea; pointer：出～ give a pointer (on). 抓到～上 get hold of the key link in work

典 diǎn〈名〉① law; canon; code ② standard work：词～ dictionary ③ literary quotation; allusion：用～ use allusions ④ ceremony：开国大～ founding ceremony of a state ⑤〈动〉mortgage; pawn

典范 diǎnfàn model; example; paragon; pattern

典故 diǎngù quotation from classics; allusion

典籍 diǎnjí ancient codes and records; ancient books and records：先秦～ pre-Qin books and records

典礼 diǎnlǐ ceremony; celebration; exercises：毕业～ graduation exercises; commencement

典型 diǎnxíng ① type; model; typicalness; specimen ② typical; representative：～示范 set an example with a model. ～试验 typical case experiment. ～塑造 representative portrayals

典押 diǎnyā mortgage; pawn

典雅 diǎnyǎ refinement; stateliness and elegance; elegant; refined：～爱情 courtly love. ～音乐 classical music

典狱 diǎnyù prison warden：～长 prison warden

典章 diǎnzhāng institutions (and statutes); decrees and regulations

碘 diǎn〈名〉iodine

碘酒 diǎnjiǔ［医］tincture of iodine

踮 diǎn〈动〉stand on tiptoe：她得～着脚才够得着架子。She had to stand on tiptoe to reach the shelf.

diàn

淀 diàn ①〈动〉form sediment; settle; precipitate ②〈名〉shallow lake

淀粉 diànfěn starch; fecula

奠 diàn〈动〉① establish; lay; found; settle ② make a libation; make offerings to the spirits of the dead

奠定 diàndìng found; settle; lay (down)：～基础 lay a foundation

奠都 diàndū establish (found) a capital

奠基 diànjī lay a foundation (of)：～人 founder; progenitor

垫 diàn〈动〉① put sth. under sth. else to raise it or make it level; lay under; pad：～路 repair a road by filling the holes ② pay for sb. and expect to be repaid later：～款 advance in cash ③〈名〉cushion; pad; mat：椅～ chair cushion

垫补 diànbu ① make up the deficiency by borrowing money or using money intended for other purposes ② have a snack

垫底儿 diàndǐr ① put sth. at the bottom ② have a bite to stave off hunger pains (before taking a regular meal) ③ do spadework; lay a foundation

垫付 diànfù pay in advance; advance

垫款 diànkuǎn ① make an advance (to sb.) ② money advanced for sb. to be paid back later; advance

垫料 diànliào padding

垫子 diànzi mat; pad; cushion：沙发～ sofa cushion. 茶杯～ teacup mat; coaster

店 diàn〈名〉shop; store：花～ florist shop

店风 diànfēng shop atmosphere

店家 diànjiā ① shopkeeper ② innkeeper; restaurateur ③ shop; store

店面 diànmiàn shop front

店铺 diànpù shop; store

店堂 diàntáng the business quarter of a shop (store); commodity section

店员 diànyuán shop assistant; salesclerk; clerk; salesman or saleswoman

店主 diànzhǔ shopkeeper; storekeeper

惦 diàn〈动〉continue to think

about; be concerned about

惦记 diànjì keep thinking about; be concerned about

惦念 diànniàn worry about; be (feel) anxious about

玷 diàn ①〈名〉flaw; defect; stain ②〈动〉disgrace; blemish

玷辱 diànrǔ humiliate; disgrace

玷污 diànwū sully; tarnish; defile: ～某人名誉 sully sb.'s reputation

电 diàn〈名〉① electricity; ② telegram: 贺～ congratulatory telegram〈动〉③ give (get) an electric shock ④ send a telegram; cable; wire: ～贺 trelegraph one's congratulations to sb.; cable a message of congratulations

电报 diànbào telegram; cable: ～挂号 cable address. ～文体 telegraphese. 打～ send a telegram; telegraph; cable

电表 diànbiǎo ① any meter for measuring electricity, such as ammeter or voltmeter ② kilowatt-hour meter; watt-hour meter; electric meter

电冰箱 diànbīngxiāng (electric) refrigerator; fridge

电唱机 diànchàngjī record player; electric gramophone (phonograph)

电车 diànchē ① tram; tramcar; streetcar ② trolleybus; trolley

电池 diànchí (electric) cell; battery: 干～ dry cell

电传 diànchuán electrical transmission; telex

电大 diàndà television college

电灯 diàndēng electric lamp; electric light: ～泡 electric (light) bulb

电动 diàndòng motor-driven; power-driven; electric: ～机 (electric) motor. ～剃须刀 electric shaver

电饭煲 diànfànbāo electric rice cooker

电风扇 diànfēngshàn electric fan

电工 diàngōng ① electrical engineering ② electrician

电焊 diànhàn electric welding: ～机 electric welding machine; electric welder

电贺 diànhè telegraph one's congratulations to sb.; cable a message of congratulations

电话 diànhuà (tele)phone: 打～ make a telephone; call; phone; ring sb. up; call sb. (up). ～号查询服务 directory assistance. ～号查询台 directory enquires. ～号码簿 telephone directory. ～会议 telephone conference

电汇 diànhuì telegraphic remittance; telegraphic money order

电机 diànjī electrical machinery: ～厂 electrical machinery plant

电吉他 diànjítā [乐] electric guitar

电教 diànjiào education based on electric audio-visual aids: ～设备 audio-visual education facilities. ～片 educational film

电烤箱 diànkǎoxiāng electric oven; electric grill; electric roaster

电力 diànlì electric power; power:～工业 power industry. ～网 electric power grid

电炉 diànlú ① electric stove; hot plate ② electric furnace:～炼钢法 electric furnace process

电路 diànlù (electric) circuit:～图 circuit diagram

电脑 diànnǎo (electronic) computer:～记帐服务 computerized accounting services

电热炉 diànrèlú electric heaters

电钮 diànniǔ push button; button:按～ press (push) a button

电气 diànqì electric:～化 electrify. ～设备 electric equipment

电器 diànqì electrical equipment (appliance):家用～ household (electrical) appliances

电褥 diànrù electric bedding

电扇 diànshàn electric fan

电视 diànshì television; TV:～大学 TV university. ～传播 TV transmissions. ～观众 television viewers. ～黄金时间 TV prime time. ～剧 TV play. ～节目 TV programme; telecast. ～商场 TV shopping. ～新闻 news on television. ～系列片 TV serial. ～制式 television system

电台 diàntái broadcasting (radio) station:那家～的收听率处于最低档。That broadcasting station was in the ratings cellar.

电梯 diàntī lift; elevator

电筒 diàntǒng (electric) torch; flashlight

电网 diànwǎng power grid; electrified wire netting; live wire entanglement

电信 diànxìn telecommunications:～局 telecommunication bureau

电刑 diànxíng electrocution

电讯 diànxùn ① (telegraphic) dispatch:《人民日报》收到世界各地发来的～。The *People's Daily* receives dispatches from all parts of the world. ② telecommunications: ～设备 telecommunication equipment

电唁 diànyàn send a telegram (message) of condolence

电邀 diànyāo send an invitation by telegraph; cable an invitation

电影 diànyǐng movie; film; motion picture; the pictures:～说明书 film synopsis. ～演员 film actor or actress. ～剧本 scenario. ～节 film festival; filmfest. ～评论 motion-picture review. ～制片厂 (film) studio. 立体～ three dimensional film; stereoscopic film. 看～去 go to the pictures (films, movies, cinema)

电源 diànyuán power supply; power source; mains:接上～ connect with the mains

电针疗法 diànzhēn liáofǎ electrical acupuncture method

电钟 diànzhōng electric clock

电子 diànzǐ electron:～秤 electronic-weighing system. ～管 electron tube; valve. ～计算机 (electronic) computer. ～窃听 electronic eavesdropping. ～玩具 electronic toys. ～邮件 electronic mail. ～游戏 electronic games; computer games. ～音乐 electronic music

佃 diàn〈动〉lease (rent) land (from a landlord)

佃耕 diàngēng tenant farming:～权 tenant right

佃户 diànhù tenant (farmer)

佃农 diànnóng tenant peasant; tenant farmer; tenants

佃权 diànquán rights of tenants

佃租 diànzū rent of the leased land; land rent

殿 diàn〈名〉① hall; temple; palace:养心～ Mind Nature Palace ②〈形〉past; rear

殿后 diànhòu bring up the rear

殿军 diànjūn ①［军］rearguard; rear ②［体］last winner in a contest

殿试 diànshì special palace examination; final imperial examination; palace examination

殿堂 diàntáng ① palace or temple buildings ② palace or temple halls

殿下 diànxià［直接称呼］Your Royal Highness;［间接称呼］His (Her) Royal Highness

靛 diàn〈名〉① indigo ② indigo-blue

靛蓝 diànlán indigo

靛青 diànqīng ① indigo-blue ② indigo

diāo

凋 diāo〈动〉wither; fade:瓶中的花～谢了。The flowers in the vase have faded.

凋敝 diāobì［生活］hard; destitute;［经］depressed:百业～。All business languished.

凋零 diāolíng ① (of flowers and plants) wither ② decline; be on the wane:百业～。All business languished. ③ die

凋落 diāoluò wither and fall

凋谢 diāoxiè ① wither; fade ② die (of old age):老成～ the passing away of worthy old people

貂 diāo〈名〉marten

貂皮 diāopí fur or pelt of marten; marten

碉 diāo pillbox; blockhouse:明～暗堡 blockhouse and bunker

碉堡 diāobǎo fort; pillbox; blockhouse

雕 diāo ①〈动〉carve; engrave; chisel:石～ stone carving ②〈名〉vulture; eagle

雕版印刷 diāobǎn yìnshuā woodblock printing; printing from engraved woodblocks; block printing

雕虫小技 diāochóng-xiǎojì insignificant skill (esp. in writing); literary skill of no higher order; petty skills comparable to the carving of insects; petty skills like the carving of insects

雕花 diāohuā ① carve patterns or designs on woodwork ② carving:～家具 carved furniture

雕刻 diāokè carve; engrave; chisel:～品 carved work; carving:～师 sculptor; engraver; carver

雕梁画栋 diāoliáng-huàdòng carved beams and painted rafters—a richly ornamented building

雕漆 diāoqī lacquer carvings

雕饰 diāoshì ① carve; engrave ② carvings; engravings ③ too elaborate; overwrought

雕塑 diāosù sculpture:～家 sculptor or sculptress

雕像 diāoxiàng statue; graven images:半身～ bust

雕琢 diāozhuó ① chisel (into) ② cut and polish; polish:～文字 polish the writing. ～性情 sculpture and polish human nature

刁 diāo〈形〉crafty; tricky; artful; cunning

刁悍 diāohàn cunning and fierce

刁难 diāonàn deliberate harassment; make trouble intentionally; make things difficult for sb.; create difficulties:百般～ put up innumerable obstacles

刁钻 diāozuān cunning; artful; wily:～古怪 sly and capricious. 发球～ tricky service

叼 diāo〈动〉hold in the mouth

叼羊 diāoyáng sheep wrestling, an entertaining game by a group of revellers on horseback contending for a lamb

diào

调 diào〈动〉① transfer; shift; move:～军队 move troops ② allot; allocate:～来一批钢材。A batch of rolled steel was allocated to us. ③ exchange:让我们～一下位子。Let's trade seats.〈名〉④ accent:南腔北～ (speak with) a moved accent ⑤ tone; tune:唱起…～子 strike up the tune of ⑥ melody; tune 另见 tiáo

调包 diàobāo stealthily substitute one thing for another

调兵 diàobīng move troops; transfer troops:～遣将 ① deploy forces ② dispose manpower

调拨 diàobō transfer and allocate (material goods or funds); allocate; appropriate:～物资 allocate supplies. ～款项 transfer and allocate funds

调查 diàochá investigate; inquire into:～报告 fact-finding report. ～表 questionnaire. ～对象 respondent; object under investigation

调动 diàodòng ① transfer; shift ② bring into play; mobilize; arouse; activate:～积极性 bring into a full play the initiative of; arouse (mobilize) the enthusiasm of; enhance one's enthusiasm

调度 diàodù ① manage; arrange; control ② [车辆] dispatch (cars):～员 dispatcher; controller

调防 diàofáng [军] relieve a garrison

调虎离山 diàohǔ-líshān lure the tiger out of the mountains; induce an enemy to go away from his base; make sb. leave his base

调回 diàohuí recall:～外汇 repatriate the foreign exchange

调集 diàojí assemble; muster:～兵力 assemble forces

调离 diàolí transfer out

调令 diàolìng transfer order

调派 diàopài allocate and dispatch:～一批干部支援大西北建设 allocate and dispatch a group of cadres to assist in the construction of the great Northwest

调配 diàopèi distribute; allocate:劳动力的合理～ rational distribution of manpower

调遣 diàoqiǎn dispatch; assign:听从～(be ready to) accept an assignment

调任 diàorèn be transferred to another post:他已～厂长。He has been transferred to be director of a factory

调研 diàoyán investigation and research; survey and study

调演 diàoyǎn transfer and perform (The management sector gathering various relevant performance groups together to perform their programmes, to view and emulate each other, to sum up experiences, and to promote the development of the arts.)

调用 diàoyòng transfer (under a unified plan):～物资 allocate materials

调阅 diàoyuè call for (documents, data, etc.) for consultation

调运 diàoyùn allocate and transport:～工业品下乡 allocate and ship industrial products to the countryside

调职 diàozhí be transferred to a new post:他奉命～。He received a horizontal promotion.

调子 diàozi tune; tone; melody:改变～ change one's tune. 定～ set the tone

掉 diào〈动〉① fall; drop:我的上衣～了一个扣子。A button has come off my coat. ② fall behind:～队 drop out; fall behind ③ lose; be missing:她把钥匙～了。She has lost her key. ④ decrease; lessen ⑤ exchange:～座位 change (exchange) seats ⑥ turn ⑦ [用在某些动词后,表示动作的完成]:洗～ wash out

掉包 diàobāo stealthily substitute one thing for another; change by trickery (into)

掉队 diàoduì drop out (off); fall behind:在急行军中,没有一个～的。No one dropped out in the forced march.

掉换 diàohuàn exchange; change; swap:～工作 be assigned a new job; be transferred to another post

掉魂 diàohún be frightened out of

one's wits

掉价 diàojià fall (drop) in price; go down in price:土豆～了。The price of potatoes has come down.

掉期资金 diàoqīzījīn funds used for changing the maturity of financial instruments in RMB

掉色 diàosè fade; discolour

掉头 diàotóu ① turn one's head ② turn round; turn back:～而去 fling off (away)

掉以轻心 diàoyǐqīngxīn let down one's guard; casual attitude; lower one's guard; treat sth. lightly

掉转 diàozhuǎn turn round; turn:～枪口 turn one's gun against

吊 diào〈动〉① hang; suspend:灯～在天花板上。The light was suspended from the ceiling. ② lift up or let down with a rope; etc. ③ condole; mourn:～丧 pay a condolence call ④ withdraw; revoke:～销 revoke (a licence, etc.)

吊膀子 diàobǎngzi〈方〉be speak love with one's eyes; carry on (with a person of the opposite sex)

吊车 diàochē crane; hoist:～梁 crane beam

吊灯 diàodēng pendent lamp

吊儿郎当 diào'érlāngdāng careless and casual; slovenly; dilly-dally

吊环 diàohuán [体] rings

吊嗓子 diàosǎngzi exercise one's voice; train one's voice; sing scales:他每天早上～。He sings scales every morning.

吊丧 diàosāng visit the bereaved to offer one's condolences; pay a condolence call

吊扇 diàoshàn ceiling fan

吊死 diàosǐ hang by the neck; hang oneself

吊胃口 diàowèikǒu tantalize

吊销 diàoxiāo revoke; withdraw; cancel:～执照 revoke a licence

吊孝 diàoxiào visit the bereaved to offer one's condolences; pay a condolence call

吊唁 diàoyàn condole; offer one's condolence:～信 letter of condolence

吊运 diàoyùn hoist and transport

钓 diào ①〈动〉fish with a hook and line; angle:～鱼去 go fishing ②〈名〉angle; fish:沽名～誉 fish for fame and praise

钓饵 diào'ěr ① bait ② lure

钓竿 diàogān fishing rod

钓钩 diàogōu fishhook

钓具 diàojù fishing tackle

钓鱼 diàoyú angle; go fishing

diē

跌 diē〈动〉① fall; tumble:～入小河 tumble into a stream ② go down; fall:河水～了。The river has sunk. ③ drop; fall:物价骤～。The prices drop sharply.

跌打损伤 diēdǎ-sǔnshāng injures from falls, fractures, contusions and strains

跌宕(荡) diēdàng free and easy; bold and unconstrained

跌倒 diēdǎo fall; tumble: ～在地 fall to the ground; fall (down)

跌跌撞撞 diēdiē-zhuàngzhuàng dodder along; stagger along: 她～地出了门。She staggered out of the house.

跌价 diējià fall (drop) in price; go down in price

跌跤 diējiāo ① trip and fall ② suffer a setback; make a mistake

爹 diē〈名〉father; dad

dié

谍 dié ①〈名〉espionage ②〈动〉spy on

谍报 diébào intelligence: ～员 intelligence agent

碟 dié〈名〉small dish; saucer

碟子 diézi small plate (dish); saucer

喋 dié

喋喋不休 diédié-bùxiū talk unceasingly (about); rattle away; an endless stream of words

喋血 diéxuè bloodshed: ～沙场 shed blood on the battlefield

蝶 dié〈名〉butterfly

蝶泳 diéyǒng butterfly stroke

牒 dié〈名〉an official document or note: ～文 notes. 最后通～ ultimatum

迭 dié ①〈动〉change; alternate: 更～ alternate ②〈副〉repeatedly; again and again: ～克名城 capture one well-known city after another

迭次 diécì repeatedly; again and again; time and again

迭句 diéjù refrain

迭起 diéqǐ happen frequently; occur repeatedly

叠 dié〈动〉① fold ② pile up; overlap: 重～ overlap

叠床架屋 diéchuáng-jiàwū unnecessary duplication or repetition

叠句 diéjù reiterative sentence

叠罗汉 diéluóhàn [体] pyramid

dīng

丁 dīng〈名〉① grown man; grown-up ② member of a family; population: ～口 population ③ cubes (of meat or vegetables): 黄瓜～ diced cucumber ④ fourth

丁当 dīngdāng〈象〉ding-dong; jingle; clatter: 铃儿～响。The bell jingled.

丁口册 dīngkǒucè household census

丁零 dīnglíng〈象〉tinkle; jingle: ～～的自行车铃声 the jingling of bicycle bells

丁宁 dīngníng urge again and again; warn; exhort

丁是丁,卯是卯 dīng shì dīng, mǎo shì mǎo keep *ding* (a Heavenly Stem) distinct from *mao* (an Earthly Branch)—be strict; be precise; be unaccommodating

丁税 dīngshuì poll tax

丁忧 dīngyōu be in mourning for a parent

丁字尺 dīngzìchǐ T-square

叮 dīng〈动〉① sting; bite:她被黄蜂~了一下。She was stung by a wasp. ② say or ask again to make sure

叮咛 dīngníng urge again and again; exhort

叮嘱 dīngzhǔ urge again and again; repeatedly advise; press advice upon; exhort:~某人要小心 exhort sb. to be careful

盯 dīng〈动〉fix one's eyes on; stare at; gaze at:~着眼睛瞧 stare fixedly at

盯(钉)梢 dīngshāo shadow sb.; tail sb.:他被警察~。He was shadowed by the police.

钉 dīng ①〈名〉nail; tack:拔出~子 draw (pull) out a nail 〈动〉② follow closely tail:贼被警察~住了。The thief was tailed by a policeman. ③ lurge; press:你一定要~着她吃药,别让她忘了。You must remind her to take her medicine, in case she forgets. ③ fix one's eyes on; gaze at

另见 dìng

钉帽 dīngmào the head of a nail

钉人 dīngrén [体] watch (mark) an opponent in a game:~防守 man-for-man (man-to-man) defence

钉是钉,铆是铆 dīng shì dīng, mǎo shì mǎo 见"丁是丁,卯是卯"

钉梢 dīngshāo follow closely behind; dog; tail

钉子 dīngzi nail:碰~ meet with a rebuff; run into snags. ~精神 spirit of the nail (metaphor for a spirit of assiduous study whereby one grasps every available minute and second). ~户 recalcitrants (Squatters who occupy construction sites and refuse to move as in accordance with government ordinances or related agreements, and who extort from state construction units.)

dǐng

顶 dǐng ①〈名〉top; peak; crown:山~ mountain top〈动〉② carry on the head:头上~着一罐水 carry a pitcher of water on one's head ③ prop; support; sustain:把门~起来 prop up the door ④ go against:~得住风浪 withstand any upheaval ⑤ retort; turn down:我~了他几句。I said a few words to him in retort. ⑥ take the place of:他~患病的工人干活。He substituted for the worker who was ill. ⑦ equal; be equivalent to ⑧ cope with; stand up to:妇女能~半边天。Women hold up half of heaven (half the sky). ⑨〈量〉:一~轿子 a sedan chair ⑩〈副〉very; most:~聪明 most intelligent

顶班 dǐngbān work on regular shifts; substituting in the ranks:李厂长经常在车间~劳动。Factory Manager Li often works as a substitute in the ranks in the workshop.

顶戴 dǐngdài ① salute; pay one's respects to ② buttons worn on Qing Dynasty officials' hats as a sign of rank

顶点 dǐngdiǎn climax; zenith; summit; culmination

顶端 dǐngduān ① top; peak; apex ② end:他们走到大桥的~。They walked to the end of the bridge.

顶多 dǐngduō at (the) most; at best

顶风 dǐngfēng ① against the wind:~冒雨 brave wind and rain; be undeterred by wind and rain; in spite of wind and rain. ~骑车 cycle against the wind ② head wind

顶峰 dǐngfēng peak; summit; pinnacle

顶好 dǐnghǎo ① very good ② had better; it would be best:你们~现在就动身回去。You'd better start going back now.

顶礼 dǐnglǐ prostrate oneself before sb. and press one's head against his feet:~膜拜 prostrate oneself before; prostrate oneself in worship; make a festish of; pay homage to; paying homage to

顶门杠 dǐngméngàng door bolt

顶球 dǐngqiú [足球] head (a ball)

顶事 dǐngshì be useful; serve the purpose:这女孩子可~啦! The girl is a great help!

顶数 dǐngshù ① serve as a fill-in; make up the number ② [通常与否定式连用] useful; effective:我说的不~。What I say carries little weight.

顶替 dǐngtì take the place of; replace; supplant:~工 replacement workers

顶天立地 dǐngtiān-lìdì upright and high-minded; indomitable; of indomitable spirit

顶头上司 dǐngtóu shàngsī one's direct (immediate) superior

顶用 dǐngyòng serve (the purpose); be of use (help):绳子太短,不~。The string is too short to serve.

顶住 dǐngzhù ① prop up ② stand up to; stand one's ground in the face of …; hold out against; weather; withstand:~错误思潮 strongly against the wrong ideological tendency

顶撞 dǐngzhuàng contradict (one's elder or superior):~父母 contradict one's parents

顶租 dǐngzū ① pay rent in kind or by labour ② rent deposit

顶嘴 dǐngzuǐ reply defiantly (usu. to one's elder or superior); answer back; talk back:你不该跟你母亲~。You shouldn't talk back to your mother.

鼎 dǐng 〈名〉 an ancient three-legged tripod or four legged cauldron for meat and cereals; tripod; quadripod

鼎鼎大名 dǐngdǐng-dàmíng of great celebrity; very famous; well-known; celebrated; the illustrious

鼎沸 dǐngfèi like a seething cauldron; noisy and confused

鼎立 dǐnglì [三个对抗势力] stand like the three legs of a tripod; exist tripartitely; tripartite confrontation

鼎力 dǐnglì your kind effort:多蒙～协助,无任感谢。We are extremely grateful to you for the trouble you have taken on our behalf.

鼎盛 dǐngshèng at its most prosperous; reaching the zenith; unsurpassed height of power; at the height of power and splendour:～时期 in a period of great prosperity

鼎新 dǐngxīn make innovations

鼎新革故 dǐngxīn-gégù discard the old ways of life and in favour of the new; drop old habits and reform

鼎足 dǐngzú the three legs of a tripod—three rival powers

鼎足之势 dǐngzúzhīshì a situation of tripartite confrontation; a situation dominated by three powerful rivals

dìng

定 dìng〈动〉① decide; fix; set: ～调子 set the tone (keynote) ② calm; stabilize:安邦～国 bring peace and stability to the country ③ subscribe to (a newspaper, etc.); book (seats, tickets, etc.); order (merchandise, etc.):～货 order goods〈形〉④ calm; stable:心神不～ be ill at ease ⑤ settled; fixed; established:～论 final verdict (conclusion); finalized ⑥〈副〉surely; certainly; definitely:～可成功 certainly will succeed

定案 dìng'àn ① decide a case; decide on a plan; make a verdict ② final decision; verdict

定编 dìngbiān personnel allocation (determining the set-up of departments, personnel quotas, and responsibility assignments)

定产、定购、定销 dìngchǎn dìnggòu dìngxiāo fixed quota system for producing, purchasing and marketing

定单 dìngdán ① order for goods; order (form) ② [书、报刊等] subscription order

定点 dìngdiǎn fixed location:物资～供应 direct supply of material at fixed location

定调子 dìngdiàozi set the tone (keynote)

定都 dìngdū choose a site for the capital; establish a capital:～北京 make Beijing the capital; decide on Beijing as the capital

定夺 dìngduó make a final decision; decide

定额 dìng'é fixed number or amount; norm; quota:～包工 job contract with quota. ～包工计酬 payment on the basis of fixed quotas; quota remuneration

定岗 dìnggǎng determining posts (it refers to the establishment of the system of responsibility for each post within a Party political organization, a mass organization, or a professional unit.)

定稿 dìnggǎo finalize a manuscript (text, etc.); final version or text

定购 dìnggòu ①［货物等］order (goods, etc.); place an order for sth. ② purchase with a quota; rationed purchase; fixed quota for purchasing

定规 dìngguī ① established rule or practice; set pattern: 并无～。There's no hard and fast rule. ② be bent on; be determined

定婚 dìnghūn be engaged (to be married); be betrothed

定货 dìnghuò place an order for goods; order goods

定级 dìngjí decide grade and level

定价 dìngjià ① fixed price; price fixing ② fix a price; set price

定金 dìngjīn earnest (money); bargain money; handsel; down payment

定居 dìngjū settle down: 在上海～ settle down in Shanghai

定局 dìngjú ① foregone conclusion; inevitable outcome. ② settle finally: 事情还没有～。The matter isn't settled yet.

定理 dìnglǐ theorem: 基本～ fundamental theorem

定量 dìngliàng fixed quantity; ration: ～分析 quantitative analysis. ～供应 supply on ration

定律 dìnglǜ (scientific) law: 万有引力～ the law of universal gravitation

定论 dìnglùn final conclusion.

定评 dìngpíng fixed assessment: 历史的～ historical conclusion

定期 dìngqī regular; at the fixed date; at regular intervals; periodical: ～存款 fixed deposit. ～交货 delivery on term. ～徒刑 penal for a fixed time

定钱 dìngqian deposit; earnest (money)

定亲 dìngqīn engagement (usu. arranged by parents); betrothal: 她已跟赵家的儿子定了亲。She is betrothed to a son of the Zhao family.

定神 dìngshén ① collect oneself; compose oneself; pull oneself together. ② concentrate one's attention: 听见有人叫我,～一看,原来是小王。I heard someone calling me and, looking hard, saw that it was Xiao Wang.

定位 dìngwèi determine position: 教师～ assign teachers to positions

定息 dìngxī fixed interest; fixed rate of interest on capital

定向 dìngxiàng determine direction: ～分配 fixed direction of allocation. ～广播 fixed direction broadcast. ～培养 fixed direction training. ～招生 directioned recruitment of students

定型 dìngxíng finalize the design; become fixed: ～的经济制度 economic system with a complete set of fixed practices

定性 dìngxìng determine (refine) the nature: ～分析 qualitative analysis

定员 dìngyuán fixed number of staff; quota system for use of labour; stipulated number of persons

定制 dìngzhì ① have sth. made to order; have sth. custom-made: ～家具 have furniture made to order ② an established rule or practice

定罪 dìngzuì determine a crime; criminate; declare sb. guilty: ～量刑 punishment fits the crime. ～量刑的标准 criterion for conviction

定做 dìngzuò [衣、鞋等] have (one's clothes, shoes, etc.) made to order (measure)

定座 dìngzuò book a seat; make reservations

碇 dìng〈名〉a heavy stone used as an anchor; killick

碇泊 dìngbó anchor; berth

锭 dìng〈动〉①〈名〉ingot-shaped tablet (of medicine, metal, Chinese ink, etc.) ②[纺] spindle ③〈量〉:一～墨 an ink stick

锭子 dìngzi spindle

订 dìng〈动〉① make; draw up; conclude: ～生产指标 set a production target ② revise; make corrections: 修～ revise ③ subscribe; order: ～一桌酒席 order a dinner ④ bind; staple together: 把报纸～在一起 bind the newspaper together

订单 dìngdān order for goods; order form

订购(货) dìnggòu (huò) order (goods); place an order for goods: ～会 orders invitation conference

订户 dìnghù subscriber (to a newspaper, periodical, etc.)

订婚 dìnghūn be engaged to (betrothed): ～戒指 engagement ring

订货 dìnghuò order goods; place an order for goods: ～确认书 confirmation of order

订立 dìnglì [合同] make (a contract); [条约] conclude (a treaty)

订约 dìngyuē conclude a contract or treaty

订阅 dìngyuè subscribe (to a newspaper, periodical, etc.)

订正 dìngzhèng correct; revise; emend; rectify; make corrections

钉 dìng〈动〉① nail: ～马掌 nail on horseshoes ② sew on: ～扣子 sew a button on
另见 dīng

diū

丢 diū〈动〉① throw; cast; toss: 把纸～在废纸篓 throw the paper away into the wastebasket ② lose; be missing: 她

的钱包～了。She has lost her purse. ③ put (lay) aside：我的英语～了好几年了，都忘得差不多了。I haven't used my English for years and have forgotten almost all of it.

丢丑 diūchǒu lose face; be disgraced

丢掉 diūdiào ① lose：她～了一支笔。She has lost her pen. ② throw away; cast away; discard：～官气 shed one's bureaucratic airs

丢盔卸甲 diūkuī-xièjiǎ throw away one's shield and armour; fly pellmell; throw away one's helmet and coat of mail; throw away everything in headlong flight

丢脸(人) diūliǎn(rén) lose face; be disgraced; bring shame (disgrace)

丢面子 diū miànzi lose face

丢人现眼 diūrén-xiànyǎn make a fool of oneself; make a spectacle of oneself

丢三落四 diūsān-làsì be always forgetting things; missing this and that; forgetful

丢眼色 diū yǎnsè tip sb. a wink; wink at sb.; shoot a glance at; give a hint with eyes

丢卒保车 diūzú-bǎojū give up a pawn to save a chariot — sacrifice minor things to save major ones

dōng

东 dōng〈名〉① east ② master; owner：股～ shareholder; stockholder ③ host：～道国 host country. 做～ stand treat (host); play the host

东半球 dōngbànqiú the Eastern Hemisphere

东奔西走 dōngbēn-xīzǒu run to and fro; move (drive) from post to pillar and from pillar to post; run around here and there; bustle about; rush about (around)

东窗事发 dōngchuāng-shìfā the plot has come to light; the secret is out

东倒西歪 dōngdǎo-xīwāi leaning; unsteady; tottering：～地在马路上走 stagger along the road

东道 dōngdào one who treats sb. to a meal; host：做～ play the host; stand treat

东方 dōngfāng ① east ② the Orient; the East：～社会理论 theory on Oriental society. ～艺术 Oriental art

东拉西扯 dōnglā-xīchě ramble (about); drag in irrelevant matters; tittle-tattle (about)

东鳞西爪 dōnglín-xīzhǎo odds and ends; bits and pieces; fragments：～地收集材料 glean scraps of information

东南亚 Dōngnányà Southeast Asia：～国家联盟 the Association of Southeast Asian Nations (ASEAN)

东欧 Dōng Ōu Eastern Europe

东拼西凑 dōngpīn-xīcòu scrape together; knock together; scissors-and-paste work; hodgepodge

东山再起 dōngshān-zàiqǐ stage a comeback; return to power

东西 dōngxī east and west:～对话 East-West dialogue

东西 dōngxi ① thing:她收拾好～就走了。She packed her things and left. 一成不变的～是没有的。Nothing is immutable. 他买～去。He's out shopping. ②[指人或动物] thing; creature:这小～真可爱。What a sweet little thing!. 真不是～! What a despicable creature!

东乡族 Dōngxiāngzú the Dongxiang (Tunghsiang) nationality, or the Dongxiangs (Tunghsiangs), inhabiting Gansu Province

东亚 Dōngyà East Asia

东一榔头,西一棒子 dōng yī lángtou, xī yī bàngzi hammer here and batter there; act or speak haphazardly; act in a hit-or-miss fashion

东瀛 dōngyíng ① the Donghai Sea; the East China Sea ② Japan

东张西望 dōngzhāng-xīwàng gaze (peer) around; glance this way and that; look in every direction

冬

dōng〈名〉winter

冬储 dōngchǔ store away in winter

冬耕 dōnggēng winter ploughing

冬季 dōngjì winter:～施工 winter construction. ～作物 winter crops

冬眠 dōngmián winter sleep; hibernation

冬闲 dōngxián slack winter season (in farming)

冬学 dōngxué winter classes

冬泳 dōngyǒng winter outdoor swimming

冬至 dōngzhì the Winter Solstice

冬装 dōngzhuāng winter dress (clothes)

dǒng

董

dǒng

董事 dǒngshì director; trustee:～会 board of directors (trustees). ～长 chairman (president) of the board (of directors)

懂

dǒng〈动〉understand; know:～政策 have a grasp of policy

懂得 dǒngde understand; know; grasp

懂行 dǒngháng know the ropes; know the business

懂事 dǒngshì sensible; perceptible; intelligent:～一点 have a little more sense

dòng

动

dòng〈动〉① move; stir:不许～! Don't move! ② act; get moving:不要轻举妄～。Don't make a rash act. ③ use:～脑筋 use one's head ④ alter; change ⑤ touch (one's heart); move:～人的情景 moving (affecting) scene ⑥〈名〉action; movement：一举一～ every movement(act)

动笔 dòngbǐ take up the pen；start writing：她最近很少～。She hasn't done much writing recently.

动不动 dòngbudòng easily；frequently；at every turn：～就发火 be apt to lose one's temper；often get into a temper

动产 dòngchǎn movable property；personal estate；movables；personal property：～抵押 pledge of movables

动词 dòngcí［语］verb：～不定式 infinitive

动荡 dòngdàng turbulence；unrest；upheaval：～不定的市面 unsettled market

动荡不安 dòngdàng-bù'ān turbulent；in turmoil

动工 dònggōng ① begin construction；start building ② construct：这里正在～，车辆不能通过。Construction site ahead. No thoroughfare.

动画片 dònghuàpiàn cartoon；animated cartoon

动机 dòngjī motive；intention；motivation：～和效果的统一 the unity of motive and effect. ～好 act with the best of intentions

动静 dòngjìng sound of people speaking or moving about；state of affairs；movement；happenings

动力 dònglì motive force；driving force；motivation；impetus：～机制 dynamic mechanism；motivational mechanism. ～心理治疗 dynamic psychotherapy

动乱 dòngluàn turmoil；turbulence；ferment：～的年代 turbulent years

动脉 dòngmài［生理］artery：～脉搏 arterial pulse

动名词 dòngmíngcí［语］gerund

动能 dòngnéng kinetic energy

动迁户 dòngqiānhù relocated households

动情 dòngqíng ①get worked up；become excited ②become enamoured；have one's (sexual) passions aroused

动人 dòngrén moving；catchy；touching：～的故事 moving story

动人心弦 dòngrénxīnxián tug at one's heartstrings；be deeply moving

动身 dòngshēn go (set out) on a journey；leave (for a distant place)

动手 dòngshǒu ① start；set to work ② touch：请勿～［揭示语］Hands off!；Please don't touch!

动手动脚 dòngshǒu-dòngjiǎo get fresh with sb.；be fresh with a gril：别～的。Keep your hands to yourself.

动手术 dòngshǒushù operate on sb.；perform an operation：为某人～切除肿瘤 operate on (upon) sb. for a tumour ② under an operation；be operated

动态 dòngtài movements；trends；tendency；development：～经济分析 analysis of dynamic economy

动弹不得 dòngtanbùdé cannot move：车里太挤，～。The bus was so crowded that nobody could move.

动听 dòngtīng interesting or pleasant to listen to

动土 dòngtǔ break ground；start building

动武 dòngwǔ use violence；resort to force；start a fight；come to blows

动物 dòngwù animal：～园 zoo. ～志 fauna. ～寓言 bestiary. ～艺术家 animalist

动向 dòngxiàng tendency；trend：改革的新～ new trends in the reform

动心 dòngxīn one's mind is perturbed；one's desire，enthusiasm or interest is aroused

动摇 dòngyáo waver；shake；falter；move：～军心 shake the morale of…

动议 dòngyì motion；proposal

动因 dòngyīn efficient cause；dynamic cause；motivating cause；cause

动用 dòngyòng employ；put to use；draw on （funds，resources，etc.）：～储备金 dissave. ～库存 draw on stock

动员 dòngyuán mobilize：～舆论 mobilize public opinion；arouse public opinion. 总～ general mobilization

动作 dòngzuò action；movement：～研究 action research

冻 dòng〈动〉freeze；congeal

冻冰 dòngbīng freeze：河上～了。The river is frozen.

冻疮 dòngchuāng chilblain：生～ have chilblains

冻僵 dòngjiāng numb with cold；frozen stiff

冻结 dòngjié freeze；congeal：～资金 freeze funds；frozen funds

冻馁之忧 dòngněizhīyōu fear of cold and starvation

冻肉 dòngròu frozen meat

冻伤 dòngshāng frostbite

冻死 dòngsǐ be frozen to death；die of cold

栋 dòng〈名〉ridge-beam（-pole）

栋梁 dòngliáng ① ridge beam；pillar ② pillar of the state：～之才 man of tremendous promise

洞 dòng〈名〉hole；cave；opening

洞察 dòngchá have an insight into；see through；see clearly；penetrate：～力 a penetrating insight into；insight；acuity；discernment. ～真理 discern the truth

洞彻 dòngchè understand thoroughly；see clearly：～事理 be sensible and perfectly aware

洞房 dòngfáng bridal chamber；nuptial chamber：～花烛 wedding festivities；wedding

洞若观火 dòngruòguānhuǒ see sth. as clearly as day；see sth. as a blazing fire

洞穴 dòngxuè cave；grotto；cavern：～岩画 cave paintings. ～艺术 cave art

洞烛其奸 dòngzhú-qíjiān know one's villainy fully；see through one's tricks

洞烛幽微 dòngzhú-yōuwēi bring to light the faintest details important

恫 dòng

恫吓 dònghè bully; intimidate; threaten: 不怕～ defy any intimidation

侗 dòng

侗族 Dòngzú Dong nationality (living in Guizhou and Hunan provinces and the Guangxi Zhuang Autonomous Region)

胴 dòng〈名〉① trunk; torso ② large intestine

胴体 dòngtǐ trunk

dōu

都 dōu〈副〉① all; both: 关于这件事,该说的我～说了。I have said all there is to be said about it. ②［跟"是"连用,说明理由］just because of: ～是你多嘴,看他生气了。Look, he is annoyed. It's all because of your unsolicited remarks. ③ even: 这种小事连小孩～知道。Even a child knows all this. ④ already: 她～80 岁了。She's already eighty.

兜 dōu〈动〉① go round; move round: 说话别～圈子。Come straight to the point. ② wrap up in a piece of cloth, etc.: 用毛巾～着一些苹果 carry some apples wrapped up in a towel ③ canvass: ～售 peddle; hawk; tout ④〈名〉pocket

兜底 dōudǐ reveal all the details (of a person's disreputable background, etc.); disclose the whole inside story

兜风 dōufēng ① take an airing; go for a drive ②［船帆等］catch the wind

兜揽 dōulǎn canvass for; solicit: ～生意 solicit business

兜圈子 dōuquānzi ① go round; revolve in a circle; revolve around ② speak in a roundabout way

兜售 dōushòu peddle; hawk: ～劣货 hawk low-quality goods

dǒu

斗 dǒu ①〈量〉*dou*, a unit of dry measure for grain (= 1 decalitre); ②〈名〉an object shape like a cup or dipper: 烟～ (tobacco) pipe
另见 dòu

斗胆 dǒudǎn make bold; be of great courage; venture: ～建议 venture to suggest

斗笠 dǒulì bamboo hat

斗篷 dǒupeng ① cape; cloak ② bamboo hat

斗室 dǒushì a small room

抖 dǒu〈动〉① tremble; shiver: 吓得发～ tremble with fright ② shake; jerk: ～掉根部的泥土 shake the earth away from the roots ③ stir up; rouse: ～起精神 pluck up one's spirits

抖擞 dǒusǒu rouse; brace up, enliven; pick up: 精神～ be high spirits; in soaring spirits; be full of energy

抖威风 dǒuwēifēng throw one's weight about

陡 dǒu ①〈形〉steep; precipitous: ～起变化 a drastic change ②〈副〉abruptly; suddenly: ～然减为 drastically fall

陡壁 dǒubì cliff; precipice; steep

陡峻 dǒujùn high and precipitous

陡立 dǒulì rise steeply

陡坡 dǒupō steep slope

陡峭 dǒuqiào steep; precipitous

陡削 dǒuxuē precipitous: ～的山崖 a sheer precipice

dòu

斗 dòu〈动〉① struggle; fight: ～争锋芒 spearhead of the struggle against ② contest with; contend with: 我～不过你。I'm not your match.
另见 dǒu

斗法 dòufǎ ① exercise magic powers against each other ② use stratagems

斗富 dòufù financial one-upmanship; vie with each other in wealth

斗牛 dòuniú bullfight: ～士 bullfighter; matador

斗殴 dòu'ōu affray; brawl

斗气 dòuqì quarrel or contend with sb. on account of a personal grudge

斗士 dòushì fighter (for a cause)

斗争 dòuzhēng ① struggle; fight; combat ② accuse and denounce at a meeting ③ strive for; fight for; 为完成第九个五年计划而～ strive for the fulfilment of the Ninth Five-Year Plan (1996—2000)

斗志 dòuzhì fighting will: ～昂扬 filled with militancy; militant; have a high morale

斗智 dòuzhì duel of wits: 外交上的～ diplomatic swordplay

豆 dòu〈名〉bean; pea

豆包 dòubāo steamed bun stuffed with sweetened bean paste

豆腐 dòufu bean curd: ～帐 bean curd account (An account which is simple and recorded at any time. It is a metaphor for simply enumerating facts and not making any deep analysis.)

豆浆 dòujiāng soya-bean milk

豆蔻年华 dòukòu-niánhuá (of a girl) in one's early teens

豆沙 dòushā sweetened bean paste

豆渣 dòuzhā residue from beans after making soya-bean milk; bean dregs

豆制品 dòuzhìpǐn bean products

痘 dòu〈名〉smallpox: ～苗 vaccine

逗 dòu〈动〉① tease; play with: ～小女孩玩 play with a little girl ② provoke; amuse; attract; charm: 这小男孩真～人喜欢。He's a charming little boy. ③ stay; stop: 在上海稍作

～留 make a short stay in Shanghai ④〈形〉funny：这话真～！What a funny remark！

逗号 dòuhào comma（，）

逗留 dòuliú stay；stop

逗弄 dòunòng tease；tantalize；make fun of

逗趣 dòuqù amuse；set people laughing（by funny remarks，etc.）

dū

都 dū〈名〉capital；city：首～capital
另见 dōu

都城 dūchéng capital（of a country）

都会 dūhuì a big city；metropolis

都市 dūshì large city；metropolis：～化 urbanization

督 dū〈动〉supervise；inspect

督办 dūbàn supervise and handle

督察 dūchá superintend；supervise

督促 dūcù supervise and urge；press；urge

督造 dūzào supervise the manufacture：～兵器 supervise arms manufacture

嘟 dū ①〈象〉toot；honk：汽车喇叭～～响。The car tooted. ②〈动〉pout：生气地～起了嘴 pout sulkily

嘟囔 dūnang mutter to oneself；mumble

dú

毒 dú〈名〉① poison；toxin：剧～ rank poison ② drug；narcotics：贩～ traffic in drugs〈形〉③ poisonous；toxic：～草 poisonous weeds ④ cruel；fierce：～打某人 beat sb. mercilessly ⑤〈动〉poison；kill with poison：受～害 be poisoned by

毒打 dúdǎ beat sb. up；flog

毒害 dúhài do harm to；poison（sb.'s mind）

毒化 dúhuà poison；spoil

毒计 dújì insidious scheme；deadly trap；venomous scheme

毒辣 dúlà pernicious and sinister；treacherous；vicious；diabolic；murderous

毒品 dúpǐn drugs；narcotics：～犯罪 drug-related crimes

毒气 dúqì poison（poisonous）gas

毒手 dúshǒu murderous plot；malicious scheme：下～ lay murderous hands on sb.；resort to murderous means：遭～ fall a victim to a malicious scheme

毒死 dúsǐ kill by means of poison；poison

毒素 dúsù poisonous substance（influence）；poison

毒药 dúyào poisonous dose；poison；toxicant

渎 dú〈动〉show disrespect or contempt：亵～ blaspheme；profane

渎职 dúzhí dereliction of duty；malfeasance；malpractice

读 dú〈动〉① read; read aloud: 你～这本小说了吗? Have you read this novel? ② read: 泛～ read extensively ③ attend school; go to school or college: ～不起书 cannot afford to go to school

读本 dúběn reader; textbook

读书 dúshū ① read; study; book-learning: ～班 study class ② go to school

读数 dúshù [物] reading: 温度计～ readings on the thermometer

读物 dúwù reading material: 通俗～ popular literature

读写能力 dúxiě nénglì [教] literacy

读音 dúyīn pronunciation

读者 dúzhě reader: ～来信 letters to the editor

牍 dú ① wooden tablets or slips for writing (in ancient times) ② documents; archives; correspondence

黩 dú〈动〉① blacken; defile ② act wantonly

黩武 dúwǔ warlike; militaristic; bellicose: ～主义者 militarist; sabre-rattler

独 dú ①〈形〉single; only; sole: ～木不成林。One tree does not make a forest; One swallow does not make a summer ②〈副〉alone; by oneself; in solitude: ～居 live a solitary existence ③〈名〉old people without offspring

独霸 dúbà dominate exclusively; monopolize: ～一方 lord it over a district; be a local despot

独白 dúbái [剧] soliloquy; soliloquize; monologue

独裁 dúcái dictatorship; autocratic rule: ～政治 autocracy

独唱(曲) dúchàng(qǔ) solo; vocal solo

独出心裁 dúchū-xīncái original; creative

独创 dúchuàng substantiality and originality; original creation; creative: ～与学习外国经验相结合 combine learning from foreign experience with our own creative efforts

独当一面 dúdǎng-yīmiàn take charge of one field of work; take charge of a department or locality; assume responsibility for a certain sector

独到 dúdào original: ～的见解 original view. ～之处 distinctive qualities; specific characteristics

独断 dúduàn arbitrary; dictatorial

独断独行 dúduàn-dúxíng indulge in arbitrary decisions and peremptory actions; take arbitrary action; decide and act arbitrarily; make dictatorial decision; act personally in all matters

独家 dújiā sole; the only one; exclusive: ～经销 sole agent. ～新闻 exclusive

独家代理 dújiā dàilǐ exclusive (sole) agency: ～人 sole agent. ～商 exclusive factory sales agent

独脚戏 dújiǎoxì one-man show; monodrama:唱～ put on a one-man show; do the work alone

独立核算 dúlì hésuàn conduct business accounting independently; independent business accounting; keep separate accounts

独立自主 dúlì-zìzhǔ maintain independence and keep the initiative in one's own hands

独揽 dúlǎn monopolize; arrogate:～经济大权 arrogate financial powers to oneself

独联体 Dúliántǐ the Commonwealth of Independent States

独龙族 Dúlóngzú the Drung (Tulung) nationality, or the Drungs (Tulungs), inhabiting Yunnan Province

独幕剧 dúmùjù one-act play

独木不成林 dúmù bù chéng lín one tree doesn't make a forest—one person alone can't accomplish much

独善其身 dúshàn-qíshēn maintain one's own integrity

独身 dúshēn ① separated from one's family:～在外 be away from home and family ② unmarried; single:～主义 celibacy. 她现在还是～。She's still single.

独生子女 dúshēng zǐnǚ only child

独树一帜 dúshù-yīzhì fly one's own colours; have a style of one's own

独特 dútè singular; distinctive; special; unique:京剧的～艺术风格 special characteristics of Beijing opera art

独行其是 dúxíngqíshì do what one thinks is right regardless of others' opinions

独一无二 dúyī-wú'èr unique; unparalleled; unmatched

独占 dúzhàn have sth. all to oneself; monopolize:～鳌头 stand first on the list; come out first. ～市场 monopolize the market

独资 dúzī investment by a sole investor; exclusive (sole) investment:～企业 ventures exclusively with one's own investment; solely foreign-owned enterprises

独自 dúzì alone; by oneself:她～一人走向电影院。She walked on alone towards the cinema.

独奏 dúzòu play a solo; instrumental solo; solo:钢琴～ piano solo. ～会 recital (of an instrumentalist)

dǔ

堵 dǔ〈动〉close; stop up; block up:～住嘴巴 silence sb.; gag sb.

堵击 dǔjī intercept and attack:～逃敌 intercept the fleeing enemy

堵塞 dǔsè stop up; block up:～税收漏洞 close tax loopholes. ～生产门路 block the channels of developing production

堵嘴 dǔzuǐ gag sb.; silence sb.:你别想堵住我的嘴。You can't stop me from speaking out.

赌 dǔ〈动〉① gamble:禁～ ban gambling ② bet; stake:我提出与他打～。I offered to bet with him.

赌本 dǔběn ① money to gamble with ② resources for risky ventures

赌博 dǔbó gambling

赌场 dǔchǎng gambling house

赌具 dǔjù gambling paraphernalia; gambling device

赌气 dǔqì feel wronged and act rashly; in a fit of pique:～走了 go away (dash off) in a fit of pique

赌钱 dǔqián gamble

赌徒 dǔtú gambler; gamester

赌咒 dǔzhòu swear; take an oath

赌注 dǔzhù a counter for gambling; stake; wager:下～ lay (make) a wager (on). ～押在…身上 put one's stakes on

笃 dǔ〈形〉① sincere; earnest; honest:～行 sincere conduct ② [病] serious; dangerous; critical:病～ be dangerously ill; be in a critical condition

笃定 dǔdìng ① certain; sure ② in a leisurely way:他们可以～取胜。They can be certain of success.

笃厚 dǔhòu sincere and magnanimous

笃信 dǔxìn have great faith in; sincerely believe in:～好学 be of unwavering good faith and love learning

笃学 dǔxué be diligent in study; devoted to study

肚 dǔ〈名〉tripe
另见 dù

dù

度 dù〈名〉① limit; extent; degree:高～的政治觉悟 a high degree of political consciousness ② linear measure ③ magnanimity; tolerance:豁达大～ open-minded and magnanimous ④ consideration ⑤〈动〉pass; spend:欢～节日 joyously celebrate a festival ⑥〈量〉occasion; time:一年一～ once a year
另见 duó

度荒 dùhuāng tide over a lean year

度假 dùjià spend one's holidays (vacation); go vacationing

度量 dùliàng capacity for tolerance; tolerance:～大 generous; magnanimous; broad-minded. ～小 ungenerous; narrow-minded

度量衡 dùliànghéng weights and measures

度日 dùrì eke out an existence; live one's life:他～如年。Time hangs heavy on his hands.; He lives a hard life.

渡 dù〈动〉① cross (a river, etc.):她东～去日本。She crossed over to Japan. ② tide over; pull through:～过经济困难 tide (get) over economic difficulties ③ ferry:～人过河 ferry people across a river

渡船 dùchuán ferryboat; ferry

渡过 dùguò ① pass; cross; sail across ② tide over:～难关 tide (bridge) over a difficulty

渡口 dùkǒu ferry; ferry crossings

渡轮 dùlún ferry steamer; ferryboat

镀 dù〈动〉plate

镀金 dùjīn ① gild; gold-plating ② get a gilding; get gilded by; win a name

镀锡 dùxī tin-plating; tinning

镀锌 dùxīn zinc-plating; galvanizing

镀银 dùyín silver-plating; silvering

杜 dù〈动〉① shut-out; stop; prevent ②［门］close (one's door)

杜绝 dùjué stop; eradicate; put an end to:～浪费 put an end to waste; eliminate waste

杜撰 dùzhuàn fabricate; invent; make up:～史实 fabricate historical facts

肚 dù〈名〉belly; abdomen; stomach

另见 dǔ

肚皮舞 dùpíwǔ hootchy-kootchy

肚子 dùzi belly; abdomen:一～气 be full of anger. 拉～ have loose bowels; have diarrhoea

蠹 dù〈名〉a kind of insect that eats into books, clothing, etc.

蠹虫 dùchóng ① moth ② a harmful person; vermin; termites

蠹害生灵 dùhài shēnglíng harming the people

蠹蛀 dùzhù be moth-eaten; be worm-eaten

妒 dù〈形〉jealous

妒忌 dùjì be jealous (envious) of; envy; turn green with envy at

妒贤忌能 dùxián-jìnéng be jealous of the worthy and able; be jealous and envious of capable men; envy sb. better or abler than oneself

duān

端 duān〈动〉① hold with both hands; serve:～饭上菜 serve a meal ② reason; cause:借～ use sth. as a pretext ③〈名〉end; termination ④〈形〉proper; upright; straight:～庄 dignified

端架子 duān jiàzi put on airs

端丽 duānlì comely; graceful:姿容～ have comely features

端倪 duānní clue; inkling:～可察 have found a clue to sth. ～已见。The clue is already there.; see an indication; have an inkling of the matter

端平 duānpíng ① fair; just; impartial ② hold sth. level with both hands

端午节 duānwǔjié the Dragon Boat Festival

端详 duānxiáng ① look sb. up and down; scrutinize:～良久 look at it for a good while ② details:解释～ explain the details ③ dignified and serene:举止～ behave with dignity

端正 duānzhèng ① proper; upright; regular: 五官～ have regular features ② clean; trim ③ set right; orientate; correct: ～业务思想 set to rights the ideas guiding all fields of work

端庄 duānzhuāng dignified; sedate

duǎn

短 duǎn ①〈形〉short; brief: 他说话简～。He is brief of speech. ②〈名〉weak point; shortcoming: 护～ shield a fault (shortcoming) ③〈动〉lack; owe; be short of: 理～ lack sound argument

短兵相接 duǎnbīng-xiāngjiē fight hand to hand; fight at close quarters; close-range fighting

短波 duǎnbō shortwave

短秤 duǎnchèng give short weight

短处 duǎnchù weak point; weakness; fault; shortcoming

短绌 duǎnchù fall short; be short of: 现金～。There is a shortage of cash.

短促 duǎncù of very short duration; very brief: 呼吸～ gasp; pant; be short of breath

短吨 duǎndūn short ton

短工 duǎngōng seasonal labourer; day-labourer

短故事片(～艺术片) duǎngùshìpiàn (～yìshùpiàn) featurette

短见 duǎnjiàn ① shortsighted view ② suicide: 自寻～ attempt suicide; commit suicide

短斤缺两 duǎnjīn-quēliǎng give short measure (weight); cheat on the scales; short on the catty and lacking on the ounce

短裤 duǎnkù shorts

短路 duǎnlù ① short circuit ② waylay; hold up

短命 duǎnmìng be short-lived; die young

短跑 duǎnpǎo short-distance run; dash; sprint: ～运动员 dash man; sprinter

短篇小说 duǎnpiānxiǎoshuō short story; short fiction

短评 duǎnpíng short review; leaderette; editorial note

短期 duǎnqī short-term; short: ～拆借 call loan; callable loan. ～贷款 short-term loans. ～投资 liquid investment. 股票指数的～波动 short-term oscillation of the share index.

短欠 duǎnqiàn ① owe; be in arrears ② be short of

短缺 duǎnquē shortage; deficiency: ～经济学 scarcity economics

短衫 duǎnshān a short Chinese-style unlined garment; a short gown

短少 duǎnshǎo deficient; short; missing: ～2页。There are two pages missing.

短视 duǎnshì ① nearsightedness; myopia ② lack foresight; be shortsighted

短途 duǎntú short distance: ～运输 short-distance transport; short haul

短线 duǎnxiàn ① short line (a relatively weak aspect): 能源交通

是～。Energy resource and transportation are short lines. ② in relative shortage：～产品 goods in short supply；undersupplied goods：～专业 specialities that are badly needed

短小精悍 duǎnxiǎo-jīnghàn［人］short and small；dapper；［文章等］condensed；compact

短讯 duǎnxùn news in brief；brief dispatch

短训班 duǎnxùnbān short-term training class（course）

短暂 duǎnzàn short；brief；of short duration：历史长河的～瞬间 a mere instant in the long history

duàn

断 duàn ①〈动〉break（off）；sever；stop：棍子～成两段。The stick broke in two. ～绝外交关系 sever（break off）diplomatic relations（with）② decide；judge：当机立～ decide promptly and opportunely ③〈副〉certainly；flatly；absolutely：～然拒绝 flatly reject

断案 duàn'àn ① settle a lawsuit ② conclusion of a syllogism

断炊 duànchuī run out of rice and fuel；can't keep the pot boiling；go hungry

断代 duàndài division of history into periods：［考］～法 method of dating. ～史 dynastic history

断档 duàndǎng［货物］be out of stock；sold out

断定 duàndìng conclude；form a judgment；decide；determine：我～机器出了毛病了。I came to the conclusion that the machine was out of order.

断断续续 duànduàn-xùxù off and on；by fits and starts：～地读了四年书 only four years of intermittent schooling

断顿 duàndùn can't afford the next meal；go hungry

断后 duànhòu ① bring up the rear；cover a retreat ② have no progeny

断交 duànjiāo ① break off a friendship ② sever（break off）diplomatic relations

断绝 duànjué break off；sever；stop：～交通 stop traffic；cut off all communications. ～往来 break off one's acquaintance（with）

断路 duànlù ①［电］open circuit；broken circuit ② waylay；hold up：一伙匪徒～拦劫旅客的钱财。A band of bandits held up the passengers and took all their money.

断念 duànniàn give up all hope；abandon oneself to despair

断气 duànqì ① breathe one's last；die ② cut off the gas

断然 duànrán ① resolute；drastic：采取～措施 take drastic measures ② absolutely；flatly；categorically：～否认 categorically deny

断送 duànsòng ruin；forfeit：～前程 ruin one's prospects；forfeit one's career. ～威信 dissipate one's prestige

断线 duànxiàn ① a string being broken② disconnect; sever; break off:有的社会学科后继乏人,面临～的危险。Certain disciplines of social sciences lack successors and face the danger of being discontinued.

断言 duànyán assert; affirm; allege

断语 duànyǔ conclusion; judgment; predication:遽下～ jump to conclusions

断章取义 duànzhāng-qǔyì take sentences out of context; quote one's words out of context; truncate; interpret out of context; distort a statement

段 duàn〈名〉portion; part; section; [文章的] paragraph

段落 duànluò ① paragraph; section:～大意 main idea of a paragraph ② [工作等] stage; phase:告一～ come to a close for the time being

煅 duàn〈动〉① forge:～铁 forge iron ② calcine

煅烧 duànshāo calcine

锻 duàn〈动〉forge

锻工 duàngōng ① forging:～车间 forging shop; forge ② forger; blacksmith

锻炼 duànliàn ① do drills; take exercise; train:～身体 have physical training; build up one's body (physical strength); toughen (harden) oneself physically. ② steel; temper:～意志 build up will power

锻炉 duànlú forge

锻模 duànmú forging die

锻冶 duànyě forging and smelting

缎 duàn〈名〉satin; [锦缎] brocade; damask:～带 ribbon

缎子 duànzi satin

duī

堆 duī ①〈动〉heap; pile; stack:把木柴～在后院里 stack the firewood in the back yard ②〈名〉pile; heap; stack:草～ haystack

堆存 duīcún store up

堆放 duīfàng pile up; stack:库房里～着许多机器。A lot of machines are piled in the storehouse.

堆积 duījī heap up; pile up:[考]～物 deposit; sediment

堆砌 duīqì ① pile up (hewn rocks, etc. to build sth.) ② load one's writing with fancy phrases:～辞藻 string together ornate phrases

堆栈 duīzhàn storehouse; warehouse

duì

兑 duì〈动〉① exchange; convert:请将这张支票～成现金。I'd like to cash this cheque in, please. ② add (water, etc.):这酒是～了水的。The wine has been watered.

兑付 duìfù cash (a cheque, etc.):

～美元 cash a cheque, etc. in U.S. dollar

兑换 duìhuàn exchange; convert: ～率 rate of exchange

兑现 duìxiàn ① cash; pay cash: ～券 convertible note ② fulfil; make real; realize; make good: 说话～ make good one's promise

对 duì〈动〉① reply; answer: ～答如流 answer without any hesitation ② cope with; treat: 正确～待 the correct way to treat ③ be directed at; face: 这房子～着大街。The house faces the street. ④ compare; check; identify: ～比今天幸福的生活 contrasting it with the happy life of today. ～笔迹 identify the handwriting ⑤ set; adjust: ～表 synchronize watches ⑥ bring (two things) into contact; fit one into the other: ～个火儿。Give me a light, please. ⑦ mix; add: 牛奶里～水了。The milk has been adulterated with water. 〈形〉⑧ correct; right: 我这样说～吗? Am I correct in saying this? ⑨ opposite; opposing ⑩〈量〉一～选手 a couple of players ⑪〈介〉[引进对象或事物的关系者]: 他～我笑了笑。He smiled at me. 水和鱼的关系正如空气～人的关系一样。Water is to fish what air is to man.

对白(话) duìbái(huà) dialogue

对比 duìbǐ compare; contrast: ～年代 [考] cross-dating. 力量的～ correlation alignment of forces

对不起 duìbuqǐ ① (I am) sorry; excuse me ② let sb. down; be unfair to

对不上号 duìbushàng hào unable to match up the numbers; have a discrepancy: 他说的和做的根本～。There are huge discrepancies between his words and his deeds.

对策 duìcè countermeasure; policies for coping with; the way to deal with; counter move: ～论 game theory

对称 duìchèng symmetry; balance: 不～ unsymmetrical

对答 duìdá answer; reply: ～不上来 can't answer the question ～如流 answer fluently; answer questions without hesitation

对待 duìdài treat; approach; handle

对得起 duìdeqǐ treat sb. fairly; not let sb. down

对等 duìděng equal; reciprocal: ～谈判 talk on an equal footing

对调 duìdiào change (with); exchange (with); trade (with); interchange: ～工作 interchange jobs

对方 duìfāng opposite side; the other side; the other party

对付 duìfu cope with; deal with; manage: 那家伙很难～。That guy is very hard to deal with.

对歌 duìgē singing in antiphonal style

对号 duìhào check the number: ～入座 take one's seat according to the number on the ticket; sit

casions:她曾～访问德国。She's visited Germany many times.

多党 duōdǎng multiparty

多发病 duōfābìng prevalent illness

多功能 duōgōngnéng multifunction(al):～集成电路 multifunctional integrated circuit. ～商业影院 cinema complex; cineplex

多国 duōguó multinational; multilateral:～公司 multinational company (corporation, firm). ～维持和平部队 miltinational peace-keeping troops

多极 duōjí multipolar:～发电机 multipolar generator. ～化 multipolarization

多口词 duōkǒucí many-mouth dialogue

多亏 duōkuī thanks to; luckily; fortunately:～你的帮助,我们按时完成了工作。Thanks to your help, we have finished our work in time.

多劳多得 duōláo-duōdé more pay for more work; more labour, more benefits

多么 duōme how; what (a):～美丽啊! How beautiful it is!; What a beautiful thing!. 她的心肠～好啊! What a good heart she has!

多面手 duōmiànshǒu versatile men (workers); able to put one's hand to anything; men of many-sided abilities; all rounder; Jack of all trades

多民族国家 duōmínzú guójiā a multinational state (country)

多谋善断 duōmóu-shànduàn sagacious and resolute; resourceful and decisive

多幕剧 duōmùjù a play of many acts; a full-length drama

多情 duōqíng full of tenderness or affection (for a person of the opposite sex); passionate:他对她很是～。He feels great affection for her.

多如牛毛 duōrú-niúmáo as many as the hairs on an ox; countless; innumerable

多少 duōshǎo amount; number; more or less; somewhat; to some extent:～不等 vary in amount (number). 我们的情况～有些改善。Our condition has more or less improved.

多少 duōshao how many; how much:你要～? How much do you want?

多事 duōshì ① meddlesome:怪他～。He shouldn't have poked his nose into this.; He shouldn't have interfered. ② eventful:～之秋 an eventful period or year; troubled times

多数 duōshù majority; most:～表决 decision by majority. ～党 the majority party; the majority. ～票 majority vote

多头 duōtóu (on the stock exchange) bull; long:～市场 bull market

多头管理体制 duōtóu guǎnlǐ tǐzhì multichannel management structure

多退少补 duō tuì shǎo bǔ (in subscribing to sth. or doing

business）refund for any overpayment or demand a supplemental payment for any difference in price

多谢 duōxiè many thanks；thanks a lot

多学科 duōxuékē multidisciplinary；cross-disciplinary：～、多层次、多方面进行研究 multidisciplinary，multilayered and multifaceted studies

多样 duōyàng〈形〉varied；diverse：～化 diversify；make varied

多一事不如少一事 duō yíshì bùrú shǎo yíshì It's better to save trouble.；the less trouble the better

多余 duōyú unnecessary；surplus；superfluous；uncalled-for：删掉～的词语 cut out superfluous words and phrases

多元 duōyuán multielement；multivariant；polybasic：～论 pluralism. ～社会 plural society

多咱 duōzan what time；when：咱们～走？When are we leaving？

多种 duōzhǒng various；diversified：～经济成份 multiple (diverse) economic sectors. ～经营 diversified business；engage in diverse economic undertakings；diversify the economy

多种多样 duōzhǒng-duōyàng varied；manifold：满足人民群众～的需要 meet the manifold needs of the people

哆 duō

哆嗦 duōsuo tremble；shiver；quiver：～着说 say in quivering voice

duó

夺 duó〈动〉① take by force；seize；wrest：～取胜利 seize victory ② force one's way：～门而出 force open the door and rush out ③ strive for；contend for；win：～高产 strive for high yields ④ deprive：～去席位 deprive of one's seat

夺标 duóbiāo win the trophy

夺得 duódé take；seize；［奖品等］win；carry off：～锦标 win championship；win the pennant

夺冠(魁) duóguàn(kuí) carry off the first prize；win first place；win the championship

夺回 duóhuí recapture；retake；seize back：～一局 win a game (after losing one or more)；pull up by a game. ～失去时间 make up for lost time

夺目 duómù dazzle the eyes；dazzling：鲜艳～ dazzlingly beautiful

夺取 duóqǔ seize；capture；take over；wrest：～政权 seize (take) state power

夺权 duóquán seize power；take over power

度 duó〈动〉surmise；estimate 另见 dù

踱 duó〈动〉pace；stroll：～来～去 pace to and fro；pace up and down

铎 duó〈名〉a kind of bell used

in ancient China when issuing proclamations or in times of war

duǒ

朵 duǒ〈量〉:一～花 a flower. 一～云 a cloud
朵儿 duǒr flower
躲 duǒ〈动〉avoid; hide; dodge: ～雨 take shelter from the rain
躲避 duǒbì ① hide (of person or animal); ② avoid; evade; dodge: ～开人群 keep away from the crowd
躲藏 duǒcáng hide (conceal) oneself; go into hiding: ～在树后 conceal oneself behind the trees; take cover behind the trees
躲躲闪闪 duǒduǒ-shǎnshǎn ① dodge about ② evasive; shifty: ～的谈话 evasive talk
躲风 duǒfēng ① take shelter from the wind ② lie low until sth. blows over
躲闪 duǒshǎn dodge; evade:
躲债 duǒzhài avoid a creditor

duò

惰 duò〈形〉lazy; idle; indolent
惰民 duòmín vagrants; fallen people
惰性 duòxìng inertia: ～影响 inertial influence
舵 duò〈名〉helm; rudder: ～手 helmsman; steersman
舵轮 duòlún steering wheel; helm
剁 duò〈动〉cut; chop: 把柳条～成 4 段 chop a willow branch into four pieces
剁碎 duòsuì mince: 把肉～。Mince the meat.
堕 duò〈动〉fall; drop; sink
堕落 duòluò be corrupted; degenerate; fall; go down hill: 受金钱的诱惑而～ degenerate under the temptation of money
堕入 duòrù sink into; lapse into
堕胎 duòtāi ① induced abortion ② have an abortion
跺 duò〈动〉stamp (one's foot)
跺脚 duòjiǎo stamp one's foot

E e

ē

阿 ē〈动〉① play up to; cater for：刚直不～ uprightness and tenacity ② be unfairly partial to 另见 ā

阿附 ēfù fawn on and echo; toady to and chime in with：～权贵 fawn on the noble

阿谀 ēyú flatter; fawn on; adulate; play up to; curry favour with：～奉承 cringe (to); curry favour with; flatter and fawn on; act the yes-man

婀 ē

婀娜 ēnuó (of a woman's carriage) lithe and graceful; supple and graceful：体态～ have a supple, graceful carriage

é

额 é〈名〉① forehead：宽～ a broad forehead ② a specific number or amount; quota：贸易～ volume of trade ③ a horizontal tablet

额定 édìng specified (number or amount); rated：～股本 authorized capital stock

额门(头) émén(tóu) forehead：～宽阔 a broad forehead

额数 éshù a specified number, figure or amount

额外 éwài extra; additional：～工作 extra work. ～发行纸币 excess issue of paper money. ～收入 additional income

俄 é ①〈副〉very soon; personally; suddenly ②〈名〉Russia

俄罗斯族 Éluósīzú the Eluosi (Russian) nationality, distributed over the Xinjiang Uygur Autonomous Region and Heilongjiang Province

俄顷 éqǐng suddenly; in an instant

俄语 éyǔ Russian language; Russian

娥 é〈名〉a pretty young woman

娥眉 éméi ① the beautiful eyebrows of a woman ② a beautiful woman

蛾 é〈名〉moth：～子 moth

峨 é〈形〉high

鹅 é〈名〉goose

鹅卵石 éluǎnshí cobblestone; cobble

鹅毛 émáo goose feather：～大雪 large snowflakes, fluffy snow; snow in big flakes

讹 é ①〈形〉erroneous; wrong：～字 wrong words ②〈名〉error：以～传～ spread an error

or a falsehood (message) ③〈动〉blackmail; extort; bluff
讹传 échuán false report (rumour); unfounded rumour
讹脱 étuō errors and missing (in a text); mistake and slip
讹误 éwù error (in a text)
讹言 éyán ① rumour ② wild talk; raving: 口出～ talk nonsense; rave
讹诈 ézhà extort under false pretences; blackmail: ～钱财 extort money under false pretences

ě

恶 ě
另见 è, wū
恶心 ěxīn feel sick (nauseated) at: 令人～的 nauseating; disgusting

è

恶 è ①〈形〉bad; evil; vicious: ～狗 vicious dog ②〈名〉evil; vice: 作～多端 commit all sorts of wickedness
另见 ě, wù
恶报 èbào retribution for evildoing (sin)
恶臭 èchòu a foul smell; stench
恶毒 èdú vicious; virulent; malicious: ～攻击 maliciously attack; make vicious attacks against
恶感 ègǎn ill feeling; malice: 对某人无～ bear sb. no malice
恶贯满盈 èguàn-mǎnyíng be guilty of countless crimes and deserve to come to judgment; be steeped in evil and deserve damnation
恶鬼 èguǐ ① evil spirit ② devil
恶棍 ègùn ruffian; scoundrel; bully
恶果 èguǒ disastrous result; evil consequence
恶狠狠 èhěnhěn fierce; ferocious:
恶化 èhuà take a bad turn; worsen; aggravate; deterioration: 形势～。The situation has taken a bad turn.
恶劣 èliè bad; odious; [态度] rough; rude; [品质] mean; base; despicable: 影响～ make a bad impression
恶人 èrén an evil person; a vile creature; villain
恶人先告状 èrén xiān gàozhuàng The villain brought suit against his victims.; The guilty party files the suit first.
恶事传千里 èshì chuán qiānlǐ Ill news runs apace.; Scandal travels fast.
恶习 èxí bad habit; evil practice: 染上～ contract a bad habit
恶行 èxíng evil-doing; vicious behaviour; bad conduct
恶性 èxìng malignant; galloping; vicious: ～循环 vicious cycle. ～案件 pernicious case. ～差错 pernicious error
恶言 èyán rude language; abusive language: 口出～ use abusive language; wag one's vicious tongue

恶意 èyì evil intentions; malice; ill will; spite: ～指责 pin the vicious charge

恶有恶报 èyǒu'èbào Evil is rewarded with evil.; Vice will have an evil recompense.

恶运 èyùn bad luck: 她交了～。Luck is against her.

恶作剧 èzuòjù mischievous tricks (action, practices); practical joke; prank; mischief: 对某人～ play pranks on (upon) sb. ～故事 trickster tale

噩 è〈形〉upsetting; shocking

噩耗 èhào evil news; sad news of the death (of one's beloved); grievous news

噩梦 èmèng horrible (frightening) dream; nightmare

厄 è〈名〉① strategic point: 险～ a strategic pass ② disaster: 遭～ meet with disaster

厄境 èjìng a difficult situation; adversity: 在～中保持乐观 remain cheerful in adversity

厄运 èyùn misfortune; adversity: 理论的～ theoretical misadventures

扼 è〈动〉① grip; clutch ② control; guard: ～住…咽喉 clutch at one's throat; secure a stranglehold on…

扼杀 èshā strangle; stifle; throttle; smother; subjugate: ～新生事物 suppress new things. ～在摇篮里 strangle … in its cradle; nip … in the bud

扼死 èsǐ strangle; throttle

扼守 èshǒu [要塞等] hold (a fortress); keep; guard

扼要 èyào to the point; concise: 简明～ brief and to the point

扼制 èzhì control; restrain; check; bring under control

遏 è〈动〉check; stop; hold back

遏抑 èyì suppress; keep down

遏止 èzhǐ stop; check; hold back: 不可～的历史潮流 an irresistible historical trend

遏制 èzhì curb; restrain; contain; repress: ～政策 policy of containment

愕 è〈形〉stunned; startled; astounded

愕然 èrán astounded; stunned: ～四顾 look around in astonishment

愕视 èshì stare in astonishment

鳄 è〈名〉crocodile

鳄鱼 èyú crocodile: ～的眼泪 crocodile tears

鄂 è〈名〉another name for Hubei Province

鄂伦春族 Èlúnchūnzú the Oroqen (Olunchun) nationality (living in Heilongjiang Province)

鄂温克族 Èwēnkèzú the Ewenki (Owenk) nationality (living in Heilongjiang Province)

饿 è〈形〉hungry

饿殍遍野 èpiǎo-biànyě People dying of starvation is a common sight.; be strewn with bodies of the starved everywhere; widespread death by starvation

饿死 èsǐ die of hunger; be starved to death

ēn

恩 ēn 〈名〉 kindness; favour; grace: 感～ feel grateful

恩爱 ēn'ài (of a married couple) be deeply in love with each other: 小两口儿十分～。The young couple love each other tenderly.

恩宠 ēnchǒng ① imperial favour ② show special favour to a minister

恩赐 ēncì bestow (favours, charity, etc.); favour, charity: ～观点 idea of bestowing sth. as a favour

恩典 ēndiǎn grace; favour

恩惠 ēnhuì kindness; favour; grace

恩将仇报 ēnjiāng-chóubào repay kindness with ingratitude; return evil for good; repay good with evil

恩情 ēnqíng loving-kindness; great kindness

恩人 ēnrén benefactor

恩师 ēnshī a teacher to whom one is greatly indebted; one's respected teacher

恩威并用 ēnwēi-bìngyòng apply the carrot and stick judiciously; justice tempered with mercy

恩怨 ēnyuàn ① feeling of gratitude or resentment ② grievance; resentment; old scores

恩重如山 ēnzhòng-rúshān sb.'s great kindness is as weighty as a mountain

ér

而 ér 〈连〉 ①[连接语意相承的成分] and: 美丽～动人 beautiful and moving ②[连接肯定和否定互相补充的成分]: 有百利～无一害 gain everything and lose nothing ③[连接事理上前后相因的成分]: 为人民～死 die for the people

而后 érhòu after that; then

而今 érjīn now; at the present time

而立之年 érlìzhīnián the year in life at which a person should be independent; thirty years of age

而且 érqiě ① and also: 这屋子很宽敞,～光线充足。The room is spacious and bright. ② but also: 他们不但战胜了灾害,～获得了丰收。They not only came through the natural calamity, but also won a bumper harvest.

而已 éryǐ that is all; nothing more (than): 如此～,岂有他哉! That's all there is to it!

儿 ér 〈名〉 ① child; boy; lad ② youngster; youth: 男～ man

儿歌 érgē nursey rhyme; children's song; nursery song

儿科 érkē ① paediatrics ② department of paediatrics: ～医生 paediatrician; children's doctor

儿女 érnǚ ① sons and daughters;

children：大儿大女 grown-up sons and daughters ② young man and woman (in love)：～情长 love between man and woman is long

儿孙 érsūn children and grandchildren; descendants

儿孙自有儿孙福 érsūn zìyǒu érsūn fú each one of your sons and your grandsons must find his own way as he ought; you cannot determine your children's fortune

儿童 értóng children：～节 Children's Day. ～读物 children's books. ～文学 children's (juvenile) literature. ～用品商店 department store specializing in children's goods. ～游戏场 adventure playground

儿媳妇儿 érxífur daughter-in-law

儿戏 érxì ① child's play ② trifling matter：视同～ regard sth. as a trifling matter

ěr

耳 ěr〈名〉ear：这音乐很刺～。The music offended our ears.

耳背 ěrbèi hard of hearing

耳鼻喉科 ěr-bí-hóukē ear-nose-throat department; E. N. T. department; otolaryngological department

耳边风 ěrbiānfēng a puff of wind passing the ear — unheeded advice; sth. goes in at one ear and out at the other

耳鬓厮磨 ěrbìn-sīmó ear to ear and temple to temple—(of a boy and a girl) have close childhood friendship

耳聪目明 ěrcōng-mùmíng have good ears and eyes—have a clear understanding (of the situation)

耳朵 ěrduo ear：～软 credulous; easily influenced; susceptible to flattery 穿～ have one's earlobes pierced (for wearing earrings)

耳根 ěrgēn ① the basal part (root) of the ear ② ear：～清净 peace of heart or mind attained by staying away from, or shutting one's ears to, worldly discord ③［佛］the ear taken as a source of sin

耳光 ěrguāng a slap on the face; a box on the ear

耳环 ěrhuán earrings; ear pendants

耳机 ěrjī earphone; headphone

耳力 ěrlì power of hearing; hearing：他的～不济了。His hearing is getting worse.

耳鸣 ěrmíng have a ringing sensation in the ears; tinnitus

耳目 ěrmù ① ears and eyes; what one sees and hears：～闭塞 uninformed; ignorant. ～一新 find everything fresh and new; (sth.) assume a new look

耳濡目染 ěrrúmùrán be imperceptibly influenced by what one sees and hears

耳生 ěrshēng unfamiliar to the ear; strange-sounding

耳熟 ěrshú familiar to the ear

耳顺 ěrshùn a docile ear

耳提面命 ěrtí-miànmìng pour exhortations into sb.'s ear; instruct with authority; give orders personally

耳听为虚,眼见为实 ěr tīng wéi xū, yǎn jiàn wéi shí what you hear may be false, what you see is true

耳闻 ěrwén hear of (about):这事略有～,不很清楚。I've heard a little about it, but I don't know the details.

耳闻不如目睹 ěrwén bùrú mùdǔ What one hears is not as reliable as what one sees.; Seeing for oneself is better than hearing from others.

耳闻目睹 ěrwén-mùdǔ what one sees and hears:其间～的事,算起来也很不少。During that time I witnessed or heard about a lot of things.

耳音 ěryīn power of hearing; hearing

耳语 ěryǔ speak in sb.'s ear; whisper to sb.

尔 ěr〈代〉① you:我无～诈。I shall not practise deception on you. ② like that; so:不过～～ just middling

尔曹 ěrcáo you people; you and your kind

尔后 ěrhòu thereafter; subsequently; henceforth:～的战斗 the subsequent battles

尔许 ěrxǔ so; such; like that:～高 just that tall (high). ～多 just that much; just so many

尔雅 ěryǎ elegant; refined; cultured

尔虞我诈 ěryú-wǒzhà mutual suspicion and deception; mutual deception; each trying to cheat or outwit the other

迩 ěr〈形〉near; close

饵 ěr〈名〉① cakes; pastry:果～ candies and cakes; confectionery ② (fish) bait ③〈动〉entice:～以重利 use great wealth as a bait; entice sb. with prospects of great wealth

饵敌 ěrdí set a trap for the enemy

饵子 ěrzi (fish) bait

èr

二 èr ①〈数〉two ②〈形〉different:不～价 one-price

二把手 èrbǎshǒu second in leadership (command); play second fiddle

二百五 èrbǎiwǔ〈口〉a stupid person:他是个～。He's a rather stupid person.; He's not all there.

二部制 èrbùzhì [教] two-shift system:～学校 two-shift school; school with two part-time shifts; platoon school

二重 èrchóng double; dual:～唱 (vocal) duet; dutto. ～性 dual character; duality. ～奏 (instrumental) duet

二传手 èrchuánshǒu setter (in volleyball)

二道贩子 èrdàofànzi two-way merchants (Merchants who take advantage of the differential between the government fixed price and the free market price, and buy from one and in turn sell in the other in order to make a profit)

二等(流) èrděng(liú) second-class; second-rate; second: ～品 second-rates; seconds

二等奖 èrděngjiǎng second prize

二等品 èrděngpǐn second-class or inferior goods; seconds

二房东 èrfángdōng sublessor (of a house or a room); sublandlord

二锅头 èrguōtóu a strong, colourless liquor distilled from sorghum (so called because it is distilled twice)

二胡 èrhú *erhu* fiddle

二话 èrhuà [多用于否定] demur; objection: ～不说 without demur

二簧 èrhuáng *erhuang* melodies

二"进宫" èrjìngōng enter the "palace" a second time (Someone with a past criminal record again commits a crime, and is indicated and put into a correctional institution.): 他因偷车～。He stole a car and entered the "palace" a second time.

二进制 èrjìnzhì binary system

二人转 èrrénzhuàn song-and-dance duet popular in Northeast China

二十四节气 èrshísì jiéqì [天] the 24 solar terms

二手 èrshǒu ① assistant: ② secondhand: ～货 secondhand goods

二心 èrxīn ① disloyalty ② half-heartedness

二氧化碳 èryǎnghuàtàn carbon dioxide

二元论 èryuánlùn [哲] dualism

二月 èryuè ① February ② the second month of the lunar year; the second moon

二者 èrzhě the two; both: ～必居其一。It must be one or the other.; There are the only alternatives.

贰 èr [二的大写] (used for the numeral 二 on cheques, banknotes, etc. to avoid mistakes or alterations)

贰臣 èrchén turncoat minister; turncoat official

贰心 èrxīn disloyality; half-heartedness

F f

fā

发 fā 〈动〉① send out; distribute:～号施令 issue orders ② launch; discharge; emit:～光 emit light ③ generate; come into being:～生问题 produce complications ④ expand; develop:～扬成绩 carry forward one's achievements ⑤ flourish:～家 build up a family fortune ⑥ become; get into a certain state:～霉 become mildewed ⑦ show one's feeling:～笑 laugh ⑧ feel; have a feeling:～懒 feel lazy ⑨ set out; start:出～ set out; start off ⑩〈量〉一～子弹 a bullet
另见 fà

发案 fā'àn case occurrence:～率 rate of case occurrence

发榜 fābǎng publish a list of successful candidates or applicants

发包 fābāo give out a contract for a project

发报 fābào transmit messages by radio, telegraphy, etc.

发表 fābiǎo publish; issue; express; put forward:～意见 express an opinion; air one's views. ～声明 issue a statement

发兵 fābīng send out troops; dispatch troops

发病 fābìng fall ill:～率 incidence of disease

发布 fābù issue; release:～命令 issue orders. ～新闻 release news

发财 fācái get rich; make a fortune (pile)

发颤 fāchàn quiver; tremble

发愁 fāchóu worry; be anxious

发出 fāchū issue; send out; give out:～阵阵清香 send forth wafts of delicate fragrance

发达 fādá ① developed; flourishing:～国家 developed country. 工商业很～。Industry and commerce are flourishing. ② promote; develop:～贸易 develop (promote) trade

发呆 fādāi stare blankly; be in a daze; be in a trance

发电 fādiàn ① generate electricity:～厂 power plant. ～机组容量 generating units with an aggregate capacity ② send a telegram; telegraph

发动 fādòng ① start; unleash; wage; launch:～战争 start a war against ② arouse; mobilize ③ put (set) in motion:～人民的积极性 arouse the people's initiative into full play

发抖 fādǒu tremble; shiver; quiver:冷得～ tremble with cold. 气得～ shake with anger

发放 fāfàng ① give out; issue;

grant ②［工资等］pay out：～贷款 grant a loan; extend a loan

发奋 fāfèn ① work energetically ② 见"发愤"

发愤 fāfèn make a firm resolution; make a determined effort：～工作 put all one's energies into one's work

发愤图强 fāfèn-túqiáng work assiduously and with vigour to make the country strong; work hard and aim high; work with a will to make the country strong

发疯 fāfēng go mad; go crazy; become insane; be out of one's mind

发福 fāfú［多用于中年以上］grow stout; put on weight：您～了。You have put on weight.

发稿 fāgǎo ① send manuscripts to the press ② distribute news dispatches

发给 fāgěi issue; distribute; grant：～护照 issue a passport

发光 fāguāng ① give off light; shine; be luminous ②［物］luminescence

发号施令 fāhào-shīlìng issue orders; order people about

发还 fāhuán return sth.［多用于上对下］; give (send) back：把作业～给学生 return the homework to the pupils

发慌 fāhuāng feel nervous; get flustered; get flurried

发挥 fāhuī ① bring sth. into play; give free rein to; give scope to; make full use of; give play to sth：充分～专长 give full play to sb.'s speciality. ～余热 devote one's remaining years to the service of the people ② expound

发昏 fāhūn ① feel giddy; feel dizzy ② be crazy; lose one's head

发火 fāhuǒ ① catch fire; ignite ② get angry; be ablaze with anger; flare up; lose one's temper

发货 fāhuò dispatch goods; send out goods; deliver goods：～单 delivery form; dispatch list

发家 fājiā build up a family fortune：～致富 build up a family fortune

发价(盘) fājià(pán) make an offer

发奖 fājiǎng award prizes：～仪式 prize-giving ceremony

发觉 fājué find; detect; discover

发掘 fājué unearth; excavate：～人才 talent-spot. ～文物 unearth cultural relics

发楞 fālèng stare blankly; be in a daze; be in a trance

发令 fālìng ① issue an order; give orders ② give a password

发闷 fāmēn ① be stuffy; be close：天气～。The weather is close. ② (of a sound) be muffled ③ fāmèn feel depressed; be in low spirits

发明 fāmíng invent; invention：～力 inventive powers. ～文学 invent writing. 物质的～ physical invention

发难 fānàn rise in revolt; launch

an attack

发排 fāpái send a manuscript to (the) press

发票 fāpiào invoice：开～ make an invoice

发起 fāqǐ sponsor；promote；initiate：～人 sponsor；initiator

发球 fāqiú serve a ball：～不过网 serve a ball into the net

发热 fārè ①have (run) a fever；have (run) a temperature ② give out heat；generate heat：③ be hotheaded；be impetuous：别头脑～！ Don't be so impetuous！

发人深省 fārénshēnxǐng thought provoking；prompt one to deep thought； provide food for thought；set people thinking

发烧 fāshāo ① run a fever；have a temperature ②［指对音乐］a frenzy for music；musical frenzy；A liking (desire) for music has reached fever-pitch.

发烧友 fāshāoyǒu［指对音乐］a person is obsessive about music；one who has an obsession with music； one's liking (desire) for music has reached fever-pitch；hi-fi fan

发射 fāshè shoot； project；launch：～人造卫星 launch a man-made satellite

发生 fāshēng arise；occur；take place；emerge；come into being；happen：～问题。Problems arose. ～了意外。Something unexpected happened.

发誓 fāshì vow；pledge；swear

发售 fāshǒu sell；put on sale

发抒 fāshū express；voice：～已见 express one's personal views

发酸 fāsuān ①turn sour；taste sour：牛奶～了。The milk has turned sour. ② feel a tingle in one's eyes or nose (when about to break down and weep)：他觉得两眼～。He felt a tingle in his eyes. ③ache slightly：腰有点～ have a slight backache

发现 fāxiàn ① find；discover ② discovery；findings；find：考古学上的一个新～ a new archaeological find

发祥地 fāxiángdì place of origin；birthplace

发饷 fāxiǎng issue pay (esp. to soldiers)

发泄 fāxiè give vent to (one's indignation)； vent (one's disgust)：～怨气 give vent to one's grievances

发薪 fāxīn pay wages or salary

发行 fāxíng ① issue；emit：～股票 float an issue of stock (share) ② publish；distribute：～报刊 publish (distribute) books and magazines. ～量 circulation. ～影片 release a film

发芽 fāyá germinate；sprout

发言 fāyán speak； make a speech；take the floor：～稿 notes of a speech. ～权 right to speak；say. ～人 spokesman. 即席～ speak offhand (extempore)

发扬 fāyáng carry forward；develop；foster；encourage：～光大 extol the excellent traditions；give greater scope to；develop；

promote; foster and enhance; carry forward. ～正气 encourage healthy trends

发洋财 fā'yángcái make a big fortune

发音 fāyīn pronounce; enunciate

发育 fāyù grow; develop:～心理学 developmental psychology

发源 fāyuán take (have) its source; originate:～地 classical home; cradle; fount; fountainhead; place of origin; source; birthplace

发运 fāyùn dispatch (goods):那批货物已提前～。That batch of merchandise has already been dispatched ahead of schedule.

发展 fāzhǎn develop; grow; expand; advance; forge ahead; surge forward; make advances; evolve into:～的观点看待历史 evolutionary view of history. ～中国家 developing countries

发颤 fāzhàn tremble; shiver; shake:气得浑身～ shake all over with rage
另见 fāchàn

发作 fāzuò ①[病] break out; be attacked with (a disease); show effect:酒性开始～。The liquor began to show its effect. ②[脾气等] have a fit of; be subject to a fit of ③ get angry; flare up

fá

罚 fá〈动〉punish; penalize:罪不当～ punish not in keep with the crime

罚不当罪 fábùdāngzuì the punishment exceeds the crime; be punished too severely

罚出场 fáchūchǎng [体] be ordered off the field for foul play; foul out

罚金 fájīn fine; penalty; amercement

罚酒 fájiǔ be made to drink as a forfeit

罚款 fákuǎn ① impose a fine (on) ② penalty; fine; amerce; peculiary penalty

罚球 fáqiú [篮球] penalty shot; [足球] penalty kick

乏 fá ①〈动〉lack; be short of; 缺～ lack ②〈形〉tired; fatigued:人困马～。The entire force was exhausted.

乏困 fákùn tired; fatigued:旅途～ tired from travelling; travelworn

乏味 fáwèi dry; dull; tasteless; flat:生活过得～ have a dull life

伐 fá〈动〉① fell; cut down:远处传来的～木声 distant thumping of the axe ② attack; strike:征～ send a punitive expedition

伐木 fámù felling; lumbering

阀 fá〈名〉established house or power group; a powerful person or family:财～ financial magnate; plutocrat

阀门 fámén valve:安全～ safety valve

筏 fá〈名〉raft:橡皮～ rubber raft

筏子 fázi raft

fǎ

法 fǎ〈名〉① law：犯～ break (violate) the law ② method; means; way：用～ use; usage ③ model; standard：效～ follow the example; take as model

法案 fǎ'àn bill; act; proposed law

法办 fǎbàn deal with (sb.) according to law; punish by law; bring to justice

法典 fǎdiǎn statute; code; legal code; statute book：～编纂 compilation of statute books

法定 fǎdìng legal; lawful：～身分(资格) legal capacity. ～汇率 legal exchange rate. ～劳动 statute labour. ～人数 quorum. ～代理人 legal (natural) representative

法度 fǎdù ① law ② moral standard

法官 fǎguān judge; justice

法规 fǎguī decrees and regulations; statute; law and regulations; rules and regulations

法纪 fǎjì law and discipline：目无～ act in complete disregard of law and discipline

法警 fǎjǐng bailiff

法老 fǎlǎo Pharaoh (the title of the ruler of ancient Egypt)

法理 fǎlǐ legal principle; theory of law：～学 jurisprudence

法令 fǎlìng decree; order; ordinance; statute

法律 fǎlǜ law; statute：～顾问 legal adviser; counsel：～范围之外 beyond judicial field or scope. ～服务机构 law offices. ～规范 legal norms. ～条款 legal provision. ～制裁 legal sanction; deal with according to law

法盲 fǎmáng legal illiterates (people who have no understanding of legal matters)

法人 fǎrén [法] legal (juridical) person

法权 fǎquán right; privilege

法庭(院) fǎtíng (yuàn) court; court house; law court; court of justice：～传票 judges' summons. ～外调解 conciliation out of court. ～判决 court decisions; judgement

法网 fǎwǎng web of justice; the arm of law

法西斯 fǎxīsī fascist：～主义 fascism

法学 fǎxué legal studies; science of law; law; jurisprudence; legal science; law studies：～家 jurist

法医 fǎyī legal medical expert：～学 medical jurisprudence; forensic medicine

法语 Fǎyǔ French (language)

法院 fǎyuàn court of justice; law court; court

法则 fǎzé law; rule

法治 fǎzhì rule by (of) law; government by law; legality

法制 fǎzhì legal system; legality; legal institutions：～建设 building of legal system

砝 fǎ

砝码 fǎmǎ weight (used on a balance); counter weight; balancing weight

fà

珐 fà
珐琅 fàláng enamel
发 fà 〈名〉 hair:假～ false hair; wig
另见 fā
发辫 fàbiàn plait; braid; pigtail
发髻 fàjì hair worn in a bun or coil
发夹 fàjiā hairpin; bobby pin
发廊 fàláng barber shop; hair dresser
发卡 fàqiǎ hairpin
发妻 fàqī first wife
发色 fàsè hair colour
发型 fàxíng hairstyle; hairdo:～设计师 hairtician; hairstylist
发油 fàyóu hair oil
发指 fàzhǐ boil (bristle) with anger

fān

帆 fān 〈名〉 sail
帆板 fānbǎn windsurfer; sailboard
帆板运动 fānbǎn yùndòng windsurfing
帆船 fānchuán sailing boat (ship, vessel); [比赛用的] yacht:～比赛 yacht racing
番 fān 〈名〉 ① a course, a turn; [次数] time:三～五次 time and again ② kind:别有一～天地 an entirely different world ③ 〈形〉 foreign
番号 fānhào [军] designation
番茄 fānqié tomato
番薯 fānshǔ sweet potato; koali
翻 fān 〈动〉 ① turn over; turn around (up, upside down):碰～ knock over. ～到第 10 页 turn up to p. 10 ② get over; cross; climb:～山越岭 travel over hill and dale ③ search; rummage:东找西～ rummage all over ④ multiply; double; increase two-fold:～两翻 quadruple ⑤ translate:把它～成法语 translate it into French
翻案 fān'àn reverse a verdict; reverse earlier (previous) correct decisions
翻版 fānbǎn reproduction; reprint; refurbished version
翻本 fānběn win back all the money lost (in gambling)
翻车 fānchē ① (of a car) overturn ② run into difficulties ③ have a row ④go back on one's word
翻番 fānfān increase by a specified number of times; double:产值不断～ double production value
翻覆 fānfù ① turn over; turn upside down ② toss and turn:～不能眠 toss and turn in bed, being unable to sleep ③ vacillate
翻改 fāngǎi remake (old clothes)
翻盖 fāngài rebuild or renovate (a house)
翻供 fāngòng retract one's testi-

mony; revoke verbal evidence

翻悔 fānhuǐ go back on; back out (of one's promise)

翻江倒海 fānjiāng-dǎohǎi holding back rivers and overturning seas — overwhelming; tremendous; earth-shaking: ～之势 with the momentum of an avalanche

翻老帐 fān lǎozhàng bring up old scores again; thumb through the records of

翻脸 fānliǎn fall out (with); quarrel with; suddenly turn hostile:～无情 turn against sb. forgetting the past

翻两番 fān liǎngfān quadruple:二十年我国工农业总产值～ quadrupling the gross output value of China's industrial and agricultural production in two decades

翻录 fānlù pirate recordings

翻拍 fānpāi [照相] reproduction (from a photograph)

翻然悔悟 fānrán-huǐwù quickly repent of one's error; be determined to make a clean break with one's past

翻砂 fānshā mould; found; cast: ～车间 foundry shop

翻身 fānshēn ① turn over ② be liberated; stand up; stand on one's feet; remake one's life

翻手为云、覆手为雨 fānshǒu wéi yún fùshǒu wéi yǔ produce clouds with one turn of the hand and rain with another — playing tricks

翻腾 fānteng ① seethe; rise; churn:波浪～ seething (turbulent) waves ② turn sth. over and over:过去的事,别再去～了。Don't rake up the past.

翻天覆地 fāntiān-fùdì world-shaking; epoch-making; titanic changes; earth-shaking

翻箱倒柜 fānxiāng-dǎoguì rummage through chests and cupboards; ransack boxes and chests

翻新 fānxīn renovate; renew; rehash; face-lift:～课程 [教] retread programme; [旧衣] turn (an old garment)

翻修 fānxiū repair; rebuild; recondition

翻译 fānyì translate; turn; render; [口译] interpret: ～片 dubbed film. 当～ serve as interpreter

翻印 fānyìn reprint; reproduce

翻阅 fānyuè look over; run through; turn over

翻造 fānzào rebuild or renovate (a building, bridge, etc.)

fán

烦 fán ①〈名〉bother; bore; trouble: 不胜其～ too much bother ②〈动〉trouble; request:～请 I beg you ③〈形〉vexed; be tired of; troubled:厌～ be fed up with

烦劳 fánláo ① trouble (sb. to do sth.): ～您带几本书给她。Would you mind taking a few books to her? ② depressed; feeling low

烦闷 fánmèn be unhappy; be depressed; be moody
烦恼 fánnǎo be worried; feel annoyed; be vexed:令人～的 annoying; vexatious; troublesome
烦扰 fánrǎo bore; bother; disturb
烦神 fánshén spend time and energy; take great trouble:这些事就不用您～了。You needn't trouble yourself about these things.
烦琐 fánsuǒ loaded down with trival details; overelaborate:～哲学 scholasticism. ～考证 scholastic textual research. ～礼节 trivial formalities
烦心 fánxīn annoying; vexatious; troublesome:他从不把～的事对人讲。He never confides his troubles to anybody.
烦躁 fánzào be in a fret; be agitated; distracted; uneasy

繁 fán 〈形〉① numerous; plenty of; in great number:～星满天 a starry sky ② luxuriant:～草茂木 a lush growth of trees and grass ③〈动〉propagate; multiply:～殖 multiplication
繁复 fánfù heavy and complicated
繁花 fánhuā full-blown flowers; flowers of different colours:～似锦 flowers in full bloom, brilliant as brocade
繁华 fánhuá flourishing; bustling; busy
繁忙 fánmáng busy:工作～ be very busy with one's work; be busily engaged
繁茂 fánmào luxuriant; exuberant
繁荣 fánróng prosperous; flourishing; boom; briskness:～市场 prosper the market; make the markets flourish. ～创作 make creative work flourish. ～经济 promote economic prosperity
繁荣昌盛 fánróng-chāngshèng thriving and prospering; flowering; a flourishing and invigorating scene
繁缛 fánrù overelaborate:～的礼节 overelaborate formalities
繁盛 fánshèng prosperous; thriving; flourishing
繁体字 fántǐzì complex characters
繁文缛节 fánwén-rǔjié overelaborate formalities; red tape; prolix style and hackneyed rites; unnecessary and overelaborate formalities
繁衍 fányǎn multiply; propagation; breeding:～人类 propagation of humanity
繁杂 fánzá complicated; intricate
繁殖 fánzhí breed; multiply:～家畜 breed cattle
繁重 fánzhòng heavy; onerous; toilsoms:～的劳动 toilsome labour

凡 fán ①〈形〉commonplace; ordinary:非～ extraordinary ②〈名〉this mortal world; the secular world; the earth:神仙下～ fairy becomes incarnate ③〈副〉whenever there is
凡尘 fánchén this world; this mortal life
凡夫俗子 fánfū-súzǐ ordinary people; the common herd

凡例 fánlì guide to the use of (a dictionary, etc.)

凡人 fánrén ① worldly people; mortal ② common people; mere man

凡是 fánshì every; any all: ～正义的事业都是不可战胜的。A just cause is invincible.

凡事 fánshì everything: ～预则立，不预则废 Preparedness ensures success and unpreparedness spells failure.

凡俗 fánsú secular; profane: ～音乐 secular music

凡响 fánxiǎng common music; ordinary music: 非同～ out of the ordinary

fǎn

反 fǎn 〈动〉① turn over: 易如～掌 as easy as turning one's hand over ② oppose; combat; turn against: ～腐败 fight against corruption ③ rebel; revolt: ～叛 rebel 〈名〉④ reverse side: 适得其～ get just the opposite ⑤ rebellion ⑥〈形〉opposite; contrary: ～面 negative side 〈副〉⑦ on the contrary; instead: ～把事情弄僵了 instead the matter got worse ⑧ back

反败为胜 fǎnbàiwéishèng turn defeat into victory; turn the tide

反比 fǎnbǐ inverse relation; inverse proportion: 与…成～ be inversely proportional to...; be in inverse proportion to...

反比例 fǎnbǐlì inverse ratio; inverse proportion

反驳 fǎnbó refute; argue against; retort; disprove

反常 fǎncháng unusual; abnormal; strange

反潮流 fǎncháoliú go against the current (tide); defiance of

反衬 fǎnchèn set off by contrast; serve as a foil to

反串 fǎnchuàn (in traditional opera) play a reversed role, i. e. a role that one is not trained for (as when a female impersonator plays a male role)

反唇相讥 fǎnchún-xiāngjī answer back; retort like for like

反动 fǎndòng ① reactionary: ～分子 reactionary element; reactionary. ～势力 reactionary forces ② reaction

反对 fǎnduì oppose; fight against; combat; fight; reject; be against: ～党 opposition party. ～票 negative vote

反而 fǎn'ér on the contrary; instead: 风不但没停，～更大了。Instead of going down, the wind blew even harder.

反复 fǎnfù ① repeatedly; again and again ② back out; chop and change: ～无常 behave capriciously; blow hot and cold; chop and change: ③ reversal; relapse: 思想上有～ have ideological relapses

反感 fǎngǎn disgusted with; repugnance: 抱～ feel repugnant (to). 令人～的 repugnant; antipathetic

反戈一击 fǎngēyījī turn one's weapon around and strike—turn against one's own side
反攻 fǎngōng launch a counteroffensive; counterattack
反光 fǎnguāng ① reflect light ② reflection of light
反话 fǎnhuà an ironic remark; irony
反悔 fǎnhuǐ change one's mind; go back on one's word (promise)
反击 fǎnjī strike back; beat back; counterattack
反间 fǎnjiān sow distrust or dissension among one's enemy; set one's enemies at odds: ～计 a stratagem of sowing distrust or discord among one's enemies
反诘(问) fǎnjié(wèn) ask a question in reply; demand in return
反抗 fǎnkàng revolt; resist ～精神 spirit of revolt; rebellious spirit
反馈 fǎnkuì feedback: 信息～ information feedback
反理性主义 fǎnlǐxìngzhǔyì irrationalism
反面 fǎnmiàn ① reverse side; back ② negative side: ～教材 lesson by negative example. ～人物 negative character. 演～人物 act a negative role (character)
反目 fǎnmù fall out (with)
反其道而行之 fǎnqídào ér xíngzhī diametrically opposed to; act in opposition to; the exact opposite of; do exactly the opposite
反射 fǎnshè ① reflex: 条件～ conditioned reflex ② reflect; reverberate: 声的～ the reflection of sound
反思 fǎnsī reflection; meditation introspection; rethink profoundly: ～文学 literature of reflection
反弹 fǎntán [经] rebound
反投机倒把 fǎn tóujī-dǎobǎ struggle against capitalist speculation and profiteering
反响 fǎnxiǎng repercussions; reverberation: 引起强烈～ evoke strong repercussions
反省 fǎnxǐng self-examination; introspection; self-questioning
反咬一口 fǎnyǎo-yīkǒu make false countercharge; trump up a countercharge against one's accuser
反应 fǎnyìng ① response; reaction ② respond; react: 作出～ make a response
反映 fǎnyìng ① reflect; mirror; portray; depict ② report: 向上级～ report to the higher level
反正 fǎnzhèng ① come over from the enemy's side ② anyhow; all the same
反证 fǎnzhèng evidence to the contrary; disproof
反作用 fǎnzuòyòng ① reaction; counteraction ② (produce an) effect contrary to what was intended

返 fǎn 〈动〉 be back; return: 往～ journey to and fro
返潮 fǎncháo get damp: 雨季里东西容易～。Things get damp

easily in the rainy season.

返工 fǎngōng do a poorly done work over again; remake

返航 fǎnháng (of ships, planes, etc.) return to base or port.

返回 fǎnhuí return; come or go back:～港口 put back to port

返老还童 fǎnlǎo-huántóng renew one's youth; rejuvenescence

返聘 fǎnpìn return to work in a work unit after one's retirement as requested by the work unit

返璞归真 fǎnpǔ-guīzhēn return to one's original simplicity (nature)

返青 fǎnqīng ［农］(of winter crops or transplanted seedlings) turn green

返任 fǎnrèn return to one's post

返销 fǎnxiāo resell to the place of production

返校 fǎnxiào return to school during the vacation to have homework checked or to take part in school activities

返修 fǎnxiū repair again sth. poorly repaired

fàn

泛 fàn〈动〉① drift; float:～舟 go boating ② flood inundate:淮河～滥。The Huaihe River was in spate. ③ be suffused with; spread:～出香味 smell sweet

泛读 fàndú extensive reading

泛泛 fànfàn generally; in general terms:～而谈 speak in general terms. ～之交 casual acquaintance; nodding acquaintance

泛化 fànhuà generalization:～媒介 generalized media

泛滥 fànlàn ① be in flood; overflow; inundate ② be rampant; be flooded by; a deluge of; run wild; be deluged; spread unchecked; open the floodgates for; unbridled growth; be swamped by

泛神论 fànshénlùn pantheism; hylotheism

泛文化 fànwénhuà pan-culture

泛溢 fànyì overflow; flood:江水～。The river overflowed.

泛指 fànzhǐ refer (to sth. or sb.) in general

范 fàn〈名〉① model; example:～本［文学］sampler ② bounds; limits:～畴 category

范本 fànběn a model for calligraphy or painting:习字～ a model for calligraphy

范畴 fànchóu ① category:这些概念属于哲学的～。These concepts belong in the field of philosophy. ② type; scope

范读 fàndú model reading

范例 fànlì example; model; paradigm:～论证 paradigm case argument

范式 fànshì paradigm;［哲］model:历史科学的～ model of historical science

范围 fànwéi sphere; scope; range; limits; field:势力～ sphere of influence

范文 fànwén model essay; anthology piece

贩 fàn ①〈动〉trade (in); buy to

resell：～毒 drug trafficking ②〈名〉pedlar；dealer

贩毒 fàndú traffic in narcotics

贩卖 fànmài traffic；sell；peddle；marketing：～牲口 deal in draught animals. ～色情 sexploitation

贩私 fànsī traffic in smuggled goods

贩运 fànyùn transport goods for sale；traffic

贩子 fànzi tradesman；dealer；trafficker

饭 fàn〈名〉① cooked rice ② meal

饭菜 fàncài ① meal；repast：～可口 tasty food ② dishes to go with rice，steamed buns，etc.

饭店 fàndiàn ① restaurant ② hotel

饭馆 fànguǎn（small）restaurant；eating house：下～ eat（dine）in a restaurant

饭盒 fànhé lunch-box；mess tin；dinner pail

饭局 fànjú dinner party；feast

饭来张口，衣来伸手 fànlái zhāngkǒu，yīlái shēnshǒu have only to open one's mouth to be fed and hold out one's hands to be dressed — lead an easy life；with everything provided

饭量 fànliàng appetite：～小 have a poor appetite

饭票 fànpiào meal ticket

饭铺 fànpù（small）restaurant；eating house

饭厅 fàntīng dining hall；dining room；mess hall

饭桶 fàntǒng ① vessel for holding rice；rice bucket ② big eater ③ good-for-nothing（persons）

饭碗 fànwǎn ① rice bowl ② job：丢了～ lose one's job

饭庄 fànzhuāng（big）restaurant

饭桌 fànzhuō dining table

犯 fàn〈动〉① break；offend（against law，etc.）：～法 break（violate）the law ② commit：～罪 commit a crime. ～错误 make a mistake ③ commit ④ attack：心脏病～了 have another heart attack ⑤〈名〉criminal；prisoner：囚～ convict；prisoner

犯案 fàn'àn（of a criminal）be found out and brought to justice

犯病 fànbìng have an attack of one's old illness

犯不着 fànbuzháo it is not worthwhile（to do，doing）

犯愁 fànchóu worry；be anxious

犯得着 fàndezháo［多用于反问］is it worthwhile：～冒这种风险吗？Is it worthwhile taking such risks？

犯嘀咕 fàndígu have misgivings；have doubts：心里直～ feel uneasy

犯法 fànfǎ violate（break）the law

犯规 fànguī ① violate the rules ②［体］foul

犯忌 fànjì violate a taboo

犯困 fànkùn feel sleepy；feel drowsy；be half asleep

犯人 fànrén criminal；prisoner；culprit；convict

犯傻 fànshǎ ① pretend to be

naive, ignorant, or stupid: 别～啦。Don't pretend not to know. ② do a foolish thing: 我真～, 竟信了他的话! What a fool I was to believe what he said. ③ be in a daze; stare blankly

犯上 fànshàng go against one's superiors

犯上作乱 fànshàng-zuòluàn defy one's superiors and start a rebellion; rebel

犯罪 fànzuì commit a crime; crime; commission of a crime; guilt; perpetrate a crime; sin; offence: ～率 crime rate. ～小说作家 crime writer

梵 fàn 〈名〉① of ancient India ② Buddhist: ～刹 Buddhist temple

梵蒂冈 Fàndìgāng the Vatican

梵宫 fàngōng Buddhist temple

梵文 Fànwén Sanskrit

梵语 Fànyǔ Sanskrit

fāng

方 fāng 〈形〉① square: ～塔 square tower ② upright; honest: 品行～正 have an upright character 〈名〉③ direction; course: 西～ the west ④ side; party: 我～ our side ⑤ way; method: 教导有～ exercise good teaching. 多～ in various ways ⑥ prescription: 验～ proved recipe ⑦〈副〉just; just then: 年～18 be just eighteen years old ⑧〈量〉short for square metre or cubic metre: 2～木材 two cubic metres of lumber

方案 fāng'àn plan; proposal; sketch; outline; scheme; programme

方便 fāngbiàn ① convenient; expedient: ～人民生活 bringing more convenience to the people in their daily life ② proper: 在这里谈话不～。It is not proper (convenient) to talk here. ③〈口〉go to the lavatory: 我要～一下。I want to wash my hands.

方便面 fāngbiànmiàn instant noodles; convenient noodles

方才 fāngcái ① just now: ～的情形, 你们都知道了。You know what has just happened. ② (only) just; not until: 等到天黑, 我～回来。I didn't come back until after dark.

方寸已乱 fāngcùnyǐluàn with one's heart troubled and in turmoil; with one's mind in a turmoil; greatly agitated

方法 fāngfǎ method; way; means: ～论 methodology

方块字 fāngkuàizì square-shaped characters—Chinese characters

方略 fānglüè general plan; policy

方面 fāngmiàn respect; aspect; side; field

方式 fāngshì way; fashion; pattern: 生活～ way (mode) of life; life style

方向 fāngxiàng direction; course; orientation: ～盘 steering wheel (gear)

方兴未艾 fāngxīng-wèi'ài rising; in the ascendant; on the upgrade; be fast unfolding

方言 fāngyán dialect

方丈 fāngzhàng Buddhist abbot

方针 fāngzhēn guiding line; policy; guiding principles; guide line

方志 fāngzhì local gazetteers; local chronicles

方子 fāngzi prescription: 开～ write out a prescription

芳 fāng 〈形〉 fragrant; sweet

芳龄 fānglíng the age of a young woman

芳名 fāngmíng ① the name of a young woman ② a good reputation

芳香 fāngxiāng sweet-smelling; fragrant

芳心 fāngxīn the heart of a young woman

坊 fāng 〈名〉 ① lane ② memorial archway: 贞节牌～ chastity arch

另见 fáng

fáng

房 fáng 〈名〉 ① house; building: 平～ bungalow; a single-storey house ② room: 客～ guest rooms

房产 fángchǎn house property

房地产 fángdìchǎn real estate: ～经纪人 estate agent (dealer); house agent; realtor. ～税 real estate tax. ～投资 real estate investment

房东 fángdōng house owner; landlord or landlady

房改 fánggǎi reform in housing

房基 fángjī foundations of (a building)

房客 fángkè tenant (of a house or room); lodger

房契 fángqì title deed for a house; property deed

房事 fángshì sexual intercourse (between a married couple)

房租 fángzū rent: ～保险 house rent insurance. ～补贴 rent subsidies

坊 fáng 〈名〉 mill; workshop; shop: 染～ dyer's workshop

另见 fāng

防 fáng 〈动〉 ① guard against; prevent: ～洪 prevent flood; control flood. ～弹汽车 bullet-proof car ② defend: ～身 defend oneself ③〈名〉 defence: 国～ national defence

防暴 fángbào antiriot; riot: ～警察 riot police

防备 fángbèi be prepared for; take precuations against: ～发生事故 take precautions against accidents

防不胜防 fángbùshèngfáng hard to guard against; cannot reckon with all eventualities

防尘 fángchén dustproof

防弹 fángdàn bulletproof; shellproof: ～背心 bulletproof vest

防盗 fángdào guard against theft; take precautions against burglars

防冻 fángdòng prevent frostbite: ～药品 frostbite preventive

防范 fángfàn guard against; provide against; be on guard; keep a lookout; keep a watchful eye on：注重～ lay stress on prevention

防风林 fángfēnglín windbreak forests

防腐 fángfǔ ① antiseptic：～纱布 antiseptic gauze ② antirot：～材料 antirot material

防旱 fánghàn take precautions against drought

防洪 fánghóng prevent or control flood：～措施 flood control measures

防护 fánghù shelter; protect; guard; shielding：～林带 shelter belts; afforested zones holding off sandstorms

防患于未然 fánghuànyú wèirán take preventive measures; provide against possible trouble

防火 fánghuǒ ① prevent fires ② fire prevention：设备 fireproof installations

防空 fángkōng air defence; anti-aircraft：～洞 air-raid shelter; hiding-place for evildoers

防涝 fánglào prevent waterlogging

防守 fángshǒu defend; guard：～阵地 defend one's position (in battle)

防暑 fángshǔ prevent heatstroke (sunstroke)：～措施 measures taken to prevent heatstroke

防微杜渐 fángwēi-dùjiàn nip (check, crush an evil) in the bud (egg); check erroneous ideas at the outset

防卫 fángwèi protect; defend：～过当 excessive defence

防务 fángwù matters pertaining to defence; defence

防险 fángxiǎn danger prevention

防锈 fángxiù rust-resist; rust-proof

防汛 fángxùn flood control (prevention)

防疫 fángyì epidemic prevention

防疫站 fángyìzhàn anti-epidemic station

防御 fángyù defend：～工事 defence works; defences

防灾 fángzāi take precautions against natural calamities

防震 fángzhèn shock-proof; [地震] quake-proof

防止 fángzhǐ prevent; guard against; forestall; avoid：～煤气中毒 guard against gas poisoning. ～浪费人力 avoid waste of manpower. ～骄傲自满 guard against conceit and complacency. ～交通事故 try to forestall traffic accidents

防治 fángzhì prevent and cure

妨 fáng 〈动〉 hinder; hamper; interfere; disturb：～碍生产的发展 hamper the growth of production

妨碍 fáng'ài hamper; impede; hinder; jeopardize：～交通 impede traffic

妨害 fánghài impair; injure; offence against; be harmful to：～婚姻家庭罪 crime of interference with marriage and the family. ～治安 disturbance; disorderly conduct. ～行为 nuisance

fǎng

访 fǎng〈动〉visit; call on:拜～ pay a visit to; call on

访查 fǎngchá go about making inquiries; investigate

访问 fǎngwèn ① visit; call on:国事～ state visit. ～学者 visiting scholar ② interview:～技巧 interview technique

访销 fǎngxiāo promotion sales

仿 fǎng〈动〉① imitate; copy:摹～ copy ② resemble:相～ be similar

仿佛 fǎngfú ① seem; as if ② resemble:我们～在哪儿见过。We seem to have met somewhere.

仿古 fǎnggǔ modelled after an antique; in the style of the ancients

仿冒 fǎngmào counterfeits:谨防～ guard against counterfeits

仿生学 fǎngshēngxué bionics

仿效 fǎngxiào imitate; follow suit; follow the example of

仿造 fǎngzào imitate; be modolled on; copy:～品 imitation; counterfeit

仿照 fǎngzhào ① imitate; follow ② after; according to

仿制 fǎngzhì imitate:～品 imitation; replica

纺 fǎng〈动〉spin:～纱厂 cotton spinning mill

纺绸 fǎngchóu a soft plain-weave silk fabric

纺绽 fǎngdìng [纺] spindle

纺纱 fǎngsha spin; spinning

纺织 fǎngzhī spinning and weaving:～厂 textile mill. ～品 textile fabrics; textiles

fàng

放 fàng〈动〉① let go; set free: ～开手脚 give … a free hand; have one's hands and feet unfettered ② put; place; lay; set:～回原处 put it where it belongs ③ give way to; let oneself go: ～声大笑 laugh a hearty laugh ④ give out; let off; ～焰火 set off fireworks ⑤ shoot: ～炮 fire guns ⑥ put out pasture; let off for prey: ～羊 let off sheep to pasture ⑦ lend money for interest:～债 make loans to ⑧ blossom:一花独～。A flower blossoms alone. ⑨ lay aside; leave alone:～在一边 put aside ⑩ extend; enlarge:～松一点 loosen it a little ⑪ readjust oneself to a certain extent: ～稳重一些。Be sedate. ⑫ show: ～录像 play a tape recorder ⑬ keep:存～银行 deposit in the bank

放长线钓大鱼 fàng chángxiàn diào dàyú throw a long line to catch a big fish — adopt a long-term plan to secure something big; angle for a large fish with a long line; go after something big with foresight

放大 fángdà enlarge; magnify;

amplify：把照片～ make enlargements of a photograph；have a photo enlarged

放荡 fàngdàng loose；dissolute；licentious；sexual exploits；profligacy：～不羁 be easy in one's morals. ～不羁的文化人 Bohemia

放毒 fàngdú ① put poison in food，water，etc.；poison ② make vicious remarks；spread poisonous ideas

放风 fàngfēng ① let in fresh air ② let prisoners out for exercise or to relieve themselves ③ leak certain information；spread news or rumours ④ be on the lookout；act as a lookout

放高利贷 fàng gāolìdài lend money at an excessively high rate of interest；practise usury

放工 fànggōng leave（work）；be off duty；knock off

放过 fàngguò let sb. off；let sth. slip by.

放活 fànghuó loosen and enliven：～经济 loosen up and enliven the economy

放火 fànghuǒ ① commit arson；set fire to ② incendiarism

放假 fàngjià have a holiday（vacation）；have a day off；［学校］break up：下星期三～。Next Wednesday is a holiday.

放开 fàngkāi ① let go ② lift the control over：～价格 decontrol of prices

放空炮 fàng kōngpào make an empty threat；talk big；brag；boast；indulge in idle boasting

放空气 fàng kōngqì circulate report；spread word；spread rumour；let it be known that…；spread talk for；drop a hint；hint at；spread a view

放宽 fàngkuān ① broaden；widen ② relax：～贷款条件 liberalize the conditions of loans. ～政策 relax policies；adopt more liberal policies ③［衣服］let out

放款 fàngkuǎn grant a loan；loan

放冷箭 fàng lěngjiàn shoot from a hidden position—injure sb. by underhand means；snipe

放马后炮 fàng mǎhòupào make comments on sth. after it is already over；a Monday morning quarterbacking：～的人 a Monday morning quarterback

放牧 fàngmù put out to pasture；graze；herd：～牛羊 herd（graze）sheep and cattle

放炮 fàngpào ① fire a gun ② run off at the mouth；shoot off one's mouth

放弃 fàngqì give up；abandon；forsake；haul down；reject；relinguish：～索赔 abandonment of claim. ～遗产 renounce inheritance

放晴 fàngqíng clear up（after rain）

放权 fàngquán transfer power to lower level

放任 fàngrèn leave sb. to himself；indulge：～自流 let things drift（by themselves）；let sb. do as he likes

放哨 fàngshào be on sentry or on patrol：站岗～ stand sentry；

stand sentinel; go on sentry duty

放射 fàngshè radiate

放声 fàngshēng at the top of one's voice; loudly; aloud: ～歌唱 sing at the top of one's voice

放手 fàngshǒu ① let go; ② leave one free to; give one a free hand to; go all out: ～发动群众 go all out to mobilize the masses

放肆 fàngsì unbridled; presumptuous; immodest; blatant; intemperate: 他这样做太～了。It is too presumptuous of him to do so.

放松 fàngsōng loosen; relax; slacken: ～警惕 relax one's vigilance

放送 fàngsòng broadcast; send out (over a loudspeaker, etc.)

放下 fàngxià lay down; let down: ～包袱 get rid of the baggage; put down one's burden. ～架子 relinquish haughty airs; get off one's high horse

放下屠刀,立地成佛 fàngxià túdāo, lìdì chéngfó The butcher who lays down his knife and at once becomes a Buddha.; A butcher becomes a Buddha the moment he drops the cleaver.

放心 fàngxīn feel at ease; set one's mind at ease; rest assured: ～不下 be anxious (about)

放行 fàngxíng let sb. or sth. pass: 申请～ request clearance. 免税～ tax-free clearance

放学 fàngxué [学校] close; [学生] leave school: 学校下午 4 点～。School closes at 4 p.m.

放眼 fàngyǎn take a broad view; scan widely: ～世界 have the whole world in view; open one's eyes to the whole world

放映 fàngyìng show (a film); project: ～队 film projection team. ～机 (film) projector. ～室 projection room. ～员 projectionist

放债 fàngzhài lend money for interest

放之四海而皆准 fàngzhīsìhǎi érjiē zhǔn valid everywhere: ～的真理 a universally applicable truth

放纵 fàngzòng ① indulge: 她～孩子。She indulges her child.; She allows her child to run wild.

fēi

非 fēi ①〈名〉wrong; mistake; error: 是与～ right and wrong ②〈形〉non-; un-, etc.: ～生产部门 non-productive branches 〈动〉③ blame; oppose; condemn: 不可厚～ excusable ④ run counter to; not conform to: ～礼 a breach of etiquette; impolite ⑤〈副〉not; no: ～同小可 no small matter ⑥ [跟"不"呼应,表示必须] insist on; must: 我～要他去不可。I insist on his going.

非暴力 fēibàolì nonviolence: ～罪犯 nonviolent offender

非…不… fēi … bù possibly only

if：～工作人员不得入内 for staff members only

非…不可 fēi … bùkě ① must; have to：你～努力学习不可。You must study hard. ② will inevitably; be bound to：非完成任务不可 be bound to fulfil the task

非常 fēicháng ① very; awfully; extremely ② unusual; special; exceptional：～时期 unusual times

非此即彼 fēicǐ-jíbǐ either this or that; one or the other

非存在 fēicúnzài nonexistence; nothingness：～物 nonbeing

非但 fēidàn not only：他们～干得好，还肯帮助别人。They not only do their own work well, but are also ready to help others. ～学生答不出，连老师也答不出。Not only the students couldn't answer, the teacher didn't know the answer either.

非党人士 fēidǎngrénshì non-Party personages

非得 fēiděi [一般跟"不"或"才"呼应] have got to; must：做校对工作～仔细才行。You've got to be very careful when you do proofreading.

非对抗性矛盾 fēiduìkàngxìng máodùn nonantagonistic contradiction

非法 fēifǎ unlawful; illegal; illicit：～贸易 illicit trade

非凡 fēifán uncommon; remarkable; extraordinary; outstanding：～的笔触 unique style

非…非… fēi … fēi neither … nor …：～驴～马 neither fish, flesh, nor fowl

非工业化 fēigōngyèhuà de-industrialization

非公莫入 fēigōngmòrù no admittance except on business

非官方 fēiguānfāng unofficial：～消息 information from unofficial sources

非婚生 fēihūnshēng illegitimacy; bastardy：～子女 child of illegitimate birth; child born out of wedlock

非…即… fēi…jì either… or…：非此即彼 either this or that

非金属 fēijīnshǔ nonmetal：～材料 nonmetallic materials

非礼 fēilǐ ① improper; indecorous; rude：～之举 improper conduct; indecorous behaviour ② assault (a woman) sexually; violate：欲行～ attempt to violate a woman

非理性 fēilǐxìng nonrationality; irrationality; unreason：～主义 irrationalism; nonrationalism

非卖品 fēimàipǐn (articles) not for sale

非贸易外汇收入 fēimàoyìwàihuì shōurù nontrade foreign currency income; foreign exchange earnings from nontrade channels

非耐用品 fēinàiyòngpǐn nondurable goods; current goods; soft goods

非难 fēinàn censure; find fault with; bring charges against

非亲非故 fēiqīn-fēigù neither relative nor friend; neither kith nor kin

非上市证券 fēishàngshì zhèngquàn unlisted securities

非生产部门 fēishēngchǎn bùmén nonproductive departments

非生产劳动 fēishēngchǎn láodòng nonproductive labour

非生产性的基本建设 fēishēngchǎnxìng de jīběn jiànshè nonproductive projects in capital construction

非同小可 fēitóngxiǎokě no small (trivial) matter

非物质论 fēiwùzhìlùn immaterialism

非物质生产部门 fēiwùzhì shēngchǎn bùmén nonproductive departments; nonmaterial production departments

非现行犯罪 fēixiànxíng fànzuì nonflagrant delict: 非现行犯 nonflagrant delictor

非虚构小说 fēixūgòu xiǎoshuō nonfiction novel

非业务费用 fēiyèwù fèiyòng nonoperational cost

非议 fēiyì [通常与否定式连用]: reproach; censure: 无可～ blameless; beyond (above) reproach

非营业资产 fēiyíngyè zīchǎn nonoperating assets

非正规学校 fēizhèngguī xuéxiào informal school

非正式 fēizhèngshì unofficial; informal: ～访问 unofficial visit

非正式婚姻 fēizhèngshì hūnyīn common-law marriage

非洲 Fēizhōu Africa: ～统一组织 the Organization of African Unity (OAU)

非主要矛盾 fēizhǔyào máodùn nonprincipal contradiction

非组织观点 fēizǔzhī guāndiǎn nonorganizational viewpoint

扉 fēi 〈名〉 door leaf: 打开心～ open one's heart

扉页 fēiyè title page; flyleaf

蜚 fēi

蜚声 fēishēng make a name; become famous: ～文坛 win renown (be famous) in literary circles

蜚语 fēiyǔ gossip; rumours

飞 fēi 〈动〉 ① fly; flit: 鸟在空中～来～去。Birds flit about in the sky. ② fly; flutter: 由北京直～广州。Fly nonstop from Beijing to Guangzhou. ③〈形〉 unexpected; accident: ～祸 unexpected calamity ④〈副〉 swiftly; speedily: ～步上楼 whisk upstairs

飞奔 fēibēn dash; tear along

飞播 fēibō sowing from air

飞船 fēichuán airship: 太空～ spacecraft; spaceship

飞地 fēidì ① land of one province or county enclosed by that of another ② enclave; exclave

飞短流长 fēiduǎn-liúcháng spread embroidered stories and malicious gossip; gossip

飞蛾扑火,自取灭亡 fēi'ér pūhuǒ, zì qǔ mièwáng seek one's own doom like moths flying into the fire

飞红 fēihóng bright red; scarlet;

crimson：她羞得满脸～。She was crimson with embarrassment.

飞黄腾达 fēihuáng-téngdá get rapid promotion；rise high in the world；climb up the social ladder rapidly；moving far up in the social scale

飞机 fēijī airplane；plane；aircraft：～上交货价 free on plane (aircraft). ～国籍标志 nationality mark of aircraft

飞快 fēikuài ① very fast；at lightning speed ② extremely sharp；razorsharp：把镰刀磨得～。Sharpen the sickles till they are like razors.

飞沙走石 fēishā-zǒushí sand flying about and stones hurtling through the air (as in a windstorm)

飞驶 fēishǐ (of vehicles) travel at a tremendous speed；speed：一辆摩托车～而过。A motorcycle sped past.

飞逝 fēishì (of time，etc.) slip by (past)；fly；elapse：时光～。Time just flies.

飞腾 fēiténg fly swiftly upward；soar：烟雾～。A smoke-laden fog rose quickly and soon filled the air.

飞舞 fēiwǔ dance in the air；flutter：雪花～。Snowflakes are dancing in the air.

飞翔 fēixiáng flight；hover；circle in the air

飞行 fēixíng (of an aircraft，missile，etc. or of a pilot) fly；make a flight：～表演 demonstration (exhibition) flight. ～管制 air traffic control. ～记录簿 flight log. ～员 pilot；aviator；flyer

飞旋 fēixuán fly in circles

飞扬 fēiyáng fly upward；rise：尘土～clouds of dust flying up

飞扬跋扈 fēiyáng-báhù presuming；arrogant and domineering；throw one's weight around

飞跃 fēiyuè ① leap ② by leaps and bounds：～发展 develop by leaps and bounds

飞越 fēiyuè ① fly over or across：～太平洋 make a flight across the Pacific ② fly upward；become elevated or uplifted：心神～ in high spirits；in an elevated mood

飞涨 fēizhàng［物价等］soar；shoot up；skyrocket：物价～。Prices were soaring.

妃 fēi 〈名〉① imperial concubine ② the wife of a prince

妃红 fēihóng light pink

妃子 fēizi imperial concubine

菲 fēi ①〈形〉(of flowers and grass) luxuriant and rich with fragrance ②［化］phenanthrene 另见 fěi

菲林 fēilín a roll of film；film

绯 fēi 〈形〉red

绯红 fēihóng bright red；crimson；scarlet：～的晚霞 rosy evening clouds. 脸羞得～ blush with shame

霏 fēi ①〈动〉(of rain or snow) fall thick and fast ②〈名〉thin，

floating clouds; mist:夕～ evening mist

féi

肥 féi 〈形〉① fat; greasy; stout:～肉 fat meat ② fertile; rich:土质很～ rich soil ③〈名〉fertilizer; manure:化～ chemical fertilizer

肥大 féidà ① loose; large:～的衣服 a loose garment ② fat; plump; corpulent:果实～ lush and plump fruit ③［医］hypertrophy:心脏(扁桃体)～ hypertrophy of the heart (tonsils)

肥厚 féihòu ① plump; fleshy:嘴唇～ have thick lips ② thick and fertile:土层～ thick and fertile topsoil ③ (of food) rich and tasty

肥力 féilì fertility:土地的～程度 degree of fertility of the land

肥料 féiliào fertilizer; manure:有机～ organic fertilizer

肥美 féiměi ①fertile; rich:～的土地 rich soil; fertile land ② luxuriant; plump; fleshy; fat:～的北京鸭 plump, tender-fleshed Beijing ducks

肥胖 féipàng fat; plump; corpulent:～症 obesity

肥缺 féiquē lucrative post

肥瘦 féishòu ① the girth of a garment ② the proportion of fat and lean:这块肉～正好。This chunk of meat is not too fat and not too lean.

肥水 féishuǐ "rich water":～外流 outflow of profits. ～不流外人田。The rich water does not fall to someone else' fields.

肥私囊 féisīnáng feather one's own nests

肥沃 féiwò fertile; rich:～的农场 productive farm

肥皂 féizào soap:～粉 soap powder. ～剧 soap opera

肥壮 féizhuàng stout and strong:牛羊～ thriving herds of sheep and cattle

fěi

诽 fěi〈动〉slander

诽谤 fěibàng traduce; vilify; slander; make the slanderous charge that…; hurl at someone the slander that…; malign; spread calumnies:～案 libel suit; case of libel. ～罪 crime of defamation; criminal libels on private person

诽谤名誉 fěibàng-míngyù defamatory libel:～侵权行为 character defamation

匪 fěi ①〈名〉bandit; brigand; robber ②〈副〉not:获益～浅 reap no little benefit

匪帮 fěibāng (bandit) gang; thugs

匪巢 fěicháo bandits' lair

匪盗影片 fěidào yǐngpiàn gangster film

匪首 fěishǒu bandit chieftain (chief)

匪徒 fěitú gangster; robber

匪夷所思 fěiyísuǒsī (of ideas) unimaginably queer; fantastic

菲 fěi 〈书〉humble; unworthy: ～礼 my humble gift
另见 fēi

菲薄 fěibó ① poor; humble ② despise; belittle: 妄自～ belittle oneself unduly; excessive humble

斐 fěi 〈形〉(of literary talent) striking; brilliant

斐然 fěirán striking; brilliant; splendid: 成绩～ (achieve) splendid results

fèi

废 fèi ①〈动〉abandon abolish; give up; discard; abrogate: ～业 abandon one's profession 〈形〉② waste; useless; disuse: ～铁 scrap iron ③ disabled; crippled: ～疾 cripplehood; disability

废弛 fèichí (of a law, custom, discipline, etc.) cease to be binding; become lax

废除 fèichú abrogate; abolish; discard; repeal; cancel: ～一切不平等条约 revocation (abolition) of all the unequal treaties

废黜 fèichù depose; abdication; dethrone: ～…的王位 discrown; dethrone

废话 fèihuà ① unnecessary (superfluous) words ② nonsense; rubbish: 从不说～ never talk nonsense

废旧货市场 fèi jiùhuò shìchǎng junk market

废料 fèiliào waste material; waste; scrap: ～堆 scrap heap; waste heap

废品 fèipǐn ① scrap; waste ② waste product; defective article; reject: ～回收 waste recovery; salvage of waste material. ～收购站 salvage point (station); waste-retrieving station

废弃 fèiqì abolish; discard; abandon; cast aside

废寝忘食 fèiqǐn-wàngshí forget to eat and sleep; neglect one's sleep and meals

废人 fèirén ①disabled person ② good-for-nothing

废水 fèishuǐ waste water; liquid waste: ～渗透 waste water infiltration

废物 fèiwù ① waste material; rubbish: ～利用 convert wastes into useful materials; materials salvage

废墟 fèixū ruins; debris: 成为～ be reduced to ruins

废学 fèixué discontinue one's schooling

废纸 fèizhǐ waste paper: 不要乱扔～。Don't litter the place with waste paper.

废止 fèizhǐ put an end to; abolish; rescind

肺 fèi 〈名〉lung

肺癌 fèi'ái carcinoma of the lungs; lung cancer

肺腑 fèifǔ the bottom of one's heart: 出自～ straight from the heart; from the depths of one's heart

肺腑之言 fèifǔzhīyán talk from the heart; words from one's heart; words from the depths (the bottom) of one's heart

肺结核 fèijiéhé pulmonary tuberculosis (TB)

肺炎 fèiyán pneumonia

沸 fèi ①〈动〉boil ②〈形〉boiling:人声鼎～ noise and shouts in great commotion

沸沸扬扬 fèifèi-yángyáng bubbling and gurgling; in a hubbub:消息～地传开了。The news spread like wildfire.

沸腾 fèiténg ① boil ② seethe with excitement; boil over:热血～ one's blood boils

沸扬 fèiyáng (of feelings, sentiments, or voices and sounds) seethe with excitement; boil over

费 fèi ①〈名〉fee; cost; charges; expenses:生活～用 living expenses ②〈动〉spend; cost; expend:～尽唇舌 do a lot of talking ③〈形〉wasteful; consuming too much:他穿鞋很～。He wears shoes quickly.

费唇舌 fèichúnshé take a lot of talking or explaining

费工(功)夫 fèigōngfu take time and energy; be time-consuming; be exacting; be demanding

费话 fèihuà take a lot of talking or explaining:一说他就明白,用不着人～。Just mention it and he'll catch on. It won't take much talking.

费解 fèijiě hard to understand; obscure; unintelligible

费劲 fèijìn need or exert great effort; be strenuous.

费尽心机 fèijìn-xīnjī take great pains; cudgel (rack) one's brains

费力 fèilì take pains; require great effort; be strenuous; toilsome; painstaking

费神 fèishén ① need or exert great mental effort ②[常用做请托时客套话] may I trouble you (to do sth.); would you mind (doing sth.):我这篇稿子您～给看看好吗? Would you mind going over this article for me?

费事 fèishì give (take) a lot of trouble

费心 fèixīn take the trouble (to do):请～捎个口信给他。May I trouble you to send him a message?

费用 fèiyòng cost; charges; expenditure; expenses

fēn

分 fēn〈动〉① divide; part; separate ② distinguish; discriminate:～别善恶 distinguish good from evil ③ distribute; allot; assign:～配土地 distribution of land〈名〉④ branch (of an organization):～公司 a branch company ⑤ fraction:三～之一 one-third ⑥ point; mark:得 80～ score 80 marks. 他们赢了 4～。They won by four points.〈量〉⑦[长度单

位] *fen*, a unit of length (=1/3 centimetre): 二尺零五～ two *chi* and half a *cun* ⑧ [时间单位] minute ⑨ [货币单位] *fen* (=1/100 of a *yuan*) ⑨ [重量单位] a unit of weight (=1/2 gram) ⑩ [地积单位] *fen*, a unit of area (=66.666 sq. metres) ⑪ [利率单位] rate of interest: 年利一～ 10% interest a year

另见 fèn

分包 fēnbāo ① subpackage ② subcontract: ～办法 subcontracting arrangement

分崩离析 fēnbēng-líxī disintegrate; fall to pieces; come (fall) apart

分辨 fēnbiàn distinguish; discern; differentiate: ～真假 distinguish truth from falsehood

分辩 fēnbiàn defend oneself (against a charge); make an excuse; give an explanation

分别 fēnbié ① part (with, from): 与朋友～ part with a friend ② distinguish ③ respectively; separately: 他们～代表自己的公司签订了合同。They signed a contract on behalf of their respective corporations.

分布 fēnbù be distributed (over an area); be dispersed; be scattered

分餐 fēncān divided meals

分成 fēnchéng percentage allotment (to be alloted a certain percentage of the total income, i.e., a portion of the money or goods.); divide into tenths

分寸 fēncuì proper limits for speech or action; sense of propriety: 发言有～ make a measured speech

分担 fēndān share (with); have a share (in): ～风险和亏损 share risks and losses

分道扬镳 fēndào-yángbiāo part company (with); go separate ways; each going his own way

分店 fēndiàn branch (of a shop)

分而治之 fēn'érzhìzhī divide and rule

分发 fēnfā ① distribute; hand out; issue (to individuals): 把课本～给同学们 hand out textbooks to the students ② assign to a post; appoint to a job

分割 fēngē cut apart; break up; carve up

分工 fēngōng ① division of labour ② divide up the work: ～负责 each person responsible for a particular field of work

分管 fēnguǎn be assigned personal responsibility for; be put in charge of

分行 fēnháng branch (of a bank, business firm, etc.): 国内～ home (domestic) branch. 国外～ overseas branch

分号 fēnhào ① semicolon (;) ② branch (of a shop, firm, etc.)

分红 fēnhóng ① share profits ② receive dividends; draw dividends

分化 fēnhuà ① become divided; break up: ～瓦解 disintegrate; divide and demoralize ② split up: ③ [生] (of cells or tissues)

differentiate

分级管理 fēnjíguǎnlǐ management (administration) at different levels

分家 fēnjiā divide up family property among children; settlement of the family fortune; break up the family and live apart

分解 fēnjiě ① resolve ② decompose; resolve ③ mediate：让我替你们～～。Let me try to mediate your dispute. ④ disintegrate; split up：促使敌人内部～ try to bring about a split-up of the enemy ⑤ explain［章回小说用语］：…，且听下回～。…, and you must listen to the explanation in the next chapter.

分界 fēnjiè ① have as the boundary; be demarcated by ② dividing line; line of demarcation：～线 line of demarcation; boundary

分居 fēnjū live apart; separate：与父母～ live apart from one's parents

分开 fēnkāi ① come apart; separate; part：弟兄俩～已经5年了。It is five years since the two brothers parted. ② cause to separate; sort：把好的和坏的～ sort out the good ones from the bad

分口管理 fēnkǒuguǎnlǐ put (place) … under separate control

分类 fēnlèi classify; sort; assort：～目录 classified catalogue

分离 fēnlí ① (of things) separate; sever ② (of people) leave; part; separate

分裂 fēnliè split; break up：反对～祖国的言论和行为 oppose any words or acts designed to split the country

分流 fēnliú by-pass flow; split-flow; branch：～企业富余人员 resettlement of the surplus labour force of the enterprises

分门别类 fēnmén-biélèi put into different categories; classify

分明 fēnmíng ① be clear; be distinct; be unmistakable：这件事情是非～。The rights and wrongs of the case are perfectly clear ② clearly; evidently; obviously

分派 fēnpài allot; allocate; assign

分配 fēnpèi ① assign; allot：～工作 assign jobs (to) ② distribute; apportion：按劳～ distribution according to work

分批 fēnpī in batches：～交货 deliver the goods in batches

分片包干 fēnpiàn bāogān divide up into pieces and assign responsibility; take responsibility for pieces; divide up the work and assign a part to each individual (group)

分期 fēnqī ① by stages ② in instalments：～付款 pay in (by) instalments

分歧 fēnqí divergence; discrepancy; difference：意见～ differences of opinion; divergence of views

分清 fēnqīng distinguish; discriminate：～大是大非 distinguish right from wrong on major issue

分散 fēnsàn ① decentralize；scatter；disperse：～经营 decentralized management ②［注意力］divert；distract：～精力 disperse one's effort；diffuse one's energies

分数线 fēnshùxiàn［教］grade cut-off point：录取～ acceptance cut-off point (this is the point on school entrance exams which delineates acceptance and nonacceptance.)

分水岭 fēnshuǐlǐng watershed；line of demarcation

分税制 fēnshuìzhì a system of tax distribution；tax-sharing system：实行中央和地方～ institute a system of tax distribution between the central and local authorities

分庭抗礼 fēntíng-kànglǐ meet as equals；stand up to (sb.) as an equal

分头 fēntóu ① separately；severally：这事咱们～去做吧。Let's go about the work separately. ② parted hair：他理了一个小～。He has a new hair parting.

分文 fēnwén a single penny：～不取 gratis；free of charge

分析 fēnxi analyse

分享 fēnxiǎng share (with)；partake of：～胜利的喜悦 share the joys of victory (with)

分销店 fēnxiāodiàn retail shop

分晓 fēnxiǎo ①［多用于"见"的后面］outcome；solution. 此事明天就见～。We'll know the outcome of the whole affair tomorrow. ② sth. seen or understood clearly：问个～ inquire about and get to the bottom of a matter ③［通常与"没"连用］reason：没～的话 unreasonable remarks

分心 fēnxīn ① divert one's attention ② claim attention

分业承包 fēnyèchéngbāo contract system is adopted in different lines of work；contract different lines of work

分忧 fēnyōu share sb.'s worries；help sb. to get over a difficulty；share sb.'s cares and burdens；help sb. to get over a difficulty

分赃 fēnzāng divide the spoils；share the loot (booty)

分灶吃饭 fēnzào chīfàn［财政］"serving meals to different diners from different pots", namely, the system of dividing revenue and expenditure between the central and local governments and holding each responsible for balancing their budgets

分支 fēnzhī subdivision；branch：银行的～机构 branches of a bank

芬

fēn〈名〉sweet smell；fragrance

芬芳 fēnfāng ① sweet-smelling；fragrant：～的花朵 sweet-smelling flowers ② sweet smell；fragrance

吩

fēn

吩咐 fēnfù tell; bid; order

纷 fēn 〈形〉① confused: ～乱 numerous and disorderly; be plunged into disorder ② numerous: 他们～～议论。This has become the subject of much discussion among them.

纷繁 fēnfán numerous and complicated; intricate

纷飞 fēnfēi (of thick-falling snowflakes, flowers, etc.) swirl in the air; fly all over: 大雪～。Snowflakes were falling thick and fast.; It was snowing hard

纷纷 fēnfēn one after another; in succession: ～提出建议 offer proposals one after another

纷纷扬扬 fēnfēn-yángyáng (of snowflakes, flowers, leaves, etc.) flying or fluttering in profusion: 鹅毛大雪～。Snowflakes were fluttering like feathers in the air.; It was snowing heavily.

纷扰 fēnrǎo confusion; turmoil

纷纭 fēnyún diverse and confused: 头绪～have too many things to attend to

纷至沓来 fēnzhìtàlái keep pouring in; come thick and fast

氛 fēn 〈名〉atmosphere

氛围 fēnwéi atmosphere: 欢乐的～ a happy and gay atmosphere

fén

坟 fén 〈名〉grave: ～地 graveyard

坟地(场) féndì (chǎng) graveyard, cemetery

坟墓 fénmù grave; tomb

坟头 féntóu grave mound

焚 fén 〈动〉burn: ～香膜拜 prayers and incense-burning

焚化 fénhuà burn off; burn up; [尸骨] cremate

焚毁 fénhuǐ burn to ashes; burn down

焚烧 fénshāo burn; set on fire

焚香 fénxiāng burn incense or joss sticks: ～拜佛 burn incense before Buddha

fěn

粉 fěn ①〈名〉powder: 漂白～ bleaching powder ②〈形〉whitewashed; white: ～色 pink colour ③〈动〉crush to powder: ～碎 smash; crush

粉笔 fěnbǐ chalk: ～画 chalk drawing

粉彩 fěncǎi [工艺] mixed glaze

粉红 fěnhóng pink; rosy: 一条～色的裙子 a pink skirt

粉末 fěnmò powder

粉墨登场 fěnmò-dēngchǎng make oneself up and go on stage; embark upon a political venture; don one's costume and appear on the stage; mount the stage in full regalia

粉身碎骨 fěnshēn-suìgǔ have one's body smashed to pieces; be crushed to a pulp; grind someone's bones to powder and make mincemeat of one's flesh

粉饰 fěnshì whitewash; gloss over; camouflage: ～太平 present a false picture of peace

粉碎 fěnsuì break to pieces; smash; crush; frustrate; shatter: ～敌人的阴谋 frustrate the plot of the enemy

fèn

粪 fèn〈名〉feces; stool; excrements; [鸟兽的] droppings

粪便 fènbiàn feces; stool; excrements: ～检验 stool test. ～学 scatology

粪车 fènchē dung-cart; night-soil cart

粪池(坑) fènchí (kēng) manure pit

粪肥 fènféi manure; dung

愤 fèn ①〈动〉resent; be filled with indignation ②〈名〉anger; resentment; indignation: 气～ angry

愤愤不平 fènfènbùpíng be indignant; feel aggrieved; be resentful

愤恨 fènhèn indignantly resent; hate; detest

愤慨 fènkǎi (righteous) indignation: 感到无比～ be overwhelmed with indignation

愤怒 fènnù indignation; anger; wrath

愤然 fènrán angry; indignant: ～离去 leave in anger; walk off in a huff

愤世嫉俗 fènshì-jísú ① be cynical; detest the world and its ways: ～的传奇故事 cynical legends ② misanthropy

奋 fèn〈动〉① put forth energy; exert oneself; rouse oneself: 兴～ be excited ② raise; lift: ～笔疾书 wield one's writing brush energetically

奋不顾身 fènbùgùshēn so eager for the safety of others as to forget about one's own; selfless heroism; dash ahead regardless of one's safety

奋斗 fèndòu struggle; fight; strive

奋发 fènfā rouse oneself; exert oneself

奋发图强 fènfā-túqiáng work hard (energetically) for the prosperity of the country; work with stamina and diligence; go all out to make the country strong

奋飞 fènfēi take off with flying speed

奋击 fènjī strike out with great force; make a spirited attack

奋激 fènjī be roused to enthusiasm: 群情～。Popular feeling runs high.

奋进 fènjìn advance courageously

奋力 fènlì do all one can; spare no effort

奋起 fènqǐ ① brace up; exert oneself; rise with force and spirit: ～抗敌 rise against the enemy. ～自卫 rise in self-defence ② raise or lift sth. with all one's strength

奋勇 fènyǒng take courage；brace oneself(up)：～前进 forge ahead valiantly； advance bravely (boldly)

奋战 fènzhàn put up a fight；hard struggle；fight：～到底 fight to the (bitter) end

分 fèn〈名〉① component：水～ moisture content ② what is within one's duty or rights：本～ one's duty
另见 fēn

分量 fènliàng weight；quantity：他的建议很有～。His suggestion carried a great deal of weight. ～不足 be short in weight；be underweight

分内 fènnèi within one's duty；duty-bound：～之事 one's duty (part)；sth. within one's duty

分外 fènwài ① beyond one's duty；outside the scope of one's duty ② particularly；extremely；exceptionally：～有趣 extremely interesting

份 fèn〈名〉① part；portion；share：股～ share；stock ② copy

份额 fèn'é portion；share

份儿饭 fènrfàn table d'hôte；set meal

份子 fènzi ① one's share of expenses for a joint undertaking, as in buying a gift for a mutual friend ② a gift of money

fēng

丰 fēng〈形〉① plentiful；abundant；rich：～硕果实 rich yields. ～富生动的语言 rich, lively language ② great；brilliant ③ fine-looking；handsome：～采 fine manners；graceful bearing

丰碑 fēngbēi monument

丰产 fēngchǎn high yield；bumper crop：～田 highyield plot；bumper harvest field

丰富 fēngfù ① plentiful；abundant；copious；rich：～多采 rich and colourful. ～的想象力 rich (fertile) imagination ② enrich：～人民群众的文化生活 enrich the cultural life of the people

丰功伟绩 fēnggōng-wěijì great achievements；signal (magnificent, immense) contributions；valiant record；great deeds；brilliant feats

丰厚 fēnghòu rich and generous

丰满 fēngmǎn ① plentiful：～的故事情节 meaty details of a story ② full and round；chubby

丰年 fēngnián abundant year；good year；year of good harvest

丰饶 fēngráo rich and fertile：～的草原 fertile grassland

丰盛 fēngshèng rich；sumptuous：～的酒席 a sumptuous feast

丰收 fēngshōu good harvest；bumper harvest：获得…双～ achieve brilliant success in both …

丰硕 fēngshuò plentiful and substantial；rich：取得～的成果 reap rich fruits；score great successes

丰衣足食 fēngyī-zúshí ample food

and clothing; be well-fed and well-clothed; secure adequate food and clothing

丰盈 fēngyíng ① full and round; well-developed: 体态～ have a full figure ② plentiful: 衣食～ have plenty to eat and wear

丰腴 fēngyú ① full and round; plump; buxom and fair ② rich and fertile: ～的草场 a rich pasture ③ sumptuous: ～的酒席 a sumptuous feast

封 fēng〈动〉① seal (up); close: 密～ seal up completely ② bank (a fire) ③ confer (a title; territory, etc.) upon: ～诸候 create principalities ③〈名〉package; envelope: 信～ envelope ④〈量〉二～信 two letters

封闭 fēngbì ① close; closed door: ～的艺术系统 closed-door artistic system ② seal up

封存 fēngcún seal up for safekeeping

封顶 fēngdǐng seal the top: 奖金上不～，下不保底。The bonus has no seal on the top (has no ceiling) and no guarantee minimum.

封官许愿 fēngguān-xǔyuàn hand out (offer) official posts and make (lavish) promises; hold out prospects of official positions; offer (promise) high posts and other favours; promise high posts

封建 fēngjiàn ① the system of enfeoffment ② feudalism ③ feudal; feudalistic: 头脑～ feudal-minded

封禁 fēngjìn ①close (a place) ② prohibit; ban: ～黄色书刊 ban pornographic books and periodicals

封口 fēngkǒu ① seal: 这封信还没～。The letter hasn't been sealed yet. ② heal: 腿上的伤已经～了。The leg wound has healed. ③ say sth. definitive so as to prevent further discussion

封面 fēngmiàn［装钉］① the title page of a thread-bound book ② the front and back cover of a book ③ front cover

封山育林 fēngshān-yùlín seal the mountain to cultivate forest

封锁 fēngsuǒ blockade; block: ～消息 block the passage of information to; prevent the leakage of news. 互相～市场 blockade the market against one another

封套 fēngtào big envelope (for holding documents, books, etc.)

封条 fēngtiáo sealing strip; paper strip seal

烽 fēng〈名〉beacon

烽火 fēnghuǒ ① beacon fire ② flames of war: ～连天 flames of war flaring up everywhere; raging flames of war

蜂 fēng〈名〉bee; wasp

蜂巢 fēngcháo honeycomb

蜂房 fēngfáng any of the six-sided wax cells in a honeycomb

蜂蜜 fēngmì honey

蜂起 fēngqǐ rise in swarms

蜂乳 fēngrǔ royal jelly

蜂王精 fēngwángjīng royal jelly

蜂拥而至 fēngyōng'érzhì swarm forward;come with a rush; come swarming

峰 fēng〈名〉① summit; peak: 群～ a group of mountain peaks ② peak-like thing:驼～ camel's hump

峰巅 fēngdiān mountain peak; summit

峰峦 fēngluán ridges and peaks: ～陡峭 rugged ridges

峰态 fēngtài kurtosis

峰值 fēngzhí peak (value):生产的～ peak in production

锋 fēng〈名〉① point or edge (of a sword, etc.):针～相对 give it tit for tat ② front; van: 先～ pioneer; vanguard

锋快 fēngkuài ①(of a knife, sword, etc.) sharp; keen ② penetrating; incisive; sharp

锋利 fēnglì sharp; keen; trenchant: ～的语言 trenchant words

锋芒 fēngmáng sharp point; keenness; spearhead:马克思主义的～ the cutting-edge of Marxism. ～毕露 make a showy display of one's abilities; be too trenchant in one's wits. ～指向 direct the spearhead against; direct the sharp edge of struggle against

锋锐 fēngruì ①(of a knife, sword, etc.) sharp; keen:～的匕首 a sharp dagger ② penetrating; incisive; sharp:～的评论 incisive comments ③ a person's impulsive force; drive; push

风 fēng〈名〉① wind; draft:～雨同舟 stand together through storm and stress ② style; mode; custom; practice:工作作～ style of work ③ scene; view:～光 scene; sight; view ④ news; information:闻～而逃 flee at the news ⑤〈动〉put out to dry or air:～干 air-dry

风暴 fēngbào ① windstorm; storm ② a violent commotion; storm; tempest:革命～ the storm of revolution

风波 fēngbō disturbance; trouble: 平地起～ a storm out of nowhere; a sudden, unexpected turn of events

风采 fēngcǎi ① elegant demeanour; graceful bearing:～动人 have a strikingly elegant and graceful bearing ② literary grace

风餐露宿 fēngcān-lùsù eat in the wind and sleep in the dew—endure the hardships of an arduous journey

风潮 fēngcháo storm; agitation; unrest; storm and stress:闹～ carry on an agitation (for or against)

风尘 fēngchén ① travel fatique: 满面～(look) travel-stained ② hardships or uncertainties in an unstable society:沦落～ be driven to prostitution

风尘仆仆 fēngchén-púpú have endured the hardships of a long journey; be travel-stained; be travel-worn and weary

风驰电掣 fēngchí-diànchè at (with) lightning speed; go by like the wind; thunder past; swift as the wind and quick as lightning

风吹草动 fēngchuī-cǎodòng the rustle of leaves in the wind—a sign of disturbance or trouble

风吹浪打 fēngchuī-làngdǎ be beaten by wind and waves; be battered by a storm

风吹雨打 fēngchuī-yǔdǎ be buffeted by wind and rain; be exposed to the weather:经不起～ cannot withstand natural calamities

风度 fēngdù bearing; carriage; mien; demeanour:～翩翩 have a graceful bearing. 个人的～ personal mien

风格 fēnggé style; genre; manner:现代西方文学的～流派 stylistic schools of modern Western literature. ～清新 striking in style

风和日丽 fēnghé-rìlì a bright sun and a gentle breeze; warm and sunny weather

风华 fēnghuá elegance and intellectual brilliance:～正茂 at life's full flowering; in one's prime

风化 fēnghuà ① public morals; decency:有伤～ corrupt public morals; be harmful to society's morals; an offence against decency. ～区 demimonde quarters ② weathering

风纪 fēngjì conduct and discipline; discipline; morale

风景 fēngjǐng scenery; landscape:～画 landscape painting. ～林 scenic forest. ～区 secnic spot

风浪 fēnglàng ① stormy waves; storm ② a stormy experience:久经～ have weathered many a storm

风凉话 fēngliánghuà sarcastic remarks:说～ make irresponsible and carping comments from the sidelines

风流 fēngliú ① distinguished and admirable; outstanding; vogue; talented and meritorious:～人物 distinguished people; truly great men ② gifted and unconventional; romantic:～才子 talented and romantic scholar. ～韵事 love affair; romantic affair; affair; affaire ③ loose; dissolute; amorous

风马牛不相及 fēng mǎ niú bù xiāng jí have absolutely nothing to do with each other; be totally unrelated; have nothing in common with; be totally unrelated; have no relationship whatsoever with

风貌 fēngmào characteristic style and features

风靡 fēngmí fashionable; popular:～一时 become fashionable for a time; be in vogue at the time; make (create) a furor

风派人物 fēngpài rénwù persons of the "wind clique"; wavering fence-sitter; trimmer; timeserver

风平浪静 fēngpíng-làngjìng The

wind has dropped and the waves have subsided.; calm and tranquil

风起云涌 fēngqǐ-yúnyǒng like a rising wind or scudding clouds; surge forward (ahead); spread like a storm; rolling on with full forces; raging; surging and fast-changing

风气 fēngqì common practice; general mood; vogue; tendency; ethos; atmosphere

风情 fēngqíng ① information about wind direction, wind-force, etc. ② bearing; demeanour ③ feelings ④ amorous feelings; flirtatious expressions ⑤ local conditions and customs

风趣 fēngqù wit; humour:～说话 be a witty talker

风尚 fēngshàng prevailing practice (custom); vogue:～喜剧 comedy of manners

风声 fēngshēng ① sound of the wind ② rumour; news

风声鹤唳,草木皆兵 fēngshēng-hèlì, cǎomù-jiēbīng a slight movement in the grass or a gust of wind is enough to make the enemy jittery; be scared by the sigh of the wind or the cry of the cranes; fear ambush at every tree and tuft of grass

风水 fēngshuǐ geomantic "spirits of wind and water"; geomancy; proper geomantic factors; geomantic advantages; geomantic omen:～先生 geomancer

风俗 fēngsú moral customs; local customs; custom:～文化 folk culture; folkways. ～小说 novel of manners

风调雨顺 fēngtiáo-yǔshùn good weather for the crops; favourable weather

风头 fēngtóu ① the trend of events ② the publicity one receives:想出～ seek publicity. ～主义 showing off; striving for the limelight; limelightism

风土 fēngtǔ natural conditions and social customs of a place:～人情 local conditions (manners) and customs

风味 fēngwèi taste; flavour:～小吃 local flavour snacks. 别有～ have a special flavour; have a distinctive taste

风险 fēngxiǎn risk:～管理 risk management

风行 fēngxíng be in fashion (vogue); be popular:～一时 be popular for a while; be all the rage for a time

风言风语 fēngyán-fēngyǔ unfounded rumour; gossip; groundless talk

风雨 fēngyǔ wind and rain; the elements; trials and hardships:～交加。It's raining and blowing hard.; It's wet and windy. ～飘摇 swaying in the midst of a raging storm; precarious; tottering. ～同舟 in the same storm-tossed boat—stand together through thick and thin

风云 fēngyún wind and cloud—a stormy or unstable situation; fast-changing situation:～变幻 constant change of events; a changeable situation. ～人物 man of the hour. ～突变 a sudden change in the situation

风韵 fēngyùn graceful bearing; charm: ～犹存 still retaining one's graceful bearing (manner); look still attractive

风烛残年 fēngzhú-cánnián old and ailing like a candle guttering in the wind

风姿 fēngzī graceful bearing; charm

枫 fēng 〈名〉 maple

枫叶 fēngyè leaves of Chinese sweet gum, maple, etc. which turn red in autumn

疯 fēng 〈形〉 mad; crazy; insane

疯癫 fēngdiān mad; insane

疯话 fēnghuà mad talk; ravings; nonsense

疯狂 fēngkuáng mad; crazy; rabid; frenzied; frantic: ～反扑 a frantic counteroffensive

疯人院 fēngrényuàn mental hospital; lunatic asylum; madhouse

疯子 fēngzi lunatic; madman

féng

逢 féng 〈动〉 meet; come across; chance upon: 生不～时 born in wrong time

逢场作戏 féngchǎng-zuòxì join in the fun on occasion; make merry as occasion arises; have fun in keeping with the occasion; act (play) according to circumstances

逢凶化吉 féngxiōng-huàjí turn calamities into blessings; turn danger into safety; turn ill luck into good

逢迎 féngyíng fawn on; curry favour with: ～感戴 fawn on and servilely thank

缝 féng 〈动〉 sew; stitch
另见 fèng

缝补 féngbǔ sew and mend: ～浆洗 mend and wash

缝纫 féngrèn sewing; tailoring: ～机 sewing machine

缝制 féngzhì make (clothes, bedding, etc.)

fěng

讽 fěng 〈动〉① satirize; mock ② recite

讽嘲 fěngcháo sneer at; taunt

讽刺 fěngcì satirize; mock; sarcasm: ～画 satirical picture; caricature. ～作家 satiric writer; satirist. ～作品 satire

讽喻 fěngyù allegory; parable: ～诗 satirical (allegorical) poems

fèng

奉 fèng 〈动〉 ① present (with respect); offer: ～上一杯清茶 present a cup of green tea ② esteem; revere: ～若神明 revere as sacred ③ ～上级指示 be instructed by higher authorities ④ believe in: 信～基督教

believe in Christianity

奉承 fèngcheng flatter; curry favour with; fawn on; toady; soft-soap

奉告 fènggào have the honour to inform; let sb. know:无可～ No comment.

奉公守法 fènggōng-shǒufǎ respect justice and abide by the laws; law-abiding

奉命 fèngmìng ① receive orders (instructions) ② by order (of); under orders:～出发 be under orders to start

奉陪 fèngpéi keep sb. company:～到底 keep sb. company to the end

奉劝 fèngquàn would like to advise; advise

奉若神明 fèngruò-shénmíng worship sb. or sth.; make a fetish of sth.

奉献 fèngxiàn dedicate; devote; offer as a tribute

奉行 fèngxíng pursue (a policy, etc.):～不结盟政策 pursue a policy of nonalignment

奉养 fèngyǎng support and wait upon (one's parents, etc.)

俸 fèng 〈名〉 pay; salary

俸禄 fènglù an official's salary; government salary

凤 fèng 〈名〉 phoenix:～凰 phoenix

凤毛麟角 fèngmáo-línjiǎo the hair of a phoenix and the horn of a giraffe — very rare; rarity of rarities

缝 fèng 〈名〉 ① seam:天衣无～ a seamless heavenly robe ② crack; chink; crevice:门～儿 slight opening in door panel 另见 féng

缝隙 fèngxì chink; crack; crevice

fó

佛 fó 〈名〉 Buddha

佛典 fódiǎn Buddhist canonical texts; Buddhist canon; Buddhist scriptures

佛法 fófǎ Buddha dharma; Buddhist doctrine; doctrine

佛教 fójiào Buddhism; Foism:～徒 Buddhist

佛经 fójīng Buddhist Scripture; Buddhist sutra; Buddhist sacred literature

佛龛 fókān niche for a statute of Buddha

佛理 fólǐ Buddhist truth

佛门 fómén Buddhism:～弟子 followers of Buddhism; Buddhists

佛事 fóshì Buddhist ceremony (service)

佛堂 fótáng family hall for worshipping Buddha

佛土 fótǔ Buddha-field; Buddha-realms

佛像 fóxiàng Buddhist images; Buddhist icons; Buddhist statues; joss

佛宗 fózōng the principles of Buddhist law

佛祖 fózǔ Buddhist patriarch

fǒu

否 fǒu ①〈动〉negate; reject; deny:～定错误论点 reject wrong theses ②〈副〉no:是～ whether or not; yes or not

否定 fǒudìng deny; negate; repudiate:～之～ negation of negation

否决 fǒujué vote down; veto; reject:～权 veto (power):提案被～。The motion was voted down.

否认 fǒurèn deny; repudiate; negate; reject; refuse:她不～事实。She didn't deny the facts.

否则 fǒuzé otherwise; if not; or; or else:要谦虚,～就要落后。Be modest, otherwise you will lag behind.

fū

夫 fū〈名〉① husband ② man

夫唱妇随 fūchàng-fùsuí the husband to sing and the wife to follow; A wife sings her husband's tune.; harmony between husband and wife

夫妇(妻) fūfù(qī) husband and wife; couple:～感情的破裂 alienation of mutual affection

夫人 fūrén ① wife ② Lady; Madam; [姓氏前] Mrs

肤 fū〈名〉skin:切～之痛 keenly felt pain

肤浅 fūqiǎn superficial; skin-deep; shallow:～的认识 a superficial understanding (knowledge) of

肤色 fūsè colour of skin

孵 fū〈动〉hatch; brood; incubate:～小鸡 hatch chicks

孵化 fūhuà hatch; incubate

孵卵 fūluǎn brood; hatch; incubate:～鸡 brooding hen

敷 fū〈动〉① apply:～药 apply medical ointment or powder ② spread; lay:～设铁路 lay a railway track ③〈副〉enough; be sufficient for:入不～出 unable to make both ends meet

敷设 fūshè ① lay (pipes, etc.): ～铁轨 lay a railway track ② lay (mines):～水雷 lay mines in water

敷衍 fūyǎn negligently; perfunctorily; be half-hearted about: ～了事 do one's work perfunctorily; muddle through one's work. ～塞责 perform one's duty in a perfunctory manner; with a perfunctory gesture; make a show of doing one's duty; perfunctoriness

fú

扶 fú〈动〉① support (with the hand); uphold:～杖 lean on a stick ② help sb. up; relieve:～危 help those in distress

扶持 fúchí ① support sb. with one's hand; help sb. to stand or walk ② help sustain:give aid to:support:荷花虽好,也要绿叶～。For all its beauty the lotus needs its green leaves to set it off.

扶老携幼 fúlǎo-xiéyòu help the aged and the young; holding the old by the arm and the young by the hand; bringing along the old and the young

扶贫 fúpín poverty alleviation; aid the poor:～项目 poverty-alleviating projects. ～救灾 support the poor and provide relief to disaster areas

扶手 fúshou ① handrail; rail; banisters ② armrest:～椅 armchair

扶养 fúyǎng support; maintain; foster:～父母 support one's parents. ～义务 duty of maintenance; duty of support

扶摇直上 fúyáo-zhíshàng rise directly to a high position; successful in one's official career; soar on the wings of a cyclone; rise steeply; skyrocket

扶植 fúzhí foster; back; prop up; patronize

扶志 fúzhì nurture the will:扶贫要先～。In aiding the poor, we must nurture the will.

扶助 fúzhù help; assist; support:～老弱 help the old and the weak

福 fú〈名〉happiness; blessing; good fortune (luck):享～ enjoy oneself or easy way of living

福分 fúfen good luck; good fortune; a happy lot:我可没有你这样的～。I don't have such good luck as you do.

福利 fúlì welfare; well-being; weal:～金 welfare fund (subsidies). ～院 welfare institutions

福气 fúqì happy lot; blessedness; good fortune (luck):有～的人(们) the blessed

福如东海 fúrúdōnghǎi happiness as boundless as the eastern seas (a stock term of congratulations)

福相 fúxiàng a face showing good fortune

福星 fúxīng lucky star; mascot:～高照。The lucky star is in the ascendant.

福音 fúyīn ①[宗] gospel ② good news; glad tidings; a blessing for

辐 fú〈名〉spoke (of a wheel)

辐合 fúhé convergency:～思维 convergent thinking. ～思维的人 converger

辐射 fúshè [物] radiation:～波 radiated wave. ～线 radiant rays

幅 fú〈名〉① width (of cloth):单～ cloth material of single width ② roll (of paper); piece; 一～肖像 a portrait

幅度 fúdù margin; range; scope; extent:大～增长 increase by a big margin. ～价格 prices fluctuating within a certain range

幅员 fúyuán area of a country's territory; the size of a country:～辽阔 have a vast territory; vast in territory

浮 fú〈动〉① float; drift: ～动工资 floating wage ② exceed: 人～于事 overstaffed〈形〉③ superficial; on the surface: ～灰 dust (ash) on the surface ④ movable: ～财 movable (portable) property ⑤ superficial; flighty: 举止轻～ behave frivolously

浮财 fúcái movable property

浮沉 fúchén now sink, now emerge; drift along: 宦海～ the ups and downs in officialdom; the vicissitudes of an official career

浮雕 fúdiāo relief (sculpture): ～像 figure in relief. ～刺绣 raised embroidery

浮动 fúdòng ① float; drift; waft: ～汇率 floating exchange rate ② fluctuate; be unsteady

浮泛 fúfàn ① float about ② superficial; general ③ display; reveal: 嘴角上～起笑意。A smile appears on his lips.

浮光掠影 fúguāng-lüèyǐng reflected light from the surface of water and a passing shadow; sth. ephemeral that leaves hardly any impression; floating right and passing shadow

浮华 fúhuá ostentatious; pompous; flashy; showy

浮夸 fúkuā boastful; untruthful; exaggerative: ～作风 boastful way of doing things; boasting and exaggeration

浮码头 fúmǎtou floating pier

浮浅 fúqiǎn superficial; shallow: 一种～的看法 a superficial view

浮土 fútǔ dust collected on furniture, clothing, etc.; surface dust

浮现 fúxiàn appear before one's eyes: 往事～在我眼前。Scenes of the past rose before my eyes.; The past came back to my mind.

浮想联翩 fúxiǎng-liánpiān thoughts or recollections flashing across one's mind; thoughts thronging one's mind

浮云 fúyún floating clouds

浮躁 fúzào rash; impetuous; impulsive: ～的学风 impetuous style of study

浮肿 fúzhǒng dropsy; edema

俘 fú ①〈名〉captive; prisoner of war ②〈动〉capture; take prisoner

俘获 fúhuò capture; seize

俘虏 fúlǔ captive; prisoner of war (P.O.W.)

伏 fú〈动〉① bend over; lie prostrate: ～地 lie on the ground ② hide: 潜～ conceal; lie low; hide ③ go down; subside: 起～ rise and fall ④ surrender; admit (defeat or guilt): ～法 be executed; be put to death ⑤〈名〉dog days; hot season: 入～ beginning of the hottest part of the summer

伏案 fú'àn bend over one's desk: ～读书 bend over one's desk reading

伏笔 fúbǐ a hint foreshadowing later developments in a story, essay, etc.; a remark suggestive of later developments in a story, etc.; foreshadowing

伏兵 fúbīng troops in ambush; ambush

伏法 fúfǎ be executed; be put to death

伏击 fújī ambush: ～圈 ring of ambush

伏天 fútiān the *fu* days—the hottest days of the year

伏帖 fútiē ① fit perfectly ② comfortable; cozy ③ submissive; obedient

伏罪 fúzuì admit one's guilt; plead guilty (to a crime)

芙 fú

芙蓉 fúróng cottonrose hibiscus: ～出水 a lotus flower just appearing above the water (said of a beautiful poem or painting or of a beautiful woman)

符 fú

① 〈名〉 sign; symbol: 音～ musical notes ② 〈动〉 tally with; square with: ～合现实 conform with reality

符号 fúhào symbol; sign; mark: ～思维 symbolic thinking

符合 fúhé conform to; conform with; be in accord with; in keeping with; live up to; be in conformity with; accord with; correspond; square with; meet: ～史实 conform to historical facts

符咒 fúzhòu charm; incantation

服 fú

① 〈名〉 clothes; dress: 礼～ formal dress 〈动〉 ② obey; be convinced: 心～口～ be sincerely convinced ③ serve: ～兵役 serve in the army ④ take (medicine): 口～ take medicine orally ⑤ be accustomed to: ～水土 acclimatization

另见 fù

服从 fúcóng obey; submit to; be subordinate to; abide by: ～国家计划 be subordinated to the state plans

服法 fúfǎ ① submit to the law: 认罪～ admit one's guilt and submit oneself to the law ② directions about how to take a medicine

服气 fúqì be convinced: 不～ refuse to give in

服丧 fúsāng be in mourning (for the death of a kinsman, etc.)

服色 fúsè the style and colour of clothes: 民族～ the styles and colours of ethnic garments

服饰 fúshì clothes and ornaments; dress and personal adornment; dress

服侍 fúshì wait upon; attend; serve

服输 fúshū acknowledge (admit) defeat: 不～ refuse to acknowledge (admit) defeat

服帖 fútiē ① be convinced ② fit; smooth: 他的上装背部有点不大～。The back of his coat is not very smooth.

服务 fúwù serve: ～性行业 service trades; catering services; public service trades: ～上门 door-to-door service. ～台 service desk (counter); information and reception desk

服刑 fúxíng serving a sentence：～期满 complete a term of imprisonment. ～者 person undergoing sentence

服役 fúyì serve in the army；be in active service

服装 fúzhuāng clothing；dress：～店 clothing store；clothes shop. ～设计 dress designing；costume designing；clothing design. ～设计师 apparel stylist

服罪 fúzuì confess (admit) one's guilt；plead guilty；acceptance of punishment

拂 fú〈动〉① flick (off)；brush off；whisk：微风～面。A breeze caresses the cheeks. ② stroke (the face) lightly；touch lightly：～泪而别 wipe tears and leave

拂荡 fúdàng sway gently；swing slightly；wave gracefully

拂动 fúdòng brush against；stroke；caress

拂拭 fúshì wipe (whisk) off

拂晓 fúxiǎo (at) dawn；(at) daybreak

拂袖而去 fúxiù'érqù leave with a flick of one's sleeve—go off in a huff

拂煦 fúxú (of the wind) be blowing warm：微风～。A light breeze is blowing warm.

fǔ

腐 fǔ ①〈名〉bean curd ②〈形〉rotten；corrupt；stale：流水不～。Running water never gets stale.

腐败 fǔbài ① rotten；putrid；decayed ② rotten；corrupt：～分子 corruptive elements

腐臭 fǔchòu emitting a smell of decay；decaying and stinking；smelly

腐恶 fǔ'è corrupt and evil：～势力 evil influences

腐化 fǔhuà become corrupt；degenerate；corruption；degeneration：～堕落 morally degenerate

腐烂 fǔlàn ① decompose；become putrid (rotten) ② corrupt；rotten

腐蚀 fǔshí ① corrode；bite ② corrupt；deprave：黄色电影～了人们的灵魂。Blue cinema corrupts the souls of people.

腐朽 fǔxiǔ rotten；decayed；decadent：～观念 decadent notions

俯 fǔ〈动〉bend own；stoop；hang (one's head)：～首 bow one's head. ～冲式轰炸 dive bombing

俯冲 fǔchōng dive：～轰炸 dive-bomb

俯伏 fǔfú lie prostrate，lie prone

俯瞰 fǔkàn overlook；survey；command；a bird's eye view：他们爬上山～城市的全景。They climbed up the mountain and enjoyed a bird's eye view of the city.

俯身 fǔshēn bend over；bend down

俯拾即是 fǔshíjíshì be easily available；can be found anywhere; be very common

俯视 fǔshì overlook; look down (at):从山上～西湖 overlook the West Lake from the hill

俯首 fǔshǒu stoop; hang one's head:～就范 meekly submit. ～帖耳 show complete submission (to); docilely obey; servile

俯首甘为孺子牛 fǔshǒu gānwéi rúzǐniú Head bowed, like a willing ox I serve the children.

俯顺民情 fǔshùn-mínqíng in deference to the feelings of the people

俯仰 fǔyǎng a bending or lifting of the head—a simple move or action:随人～ be at sb.'s beck and call

辅 fǔ ①〈动〉assist; complement; supplement:相～相成 complement each other ②〈形〉supplementary; subsidiary; auxiliary:～助作用 supplementary role

辅币 fǔbì fractional currency;[硬币] subsidiary coin;[纸币] subsidiary note

辅导 fǔdǎo give guidance (to); coach; tutor:～学习有困难的学生 tutor a pupil who was having difficulty with his lessons. ～课 coaching hour

辅料 fǔliào supplemental materials

辅音 fǔyīn consonant

辅助 fǔzhù ① assist ② supplementary; subsidiary:～读物 supplementary reading material. ～劳动力 subsidiary labour power. ～性机构 support units

辅佐 fǔzuǒ assist a ruler in governing a country

抚 fǔ〈动〉① console; comfort:～慰 comfort; console ② bring up; foster:～孤 nurse orphan ③ stroke

抚爱 fǔ'ài caress; fondle

抚摩 fǔmó stroke:我轻轻地～着他的头发。I was gently stroking his hair.

抚弄 fǔnòng stroke; fondle:她双手不停地～着她的辫子。She kept on stroking her braids.

抚慰 fǔwèi console; soothe; comfort

抚心自问 fǔxīn-zìwèn examine one's own conscience

抚恤 fǔxù comfort a bereaved family:～金 pension for the disabled or for the family of the deceased; consolation money

抚养 fǔyǎng bring up; raise; rear; foster:～成人 bring sb. up

抚育 fǔyù foster; nurture; tend:～烈士子女 bring up the children of revolutionary martyrs

斧 fǔ〈名〉axe; hatchet:～头 axe; hatchet

斧正 fǔzhèng (please) make corrections

府 fǔ〈名〉① seat of government; government office ② official residence; mansion:王～ a prince's residence ③ prefecture:知～ magistrate of a prefecture ④〈敬〉your home:贵～ your home

府绸 fǔchóu poplin：山东～ Shandong pongee；shantung

府第 fǔdì (of nobles. high officials，big landlords，etc.)；mansion house

府上 fǔshang ① your home；your family：改日再来～拜访。I'll pay a visit to your home some other day. ②your native place：您～哪里？Where are you from？

釜 fǔ〈名〉cauldron

釜底抽薪 fǔdǐ-chōuxīn take away (extract) the firewood from under the cauldron — a fundamental solution；remove the ground on which someone stands

fù

富 fù ①〈名〉wealth：致～ build up a fortune〈形〉② rich；wealthy：～商 wealthy merchant ③ opulent；affluent；abundant：年～力强 in one's prime

富贵 fùguì riches and honour；wealth and rank：～不能淫 not to be corrupted by riches and honour

富豪 fùháo rich and powerful people；millionaire

富丽堂皇 fùlì-tánghuáng beautiful and imposing；splendid；magnificent；grand

富强 fùqiáng strong and prosperous；rich and mighty：繁荣～ prosperous and powerful

富饶 fùráo rich；fertile；abundant；affluent

富人 fùrén the rich；rich people

富翁 fùwēng man of wealth；moneybags

富有 fùyǒu ① rich；wealthy ② be full of；be rich in：～艺术魅力的作品 works which have a good artistic appeal

富余 fùyu have more than needed；have enough and to spare：我还～两张票。I have two tickets to spare.

富裕 fùyù rich；wealthy；well-to-do：走共同～的道路 take the road to common prosperity

富足 fùzú plentiful；abundant；rich

副 fù〈形〉① deputy；assistant；vice；associate：～总经理 deputy general manager. ～主席 vice president. ～编审 associate senior editor. ～译审 associate senior translator. ～研究员 associate research fellow ② secondary；auxiliary：～食品 nonstaple food ③〈量〉pair；set：两～手套 two pairs of gloves

副本 fùběn duplicate (copy)；transcript；copy

副标题 fùbiāotí subheading

副产品(物) fùchǎnpǐn (wù) by-product

副官 fùguān adjutant；aide-de-camp

副教授 fùjiàoshòu associate professor

副刊 fùkān supplement：文学～ literary supplement

副品 fùpǐn substandard goods; second-class goods; seconds

副食 fùshí nonstaple food:～加工厂 nonstaple food processing factory. ～商店 grocer's; grocery

副手 fùshǒu assistant; secondary

副研究员 fùyánjiūyuán associate research fellow

副业 fùyè bywork; sideline:～生产 sideline production

副职 fùzhí the position of a deputy to the chief of an office, department, etc.

副作用 fùzuòyòng by-effect; side effect; aftereffect

讣 fù 〈名〉 announcement of death; obituary

讣告 fùgào obituary (notice)

赴 fù 〈动〉 go to; leave for:～宴 attend a banquet. 离京～广州 leave Beijing for Guangzhou

赴会 fùhuì attend a meeting; keep an appointment (to meet sb.)

赴任 fùrèn proceed to take up one's post; go to one's post; leave for an assignment

赴汤蹈火 fùtāng-dǎohuǒ go through fire and water; take all risks; through thick and thin; undaunted by danger

赴宴 fùyàn go to a feast; attend a banquet

赴约 fùyuē fulfil an engagement; keep an appointment

赋 fù 〈名〉 ① tax; levy:田～ land tax ② *fu*, a descriptive poetic prose interposed with verse; rhymed prose 〈动〉 ③ bestow; endow with:天～之才 God-given talent ④ compose:～诗一首 compose a poem

赋税 fùshuì taxes; levy

赋役 fùyì taxes and corvee

赋有 fùyǒu be endowed with (qualities or characteristics)

赋予 fùyǔ give; grant; endow (with); entrust:～新的使用价值 endow sth. with new use value

父 fù 〈名〉 father

父辈 fùbèi people of father's generation

父老 fùlǎo elders (of a country or district):～兄弟 elders and brethren

父母 fùmǔ father and mother; parents:～保护子女的责任 parent's duty to protect child. ～对子女侵权行为的责任 parent's liability for child's torts

父亲 fùqin father

父系 fùxì paternal line; patriline; paternity; patrilineal:～家庭 patrilineral family. ～亲属 relatives on the paternal side

复 fù 〈动〉 ① turn around; turn over; repeat:反～无常 changeable. 在床上翻来～去 toss in bed ② reply; answer:电～ reply by telegram ③ restore; recover:康～ restored to health ④ revenge:～仇 revenge; avenge ⑤ 〈形〉 repeated; double:～试 second examination ⑥ 〈副〉 repeatedly; again:故态～

萌 return to one's habit

复本位制 fùběnwèizhì ［经］ bimetallism; bimetallic standard

复辟 fùbì restore a dethroned monarch or the old order

复查 fùchá check; reexamine: 一个星期后到医院～。Come back to the hospital for a check in a week's time.

复仇 fùchóu revenge; avenge: ～主义 revanchism

复发 fùfā recurrence; relapse: 旧病～ have a relapse

复工 fùgōng return to work (after a strike or layoff)

复古 fùgǔ restore old order; restore ancient ways; yearning for the past

复合 fùhé compound; complex: 感觉的～ complex of sensation

复核 fùhé reexamine; check

复会 fùhuì resume a session (sitting)

复婚 fùhūn ① (of a divorced couple) remarry each other ② restoration of a marriage

复活 fùhuó revive; resurgence; bring back to life: ～节 Easter; Easter Sunday (day)

复交 fùjiāo ① resume (once broken) relations ② reestablish (resume) diplomatic relations

复旧 fùjiù restoration of the old; return to the past

复利(息) fùlì(xī) compound interest

复刊 fùkān (of magazines or newspapers) resume publication

复课 fùkè resume classes

复赛 fùsài ［径赛］ intermediary heats; ［球赛］ semifinals

复审 fùshěn ① recheck; reexamine ② ［法］ rehear; retrial: ～请求书 petition for rehearing

复苏 fùsū ① come back to life or consciousness; resuscitate ② recovery; resurgence: 经济～ economic resurgence

复习 fùxí review; revise: ～功课 review (revise) lessons

复线 fùxiàn ［铁路］ alternate lines

复信 fùxìn ① write a letter in reply; reply ② a letter in reply

复兴 fùxīng revive; rehabilitate; resurrect: 民族～ national revival. 文艺～ the Renaissance

复姓 fùxìng two-character surname; compound surname

复学 fùxué go back to school (after prolonged absence for health reasons, etc); resume one's interrupted studies

复业 fùyè ① take up one's old trade again ② reopen or restart business

复印 fùyìn duplicate; photocopy; xerox: ～机 xerox machine

复员 fùyuán ① return to peacetime conditions ② (of servicemen) be demobilized: ～费 demobilization pay. ～军人 a demobilized serviceman; an ex-serviceman

复原 fùyuán ① be restored to health; recuperate (from) ② put sth. back into the original state; restore

复杂 fùzá complicated; complex:

故事情节～。The story is very complicated.

复职 fùzhí resume one's post

复制 fùzhì reproduce; duplicate: ～品 reproduction; duplication; replica

复种 fùzhòng multiple crops: ～面积 multiple-cropping area; multiple crop area

复转军人 fùzhuǎnjūnrén armymen demobilized or transferred to civilian work

覆 fù 〈动〉① cover ② overturn

覆被 fùbèi cover: 森林～率 forest cover

覆盖率 fùgàilǜ ①[电视] coverage ② rate of ground cover (the ratio of land area which is covered with vegetation)

覆灭 fùmiè destruction; downfall; complete collapse

覆没 fùmò ① sink and capsize ② be wiped out; be annihilated

覆辙 fùzhé the track of an overturned cart: 重蹈～ take the same disastrous road

腹 fù 〈名〉 belly; abdomen

腹背受敌 fùbèi-shòudí be attacked front and rear

腹地 fùdì interior; inland

腹稿 fùgǎo general outline of an article in one's mind

腹痛 fùtòng abdominal pain

腹心 fùxīn ① vital organs; key parts: ～之患 disease in one's vital organs—danger from within; serious hidden trouble ② trusted subordinate; reliable agent

付 fù 〈动〉① pay: 预～ pay in advance ② turn (hand) over to; give; commit: ～诸行动 put into practice

付出 fùchū ① pay: ～代价 pay the cost ② expend ～劳动量 expend the quantity of labour; contribute the amount of labour

付方 fùfāng [簿记] credit side; credit

付还 fùhuán pay back; repay

付款 fùkuǎn pay a sum of money; make payment; pay: 货到～ cash on delivery (COD). ～人 payer. ～条件 terms of payment

付讫 fùqì paid

付清 fùqīng pay in full; pay off; clear (a bill): 一次～ pay off in one lump sum

付息 fùxī pay interest

付现 fùxiàn pay in cash

付印 fùyìn ① send to (the) press; go to (the) press ② put into print: ～校样 final proof

付帐 fùzhàng pay expenses; pay (foot) a bill

付之一炬 fùzhī-yījù commit to the flames

付之一笑 fùzhī-yīxiào dismiss with a laugh

付诸东流 fùzhū-dōngliú (of efforts) have proven futile; thrown into the eastward flowing stream — all one's efforts wasted; irrevocably lost; cast to the winds; bury in oblivion

附 fù 〈动〉① add; attach; enclose: 信中～上几笔 add a few

words in a letter ② get close to;be near to:～耳交谈 talk in whispers

附带 fùdài ① in passing; incidentally:～说一下 by the way; incidentally. ～民事诉讼 incidental civil action ② supplementary; extra:～收入 extra income

附和 fùhè join one's voice to; parrot; chime in with; echo:随声～ echo others thoughtlessly

附会 fùhuì drawing wrong conclusions by false analogy; drawing incorrect conclusions by the use of false analogies; false analogy

附加 fùjiā additional; extra:～工资 supplemental wages. ～费 extra charges; surcharge. ～税 supertax; surtax; additional tax

附件 fùjiàn ① appendix; annex ② annexed document; proviso

附录 fùlù appendix; addendum; supplement

附上 fùshàng be enclosed herewith:随信～产品目录一份。A catalogue of products is enclosed herewith.

附设 fùshè have as an attached institution:这所大学～一所中学。There is a middle school attached to the university.

附属 fùshǔ attached; affiliated; accessory:～公司 affiliated company. ～医院 affiliated (attached) hospital. ～中学 affiliated (attached) middle school

附言 fùyán postscript (PS)

附议 fùyì second a motion or proposal

附则 fùzé supplementary provisions

服

fù〈量〉(for Chinese medicine) dose:一～中药 a dose of Chinese medicine
另见 fú

驸

fù〈名〉a horse hitched up by the side of the shaft-horse (to assist the pulling of a vehicle)

驸马 fùmǎ husband of an emperor's daughter or sister; emperor's son-in-law or brother-in-law

负

fù〈动〉① carry on the back; bear:～重荷 bear (carry) a heavy burden ② owe:～债 be in debt ③ fail in one's duty or obligation; betray:辜～ fail to live up to ④ shoulder; take on; bear:～责任 assume responsibility ⑤ lose (a battle; game, etc.); be defeated:～于对手 lose the match ⑥ suffer:～伤 be wounded; be injured ⑦ enjoy:久～盛名 have long enjoyed a good reputation〈形〉⑧ negative; minus:～效应 negative effects

负担 fùdān ① bear; shoulder:～损失 bear a loss ② burden; load

负荷 fùhè ① carry on one's back and shoulder; bear; shoulder ② load (that a person or machine is expected to perform); work load:超～ overload

负荆请罪 fùjīng-qǐngzuì proffer a

birch and ask for a flogging—offer a humble apology

负片 fùpiàn negative

负气 fùqì (in a fit of) pique:～出走 leave home in a fit of pique

负伤 fùshāng be wounded; be injured:负重伤 be badly wounded. 光荣～ be wounded in action

负心 fùxīn faithless; ungrateful (esp. in love); conscienceless; heartless:～汉 unfaithful lover (husband)

负盈不负亏 fùyíng bù fùkuī [经] share only the profits and shoulder no responsibility for losses

负有罪责 fùyǒu-zuìzé answer for a crime

负隅顽抗 fùyú-wánkàng resist desperately; make a last-ditch fight; With their backs to the wall, they fight stubbornly.; Cornered as they are, they continue to put up a stiff resistance.; put up a desperate struggle

负约 fùyuē fail to keep a promise; break one's engagement

负责 fùzé be responsible for; be in charge of:～干部 responsible cadre; cadre in charge. ～人 person in charge; leading person

负债 fùzhài run (get) into debt; be in debt:～额 amount of obligation. ～累累 be over head and ears in debt; be heavily in debt; be up to one's eyes in debt

负罪 fùzuì bear the blame

妇 fù 〈名〉 woman:～幼保健站 women and children's health station

妇产科 fùchǎnkē (department of) gynaecology and obstetrics; (department of) gynaecology:～医生 gynaecologist

妇产医院 fùchǎn yīyuàn a hospital for gynaecology and obstetrics

妇联 fùlián women's federation:全国～ All-China Women's Federation

妇女 fùnǚ woman:～半边天。Women make up half of the sky. ～节 International Working Women's Day. ～社团 sorority

妇人 fùrén married woman

妇孺 fùrú women and children:～皆知 known even to women and children

妇婴 fùyīng women and infants; mothers and babies:～卫生 maternity and infant hygiene

妇幼 fùyòu women and children:～保健站 health centre for women and children; maternity and child-care centre. ～卫生 maternity and child hygiene

G g

gā

嘎 gā〈象〉a loud, high-pitched sound：汽车～的一声刹住了。The car screeched to a halt.

嘎吱 gāzhī〈象〉[多重叠用]the creaking sound of objects that are under great stress：行李压得扁担～～直响。The shoulder pole creaked under the weight of the luggage.

咖 gā
另见 kā

咖喱 gālí curry：～粉 curry powder

gá

轧 gá〈动〉① press hard against each other ② associate with; make (friends) with：～朋友 make friends with sb. ③ check; audit
另见 yà，zhá

轧帐 gázhàng check the accounts

gāi

该 gāi ①〈助动〉should; ought to：～罚 should be punished〈动〉② be one's turn to do sth.：～他了。It's his turn now. ③ owe：你～他多少钱？How much do you owe him? ④〈代〉this; that; it：～案 that case ⑤〈副〉probably; most likely：他们如果是一点出发的，现在～到那儿了。If they had started at one o'clock, they ought to have got there by now.

该死 gāisǐ ①[咒语] Damn! Damn it (you)! Go to hell! Blast it (him)! ② damned; cursed：～的老鼠！That damned mouse!

该帐 gāizhàng be in debt：～该多了，就不好还了。If you run up your bills, you'll have difficulty paying them.

该证人 gāizhèngrén the said witness

gǎi

改 gǎi〈动〉① change; transform：～荒山为果园 transform barren hills into orchards ② revise; alter：删～ amend and correct ③ correct; rectify：～错 correct mistakes

改编 gǎibiān ① adapt; rearrange; rewrite：这部小说～成剧本。This novel was adapted for the stage. ② reorganize; reform

改变 gǎibiàn change; alter; transform:三年不见,她的样子看来没有多大的~。It's been three years since I last saw her but she hasn't changed much.

改朝换代 gǎicháo-huàndài dynastic changes; changes of dynasties

改动 gǎidòng change; alter; modify:这篇文章他只~了一些词句。He just polished a few sentences in this essay.

改革 gǎigé reform; reorganize:~开放 reform and opening to the outside world. 经济体制~ economic structure reform. ~文学 literature of reform

改观 gǎiguān change in appearance; take on a new look

改过 gǎiguò reform (oneself); mend one's ways:~自新 make a new man of oneself; turn over a new page (leaf); mend one's ways

改行 gǎiháng change one's occupation (profession)

改换 gǎihuàn change over to; change

改悔 gǎihuǐ repent; mend one's ways

改嫁 gǎijià (of a woman) remarry

改建 gǎijiàn reconstruct; rebuild:把仓库~为厂房 remodel a storehouse for use as a workshop

改进 gǎijìn improve; make better:服务态度有很大的~。The service has improved a lot.

改口 gǎikǒu withdraw or modify one's previous remark; correct oneself

改良 gǎiliáng ① improve; ameliorate:~土壤 improve (ameliorate) the soil ② reform:~主义 reformism

改判 gǎipàn amend (revise) a judgement; change the original sentence

改期 gǎiqī change the date; postpone:会议~至下星期一举行。The meeting is postponed until (to) next Monday.

改任 gǎirèn change to another post:他从上月起~车间主任。He has been at his new post as workshop superintendent since last month.

改善 gǎishàn improve; better; ameliorate:~环境 improve the environment

改天 gǎitiān some other day; another day:~见!See you later. ~换地 gǎitiān-huàndì transform heaven and earth; change the world

改头换面 gǎitóu-huànmiàn change the appearance but not the substance; make only superficial changes; dish up in a new form

改弦更张 gǎixián-gēngzhāng start afresh; make a fresh start

改弦易辙 gáixián-yìzhé change one's course; strike out on a new path

改选 gǎixuǎn reelect. 班委会每年~一次。A new class committee is elected every year.

改邪归正 gǎixié-guīzhèng forsake evil ways and return to the right path; turn over a new leaf; mend one's ways
改写 gǎixiě rewrite; adapt: ～本 adapted version
改造 gǎizào remake; reform; remould; reconstitute; transform: ～罪犯 reform criminals. ～中低产田 transform medium and low-yielding land
改正 gǎizhèng correct; rectify; amend: ～错误 correct one's mistakes
改制 gǎizhì change a social system; reform
改组 gǎizǔ reorganize; restructure; reshuffle: ～机构 reorganize the setup. ～内阁 reshuffle the cabinet. ～现有企业 revamping the existing enterprises

gài

盖 gài ①〈名〉cover; lid: 盒～ the lid of a box〈动〉② cover; shield: ～好被子 tuck the quilt ③ surpass; excel; overwhelm: 力大～人 excel all others in strength ④ affix a seal; seal: ～手印 take finger prints ⑤ build: ～房子 build houses
盖棺论定 gàiguān-lùndìng Only when a person is dead can he be finally judged and assessed.
盖世 gàishì unparalleled; matchless; peerless: ～无双 without a match; unparalleled in the world. ～英雄 a peerless (matchless) hero
盖章 gàizhāng affix one's seal to; seal
盖子 gàizi ① lid; cover; cap; top: 水壶～ the lid of a kettle ② shell (of a tortoise, etc.)
概 gài ①〈名〉general outline: 梗～ main idea; broad outline ②〈形〉general; approximate: ～算 a rough estimate ③〈副〉without exception; categorically: ～而论之 generally speaking
概不追究 gàibùzhuījiū no action will be taken against
概况 gàikuàng general condition (situation); survey
概括 gàikuò summarize; generalize; epitomize: ～的表现 summary expression
概率 gàilǜ probability; chance
概貌 gàimào general picture: 反映人民生活的～ give a general picture of the life of the people
概念 gàiniàn concept; notion; idea: ～化 deal in abstract terms; generalize; conceptualization. ～艺术 conceptual art
概数 gàishù approximate number; round number
概算 gàisuàn[经] budgetary estimate; financial estimates
概要 gàiyào outline; summary; essentials

gān

干 gān〈形〉① dry; dried: 晒～ sun dry ② empty; hollow: 外强中～ outwardly strong and in-

wardly weak ③ adopted; relative not linked by blood: ～女儿 adopted daughter 〈动〉④ offend ⑤ be concerned with; have to do with: 与你何～? What has this to do with you? ⑥ seek; request; pursue: ～禄 seek official position 〈副〉⑦ with no result; in vain: ～嚎 howling without tears ⑧ only; with nothing else: ～凭这点本事 have only this bit of skill
另见 gàn

干巴巴 gānbābā dull and dry; insipid; wizened

干杯 gānbēi ① drink a toast: 为两国人民的友谊～! Let's toast the friendship between the people of our two countries! ② Bottoms up!; Cheers!

干瘪 gānbiě ① dry ② shrivelled; wizened: ～老太婆 a wizened old woman ③ (of writing) dull; drab; dryasdust

干脆 gāncuì ① simply; just ② straightforward; frank: 办事～ be straigftforward in doing things

干瞪眼 gāndèngyǎn stand by anxiously, unable to help; look on in despair

干电池 gāndiànchí dry cell

干爹 gāndiē (nominally) adoptive father; godfather

干儿子 gān'érzi (nominally) adopted son

干戈 gāngē weapons of war — war: 动～ take up arms; go to war

干货 gānhuò dried food and nuts (as merchandise)

干净 gānjìng ① clean: 把房间打扫～ clean up the room ② wholly; completely: ～利落 neat and tidy; neat

干刻法 gānkèfǎ drypoint

干枯 gānkū dried-up; withered; sear; shrivelled; wizened

干粮 gānliang solid food (prepared for a journey); field rations; rations for a journey

干女儿 gānnǚ'ér (nominally) adopted daughter

干扰 gānrǎo ① disturb; obstruct; interfere (with): ～婚姻自由 interference with the freedom of marriage. ～证人 interference with witness ② [无] jamming; interference

干涉 gānshè interfere (in); intervene (in): ～别国内政 interfere in the internal affairs of other countries

干洗 gānxǐ dry-cleaning

干薪 gānxīn salary drawn for a sinecure: 领～ hold a sinecure

干预 gānyù interfere (in); meddle (in); poke one's nose into: ～其事 have a finger in the pie

干着急 gānzháojí be anxious but unable to do anything: 这件事他～没办法。He had to stand by helplessly and couldn't do anything about it.

干租约 gānzūyuē dry rent

杆 gān 〈名〉 pole; post; staff: 旗～ flagstaff; flagpole
另见 gǎn

肝 gān 〈名〉 liver: ～功能 the

function of the liver

肝癌 gān'ái cancer of the liver

肝胆 gāndǎn ① open-heartedness; sincerity ② heroic spirit; courage

肝胆过人 gāndǎn-guòrén far surpass others in daring

肝胆相照 gāndǎn-xiāngzhào treat each other with all sincerity; be openhearted to each other; loyal-hearted

肝脑涂地 gānnǎo-túdì spill one's liver and brains on the ground—lay down one's life (in fighting for one's sovereign)

肝炎 gānyán hepatitis

甘 gān 〈形〉 ① sweet; delicious: ～甜 sweet ② willing: ～当群众的小学生 make oneself a willing pupil of the masses

甘拜下风 gānbàixiàfēng willingly acknowledge one's inferiority; candidly admit defeat

甘苦 gānkǔ sweetness and bitterness; weal and woe; joys and sorrows: 同～ share joys and sorrows (with)

甘心 gānxīn ① willingly; readily ② be reconciled to: 不～ be not reconciled to; not resign oneself to

甘休 gānxiū be willing to give up: 不达目的决不～ will never give up till the aim is achieved

泔 gān 〈名〉 swill; slops; hogwash

泔水 gānshuǐ swill; slops; hogwash

柑 gān 〈名〉 mandarin orange; tangerine

柑橘 gānjú ① oranges and tangerines; mandarin ② citrus

竿 gān 〈名〉pole; rod: 钓～ fishing rod

竿子 gānzi bamboo pole

尴 gān

尴尬 gāngà awkward; bewildered; embarrassed: 感到～ feel awkward (embarrassed)

gǎn

赶 gǎn 〈动〉 ① catch up with; overtake: ～上时代 catch up with the times ② hurry; rush: ～班车 try to catch the regular bus . ～任务 rush through one's work ③ drive: ～驴 drive donkey ④ drive away; expel: 把侵略者～走 drive the aggressors away ⑤ happen to: ～上了一场雨 be caught in the rain

赶不及 gǎnbují there's not enough time (to do sth.); it's too late (to do sth.): 火车6点开，动身晚了就～了。The train leaves at six, and we won't catch it if we start off too late.

赶不上 gǎnbushàng ① be unable to catch up with ② there's not enough time (to do sth.); it's too late (to do sth.): 离开车只有30分钟，恐怕～了。The train is going to leave in thirty minutes. I'm afraid we'll be too late. ③ be unable to meet with or chance upon: 几个星期天都

～好天气。We never met with good weather these past few Sundays.

赶场 gǎncháng ① go to the village fair or market ② gǎnchǎng (of a performer) hurry from one performance to a second one in another place

赶超 gǎnchāo catch up and surpass:～先进 catch up with and surpass the advanced

赶得及 gǎndejí there is still time; be able to do sth. in time; be able to make it

赶得上 gǎndeshàng ① be able to catch up ② there is still time; be able to do sth. in time; be able to make it

赶集 gǎnjí go to the fair (market)

赶紧 gǎnjǐn hastily; without losing time:～刹车 quickly put on the brakes

赶快 gǎnkuài at once; quickly:～跟我走。Come along with me at once

赶路 gǎnlù push (hurry) on with one's journey

赶前不赶后 gǎnqián bù gǎnhòu It's better to hurry at the beginning than to do things in a rush at the last moment.

赶巧 gǎnqiǎo happen to; it so happened that

赶上 gǎnshàng ① overtake; catch up with; keep pace with:～时代的发展 keep abreast of the times ② run into (a situation); be in time for:他到北京那天正～过国庆。It happened to be National Day when he arrived in Beijing.

赶时髦 gǎnshímáo keep up with the Jones; try to be in style; follow the fashion:～的人 fashion-lovers

赶鸭子上架 gǎnyāzi shàngjià drive a duck onto a perch — try to make sb. do something entirely beyond him; force a donkey to dance

杆 gǎn〈名〉shaft; rod; bar:枪～ the barrel of a rifle

杆秤 gǎnchèng steelyard

感 gǎn〈动〉① feel; sense:他深～力不从心。He feels keenly that his ability falls short of his wishes. ② move; touch:深有所～ be deeply moved ③ be obliged; be grateful ④〈名〉sense; feeling:责任～ sense of responsibility

感触 gǎnchù ① thoughts and feelings; feeling ② be touched (stirred):～很深 be deeply touched

感到 gǎndào feel; sense:他～自己错了。He sensed that he himself was wrong.

感动 gǎndòng move; touch; impress:深受～ be deeply moved; be greatly touched

感恩 gǎn'ēn be grateful (to sb. for sth.); be indebted (to sb. for sth.)

感官 gǎnguān sense organ:～刺激 sensory stimulation

感化 gǎnhuà help sb. to change (by education and persuasion)

感激 gǎnjī be grateful (thankful)

(to sb. for sth.); feel indebted:不胜～ be deeply grateful

感觉 gǎnjué ①[哲] sense perception; sensation; feeling ② feel; be aware of; perceive

感慨 gǎnkǎi be deeply touched with regret; express sorrow (over, for)

感情 gǎnqíng feelings; emotion; passion; sentiment:～不和 incompatibility. ～用事 give way to one's feelings; be blinded by one's emotions; be thrall to one's passions. ～主义 sentimentalism

感染 gǎnrǎn ①[病] catch; be infected (with) ② influence; affect:艺术～力 artistic appeal

感人肺腑 gǎnrénfèifǔ touch one deeply in the heart; pull at one's heartstrings

感伤 gǎnshāng sentimental; pathetic; touching:～主义 sentimentalism

感受 gǎnshòu ① feel; experience ② impression:～很深 be deeply impressed (by, with)

感想 gǎnxiǎng impressions; reflections; thoughts:谈谈自己的～ talk about one's impressions (of)

感谢 gǎnxiè thank; be grateful:～信 letter of thanks. 表示衷心的～express heartfelt thanks

感性 gǎnxìng sensuality; sensuousness; perceptivity; (sense) perception:～认识 perceptual knowledge

感应 gǎnyìng ① response; reaction; interaction ②[生] irritability ③[电] induction:电磁～ electromagnetic induction

感召 gǎnzhào move and inspire; impel:在政府政策的～下 under the influence of the government's policy

敢

敢 gǎn 〈动〉① dare:～干 dare to act ② have the confidence; be certain; be sure ③〈形〉 bold; courageous; daring:果～ courageous and resolute

敢怒而不敢言 gǎnnù ér bù gǎnyán be forced to keep one's resentment to oneself; choke with silent fury

敢为 gǎnwéi take the bull by the horns; march up to the cannon's mouth; go through fire and water; dare to do

敢于 gǎnyú dare (to do); have the courage; be bold enough:～革新 have the courage to renovate sth.

敢在太岁头上动土 gǎn zài tàisuì tóushàng dòngtǔ dare to leap on an earth god's head to make trouble; dare to scratch Buddha's head; beard the lion in his den

敢作敢当 gǎnzuò-gǎndāng have the courage to take the blame for what one does

敢作敢为 gǎnzuò-gǎnwéi bold and decisive in action

橄

橄 gǎn

橄榄 gǎnlǎn ① Chinese olive (Canarium album); the fruit of the canary tree ② olive

橄榄球 gǎnlǎnqiú rugby; American football

橄榄枝 gǎnlǎnzhī olive branch—a symbol of peace

擀 gǎn 〈动〉① roll (dough, etc.): ~饺子皮 roll out dumpling wrappers ② polish; shine

擀面杖 gǎnmiànzhàng rolling pin: ~吹火——一窍不通 try to blow the fire with a rolling pin—know nothing about sth.

gàn

干 gàn 〈名〉① trunk; stem; main part: 躯~ trunk ② short for cadre: ~群关系 relations between cadres and masses ③ 〈动〉do; work: 苦~ work hard 〈形〉④ main: ~线 main line; trunk line ⑤ able: 真能~ really capable

另见 gān

干部 gànbù cadre

干才 gàncái ① capability; ability ② able (capable) person

干活 gànhuó work; work on a job: 我们都在~呢。We are all at work (on the job). 今儿你干什么活啊? What's your job for today?

干架 gànjià ① quarrel ② come to blows

干将 gànjiàng capable person; go-getter

干劲 gànjìn vigour; drive; energy: ~十足 be full of drive

干警 gànjǐng public security cadres and police; police officers

干练 gànliàn capable and experienced; competent

干吗 gànmá ① why on earth; whatever for: ~这么大规矩? Why all this formality? ② what to do: 你想~? What are you up to?

干事 gànshì secretary (staff member, clerical worker) in charge of sth.

干线 gànxiàn main line; trunk line; artery: 交通~ main lines of communication (transportation)

干休所 gànxiūsuǒ cadres' sanitoriums

gāng

冈 gāng 〈名〉ridge (of a hill)

扛 gāng 〈动〉① lift with both hands: 力能~鼎 strong enough to lift a tripod ② carry (by two or more persons)

另见 káng

缸 gāng 〈名〉large crock; vat; jar: 水~ water vat. 鱼~ fish bowls

缸盆 gāngpén glazed earthen basin

缸瓦 gāngwǎ a compound of sand, clay, etc. for making earthenware

肛 gāng 〈名〉anus

肛门 gāngmén anus

刚 gāng ① 〈形〉hard; rigid;

strong; unyielding:柔能克～。The soft can overcome the hard. 〈副〉② just; exactly:～合适 fit perfectly ③ barely; only:～成年 be barely of age ④ only a short while ago; just:～到 have just arrived ⑤ just; only at this moment:他～进屋就下雨了。He had hardly come into the room when it began to rain.

刚愎自用 gāngbì-zìyòng obstinate and self-opinionated; self-willed

刚才 gāngcái a moment ago; just now:～她在这里。She was here just now.

刚刚 gānggāng ① just; only; exactly:上次讨论会到现在～一个星期。It's only a week since the last discussion. ② a moment ago; just now:报纸～到。The newspaper came just now.

刚好 gānghǎo ① just; exactly:他们～赶上末班车。They just managed to catch the last bus. ② by chance; by coincidence:他们两人～编在一个班里。The two of them happened to be in the same class.

刚…就… gāng…jiù as soon as; no sooner than; immediately

刚强 gāngqiáng tough; staunch; unyielding

刚巧 gāngqiǎo by chance; by coincidence:明天～有车进城。It just so happens that there's a bus going to the city tomorrow.

刚毅 gāngyì resolute and steadfast

刚正 gāngzhèng staunch and upright

刚直 gāngzhí inflexible; upright:～不阿 uprightness and tenacity; upright and outspoken; frank and straight-forward; standing on principles and not yielding to pressure

钢

gāng 〈名〉 steel:不锈～ stainless steel

钢板 gāngbǎn ① steel plate ② stencil steel board

钢笔 gāngbǐ fountain pen; pen:～画 pen drawing

钢材 gāngcái steels; rolled steel:～制品 steel product

钢锭 gāngdìng steel ingot

钢管 gāngguǎn steel tube (pipe):无缝～ seamless steel tube

钢轨 gāngguǐ rails (for trains, etc.); tracks

钢号 gānghào [冶金]steel grade

钢化玻璃 gānghuà bōli toughened glass

钢筋水泥 gāngjīn shuǐní reinforced concrete

钢盔 gāngkuī (steel) helmet

钢坯 gāngpī [冶金] billet:大～ bloom

钢琴 gāngqín piano:弹～ play the piano

钢水 gāngshuǐ molten steel; liquid steel

钢丝 gāngsī steel wire:走～ walk the wire

钢铁 gāngtiě iron and steel; steel:～厂 steelworks. ～工业股票 steels. ～意志 iron will

钢印 gāngyìn ① steel seal; embossing seal ② embossed stamp

纲 gāng〈名〉① the headrope of a fishing net ② key link; programme; outline: 总～ the general programme

纲纪 gāngjì law and order; discipline

纲举目张 gāngjǔ-mùzhāng Once the key link is grasped, everything falls into place.; Once the headrope of a fishing net is pulled up, all its meshes open.

纲领 gānglǐng programme; guiding principle: ～性文件 programmatic document

纲目 gāngmù detailed outline (of a subject); outline

纲要 gāngyào ① outline ② essentials; compendium: 哲学～ compendium of philosophy

gǎng

港 gǎng〈名〉① port; harbour: 不冻～ an ice-free port ② Hong Kong

港澳同胞 Gǎng-Ào tóngbāo compatriots from (in) Hong Kong and Macao:《～回乡证》Home Visit Certificate for Hong Kong and Macao Compatriots

港币 gǎngbì Hong Kong dollar

港口 gǎngkǒu port; harbour: ～吞吐量 handling capacity of ports; capacity of ports

港湾 gǎngwān harbour

港务局 gǎngwùjú harbour bureau; port office

岗 gǎng〈名〉① mound ② sentry; post

岗警 gǎngjǐng policeman on point duty

岗哨 gǎngshào ① watch-post ② sentry post; sentry: 布置～ post sentries

岗亭 gǎngtíng sentry box; police box

岗位 gǎngwèi post: ～津贴 job subsidies. ～责任制 system of post responsibility (for the work done by each individual at his post)

gàng

杠 gàng〈名〉① thick carrying pole ② bar

杠杆 gànggǎn lever: ～作用 leverage

杠铃 gànglíng [体]barbell

gāo

高 gāo〈形〉① high; tall: ～山 high mountain ② above the average; advanced; superior: ～标准 higher standard ③ high-priced; dear; expensive: 要价太～ ask too high a price

高昂 gāo'áng ① high; elated: 情绪～ be in high spirits ② dear; costly

高傲 gāo'ào haughty; arrogant; insolent

高保真音响 gāobǎozhēn yīnxiǎng hi-fi (= high fidelity)

高不可攀 gāobùkěpān ① too high to reach; unattainable ② [态

度] unapproachable; inaccessible:她是～的那种人吗? Is she an unapproachable sort of woman?
高才生 gāocáishēng a brilliant (outstanding) student
高参 gāocān ① senior staff officer ② counsellor; mentor
高产 gāochǎn high yield:～稳产 high production, steady production
高唱 gāochàng ① sing loudly; sing with spirit:～战歌 sing battle songs ② talk glibly about; call out loudly for
高超 gāochāo remarkable; superb; exquisite:～的技术 superb skill
高潮 gāocháo ① high tide (water) ② high tide; upsurge ③ climax:故事的～ climax of the story
高大 gāodà ① tall and big; stalwart ② great; lofty:～形象 lofty image
高蛋白 gāodànbái high protein
高档 gāodàng high-grade:～消费品 high-grade consumer goods
高等 gāoděng of a higher grade; higher:～教育 higher education. ～学位 advanced degree. ～院校 institutions of higher learning; colleges and universities
高低 gāodī ① height:声调的～ the pitch of a voice ② relative superiority or inferiority:难分～ hard to tell which is better ③ sense of propriety; discretion:不知～ not know what's proper; have no sense of propriety ④ on any account; just; simply:不管我怎么劝说,她～不听。No matter how hard I tried to persuade her, she just wouldn't listen.
高调 gāodiào ① lofty tone; high-sounding words ② high tone
高度 gāodù ① altitudes; height:山的～ the height of a mountain ② a high degree:～赞扬 pay high tribute to; speak highly of
高尔夫球 gāo'ěrfūqiú ① golf:～场 golf course; golf links ② golf ball
高峰 gāofēng peak; summit; height:～时间[交通、用电等] peak hours; [公共车辆等] rush hours
高高在上 gāogāo-zàishàng stand high above the masses; be high up in the air; live in the clouds; hold oneself aloof from the masses
高跟鞋 gāogēnxié high-heeled shoes
高官厚禄 gāoguān-hòulù high position and handsome salary; high position with high pay
高贵 gāoguì ① noble; high-minded ② privileged:～的品质 noble character
高级 gāojí ① high-class; high-grade; advanced:～化妆品 de luxe cosmetics ② high; high-ranking; senior:～官员 high(-ranking) official:～干部 senior cadre. ～人民法院 higher people's court; superior

people's court. ～学位 higher degree; advanced degree

高技术 gāojìshù high-technology; high-tech

高价 gāojià high price: ～收买 buy over at a high price

高见 gāojiàn your brilliant idea; your opinion: 不知～以为如何? I wonder if you would be kind enough to enlighten us on this matter.

高精尖 gāojīngjiān high-grade, precision and advanced; high, refined, peak: ～产品 high, refined and peak products

高举 gāojǔ hold high; hold aloft: ～着奖杯向观众致意 hold the cup high for all the audience to see

高考 gāokǎo college entrance examination

高科技 gāokējì high technology; high-tech

高空 gāokōng upper air; high altitude: ～作业 work in high altitudes; work high above the ground

高利 gāolì very high interest (on a loan)

高利贷 gāolìdài usury: 放～ practise usury

高龄 gāolíng advanced age; advanced in years: ～化社会 aging society

高楼大厦 gāolóu dàshà high buildings and large mansions

高炉 gāolú [冶金] blast furnace

高明 gāomíng wise; clever; superior: 医术～ high degree of medical skill. 另请～。Please get someone better qualified.

高能燃料 gāonéngránliào high-energy fuel

高攀 gāopān make friends or claim ties of kinship with someone of a higher social position: ～婚 hypergamy

高朋满座 gāopéng-mǎnzuò a great gathering of distinguished guests

高频 gāopín [收音机] high frequency: 甚～ very high frequency (vhf). 超～ ultrahigh frequency (uhf)

高人一等 gāorényīděng stand head and shoulders above others; tower above the rest

高山族 Gāoshānzú the Gaoshan (Kaoshan) nationality, or the Gaoshans (Kaoshans), inhabiting Taiwan Province

高尚 gāoshàng noble; high; high-minded: 人格～ be noble-minded; be of high character. ～的思想 elevated mind; elevated ideas. ～音乐 grand music

高烧 gāoshāo high fever: 发～ have (run) a high fever

高寿 gāoshòu ① longevity; long life ② your venerable age: 老奶奶，您今年～? May I ask how old you are, Grandma?

高耸 gāosǒng (stand) tall and erect; towering: ～入云 reach to the sky; tower into the clouds

高速 gāosù high speed: ～公路 expressway; superhighway. 信息～公路 information superhighway

高抬贵手 gāotái-guìshǒu be magnanimous;be generous; not be too hard on sb.

高谈阔论 gāotán-kuòlùn indulge in loud and empty talk; talk volubly (bombastically); harangue

高徒 gāotú ① your (brilliant) student ② a brilliant student

高屋建瓴 gāowū-jiànlíng pour water off a steep roof—sweep down irresistibly from a commanding height; operate from a strategically advantageous position

高消费 gāoxiāofèi high (level of) consumption

高薪 gāoxīn high salary; high pay

高兴 gāoxìng ① glad; happy; cheerful ② be willing to; be happy to:你不～去就甭去了。You needn't go if you don't feel like it.

高血压 gāoxuèyā [医] hypertension; high blood pressure

高压 gāoyā high pressure:～手段 highhanded measures

高雅 gāoyǎ elegant and in good taste; noble and graceful:～艺术 art of refined taste and style

高瞻远瞩 gāozhān-yuǎnzhǔ be far-sighted and aim high; take a broad and long view; stand high and see far; show great foresight

高招 gāozhāo clever move; brilliant idea:你有什么～,快说说。What have you got up your sleeve? Out with it!

高枕无忧 gāozhěn-wúyōu shake up the pillow and have a good sleep; sit back and relax

高指标 gāozhǐbiāo setting unrealistic production target; high target

羔 gāo 〈名〉lamb; kid; fawn

羔羊 gāoyáng lamb—an innocent and helpless person or a scapegoat

膏 gāo 〈名〉① fat; grease; oil ② paste; cream; ointment
另见 gào

膏药 gāoyao medicated plaster, plaster:贴～ apply a plaster to

糕 gāo 〈名〉 cake:年～ New Year cake (made of glutinous rice)

糕点 gāodiǎn pastry; cake

gǎo

搞 gǎo 〈动〉① do; make; practise:～好了吗? Is it done? ② engage in; go in for:～科学研究 be engaged in scientific research ③ draw up; work out:～个计划 draw up a plan ④ get hold of; secure:咱们先给他们～点东西吃。Let's first get them something to eat.

搞不懂 gǎobùdǒng be at a loss to understand; be puzzled

搞对象 gǎoduìxiàng be occupied with finding a match; go steady

搞鬼 gǎoguǐ play a (dirty) trick (on)

搞好 gǎohǎo ① do sth. well; do a good job of:～经济建设 do

well in economic construction ②get sth. done; carry out

搞活 gǎohuó enliven; vitalize; invigorate: ～国有经济 enliven the state economy

搞乱 gǎoluàn mix up; muddle up; upset; end up in a mess

搞通思想 gǎotōng sīxiǎng arrive at a right perception of; get through to someone's thought; straighten out one's ideas

搞小动作 gǎo xiǎodòngzuò indulge in petty and mean actions

搞小圈子 gǎo xiǎoquānzi be involved in a small circle

搞糟 gǎozāo make a mess (of); mess up

镐 gǎo 〈名〉 pick; pickaxe

镐头 gǎotou pick; pickaxe

稿 gǎo 〈名〉 ① stalk of grain; straw ② draft; sketch: 草～ rough draft ③ manuscript; original text: 底～ original copy of a published article

稿本 gǎoběn manuscript

稿费 gǎofèi payment for an article or book published or accepted; copy money; contribution fees; royalty from a book or aritcle

稿件 gǎojiàn contribution; manuscript

稿纸 gǎozhǐ manuscript (copy) paper

稿子 gǎozi ① draft; sketch: 起个～ make a draft ② manuscript; contribution ③ idea; plan: 他心里还没个准～。He hasn't got any definite plan yet.

gào

告 gào 〈动〉 ① tell; inform; notify: 电～ inform by telegraph; cable ② ask for; request; solicit: ～援 ask for help ③ accuse; sue: ～状 file a suit ④ make known; announce: ～一段落 be brought to a temporary close

告别 gàobié take leave (of); say good-bye (to); bid farewell (to): ～仪式 a ceremony held to pay last respects to

告吹 gàochuī fizzle out (a relationship falls apart or a matter fails): 恋爱～。The romance has fallen apart.

告辞 gàocí take leave (of one's host)

告贷 gàodài ask for a loan: 奔走～ run around trying to raise money

告发 gàofā inform against; accuse sb. (of an offence); report sb. to; peach against; lodge accusation (information) against; bring sb. to trial: ～同案犯 split on an accomplice

告急 gàojí report an emergence; ask for emergence help

告假 gàojià ask for leave: ～一天 ask (sb.) for a day's leave

告捷 gàojié win; gain a victory (over)

告诫 gàojiè warn; admonish; enjoin; exhort

告密 gàomì peach against; inform against: ～者 informer

告罄 gàoqìng run out; be ex-

hausted:库存～ be out of stock
告饶 gàoráo beg for mercy; ask pardon:求情～ plead for mercy
告示 gàoshì notice; announcement; bulletin
告诉 gàosu ① tell; let (make) know ②[法] complain; bring a complaint
告退 gàotuì ask for leave to withdraw from a meeting, etc.
告慰 gàowèi ① comfort; console ② feel relieved
告知 gàozhī inform; notify:我将这事～了有关人员。I informed those concerned of this matter.
告终 gàozhōng come to an end; end (up):以失败～ end up in failure
告状 gàozhuàng ① go to law against sb.; bring a lawsuit against sb. ② lodge a complaint against sb. (with his superior)

膏 gào 〈动〉① lubricate:在轴上～点儿油 put some lubricant on the axle ② dip a writing brush in ink and smooth it on an inkstone before writing:～笔 smooth a (ink-dipped) writing brush on the edge of an inkstone
另见 gāo

gē

戈 gē 〈名〉① dagger-axe (an ancient weapon) ② (Gē) a surname
戈壁 gēbì ①[地质] gobi ② (Gēbì) the Gobi Desert

割 gē 〈动〉cut:～断价格联系 sever the relationship in prices
割爱 gē'ài give up what one treaures; part with a beloved object
割地 gēdì cede territory
割断 gēduàn cut off; sever; isolate:～历史 lop off history; segment history
割据 gējù form (set up) a separatist regime by force of arms
割裂 gēliè split; (of abstract matters) cut apart; separation; carve up; partition
割让 gēràng cede; cession:～领土 cede territory

哥 gē 〈名〉elder brother; brother
哥哥 gēgē (elder) brother
哥老会 gēlǎohuì Elder Brothers Society
哥们儿 gēmenr ①〈口〉brothers ② pals; buddies:～义气 brotherhood loyality; gang spirit

歌 gē ①〈名〉song ②〈动〉sing
歌唱 gēchàng ① sing ② praise (through songs, poems, etc.):～祖国的繁荣昌盛 sing (in praise) of the prosperity of our country
歌词 gēcí words of a song; song; the lyrics of a song
歌功颂德 gēgōng-sòngdé chant one's praises and sing of someone's virtue; eulogize one's virtues and achievements; sing the praises of sb.
歌喉 gēhóu (singer's) voice;

singing voice

歌剧 gējù opera：～院 opera house

歌片儿 gēpiānr song sheet

歌谱 gēpǔ music score of a song；music of a song

歌曲 gēqǔ song：主打～ hit songs；hits

歌声 gēshēng sound of singing；singing

歌手 gēshǒu singer；vocalist

歌颂 gēsòng sing the praises of；praise；eulogize；extol

歌坛 gētán the circle of singers：～新秀 a new singing star

歌舞 gēwǔ singing and dancing：～影片 musical film. ～团 song and dance troupe

歌星 gēxīng singing star；star singer

歌谣 gēyáo folk (popular) song；ballad；folk rhymes；ditty

歌咏 gēyǒng singing：～队 singing group

搁

gē〈动〉① put；lay (down)：这菜里你～盐太多了。You put too much salt in this dish. ② put (set) aside：～起不说 leave over

搁浅 gēqiǎn ① run aground (ashore)；be stranded；be grounded ② be suspended；be held up；come to a deadlock：会谈～了。The talks were held up.

搁置 gēzhì lay aside；shelve；pigeonhole；lay on the shelf

疙

gē

疙瘩 gēda ① pimple；lump ② problem；difficulty；knot：解开某人心上的～ dispel one's misgivings. 解除思想～ dispel a burden from one's mind

鸽

gē〈名〉dove；pigeon：信～ carrier pigeon

鸽派 gēpài dove faction；dove

鸽子 gēzi pigeon，dove：～笼 dovecote；pigeon house；loft

格

gē

另见 gé

格格 gēgē〈象〉the sound of laughing；chuckle；titter

胳

gē〈名〉～膊 arm

胳臂 gēbei arm

胳膊 gēbo arm：～扭不过大腿。The arm is no match for the thigh—the weaker can't contend with the stronger.

gé

革

gé ①〈名〉leather；hide：皮～ leather；hides〈动〉② dismiss；abolish：～除陋习 elimination of bad customs ③ reform；transform；change：洗心～面 turn over a new leaf；reform oneself thoroughly

革除 géchú ① do away with；get rid of；abolish ② dispel；dismiss；excommunicate

革命 gémìng revolution：～残废军人 disabled military personnel of the revolution. ～化 revolutionize. ～前辈 revolutionaries of the older generation. ～英雄主义 revolutionary heroism

革新 géxīn reform；innovate：技

术～ technical innovation

革职 gézhí discharge (dismiss) sb. from office; remove from office; sack: ～留任 dismissal from one's post while being allowed to carry on his duties; dismissal from sb.'s post while retaining his duties

革制品 gézhìpǐn leather goods

隔 gé 〈动〉① separate; part; partition: ～江相望 face each other across the river ② be at a distance from; after or at an interval of ③〈形〉next; alternate: ～壁 next door to. ～壁的～壁 two doors away

隔壁 gébì next door: ～邻居 next-door neighbour

隔行 géháng of different trades or professions: ～如隔山 different trades are separated as by mountains (i. e., the outsider knows no more of the secrets of the craft than he knows of another country)

隔阂 géhé misunderstanding: 消除～ remove the misunderstanding. 制造～ foment feelings of estrangement

隔绝 géjué isolate; seclude; completely cut off

隔开 gékāi separate; partition (off): 把房间～ partition a room

隔离 gélí keep apart; isolate; separate; seclude; segregate: ～病房 isolation ward

隔膜 gémó lack of understanding (each other); be unfamiliar with

隔墙 géqiáng partition (wall)

隔墙有耳 géqiāng-yǒu'ěr walls have ears; beware of eavesdroppers

隔日 gérì ① the next day ② every other day: ～吃一片 take a tablet every other day

隔靴搔痒 géxuē-sāoyǎng scratch an itch through one's boot — a useless attempt

隔夜 géyè of the previous night: ～的茶最好别喝。You'd better not drink last night's tea.

隔音 géyīn soundproof; sound insulation: ～室 soundproof room

阁 gé 〈名〉① pavilion ② cabinet: ～员 members of the cabinet

阁僚 géliáo official family: 总统和他的～ the President and his official family

阁楼 gélóu loft; attic; garret

阁下 géxià (Your, His, Her) Excellency; (Your, His Her) Honour

格 gé 〈名〉① square; check: 方～纸 squared paper ② shelf; division: 这书架有四～。This bookcase has four shelves. ③ standard; form; pattern: ～式 pattern ④ case: 所有～ the possessive case

格调 gédiào ① (literary or artistic) style; ② one's style of work as well as one's moral quality: 作者～不高 the underdeveloped moral views of the authors

格斗 gédòu wrestle; fishfight;

grapple

格格不入 gégébùrù misfits; like square pegs in round holes; incompatible with; be ill-adapted to; alien to

格局 géjú pattern; framework; structure; setup

格律 gélǜ [诗歌] rules and forms of classic poetic composition (with respect to tonal pattern, rhyme, scheme; etc.): ～诗 metrical poetry. ～诗词 poetrical meter; metrical pattern of poetry

格式 géshì form; style; pattern

格外 géwài ① especially; particularly; all the more: 雪地上骑车要～小心。You've got to be especially careful when you cycle on snow. ② additionally

格言 géyán maxim; motto; aphorism; proverb: ～诗 aphoristic poetry; gnomic poetry; epigrams

葛 gé 〈名〉① kudzu vine ② poplin ③ (Gě) a surname

葛布 gébù ko-hemp cloth

gè

个 gè 〈量〉① [用于没有专用量词的名词]: 4～梨 four pears ② [用于带宾语的动词后面]: 说～话儿 have a talk ③ [用于约数的前面]: 差～两三岁 about two or three years short ④〈助〉[用于动词和补语之间]: 笑～不停 keep on laughing ⑤〈形〉individual: ～人计算机 personal computer

个案分析 gè'ànfēnxì case study

个别 gèbié ① a few; very few ② specific; individual: 作～谈话 have a private (an individual) talk (with)

个把 gèbǎ one or two; a couple of: 再过～月,她就要回国了。In a couple of months, he'll be going back to his country.

个个 gègè each and every one; all

个儿 gèr ① size; height; stature; 别看他～不大,劲儿可不小。He's not big, but he's strong. ② persons or things taken singly: 论～卖 be sold by the piece

个人 gèrén individual; personal;: ～收入调节税 individual income regulatory taxes. ～自谋职业 seeking of new job opportunities by the individual. ～帐户 individual accounts

个体 gètǐ individual: ～户 self-employed households; privately-owned small businesses; individual businessperson; self-employed businessperson. ～工商业者 individual industralists and businessmen. ～经济 individual economy. ～经营户 individually-managed establishments. ～营业执照 individual licence

个性 gèxìng individuality; personality; individual character

各 gè 〈形〉① each; every; all: ～位来宾 every guest. ～行～业 all trades and professions ② different; various: ～种原材料

various raw materials

各半 gèbàn half and half; fifty-fifty:成败的机会～。The chances of success are fifty-fifty.

各奔前程 gèbèn-qiánchéng each pursues his own course; each goes his own way

各别 gèbié ① distinct; different: ～对待 treat differently; treat each on its (his, etc.) own merits ② out of the ordinary; peculiar:这只钟式样很～。This clock is quite unusual-looking. ③ odd; eccentric; funny:她这人的脾气真～。She's a really eccentric character.

各别教练 gèbié jiàoliàn individual training

各不相让 gèbùxiāngràng neither is willing to give ground, each is trying to outdo the other

各不相同 gèbùxiāngtóng have nothing in common with each other; differ from one another

各持己见 gèchí-jǐjiàn each sticks to his own view

各打五十大板 gè dǎ wǔshí dàbǎn a balance of blame; blame both sides without discrimination; punish the innocent and the guilty alike

各得其所 gèdé-qísuǒ Everyone is properly placed and keeping to his place.; Each plays his proper role and gets his due.

各个 gège ① each; every; various ② one by one

各个击破 gègè-jīpò destroy (crush) one by one

各行各业 gèháng-gèyè all trades and professions; all walks of life

各级 gèjí different levels:～领导 leaders at different levels

各界 gèjiè all (various) walks of life; all circles:～人民 people in all walks of life; all sections of the people

各尽所能,按劳分配 gèjìn-suǒnéng, ànláo-fēnpèi from each according to his ability, to each according to his work—the socialist principle of distribution

各尽所能,按需分配 gèjìn-suǒnéng,ànxū-fēnpèi from each according to his ability, to each according to his needs—the communist principle of distribution

各取所需 gèqǔ-suǒxū Each takes what he needs.

各人 gèrén everybody; everyone; each one:～自扫门前雪。Each minds his own business.; Each hoes his own row.

各色 gèsè different kinds of; of every description:～各样 of all kinds

各抒己见 gèshū-jǐjiàn Each expresses his opinion; Each airs his own views.

各显神通 gèxiǎn-shéntōng Each shows his special skill.; each trying for all one's worth

各行其是 gèxíng-qíshì Each acts as he pleases.; Each takes (goes) his own way.

各有千秋 gèyǒu-qiānqiū Each has his own merits.

各有所好 gèyǒu-suǒhào Everyone has his hobby.; Everyone has his own particular taste.

各执一词 gèzhí-yīcí Each sticks to his argument.; Each has his own opinion.

各种 gèzhǒng different kinds of; various sorts of: ～各样 all kinds of; of all sorts; of every description

各自 gèzì each; respective; separate: ～为政。Everyone goes his own way.; Each acts wilfully regardless of overall interest.

gěi

给 gěi〈动〉① give: ～父亲一件礼物 give father a gift ② let; allow: 不要～他看。Don't allow him to have a look.〈介〉③ for; to: 你～我唱首歌好吗? Will you sing a song for me? ④ by: 报纸～风吹走了。The newspaper was blown away by the wind. ⑤〈助〉[用在表示被动、处置等意思的谓语动词前,以加强语气]: 我把那件事～忘了。I've forgot the matter.
另见 jǐ

给…记过处分 gěi…jìguò chùfèn give sb. a demerit

给脸不要脸 gěiliǎn bùyào liǎn be fool enough to reject a face-saving offer

给牵着鼻子走 gěi qiānzhe bízǐ zǒu be led by the nose

给人穿小鞋 gěirén chuan xiǎoxié give sb. tight shoes to wear — put sb. on the spot behind his back

给以 gěiyǐ ① give; render (help, etc.) to: ～协助 render assistance to ② pay (attention) to: ～影响 exert influence on ③ show (consideration) for: ～适当照顾 show due consideration for

gēn

根 gēn〈名〉① root: 树～ the root of a tree ② foot; base; root: 墙～ the foot of a wall ③ source; origin; root: 思想～源 ideological root-cause ④ foundation; basis: 扎～于群众 have one's roots among the masses ⑤〈副〉completely; thoroughly: ～除 completely do away with

根本 gēnběn ① root; foundation; base: ～动摇 shake ... to its foundations ② basic; fundamental: ～大法 fundamental law ③ totally; completely; utterly: ～对立 be diametrically opposed to

根除(绝) gēnchú (jué) uproot; eradicate; root out

根底 gēndǐ ① foundation; grounding; basis: 她的英语～好。She has a good foundation in English. ② root: 事情的～ root of a matter

根雕 gēndiāo tree-root carving

根基 gēnjī foundation; basis: 打下结实的～ lay a solid foundation

根据 gēnjù ① basis; foundation; grounds ② according to; in line with; on the basis of; based on; in keeping with; in the light of: ～情节轻重 in accordance with the seriousness of the case

根绝 gēnjué stamp out; eradicate; exterminate

根深蒂固 gēnshēn-dìgù deep-rooted; deep-seated; inveterate

根深叶茂 gēnshēn-yèmào have deep roots and luxuriant leaves—be well established and vigorously developing

根源 gēnyuán origin; source; root: 错误观点的～ the source of erroneous views

根治 gēnzhì effect a real cure; cure radically of: ～水患 permanent control of floods

跟 gēn ①〈名〉heel: 鞋后～ the heel of a shoe ②〈动〉follow: ～着某人的脚印走 follow in someone's footsteps 〈介〉③ [和、与] with; and: 我～她一样高。She and I are of the same height. ～你谈话 have a talk with you ④ [对、向] towards; to: 我正在～他谈话。I am talking to him.

跟不上 gēnbushàng fall (lag) behind: ～形势 fall behind the current situation

跟单汇票 gēndān huìpiào documentary bill of exchange

跟前 gēnqián ① the area in front of sb. or sth.: 她把我叫到～又讲了几句。She told me to come closer and said a few more words. ② the time just before: 春节～ shortly before the Spring Festival ③ gēnqian (of one's children) living with one: 她～有一儿一女。She has a son and a daughter living with him.

跟上 gēnshàng keep pace with; keep abreast of

跟头 gēntou ① somersault: 翻～ turn a somersault ② fall: 摔～ have a fall

跟踪 gēnzōng trail; tail after; shadow; follow on the heels of: ～研究 follow-up study. ～追击 go in hot pursuit of

gēng

庚 gēng〈名〉① the seventh of the ten Heavenly Stems ② age

耕 gēng〈动〉plough; till; cultivate: ～田队 ploughing team

耕畜 gēngchù farm animal

耕地 gēngdì ① arable (land): ～面积 cultivated acreage; area under cultivation ② plough (land); till

耕牛 gēngniú farm cattle

耕田 gēngtián plough; till

耕耘 gēngyún ploughing and weeding; cultivation: 一分～，一分收获。The more ploughing and weeding, the better the crop.

耕种 gēngzhòng till; cultivate

耕作 gēngzuò farming; cultivation; tillage: ～机械 tillage machine

羹 gēng〈名〉a thick soup: 鸡蛋～ egg custard (usu. salty)

羹匙 gēngchí soup spoon; tablespoon

更 gēng ①〈动〉change; replace; alter: ～改计划 make some changes in the plan ②〈名〉one of the five two-hour periods into which the night was formerly divided; watch: 打～ beat the watches
另见 gèng

更迭 gēngdié alternate; change: 内阁～ a change of cabinet

更动 gēngdòng change; alter: 人事～ personnel changes

更改 gēnggǎi change, alter

更换 gēnghuàn change; shift; replace

更年期 gēngniánqī climacteric; menopause; change of life: 处于～的妇女 women at the change of life

更名 gēngmíng change one's name

更替 gēngtì replace (by); substitute (for): 用甲～乙 substitute A for B

更新 gēngxīn renew; renovate; rehabilitation: ～改造 renovation (replacement) and transformation. ～设备 renovate equipment

更衣 gēngyī ① change one's clothes: ～室 changeroom; locker room ②［婉辞］go to the toilet

更正 gēngzhèng make corrections; correct

gěng

埂 gěng〈名〉① a low bank of earth between fields ② a long, narrow mound: 山～ a hill mound ③ an earth dyke (embankment)

耿 gěng〈形〉① bright ② candid

耿耿 gěnggěng ① faithful; devoted: 忠心～ with utter devotion; wholeheartedly ② be uneasy in mind (about): ～于怀 keep unforgettably in mind; stick in one's throat; brood on

耿直 gěngzhí candid; straightforward; upright; honest and frank

梗 gěng ①〈名〉stalk; stem ②〈动〉hinder; obstruct; block: 作～ place obstacles in the way

梗概 gěnggài outline; summary; gist

梗塞 gěngsè ① block up (with): 交通～ traffic jam ②［医］infarction: 心肌～ myocardial infarction

梗阻 gěngzǔ hinder; obstruct; block

哽 gěng〈动〉choke (with emotion): ～咽 (choke with) sobs

gèng

更 gèng〈副〉① more; even; still more ② again
另见 gēng

更加 gèngjiā still more; more

更进一步 gèngjìn yībù go a step further; further

更上一层楼 gèng shàng yīcénglóu strive for further improvement;

scale new heights

gōng

宫 gōng〈名〉palace
宫灯 gōngdēng palace lantern
宫殿 gōngdiàn palace
宫女 gōngnǚ maid in an imperial palace; maid of honour
宫阙 gōngquè 〈书〉 imperial palace
宫廷 gōngtíng palace: ～政变 palace coup
宫外孕 gōngwàiyùn [医] extrauterine pregnancy; ectopic pregnancy
工 gōng〈名〉① work; job; labour: 做～ do manual labour ② worker: 青～ young worker ③ (construction) project: 竣～ complete a project ④ industry: ～交系统 industry and communications ⑤ man-day ⑥〈形〉be good at; be versed in
工本 gōngběn cost (of production)
工兵 gōngbīng engineer (in an army): 坑道～ sapper. 轻～ pioneer
工厂 gōngchǎng factory, mill; plant; works
工场 gōngchǎng workshop; shop: ～经济 workshop economy
工潮 gōngcháo workers' demonstration or protest movement; strike movement: 闹～ go on strike
工程 gōngchéng engineering; construction work; project: ～项目 project. ～师 engineer
工代会 gōngdàihuì workers' representatives conference
工地 gōngdì worksite; building (construction) site
工读学校 gōngdúxuéxiào work-study school (reformatory)
工段 gōngduàn workshop section; section of a construction project
工夫 gōngfu ① time: 他2天～就学会了游泳。It took him only two days to learn to swim. ② at that time: 她当闺女那～,连大门都不敢出。When she was a girl, she didn't even dare to go outdoors. ③ workmanship; skill; art: 练～ (of actors, athletes, etc.) practise ④ effort; work: 花了好大～ put in a lot of work
工会 gōnghuì trade union; labour union
工技贸相结合 gōng-jì-mào xiāng jiéhé integration of industry, technology and trade
工间操 gōngjiāncāo workbreak calisthenics (exercises)
工交口 gōngjiāokǒu industrial, communications offices
工具 gōngjù tool; instrument; implement: ～书 reference book
工科 gōngkē engineering (course): ～大学 engineering college
工矿 gōngkuàng industry and mining: ～企业 industrial and mining enterprises
工料 gōngliào labour and materials (for a building project)
工龄 gōnglíng length of service; length of the time employed

工农 gōngnóng workers and peasants：～差别 the difference between industry and agriculture. ～联盟 alliance of workers and peasants； worker-peasant alliance. ～大众 the broad masses of workers and peasants. ～干部 cadres of worker-peasant origin； worker and peasant cadres

工农业总产值 gōngnóngyè zǒngchǎnzhí gross output value of industry and agriculture

工棚 gōngpéng builders' temporary shed； work shed

工期 gōngqī time limit for a project：提高效率，缩短～。Increase efficiency and shorten the time limit for the project.

工钱 gōngqián charge for a service； money paid for odd jobs

工区 gōngqū work area (a grass-roots unit of an industrial enterprise)

工人 gōngrén worker； workman：产业～ industrial worker

工伤 gōngshāng injury incurred during work：～事故 work (labour) accident； accidental work injury

工商 gōngshāng industry and commerce：～登记 industrial and commercial registration. ～行名录 directory. ～户 industrial and commercial units. ～界 industrial and commercial circles； business circles. ～业 industry and commerce. ～业统一税 industrial and commercial consolidated tax

工时 gōngshí man-hour

工头 gōngtóu overseer； foreman

工效 gōngxiào work efficiency：提高～ raise (improve) work efficiency

工薪族 gōngxīnzú salarist； salaryman； wage-earners

工休日 gōngxiūrì day off； holiday

工序 gōngxù (working) process； production process； procedure

工业 gōngyè industry：～大学 polytechnical university. ～化 industrialization. ～基础结构 industrial infrastructure. ～总产值 gross value of industrial output

工艺 gōngyì ① technology ② craft：～美术 arts and crafts. ～品 handicraft wares. ～设计 technological design

工长 gōngzhǎng section chief (in a workshop, or on a building site)； foreman

工整 gōngzhěng careful and neat：字迹～ neatly lettered

工种 gōngzhǒng type of work in production； branch (type) of work； kind of work

工转干 gōng zhuǎn gàn worker turned cadre

工资 gōngzī wages； pay； salary：～级别 pay scale； wage scales. ～纠纷 pay dispute. 领～ draw one's pay. 附加～ supplementary wages

工作 gōngzuò work； job：～单位 work unit. ～会议 work conference. ～述职 report one's work. ～效率 working efficiency. ～证 identity card； ID card. ～座谈会 symposium on work

攻 gōng〈动〉① attack; storm: 主～方向 the main direction of the offensive ② reproach; censure; charge ③ study; work at; specialize in: 专～医学 major in medicine

攻打 gōngdǎ attack; assault

攻读 gōngdú ① study (hard) ② specialize in; major in: ～物理学 specialize in physics

攻关 gōngguān tackle a critical point

攻击 gōngjī ① attack; assail ② charge; accuse: 恶毒～ level malevolent attacks on; accuse. 人身～ make personal abuse

攻坚 gōngjiān storm fortifications; assault fortified positions: ～部队 assault troops

攻克 gōngkè ① capture; conquer; take ② overcome: ～难关 overcome a serious difficulty. ～科学难关 breaking deadlocks in academic research

攻破 gōngpò make a breakthrough; breach

攻其不备 gōngqíbúbèi attack by surprise; take sb. by surprise; catch sb. unawares

攻势 gōngshì offensive: 采取～ take (assume) the offensive

攻守同盟 gōngshǒu-tóngméng an offensive and defensive alliance—an agreement between partners in crime not to give each other away; a pact to shield each other

攻陷 gōngxiàn take by storming; capture; storm

攻心 gōngxīn try to persuade an offender to confess; make a psychological attack

攻占 gōngzhàn attack and occupy; storm and capture

功 gōng〈名〉① meritorious deed; merit; exploit: 立～ render meritorious service ② effect; result: 劳而无～ work hard but to no avail ③ skill: 基本～ basic skill

功败垂成 gōngbài-chuíchéng suffer defeat when victory is within one's grasp; fail in a great undertaking on the verge of success

功臣 gōngchén meritorious person; hero

功成业就 gōngchéng-yèjiù (of a person's career) be crowned with success

功到自然成 gōngdào zìrán chéng constant effort yields sure success.

功德 gōngdé ① merits and virtues: ～无量 boundless beneficence; great service ② [佛] charitable and pious deeds; benefaction; beneficence; works

功夫片 gōngfupiàn *gongfu* film

功过 gōngguò merits and faults (demerits)

功绩 gōngjì meritorious deeds; achievements; exploit; great services; merits

功课 gōngkè lessons; studies; homework: ～好 do well in one's studies

功亏一篑 gōngkuīyīkuì fall through when success is in sight; abandon work that has been seriously undertaken

功劳 gōngláo merit; contribution; credit: 立下了伟大的～ have great achievements to its credit

功利 gōnglì material gain; utility: ～主义 utilitarianism

功名 gōngmíng scholarly honour or official rank (in feudal times)

功能 gōngnéng function

功效 gōngxiào efficacy; effect: 此药～非常显著。This medicine is most efficacious.

功勋 gōngxūn great deed; exploit; meritorious service (deeds); contribution

功业 gōngyè achievements; exploits

功用 gōngyòng use; function

供 gōng 〈动〉 supply; provide; furnish: ～不应求的商品 undersupplied commodities. ～电 power supply
另见 gòng

供不应求 gōngbùyìngqiú supply falls short of demand; demand exceeds supply

供电 gōngdiàn supply electricity; supply power

供过于求 gōngguòyúqiú supply exceeds demand

供给 gōngjǐ supply; provide; furnish: ～制 free supply system

供暖 gōngnuǎn heating: ～系统 heating system. 热水～ hot water heating

供求 gōngqiú supply and demand: ～平衡 balance between supply and demand. 供不应求。Supply falls short of demand. 供过于求。Supply exceeds demand.

供销 gōngxiāo supply and marketing: ～合作社 supply and marketing cooperatives

供养 gōngyǎng support (one's parents or elders); provide for

供应 gōngyìng supply; provide: ～点 supply centre. ～学派［经］ the supply school of economy

恭 gōng 〈形〉 respectful; polite; reverent: 洗耳～听 listen with respectful attention

恭贺 gōnghè congratulate: ～新禧! (I wish you a) happy New Year!; With best wishes for a happy New Year!

恭候 gōnghòu 〈敬〉 await respectfully: ～光临。We request the pleasure of your company.

恭敬 gōngjìng respectful

恭请 gōngqǐng invite respectfully: ～光临。We request the honour of your presence.

恭维 gōngwei say sth. polite about; flatter; compliment: ～话 compliments; flattery

恭喜 gōngxǐ congratulate sb. on (upon) sth; congratulations

公 gōng 〈形〉 ① public; common; general ② just; fair: 大～无私 unselfish ③ male ④〈动〉 publish; make known; make public: ～开申明 openly announce 〈名〉⑤ public affairs; official affairs: ～事～办。A public business should be done with strictness. ⑥ collective; authority:交～ turn over to the authorities

公安 gōng'ān public security:～局 public security bureau. ～人员 public security personnel (officers). ～分局 public security subbureau. ～派出所 public security stations

公办 gōngbàn publicly administered:～教师 publicly administered teachers

公报 gōngbào communiqué; bulletin

公报私仇 gōngbào-sīchóu avenge personal wrongs in the name of public interests; abuse public power to retaliate against a personal enemy

公布 gōngbù announce; publish; make public; promulgate:～施行 come into effect upon promulgation

公产 gōngchǎn public property

公道 gōngdào ①〈名〉justice:讨回～ seeking legal redress for an accident. 主持～ uphold justice ②gōngdao〈形〉fair; just; reasonable; impartial:价钱～。The price is reasonable.

公德 gōngdé public morals; social morality:～心 sense of public morals; public spirit

公断 gōngduàn ① arbitrate ② consider and decide impartially

公吨 gōngdūn metric ton (MT)

公费 gōngfèi at public expense:～医疗 free medical service; medical service at state expense

公愤 gōngfèn general indignation:引起～ arouse general (public) indignation

公干 gōnggàn official business

公告 gōnggào notice; announcement; proclamation

公公 gōnggōng ① husband's father; father-in-law ② (paternal) grandfather ③ (maternal) grandfather

公共 gōnggòng public; common:～财产 public property. ～财物 article of public property. ～事业 public utilities. ～秩序 public order

公股 gōnggǔ government share (in a joint state-private enterprise)

公关 gōngguān public relations

公海 gōnghǎi high seas

公害 gōnghài ① environmental pollution ② public harm; public nuisance

公会 gōnghuì trade council; trade association; guild

公积金 gōngjījīn accumulation fund (of a socialist collective); public accumulation fund

公检法 gōng-jiǎn-fǎ judicial and public security organs, people's procuratorate and people's court

公斤 gōngjīn kilogram (kg.); kilo

公举 gōngjǔ elect by public nomination

公爵 gōngjué duke:～夫人 duchess

公开 gōngkāi ① open; public; overt:～课 open class; demonstration class ② make public

公款 gōngkuǎn public money (fund); government money

公理 gōnglǐ ① universally accepted truth ②[数] axiom

公立 gōnglì established and maintained by the government; public

公粮 gōngliáng agricultural tax paid in grain; grain delivered to the state; public grain: 交～ deliver tax grain to the state

公路 gōnglù highway: 高速～ expressway; superhighway

公买公卖 gōngmǎi-gōngmài be fair in buying and selling; buy and sell at reasonable prices

公民 gōngmín citizen: ～权 civil rights; citizenship. ～私人所有的合法财产 citizen's lawful privately-owned property

公判 gōngpàn ① pronounce judgment in public ② verdict of the public

公平 gōngpíng fair; just; impartial; equitable; 买卖～ be fair in buying and selling; buy and sell at reasonable prices

公平秤 gōngpíngchèng fair scales

公婆 gōngpó husband's father and mother; parents-in-law ② husband and wife: 两～ the husband and his wife; the couple

公仆 gōngpú public servant: 人民的～ a servant of the people

公勤人员 gōngqín rényuán office attendants

公然 gōngrán openly; undisguisedly; brazenly: ～背叛 openly betray

公认 gōngrèn generally acknowledge (recognize); universally accept; establish

公审 gōngshěn open (public) trial

公使 gōngshǐ minister: ～馆 legation

公事 gōngshì ① public affairs; official business: ～公办。Business is business.

公署 gōngshǔ government office

公说公有理,婆说婆有理 gōng shuō gōng yǒulǐ, pó shuō pó yǒulǐ each says he is right; both parties claim to be in the right

公私合营 gōngsī-héyíng joint public and private ownership of individual enterprises; state-private joint operations

公私兼顾 gōngsī-jiāngù take both public (state) and private interests into account; give consideration to both public and private interests

公司 gōngsī company; corporation; firm: 股份～ joint-stock company. 母～ parent company (firm). 信托～ trust company. 子～ subsidiary company (corporation); subsidiary

公诉 gōngsù public prosecution; public action: ～人 official (public) procurator; prosecuting officer

公文 gōngwén official document: ～旅行 travel of documents; bureaucratic red-tape

公务 gōngwù public affairs (services); official business

公演 gōngyǎn perform in public; give a performance

公益 gōngyì public welfare (good): ～金 public welfare

fund. ～劳动 volunteer labour. ～性单位 welfare services

公营 gōngyíng publicly-owned; publicly-operated; public: ～经济 the public sector of the economy; public economy

公用 gōngyòng for public use; public: ～电话 public telephone. ～事业 public utilities. ～月票 public monthly ticket

公有 gōngyǒu publicly-owned; public: ～化水平 level of socialist public ownership. ～制经济 publicly-owned economy

公寓 gōngyù ① block of flats; apartment house ② lodging house

公元 gōngyuán A.D. (Anno Domini); the Christian era: ～104年 A.D. 104. ～前221年 221 B.C. (Before Christ)

公约 gōngyuē ① pact; compact ② joint pledge: 服务～ service pledge (given by workers in the service trades)

公债 gōngzhài public loan; bonds: 发行～ float bonds

公章 gōngzhāng official seal: 盖～ affix an official seal

公正 gōngzhèng just; fair; impartial; fair-minded

公证 gōngzhèng notarization: ～机关 notary bodies. ～人 notary (public)

公职 gōngzhí public employment; public office: ～人员 government employees

公众 gōngzhòng the public: ～领袖 leader of the public

弓 gōng ① 〈名〉 bow: ～箭 bow and arrow ② 〈动〉 arch; bend

弓箭 gōngjiàn bow and arrow

弓琴 gōngqín musical bow

弓形竖琴 gōngxíng-shùqín arched harp

弓弦 gōngxián bowstring: ～乐器 bowed stringed (string) instrument; bowed instrument

躬 gōng 〈动〉 bend forward; bow: ～身 bend at the waist

躬亲 gōngqīn attend to personally

gǒng

巩 gǒng 〈动〉 consolidate: ～固根本 strengthen the root

巩固 gǒnggù ① strengthen; consolidate; fortify: ～国防 strengthen the national defence ② strong; stable; consolidated

拱 gǒng 〈动〉 ① cup one hand in the other before the chest ② encircle; surround: 四山环～的大湖 a great lake surrounded by mountains ③ arch; hump: ～着腰 arch one's back ④ 〈名〉 arch: 圆～ circular arch

拱门 gǒngmén arched door

拱桥 gōngqiáo arched bridge

拱手 gōngshǒu bow with clasped hands: ～让人 surrender sth. submissively; hand over with a bow

gòng

贡 gòng 〈动〉 tribute: 进～ pay tribute

贡品 gòngpǐn articles of tribute; tribute

贡税 gòngshuì tribute and taxes

贡献 gòngxiàn ① contribute; dedicate; devote ② contribution: ~自己的一份力量 contribute one's share (to); do one's bit (for). 为…作出更大的~ make greater contributions to…

共 gòng ①〈形〉common; joint; mutual: ~有 joint possession ②〈动〉share with: 休戚与~ share weal and woe〈副〉③ together: 同生~死 live and die together ④ altogether; in all: ~50人 altogether fifty people

共产党 gòngchǎndǎng Communist Party: ~员 member of the Communist Party; Party member; Communist

共产主义 gòngchǎnzhǔyì communism: ~青年团 Communist Youth League

共处 gòngchǔ coexist: 和平~ peaceful coexistence

共存 gòngcún coexist

共犯 gòngfàn accomplice; joint offenders; participant in a crime

共负盈亏 gòngfù-yíngkuī sharing profits and losses; joint responsibility for profits and losses

共计 gòngjì add up to; total; amount to

共聚一堂 gòngjù-yītáng gather in the same hall; gather together: 全国人民代表大会代表~,商讨国家大事。Deputies to the National People's Congress gather in the same hall to discuss affairs of state.

共勉 gòngmiǎn encourage each other: 愿~之。Let us encourage each other in our endeavours.

共鸣 gòngmíng ① resonance ② sympathy; echo: 引起~ arouse sympathy

共青团 gòngqīngtuán Communist Youth League

共事 gòngshì work together (at the same organization); be fellow workers

共同 gòngtóng common; joint: ~富裕 common (collective) prosperity. ~市场 Common Market. ~体 community. ~投资 joint venture. ~关心的问题 question of common concern. ~刑事被告 joinder of defendants

共享 gòngxiǎng share (with); partake (with)

共性 gòngxìng common (general) character

供 gòng〈动〉① offer; lay (offerings); dedicate ② confess; admit: 逼~ extort a confession 另见 gōng

供词 gòngcí statement; confession

供品 gòngpǐn offerings

供认 gòngrèn confess; admit; avow; avowal: ~者 confessor

供认不讳 gòngrènbùhuì candidly confess; confess everything

供述 gòngshù confess; declare; statement

供养 gòngyǎng make offerings to; offer sacrifices to; enshrine and worship

供职 gòngzhí hold a post; work
供状 gòngzhuàng confessions; admission
供桌 gòngzhuō altar

gōu

篝 gōu 〈名〉 bamboo cage; cage
篝火 gōuhuǒ bonfire; campfire:宿营地上燃起熊熊的～。A bright bonfire was built at camp.
勾 gōu 〈动〉 ① cancel; cross out; tick; strike out:～销 expunge; erase; delete ② draw:～画出…的蓝图 map out the blueprints for ③ induce; evoke; call to mind:～起对过去的回忆 evoke memories of the past ④ gang up with; collude with:～～搭搭 team up with; hitch up with
勾搭 gōuda ① flirt with; court ② gang up with
勾画 gōuhuà sketch out
勾魂 gǒuhún captivate sb.'s soul—enchant; bewitch
勾结 gōujié connive with (at); collaborate with; gang up with; conspire with; collude with; in collusion with; work in collusion; work in league; work hand in glove with
勾留 gōuliú make a short stay; stop over:在北京稍作～ stop over at Beijing
勾通 gōutōng work in collusion with; work hand in glove with; collaborate with
勾销 gōuxiāo cancel; liquidate; strike out; write off:一笔～ write off at one stroke; wipe out all
勾引 gōuyǐn seduce; cajoke; induce; allure; lure
沟 gōu 〈名〉 ① ditch; channel; trench:排水～ drainage ditch ② groove; rut; furrow
沟渠 gōuqú irrigation canals and ditches
沟通 gōutōng link up (with); communicate (with):～感情 communicate feelings. ～思想 get to know each other's viewpoints better
钩 gōu 〈名〉 ① hook:衣～ a coat hanger ② hook stroke in Chinese characters 〈动〉 ③ hook:～住 get hooked
钩损险 gōusǔnxiǎn risk of hook damage
钩心斗角 gōuxīn-dòujiǎo play tricks on each other; plot against each other; scheme (manoeuvere, conspire) against each other
钩针 gōuzhēn crotchet hook (needle)

gǒu

苟 gǒu ①〈形〉 careless; negligent; heedless:不～言笑 be discreet (serious) in speech and manner ②〈连〉 if:～能如此 if it could be so
苟安 gǒu'ān be content with temporary tranquility; seek mo-

mentary ease

苟合 gǒuhé illegal sexual relations

苟且偷安 gǒuqiě-tōu'ān seek ease and comfort at the expense of principles

苟且偷生 gǒuqiě-tōushēng drag out an ignoble existence; seek a moment's peace however one can

苟延残喘 gǒuyán-cánchuǎn try to prolong one's exhausted panting; merely prolong one's death throes; brief respite; prolong one's moribund (feeble, precarious) life; eke out a meagre (miserable) existence; win some time in one's death-bed struggle

狗 gǒu ①〈名〉dog ②〈形〉damned; cursed

狗胆包天 gǒudǎn-bāotiān monstrously audacious

狗急跳墙 gǒují-tiàoqiáng A cornered dog tries to jump over a high wall.; just as a dog will leap over a wall in desperation; be driven to extremities; A cornered beast will do something desperate.

狗拿耗子,多管闲事 gǒu ná hàozi, duō guān xiánshì a dog trying to catch mice; poke one's nose into other people's business

狗屁不通 gǒupìbùtōng unreadable rubbish; mere trash: 这篇文章写得～。This article is mere trash.

狗头军师 gǒutóu-jūnshī vicious (sinister) adviser

狗腿子 gǒutuǐzi hired thug; lackey; henchman

狗眼看人低 gǒuyǎn kàn rén dī be a bloody snob

狗咬狗 gǒu yǎo gǒu a dog-eat-dog; dog-fight; dog-eat-dog strife between

狗仗人势 gǒuzhàngrénshì play the bully with the backing of a powerful person

gòu

够 gòu ①〈形〉enough; adequate; sufficient: 5个人足～了。Five men will be quite enough. ②〈动〉reach; be up to (a certain standard, etc.): 你能～到书架上那一格上的书吗? Can you reach those books on the upper shelf? ③〈副〉really; quite; enough; rather: 她今天～累的了。She is rather tired today.

够本 gòuběn make enough money; cover the cost; break even: 刚～ barely covered costs

够格 gòugé be up to standard; be qualified

够交情 gòujiāoqing be on enough good terms; be in the graces of sb. enough

够劲儿 gòujìnr ① (of an onerous task, etc.) almost too much to cope with. 她一个人担任那么多工作,真～。She really has a tough job having to attend to so many things. ② strong (in taste, strength, etc.) 这酒真～。This wine is certainly powerful stuff.

够朋友 gòu péngyou deserve to be called a true friend; be a friend indeed

够呛 gòuqiàng really terrible; simply unbearable

够瞧的 gòuqiáode really awful; too much: 天热得真～。The weather is terribly hot.; The weather is really scorching.

够受的 gòushòude hard to bear; quite an ordeal; unbearable

够数 gòushù sufficient in quantity; enough

够意思 gòu yìsi ①〈口〉really sth.; terrific ② generous; really kind: 不～ unfriendly; ungraceful

媾

gòu〈动〉① wed: 媒～ serve as a go-between in marriage ② reach an agreement ③〈名〉coition

媾和 gòuhé make peace: 单独～ make peace without consulting one's allies; make a separate peace

勾

gòu

另见 gōu

勾当 gòudàng deal; trick: 肮脏～ dirty deal

构

gòu〈动〉form; construct; make up: ～成…学说 formulate

构成 gòuchéng make up; compose; constitute; form: ～犯罪的要件 requisites to constitute a crime

构件 gòujiàn ①［建筑］(structural) member; component ②［机械］component (part)

构思 gòusī conceive; compose; (of a writer or artist) work out the plot of; conception: ～巧妙 be skilfully composed. ～剧本 mediate on the plot of a play

构想 gòuxiǎng concept; conception; idea

构造 gòuzào structure; construction: ～心理学 structural psychology

构筑 gòuzhù construct (military works); build: ～工事 construct field works (fortifications); build defences; dig in

购

gòu〈动〉buy; purchase

购办 gòubàn buy (goods, supplies, etc.)

购货单 gòuhuòdān order form; order

购买 gòumǎi buy; purchase: ～力 purchasing (buying) power

购物 gòuwù buy things; do shopping: ～狂 a shopping frenzy; a buying frenzy. 她是个～狂。She is obsessive about shopping.

购销 gòuxiāo purchase and sale: ～政策 purchase-market policy. ～倒挂。The purchasing price exceeded the selling price. ～两旺。Both purchasing and marketing are brisk.; brisk buying and selling

gū

沽

gū〈动〉buy ② sell: 待价而～ wait to sell at good price

沽名钓誉 gūmíng-diàoyù angle

(fish) for fame and compliments;seek publicity; cater to publicity by sordid methods; réclame

辜 gū〈名〉guilt; crime:无～ free from guilt

辜负 gūfù fail to live up to; let down; be unworthy of; disappoint:～某人的期望 fail to live up to sb's. expectations

咕 gū〈象〉the clucking of a hen; the cooing of a pigeon

咕咚 gūdōng the sound of a heavy thing falling down; thud; splash; plump:一块石头～一声掉到水里去了。A stone fell into the water with a splash.

咕嘟 gūdū ① bubble; gurgle:他端起一碗水,～～地喝了下去。He took up a bowl of water and gulped it down. ② gūdu boil for a long time ③ purse (one's lips):不高兴地～着嘴 purse one's lips in displeasure

咕噜 gūlū rumble; roll:她的肚子～～直响。Her stomach kept rumbling.

咕哝 gūnong murmur; mutter; grumble:你在～些什么? What are you muttering about?

估 gū〈动〉estimate; appraise; figure:低～ underestimate

估产 gūchǎn ① estimate the yield ② appraise the assets; assess:～定息 payment of a fixed rate of interest on the basis of an appraisal of the assets

估计 gūjì estimate; reckon; appraise; calculate; take into account:～到 take into account (consideration). ～纯利 estimated net profit. ～的数字 estimative figure

估价 gūjià appraised (estimated) price; estimate price; evaluate:～员 assessor

估量 gūliang appraise; estimate; assess; reckon:～双方力量的对比 assess the balance of strength between the two sides. 你～她挣多少? How much do you reckon she earns?

估算 gūsuàn estimate; appraise; reckon:～产量 estimate the yield. ～到几种可能性 reckon with several possibilities

姑 gū〈名〉① father's sister; aunt ② husband's sister; sister-in-law ③ nun:道～ Taoist priestess〈副〉④ for the time being; for the moment; tentatively

姑表 gūbiǎo the relationship between the children of a brother and a sister; cousinship:～兄弟 male cousins (the father of one and the mother of the other being brother and sister)

姑夫 gūfu husband of father's sister; uncle-in-law

姑姑 gūgu father's sister; aunt

姑母 gūmǔ father's sister; aunt

姑娘 gūniang ① girl ② daughter

姑且 gūqiě for the time being; tentatively; just; for the moment:～不谈 leave aside for the moment

姑嫂 gūsǎo a woman and her

brother's wife; sister-in-law
姑妄听之 gūwàngtīngzhī just listen to (sth.) without taking it seriously; take sth. with a grain (pinch) of salt
姑妄言之 gūwàngyánzhī just talk for the sake of talking; tell sb. sth. for what it is worth
姑息 gūxī tolerate; appease; indulge:～养奸。Overindulgence encourages evildoers.; To condone evil is to foster its growth.; foster evil propensities by being overlenient
姑置不论 gūzhìbùlùn (just) leave it for the time being

孤 gū〈形〉① fatherless ② single; solitary; isolated; alone: ～独的人群 lonely crowd ③〈名〉orphan:～儿院 orphanage
孤傲 gū'ào be too proud to associate with others; aloof and arrogant
孤本 gūběn the only existing copy; the only extant
孤单 gūdān ①alone; lonely:孤孤单单一个人 all alone; all by oneself; a lone soul ② weak:力量～ weak and helpless
孤独 gūdú solitary; isolated; lonely:～性(症) autism
孤儿 gūér orphan
孤苦伶仃 gūkǔ-língdīng orphaned and helpless; alone and uncared for; friendless and wretched
孤立 gūlì ① isolated; detached; solitary ② isolate:～无援 isolated and cut off from help; isolated and without help
孤陋寡闻 gūlòu-guǎwén ignorant and scant of information; superficial and ill-informed
孤僻 gūpì unsocial; uncommunicative:性情～ have an unsocial disposition
孤掌难鸣 gūzhǎng-nánmíng One can't clap with one hand.; He who stands alone has no power.; It is difficult to succeed without support.
孤注一掷 gūzhù-yīzhì make a last desperate effort; stake everything on; risk it all on a single throw; risk everything on a single throw; put all one's eggs in one basket; stake all one has

骨 gū
另见 gǔ
骨碌 gūlu roll:她一～从床上爬起来。She rolled out of the bed.

gǔ

鼓 gǔ ①〈名〉drum:～手 timpanist; drummer〈动〉② beat; clap; strike:～掌 clap one's hands ③ rouse; agitate:～起勇气 pluck up one's courage ④ blow with bellows; fan:～风 work a bellows; make a blast
鼓包 gǔbāo ① bulge; swell ② swelling; lump; bump
鼓吹 gǔchuī ① advocate; propagate; publicize; ② preach; advertise; beat the drums for; trumpet about
鼓槌 gǔchuí drumstick
鼓词 gǔcí storytelling to the accompaniment of rhythmic

drumming

鼓动 gǔdòng agitate; encourage; rouse; drum up; incite; instigate:～成千上万的群众 rouse the people in their millions

鼓励 gǔlì encourage; stimulate; inspire; urge

鼓楼 gǔlóu drum-tower

鼓起 gǔqǐ pluck up; muster up; bolster up:～勇气 pluck up one's courage; bolster up the morale

鼓手 gǔshǒu drummer

鼓舞 gǔwǔ encourage; inspire; rouse; stimulate:～人心 set the hearts of people aflame

鼓噪 gǔzào make a great deal of noise; make a great to-do; clamour

鼓掌 gǔzhǎng clap one's hands; applaud:热烈～ warmly applaud. ～通过 approve by acclamation

古

gǔ 〈形〉ancient; old; olden; antique:～代 ancient times; antiquity

古代 gǔdài ① the period in Chinese history from remote antiquity down until the mid-19th century ② the age of slave society; ancient times; antiquity ～史 ancient history

古典 gǔdiǎn ① classical:～文学艺术研究(教育) classical studies (education) ② classical allusion

古董 gǔdǒng curio; antique; rarities:～商 antiquarian

古怪 gǔguài strange; quaint; odd; eccentric:性情～ have an eccentric disposition

古话 gǔhuà saying

古籍 gǔjí ancient books

古迹 gǔjì historic spot (site); place of historic interest

古今中外 gǔjīn-zhōngwài in ancient or modern times, in China or abroad; past and present, at home and abroad; both ancient and modern, Chinese and foreign

古老 gǔlǎo ancient, time-honoured; age-old

古朴 gǔpǔ (of art, architecture, etc.) simple and unsophisticated; of primitive simplicity

古人 gǔrén the ancients; our forefathers

古色古香 gǔsè-gǔxiāng ancient elegance and delicacy; classic beauty; quaint; antique

古诗 gǔshī ancient poetry; ancient-style verse; ancient verse; ancient-style poem; ancient-style poetry

古玩 gǔwán curios; antiques:～店 antique store

古往今来 gǔwǎng-jīnlái from ancient times to modern times; from time immemorial through the ages

古为今用 gǔwéijīnyòng make the past serve the present

古文 gǔwén classical form of prose; classic style of prose-writing; archaic prose; prose written in the classical literary style:～作家 writer of archaic prose

古物 gǔwù ancient objects; historical relics; antiquities

古稀 gǔxī seventy years of age: 年近～ getting on for seventy

古训 gǔxùn an old maxim (adage)

古雅 gǔyǎ (of material things, literary works, etc.) of classic beauty and in elegant taste; of classic elegance

古语 gǔyǔ ① archaism ② an old saying

古装 gǔzhuāng ancient costume

谷 gǔ 〈名〉① valley; gorge: 深～ a deep valley ② grain; cereal: 稻～ paddy rice

谷仓 gǔcāng barn; cereals granary; granary

谷壳 gǔké husk (of rice)

谷类作物 gǔlèi zuòwù general name for rice, wheat, millet, sorghum, maize, etc.; cereal crops

谷物 gǔwù grain; cereal: ～法 corn law

谷子 gǔzi ① millet ② unhusked rice

蛊 gǔ 〈名〉 a legendary venomous insect

蛊惑人心 gǔhuò-rénxīn blind (befog) the minds of the people; instil poisonous suspicions into men's minds; beguile people out of the right way; confuse and poison people's minds; resort to demagogy

骨 gǔ 〈名〉① bone ② backbone; integrity: 硬～ person of unyielding integrity ③ rib; skeleton

另见 gú

骨干 gǔgàn backbone; core; mainstay; key: ～队伍 backbone force. ～企业 backbone enterprise

骨灰 gǔhuī ashes of the dead: ～盒 cinerary casket

骨科 gǔkē (department of) orthopaedics: ～医生 orthopaedist

骨牌 gǔpái dominoes

骨气 gǔqì moral integrity; backbone: 有～的人 man of integrity

骨肉 gǔròu one's own flesh and blood; blood relations; kindred; kin: ～团聚 reunite with one's family; enjoy one's family reunion. ～之亲 blood relatives (relations)

骨瘦如柴 gǔshòu-rúchái as thin as a rail; only skin and bone; bag of bones

骨头 gǔtou ① bone ② moral character: 他～很硬。He is a person of great moral integrity. ③ sharpness; bitterness: 她话里有～。Her words had a bite to them.

骨子里 gǔzilǐ in one's heart; at bottom

股 gǔ 〈名〉① thigh ② section (of an organization): ～长 section chief ③ share; stock: ～金 share capital ④ strand; ply: 把线捻成～儿。Twist thread into strand. 〈量〉⑤ [用成条的东西]: 一～头发 a strand of hair ⑥ [用于气体、气味、力气等]: 一～新鲜空气 a whiff of fresh air

股本 gǔběn capital stock; the

money invested

股东 gǔdōng shareholder; stockholder

股份 gǔfèn share; stock: ～有限公司 limited-liability company; limited company (Ltd.). ～制公司 joint-stock company. ～合作制 system of joint-stock and cooperation

股金 gǔjīn money paid for shares (in a partnership or cooperative)

股利(息) gǔlì(xī) dividend

股票 gǔpiào share (certificate); stock: ～成交金额 equity turnover. ～交易所 stock exchange. ～经纪人 stockbroker; stockjobber

股权 gǔquán stock right; stock ownership; stockholders' right; contribution; interest; equity: 他买下了一条帆船三分之一的～。He purchased a third interest in a schooner.

股长 gǔzhǎng section chief

gù

雇 gù 〈动〉 hire; employ; engage: ～保姆 employ a housekeeper

雇工 gùgōng ① hire labour; hire hands ② hired labourer

雇请 gùqǐng hire or employ (a person)

雇"托儿" gùtuōr hiring of a silent partner or side kick by a peddlar in order to cheat customers

雇佣 gùyōng hire; employ: ～军 mercenary troops; mercenaries. ～劳动 hired labour; wage labour

雇用 gùyòng employ; hire: ～合同(契约) contract of employment (service)

雇员 gùyuán hired workers; employees

雇主 gùzhǔ employer: ～责任保险 employer's liability insurance

顾 gù 〈动〉 ① look round and look at; look back: 环～ look around ② attend to; take care of; consider: 照～ take good care of ③ call on; visit

顾此失彼 gùcǐ-shībǐ attend to one thing and lose sight of another; have too many things to take care of at the same time; be unable to attend all its troubles at the same time; be unable to attend to everything at once

顾大局 gùdàjú give due consideration to the overall situation; take the interests of the whole into account; out of consideration for the general interest; take the whole situation into consideration

顾及 gùjí attend to; take into account; consider: 无暇～ have no time to attend to

顾忌 gùjì have scruples (misgivings) (about): ～舆论 pay heed to public opinion

顾客 gùkè [商店的] customer; shopper; [银行、理发店等的] client

顾虑 gùlǜ ① scruples; misgivings; apprehension: ～重重 full of misgivings ② have scruples (about); entertain apprehensions(for)

顾面子 gùmiànzi ① save face; keep up appearances ② spare sb.'s feelings

顾名思义 gùmíng-sīyì as the name implies; as the term suggests (indicates)

顾前不顾后 gùqián bù gùhòu drive ahead without considering the consequences; act rashly

顾全 gùquán show consideration for and take care to preserve: ～大局 take the interests of the whole into account; consider the situation as a whole

顾问 gùwèn adviser: ～委员会 advisory commission

顾主 gùzhǔ customer; client; patron

故 gù 〈名〉① reason; cause: 托～离开 make an excuse and leave ② accident; incident; event: 变～ unforeseen event ③ friend; acquaintance: 非亲非～ neither relative nor friend ④ 〈动〉die: 亡～ pass away 〈形〉⑤ old; former; ancient: ～都 ancient capital ⑥ native: ～乡 native land; home town 〈副〉⑦ intentionally; purposely: ～意刁难 deliberately make things difficult for others

故步自封 gùbù-zìfēng stick to the beaten track; be satisfied with old practices; hold fast to established ideas

故地 gùdì an old haunt: ～重游 revisit an old haunt

故都 gùdū onetime capital

故宫 gùgōng Imperial Palace

故宫博物院 Gùgōng bówùyuàn the Palace Museum (in Beijing)

故伎 gùjì stock trick; old tactics: ～重演 be up to one's old tricks; play the same old trick

故居 gùjū former residence (home)

故里 gùlǐ native place; hometown: 荣归～ return home with honours

故弄玄虚 gùnòng-xuánxū purposely make a mystery of simple things; be deliberately mystifying

故事 gùshi story; tale: ～片 feature film; feature. 这本小说～性强。The novel has an interesting plot. ～员 storyteller

故态复萌 gùtài-fùméng revert to one's old ways; return to one's old vices; one's old manners restored

故土 gùtǔ native land; native place; birthplace; hometown: 怀念～ long for home

故乡 gùxiāng home; native place; birthplace

故意 gùyì purposely; intentionally; deliberately: ～犯罪 intentional crime (offence); calculated crime

故障 gùzhàng trouble; breakdown; hitch: ～检修 corrective maintenance; trouble shooting

故作姿态 gùzuò-zītài strike a pose; put on airs

固 gù ①〈形〉strong; firm; solid: 稳～ stable; firm 〈副〉② resolutely; firmly: ～请 firmly invite ③ originally; in the first place:～当如此。It is just as it should be.

固步自封 gùbù-zìfēng stick to the beaten track; be satisfied with old practices

固定 gùdìng fixed; steady; regular:～收入 regular income. ～摊位执照 fixed pitch licence. ～资产 fixed assets

固然 gùrán [表示承认某个事实,引起下文转折] of course; admittedly; no doubt; it is true:他～不对,可是你也不对。He's not right, it's true; but you aren't either.

固若金汤 gùruòjīntāng strongly fortified; impregnable

固守 gùshǒu ① defend tenaciously; be firmly entrenched in ② stick to:～老一套的办法 stick to the old ways

固体 gùtǐ solid:～饮料 solid drinks

固有 gùyǒu inherent; original; innate:～机制 innate mechanism

固执 gùzhì ① obstinate; stubborn ② stick to; adhere to:～己见 adhere stubbornly to one's own opinion; stick to one's view

guā

刮 guā 〈动〉① scrape:～锅子 scrape a pot clean ② shave:～胡子 shave one's beard (whiskers) ③ blow:门～开了。The door blew open. ④ fleece; extort

刮刀 guādāo scraping cutter; scraper

刮脸 guāliǎn shave (the face):～刀 razor

刮目相看 guāmù-xiāngkàn treat sb. with increased respect; have a completely new appraisal of sb.; look at sb. with new eyes

瓜 guā 〈名〉melon; gourd

瓜分 guāfēn partition; carve up; divide

瓜葛 guāgé connection (with); entanglement (with); involvement (in):与某事有～ be involved in sth.

瓜熟蒂落 guāshú-dìluò Things will be easily settled when conditions are ripe.; At the right time everything comes easy.; Fruits fall off when ripe.

瓜子 guāzǐ melon seeds; 嗑～儿 crack melon seeds

呱 guā

呱呱叫 guāguājiào ① first-rate; excellent ② Thumbs up!; Great!; Terrific!

guǎ

寡 guǎ 〈形〉① few; little; scant:孤陋～闻 ignorant and ill-informed ② tasteless; insipid:索然～味 dull and monotonous ③〈名〉widowhood

寡不敌众 guǎbùdízhòng A few are no match for the many.; be hopeless outnumbered

寡断 guǎduàn indecisive; irresolute

寡妇 guǎfù widow

寡欢 guǎhuān joyless; unhappy: 郁郁～ joyless; depressed; melancholy

寡廉鲜耻 guǎliánxiǎnchǐ have no sense of shame (dishonour, disgrace); infamy; unprincipled; lost to shame; shameless

寡头 guǎtóu oligarch: ～政治 oligarchy; aristocracy. 财政资本～ oligarchy of financial capital

寡言 guǎyán taciturn: 沉默～ taciturn; reticent

寡欲 guǎyù have few desires; be ascetic: 清心～ be pure of heart and have few desires; purify one's heart and reduce the number of one's desires

guà

挂 guà 〈动〉 ① hang; suspend: 把帽子～在衣架上 hang (put) the cap on the coat hanger ② hitch; get caught: 把拖车～上 hitch up the trailer ③ ring off; hang up: 请别～上电话。Hold the line, Please! ④ ring up; phone; call: 我要给她～电话。I'll phone her up. ⑤ be anxious about; be concerned about: 她总是～念着母亲的病。She's very worried about her mother. ⑥ register; put on record: 他要～外科。He wants to register for surgery.

挂彩 guàcǎi ① decorate with coloured silk festoons; decorate for festive occasions ② be wounded in action

挂档 guàdàng engage a gear; put into gear

挂钩 guàgōu establish links with; link up: 产销～ establish a link between producer and seller; link up production with marketing

挂号 guàhào register: ～费 registration fee; [医院] check-in fee. ～处 registration office; registry

挂历 guàlì monthly calendar hung up on the wall; hanging calendars; wall calendar

挂面 guàmiàn fine dried noodles

挂名 guàmíng in name; nominal: ～党员 be Party member only in name

挂念 guàniàn worry about sb. who is absent; miss: ～亲人 miss one's folks at home. 我身体很好，请勿～。I'm in good health. Please don't worry.

挂牌 guàpái hang out one's shingle; put up one's brass plate; hang signs: ～律师 regular practitioner. ～售货 hang signs in selling goods. ～证券 quoted securities

挂失 guàshī give notice of the loss of sth. (to): 支票～ report the loss of check; check replacement

挂帅 guàshuài be in command; take command (of): 政治～ politics in command

挂毯 guàtǎn tapestry

挂靴 guàxuē hang up shoes: 这支

女排由于三位主将～，实力大减。 Because three star players in the women's volleyball team have hung up their shoes, the strength of the team has manifestly diminished.

挂羊头，卖狗肉 guà yángtóu, mài gǒuròu hang up a sheep's head and sell dog-meat— try to palm off something inferior to what it purports to be; selling horse-meat as beefsteak; sell dog-meat as mutton; put up sign-board of something behind which one sells other things

挂一漏万 guàyī-lòuwàn For one thing cited, ten thousand may have been left out — the list is far from being complete; the list is by no means exhaustive

挂衣钩 guàyīgōu clothes-hook

挂钟 guàzhōng wall clock

褂 guà 〈名〉a Chinese-style unlined garment; gown：短～儿 short gown

guāi

乖 guāi 〈形〉① (of a child) well-behaved; lovely; good：～儿子 good son ② clever; quick-witted：学～了 become a little wiser ③ contrary to reason

乖乖 guāiguāi ① tractable; well-behaved; obedient：～地听 submit to someone's will ② darling; little dear

乖僻 guāipì eccentric; queer; odd：性情～ have a queer disposition

乖巧 guāiqiǎo ① clever; smart ② cute; lovely

guǎi

拐 guǎi 〈动〉① turn：向右～ turn to the right ② limp：一～一～地走 limp along; ③ abduct; swindle; kidnap：～骗 kidnap; swindle

拐带 guǎidài kidnap (women or children); abduct

拐带儿童 guǎidài értóng child-stealing

拐卖 guǎimài abduct and traffic：～妇女儿童 abduction and sale of women and children. ～人口 abduct and sell people

拐骗 guǎipiàn ① abduct; swindle：～罪 kidnaping ② [金钱] cheat (money out of sb.)

拐弯 guǎiwān turn (a corner)：～抹角 (talk) in a roundabout way; beat about the bush

拐杖 guǎizhàng walking stick

guài

怪 guài ①〈形〉strange; odd; curious：～现象 strange phenomenon 〈动〉② wonder (at); find sth. strange ③ blame：我必须说都～我不好。I must say that I am very much to blame. ④〈名〉monster; demon; devil：鬼～ demons; ghosts ⑤〈副〉quite; rather：～不好意思的 be very embarassed

怪不得 guàibude ① (it is) no wonder that…; not without good cause ② be not to blame: 这～她。She is not to blame.; You can't blame her.

怪诞 guàidàn strange; grotesque; weird: ～不经 crazy; fantastic

怪话 guàihuà ① cynical remark; absurdity: 说～ make cynical remarks ② grumbling

怪里怪气 guàiliguàiqì eccentric; peculiar; queer: ～的人 an eccentric fellow

怪模怪样 guàimú-guàiyàng grotesque; queer-looking

怪僻 guàipì eccentric; erratic: 性情～ have an erratic disposition; be eccentric

怪声怪气 guàishēng-guàiqì (speak in) a strange voice or an affected manner

怪事 guàishì strange thing

怪物 guàiwù ① monster; chimera; freak ② eccentric person; queer fish

怪异 guàiyì ① monstrous; strange; unusual ② strange phenomenon; portent; prodigy

怪罪 guàizuì blame sb.

guān

官 guān 〈名〉 ① government official; officer; functionary: 文～ civil official. ～办企业 enterprises operated by the official bodies ② organ; sense: 五～ the five sense organs (ears, eyes; lips, nose and tongue)

官办 guānbàn run by the government; operated by official bodies: ～企业 enterprises operated by the official bodies

官兵 guānbīng ① officers and men

官场 guānchǎng officialdom; official circles

官邸 guāndǐ official residence; official mansion: 首相～ prime minister's residence

官方 guānfāng official: ～机密 official secrecy; official secrets. ～人士 official circles (quarters)

官官相护 guānguān-xiānghù officials protect each other; bureaucrats shield one another

官价 guānjià official price (rate)

官架子 guānjiàzi the airs of an official; bureaucratic airs: 摆～ put on bureaucratic airs

官吏 guānlì government officials

官僚 guānliáo bureaucrat: ～作风 bureaucratic style (of work); officialism

官迷 guānmí devotee of officialdom; title crazy; mad for official position

官能 guānnéng (organic) function; sense

官气 guānqì bureaucratic airs; bureaucratism: ～十足 full of bureaucratic airs

官腔 guānqiāng official jargon: 打～ use official jargon

官商作风 guānshāng-zuòfēng style of government monopoly of commerce

官司 guānsi lawsuit: 打～ go to law (against sb.); bring an action (against sb.)

官衔 guānxián official rank; official title

官样文章 guānyàng-wénzhāng mere formalities; bureaucratic red tape

官员 guānyuán official

官制 guānzhì government institutions; government system

关 guān 〈动〉① shut; close; [水、电等] turn off: 关门 shut the door. ～电灯 turn off the light ② shut in; lock up: 她把自己～在房里一整天。She locked herself in the room for a whole day. ③ close down: 昨天又有三家店铺～了。Three more shops closed down yesterday. ④ concern; involve: ～心不足 lack of concern for 〈名〉⑤ pass; check point: 把～ guard the pass ⑥ barrier; critical juncture: 突破难～ break through the barrier

关隘 guān'ài (mountain) pass

关闭 guānbì ① close; shut ② (of a shop or factory) close down; shut down

关怀 guānhuái be concerned about; show concern for: ～备至 show every concern for (towards)

关键 guānjiàn ① door bolt; door bar ② key; hinge; crux: 问题的～ the key to the question; the crux (heart) of the matter

关节 guānjié [生理] ① joint: 指～ finger joints ② a key (crucial) link; a key (crucial) point

关贸总协定 guānmào zǒngxiédìng General Agreement on Tariffs and Trade (GATT)

关门 guānmén ① (of a shop, etc.) close; close the door: 展览馆下午六点～。The exhibition centre closes at 6 p. m. ② (of a business) close down ③ refuse discussion or consideration; slam the door on sth ④ be behind closed doors: 我们不能～办报。We must not run a newspaper behind closed doors.

关切 guānqiè ① be deeply concerned (about, over) ② concern; anxiety: 对某事表示～ express concern over sth.

关税 guānshuì customs duties; tariff

关停并转 guāntíng bìngzhuǎn closing, suspension, and merging of enterprises and the shifting of their lines of production

关系 guānxì ① relation; relationship; connection: 外交～ diplomatic relations. ～户 parties of connection; a well-connected individual or group ② matter: ～不大。It doesn't matter much. 由于时间～ owing to limited time; for reasons of time ③ bearing; affect: ～到全世界局势 affect the whole world

关心 guānxīn care for; be concerned about (with); show concern for; be interested in: ～群众疾苦 be concerned about the well-being of the people

关押 guānyā take sb. into custody; custody; imprison; quod

关于 guānyú concerning; about; on;with regard to
关照 guānzhào ① attend to; look after ② notify (by word of mouth); tell
关注 guānzhù pay close attention to; show concern for; follow with interest

鳏 guān 〈形〉 wifeless; widowered:～居 live as a widower
鳏夫 guānfū an old wifeless man; bachelor or widower

冠 guān 〈名〉 ① hat:免～照片 bare-headed photo ② crown; crest:花～ corolla
另见 guàn
冠礼 guānlǐ capping ceremony
冠冕堂皇 guānmiǎn-tánghuáng ostentatious; high-flown; high-falutin(g); high-sounding; pretentious; turgid:～的谬论 pretentious hotchpotch
冠心病 guānxīnbìng [医] coronary heart disease

倌 guān 〈名〉① a keeper of domestic animals; herdsman:马～儿 groom ② a hired hand in certain trades

棺 guān 〈名〉coffin
棺材 guāncai coffin
棺架 guānjià bier
棺木 guānmù coffin

观 guān ① 〈动〉 watch; look at; watch:纵～ make a general observation 〈名〉 ② view; sight:壮～ a grand view ③ outlook; conception of the nature of things:世界～ world outlook
观测 guāncè observe and survey:～天象 astronomical observation
观察 guānchá observe; survey:～的理性 observation as a process of reason. ～员 observer. ～室[医院] observation ward
观点 guāndiǎn point of view; standpoint
观感 guāngǎn impression of a visit; view:对上海的～ impressions of Shanghai
观光 guānguāng go sightseeing; see the sights; be on a sightseeing trip; tour; visit:到各地～ go to different places to see the sights
观礼 guānlǐ attend a ceremony:～台 reviewing stand; rostrum
观摩 guānmó inspect (watch) and learn from each other's work; view (watch) and emulate:～教学 demonstration lecture
观念 guānniàn idea; notion; concept; sense:组织～ sense of organization. ～形态 ideology
观赏 guānshǎng enjoy the sight of; view and admire; feast one's eyes on:～花卉 ornamental flower
观望 guānwàng wait and see; hesitate:～态度 wait-and-see attitude
观瞻 guānzhān the appearance of a place and the impressions it leaves; sight; view
观众 guānzhòng spectator; audience; [电视的] viewer

guǎn

管 guǎn ①〈名〉tube; pipe:水～water pipe〈动〉② take care of; manage; control; be in charge of:～好骨干企业 keep tabs on the key enterprises ③ mind; attend to:别～她 leave her alone

管保 guǎnbǎo guarantee; assure 他～不知道。I'm sure he doesn't know.

管得宽 guǎndekuān make everything one's own business

管饭 guǎnfàn include board; have free meals provided

管护 guǎnhù caretaking (of horticulture):～任务 the duty of taking care of the grounds

管家 guǎnjiā ① manage a household; run a house ② steward; butler ③ manager (of a work unit); housekeeper

管教 guǎnjiào ① bet; be certain:～你满意。I bet you will be satisfied. ② teach (a child) to behave:缺父母～ lack parental control ③ [法]subject to discipline:～所 reformatory

管理 guǎnlǐ administer; manage; control:企业～ business management. ～经济学 managerial economics

管事 guǎnshì ① effective; useful:针灸很～。Acupuncture is quite effective. ② run affairs; take care of things; be in charge

管辖 guǎnxiá have jurisdiction over; under the jurisdiction of; control over:在～范围之内 come within the jurisdiction

管弦乐 guǎnxiányuè orchestral music:～队 orchestra

管闲事 guǎnxiánshì be meddlesome; be a busybody:她爱～。She's a real busybody.

管押 guǎnyā take sb. into custody; keep in custody; detain

管乐器 guǎnyuèqì wind instrument

管制 guǎnzhì ① control:～的物价 control price ② [法]put under surveillance:～处分 punishment of control. ～劳动 labour under surveillance

管中窥豹,可见一斑 guǎnzhōngkuībào, kějiàn-yībān look at one spot on a leopard and you can visualize the whole animal; conjure up the whole thing through seeing a part of it

馆 guǎn〈名〉① accommodation for guests:旅～ hotel ② embassy; legation or consulate ③ (of service trades) shop:茶～ teahouse ④ a place for cultural activities:博物～ museum

馆藏 guǎncáng (of a library or a museum) ① have a collection of:～图书五十万册 have a collection of 500,000 volumes ② collection:～丰富 have a fine library; have a fine collection of books, paintings, etc.

馆子 guǎnzi restaurant; eating house:下～ eat at a restaurant

guàn

冠 guàn〈动〉① put on a hat ② crown with; precede with (by):～以她"爱民模范"称号 crown her with the title of "model of cherishing the people" ③〈名〉first place
另见 guān

冠军 guànjūn champion:上届～ defending champion

盥 guàn wash

盥漱 guànshù wash one's face and rinse one's mouth

盥洗 guànxǐ wash one's hands and face:～用具 toilet articles

盥洗室 guànxǐshì toilet (-room); lavatory

盥洗台 guànxǐtái washstand

灌 guàn〈动〉① irrigate:～溉面积 irrigated area ② pour; fill:～热水瓶 pour boiling water into a thermos flask

灌唱片 guànchàngpiàn make a gramophone record; cut a disc

灌溉 guàngài irrigate:～渠网化 a network of irrigation canals

灌迷魂汤 guànmíhúntāng try to ensnare sb. with honeyed words

灌输 guànshū instil sth. into the minds of; indoctrinate sb. with; imbue sb. (with):～新思想 imbue (sb.) with new ideas; instil new ideas into sb.

灌音 guànyīn have one's voice recorded

灌装 guànzhuāng bottle:～液化石油气钢瓶 bottle liquefied petroleum gas (LPG) in steel bottles

罐 guàn〈名〉jar; pot; tin; can

罐头 guàntou tin; can:～食品 tinned (canned) food

贯 guàn〈动〉① pass through; run through:～穿于一切过程的始终 run through all processes from beginning to end ② be linked together; follow in a continuous line:鱼～ one following the other

贯彻 guànchè carry out; carry through; put into effect:～…的精神 be permeated with the spirit of…

贯穿 guànchuān pass through; run through; penetrate

贯串 guànchuàn spread through; run through; permeate

贯通 guàntōng ① join up; link up ② have a thorough knowledge; understand thoroughly:豁然～ understand thoroughly at last

贯注 guànzhù concentrate on; be absorbed in:全神～ be fully absorbed in; concentrate one's attention on

惯 guàn〈动〉① be in the habit of; be used to:她过不～这里的生活。She's not used to the life here. ② spoil:他承认是妈妈把他～坏了。He admitted that his mother had spoilt him. ③〈形〉habitual; customary:～犯 confirmed (habitual, inveterate)

criminal
惯犯 guànfàn habitual offender; hardened criminal; recidivist; repeater
惯技 guànjì old trick; customary trick
惯例 guànlì (usual) practice; convention; usage; praxis:～抵押 conventional mortgage. ～折旧 conventional depreciation
惯骗 guànpiàn habitually swindle
惯窃 guànqiè habitual (confirmed) thief; habitually steal
惯偷 guàntōu hardened thief
惯用 guànyòng ① habitually practise; consistently use:～两面派的手法 consistently use double-faced tactics ② habitual; customary:～手法 habitual practice
惯于 guànyú get (be) used to (doing); be accustomed to doing
惯纵 guànzòng pamper; spoil; indulge

掼 guàn 〈动〉throw away; cast away
掼纱帽 guànshāmào throw away one's official hat in a huff; refuse to continue one's work; resign in resentment

guāng

光 guāng 〈名〉① light; ray:日～ sunlight; sunshine ② scenery:风～ sight; view; scene ③ honour; glory:～荣榜 honour roll (board)〈形〉④ smooth:这纸不太～。This paper is not smooth enough. ⑤ naked; bare:他～着脊梁。He stripped to the waist. ⑥ used up:她把钱都用～了。She has spent all her money. ⑦〈副〉only; solely; merely:他～吃青菜,不吃肉。He eats only vegetables and abstains from eating meat.
光彩 guāngcǎi splendour; brilliance; radiance:～夺目 dazzlingly brilliant; brightness; dazzle the eyes
光大 guāngdà ① glorify; carry forward; develop ② wide; extensive
光导纤维 guāngdǎo xiānwéi light-guide fibre; optical fibre
光电话 guāngdiànhuà photophone
光电技术 guāngdiàn jìshù photoelectric technology
光杆儿 guānggǎnr ① a bare trunk or stalk ② a man who has lost his family
光杆儿司令 guānggǎnr sīlìng commander without troops; single commander
光顾 guānggù patronize:如蒙～,不胜欢迎。Your patronage is cordially invited.
光怪陆离 guāngguàilùlí grotesque in shape and gaudy in colour; bizarre and motley:～的广告 grotesque and gaudy advertisements
光棍 guānggùn unmarried man; bachelor
光滑 guānghuá smooth; glossy; sleek

光辉 guānghuī ① brilliant; splendid; shining; magnificent: ～形象 splendid image ② brilliance; glory

光景 guāngjǐng〈名〉① view; scene ② circumstances; condition ③ about; around: 她母亲有 60 岁～。Her mother is about 60 years old.

光缆 guānglǎn optical cable (fibre): ～通讯 optical fibre communications

光亮 guāngliàng bright; luminous; shiny

光临 guānglín〈谦〉gracious presence (of a guest, etc.); honour sb. with one's presence (a visit): 敬请～ request the honour of your presence; Your presence is cordially requested.

光芒 guāngmáng rays of light; brilliant rays; radiance: ～万丈 shining with boundless radiance; gloriously radiant; resplendent

光明 guāngmíng ① light: 黑暗中的一线～ a streak of light in the darkness ② bright; promising ③ openhearted; guileless: 心地～ upright and pure in mind

光明磊落 guāngmíng-lěiluò completely open; frank and forthright; open and aboveboard

光明正大 guāngmíng-zhèngdà just and honourable; open and aboveboard

光盘 guāngpán［计］compact disc (disk). ～只读存储器 CD-ROM (compact disc ready-only memory)

光荣 guāngróng ① honourable; honoured; glorious: ～传统 a glorious tradition ② honour; glory; credit: ～榜 honour roll; roster of honour

光天化日 guāngtiān-huàrì (in) broad daylight; the light of day

光纤通讯 guāngxiān tōngxùn optical fiber communications

光线 guāngxiàn light; ray

光学 guāngxué optics: ～纤维 light guide; optical fibre. ～仪器 optical instrument

光阴 guāngyīn time: ～似箭。Time flies (like an arrow).

光泽 guāngzé lustre; polish; gloss; sheen

光宗耀祖 guāngzōng-yàozǔ bringing honour to one's ancestors; make one's ancestors illustrious

guǎng

广 guǎng〈形〉① vast; broad; extensive: 我国～大地区 the vast areas of our country ② general; numerous: ～众 a huge crowd ③〈动〉broaden; expand: 推～ extend; spread; popularize

广播 guǎngbō broadcast: ～电视节目制作人 radio and television packager. ～剧 radio play. ～体操 setting up exercises to radio music; broadcast calisthenics. 实况～ live broadcast

广博 guǎngbó (of a person's

knowledge) extensive; wide:具有～的知识 have extensive knowledge

广场 guǎngchǎng public square; square:天安门～ Tian'anmen Square

广大 guǎngdà ① (of an area or space) vast; wide; extensive:幅员～ vast in territory. ② large-scale; widespread:掀起～的增产节约运动 set off a large-scale emulation drive to increase production and practise economy ③ (of people) numerous:～人民群众 the broad masses of the people

广泛 guǎngfàn broad; wide-ranging; extensive:～讨论 discuss extensively (at length). ～征求意见 solicit opinions from all sides

广告 guǎnggào advertisement; advertising; ad:～的样本 preprints of an advertisement. ～价格 advertising rate. 登～ put an ad in the newspaper; advertise (for sth.)

广交会 guǎngjiāohuì China Guang-
zhou Export Commodities Fair

广开才路 guǎngkāi-cáilù open all avenues for people of talent

广开言路 guǎngkāi-yánlù encourage the free airing of views; encourage freedom of speech

广阔 guángkuò vast; wide; broad:～的前景 broad prospects. ～天地,大有作为 a vast world where much can be accomplished; a vast field for using one's talents

广义 guǎngyì broad sense:～地说 broadly speaking; in a broad sense. ～相对论 general theory of relativity

广种薄收 guǎngzhòng-bóshōu extensive cultivation

犷 guǎng 〈形〉rustic; uncouth; boorish

犷悍 guǎnghàn tough and intrepid

guàng

逛 guàng 〈动〉walk about; stroll; roam:～书店 roam about the bookstores. 闲～ stroll; saunter

逛荡 guàngdang linger idly; loiter; loaf about; gad about

guī

规 guī ①〈名〉rule; regulation:厂～ factory regulations 〈动〉② plan; map out:～定适当的积累和消费基金的比例 work out a proper ratio between accumulation fund and consumption fund ③ advise:～劝 admonish

规避 guībì evade; evasion; shirk; dodge:～纳税 tax avoidance

规程 guīchéng rules; regulations:操作～ rules of operation

规定 guīdìng ① regulate; stipulate; formulate; define; provide:～经济发展方向 define the orientation of economic development ② fix; set:在～的时间内 within the fixed time. ～性 determination; definiteness

规范 guīfàn model; standard; norm:～导向 normative orientation. ～现有的股份制公司 standardize the existing joint-stock companies. ～用法 prescriptive usage

规格 guīgé standards; norms; specifications:符合～ conform to specifications

规划 guīhuà plan; project; programme:订出全面～ map out a comprehensive plan

规矩 guīju ①〈名〉rule; established practice; custom ②〈形〉well-behaved; proper; honest:守～ behave oneself. 没～ have no manners; be impolite

规律 guīlǜ law; regular pattern:～发生作用 bring laws into operation. ～性 regularity; law

规模 guīmó scale; scope:～经济 economics of scale

规劝 guīquàn remonstrate; admonish; advise

规约 guīyuē stipulations of an agreement

规则 guīzé rule; regulation:守～ keep the rules

规章 guīzhāng rules and regulations

闺 guī〈名〉young lady's chamber; boudoir

闺房 guīfáng lady's chamber; boudoir

闺女 guīnü ① girl; maiden ② daughter

闺秀 guīxiù young lady:大家～ girls from prominent families

硅 guī〈名〉[化] silicon

硅谷 guīgǔ silicon valley

归 guī〈动〉① return; be back:荣～故里 return to one's native place with high honour ② give back to; return sth. to:物～原主 return sth. to its original owner ③ converge; come together:～档 filing; file documents ④ turn over to; put under sb.'s care:～国家所有 be turned over to the state ⑤ attribute to; ascribe to:荣誉～功于党。The credit goes to the Party.

归案 guī'àn bring to justice:～法办 bring sb. to trial and punishment

归并 guībìng merge into (with); incorporate into

归档 guīdàng place on file; file away:把文件～ place a document on file; file a document

归根结底(蒂) guīgēn-jiédǐ(dì) in the last (final) analysis; all in all; in the long run; in the end

归功 guīgōng give (ascribe) the credit to; attribute the success to; owe to:把成就～于某人的帮助 attribute one's achievements to sb.'s help

归国 guīguó return to one's country:～华侨 returned overseas Chinese

归还 guīhuán return; revert:向阅览室借的杂志要按时～。Magazines borrowed from the reading-room should be returned on time.

归咎 guījiù put (lay) the blame on; ascribe the blame to

归口 guīkǒu channel to the proper authorities (on the basis of jurisdiction): ～部门 the department with jurisdiction (over certain matters). ～管理 channel to the appropriate department for management. ～包干 channel certain matters and entrust full responsibility for them to the appropriate department

归类 guīlèi sort out; classify

归纳 guīnà ① sum up; generalize ② induce: ～法 inductive method; induction. ～社会学 inductive sociology

归侨 guīqiáo returned overseas Chinese

归属 guīshǔ ownership; belong to; come under the jurisdiction of: ～地位 ascribed status. ～感 sense of belonging

归宿 guīsù end result; a home to return to: 人生～ destination of one's life voyage

归心似箭 guīxīn-sìjiàn be eager to dart homeward; wish to wing one's way home; be anxious to return; impatient to get back

归因 guīyīn ascribe to; attribute to: 他们把他们的成功～于努力工作。They attributed their success to hard work. ～理论 attribution theory

归于 guīyú belong to; be ascribed to; put down to; set down to; bring home to: 不同意见～一致。The dissenting views have given way to agreement.

归正 guīzhèng reform (oneself); mend one's ways

归罪 guīzuì put the blame on; impute to: ～于人 lay the blame on others

归罪于 guīzuìyú incriminate; impute; inculpate

瑰 guī 〈形〉 rare; marvellous

瑰宝 guībǎo (rich) treasure; rarity; gem

瑰丽 guīlì surpassingly beautiful; magnificent

龟 guī 〈名〉 tortoise: ～甲 tortoise shells

龟卜 guībǔ divination by the shell of the tortoise; scapulimancy

龟甲 guījiǎ tortoise-shell

龟缩 guīsuō withdraw to passive defense; hole up; entrench oneself in: ～在据点里 hole up in a stronghold

guǐ

鬼 guǐ 〈名〉 ① ghost; devil; spirit: ～神 spiritual beings ② used to form a term of abuse for ignoble character: 胆小～ coward ③ dirty trick; sinister plot: 心中有～ have a bellyfull tricks; have a guilty conscience ④〈形〉clever; smart: 这孩子真～。The boy is very clever.

鬼把戏 guǐbǎxì dirty trick; (wicked) game; got-up affair:

玩弄～ play a dirty trick

鬼点子 guǐdiǎnzi wicked idea; devilish trick:出～ give devilish advice; make a wicked suggestion

鬼怪 guǐguài ghosters and monsters; forces of evil:～论 demonism

鬼鬼祟祟 guǐguǐ-suìsuì furtive; sneaking; stealthy; surreptitious

鬼话 guǐhuà utter nonsense; nonsense lie; a cock-and-bull story

鬼话连篇 guǐhuà-liánpiān a pack of lies; lies from start to finish

鬼混 guǐhùn muddle on (along); fool around; lead an aimless or irregular existence

鬼迷心窍 guǐmíxīnqiào be possessed by ghosts; be haunted by ghosts

鬼头鬼脑 guǐtóu-guǐnǎo thievish; stealthy; furtive:有几个人～地从山洞里钻了出来。Several suspicious-looking people sneaked out of the cave.

鬼蜮伎俩 guǐyù-jìliǎng a devilish stratagem; evil tactics; dirty underhanded tricks

鬼主意 guǐzhǔyì evil plan; wicked idea:打～ form an evil plan

诡 guǐ〈形〉crafty; deceitful; wily; tricky:～称 pretend to state…

诡辩 guǐbiàn sophistry; sophism; quibbling; syllogism; philosophism:～言词 pretentious devices; verbal artifices

诡称 guǐchēng falsely allege; pretend

诡计 guǐjì craft plot; cunning scheme; trick; guile:～多端 full of craft and cunning; be full of wiles; guileful

诡谲 guǐjué ① strange and changeful ② weird; eccentric; odd:言语～ speak cryptically ③ crafty; cunning; treacherous

诡秘 guǐmì furtive; surreptitious; secretive:行踪～ surreptitious in one's movements

诡诈 guǐzhà crafty; deceitful; cunning

轨 guǐ〈名〉① rail; track ② way; rule

轨道 guǐdào ① rail; track ② way; path; orbit; course:空间～站 outer space orbit station

轨迹 guǐjì ①[天] orbit ②[数]locus

guì

桂 guì〈名〉①[肉桂] cassia; Chinese cinnamon ②[木犀] sweet osmanthus

桂冠 guìguān laurel:～诗人 poet laureate

桂花 guìhuā [植] sweet-scented osmanthus

桂皮 guìpí cassia bark; Chinese cinnamon

桂圆 guìyuán longan:～肉 dried longan pulp

柜 guì〈名〉① chest; cabinet:保险～ safe ② counter

柜台 guìtái counter; bar:～租赁

counters leasing. 站～ serve behind the counter

柜子 guìzi chest; cabinet; [衣柜] wardrobe; [食柜] cupboard; [书柜] bookcase

贵 guì 〈形〉 ① costly; dear; expensive: 昂～ very expensive ② precious; valuable: 春雨～如油。Spring rain is as precious as oil. ③ noble; honourable: ～族子弟 descendents of the noble families ④ 〈敬〉 your: ～姓 May I know your name? ⑤ 〈动〉 respect

贵宾 guìbīn guest of honour; distinguished guest

贵妃 guìfēi highest-ranking imperial concubine

贵干 guìgàn honourable business; noble errand: 有何～? What honourable business (noble errand) brings you here?

贵金属 guìjīnshǔ precious (noble) metal

贵客 guìkè honoured guest

贵人 guìrén ① a high official: ～多忘事 a man of your eminence has a short memory (said with good-natured sarcasm); important people have short memories ② a high-ranking imperial concubine

贵重 guìzhòng precious; valuable: ～物品 valuables

贵族 guìzú noble; aristocrat; peers; aristocracy; nobility

跪 guì〈动〉 kneel

跪拜 guìbài kowtow; worship on bended knees

跪倒 guìdǎo prostrate… before; throw oneself on one's knees; grovel

刽 guì 〈动〉 cut off

刽子手 guìzishǒu executioner; slaughter; butcher

gǔn

滚 gǔn 〈动〉 ① roll; tumble: ② get away: ～开 get out; scram ③ boil: 锅里汤～了。The soup is boiling in the pot.

滚蛋 gǔndàn beat it; scram

滚动 gǔndòng roll; trundle

滚瓜烂熟 gǔnguālànshú (recite, etc.) fluently; be extremely fluent; (know sth.) pat; (have sth.) at one's fingertips

滚滚 gǔngǔn roll; surge: 历史车轮～向前。The wheel of history rolls forward.

滚热 gǔnrè piping hot; burning hot; boiling hot

滚烫 gǔntàng boiling hot; burning hot

滚雪球 gǔnxuěqiú (of a business, project, etc.) get bigger and bigger as it proceeds; snowball

gùn

棍 gùn 〈名〉 ① stick; club; rod ② scoundrel; rascal: 恶～ ruffian; scoundrel; villain

棍棒 gùnbàng ① club; cudgel; bludgeon ② a stick or staff used in gymnastics

棍子 gùnzi rod; stick

guō

郭 guō 〈名〉① the outer wall of a city:东～ the east wall of a city ② (Guō) a surname

锅 guō 〈名〉(cooking) pot; pan:《～碗瓢盆交响曲》Song of the Kitchen

锅巴 guōba rice crust; crust of cooked rice

锅铲 guōchǎn slice (a kitchen utensil)

锅盖 guōgài the lid of a cooking pot

锅炉 guōlú boiler

锅台 guōtái the top of a kitchen range

guó

国 guó 〈名〉country; nation; state:东道～ host country

国宝 guóbǎo national treasure

国宾 guóbīn state guest: ～馆 state guesthouse

国策 guócè basic policy of a state; national (state) policy

国产 guóchǎn made in one's own country; made in China: ～品 home (domestic, national) products

国耻 guóchǐ national humiliation

国粹 guócuì the quintessence of Chinese culture; Chinese cultural quintessence

国都 guódū national capital; capital

国法 guófǎ national law; the law of the land; law: ～难容 punishable by law

国防 guófáng national defence: ～意识 awareness of the importance of national defence

国歌 guógē national anthem

国格 guógé national honour; national prestige:不做有损～的事 will do nothing that would undermine national prestige

国画 guóhuà traditional Chinese painting

国徽 guóhuī state emblem; national emblem

国会 guóhuì parliament; [美国] Congress; [日本] the Diet

国货 guóhuò China-made goods; Chinese goods

国籍 guójí nationality; citizenship:双重～ dual nationality

国计民生 guójì-mínshēng national economy and the people's livelihood; national welfare and people's livelihood

国际 guójì international: ～法 international law. ～惯例 international practice (convention). ～互联网络 Internet. ～消费者权益日 World Consumer Rights Day. ～刑警组织 International Criminal Police Organization; Interpol

国家 guójiā country; nation; state: ～财政收入 state revenue. ～控股公司制度 state-controlled holding company system. ～权力机关 organ of state power. ～外汇储备

state's foreign exchange reserve
国脚 guójiǎo football player on the national team; national feet
国界 guójiè national boundaries
国境 guójìng national territory:～卫生检疫 national border health and quarantine. 偷越～ cross the border illegally
国库 guókù state (national) treasury:～券 treasury bill (T.B.); state treasury bonds; treasury bonds
国力 guólì national power (strength, might):～雄厚 have solid national strength
国立 guólì state-maintained; state-run:～大学 national university
国民 guómín ① the people of a nation; a member of a nation ② national:～经济持续、快速、健康发展 maintain the sustained (steady), rapid and sound development of the national economy. ～收入 national income. ～生产总值 gross national product (GNP)
国内 guónèi domestic; internal; home:～贸易 domestic (home) trade. ～市场 domestic market
国旗 guóqí national flag
国情 guóqíng the condition (state) of a country; national conditions
国庆节 Guóqìngjié National Day
国事 guóshì national (state) affairs:～访问 state visit
国书 guóshū letter of credence; credentials:递交～ present credentials
国术 guóshù traditional Chinese boxing and fencing (martial arts)
国泰民安 guótài-mín'ān The country is prosperous and the people live in peace
国体 guótǐ ① state system; the form of the state; the form of government ② national prestige
国土 guótǔ territory:～规划 programme for national lands. ～经济学 economics of national lands
国外 guówài external; overseas; abroad:～市场 overseas (foreign) market
国王 guówáng king
国威 guówēi national ascendancy
国务 guówù state affairs
国务委员 guówù wěiyuán [中国] member of the State Council; State Councillor
国务院 guówùyuàn ① [中国] State Council:～总理 Premier of the State Council ② [美国] the State Department
国宴 guóyàn state banquet
国营 guóyíng state-owned; state-run:～经济为主体 leading position of the state-owned economy. ～企业 state enterprises
国优 guóyōu (of a product) national best
国有 guóyǒu state-owned:～化 nationalization. ～流通企业 state-owned circulation enterprises. ～资产评估 evaluate the state's assets
国债 guózhài national debts

guǒ

果 guǒ〈名〉① fruit：鲜～ fresh fruit② result；effect；consequence：恶～ a disastrous result ③〈形〉resolute；determined：行必～ be firm in action ④〈副〉really；as expected；actually：～然如此。It has indeed turned out as expected.

果断 guǒduàn resolute；unwavering；decisive

果敢 guǒgǎn courageous and resolute；daring；undaunted；bold：采取～行动 take bold actions

果木 guǒmù fruit tree

果农 guǒnóng fruit grower

果皮 guǒpí the skin of fruit；peel；rind：～箱 litterbin

果然 guǒrán really；indeed；actually；as expected；sure enough；true to one's words

果实 guǒshí gain；fruit：劳动～ fruits of labour

果园 guǒyuán orchard；garden

果真 guǒzhēn ① really；as expected；sure enough ② if indeed；if really：～如此，我就放心了。If this is really true，it'll take a load off my mind.

果汁 guǒzhī fruit juice

裹 guǒ〈动〉bind；wrap：把毯子～在身上 wrap oneself in a blanket

裹挟 guǒxié （of circumstances，trends，etc.）sweep sb. along

裹胁 guǒxié force to take part (in bad things)；coerce

裹足不前 guǒzúbùqián timidity and hesitancy；come (bring) to a standstill；hesitate to move forward

guò

过 guò〈动〉① pass；cross：～街 cross the street ② spend (time)；pass (time)：她在大连～夏天。She spent the summer in Dalian. ③ past；after：～了好几个月 several months have passed ④ exceed；go beyond：年～70 over seventy (years old) ⑤［用在动词后面，表示趋向］：跳～篱笆墙 jump over a fence ⑥［用在动词后面，跟“得”或“不”连用，表示胜过或通过］：我说不～他。I can't outargue him. ⑦ live：他～着流亡生活。He lived the life of an exile. ⑧ celebrate：～生日 celebrate one's birthday ⑨〈副〉too；excessively；unduly：～早宣布 prematurely declare that … ⑩〈名〉fault；mistake；error：改～ correct one's mistakes〈助〉⑪［用在动词后面，表示完毕］：钱已付～了。The bill has been paid. ⑫［用在动词后面，表示行为曾经发生，但未继续到现在］：你去～广州吗？Have you ever been to Guangzhou？

过磅 guòbàng weigh (on the scales)

过不去 guòbuqù ① be impassable；be unable to get by ② find fault with；be hard on sb.；

make things difficult for sb.：他们有意跟我～。They deliberately made things difficult for me.

过程 guòchéng process；course：～教育 process education. ～型激励理论 process theory of motivation

过错 guòcuò fault；mistake

过道 guòdào passageway；corridor

过得去 guòdeqù ① be able to pass；passable ② so-so；not too bad；tolerable：她的身体还～。Her health is not bad.

过渡 guòdù transition：～时期的政府 caretaker government. ～时期总路线 general line for the transition period

过度 guòdù excessive；undue；over：～兴奋 be overexcited

过房 guòfáng adopt a young relative

过分 guòfèn excessive；undue；over：～的要求 excessive demands

过关 guòguān ① go through a pass (an ordeal)② pass a test；reach a standard；be up to standard：这项产品的质量已～。The quality of this product is up to standard.

过河拆桥 guòhé-chāiqiáo remove the plank after crossing the bridge — leave one in the lurch；pull down the bridge after crossing the river — cold-shoulder a person who has helped one tide over a difficulty；be ungraceful

过户 guòhù change the name of the owner in a register；transfer ownership；transfer：～代理 transfer agent

过活 guòhuó make a living；live：勉强～ just manage to make a living

过火 guòhuǒ go (run) to excess (extremes)；go too far；carry things too far；overdo：～政策 the policy carried to excess

过激 guòjī too drastic；extremist：～的言论 extremist opinions

过继 guòjì ① adopt a young relative ② have one's child adopted by a relative

过街老鼠，人人喊打 guòjiē lǎo shǔ，rénrén-hǎndǎ rats scurrying across the street with everyone yelling："Kill them，kill them!"；the object of universal condemnation

过街天桥 guòjiē tiānqiáo pedestrian overpass

过节 guòjié celebrate a festival

过境 guòjìng pass through the territory of a country；be in transit：～贸易 transit trade. ～签证 transit visa

过来 guòlái ① come over；come up：快～！Come over here，quick！②[用在动词后，多跟"得"或"不"连用，表示时间、能力、数量充分或不足]：你一个人忙得～吗？Can you manage by yourself？③ [用在动词后，表示来到说话者所在的地方]：一队学生正朝我们走～。A contingent of students was marching towards us. ③[用在动词后，表

示正面对着说话者]:他转过脸来,我才认出是位老同学。He turned around, and then I recognized him as a former classmate of mine. ④[用在动词后,表示回到正常的状态]:她的坏习惯一定得改~。Her bad habits must be changed

过来人 guòláirén a person who has had experience; an experienced hand

过量 guòliàng excessive; over-:饮食~ excessive eating and drinking

过磷酸钙 guòlínsuāngài calcium superphosphate

过路 guòlù pass by one's way:~人 passerby

过门 guòmén move into one's husband's household upon marriage

过年 guònián celebrate the New Year

过目 guòmù have a look (at); look over (for check or approval)

过期 guòqī ① overdue; past due:~票据 overdue note ② expire:~无效 be invalid on expiry

过去 guòqù ① (in or of) the past; formerly; previously:她比~胖多了。She's much fatter than she used to be. ② go over; pass by:你在这里等着,我~看看。You wait here, I'll go over and see. ③ [用在动词后,表示离开或经过说话者所在的地方]:把车开~。Drive the car over (there). ④ [用在动词后,表示后面对着说话者]:先别把这一页翻~。Don't turn over the page yet. ⑤ [用在动词后,表示失去原来的、正常的状态]:他晕~了。He has fainted. ⑥ [用在动词后,表示通过]:企图蒙混~ try to get by under false pretences. 老头脑子很清楚,你休想骗~。The old man is sharp-witted. You won't fool him. ⑦ [用在形容词后多跟"得"或"不"连用,表示超过]:鸡蛋还能硬得过石头去! How can an egg be harder than a stone?

过日子 guòrìzi live; get along:勤俭~ live industriously and frugally

过失 guòshī fault; defect; negligence; delinquency:~犯罪 negligent crime. ~伤害他人 negligently injure another

过时 guòshí out-of-date; outmoded

过世 guòshì die; pass away

过手 guòshǒu take in and give out (money, etc.); receive and distribute; handle

过头 guòtóu go beyond the limit; overdo:聪明~ be too clever by half

过往 guòwǎng ① come and go:~的车辆 vehicular traffic ② have friendly intercourse with; associate with

过问 guòwèn look into; take an interest in; intervene (in):~政治 take an interest in politics. 亲自~ look into a matter personally

过夜 guòyè put up for the night; stay overnight; pass the night

过意不去 guòyìbúqù feel uneasy (about); feel sorry (for); feel apologetic

过瘾 guòyǐn do sth. to one's heart's content; enjoy oneself to the full; satisfy a craving

过硬 guòyìng become really proficient in sth.; be able to pass the stiffest test; have a perfect mastery of sth.

过帐 guòzhàng transfer items (as from a daybook to a ledger); posting of account; carry to:～根据 posting medium

过重 guòzhòng excess weight; overweight:减轻中小学生～的课业负担 reduce the workload of middle and primary school students

H h

hā

哈 hā〈动〉① blow one's breath; breathe out: ～了一口气 breathe out a breath ② bend ③〈叹〉aha; ha
另见 hǎ

哈雷彗星 hāléihuìxīng Halley's Comet; the Halley Comet

哈尼族 Hānízú the Hani nationality (living in Yunnan Province)

哈欠 hāqian yawn: 打～ give a yawn

哈萨克族 Hāsākèzú the Kazak (Kazakh) nationality (living in the Xinjiang Uygur Autonomous Region, Gansu and Qinghai Provinces)

哈腰 hāyāo ① bend one's back; stoop ② bow slightly: 点头～ bow and scrape; bow unctuously

hǎ

哈 hǎ
另见 hā

哈达 hǎdá hata (ceremonial silk scarf)

hāi

咳 hāi〈叹〉①［表示懊悔，惊奇等］oh: ～，我多么愚蠢！Oh, how foolish I was! ②［提醒别人注意］hey; hi: ～，到这里来！Hi, come over here!
另见 ké

hái

还 hái〈副〉① still; yet: 夜深了，她～在做作业。It was late and she was still working away at her homework. ② still more; even more: 今天比昨天～冷。Today is even colder than yesterday. ③ too; also; as well: 我们参观了这家工厂，～参观了学校和医院。We visited some schools and hospitals as well as the factory. ④ fairly; rather: 屋子收拾得倒～干净。The room is kept quite tidy. ⑤ even: 大人～举不起来，更别说小孩了。Even grown-ups can't lift it, to say nothing of children. ⑥［用以加强语气］: 她～真有办法。She really is resourceful.
另见 huán

还好 háihǎo ① not so bad; passable ② luckily; fortunately: ～，他们赶上了火车。Luckily, they caught the train.

还是 háishi ① or: 你早上去，～下午去？Are you going in the

morning or in the afternoon? ② still; all the same:尽管如此,～要谢谢你。Thank you all the same. ③ remain:虽然年老,但她～热心公益。Though old, she remains public-spirited. ④ had better:我们～休息一下。We had better take a rest.

孩 hái〈名〉child

孩童 háitóng child

孩子 háizi child:男～ boy. 女～ girl. ～气 childish

孩子头 háizitóu ① a person who is very popular with children ② leader of a group of children

骸 hái〈名〉① bones of the body; skeleton ② body

骸骨 háigǔ bones of the dead

hǎi

海 hǎi〈名〉sea:渤～ Bohai Sea ② a great number of people or things gathering together:林～ a vast stretch of forest

海岸 hǎi'àn seacoast; coast; seashore:～线 coastline

海拔 hǎibá (height) above sea level:～1000 米 1000 metres above sea level

海报 hǎibào poster; playbill:张贴～ put up a poster

海滨 hǎibīn seaside; seashore:～浴场 seaside resort

海产 hǎichǎn marine products

海带 hǎidài kelp

海岛 hǎidǎo island (in the sea)

海盗 hǎidào pirate; corsair; sea rover:～商人 marauding merchant. ～行为 piracy

海底 hǎidǐ seabed:～电缆 submarine cable. ～捞针 look for a needle in the ocean; hunt for a needle in a haystack

海防 hǎifáng coastal defence:～前线 coastal frontiers

海港 hǎigǎng harbour; seaport:～设备 harbour accommodation; harbour installations

海关 hǎiguān customhouse; customs; marine customs:～检查 customs inspection (examination). ～担保 customs guarantee. ～放行 customs clearance

海货 hǎihuò marine products

海疆 hǎijiāng coastal areas and territorial seas

海军 hǎijūn navy:～基地 naval base

海枯石烂 hǎikū-shílàn (even if) the seas run dry and the rocks crumble.

海量 hǎiliàng ① magnanimity; ② great capacity for liquor:您是～,再来一杯。Have another one. You can hold your liquor.

海路 hǎilù sea route:走～ go by sea

海绵 hǎimián ① sponge ② foam rubber or plastic; sponge

海面 hǎimiàn sea surface

海难 hǎinàn perils of the sea

海商法 hǎishāngfǎ law of maritime commerce; maritime law

海上 hǎishàng ① on the sea ② marine; maritime:～保险 marine (maritime) insurance. ～救助 salvage. ～文化队 sea-borne cultural team. ～事故 maritime casualty

海参 hǎishēn sea cucumber; sea slug; trepang

海事 hǎishì maritime affairs:～保险 maritime insurance. ～法 admiralty law; maritime law. ～纠纷 admiralty dispute. ～仲裁 maritime arbitration

海市蜃楼 hǎishì-shènlóu mirage; castle in the air; castle in Spain

海誓山盟 hǎishì-shānméng (make) a solemn pledge of love

海损 hǎisǔn average; sea damage:单独～ particular average. ～理算 adjustment of average; adjustment. ～理算人 average adjuster

海滩 hǎitān seabeach; beach

海外 hǎiwài overseas; abroad:～华侨 overseas Chinese. ～关系 overseas connections (social relationships between people in China and people overseas); relative abroad

海湾 hǎiwān bay; gulf

海味 hǎiwèi seafood; sea delicacies; marine products:山珍～ all sorts of delicacies

海峡 hǎixiá strait; channel:～两岸经贸联系 economic and trade relations between the two sides of the Taiwan Straits

海鲜 hǎixiān seafood

海啸 hǎixiào seaquake; tsunami; tidal wave

海牙规则 hǎiyá guīzé Hague Rules

海洋 hǎiyáng seas and oceans; sea:～性气候 marine climate. ～权 maritime rights. ～渔业基地 marine fishing ground

海洋石油 hǎiyáng shíyóu offshore oil:～钻井平台 offshore oil drilling platform

海域 hǎiyù sea area; maritime (ocean) space:南海～ Nanhai Sea waters

海员 hǎiyuán seaman; sailor:～俱乐部 seamen's club

海运 hǎiyùn ocean shipping; marine transportation; ocean carriage:～业 shipping industry

海战 hǎizhàn sea warfare; naval battle

hài

骇 hài〈动〉be startled; be astonished; be shocked

骇然 hàirán gasping with astonishment; struck dumb with amazement

骇人听闻 hàirén tīngwén shocking; terrifying; sensational; astounding

害 hài〈动〉① do harm to; impair:～人不浅 inflict a person not shallowly; do people great harm ② kill; murder:她被～了。She was murdered. ③ suffer from; contract (an illness):～眼 suffer from eye disease ④ feel (ashamed, afraid, etc.):～怕 be afraid of; be scared to; fear ⑤〈名〉evil; harm:为民除～ rid the people of a scourge ⑥〈形〉harmful; injurious:～人的政策 pernicious policy

害病 hàibìng be ill (with); fall sick (ill)

害虫 hàichóng destructive (injurious) insect; pest

害处 hàichu harm:吸烟过多对身体有～。Excessive smoking is harmful to one's health.

害怕 hàipà be afraid; be scared

害群之马 hàiqúnzhīmǎ an evil member of the herd; one who brings disgrace on his group; black sheep

害人不浅 hàirénbùqiǎn no small harm is done; do people great harm

害人虫 hàirénchóng an evil creature; pest; vermin

害人反害己 hàirén fǎn hàijǐ be hoist with (by) one's own petard; harm set, harm get; harm watch, harm catch

害臊 hàisào feel ashamed; be bashful; be shy

害羞 hàixiū shy; bashful; coy

hān

鼾 hān 〈动〉 snore

鼾声 hānshēng snore; stertor:～如雷 snore thunderously

鼾睡 hānshuì sound, snoring sleep

憨 hān 〈形〉 ① silly; foolish ② naive

憨厚 hānhòu straightforward and good-natured; simple and honest

憨态可掬 hāntàikějū charmingly naive

憨笑 hānxiào smile fatuously; simper

憨直 hānzhí honest and upright (straightforward)

憨子 hānzi fool; blockhead; simpleton

酣 hān 〈形〉 (drink, etc.) to one's heart's content; be given to hearty drinking:半～ half drunk

酣睡 hānshuì sleep soundly; be fast asleep

酣饮 hānyǐn drink to the full; carouse

酣战 hānzhàn fight bitterly; be in the thick of battle; fierce battle; hard-fought battle

酣醉 hānzuì be dead drunk

hán

寒 hán 〈形〉 ① cold; chilly:受了一点风～ catch a slight cold ② afraid; fearful; tremble (with fear):～颤 shiver; shaking ③ poor:～士 poor intellectuals

寒潮(流) háncháo(liú) cold wave (current)

寒碜 hánchen ① ugly; unsightly:长得不～ not bad-looking ② shabby; disgraceful:穷并不～。Being poor is no disgrace. ③ ridicule; make fun of:叫人～了一顿 be ridiculed by sb.

寒带 hándài frigid zone

寒风 hánfēng cold wind:～凛冽 a piercing wind

寒假 hánjià winter vacation
寒噤 hánjìn shudder (tremble, shiver) (with cold or fear)
寒冷 hánlěng cold; frigid
寒流 hánliú cold current
寒热 hánrè fever; high temperature: 发～ have (run) a temperature. ～病似的发展 chills-and-fever type development
寒暑表 hánshǔbiǎo thermometer: 摄氏～ centigrade thermometer
寒酸 hánsuān shabby; pitiful: 看上去～相 look shabby
寒心 hánxīn be bitterly disappointed
寒暄 hánxuān exchange of conventional greetings; exchange of compliments (amentities): 她同我～了几句。She exchanged a few words of greeting with me.
寒衣 hányī winter clothing
寒意 hányì a nip (chill) in the air
寒战 hánzhàn shiver (with cold or fear)

韩

Hán a surname
韩国 hánguó The Republic of Korea

含

hán 〈动〉 ① keep in one's mouth: ～着润喉片 have a throat tablet in the mouth ② contain; comprise; imply ③ nurse; harbour; cherish
含苞 hánbāo in bud: ～待放 a bud just ready to burst
含垢忍辱 hángòurěnrǔ endure contempt and insults; bear shame and humiliation
含恨 hánhèn nurse a grievance or hatred
含糊 hánhu ambiguous; vague; equivocal: ～其词 make ambiguous remarks; talk in vague terms; mention vaguely
含混 hánhùn vagueness; ambiguity
含金量 hánjīnliàng gold content
含量 hánliàng content
含情 hánqíng harbour emotions
含情脉脉 hánqíng-mòmò (soft eyes) exuding tenderness and love
含沙射影 hánshā-shèyǐng attack by innuendo; make insinuations; with insidious language
含辛茹苦 hánxīn-rúkǔ suffer bitter hardships; suffer hardships and privations
含羞 hánxiū shyly; bashfully; with a shy look: ～不语 be silent with a shy look. ～草 sensitive plant
含蓄 hánxù ① contain; imply; embody ② implicit; implied; reserved: ～的契约 implicit contract
含义 hányì meaning; implication; sense
含冤 hányuān suffer a wrong: ～而死 die uncleared of a false charge
含怨 hányuàn nurse a grievance; suffer a gross injustice

函

hán 〈名〉 letter
函电 hándiàn letters and cables
函调 hándiào ① correspondence investigation ② transfer of a person through letter
函复 hánfù reply by letter; write

a letter in reply
函告 hángào write to inform; inform by letter
函购 hángòu purchase by mail; mail order
函授 hánshòu teach by correspondence; give a correspondence course:～大学 correspondence university. ～讲授 postal tuition. ～课程 postal course; correspondence course
函数 hánshù [数] function
涵 hán〈动〉① contain; imply ② tolerate:～养功夫 virtue of patience ③〈名〉culvert
涵洞 hándòng culvert
涵化 hánhuà [社会学]acculturation:～式现代化 acculturated modernization
涵容 hánróng excuse; forgive; bear with
涵养 hányǎng ① self-control; self-command; ability to control oneself:很有～ know how to exercise self-control ② moral cultivation

hǎn

罕 hǎn〈副〉rarely; uncommonly; seldom
罕见 hǎnjiàn seldom; rare:～见的机会 an opportunity very seldom to be met with
罕事 hǎnshì rare event
罕闻 hǎnwén seldom heard of
罕物 hǎnwù rare thing;
喊 hǎn〈动〉① shout; cry out: ～叫声 shouting ② call
喊叫 hǎnjiào shout; cry out
喊救 hǎnjiù cry for help
喊嗓子 hǎnsǎngzi ① shout ② train (exercise) one's voice (as opera singers do in an open space early in the morning)
喊冤叫屈 hǎnyuān-jiàoqū complain loudly about an alleged injustice; call for redressing grievance

hàn

汉 hàn〈名〉① Han nationality ② Chinese (language):一本～英词典 a Chinese-English dictionary ③ the Han Dyansty (206 B. C. — A. D. 220) ④ man:老～ an old man
汉堡包 hànbǎobāo hamburger
汉人 hànrén the Han people; the Hans
汉学 hànxué Sinology:～家 Sinologist
汉语 hànyǔ Chinese (language): ～拼音字母 Chinese phonetic alphabet
汉字 hànzì Chinese character:～信息处理 Chinese character coding
汉族 hànzú the Han nationality, China's main nationality, distributed all over the country; the Hans
汗 hàn〈名〉sweat; perspiration:出～ perspire; sweat. 擦去～水 wipe one's perspiration; mop sweat from one's face

汗斑 hànbān sweat stain

汗背心 hànbèixīn sleeveless undershirt; vest; singlet

汗淋淋 hànlīnlīn dripping with perspiration; soaked with sweat

汗流浃背 hànliú-jiābèi sweat (perspire) all over; be wet through with sweat

汗马功劳 hànmǎ-gōngláo achievements in war; war exploits; laboriously achieved merit; toil and hardship in the wars; distinctions won in battle: 立下了～ perform deeds of valour in battle

汗衫 hànshān ① undershirt; T-shirt ② shirt

汗水 hànshuǐ sweat (esp. in large amounts): ～湿透了我的衣衫。My shirt was soaked through with sweat.

汗颜 hànyán blush with shame; feel deeply ashamed

汗渍 hànzì ① sweat stain ② be soaked with sweat

旱 hàn ①〈名〉drought ②〈形〉dry; arid: ～季 dry season ③ on land

旱冰场 hànbīngchǎng dry ice rink

旱冰鞋 hànbīngxié dry ice shoes (roller skates)

旱稻 hàndào upland rice; dry rice

旱地 hàndì nonirrigated farmland; dry land: ～耕作 dry farming

旱季 hànjì dry season

旱涝保收 hànlào-bǎoshōu ensure good harvests despite drought or excessive rain; guaranteed harvest despite drought and flood

旱桥 hànqiáo overpass; viaduct

旱情 hànqíng damage to crops by drought; ravages of a drought: ～严重 be afflicted with a severe drought

旱田 hàntián dry farmland; dry land

旱鸭子 hànyāzi ① ducks raised on dry land as opposed to ducks raised by rivers and ponds ② nonswimmer

旱烟 hànyān tabacoo (smoked in a long-stemmed Chinese pipe)

旱灾 hànzāi drought

悍 hàn〈形〉① daring; bold; brave: 强～ intrepid; doughty ② wild; fierce; ferocious

悍妇 hànfù shrewish woman; shrew

悍然 hànrán brazenly; blatantly; flagrantly; brashly; without any scruples: ～入侵 outrageously invade

捍 hàn〈动〉defend; guard

捍卫 hànwèi defend; safeguard; protect: ～马克思主义根本原则 defend the fundamental principles of Marxism

捍御 hànyù defend; guard; protect

焊 hàn〈动〉weld; solder: 电～ electric(al) welding; electric soldering

焊工 hàngōng ① welding; soldering ② welder; solderer

焊接 hànjiē weld; solder

焊条 hàntiáo welding rod

焊锡 hànxī soldering tin; tin solder

翰 hàn 〈书〉① writing brush: 挥～ wield one's writing brush ② writing

翰林 hànlín member of the Imperial Academy. ～院 Hanlin Academy; Imperial Academy

撼 hàn 〈动〉 shake: ～动 shake; vibrate

撼天动地 hàntiān-dòngdì shake heaven and earth

瀚 hàn〈形〉vast

瀚海 hànhǎi big desert

憾 hàn 〈动〉 regret

憾事 hànshì a matter for regret; pity: 昨天你不能来,这真是件～! What a pity you couldn't come here yesterday!

háng

杭 Háng ① short for 杭州 ② (Háng) a surname

航 háng ①〈名〉ship; boat ②〈动〉sail; navigate: 出～ set out on a voyage

航班 hángbān scheduled flight; flight number

航标 hángbiāo navigation mark; buoy

航程 hángchéng passage; voyage: ～保险单 voyage policy

航船 hángchuán boat that plies regularly between inland towns

航次 hángcì ① the sequence of voyages or flights; voyage or flight number ② the number of voyages or flights made

航道 hángdào channel; waterway; lane

航海 hánghǎi navigation: ～证明书 navicert

航空 hángkōng aviation: ～公司 airline (company); airways: ～信 airmail; air letter. ～货运 airfreight. ～货运单 airway bill (of lading)

航路 hánglù sea route; air route; airway

航天 hángtiān spaceflight: ～飞机 space shuttle. ～工业 space engineering

航务 hángwù navigational matters

航线 hángxiàn ① line; route; course; ② air or shipping line

航向 hángxiàng course (of a ship or plane): 船的～正确。The ship is on her right course.

航行 hángxíng navigate; run; sail; [航空] fly: ～权 right of navigation

航运 hángyùn shipping: ～保险 shipping insurance

行 háng 〈名〉① line; row: 站成一～ stand in a row ② seniority among brothers and sisters: 他～几? 他～三。Where does he come among his brothers and sisters? — He's the third. ③ line of business; trade; profession: 各～各业 all trades and professions ④ firm and bank: ～号 firms; companies
另见 xíng

行帮 hángbāng trade association;

guild

行当 hángdang ① trade; profession; line of business ② type of role (in traditional Chinese operas)

行贩 hángfàn pedlar

行行出状元 hángháng chū zhuàngyuan every profession produces its own leading authority

行话 hánghuà professional jargon; cant

行会 hánghuì guild: ～制度 the guild system

行家 hángjiā ① expert; specialist ② cognoscente; connoisseur

行间 hángjiān ① in the ranks ② between lines; ③ between rows

行距 hángjù row spacing

行列 hángliè ① line; ranks; [进行中的] procession ② matrices

行情 hángqíng market price; quotations (on the market): ～看涨。The market prices are expected to rise.

行市 hángshi quotations (on the market); prices: 一天一个～。The prices change from day to day.

行业 hángyè trade; industry; profession: 纠正～不正之风 correct shameful practice in government departments, trades and professions

行长 hángzhǎng president (of a bank)

hàng

沆 hàng〈名〉a vast expanse of water

沆瀣 hàngxiè evening mist: ～一气 be congenial to each other; act in collusion with; wallow in the mire with

巷 hàng〈名〉tunnel
另见 xiàng

háo

豪 háo ①〈名〉a person of extraordinary powers or endowments〈形〉② bold and unconstrained; forthright: ～情壮志 lofty aspirations ③ despotic; bullying: 土～ local despots

豪放 háofàng unbridled; unconstrained; powerful and free: 性格～ be unbridled in character

豪华 háohuá luxurious; luxury; splendid; sumptuous: 过～的生活 lead a luxurious life

豪杰 háojié hero; warrior; person of exceptional ability

豪举 háojǔ ① a bold move ② a munificent act

豪迈 háomài heroic; bold and generous: ～的召唤 gallant call

豪门 háomén rich and powerful family; wealthy and influential clan: ～子弟 sons of the rich

豪气 háoqì heroism; heroic spirit

豪情 háoqíng lofty sentiments; heroic feelings; pride and enthusiasm: ～满怀 be full of pride

豪商 háoshāng wealthy and powerful merchant

豪绅 háoshēn powerful gentry;

despotic gentry

豪言壮语 háoyán-zhuàngyǔ brave words; proud words

壕 háo〈名〉① [军] moat; ② ditch; trench

壕沟 háogōu ① trench ② ditch

嚎 háo〈动〉howl:一声长～ give a long howl

号 háo〈动〉① shout; yell; howl:北风怒～。A north wind is howling. ② cry; wail

另见 hào

号叫 háojiào howl; yell:她疼得～起来。She yelled (cried out) with pain.

号啕大哭 háotáo-dàkū cry bitter tears; wail; bewail mournfully; burst into a storm

毫 háo〈名〉① fine long hair:羊～笔 a writing brush made of goat's hair ② writing brush ③〈副〉a bit:～不费力 without the slightest effort

毫不 háobù not in the least; not at all; not a bit:～动摇 unswervingly; unshaken in one's conviction; without vacillation

毫克 háokè milligram (mg.)

毫厘 háolí the least bit; an iota:～不差 without the slightest error; just right

毫毛 háomáo soft hair on the body:不准你动她一根～。You are not allowed to do the least harm to her.

毫米 háomǐ millimetre (mm.):～波 millimetre wave

毫末 háomò the tip of a hair—an extremely small thing:合抱之木,生于～ a tree that can fill the span of a man's arms grows from a downy tip

毫升 háoshēng millilitre (ml.)

毫无 háowú without; without a grain of; beyond:～共同之处 have nothing in common (with):～疑问 beyond (all) question; without the least doubt; undoubtedly

hǎo

好 hǎo〈形〉① good; fine; nice:～消息 good news ② get well; be in good health:她的病～了。She is well (all right) now. ③ friendly; kind:～朋友 good friend ④ [用在动词后,表示完成或达到完善的地步]:文章写～了。The article has been finished. ⑤ [表示赞许、同意或结束等语气]:～了。不要再说了。All right, no need to say any more.〈副〉⑥ so as to; so that:把他的地址告诉我,我～找他。Tell me his address so that I can go and see him. ⑦ [用在数量词、时间词的前面,表示多或久]:～半天 quite a while ⑧ [用在形容词、动词前,表示程度深,并带有感叹语气]:～冷啊! How cold it is!〈名〉⑨ [指表扬的话或喝彩声]:观众连声叫～。The audience broke into loud cheers. ⑩ [表示问候]:你去见她,别忘了给我捎个～儿。Don't forget to convey my regards when you see her. 另见 hào

好办 hǎobàn easy to handle:这件事～。That can be easily arranged.

好比 hǎobǐ may be likened to; can be compared to; be just like

好不 hǎobù [表示程度深,并带感叹语气] very; quite; so:我们见了面,～欢喜。How happy we were to see each other.

好端端 hǎoduānduān in perfectly good condition; when everything is all right:～的,怎么生起气来了? Why are you angry when everything is perfectly all right?

好处 hǎochù good; benefit; advantage; profit:空谈有什么～? What's the good of empty talk? ～费 favour fees; pickings

好歹 hǎodǎi ① what's good and what's bad:不识～ not know what is good and what is bad; unable to appreciate a favour ② anyhow; at any rate

好感 hǎogǎn good (favourable) impression:对某人有～ have a good impression of sb. 给人～ make a good impression on people

好汉 hǎohàn brave man; true man; hero:～不吃眼前亏。A wise man will not fight when the odds are obviously against him.; A wise man doesn't fight against impossible odds.

好话 hǎohuà good word; word of praise; fine words:说～ say a good word (for sb.); fine words

好话说尽,坏事做绝 hǎohuà shuōjìn, huàishì zuòjué say every fine word and do every foul deed

好家伙 hǎojiāhuo good god; good lord; good heavens:～他一天足足走了一百里! Good lord, he walked a hundred *li* in a day!

好景不长 hǎojǐngbùcháng good times don't last long

好看 hǎokàn ① beautiful; prety; nice-looking ② interesting; delightful:电影很～。The film is very interesting. ③ proud; honoured ④ an embarrasing situation

好了疮疤忘了疼 hǎole chuāngbā wàngle téng forget the pain once the wound is healed—forget the bitter past when released from one's suffering

好评 hǎopíng favourable comment; high opinion; commendation:得到某人～ receive favourable comments from sb.

好人 hǎorén fine fellows; honest people; nice-guy:～主义 seeking good relations with all and sundry at the expense of principle. ～好事 good people (personalities) and good deeds

好日子 hǎorìzi ① auspicious day:他拣个～开张。He chose an auspicious day to start the business. ② wedding day:今天是她的～。Today is her wedding day. ③ good days; happy life:过～ live a happy life; live well；live in happiness

好商量 hǎoshāngliang can be settled through discussion：这事～。That can be settled through discussion.

好事 hǎoshì good deed：做～ do a good deed；do good. ～多磨。The road to happiness is strewn with setbacks.

另见 hàoshì

好手 hǎoshǒu good hand；expert；adept；past master：烹调～ a good hand at cooking

好受 hǎoshòu feel better；feel more comfortable：他吃了药以后～多了。He felt much better after taking the medicine.

好说 hǎoshuō ①［用在别人向自己致谢或恭维自己时，表示不敢当］：～，～！您太夸奖了。It's very good of you to say so，but I don't deserve such praise. ② no problem

好说歹说 hǎoshuō-dǎishuō try every possible way to persuade sb：我～，他总算答应了。He agreed，but only after I had pleaded with him in every way I could.

好似 hǎosì seem；be like

好听 hǎotīng ① pleasant to the ear；plausible ② interesting；amusing：～的故事 interesting story

好玩儿 hǎowánr amusing；interesting：这可不是～的！This is no joking matter.

好戏 hǎoxì good topical play；fascinating perfomances

好像 hǎoxiàng ① seem；appear；look；be like：天～要下雨。It looks like rain. ② as if，as though：她谈起来～是个理论家。She talks as if she were a theorist.

好心 hǎoxīn good intentions；kindness：她的～却受到了恶报。Her good intentions were repaid by evil results.

好样的 hǎoyàngde fine person；quite a man：如果你是～ if you are man enough

好意 hǎoyì goodwill；kindness；favour

好意思 hǎoyìsi how can one have the face (nerve) to do sth：他请我喝酒，我～不喝吗？When he offered me a drink，how could I have the face to refuse it？

好在 hǎozài fortunately；luckily

好转 hǎozhuǎn improve；take a turn for the better；take a favourable turn；change for the better：形势正～。The situation is taking a favourable turn.

好自为之 hǎozìwéizhī look out for yourself：有这样的机会不容易，希望你～。An opportunity like this is not easy to come by，so I hope you'll make best use of it.

hào

耗 hào ①〈动〉expend；cost；consume：～费劳动 expend labour ②〈名〉(bad) news：噩～ the sad news of the death of one's beloved

耗费 hàofèi waste；consume；

spend：～精力 spend one's energies
耗尽 hàojìn exhaust；use up；expend
耗能 hàonéng energy consumption
耗损 hàosǔn waste；consume；lose；detrition
耗子 hàozi mouse；rat

号 hào〈名〉① name：法～ Buddhist monastic name ② mark；sign：加～ plus sign ③ number ④ business house：分～ branch (of a firm，etc.) ⑤ size：这鞋小了两～。These shoes are two sizes too small. ⑥ date：今天几～？What date is it today？ ⑦ order：发～施令 issue orders ⑧ any brass-wind instrument ⑨ anything used as a horn
另见 háo
号兵 hàobīng bugler；trumpeter
号称 hàochēng be called；be known as；reputedly：～强大 reputedly powerful
号角 hàojiǎo horn；bugle；bugle call：～齐鸣 fanfare
号码 hàomǎ number：电话～ telephone number
号脉 hàomài feel the pulse
号外 hàowài (of a newspaper) extra；special
号召 hàozhào call on；call；appeal：发出～ send out a call
号子 hàozi work song

好 hào〈动〉① like；be fond of：～表现 like to get into the limelight ② be liable to：～晕船 be liable to seasickness
另见 hǎo
好吃懒做 hàochī-lǎnzuò be fond of eating and averse to work；be gluttonous and lazy
好大喜功 hàodà-xǐgōng crave for greatness and success；be ambitious for great achievements；have a passion for the grandiose
好高务(骛)远 hàogāo-wùyuǎn crave for (after) sth. high and out of reach；run after far-off things
好客 hàokè be hospitable；keep open house
好奇 hàoqí curious；inquisitive：～心 curiosity；inquisitiveness
好强 hàoqiáng eager to do well in everything
好色 hàosè love woman's beauty；be fond of women：～之徒 lecher；libertine
好胜 hàoshèng have a desire to excel in everything；try to be preeminent；seek to do others down
好事 hàoshì meddlesome；officious：～者 busybody；meddler
好为人师 hàowéirénshī be fond of teaching others；have a tendency to sermonize people；presumptuously lecture people
好恶 hào-wù likes and dislikes
好学 hàoxué studious；assiduous；diligent
好逸恶劳 hàoyì-wùláo dislike work and love leisure；love ease and comfort but hate to work
好战 hàozhàn warlike；bellicose

浩 hào〈形〉great；grand；vast：～瀚的沙漠 a vast expanse of desert

浩大 hàodà ① huge; gigantic ② heavy; very great

浩荡 hàodàng vast and mighty: 浩浩荡荡的大军 a mighty contingent

浩繁 hàofán vast and numerous: ～的开支 heavy expenditure

浩翰 hàohàn vast: ～的沙漠 a vast expanse of desert

浩劫 hàojié havoc; disaster; holocaust

浩气 hàoqì noble spirit: ～凌云 fully display one's noble spirit

浩如烟海 hàorúyānhǎi as vast as the smoke and sea - multitude; as vast as the open sea; tremendous amount of; voluminous

皓 hào〈形〉① white ② bright; luminous

皓白 hàobái white; pure white

皓月当空 hàoyuè-dāngkōng a bright moon hung in the sky

hē

呵 hē〈动〉① exhale ② scold

呵斥 hēchì scold; berate; excoriate; rebuke

呵呵 hēhē the sound of laughing: ～大笑 laugh loudly; roar with laughter

呵欠 hēqiàn yawn; gape

呵责 hēzé berate; excoriate

喝 hē〈动〉drink: ～茶 drink tea. ～酒 drink wine; drinking 另见 hè

喝水不忘掘井人 hēshuǐ bù wàng juéjǐngrén When you drink the water, think of those who dug the well.

喝西北风 hē xīběifēng feed on the winter's northwestern wind; go hungry; have to live on air

喝醉 hēzuì get (be) drunk; become intoxicated

嗬 hē〈叹〉ah; oh: ～,这小伙子真棒! Oh, what a fine young chap!. ～怎么这么贵! Wow, how expensive!

hé

禾 hé〈名〉standing grain (esp. rice)

禾场 hécháng threshing floor

禾苗 hémiáo seedlings of cereal crops

核 hé〈名〉① stone; pit; kernel: 桃～ peach-pit. ～心力量 the force at the core ② nucleus: ～子能 nuclear energy ③〈动〉examine; check: ～准 check and approve

核爆炸 hébàozhà nuclear explosion

核裁军 hécáijūn nuclear disarmament

核导弹 hédǎodàn nuclear ballistic missiles

核电站 hédiànzhàn nuclear power station; nuclear power plant

核定 hédìng check and ratify; ratify: ～地价 appraise and fix land prices. ～股份 authorized share

核动力 hédònglì nuclear power

核对 héduì check (up); verify: ～帐目 check the accounts
核讹诈 hé'ézhà nuclear blackmail
核扩散 hékuòsàn nuclear proliferation
核实 héshí verify; confirm; check up: ～数字 verify the figures
核算 hésuàn ① examine and calculate; adjust accounts ; assess ② (business) accounting: ～成本 cost accounting. ～单位 accounting unit
核桃 hétao walnut
核心 héxīn nucleus; core; kernel; centre: ～家庭 nuclear family. ～内阁 inner cabinet
核战争 hézhànzhēng nuclear war; N-war
核准 hézhǔn check and approve; approve; ratify; examine and approve

河

hé 〈名〉 river
河岸 hé'àn river bank
河床 héchuáng riverbed
河道 hédào river course; channel; waterway
河堤 hédī river embankment; dyke
河防 héfáng flood-prevention work done on rivers, esp. the Huanghe (Yellow) River
河肥 héféi river fertilizer
河沟 hégōu stream; brook
河口 hékǒu river mouth; outfall; [与海相连的] estuary
河狸 hélí beaver
河流 héliú rivers
河曲 héqū bend (of a river); meander
河山 héshān rivers and montains; land; territory: 锦绣～ beautiful rivers and mountains; beautiful land
河套 hétào ① the bend of a river ② the Great Bend of the Huanghe (Yellow) River
河西走廊 Héxīzǒuláng the Hexi (Gansu) Corridor (in northwestern Gansu, so called because it lies to the west of the Yellow River)
河蟹 héxiè river crab
河沿 héyán river bank; riverside
河鱼 héyú freshwater fish
河运 héyùn transport by boat on the river; river transport

何

hé ① 〈代〉 [表示疑问]: ～时 when; what time; what ② [表示反问]: 有～不同? What is the difference? ③ (Hé) a surname
何必 hébì Why (should you)…? What's the need to…?; there is no need: ～问她? What's the need to ask her?
何不 hébù Why not…?: ～再试一下? Why not try once more?
何尝 hécháng [用反词的语气表示未曾或并非]ever so: 我～不想去,只是没工夫罢了。No that I don't want to go; I just haven't got the time.
何等 héděng ① what kind of: ～人物 what kind of person ② how; what: 他～高尚! How noble he is!; What a noble man he is!
何妨 héfáng might as well; why not: 你～试一试。You might as well have a try.; Why not have

a try?

何苦 hékǔ Why should you take the trouble to…?; Is it worthwhile to…?; why bother:～乃尔? Why bother like this?

何况 hékuàng let alone; much less:他们死都不怕,～困难? They fear no death, let alone difficulties?

何乐而不为 hélè'érbùwéi why not do it; one would be only too glad to do it

何其 héqí (used in exclamations to express disapproval) what; how:～相似 what a striking likeness (similarity)

何去何从 héqù-hécóng what course to follow

何如 hérú ① it would be better:与其求人,～求己。It would be better to rely on ourselves than on others. ② What about…?; How about…?:请君试一试,～? What about you having a try?

何以 héyǐ why; how:～自解? How are you to justify yourself?

何止 hézhǐ far more than; not only:～十万八千里 as far as can be. 例子～这些。There are far more instances than we have just enumerated.

何足挂齿 hézúguàchǐ Don't mention it.; not worth bothering (talking) about

荷

hé 〈名〉 lotus

荷包 hébāo ① small bag (for carring money and odds and ends); pouch ② pocket (in a garment)

荷包蛋 hébāodàn poached or fried eggs

荷尔蒙 hé'ěrméng hormone

荷花 héhuā lotus flower; lotus

荷叶 héyè lotus leaf

合

hé 〈动〉 ① shut; close:请把书～上。Close your book, please. ② join; combine:～力 combined strength, make a joint effort ③ suit; agree; confirm to:～乎事实 tally with facts ④ be equal to; add up to:一公尺～三市尺。One metre is equal to three *chi*.

合办 hébàn operate or run jointly:～企业 a joint enterprise; a joint venture

合编 hébiān ① compile in collaboration with:这本书是他们两位～的。They are the two joint compilers of this book. ② merge and reorganize (army units, etc.)

合并 hébìng merge; unite; combine

合不来 hébulái not get along well; be incompatible

合唱 héchàng chorus:～曲 (music for) chorus. ～团 chorus (a group of singers). ～指挥 chorus master. 混声～ mixed chorus

合成 héchéng ① compose; compound:～工业 compound industry. ② synthetize; synthesize:～革 synthetic leather. ～纤维 synthetic fibre

合得来 hédelái get along well; be compatible

合订本 hédìngběn one-volume edition; file: 报纸的～ a file of newspapers

合二为一 hé'èrwéiyī unite two into one

合法 héfǎ lawful; legal; legitimate: ～化 legalize. ～斗争 legal struggle. ～经营 lawful operation

合格 hégé up to standard; qualified: ～试验 qualification test. ～证 certificate of quality

合股 hégǔ ① pool capital; form a partnership: ～公司 joint-stock company ② [纺] plying: ～线 ply (plied) yarn

合乎 héhū conform with (to); be in keeping with: ～规格 meet the specifications

合伙 héhuǒ form a partnership: ～人 partner

合计 héjì ① amount to; add up to; aggregate; total② héji figure out; think over; consult; lay one's heads together; confer with sb.

合家 héjiā the whole family: ～欢 a family group photo. ～团圆 a reunion of the whole family

合理 hélǐ reasonable; rational; equitable: ～化建议 rationalization proposal

合力 hélì ① join forces; pool efforts: ～修建水库 pool efforts to build a reservoir ② [物] resultant of forces

合流 héliú ① [河流] confluence ② joint forces with; cast one's lot with; collaboration

合谋 hémóu conspire; collude; plot together

合拍 hépāi ① be in time (with): 与音乐～ be in time with the music ② be in harmony (with)

合情合理 héqíng-hélǐ fair and reasonable; fair and sensible: 这个建议～。The proposal is fair and reasonable.

合群 héqún ① get on well with others; be sociable ② be gregarious

合身 héshēn fit; suit; become: 这件上衣对你很～。This coat fits you well.

合时 héshí fashionable; in vogue: 穿戴～ dress fashionably

合十 héshí [佛] put the palms together (a Buddhist greeting)

合适 héshì appropriate; suitable; becoming right

合算 hésuàn paying; worthwhile: 买这种钟不～。It doesn't pay to buy such a clock.

合同 hétóng contract: ～工 contract worker; contract job. ～期限 contract period; ～当事人的一方 one contracting party. 订～ sign (make) a contract (with sb.). 撕毁～ tear up a contract.

合演 héyǎn appear in the same play, dance, etc.; costar

合页 héyè hinge

合议 héyì panel discussion: [法] ～庭 collegial panel (bench)

合营企业 héyíng qǐyè joint venture

合影 héyǐng have a group photo taken; group photo

合约 héyuē contract

合帐 hézhàng make up accounts; figure out accounts

合著 hézhù write in collaboration with; coauthor

合资 hézī pool capital; enter into partnership

合资经营 hézī jīngyíng jointly operated (owned): ～企业 joint venture

合作 hézuò cooperate: ～流通企业 cooperative circulation enterprise. ～银行 cooperative bank

盒 hé〈名〉box; case

盒饭 héfàn boxed meals; box lunch

盒式 héshì cassette: ～磁带 cassette tape. ～录像带 videocassette. ～录音机 cartridge recorder

阖 hé ①〈形〉entire; whole: ～城 the whole town ②〈动〉shut; close: ～户 close the door

阖家 héjiā the whole family

阖眼 héyǎn close one's eyes

和 hé〈形〉① harmonious; on good terms: 天时、地利、人～ favourable climatic, geographical and human conditions ② mild; gentle; kind: 兄弟不～ brothers on bad terms with each other〈名〉③ peace: ～亲 peace through marriage ④ tie; draw: 那盘棋～了。That game of chess ended in a draw. ⑤〈副〉together with: ～衣而卧 sleep with one's clothes on ⑥〈介〉[表示相关、比较等] with; too: ～这件事有些关系 have something to do with it
另见 huó, huò

和蔼 hé'ǎi genial; kindly; amiable; affable; good-natured: ～可亲 affable; amiable

和风 héfēng gentle breeze; soft wind: ～细雨 in a mild and gentle way; gentle winds and fine rain

和好 héhǎo become reconciled (with); make (one's) peace (with); be at peace (with): ～如初 be on good terms again as before; become friends again as before

和缓 héhuǎn ① mild; gentle: 用～语气说话 speak in a mild tone ② relax; relieve; alleviate: 局势～了。The tension was relieved.

和会 héhuì peace conference

和解 héjiě ① be reconciled (with); conciliate; make compromise with; reconciliate: ～条款 compromise clause. 采取～态度 adopt a reconciliatory attitude (towards). ②[法] arrange a settlement; conciliation; reconcil; composition

和局 héjú draw; drawn game; tie: 比赛以～结束。The game ended in a draw.

和美 héměi harmonious: 小两口儿日子过得挺～。The young couple are living together in perfect harmony.

和睦 hémù harmony; amity; concord: 家庭～ family harmony; domestic peace

和平 hépíng peace：～共处五项原则Five Principles of Peaceful Coexistence

和气 héqì ① kind; polite; gentle：说话～ speak politely (gently) ② harmonious; friendly; amiable ③ friendship; harmonious relations：伤～ impair harmonious relations (between); hurt sb.'s feelings

和洽 héqià harmonious; on friendly terms：相处～ live in harmony

和善 héshàn kind and gentle; genial：性情～ be kind-hearted

和尚 héshang Buddhist monk

和事老 héshìlǎo peacemaker (esp. one who is more concerned with stopping the bickering than settling the issue)

和祥 héxiáng kindly; affable; amiable：面貌～ a kindly face

和谐 héxié harmonious; melodious：～的气氛 harmonious atmosphere

和煦 héxù pleasantly warm; sunny; genial：～的阳光 genial sunshine

和颜悦色 héyán-yuèsè benign (pleasant) countenance; be kindly and genial; have a pleasing, gracious face

和约 héyuē peace treaty

和悦 héyuè kindly; affable; amiable

和衷共济 hézhōng-gòngjì work together with one heart; pull together for a common cause; cooperate harmoniously

hè

鹤 hè〈名〉crane

鹤发 hèfà white hair：～童颜 have white hair and a youthful face (complexion)

鹤立鸡群 hèlì-jīqún like a crane standing among chickens — stand head and shoulders above others; be distinguished among the rest

赫 hè〈形〉grand; conspicuous：～～一世的大人物 a bigwig in his day

赫赫 hèhè illustrious; very impressive：～战功 illustrious military exploits; brilliant military success

赫赫有名 hèhè-yǒumíng have a great reputation; illustrious; of great celebrity; of high reputation：～的社会科学家 social socientist of high reputation

赫然 hèrán ① impressively ② terribly (angry)：～震怒 fly into a passion (rage); get into a terrible temper

赫哲族 Hèzhézú the Hezhen (Hoche) nationality, or the Hezhens (Hoches), inhabiting Heilongjiang Province

褐 hè ①〈名〉coarse cloth or clothing ②〈形〉brown：～土 brown earth

褐煤 hèméi brown coal; lignite

褐铁矿 hètiěkuàng brown iron ore; limonite

喝 hè 〈动〉shout loudly
另见 hē
喝彩 hècǎi acclaim; applaud; cheer
喝倒彩 hè dàocǎi make catcalls; hoot; boo
喝令 hèlìng shout one's order
贺 hè 〈动〉congratulate：可喜可～。You are to be congratulated.
贺匾 hèbiǎn congratulatory plaque
贺词 hècí message (speech) of congratulation; congratulations; greetings
贺电 hèdiàn congratulatory telegram; message of congratulation
贺礼 hèlǐ congratulatory gift
贺年 hènián extend New Year greetings; pay a New Year call：～卡 New Year card
贺喜 hèxǐ congratulate sb. on a happy occasion (e.g. a wedding, the birth of a child, etc.); offer congratulations
贺信 hèxìn congratulatory letter; letter of congratulation
荷 hè ①〈动〉carry on one's shoulder or back：～锄 carry a hoe on one's shoulder ②〈名〉burden; responsibility
另见 hé
荷枪实弹 hèqiāng-shídàn (of soldiers or policemen) carry loaded rifles—ready for an emergency
荷载 hèzài load
荷重 hèzhòng the weight a building can bear; load

hēi

黑 hēi 〈形〉① black：～发 black hair ② dark：天～了。It is getting dark. ③ sinister; wicked：～暗势力 forces of darkness; sinister forces ④ secret; shady：～交易 shady deal. ～幕 dark secret; inside story of a plot; sinister plot
黑暗面 hēi'ànmiàn undesirable phenomena; seamy side：暴露～ expose these sinister phenomena
黑白 hēibái black and white; right and wrong：～不分 make no distinction between right and wrong. ～分明 with black and white sharply contrasted. 混淆～ confuse right and wrong; confound black and white
黑道 hēidào ① dark road：拿着电筒，省得走～。Take a torch, or you'll be groping your way in the dark. ② dark deeds (as of robbers)
黑点 hēidiǎn stain; blemish; smirch
黑糊糊 hēihūhū ① black; blackened ② rather dark; dusky：屋子里～的。It's rather dark in the room. ③ indistinctly observable in the distance：远处是一片～的树林。A dark mass of trees loomed in the distance.
黑话 hēihuà ① sinister (mali-

cious) words ②［盗贼用的］cant; argot; patter

黑货 hēihuò smuggled goods; contraband

黑经济 hēijīngjì black economy

黑面包 hēimiànbāo black bread; brown bread; rye bread

黑幕 hēimù inside story of a plot, shady deal, etc.：揭穿～ expose a sinister project; tell the inside story of a plot, etc.

黑啤酒 hēipíjiǔ dark beer; black beer; stout

黑人 hēirén Black people; Black：美国～ Black American

黑色 hēisè black (colour)：～火药 black powder. ～人种 the black race

黑色金属 hēisèjīnshǔ ferrous metal

黑社会 hēishèhuì black society; gangsterdom; gangland; roguery; criminal syndicate; crookery：～头子 gang leader. ～性质的犯罪团伙 underground gangsters

黑市 hēishì black market; illicit market：～价 black rate. ～交易 black market operations; off-the-books deal. ～商人 black marketer. ～投机买卖 speculative trading; black market

黑手 hēishǒu sinister hand：～党 Mafia

黑匣子 hēixiázi black box

黑心 hēixīn black heart; evil mind

黑压压 hēiyāyā a dense or dark mass of

黑油油 hēiyōuyōu jet-black; shiny black：～的头发 shiny black hair

黑黝黝 hēiyōuyōu dim; dark：四周～的。It's dark all around.

黑云 hēiyún black clouds; dark clouds

嘿 hēi〈叹〉①［表示招呼或提起注意］hey：～！当心点！Hey! Be careful! ②［表示得意］：～，你看庄稼长得多好！Hey! Look! How well the crops grow! ③［表示惊异］：～，下雨了！Why, it is raining!

hén

痕 hén〈名〉mark; trace; scar：伤～ a scar from a wound

痕迹 hénjì mark; trace; imprint; vestige：古代文明的～ the vestiges of an ancient civilization

hěn

很 hěn〈副〉very; quite; awfully：～不愉快 not at all happy about

狠 hěn〈形〉① ruthless; relentless; cruel：心～手辣 cruel and evil ② firm; resolute：我们必须～抓队伍的建设。We must endeavour to build up our ranks. ③〈副〉retentlessly; severely

狠毒 hěndú vicious; spiteful

狠狠 hěnhěn severely; relentlessly; roundly：～打击 hit hard; deal heavy blows to

狠心 hěnxīn ① harden one's heart

② heartless

hèn

恨 hèn ①〈动〉hate；detest：～得要命 bitterly hate；hate intensely ②〈名〉regret：抱～ have a gnawing regret

恨不得 hènbude be very anxious (to do)；itch (to do)；how one wishes one could：我～马上去那儿。How I wish I could go there right now.

恨铁不成钢 hèn tiě bù chéng gāng be exasperated at sb.'s failure to make good；regret that one's offspring does not live up to one's expectations

恨之入骨 hènzhīrùgǔ harbour a bitter hatred for sb.；hate someone to the core (marrow)；consumed with hatred for

hēng

亨 hēng go smoothly

亨通 hēngtōng go smoothly；be prosperous：万事～。Everything is going smoothly.

哼 hēng〈动〉① moan；groan：轻蔑地～了一声 give a snort of contempt ② hum；croon：他独自～着歌。He was humming a song to himself.
另见 hng

哼哧 hēngchī puff hard：她跑得～～地直喘。She was puffing and blowing from running.

哼哼唧唧 hēnghēng-jiji mumble：这孩子～的叫人心烦。The child's mumbling is so annoying.

héng

恒 héng〈形〉① permanent；lasting：～久的可能性 permanent possibility ② usual；common：～言 common saying ③〈名〉perseverance

恒产 héngchǎn immovable property；immovables；real estate

恒久 héngjiǔ permanent；lasting；enduring

恒温 héngwēn constant temperature

恒心 héngxīn perseverance；constancy of purpose：有～的人 a person of perseverance

恒星 héngxīng [天](fixed) star

恒性 héngxìng perseverance；persistence：他干什么都没个～。He lacks perseverance in whatever he does.

横 héng〈形〉① transverse；horizontal：～耕 transverse ploughing ② across；sideways：～过街道 across the street〈副〉③ unrestrainedly；turbulently：老泪～流 tears flowing from aged eyes ④ wilfully；violently；fiercely：～加批判 wilfully criticize
另见 hèng

横冲直撞 héngchōng-zhízhuàng rampage about；run amuck

横渡 héngdù cross a river, etc.:～太平洋的飞行 a trans-Pacific flight

横断学科 héngduàn-xuékē cross-disciplinary science; transverse science

横幅 héngfú ① horizontal scroll of painting or calligraphy ② streamer; banner

横亘 hénggèn lie across; span:一座大桥～在江上。A bridge spans the river.

横贯 héngguàn cross over; traverse:这条铁路～全国。The railway traverses the whole country.

横祸 hénghuò unexpected calamity; sudden misfortune

横加 héngjiā do sth. to sb. unreasonably, forcibly, wilfully, etc.:～指责 make unwarranted charges

横跨 héngkuà [桥等] stretch across; span

横梁 héngliáng ①[建] crossbeam ②[汽车]cross member

横眉 héngméi scowl; frown in anger:～冷对千夫指,俯首甘为孺子牛 Fierce-browed, I coolly defy a thousand pointing fingers. Head bowed, like a willing ox I serve the children.

横七竖八 héngqī-shùbā in utter disorder; at sixes and sevens

横扫 héngsǎo sweep across or over; sweep away

横竖 héngshù 〈口〉 anyway; in any case

横挑鼻子竖挑眼 héng tiāo bízi shù tiāo yǎn find fault in a petty manner; pick holes in sth.; nitpick

横向 héngxiàng horizontal; crosswise; transverse:～经济联系 horizontal economic ties (with). ～研究 horizontally study; cross-sectional study

横心 héngxīn steel one's heart; become desperate:横下一条心 resolve to do sth. in desperation

横行霸道 héngxíngbàdào ride roughshod over; run wild; play the bully; lord it over; act violently; tyrannize over; acting like an overlord; play the tyrant

横溢 héngyì ① (of a river) overflow; be in flood:江河～ turbulent waters overflowing their banks ② (of talent, enthusiasm, etc.) brimming; overflowing; abundant:才气～ brimming with talent

横征暴敛 héngzhēng-bàoliǎn exact taxes in an arbitrary manner; exorbitant taxes; extort excessive taxes and levies; levy exorbitant taxes

衡 héng ①〈名〉 weighing apparatus 〈动〉② weigh ③ consider; judge:权～利害 weigh the advantages and disadvantages

衡量 héngliáng weigh (up); measure; consider; judge:～得失 weigh up the gains and losses

hèng

横 hèng 〈形〉 ① harsh and un-

reasonable; perverse: 蛮～harshand unreasonable; perverse ② accidental; unexpected
另见 héng

横暴 hèngbào perverse and violent

横财 hèngcái a fortune which one doesn't deserve; ill-gotten wealth (gains); windfall: 发～get a windfall

横祸 hènghuò unexpected calamity; sudden misfortune

横蛮 hèngmán rude and unreasonable: 他是个～不讲理的人。He's most rude and unreasonable man.

横事 hèngshì an untoward accident

横死 hèngsǐ die a violent death; be killed in an accident

hng

哼 hng 〈叹〉[表示满意或不相信] humph; umph; tut: ～! 你也配? Humph! Do you think you are qualified?
另见 hēng

hōng

烘 hōng 〈动〉① warm or dry by the fire; roast; bake ② set off: ～衬 serve as a foil to

烘焙 hōngbèi cure (tea or tobacco leaves)

烘干 hōnggān get dried by the fire; dry beside or over a fire

烘烤 hōngkǎo toast; bake: ～面包 bake bread

烘托 hōngtuō set off by contrast: ～作用 serve as contrast

哄 hōng ①〈象〉roars of laughter or hubbub ②〈动〉clamour; roar
另见 hǒng, hòng

哄传 hōngchuán (of rumours) circulate widely

哄抢 hōngqiǎng open plunder of; looting: ～事件 a looting incident

哄抬 hōngtái force up; drive up: ～物价 force up prices; jacking up prices; inflate prices

哄堂大笑 hōngtángdàxiào set the whole room roaring (in an uproar); explode into loud laughter; burst out into laughter; fit of laughter

轰 hōng ①〈象〉bang; boom: ～的一声炮响 a bang of a cannon 〈动〉② rumble; bombard; explode: 雷～电闪。Thunder rumbled and lightning flashed. ③ drive off; shoo away: ～下台 hoot sb. off the platform; oust sb. from office; hoot down

轰动 hōngdòng create (make) a stir; cause a sensation: ～文坛 create a stir among the men of letters

轰动一时 hōngdòng-yīshí create (make) a furore; make a great stir; cause a great sensation: 这部电影曾～。The film was a great hit.

轰轰烈烈 hōnghōng-lièliè on a grand and spectacular scale;

vigorous; amid fire and thunder;with vigour and vitality; stormy and heroic; rousing; stirring and seething; dynamic; resounding

轰鸣 hōngmíng thunder; roar:马达～。Motors roared.

轰炸 hōngzhà bomb; bombard:～机 bomber

hóng

鸿 hóng〈名〉① swan; goose:轻如～毛 lighter than a goose feather; as light as a goose feather ② letter:远方来～ a letter from afar ③〈形〉grand; great

鸿沟 hónggōu wide gap; gulf; chasm:不可逾越的～ impassable gulf; insurmountable barrier

鸿基 hóngjī foundation for a great undertaking

鸿门宴 hóngményàn a dinner at Hongmen where treachery (murder of invited guest) was planned; Hongmen feast — a meeting contrived as a trap

鸿雁 hóngyàn swan (wild) goose: ～传书 keep on shuttlecocking letters; a letter from afar

鸿运 hóngyùn good luck

鸿运高照 hóngyùn-gāozhào bring sb. good luck and success in life

虹 hóng〈名〉rainbow:彩～ rainbow

红 hóng〈形〉① red:～领巾 red scarf ② luck; symbol of success:～运 good luck ③ revolutionary:～色专家 socialist-minded expert ④〈名〉bonus; dividend:分～ distribute (draw) dividends

红白脸 hóngbáiliǎn with some wearing the white make-up of the stage villain and others the red make-up of the hero

红包 hóngbāo red packet (money inside a red paper envelope given by elders to their unmarried juniors on lunar New Year's eve or to newly-wed couples at their first meeting. Now sometimes it is also used for a bonus or commission.); a red paper envelope containing money as a gift, tip, or bonus

红茶 hóngchá black tea:～菌 fermented tea

红蛋 hóngdàn red eggs (eggs dyed red on the happy occasion of the birth of a child and given as gifts to friends and relatives)

红得发紫 hóngdefāzǐ (of a person) extremely popular

红股 hónggǔ bonus stock:～发行 bonus issue

红火 hónghuo flourishing; prosperous:我们的日子越过越～。Our days are becoming better and better.

红极一时 hóngjíyīshí be well-known for a time; enjoy popularity for a time

红利 hónglì bonus; extra (bonus) dividend:～工资 bonus wage

红脸 hóngliǎn ① blush ② flush

with anger; get angry:我俩从来没有红过脸。There has never been a cross word between the two of us. ③red face, face painting in Beijing opera, etc., traditionally for the heroic or the honest

红领巾 hónglǐngjīn ① red scarf ② Young Pioneer

红领章 hónglǐngzhāng red collar tab (as on PLA uniforms)

红绿灯 hónglǜdēng traffic light

红木 hóngmù red sandalwood; mahogany; padauk

红牌 hóngpái [体] red card

红皮书 hóngpíshū red paper; red book

红旗 hóngqí red flag or banner:～单位 red-banner unit; advanced unit. ～手 red-banner pacesetter; advanced worker

红人 hóngrén favourite with sb. in power; fair-haired boy:处长的～ a favourite with the head of the department

红润 hóngrùn ruddy; rosy

红十字会 hóngshízìhuì the Red Cross

红糖 hóngtáng brown sugar

红彤彤 hóngtōngtōng bright red; glowing

红头文件 hóngtóuwénjiàn red-heading documents

红外线 hóngwàixiàn [物] infrared ray

红星 hóngxīng red star:～帽徽 red star cap insignia (of PLA soldiers)

红颜 hóngyán a pretty face — a beautiful woman:～薄命 beautiful women suffer unhappy fates

红眼 hóngyǎn ① inflammation of the eye; pinkeye:～病 red eye disease ② get angry; become infuriated ③ be jealous of; feel envy at

红叶 hóngyè red autumnal leaves (of maple, etc.)

红运 hóngyùn good luck:走～ have a spate of good luck

红晕 hóngyùn blush; flush:脸上泛出～ one's face blushing scarlet

红枣 hóngzǎo red date

红涨 hóngzhàng (of one's face) be swelled with blood

红肿 hóngzhǒng red and swollen; swollen:～的手指 swollen finger

洪

hóng ①〈形〉big; vast:～流 powerful current ②〈名〉flood

洪峰 hóngfēng peak of flow; flood peak

洪福 hóngfú great blessing:～齐天 limitless blessing

洪亮 hóngliàng loud and clear; sonorous:嗓音～ a sonorous voice

洪流 hóngliú powerful current; giant (mighty) torrent:时代的～ powerful current of the times

洪水 hóngshuǐ flood-water; flood:～猛兽 fierce floods and savage beasts; terrible scourge; dreadful monster. ～位 flood level

宏

hóng〈形〉great; grand; vast:～大的计划 grandiose

plan

宏大 hóngdà great; grand; grandiose:～志愿 great aspirations

宏观 hóngguān ① [物] macroscopic ② macro-:～调控 macrocontrol. ～经济学 macroeconomics

宏图 hóngtú great plan

宏伟 hóngwěi grand; splendid; magnificent:～的前景 grand prospects

宏愿 hóngyuàn great aspirations; noble ambition:改造自然的～ the great aspirations to reshape nature

宏旨 hóngzhǐ main idea (theme):无关～ be irrelevant to the main idea

弘 hóng ①〈形〉grand; great; magnificent ②〈动〉promote; expand

弘扬 hóngyáng carry forward; develop; carry on and promote:～我们时代的主旋律 give full scope to the central theme of our times

hǒng

哄 hǒng〈名〉① fool; kid; humbug:不要～我。Don't fool me. ② coax; humour:～孩子吃药 coax a child to take medicine 另见 hōng,hòng

哄逗 hǒngdòu keep (esp. a child) in good humour; coax:她很会～孩子。She knows how to handle children.; She has a way with children.

哄骗 hǒngpiàn humbug; coax; cheat; cajole:～某人做某事 humbug sb. into doing sth.

哄劝 hǒngquàn coax:～孩子吃药 coax a child to take medicine

hòng

讧 hòng〈名〉strife; conflict

哄 hòng〈动〉uproar; horseplay 另见 hōng,hǒng

哄场 hòngchǎng make catcalls; hoot; boo

hóu

侯 hóu〈名〉① marquis ② a noble man or a high official ③ (Hóu) a surname

侯爵 hóujué marquis:～夫人 marquise

侯门似海 hóuménsìhǎi the gate of a noble house is like the sea—impassable to the common man

喉 hóu〈名〉throat

喉咙 hóulóng ① throat ② voice:～痛 have a sore throat

喉舌 hóushé mouthpiece; spokesman; speaker; voice:人民的～ mouthpiece (voice) of the people.

喉头 hóutóu larynx; throat

喉炎 hóuyán laryngitis

猴 hóu〈名〉monkey

猴戏 hóuxì a show by a performing monkey; monkey show

hǒu

吼 hǒu〈动〉roar; howl: ～声 roar

吼叫 hǒujiào roar; howl; shout

hòu

厚 hòu〈形〉① thick: ～木板 a thick plank ② profound: 深情～谊 profound friendship ③ kind; magnanimous: ～道人 a decent sort ④ large; generous: ～薪 high pay ⑤ rich or strong in flavour: 酒味很～。The wine tastes strong. ⑥〈动〉stress; favour: ～今薄古 lay more stress on the present than on the past; stress the present over the past

厚爱 hòu'ài your kind thought; your kindness: 承蒙～, thank you for your kindness

厚薄 hòubó thickness: ～合适。It's just the right thickness.

厚此薄彼 hòucǐ-bóbǐ favour one and be prejudiced against the other; favour one and discriminate against the other

厚待 hòudài treat sb. kindly

厚道 hòudao honest and kind; kind and sincere; tolerant

厚古薄今 hòugǔ-bójīn stress the past, not the present

厚今薄古 hòujīn-bógǔ stress the present, not the past

厚金 hòujīn handsome reward; liberal remuneration

厚礼 hòulǐ generous gifts

厚脸皮 hòuliǎnpí brazen; thick-skinned; cheeky: 厚着脸皮说 have the nerve to say

厚禄 hòulù handsome salary; high government pay

厚实 hòushi ① thick; strong ② abundant; well-off

厚望 hòuwàng great expectations: 不负～ live up to sb.'s expectations; not let sb. down

厚谢 hòuxiè give sb. a rich reward: 事成之后,必当～。When the thing is done, there will be a rich reward for you.

厚颜无耻 hòuyán-wúchǐ be lost to shame; have no shame; shameless; brazen-faced; have a nerve

厚意 hòuyì kindness; good will; great cordiality: 多谢你的～。Thank you for your kindness.

厚葬 hòuzàng ① bury with full honours ② a lavish funeral

候 hòu〈动〉① wait for; await: 恭～ await respectfully ② inquire after: 致～ send one's regards〈名〉③ time; season: 时～ time ④ condition; state

候补 hòubǔ be an alternate; be a candidate (for a vacancy): ～委员 alternate member (of a committee)

候车 hòuchē wait for a train, bus, etc.: ～室 waiting room (in a bus or railway station)

候机室 hòujīshì airport lounge or waiting room

候鸟 hòuniǎo migratory bird; migrant

候审 hòushěn [法] await trial
候选人 hòuxuǎnrén candidate
候诊 hòuzhěn wait for one's turn to see the doctor: ～室 clinic waiting room
后 hòu 〈名〉① back; behind; rear: 敌～ the enemy's rear ② offspring: 无～ without issue; without male offspring ③ queen; empress ④〈副〉after; afterwards; later: 不久以～ soon afterwards; before long
后半生 hòubànshēng the latter half of one's life
后半叶 hòubànyè latter half of a century: 20 世纪～ the latter half of 20th century
后辈 hòubèi ① younger generation; juniors ② posterity
后备 hòubèi reserve: ～基金 reserve fund. ～力量 reserve force
后代 hòudài ① later periods (in history); future ages ② later generations; descendants; posterity; offspring
后发制人 hòufāzhìrén gain mastery by striking only after the enemy has struck
后福 hòufú ① future blessings ② blessings in one's old age
后顾 hòugù turn back (to take care of sth.: ～之忧 any menace from the "rear"; fear of attacks from behind; drawing attention away from one's own work; have extraneous worries to distract one. 无暇～ have no time to look after things one has left behind
后果 hòuguǒ consequence; aftermath: 前因～ cause and effect
后话 hòuhuà part of a story to be recounted later; part of a story that is to come: 这是～,暂且不提。That's what happened later, so no more of it now.
后患 hòuhuàn future trouble: ～无穷。There will be no end of trouble.; a source of endless trouble
后悔 hòuhuǐ regret; repent: ～莫及 too late for regrets; repent bitterly; no use crying over spilt milk
后会有期 hòuhuì-yǒuqī we'll meet again some day
后继无人 hòujì-wúrén leave no successor (to carry on a tradition, transmit an art or craft, etc.)
后继有人 hòujì-yǒurén have qualified successors; there will people who can carry on…
后进 hòujìn ① those who lag backward; laggard ② junior member of a profession
后劲 hòujìn ① delayed effect; aftereffect: 这酒～大。This wine has a strong delayed effect. ② reserve strength; stamina: 她干活有～。She has staying power when she's doing a job.
后来居上 hòuláijūshàng late-comers surpassing old timers; The newcomers have outdone the old hands.; Later comers become the first.
后路 hòulù ① route of retreat; line of retreat ② room for ma-

noeuvre：留～ make room for manoeuvre;leave someone leeway

后门 hòumén ① back door ② "backdoor"(dealings)

后面 hòumian ① at the back; in the rear; behind ② later：这个问题我～还要讲。I'll come back to this question later.

后母 hòumǔ stepmother

后怕 hòupà fear after the event：事过之后，我倒真有些～。After it was all over, I became really scared.

后期 hòuqī later stage; later period

后起 hòuqǐ (of people of talent) of new arrivals; of the younger generation：～之秀 an up-and-coming youngster; a promising (remarkable) young person

后勤 hòuqín ① rear service; logistics：～保障 logistical requirements ② supporting work; backup service

后人 hòurén ① people of future generations ② descendant; offspring; posterity

后生可畏 hòushēng-kěwèi The young are to be regarded with respect (awe).; The younger generation will grow up one day to surpass the older.

后世 hòushì ① later ages ② future generations; posterity

后事 hòushì ① what happened afterwards; subsequent event ② arrangements after one's death; funeral affairs

后台 hòutái ① backstage; behind-the-scenes ② backer; supporter：～老板 backstage boss; behind-the-scenes backer

后天 hòutiān ① day after tomorrow ② postnatal; acquired：知识是～获得的，不是先天就有的。Knowledge is acquired, not innate.

后退 hòutuì draw back; fall back; retreat

后续 hòuxù ① follow-up：～部队 follow-up units ② remarry after the death of one's wife

后遗症 hòuyízhèng ①［医］sequelae ②［后果］aftermath

后裔 hòuyì descendant; offspring

hū

乎 hū ①〈助动〉[表示疑问]：成败之机，其在斯～？Does not success or failure hinge on this? ②[动词后缀]：出～意料 be beyond one's expectations ③[形容词或副词后缀]：确～重要 very important indeed

呼 hū〈动〉① breathe out; exhale：～出一口气 exhale a breath ② cry out; shout：大声疾～ cry (shout) at the top of one's voice ③ call：一～百应。Hundreds respond to a single call.

呼风唤雨 hūfēng-huànyǔ summon wind and rain—exercise magic powers; stir up trouble.

呼喊 hūhǎn shout; call out; cry

呼号 hūháo wail; cry：奔走～ go round crying for help

呼吼 hūhǒu whistle; roar: 北风～。The north wind howled.
呼唤 hūhuàn call; shout to
呼机 hūjī pager; beeper
呼救 hūjiù cry (call) for help
呼哨 hūshào whistle: 打～ give a whistle
呼声 hūshēng cry; shout; voice: 发出～ give (utter) a cry
呼吸 hūxī breathe; respire; exhale and inhale
呼啸 hūxiào whistle; scream; whizz: 子弹～而过。A bullet whizzed past.
呼应 hūyìng echo; chime in with; in concert with
呼吁 hūyù appeal (to); call on: 发出～ make an appeal

忽 hū ①〈动〉neglect; ignore; overlook: ～明～灭 flicker ②〈副〉suddenly: ～生奇念 suddenly have a strange idea
忽地 hūdì suddenly; all of a sudden;
忽而…忽而… hū'ér…hū'ér… now…, now…: ～南～北 appearing now in the south and now in the north
忽…忽… hū…hū… now..., now...: 情绪忽高忽低 be in high spirits one moment and in low spirits the next; be subject to sudden changes of mood
忽略 hūlüè neglect; ignore; overlook; lose sight of
忽然 hūrán suddenly; all of a sudden; unexpectedly
忽视 hūshì overlook; disregard; ignore; neglect
忽左忽右 hūzuǒ-hūyòu suddenly left, suddenly right — now one extreme, now the other

hú

壶 hú〈名〉pot; kettle: 茶～ tea pot

胡 hú ①〈名〉beard; whiskers; moustache ②〈副〉at random; recklessly: ～说 sheer nonsense; talk nonsense
胡扯 húchě talk nonsense; chatter idly
胡吹 húchuī boast outrageously; talk big
胡搞 húgǎo ① make a muddle of sth.; mess things up ② carry on an affair with sb.
胡椒 hújiāo pepper
胡搅 hújiǎo ① pester sb.; be mischievous ② argue tediously and vexatiously; wrangle: ～蛮缠 argue tediously and vexatiously; plague sb. with unreasonable demands
胡来 húlái ① mess things up; fool with sth. ② run wild; act irresponsibly or recklessly
胡乱 húluàn ① carelessly; casually: ～花钱 squander money ② wild; at random
胡萝卜 húluóbo carrot
胡闹 húnào run wild; make trouble; get into mischief
胡琴 húqín *huqin*, two-stringed Chinese fiddle: 拉～ play the Chinese fiddle
胡说 húshuō talk through one's hat; talk nonsense; blather: ～

八道 talk (sheer) nonsense; rubbish; humbug; stuff and nonsense

胡思乱想 húsīluànxiǎng imagine things; give oneself up to daydreams; give free rein to fancy

胡同 hútòng alley; lane

胡言乱语 húyán-luànyǔ talk nonsense (rubbish); babble (about); talk arrant nonsense; rave

胡子 húzi beard, moustache or wiskers

胡作非为 húzuò-fēiwéi commit all manner of evil; act wantonly; run amuck

湖 hú 〈名〉lake

湖滨 húbīn lakeside

湖光山色 húguāng-shānsè a beautiful scenery of lakes and mountains

湖泊 húpō lakes

湖泽 húzé lakes and marshes

糊 hú 〈动〉① stick (with paste); paste ② (of food) burnt

糊糊 húhu ① mush; paste ② trouble.

糊口 húkǒu eke out a living; keep body and soul together; make ends meet

糊里糊涂 húlǐhútu confused in thinking; muddle-headed; with minds in a haze: ～地活下去 muddle along

糊涂 hútu ① muddle-headed; muddled: ～观念 muddled ideas ② chaotic; messy: ～帐 messy accounts ③ not clear; blurred

葫 hú

葫芦 húlu bottle gourd; calabash

蝴 hú

蝴蝶 húdié butterfly

囫 hú

囫囵 húlún whole: ～吞下 swallow sth. whole

囫囵吞枣 húlún-tūnzǎo swallow a date whole — read hastily and without thinking; gulp down without thought

猢 hú

猢狲 húsūn macaque; monkey

煳 hú〈形〉(of food) burnt: 饭～了。The rice is burnt.

煳锅 húguō burnt in a pot

核 hú

另见 hé

核儿 húr ① stone; pit; core: 杏～ apricot stone ② sth. resembling a fruit stone: 煤～ partly-burnt coals or briquets; cinders

狐 hú 〈名〉fox

狐臭 húchòu body odour; bromhidrosis

狐假虎威 hújiǎ-hǔwēi The fox borrows the tiger's terror (influence) — bully people by flaunting one's powerful connections.; the fox "borrowing" the awe of the tiger; assume someone else's authority as one's own

狐狸尾巴 húli wěiba fox's tail—something that gives away a person's real character or evil intentions; cloven hoof

狐群狗党 húqún-gǒudǎng gang of rogues (scoundrels); despicable gang

狐疑 húyí doubt; suspicion: 满腹～ be very suspicious; be full of misgivings

弧 hú 〈名〉arc: ～灯 arc lamp (light)

弧度 húdù [数] radian

弧光 húguāng arc light; arc: ～灯 arc lamp; arc light

弧圈球 húquānqiú [乒乓球] loop drive

弧形 húxíng arc; curve

hǔ

虎 hǔ ①〈名〉tiger ②〈形〉vigorous; brave

虎虎有生气 hǔhǔ yǒu shēngqì be full of vim and vigour

虎劲 hǔjìn dauntless drive; dash: 有一股子～ be full of drive and daring; have plenty of dash

虎口 hǔkǒu tiger's mouth — jaws of death; dangerous place: ～余生 narrowly escape death

虎视眈眈 hǔshì-dāndān glare like a tiger eyeing its prey; eye covetously; the hostile eyes of; eye with hostility; cast greedy eyes on

虎头虎脑 hǔtóu-hǔnǎo [多指儿童] looking strong and good-natured: 他儿子长得～,非常可爱。His son's a lovely boy, so strong and good-natured.

虎头蛇尾 hǔtóu-shéwěi begin with tigerish energy but peter out towards the end; do things by halves; come in like a lion, go out like a lamb; fine start and poor finish

虎穴 hǔxuè tiger's lair (den): 不入～,焉得虎子? How can you catch tiger cubs without entering the tiger's lair?; Nothing venture, nothing have.

hù

户 hù 〈名〉① door ② family; household ③ account: 帐～ account

户籍 hùjí ① census register; household register ② registered permanent residence: ～警 census policeman

户均 hùjūn household average: ～收入一万元。The average per household income is 10,000 yuan

户口 hùkǒu ① census registration ② one's registered residence; one's domicile: ～簿 household register; residence booklet. 报(销,迁)～ register (cancel, change) one's residence. ～管理制度 domiciliary control system

户售 hùshòu household sale: 平均～粮食 1,500 公斤。The average per household grain sale is 1,500 kg.

户枢不蠹 hùshū-bùdù A door-hinge is never worm-eaten.

户头 hùtóu bank account: 开～ open an account

户外 hùwài outdoor：～运动 outdoor games；outdoor sports

户主 hùzhǔ head of a household (family)

沪 Hù short for 上海

沪剧 hùjù Shanghai opera

护 hù〈动〉① protect；guard：～田林 field-protection woods ② shield from censure；be partial to：官官相～ Bureaucrats shield one another.

护岸 hù'àn bank revetment

护短 hùduǎn cover up one's shortcomings；shield one's mistakes；attempt to justify one's mistakes

护发素 hùfàsù hair conditioner

护封 hùfēng cardboard jacket；book jacket；jacket

护肤霜 hùfūshuāng face cream

护航 hùháng escort；convoy：由 3 艘军舰～ be convoyed by three warships；have an escort of three warships

护理 hùlǐ nurse；look after；tend：～人员 nursing staff；paramedical worker；paramedic

护林 hùlín protect a forest

护身符 hùshēnfú ① amulet；protective talisman ② a person or thing that protects one from punishment or censure；shield

护士 hùshì nurse：～长 head (chief) nurse

护送 hùsòng escort；convoy：～回家 escort (sb.) home

护卫 hùwèi ① protect；guard ② bodyguard

护照 hùzhào passport

戽 hù ①〈名〉bailing bucket ②〈动〉bail：～水灌田 bail water to irrigate fields

戽斗 hùdǒu bailing bucket；dredging box

怙 hù〈动〉depend (rely) on

怙恶不悛 hù'èbùquān be incorrigible；remain impenitent；be steeped in evil and refuse to repent

互 hù〈形〉mutual；reciprocal；each other：～相转化 reciprocal transformation

互不侵犯条约 hù bù qīnfàn tiáoyuē nonaggression treaty (pact)

互访 hùfǎng exchange visits；reciprocal visits

互…互 hù…hù… mutual；each other：互谅互让 mutual understanding and (mutual) accommodation

互换 hùhuàn exchange；interchange：～货币 currency swap. ～批准书 exchange of instruments of ratification. ～照会 exchange notes

互惠 hùhuì mutually beneficial；reciprocal：～条约 reciprocal treaty. ～关税 reciprocal tariff. ～政策 give-and-take policy

互教互学 hùjiāo hùxué teach and learn reciprocally

互利 hùlì mutual benefit

互让 hùràng yield to each other；give in to each other

互通有无 hùtōng-yǒuwú help supply each other's needs；each

supplies what the other needs; make up for each other's shortages

互为因果 hùwéi-yīnguǒ interact as both cause and effect

互相 hùxiāng mutually; each other:～扯皮 wrangle endlessly with each other. ～配合,～制约 coordinate with each other and restrain each other

互助 hùzhù help each other:～条约 treaty of mutual assistance

huā

花 huā〈名〉① flower; blossom:开～ come into blossom ② anything resembling a flower:浪～ spray ③ fireworks:放～ let off fireworks ④ design; pattern:白地蓝～ blue patterns on a white surface〈形〉⑤ coloured; multicoloured:～～绿绿的衣服 gaudy clothes ⑥ (of eyes) blurred; dim:老眼昏～ dim-sighted from old age ⑦〈动〉expend; spend:这项工程我们～了三年时间。We spent over three years on this project.

花白 huābái (of hair or beard) grey; grizzled:头发～ with grey (grizzled) hair; grey-haired

花边 huābiān lace:～文学 decorative literature. ～新闻 news in box; titbits (of news)

花布 huābù cotton print; print

花草 huācǎo ① flowers and plants ② Chinese milk vetch

花茶 huāchá scented tea:茉莉～ jasmine tea

花朵 huāduǒ flower:盛开的～ flowers in full bloom. 儿童是祖国的～。Children are the flowers of our country.

花房 huāfáng greenhouse

花费 huāfèi ① spend; expend; cost:～金钱 spend money (on a project, etc.) ② money spent; expenditure; expenses:这笔～我担负不了。I can't afford the expense.

花好月圆 huāhǎo-yuèyuán blooming flowers and full moon — perfect conjugal bliss (felicity); The flowers are in full bloom and the moon is full.

花红柳绿 huāhóng-liǔlǜ red flowers and green willows—a beautiful spring scene

花花公子 huāhuā-gōngzǐ playboy; dandy; coxcomb; fop

花花绿绿 huāhuā-lǜlǜ brightly coloured; colourful:穿得～的 be colourfully dressed. ～的招贴画 poster in colour

花花世界 huāhuā-shìjiè the dazzling human world with its myriad temptations; the glittering world; vanity fair

花卉 huāhuì flowers and plants:～画 flower piece

花会 huāhuì flower fair

花甲 huājiǎ a cycle of sixty years:～之年 sixty (years of age)

花架子 huājiàzi pretty appearance (metaphor for a work style that seeks superficial form and pays no actual accomplishments)：不追求～ do not seek only a pretty appearance

花剑 huājiàn［体］foil：～运动员 foil fencer

花匠 huājiàng gardener

花镜 huājìng presbyopic glasses

花篮 huālán ① a basket of flowers ② gaily decorated basket

花里胡哨 huālihúshào ① gaudy；garish；showy：穿得～的 be gaudily dressed ② without solid worth：她吹得～的，不能信。Don't believe her florid words.

花柳病 huāliǔbìng venereal disease (V.D.)

花名册 huāmíngcè register (of names)；membership roster；roster

花鸟 huāniǎo painting of flowers and birds in traditional Chinese style：～画 flower-and-bird painting

花农 huānóng flower grower

花瓶 huāpíng ① flower vase；vase ② a woman employed for her beauty only，usu. installed as secretary in an office for decorative purposes ③ a woman who only knows how to make herself up and can do no useful work

花圃 huāpǔ flower nursery；flowerbed

花圈 huāquān wreath (of flowers)：送～ present a wreath. 敬献～ respectfully lay a wreath (at the tomb of…)

花容月貌 huāróng-yuèmào flower-like features and moonlike face—a great beauty

花色 huāsè design and colour：～品种 variety and specifications. ～繁多 a great variety (of sth.)

花哨 huāshao ① garish；gaudy：她打扮得太～。She was gaudily dressed. ② full of flourishes；flowery

花生 huāshēng peanut；groundnut

花饰 huāshì ornamental design

花束 huāshù bunch of flowers；bouquet：献～ present sb. with a bouquet

花天酒地 huātiān-jiǔdì indulge in dissipation；lead a life of debauchery；lead a fast life；guzzle and carouse to one's heart's content；lead a gay life

花团锦簇 huātuán-jǐncù bouquets of flowers and piles of silks—rich multicoloured decorations

花纹 huāwén decorative pattern；figure

花絮 huāxù［报刊上的］supplementary story；titbits；interesting sidelights

花言巧语 huāyán-qiǎoyǔ fine words；honeyed words；luring speech；seductive speech；blandishment；verbal tricks；flowery words

花样 huāyàng pattern；sample；variety：～滑冰 figure skating. ～游泳 synchronized swimming

花帐 huāzhàng padded bills or accounts：开～ pad accounts；make out a padded account

花招 huāzhāo ① game；trick；trickery ②［武术］apparently skilful movement

花枝招展 huāzhī-zhāozhǎn (of women) be gorgeously dressed：打扮得～的 freshly made up and as pretty as a flower

huá

划 huá〈动〉① row；paddle：～船 row (paddle) a boat ② scratch；cut：他手～破了。His hands were scratched. ③ to one's profit；pay：～得来。It is worthwhile.
另见 huà

划不来 huábùlái be not worth it；do not pay

划得来 huádelái be worth it；pay：还是买质量好的东西～。It always pays to buy good quality products (goods).

划算 huásuàn ① calculate；weigh ② be profitable；be to one's profit；pay

滑 huá〈形〉① smooth；slippery；sleek：雨后路～。The road is slippery after rain. ② sly；cunning；crafty：又奸又～ mean and crafty ③〈动〉slip；slide：～到…轨道 slide onto a track

滑冰 huábīng ice-skating；skating：～场 skating rink. ～运动员 skater

滑旱冰 huáhànbīng roller-skate

滑稽 huájī funny；ridiculous farcical；comical：～剧 farce. ～模仿 parody；travesty

滑坡 huápō ① landslide；landslip ② be on the slippery slope；decline；come down；drop：财政收入连续 3 年～。State revenue declined for three years in succession.

滑天下之大稽 huá tiānxià zhī dàjī be the biggest joke in the world；be the laughingstock of the world；be the object of universal ridicule

滑头 huátóu ① mischievous (slippery) fellow；sly old fox ② foxy；cunning

滑行 huáxíng slide；coast；taxi (along)：飞机降落，在跑道上～。The plane came in and taxied along the runway.

滑雪 huáxuě skiing：～运动员 skier

华 huá〈形〉① splendid brilliant；magnificant：～丽 gorgeous；magnificent ② flourishing；prosperous：繁～ flourishing；thriving ③ extravagant；flashy〈名〉④ best part；essence：精～ the cream；the essence ⑤ China：～南 South China

华表 huábiǎo ornamental column (erected in front of palaces, tombs, etc.)

华诞 huádàn your birthday

华灯 huádēng colourfully decorated lantern；light：～初上 when the evening lights are lit

华而不实 huá'érbùshí flashy and without substance；superficially clever

华贵 huáguì ① luxurious；sumptuous；costly：～的地毯 luxurious carpet ② wealthy：～之家 a wealthy family

华丽 huálì splendid; gorgeous: ～的客厅 magnificent parlour; flamboyantly furnished guest-room

华侨 huáqiáo overseas Chinese: 归国～ returned overseas Chinese

华人 huárén Chinese: 美籍～ an American Chinese

华裔 huáyì foreign citizen of Chinese origin; a person of Chinese descent

华语 huáyǔ Chinese (language)

华章 huázhāng your brilliant work; your beautiful writing

哗 huá 〈动〉 clamour; make noise

哗变 huábiàn mutiny

哗然 huárán in an uproar; in commotion: 舆论～。There was a public outcry (clamour).

哗众取宠 huázhòng-qǔchǒng curry favour by claptrap; talk big to impress people

猾 huá 〈形〉 cunning; crafty; sly: ～吏 a cunning and unscrupulous official

huà

话 huà ①〈名〉word; remark; speech: 说几句～ say a few words ②〈动〉talk about; speak about: ～家常 exchange small talk; chitchat

话本 huàběn text of a story; prompt book; script for story-telling: ～小说 story-teller's script; vernacular tales

话别 huàbié say good-bye (to); take one's farewell (of); bid farewell

话柄 huàbǐng subject for ridicule; proverb handle: 传为～ pass into a proverb; become a subject for ridicule

话不投机 huàbùtóujī mistime one's remarks; not to talk to the point

话茬儿 huàchár ① thread of discourse: 接上～ take up the thread of a conversation ② tone of one's speech: 听她的～, 这件事不好办。From what she says, that can't be easily done. ③ a cause for dispute; quarrel

话锋 huàfēng thread of discourse; topic of conversation

话家常 huàjiācháng chitchat; exchange small talk

话剧 huàjù modern drama; stage play: ～团 modern drama troupe; theatrical company

话里有话 huàlǐ-yǒuhuà The words mean more than they say.; There is more to it than what is said.; There is something behind what he said.

话题 huàtí topic of conversation; subject of a talk; theme: 换个～ change the subject

话筒 huàtǒng ① microphone ② telephone transmitter

话务员 huàwùyuán switchboard operator

话音 huàyīn ① one's voice in speech: ～儿未落 when one has

hardly finished speaking ② tone;implication:听她的～儿,准是另有打算。Her tone suggests that she has something else in mind.

话语 huàyǔ what one says; words:他～不多,可句句中听。His words are few, but everything he says makes good sense.

画 huà ①〈动〉paint; draw:～素描 make a sketch; sketch ②〈名〉painting; drawing; picture:水彩～ water-colour painting ③〈形〉be decorated with paintings or pictures:～珐琅 painted enamel

画报 huàbào illustrated magazine or newspaper; pictorial

画笔 huàbǐ painting brush; brush

画饼充饥 huàbǐng-chōngjī draw a cake to satisfy (allay) (one's) hunger—feed on illusions; draw a cake and call it a dinner

画册 huàcè album of paintings; picture album

画法 huàfǎ technique of painting or drawing:～新颖 a novel technique in painting or drawing

画舫 huàfǎng gaily-painted pleasure boat

画稿 huàgǎo a preliminary sketch to be painted over; painter's sketch

画家 huàjiā painter; artist

画架 huàjià easel

画刊 huàkān ① pictorial section of a newspaper ② pictorial

画廊 huàláng picture gallery; gallery

画龙点睛 huàlóng-diǎnjīng give (put) the finishing touch to a piece of writing; bring life to an article by adding a few words to it; add the finishing touch

画蛇添足 huàshé-tiānzú draw a snake and add feet to it — ruin the effect by adding something superfluous; To overreach the mark is just as bad as not reaching it.

画师 huàshī ① painter; artist ② artisan-painter

画室 huàshì painting room; studio

画坛 huàtán art circle

画图 huàtú ① draw designs, maps, etc. ② picture (fig.):构成一幅农村生活多彩的～。give a colourful picture of country life

画像 huàxiàng ① portrait; picture ② paint (draw) a portrait; portray

画页 huàyè page with illustrations (in a book or magazine); plate

画展 huàzhǎn art exhibition; exhibition of paintings; picture show

划 huà〈动〉① delimit; divide; differentiate:～定边界 delimit the boundary line ② assign; transfer:～款 transfer money ③〈名〉plan:规～ programme; plan

另见 huá

划拨 huàbō transfer:这笔款子由银行～。This sum of money will be transferred by the bank.

划定 huàdìng delimit；designate：～边界 delimit a boundary line

划分 huàfēn ① divide：～势力范围 carve out spheres of influence；divide into spheres of influence. ～界限 draw a clear demarcation line between；draw a clear-cut line of demarcation between ② classify；differentiate

划归 huàguī put under（sb.'s administration，etc.）；incorporate into：这家工厂已～地方管理。The factory has been put under local administration.

划价 huàjià have a prescription priced（in a hospital dispensary）

划清 huàqīng draw a clear line of demarcation；make a clear distinction：～政策界限 draw distinctions in accordance with the policy

划时代 huàshídài epoch-making；epoch-marking：～的大事 epoch-making event

划线支票 huàxiànzhīpiào crossed check

化

huà〈动〉turn，change；transform：～悲痛为力量 turn grief into strength ② dissolve；melt：～冻 thawing ③ digest：～食 help digestion ④ burn up：～为灰烬 be reduced to ashes ⑤［后缀，加在名词或形容词后构成动词］：-ize；-ify：工业～ industrialize. 电气～ electrify

化冻 huàdòng thaw；melt

化干戈为玉帛 huà gān gē wéi yùbó turn hostility into friendship；bury the hatchet

化公为私 huàgōng-wéisī appropriate public property for private use；turning of public property into private property

化合 huàhé chemical combination：～物 chemical compound

化名 huàmíng assumed name；alias；pseudonym

化身 huàshēn embodiment；personification；incarnation：勇敢的～ embodiment of courage

化石 huàshí fossil

化为乌有 huàwéiwūyǒu come to naught；go up in smoke；dissolve into thin air

化纤 huàxiān chemical fibre；man-made fibre

化险为夷 huàxiǎnwéiyí turn danger into safety；head off a disaster

化学 huàxué chemistry：～鉴定 chemical analysis. ～污染 chemical pollution

化验 huàyàn（laboratory）test；chemical examination：～室 laboratory；lab. ～员 laboratory technician

化缘 huàyuán（of Buddhist monks or Taoist priests）beg alms

化装 huàzhuāng ① make up：～室 dressing room ② disguise oneself：～舞会 fancy dress ball；masquerade

化妆 huàzhuāng put on makeup；make one's toilet；make up；prink（up）：～品 cosmetics；makeup

huái

怀 huái〈名〉① bosom：抱在～里carry in the bosom ② mind; heart：襟～坦白 frank and open-minded〈动〉③ cherish; keep in mind：～着崇敬的心情 hold in high esteem ④ yearn for; think of：～乡 yearn for one's native place ⑤ conceive (a child)：～了孩子 become pregnant; be with child

怀抱 huáibào ① bosom; embrace ② cherish; nourish; entertain：回到…的～ return to the embrace of…

怀表 huáibiǎo pocket watch

怀才不遇 huáicáibùyù be frustrated for one's talent; have unrecognized talents; One's talents remained unrecognized.

怀鬼胎 huái guǐtāi have evil intentions; harbour sinister designs

怀恨在心 huáihèn zài xīn harbour a grudge against; have resentment rankling in one's mind; nurse (harbour) hatred against

怀旧 huáijiù remember past times or old acquaintances (usu. with kindly thoughts)

怀恋 huáiliàn think fondly of (past times, old friends, etc.); look back nostalgically：我深深地～童年的生活。I felt a great nostalgia for my childhood.

怀念 huáiniàn ① long for; yearn for ② think of; miss; cherish the memory of

怀疑 huáiyí suspect; doubt

怀孕 huáiyùn become (be) pregnant; be (heavy) with child; be in the family way

淮 huái

淮北 Huáiběi the area north of the Huaihe River; specifically, northern Anhui Province

淮剧 huáijù Huai opera, popular in northern Jiangsu Province

踝 huái〈名〉ankle

踝骨 huáigǔ anklebone

huài

坏 huài ①〈形〉bad; evil：～书 inferior books ②〈动〉spoil; ruin; go bad：她的身体～了。Her health has broken down. ③〈名〉dirty trick; evil idea：一肚子～水 full of tricks

坏处 huàichu harm; disadvantage

坏掉 huàidiào ①［食品等］go bad：鱼～了。The fish has gone bad. ②［机件等］be out of order; break down：冰箱～了。The frig is out of order.

坏话 huàihuà malicious words; scandal：不要背后讲人～。Don't speak ill of others behind their backs.; Don't backbite people.

坏人 huàirén bad person; evildoer; scoundrel

坏事 huàishì ① evil deed; evildoing; bad thing：～变好事。Bad things can be turned into good things. ② spoil the game

(thing)

坏透 huàitòu downright bad; rotten to the core

坏心眼儿 huàixīnyǎnr 〈口〉 ill will; evil intention

坏帐 huàizhàng bad debt; uncollectible debt

huān

欢 huān 〈形〉 joyous; merry; jubilant: ～声笑语 merry laughter 〈副〉 ② joyfully; merrily: ～唱 sing merrily ③ cheerfully; in full swing: 火着得很～。The defire is burning cheerfully.

欢蹦乱跳 huānbèng-luàntiào healthy-looking and vivacious

欢唱 huānchàng sing merrily

欢度 huāndù spend (an occasion) joyfully; celebrate: ～春节 celebrate the Spring Festival

欢呼 huānhū shout for (with) joy; cheer; hail; acclaim

欢聚 huānjù happy get-together; happy reunion: 国庆节到了,全家老小～在一起。The whole family got together happily for the National Day.

欢聚一堂 huānjù-yītáng happy gathering (union); get together joyously; enjoy a nice get-together

欢快 huānkuài cheerful and light-hearted; lively

欢乐 huānlè joyous; gay; happy: ～的人群 happy crowds

欢庆 huānqìng celebrate with jubilation

欢声雷动 huānshēng-léidòng cheers resound like peals of thunder

欢声笑语 huānshēng-xiàoyǔ happy laughters and cheerful voices.

欢送 huānsòng see (send) sb. off: ～会 farewell meeting; send-off

欢腾 huānténg great rejoicing; jubilation; be transported with joy: 万众～。All the people were transported with joy.

欢天喜地 huāntiān-xǐdì with boundless joy; wild with joy; overjoyed

欢喜 huānxǐ ①joyful; happy; delighted: 欢欢喜喜过春节 spend a joyful Spring Festival ② like; be fond of; delight in: 他～拉手风琴。He likes to play the accordion.

欢喜若狂 huānxǐ-ruòkuáng tread (walk) on air; gloat over; gleefully

欢笑 huānxiào laugh heartily

欢心 huānxīn favour; liking; love: 博取某人的～ win sb.'s favour

欢欣鼓舞 huānxīn-gǔwǔ dance with (for) joy; be filled with exultation; be jubilant; be elated

欢宴 huānyàn entertain at a banquet on some happy occasion; welcome feast

欢迎 huānyíng welcome; greet: ～词 address of welcome; welcome speech. ～惠顾 welcome to enjoy sb.'s service. ～会 welcome party (meeting)

huán

还 huán 〈动〉 ① go (come) back; return: ～家 return home ② return; give back; repay: 把它～给我。Return it back to me. ③ give or do sth. in return: 以其人之道，～治其人之身 deal with a man as he deals with you; pay sb. back in his own coin
另见 hái

还本 huánběn repayment of principal (capital)

还本付息 huánběn fùxī repay capital with interest; pay principle and interest; debt servicing

还魂 huánhún return from the grave; revive after death

还价 huánjià beat a bargain; give a counter-offer

还礼 huánlǐ ① return a salute; acknowledge a salute ② give a gift in return

还清 huánqīng pay up; pay off: ～旧帐 pay off old scores; settle an old score. ～债务 extinction of debt

还俗 huánsú (of Buddhists) return to (resume) secular life; return to the laity; secularization

还原 huányuán ① be restored to the original state or shape: ～主义 reductionism ② [化] reduction ③ [数] return to original equation

还愿 huányuàn ① redeem a vow to a good ② fulfil one's promise

还债 huánzhài pay one's debt; repay a debt; meet one's engagement; pay a debt

还帐 huánzhàng pay one's debt; settle accounts

还嘴 huánzuǐ answer (talk) back; retort

环 huán 〈名〉 ① ring; loop: 耳～ earring ② link: 薄弱的一～ a weak link ③ 〈动〉 encircle; surround; hem in: 这个国家四面～海。The country is encircled by the sea.

环保 huánbǎo environmental protection

环抱 huánbào embrace; encircle; surround: 一个群山～的村庄 a village surrounded by mountains

环城 huánchéng around the city: ～公路 ring road; belt highway; beltway

环节 huánjié ① link; sector: 减少～，提高效率 reduce the number of intermediate links and raise efficiency ② [动物学] segment

环境 huánjìng ① surroundings; environment: ～保护 environmental protection. ～卫生 environmental sanitation. ～污染 environmental pollution. ～噪音 ambient noise. ② circumstances; setting; milieu

环球 huánqiú ① round the world: ～旅行 travel round the world; a round-the-world tour ② the earth; the whole world

环绕 huánrào ① surround; encircle ② revolve around: ～着中心

任务 revolve around one's central task

环卫 huánwèi environmental sanitation：～工人 environmental sanitation workers

环行 huánxíng going in a ring：～公共汽车 bus with a circular route. ～铁路 circuit railway；belt line

huǎn

缓 huǎn ①〈形〉slow；unhurried：～步而行 walk unhurriedly〈动〉② delay；put off；postpone：刻不容～ sth. must be done without delay ③ revive；recuperate；come to：～过劲来 feel refreshed after a breathing spell

缓兵之计 huǎnbīngzhījì delaying (stalling) tactics；stratagem to gain a respire

缓冲 huǎnchōng cushion；buffer：～国 buffer state. ～作用 cushioning effect

缓和 huǎnhé ① relax；alleviate；mitigate：～紧张气氛 relieving the tension ②［国际关系等的］détente

缓急 huǎnjí ① pressing or otherwise；of greater or lesser urgency ② emergency

缓建 huǎnjiàn postpone (delay) construction：～工程 a delayed construction project

缓解 huǎnjiě ease；relax；alleviate

缓慢 huǎnmàn slow：进展～ make slow progress

缓期 huǎnqī postpone a deadline；defer：～执行 suspension of execution

缓刑 huǎnxíng probation；reprieve；suspension of sentence：～2年 be put on two years' probation

缓行 huǎnxíng ① walk or drive slowly ② postpone implementation

huàn

豢 huàn

豢养 huànyǎng keep；feed；groom：～家禽 rear poultry

患 huàn ①〈名〉trouble；disaster；peril：～难之中 in the midst of troubles ②〈动〉be ill with；suffer from：他～了癌症。He was suffering from cancer.

患病 huànbìng be ill；fall sick；suffer from an illness

患得患失 huàndé-huànshī worry about personal gain and loss；think in terms of personal gain and loss；be swayed by considerations of gain and loss

患难 huànnàn trials and tribulations；adversity；trouble：～夫妻 husband and wife who have gone through difficult times together

患难与共 huànnànyǔgòng share weal and woe (joy and sorrow)；come (go) together through thick and thin

患难之交 huànnànzhījiāo friends in adversity；tested friend

患者 huànzhě sufferer；patient：结

核病～ a person suffering from tuberculosis;a TB patient

涣 huàn

涣然 huànrán vanish; disappear

涣散 huànsàn slack; lose; lax; dissipate; sap:士气～ be lax in morale

焕 huàn

焕发 huànfā radiate; shine; glow:容光～ (one's face) glow with health

焕然一新 huànrányīxīn take on an entirely new look; look brand-new; spick and span; take on an altogether new aspect

换 huàn 〈动〉① exchange; barter; trade: ～工 exchange work ② change; replace; relieve:中途～马 change (swop) horses in mid-stream

换班 huànbān ① change shifts ② relieve sb. on duty

换车 huànchē change trains or buses:从工厂回家一路上要换三趟车。I have to change buses three times going home from factory

换代 huàndài replace; regenerate:产品更新～ replace the older generations of products by new ones

换防 huànfáng relieve a garrison

换房 huànfáng exchange houses: ～站 housing exchange office

换工 huàngōng exchange labour

换汇 huànhuì exchange currency: ～成本 costs in terms of foreign exchange

换货 huànhuò exchange commodities; barter: ～和付款协定 goods exchange and payments agreement

换季 huànjì change garments according to the season; wear different clothes for a new season

换钱 huànqián ① change money ② sell sth. for money

换取 huànqǔ exchange (barter) sth. for:～外汇 earning of foreign exchange from

换算 huànsuàn conversion: ～表 conversion table

换汤不换药 huàntāng bù huànyào change in form but not in content; make no change in substance; old wine in new bottle

换文 huànwén exchange notes (letters)

换洗 huànxǐ change clothes (for washing):带一套～衣服。Take along a change of clothes.

换休 huànxiū change the day off

换药 huànyào change dressing; redress (a wound)

换衣 huànyī change one's clothes; change oneself

换约 huànyuē exchange of ratifications

唤 huàn 〈动〉call out:召～ call; summon

唤起 huànqǐ ① arouse:～国民精神 inspire the morale of the people ② call; recall; attract: ～人们的注意 call the people's attention to

唤醒 huànxǐng wake up; awaken; rouse

幻 huàn 〈形〉① magic；unreal；illusive：～想 illusion ② changeable；magic：变～ change irregularly ③〈动〉undergo a surprising change

幻灯 huàndēng slide show；diascope：～机 slide projector；epidiascope. 放～ show slides

幻景 huànjǐng illusion；mirage；phantasm

幻境 huànjìng dreamland；fairyland

幻觉 huànjué hallucination；illusion：～论证 arguments from illusion

幻灭 huànmiè disillusion；vanish into thin air

幻术 huànshù magic；conjuring

幻想 huànxiǎng ① illusion；fantasy；fancy ② dream；figment of one's imagination

幻象 huànxiàng phantasm；mental image；mirage；apparition

huāng

荒 huāng 〈形〉① waste；uncultivated：地～了。The land lies waste (uncultivated). ② desolate；barren：～漠草原 barren grassland ③〈动〉neglect：别把功课～了。Don't neglect your lessons. 〈名〉④ uncultivated land；wasteland：垦～ open up (reclaim) wasteland ⑤ shortage：水～ water shortage ⑥ famine；crop failure

荒草 huāngcǎo weeds

荒诞 huāngdàn fantastic；absurd；preposterous；incredible：～小说 absurdist fiction. ～派作家 absurdist

荒诞无稽 huāngdànwújī fantastic；absurd；incredible：～之谈 a tall story；a preposterous statement

荒地 huāngdì wasteland；uncultivated (undeveloped) land

荒废 huāngfèi ① lie waste；leave uncultivated ② neglect：～学业 neglect one's studies

荒凉 huāngliáng desolate；deserted：满目～ a scene of desolation

荒谬 huāngmiù absurd；ludicrous；preposterous；ridiculous：～绝伦 absurd to the extreme；absolutely preposterous；sheer nonsense. ～的指责 ridiculous charge

荒年 huāngnián year of bad harvest；famine (lean) year

荒疏 huāngshū be out of practice；become rusty：她的法语～了。Her French has become rusty.

荒唐 huāngtáng ① absurd；fantastic；ludicrous；preposterous ② loose；wild：过～生活 lead a loose life

荒无人烟 huāngwú-rényān desolate and uninhabited：～的地带 a region with no sign of human habitation

荒芜 huāngwú lie waste；go out of cultivation

荒淫 huāngyín dissolute；debauched；licentious：～奢侈的生活 an idle (debauched) and extravagant life. ～无耻 dissipated and unashamed；given to debauchery; be dissolute in conduct

慌 huāng 〈形〉① flurried; confused: 心～意乱 mentally confused ② be scared; get flustered: ～作一团 be thrown into utter confusion

慌慌张张 huānghuāng-zhāngzhāng in a flurry; helter-skelter

慌乱 huāngluàn become alarmed and bewildered; get confused; fall into a flutter; flurried; alarmed and bewildered

慌忙 huāngmáng in a great rush; in a flurry; hurriedly: ～起身迎客 hurriedly rise to greet one's guest

慌手慌脚 huāngshǒu-huāngjiǎo in a rush; in a flurry

慌张 huāngzhāng flurried; confused; flustered: 神色～ look flustered (flurried)

huáng

黄 huáng ①〈形〉yellow; sallow: ～酒 yellow rice wine ②〈动〉fall through; fizzle out: 那笔买卖～了。The deal is off.

黄包车 huángbāochē rickshaw

黄豆 huángdòu soya bean; soybean

黄瓜 huángguā cucumber

黄河 huánghé Huanghe (Yellow) River

黄褐色 huánghèsè brownish yellow; tan; tawny

黄花菜 huánghuācài day lily

黄花鱼 huánghuāyú yellow croaker

黄昏 huánghūn dusk

黄金 huángjīn gold: ～储备 gold reserve. ～时代 golden age. ～时间[电视] prime time; good TV time; peak viewing time

黄酒 huángjiǔ yellow rice or millet wine; Shaoxing wine

黄历 huánglì almanac

黄粱美梦 huángliáng-měimèng Golden Millet Dream; fond dream; pipe dream; heady dream

黄梅戏 huángméixì Huangmei opera

黄牌 huángpái [体] yellow card

黄色 huángsè ① yellow (colour) ② blue; obscene; pornographic: ～报刊 scandal sheet. ～小说 pornographic novel. ～影片 blue film; sexy movie

黄色人种 huángsè rénzhǒng yellow race

黄鳝 huángshàn ricefield eel; finless eel

黄铜 huángtóng brass: ～制品 brass work. ～工艺制品厂 brazier

黄土 huángtǔ loess: ～高原 loess high-land (plateau)

黄油 huángyóu butter

磺 huáng [化] sulphur

簧 huáng 〈名〉① [乐] reed ② spring: 闹钟的～断了。The main spring of the alarm clock is broken.

簧乐器 huángyuèqì reed instrument

皇 huáng 〈名〉emperor: 女～

empress
皇朝 huāngcháo feudal dynasty
皇储 huángchǔ crown prince; designated heir to the throne; heir apparent
皇帝 huángdì emperor: ～的谕旨 imperial edicts
皇宫 huánggōng imperial palace
皇冠 huángguān imperial crown
皇后 huánghòu empress
皇家 huángjiā royal (imperial) family (house): ～家谱 records of the imperial family
皇陵 huánglíng imperial mausoleum
皇母 huángmǔ imperial mothers
皇亲国戚 huángqīn-guóqì relatives of the emperor
皇权 huángquán imperial authority; power in the royal house; regal authority
皇室 huángshì ruling house; royal house; imperial family
皇太后 huántàihòu empress dowager
皇太子 huángtàizǐ crown prince; heir apparent

惶 huáng 〈名〉 fear; anxiety
惶惶 huánghuáng in anxiety; in alarm: ～不可终日 be in a state of constant anxiety; be on tenterhooks all the time; be kept perpetually in a state of tension
惶惑 huánghuò perplexed and alarmed; apprehensive: ～不安 perplexed and uneasy
惶恐 huángkǒng frightened; terrified: ～万状 be frightened out of one's wits; be seized with fear
惶恐不安 huángkǒng-bù'an in a state of alarm (trepidation)

煌 huáng 〈形〉 bright; brilliant

蝗 huáng 〈名〉 locust
蝗灾 huángzāi plague of locusts

huǎng

谎 huǎng 〈名〉 lie
谎报 huǎngbào lie about; give false information: ～年龄 lie about one's age
谎称 huǎngchēng falsely claim to be; pretend to be
谎话 huǎnghuà lie; falsehood
谎言 huǎngyán lie; falsehood

恍 huǎng
恍惚 huǎnghū ① dimly; vaguely ② in a trance: 精神～ be in a trance
恍然大悟 huǎngrándàwù realize all of a sudden; be suddenly aware (of); dawn on; suddenly see the light

晃 huǎng 〈动〉 dazzle: 亮得～眼 dazzingly bright ② flash past: 一～一年过去了。A year passed in a flash.
另见 huàng

幌 huǎng
幌子 huǎngzi ① shop sign; signboard ② cover; smokescreen; guise; pretence

huàng

晃 huàng 〈动〉 shake; sway 另见 huǎng

晃动 huàngdòng sway; rock:别～桌子。Don't wobble the desk.

晃悠 huàngyou shake from side to side; stagger; wobble

huī

挥 huī 〈动〉 wave; wield:～笔 wield the brush ② wipe off:～泪 wipe away tears; wipe one's eyes ③ scatter; disperse:～霍国家财产 squander the state's property

挥动 huīdòng wave; brandish:～拳头 shake one's fist

挥发 huīfā volatilize:瓶盖没拧紧,里面的酒精都～光了。Because the top is loose, the alcohol inside has volatilized. ～性 volatility

挥霍 huīhuò spend freely (lavishly); squander:～国家资金 squander state funds

挥金如土 huījīn-rútǔ spend money like dirt (water); throw money about like water; money burning one's pocket

挥泪 huīlèi wipe away tears; wipe one's eyes:～而别 take a tearful leave

挥师 huīshī command an army:～北上 command an army to march north

挥手 huīshǒu wave one's hand:～告别 wave good-bye (to); wave farewell (to):～致意 wave greetings to sb.

挥舞 huīwǔ wave; flourish; brandish:～花束表示欢迎 wave bouquets (to sb.) in welcome

辉 huī ①〈名〉 brightness; splendour; brilliance ②〈动〉 shine:互相～映 shine by reflected glory

辉煌 huīhuáng splendid; brilliant; glorious:～胜利 brilliant (signal) victory

辉耀 huīyào shine; illuminate

辉映 huīyìng reflect; illuminate; shine:交相～ reflect radiance to each other; vie with each other for radiance

灰 huī 〈名〉 ① ash:草～ straw ashes ② dust:一层～ a layer of dust 〈形〉 ③ grey:～马 a grey horse ④ disheartened; despondent:～溜溜地 down in the mouth

灰暗 huī'àn dark; gloomy

灰白 huībái pale; grey; greyish white:他脸色～。He looks pale.

灰尘 huīchén dust; dirt

灰溜溜 huīliūliū ① dull grey ② gloomy dejected; crestfallen:他看起来有点～的样子。He looked a little crestfallen (depressed).

灰蒙蒙 huīmēngmēng dusky; overcast

灰色 huīsè ① grey; ashy ② pessimistic; gloomy:～人生观 a pessimistic (grey) outlook on life ③ obscure; ambiguous

灰心 huīxīn be (feel) discouraged; lose heart:～丧气 downhearted; downcast

恢 huī

恢复 huīfù recover; restore; resume; regain:～健康 recover one's health; recuperate. ～名誉 rehabilitate one's reputation. ～元气 recover one's impaired energy; recuperate

恢恢 huīhuī extensive; vast:天网～,疏而不漏。The net of Heaven has large meshes, but it lets nothing through.

诙 huī

诙谐 huīxié ① humorous; jocular:～曲[乐] humoresque; scherzo. ～作品[文学] burlesque

徽 huī 〈名〉 badge; emblem

徽号 huīhào title of honour; good name

徽记 huījì sign; mark

徽章 huīzhāng badge; insignia

huí

回 huí 〈动〉 ① go back; return:～故乡 return to one's hometown ② turn round:～过身来 turn round ③ answer; reply:～信 send a letter in reply; write back 〈名〉 ④ chapter:这部小说有一百～。This novel has a hundred chapters. ⑤ time:来过一～ have been here once

回拜 huíbài return a visit

回报 huíbào ① report back on what has been done ② repay; requite; reciprocate:～他的盛情 repay him for his hospitality or kindness ③ retaliate; get one's own back

回避 huíbì ① evade; shun; avoid; get round; parry; sidestep:～要害问题 steer clear of the crucial question ②[法] withdrawal

回潮 huícháo ① turn damp again ② relapse; tide reversion; reversion

回程 huíchéng way back; return trip; return:～运费 backfreight

回答 huídá answer; reply; response

回单 huídān a short note acknowledging receipt of sth.; receipt

回电 huídiàn ① reply by telegram; wire back:～费已付 reply paid ② call back; phone back:要我～吗? Shall I call back?

回复 huífù ① reply (to a letter) ② restore; recover:～原状 restore to its original shape

回顾 huígù ① look back ② review; retrospect:～过去 review the past. ～展 retrospective show (exhibition)

回归 huíguī ① regression; reconciliation; retreat:～教育 regression education ② return; revert

回教 huíjiào Islam:～徒 Moslem

回敬 huíjìng ① return a compliment; do or give sth. in return：～一杯 drink a toast in return ② give sb. tit for tat

回绝 huíjué refuse；decline

回扣 huíkòu commission；kickback；sales commission；rebates

回礼 huílǐ ① return a compliment or a salute ② give a present in return

回笼 huílóng ① steam again ② withdraw；recall：～货币 withdraw surplus paper money

回民 huímín the Huis；the Hui people

回去 huíqù ① return；go back；be back：她明天回广州去。She will return to Guangzhou tomorrow. ②［用在动词后面］back (there)：请把这封信给她退～。Please return the letter to her.

回升 huíshēng go up (rise) again；pick up：产量～。The output is picking up.

回收 huíshōu recover；retrieve；reclaim：～废品 collect waste material. ～率 rate of recovery. ～值 recovery value

回首 huíshǒu ① turn one's head ② look back upon；recall：不堪～ can't bear to think of the past

回溯 huísù recall；review；look back to (upon)：～过去 recall the past

回条 huítiáo ① receipt ② note of reply；short reply

回头 huítóu ① turn round；look back ② repent ③ by and by；soon；later：～见！See you later!

回头是岸 huítóushì'àn turn from one's evil ways；turn back to safety；Repentance is salvation.；There is yet time for you to mend your ways.；It is never too late to mend.

回味 huíwèi ① aftertaste ② call sth. to mind and ponder over it：～他说的话 ponder over what he has said

回乡 huíxiāng return to one's native place：～知青 educated youths who return to the countryside

回想 huíxiǎng recall；recollect；think back

回响 huíxiǎng reverberate；echo；resound

回心转意 huíxīn-zhuǎnyì turn back one's heart and change one's mind；change one's views；come around to the correct way of thinking

回信 huíxìn ① write in reply；write back：望早日～。I'm looking forward to hearing from you soon. ② a letter in reply ③ a verbal message in reply；reply

回旋 huíxuán ① circle round：飞机在上空～。The airplane is circling overhead. ② manoeuvre：～余地 room for manoeuvre

回忆 huíyì recollect；recall；look back upon；call to mind：～录 recollections；reminiscences；memoirs. ～论证 argument from recollections

回音 huíyīn ① echo ② reply

回赠 huízèng send a present in return;present a gift in return

回执 huízhí a short note acknowledging receipt of sth. ; receipt

回族 Huízú the Hui nationality, or the Huis, mainly distributed over the Ningxia Hui Autonomous Region, Gansu, Henan, Hebei, Qinghai, Shandong, Yunnan, Anhui, the Xinjiang Uygur Autonomous Region, Liaoning, Beijing and Tianjin

huǐ

悔 huǐ〈动〉repent; regret:追～莫及 too late to repent

悔不当初 huǐbùdāngchū regret a previous mistake; regret having done sth.

悔改 huǐgǎi repent and mend one's ways; repent:～程度 extent of repentance. ～态度 attitude towards repentance

悔过 huǐguò repent one's error; be repentant

悔过自新 huǐguò-zìxīn repent and turn over a new leaf; repent and make a fresh start

悔恨 huǐhèn deeply regret; feel bitter remorse (for); be filled with remorse:～交加 be stung by remorse

悔悟 huǐwù realize one's error and show repentance

悔罪 huǐzuì show repentance

毁 huǐ〈动〉① destroy; ruin; damage:～于一旦 be destroyed in one day ② burn to ashes; burn up:焚～ destroy by fire ③ defame; slander:诋～ slander; vilify

毁谤 huǐbàng slander; malign; calumniate; disparagement:～名誉 character assassination

毁坏 huǐhuài destory; ruin; demage; demolish:～公共财物 deface public property.

毁灭 huǐmiè wipe out; wreck; destory:～物证 destroy the material evidence. ～罪证 destroy criminal evidence

毁容 huǐróng disfigure one's face

毁伤 huǐshāng injure; hurt; damage

毁损 huǐsǔn impair; damage; spoil:～赔偿 indenmity for damage. 很多古代建筑遭到～。Many ancient buildings have been damaged

毁誉 huǐyù praise or blame; praise or censure (condemnation)

毁约 huǐyuē scrap a contract (treaty); breach of promise

huì

汇 huì〈动〉① converge:人类知识的～流 convergence of human knowledge ② gather together ③ remit:电～ telegraphic transfer

汇报 huìbào briefing; report; give an account of:～会 report-back meeting. ～思想 report one's own thoughts to. ～演出 report-back performance

汇编 huìbiān compilation; corpus; collection: 文件～ a collection of documents

汇拨支付 huìbō-zhīfù payment by remittance

汇兑 huìduì remittance: 国内～ domestic remittance. ～率 rate of exchange. ～银行 exchange bank

汇费 huìfèi remittance charge (fee); charge for remittances

汇合 huìhé converge; join: 四条支流的～口 the confluence of four tributaries

汇寄 huìjì remit: 通过邮局～款项 remit (send) money by post

汇价 huìjià rates of exchange; conversion rate

汇款 huìkuǎn ① remit money; make a remittance ② remittance: ～单 money order. ～人 remitter. ～收款人 beneficiary of remittance

汇率 huìlǜ exchange rate: ～并轨 official rate of exchange for *Renminbi* was made uniform with the market rate. ～下跌 exchange rate depreciation

汇票 huìpiào money order; draft; bill of exchange: 邮政～ postal order; (postal) money order. ～到期 bill to fall due. ～贴现 discount of bill

汇(会)演 huìyǎn joint performance (Various units from various localities pull together their theatrical programmes and perfrom them singly or together. It serves the function of reporting, learning from each other, and exchanging experience.)

汇总 huìzǒng gather; collect; pool: 把材料～上报 collect data for the higher level; present an itemized report to the higher level

汇总缴纳 huìzǒng jiǎonà pay on a consolidated basis

讳 huì ①〈动〉avoid as taboo: 无庸～言 no need for reticence; it is no secret that… ②〈名〉taboo; forbidden word

讳疾忌医 huìjíjìyī conceal one's sickness for fear of treatment; conceal a malady for fear of taking medicine; hide one's mistakes for fear of criticism

讳莫如深 huìmòrúshēn carefully conceal (avoid) mentioning (scandal); keep sth. dark; not breathe a single word to a soul

讳言 huìyán avoid mentioning sth.; dare not or would not speak up

彗 huì〈名〉broom

彗星 huìxīng comet

贿 huì〈动〉bribe: 行～ practise bribery; bribe

贿赂 huìlù ① offer bribes to sb.; butter up; bribe ② bribery: ～物 bribe

贿通 huìtōng buy over; buy off; bribe

秽 huì〈形〉① dirty: 污～ filthy ② ugly; abominable: ～行 immoral conduct; abominable behaviour; scandalous conduct

秽亵 huìxiè ① filthy; foul ② obscene; salacious; bawdy

秽语 huìyǔ obscene words; lewd speech

会 huì 〈动〉① get together; assemble: ～战 join in a battle ② meet; see: 昨天我没有～着她。I didn't see her yesterday. ③ understand; grasp: 心领神～ understand tacitly ④ can; be able to: 她～游泳。She can swim. ⑤ be good at; be skilful in: 挺～过日子 can manage to get along quite well ⑥ be likely to; be sure to: 他们不～不来。They are sure to come. 〈名〉⑦ meeting; gathering; party: 欢送～ send-off party ⑧ society; association: ～馆 provincial guild ⑨ chief city; capital: 省～ provincial capital ⑩ opportunity; occasion
另见 kuài

会餐 huìcān dine together; have a dinner party

会费 huìfèi membership dues (fees)

会馆 huìguǎn guild hall; provincial or county guild

会合 huìhé join forces; meet; assemble

会话 huìhuà conversation (as in a language course)

会见 huìjiàn meet with; interview

会聚 huìjù assemble; flock together: 游园群众～于各个公园，欢庆五一节。Holidaymakers flocked to the parks to celebrate May Day.

会客 huìkè receive visitors (guests): ～室 reception room (chamber)

会面 huìmiàn meet

会期 huìqī ① date for a meeting ② duration of a meeting; session: ～一个星期。The meeting will last a week.

会签 huìqiān countersign; countersignature; (of two or more than two units) jointly sign an official document

会商 huìshāng confer (with sb. on sth.); talk (sth. over with sb.)

会审 huìshěn joint hearing; joint trial

会谈 huìtán talk; negotiation: 与某人举行～ hold talks with sb.. ～纪要 minutes of talks

会同 huìtóng (handle an affair) jointly with other organizations concerned: 这件事由计委～对外贸易经济合作部审批。This matter is subject to joint examination and approval by the State Planning Commission and the Ministry of Foreign Trade and Economic Cooperation

会务 huìwù administrative matters concerning a meeting

会晤 huìwù meet: 两国外长定期～。The foreign ministers of the two coutries meet regularly.

会演 huìyǎn joint performance; festival: 文艺～ theatrical festival

会议 huìyì ① meeting; conference: 正式～ official meeting

会战 huìzhàn ① decisive battle

(between the opposing armies) ②battle; campaign; join in a battle

会诊 huìzhěn (hold a) joint conference to diagnose a case; (have a) consultation of doctors; join in treatment

荟 huì 〈形〉 luxuriant growth (of plants)

荟萃 huìcuì (of distinguished people or exquisite objects) gather together; assemble: 人才～ a galaxy of talent. ～一堂 a distinguished gathering; gather together in one hall

绘 huì 〈动〉 draw; paint

绘画 huìhuà painting; drawing: ～陈列馆 picture gallery. ～艺术 pictorial art

绘声绘色 huìshēng-huìsè vivid; lifelike; lively: ～的描述 a vivid description

绘制 huìzhì drawing (chart or diagram)

烩 huì 〈动〉① braise: ～虾仁 braised shrimp meat ② cook (rice or shredded pancakes) with meat, vegetables and water

诲 huì 〈动〉 teach

诲人不倦 huìrénbùjuàn be tireless in teaching; be never tired of teaching; teach with tireless zeal

诲淫诲盗 huìyín-huìdào propagate sex and violence; stir up the base passions

晦 huì ①〈形〉 dark; dim; obscure ②〈名〉 night: 风雨如～。 It blows and rains like a dark night.

晦暗 huì'àn dark and gloomy

晦气 huìqì unlucky; unfortunate; bad luck: 真～! What bad luck!

晦涩 huìsè hard to understand; obscure; unclear in meaning: 一篇充满～文字的哲学文章 a philosophical essay full of obscurities

惠 huì ①〈名〉favour; kindness; benefit ②〈形〉kind; gracious ③ (Hui) a surname

惠存 huìcún please keep (this photograph, book, etc. as a souvenir); to so-and-so.

惠顾 huìgù your patronage: 欢迎～。 (used by shopkeepers) Your patronage is solicited.

惠临 huìlín your gracious presence: 敬请～。 Your presence is requested.

惠允 huìyǔn be kind enough to allow one (to do sth.)

慧 huì 〈形〉 intelligent; bright

慧心 huìxīn wisdom

慧眼 huìyǎn ① [佛] a mind which perceives both past and future ② mental discernment (perception); insight; acumen: 独具～ have exceptional insight

hūn

荤 hūn 〈名〉 meat or fish

荤菜 hūncài meat dishes

昏 hūn〈名〉① dusk：～暗的暮色中 in the gathering dusk〈形〉② dark：天～地暗 a murky sky over a dark earth ③ muddled；confused：～头～脑 become muddled ④〈动〉faint；lose consciousness：她～过去了。She fainted away.

昏暗 hūn'àn dim；dusky：～的灯光 a dim light

昏沉 hūnchén ① murky ② dazed；befuddled

昏倒 hūndǎo fall into a swoon；faint

昏昏欲睡 hūnhūn-yùshuì drowsy；sleepy

昏厥 hūnjué faint；swoon：～过去 fall into a coma；faint away

昏迷 hūnmí lose one's consciousness；faint；coma；stupor：～不醒 remain unconscious

昏天黑地 hūntiān-hēidì ① heaven and earth in darkness ② be in a state of delirium；lose consciousness：当时我流血过多，觉得～的。I blacked out through loss of blood. ③ dissipated：过着荒淫无耻、～的生活 lead an immoral life，given to dissipation and sensuality ④ dark rule and social disorder

昏头昏脑 hūntóu-hūnnǎo ① utterly confused；muddle-headed；addleheaded ② forgetful；absentminded

昏眩 hūnxuán feel dizzy (giddy)

昏庸 hūnyōng stupid；fatuous；muddleheaded

婚 hūn ①〈动〉wed；marry：已～ married ②〈名〉marriage；wedding

婚假 hūnjià marriage leave

婚嫁 hūnjià marriage

婚礼 hūnlǐ wedding（marriage；matrimonial）ceremony；wedding

婚龄 hūnlíng（legally）marriageable age

婚配 hūnpèi married：子女两人，均未～。Both son and daughter are unmarried.

婚外恋 hūnwàiliàn extramarital affair (love)

婚姻 hūnyīn marriage；matrimony：～登记 registration of marriage. ～介绍所 matrimonial agency；match-making service. ～法 marriage law. ～纠纷 marital (marriage) dispute. ～自由 freedom of marriage

婚育期 hūnyùqī marriage and childbirth period

婚约 hūnyuē engagement；marriage contract

hún

浑 hún〈形〉① muddy；turbid：～水 muddy water ② stupid；foolish：你这人好～啊！How stupid you are！③ unsophisticated；simple and natural ④ whole；all over：～身是胆雄赳赳 be filled with courage and strength

浑厚 húnhòu ① simple and honest；honest-minded ②［书画等］natural and powerful：笔力～ with natural and powerful strokes

浑话 húnhuà impudent remark

浑浑噩噩 húnhún-è'è muddle-headed;muddle along;ignorant

浑朴 húnpǔ simple and natural; unsophisticated

浑身 húnshēn all over the body: ～湿透 sopping wet; be drenched to the skin; be wet all over. 那女演员施展～解数来表演。The actress emoted for all she was worth.

浑水摸鱼 húnshuǐ-mōyú fish in troubled waters

浑圆 húnyuán perfectly round:～的珍珠 a perfectly round pearl

浑浊 húnzhuó dirty; turbid

魂

hún〈名〉① soul ② mood; spirit:失～落魄 be scared out of wits

魂不附体 húnbùfùtǐ be frightened out of one's wits; as if the soul had left the body

魂不守舍 húnbùshǒushè be scared out of one's wits; have lost one's mind

魂飞魄散 húnfēipòsàn be scared out of one's wits; be half dead with fright

魂魄 húnpò soul

馄

hún

馄饨 húndùn *wonton* (huntun); dumpling soup

hùn

诨

hùn〈名〉joke; jest

诨名 hùnmíng nickname

混

hùn〈动〉① mix; mingle; confuse:～淆是非 confuse right and wrong ② pass off as; pass for:鱼目～珠 pass off fish eyes as pearls ③ muddle along; drift along:依靠说谎～日子 muddle through deception ④ get along with sb.: ～熟 get to know sb.; mix with sb.

混充 hùnchōng pass oneself (sth.) off as:～内行 pass oneself off as an expert

混沌 hùndùn chaos:～运动 chaotic movement (motion)

混饭吃 hùnfàn chī engage in a job for the sake of making a living (without having any real interest in it)

混纺 hùnfǎng mixture fabric; mixed fibres; be woven of mixed fibres

混关 hùnguān smuggle through customs (i. e., violate regulations and smuggle items through customs)

混合 hùnhé mix; blend; mingle: ～成本 mixed cost. ～法庭 mixed court. ～经济 mixed economy. ～家庭 composite family. ～诉讼 mixed action.

混进 hùnjìn infiltrate; sneak into; worm one's way into

混乱 hùnluàn confusion; mess; turmoil; disorder:～不堪 be in utter disorder

混凝土 hùnníngtǔ concrete:～搅拌机 concrete mixer

混日子 hùnrìzi dawdle (potter) away one's time; loaf

混同 hùntóng confuse; mix up

混为一谈 hùnwéiyītán equate…with; lump together; confuse (with); confound… with; mix; jumble together

混淆 hùnxiáo mix up; confuse; blur: ～黑白 confuse black and white; juggle (mix up) black and white; obliterate difference between black and white. ～视听 confuse the public

混血儿 hùnxuè'ér a person of mixed blood; half-breed

混战 hùnzhàn tangled warfare: 军阀～ tangled warfare among warlords; tangled fighting between warlords. 球门前一场～,球被捅进了球门。In a scramble in front of the goal, the ball was kicked in.

混浊 hùnzhuó muddy; dirty; turbid

huō

豁 huō 〈动〉① split; break; crack: 墙上～了一个口子。There is a breach in the wall. ② give up; abandon; sacrifice 另见 huò

豁出去 huōchūqu go ahead regardless; be ready to risk everything

豁口 huōkǒu crack; opening; breach

huó

活 huó ①〈动〉live: 他～到 90 岁。He lived to be ninety. 〈形〉② living; live: ～的榜样 living example ③ active; lively; vivid: 脑子很～ have a quick mind ④ movable; moving: ～动资本 liquid capital ⑤〈副〉simply; exactly: ～像 look exactly ⑥〈名〉work: 零～ odd jobs

活宝 huóbǎo a funny fellow; a bit of a clown

活蹦乱跳 huóbèng-luàntiào skip and jump about; gambol; frolic: 孩子们在雪地里～。The children were frolicking happily in the snow.

活标本 huóbiāoběn living specimen

活到老,学到老 huódào lǎo, xuédào lǎo keep on learning as long as you live; one is never too old to learn

活动 huódòng ① activity; manoeuvre: ～成本 cost of activities. ～教学 activity teaching ② movable; mobile; active: ～机能 active function ③ exercise one's influence unfairly; use irregular means

活佛 huófó [宗] Living Buddha

活化石 huóhuàshí living fossil

活计 huóji ① handicraft work; manual labour: 针线～ needlework ② handiwork; work: 她拿着～给大家看。She showed her work to everybody.

活教材 huójiàocái live teaching material

活口 huókǒu ① a survivor of a murder attempt ② a prisoner who can furnish information ③ keep body and soul together;

eke out an existence ④ flexible tone;flexible words

活力 huólì vitality; vigour:充满～ be full of vigour. ～论[哲] vitalism

活灵活现 huólíng-huóxiàn life-like; vivid:说得～ give a vivid description; make it come to life

活龙活现 huólóng-huóxiàn vivid; lively:说得～ give a vivid description (of); describe vividly

活路 huólù ① means of subsistence; way out ② workable method

活泼 huópo ① lively; vivacious; vivid:天真～的孩子 lively children ② [化]reactive

活期 huóqī current:～存款 current deposit. ～利息 current interest

活生生 huóshēngshēng ① real; living:～的例子 a living example ② while still alive

活受罪 huóshòuzuì suffer a living hell; have a hell of a life

活样板 huóyàngbǎn living example

活页 huóyè loose-leaf:～笔记本 loose-leaf notebook

活跃 huóyuè ① active; animated; brisk ② animate; enliven:～市场 enliven the market; liven up the market

活捉 huózhuō capture alive

活字典 huózìdiǎn a walking dictionary

和 huó 〈动〉 mix (powder) (with water, etc.)
另见 hé, huò

和面 huómiàn knead dough

huǒ

火 huǒ 〈名〉 ① fire; blaze:文～ soft (slow) fire ② firearms; ammunition:停～ cease fire ③ anger; temper:冒～ get angry; burn with anger 〈形〉 ④ fiery; flaming:～红 red as fire ⑤ pressing; urgent:～速回电。Cable reply immediately.

火把 huǒbǎ torch:～节 Torch Festival

火暴(爆) huǒbào ① fiery; irritable:～性子 a hot temper ② vigorous; exuberant; lively; exploding; burgeoning:～的球市 exploding (burgeoning) football market

火并 huǒbìng open fight between factions; internecine warfare

火柴 huǒchái match:划根～ strike a match. ～盒 matchbox

火车 huǒchē train:～上交货价 free on rail. ～票 railway (train) ticket. ～站 railway station

火罐 huǒguàn [中医] cupping jar (glass)

火锅 huǒguō chafing dish

火红 huǒhóng red as fire; fiery; flaming:～的太阳 a flaming sun

火候 huǒhou ① duration and degree of heating, cooking, smelting, etc.:炒菜掌握～很重要。Heat control is very important in stir-frying. ② level of attainment; ③ a crucial moment

火花 huǒhuā spark; sparkle; fire

火化(葬) huǒhuà(zàng) cremate; cremation

火鸡 huǒjī turkey

火箭 huǒjiàn rocket: 发射~ launch (fire) a rocket

火警 huǒjǐng fire alarm

火炬 huǒjù torch: ~计划 Torch Plan (to promote the commercialization of research results in the areas of high and new technology, and the formation and development of new and advanced technological industries)

火炕 huǒkàng heated brick bed; heated *kang*

火坑 huǒkēng living hell; abyss of suffering: 跳出~ escape from the living hell

火力 huǒlì firepower; fire: ~发电站 thermal power station (plant)

火气 huǒqì anger; temper: ~很大 have a bad temper

火热 huǒrè ① burning hot; fervent; fiery: ~的斗争 fiery struggle ② intimate

火山 huǒshān volcano: ~爆发 volcanic eruption

火上加油 huǒshàng-jiāyóu pour oil over the flames; add fuel to the fire; add fuel to the flames (fire); aggravate the situation; stir things up

火烧火燎 huǒshāo-huǒliǎo ① feeling terribly hot; ② restless with anxiety.

火速 huǒsù at top speed; posthaste: ~增援 rush up reinforcements

火险 huǒxiǎn fire insurance: 给房子保~ insure one's house against fire

火星 huǒxīng ① spark ② [天文] Mars

火眼金睛 huǒyǎn-jīnjīng fiery eyes and diamond pupils—discerning eyes

火药 huǒyào gunpowder; powder explosives: ~库 magazine. ~味 gunpowder odour

火灾 huǒzāi fire; conflagration: ~保险 fire insurance. ~保险公司 fire office. ~损失评定 fire loss adjustment

火葬场 huǒzàngchǎng crematorium; crematory

火中取栗 huǒzhōng-qǔlì pull (sb. 's) chestnuts out of the fire; act as a cat's paw

火种 huǒzhǒng ① kindling material; kindling; tinder ② live cinders kept for starting a new fire: 革命的~sparks of revolution; seeds of revolution

伙

huǒ 〈名〉① mess; meals; board: 在校入~ board at school ② partner; mate ③ partnership; company: ~耕 plough the fields in partnership ④ group; band: 一~强盗 a band of robbers

伙伴 huǒbàn parther; companion; co-worker

伙计 huǒji ① [旧] shop assistant; salesman ② partner

伙食 huǒshí mess; meals; food

伙食科 huǒshíkē catering office

伙同 huǒtóng gang up with; collude with; in league with; in collusion with

huò

豁 huò ①〈形〉open clear; open-minded ②〈动〉exempt; remit
另见 huō

豁达 huòdá open-minded; open and clear; sanguine; optimistic: ～达大度 open-minded and magnanimous

豁朗 huòlǎng high-spirited; broad-minded

豁亮 huòliàng ① roomy and bright: 这屋子又干净,又～。The room is clean, bright and spacious. ② sonorous; resonant: 嗓音～ have a sonorous voice

豁免 huòmiǎn exempt (from); remit: ～捐税 exempt sb. from duties

豁然 huòrán suddenly; all of a sudden: ～开朗 suddenly see the whole thing clearly; be enlightened all of a sudden

祸 huò ①〈名〉misfortune; calamity: 大～临头 disaster strikes ②〈动〉bring calamity to (upon); ruin

祸不单行 huòbùdānxíng Misfortunes never come alone.; An evil chance seldom comes alone.

祸从口出 huòcóngkǒuchū trouble comes out of the mouth (i. e. from a loose tongue)

祸从天降 huòcóngtiānjiàng a disaster descends from heaven (i. e. befalls sb. unexpectedly)

祸端 huòduān the source of the disaster; the cause of ruin

祸根 huògēn root of the trouble; source of disaster; bane

祸国殃民 huòguó-yāngmín bring calamity to the country and the people; be a bane to the state and the people

祸害 huòhài disaster; scourge; evil; vice

祸患 huòhuàn disaster; calamity

祸乱 huòluàn disastrous disorder; turmoil; social upheaval

祸首 huòshǒu chief culprit; arch-criminal

祸心 huòxīn evil intent; malicious intentions

祸殃 huòyāng disaster; calamity; catastrophe

霍 huò〈副〉① suddenly ② quickly; rapidly

霍地 huòdì suddenly: ～立起身来 suddenly stand up; spring to one's feet

霍乱 huòluàn［医］cholera

霍然 huòrán ① quickly; suddenly ② recover quickly (from an illness); be cured quickly

获 huò〈动〉① catch; capture: 捕～ capture ② get; obtain: ～得称赞 win acclaim ③ reap; get: 收～ harvest; bring in the crops

获得 huòdé get; gain; obtain; achieve: ～新生 get a new lease of life; turn over a new leaf

获奖 huòjiǎng win a prize; be awarded a prize: ～作品 an award-winning work
获利 huòlì make a profit; reap profits: ～年度 profit-making year. ～万元 make a profit of 10,000 *yuan*
获取 huòqǔ procure; obtain; gain; reap: ～暴利 reap staggering (colossal) profits
获胜 huòshèng gain (win) a victory; triumph
获释 huòshì be set free; be released; get-off
获悉 huòxī learn (of an event)
获准 huòzhǔn get (obtain) permission

或 huò ①〈副〉perhaps; maybe: 他们明晨～可到达。They may arrive tomorrow morning. ②〈连〉or; either… or…: 你～我必须参加这个会。Either you or I must attend the meeting.
或多或少 huòduō huòshǎo more or less; to a greater or lesser extent
或许 huòxǔ perhaps; maybe; probably
或者 huòzhě perhaps; maybe: 说他们的工作样样都好～一无是处,都是错误的。It is wrong to regard their work either as totally good or as completely bad.

和 huò〈动〉mix; blend: 豆沙里～点儿糖 mix a little sugar into the bean paste
另见 hé, huó
和稀泥 huòxīní ① mix mud ② reconcile differences regardless of principles; settle a difference by way of compromise; try to mediate differences at the sacrifice of principles; try to smooth things over

货 huò〈名〉① money: 通～ currency ② goods; commodity: 接～ receive goods ③ blockhead: 蠢～ idiot; blockhead
货币 huòbì money; currency; [硬币] coin: ～流通量 currency in circulation. ～回笼 withdrawal of currency from circulation. ～主义学派 currency doctrine school of economics. 储备～ reserve currency
货舱 huòcāng (cargo) hold; cargo bay (of a plane)
货场 huòchǎng freight yard; goods yard
货车 huòchē ① goods (freight) train ② freight car (wagon); goods van (wagon) ③ truck; lorry
货船 huòchuán cargo steamer (ship, vessel); freighter
货单 huòdān manifest; waybill; shipping list
货到付款 huòdào fùkuǎn cash on delivery (COD); cash against delivery; pay on delivery
货方 huòfāng cargo interests
货柜 huòguì ① counter; bar ② container
货机 huòjī cargo aircraft (plane); air freighter
货价 huòjià commodity price; price of goods
货款 huòkuǎn money for buying

or selling goods; payment for goods

货款两清 huòkuǎn liǎngqīng collected and delivered

货品 huòpǐn kinds or types of goods

货色 huòsè ① goods :上等～ first-rate goods; quality goods. ～齐全。Goods of every description are available. ② stuff; rubbish

货摊 huòtān stall; stand

货物 huòwù goods; wares; commodity; [船货] cargo:～保险 cargo insurance. ～托运 consignment of goods. ～税 commodity tax

货箱 huòxiāng packing box

货样 huòyàng samples of goods; sample

货源 huòyuán source of goods; supply of goods

货运 huòyùn transportation of goods; freight transport:～标签 shipping tag. ～量 volume of goods transported. ～列车 freight train; goods train. ～业 carrying trade

货栈 huòzhàn warehouse; storehouse

货真价实 huòzhēn-jiàshí ① genuine goods at a fair price; supply honest goods at honest price ② out-and-out; through and through

货主 huòzhǔ owner of cargo:～不明的货物 unclaimed goods

嚯 huò ①〈叹〉[表示惊讶或赞叹]: wow; gee:～,怎么这么贵! Wow! How come it is so expensive! ②〈象〉ho-ho:～～一笑 give a hearty laugh

J j

jī

激 jī〈动〉① surge；dash：一石～起千层浪。A tossed stone raises a thousand ripples. ② stimulate；excite；arouse ③〈形〉fierce；sharp；violent：～烈的论战 fierce debate (controversy, polemics)

激昂 jī'áng excited；fervent；impassioned；aroused：～慷慨 fervent and excited；speak vehemently with a distinctly moral tone

激动 jīdòng get excited；be moved：～人心的 exciting；stirring

激发 jīfā arouse；stimulate；kindle；work up；evoke：～群众的热情 kindle the masses' enthusiasm

激光 jīguāng [物] laser：～唱机 CD (compact disc)player. ～唱片 compact disc (CD). ～视盘 laser disc (LD)；video compact disc (VCD). ～通讯 laser communication

激化 jīhuà sharpen；intensify；aggravate；become acute

激进 jījìn radical：～派 radicals

激励 jīlì encourage；urge；impel；inspire

激烈 jīliè keen；sharp；fierce；intense：～的贸易竞争 keen trade competition

激怒 jīnù infuriate；enrage；exasperate；irritate

激情 jīqíng intense (strong) emotion；passion；enthusiasm：满怀～ be filled with enthusiasm. ～主义 sensationalism

激增 jīzēng increase rapidly (sharply)；shoot up；rise steeply；jump from

激战 jīzhàn hard (fierce) fighting；stiff fighting；in the thick of a battle

积 jī ①〈动〉store；accumulate；amass：～蓄力量 accumulate strength ②〈名〉[数] product

积案 jī'àn accumulated cases；a long-pending case

积弊 jībì age-old malpractice；long-standing abuse

积极 jījí ① active；enthusiastic：～参加 take an active part (in). ～防御 active defence ② positive：～因素 positive factor

积聚 jījù accumulate；amass；gather；build up

积劳成疾 jīláo-chéngjí fall sick from overwork；break down from constant overwork；suffer from poor health because one works tirelessly

积累 jīlěi accumulate：～资金 accumulate funds

积习 jīxí inveterate (ingrained) habit；long-standing practice；

old habit：～难改。Ingrained habits cannot be cast off overnight.

积蓄 jīxù ① savings ② accumulate；save

积压 jīyā overstock；pile up：物资的～ overstocking of materials. ～物品 overstocking of goods

积重难返 jīzhòng-nánfǎn Confirmed habits are hard to get rid of.；Bad practices die hard.；do not readily break oneself of the habit

击 jī〈动〉① hit；beat；strike：～中痛处 hit one squarely in a sore spot ② attack；assault：痛～敌人 attack the enemy mercilessly

击败 jībài vanquish；defeat；beat

击毙 jībì shoot dead；kill

击剑 jījiàn［体］fencing：～衫 fencing shirt

击溃 jīkuì utterly defeat；rout；crush

击落 jīluò［飞机］bring down；shoot down；down：～敌机2架 down two enemy planes

击破 jīpò destroy；rout；crush：各个～ crush (enemy forces) one by one

击中 jīzhòng hit；hit the mark：～要害 hit (strike) home；hit the nail on the head

基 jī ①〈名〉foundation；base：工业～地 industrial base ②〈形〉fundamental；basic：～本功 basic (essential) skill

基本 jīběn basic；principal；fundamental；cardinal；essential：～工资 basic wages. ～核算单位 basic accounting unit. ～路线 basic line. ～建设重点 priorities of capital construction

基层 jīcéng basic level；grass-roots level：～人民法院 basic people's court. ～商店 grass-roots commercial agencies

基础 jīchǔ foundation；base：加强～工作 be strict in supporting measures. ～工业 basic industries. ～结构 infrastructure. ～医疗 basic medical treatment

基调 jīdiào keynote；basic idea

基督教 jīdūjiào Christian religion；Christianity：～徒 Christian

基金 jījīn fund

基数 jīshù ① cardinal number ② base：以1994年的产量为～ taking the output of 1994 as the base

基于 jīyú on the ground(s) of；owing to；in view of

缉 jī〈动〉arrest；seize

缉拿 jīná arrest；apprehend；seize：～归案 bring (a criminal) to justice

缉私 jīsī seize smugglers (smuggled goods)；suppress smuggling

畸 jī〈形〉① unbalanced；lopsided：～形发展 lopsided development ② abnormal；irregular

畸形 jīxíng abnormality；deformity；malformation：～现象 abnormal phenomenon. ～艺术 funk art

羁 jī ①〈名〉bridle；headstall

②〈动〉control；restrain：放荡不～ unconventional and uninhibited

羁绊 jībàn fetters；trammels；yoke

羁押 jīyā custody；detention；detain；hold in custody：～候审 custody for trial；committed for trial

稽 jī〈动〉check；examine；investigate：有案可～ be on record

稽查 jīchá ① check；inspect ② inspector：海关～ customs officer

稽核 jīhé examine；check；audit：～帐目 audit accounts

稽私 jīsī prevention of smuggling

几 jī ①〈名〉small table：茶～ tea table ②〈副〉almost；nearly：到会者～乎达到 2,000 人。Nearly 2,000 people came to the meeting.

讥 jī〈动〉laugh at；satirize；ridicule

讥讽 jīfěng satirize：～的评论 ironical remark

讥笑 jīxiào laugh at；sneer at；ridicule

饥 jī ①〈形〉hungry；starving ②〈名〉famine：～民 victims of famine

饥不择食 jībùzéshí When one is hungry one does not choose one's food.；Hunger is the best sauce.

饥肠辘辘 jīcháng-lùlù one's stomach rumbling with hunger

饥饿 jī'è hungry；starved：挣扎在～线上 struggling along on the verge of starvation

饥寒交迫 jīhán-jiāopò live in cold and hunger；be miserable with cold and hunger；misery of starvation and poverty

饥荒 jīhuāng famine；crop failure：发生了～。A famine broke forth.

饥馑 jījǐn famine；crop failure

饥渴 jīkě hunger and thirst：～难耐 unbearable hunger and thirst

机 jī〈名〉① machine：洗衣～ washing machine ②（air）plane；aeroplane：客～ passenger plane ③ pivot；crucial point；key link：转～ a turn for the better ④ occasion；chance；opportunity：见～行事 do as one sees fit ④〈形〉organic：有～化学 organic chemistry

机不可失，时不再来 jī bù kěshī，shí bù zàilái don't let slip an opportunity as it may never come again；opportunity knocks but once

机场 jīchǎng airport；airfield；aerodrome

机动 jīdòng ① power-driven；motor-driven ② mobile；flexible：～汇率 flexible exchange rate ③ kept in reserve：～车辆 motor vehicles. ～权 right of independent action. ～资金 fund kept in reserve；reserve fund

机房 jīfáng ① generator or motor room ② engine room（of a ship）

机构 jīgòu ① organization；structure; setup:～重叠 organizational overlapping. 精简行政～ simplify (streamlining) the administrative structure ② mechanism

机关 jīguān ① organ; (government) office; institution:～事务科学 cameralistic science ② machine; gear:起动～ starting gear ③ craft; machination

机会 jīhuì chance; opportunity:～主义 opportunism

机警 jījǐng sharp; dexterous; alert:～地监视敌人 keep watch alertly on the enemy

机灵 jīling clever; smart; sharp; intelligent

机密 jīmì secret; confidential; classified:～等级 degree of secrecy. ～文件 confidential documents; classified papers

机敏 jīmǐn quick-witted; alert and resourceful; ingenious; tactful

机能 jīnéng function:～失调 dysfunction

机器 jīqì machine:machinery; apparatus

机器人 jīqìrén robot

机务人员 jīwùrényuán ① maintenance personnel ② flight personnel

机械 jīxiè ① machine; mechanism:～电子产品 mechanical and electrical products. ～工业 machine-building industry. ～手 mechanical hand ② inflexible; mechanical:～地搬用外国经验 mechanically apply foreign experience

机型 jīxíng ① type (of an aircraft) ② model (of a machine)

机要 jīyào confidential:～部门 departments in charge of confidential or important work

机宜 jīyí principles of action; guidelines

机油 jīyóu engine oil; machine oil

机遇 jīyù chance; opportunity

机缘 jīyuán good luck; lucky chance:～凑巧 as luck would have it; by a lucky coincidence; by chance

机制 jīzhì ① machine-made; machine-processed ② mechanism:市场～ market mechanism

机智 jīzhì quick (ready-witted) tactful; resourceful:～勇敢的 brave and resourceful

机组 jīzǔ ① set; unit:水力发电站～容量 capacity of generator sets of hydroelectric power station ② flight crew:～人员 personnel of flight crew

肌 jī muscle; flesh:～肉抽动 the muscles drawn

肌肤 jīfū (human) skin and muscle

肌肉 jīròu muscle:～发达的 muscular

肌体 jītǐ body; organism

鸡 jī 〈名〉 hen or cock; fowl; chicken:养～场 chicken farm

鸡蛋 jīdàn (hen's) egg

鸡蛋里挑骨头 jīdàn li tiāo gútou look for a bone in an egg—look for a flaw where there's none to be found; find fault; nitpick

鸡蛋碰石头 jīdàn pèng shítou (like) an egg striking a rock—attack sb. far stronger than oneself; court destruction

鸡飞蛋打 jīfēi-dàndǎ the hen has flown away and the eggs in the coop are broken—all is lost

鸡冠 jīguān cockscomb

鸡肋 jīlèi chicken ribs—things of little value or interest: 味同～ taste like chicken ribs—be of little or no value

鸡毛 jīmáo chicken feather

鸡毛蒜皮 jīmáo-suànpí chicken feathers and garlic skins; trifles; trivialities

鸡皮疙瘩 jīpí gēda goose pimples (flesh; skin)

鸡犬不留 jīquǎn-bùliú not a chicken or dog left

鸡犬不宁 jīquǎn-bùníng cause such utter confusion as to make everybody nervous; great tumult: 闹得家内～ stir the whole family into a tempest

鸡尾酒 jīwěijiǔ cocktail: ～会 cocktail party (reception)

鸡窝里飞出金凤凰 jīwō li fēichū jīnfènghuáng a golden phoenix flying out of a henhouse—a person of humble origin rising to prominence

奇 jī ①〈形〉odd ②〈名〉a fractional amount (over that mentioned in a round number); odd lots

奇数 jīshù odd number

jí

疾 jí〈名〉① illness; sickness: 积劳成～ fall sick from overwork ② suffering; difficulty; pain ③〈形〉swift; rapid: ～驰而过 speed past

疾病 jíbìng disease; illness; sickness: ～保险 sickness insurance; insurance against sickness. 防治～ prevent and cure disease

疾恶如仇 jí'è-rúchóu hate evil like an enemy

疾风扫落叶 jífēng sǎo luòyè like a strong wind sweeping away dead leaves — carrying everything before one

疾患 jíhuàn illness; disease

疾苦 jíkǔ sufferings; miseries; difficulties; weal and woe: 关心人民的～ be concerned about the sufferings of the people

疾驶 jíshǐ (of vehicles) speed along

疾言厉色 jíyán-lìsè look fierce and talk boisterously; harsh words and stern looks

吉 jí〈形〉lucky; auspicious

吉利 jílì lucky; auspicious; propitious

吉庆 jíqìng propitious; auspicious; happy

吉人天相 jíréntiānxiàng Heaven stands by the good man

吉日 jírì auspicious day; lucky day

吉祥 jíxiáng lucky; auspicious;

propitious

吉星高照 jíxīng-gāozhào be blessed by a lucky star

吉凶 jíxiōng good or ill luck; fate：～未卜。No one can tell how it will turn out.

吉兆 jízhào good omen; auspice; propitious sign

籍 jí〈名〉① book; record ② record; register ③ native place

籍贯 jíguàn native place; the place of one's birth orgin; birthplace

棘 jí〈名〉thorny bushes

棘手 jíshǒu thorny; ticklish; vexing; hard to deal with：～的问题 thorny problem; hard nut to crack

集 jí ①〈动〉gather; assemble; collect：聚～ gather together〈名〉② collected works; collection：鲁迅选～ Selected Works of Lu Xun ③ fair; market：赶～ go to a country fair

集成电路 jíchéngdiànlù integrated circuit

集合 jíhé gather; assemble; muster; call together

集会 jíhuì meeting; gathering; assembly; rally

集结 jíjié concentrate; assemble; mass：～军队 mass troops

集锦 jíjǐn a collection of choice specimens

集聚 jíjù gather; collect; assemble

集散地 jísàndì collecting and distributing centre; distributing centre

集市 jíshì (country) fair; market：～贸易 market fairs; country markets

集思广益 jísī-guǎngyì draw upon all useful opinions; pool the wisdom of the collective

集体 jítǐ〈形，名〉collective：～化 collectivization. ～经济 collective economy. ～所有制 collective ownership. ～消费 collective consumption. ～提留 accumulation and retention of common funds by the collective

集团 jítuán group; bloc; clique：企业～ enterprise group

集团购买力 jítuán gòumǎilì the purchasing power of institutions; institutional purchases

集训 jíxùn assemble for training

集腋成裘 jíyèchéngqiú Many drops of water make an ocean.; Many a little makes a mickle.

集邮 jíyóu stamp collecting; philately：～者 stamp-collector; philatelist

集约经营 jíyuējīngyíng intensive management

集中 jízhōng concentrate; focus; centralize：～注意力 concentrate one's attention (on). ～体现 epitomize

集装箱 jízhuāngxiāng container：～船 container ship. ～堆放场 container yard (pool). ～提单 container bill of lading

集资 jízī raise funds; collect money

辑 jí ①〈动〉collect; compile;

edit ②〈名〉part；volume；division：新闻简报第一～ Newsreel No. 1

嫉 jí〈动〉① be jealous；be envious ② hate

嫉妒 jídù envy；be envious (jealous)

嫉恨 jíhèn envy and hate；hate out of jealousy

及 jí ①〈动〉reach；come up to：力所能～ within one's power；what is in power ②〈副〉be in time for：这场雪很～时。This snow has come at the right time. ③〈连〉and：工人、农民～士兵 workers，peasants and soldiers ④〈介〉to：由南～北 from south to north

及格 jígé pass (an examination)；get through：～分数 pass mark. 考试不～ fail (in) the examination. ～赛 qualifying event (trial)

及时 jíshí ① in time；timely ② promptly；without delay；at once：必须～处理 must be handled without delay

及时行乐 jíshí-xínglè enjoy pleasure in good time；enjoy life while one is young

及早 jízǎo as early as possible；at an early hour：～回头 make haste to reform

汲 jí〈动〉draw (water)：从井里～水 draw water from a well

汲取 jíqǔ draw；derive：他们可以～其他地方的经验。They can draw on the experience of other regions.

极 jí ①〈名〉extreme；the utmost point：无所不用其～ go to any extreme ②〈动〉reach the end of；push to extremes ③〈副〉extremely；exceedingly：高兴～了 extremely happy

极地 jídì polar region：～航行 arctic navigation；polar air navigation

极点 jídiǎn the extreme；the limit：发展到～ reach one's culmination

极度 jídù ① extremely；exceedingly；to the utmost：～疲劳 be extremely tired；be overcome with fatigue ② the limit；the extreme；the utmost

极端 jíduān ① extremes：走～ go to extremes. ～主义 extremism ② extreme；exceeding：～孤立 extreme isolation. ～重要性 paramount importance

极力 jílì do one's best；make every effort；spare no effort；go to great lengths

极目 jímù look as far as the eye can see：～远眺 gaze far into the distance (from a high place，as a mountaintop)

极品 jípǐn highest grade；best quality

极盛 jíshèng zenith；heyday；acme：～时期 the most glorious era

极限 jíxiàn ① the limit；the maximum ② limit

极刑 jíxíng death penalty；capital punishment；extreme penalty：处以～ give sb. the death penalty; put sb. to death

极右 jíyòu ① extreme right ② ultra Right

极致 jízhì ultimate attainment; highest achievement

极左 jízuǒ ① extreme left ② ultra "Left"

岌 jí〈形〉① high; lofty ② imminent

岌岌可危 jíjí-kěwēi in imminent danger; in a precarious situation; in great peril

级 jí〈名〉① level; grade; rank:高～干部 high-ranking cadres ② grade; class; form:升留～制度 system of promoting or holding back students ③ step; stage:石～ stone steps ④［语］degree

级别 jíbié rank; grade; scale:工资～ wage scales

级差收入 jíchāshōurù differential income

急 jí〈形〉① urgent; pressing:当务之～ the urgent task at present ② anxious; impatient:～性病 impetuosity ③ irritated; annoyed ④ rapid; fast:雨下得～。It's raining hard. ⑤〈名〉emergency; urgency:应～ meet an emergency ⑥〈动〉be eager to help:～人之难 be eager to help those in need

急不可待 jíbùkědài too impatient to wait; extremely anxious

急茬儿 jíchár urgent matter

急促 jícù ① hurried; rapid:～的脚步声 hurried footsteps ②（of time）short; pressing:时间很～,不要再犹豫了。Time is running short. Stop hesitating

急风暴雨 jífēng-bàoyǔ violent storms; hurricane; tempest

急公好义 jígōng-hàoyì zealous for public interests; be public-spirited and kindhearted

急功近利 jígōng-jìnlì quick for success and instant benefits; be anxious to achieve quick success and get instant benefits

急件 jíjiàn urgent dispatch (document)

急救 jíjiù emergency treatment; first aid:采取～措施 take first-aid measures

急剧 jíjù sharp; rapid; abrupt

急来抱佛脚 jílái bào fójiǎo ask for help at the last moment; do nothing until the last minute; seek help when it is very late

急流 jíliú torrent; swift; rapid stream; rapids:～勇进 advance through the rapids; press on in the teeth of difficulties. ～勇退 resolutely retire at the height of one's official career; make a quick retreat before a crisis

急忙 jímáng in a hurry; in haste; hurriedly; hastily

急迫 jípò urgent; pressing

急起直追 jíqǐ-zhízhuī make a big effort to catch up; make haste to catch up (with)

急切 jíqiè ① urgent; eager ② in a hurry; in haste

急人所急 jírén-suǒjí be anxious to help those in grave danger; be eager to meet the needs of others

急刹车 jíshāchē ① bring to a halt ② slam the brakes on

急需 jíxū need badly; be badly in need of; urgent need

急眼 jíyǎn be taken aback; feel anxious

急于 jíyú be eager (to do, for); be impatient (to do, for):～求成 be impatient for success; overanxiety to make achievements

急躁 jízào ① irritable; irascible:他性情～。 He has an irascible temperament. ② impetuous; rash; impatient:～冒进 advance impetuously

急诊 jízhěn emergency treatment (call):～室 emergency room

急中生智 jízhōng-shēngzhì have quick wits in emergency; hit upon an idea in peril; think up a device in an emergency

急转直下 jízhuǎn-zhíxià suddenly take an unexpected turn; go into a precipitous decline; develop rapidly after a sudden change

即 jí 〈动〉① reach; be near; approach:可望而不可～ be within sight but inaccessible ② assume; undertake:～位称帝 ascend the throne to become emperor ③ be; mean:春节～农历新年。The Spring Festival is the lunar New Year. 〈形〉④ at present; immediate:～时消费品 current goods ⑤ prompted by occasion:～景诗 occasional verse ⑥〈副〉promptly; at once:黎明～起 get up as soon as it dawns

即便 jíbiàn even; even if; even though

即付票据 jífù piàojù note on demand

即将 jíjiāng ① soon; before long ② be about (to do):新年～来临. New Year is drawing near.

即决裁判 jíjué-cáipàn summary justice

即景生情 jíjǐng-shēngqíng The landscape evokes memories of the past.; The scene touches a responsive chord in one heart.; The circumstances excited one's feeling.

即刻的处罚 jíkè de chùfá [法] summary punishment

即期 jíqī immediate; on demand; spot:～付款 payment at sight. ～交货 delivery on spot; immediate delivery. ～装运 prompt shipment

即日 jírì ① this day; today ② within a few days; soon

即时 jíshí immediately; forthwith

即使 jíshǐ even if; even though; even

即位 jíwèi ascend the throne

即席(兴) jíxí(xìng) impromptu; extemporaneous:～赋诗 extemporize in verse

jǐ

脊 jǐ〈名〉① backbone; spine ② ridge

脊髓灰质炎 jǐsuǐhuīzhìyán poliomyelitis; polio

脊柱 jǐzhù spinal column; vertebral column; backbone; spine

脊椎 jǐzhuī vertebra:～动物 vertebrate

挤 jǐ 〈动〉 ① crowd; cram; pack:房间里～满了人。The room was crammed with people. ② squeeze; press:～牛奶 milk a cow ③ push against; jostle:～进行列 squeeze oneself into the ranks of

挤出 jǐchū squeeze out; crowd out; [时间]find (time):～时间做某事 try to find time to do sth.; squeeze in every possible minute to do sth.

挤兑 jǐduì a run on a bank

挤对 jǐdui ① force into submission ② push aside; push out; squeeze out; elbow out ③ make fun of; poke fun at

挤过 jǐguò squeeze (jostle) one's way through

挤进 jǐjìn squeeze into; pack into; wedge oneself into

挤满 jǐmǎn be crowded (packed) with; be filled to capacity

挤眉弄眼 jǐméi-nòngyǎn wink and make signs to one another; give sb. a surreptitious wink now and then; make eyes (at); wink (at)

挤牙膏 jǐyágāo squeeze toothpaste out of a tube—be forced to tell the truth bit by bit

几 jǐ 〈形〉 ① how many:你有～本书? How many books do you have? ② some; several; a few: 30～个人 thirty odd people. 相差无～ not much difference

另见 jī

几分 jǐfēn a bit; somewhat; rather:有～醉意 a bit merry; a bit tipsy

几何 jǐhé ① how many; how much ② [数] geometry

几起几落 jǐqǐ-jǐluò several ups and downs; slumps:国民经济～ several ups and downs appeared in the national economy

几上几下 jǐshàng-jǐxià go up and step down many times:经得起～的考验 stand the test of going up and stepping down many times

几时 jǐshí ① what time; when ② any time; when:你～有空～来。Come when you are free.

几许 jǐxǔ how much; how many

己 jǐ 〈代〉 one's own; oneself; personal:坚持～见 stand to one's assert

己方 jǐfāng one's own side

己所不欲,勿施于人 jǐ suǒ bùyù, wù shī yú rén Do not do to others what you don't want others to do to you

给 jǐ ①〈动〉 supply; provide; furnish:配～ ration ②〈形〉 abundant; ample; plentiful:家～户足。Every household is well provided for.

另见 gěi

给养 jǐyǎng supplies; provisions; victuals

给予 jǐyǔ give; offer; render:～协助 render assistance to

jì

寂 jì 〈形〉 silent；quiet

寂静 jìjìng still；quiet；silent

寂寞 jìmò lonely；solitary；lonesome

寂然 jìrán quiet；still；silent：～不动 quiet and inactive

绩 jì ①〈动〉 twist hempen thread：～麻 twist threads ②〈名〉merit；achievement；accomplishment：功～ merits and achievements

计 jì〈动〉① count；calculate；reckon；compute：～算每股收益 computing earnings per share ② plan；plot：～划经济 planned economy〈名〉③ plan；meter；gauge：体温～ thermometer ④ plan；stratagem

计策 jìcè plan；device；stratagem

计酬 jìchóu work out or calculate payment

计划 jìhuà plan；scheme；project：～调拨 planned allocation (transfer). ～供应 planned supply. ～生育 family planning；planned parenthood. ～市场 planned market. ～收购 planned state purchase

计件 jìjiàn reckon by the piece：～付酬 pay by the piece. ～工资 piece rate wage；piece wage；piece work wage

计较 jìjiào ① care about；bother about：～小事 fuss over trifles ② dispute；argue：我现在不和她～。I won't dispute (argue) with her now. ③ plan；think over

计量 jìliàng calculate；measure；estimate：～经济学 econometrics

计谋 jìmóu plot；scheme；stratagem

计时 jìshí reckon by time：～工资 time wage；payment by the hour. ～员[体] timekeeper

计算 jìsuàn compute；calculate；count

计算机 jìsuànjī calculator；computer：～病毒 computer virus. ～处理的数据文件 computerized data file. ～犯罪 computer crime. ～辅助设计 computer aid design (CAD). ～软件 computer software. ～硬件 computer hardware. ～中央处理器 central processing unit (CPU)

计委 jìwěi State Planning Commission

技 jì〈名〉 skill；ability；technique；trick：～术变革 technological change

技工 jìgōng ① mechanic ② skilled worker：～学校 technical school for workers

技击 jìjī the art of attack and defence in *wushu*

技能 jìnéng skill；abilities：～库 skills tank

技贸结合 jìmào jiéhé combine foreign trade with the introduction of new technology

技巧 jìqiǎo ① skill；technique ② (sports) acrobatics：～运动 acrobatic gymnastics. 写作～ writing technique

技术 jìshù technique;technology; craftsmanship:～革新 technical innovation. ～工人 skilled worker. ～交流 technological exchanges. ～封锁 blockade on new techniques. ～经济指标 technological and economic indicators. ～密集型产品 technology-intensive products. ～市场 markets for technology. ～转让 transfer of technology. ～职称 technical titles

技艺 jìyì artistry; skill; craftsmanship; feat

伎 jì〈名〉skill; trick

伎俩 jìliǎng trick; trickery; artifice:玩弄卑劣～ play a dirty trick (on)

妓 jì〈名〉prostitute

妓女 jìnǚ prostitute; whore; party girl:～改造所 reformatory

妓院 jìyuàn brothel

寄 jì〈动〉① send; post:～信 send a letter; mail (post) a letter ② deposit; place:～希望于他们 place hopes on them

寄存 jìcún deposit; consign; check:～处 depository. ～手提包 check one's bag

寄存器 jìcúnqì [计] register

寄放 jìfàng leave with; leave in the care of

寄居 jìjū live away from home

寄卖 jìmài consign for sale on commission; put up for sale in a secondhand shop

寄人篱下 jìrén-líxià be under sb. else's roof — depend (rely) on other people for a living; live (be) under someone's thumb; live under subjugation

寄生 jìshēng ① parasitism ② parasitic:过着～生活 lead a parasitic life

寄售 jìshòu consign (for sale on commission); consignment sale:～商店 commission shop

寄宿 jìsù ① put up; lodge ② [学生] board:～学校 boarding school. ～生 boarder

寄托 jìtuō ① leave with sb.; entrust ② pin (place) on; find sustenance:精神～ spiritual sustenance. 把希望～于年轻一代 pin one's hope(s) on the younger generation

寄养 jìyǎng entrust one's child to the care of sb.; ask sb. to bring up one's child:把孩子～在朋友那里 leave a child in the care of a friend

寄予 jìyǔ ① place on:党对我们～很大的希望。The Party places great hopes on us. ② show; give; express

寄语 jìyǔ send word

季 jì〈名〉season

季度 jìdù quarter:第二～ second quarter of a year

季风 jìfēng monsoon

季节 jìjié season:～性行业 seasonal trade. ～差价 seasonal price difference

季刊 jìkān quarterly

系 jì〈动〉tie; fasten; do up;

button up：～鞋带 tie shoe lace 另见 xì

既 jì ①〈副〉already：～得利益 vested interest ②〈连〉since：～然如此，我们不用再谈了。Since it is so, we don't have to talk about in any more.

既成事实 jìchéng shìshí established (accomplished) fact; *fait accompli*

既得利益 jìdélìyì vested interest

既定 jìdìng fixed; set; established：～方针 established principle

既来之，则安之 jì láizhī, zé ānzhī Since this is so, it's better to accept it.; Since we are here, we may as well stay and make the best of it.

既然 jìrán since; as; now that：～这个方法不行，我们试试另一个。Since this method doesn't work, let's try another.

既遂犯 jìsuìfàn one who consummates a crime

既往不咎 jìwǎng-bùjiù forgive sb.'s past misdeeds; be let off for one's past misdeeds; Let bygones be bygones.

既…又 jì…yòu… both… and…：他既懂政治又懂业务。He is both politically good and professionally efficient.

记 jì〈动〉① remember; commit to memory; keep in mind：～在心里 make mental notes. ～下电话号码 jot down the telephone number ② write (take, jot) down; record〈名〉③ mark; sign ④ notes; record：～载在史册上 go down in history

记得 jìde remember

记分 jìfēn ①[比赛成绩]keep the score ②[学生的分数]record the marks：～制 mark system ③ record workpoints

记功 jìgōng cite sb. for meritorious service; record a merit

记挂 jìguà be concerned about; keep thinking about; miss

记过 jìguò record a demerit; give a bad mark：他已～2次。He already has two demerits on his record.

记号 jìhao mark; sign

记录 jìlù ①〈动〉write down; record; take notes ②〈名〉minutes; notes; record：～簿 minute book. 做～ take minutes. 世界～ world record

记名 jìmíng put down one's name; sign：无～投票 secret ballot. ～证券 inscribed securities; inscriptions. ～支票 order check; specific check (cheque)

记取 jìqǔ remember; bear in mind：～这个血的教训 bear firmly in mind this lesson learned at the cost of blood

记述 jìshù relate; give an account of; record and narrate

记性 jìxing memory：～好 have a good (tenacious, retentive) memory. ～坏 have a bad (poor, short) memory

记忆 jìyì remember; recollect：～力 memory. ～犹新 be still fresh (green) in one's memory (mind)

记载 jìzǎi put down in writing; record:他作为伟大的先行者～在史册上。He goes down in history as a great pioneer.

记帐 jìzhàng keep accounts; keep books; charge to one's account:～人 bookkeeper. ～结算 settlement on account. ～外汇 foreign exchange remittances through a clearing account

记者 jìzhě reporter; correspondent:～招待会 press (news) conference. ～席[议会等处的] press gallery;[比赛场所看台上的] press stand;[法庭上的] press table. ～证 press card. 新闻～ newsman; newspaper reporter. 特派～ special correspondent

记住 jìzhu remember; take to heart; learn by heart; commit to memory

忌 jì〈动〉① be jealous of envy:猜～ be suspicous and jealous of ② dread; fear:横行无～ run amuck; ride roughshod ③ avoid; refrain from:～带主观性 shun subjectivity

忌辰(日) jìchén(rì) the anniversary of the death of a parent, ancestor, or anyone else held in esteem

忌惮 jìdàn dread; fear; scruple

忌妒 jìdù be jealous of; envy:出于～ out of jealousy

忌讳 jìhuì ① taboo:触犯～ violate a taboo ② avoid; shun; refrain from

纪 jì〈名〉① age; epoch:中世～ the Middle Ages ② discipline:～律松弛 laxity in discipline ③〈动〉put down in writing; record:～事体裁 chronology genre

纪检 jìjiǎn discipline inspection:～部门 discipline inspection departments

纪律 jìlǜ discipline:～性 sense of discipline. ～严明 strict discipline; be highly disciplined. 守～ observe discipline

纪念 jìniàn ① commemorate; observe; mark ② commemoration; anniversary:～册 autograph album. ～品 souvenir; keepsake; token. ～日 commemoration day;[周年的] anniversay. ～邮票 commemorative stamp

纪实 jìshí record of actual events; on-the-spot report:～小说 document novel

纪委(纪律检查委员会) jìwěi (jìlǜjiǎncháwěiyuánhuì) discipline inspection commission

纪要 jìyào summary:讨论～ summary minutes of discussion

纪元 jìyuán ① beginning of an era ② era; epoch:新～ new era

纪传体 jìzhuàntǐ history presented in a series of biographies:～史书编纂 history books compiled in biographical style

际 jì〈名〉① border; boundary; edge ② occasion; time:～此盛会 on the occasion of this grand gathering〈介〉③ between ④ inside:脑～ in one's head

际遇 jìyù favourable turns in life;

spells of good or bad fortune

剂 jì 〈名〉 ① a pharmaceutical or other chemical preparation ② (for herbal medicine)：一～中药 a dose of Chinese herbal medicine

剂量 jìliàng dosage；dose

济 jì 〈动〉 ① cross a river ② aid；relieve；help ③ be of help；benefit

济贫 jìpín aid the poor；relieve the poor

济世 jìshì benefit mankind；do good to society

济事 jìshì ［通常用于否定式］be of use (help)：空谈不～。Empty talk doesn't help matters.

迹 jì 〈名〉 ① mark；trace ② remains；vestige；ruins

迹象 jìxiàng sign；indication；token：可喜的～ a welcome indication. 有～表明两国的外交关系将得到改善。There are indications that the two countries are going to improve their diplomatic relations.

继 jì ①〈动〉 continue；succeed；follow：～续深入 continue to develop in depth ②〈副〉 then；afterwards：她初感头晕，～又呕吐。Feeling dizzy and then she began to vomit.

继承 jìchéng ① succeed (to)；inherit：～法 inheritance act；law of succession. ～权 right of inheritance (succession). ～人 successor；inheritor. ～遗产 inherit a fortune；heritage ② carry forward；carry on；follow：～前人成果 carrying forward the results of our predecessors

继电器 jìdiànqì relay

继任 jìrèn succeed sb. in office；take over sb.'s job

继嗣 jìsì ① adopt a son ② heir

继往开来 jìwǎngkāilái carry forward the work of our predecessors and open up a way for the future；carry on the fine traditions of the past and open up a way for those who follow

继位 jìwèi accede to the throne；inherit the throne

继续 jìxù go on；continue；keep on：～犯罪 continuing offence. ～教育 further education；continuing the eduction. ～有效 continue in force

祭 jì 〈动〉 ① hold a memorial ceremony for ② offer a sacrifice to ③ wield

祭奠 jìdiàn hold a memorial ceremony for

祭品 jìpǐn sacrificial offerings；oblation

祭扫 jìsǎo offer sacrifices at and sweep (the ancestral tomb)

祭祀 jìsì offer sacrifices to gods or ancestors

祭文 jìwén funeral oration；elegiac address

jiā

家 jiā 〈名〉 ① family；household：～政学 home economics

② home：呆在～里 stay at home③ a person or family engage in a centain trade：农～ peasant (farm) family ④ a specialist in a certain field：作～ writer ⑤ a school of thought：墨～学说 Mohism ⑥ nationality：苗～ the Miao nationality ⑦〈量〉2～电影院 two cinemas

家产 jiāchǎn household effects; family property

家常 jiācháng ① home affairs; domestic trivia：～便饭 homely meals ② common occurrence (practice)：～话 small talk

家丑 jiāchǒu family scandal; domestic shame：～不可外扬。Family scandals shouldn't be made known in public.; Don't wash your dirty linen in public.

家传 jiāchuán handed down from the older generations of the family

家当 jiādàng family property (belongings); property

家底 jiādǐ ① family property accumulated over a long time ② resources

家法 jiāfǎ ① domestic discipline exercised by the head of a feudal household ② a rod for punishing children or servants in a feudal household

家访 jiāfǎng visit to the parents of schoolchildren or young workers

家风 jiāfēng family tradition; family trait

家伙 jiāhuo ① tool; utensil; weapon ② fellow; guy：小～ little chap; kid

家教 jiājiào ① domestic discipline; family education; upbringing ② home tutor; private teacher

家境 jiājìng family circumstances; family financial situation：～清寒 come from a poor family

家具 jiājù furniture

家眷 jiājuàn ① wife and children; one's family ② wife

家破人亡 jiāpò-rénwáng with one's family ruined and its members killed; family ruined; One's family was broken up and its members died (killed).

家谱 jiāpǔ family tree; family pedigree; genealogical tree; genealogy

家事 jiāshì family matters; domestic affairs

家属 jiāshǔ member(s) of a family; family：～工厂 family dependents' factory. ～委员会 dependents' committee

家庭 jiātíng family; household; home：～病床 home sickbeds. ～暴力 domestic (family) violence. ～教师 home tutor; tutor. ～教育 family education; home education. ～联产承包责任制 system of contracted responsibilities on the household basis with remuneration linked to output; system of contracted household responsibility related to output. ～破裂 breakdown of a family

家徒四壁 jiātúsìbì have nothing but the bare walls in one's

house—be utterly destitute

家务 jiāwù domestic (household) chores; household affairs (duties): ～劳动 housework; chores

家乡 jiāxiāng hometown; native place

家信 jiāxìn a letter to or from home

家畜 jiāxù [总称] livestock; domestic animal

家业 jiāyè family property; property

家用 jiāyòng ① household (domestic, family) expenses ② household: ～电器 household electrical appliances

家喻户晓 jiāyù-hùxiǎo make known to every family

家长 jiāzhǎng head of a household (family); parent of a child: ～制 patriarchy; patriarchism

家族 jiāzú family; clan: ～主义的社会 familistic society

夹

jiā 〈动〉① press from both sides; place in between; clamp: 她的手指头被门～了一下。Her fingers got squeezed in the door. ② mingle; mix; intersperse: 风～着雨 wind accompanied by rain ③〈名〉clip: 发～ hairpin

另见 jiá

夹板 jiābǎn ① boards for pressing sth. or holding things together ② splint

夹板气 jiābǎnqì the state of being between two fires

夹层 jiācéng double layer

夹带 jiādài ① carry secretly; smuggle ② notes smuggled into an examination hall

夹道 jiādào ① line the streets: ～欢迎 line (throng) the streets to welcome sb.; a grand roadside welcome; welcoming crowds lining the streets ② a narrow lane

夹缝 jiāfèng a narrow space between two adjacent things; crack; crevice

夹攻 jiāgōng attack from both sides; under the crossfire; converging attack; hold in pincers: ～敌人 hold the enemy in pincers; pincers around the enemy

夹具 jiājù clamping apparatus; fixture; jig

夹生 jiāshēng half-boiled; half-done; half-baked: ～饭 half-cooked rice

夹心 jiāxīn with filling

夹杂 jiāzá be mixed up with; be mingled with: 歌声～着笑声。The singing mingled with laughter.

夹子 jiāzi clip; clamp; tongs: 皮～ wallet; pocketbook. 文件～ folder

佳

jiā 〈形〉good; fine; beautiful; fair; nice: 成绩甚～ achieve very good results

佳话 jiāhuà a much-told story; deed praised far and wide; story on everybody's lips: 传为～ become an interesting story on everybody's lips

佳节 jiājié happy festival time; joyous festival; festive occasion: 每逢～倍思亲。On every festive occasion more than ever one thinks of one's dear ones far away.

佳境 jiājìng pleasant (delightful) stage：渐入～ become more and more delightful

佳丽 jiālì ① beautiful ② beautiful woman

佳偶 jiā'ǒu well-assorted couple; happily married couple

佳品 jiāpǐn excellent product; famous produce

佳人 jiārén beautiful woman; beauty：才子～ gifted scholars and beautiful ladies

佳音 jiāyīn welcome news; good (glad) tidings; favourable reply

佳作 jiāzuò fine piece of writing; excellent work

加 jiā 〈动〉 ① add; plus：3～3等于6。Three plus three makes six. ② increase; augment：～大打击犯罪活动的力度 implement harsher measures to combat criminal activities. ～倍努力 redouble one's efforts ③ put in; add：菜里～点盐 put some salt in the dish ④ [表示施以某种动作]：大～赞扬 lavish praise on

加班 jiābān work overtime：～费 overtime pay

加倍 jiābèi double; redouble

加餐 jiācān add a snack：课间～，关系到孩子的成长。A snack between classes has an impact on the growth of children.

加法 jiāfǎ [数] addition

加封 jiāfēng grant additional titles and territories (to the nobles)

加工 jiāgōng process：～出口区 export processing zone. 来料～ made to order with customer's own material. ～订货 processing and ordering goods. [解放初期] placing state orders with private enterprieses; work on government orders. ～工业品 manufactured goods

加固 jiāgù reinforce; consolidate

加害 jiāhài injure; do harm to

加价(～码,～值) jiājià(～mǎ,～zhí) [金] markup

加紧 jiājǐn step up; speed up; intensify

加剧 jiājù aggravate; sharpen; intensify：～阶级分化 acceleration of class polarization

加快 jiākuài quicken; speed up; expedite：～改革步伐 quicken the pace of the reforms

加码 jiāmǎ ① raise the price of commodities; overcharge ② raise the stakes in gambling ③ raise the quota：层层～ raise the quota at each level

加盟 jiāméng become a member of an alliance or union

加冕 jiāmiǎn coronation

加强 jiāqiáng strengthen; intensify; make greater efforts; increase; reinforce; improve：～社会主义精神文明建设 make greater efforts to improve socialist culture and ideology. ～社区文化建设 increase the cultural activities in communities

加权 jiāquán weighting; weighted：～指数 weighted index number

加入 jiārù ① add; mix; put in ② join; accede to

加塞儿 jiāsāir jump the queue; butt in line

加上 jiāshàng ① add; give ② moreover; in addition

加深 jiāshēn deepen; exacerbate; aggravate: ～理解 get a deeper understanding. ～矛盾 aggravate contradiction

加生饭 jiāshēngfàn ① half-cooked rice ② a job not thoroughly done

加速 jiāsù quicken; hasten; accelerate; expedite; speed up: ～社会主义建设 accelerate socialist construction. ～折旧 accelerated depreciation

加薪 jiāxīn get an increase in pay; have a pay rise

加油 jiāyóu ① oil; grease; lubricate ② refuel: ～站 filling station; gas station ③ work with more zeal; zip up; [呼声]Hurry up!; Let's put on a spurt!; Step on the gas!

加重 jiāzhòng ① increase the weight (of); increase: ～他的责任 increase his responsibility. 为了～份量，他补充说道："……"。In order to strengthen his point, he added: "……".

嘉

嘉 jiā ①〈形〉good; fine; nice: ～偶 a happily married couple ②〈动〉commend; praise; admire: 精神可～ a praiseworthy spirit

嘉宾 jiābīn honoured guest

嘉奖 jiājiǎng commend and praise; bestow praise; cite; commend: 传令～ cite sb. for his meritorious service. ～令 order of commendation; citation

嘉勉 jiāmiǎn praise and encourage

嘉许 jiāxǔ praise; approve

茄

茄 jiā
另见 qié

茄克衫 jiākèshān jacket

枷

枷 jiā〈名〉cangue; shackles

枷锁 jiāsuǒ shackles; fetters; chains; yoke: 摆脱…的～ throw off (shake off; cast off) yoke of…

jiá

夹

夹 jiá〈形〉lined: ～衣 lined clothes
另见 jiā

jiǎ

甲

甲 jiǎ〈名〉① the first of ten Heavenly Stems ② shell: 龟～ tortoise shell ③ armour: 装～车 armoured car ④〈动〉occupy first place; stand first: 桂林山水～天下。The mountains and waters of Guilin are the finest under heaven.

甲板 jiǎbǎn deck

甲醇 jiǎchún methyl alcohol; methanol; wood spirit; wood alcohol

甲骨文 jiǎgǔwén oracle-bone inscriptions; inscriptions on animal bones or tortoise shells

甲级 jiǎjí first-rate; first-class; top-grade
甲烷 jiǎwán methane
甲午战争 Jiǎwǔ-zhànzhēng the Sino-Japanese War of 1894—1895 (launched by Japanese imperialism to annex Korea and invade China)
甲型肝炎 jiǎxínggānyán hepatitis A
甲鱼 jiǎyú soft-shelled turtle
甲胄 jiǎzhòu armour
甲状腺 jiǎzhuàngxiàn thyroid gland
甲子 jiǎzǐ cycle of sixty years

钾

jiǎ 〈名〉potassium
钾肥 jiǎféi potash fertilizer
钾盐 jiǎyán sylvite

假

jiǎ ①〈形〉false; fake; artificial; phoney; sham:～恶丑 the false; the evil and the ugly ②〈动〉borrow; avail oneself of:～借革命之名 usurp the name of revolution ③〈连〉if; suppose:～定 supposition
另见 jià
假案 jiǎ'àn feigned case
假扮 jiǎbàn disguise oneself as; dress up as
假定 jiǎdìng ① suppose; presume; assume:～成本 assumed (hypothetical) cost ② hypothesis ③ if; even if
假公济私 jiǎgōng-jìsī gain private ends in a public cause; use public office for private gain; act in the public service for one's own ends; seek one's own profit in public affairs; practise jobbery
假话 jiǎhuà lie; falsehood:说～ tell lies
假冒 jiǎmào ① pretend to be; falsely pass off ② counterfeit; falsify; imitate:～商标 counterfeit trademark. ～他人专利的人 person passes off the patent of another person. ～伪劣商品 fake or poor quality commodities
假面具 jiǎmiànjù false face; mask:揭穿某人的～ tear off sb.'s mask; unmask sb.
假票据 jiǎ piàojù fictious bill
假仁假义 jiǎrén-jiǎyì pretended benevolence and righteousness; hypocrisy; don a pious mask
假如 jiǎrú if; supposing; in case
假若 jiǎruò if; supposing; in case
假设 jiǎshè hypothesis; assume; presume; hypothesize; conjecture:～演绎法 hypothetico-deductive method
假使 jiǎshǐ if; in case; in the event that
假释 jiǎshì[法] release on parole; parole:～犯 parolee
假手 jiǎshǒu do sth. through sb. else:～于人 make a cat's paw of sb.; make use of sb. to achieve one's maclicious purpose
假托 jiǎtuō ① make a pretext; on the pretext of:～有病 on the pretext of illness ② under sb. else's name:～伪名的著作 allonym ③ through the medium of; by means of
假惺惺 jiǎxīngxīng falsely; pretentiously; hypocritically:～的

眼泪 shed crocodile tears

假想 jiǎxiǎng ① hypothesis; supposition; imagination ② hypothetical; imaginary; suppositious: ~合约 suppositious contract. ~战 mock battle

假象 jiǎxiàng semblance; mere appearance; false (misleading) appearance; facade; false impression; false front

假牙 jiǎyá dental prosthesis; false tooth; denture

假药 jiǎyào bogus medicine

假意 jiǎyì ① unction; insincerity; hypocrisy ② pretend; put on

假造 jiǎzào ① forge; counterfeit; falsify: ~舆论 manufacture public opinion ② fabricate; invent

假帐 jiǎzhàng false account

假正经 jiǎzhèngjǐng pretend to be serious; be mock-serious

假支票 jiǎ zhīpiào forged (counterfeit) cheque; stumer

假装 jiǎzhuāng pretend; feign; simulate; make believe

jià

嫁 jià 〈动〉 ① (of a woman) marry: ~给某人 take sb. in marriage. 把自己的女儿~给一位作家的儿子 marry one's daughter to a writer's son ② transfer; shift

嫁祸于人 jiàhuòyúrén shift the blame onto; transfer the evil to another; shift the misfortune onto sb. else

嫁妆 jiàzhuang dowry; marriage portion; trousseau

价 jià 〈名〉 price; cost: 零售~格 retail price ② value; worth: 使用~值 use value ③ valence

价格 jiàgé price; cost: ~补贴 subsidized price; price subsidy. ~倒挂 price inversion. ~公道 (sell) at a fair price. ~战 price war

价廉物美 jiàlián-wùměi cheap but good; inexpensive but elegant

价目 jiàmù marked price; price: ~表 price list. ~标签 price tag

价值 jiàzhí ① value: ~工程 value engineering. ~观 concept of value. ~规律. law of value. ~取向 value orientation ② vlaue; worth: ~500万元的援助 five million yuan worth of aid

假 jià 〈名〉 ① holiday; vacation: 寒~ winter vacation ② leave of absence: 病~ sick leave. 请病~ ask for leave
另见 jiǎ

假期 jiàqī holiday; vacation; recess: ~学校 vacation school

假日 jiàrì holiday; day of rest; day off

假条 jiàtiáo ① absence slip; application for leave ② leave certificate: 病~ doctor's certificate for sick leave

驾 jià 〈动〉 ① harness; draw (a cart; etc.): ~上牲口耕地 harness cattle to plough the fields ② [车]drive; [船、车] steer;

［飞机］pilot：他～车走了。He drove away in a car.

驾临 jiàlín your arrival；your esteemed presence

驾轻就熟 jiàqīng-jiùshú take (drive) a light carriage on a familiar road；do some familiar work with ease and dexterity；do sth. with ease through experience；in one's element；be versed in

驾驶 jiàshǐ drive (a car)；pilot (a ship or plane)；sail (a boat)：～许可证(执照) driving licence；driving permit. ～员［火车、汽车等的］driver；［飞机的］pilot

驾驭 jiàyù ① drive (a horse, carts, etc.) ② control；master；keep hold of the reins：人们～自然的能力 people's capability to control nature

架 jià 〈名〉① frame；shelf；stand；rack：书～ bookshelf ② fight；quarrel：打～ come to blows；fight 〈动〉③ erect；put up：～起桥梁 erect (span) a bridge ④ ward off；fend off ⑤ prop；support；help：～着拐走 walk on crutches ⑥ take sb. away forcibly；kidnap：他的爹被～走了。His dad was hustled away.

架不住 jiàbuzhù ① cannot sustain (the weight)；cannot stand (the pressure)；cannot stand up against

架得住 jiàdezhù be able to bear or endure：小学生怎么～这么多家庭作业？How can the pupils cope with so much homework？

架空 jiàkōng ① built on stilts；prop up in mid-air ② impracticable；unpractical ③ make sb. a mere figurehead

架设 jiàshè build；erect；set up：～电话线 set up telephone lines

架势 jiàshi posture；pose：他那如临大敌的～。He positioned himself as if he were encountering the enemy.

架子 jiàzi ① framework；frame ② airs：摆～ put on airs

jiān

煎 jiān 〈动〉① fry in shallow oil：～鸡蛋 fried eggs ② decoct；brew；simmer in water

煎熬 jiān'áo suffering；torture；torment

煎饼 jiānbing thin pancake made of millet flour, etc.

煎药 jiānyào decoct (brew) medicinal herbs

兼 jiān 〈形〉① twice；double ② concurrent；simultaneous：～任 hold a concurrent post；concurrently ③〈动〉hold two or more jobs concurrently：～课 hold two or more teaching jobs concurrently

兼备 jiānbèi have both… and…：德才～ have both political integrity and ability；combine ability with political integrity

兼并 jiānbìng merge；annex (property；territory, etc.)：～企业 merge with the enterprises. ～战争 war of annexation

兼程 jiānchéng travel at double speed

兼而有之 jiān'éryǒuzhī have both at the same time

兼顾 jiāngù give consideration to both… and …：公私～ give consideration to both public and private interests

兼任 jiānrèn ① hold a concurrent post；work concurrently as ② part-time：～教师 part-time teacher. ～教学工作的研究员 teaching fellow

兼容 jiānróng compatible

兼收并蓄 jiānshōu-bìngxù incorporate things of diverse nature；taking in everything；swallow anything and everything

兼听则明，偏听则暗 jiāntīngzémíng，piāntīngzé'àn Listen to both sides and you will be enlightened，heed only one side and you will be benighted.

兼业户 jiānyèhù households with combined occupations

兼职 jiānzhí ① hold two or more posts concurrently；concurrent jobs：～教授 adjunct professor ② moonlighting

间 jiān ①〈介〉between：劳资之～ between labour and capital ②〈副〉within a definite time or space：世～（in）the world ③〈名〉room：外～ outer room ④〈量〉2～门面房 a two-bay shop front

另见 jiàn

间不容发 jiānbùróngfà a narrow（near，close，tight）escape（squeak）；be in immediate danger

间架 jiānjià ① framework of a house ② form of a Chinese character ③ structure of an essay

间距 jiānjù interval；separation；space；range；step：出生～ birth interval. 开放～ open interval

间奏曲 jiānzòuqǔ intermezzo；entracte

肩 jiān ①〈名〉shoulder：～挑叫卖 peddle wares around on a shoulder-pole ②〈动〉bear；undertake：～负革命重担 bear heavy burdens for the revolution

肩膀 jiānbǎng shoulder

肩并肩 jiānbìngjiān shoulder to shoulder；side by side：与某人～作战 fight shoulder to shoulder with sb.

肩负 jiānfù bear；undertake；shoulder；take on：～光荣任务 undertake a glorious task

肩摩踵接 jiānmó-zhǒngjiē rubbing the shoulder and following the steps；crowded

肩章 jiānzhāng ① shoulder loop；shoulder strap ② epaulet

歼 jiān〈动〉annihilate；wipe out；exterminate

歼击机 jiānjījī fighter plane；fighter；pursuit plane

歼灭 jiānmiè annihilate；destroy：～战 battle（war）of annihilation

缄 jiān〈动〉shut；seal；close

缄口 jiānkǒu keep one's mouth shut;remain silent; hold one's tongue

缄默 jiānmò keep silent; be reticent:保持～ remain silent; keep mum (about)

笺 jiān 〈名〉① writing paper:便～ note paper; memo ② letter ③ commentary; annotation

笺注 jiānzhù notes and commentary on ancient texts; annotations of ancient works

监 jiān ①〈动〉supervise; watch; inspect; oversee:～督权 authority to supervise ②〈名〉prison; jail:收～ put sb. into jail

监察 jiānchá control; supervise:～委员会 supervisory committee (commission). ～制度 supervisory system. ～主任 inspector general

监测 jiāncè monitor

监督 jiāndū supervise; control; superintend:～劳动改造 labour reform under surveillance

监管人犯 jiānguǎn rénfàn supervise and control offenders

监护 jiānhù guardianship; in care; custody; tutelage:～人 guardian; custodian; keeper. ～人与被～ guardian and ward

监禁 jiānjìn put (hold) in prison; imprison; confine; custody:～处罚 punishment of imprisonment

监考 jiānkǎo invigilate:～人 invigilator; examiner

监控 jiānkòng supervisory control; supervise and control; control

监牢 jiānláo prison; jail

监理 jiānlǐ inspect and control; manage

监票人 jiānpiàorén scrutineer

监事会 jiānshìhuì supervisory commission; board of supervisors

监视 jiānshì keep watch on; keep an eye on; surveillance; guard:～居住 live at home under surveillance

监守自盗 jiānshǒu-zìdào steal what is entrusted to one's care; embezzle; defalcate

监听 jiāntīng monitor

监外执行 jiānwài zhíxíng execute (sentence) outside prison; executing a sentence outside of jail; serving sentence outside the prison under surveillance

监狱 jiānyù prison; jail; goal; jailhouse:～看守 guard

监制 jiānzhì supervise the manufacture of

坚 jiān ①〈形〉hard; strong:～冰 hard (solid) ice ②〈名〉a heavily fortified point; stronghold; fortification:无～不摧 overrun all fortification ③〈副〉resolutely; firmly; steadfastly:～持真理 hold firmly to the truth; uphold the truth

坚壁 jiānbì hide supplies to prevent the enemy from seizing them; place in a cache; cache

坚持 jiānchí persist in; adhere to; hold fast to; cling to; stick to:～不懈的斗争 a determined struggle. ～到底 stick it out; hold on to the last. ～原则 adhere to principle

坚定 jiāndìng firm; staunch; stout; steadfast: ～不移 unswerving; unshakable; unflinching: ～决心 strengthen one's resolve

坚固 jiāngù strong; firm; solid; sturdy: ～的大厦 a substantial building

坚决 jiānjué firm; resolute; determined

坚苦 jiānkǔ steadfast and assiduous

坚强 jiānqiáng ① strong; firm; staunch ② strengthen

坚忍不拔 jiānrěnbùbá firm and indomitable; stubborn and unyielding; unswerving: ～的意志 unyielding will

坚韧 jiānrèn tough and tensile; firm and tenacious

坚如磐石 jiānrú-pánshí rock-firm; as firm as a rock; monolithic; solid as a rock

坚实 jiānshí ① solid; substantial ② strong; robust

坚守 jiānshǒu keep to; hold fast to: ～岗位 keep to one's post; stand fast at one's post; keep to work post

坚挺 jiāntǐng strong; firm; robust: 美元～。The American dollar is robust. ～趋涨 firm with an upward tendency

坚信 jiānxìn firmly believe

坚毅 jiānyì firm and persistent; with unswerving determination; tenacious of purpose

坚硬 jiānyìng hard; solid

坚贞 jiānzhēn faithful; firm; constant: ～不屈 remain faithful; stand firm and unyielding

尖

尖 jiān 〈形〉 ① pointed; tapering ② piercing; shrill: ～叫 scream ③ sharp; acute: 眼～ have sharp eyes. ～锐的争端 sharp debate ④〈名〉point; tip: 针～ the point of needle

尖兵 jiānbīng ① [军] point; vanguard: 战斗的～ vanguard ② trailblazer; pioneer; pathbreaker

尖端 jiānduān ① point; tip ② top; most advanced; sophisticated: ～产品 top-notch products. ～科学 most advanced science; frontiers of science; top sciences. ～技术 sophisticated technique

尖刻 jiānkè sharp; pungent; biting; caustic: 讲～话 make caustic remarks; speak with sarcasm

尖锐 jiānruì 〈形〉① sharp-pointed ② incisive; penetrating; sharp: ～的批评 incisive ciriticism ③ shrill; piercing ④ acute; intense; sharp: ～的思想斗争 sharp mental conflicts

尖子 jiānzi ① ace; élite ② top; top-notch; best; cream of the crop: ～班 advanced class. 技术～ the one with highest skills. 业务～ professionally the best

艰

艰 jiān〈形〉 hard; difficult; arduous: ～苦努力 unrelenting and strenuous efforts

艰巨 jiānjù arduous; formidable

艰苦 jiānkǔ hard; arduous; difficult: ～奋斗 plain living and hard struggle. ～卓绝的斗争 extremely hard and bitter struggle; most arduous struggle

艰难 jiānnán difficult; hard; arduous: ～困苦 difficulties and hardships. ～路程 travel a hard stretch of road. ～险阻 difficulties and dangers

艰深 jiānshēn difficult to understand; abstruse

艰险 jiānxiǎn difficulties and perils;; hardships and dangers: 不避～ in spite of all difficulties and perils (dangers)

艰辛 jiānxīn hardships; tribulations: 历尽～ have gone through all kinds of tribulations

奸 jiān 〈形〉① wicked; evil; treacherous: ～佞小人 wicked and treacherous courtiers ② self-seeking and wily 〈名〉③ traitor: 内～ hidden traitor ④ adultery: 男女间的～情 adulterous relation between a man and a woman

奸臣 jiānchén treacherous court official

奸猾 jiānhuá sly; crafty; deceitful; treacherous

奸计 jiānjì trick; scheme; wiles; evil plot; sinister trap

奸商 jiānshāng unscrupulous merchant; profiteer; profiteering merchant

奸污 jiānwū rape; dishonour; seduce; debauchery: ～处女 defloration

奸笑 jiānxiào sinister (villainous) smile

奸雄 jiānxióng person who achieves high position by unscrupulous scheming; arch-careerist

奸淫 jiānyín adultery; illicit sexual relations: ～少女罪 crime of fornication with an underage girl

奸诈 jiānzhà crafty; roguery; cunning

jiǎn

简 jiǎn ①〈形〉simple; brief; simplified: ～单的多数 a simple majority 〈名〉② letter: 书～ letters ③ bamboo slips (used for writing on in ancient times): 木～ inscribed wooden slip ④〈动〉choose; select

简报 jiǎnbào preliminary report; brief report; bulletin: 新闻～ (news) bulletin

简便 jiǎnbiàn simple and convenient; handy

简称 jiǎnchēng ① be called… for short ② abbreviated form

简单 jiǎndān simple; brief; plain: ～的历史回顾 brief historical retrospect. ～劳动 simple labour

简短 jiǎnduǎn brief

简而言之 jiǎn'éryánzhī in brief; in short; to put it in a nutshel

简化 jiǎnhuà simplify: ～法 reductionism. ～工序 simplify working process. ～汉字 simplifed

Chinese characters. ～多头管理体制 streamline the multichannel management structure

简洁 jiǎnjié brief; succinct; concise; terse; pithy: 文章写得很～。The essay was pithily written.

简介 jiǎnjiè brief (short) introduction; [书、剧本等的] synopsis: 剧情～ the synopsis of a drama

简历 jiǎnlì résumé; curriculum vitae; biographical notes; concise biography; brief of service

简练 jiǎnliàn terse; succinct; pithy

简陋 jiǎnlòu simple and poor (crude); miserable: 设备～ simple and crude equipment

简略 jiǎnlüè simple (in content); brief; sketchy

简明 jiǎnmíng concise; simple and clear; succinct: ～扼要 concise and to the point. ～新闻 news in brief. ～资产负债表 condensed balance sheet

简谱 jiǎnpǔ [乐] numbered musical notation; so-fa notation

简朴 jiǎnpǔ simple and unadorned; plain: 生活～ a simple and frugal life; plain living

简写 jiǎnxiě write a Chinese character in simplified form; simplified writing: ～本 simplified edition

简讯 jiǎnxùn news in brief; newsflash

简要 jiǎnyào concise and to the point; brief

简易 jiǎnyì ① simple and easy; simple: ～人身保险 simple life insurance. ～审判 summary jurisdiction. ～审判庭 summary court; petty session ② simple constructed; simple equipped; unsophisticated

简章 jiǎnzhāng general regulations

简政 jiǎnzhèng streamline the administration

简政放权 jiǎnzhèng fàngquán streamline administration and institute decentralization

简直 jiǎnzhí simply; just; at all: 她的成功～是奇迹。Her success is little short of miraculous.

简装 jiǎnzhuāng simple packing

剪 jiǎn ①〈名〉scissors; clippers; shears〈动〉② cut (with scissors); clip; trim: ～开 cut open. ～毛机 shearing machines ③ do away with; wipe out: ～除 annihilate; wipe out

剪报 jiǎnbào newspaper clippings; clippings: ～服务社 clipping bureau

剪彩 jiǎncǎi cut the ribbon (at a ceremony); snip a red ribbon

剪除 jiǎnchú wipe out; annihilate; exterminate

剪刀 jiǎndāo scissors; shears: ～差 [经] scissors differential (difference): 工农业～差 scissors difference between industrial and agricultural prices

剪辑 jiǎnjí [影片的]cutting; film editing; montage; [报纸等] clipping: ～录音磁带 edit the tape recording. ～错了的故事 a

badly edited story
剪贴 jiǎntiē ① clip and paste (sth. out of a newspaper, etc.) in a scrapbook or on cards ② cutting out (as schoolchildren's activity)
剪影 jiǎnyǐng ① paper-cut shilhouette ② sketch; outline
剪纸 jiǎnzhǐ paper-cut; scissor-cut
剪子 jiǎnzi scissors; shears; clippers

茧 jiǎn 〈名〉① cocoon: 蚕～ silkworm cocoon ② callus
茧绸 jiǎnchóu pongee

拣 jiǎn 〈动〉select; choose; sort out
拣选 jiǎnxuǎn select; choose; pick

减 jiǎn 〈动〉① subtract; deduct: 8～5得3。Eight minus five is three. ② reduce; lessen; decrease; cut: ～轻人民负担 lighten the burden on the people
减产 jiǎnchǎn drop in production; falling yields
减低 jiǎndī reduce; lower; bring down; cut
减肥 jiǎnféi reduce weight: ～法 reducing. ～者 weight watcher. ～中心 health spa
减缓 jiǎnhuǎn reduce and decelerate; retard; slow down
减价 jiǎnjià reduce (lower) prices: ～出售 sell at a reduced price
减免 jiǎnmiǎn ① reduce or remit (taxation); reduction and exemption ② mitigate a punishment; annul a punishment
减轻 jiǎnqīng ① lighten; reduce; lessen; alleviate: ～赋税负担 ease the tax burden. ～刑罚 reduction of punishment; commutation of penalty ② mitigate; extenuate; reduce: ～处罚 mitigated punishment. ～责任 diminished responsibility. ～罪责 extenuate guilt
减弱 jiǎnruò weaken; abate
减色 jiǎnsè lose lustre; impair the excellence of; detract from the merit of
减少 jiǎnshǎo lessen; decrease; cut down; reduce: ～流通环节 cut down on circulation intermediates
减税 jiǎnshuì reduce taxes; derate; abate a tax
减速 jiǎnsù slow down; decelerate; retard
减退 jiǎntuì drop; go down
减刑 jiǎnxíng reduce a penalty (sentence); commute a sentence
减员 jiǎnyuán depletion of numbers (in the armed forces); personnel (staff) reduction
减灾 jiǎnzāi reduce natural disasters
减震 jiǎnzhèn shock absorption; damping

碱 jiǎn 〈名〉① alkali: 盐～地 alkaline land ② soda
碱化 jiǎnhuà alkalization; basification
碱性 jiǎnxìng basicity; alkalinity

检 jiǎn 〈动〉① check; examine; inspect:～查孩子的功课 hear a boy's lesson. ～查和纠正贪污现象 investigate and clean up the petty graft ② restrain oneself:～点行为 keep watch over one's actions

检测 jiǎncè check; test; check out; detecting; measuring:进行～ give a test

检查 jiǎnchá ① examine; check up; inspect:～机关 investigating and prosecuting apparatus. ～员 inspector ② audit:～帐目 audit accounts

检察 jiǎnchá procuratorial work; prosecute:～委员会 procuratorial committee. ～院 procuratorate. ～院院长 chief procurator; public procurator-general. ～员 procurator; government attorney

检点 jiǎndiǎn ① check; examine ② be cautious (about what one says or does); keep watch over; be careful about:他说的话有失～。He was careless about his words.

检举 jiǎnjǔ report an offence to the authorities; inform against an offender; bring sb. to trial; prosecute; accuse; impeach:～案件 impeachment cases. ～某人盗窃 prosecute sb. for theft. ～人 accuser; offence-reporter. ～失实 accusation at variance with the facts. ～箱 accusation letter box

检录 jiǎnlù call the roll of the contestants in athletic events

检索 jiǎnsuǒ search; retrieve

检讨 jiǎntǎo ① examine; inspect ② self-criticism

检修 jiǎnxiū check (examine) and repair; overhaul; maintain; service:～成本 cost of overhaul. ～打字机 service a typewriter

检验 jiǎnyàn examine; check; test; inspect:商品～ commodity inspection

检疫 jiǎnyì quarantine:～所 quarantine station. ～员 quarantine officer

检阅 jiǎnyuè review; inspect:～台 reviewing stand

捡 jiǎn 〈动〉pick up; gather; collect:～煤渣 scavenge bits of coal

捡了芝麻,丢了西瓜 jiǎnle zhīma, diūle xīguā pick up the sesame seeds but overlook the watermelons—concentrate on minor matters to the neglect of major ones

捡漏 jiǎnlòu repair the leaky part of a roof; plug a leak in the roof

捡起 jiǎnqǐ pick up; take up

俭 jiǎn 〈形〉frugal; thrifty:～省 economical; thrifty

俭朴 jiǎnpǔ plain and thrifty; frugal:生活～ lead a plain and thrifty life

jiàn

渐 jiàn 〈副〉by degrees; gradually

渐次 jiàncì one after another; gradually

渐渐 jiànjiàn gradually; by degrees; little by little

渐进 jiànjìn ① proceed step by step ② gradual:循序～ proceed step by step in due order. ～主义 incrementalism; gradualism

渐入佳境 jiànrùjiājìng (of a situation) be improving; be getting better

渐悟 jiànwù gradual enlightement

间 jiàn ①〈名〉space in between; opening:亲密无～ on intimate terms〈动〉② separate:把一间房～成两间 partition a room into two ③ sow discord:挑拨离～ sow dissension

另见 jiān

间谍 jiàndié spy; espionage agent:～活动 espionage. ～行为 act of espionage

间断 jiànduàn ① be disconnected; be interrupted ② intermittent

间隔 jiàngé interval; space:～练习 spaced practice; distributed practice

间接 jiànjiē indirect:～选举 indirect election

间隙 jiànxì ① interval; gap; space ②［机］clearance:齿轮～ gear clearance

间歇 jiànxiē intermittent:～性精神病 mental illness of an intermittent nature; intermittent insanity

间作 jiànzuò［农］inter-cropping

谏 jiàn〈动〉remonstrate with (one's superior or freind); admonish:～阻 admonition. 进～ remonstrance

践 jiàn〈动〉① tread; trample ② fulfil; carry out:～诺 keep one's word

践诺 jiànnuò keep one's promise

践踏 jiàntà trample (on); tread (on):～原则 trample a principle

践约 jiànyuē keep a promise; fulfil one's engagement

贱 jiàn〈形〉① cheap:～买贵卖 buy cheap and sell dear ② lowly; humble:贫～ poor and lowly ③ mean; base:下～ base; shameless

贱骨头 jiàngútou miserable wretch; worthless creature; rotter

贱货 jiànhuò ① cheap goods ② miserable (contemptible) wretch

贱买贱卖 jiànmǎi-jiànmài buy and sell at low prices

贱民 jiànmín outcaste; mean people; the untouchables

溅 jiàn〈动〉splash; spatter

溅落 jiànluò (of a space vehicle, etc.) splash down

饯 jiàn ①〈动〉give a farewell dinner ②〈名〉candied fruit:蜜～ preserved fruit

饯别 jiànbié give a farewell dinner

饯行 jiànxíng give a farewell dinner

荐 jiàn〈动〉recommend：～举 recommend sb. for a post (an office)；recommend

鉴 jiàn〈名〉① ancient bronze mirror ② warning；object lesson：～戒 take warning from〈动〉③ reflect；mirror：水清可～。The water is so dear that you can see your reflection in it. ④ scrutinize；examine；inspect：～别好坏 distinguish the good from the bad

鉴别 jiànbié identify；differentiate；distinguish：～能力 ability to differentiate；discernment. ～真伪 distinguish between genuine and false

鉴定 jiàndìng appraise；determine；authenticate：～笔迹 identify handwriting. ～产品质量 appraise the quality of a product. ～家 connoisseur. 通过国家～ pass state appraisal. ～人[法]expert；expert witness；identifier. ～意见书 verified written opinion

鉴赏 jiànshǎng appreciate：～家 connoisseur

鉴于 jiànyú in view of；in consideration of：～这些事实 in view of these facts

见 jiàn〈动〉① see；catch sight of：～物不～人 ignore the human factor and see only the material factor ② meet with；be exposed：～不得天日 cannot bear the light of day ③ appear to be；show evidence：日久～人心。Time reveals a person's heart. ④ refer to；see：～第26页 see p. 26. ～后 vide post；see after ⑤ call on；see；visit：下午～。See you afternoon. ⑥ view；opinion：～识高的人 a man of broad vision

见不得人 jiànbudérén cannot stand scrutiny；unpresentable；disreputable；cannot bear the light of day；shameful；scandalous

见财起意 jiàncái-qǐyì entertain evil thoughts at the sight of money

见长 jiàncháng be good at；be expert in

见地 jiàndì insight；judgement：深有～的人 man of deep insight

见多识广 jiànduō-shíguǎng well-informed and well-grounded；have great experience；have a mind of wide scope

见风使舵 jiànfēng-shǐduò sail with the wind (current)；trim one's sail；act as the occasion dictates；temporizing

见缝插针 jiànfèng-chāzhēn insert a needle wherever a crevice is seen — utilize every bit of space；make use of every second

见怪 jiànguài take amiss；mind；take offence (at)：我的话请勿～。Please don't take my words amiss.

见鬼 jiànguǐ ① fantastic；preposterous；absurd ② go to hell

见机行事 jiànjī-xíngshì act according to circumstances；do as one sees fit

见教 jiànjiào favour me with your advice; instruct me

见解 jiànjiě view; viewpoint; opinion

见景生情 jiànjǐng-shēngqíng one sees a scene that arouses his emotions; be moved by what one sees; The scene evokes memories of the past.; Memories revive the sight of familiar places

见面 jiànmiàn meet; see:他们俩经常～。They see a lot of each other.

见面礼 jiànmiànlǐ present given to sb. on first meeting him

见票 jiànpiào [商] demand:～付款 payable on demand. ～即付 payable at sight; payable to bearer

见世面 jiànshìmiàn face (see) the world; enrich one's experience

见仁见智 jiànrén-jiànzhì different people have different views even about the same question; personal differences of opinion; different people, different views; opinions differ

见识 jiànshí ① widen one's knowledge ② knowledge; insight; experience: 有～的 knowledgeable; intelligent. 长～ enrich one's knowledge; broaden one's horizons

见世面 jiànshìmiàn see the world; enrich one's experience

见外 jiànwài regard sb. as an outsider

见闻 jiànwén what one sees and hears; information; knowledge: ～广 well-informed. ～录 sketchbook

见习 jiànxí be on probation:～教师 teacher intern. ～期间 probationership. ～生 probationer

见效 jiànxiào take effect; be effective; produce the desired result

见笑 jiànxiào ① laugh at (me or us): 您可别～。Now don't laugh at me. ② incur ridicule (by one's poor performance)

见义勇为 jiànyìyǒngwéi gallantly rise to the occasion; do boldly what is righteous; act bravely for a just cause

见异思迁 jiànyì-sīqiān change one's mind the moment one sees something new; be inconstant; wish to change one's work the moment someone sees something different

见长 jiànzhǎng grow perceptibly

见证 jiànzhèng witness; testimony:～人 eyewitness; witness

舰 jiàn 〈名〉 warship; naval vessel; battleship

舰队 jiànduì fleet; naval force

舰旗 jiànqí ensign

舰艇 jiàntǐng naval ships and boats; naval craft (vessels)

舰载 jiànzài carrier-borne; carrier-based; ship-bassed

舰长 jiànzhǎng captain

舰只 jiànzhī warships; naval vessels

剑 jiàn 〈名〉 sword; sabre

剑拔弩张 jiànbá-nǔzhāng with swords drawn and bows bent;

at daggers drawn; sabre-rattling;in a blustering and aggressive manner

剑术 jiànshù art of fencing

剑舞 jiànwǔ sword dance

箭 jiàn〈名〉arrow

箭步 jiànbù a sudden big stride forward

箭楼 jiànlóu embrasured watchtower over a city gate

箭在弦上 jiànzàixiánshàng like an arrow on the bowstring — there can be no turning back

件 jiān〈名〉① piece; article; item: 2～行李 two pieces of luggage ② letter; correspondence; document; paper: 急～ urgent document or dispatch ③〈量〉[指可以一一计算的事物]: 案～ case

件次 jiàncì total number of items from successive events

件工 jiàngōng piece rate

建 jiàn〈动〉① build; construct; erect: ～水力发电站 build a hydropower station ② establish; set up; found: ～国 found a state ③ propose; advocate

建材工业 jiàncái gōngyè building materials industries

建交 jiànjiāo establish diplomatic relations (with)

建军 jiànjūn build an army: ～节 August First Army Day; Army Day

建立 jiànlì build (up); establish; set up; found; form; create: ～功勋 perform meritorious deeds. ～广泛的统一战线 form an most extensive united front

建设 jiànshè build; construct: ～公债 public bonds for construction. ～社会主义精神文明 promote (build) socialist culture and ethics. ～有中国特色的社会主义 building socialism with Chinese characteristics. ～周期 construction cycle

建树 jiànshù make contributions to; contribute to (towards)

建议 jiànyì propose; suggest: ～价格 suggested price

建造 jiànzào build; construct; make

建制 jiànzhì organizational system: ～镇 official status of township; county town whose status as town has been established by the government. 部队～ the organizational system of the army

建筑 jiànzhù ① construct; build; erect: ～包工队 construction teams on contract. ～高楼 erect a tall building ② building; structure; edifice: 拆除违章～ level illegal buildings to the ground. ～楼比 ratio of space allotted to buildings. ～造型艺术 art of architectural modelling

键 jiàn〈名〉key: 琴～ a piano key

键盘 jiànpán keyboard; fingerboard: ～练习曲 [乐] keyboard practice. ～乐器 keyboard instrument; clavier

健 jiàn ①〈形〉strong; healthy; robust:～步来到 walk with firm strides into …〈动〉② strengthen; invigorate; toughen:～脾 invigorate the function of the spleen ③ be good at; be strong in:～谈 be a good talker

健步 jiànbù walk at a brisk pace; walk with firm steps:～如飞 walk fast and vigorously

健将 jiànjiàng ①［田径等的］master sportsman or sportswoman ②［球类等的］top-notch player

健康 jiànkāng health; physique:～保险 health insurance. ～文明的生活方式 healthy and cultured life-styles. ～证明书 health certificate; medical certificate

健美 jiànměi strong and handsome; vigorous and graceful:～操 eurythmics; aerobics. ～运动 body building

健全 jiànquán ①〈形〉sound; healthy; sturdy ②〈动〉strengthen; improve; put… on a sound footing; consolidate; perfect:～理智 intellectual integrity. ～法制 perfect the legal system

健身操 jiànshēncāo setting-up exercise; callisthenics

健身房 jiànshēnfáng gymnasium; gym

健谈 jiàntán be a good talker; be a brilliant conversationalist

健忘 jiànwàng forgetful; oblivious:～的人 man who has short memory

健在 jiànzài (of a person of advanced age) be still living and in good health

健壮 jiànzhuàng healthy and strong; robust

jiāng

将 jiāng〈动〉① do sth.; handle (a matter):慎重～事 handle a matter with care. ～某人捉拿归案 bring sb. to justice ② check［象棋］:"～一军"的局面 in a position of being checkmated ③ incite sb. to action; challenge; checkmate:他可～了我的军。He had pushed me to a corner. ④ be going to; be about to:革命～要胜利。The revolution was approaching victory.〈介〉⑤［拿、用,多见于成语］with; by; by means of:恩～仇报 repay kindness with ingratitude ⑥［把］:～窗关上 shut the window ⑦〈助〉［用在动词和"进来"、"出去"等表示趋向的补语中间］:～走进去 get into (the room)
另见 jiàng

将次 jiāngcì be going to; will; shall

将错就错 jiāngcuò-jiùcuò make the best of a mistake; take the wrong and make the best of it

将功补过 jiānggōng-bǔguò make amends for one's previous faults (mistakes) by giving good service

将功赎罪 jiānggōng-shúzuì atone for a crime by meritorious service; expiate faults by good services; make amends for one's crimes by good deeds

将计就计 jiāngjì-jiùjì reply to sb.'s trick with one's own; meet another's scheme with one's own; turn sb.'s trick against himself

将将 jiāngjiāng just; barely; only

将近 jiāngjìn ① nearly; almost; close to ② be getting on for; be close on: 他~60岁了。He is getting on for sixty.

将就 jiāngjiu make do with; make the best of; put up with

将军 jiāngjūn ① general ② [象棋] check ③ embarrass; put sb. on the spot

将来 jiānglái future

将信将疑 jiāngxìn-jiāngyí half believe; be half in doubt; with reservations

将养 jiāngyǎng rest; recuperate

将欲取之，必先与之 jiāng yù qǔzhī, bì xiān yǔzhī In order to take, one must first give.; Give in order to take.

浆

jiāng ①〈形〉thick liquid ②〈动〉starch

另见 jiàng

浆洗 jiāngxǐ wash and starch

姜

jiāng〈名〉ginger

姜还是老的辣 jiāng háishi lǎode là old ginger is hotter than new—veterans are abler than recruits

姜太公钓鱼，愿者上钩 jiāngtàigōng diàoyú, yuànzhě shànggōu (like) the fish rising to Jiang Tai Gong's hookless and baitless line — a willing victim letting himself be caught; willingly to fall into the snare

姜汤 jiāngtāng ginger decoction

江

jiāng〈名〉river: ~岔 river arm

江河日下 jiānghé-rìxià go from bad to worse; deteriorate with each passing day; fall away; be on the decline

江湖 jiānghú ①rivers and lakes ② itineracy: ~与中国雅文化 itineracy and Chinese culture of elegance ③ itinerant entertainers, quacks, etc. ④ trade of such people: ~医生 quack; mountebank; charlatan. ~艺人 wandering performers; itinerant entertainers

江山 jiāngshān ① rivers and mountains ② land; country: ~如画。The land is picturesque. ~易改本性难移。Rivers and mountains may be changed but it is hard to alter a man's nature.; A fox may grow grey, but never good.; The leopard can never change its spots.

僵

jiāng〈形〉① stiff; rigid numb: ~化的公式 rigid formula ② deadlocked; have reached a stalemate: 打破~持 break the stalemate

僵持 jiāngchí be at a deadlock; be stalemated; reach a deadlock; stalemate

僵化 jiānghuà rigid; ossified; petrified; inflexible; stiffened: 思

想～ have a rigid way of thinking

僵局 jiāngjú impasse; stalemate; deadlock:谈判陷入～。The negotiations have reached (come to) a deadlock.

僵死 jiāngsǐ ① stagnate; petrify ② stiff and dead; rigid:～的东西 something rigid

僵硬 jiāngyìng ① stiff ② rigid; inflexible

缰 jiāng〈名〉reins; halter:～绳 reins; halter

疆 jiāng〈名〉boundary; border; bounds; limits

疆场 jiāngchǎng battlefield:～捐躯 lay down one's life on the battlefield

疆臣 jiāngchén high-ranking officials

疆界 jiāngjiè border; boundary; confines

疆域 jiāngyù territory; domain

jiǎng

奖 jiǎng ①〈动〉praise; encourage; reward:～励先进 rewarding the advanced ②〈名〉prize; award; premium:～金 bonus; premium

奖杯 jiǎngbēi (challenge) cup:～保持者 cup holder

奖惩 jiǎng-chěng rewards and penalties; rewards and disciplinary sanctions

奖金 jiǎngjīn bonus; premium; money award:年终～ year-end bonus

奖券 jiǎngquàn lottery ticket

奖励 jiǎnglì ① encourage and reward; give awards (to) ② reward; award; citation:～工资 reward wages

奖勤罚懒 jiǎngqín-fálǎn reward the diligent and punish the lazy

奖品 jiǎngpǐn prize; award; trophy

奖赏 jiǎngshǎng ① reward; prize; premium ② reward (with, for)

奖售 jiǎngshòu awarding those who overfulfil their state purchase quotas; premiums for sale; reward sale

奖学金 jiǎngxuéjīn scholarship; monetary academic prize; fellowship; grant-in-aid:～考试 scholarship examination

奖章 jiǎngzhāng medal; decoration:金质～ gold medal

奖状 jiǎngzhuàng ① honour certificate; certificate of merit; commendation; citation ②［学校］testimonial (of good conduct and progress)

桨 jiǎng〈名〉oar; paddle

桨板 jiǎngbǎn paddle board

讲 jiǎng〈动〉① say; speak; talk; tell:～的是一套,做的是另一套 say (talking about) one thing and do another ② explain; elaborate; make clear:～明立场 state one's stand in explicit terms ③ discuss; bargain; negotiate:～道理 reason things out. ～价钱 negotiate terms; bargain over the pirce ④stress; pay attention to:～究卫生 pay attention to hygiene ⑤〈名〉lecture; discoure:～义 lecture sheets; teaching materials

讲道 jiǎngdào ① moralization; preaching; preachment ② preach a sermon; deliver a sermon; sermonize

讲道理 jiǎng-dàolǐ reason things out; discuss … rationally; be reasonable

讲稿 jiǎnggǎo lecture notes; [演讲稿] the text (draft) of a speech

讲和 jiǎnghé make peace (with); settle a dispute

讲价 jiǎngjià bargain; haggle over the price

讲解 jiǎngjiě explain; expound; interpret:～式教学 expository teaching. ～员[展览会的] interpreter; [游览的] guide

讲究 jiǎngjiu ① be particular about; pay (special) attention to:～工作方法 make efforts to study and perfect the method of work ② elegant; tasteful

讲课 jiǎngkè teach; lecture; give a lesson; give lectures:～时数 teaching hours

讲理 jiǎnglǐ ① reason with sb.; argue ② listen (be amenable) to reason; be reasonable; be sensible

讲求 jiǎngqiú pay (special) attention to; stress; strive for:～经济效果 stress better economic results; take into consideration the economic effect. 办事～效率 strive for efficiency in work

讲排场 jiǎngpáichǎng go in for pomp; love ostentation

讲评 jiǎngpíng comment on and appraise:～学生作业 comment on students' work. ～作文 description and critiquie of an essay

讲情 jiǎngqíng plead for sb.; intercede; put in a good word for sb.; ask for leniency:她为儿子～。She pleaded for her son.

讲师 jiǎngshī lecturer; instructor:～团 lecture teams

讲授 jiǎngshòu [教]lecture; instruct; teach

讲述 jiǎngshù tell about; relate; narrate

讲坛 jiǎngtán ① (speaker's) platform; rostrum ② forum (for public discussion)

讲演 jiǎngyǎn lecture; speech; make a speech (on); give a lecture (on)

讲义气 jiǎngyìqi set store by gallantry

讲座 jiǎngzuò ① course of lectures; series of lectures ② chair

jiàng

匠 jiàng〈名〉craftsman; artisan

匠人 jiàngrén artisan; craftsman

匠心独运 jiàngxīn-dúyùn consummate craftsmanship

酱 jiàng ①〈名〉sauce; paste; [果酱]jam ②〈形〉pickled;

marinated:～鸭 marinated duck

酱菜 jiàngcài pickled vegetables; pickles

酱油 jiàngyóu soy sauce; soy

酱园 jiàngyuán shop making and selling sauce, pickles, etc.; sauce and pickle shop

降 jiàng 〈动〉fall; come (go) down; drop; descend; lower: ～低生产成本 reduce (lower) production costs. 地位～低 a decline in the standing of

另见 xiáng

降低 jiàngdī lower; cut down; drop; debase; reduce:～生产增长速度 holding up the growth of production

降格 jiànggé lower one's standard or status

降级 jiàngjí demote; degrade

降临 jiànglín befall; arrive; come

降落 jiàngluò fall; drop; [飞机] land:一架喷气式客机～在空军基地。A jetliner touched down at the air force base.

降落伞 jiàngluòsǎn parachute

降水量 jiàngshuǐliàng precipitation

降温 jiàngwēn ① lower the temperature ② drop in temperature

降值 jiàngzhí depreciation

将 jiàng 〈名〉① general ② commander in chief, the chief piece in Chinese chess

另见 jiāng

将才 jiàngcái as a field commander

将领 jiànglǐng high-ranking military officer; general

将士 jiàngshì commanders and fighters; officers and soldiers

浆 jiàng 〈名,动〉starch

另见 jiāng

浆糊 jiànghu paste; starch

jiāo

浇 jiāo 〈动〉① sprinkle on; pour liquid on:大雨～得她全身都湿透了。She was drenched with rain. ② water; irrigate: ～地 irrigate the fields

浇灌 jiāoguàn ① irrigate; irrigation: ～面积 irrigated acreage ② pour: ～混凝土 pour concrete

浇注 jiāozhù pour into a mould

交 jiāo 〈动〉① hand in; give; deliver; turn over: ～货 deliver the goods ② (of places or periods of time) meet; join:秋冬之～ when autumn is changing into winter ③ reach (a certain hour or season):去年～春早。Spring set in early last year. ④ insert; cross: ～叉分类 cross-classification ⑤ associate with; make friends; be on good terms with ⑥ breed; mate:杂～ cross breed 〈名〉⑦ friendship; acquaintance; relationship: 点头之～ nodding acquaintance ⑧ business transaction:成～不旺的市场 thin market ⑨〈形〉mutual; reciprocal:～换 exchange

交班 jiāobān turn over one's duty (to); change shift

交保 jiāobǎo [法] let go on bail; deliverance:～者 deliverer

交叉 jiāochā ① intersect; cross; crisscross ② overlapping:③ alternate; stagger

交差 jiāochāi report to the leadership after accomplishing a task

交出 jiāochū surrender; hand over

交错 jiāocuò ① interlock; crisscross ② staggered

交代(待) jiāodài ① hand over; transfer:～工作 hand over work to one's successor; brief one's successor on his owrk ② explain; expound ③ tell; bid; instruct:～任务 brief sb. on his task ④ confess; make a clean breast; give an account of:～问题 give an account of the problem. ～罪行 confess a crime

交底 jiāodǐ tell sb. what one's real intentions are; keep sb. well-informed:他们相互～。They have confided to each other what they have in mind.

交锋 jiāofēng cross swords; engage in a battle or contest

交付 jiāofù ① pay:～租金 pay rent ② hand over; deliver; consign

交割 jiāogē complete a business transaction:～日 prompt day; pay day; settlement day

交还 jiāohuán give back; return

交换 jiāohuàn exchange; interchange:～留学生 exchange students. ～意见 exchange views; compare notes. ～批准书 exchange of ratification

交货 jiāohuò ① deliver the goods ② delivery:～单 delivery order. ～前付款 cash before delivery. ～日期 date of delivery

交际 jiāojì social intercourse; contacts; communication:～舞 social dancing; ballroom dancing. ～应酬费 business entertainment expense

交加 jiāojiā (of two things) accompany each other; occur simultaneously

交接 jiāojiē ① join; connect ② hand over and take over:保证顺利～ ensure a smooth transfer

交口称誉 jiāokǒu-chēngyù praise with one voice; unanimously praise; be held in high esteem

交流 jiāoliú ① exchange:～经验 exchange (share, swop) experience; compare notes with ② alternating:～电 alternating current

交流电 jiāoliúdiàn alternating current (AC)

交纳 jiāonà pay (to the state or an organization); hand in

交配 jiāopèi mating; copulation

交情 jiāoqing friendship; acquaintanceship; friendly relations:与某人有～ be on good terms with sb.

交涉 jiāoshè negotiate (with); make negotiations:办～ carry on negotiations; take up a matter with

交手 jiāoshǒu fight hand to hand; be engaged in a hand-to-hand fight; come to grips

交谈 jiāotán talk with each other; converse; chat

交替 jiāotì ① supersede; replace 新旧体制的～ the transition from the old structure to the new ② alternately; in turn

交通 jiāotōng communication; traffic:～工具 means of communication. ～规则 traffic regulations. ～警 traffic police. ～干线 the main line of communications. ～极为便利 have excellent communications. ～事故现场 scene of a traffic (road) accident

交头接耳 jiāotóu-jiē'ěr speak in each other's ears; whisper to each other

交往 jiāowǎng intercourse; contacts; dealings:和某人有(没有)～ have (no) dealings with sb.

交响乐 jiāoxiǎngyuè symphony; symphonic music:～团 symphony orchestra

交心 jiāoxīn open one's heart to; reveal what's in his heart; confide what one has in mind:相互～ have a heart-to-heart talk

交易 jiāoyì trade; business; transaction; deal:～额 volume of trade; turnover. ～会 commodities fair; trade fair. 一揽子～ package deal

交易所 jiāoyìsuǒ exchange:商品～ commodity exchange. 证券～ stock exchange

交游 jiāoyóu make friends

交战 jiāozhàn be at war (with); wage war; fight a war (with, against):～国 combatant (belligerent) nation

交帐 jiāozhàng ① hand over the accounts ② account for:他实在交不了帐 when it became impossible for him to drag on

交织 jiāozhī interweave; intertwine; mingle

胶

胶 jiāo 〈名〉① glue; gum ② rubber:～皮带 rubber belt ③〈动〉stick with glue; glue

胶版 jiāobǎn offset plate

胶布 jiāobù ① adhesive plaster (tape) ② rubberized fabric

胶带 jiāodài adhesive tape; gummed tape

胶合板 jiāohébǎn plywood; veneer board

胶卷 jiāojuǎn roll film; film

胶皮 jiāopí rubber:～轱辘车 rubber-wheeled cart

胶片 jiāopiàn film:正色～ orthochromatic film

胶水 jiāoshuǐ mucilage; glue

胶鞋 jiāoxié ① rubber overshoes; galoshes; rubbers ② rubber-soled shoes; tennis shoes; sneakers

胶印 jiāoyìn offset printing; offset print:彩色～ offset print in colour

胶着 jiāozhuó deadlocked; stalemated:～状态 deadlock; stalemate; impasse

郊

郊 jiāo 〈名〉suburbs; outskirts

郊区 jiāoqū suburban area; suburbs:～居民 suburbanite. ～县 suburban counties. 北京～ in the suburbs of Beijing

郊外 jiāowài (in the) suburbs; (on the) outskirts

郊游 jiāoyóu outing; excursion: 去～ go outing

教 jiāo 〈动〉teach; instruct
另见 jiào

教给 jiāogěi impart (knowledge, skill) on someone

教书 jiāoshū teach: ～育人 impart knowledge and educate (cultivate) people

娇 jiāo 〈形〉① tender; lovely; charming ② fragil; frail; delicate: 这女孩子身体太～嫩了。The girl's health is fragile. ③ finicky; squeamish. ④〈动〉spoil; pamper: ～惯孩子 pamper a child

娇嗔 jiāochēn grumble in a flirtish manner

娇惯 jiāoguàn pamper; coddle; spoil

娇嫩 jiāonèn ① tender and lovely ② fragile; delicate

娇气 jiāoqì finicky (finical) airs: ～十足 be full of finicality

娇生惯养 jiāoshēng-guànyǎng be accustomed to delicate living; be brought up in clover; be spoiled; be pampered

娇小 jiāoxiǎo petite; delicate

娇纵 jiāozòng pamper; indulge: ～孩子 pamper a child

骄 jiāo 〈形〉① proud; arrogant; conceited: ～傲自持 overconfidence and conceit ② fierce; strong: ～阳 the blazing sun

骄傲 jiāo'ào arrogant; conceited: ～自满 become conceited and complacent; be conceited and self-satisfied; self-exaltation and self-complacency

骄兵必败 jiāobīng-bìbài The self-conceited troops are destined to fail (failure).; An army puffed up with pride is bound to lose.

骄横 jiāohèng arrogant and imperious; overbearing: ～得不可一世 insufferably arrogant; extremely overbearing; unberably conceited

骄奢淫逸 jiāoshē-yínyì lordly, luxury-loving, loose-living and idle; wallowing in luxury and pleasure; extravagant and dissipated; live a licentious, extravagant life

骄阳 jiāoyáng blazing sun: ～似火 a scorching sun beating down

焦 jiāo 〈形〉① scorched; burnt: ～土 the scorched earth ② anxious; worried: ～急万状 much worried; in hot haste ③〈名〉coke: 炼～ coking

焦点 jiāodiǎn ① focus; focal point ② point at issue; central issue: 问题～所在。Herein lies the heart of the matter.

焦急 jiāojí anxious; worried

焦虑 jiāolǜ ① anxiety ② be very anxious about; distress oneself about

焦头烂额 jiāotóu-làn'é in a terrible fix; in dire straits; be bruised and battered: 打得敌人

～ beat the enemy black and blue

焦油 jiāoyóu tar

焦躁 jiāozào ① feel vexed; be in a fret ② restless with anxiety; fretful; impatient

焦灼 jiāozhuó deeply worried; very anxious

礁 jiāo 〈名〉 reef: 触～ run up on arock; strike a reef

礁石 jiāoshí (sunken) rock; reef

jiáo

嚼 jiáo 〈动〉chew; masticate; munch: 细～慢咽 chew carefully and swallow slowly

嚼舌 jiáoshé ① wag one's tongue; chatter; gossip ② argue meaninglessly; squabble

jiǎo

佼 jiǎo 〈形〉 beautiful; handsome

佼佼 jiǎojiǎo above average; outstanding: ～者 outstanding figure

皎 jiǎo 〈形〉 bright and clear: ～月当空。A bright moon hung in the sky.

皎洁 jiǎojié (of moonlight) bright and clear

狡 jiǎo 〈形〉 cunning; crafty; foxy

狡辩 jiǎobiàn quibble; indulge in sophistry

狡猾 jiǎohuá sly; cunnintg; crafty

狡赖 jiǎolài deny (by resorting to sophistry); play the fox; prevaricate

狡兔三窟 jiǎotù-sānkū a wily hare has three burrows — a crafty person has more than one hideout

狡诈 jiǎozhà cunning; deceitful; falsehearted

饺 jiǎo 〈名〉 dumpling: 水～ boiled dumplings

饺子 jiǎozi dumpling (with meat and vegetable stuffing): ～皮 dumpling wrappper. ～馅 filling for dumplings

绞 jiǎo 〈动〉 ① twist; wring: ～动吊车 turn a windlass ② hang: ～架 gallows ③〈量〉 skein; hank: 2～毛线 two skeins of woolen yarn

绞尽脑汁 jiǎojìn-nǎozhī rack (cudgel) one's brains

绞痛 jiǎotòng ① colicky pain; colic ② angina: 心～ angina pectoris

绞刑 jiǎoxíng punishment by strangling; death by hanging: 上～ be hanged by the neck

搅 jiǎo 〈动〉 ① mix; stir: 用匙～咖啡 stir one's coffee with a spoon ② disturb: 他在工作，别打～他。He is working. Don't disturb him.

搅拌 jiǎobàn stir; mix

搅动 jiǎodòng mix; stir

搅浑 jiǎohún stir and make muddy; deliberately create confusion

搅和 jiǎohuo ① mix; blend; mingle ② mess up; spoil

搅乱 jiǎoluàn confuse; disarrange; mess up; throw into disorder: ～全部计划 mess up the whole scheme

矫 jiǎo 〈动〉① straighten out; rectify; correct: ～正教育教师 remedial teacher ② feign; pretend ③〈形〉strong; brave

矫健 jiǎojiàn strong and vigorous; robust: ～的身影 robust physique

矫揉造作 jiǎoróu-zàozuò artificial; affected; mannered; too-too; tortuous: ～的文体 mannered style of writing. 这部电影～。The movie was simply too-too.

矫饰 jiǎoshì feign in order to conceal sth.; dissemble: ～的文体 ambitious style

矫枉过正 jiǎowǎng-guòzhèng exceed the proper limits in righting a wrong; overcorrect; overdo in rectifying behaviour; straighten the crooked beyond the straight

矫正 jiǎozhèng set right; correct; remedy: ～教学 remedial teaching. ～院 house of correction

侥 jiǎo

侥幸 jiǎoxìng luckily; by luck; by a fluke: ～取胜 win by a stroke of luck; win by a fluke; winning easy victories through good luck. ～心理 the idea of leaving things to chance

缴 jiǎo 〈动〉① pay; turn over (to): ～纳罚款 pay the penalty ② capture: ～获归公 hand (turn) in everything captured

缴费 jiǎofèi pay a fee (to): ～图书馆 subscription library

缴获 jiǎohuò capture; seize

缴库 jiǎokù pay into the treasury; turn the taxes over to the state treasury

缴款 jiǎokuǎn make payment: ～通知 pay notice

缴纳 jiǎonà hand in; pay: ～使用费 pay for the use of

缴税 jiǎoshuì pay taxes

缴销 jiǎoxiāo hand in for cancellation: ～营业执照 hand in the business licence for cancellation

缴械 jiǎoxiè surrender one's arms; be disarmed

脚 jiǎo 〈名〉① foot: ～步声 the tramp of feet ② base; foot: 山～ the foot of a hill

脚本 jiǎoběn acting copy; acting version; acting script; script; scenario

脚步 jiǎobù footstep; step; pace: ～一致 keep (in) step with

脚夫 jiǎofū ① porter ② one who hires out his donkey or horse to riders and leads or follows it on foot

脚手架 jiǎoshǒujià scaffold; scaffolding

脚踏两条船 jiǎo tà liǎng tiáo chuán sit on the fence; straddle two boats; have a foot in either camp; a fence-sitter

脚踏实地 jiǎotà-shídì have one's feet planted on solid ground — earnest and down-to-earth; down-to-earth; conscientious and practical:～的工作作风 down-to-earth style of work

脚印 jiǎoyìn footprint; footmark; track

脚正不怕鞋歪 jiǎozhèng bú pà xié wāi A straight foot is not afraid of a crooked shoe.

脚注 jiǎozhù footnote

角 jiǎo 〈名〉① horn:牛～ ox horn ② corner:眼～ corner of the eye ③ angle:钝～ obtuse angle ④ ten *fen*; *jiao*
另见 jué

角尺 jiǎochǐ angle square

角度 jiǎodù ①[数]angle ② point of view; angle:从不同～来看这问题 view the problem from a different angle

角落 jiǎoluò ① corner; nook:在教室～里 in a corner of the classroom. 在我国每一～里 in the remote parts of our country

角膜 jiǎomó cornea

剿 jiǎo 〈动〉send armed forces to suppress; annihilate; put down

剿匪 jiǎofěi suppress bandits

剿灭 jiǎomiè wipe out; extirpate

jiào

校 jiào 〈动〉① check; proofread; collate:～长条样 read galley proofs ② contrast; compare
另见 xiào

校订 jiàodìng ① check; collate; emend ② manuscript reader

校对 jiàoduì proofread; read; check; collate:～室 proofroom. ～员 proofreader; press corrector; corrector

校改 jiàogǎi read and correct proofs

校勘 jiàokān textual criticism; textual evaluation; collation:～学 textualism; critical scholarship

校样 jiàoyàng proof (sheet):长条～ galley proof. 付印～ final proof

校阅 jiàoyuè read and revise

校正 jiàozhèng proofread and correct; rectify:～错字 correct misprints

校准 jiàozhǔn adjust; calibrate:～器 calibrator; regulator

较 jiào 〈动〉① compare:～一～劲 have a trial of strength ② dispute:锱铢必～ equibble over every penny ③〈副〉comparatively; relatively:～好的经济效果 better economic results

较劲 jiàojìn match strength

较量 jiàoliàng have a test (contest, trial) of strength between …; match strength with; measure one's strength

较真 jiàozhēn serious; earnest

教 jiào ①〈动〉teach; instruct:有件事对他～育很深。An incident taugh him a serious lesson. 请～ ask for advice; consult ②〈名〉religion:信～ be-

lieve in a religion. 佛～ Buddhism
另见 jiāo

教案 jiào'àn lesson plan; teaching plan

教材 jiàocái teaching material

教程 jiàochéng ① course of study ② (published) lectures

教导 jiàodǎo ① teach; instruct ② teachings; give guidance; instruction:～文学 didactic literature

教工 jiàogōng teachers and staff; teaching and administrative staff

教皇 jiàohuáng pope; pontiff

教会 jiàohuì church:～学校 missionary (church) school

教诲 jiàohuì teaching; instruction; edification; tuition: 谆谆～ earnest teachings

教具 jiàojù teaching aid; classroom aid; instructional media

教科书 jiàokēshū textbook

教练 jiàoliàn ① train; coach ② coach; trainer:～兼队员 player-coach

教师 jiàoshī teacher; mentor; instructor:～节 Teacher's Day (September 10). 家庭～ private teacher; tutor

教授 jiàoshòu ① teach; give lessons (in):～法 methods of teaching; pedagogics ② professor:副～ associate professor. 客座～ guest (visiting) professor

教唆 jiàosuō abet; instigate:～犯 abettor; instigator. ～犯罪 subornation

教堂 jiàotáng church; cathedral

教务 jiàowù educational administration:～处 office of the dean of studies; dean's office. ～长 dean (of studies)

教学 jiàoxué ① teaching and studying ② teaching:～大纲 teaching programme; syllabus. ～工作量 teaching load. ～技术 instructional technology; pedagogic techniques. ～质量 teaching quality

教学相长 jiàoxué-xiāngzhǎng Teaching benefits teachers as well as students.; Both teachers and students make progress by learning from each other.

教训 jiàoxùn ① lesson; moral:吸取～ draw a lesson from sth. ② chide; give sb. a talking-to; lecture sb. (for):～某人 read someone a lecture

教研室 jiàoyánshì teaching and research section (division)

教养 jiàoyǎng ① bring up; educate; train ② culture; (good) breeding; cultivation:有～的 cultured ③ correction:～处分[对少年犯等的] corrective training. ～院 house of correction; reform school [美国]; reformatory [英国]

教育 jiàoyù ① education ② educate; teach:～程度 level of education. ～家 educationist; educator. ～改造[法] reformatory education. ～戏剧 drama in education

教职员 jiàozhíyuán teaching and administrative staff

叫 jiào〈动〉① cry; shout; yell:大～一声 give a loud cry ② call; greet:她被～出城了。She was called out of town. ③ hire; order:～卖 cry one's wares. ～一辆出租车 call (hire) a taxi ④ call; name:你～什么名字? What's your name? 他～张明。He is called Zhang Ming. ⑤ ask; order; bid:他们～她进去。They bade her enter. ⑥〈介〉[用在被动式里引进主动者]:书～小张拿走了。The book was taken by Xiao Zhang.

叫菜 jiàocài choose dishes from a menu; order dishes (in a restaurant)

叫喊 jiàohǎn cry out; shout; yell; howl; call out

叫好 jiàohǎo applaud

叫花子 jiàohuāzi beggar:～主义 beggarism (The philosophy of relying on other's charity to live.); theory of begging for handouts

叫苦 jiàokǔ complain; moan and groan:～不迭 pour out endless grievances; constantly complain; complain to high heaven; ventilate one's endless grievances

叫卖 jiàomài peddle; hawk:沿街～ peddle one's wares in the street

叫门 jiàomén call at the door to be let in

叫屈 jiàoqū complain of being wronged

叫响 jiàoxiǎng loudly lauded (to receive commendation due to outstanding performance)

叫嚣 jiàoxiāo clamour about; raise a hue and cry; raise a hullabaloo

叫座 jiàozuò draw a large audience; draw well:这出戏很～。The play draws well.

窖 jiào ①〈名〉cellar or pit for storing things ②〈动〉store sth. in a cellar or pit

窖藏 jiàocáng store sth. in a cellar or pit

酵 jiào〈动〉ferment; leaven

酵母 jiàomǔ yeast

轿 jiào〈名〉sedan (chair):小～车 car; limousine

轿车 jiàochē bus; (sedan) car

轿子 jiàozi sedan (chair)

jiē

结 jiē〈动〉bear (fruit); form (seed):～果 bear fruit. 这些花～子儿了。These flowers have gone to seed.
另见 jié

结巴 jiēba stammer; stutter; falter; stumble:～地回答 falter out a reply

结实 jiēshi ① strong; sturdy; robust:～的人 man of strong build ② durable:这张椅子很～。This is a very solid chair.

皆 jiē〈副〉all; each and every:尽人～知 It is known to all.

皆大欢喜 jiēdàhuānxǐ everybody

is happy; to the satisfaction of all

接 jiē 〈动〉① come into contact with; come close to:～触 come into contact with ② connect; join; put together:我国与国际经济～轨 interconnection between Chinese and international economies ③ catch; take hold of:～球 catch a ball ④ receive:～电话 answer the phone ⑤ meet; welcome:到火车站～一个代表团 meet a delegation at the railway station

接班 jiēbān ① take sb.'s place; take one's turn on duty ② succeed:～人 successor; heir

接待 jiēdài receive; entertain:～单位 host organization. ～日 reception day; open day [学校]

接济 jiējì give (render) material assistance to; offer pecuniary aid to; give financial help to

接见 jiējiàn grant sb. an audience; receive

接近 jiējìn be close to; be near; approach:～国际水平 approach the international level. ～理论 theory of contiguity

接力 jiēlì work by relays

接连 jiēlián on end; in a row; in succession

接纳 jiēnà admit (into an organization); accept:～新会员 admit new members

接洽 jiēqià consult with; take up a matter with; arrange (sth.) with:她来～工作。She is here on business. ～业务 arrange business with sb.

接壤 jiērǎng border on; be contiguous to; be bounded by

接任 jiērèn take over a job; replace; succeed

接生 jiēshēng deliver a child; practise midwifery

接手 jiēshǒu ① take over (duties, etc.):这项工作我刚～,还不熟悉。I'm new to the job; in fact, I've just taken over. ② catcher

接收 jiēshōu ① take over ② receive ③ admit; take in

接受 jiēshòu accept; take; embrace:～传票人 person summoned. ～定货 accept (execute) an order. ～教训 learn a lesson (from). ～新思想 receive new ideas; receptive of new ideas

接送货物服务 jiēsòng huòwù fúwù pick up and delivery service

接替 jiētì take over; replace

接头 jiētóu ① get in touch with; contact ② know about:这事情他不～。He knows nothing about it.

接吻 jiēwěn kiss

接续 jiēxù continue; follow

接应 jiēying ① come to sb.'s aid; coordinate with ② supply:食品不再～不上。Food is no longer in short supply.

接踵而来 jiēzhǒng'érlái follow hard at heel

接种 jiēzhòng have an inoculation; inoculate

揭 jiē 〈动〉① uncover; lift (the lid, etc.):～盖子 take the lid off ② take off; tear off:他把墙上那幅画～下来。He took that picture off the wall. ③ expose; reveal; bring to light:～开某人的真面目 expose sb. in his true colours ④〈书〉hoist; raise:～竿而起 rise up in arms

揭不开锅 jiēbukāiguō have nothing in the pot; have nothing to eat; go hungry

揭穿 jiēchuān expose; disclose; lay bare; show up:～骗局 show up a fraud

揭短 jiēduǎn rake up sb.'s faults, shortcomings or weaknesses

揭发 jiēfā expose; unmask; reveal; bring to light:～阴谋 expose (disclose) a secret plot

揭开 jiēkāi open up; uncover; disclose:～内幕 reveal the inside story; get to the bottom of

揭露 jiēlù expose; unmask; lay bare; uncover; ferret out:～非法活动 lay bare illegal activities

揭幕 jiēmù raise the curtain; unveil; inaugurate:～式 unveiling ceremony; inaguration

揭示 jiēshì ① announce ② reveal; bring to light; put forth:～资本主义生产关系的本质 bring to light the essence of the capitalist relations of production. 马克思～的社会劳动分配规律 the law of distribution of social labour put forth by Marx

揭晓 jiēxiǎo announce; publish; announce the results; make known:考试成绩已～。The result of the examination has been announced.

阶 jiē〈名〉stairs; steps:石～ stone stairs ② rank; grade:军～ military rank

阶层 jiēcéng (social) stratum:～意识 stratum consciousness

阶段 jiēduàn stage; period; phase:历史～ historical period

阶级 jiējí class:～差别 class distinctions. ～分化 class differentiation; class polarization. ～阶层结构 class hierarchy. ～特点 class traits. ～性 class character

阶梯 jiētī ① steps; ladder ② stepping stone

阶下囚 jiēxiàqiú prisoner; captive

街 jiē〈名〉street:～道服务站 street service stations

街道 jiēdào ① street ② neighbourhood:～办的集体企业 collective enterprises run by urban communities; community-run collectives; neighbourhood enterprises. ～办事处 subdistrict offices; street agencies. ～工厂 neighbourhood factory; community-run workshops. ～社区 urban communities. ～社会工作者 street workers. ～居民委员会 neighbourhood committee

街谈巷议 jiētán-xiàngyì the talk of the town; street gossip

街头剧 jiētóujù street-corner skit; street performance

街头巷尾 jiētóu-xiàngwěi streets and lanes

jié

孑 jié〈副〉all alone; lonely

孑然一身 jiéranyīshēn all alone in

the world; be left quite desolate

洁 jié〈形〉clean: 纯～ clean and honest

洁白 jiébái spotlessly white; pure white

洁白无瑕 jiébái-wúxiá spotless and flawless; spotless white

洁净 jiéjìng clean; spotless

洁癖 jiépǐ unhealthy obsession with cleanliness; mysophobia

洁身自好 jiéshēn-zìhào preserve one's purity; lead an honest and clean life

拮 jié

拮据 jiéjù short of money; in dire straits; hard up; in straitened circumstances: 经济～ in financial straits. 手头～ be hard up for money

结 jié〈动〉① knit; weave; knot; tie: 把毛线～成毛线衫 knit wool into a sweater ② form; connect; forge; cement; congeal: ～成一定的生产关系 enter into definite relations of production with ③ conclude; settle: ～清债务 settle a debt ⑤〈名〉knot: 打～ tie a knot

结案 jié'àn wind up a case; settle a lawsuit

结拜 jiébài become sworn brothers or sisters

结伴 jiébàn go with: ～而行 go or travel in a group

结草衔环 jiécǎo-xiánhuán pay a debt of gratitude

结成 jiéchéng form; make up: 与……～同盟 form an alliance with…

结党营私 jiédǎng-yíngsī gang up for selfish interests; form a clique for selfish purposes; form cliques for private gains

结发夫妻 jiéfà-fūqī husband and wife by the first marriage

结构 jiégòu structure; frame; [小说等的]design: ～布局 structural arrangement (layout). ～严谨 be tight in structure

结果 jiéguǒ ① result; outcome ② finally; at last: ～问题解决了。Finally the question was settled. ③ kill; finish off

结合 jiéhé ① combine (with); integrate (with); link: 理论与实践相～ combine theory with practice ② marry; be united in wedlock

结核 jiéhé ① tubercle ② tuberculosis ③ nodule: 锰～ manganese nodule

结汇 jiéhuì settle foreign exchange account; convert foreign exchange; settlement of exchange; surrender of exchange: ～售汇制度 system for buying and selling foreign exchange

结婚 jiéhūn marry; get married: ～登记 register of marriage. ～证书 marriage certificate; marriage lines

结伙 jiéhuǒ gang: ～斗殴 gang fighting. ～抢劫 gang robbery. ～盗窃 gang stealing

结交 jiéjiāo make friends with; associate with

结晶 jiéjīng ① crystallize ② crystal ③ crystallization: 智慧的～

a crystallization of wisdom
结局 jiéjú final result; conclusion; outcome
结论 jiélùn conclusion: 得出～ come to the conclusion; draw a conclusion; conclude
结盟 jiéméng conclude an alliance (with): 不～国家 nonaligned countries
结膜 jiémó conjunctiva
结亲 jiéqīn ① marry; get married ② (of two families) become related by marriage
结清 jiéqīng clear off; settle; square (up): ～帐目 get one's accounts squared; even up accounts with
结识 jiéshí get acquainted with; pick up an acquaintance with
结束 jiéshù end; finish; conclude; wind up; close
结算 jiésuàn close an account; settle accounts: ～贷款 loan for the settlement of accounts
结尾 jiéwěi ① ending; winding-up stage ② coda
结业 jiéyè finish a course; complete one's studies
结余 jiéyú surplus; balance
结缘 jiéyuán form ties; become attached to
结怨 jiéyuàn contract enmity; incur hatred
结扎手术 jiézhāshǒushù [计生] ligation operation
结帐 jiézhàng settled accounts; square accounts; strike a balance; balance the books

睫 jié〈名〉eyelash; lash
睫毛 jiémáo eyelash; lash

截 jié〈动〉① cut; sever: ～断 cut off ② intercept; stop; check: ～流 stop the flow; dam a river ③〈介〉by (a specified time): ～至下个月底 by the end of next month
截长补短 jiécháng-bǔduǎn make up a deficiency by the surplus; take from the long to add to the short; draw on the strength of each to offset the weakness of the other
截断 jiéduàn cut off; intercept: 敌人的退路已被～。The enemy's line of retreat was cut off.
截稿时间 jiégǎo shíjiān [新闻] press time
截获 jiéhuò intercept and capture
截击 jiéjī intercept
截流 jiéliú dam a river
截留 jiéliú hold back; retain for one's own use: ～应上交的收入 withholding state revenue
截然 jiérán distinctly; sharply; completely; strikingly; entirely: ～不同 entirely different
截瘫 jiétān paraplegia: ～病人 paraplegics
截肢 jiézhī amputation
截止 jiézhǐ ① stop; close; end: ～期 deadline (for). ～时间[新闻]press time
截趾适履 jiézhǐ-shìlǚ cut one's toes (feet) to fit the shoes
截至 jiézhì by (a specified time); up to

劫 jié〈动〉① plunder; rob; raid: 打～ loot; rob ② coerce; compel ③〈名〉disaster;

calamity：浩～ a great calamity

劫持 jiéchí hijacking；abduction：～飞机 hijacking of aircraft；air piracy. ～飞机者 skyjacker

劫富济贫 jiéfú-jìpín rob the rich to give to the poor

劫后余生 jiéhòu-yúshēng be a survivor of a disaster

劫掠 jiélüè looting and vandalism；sack；plunder

劫数 jiéshù predestined fate；inexorable doom

劫狱 jiéyù gaol delivery；prison raid

节 jié〈名〉① joint；node；knob：竹～ bamboo joint ② part；division：音～ syllable ③ festival；red-letter day；holiday：～日气氛 festival atmosphere ④ item：生活小～ trifling personal matters ⑤ moral integrity；chastity：～操 moral integrity〈动〉⑥ save；economize：～衣缩食 save on food and clothing ⑦ abridge：畅销小说的～略 condensation of a popular novel

节哀 jié'āi restrain one's grief

节假日 jiéjiàrì festivals and holidays

节俭 jiéjiǎn thrift；frugality：提倡～ encourage frugality

节节 jiéjié steadily；continually；one after another：～胜利 win (gain) victory after victory；go from victory to victory

节令 jiélìng climate and other natural phenomena of a season

节流 jiéliú reduce expenditure

节录 jiélù excerpt；extract

节目 jiémù programme；item：～部主任 programme director. ～主持人[电台或电视台] host. ～受欢迎程度 rating. 剧场～单 playbill

节拍 jiépāi metre；rhythm

节日 jiérì festival；holiday：～气氛 festive air；festival atmosphere. ～盛装 holiday clothes

节省 jiéshěng save；economize；retrench；cut down：～开支 cut down expenses

节食 jiéshí be moderate in eating and drinking；be (go) on a diet

节外生枝 jiéwài-shēngzhī create side issues；cause complications；raise unexpected side issues

节育 jiéyù birth control

节约 jiéyuē save；be thrifty with；practise economy (on)；economize：～能源 save energy

节制 jiézhì ① control；regulate；check：～饮食 be moderate in eating and drinking. ～资本 the regulation of capital ② command；direct；control：～各军 in command of the armies

节奏 jiézòu rhythm：小说～ rhythm of a novel

捷 jié ①〈形〉prompt；quick；nimble：敏～ agile；nimble；quick ②〈名〉victory：大～ a great victory

捷报 jiébào triumphant news；news of victory；report of success：～频传。Reports of success (Triumphant news) keep pouring in.

捷径 jiéjìng shortcut：走～ take a

shortcut

捷足先登 jiézúxiāndēng The nimble foot gets there first.; Victory belongs to the swift-footed.; The early bird catches (gets) the worm.; outstrip everyone else

竭 jié〈动〉exhaust; use up; wear out

竭诚 jiéchéng with all one's heart; heart and soul; wholeheartedly:～为顾客服务 serve the clients wholeheartedly

竭尽全力 jiéjìn-quánlì spare no effort; do one's utmost; do all one can

竭力 jiélì do one's utmost (best) to; do everything in one's power to; do all one can to…; try one's best:～支持 give all-out support

竭泽而渔 jiézé'éryú catch the fish by draining the pool; drain a pond to catch all the fish; sacrifice future profit to present gains

杰 jié ①〈名〉outstanding person; talented man; hero:俊～ person of outstanding talent; hero ②〈形〉distinguished; eminent

杰出 jiéchū prominent; outstanding; distinguished; remarkable:～的代表 noted representative

杰作 jiézuò masterpiece; masterwork; classics

诘 jié〈动〉closely question; interrogate

诘问 jiéwèn closely question; interrogate; crossexamine

诘责 jiézé censure; rebuke; denounce

jiě

解 jiě〈动〉① divide; separate:～体 disintegrate ② untie; undo; unbind:～鞋带 undo shoelaces ③ ease; dispel; dismiss:～除戒备 relax one's vigilance. ～痛 alleviate pain. ④ explain:～释性分析 explanatory analysis ⑤ comprehend; understand:费～ hard to understand

解馋 jiěchán satisfy a craving for good food

解除 jiěchú dismiss; dissolve; remove; get rid of; relieve; renounce:～管制[法] termination of control. ～合同 rescind a contract; dissolution of contract. ～某人职务 dismiss sb. from his post. ～婚姻关系 dissolution of marriage. ～教养[法] release from rehabilitation. ～顾虑 relieve misgivings

解答 jiědá explain; solve; answer:～习题 explain a problem

解冻 jiědòng ① thaw; melt the ice of (in) ② unfreeze; release:银行存款～ release of bank accounts

解毒 jiědú ① detoxify; detoxicate ② relieve internal heat or fever

解乏 jiěfá ① recover from fatigue ② refreshing

解放 jiěfàng liberate；free；emancipate：～思想 emancipate one's mind；emancipation of minds

解雇 jiěgù discharge；sack；fire；dismiss from office：被～ be dismissed；get the sack

解恨 jiěhèn vent one's hatred；have one's hatred slaked

解禁 jiějìn lift a ban

解酒 jiějiǔ neutralize the effect of alcoholic drinks

解救 jiějiù save；rescue；deliver

解决 jiějué solve；settle；resolve；do away with；finish off：通过内部讨论～分歧 solve the differences through internal discussions

解开 jiěkāi untie；undo ～疑团 clear up suspicions

解渴 jiěkě quench one's thirst

解闷 jiěmèn divert oneself (from boredom)

解囊相助 jiěnáng-xiāngzhù help sb. generoulsy with money

解聘 jiěpìn dismiss (an employee)

解剖 jiěpōu anatomize；dissect；autopsy：～学 anatomy

解气 jiěqì vent one's spleen；work off one's anger

解散 jiěsàn ① break up；dismiss ② dissolve；disband：～法人团体 disincorporate. ～公司 wind up a company

解释 jiěshì explain；expound；elaborate；interpret；elucidate；construe：～法律条文 explain legal provisions

解手 jiěshǒu relieve oneself；go to the toilet (lavatory)

解说 jiěshuō explain orally；comment

解说词 jiěshōcí (oral) commentary；(written) caption

解体 jiětǐ disintegration；collapse；fall apart

解脱 jiětuō free (extricate) oneself；detachment

解围 jiěwéi ① raise a siege ② save sb. from embarrassment；help sb. out of his predicament

解约 jiěyuē terminate an agreement；cancel (rescind) a contract；break off an engagement

解职 jiězhí dismiss (remove) from office；relieve sb. of his post；discharge

姐 jiě 〈名〉elder sister；sister

姐夫 jiěfu elder sister's husband；borther-in-law

姐妹城 jiěmèichéng twinning of sisters；twin cities；sister cities

姐妹篇 jiěmèipiān companion piece；companion volume

jiè

戒 jiè 〈动〉① guard against：力～浮夸 strictly avoid boasting and exaggeration ② exhort；admonish；warn：引以为～ take sth. as an object lesson ③ give up：～烟 leave off (stop) smoking；wean oneself from smoking (tobacco) ④〈名〉Buddhist monastic discipline：～杀生 abstain from taking life

戒备 jièbèi guard；be on the alert；take precautions：～森严 be closely guarded

戒尺 jièchǐ teacher's ruler for beating pupils

戒除 jièchú give up; abstain from; stop: ～恶习 abstain from a bad habit

戒惧 jièjù be frightened and watchful

戒律 jièlǜ religious discipline; commandment; discipline

戒骄戒躁 jièjiāo-jièzào be on guard (to guard) against conceit and impetuosity; shun complacency and impetuosity; guard against pride and haste; avoid conceit and impetuosity; guard against arrogance and rashness

戒心 jièxīn caution; vigilance; wariness: 对某人或某事存有～ be wary of sb. or sth.

戒烟 jièyān give up smoking; swear off smoking

戒严 jièyán enforce (proclaim) martial law; impose a curfew; place guards around

戒指 jièzhi (ginger) ring

诫 jiè ①〈动〉warn; admonish: 告～ give warning; admonish ②〈名〉commandment

介 jiè〈动〉① lie between; interpose: 这座山～于两省之间。The mountain lies between the two provinces. ② take seriously; care; mind: 他不～意你说的话。He doesn't care a rap for what you say.

介词 jiècí preposition

介入 jièrù intervene (in); interpose: ～别国的事务 intervene in the affairs of another country. ～诉讼当事人 intervenient party; intervening party

介绍 jièshào ① introduce; present: ～信 letter of introduction ② recommend; suggest: 为某人～工作 recommend sb. for a position ③ give an account of; brief: 向某人简要地～某事 brief sb. on sth.

介意 jièyì care; mind; care about; get annoyed; take offence (at sth.): 他不懂礼貌，请勿～。Please don't take offence at his impoliteness.

介质 jièzhì medium: 工作～ actuating medium

界 jiè〈名〉① boundary: ～桩 boundary marker ② scope; extent: 眼～ field of vision ③ circles; world: 文艺～ circles of literature and art

界碑 jièbēi boundary tablet

界限 jièxiàn dividing line; demarcation line; bounds; limit

界线 jièxiàn ① boundary line ② demarcation line; dividing line

借 jiè〈动〉① borrow: 我向他～钱。I borrowed money from him. ② lend: 你能把小刀～我吗? Will you lend your knife to me? ③ take advantage of sth.; make use of: ～此机会 take this opportunity (occasion) to ④ use as a pretext: ～端滋事 use … as a text to make trouble

借贷 jièdài borrow or lend money: ～抵押证书 bill of goods adventure

借刀杀人 jièdāo-shārén kill sb. by another's hand; make use of another person to get rid of an adversary; harm sb. through a third party

借调 jièdiào transfer on loan (temporarily):～干部 transfer a cadre on loan. 他～到这家出版社工作。He is on loan to the publishing house.

借读 jièdú study at a school on a "loan" basis (on a temporary basis)

借故 jiègù find an excuse:～推托 find an excuse to refuse

借光 jièguāng excuse me

借花献佛 jièhuā-xiànfó present Buddha with flowers given by another — make a gift of sth. given by another

借鉴 jièjiàn draw lessons from; use for reference; benefit by another person's experience; learn from; use the experience of:外国的经验可供我们～。The experience of other countries can be used for our reference.

借酒浇愁 jièjiǔ-jiāochóu drown one's sorrows in liquor

借据 jièjù debt on bond; certificate of indebtedness

借口 jièkǒu on the pretext of; under the pretence of

借款 jièkuǎn ①[向人借钱] borrow money; ask for a loan:～企业 borrowing enterprise (venture) ②[借钱给人] offer a loan; lend money

借取 jièqǔ borrowing:科技～technological borrowing. 文化～cultural borrowing

借宿 jièsù stay overnight at sb. else's place; put up for the night

借题发挥 jiètí-fāhuī play on the theme of; make use of the subject under discussion to put over one's own ideas; seize on an incident to exaggerate matters

借条 jiètiáo receipt for a loan (IOU)

借用 jièyòng ① borrow; have the loan of ② use sth. for another purpose

借债 jièzhài borrow money; raise (contract) a loan

借重 jièzhòng rely on for support; enlist sb.'s help

借助 jièzhù with the help; have the aid of:～词典阅读英文小说 read an English novel with the help of a dictionary

届

jiè ①〈动〉fall due:～期 on the appointed date; when the day comes ②〈名〉[会议] session; convocation; [毕业班级] year of graduation:他是北京大学1956年～毕业生。He was graduated from Beijing University in the class of 1956. 本～毕业生 this year's graduates

届满 jièmǎn expire; expiration; end of tenure:在任期～时 at the expiration of one's term of office

届期 jièqī when the day comes; on the appointed date

届时 jièshí at the appointed time;

on the occasion by that time

jīn

津 jīn〈名〉saliva

津津乐道 jīnjīn-lèdào take delight in talking about; indulge in elaborating on; delight in talking about; dwell upon … with great relish

津津有味 jīnjīn-yǒuwèi with (great) relish; with gusto; with keen pleasure; with great interest: 听得～ listen with great interest

津贴 jīntiē subsidy; allowance: 岗位～ subsidies appropriate to particular jobs; job subsidies. 物价～ price (dearness) allowance

津液 jīnyè ① body fluid ② saliva

禁 jīn〈动〉① bear; stand; endure: 弱不～风 too weak to stand a gust of wind ② contain (refrain) from: 不～哑然失笑 can't help laughing

另见 jìn

禁不起 jīnbuqǐ be unable to stand (tests, trials, etc.): ～考验 fail to stand the test

禁不住 jīnbuzhù ① be unable to bear or endure ② can't help (doing); can't refrain from: ～流下了眼泪 can't refrain from shedding tears

襟 jīn〈名〉front of a garment

襟怀 jīnhuái bosom; (breadth of) mind: ～坦白 largeness of mind; openminded; open and aboveboard

巾 jīn〈名〉a piece of cloth (as used for a towel, scarf, kerchief, etc.): 餐～ napkin

巾帼 jīnguó woman: ～英雄 heroine; female hero

今 jīn〈形〉① modern; present-day: ～人 contemporaries; this generation; moderns ② today: ～晚 this evening; tonight ③ of this year; this (year): ～春 this (coming) spring

今儿 jīnr today

今非昔比 jīnfēixībǐ Today we are no longer as we have been.; be no longer what one was; The present cannot compare with the past.

今后 jīnhòu from now on; in the days to come; henceforth; hereafter; in future

今日 jīnrì ① this day; today ② present; now

今世 jīnshì this life

今天 jīntiān ① this day; today ② the present time or age; today

今昔 jīnxī the present and the past; today and yesterday: ～对比 contrast the present with the past; contrast past suffering with present happiness

今宵 jīnxiāo tonight

今夜 jīnyè this evening; tonight

今朝 jīnzhāo ① today ② the present; now

金 jīn〈名〉① metals: ～属加工业 metal-working industry ②

money; ～融问题 monetary problems③ gold: ～币 gold coin; gold money

金榜 jīnbǎng a list of successful candidates in the imperial examinations

金不换 jīnbuhuàn not to be exchanged even for gold; invaluable

金本位制 jīnběnwèizhì gold standard

金蝉脱壳 jīnchán-tuōqiào slip out of a predicament like a cicada sloughing its skin; escape by cunning manoeuvring; escape like a cicada by casting off its skin

金刚钻 jīngāngzuàn diamond

金婚 jīnhūn golden wedding

金科玉律 jīnkē-yùlǜ golden rule; infallible law; unalterable rule

金库 jīnkù state (national) treasury; coffers

金兰之交 jīnlánzhījiāo intimate friendship; sworn brotherhood

金迷纸醉 jīnmí-zhǐzuì be given to sensual pleasures; live an extravagant life

金牌 jīnpái [体] gold medal; gold: 赢得2枚～ win two golds

金钱 jīnqián money: ～万能的社会 a society where money talks

金融 jīnróng finance; banking: ～公司 financial company. ～市场 money (financial) market. ～中心 banking centre; financial centre. ～诈骗 financial swindling

金嗓子 jīnsǎngzi golden voice—beautiful voice

金属 jīnshǔ metal

金条 jīntiáo gold bar

金鱼 jīnyú goldfish

金玉良言 jīnyù-liángyán golden saying; precious words; wise counsel

金子 jīnzi gold

金字塔 jīnzìtǎ pyramid: ～式等级制度 hierarchic pyramid

金字招牌 jīnzì-zhāopái ① a gilded signboard; gold-letter signboard ② (of a business firm) of good repute; most realiable; well established

筋

jīn〈名〉① muscle ② sinew: 扭了～ get one's sinew (tendon) sprained ③ vein

筋斗 jīndǒu ① somersault ② tumble (over); fall: 翻～ turn a somersault. 摔～ trip over sth. and fall; have a fall; tumble over

筋骨 jīngǔ ① muscles and bones ② physique; sinews: 强壮～ strengthen the physique

筋疲力尽 jīnpí-lìjìn be used up; be tired out; be completely exhausted; be dead tired

斤

jīn〈量〉*jin*, Chinese unit of weight (=1/2 kilogram)

斤斤计较 jīnjīn-jìjiào square accounts in every detail; be very calculating; be bother about trifling matters; think about personal gains and losses; worry about petty gain or loss

斤两 jīnliǎng weight: ～不足 underweight

jǐn

谨 jǐn 〈形〉① careful; cautious; circumspect: ～慎对待 must be circumspect in ② sincere; respectful: ～启 yours respectfully

谨防 jǐnfáng be cautious of; guard against; beware of: ～扒手 beware of pickpockets (pilferers)

谨慎 jǐnshèn cautious; prudent; discreet: ～谦虚 be modest and prudent

谨小慎微 jǐnxiǎo-shènwēi cautious and meticulous; timid and overcautious; timorous and punctilious

紧 jǐn 〈形〉① tight; taut: 把绳子拉～ pull the rope taut ② fast; firm: 把门关～ make the door fast ③ pressing; urgent; tense: ～任务 urgent task ④ strict; stringent: 管得～ exercise strict control over ⑤ short of money; hard up: ～缩支出 drastically reduce budget expenditure

紧逼 jǐnbī press hard; close in on

紧凑 jǐncòu compact; terse; closely arranged; well-organized; well-knit: ～的情节 well-knit plot. 写得～和深刻 write with intensity and insight

紧跟 jǐngēn follow closely; keep in step with: ～时代的步代 keep in step with the times

紧急 jǐnjí urgent; pressing; emergent; critical: ～避险 urgent danger prevention. ～法令 emergency act. ～会议 emergency meeting. ～追捕 hot pursuit. ～治罪条例 emergency penal ordinance

紧邻 jǐnlín close neighbour; next-door neighbour

紧密 jǐnmì ① close together; inseparable ② thick and fast; rapid and intense: ～的雨点 a heavy rain

紧迫 jǐnpò pressing; urgent; imminent: ～感 feeling (sense) of urgency; awareness of the urgent need; feel the urgent need to

紧俏 jǐnqiào in short supply; currently popular; hot: ～商品 commodities (goods) in short supply; goods in great demand; high demand merchandise

紧缺 jǐnquē shortage: ～物资 materials in shortage

紧身儿 jǐnshenr close-fitting undergarment

紧缩 jǐnsuō cut down; reduce; curtail: ～开支 cut down expenses. ～通货 deflate currency

紧要 jǐnyào ① critical; imminent ② important; momentous: ～关头 (at the) critical moment (juncture)

紧张 jǐnzhāng ① nervous; excited: 心情有些～ be in an excited mood. ～动人的情节 an exciting and moving plot ② tense; strained: 他们之间的关系相当～。 The relations between them are rather strained. ③ [货物等] run short; be in great demand：供应～ be in short supply. 物资供应～。Material goods are in shortage.

紧追 jǐnzhuī in hot pursuit

锦 jǐn ①〈名〉brocade ②〈形〉bright and beautiful：～绣河山 beautiful land；land of charm and beauty

锦标 jǐnbiāo prize；title；trophy：～赛 championship contest；cup event；championships. ～主义 win medals at the expense of sportsmanship；trophies above all

锦缎 jǐnduàn brocade

锦纶 jǐnlún polyamide fibre

锦囊妙计 jǐnnáng-miàojì instructions for dealing with an emergency；wise counsel

锦上添花 jǐnshàng-tiānhuā add flowers to brocade — make perfection still more perfect；put more flowers on the brocade；make beautiful things more beautiful

锦绣 jǐnxiù ① beautiful；fine ② bright；rosy：～前程 bright prospects；glorious future

仅 jǐn〈副〉only；merely

仅仅 jǐnjǐn only；merely；simply

仅识皮毛 jǐnshípímáo only acquainted with skin and hair；have scrappy (a superficial) knowledge

仅以糊口 jǐnyǐhúkǒu live from hand to mouth；pick up a bare livelihood

尽 jǐn ①〈副〉to the great extent：～早 at the earliest possible time (date)；as early as possible ②〈介〉within the limits of：～着一个星期把事情办好。Get the job done properly within a week. ③〈动〉give priority to：～着年纪大的坐。Let the older people sit down first.

尽管 jǐnguǎn ① feel free to；not hesitate to：你～直说。Just speak out. ② in spite of；notwithstanding；even though；though：～下雪，我们还是要动身。We shall start in spite of the snow.

尽可能 jǐnkěnéng as … as possible；to the best of one's ability；in every possible way：～早作准备 get prepared as early as possible

尽快 jǐnkuài as soon (early, quickly) as possible：～投入生产 put into production as soon (early) as possible

尽量 jǐnliàng as far as possible；to the greatest possible extent；to the best of one's ability；in every possible way：～解决 be possible of solution

尽然 jǐnrán entirely so：也不～ not exactly so；not exactly the case

尽先 jǐnxiān〈副〉give first priority to：～考虑住房问题 give first priority to the housing problem

jìn

进 jìn〈动〉① get (go) into；enter：～屋 enter a house or room

② advance; proceed; move forward: ～程 progress; course ③ receive: ～了一批货 have laid in a new stock of goods ④ eat; drink; take: ～食 food intake ⑤ submit; present: ～一言 give a word of advice

进步 jìnbù ① 〈动〉progress; advance; improve ② progress; improvement: 他法语～很快。He has made rapid progress in French.

进餐 jìncān have a meal

进城 jìnchéng ① go into town; go to town ② enter the big cities (to live and work)

进出 jìnchū ① pass in and out ② (business) turnover

进出口 jìnchūkǒu improts and exports: ～货物报关单 customs declaration for imports and exports. ～申报单 import and export declaration. ～商品检验局 import and export commodities inspection bureau. ～总额 total volume of foreign trade

进抵 jìndǐ (of troops) reach (a place)

进度 jìndù ① rate of progress: ～表 progress chart (schedule) ② schedule; planned speed: 按照～完成这项工程。The project is to be completed according to plan.

进而 jìn'ér and then; after that

进发 jìnfā set out; start

进攻 jìngōng attack; assault; offensive

进化 jìnhuà evolution

进货 jìnhuò replenish one's stock (of goods); purchase of merchandise: ～成本 purchase cost; cost of goods purchased

进见 jìnjiàn call on (sb. holding high office); have an audience with

进口 jìnkǒu ① import: ～货 imported goods. ～税 import duty; impost. ～商 importer ② entrance

进来 jìnlái come (get) in; enter

进料加工 jìnliào jiāgōng processing imported materials

进取 jìnqǔ ① be up-and-coming; be enterprising: ～心 enterprising spirit ② achieve; achievement: ～的社会 achieving society. ～动机 achievement motivation

进入 jìnrù enter; get into

进食 jìnshí take food; have one's meal

进退两难 jìntuì-liǎngnán difficult to advance or to retreat — in a dilemma; on the horns of a dilemma; in a dilemma; in a quandary; be between two fires

进香 jìnxiāng offer incense in a temple; worship in a temple

进项 jìnxiang income; receipts

进行 jìnxíng ① go on; be in progress; be under way; enter into: ～辩论 enter into a debate ② carry on; carry out; conduct: ～科研工作 engage in scientific research. ～民事诉讼 sue in civil action. ～刑事诉讼 institute penal proceedings ③ be on the march; march; advance: ～曲 march

进修 jìnxiū advance one's study; engage in advanced studies; take a refresher course:～教育 continuing education. ～课程 refresher course; upgrading course. 出国～ go abroad for further studies

进言 jìnyán offer a piece of advice or an opinion

进展 jìnzhǎn make progress; advance; make headway:～良好 proceed well. 取得巨大～ make great progress

进站 jìnzhàn (of a train) get into (draw into, pull into) a station

进帐 jìnzhàng income; receipts

进驻 jìnzhù enter and be stationed in; enter and garrison

晋

jìn〈动〉① advance; ② promote:加官～爵 be promoted to a higher post and rank

晋级 jìnjí rise in rank; be promoted

晋见 jìnjiàn call on (sb. holding high office); have an audience with

晋升 jìnshēng promote to a higher office:～的阶梯 ladder of success

晋谒 jìnyè call on (sb. holding high office); have an audience with

晋职 jìnzhí promotion (to a higher office)

觐

jìn〈动〉present oneself before (a monarch)

觐见 jìnjiàn present oneself before (a monarch); have (ask for) an audience with

禁

jìn〈动〉① forbid; prohibit:～止贪污 forbid corrupt practices ② imprison; detain:监～ imprison ③〈名〉what is forbidden by law or customs:～运品 contraband

另见 jīn

禁闭 jìnbì confinement (as a punishment); keep in custody; incarcerate:关～ be placed in confinement

禁地 jìndì forbidden area; restricted area; out-of-bounds area

禁锢 jìngù ① debar from holding office (in feudal times) ② keep in custody; imprision; under arrest; put in jail ③ confine

禁忌 jìnjì ① avoid; abstain from ② taboo; ban

禁令 jìnlìng ban; prohibition; injunction:取消～ lift a ban

禁区 jìnqū ① prohibited area; forbidden zone:军事～ military forbidden zones. 思想～ ideological forbidden zone ②[自然保护区] natural park; preserve; reserve

禁书 jìnshū officially banned books

禁运 jìnyùn embargo:解除～ lift the embargo (on). 实行～ lay embargo on

禁止 jìnzhǐ prohibit; ban; forbid:～记者采访 be barred to the press

近

jìn〈形〉① close; near:～在咫尺 near at hand ② approaching; close to:年～70 approaching seventy; getting on for seventy③ intimate; closely related: 两家关系挺～。The two families are on intimate terms ④ easy to understand: 浅～ simple and easy to understand

近处 jìnchù vicinity; neighbourhood

近代 jìndài modern times: ～史 modern history

近海 jìnhǎi offshore; inshore; coastal waters: ～石油钻探 offshore oil drilling

近乎 jìnhu ① close to; little short of ② intimate; friendly

近郊 jìnjiāo outskirts of a city; suburbs; environs

近景 jìnjǐng close shot

近况 jìnkuàng recent development; current situation: 你～如何? How are you getting along? How are things with you?

近来 jìnlái recently; of late; lately

近期 jìnqī in the near feature; recent; short-term: ～交货 near delivery. ～经济增长速度 economic growth rate in the near future

近亲 jìnqīn near relation; close relative; proximity of blood; be akin to: ～通婚 intermarriage; consanguineous marriage. ～收养 adoption by close relative

近日 jìnrì ① recently; in the past few days ② within the next few days: 这项工程～即将完工。The project will be completed within the next few days.

近视 jìnshì shortsighted; near-sighted; myopia

近似 jìnsì be similar to; closely resemble; approximate: ～值 approximate value

近因 jìnyīn immediate cause

近于 jìnyú be little short of; border on: ～奇迹 be little (nothing) short of miraculous. ～粗暴 border on rudeness

近在咫尺 jìnzàizhǐchǐ close at hand; well within reach

近朱者赤,近墨者黑 jìnzhūzhě chì, jìnmòzhě hēi he who stays near vermilion gets stained red, and he who stays near ink gets stained black—one takes on the colour of one's company; Near vermilion, one gets stained pink; near ink, one gets stained black. ; One takes the colour of one's company.

尽 jìn 〈动〉① exhaust; use up: 人～其才 make the best possible use of men ② put to the best use; try one's best: ～心竭力 exert one's heart and strength to the utmost 〈形〉③ exhausted; finished: 无穷无～ boundless; endless; inexhaustible ④ to the limit; to the utmost: 用～力气 exert oneself to the utmost ⑤〈副〉all; exhaustive: ～收眼底 have a panoramic view

另见 jǐn

尽力 jìnlì do all one can; make every effort; do (try) one's best: ～而为 do one's best; do every thing in one's power

尽情 jìnqíng to one's heart's content：～歌唱 sing to one's heart's content；sing lustily

尽人皆知 jìnrénjiézhī be known to all；be common knowledge；be widely known

尽善尽美 jìnshàn-jìnměi leave nothing to be desired；attain (to) perfection；reach the acme of perfection；perfectly good and beautiful

尽头 jìntóu end

尽心 jìnxīn with one's whole heart：～竭力 with all one's mind and energy；put one's heart and soul；do one's best

尽兴 jìnxìng to one's heart's content：～而归 come back in perfect content

尽义务 jìnyìwù do one's duty；fulfil one's duty (obligation)

尽责 jìnzé do one's duty (part)；fulfil one's trust

尽职 jìnzhí fulfil one's duty

劲 jìn〈名〉① strength；energy；might：用～ put forth strength ② vigour；drive；spirit：干得非常起～ work with great zeal ③ interest：下棋没～，还是去打篮球吧。Playing chess is no fun；let's go to play basketball.
另见 jìng

劲头 jìntóu ① strength；energy ② vigour；drive；zeal；spirit：～十足 be full of vigour；be all energy

浸 jìn〈动〉soak；immerse：他把面包～在牛奶里。He soaked bread in milk.

浸泡 jìnpào soak；immerse

浸湿 jìnshī soak；wet

浸透 jìntòu get soaked；be drenched through；saturate；steep：她的衬衫～了汗水。Her shirt was steeped with sweat.

jīng

京 jīng〈名〉① capital of a country ② Beijing：～九铁路 Beijing-Kowloon Railway

京华 jīnghuá the capital of a country

京剧 jīngjù Beijing (Peking) opera：～清唱 arias drawn from Beijing opera

京韵大鼓 jīngyùndàgǔ storytelling in Beijing dialect with drum accompaniment

京族 Jīngzú the Jing (Ching) nationality (living in the Guangxi Zhuang Automomous Region)

惊 jīng〈动〉① be frightened；startle：大～失色 grow alarmed and turn colour ② shock；alarm；surprise：～动全国 shock the whole nation ③ shy；stampede：一匹～马 a shying horse

惊诧 jīngchà surprised；amazed；astonished

惊动 jīngdòng ① trouble；disturb ② startle；alarm

惊愕 jīng'è be staggered (by)；terror-stricken；stunned；be stupefied (at)：令人～的 staggering；shocking

惊弓之鸟 jīnggōngzhīniǎo a bird startled by the mere twant of a bow-string; a badly frightened person; a bird that starts at the sight of a bow; nervously alert; Burned child fears fire

惊骇 jīnghài frightened; panic-stricken

惊慌 jīnghuāng become alarmed; be terrified; panic-striken:～失措 be terrified out of one's wits; be panic-stricken; be thrown into a panic; thunder-struck

惊魂 jīnghún the state of being frightened

惊恐 jīngkǒng terrified; panic-stricken; be alarmed (at):～万状 be in a great panic

惊奇 jīngqí be surprised (at); be amazed; wonder (at):令人～的 surprising; amazing; astonishing

惊扰 jīngrǎo alarm; agitate

惊人 jīngrén alarming; wonderful; astonishing; amazing:～的成就 amazing success; howling success

惊世骇俗 jīngshì-hàisú astounding the world with extraordinary ideas

惊叹 jīngtàn wonder at; marvel at; exclaim (with admiration)

惊涛骇浪 jīngtāo-hàilàng ① tempestuous storm (wave); fierce and frightening storm; terrifying waves; stormy waves ② a sea of trouble

惊天动地 jīngtiān-dòngdì earth-shaking; world-shaking: ～的事业 earth-shaking undertaking

惊悉 jīngxī be shocked to learn

惊喜 jīngxǐ pleasantly surprised

惊吓 jīngxià frighten; scare

惊险 jīngxiǎn thrilling:～的表演 breathtaking performace. ～小说 thriller; chiller

惊心动魄 jīngxīn-dòngpò soul-stirring; thrilling; exciting

惊醒 jīngxǐng sleep lightly; be a light sleeper

惊讶 jīngyà be surprised (amazed) at; wonder at

惊异 jīngyì surprised; amazed; astonished:令人～的 surprising; amazing; astonishing

惊蛰 jīngzhé the Waking of Insects

鲸

jīng〈名〉whale

鲸吞 jīngtūn swallow like a whale; annex (territory):～蚕食 swallow as a whale and gnaw as a silkworm; gulp down or eat up by degrees

鲸鱼 jīngyú whale

旌

jīng

旌旗 jīngqí banners and flags

精

jīng〈形〉① refined; picked; choice:～锐部队 picked troops ② excellent; perfect:少而～ smaller quantity and better quality ③ meticulous; fine; precise:～密机床 precision machine tool ④ skilled; proficient; conversant: ～于绘画 skilled in painting ⑤ smart; clever and able:～明强干 able and clear-headed〈名〉⑥ energy, spirit:聚～会神 concentrate one's attention ⑦ extract;

essence：~髓 quintessence

精兵简政 jīngbīng-jiǎnzhèng better troops and simpler administration；streamline troops and simplify administration；streamline the administrative structure；better staff and simpler administration；streamlined administration

精彩 jīngcǎi excellent；marvellous；wonderful：~的表演 wonderful performance. 择其~者 select the prize ones

精诚 jīngchéng absolute sincerity；good faith

精粹 jīngcuì succint；pick；terse；cream：民族文化~ cream of national culture

精打细算 jīngdǎ-xìsuàn count every cent and make every cent count；careful calculation and strict budgeting；operate within a tight budget

精雕细琢 jīngdiāo-xìzhuó work at sth. with utmost care；work elaborately (at)

精干 jīnggàn ①（of a body of troops，etc.）small in number but well-trained；crack ② capable；able-minded；keen witted and capable：工作队力求~。The working teams should be efficient.

精悍 jīnghàn ① capable and vigorous ② pithy and poignant

精华 jīnghuá essence；pick；cream；quintessence

精加工 jīngjiāgōng finish machining；precision work

精简 jīngjiǎn simplify；condense；cut；reduce；retrench；streamline：~机构 simplify the administrative structure；streamline the organization. ~节约 simplify administration and practise economy；retrench and economize

精力 jīnglì energy；vigour；vim：~充沛 full of energy；very energetic

精练 jīngliàn terse；succinct；concise；refined：语言~ refined language

精良 jīngliáng excellent；superior；of the best quality

精美 jīngměi exquisite；elegant

精密 jīngmì accurate；precise：~仪器 precision instruments (tools)

精妙 jīngmiào exquisite

精明 jīngmíng shrewd；astute；sagacious；intelligent：~强干 intelligent and capable；able and efficient：~强干的企业家 competent entrepreneurs

精疲力竭 jīngpí-lìjié be tired out；be absolutely exhausted；be fagged out；be worn out

精辟 jīngpì incisive；penetrating；pithy：~的分析 incisive analysis. ~的指示 pithy instructions

精品 jīngpǐn ① fine works (of art) ② quality goods；articles of fine quality

精巧 jīngqiǎo subtle；exquisite；ingenious：~的机器 ingenious machine

精确 jīngquè accurate；exact；precise

精锐 jīngruì crack; picked
精深 jīngshēn profound
精神 jīngshén ① spirit; mind: ～文明 culture and ethics (ideology). ～面貌 mental outlook. ～公害 public spiritual poison. ～贵族 intellectual aristocracy. ～食粮 spiritual (mental) food. ～支柱 spiritual pillars ② [文件等] gist; essence: 领会文件的～ try to understand the gist of the document
精神 jīngshen ① vigour; vitality ② lively; vigorous: ～抖擞 in high spirits; in soaring spirits; be full of vigour
精髓 jīngsuǐ marrow; pith; quintessence
精通 jīngtōng be versed in; be proficient in; master; have a thorough understanding (command) of: ～德语 be proficient in German
精细 jīngxì fine; delicate; careful; meticulous: ～分工 a fine division of labour
精心 jīngxīn painstakingly; elaborately; meticulously: ～筹划、～设计、～施工 plan, design and build meticulously
精选 jīngxuǎn ① concentration ② carefully chosen; choice
精养 jīngyǎng [畜] punctilious animal husbandry
精液 jīngyè seminal fluid; semen
精义 jīngyì essential ideas; essentials
精益求精 jīngyì-qiújīng constantly improve sth., become better and better; strive for perfection: 对技术～ perfect one's skill constantly; constantly improve one's skill
精英 jīngyīng ① essence; cream ② elite; flower
精于 jīngyú be skilful in (at); be expert in (at): ～音乐 be expert in music
精湛 jīngzhàn consummate; superb; exquisite: ～的工艺 exquisite craftsmanship
精致 jīngzhì fine; delicate; exquisite
精制 jīngzhì make with extra care; refine: ～品 finely made items. ～盐 refined salt
精装 jīngzhuāng clothbound; hard-cover; hardback: ～本 *de luxe* edition; fined edition; standard edition
精子 jīngzǐ sperm; spermatozoon

荆

荆 jīng 〈名〉 vitex; chaste tree: ～棘之地 place of briers and brambles
荆棘 jīngjì thorny undergrowth; thistles and thorns; brambles; thorns

兢

兢 jīng
兢兢业业 jīngjīng-yèyè ① be cautious and conscientious; be conscientious and earnest; do sth. in a careful manner ② cautiously; assiduously; conscientiously

晶

晶 jīng ① 〈名〉 crystal ② 〈形〉 brilliant; bright; glittering: 亮～～ glistening; shining
晶体管 jīngtǐguǎn transistor: ～收音机 transistor set (radio)

晶莹 jīngyíng crystalline; sparkling and crystal-clear; glittering and translucent

腈 jīng [化]〈名〉nitrile

腈纶 jīnglún acrylic fibres

茎 jīng〈名〉stem (of a plant); stalk

泾 jīng river rising in Ningxia and flowing into central Shaanxi where it empties into the Weihe

泾渭分明 jīngwèi-fēnmíng as different as the waters of the Jinghe and the Weihe—entirely different

经 jīng〈名〉① longitude:西～ west longitude ② classics; scripture; canon:佛～ Buddhist scripture (surta)〈动〉③ pass through; undergo:途～上海 pass through Shanghai ④ engage in; manage; deal in:～营活动 business activities. ～商 engage in trade ⑤ bear; stand; endure:～得起风浪的考验 able to stand all tests of storm and stress ⑥〈介〉as a result of; after; through:～某人建议 upon sb.'s proposal

经办 jīngbàn handle; deal with

经常 jīngcháng ① often; frequently; regularly ② daily; day-to-day:～工作 day-to-day work; daily routine

经典 jīngdiǎn ① classics; calssical:～作家 authors (writers) of classics; classical writers ② scriptures; canons

经费 jīngfèi funds; outlay; appropriations:～包干 take responsibility for one's surplus or deficits. ～结余 cash surplus from the funds of the government

经管 jīngguǎn be in charge of; manage

经过 jīngguò ① go through; pass; go past; undergo:这汽车～公园吗? Does this bus pass the park? ② as a result; through; after:事件的全部～ the whole course of the incident; the whole process from beginning to end ③ course; process

经济 jīngjì ① economy; economic:～核算 economic accounting. ～开发区 economic development zones. ～立法 economic legislation. ～实体 economic entity. ～体制改革 economic restructuring. ～特区 special economic zone (SEZ). ～效益好 sound economic performance. ～基础 economic base (basis) ② of industrial or economic value:～作物 industrial crop; cash crop ③ financial condition; income:～拮据 be hard up ④ economical:～地使用 use economically

经济联合体 jīngjì liánhétǐ economic coalition (association)

经济区划 jīngjìqūhuà division into economic districts

经济协作区 jīngjì xiézuòqū economically coordinated regions

经纪人 jīngjìrén ①［股票、公债等

的]broker ② middleman; agent

经久 jīngjiǔ ① prolonged ② durable

经理 jīnglǐ ① manage; handle ② manager; director: ～负责制 system of manager assuming chief responsibility; manager takes responsibility for production

经历 jīnglì ① career; (work) record; antecedents ② undergo; experience: ～巨大的变化 experience great changes

经络 jīngluò main and collateral channels, regarded as a network of passages, through which vital energy circulates and along which the acupuncture points are distributed

经商 jīngshāng engage in trade; go into business

经手 jīngshǒu handle; deal with; be responsible for: ～家用开支 handle the household accounts

经售(销) jīngshòu(xiāo) sell on commission; distribute; deal in; sell

经受 jīngshòu stand; bear; undergo; experience; withstand; be subjected to: ～住任何考验 withstand any storm

经销专业户 jīngxiāozhuānyèhù households specializing in marketing

经验 jīngyàn experience: ～主义 empiricism. ～丰富(缺乏) have much (little) experience (in)

经营 jīngyíng manage; operate; run; engage in: ～承包制 management contract system. ～层次 management tiers. ～方向 management direction. ～思想 management philosophy. ～范围 business scope. ～好坏 level of managerial competence; success or failure of enterprise operation. ～性亏损 run at a loss due to poor operation. 中外合资～企业 joint ventures involving Chinese and foreign investment

经由 jīngyóu by way of; via: ～上海去广州 go to Guangzhou via Shanghai

经传 jīngzhuàn classical works; Confucian classics and commentaries; Confucian canon

jǐng

井 jǐng 〈名〉 ① well: 打～ drill a well; sink a well ② sth. in the shape of a well: 油～ an oil well

井底之蛙 jǐngdǐzhīwā frog in a well — a person with a very limited outlook; a person with a narrow view of the world

井架 jǐngjià ① derrick ② headframe; headgear; pitheadframe

井井有条 jǐngjǐng-yǒutiáo methodical; in a good order; in perfect order; shipshape and orderly: ～地工作 work methodically

井喷 jǐngpēn blowout

井然 jǐngrán in good order; orderly: 旅客上飞机秩序～。The passengers boarded the plane in good order.

井水不犯河水 jǐngshuǐ bù fàn

héshuǐ The well water does not interfere with (intrude into, mix with) the river water — each one minds his own business; each going his own way (without interfering with the other)

警 jǐng ①〈动〉warn; guard against; garrison: ～戒 be on guard against ②〈形〉alert; vigilant: ～醒 be a light sleeper 〈名〉③ alarm: 火～ fire alarm ④ police: ～察分局 police office

警报 jǐngbào alarm; warning; alert

警备 jǐngbèi guard; garrison: ～司令部 garrison headquarters

警察 jǐngchá police; policeman: 人民～ a people's policeman

警车 jǐngchē patrol wagon; paddy wagon; black maria

警告 jǐnggào ① warn; admonish; caution against; caution ② warning: ～处分 disciplinary warning; punishment of warning

警戒 jǐngjiè warn; guard against; take precautions against: ～责任 duty of vigilance. ～线 cordon

警句 jǐngjù epigram; aphorism; apothegm

警觉 jǐngjué vigilance; alertness; on the alert: ～地看了一眼 give sb. a guarded glance

警惕 jǐngtì be vigilant; be on guard against; maintain vigilance against: 提高～ heighten one's vigilance

警亭 jǐngtíng police box (kiosk)

警卫 jǐngwèi guard: ～森严 be heavily (closely) guarded. ～人员 guard personnel

警务 jǐngwù police affairs; police service

警钟 jǐngzhōng alarm bell; tocsin

景 jǐng 〈名〉① scene; scenery; view: 山～ mountain scenery ② state; condition; situation: 好～不长。Good times do not last long ③ scenery (of a film or play): 换～ change of scenery ④〈动〉revere; respect; admire: ～慕 revere; esteem

景德镇 Jǐngdézhèn Jingdezhen (a town in Jiangxi Province, one of China's leading porcelain-manufacturing centres)

景观 jǐngguān landscape: 自然～ natural landscape

景况 jǐngkuàng condition; situation; circumstances; state of affairs: 他们的～在好转。Their situation is getting better.

景颇族 Jǐngpōzú the Jingpo (Chingpo) nationality (living in Yunnan Province)

景气 jǐngqì boom; prosperity: 不～ depression; slump

景色 jǐngsè scene; scenery; view: ～宜人。The beautiful scenery is pleasing. ; attractive scenery

景泰蓝 jǐngtàilán *cloisonné* enamel

景物 jǐngwù scenery

景象 jǐngxiàng scene; sight; picture: 美丽的～ a beautiful sight

景仰 jǐngyǎng hold in high respect; respect and admire; cherish: 千百万人～的光荣名字 the glorious name cherished by millions of people

景致 jǐngzhì view; scenery; scene

jìng

颈 jìng〈名〉neck

颈椎 jìngzhuī cervical vertebra

竟 jìng ①〈动〉complete; finish: 未～之业 unfinished task; unaccomplished cause ②〈形〉whole; all: ～夜 the whole night〈副〉③ at last; in the end; eventually: 有志者事～成。Where there's a will there is a way. ④ unexpectedly; actually: 这么大的事她～会不知道? I'm surprised that she didn't know of such an important event. ⑤ go so far as to; go to the length of; have the impudence to: ～当面撒谎 go so far as tell a bare-faced lie

竟敢 jìnggǎn have the audacity (to do); dare: 她～在我的家里如此放肆! She dares to behave like that in my house!

竟然 jìngrán ① unexpectedly; actually; to one's surprise: 实验～成功。To our surprise, the experiment came out successful. ② have the cheek (to do): ～当众说谎 have the cheek to tell lies before the public

竟自 jìngzì unexpectedly; to one's surprise; actually

境 jìng〈名〉① boundary; border: 在我国～内 within our borders ② place; territory; area: 敌～ enemy territory ③ condition; circumstances; situation: 家～ family financial situation

境地 jìngdì condition; situation; circumstances: 处于贫困的～ be in reduced circumstances

境界 jìngjiè bounds; boundary; realm; world: ～说 [佛] doctrine of Buddhist realm

境况 jìngkuàng condition; circumstances; situation; [困难的] plight: ～(不)好 be well (badly) off

境内机构 jìngnèi jīgòu domestic institution

境遇 jìngyù circumstances; situation; one's lot: 各人～不同。Everybody has his own lot. ～伦理学 situation ethics

镜 jìng〈名〉mirror; looking glass: ～中自我 looking-glass self

镜框 jìngkuàng ① picture frame ② spectacles frame

镜片 jìngpiàn lens

镜头 jìngtóu ① camera lens ② shot: 特写～ close-up

镜子 jìngzi ① mirror; looking glass ② glasses; spectacles

竞 jìng〈动〉compete; contend; contest; vie

竞标 jìngbiāo competitive bidding; competitive tender

竞技 jìngjì sports; athletics: ～状态良好 be in top form. ～伦理教育 ethical education in sports

竞赛 jìngsài contest; emulation; competition: ～运动 emulation drive

竞选 jìngxuǎn run for; stand for; campaign:～总统 run for president

竞争 jìngzhēng compete (with sb. for sth.); contest:～价格 competitive price. ～力 competitive power; competitiveness. ～性节目安排[电视台] counter programming. ～者 rival

竞走 jìngzǒu (heel-and-toe) walking race

净 jìng 〈形〉① clean; pure:～水 clean water ② net:～利润 net profits 〈副〉③ completely; all:～说不干 all talk, no action ④ only, merely; nothing but:这几天～下雪。It has been snowing for the past few days.

净化 jìnghuà ① purify ②[文艺评论用语] catharsis

净价 jìngjià net price

净收入 jìngshōurù net income; net revenue; net receipt

净手 jìngshǒu ① wash one's hands ② relieve oneself

净水器 jìngshuǐqì water purifier; filter

净土 jìngtǔ the Pure Land

净土宗 jìngtǔzōng [佛] the Pure Land Sect

净增 jìngzēng net increase; net growth

净值 jìngzhí net value; net worth

净重 jìngzhòng net weight

净赚 jìngzhuàn make a net profit of; clear

静 jìng 〈形〉quiet; calm; silent:～止轨道 static orbit

静电 jìngdiàn static electricity:～复印 xerox

静观 jìngguān ① wait-and-see:～的态度 wait-and-see attitude ② contemplation[美学]:～自然 contemplation of Nature

静默致哀 jìngmò-zhì'āi mourn in silence; observe a moment's silence in mourning (for)

静悄悄 jìngqiāoqiāo very quiet

静态 jìngtài static state:～雕刻 stabile. ～经济学 static economics. ～社会学 static sociology

静物 jìngwù still life

静养 jìngyǎng have a rest-cure; convalesce

静园 jìngyuán stilling the park

静止 jìngzhǐ still; stationary; motionless:～镜头[电影] freeze frame; frozen frame

静坐 jìngzuò meditating; meditation; quiet-sitting; sit-in:～示威 sit-in demonstration; sit-in

靖 jìng ①〈形〉peaceful; tranquil ②〈动〉pacify

靖边 jìngbiān pacify the border regions

敬 jìng 〈动〉① respect; honour:尊～ esteem; respect ② present; offer:～烟 offer a cigarette ③〈副〉～候光临 respectfully await your presence

敬爱 jìng'ài respect and love; respected and beloved

敬而远之 jìng'éryuǎnzhī keep someone at a respectful distance

敬告 jìnggào beg to inform

敬贺 jìnghè congratulate with respect; send respectful greetings to

敬候 jìnghòu await respectfully: ～佳音。We are waiting to hear the good news.

敬酒 jìngjiǔ toast: ～不吃吃罚酒 refuse a toast only to drink a forfeit — submit to sb.'s pressure after first turning down his request; be constrained to do what one at first declined; rather do things under compulsion than of one's own accord

敬老院 jìnglǎoyuàn homes for the aged

敬礼 jìnglǐ ① salute; give a salute

敬佩 jìngpèi esteem; admire

敬请 jìngqǐng invite respectfully

敬畏 jìngwèi hold in awe and veneration; revere

敬仰 jìngyǎng hold in reverence; revere; have the greatest admiration for

敬意 jìngyì regards; respects; tribute; compliments

敬重 jìngzhòng honour; revere; deeply respect; esteem

痉 jìng

痉挛 jìngluán cramps; spasm; convulsions: 面部～ facial spasm

径 jìng

〈名〉① footpath; track: 山～ mountain path ② diameter: 半～ radius ③ means; way: 捷～ shortcut; an easy way ④〈副〉straightly; driectly: ～回沈阳 go straight back to Shenyang

径情直遂 jìngqíngzhísuì have got one's wish; achieve what one wishes; meet (answer, come up to) one's expectation; follow a straight line

径赛 jìngsài track: ～项目 track events

径直 jìngzhí directly; straight; straight-way: 客机～飞往广州。The liner flew directly (straight) to Guangzhou.

径自 jìngzì without consulting anyone; without leave: 他没打招呼,～走了。He turned away without leave.

劲 jìng

〈形〉strong; sturdy; powerful: ～松 sturdy pines

另见 jìn

劲敌 jìngdí ① strong rival; formidable adversary; ② powerful enemy

劲旅 jìnglǚ ① crack troops ② strong (crack) force; strong contingent

jiǒng

窘 jiǒng

〈形〉① hard up; in straitened: 她一度生活很～。She was rather hard up for a time. ② awkward; embarrassed: 露出～态 show signs of embarrasment ③〈动〉embarrass; disconcert

窘境 jiǒngjìng plight; predicament: 处于～ be in a tight situation

窘迫 jiǒngpò straitened; hard up; poverty-stricken

窘态 jiǒngtài embarrassed look

炯 jiǒng〈形〉bright; shining

炯炯 jiǒngjiǒng bright; shining; sparkling: 目光～ sparkling eyes; piercing eyes

迥 jiǒng〈形〉① far away ② widely different

迥然不同 jiǒngránbùtóng utterly (totally; entirely) different (from)

迥异 jiǒngyì totally different

jiū

揪 jiū〈动〉seize; grip; hold tight: ～住不放 be held in a tight grip; tie up in knots

揪辫子 jiūbiànzi seize sb.'s queue; catch sb. in the wrong; seize upon sb.'s mistakes or shortcomings

揪心 jiūxīn ① anxious; worried ② heartrending; agonizing; gnawing

究 jiū ①〈动〉study carefully; investigate; examine: ～其根源 trace sth. to its source ②〈副〉actually; really; after all: ～竟如何办理? How should this really be dealt with?

究办 jiūbàn investigate and deal with; prosecute

究竟 jiūjìng ① outcome; what actually happened: 他们都想知道个～。They want to know what actually happened. ② exactly; actually: 你们～要干什么? What exactly do you want? ③ [放在疑问词 who, what, where 等之后用以加强语气] ever; on earth; in the world: 这～是怎么一回事? What on earth is the matter?

纠 jiū〈动〉① entangle: ～缠不清 become entangled ② gather together; gang up: 他们～合在一起。They were drawn together. ③ correct; rectify: ～正偏差 correct deviations

纠察 jiūchá ① uphold (maintain) order (at a public meeting, etc.) ② pick; patrol; [维持交通的] traffic monitor

纠缠 jiūchán ① entangle; implicate: ～不清的事情 entangled affair ② worry; annoy; bother; nag: 她还有事,别～她。She is busy, stop nagging at her.

纠纷 jiūfēn trouble; complication; conflict; friction; dispute: 这问题会引起～。The problem will give rise to troubles. ～的起因 [法] occasion of trouble

纠葛 jiūgé entanglement; dispute; complication [戏剧或小说]

纠集 jiūjí get together; muster

纠正 jiūzhèng correct; rectify; redress; put right: ～忽视法律的现象 remedy the tendency to ignore laws. ～机关 correctional institution

jiǔ

酒 jiǔ〈名〉wine; spirits

酒吧间 jiǔbājiān bar

酒厂 jiǔchǎng winery

酒德 jiǔdé propriety in drinking

酒店 jiǔdiàn wineshop; public house
酒馆 jiǔguǎn public house; pub
酒后 jiǔhòu after drinking; under the influence of wine (alcohol): ～驾驶[汽车] drunk driving
酒会 jiǔhuì cocktail party
酒精 jiǔjīng ethyl alcohol; alcohol
酒量 jiǔliàng one's drinking capacity; capacity for liquor
酒肉朋友 jiǔròu péngyǒu wine-and-meat friend; brother in debauchery; fair-weather friend
酒神 jiǔshén Dionysia: ～文化 Dionysian culture. ～型人格 Dionysian personality
酒文化 jiǔwénhuà spirits culture
酒席 jiǔxí feast; banquet
酒醉 jiǔzuì durnkenness

韭 jiǔ

韭菜 jiǔcài (Chinese) chives; fragrant-flowered garlic
韭黄 jiǔhuáng hotbed chives

九 jiǔ 〈数〉 nine

九九归一 jiǔjiǔguīyī when all is said and done; in the last analysis; in the final analysis
九年义务教育 jiǔnián yìwù jiàoyù nine-year compulsory education
九牛二虎之力 jiǔ niú èr hǔ zhī lì tremendous effort; herculean effort: 费尽～ work overtime to; make herculean efforts; strain oneself to the limit
九牛一毛 jiǔniú-yīmáo a hair from nine cows — the least particle; a drop in the ocean
九泉之下 jiǔquánzhīxià in the nether world; in the lower (next) world; under the clod (sod)
九死一生 jiǔsǐ-yīshēng have a narrow escape from death; a close shave; escape with one's neck
九五之尊 jiǔwǔzhīzūn the imperial throne
九霄云外 jiǔxiāoyúnwài be flung to the four winds; beyond the highest heavens; cast… to the winds:把个人安危抛到～ cast personal safety to the winds; in total disregard of personal safety
九州 jiǔzhōu ① the nine divisions of China in remote antiquity ② a poetic name for China

久 jiǔ 〈副〉 ① for a long time; long:很～以前 long ago ② of a specific duration:三个月之久 for as long as three months

久别重逢 jiǔbié chóngféng meet again after a long separation; meet sb. after being apart a long time; reunite with sb. after a long separation
久等 jiǔděng wait for a long time
久而久之 jiǔ'érjiǔzhī in the course of time; as time goes on
久负盛名 jiǔfùshèngmíng have long enjoyed a good reputation
久经考验 jiǔjīng kǎoyàn steeled; seasoned; long-tested: ～的战友 the tried and trusted comrade-in-arms
久留 jiǔliú stay long
久违 jiǔwěi 〈套〉 how long it is since we last met; I haven't seen you for ages.

久仰 jiǔyǎng〈套〉I've long been looking forward to meeting you; I have long desired to know you

久远 jiǔyuǎn far back; ages ago; remote

jiù

就 jiù〈动〉① get near to; move towards:避繁~简 take the simple, less complicated way ② engage in; enter upon; undertake:~学 go to school ③ make; accomplish:一蹴而~ accomplish in one move ④ accommodate oneself to; fit; suit:~我记忆所及 to the best of my memory ⑤ eat with; go with:花生仁~酒 have peanuts to go with liquor ⑥〈介〉with regard to; concerning:~我所知 so far as I know〈副〉⑦ at once; exactly; right away:她~来。She will come right away. ⑧ as early; already; long since:雨早晨~停了。The rain has stopped in the morning. ⑨ as soon as; right after:说干~干。Let's start working at once. ⑩ only; merely; just:~等他一个人了。He is the only one we are waiting for. ⑪〈连〉even if:你~不说,我们也会知道。Even if you won't tell us, we'll know anyway.

就便 jiùbiàn at sb.'s convenience; while you're at it

就餐 jiùcān have a meal; eat; dine

就此 jiùcǐ at this point; here and now; thus

就地 jiùdì on the spot; locally:~取材 make use of local materials; draw on local resources. ~诉讼 local action. ~审判 on-the-spot trial

就读 jiùdú attend school

就范 jiùfàn submit; give in

就近 jiùjìn (do or get sth.) nearby; in the neighbourhood; without having to go far

就擒 jiùqín be seized; be captured

就寝 jiùqǐn retire for the night; go to bed

就任 jiùrèn assume office; take office; entrance into office

就事论事 jiùshì-lùnshì consider (judge) something as it stands; consider a matter as it stands

就是 jiùshì ① just; exactly; simply:她~不肯来。She simply refused to come. ② even; even if:~小孩子也知道这点。Even a child knows it.

就手 jiùshǒu while you're at it

就算 jiùsuàn granted that; even if:~他对,他也不该这样无礼。Granted that he is right, he should not be so impolite.

就席 jiùxí take one's seat (at a banquet, etc.); be seated at the table

就绪 jiùxù be comlpeted; be arranged; be ready:布置~。Disposition was completed.

就要 jiùyào be about to; be going to; be on the point of:~下雪了。It's going to snow.

就业 jiùyè obtain employment;

take up an occupation; get a job:～登记 employment registration. ～指导 careers guidance; placement guidance

就职 jiùzhí assume office; entrance into office:～演说 inaugural address

就座 jiùzuò take one's seat; be seated

救

jiù 〈动〉① rescue; save; salvage:～国正义战争 the just war for national salvation ② relieve; help:～济灾荒 provide disaster relief

救兵 jiùbīng relief troops; reinforcements

救场 jiùchǎng go on stage as a last-minute understudy

救国 jiùguó save the country; national salvation

救护 jiùhù relieve a sick or injured person; give first-aid (to); come to the rescue of; rescue:～伤员 give first-aid to the wounded

救火 jiùhuǒ fight a fire; try to put out a fire

救急 jiùjí help sb. to cope with an emergency; help meet an urgent need

救济 jiùjì relieve; give relief to:～金 relief fund; relief payment. ～饥民 provide relief for victims of famine. ～物资 relief supplies

救死扶伤 jiùsǐ-fúshāng heal the wounded and rescue the dying

救星 jiùxīng saviour; liberator; emancipator

救援 jiùyuán come to sb.'s rescue (help); rescue:～车 rescue vehicle

救灾 jiùzāi disaster relief; relieve the people in a disaster area; provide disaster relief:～基金 calamity fund

救助 jiùzhù help sb. in danger or difficulty; succour

旧

jiù 〈形〉① past; old; bygone; former:～币 old currency ② secondhand; used:～衣服 used clothes ③〈名〉old friendship; old friend:故～ old acquaintances

旧地 jiùdì once visited place

旧调重弹 jiùdiào-chóngtán harp on the same old tunes; sing the same old tunes

旧故 jiùgù acquaintance; old friend

旧货 jiùhuò ① old things; old stuff ② secondhand (goods):～店 secondhand shop [寄售的]; commission shop

旧交 jiùjiāo old friendship; old acquaintance

旧历 jiùlì lunar calendar

旧情 jiùqíng old or former friendship; former affection

旧石器时代 jiùshíqì shídài Paleolithic age; Old Stone Age

旧式 jiùshì old-style:～服装 old-style clothes. ～文人 old-style men of letters (literati)

旧体诗 jiùtǐshī old-type poetry; classical poetry

旧现代主义 jiùxiàndàizhǔyì older modernism

旧学 jiùxué old learning

旧业 jiùyè ① old trade or profession ② ancestral estate; family fortune

旧址 jiùzhǐ site (of a former organization, building, etc.)

旧制 jiùzhì ① old system ② the old system of weights and measures

舅 jiù 〈名〉 mother's brother; (maternal) uncle; wife's brother

舅父 jiùfù mother's brother; uncle

舅母 jiùmǔ wife of mother's brother; aunt

舅甥关系 jiùshēng guānxì avunculate

舅子 jiùzi wife's brother; brother-in-law

咎 jiù ①〈名〉 fault; blame: 引~辞职 take the blame and resign ②〈动〉censure; punish; blame: 既往不~ forgive sb.'s past misdeeds; let bygones be gyones

咎由自取 jiùyóuzìqǔ bring trouble to oneself; have only oneself to blame; He is bringing the trouble on himself.

jū

狙 jū

狙击 jūjī snipe: ~战 sniping action

鞠 jū 〈动〉 bring up; rear

鞠躬 jūgōng bow: ~致谢 bow one's thanks

鞠躬尽瘁 jūgōng-jìncuì bend one's body and exhaust his energy; devote oneself entirely to; devote one's life to; bend oneself to a task and exert oneself to the utmost; spare no effort in the performance of one's duty: ~死而后已 devoting oneself to … until one's death; bend oneself to the task unto death

拘 jū 〈动〉 ① seize; arrest; detain: ~禁 detain ② restrain; restrict; constraint: 无~无束 unconstrained; free and easy ③〈形〉 inflexible; rigid: ~泥于马克思的个别结论 confine oneself to the specific theoretical conclusion made by Marx

拘捕 jūbǔ arrest

拘传 jūchuán summon for detention

拘谨 jūjǐn formal; stiff; overcautious; reserved: 态度~ be stiff in manner

拘禁 jūjìn take into custody; imprison; detain; detention

拘礼 jūlǐ be punctilious; stand on ceremony

拘留 jūliú keep (hold) in custody; detain; under arrest; commitment: ~处分 punishment of detention. ~查讯 detention for questioning. ~所 remand centre (home); detention home (house); bridewell. ~证 detention warrant

拘泥 jūní rigidly adhere to; stick to; confine oneself to; adhere dogmatically to; be nice about: ~小节 stand on trifles

拘束 jūshù ① restrain; restrict ② ill at ease; awkward; constrained:感到～ feel ill at ease

拘押 jūyā take into custody; detain

拘役 jūyì criminal detention

居 jū〈动〉① live; reside; dwell: ～住权利 right to reside ② be (in a certain position); occupy (a place): ～于第二位的地位 take second place ③ assert; claim: ～功 claim credit to oneself ④ store up; lay by: 囤积～奇 hoarding and profiteering ⑤〈名〉house; residence: 故～ former residence

居安思危 jū'ān-sīwēi think of danger in time of peace; be prepared for danger in times of peace; be vigilant in peace time

居处 jūchù residence; house; dwelling(-place)

居多 jūduō be in the majority

居高临下 jūgāo-línxià look down from a height; be at a commanding position; have a commanding view from a good vantage point: 在这座塔上～可望全城。The pagoda offers a commanding view of the whole city.

居留 jūliú reside; residence; inhabitation: ～签证 residence visa. ～证 residence permit

居民 jūmín resident; inhabitant: ～大院 large residential compounds. ～调解委员会 neighbourhood mediation committee. ～委员会 residents' committee; neighbourhood committee

居然 jūrán ① unexpectedly; actually; to one's surprise: 她～能讲德语。To my surprise, she can speak German. ② have the impudence (cheek) (to do); go so far as (to do): ～做这种事 have the cheek to do such a thing

居心 jūxīn harbour (evil) intentions: ～叵测 with malicious intent; with ulterior motive; insidious

居住 jūzhù live; reside: ～地迁徙 residential mobility. ～条件 housing conditions. ～面积 floor (living) space

jú

菊 jú〈名〉chrysanthemum

菊花 júhuā chrysanthemum

桔 jú〈名〉同"橘"

局 jú〈名〉① bureau; administration; department: 人事～ the bureau of personnel ② situation; position; state of affairs: 政～ political situation ③ trap; ruse: 骗～ fraud; trap; swindle ④ part; portion: ～部立场 partial stand ⑤ limit; confine: ～限性 limitation ⑥ game; set; innings: 第二～［乒乓球等］the second game (set) ⑦ chessboard

局部 júbù ① part: ～利益 the interests of the part ② partial; local: ～的调整 partial readjustments

局促 júcù ① (of place) narrow; small ② (of time) pressing;

urgent ③ feel or show constraint:～不安 be ill at ease; feel uneasy

局面 júmiàn situation; aspect; phase; prospect:打开新～ open up a new prospect

局势 júshì situation:缓和紧张～ relax the tense situation; ease tensions

局限 júxiàn be limited; be confined to:～性 limitations

焗 jú〈方〉① steam food in a sealed container ② feel smothered; be stifling

焗油 júyóu ① treatment of the hair with a cream to make it soft and shiny ② hair treatment cream

橘 jú〈名〉tangerine

橘黄(色) júhuáng(sè) orange (colour)

橘汁 júzhī orange juice

橘子 júzi tangerine; orange

jǔ

矩 jǔ〈名〉① carpenter's square; square ② rules; regulations ③[物] moment

矩形 jǔxíng rectangle

矩阵 jǔzhèn[数] matrix

举 jǔ〈动〉① raise; lift; hold up:～杯 raise one's glass (to propose a toast) ② elect; choose:公～她当人民代表 choose her as a deputy to the people's congress ③ start:～义 rise in revolt ④ cite; enumerate:他可以～出好几件事来说明。He can cite quite a few instances to illustrate. ⑤〈名〉act; deed; move:～止适度 act in an appropriate manner

举办 jǔbàn run; hold; sponsor; conduct:～展览会 hold an exhibition

举报 jǔbào report; tip-off:～室 reception room for people who have things to report. ～箱 offence-reporting box. 群众～ public tip-offs

举动 jǔdòng act; move; movement; deed:～迅速 quick in movement

举荐 jǔjiàn recommend (a person)

举例 jǔlì give an example

举目无亲 jǔmù-wúqīn be a stranger in a strange land; live alone far away from one's family; have no kith or kin in the world

举棋不定 jǔqí-bùdìng hesitate about (over) what move to make; waver; be in two minds (about); change one's mind often; indecisive; be unable to make up one's mind

举世 jǔshì all over the world:～公认 be established and accepted by the whole world; universally acknowledged. ～闻名 be known to all the world; world-famous. ～瞩目 attract the attention of the world

举手 jǔshǒu raise one's hand:～表决 vote by a show of hands. 赞成的请～。Those in favour please put up their hands.

举行 jǔxíng ① hold; stage; give: ～宴会 give a banquet ② take place

举一反三 jǔyī-fǎnsān infer other things from one fact; learn by analogy; infer from what is already known

举债 jǔzhài borrow; float a loan; contract a loan: ～筹资 debt financing. ～国 credit countries. ～经营 gearing[英国]; leverage[美国]

举证 jǔzhèng put to the proof: ～方法 means of proof. ～责任 burden of proof

举止 jǔzhǐ bearing; behaviour; manner: ～大方 be decent in manner; behave in a decent manner; bear oneself well

举足轻重 jǔzú-qīngzhòng play a decisive role; hold the balance; carry a big weight in; prove decisive: 处于～的地位 occupy a pivotal position

沮 jǔ 〈动〉 prevent; stop

沮丧 jǔsàng dejected; despondent; crestfallen: 神色～ look dejected. 令人～的 depressing; discouraging; mournful

咀 jǔ 〈动〉 chew

咀嚼 jǔjué ① chew; ② chew (over, upon); mull over; ruminate

jù

聚 jù 〈动〉 assemble; gather; get together; amass: ～众滋事 gather a crowd and make disturbances

聚变 jùbiàn fusion: 核～ nuclear fusion

聚餐 jùcān dine (mess) together (usu. on festive occasions)

聚赌 jùdǔ gambling in group; group gambling

聚合 jùhé ① get together ② polymerization

聚会 jùhuì ① get together; meet ② get-together

聚积 jùjī accumulate; collect; build up

聚集 jùjí assemble; gather: ～力量 accumulate strength

聚精会神 jùjīnghuìshén concentrate one's attention (and energy) on; with great concentration; be absorbed; be all attention

聚居 jùjū inhabit a region (as an ethnic group); live in a compact community

聚沙成塔 jùshāchéngtǎ The sand accumulates to form a pagoda—many a little makes a mickle.; A great many grains of sand grouped together to form a pagoda.

聚众 jùzhòng gather a crowd: ～斗殴罪 crime of affray. ～犯罪 assemble a crowd to commit a crime. ～闹事 mob. ～叛乱 mass rebellion

巨 jù 〈形〉 large; huge; colossal; enormous: 文坛～擘 literary mogul

巨变 jùbiàn great change; tremendous change

巨大 jùdà large; great; huge; tremendous; enormous; gigantic: ~的物质力量 tremendous material force. ~作用 play a crucial role in

巨额 jù'é big amount; huge sum: ~利润 enormous (large) profits. ~投资 huge investments

巨匠 jùjiàng great master; consummate craftsman; giant

巨款 jùkuǎn huge sum of money

巨轮 jùlún ① large wheel (fig.) ② large ship

巨人 jùrén colossus; giant: 文学界~ literary giant

巨头 jùtóu magnate; tycoon; bigwig; big-gun

巨著 jùzhù great work; monumental work

炬 jù 〈名〉① torch ② fire

拒 jù 〈动〉① repel; resist: ~敌 resist the enemy ② refuse; reject: ~不交代 refuse to give an accounting; refuse to own up

拒捕 jùbǔ resist arrest; resisting arrest: ~的罪犯 offender resisting arrest

拒腐防变 jùfǔ-fángbiàn combat corruption

拒付 jùfù repudiate; dishonour; refuse payment; protest: ~税金 pay duty under protest. ~支票 dishonour check; protest check

拒绝 jùjué refuse; reject; turn down; exclude: ~无理要求 reject an unreasonable demand. ~考虑一项建议 turn down a suggestion. ~执行 refusal of enforcement

拒赔 jùpéi claims rejected

距 jù ①〈名〉distance: 行~ the distance between rows of plants ②〈动〉be apart from; be at a distance from: 两地相~20公里。The two places are 20 kilometres apart.

距离 jùlí ① distance; range; space: 扩大(缩小)~ increase (reduce) the distance ② be apart (away) from; be at a distance from: ~北京约 60 公里 be about 60 kilometres away from Beijing

具 jù ①〈名〉utensil; tool; instrument: 文~ writing materials; stationery ②〈量〉2~尸体 two corpses ③〈动〉have; possess: ~有光荣传统的人民 the people reared in the glorious tradition. ~有内部规律 be governed by inner laws

具备 jùbèi possess; have; be provided with: ~申请条件 have qualifications for application. ~入党条件的人们 those who measure up to the requirements of the Party membership

具结 jùjié recognizance: ~悔过 make a statement of repentance. ~随传随到 enter into recognizances

具名 jùmíng sign one's name: ~盖章 sign and seal

具体 jùtǐ concrete; specific: ~入微 similar in shape but smaller in proportions; miniature. ~规定 specifying the details of. 按

照～情况 take each case on its merits. 谈得很～ speak in concrete terms

具有 jùyǒu possess; have; be provided with; with:～法律约束的文件 legally binding instrument. ～重大意义 be of great significance (importance). ～证人资格 qualified as a witness. ～中国特色的社会主义 socialism with Chinese characteristics

惧 jù〈动〉fear; be afraid of; dread:临危不～ face danger fearlessly

惧内 jùnèi henpecked

惧怕 jùpà fear; dread; be afraid of

惧色 jùsè scared look:面无～ look undaunted

俱 jù〈形〉complete; all:面面～到 considerate in all respects; attend to each and every aspect of matter

俱乐部 jùlèbù club:～会员 cluber

俱全 jùquán complete in all varieties:一应～。Everything needed is there.

飓 jù

飓风 jùfēng hurricane

句 jù〈名〉sentence

句法 jùfǎ syntax:～分析 syntactic analysis

句号 jùhào full stop; period

句型 jùxíng sentence pattern:～教学 the teaching of sentence patterns

据 jù ①〈介〉according to; on the grounds of; in accordance with:～我看来 in my opinion; as I see it ②〈名〉proof; evidence; certificate:凭～ proof; evidence〈动〉③ occupy; possess; seize ④ rely on; depend on

据称 jùchēng it is said; they say; allegedly

据传 jùchuán story is going around that; rumour has it that

据此 jùcǐ on these grounds; in view of the above; accordingly

据点 jùdiǎn fortified point; stronghold; strongpoint

据理力争 jùlǐ-lìzhēng argue on the basis of reason

据实招认 jùshí-zhāorèn factual admission

据守 jùshǒu hold; guard:～要塞 hold a fort

据说 jùshuō It is said (that…); they say:～是用于和平目的的核装置 a nuclear device allegedly for peaceful purpose

据悉 jùxī it is reported:～,他将于明天辞职。He is reportedly going to resign tomorrow.

剧 jù ①〈名〉play; theatrical work; drama; [歌剧] opera:京～ Beijing opera ②〈形〉violent; intense; severe; acute:～增 a sharp increase; sudden increase

剧本 jùběn drama; play; playbook; [影、剧 script; librettos; [影视]scenario:～作者 script writer

剧变 jùbiàn violent (drastic) change

剧场 jùchǎng theatre; stage

剧烈 jùliè violent; intense; drastic; acute; fierce: ～的社会变动 radical social changes. ～运动 strenuous exercise

剧评 jùpíng drama critique; dramatic criticism

剧情 jùqíng story; plot: ～发展 unfolding of plot. ～简介 synopsis

剧团 jùtuán theatrical company; drama troupe; troupe; ensemble

剧院 jùyuàn theatre: ～布景设计师 theatre set designer. ～经理 artistic director

剧照 jùzhào stage photo; still

剧中人(物) jùzhōngrén (wù) dramatis persona; characters in a play or opera

剧种 jùzhǒng type (genre) of drama; operatic forms

剧组 jùzǔ theatre group: ～全体人员 all persons of the theatre group

剧作家 jùzuòjiā playwriter; playwright; dramatist

踞 jù ① crouch; squat ② sit ③ occupy: 盘～ illegally or forcibly occupy

锯 jù 〈名,动〉 saw

锯齿 jùchǐ sawtooth: ～形 indented; sawtoothed

锯床 jùchuáng [机] sawing machine

juān

涓 juān ①〈名〉a tiny stream 〈动〉② clear ③ choose

涓涓 juānjuān trickling sluggishly: ～流水 a sluggish trickle of water

涓流 juānliú trickle: ～效应 [经] trickling-down effect

捐 juān 〈动〉 ① give up; abandon; relinquish ② donate; contribute; subscribe: ～钱 contribute money ③〈名〉duty; tax: ～税繁重。Taxes are innumerable and crushing.

捐款 juānkuǎn ① contribute money (to) ② contribution; donation: 为救灾基金～ make contributions to the calamity fund

捐弃 juānqì abandon; relinquish: ～前嫌 forget past grievances; bury the hatchet; let bygones be bygones. ～旧怨 sink a feud

捐躯 juānqū sacrifice one's life; lay down one's life

捐税 juānshuì duties; taxes and levies

捐献 juānxiàn contribute (to an organization); donate; present

捐赠 juānzèng donate; present; contribute (as a gift): ～图书 present books

捐助 juānzhù offer financial assistance; contribute; donate

娟 juān 〈形〉 graceful; beautiful

娟秀 juānxiù graceful; beautiful: 字迹～ a graceful hand; beautiful writing

镌 juān 〈副〉 engrave

镌刻 juānkè engrave

juǎn

卷 juǎn〈动〉① roll up：～起袖子roll (tuck) up one's sleeves ② sweep off；carry along：～入旋涡 be pulled into the whirlpool〈名〉③ roll：～轴画 rolled paintings；scroll paintings ④ spool
另见 juàn

卷尺 juǎnchǐ tape measure；band tape

卷入 juǎnrù be drawn into；be involved in：～纠纷 be involved in a dispute

卷土重来 juǎntǔ-chónglái ① make (stage) a comeback ② renew an effort after failure

卷心菜 juǎnxīncài cabbage

卷烟 juǎnyān ① cigarette ② cigar

juàn

眷 juàn ①〈名〉family member (dependent)：女～ female members of a family ②〈动〉have an affection for；have tender feeling for；be regardful of

眷恋 juànliàn be sentimentally attached to (a person or place)

眷念 juànniàn think fondly (affectionately) of；feel nostalgic about；miss

眷属 juànshǔ family dependents (members)；family

卷 juàn〈名〉① book：手不释～ always have a book in one's hand ② volume：该书分上、中、下三～。This book consists of three volumes. ③ file；archives ④ examination paper：交～ hand in an examination paper
另见 juǎn

卷子 juànzi examination paper：看～ mark examination papers

卷宗 juànzōng file；archives dossier：律师经办讼案的～ lawyer's dossier of a case in court

圈 juàn〈名〉pen；[猪的]sty；[羊的]fold：～肥 barnyard manure
另见 quān

圈养 juànyǎng rear livestock in pens

倦 juàn ①〈形〉tired；weary：十分疲～ very tired ②〈动〉be tired of；be weary of：诲人不～ teach with tireless zeal；be tireless in teaching

倦怠 juàndài languid；sluggish

倦容 juànróng tired look

倦意 juànyì feeling of tiredness

绢 juàn〈名〉thin tough silk；pongee silk

绢本 juànběn silk cloth (scroll)：～画幅 pictures on silk cloth

绢裱 juànbiǎo front mounting of ordinary silk

绢画 juànhuà silk painting

绢丝 juànsī spun silk (yarn)

隽 juàn
另见 jùn

隽永 juànyǒng meaningful；witty

隽语 juànyǔ witty remark；witticism

jué

觉 jué 〈动〉 ① feel; find: 最近他一直～着身体不适。He hasn't been feeling up to the mark lately. ② wake (up); awake: 新的～醒 a new awakening ③ 〈名〉feel; sense: 听～ sense of hearing

觉察 juéchá discern; detect; perceive; become aware of

觉得 juéde ① feel ② find; think; feel: 这部电影你～怎样? What do you think of the film?; How do you like the film?

觉悟 juéwù ① consciousness; political consciousness ② become conscious of; become politically awakened

觉醒 juéxǐng awaken

矍 jué

矍铄 juéshuò hale and hearty: ～的老人 hale old man

攫 jué 〈动〉 seize with claws; snatch; grab: ～取各种特权 seize all kinds of privileges

攫取 juéqǔ seize; snatch away; grab: ～高额利润 rake in enormous profits from

角 jué ①〈动〉 contend; struggle; wrestle: 口～ quarrel 〈名〉 ② part; role: 不光彩的～色 a contemptible role ③ actor or actress: 名～ a famous actor or actress ④ type of role: 丑～ clown

另见 jiǎo

角斗 juédòu wrestle (with): ～场 wrestling ring

角色 juésè part; role; character: 正面(反面)～ positive (negative) character

角逐 juézhú contend (with, for); tussle (with): ～场所 arenas of contention

决 jué 〈动〉 ① decide; determine: 悬而未～ be awaiting decision; be undecided ② execute a person: 处～ put to death; execute ③ (of a dyke, etc.) be breached; burst: ～堤 breach dykes (dikes) ④〈副〉certainly; definitely; decidedly: ～不宽待。On no account will leniency be shown.

决标 juébiāo award of bid

决不 juébù never; on no account; by no means: ～食言 never go back on one's word

决策 juécè ① make policy; make decision ② decision making; policy making: ～机构 policy-making body. ～民主化和科学化。The decision-making is more democratic and scientific. ～者与被～者 those making decisions and those for whom the decisions are made

决出 juéchū contest (prizes); fight for: 明天将～5块金牌。Five gold medals will be contested and awarded tomorrow.

决定 juédìng ① decide; resolve; determine: ～工资的级别 determine wage scale ② decision; resolution: ～因素 decisive factor; deciding factor. ～权 power to make decisions

决斗 juédòu ① duel ② decisive struggle

决断 juéduàn ① make a decision ② resolve; decisiveness; determination: 有～的人 man of determination

决计 juéjì ① have made up one's mind; be determined (resolved) (to do) ② definitely; surely: ～不会错 definitely can't be wrong

决裂 juéliè break (off) with; rupture: 同机会主义～ break with opportunism

决赛 juésài [体]finals: 进入～ enter the finals. 半～ semifinals

决胜 juéshèng decide the issue of the battle; determine the victory

决算 juésuàn final accounting of revenue and expenditure; closing account; final accounts: 国家～ final state accounts

决心 juéxīn ① determination; resolution: 表～ express one's determination. ～书 written pledge ② be determined; make up one's mind

决议 juéyì resolution; decision: 通过(撤销)～ adopt (revoke) a resolution

决意 juéyì make up one's mind; decide; be fixed or determined; be set on; form the fixed resolution

诀

jué 〈名〉① rhymed formula: 十六字～ sixteen-character formula ② secret; knack; trick: 秘～ secret of success; key to success ③〈动〉part; bid farewell: ～别 part; bid farewell

诀窍 juéqiào secret; tricks; knack; know-how: 做人的～ secret success in life. 做生意的～ tricks of the trade

抉

jué 〈动〉pick out; single out

抉择 juézé select; choose: 作出～ make one's choice

掘

jué 〈动〉dig: ～井 dig (sink) a well

掘进 juéjìn tunnelling; driving; drilling: ～工作面 driving face

掘墓 juémù excavating tombs; exhumation: ～人 gravedigger

掘取古物 juéqǔ gǔwù exhuming antiquities

崛

jué 〈动〉rise

崛起 juéqǐ [山峰等] rise abruptly; suddenly appear on the horizon; [势力等] rise; spring up

倔

jué

倔强 juéjiàng stubborn; stiff-necked unyielding; unbending: 她的～的朋友 her stubborn friend

绝

jué ①〈动〉break; cut off; sever: 断～外交关系 sever diplomatic relations〈形〉② used up; finished; exhausted: ～版的图书 out-of-print books ③ hopeless; desperate: ～境 in desperate (hopeless) straits; impasse ④ superb; unique: ～

妙的画像 an excellent protrait 〈副〉⑤ [用在否定句前面]absolutely; in the least; on any account: ～不是偶然的。It is by no means fortuitous. ⑥ extremely; most: ～大的错误 gross mistake; a grievous fault

绝版 juébǎn out of print; out of the press

绝笔 juébǐ ① last words written before one's death ② the last work of an author or painter

绝不 juébù ① never; on no account; not at all; by no means: ～甘心 never reconcile oneself to ② be anything but: 她～自私。She is anything but selfish.

绝对 juéduì absolute: ～平均主义 absolute equalitarianism. ～优势 absolute advantage

绝迹 juéjì disappear; vanish; extinct; be completely wiped out: ～字 defunct characters

绝技 juéjì unique skill; *tour de force*

绝交 juéjiāo break off (with); sever relations (with); [外] sever diplomatic relations (with)

绝境 juéjìng ① isolated condition ② hopeless situation; impasse; blind alley

绝句 juéjù [古典文学] *jueju*; poem of four lines, each containing five or seven characters, with a strict tonal pattern and rhyme scheme

绝路 juélù road to ruin; blind alley: 走上～ take the road to ruin; go farther and farther down the road of destruction; heading for one's doom

绝伦 juélún unsurpassed; unequalled; peerless; matchless: 精美～ exquisite beyond compare; superb

绝密 juémì strictly confidential; top-secret

绝妙 juémiào extremely clever (wonderful); marvellous; excellent; perfect: ～的讽刺。This sarcasm about … is very much to the point.

绝食 juéshí go on a hunger strike

绝望 juéwàng ① lose all hope (of); have no hope of; despair (of) ② hopeless; in the depths of despair; desperate: 作～挣扎 conduct a desperate struggle

绝响 juéxiǎng lost art; inimitable art

绝育 juéyù sterilization

绝招 juézhāo ① unique skill ② unexpected tricky move (as a last resort)

绝症 juézhèng incurable disease; fatal illness

绝种 juézhǒng die out; become extinct

爵 jué 〈名〉① the rank of nobility; peerage ② an ancient wine vessel with three legs and a loop handle

爵禄 juélù ranks and stipends; titles and stipends; dignities and emoluments

爵士音乐 juéshìyīnyuè jazz

爵位 juéwèi the rank (title) of nobility

jūn

军 jūn〈名〉① armed forces; army; troops: 参～ join the army ② army; contingent: 劳动大～ labour army; contingent of labour forces ③ army: 红～ the Red Army

军备 jūnbèi armament; arms: ～竞赛 armament (arms) race

军队 jūnduì armed forces; army; troops

军法 jūnfǎ military criminal code; military law

军费 jūnfèi military expenditure

军服 jūnfú military (army) uniform; uniform

军功 jūngōng military merit; military exploit

军工 jūngōng military industry

军管 jūnguǎn military control

军婚 jūnhūn soldier's (military) marriage(s)

军火 jūnhuǒ munitions: ～商 munitions merchant; arms dealer; merchant of death

军纪 jūnjì military discipline

军舰 jūnjiàn warship; naval vessel

军阶(衔) jūnjié (xián) military rank

军力 jūnlì military power (strength)

军令 jūnlìng military orders: ～状 military command contract

军民共建 jūnmín gòngjiàn the army and the people should join in efforts to make cultural and ideological progress

军区 jūnqū military region; (military) area command

军权 jūnquán military leadership; military power

军事 jūnshì military affairs: ～基地 military base. ～委员会 military commission. ～演习 military manoeuvre

军属 jūnshǔ armyman's family; soldier's dependents

军务 jūnwù military affairs; military task

军饷 jūnxiǎng soldier's pay and provisions

军校 jūnxiào military school; military academy

军心 jūnxīn army's morale; morale of the troops

军需 jūnxū ① military supplies ② quartermaster

军训 jūnxùn military training

军医 jūnyī medical officer; military surgeon

军衣 jūnyī military (army) uniform; uniform

军用 jūnyòng for military use; military: ～地图 military map. ～物资 military supplies; war materiel; supplies. ～飞机 warplane

军乐 jūnyuè military music: ～队 military band

军装 jūnzhuāng military (army) uniform; uniform

均 jūn ①〈形〉equal; even; balanced: ～分继承 egalitarian inheritance ②〈副〉all; without exception: 各项准备工作～已就绪。All the preparatory work has been completed.

均等 jūnděng equal; impartial;

fair：机会～ equal opportunity for all

均分 jūnfēn divide equally；go snacks：作 10 股～ divide into ten equal parts. ～到货 split delivery

均衡 jūnhéng balance；equilibrium：～利率 equilibrium rate of interest

均势 jūnshì balance of power；relative equilibrium of forces between

均摊 jūntān share（apportion）equally：～费用 share the expenses equally

均匀 jūnyún even；well-distributed

君 jūn〈名〉① sovereign；monarch；supreme ruler；king；lord ② gentleman：诸～ gentlemen

君主 jūnzhǔ sovereign；monarch：～立宪制度 constitutional monarchy

君子 jūnzǐ man of character；gentleman

君子兰 jūnzǐlán scarlet kafirlily

君子协定 jūnzǐ xiédìng gentlemen's agreement

君子一言，快马一鞭 jūnzǐ yì yán，kuàimǎ yì biān A word spoken is past recalling.；A word spoken（A word once said）can never be taken back.

jùn

竣 jùn〈动〉finish；complete；accomplish：告～ have been completed

竣工 jùngōng be completed；be brought to completion：～面积 floor space completed

峻 jùn〈形〉① high；steep：高山～岭 high mountains ② harsh；stern；severe：～法 harsh law

峻峭 jùnqiào steep；precipitous

俊 jùn〈形〉① beautiful；handsome：这小伙子长得挺～的。That lad is very handsome. ② remarkable；distinguished；talented；smart ③〈名〉a person of outstanding talent

俊杰 jùnjié person of distinguished（outstanding）talent；hero：识时务者为～。Those who suit their actions to the times are wise.；He is wise who understands the times.；Whosoever understands the signs of the times is a great man.

俊俏 jùnqiào pretty and charming

俊秀 jùnxiù handsome；comely

郡 jùn〈名〉[古代的行政区划] prefecture

骏 jùn

骏马 jùnmǎ fine horse；noble（gallant）horse；steed

K k

kā

咖 kā
另见 gā
咖啡 kāfēi coffee：速溶～ instant coffee
咖啡馆 kāfēiguǎn coffee house；café
咖啡因 kāfēiyīn caffeine

kǎ

卡 kǎ〈名〉card：～片 card ②〈动〉check；block
卡车 kǎchē truck；lorry：～上交货价 free on truck
卡介苗 kǎjièmiáo［药］BCG vaccine (Bacille Calmette-Guérin)
卡拉 OK kǎlā'ok karaoke：～酒吧 karaoke bar
卡路里 kǎlùlǐ［物］calorie
卡片 kǎpiàn card：～目录 card catalogue. ～索引 card index
卡通 kǎtōng cartoon：～片（animated）cartoon；animated drawing. ～片绘制者 animator
咯 kǎ〈动〉cough up
咯痰 kǎtán cough up phlegm
咯血 kǎxiě［医］spit blood

kāi

开 kāi〈动〉① open；turn；switch on：～门 open the door. ～灯 turn on the light ② make an opening；open up；reclaim：～埠通商 open trading cities. ～垦荒地 open up wasteland ③ open out；come loose：花都～了。The flowers are all open. ④ lift (a ban, restriction etc.)：～禁 lift a ban ⑤ start；begin：开演。The curtain rises. ⑥ (of troops, etc.) set out；move：～拔令 marching order ⑦ set up；run：～工厂 set up a factory ⑧ start；operate：～工 put (go) into operation ⑨ hold (a meeting, exhibition, etc.)：～庭审理 hold hearings ⑩ make a list of；write out：～支票 make out a check. ～一个户头 open an account ⑪ pay (wages, fares, etc.)：～工资 pay out wages ⑫［用在动词后，表示扩大或扩展］：消息传～了。The news got about. ⑬［用在动词后，表示分开或离开］：把窗户推～ push the window open
开办 kāibàn open；set up；establish；start：～训练班 run a training corse. ～费用 initial expenditure；organization expenses
开本 kāiběn format；book size
开标 kāibiāo open sealed tenders
开采 kāicǎi mine；extract；exploit：～金矿 gold mining. ～石

油 recover petroleum

开衩 kāichà make a slit or vent (at the sides or back of a garment); slit

开场 kāichǎng ① begin; start:戏已经~了。The play has started. ② beginning; opening:~白 opening remarks; preliminary (introductory) remarks; [剧] prologue

开车 kāichē drive (start) a car, train, etc.

开诚布公 kāichéng bùgōng speak frankly and sincerely; be frank and aboveboard; in all sincerity and frankness

开除 kāichú expel; dismiss; discharge; sack; expel:~公职 discharge sb. from public employment. ~学籍 expel sb. from school

开船 kāichuán set sail; sail

开创 kāichuàng start; set up; initiate; open:~新纪元 open a new epoch; usher in a new epoch

开春 kāichūn beginning of spring; in early spring

开刀 kāidāo ① operate (on); perform an operation (on, upon):他明天~。He will be operated on tomorrow. ② make sb. or sth. the first target of attack

开导 kāidǎo help sb. to see what is right or sensible; help sb. to straighten out his wrong or muddled thinking; enlighten

开倒车 kāidàochē turn the clock back; return to the past; turn back the wheel of history; slide back; backsliding

开动 kāidòng ① [机器等] set in motion; operate:~脑筋 use one's brains ② march; move; be on the move

开端 kāiduān beginning; start

开恩 kāi'ēn show mercy; bestow favours

开发 kāifā develop; exploit; tap:~成本 cost of development. 经济~区 economic development zone. ~性承包 developmental contract. ~性项目 exploration projects

开放 kāifàng ① [公园等] open (to the public); [对外] open to the outside world:~城市 open cities. 改革~ reform and opening up ② lift the ban (on) ③ [花] bloom

开工 kāigōng ① start work (working) ② [工厂等] operate; go into operation:~不足 be operating under capacity. ~率 utilization of capacity

开航 kāiháng ① set sail; sail:去上海的船上午9点~。The boat for Shanghai sails at 9 a.m. ② become open for navigation

开后门 kāihòumén sell things by underhand methods; let in by the back door; abusing one's powers to secure advantages for others; open a back door

开户 kāihù open an account:在银行~ open an account with the bank

开花 kāihuā flower; bloom; [树] blossom:~结果 blossom and

bear fruit; yield good results

开化 kāihuà become (be) civilized (enlightened): 未～的 uncivilized

开荒 kāihuāng reclaim wasteland; open up barren land

开会 kāihuì ① hold a meeting ② attend a meeting

开火 kāihuǒ open fire

开价 kāijià state a price; opening price; quote a price; initial price

开架式 kāijiàshì open-shelf: ～图书馆 open-shelf library. ～阅览[图书馆] open access

开胶 kāijiāo come unglued; come unstuck

开金 kāijīn karat gold: 12～ 12 karat gold; gold 12 karats fine

开禁 kāijìn lift a ban

开卷 kāijuàn open a book: ～考试 open-book examination

开课 kāikè ① start a class at the beginning of a new semester ② give a course; teach a subject; deliver a course

开垦 kāikěn open up; exploit; reclaim: ～荒地 open up wasteland for farming; bring wasteland under cultivation; exploit the virgin land

开口 kāikǒu ① open one's mouth; start to talk ② put the first edge on a knife

开矿 kāikuàng open (up) a mine; exploit a mine

开阔 kāikuò ① open; wide ② tolerant; broad-minded ③ widen

开朗 kāilǎng ① sanguine; optimistic ② open and clear: 豁然～ suddenly see the light

开列清单 kāiliè qīngdān draw up a list; make an inventory

开路 kāilù ① open a new road; clear the way: ～先锋 pathbreaker; pioneer ② [电视或无线电广播] open channel; open circuit

开绿灯 kāilǜdēng give sb. the green light; give sb. the go-ahead; turn on the green light

开门 kāimén open the door: ～办学 open-door school management. ～红 make a good (flying) start; off to a good start; let the beginning of the year be crowned with the achievements

开门见山 kāimén-jiànshān come straight to the point; declare one's intention immediately; put it bluntly

开幕 kāimù ① [演出] raise the curtain; begin the performance ② be inaugurated; open: ～词 opening speech. 展览会下星期～。The exhibition will be inaugurated next week.

开盘 kāipán opening quotation: ～价格 opening price

开辟 kāipì open up; pioneer; start

开票 kāipiào ①[选举]count the ballots ② [发票]make out an invoice: ～人 drawer

开启 kāiqǐ open

开窍 kāiqiào ① have one's ideas straightened out ② (of a child) begin to know things ③ open one's eyes; widen one's view (horizons); broaden one's mind

开球 kāiqiú [足球] kick off

开设 kāishè ① open (a shop, factory, etc.); set up ② offer (a course in college, etc.)

开审 kāishěn sit at session

开始 kāishǐ begin; start: ~审理案件 open a case. ~生效 come into effect (force); take effect; carry into effect

开释 kāishì acquit; release; set free

开市行情 kāishìhángqíng opening quotation

开水 kāishuǐ ① boiling water ② boiled water

开天辟地 kāitiān-pìdì ① when the earth was in its making ② since the dawn of history; from the very beginning; since the beginning of time

开庭 kāitíng hear the case; hold hearings; open the court session: ~通知 notice of trial. 本案将于下星期一~。The court will hear the case next Monday.

开通 kāitōng ① remove obstacles from; dredge ② [kāitong] enlightened; open-minded; liberal

开头 kāitóu begin; start; beginning

开脱 kāituō absolve; exonerate

开拓 kāituò open up; reclaim; exploit; pioneer: ~精神 frontier spirit; pioneering spirit. ~性的研究 trial-blazing research. ~者 builders; pioneers

开玩笑 kāiwánxiào make fun of; crack a joke; joke

开往 kāiwǎng leave for; be bound for; [船] sail for

开销 kāixiāo ① pay (expenses) ② expenses: 日常~ daily expenses; running expenses

开小差 kāixiǎochāi ①[兵]desert one's post; decamp ②[思想] be absent-minded; be wool-gathering

开小灶 kāixiǎozào favoured treatment (lit. "open a private kitchen," a metaphor for giving special support to a certain project or constituency)

开学 kāixué school opens; term begins

开演 kāiyǎn (of a play, movie, etc.) begin: 今晚节目 7 点~。The performance begins at seven this evening.

开眼界 kāiyǎnjiè widen one's horizon (vision); increase one's experience

开业 kāiyè ①[商店] open for business; start business; opening of a business: ~大廉价 opening sales ②[医生等]practise: ~行医 practise medicine

开夜车 kāiyèchē sit up late at work; work late into the night; burn the midnight oil

开源节流 kāiyuán-jiéliú tap new resources and cut down expenses; increase income and cut down expenditure; broaden sources of income and reduce expenditure

开展 kāizhǎn develop; unfold; launch; open up; carry out; extend; organize: ~丰富多采的群众性文化活动 organize a variety of cultural activities with mass participation. ～技术革新 carry out technical innovation. ～城乡交流 develop rural-urban trade

开战 kāizhàn make war (on); open hostilities

开张 kāizhāng ① open a business; begin doing business ② conduct the first transaction of a day's business ③ (of certain activities) begin; start

开帐 kāizhàng make out a bill: ～单 state an account

开支 kāizhī expenses; outlay: ～标准 spending standards

开宗明义 kāizōngmíngyì state one's central ideas at the outset in writing or speaking; make clear the purpose and main theme from the very beginning: ～地肯定 openly assert

揩 kāi 〈动〉 wipe

揩汗 kāihàn wipe sweat

揩油 kāiyóu get petty advantages at the expense of other people or the state; sponge on; pocket: 他～了一部分公款。He pocketed a portion of public funds.

kǎi

慨 kǎi 〈形〉 ① indignant: 愤～ righteous indignation ② deeply touched: 感～ sign with emotion ③ generous: ～允 kindly promise

慨然 kǎirán ① generously; unsparingly; without stint ② with emotion; with deep feeling: ～相助 help without stint

慨允 kǎiyǔn give one's consent without stint; consent readily; generously promise

楷 kǎi 〈名〉 ① model; pattern ② *kai*, regular script

楷模 kǎimó model; example; paragon; pattern: 国际主义精神的～ a pattern of internationalism

楷书 kǎishū (in Chinese calligraphy) regular script; standard script of handwriting; formal script: 楷隶相兼 in official and standard scripts

凯 kǎi 〈形〉 triumphant; victorious

凯歌 kǎigē song of triumph; paean of victory

凯旋 kǎixuán triumphant return; return with glory: ～交响曲 triumphal symphony. ～归来 return in triumph (victory); return with drums beating and banners flying

kān

刊 kān ①〈名〉 publish; publication; print: 停～ suspend publication. 报～ newspapers and magazines ② 〈动〉 correct; delete: ～误 correct errors in printing

刊登(载) kāndēng(zǎi) publish; carry: ～广告 advertise

刊授大学(刊大) kānshòu dàxué (kāndà) university taught (offering) through periodicals; publications university

刊头 kāntóu masthead of a newspaper or magazine

刊物 kānwù publication; [定期的] periodical

刊载 kānzǎi publish (in a newspaper or magazine); carry

堪 kān 〈动〉① may; can: ～称佳作 may be rated a good piece of writing or a fine work of art ② endure; bear: 不～一击 cannot withstand a single blow

勘 kān 〈动〉① read and correct the text of; collate: 校～ collate ② survey; investigate: ～查 survey; prospect; inquest [法] ③ suppress: ～平叛乱 suppress (put down) a rebellion

勘测 kāncè survey: ～员 surveyor

勘察 kānchá investigate; examine: ～地形 investigate the terrain

勘界 kānjiè survey: ～立标 conduct boundary survey and erect boundary markers

勘探 kāntàn prospect; explore: 地质～ geological prospecting

勘误 kānwù correct errors in printing: ～表 errata; corrigenda

勘验 kānyàn [法]inspection; (of judicial workers) examine on the spot; hold an inquest

看 kān 〈动〉① look after; take care of ② keep under surveillance ——

另见 kàn

看管 kānguǎn ① take care of; look after ② watch; guard; subject to surveillance: ～犯人 guard a prisoner

看孩子 kānháizi look after children

看护 kānhù look after; nurse: ～病人 look after the patient; nurse the sick

看家 kānjiā ① look after the house; mind the office ② special (skill); outstanding (ability): ～本领 one's speciality (special skill)

看门 kānmén ① guard the entrance; act as doorkeeper ② look after the house

看守 kānshǒu ① guard; watch; [犯人] guard (prisoners) ② warder; gaoler; turnkey: ～内阁(政府) caretaker cabinet (government)

看押 kānyā [法] keep under detention

kǎn

侃 kǎn 〈形〉 straightforward

侃大山 kǎndàshān grand chatting; chat idly

侃侃而谈 kǎnkǎn'értán talk with ease and fluency (sincerity); speak freely and frankly; speak with fervour and assurance

坎 kǎn 〈名〉① ridge and bank: 田～儿 a raised path through fields ② pit; hole

坎儿 kǎnr insinuating language; professional jargon

坎儿井 kǎnrjǐng underground canals (*karez*); underground irrigation system

坎坷 kǎnkě ① rugged; uneven; bumpy ② full of frustrations; misforture; bad luck:～的一生 a life (lifetime) of frustrations; tribulations of life

砍 kǎn〈动〉cut; hack; chop; fell:把树～倒 fell a tree

砍倒 kǎndǎo cut (chop) down; fell:把树枝砍下来 cut (lop) off a branch

砍掉 kǎndiào cut (lop) off; slash; dissolve; strike out:～资本主义尾巴 cutting off the tails of capitalism

砍伐 kǎnfá [林]fell (tree)

砍价 kǎnjià haggle over prices; barter

砍伤 kǎnshāng chop wound

kàn

看 kàn〈动〉① see; look at; watch:～球赛 watch a ball game ② read:～校样 read the proof ③ think; observe; consider:～清形势 size up the situation; have a correct appraisal of the situation ④ visit; call on; see:～望朋友 call on (visit) a friend ⑤ regard; look upon:和地主一律～待 be put in the same category of landlords ⑥ treat:他正在～病。He is under medical treatment. ⑦ look after:～孩子 look after children ⑧ depend on:明天是否去颐和园,得～天气情况。Whether we'll make a trip to the Summer Palace tomorrow depends on the weather. ⑨[用在动词或动词结构后面,表示试一试]:尝尝～。Just taste this. 另见 kān

看病 kànbìng ① (of a doctor) see (receive) a patient ② (of a patient) see (consult) a doctor

看不惯 kànbuguàn cannot bear the sight of; detest; hate to see; be intolerant of

看不起 kànbuqǐ despise; look down upon; scorn; disdain

看出 kànchū find out; be aware of; perceive; make out:～苗头 have seen a sign (of sth.); have smelt a rat

看穿 kànchuān see through; penetrate:一眼～ see through at a glance

看待 kàndài treat (as); regard (as):把某人当自家人～ treat sb. as a member of one's own family

看到 kàndào catch sight of; see

看得起 kàndeqǐ have a high (good) opinion of; have respect for; think much of; think highly of

看法 kànfǎ view; idea; perspective:照我的～,她是对的。In my opinion she is right.

看风使舵 kànfēngshǐduò steer according to the wind; sail with the current; see how the wind blows; trim one's sails

看风水 kànfēngshuǐ practise geomancy for selecting a site for a tomb, house, etc.

看见 kànjiàn catch sight of; see

看开 kànkāi accept (resign oneself to) an unpleasant fact or situation

看来 kànlái it seems (appears); it looks as if

看破 kànpò see through:～红尘 disillusionment with the mortal world. ～骗局 see through a trick

看起来 kànqilai it seems (appears); it looks as if

看轻 kànqīng make light of; underestimate; take lightly

看热闹 kànrènao watch the excitement; watch the fun

看台 kàntái [体]stand; bleachers

看透 kàntòu see through; have an insight into; understand thoroughly:～某人心思 have an insight into sb.'s mind

看图识字 kàntú shízì learn to read with the aid of pictures; learn reading by way of pictures; look-and-say

看望 kànwàng visit; call on; see

看问题 kànwèntí look at problems; in one's approach to problems; approach problems

看涨 kànzhǎng (of market prices) be expected to rise

看中 kànzhòng become fond of; take a fancy to; settle on (sth.):他～了这个姑娘。He took a fancy to the girl.

看重 kànzhòng think highly of; regard as important; have a high opinion of; appreciate; value; set store by (sth.):～理论 emphasize the importance of theory

看做 kànzuò look upon as; regard as

kāng

康 kāng 〈形〉① well-off; prosperous:我国人民物质和文化生活达到小～水平。Chinese people will be comparatively well-off both materially and culturally. ② healthy

康复 kāngfù recover from illness; restore to health; rescue; recuperate one's health:～中心 health recovery centre; rehabilitation centre

康健 kāngjiàn be in (good) health; be healthy

康庄大道 kāngzhuāngdàdào broad road (path); main road

慷 kāng

慷慨 kāngkǎi ① generous; magnanimous ② fervent; vehement:～激昂 with strong emotion; impassioned; vehement. ～陈词 air one's views vehemently. 慷他人之慨 be generous at the expense of others; make free with other's money

糠 kāng 〈名〉bran; chaff; husk:～秕 rice bran; chaff

káng

扛 káng 〈动〉 carry (on the shoulder):～枪放哨 carry rifles and perform guard duty
另见 gāng

扛活 kánghuó work as a farm labourer

kàng

亢 kàng 〈形〉 ① high ② haughty: 不～不卑 neither haughty nor humble ③ extreme; excessive

亢奋 kàngfèn extremely excited; stimulated

炕 kàng ①〈名〉*kang*, (brick bed which is kept warm in winter by piping heat under it) ②〈动〉 dry by the heat of a fire

炕肥 kàngféi fertilizer from a heatable brick bed

炕桌 kàngzhuō a small short-legged table for use on a *kang*; *kang* table

抗 kàng 〈动〉 ① resist; fight; combat:～灾能力 the capacity to combat natural calamities ② defy; refuse:～捐～税 refuse to pay levies and taxes ③ contend with; be a match for:分庭～礼 stand up to sb. as an equal

抗爆 kàngbào antiknock

抗辩 kàngbiàn ① reject charges and plead not guilt; speak out in one's own defense ②［法］counterplea; demurrer; plea:～者 opposing counsel

抗旱 kànghàn fight (combat) drought

抗衡 kànghéng rival; match; contend a challange with; compete; challenge against

抗洪 kànghóng resist floods:～排涝 fight the flood and drain waterlogged areas

抗击 kàngjī resist and fight back

抗拒 kàngjù defy; resist; refuse: ～从严 severe punishment to those who refuse to confess their crimes; be strict with those who resist. ～逮捕 resist arrest

抗命 kàngmìng defy orders; disobey

抗税 kàngshuì refuse to pay tax; resist tax

抗诉 kàngsù protest: ～案件 protested case. ～书 written protest

抗体 kàngtǐ antibody

抗议 kàngyì protest (against); lodge a protest (against; with):～书 protest letter

抗原 kàngyuán antigen

抗战 kàngzhàn ① war of resistance against aggression ② War of Resistance Against Japan

抗震救灾 kàngzhèn jiùzāi combat the earthquake and do relief work

抗争 kàngzhēng take a stand against; resist

伉 kàng 〈动〉 be equal to; be well matched

伉俪 kànglì husband and wife; married couple

kǎo

考 kǎo 〈动〉① examine; give (take) an examination; test: 统～ the unified state examination ② check; inspect: ～勤 check on work attendance ③ study; research: ～订 do textual research

考辨 kǎobiàn textual research on; enquiry into

考查 kǎochá test; examine; check

考察 kǎochá investigate; inspect; examine; consider: 到某地去～ go (somewhere) on a tour of investigation. ～团 observation (inspection, investigation) group; exploratory mission

考场 kǎochǎng examination hall or room

考订 kǎodìng do textual research; examine and correct; collate

考古 kǎogǔ ① engage in archaeological studies ② archaeology

考古学 kǎogǔxué archaeology: ～材料 archaeological findings. ～发掘 archaeological excavation. ～工作者 archaeological worker

考核 kǎohé examine; check; assess: ～标准 assessment criteria. ～成绩 results of rating. ～企业 make assessments of the performance of each enterprise; examine the economic performance of a factory

考绩制 kǎojìzhì merit system

考究 kǎojiū ①observe and study; investigate ② be particular about; care about; fastidious: ～的需要 refined needs

考据 kǎojù textual research; textual criticism; collation

考卷 kǎojuàn examination paper

考虑 kǎolǜ consider; think over; take into account

考评 kǎopíng evaluation (of one's professional work)

考勤 kǎoqín check on work attendance: ～簿 attendance book (record); sign-in book

考取 kǎoqǔ succeed in (pass) an entrance examination; be admitted to (middle school, college, etc.)

考生 kǎoshēng examinee; candidate for an extrance examination

考试 kǎoshì examination; test: ～不及格 fail (in) an examination; flunk in one's examination; be (get) plucked (in an examination.) ～及格 pass (get through) an examination. 数学～成绩优异 pass with honour in mathmatics

考题 kǎotí examination questions (paper): 出～ set examination questions

考验 kǎoyàn test; trial: 久经～的 long-tested. ～期限[法] probation period

考证 kǎozhèng textual research (criticism); enquiry; critical study: 历史～ historical enquiry

考中 kǎozhòng pass an examination or test

烤 kǎo〈动〉bake；roast；toast

烤电 kǎodiàn diathermy

烤火 kǎohuǒ warm oneself by the fire

烤面包 kǎomiànbāo bake bread；toast：一片～ a slice of toast

烤箱 kǎoxiāng oven

烤鸭 kǎoyā roast duck

烤烟 kǎoyān flue-cured tobacco

烤羊(牛)肉串 kǎoyáng (niú) ròuchuàn shashlik；shish kebab

拷 kǎo〈动〉beat；flog；torture

拷贝 kǎobèi［电影］copy；replica

拷打 kǎodǎ beat；torture；flog：严刑～ torture sb. cruelly；subject sb. to severe torture

拷问 kǎowèn interrogate；cross-examine；excruciate

kào

靠 kào〈动〉① lean against；lean on：把梯子～在墙上 lean a ladder against a wall ② keep to；get near；come up to：疗养院～山。The sanatorium stands by the mountain. ③ rely on；depend on：～卖劳力生活 live by selling one's labour power. 依～自力更生 rely on one's own efforts ④ trust：可～ trustworhy；reliable

靠岸 kào'àn draw alongside；pull in to shore

靠边 kàobiān ① keep to the side；step aside ② sensible；reasonable

靠边儿站 kàobiānrzhàn step aside；stand aside

靠得住 kàodezhù reliable；trustworthy；dependable：她这人～。She is a woman to be relied upon.；She is reliable.

靠垫 kàodiàn cushion (for leaning on)

靠拢 kàolǒng ① keep close to；come over to；draw close (to) ②［倾向于］lean towards (to)

靠山 kàoshān patron；supporter；protector；mainstay；backer

kē

磕 kē〈动〉knock (against sth. hard)：碗边儿～掉了一块 chip the edge of a bowl

磕碰 kēpèng ① collide with；knock against；bump against ② squabble；clash

磕头 kētóu kowtow：～赔罪 give sb. a grand kowtow and apologize

瞌 kē

瞌睡 kēshuì sleepy；drowsy；doze：看书打～ doze over a book

苛 kē〈形〉harsh；severe；exacting：～法 harsh laws

苛捐杂税 kējuān záshuì exorbitant taxes and miscellaneous levies

苛刻 kēkè harsh；onerous；severe：～的条件 harsh terms；exacting terms. 待人～ be hard on others

苛求 kēqiú make excessive demands;ask too much; be overcritical; be hypercritical

苛政 kēzhèng harsh (oppressive) government; tyranny

柯 kē〈名〉① stalk or branch ② helve; axe-handle ③ (Kē) a surname

科 kē〈名〉① a branch of academic or vocational study:文～ the humanities; the liberal arts ② section; department:销售～ sales department ③ family:豆～植物 bean family ④〈动〉inflict (a penalty) on; impose (a fine) on; pass a sentence:～以重刑 mete out heavy punishment

科班 kēbān ① opera school of old type ② regular professional training:～出身 people who have undergone professional training; be a professional by training

科层(组织) kēcéng (zǔzhī) bureaucracy:工业～ industrial bureaucracy. ～制的集体主义 bureaucratic collectivism

科幻小说 kēhuànxiǎoshuō science fiction; sci-fi

科技 kējì science and technlogy:～示范户 science-technology model household. ～咨询活动 scientific and technological consulting services. 促进～成果向现实生产力转化 promote the translation of research results into real productive force

科教片儿 kējiàopiānr science and educational film; popular science film; science education films

科盲 kēmáng blind to science

科目 kēmù ① branch of study; subject; course ②[会计]account

科普 kēpǔ dissemination of science; popularization of science:～读物 popular science readings

科室 kēshì administrative or technical offices; departments and offices; offices; departments:～人员 office worker (staff, personnel)

科协(中国科学技术协会) kēxié (zhōngguó kēxué jìshù xiéhuì) China's Science and Technology Association (CSTA)

科学 kēxué ① science; scientific knowledge:～城 science town. ～技术是第一生产力。Science and technology are the primary productive forces. ～学说 teaching of science ② scientific

科学院 kēxuéyuàn academy of sciences:中国社会～ Chinese Academy of Social Sciences

科研 kēyán scientific research:～讨论 research seminar

科员 kēyuán member of an administrative section; section member

科长 kēzhǎng section chief

棵 kē (usu. for plants):一～树 a tree

颗 kē (usu. for anything small and roundish):一～黄豆 a soya bean

颗粒 kēlì ①anything small and roundish(as a bean, pearl, etc.); pellet ②a grain (of rice, wheat, etc.):～肥料 pellet fertilizer; granulated fertilizer

ké

咳 ké〈动〉cough
另见 hāi

咳嗽 késou cough:干～ dry cough

壳 ké〈名〉shell; husk:核桃～ walnut shell

kě

渴 kě ①〈形〉thirsty:感到有些～ feel more or less thirsty ②〈副〉eagerly

渴念 kěniàn be very anxious about; miss terribly; yearn for

渴求 kěqiú eagerly desire; crave for

渴望 kěwàng long for; crave for; yearn for; hanker after; eagerly hope for; thirst for:～爱情 starve for affection

可 kě〈动〉①approve:不置～否 decline to comment ②may; can:由此～见 thus it can be seen that ③be worth (doing); need (doing) ④〈副〉[表示强调]:～别忘了。Be sure to remember it. ⑤[表示加强疑问语气]:你～曾跟她谈过这个问题? Did you ever talk it over with her?

可爱 kě'ài lovely; lovable; adorable; amiable; beloved:～的小孩 adorable kids

可保 kěbǎo insurable:～财产 insurable property. ～权益 insurable interest

可悲 kěbēi sad; deplorable; lamentable; pitiable:～的表现 a pitiable display of…

可比 kěbǐ comparable:～产品 comparable products. ～价格 comparable price. ～经济指标 comparable economic targets. ～能耗 comparable energy consumption

可变 kěbiàn changeable; variable:～资本 variable capital

可耻 kěchǐ shameful; disgraceful; ignominious:遭到～的失败 meet with an ignominious defeat

可兑换 kěduìhuàn exchangeable; convertible:～证券 convertible bond

可付外币 kě fù wàibì foreign currency bills payable

可歌可泣 kěgē-kěqì inspiring; heroic and moving; move one to song and tears; stirring:～的斗争 an epic struggle

可更新资源 kěgēngxīn zīyuán renewable resources

可观 kěguān handsome; considerable:～的收入 handsome income

可贵 kěguì valuable; precious; worthy; noble:～的品质 fine (noble) quality

可恨 kěhèn hateful; detestable; abominable

可嘉 kějiā praiseworthy; commendable

可见 kějiàn it is thus clear (evident, obvious) that; it shows; that proves; so

可敬 kějìng honourable; respected; venerable

可靠 kěkào reliable; dependable; trustworthy:～投资 sound investment. ～帐户 reliable account

可口 kěkǒu good to eat; nice; tasty; palatable

可乐 kělè ① laughable; funny; amusing ② cola (a type of non-alcoholic drink):可口～ Coca Cola

可怜 kělián pitiable; pitiful; wretched:～虫 poor fellow; wretch

可能 kěnéng ① possible; probable:likely ② probably; maybe ③possibility

可怕 kěpà fearful; frightful; terrible; terrifying

可欺 kěqī ① gullible; easily duped ② easily cowed or bullied

可气 kěqì annoying; exasperating:这孩子刚换的衣服就弄脏了，真～! The child just changed his clothes and now he's got them dirty again. How annoying!

可取 kěqǔ desirable; advisable; recommendable:一无～ nothing to recommend

可是 kěshì but; yet; however

可体 kětǐ be a good fit; fit nicely

可谓 kěwèi one may well say; it may be said; it may be called

可恶 kěwù abominable; hateful; odious; loathsome

可惜 kěxī It is a pity (that…); alas for; unfortunately:～他们昨天没有来。It is a pity that they didn't come yesterday.

可喜 kěxǐ ① joyful; delightful ② encouraging; gratifying; heartening:～可贺 be congratulated. 取得～的成绩 achieve gratifying (encouraging) results

可笑 kěxiào laughable; ludicrous; ridiculous:可怕到这种～程度 carry one's fear to such absurd lengths

可行 kěxíng feasible; practicable:～性研究报告 feasibility study report

可疑 kěyí doubtful; dubious; questionable; suspicious:形迹～ look suspicious

可以 kěyǐ ① can; may ② be worth (doing):这些问题很～研究一番。These questions are worth looking into. ③ passable; pretty good; not bad ④ terrible; awful:他这张嘴真～! What a sharp tongue he's got!

可用现金 kěyòngxiànjīn available cash

可有可无 kěyǒukěwú not essential; may or may not be needed; not indispensable

可征税收入 kězhēngshuì shōurù taxable income

可转让信用证 kězhuǎnràng xìnyòng zhèng transferable letter of credit

kè

刻 kè ①〈动〉carve; cut; engrave:木～ woodcut. ～图章 engrave a seal〈名〉② quarter (of an hour):3点1～ a quarter past three ③ moment:此～ at the moment〈形〉④ cutting; penetrating:～薄语言 acrimonious phrases ⑤ in the highest degree:深～ profound; penetrating; deep-going

刻板 kèbǎn ① inflexible; mechanical ② cut blocks for printing:～印书业 wood-block printing

刻本 kèběn block-printed edition

刻薄 kèbó unkind; harsh; caustic; tart; mean:～话 make caustic remarks; speak unkindly. ～成家 become rich by harsh (unsuitable, inappropriate) means

刻不容缓 kèbùrónghuǎn brook no delay; demand immediate attention; be of great importance:此事～。The matter brooks no delay.

刻刀 kèdāo burin; graver

刻毒 kèdú venomous; spiteful

刻度 kèdù graduation (on a vessel or instrument)

刻骨 kègǔ deep-rooted; deep-ingrained:～仇恨 deep-seated hatred for; bitter hatred; inveterate hatred. 怀着～的阶级仇恨 nourish irreconcilable (bitter) class hatred for…

刻画 kèhuà delineate; depict; portray:～入微 portray to the life

刻苦 kèkǔ ① arduous; assiduous; painstaking ② simple and frugal:～钻研 study assiduously; mug (up)

刻纹 kèwén carving

刻意 kèyì painstaking; sedulous:～的技巧 conscious technical skill. ～求工 sedulously strive for perfection

克 kè〈动〉① can be able to:不～分身 be unable to leave what one's doing at the moment ② control; restrain:～制 exercise restraint ③ subdue; capture; overcome:～服邪气 overcome all that is evil. 无攻不～ be invincible ④ set a time limit:～期完工 set a date for completing the work; complete the work on a set date ⑤〈名〉gram (g.)

克服 kèfú overcome; surmount; conquer; get over:～困难 overcome (surmount) difficulties

克己 kèjǐ restrain one's selfishness; self-restraint; self-control:～奉公 be wholeheartedly devoted to public duty; work selflessly for the common good (public interest)

克扣 kèkòu make an illegal cut (on); embezzle part of what should be issued (on); deduct illegally:～军饷 pocket a portion of the soldiers' pay; make an illegal cut on the soldiers' pay

克拉 kèlā carat

克隆 [指生物体的无性繁殖] kèlóng clone

克勤克俭 kèqín-kèjiǎn hard work and thrift; be industrious and frugal; industry and frugality; save and be economical; practise economy and diligence

克制 kèzhì restrain; control; exercise restraint

课

kè〈名〉① lesson:第 5 ~ Lesson Five ② class:上 3 节~ have three classes ③ subject; course:~程要精简。Courses should be fewer and better. ④〈动〉impose; levy:~税 levy taxes

课本 kèběn textbook

课表 kèbiǎo school timetable

课程 kèchéng curriculum; course; lessons; schedule; studies:~表 curriculum schedule. ~研究 curriculum studies. ~组 course team

课间餐 kèjiāncān recess snack

课间操 kèjiāncāo recess calisthenics; setting-up exercises during the break

课时 kèshí class hour; period

课税 kèshuì levy tax (duty); charge duty:~单位 taxable unit. ~品 object of taxation; dutiable goods

课堂 kètáng classroom; schoolroom:~教学 classroom instruction (teaching). ~作业 classwork

课题 kètí ① task; problem:提出新的~ pose a new problem; set a new task ② research subject; project:~承包制 contract system for research job. ~组 project group; research (study) group

课外 kèwài outside class; extracurricular; outside; after school (class):~活动 extracurricular activities. ~阅读 outside reading. ~作业 homework

课余 kèyú after class; after school

课桌 kèzhuō (school) desk

客

kè〈名〉① guest; visitor:贵~ distinguished guest ② passenger; traveller:~机 passenger plane; airliner ③ customer:乘~ passenger ④ settle or live in a strange place; be a stranger:作~他乡 live in a strange land ⑤ a person engaged in a particular pursuit:政~ politician ⑥〈形〉objective ⑦〈量〉portion; helping:要一~煎蛋 order a portion of fried eggs

客船 kèchuán passenger ship (boat)

客串 kèchuàn be a guest performer:上台~表演 mount the stage for a guest performance

客地 kèdì place far away from home; alien land

客队 kèduì [体] visiting (guest) team

客饭 kèfàn meal specially prepared for visitors at a canteen; set meal

客房 kèfáng guest room

客观 kèguān objective:~规律 objective law. ~外界的现象 phenomena of the objective external world

客户 kèhù client; customer

客居 kèjū live in a place other than one's hometown; stay in a strange land

客流 kèliú the flow of passengers

客满 kèmǎn ① full house ② be filled to capacity:电影院已～。The cinema is filled to capacity.

客气 kèqi ① courteous; polite; civil[对客人说时用]: Please don't stand on ceremony. [对主人说时用]: Please don't bother ② modest:你太客气了。You are too polite. 别～。[回答别人的感谢语] Don't mention it.; You are welcome.

客人 kèrén ① visitor; guest ② guest (at a hotel, etc.); traveller

客商 kèshāng investor; foreign trader

客随主便 kèsuízhǔbiàn A guest should suit the convenience of the host (hostess); do as one's host thinks fit.

客套 kètào civilities; formalities: ～话 conventional phrase; polite greetings. 不讲～ do away with formalities; not stand on ceremony

客厅 kètīng drawing room; parlour; living room; sitting room

客运 kèyùn passenger transport; passenger traffic

客座教授 kèzuò jiàoshòu visiting professor; guest professor

恪 kè 〈副〉 scrupulously and respectfully

恪守 kèshǒu scrupulously abide by (a treaty, promise, etc.); adhere faithfully to: ～本分 scrupulously abide by one's duty. ～不渝 submissively obey

kěn

肯 kěn 〈动〉 ① agree; consent: 首～ nod assent ② be willing (to do); be ready:～干 be willing to do hard work

肯定 kěndìng ① affirmative; positive ② affirm; confirm:～成绩 affirm the achievements

啃 kěn 〈动〉 ① bite; gnaw; nibble ② take great pains with one's studies

啃骨头 kěngútou pick a bone; [动物]gnaw (at) a bone

啃书本 kěnshūběn make laborious efforts to read; delve into a book; read with great difficulty but with little understanding

恳 kěn ① 〈动〉beseech; entreat; implore: 敬～ respectfully request ② 〈副〉 earnestly; cordially:～谢 thank sincerely

恳切 kěnqiè earnest; sincere; cordial

恳求 kěnqiú entreat; implore; plead

恳请 kěnqǐng earnestly beseech; cordially invite

恳谈会 kěntánhuì frank discussion meeting

垦 kěn 〈动〉 reclaim; cultivate; subdue

垦荒 kěnhuāng open up (upturn)

virgin soil; reclaim wasteland; bring wasteland under cultivation

垦区 kěnqū reclamation area

kēng

坑 kēng 〈名〉① pit; hollow; hole:土～ (sunken) pit ② tunnel: ～道作业 tunnel operations 〈动〉③ entrap; cheat:奸商净～人。The profiteers cheat people right and left. ④ bury alive:焚书～儒 burning books and burying the literati

坑道 kēngdào tunnel

坑害 kēnghài lead into a trap; frame (sb.) up; entrap; scheme to do harm

坑骗 kēngpiàn entrap; cheat

吭 kēng 〈动〉 utter

吭声 kēngshēng utter a word (sound)

铿 kēng 〈象〉 clang; clatter

铿锵 kēngqiāng ① ring; clang; jingle ② clangorous; sonorous: 这首诗读起来音调～。This poem reads sonorous.

kōng

空 kōng ①〈形〉 empty; hollow; void: ～瓶子 an empty bottle. ～洞的理论 an empty theory ②〈名〉sky; air:天～ sky ③〈副〉 for nothing; in vain: ～忙 make fruitless efforts

另见 kòng

空播 kōngbo aerial sowing

空舱费 kōngcāngfèi dead freight

空城计 kōngchéngjì a stratagem to present a bold front to conceal unpreparedness (a weakly defended); "undefended-city" stratagem — to bewilder and keep away the enemy by openig the gate of a city actually left unguarded

空洞 kōngdòng devoid of sense; empty; hollow; pointless:内容～的文章 article empty of matter

空翻 kōngfān somersault; flip:后～ backward somersault; backflip

空腹 kōngfù on an empty stomach

空喊 kōnghǎn loud empty talk

空话 kōnghuà empty talk (verbiage); idle talk: ～连篇,言之无物。It fills endless pages with empty verbiage.

空间 kōngjiān space: ～布局 spatial distribution. ～科学 space science

空军 kōngjūn air force

空口无凭 kōngkǒu-wúpíng mere verbal statement is no guarantee

空旷 kōngkuàng open; spacious

空难 kōngnàn space disaster

空气 kōngqì ①air ②atmosphere: 紧张～ tense atmosphere. ～污染 air pollution

空前 kōngqián unprecedented; unparalleled; as never before: ～繁荣 be thriving as never before

空勤 kōngqín air duty

空手 kōngshǒu empty-handed
空谈 kōngtán ① indulge in empty talk ② empty talk; idle talk; prattle
空调 kōngtiáo air conditioning:～机 air conditioner
空头 kōngtóu ① nominal; in name:～支票 dishonoured cheque; dud cheque; bad (false) cheque; rubber cheque ② empty (false) promise; pay lip service to. ～政治 phony politics ③[投机]short; bear
空投 kōngtóu air-drop:～物资 air-dropped supplies
空袭 kōngxí make an air attack (raid)
空想 kōngxiǎng fantasy; pipe-dream; (idle) dream:耽于～ indulge in idle dreams. ～社会主义 utopian socialism
空虚 kōngxū empty; void; hollow
空运 kōngyùn ① air transport ② airlift:～单 airway bill of lading. ～救灾物资 airlift relief supplies. ～保险 air transportation insurance
空中 kōngzhōng ① in the air ② aerial; air:～预警飞机 air warning planes. ～劫持飞机 hijacking. ～小姐 air hostess; stewardess
空转 kōngzhuàn ① (of a motor, etc.) idle; race ② (of a wheel) turn without moving forward; spin

kǒng

恐 kǒng〈动〉① fear; dread; be afraid of:～惧 dread; fear; be afraid of ② threaten; terrorize; terrify:～吓 intimidate; threaten
恐怖 kǒngbù terror; fright:～电影 horror movies
恐高症 kǒnggāozhèng acrophobia
恐吓 kǒnghè threaten; frighten; intimidate:～索财(罪) blackmail. ～信 threating letter
恐慌 kǒnghuāng panic; scare:[危机]crisis:～万状 panic-stricken. 经济～ economic crisis. ～价格 panic price
恐惧 kǒngjù fear; dread
恐龙 kǒnglóng dinosaur
恐怕 kǒngpà ① I'm afraid:今晚～他们不会来。I'm afraid they won't come tonight. ② perhaps; probably:～她忘了。It is probable that she forgot.

孔 kǒng〈名〉hole; opening; aperture:钥匙～ keyhole
孔孟之道 kǒngmèngzhīdào the doctrine of Confucius and Mencius
孔庙(府) kǒngmiào (fǔ) Confucian Temple (Kongs' Residence)
孔雀 kǒngquè peacock
孔隙 kǒngxī small opening; hole

kòng

空 kòng ①〈形〉unoccupied vacant; blank:～座 a vacant seat ②〈动〉leave empty; vacate:～出一个抽屉 empty a drawer 〈名〉③ empty space:各行之间

多留点～儿。Leave a little more space between the rows. ④ free time; spare time: 他有～儿? Is he free?
另见 kōng

空白 kòngbái space; blank gap: ～承兑 acceptance in blank. ～点 blank spot; blank. ～支票 blank cheque (check). 填补～ fill a gap

空地 kòngdì vacant lot; open ground; open space

空格 kònggé blank space (on a form)

空缺 kòngquē vacant post; vacancy

空隙 kòngxì ① interval ② space; gap; clearance

空闲 kòngxián ① idle; free ② free time; spare time; leisure: 他很少有～。He is seldom at leisure.

空余 kòngyú free; vacant; unoccupied

空子 kòngzi opening; loophole: 钻～ avail oneself of loopholes (in a law, a statute, a contract, etc.)

控 kòng 〈动〉 ① accuse; charge: ～诉 accuse ② control; dominate: ～制观察 controlled observation

控方证人 kòngfāng zhèngrén [法] prosecution witness

控告 kònggào accuse (of); charge (with); bring an action against; complain; bring a complaint: ～某人 take action against sb.; bring a suit (charge) against sb.; charge a crime upon sb.; level a charge against sb. 被～偷窃 be charged with theft. ～人 complainant. ～违约 sue for a breach of promise

控股公司 kònggǔ gōngsī holding company

控诉 kòngsù accuse; complain; delate; make a complaint against; ～人 accusing party; complainant. ～会 accusation meeting. ～要点 gravamen

控制 kòngzhì control; contain: ～不住自己的感情 can't contain one's feelings. ～固定资产投资规模 scale of investment in fixed assets should be brought under control. ～经济 command economy. ～论 cybernetics

kōu

抠 kōu 〈动〉 ① dig or dig out with a finger or sth. pointed; scratch ② carve; cut ③ delve into; study meticulously ④ stingy; miserly: 这人真～! How stingy he is!

抠门儿 kōuménr stingy; miserly

抠字眼儿 kōuzìyǎnr pay too much attention to wording; find fault with the choice of words

kǒu

口 kǒu 〈名〉 ① mouth ② opening; entrance; mouth: 洞～ the mouth of a cave ③ cut; hole: 伤

～ wound ④ the edge of a knife:刀～ the edge of a knife ⑤ department; section:文教～ cultural and educational departments ⑥〈量〉[用于人]他家有4～人。There are four people in his family.

口岸 kǒu'àn port:通商～ trading port. ～检查机关 inspection office at the port

口碑 kǒubēi public praise

口才 kǒucái talent for speaking; eloquence:～好 be eloquent

口吃 kǒuchī stammer; stutter:说话有点～ speak with a slight stammer

口齿 kǒuchǐ ① enunciation:～清楚 have clear enunciation ② ability to speak

口臭 kǒuchòu bad breath; halitosis

口袋 kǒudài ① pocket ② kǒudai bag; sack

口风 kǒufēng one's intention or view as revealed in what one says

口福 kǒufú gourmet's luck; the luck to get sth. very nice to eat

口服 kǒufú ① take orally:不得～ not to be taken orally ② profess to be convinced:～心服 be sincerely (utterly) convinced

口供 kǒugòng testimony; a statement made by the accused under examination; deposition; oral (verbal) confession; confession:～记录 record of testimony. ～证据 testimonial proof

口号 kǒuhào slogan; watchword

口红 kǒuhóng lipstick

口技 kǒujì art of imitating sounds; ventriloquism

口径 kǒujìng ① bore; calibre ② requirements; specifications; line of action

口诀 kǒujué (arithmatic) tables which should be committed to memory for ready use, as the multiplication table, etc.; oral formula

口口声声 kǒukǒu-shēngshēng say again and again; repeatedly declare; keep on saying; go on prating; talk glibly about

口粮 kǒuliáng ration (of grain): ～田 fields for growing grain rations

口蜜腹剑 kǒumì-fùjiàn honey-mouthed and dagger-hearted; hypocritical and malignant; honey in mouth, dagger in heart; a mouth that praises and a hand that kills; play a double game; honey on one's lips and murder in one's heart

口气 kǒuqì ① tone; tune ② the way one speaks; manner of speaking: ～强硬 in strong terms

口若悬河 kǒuruòxuánhé be eloquent; speak with a flow of eloquence; let loose a flood of eloquence

口实 kǒushí ① pretext; pretence; a cause for gossip:以…为～ on the pretence of… ② handle:贻人～ provide one's critics with a handle

口试 kǒushì oral test; oral examination; oral:参加～ take an oral (examination)

口是心非 kǒushì-xīnfēi say one thing and mean another; play a double game; right with the mouth but wrong at heart; outwardly agree but inwardly disagree; affirm… with one's lips but deny in one's heart

口授 kǒushòu ① instruct orally: ～语言教学法 oral method of teaching languages ② dictate: ～遗嘱 oral testament

口述 kǒushù give an oral account

口水 kǒushuǐ saliva: 流～ slobber. 令人流～ make sb. 's mouth water

口说无凭 kǒushuō wúpíng Words of mouth alone don't carry conviction.; Words alone are no proof.; Oral expressions cannot be taken as evidence.

口头 kǒutóu oral; verbal; in word: ～练习 oral practice. ～表决 voice vote; acclamation. ～禅 commonplace sayings; conventional expressions; pet phrase. ～起诉 oral complaint. ～契约 parol contract. ～文学 oral literature; unwritten literature. ～证据 oral evidence

口味 kǒuwèi taste; flavour: 本地～ local flavour

口误 kǒuwù ① make a slip of the tongue ② a slip of the tongue; an oral slip

口音 kǒuyīn accent: 说话带天津～ speak with a Tianjin accent

口语 kǒuyǔ ① spoken language ② colloquial language; colloquialism

口罩 kǒuzhào breathing mask; mask; gauze mask

口重 kǒuzhòng ① salty ② be fond of salty food

kòu

叩 kòu ① knock ② kowtow ③ inquire; ask

叩见 kòujiàn visit (one's superior); call on (one's superior)

叩首 kòushǒu kowtow

叩谢 kòuxiè kowtow in thanks; offer earnest thanks

扣 kòu 〈动〉 ① buckle; clasp; button: ～～子 do up the buttons ② arrest; take into custody; detain: 把罪犯～起来。Keep the criminal in custody. ③ deduct: ～奖金 make bonus deductions ④ discount: 打 8～ give a 20 percent discount ⑤ hit: 猛～一球 smash the ball forcefully

扣除 kòuchú deduct; set apart; carry back: ～价格因素增长 allowing for price rises

扣工资 kòu gōngzī dock one's wages

扣缴 kòujiǎo withhold: ～所得税报告表 withholding income tax return

扣留 kòuliú detain; arrest: ～船舶 detention of ship. ～驾驶执照 suspend a driving card

扣帽子 kòumàozi put (pin) a label on sb.; put a hat on sb.; label sb.; tag sb. with the label of

扣球 kòuqiú smash (a ball)

扣人心弦 kòurénxīnxián soul-stirring; thrilling; exciting

扣压 kòuyā hold up; withhold: ～文章 pigeonhole articles

扣押 kòuyā ① [人]detain; hold in custody ② [法] distrain (upon): ～家产抵偿债务 distrain upon sb.'s property for debt. ～财产 seize property

kū

窟 kū 〈名〉① cave; grotto ② den; lair

窟窿 kūlong hole; opening; cavity

枯 kū 〈形〉① (of a plant, etc.) withered: ～叶 dead leaves ② (of a well, river, etc.) dried up: 河～了。The river has run dry. ③ dull; uninteresting: ～燥无味的宣传 dry and dull propaganda

枯肠 kūcháng impoverished mind: 搜索～ rack one's brains (for ideas or expressions)

枯干 kūgān dried-up; withered; wizened

枯黄 kūhuáng withered and yellow

枯竭 kūjié be dried up; be exhausted: 资金～。The capital has been exhausted.

枯木逢春 kūmùféngchūn like a dry tree reviving in spring; good fortune that comes after a long spell of bad luck

枯燥 kūzào dry; tedious; insipid: ～无味 dry and dull; tedious

骷 kū

骷髅 kūlóu ① human skull; death's head ② human skeleton

哭 kū 〈动〉cry; weep

哭泣 kūqì cry; weep; sob

哭穷 kūqióng go about telling people how hard up one is; complain of being hard up

哭丧着脸 kūsangzhe liǎn ① put on (wear) a long face; go around with a long face; ② a woe-begone look; with an ugly grimace

哭声 kūshēng cry; tearful voice

哭诉 kūsù accuse in tears; complain tearfully

哭天抹泪 kūtiān-mǒlèi wail and whine

哭笑不得 kūxiào-bùdé find sth. both funny and annoying; be at a loss whether to cry or laugh; hard to make up one's mind whether to laugh or cry: ～的小伙子 a happy-go-lucky-fellow

kǔ

苦 kǔ 〈形〉① bitter: ～药 bitter medicine ② difficult ③〈形,副〉hard: ～干 work hard ④〈名〉suffering; hardship; pain: ～水中长大 grow up amidst sufferings ⑤〈动〉cause sb. suffering; give sb. a hard time: 他们在旧社会受尽了～。They went through all kinds of hardships in the old society. ⑤〈副〉painstakingly; do one's utmost:

～心经营 painstakingly build up

苦处 kǔchù suffering; difficulty; hardship

苦干 kǔgàn work hard; be painstaking with one's work:～实干 work in a down-to-earth way

苦功 kǔgōng painstaking efforts; pains; harwork:下～ take pains

苦工 kǔgōng ① hard (manual) work; hard labour ② a person doing hard (manual) work

苦果 kǔguǒ bitter fruit

苦海 kǔhǎi abyss of misery; sea of bitterness:脱离～ get out of the abyss of misery

苦尽甘来 kǔjìn-gānlái when bitterness is finished, sweetness begins; After suffering comes happiness.; Sweet after sweat.; After rains comes fair weather

苦口良药 kǔkǒu-liángyào A good medicine tastes bitter.; Though bitter-tasting, it is still the best medicine for

苦口婆心 kǔkǒu-póxīn advise in earnest words and with good intention; admonish sb. earnestly; urge sb. time and again with good intentions

苦乐不均 kǔ lè bù jūn much disparity in material well-being; inequality of benefits; unfair treatment:企业～。Enterprises were not equally treated in terms of benefits and obligations.

苦闷 kǔmèn depressed; distressed; down-hearted:感到～ feel depressed

苦难 kǔnàn bitterness; hardships; misery; sufferings:～的岁月 years of darkness. ～深重的历史 a history of untold suffering

苦恼 kǔnǎo worried; distressed; vexed:令人～的 distressing; annoying

苦涩 kǔsè ① bitter and astringent ② pained; agonized; anguished

苦水 kǔshuǐ ① bitter water ② gastric secretion, etc. rising to the mouth ③suffering (in the old society)

苦思 kǔsī think hard; be lost in hard thinking; cudgel one's thinking

苦痛 kǔtòng pain; suffering

苦头 kǔtóu suffering; bitterness: 吃尽～ go through all kinds of sufferings. 我们都尝过…的～。We have all suffered from …

苦笑 kǔxiào force a smile; make a wry smile

苦心 kǔxīn painstaking efforts; take great pains; trouble taken:～经营 painstakingly build up (an enterprise, etc.); work out with unsparing efforts. 煞费～ rack one's brains

苦役 kǔyì hard labour; penal servitude; drudgery

苦于 kǔyú ① suffer from (a disadvantage) ② be harder than; be worse off than

苦衷 kǔzhōng difficulties that one is reluctant to bring to the notice of others; difficulties that one is reluctantly to discuss or mention; difficulties

kù

库 kù〈名〉storehouse; depot

库藏 kùcáng have in storage

库存 kùcún stock (of goods); [金钱]reserves (of money):～物资 stock in storage; goods kept in stock. ～现金 cash holding; cash in treasury

库容 kùróng storage capacity (of a reservoir, warehouse, etc.)

裤 kù〈名〉trousers; pants:短～ shorts. 棉～ cotton-padded trousers

裤衩 kùchǎ underpants; undershorts

裤带 kùdài trouser belt; waist belt (band):各国政府都试图"束紧～"而不想采取通货再膨胀政策。Various governments tried to "tighten their belts" in stead of reflating.

酷 kù ①〈形〉cruel; ruthless ②〈副〉very; extremely

酷爱 kù'ài be very fond of; be keen on:～自由 ardent love of freedom

酷好 kùhào have a deep love for (art, music, etc.); be very keen on

酷热 kùrè (of weather) extremely hot

酷似 kùsì bear a close resemblance to; be just like

酷肖 kùxiào closely resemble; be the very image of; be exactly like

酷刑 kùxíng savage (cruel) torture; excruciation; cruel punishment

kuā

夸 kuā〈动〉① speak highly of; praise; commend:自～ sing one's own praise ② boast; exaggerate; overstate:～口 brag; boast

夸大 kuādà exaggerate; overstate; magnify:把部分真理～为普遍真理 magnify partial truth into universal truths

夸奖 kuājiǎng praise; speak favourably of; commend

夸口 kuākǒu boast; brag; talk big

夸夸其谈 kuākuā-qítán indulge in verbiage; talk big; become bombastic

夸耀 kuāyào make a display of; flaunt; brag about; show off

夸张 kuāzhāng exaggerate; overstate:艺术～ artistic exaggeration ②[语言]hyperbole

kuǎ

垮 kuǎ〈动〉fall; break (tumble) down; collapse:洪水冲～了堤坝。The flood waters burst the dyke. 她的身体～了。She has broken down (in health).

垮台 kuǎtái collapse; disintegrate; fall from power; downfall:反动派～了。It was all up with reactionaries.

kuà

挎 kuà〈动〉① carry on one's arm ② carry sth. over one's shoulder or at one's side

挎包 kuàbāo satchel;［旅行时用的］haversack

跨 kuà〈动〉stride; step:向前～一步 take a step forward ② straddle; bestride:横～黄河的大桥 a gigantic bridge spanning the Huanghe (Yellow) River

跨度 kuàdù span

跨国公司 kuàguó gōngsī transnational (supranational) corporation; multinational corporation

跨行业、跨地区 kuà hángyè, kuà dìqū intertrade and transregion; transcending the barriers between industries and regions:～经营 extend operations beyond the limits of respective industries and regions; intertrade and transregional operations

跨世纪 kuà shìjì transcentury:～蓝图 a transcentury blueprint

跨系 kuàxì interdepartmental:～专业学生 interdepartmental major

跨学科 kuà xuékē interdiscipline

跨越 kuàyuè stride across; leap over; span:铁路～高山。Rails span mountains.

kuài

会 kuài
另见 huì

会计 kuàijì ① accounting:～法 accountancy law. ～管理 management through accounting. ～监督 accounting control. ～年度 fiscal (financial) year ② accountant; bookkeeper:～师 chartered accountant

脍 kuài〈名〉fine minced meat

脍炙人口 kuàizhì-rénkǒu be on everybody's lips; enjoy great popularity; be widely quoted; popular

块 kuài〈名〉① piece; cube; chunk; lump; block:石～ blocks of stone ②［肥皂等］cake;［土地］lot; plot〈口〉［人民币］*yuan*

块块 kuàikuài ① squares; blocks ② a system of enterprise management by various levels of local governments:以～为主的财政体制 local governments are responsible for balancing their own budgets

快 kuài〈形〉① fast; rapid; quick:～速 high speed ②［刀］sharp ③ quick-witted; ingenious ④ glad; happy pleased:心中不～ feel bad ⑤ frank; straightforward〈副〉⑥ quickly:～来! Come here quickly! ⑦ soon; before long:他们～要回来了。They'll be back soon.

快班课程 kuàibān kèchéng accelerated course; accelerated programme; accelerated studies

快板 kuàibǎn *kuaiban* — clapper verses accompanied by bamboo castanets; song to quick patter; clapper talk; *kuaiban* ballad

快报 kuàibào wall bulletin; bulletin

快步 kuàibù ① walk at a quick pace ② [军]half step; trot

快餐 kuàicān quick (fast) meal; snack; buffet: ～馆 fast-food restaurants

快车 kuàichē express (train): ～道 fast traffic lane

快递公司 kuàidì gōngsī express company

快感 kuàigǎn pleasant feeling; delight

快活 kuàihuo happy; merry; cheerful

快货 kuàihuò quick-selling merchandise

快乐 kuàilè happy; joyful; cheerful; gay: 祝你新年～。(I wish you a) Happy New Year!

快速 kuàisù quick; high-speed: ～市际公共交通系统 high-speed, intercity public transit. ～切削(机) high-speed cutting

快慰 kuàiwèi feel reassured and happy; be extremely pleased

快信 kuàixìn express letter

快讯 kuàixùn newsflash; flash

快要 kuàiyào be about to; be going to: 她～60岁了。She is going to be sixty.; She is getting on for sixty.

快照 kuàizhào ① snapshot; snap ② [即时可取的]instant prints: 为某人拍～ take snap of sb.

快装费 kuàizhuāngfèi dispatch money

筷 kuài 〈名〉 chopsticks

筷子 kuàizi chopsticks: 一双～ a pair of chopsticks

kuān

宽 kuān 〈形〉 ① wide; broad: 眼界放～ have a broad outlook ② liberal; generous; lenient: ～以待人 be lenient with others ③ well-off; comfortably off: 她手头比过去～多了。She's much better off than before. 〈动〉④ relax; relieve: 把心放～一点。Don't take it too hard. ⑤ extend: 限期能再～几天吗? Can the deadline be extended a few more days? ⑥〈名〉breadth; width: 这个大厅10米～。The hall is ten metres in breadth.

宽敞 kuānchǎng spacious; roomy: ～的客厅 spacious parlour

宽畅 kuānchàng free from worry; happy

宽大 kuāndà ① lenient; liberal; clement: ～处理 deal with leniently; be accorded lenient treatment; be treated with leniency ② spacious; [衣服等] loose; wide: ～为怀 magnanimity (leniency; clemency)

宽度 kuāndù width; breadth: 领海～ the extent of the territorial sea

宽宏大量 kuānhóng-dàliàng

broad-minded and generous; big-hearted; generous

宽厚 kuānhòu generous; clement: ～待人 be generous to people

宽阔 kuānkuò broad; wide

宽容 kuānróng leniency; tolerance; clemency

宽恕 kuānshù forgive; pardon

宽松 kuānsōng loose and confortable: ～的宏观经济环境 nonconstricting macro-economic environment

宽慰 kuānwèi ① soothe; console; comfort ② be relieved: 感到～ feel relieved

宽限日期 kuānxiàn rìqī days of grace; grace period

宽衣 kuānyī take off your coat

宽银幕 kuānyínmù wide movie screen: ～电影 wide-screen film; cinemascope. 全景～ cinepanoramic

宽裕 kuānyù ① well-off; well-to-do: 手头～ be quite well off; be in easy circumstances ② [时间]plenty (of time)

宽窄 kuānzhǎi width; breadth; size

kuǎn

款 kuǎn 〈名〉① a sum of money; fund: 申请国家拨～ apply for a financial grant from the state ② section of an article in a legal document, etc.; paragraph ③〈动〉entertain; receive with hospitality: ～客 entertain guests〈形〉④ sincere ⑤ slow; leisurely

款待 kuǎndài treat (receive) cordially; entertain

款款 kuǎnkuǎn ① sincere; faithful ② slowly; leisurely

款留 kuǎnliú cordially urge (a guest) to stay

款式 kuǎnshì pattern; style; design

款项(子) kuǎnxiàng(zi) fund; a sum of money

kuāng

框 kuāng
另见 kuàng

框框 kuāngkuang ① frame; circle ② convention; stereotype: 打破旧～ break through the conventions. 摆脱小农经济的～ be free from the limitations of a small-scale peasant economy

筐 kuāng 〈名〉 basket: ～子 basket

kuáng

狂 kuáng 〈形〉① mad; crazy: 高兴得发～ be crazy with delight ② violent; wild: ～风 strong fast wind ③ wild; delirious; raving: ～喜 be wild with job ④ arrogant; overbearing: 口出～言 talk wildly

狂暴 kuángbào violent; wild

狂奔 kuángbēn run wildly; run like mad

狂草书 kuángcǎoshū [书法]uninhibited, free-flowing wild grass style

狂风 kuángfēng violent wind; gale: ～暴雨 violent storm; tempest; hurricane

狂欢 kuánghuān revelry; spree; carnival; lively celebration; public merrymaking: ～节 carnival

狂澜 kuánglán furious waves: 力挽～ save a critical situation

狂怒 kuángnù be furious with anger; boil with rage

狂热 kuángrè crazy; feverish; fanatical; frantic; frenized; violently; delirious: ～的信徒 a fanatical follower

狂妄 kuángwàng arrogant; presuming; unbridled; preposterous: ～的野心 unbridled ambition. ～自大 wildly arrogant; arrogant and conceited

狂喜 kuángxǐ be mad with joy; be enraptured; throw one into raptures

狂想曲 kuángxiǎngqǔ [乐] rhapsody

狂言 kuángyán crazy remarks; wild language; ravings: ～大语 in wild phraseology

kuàng

矿 kuàng 〈名〉① mine ② ore

矿藏 kuàngcáng mineral wealth; mineral resources (deposits): ～丰富 be rich in mineral deposits (resources)

矿层 kuàngcéng ore bed; ore horizon; seam

矿产 kuàngchǎn mineral products; minerals: ～普查 survey for the purpose of locating mineral resources

矿车 kuàngchē mine car; tub; tram

矿工 kuànggōng miner; [煤矿的] collier; pitman

矿井 kuàngjǐng pit; shaft

矿区 kuàngqū mining area

矿泉 kuàngquán mineral spring: ～水 mineral water

矿山 kuàngshān mine: ～开发 mine development

矿石 kuàngshí ore

矿物 kuàngwù mineral: ～油 mineral oil

矿务局 kuàngwùjú mining bureau

旷 kuàng 〈形〉① spacious; vast; open: 地～人稀 a vast territory with a sparse population ② free from worries and petty ideas; broad-minded: 心～神怡 carefree and happy ③ 〈动〉be absent (from work, etc.) without leave

旷达 kuàngdá big-hearted; broad-minded; open-minded

旷工 kuànggōng be absent from work without leave; deliberately stay away from work

旷课 kuàngkè be absent from school without leave; cut classes; skip school; play traunt

旷日持久 kuàngrì-chíjiǔ protracted; prolonged; long-drawn-out

旷世 kuàngshì unequalled in one's time; unrivalled; unique

旷野 kuàngyě open field; wilderness: ～荒郊 deserted countryside

旷职 kuàngzhí be absent from duty without leave

框 kuàng 〈名〉 frame; sash; case; [眼镜的] rim
另见 kuāng

框架 kuàngjià framework

况 kuàng ①〈名〉condition; situation; state: 近～如何? How have you been recently? ②〈动〉 compare (with, to): 以古～今 draw parallels from history ③〈副〉 moreover; besides

况且 kuàngqiě moreover; besides; in addition: 现在去看足球太晚了,～天又开始下雨了。It's too late to go to the football match now, besides, it's beginning to rain.

kuī

窥 kuī〈动〉 peep (at, into); spy

窥测 kuīcè spy out: ～方向 keep an eye on which direction the wind blows; watch (see) how the wind blows. ～时机 bide one's time

窥见 kuījiàn detect; get (catch) a glimpse of

窥视 kuīshì spy on; peep at

窥伺 kuīsì be on watch for; lie in wait for

窥探 kuītàn spy upon; pry into (about)

窥听 kuītīng eavesdrop

亏 kuī ①〈名〉 loss; deficit: ～损企业 deficit-ridden firms 〈动〉 ② lose (money, etc.); have a deficit: ～本 lose one's capital ③ treat unfairly: 理～ be in the wrong. 我～不了你们。I'll never let you go empty-handed. ④〈副〉 thanks to; fortunately; luckily: ～得… it is fortunate that…

亏本 kuīběn lose one's capital; suffer a loss; lose; lose money in business: ～卖出 sell sth. at a loss

亏秤 kuīchèng give short weight

亏待 kuīdài treat unfairly; be short with sb.

亏空 kuīkōng be in debt; deficit; debt

亏欠 kuīqiàn be in arrears; have a deficit

亏损 kuīsǔn loss; deficit: ～包干 system of responsibility for fixed profits and losses; loss contract system ② general debility

亏心 kuīxīn guilty conscience; conscience-stricken: 做～事 do sth. against one's conscience

盔 kuī 〈名〉 helmet

盔甲 kuījiǎ a suit of armour; helmet and armour; brace

岿 kuī

岿然 kuīrán towering; lofty; loftily; steadfastly: ～不动 steadfastly stand on one's ground; remain unmoved. ～屹立 stand towering; tower

kuí

魁 kuí 〈名〉 chief; head

魁首 kuíshǒu a person who is head and shoulders above others; the brigtest and best

魁伟 kuíwěi big and tall; strapping; stalwart; strong-built: 体格～的人 man of strong build

魁梧 kuíwú big and tall; stalwart

葵 kuí

葵花 kuíhuā sunflower: ～子 sunflower seeds

傀 kuí

魁儡 kuílěi puppet: ～戏 puppet show (play). ～政权 puppet regime

kuì

愧 kuì 〈动〉 be ashamed (of); conscience-stricken: 问心无～ have a clear conscience; have nothing on one's conscience

愧恨 kuìhèn be ashamed and remorseful; feel remorseful: ～交集 be overcome with shame and remorse

愧悔 kuìhuǐ repent with shame

愧疚 kuíjiù feel remorseful and uneasy; be conscience-stricken

愧色 kuìsè look of shame; ashamed look: 面有～ look ashamed

溃 kuì 〈动〉 (of a dyke or dam, etc.) burst: ～堤 burst the dyke ② break through (a circlement) ③ be routed: ～不成军 be almost (utterly) routed

溃败 kuìbài be put to rout; be routed

溃烂 kuìlàn fester; ulcerate

溃散 kuìsàn stampede; break: 敌人～而逃。The enemy broke and fled.

溃逃 kuìtáo escape in disorder; fly pell-mell; flee helter-skelter

溃退 kuìtuì retreat in disorder; in pell-mell flight; retreat helter-skelter

溃疡 kuìyáng ulcer

匮 kuì 〈形〉 deficit

匮乏 kuìfá short (of supplies); defficient: 资源～ want of natural resources

馈 kuì 〈动〉 make a present of

馈电 kuìdiàn feed: ～线 feed line; feeder

馈赠 kuìzèng give as a present; make a present of sth.; present (a gift)

kūn

坤 kūn 〈形〉 female; feminine: ～表 woman's watch

昆 kūn

昆虫 kūnchóng insect

昆腔 kūnqiāng melodies which originated in Kunshan, Jiangsu Province, in the Ming Dynasty; Kunshan tune; *kun qiang* (Kunshan drama)

昆曲 kūnqǔ *kunqu* opera

kǔn

捆 kǔn ①〈动〉 tie together;

bind; bundle up: ～住手脚 bound hand and foot ②〈名〉bundle; bunch: 一～柴火 a bundle of firewood

捆绑 kǔnbǎng tie up; bind; truss up

捆装 kǔnzhuāng in bundle: ～货物 cargo in bundle

kùn

困 kùn〈动〉① be hard pressed; be stranded: ～而学之 those who learn when they are hard pressed ② surround; besiege: 把敌人～死在据点里。Bottle up the enemy in his stronghold.〈形〉③ hard; difficult: ～难处境 the difficult plight ④ tired: ～乏 fatigued; tired

困处 kùnchǔ ① difficult position; predicament; straits ② be stranded in; be in a fix

困顿 kùndùn ① tired out; exhausted ② be in financial straits

困乏 kùnfá ① tired; fatigued ② financially difficult; straitened economically

困惑 kùnhuò ① dilemma; perplexity; ② puzzled; bewildered; perplexed: 感到～ feel puzzled (about); be bewildered

困境 kùnjìng difficult position; dilemma; impasse; straits; (sad) plight; predicament: 陷于～ find oneself in an awkward predicament

困窘 kùnjiǒng embarrassed; be in straitened circumstances; untoward circumstances

困苦 kùnkǔ ① miserable; distressed ② (live) in hardship; privation: ～备尝 suffer privations

困难 kùnnan ① hard; difficult: ～重重 be beset with difficulties ② straitened circumstances; financial difficulties: 生活～ live in straitened circumstances

困扰 kùnrǎo perplex; puzzle

困守 kùnshǒu defend against a siege; stand a siege; be hemmed in; besieged: ～在几座孤立的城市里 be holed up in a few isolated cities

困兽犹斗 kùnshòu-yóudòu A cornered beast will still fight.; Even a trapped beast struggles.; Beasts at bay put up a desperate fight.

困知 kùnzhī knowledge attained through painful efforts

kuò

廓 kuò〈形〉wide; extensive; boundless ②〈名〉exterior features: 轮～ outline

廓清 kuòqīng sweep away; clean up: ～理论上的混乱 remove the confusion of theory

扩 kuò〈动〉expand; extend; spread: ～大家庭 extended (expanded) family

扩编 kuòbiān enlarge the establishment of an army unit

扩充 kuòchōng enlarge; expand; extend; augment: ～业务范围

branch out business

扩大 kuòdà enlarge; expand; broaden:~财源 open up new sources of revenue. ~就业面 expand employment. ~企业自主权 expand enterprise's autonomy

扩建 kuòjiàn expand; extend:~工厂 expand a factory

扩军 kuòjūn expand armaments:~备战 arms expansion and war preparations

扩散 kuòsàn spread; diffuse:[核、病菌等]proliferate:~税论 diffusion tax theory. 核~ nuclear proliferation. 癌~ proliferation of cancer

扩展 kuòzhǎn expand; extend; develop:~对外贸易 expand foreign trade. ~意义 extended meaning; extensional meaning

扩张 kuòzhāng expand; extend; enlarge; amplify; spread out; magnify:~冲动 impulse for expansion

阔 kuò 〈形〉① wide; vast; broad ② wealthy; rich:摆~ flaunt one's wealth

阔步 kuòbù take big strides; make great strides; walk in big strides:~前进 stride forward; advance with giant strides

阔别 kuòbié long separated; long parted; separate for a long time; have not seen each other for a long time

阔绰 kuòchuò liberal with money; ostentatious; extravagant:~的生活 extravagant life

阔气 kuòqi airs of extravagance; extravagant in spending habits; showily rich:花钱~ spend money freely; spend lavishly

阔叶树 kuòyèshù broadleaf trees

括 kuò 〈动〉① draw together (muscles, etc.); contract ② include

括号 kuòhào brackets; parentheses:大~ braces. 圆~ parentheses

括弧 kuòhú parentheses;brackets;braces

L l

lā

垃 lā

垃圾 lājī garbage; rubbish; refuse; dust; raffle: ～堆 garbage heap. ～车 dustcart. ～箱 dustbin. 清除～ remove refuse

拉 lā 〈动〉① pull; draw; drag: ～线搭桥 pull strings and make contacts ② haul; convey by vehicles; transport: 开卡车～货 drive a truck to carry cargo ③ play (certain musical instruments): ～小提琴 play the violin ④ drag out; draw out; space out: ～开距离 leave distances in between; space out ⑤ give (lend) a hand; help: ～他们一把 give (lend) them a helping hand ⑥ draw in; solicit; win over: ～拢 pull over to one's side ⑦ try to establish; claim

另见 lá

拉帮结派 lābāng-jiēpài form cliques

拉扯 lāchě ① pull; draw; drag: 孩子～着妈妈的外衣。The child is pulling his mother's coat. ② take great pains to bring up (a child): 她自己把孩子～大的。She raised the children by herself. ③ drag in; implicate: 干嘛把他也～进来? Why drag him in? ④ chat

拉倒 lādǎo forget about it; leave it at that; drop it

拉肚子 lādùzi suffer from diarrhoea; have loose bowels

拉关系 lā guānxi try to establish a relationship with sb.; establish unprincipled connections; trying to establish underhand connections for the sake of personal gain

拉过来 lā guòlái ① pull back ② win over; gain over

拉后腿 lā hòutuǐ hold sb. back; be a drag on sb.

拉架 lājià try to stop people from fighting each other

拉开 lākāi ① pull open; open ② pull apart; draw apart ③ widen the gap: 比分逐渐～。The gap in the score was gradually widening.

拉客 lākè ① solicit guests or dinners ② take on passengers ③ solicit patrons

拉拉扯扯 lālā-chěchě pull (drag) someone about; trafficking in mutual flattery and commendation; resort to boasting, flattery and touting; exchange flattery and favours

拉拉队 lālāduì cheer team; cheering squad; rooters: ～鼓动

运动员的呼喊声 yell. ～队员 rooter. ～队长 yell leader; cheerleader; rooter king

拉拢 lālǒng draw sb. over to one's side; pull over to one's side; drag over; draw in; woo; curry favour with; rope in

拉买卖 lā mǎimai canvass business orders; drum up trade

拉皮条 lā pítiáo act as a procurer or pimp

拉平 lāpíng even up; make even (equal):～收入 even up the incomes

拉山头 lā shāntóu factionalism

拉下马 lāxià mǎ pull off the horse; depose

拉下水 lāxià shuǐ pull into the water; drag… into the mire; make an accomplice of sb.; corrupt sb.:被资产阶级～ be pulled into the water by the bourgeoisie

拉主顾 lā zhǔgù solicit customers; attract customers

邋 lā

邋遢 lātā sloppy; shaggy; tatty; slovenly: 衣服～ be slovenly dressed

lá

拉 lá〈动〉cut; slash; slit:～玻璃 cut a piece of glass
另见 lā

lǎ

喇 lǎ

喇叭 lǎba ① bugle; trumpet; horn: 吹～ blow a trumpet ② loudspeaker:～筒 megaphone. ～裤 bell-bottom pants (trousers)

喇嘛 lǎma lama: 达赖～ Dalai Lama. ～教 Lamaism; Lamaist Buddhism. ～庙 lamasery; monastery; lama monastery

là

落 là〈动〉① miss; leave out: 你把字母"a"～了。You've left the letter "a". ② forget to bring: 对不起,我把信用卡～在家里了。Sorry, I left my credit card at home. ③ lag behind: 他～了2个星期的课。He missed two weeks' lessons.
另见 luò

蜡 là〈名〉① wax ② candle

蜡笔 làbǐ wax crayon; pastel: ～画 pastel drawing

蜡画法 làhuàfǎ encaustic painting

蜡黄 làhuáng wax yellow; waxen: 面色～ wear a waxen complexion; look sallow

蜡染 làrǎn ① wax printing ② wax prints

蜡像 làxiàng wax figure; wax work

蜡纸 làzhǐ ① wax paper ② stencil paper; stencil

蜡烛 làzhú candle: 点～ light a candle

腊 là〈形〉cured

腊八 làbā the eighth day of the

twelfth lunar month：～粥 rice porridge with nuts and dried fruit eaten on the eighth day of the twelfth lunar month

腊味 làwèi cured delicacies

腊月 làyuè the twelfth month of the lunar year；the twelfth moon

辣 là〈形〉① peppery；pungent；hot；biting：这咖喱太～了。This curry is too hot. ② cruel；relentless：毒～ sinister；diabolic ③〈动〉(of smell or taste) burn；bite；sting：～得舌头发麻。The hot taste burns the tongue.

辣椒 làjiāo hot pepper；chilli；cayenne：～粉 chilli powder；cayenne pepper

辣手 làshǒu ① relentless；ruthless ② hard to deal with；troublesome；thorny：一个～问题 a thorny problem；a hard nut to crack；a hot potato

辣子 làzi hot pepper；cayenne pepper；chilli

lái

来 lái〈动〉① come；arrive：他还没有～。He has not come yet. ② crop up；take place；come up：问题～了。Problems have cropped up. ③［做某个动作，代替意义更具体的动词］：你歇歇，让我～吧。You take a rest. Let me do it. ④［跟"得"或"不"连用，表示可能或不可能］：坡太陡，车子上不～。The car can't come up as the slope is so steep. ⑤［用在另一动词前面，表示要做某件事情］：咱们～试试，看它会不会折断。Let's try whether it will break. ⑥［用在动词结构或介词结构与动词或动词结构之间，表示后面是目的］：你能用什么办法～帮助她呢？How are you going to help her？⑦［用在动词后面，表示动作朝着说话人所在的地方］：拿把尺～。Bring me a ruler. ⑧［用在动词后面，表示动作的结果］：一觉醒～ when one wakes up after a sound sleep ⑨［从过去到现在］ever since：十年～ for a decade

来宾 láibīn guest；visitor

来得及 láidejí have time (for；to do)；be in time (for；to do)；there is still time for one (to do)：你要赶火车还～。There is still time for you to catch the train.

来而不往非礼也 lái ér bù wǎng fēi lǐ yě It is impolite not to reciprocate.；It is impolite not to make a return for what one receives.

来访 láifǎng come to visit；come to call

来复枪 láifùqiāng rifle

来回 láihuí ① go there and back；make a round trip ② back and forth；to and fro：～票 return ticket；round-trip ticket

来劲 láijìn ① full of enthusiasm；in high spirits ② exhilarating；exciting；thrilling

来历 láilì source；background；

antecedents:～不明[指人] dubious background or questionable antecedents; [指事] of unknown source (origin). 查明～ trace sth. to its source; ascertain a person's antecedents

来料加工 láiliào jiāgōng processing of materials supplied by the foreign businessmen; processing raw materials on clients' demands; processing imported materials

来临 láilín come; arrive; advent; approach

来龙去脉 láilóng-qùmài ins and outs; whence and whither; origin and development; the entire process; cause and effect:明白问题的～ be clear about the ins and outs of a problem

来去自由 lái-qù zìyóu freedom to come and go; freedom of movement

来势 láishì the force with which sth. breaks out; oncoming force

来头 láitou ① backing; background:～不小 have plenty of backing from influential quarters; have powerful backing ② the motive behind; cause:说话有～ say sth. with a motive

来往 lái-wǎng ① come and go:～车辆 vehicles coming and going ② dealings; contact; intercourse:促进商业～ promote commercial intercourse

来信 láixìn ① send a letter here ② incoming letter; your letter

来样加工 láiyàng jiāgōng processing according to buyer's samples; processing according to foreign specimen

来意 láiyì one's purpose in coming

来由 láiyóu reason; cause

来源 láiyuán ① source; origin:税收～ source of revenue ② [后面跟"于"] originate; stem from

来者不善,善者不来 láizhě bù shàn, shànzhě bù lái He who has come is surely strong or he'd never have come along.; He who has come, comes with ill intent, certainly not on virtue bent.; The one who is coming surely has bad intentions.; He could not have come with good intentions.

来之不易 láizhī-bùyì not easily come by; hard-earned

莱 lái 〈名〉① pigweed; goosefoot ② fields overgrown with grass; fields lying fallow in rotation

lài

赖 lài 〈动〉① rely on; depend on:有～于他的帮助 rely upon him for help ② hang on (in a place); drag one's stay in a place:～着不走 overstay one's visit; hang on; continue to stay in a place ③ repudiate; deny:～婚 repudiate a marriage contract; deny marriage ④ lay the blame on sb. else:～她偷东西 falsely accuse her of being a

thief
赖皮 làipí rascally; shameless; unreasonable：耍～ act shamelessly; play the rascal
赖学 làixué play truant; play (the) wag
赖债(帐) làizhài(zhàng) ① repudiate one's debt：～者 repudiator ② go back on one's word
癞 lài〈名〉① leprosy ② favus of the scalp
癞蛤蟆想吃天鹅肉 làiháma xiǎng chī tiān'éròu a toad wanting to eat swan meat — daydreaming; a toad wishing to eat swan meat — to crave for what one is not worthy of; An ugly man hopes to marry a pretty girl.
癞皮狗 làipígǒu ① mangy (scabby) dogs ② loathsome creature
籁 lài〈名〉① an ancient musical pipe; flute ② sound; noise：天～ sounds of nature

lán

阑 lán ①〈形〉late ②〈名〉railing; balustrade：～干 crisscross
阑尾炎 lánwěiyán appendicitis
谰 lán〈动〉calumniate; slander; deny
谰言 lányán slander; calumny：～无耻 shameless slander
兰 lán orchid：～花 orchid
栏 lán〈名〉① railing; balustrade; fence; hurdle：跨～赛跑 hurdle race ② column：专～作家 columnist ③［牛、羊等的］pen：羊～ sheep pen
栏杆 lángān railing; balustrade：路的两旁铁索～ concrete balusters linked with iron chains
拦 lán〈动〉stop; block; bar; obstruct：～住去路 block (bar) the way
拦河坝 lánhébà dam (across a river); diversion dam
拦洪 lánhóng hold back a flood; flood retention：～坝 regulating dam; flood-control dam
拦劫 lánjié waylay and rob; mug
拦截 lánjié intercept
拦路 lánlù block the way：～抢劫 block the road and rob the passers-by; hold-up; waylay; highway robbery
栏目 lánmù the heading or title of a column (in a magazine, etc.)
拦阻 lánzǔ block; obstruct; hold back; prevent
褴 lán
褴褛 lánlǚ ragged; tattered; shabby：衣衫～ be in rags; be shabbily dressed; dressed in rags
蓝 lán〈形〉blue：蔚～ sky blue; azure
蓝本 lánběn ① the source material on which later work is based on; chief (primary) source ② original version (of a literary work)

蓝鲸 lánjīng blue whale
蓝领工人 lánlǐng gōngrén blue-collar worker
蓝田人 lántiánrén Lantian (Lantien) Man (*Sinanthropus lantianensis*)
蓝图 lántú blueprint：跨世纪～ transcentury blueprint

篮 lán〈名〉basket
篮球 lánqiú basketball：～场 basketball court
篮子 lánzi basket

lǎn

览 lǎn〈动〉① see；look at；view：游～ tour；go sight-seeing ② read：阅～ read
览胜 lǎnshèng visit scenic spots

揽 lǎn〈动〉① pull sb. into one's arms；take into one's arms：把孩子～在怀里 clasp a child to one's bosom ② fasten with a rope，etc. ③ take upon oneself；take on；canvass：～买卖 canvass business order ④ monopoly；grasp
揽笔 lǎnbǐ take up one's pen；write
揽承 lǎnchéng contract (agree) to do a job
揽活 lǎnhuó take on work

懒 lǎn〈形〉① lazy；indolent；idle：～惰 sloth ② languid；sluggish：伸～腰 stretch oneself
懒得 lǎnde not feel like (doing)；be not inclined (to do)：～出去 not feel like going out
懒惰 lǎnduò lazy；indolent；idle
懒汉 lǎnhàn lazy fellow；idler；sluggard：～鞋 loafers
懒散 lǎnsǎn negligent；sluggish；indolent
懒洋洋 lǎnyángyáng languid；listless；listlessly；languidly：～地躺在沙发上 lounge on a sofa

缆 lǎn〈名〉① mooring rope；hawser ② cable；thick rope：电～ power cable；cable
缆车 lǎnchē cable car

làn

滥 làn ①〈动〉flood；overflow ②〈形〉excessive；indiscriminate：～赐 excessive grants ③〈副〉excessively；lavishly；indiscriminately：～炸 bomb indiscriminately
滥调 làndiào hackneyed tune；worn-out tune (theme)；platitude；shop-worn theme：陈词～ hackneyed expressions；*clichés*
滥发 lànfā overissue：～奖金 overissue of bonuses
滥伐 lànfá excessive cutting；illegal felling：～林木 excessive cutting of trees
滥觞 lànshāng origin；source；fountainhead：五四"人的文学"之～ the origin of the May 4th "literature of man"
滥用 lànyòng abuse；misuse；stretch；use indiscriminately：～法律 stretch the law. ～国家资金 misappropriating the state funds. ～职权 abuse one's pow-

er (authority); misuse one's power; override one's commission

滥竽充数 lànyú-chōngshù pretend to play the *Yu* (a wind instrument) in order to make up the number for an orchestra — to be included in a group; just to fill in a vacancy; be a layman who passes himself off an expert; be an incompetent person or a person unequal to his task

烂 làn〈形〉① mashed; sodden; pappy: 肉烧得太～了。The meat is overdone. ② rotten; decayed: ～掉 become rotten ③ worn-out; torn to pieces: 衣服穿～了。The clothes are worn-out. ④ messy: 一本～帐 a messy account

烂漫 lànmàn ①brightly coloured; brilliant ②[天真的] simple; naive: 天真～ innocent; naive

烂熟 lànshú ① thoroughly cooked ② know sth. thoroughly: 所有的课文她都背得～。She learned all the texts by heart.

烂摊子 làntānzi rotten (trashy) legacy; broken-down stall; awful mess; dreadful (hopeless) mess; shambles

láng

榔 láng

榔头 lángtóu hammer

琅 láng

琅琅 lángláng the sound of tinkling; reading aloud: ～的读书声 read in ringing tones; the sound of reading aloud

锒 láng

锒铛 lángdāng ① iron chains: ～入狱 be chained (fettered) and thrown into prison; be put in jail ② clang; chank

郎 láng〈名〉an ancient official title: 侍～ vice minister ② form of address to some persons: 货～ street vendor

郎才女貌 lángcái nǚmào a perfect match between a man and a girl

郎舅 lángjiù a man and his wife's brother

郎中 lángzhōng ① a physician trained in herbal medicine; doctor ② an ancient official title

廊 láng〈名〉corridor; porch veranda: 万里边疆文化长～ Cultural Corridor along Our Ten Thousand *Li* Border. 画～ picture gallery

狼 láng〈名〉wolf

狼狈 lángbèi be in an awkward position; in a tight corner: ～不堪 be thrown into a panic; be in an extremely awkward position (predicament); in a dilemma; in an embarrassing (helpless) situation. ～为奸 collude with sb. in doing evil; work hand in glove with; work in collusion with sb. for some evil purpose; band together

狼籍 lángjí in disorder; scattered about in a mess; at sixes and sevens; promiscuously:声名～ infamous; notorious; discredited

狼吞虎咽 lángtūn-hǔyàn gulp; gorge; gobble up; wolf down; devour ravenously

狼心狗肺 lángxīn-gǒufèi ① be as cruel as a wolf; be cruel and unscrupulous; brutal and cold-blooded ② ungrateful

狼烟 lángyān the smoke of wolves' dung burnt at border posts in ancient China to signal alarm

狼子野心 lángzǐ-yěxīn wolfish ambition; designs of the wolves; wild ambition

lǎng

朗 lǎng 〈形〉 ① light; bright; clear:明～ clear and bright ② clear and loud

朗读 lǎngdú read aloud

朗诵 lǎngsòng recite; read aloud with expression; declaim:～一首诗 recite a poem

làng

浪 làng 〈名〉 wave; billow; breaker:～峰波谷 the crests and troughs of waves

浪潮 làngcháo wave; tide:第三～ the Third Wave

浪荡 làngdàng ① loiter about; loaf about ② dissipated; dissolute:～伙伴 fellow waster

浪费 làngfèi waste; squander; dissipate:～青春 waste one's youth. ～者 spend thrift. 反对～ combat waste

浪花 lànghuā ① the foam of breaking waves ② episodes in one's life

浪漫 làngmàn ① romantic:～式爱情 romantic love. ～主义 romanticism ② loose; licentious; dissolute

浪头 làngtóu ① wave ② tide; trend:赶～ go with the tide; follow the trend

浪子 làngzǐ prodigal (son):～回头 return of the prodigal (son); return to the fold; turn over a new leaf

浪子回头金不换 làngzǐ huítóu jīn bù huàn A prodiagal who returns is more precious than gold.

lāo

捞 lāo 〈动〉 ① drag for; pull out (from the water); fish for; scoop up:在河里～水草 dredge up water plants from the river ② pick; reap; catch at; gain

捞本 lāoběn win back lost wagers; recover one's losses; recoup oneself

捞救命稻草 lāo jiùmìng dàocǎo a drowning person clutching (catch, grasp) at a straw; take advantage of something:她那样做就像是一个快要淹死的人～似的。She acted like a drowning person trying to catch a straw.

捞取 lāoqǔ gain；reap；fish for：～实惠 reap gains. ～政治资本 gain (pocket) political capital；fish for political advantage

捞一把 lāoyībǎ reap some profit；cash in on sth.；profiteer

捞油水 lāo yóushui make a side profit；get a squeeze

捞资本 lāo zīběn dredge for capital；make capital for oneself

láo

牢 láo〈名〉① prison：～房 prison；prison house；jail ② pen；fold：亡羊补～ mend the fold after a sleep is lost ③〈形〉strong；fast；durable：绳子系～。The rope has been tied fast.

牢不可破 láobùkěpò indestructible；unbreakable：～的友谊 unbreakable friendship

牢房 láofáng prison cell

牢固 láogù firm；secure

牢记 láojì remember well；firmly bear (keep) in mind

牢靠 láokao ① firm；strong；sturdy ② dependable；reliable

牢笼 láolóng ① cage ② bonds；shackles：冲破～ shake off the bonds ③ trap；snare：陷入～ fall into (be caught in) a trap

牢骚 láosāo complaint；grievance；discontent：～满腹 be full of complaints (about). 发～ grumble (at)；voice one's discontent

牢狱 láoyù prison；jail

劳 láo〈动〉① work；labour：不～动者不得食。He who does not work，shall not eat either. ② put sb. to the trouble of；trouble sb. with sth.：～您费心了。I'm sorry to trouble you a lot. ③ express one's appreciation (to the performer of a task)：犒～ reward with food and drink〈名〉④ work；labour：～逸结合 alternate work with rest ⑤ merits；achievements；service：～苦功高 with toilsome labour and distinctive merits. 勋～ meritorious service

劳保 láobǎo ①[劳动保险] labour insurance：享受～待遇 enjoy the benefit of labour insurance. ～福利 labour insurance and welfare ②[劳动保护] labour protection：～医疗 labour-protection medical care

劳动 láodòng labour；work：～服务公司 employment service company. ～合同制 labour contract system. ～改造 reform through (forced) labour. ～管理体制 labour control system. ～介绍所 employment agency. ～教养 rehabilitation (indoctrination，reeducation) through labour. ～节 International Labour Day；May Day. ～竞赛 labour emulation. ～力 labour power；man-power；capacity for labour；ability to work；able-bodied worker

劳顿 láodùn fatigued；wearied

劳方与资方 láofāng yǔ zīfāng

labour and capital

劳改 láogǎi reform through labour; labour reform: ～场所 labour reform site. ～犯 offenders under labour reform; criminals undergoing reform through labour

劳工关系 láogōng guānxi labour relations

劳驾 láojià ①[要求让路等] Excuse me. ②[请求办事]May I trouble you (to do)?; Would you mind (doing sth.)?; have the goodness to do sth.

劳教 láojiào education (rehabilitation) through labour: ～人员 person undergoing rehabilitation through labour. ～所 labour education and rehabilitation school; labour education institution

劳苦 láokǔ laborious; toilsome; painstaking: ～功高 have achieved great success through hard work; have performed a valuable service with high merits

劳力 láolì ① labour; labour force ② labour with one's strength; work with one's brawn

劳碌 láolù work hard; toil

劳民伤财 láomín-shāngcái waste money and labour; spend blood and money; harass the people and waste money

劳模 láomó labour model

劳务 láowù labour service; service profession; personal service: ～出口 exporting service; export services. ～合作 cooperation in the field of labour service; service cooperation

劳心者治人,劳力者治于人 láoxīnzhě zhìrén, láolìzhě zhìyúrén Those who work with their minds govern, while those who toil with their hands are governed.

劳役 láoyì corvée; forced labour; servitude

劳资 láozī labour and capital: ～纠纷 trouble between labour and management; industrial dispute

劳作 láozuò ① manual work ② do manual labour

唠 láo

唠叨 láodao wag one's chin; chatter; be garrulous

唠唠叨叨 láoláo-daodao babble on and on; talk nineteen to the dozen; nag; constantly repeat

lǎo

老 lǎo〈形〉① old; aged: ～弱病残 those who are old, weak, ill or disabled ② of long standing; old: ～前辈 veteran; predecessor ③ out-dated; old: ～一套 the old set of practice ④ overgrown; tough: ～笋 tough bamboo shoots 〈副〉⑤ for a long time: 她～没来。She hasen't been here for a long time. ⑥ always (doing sth.): 她～念叨着孩子们。She is always talking about her children. ⑦〈动〉become old: 他～

得很快。He was aging rapidly.

老百姓 lǎobǎixìng common (ordinary) people; civilians

老板 lǎobǎn boss; proprietor; shopkeeper; master:后台～ backstage boss

老本 lǎoběn original capital; principal:把～输光 lose one's last stakes

老成 lǎochéng experienced; steady; practised:～持重 experienced and steady

老当益壮 lǎodāngyìzhuàng old but vigorous; be old in age, but young in spirit; become more vigorous with age

老底 lǎodǐ sb.'s past; sb.'s unsavoury background

老调 lǎodiào old tune; hackneyed theme; play the same old tune: ～重弹 harp on the same string; sing the same song again

老公 lǎogōng husband

老规矩 lǎoguīju old rules and regulations; convention; established custom or practice

老虎屁股 lǎohǔ pìgǔ tiger's rump:～摸不得 like a tiger whose backside no one dares to touch. 不能听批评的～摸不得的作风 turn like a wounded tiger on those who raise criticism

老花眼 lǎohuāyǎn old-sightedness; presbyopia:～镜 presbyopic glasses

老化 lǎohuà ag(e)ing:知识～ the ag(e)ing of knowledge

老奸巨猾 lǎojiān-jùhuá old crafty person; sly old fox; crafty old scoundrel; old hand at trickery and deception

老交情 lǎojiāoqing long-standing friendship; an old friend

老框框 lǎokuàngkuàng old conventions

老老实实 lǎolǎo-shishi ① honest; unpretentious; unassuming; in earnest; without affectation:～向…学习 learn in earnest from … ② play no tricks; behave oneself

老练 lǎoliàn seasoned; experienced; practised; tactful:他办事～。He is experienced and do a good job of work.

老马识途 lǎomǎ-shítú old horse knows the way; old hand is a good guide

老毛病 lǎomáobìng old trouble; old weakness

老年 lǎonián old age:～化 ag(e)ing. ～社会保障措施 measures to provide social security to the elderly. ～医药保险 medicare for the aged

老农 lǎonóng old farmer; experienced peasant

老气 lǎoqì ① mature and steady ②(of clothes) dark and old-fashioned

老前辈 lǎoqiánbèi one's senior; one's elder

老弱 lǎoruò ① the old and the young ② the old and the weak

老三届 lǎosānjiè junior or senior students who graduated in 1966, 1967 and 1968

老生常谈 lǎoshēng-chángtán

commonplace talk of an old scholar;bromides; platitudes; shopworn phrases

老师 lǎoshī teacher

老师傅 lǎoshīfu master worker (craftsman); experienced worker; master

老实 lǎoshi honest; frank; well-behaved; simple. ～说 to tell the truth; to be frank. ～交代 make a clean breast of everything

老式 lǎoshì old style:～家具 old-fashioned furniture

老手 lǎoshǒu old hand; old-timer; veteran; expert

老鼠过街,人人喊打 lǎoshǔ guò jiē,rénrén hǎn dǎ rats scurrying across the street with everyone yelling:"Beat (kill) them! Beat (kill) them!"; rats running across the street and being chased by all (passers-by); An extremely unpopular figure is hated by everyone.

老态龙钟 lǎotài-lóngzhōng look old and clumsy; be old and shaky; senile

老乡 lǎoxiāng ① fellow-townsman; fellow-villager ② a friendly form of address to a man in the countryside

老羞成怒 lǎoxiū-chéngnù fly into a rage out of shame; become angry and red-faced; be furious at being disgraced; angry at one's humiliation

老朽 lǎoxiǔ old and useless; decrepit and behind the times

老一套 lǎoyītào old practice; the same old stuff (story); old rut; the old set of practices

老油子 lǎoyóuzi wily old bird; old campaigner

老有所养 lǎoyǒu-suǒyǎng Elderly will be looked after properly.

老玉米 lǎoyùmi ① maiz; Indian corn; corn ② ear of maize (corn)

老资格 lǎozīgé ① old-timer; old head; veteran ② seniority

老字辈 lǎozìbèi the elder generation

老字号 lǎozìhào old name in business—an old firm or shop

lào

涝 lào〈名〉waterlogging:防～ prevent waterlogging

烙 lào〈动〉① bake; sear:～火烧 bake wheaten cakes ② brand; iron:～衣服 iron clothes

烙饼 làobǐng pancake

烙铁 làotie ①[焊接用的]soldering iron ②[烫衣服用的]iron

烙印 làoyìn brand; stigma:不同阶级思想的～ bear the impress of various class ideologies

酪 lào〈名〉① junket:乳～ cheese ② thick fruit juice; fruit jelly ③ sweet paste made from crushed nut; sweet nut paste:杏仁～ almond cream

lè

乐 lè ①〈形〉 happy; joyful; glad; cheerful: 欢～ happy and gay ②〈名〉happiness; pleasure; joy: ～而不淫 pleasure without lasciviousness 〈动〉③ be glad to; enjoy; love; find pleasure in: ～善好施 love to do philanthropic work ④ be amused; laugh: 你～什么? What are you laughing at?. 你可别～坏了。Don't go off your head with joy.
另见 yuè

乐不思蜀 lèbùsīshǔ so happy as to forget home and duty

乐观 lèguān optimistic; sanguine: ～向上 be optimistic and have a desire for progress

乐极生悲 lèjí-shēngbēi Extreme joy begets sorrow.; Joy at its height engenders sorrow.; After joy comes sadness.; Too great pleasure will bring about sadness.

乐趣 lèqù joy; delight; pleasure; taste

乐土 lètǔ land of happiness; paradise

乐意 lèyì ① be willing (to do); be ready (to do) ② pleased; delighted: ～的神色 delighted look

乐于 lèyú be glad (to do); be ready (to do): ～助人 be ready to help others

乐园 lèyuán paradise; playground; amusement park

勒 lè 〈动〉① bridle; rein in: 悬崖～马 rein in one's horse at the brink of the precipice ② compel; force; coerce: ～捐 compel sb. to make monetary contributions
另见 lēi

勒交 lèjiāo force sb. to hand sth. over

勒令 lèlìng enforce; order: ～退学 sent down. 被～停业 be ordered to close down

勒索 lèsuǒ exact; extort; squeeze; blackmail

了 le 〈助动〉①[用在动词或形容词后,表示动作或变化已经完成]: 读～两遍 read twice ②[用在句子的末尾或句中停顿处,表示出现新的情况,用作催促或劝止]: 好～, 别再提那件事～。Well, don't bring that up again.
另见 liǎo

lēi

勒 lēi 〈动〉 tighten (up); tie or strap sth.
另见 lè

勒紧 lēijǐn tighten: ～裤带 tighten one's belt

勒死 lēisǐ jugulate; strangle

léi

雷 léi 〈名〉① thunder: ～电崇拜 thunder cult ② mine: 布～ lay mines

雷达 léidá radar:～兵 radar operator;radarman

雷打不动 léidǎ-bùdòng unshakable; not to be altered under any circumstances:～的天天学习制度 an inviolable daily system of studying

雷管 léiguǎn detonator; detonating cap; blasting cap; primer

雷击 léijī be struck by lightning

雷厉风行 léilì-fēngxíng carry out … with the power of a thunderbolt and the speed of lightning; vigorously and speedily; with an all-out effort; with thunder-like violence and wind-like swiftness; rigorously and effectively; enforcement in a sweeping manner

雷鸣 léimíng ① thunder ② thunderous

雷声 léishēng peal of thunder; thunder:～大,雨点小。Loud thunder but small raindrops.; much said but little done; Much cry and little wool.

雷同 léitóng ① echo the views of others ② identical; duplicate

雷雨 léiyǔ thunderstorm

镭 léi〈名〉radium

镭射电影 léishè diànyǐng laser video

累 léi

另见 lěi,lèi

累累 léiléi in clusters:果实～ fruit hanging in clusters

另见 lěilěi

累赘 léizhuì ① bothersome; burdensome; cumbersome;[句子] verbose; ② burden; encumberance;[文字]verbiage; verbosity:行李带的多了,真～。Too much luggage is a nuisance.

lěi

磊 lěi

磊落 lěiluò open and upright:胸怀～ openhearted and upright. 光明～ open and aboveboard

累 lěi〈动〉① accumulate; pile up:日积月～ accumulate day by day and month by month; accumulate gradually ② involve; implicated:拖～ get sb. into trouble ③〈形〉repeated; continuous

累次 lěicì time and again; repeatedly

累犯 lěifàn habitual criminal; recidivist; offender with old records

累积 lěijī acumulate:～得 4 胜 2 负的纪录 complile a record of four wins and two losses. ～服刑判决 accumulative sentence. ～资本 accumulating capital

累及 lěijí entangle; involve; implicate:～无辜 involve the innocent

累计 lěijì ① add up ② accumulative total; grand total

累教不改 lěijiào-bùgǎi refuse to correct errors after repeated education; refuse to mend one's ways after repeated education

累进 lěijìn progression

累累 lěilěi ① innumerable ② again and again; repeatedly: 罪行～ commit innumerable crimes

累卵之危 lěiluǎnzhīwēi as precarious as a stack of eggs; in an extremely precarious situation; the peril of piled eggs

垒 lěi 〈动〉① build by piling bricks, stones, earth, etc.: ～坝 make embankments ②〈名〉rampart; barrier

垒球 lěiqiú softball: ～棒 softball bat. 打～ play softball

lèi

泪 lèi 〈名〉tear; teardrop

泪痕 lèihén traces of tears; tear stains

泪如雨下 lèirúyǔxià tears raining down one's cheeks; tears streaming down like raindrops

泪汪汪 lèiwāngwāng tearful; (one's eyes) swimming with tears: ～地诉说 complain tearfully

泪珠(水) lèizhū(shuǐ) teardrop

类 lèi 〈名〉① class; kind; category; type: ～别 classification ②〈动〉resemble; be similar to: 以～似的方法 on a similar plan

类比 lèibǐ analogy: 作历史～ draw a historical analogy

类别 lèibié sort; classification; category; genre

类似 lèisì ① resemblance; similarity: ～联想 association by similarity ② similar; analogous: ～案例的量刑 measurement of penalty in similar cases

类推 lèituī reason by analogy; analogy; analogize: 用～法辩论 argue by analogy

类型 lèixíng type; genre; form; mould: ～论 theory of types

擂 lèi 〈动〉beat a (drum)

擂台 lèitái ring (for material contest); arena: ～赛 an arena match (contest). 摆～ give an open challenge. 打～ take up the challenge; pick (take) up the gauntlet

累 lèi 〈形〉tired; fatigued: ～乏 tired out with too much exertion

另见 léi, lěi

累坏 lèihuài be tired out; be dead tired

累活 lèihuó heavy work; tiring work; toil

肋 lèi 〈名〉rib

肋骨 lèigǔ rib

肋条 lètiáo ① rib ② pork ribs; spareribs

léng

棱 léng 〈名〉① arris; edge ② ridge; raised angle: 瓦～ rows of tiles on a roof

棱角 léngjiǎo ① edges and corners ② sharp point; pointedness; sharp-wittedness; incisiveness: 她的批评颇有～。Her criticism is rather incisive.

lěng

冷 lěng〈形〉① cold; chilly: 天气～飕飕。There is a nip in the air. ② cold in manner: 受到～遇 receive a cold response from ③ unfrequented; desolate: ～清清 cold and dreary ④ deserted; out-of-the-way: ～僻 deserted ⑤ rare; strange: ～字 unfamiliar word

冷板凳 lěngbǎndèng cold bench—an indifferent post or a cold reception

冷背商品 lěngbèi shāngpǐn unsaleable goods

冷冰冰 lěngbīngbīng ice-cold; frosty; icy: ～的脸色 frosty looks

冷餐 lěngcān buffet: ～招待会 buffet reception

冷藏 lěngcáng keep in cold storage; refrigerate; chill: ～库 cold storage; refrigerator

冷场 lěngchǎng ① awkward silence on the stage when an actor enters late or forgets his lines ② awkward silence at a meeting

冷嘲热讽 lěngcháo-rèfěng jeer and sneer at; heap burning (scorching) satire and freezing irony; pour ridicule on; give sb. a dig

冷淡 lěngdàn ① cold; indifferent; cheerless; desolute: 反映～ a faint (cold) response ② cold shoulder; treat coldly: ～待人 give the cold shoulder to; treat sb. coldly; give sb. a cold reception

冷点 lěngdiǎn cool spots (i. e., places or things that have not yet attract popular attention): 开辟旅游～ develop cool spots for tourism

冷箭 lěngjiàn arrow shot from hiding; sniper's shot

冷静 lěngjìng cool; sober; calm: 头脑～ coolheaded

冷酷 lěngkù grim; cold; unfeeling: ～无情 unfeeling; hardhearted

冷冷清清 lěnglěng-qīngqīng coolly and quietly; cold and dreary (lonely, cheerless); desolate

冷落 lěngluò ① desolute; unfrequented ② leave sb. out in the cold; cold-shoulder; treat coldly

冷门 lěngmén ① a profession, trade or branch of learning that receives little attention; not in great demand; unpopular: ～货 unpopular goods; dull goods ② unexpected winner; dark horse: 比赛出了～。A dark horse emerged in the contest.

冷漠 lěngmò indifferent; nonchalant; apathy

冷僻 lěngpì ① out-of-the-way; unfrequented ② rare; uncommon: ～字 rarely used word

冷清 lěngqing cold and cheerless; desolate; lonely; deserted

冷却剂 lěngquèjì coolant; cooler

冷却塔 lěngquètǎ cooling tower

冷热病 lěngrèbìng capricious changes in mood; sudden waxing and waning of enthusiasm

冷色 lěngsè cool colour
冷笑 lěngxiào laugh scornfully; sneer; give a disdainful laugh
冷言冷语 lěngyán-lěngyǔ mocking words; cold words; sarcastic comments; ironical remarks
冷饮 lěngyǐn cold drink
冷战 lěngzhàn cold war

lèng

愣 lèng 〈形〉① distracted; stupefied; dumb-founded; stunned; blank: 吓～了 be struck (stunned) dumb ② reckless; rash; rude: ～小子 a rash young fellow
愣干 lènggàn do things rashly (recklessly); persist in going one's own way
愣神儿 lèngshénr stare blankly; be in a daze
愣头愣脑 lèngtóu-lèngnǎo rash; impetuous; reckless
愣住 lèngzhù be struck dumb: 吓得～了 be struck dumb with fear; be dumbfounded

lí

离 lí 〈动〉① leave; part from: ～北京赴上海 leave Beijing for Shanghai ② go against: 叛～ desert and rebel ③ dispense with; go without: 鱼儿～不开水。Fish can not live without water. ④〈副〉off; away; from: 开发区～机场不远。The development zone is not far from the airport.
离岸价 lí'ànjià free on board
离别 líbié leave; part (from, with)
离队 líduì leave the ranks; leave one's post
离轨 líguǐ deviance; deviancy: 社会～ social deviance. 心理～ mental deviance
离合 líhé separation and reunion
离婚 líhūn divorce: ～率 divorce rate. 他跟妻子～了。He was divorced from his wife. ～者 divorcee; repudiator
离间 líjiān sow dissension; estrange
离经叛道 líjīng-pàndào rebel against orthodoxy; discard (depart from) the classics and rebel against orthodoxy; heretical and deviating from the true teachings: ～的《十日谈》perpetually profane *Decameron*
离境 líjìng leave a country or a place: ～签证 exit visa. ～许可证 exit permit
离开 líkāi leave; depart from; deviate from
离奇 líqí fantastic; odd; weird: ～曲折的情节 present bizarre and complicated plots
离群索居 líqún-suǒjū live in solitude; live all alone
离任 lírèn leave a post
离散 lísàn ① be separated from; be dispersed; be scattered: 骨肉～。The family were scattered in different places. ② estrangement; divergence; dissolution
离世 líshì ① cut oneself off from

the world; keep aloof from wordly affairs ② depart this life; pass away

离题 lítí digress (from); wander (from):～太远 digress too far from the subject

离土不离乡 lítǔ bù líxiāng leave the land but not the home (i.e., peasants who engage in industrial, commercial, mining, transport, and other professions, but still reside in the rural villages)

离乡背井 líxiāng-bèijǐng be compelled to leave one's own village (home); leave one's native place reluctantly; desert one's home and leave the place where one used to live

离心 líxīn centrifugal:～力 centrifugal force. ～离德 dissension and discord; disunity

离休 líxiū leave position to rest; retire on preferential terms (it is a system for settling retiring old cadres who took part in revolutionary work before the founding of PRC, or who lose working ability. After cadres retire, their basic political treatments remain unchanged, and they receive favourable welfare benefits. When they retire, old cadres receive honourary retirement certificates.):～干部 retired cadres

离异 líyì divorce

离职 lízhí leave one's post; leave one's job:～率 separation rate. ～休养 leave one's job in order to recuperate

离子 lízǐ [物] ion

篱 lí hedge; fence:竹～ bamboo fence

篱笆 líba hedge; bamboo (twig) fence; hurdle; wattle

厘 lí 〈名〉① *li*, a unit of length (=1/3 millimetre) ② *li*, a unit of weight (=0.05 grams) ③ *li*, a unit of area (=0.666 square metres) ④ *li*, one thousandth of a *yuan* ⑤ *li*, a unit of monthly interest rate (=0.1%) ⑥ *li*, a unit of annual interst rate (=1%) ⑦ a traction; the least:分～不差 without the slightest error

厘金 líjīn [史] likin (tax of a thousandth):～过境税 likin transit tax; internal tax on the transit goods

狸 lí 〈名〉 racoon dog

狸猫 límāo leopard cat

罹 lí 〈动〉 meet with a misfortune; be caught in; suffer from:～祸 be killed in an accident

罹难 línàn ① meet with a misfortune; be killed ② die in a disaster or an accident

梨 lí 〈名〉 pear

梨园 líyuán *liyuan*, theatrical troupe; the operatic circle:～世家 come from a family of opera artists. ～戏 *liyuan* opera

犁 lí 〈名,动〉 plough

犁田 lítián plough the land (fields)

喱 lí 见“咖喱”(gālí)

黎 lí〈名〉multitude; host:～庶 the multitude

黎明 límíng (at) dawn (at); daybreak:～即起 rise (get up) at dawn

黎族 Lízú the Li nationality (living in Hainan province)

lǐ

礼 lǐ〈名〉① ceremony; rite:～崩乐坏 disintegration of rites and deterioration of music happiness ② courtesy; etiquette; manners:行～(give a) salute. ～宾司 protocol department ③ gift; present:～券 gift certificate

礼拜 lǐbài ① week ② religious service:做～ go to church; be at church. ～式音乐 liturgical music

礼单 lǐdān list of presents

礼服 lǐfú ceremonical robe; full dress; formal attire

礼花 lǐhuā fireworks display

礼教 lǐjiào the Confucian (feudal) ethical code; feudal ethics

礼节 lǐjié courtesy; formalities; protocol; ceremony; etiquette:～性拜访 courtesy (duty) call. ～制度 ceremonial institution

礼貌 lǐmào manners; courtesy; politeness:有～的 polite; courteous; civil

礼炮 lǐpào (gun) salute; salvo:鸣～21响 fire a 21-gun salute; fire a salvo of 21 guns

礼品(物) lǐpǐn(wù) gift; present:～交换 gift exchange

礼器 lǐqì ritual vessels; items used for ceremony and ritual

礼让 lǐràng give precedence to sb. out of courtesy or thoughtfulness; comity:安全～ yield right of way for safety's sake

礼尚往来 lǐshàng-wǎnglái ① Courtesy requires a return of visits received.; Etiquette (courtesy) demands reciprocation.; ② deal with sb. as he deals with you

礼堂 lǐtáng assembly hall; auditorium

礼仪 lǐyí ceremony; rites; ritual:～之邦 a land of propriety and righteousness; a land where etiquette prevails. ～之争 rites controversy

礼遇 lǐyù polite (courteous) reception:受到～ be received with courtesy

李 lǐ〈名〉① plum:～子 plum ② plum tree

李代桃僵 lǐdài-táojiāng palm off a substitute for the real things; sacrifice oneself for another person; have punished a wrong man

李下瓜田(瓜田李下) lǐxià-guātián (guātián-lǐxià) in a melon patch or under a plum tree; liable to lay oneself open to suspicion

里 lǐ〈名〉① lining; inside:被～儿 the underneath side of a quilt ② neighbourhood:邻～ people of the neighbourhood ③ lane; alley ④ hometown; native place:故～ one's native place ⑤ *li*, a Chinese unit of length (＝1/2 kilometre) ⑥〈介〉inside; in:屋～ in the room

里边 lǐbian inside; in; within

里程 lǐchéng ① mileage:通车～ traffic mileage ② course of development; course:历史～碑 a milestone in history

里面 lǐmiàn inside; interior

里弄 lǐnòng lane; alley; neighbourhood:～干部 neighbourhood cadres

里通外国 lǐtōng-wàiguó have (maintain) illicit (traitorous) relations with a foreign country

里头 lǐtou inside; interior

里应外合 lǐyìng-wàihé act from inside in coordination with forces attacking from outside; attack the enemy from within in coordination with operations from without; strike from both without and within; collaborate from within with forces from without; work in collusion, one from without and the other from within

理 lǐ〈名〉① texture; grain (in wood, skin, etc.):肌～ skin texture ② reason; truth; logic:他不讲道～。He is not amendable to reason. ③ natural science; esp. physics:～工科学院 college of science and engineering〈动〉④ run; manage:处～ cope or deal with ⑤ put in order; tidy up:～发 have a hair cut. 梳～ comb hair; arrange in proper order ⑥ take notice of; pay attention to:没人～ be left out in the cold

理财 lǐcái manage money matters; conduct financial transactions

理睬 lǐcǎi [多用于否定] pay heed to; take notice of:不予～ pay no heed to

理发 lǐfà haircut; hairdressing:～店 barbershop; hairdressing saloon. ～师 barber; [为女子服务的] hairdresser

理会 lǐhuì ① understand; perceive ② [多用于否定] pay heed to; take notice of:不要去～他的话。Don't take any notice of what he says.

理解 lǐjiě understand; comprehend; grasp:～力 comprehensive faculty; comprehension

理科 lǐkē ① natural science ② [大学] science department

理亏 lǐkuī be in the wrong; be unjustifiable:～心虚 have a guilty conscience; Justice is not on his side.

理论 lǐlùn theory

理赔 lǐpéi settlement of claim; settle a claim

理屈词穷 lǐqū-cíqióng have nothing to say to justify oneself; find one's arguments indefensible; find oneself devoid of all arguments; be unable to advance any further arguments

理事 lǐshì member of a council; director:～会 board of directors; council

理顺 lǐshùn straighten (smooth) out; bring into better balance: ～价格关系 balancing (smoothing out) price relationships

理算 lǐsuàn adjustment:海损～人 adjuster

理所当然 lǐsuǒdāngrán as a matter of course; naturally; as it ought to be; what propriety requires; it goes without saying that…

理想 lǐxiǎng ideal:有～ foster high ideals. 有～的人 man with lofty ideals

理性 lǐxìng reason; senses:～认识［哲］rational knowledge; conceptual knowledge

理应 lǐyīng ought to; should

理由 lǐyóu reason; ground; argument

理直气壮 lǐzhí-qìzhuàng (speak) with great confidence; be bold and straight; be in the right and self-confident

理智 lǐzhì reason; intellect; senses:丧失～ lose one's senses

俚 lǐ〈形〉vulgar

俚语 lǐyǔ slang

鲤 lǐ〈名〉carp

鲤鱼 lǐyú carp

lì

立 lì〈动〉① stand:直～ stand straight ② erect; set up:～界标 erect boundary markers ③ establish; found:～德 establish one's virtue. ～合同 sign a contract ④ live; exist:自～ live one's own; be on one's feet ⑤〈形〉erect; upright; vertical: ～式发动机 an upright engine ⑥〈副〉immediately; at once: ～即处决 execute summarily

立案 lì'àn file a case; put a case on file; put on record

立场 lìchǎng stand; standpoint; position

立法 lìfǎ ① enact laws; make laws ② legislation; legislature: ～机关 legislative body. ～机关调查权 legislative investigative powers

立功 lìgōng perform a meritorious deed; do a deed of merit; render meritorious service; win honour; make contributions:～赎罪 perform merits to atone for one's crimes

立即(刻) lìjí(kè) at once; immediately:～付款 at-once-payment; prompt payment. ～支付 immediate payment

立交桥 lìjiāoqiáo interchange; cloverleaf bridge:多层～ multilevel three dimensional interchange bridge

立据 lìjù deed

立刻 lìkè immediately; at once; right away

立论 lìlùn ① set forth one's view; present one's arguments ② argumentation; argument; position

立式 lìshì vertical; upright
立体 lìtǐ ① solid ② stereoscopic; three-dimensional: ～电影 stereoscopic film. ～画法[美] stereography. ～交叉工程 grade separation engineering. ～主义[美] cubism
立体声 lìtǐshēng sterophony; stero: ～收录机 stereo radio-tape player. ～音响设备 stero component system; stero
立宪 lìxiàn constitutionalism: ～国家 constitutional state. ～会议 Constituent Assembly. ～君主 constitutional monarch (ruler). ～政府 constitutional government
立项 lìxiàng [投资] approval of the project proposal
立言 lìyán establish one's words; established words
立遗嘱 lìyízhǔ make a will; draw up a will: ～人 testator; legator
立意 lìyì ① make up one's mind; be determined ② approach; conception: ～新颖 show an interesting new approach; novel ideas
立于不败之地 lìyú bùbài-zhīdì establish oneself in an unassailable position; be in an impregnable position; remain invincible (unconquerable)
立约 lìyuē conclude a treaty; draw up an agreement (a contract)
立志 lìzhì resolve; be determined; make up one's mind: ～攀登科技高峰 aim to scale new heights of science and technology
立足 lìzú gain a footing (foothold): ～点 footing; foothold

粒

lì 〈名〉 gain; granule
粒子 lìzǐ particle: ～的 corpuscular

莅

lì 〈动〉 be present; attend: ～会 attend the meeting; be present at the meeting
莅临 lìlín come; arrive; attend; be present: 敬请～指导。Your presence and guidance are welcome.

笠

lì 〈名〉 a large bamboo or straw hat with a conical crown and broad brim: 斗～ bamboo hat

栗

lì ① 〈名〉 chestnut: ～子 chestnut ② 〈动〉 tremble; shiver: 不寒而～ make one's flesh creep

吏

lì 〈名〉 ① clerk; lesser functionary ② official; mandarin: 贪官污～ corrupt officials
吏员 lìyuán clerk; clerical official
吏治 lìzhì civil administration (government)

厉

lì 〈形〉 ① strict; rigorous: ～禁 strictly forbid ② severe; stern; grim: 他立即露出一副～害的嘴脸。He abruptly screwed his face into a scowl.
厉兵秣马 lìbīng-mòmǎ groom the horses and drill the troops — get ready for battle; sharpen

the war weapons and feed the horses;maintain combat readiness

厉害 lìhài ① formidable; tough; fierce ② serious; critical:病得很～ be seriously ill

厉行 lìxíng strictly execute; enforce; make great efforts to:～节约 practise strict (rigid) economy

励 lì〈动〉encourage; exert oneself:鼓～ encourage

励精图治 lìjīng-túzhì make great efforts to build a strong state; exert oneself to make the country prosperous; brace oneself up and run one's country well

励志 lìzhì pursuit a goal with determination

丽 lì〈形〉beautiful; pretty:绮～ beautiful; gorgeous. 风和日～。The wind is gentle and the sun radiant.; a beautiful day with a gentle breeze blowing

丽人 lìrén a beautiful woman; a beauty

丽质 lìzhì beauty (of a woman):天生～ natural beauty

俪 lì〈名〉husband and wife; couple:结成伉～ become married couple

俪句 lìjù parallel sentences

俪影 lìyǐng a husband and wife appearing in public or in a photograph

利 lì〈形〉① sharp:～刃 a sharp sword or blade ② favourable; convenient:有～形势 favourable situation〈名〉③ advantage; benefit ④ profit; interest:根本～益 basic interests. ～息成本 interest cost. ～润指标 profit norm (index) ⑤〈动〉～国～民 benefit the country and its people

利弊 lìbì advantages and disadvantages; merits and demerits:利多弊少。The advantages outweigh the disadvantages.

利改税 lìgǎishuì replace profit delivery with tax payments; replacement of profits by taxes

利害 lìhài merits and demerits; gains and losses; interests:～关系人 interested party (person). ～攸关 be closely related to one's interests

利害 lìhai formidable; terrible:这着棋十分～。That's a cunning (devastating) move.

利己主义 lìjǐzhǔyì individualism; egoism

利令智昏 lìlìngzhìhūn be blinded by lust for gain; be fuddled by the desire for gain; Gain blinds one's better judgement

利率 lìlǜ [经] rate of interest; interest rate:～机动权 have the power to regulate interest rate

利落 lìluo ① agile; nimble; dexterous ② neat; orderly:他做事干净～。He is a neat worker. ③ settled; finished

利民活动 lìmín huódòng people-benefiting activities

利钱 lìqian interest

利润 lìrùn profit:～分成 shared proportion of the profit. ～留成

retained proportion of the profit; set aside a portion of the profit to be placed at the disposal of the enterprise. ～提成制 profits retention system; profit-sharing system

利市 lìshì ① profits ② a good market ③ lucky

利息 lìxī interest: ～补贴 interest subsidization

利益 lìyì interests; benefit; advantage; profit: 长远(眼前)～ long-term (immediate) interests. ～所有人 beneficial owner

利用 lìyòng ① utilize; make (good) use of: ～废物 make use of waste materials ② take advantage of; exploit: ～职权 abuse one's powers; take advantage of one's power; exploit one's office

利诱 lìyòu lure (sb.) by promise of gain: 威逼～ lure by money and oppress with power

利于 lìyú be of advantage to; benefit

利欲 lìyù lust for gain: ～熏心 be blinded by the lust for gain; be reckless with greed; be obsessed with the desire for gain

痢 lì 〈名〉 dysentery

痢疾 lìji dysentery: 细菌性～ bacillary dysentery

例 lì 〈名〉 ① example; instance: 实～ instances ② precedent: 无先～可援 have no precedent to go by ③ case; instance: 案～ law case ④ rule; regulation: 不在此～。That is an exception. ⑤〈形〉regular; routine: ～会 regular (routine) meetings

例案 lì'àn established case

例会 lìhuì regular meeting

例假 lìjià regular holiday; official holiday

例句 lìjù illustrative sentence; example sentence

例如 lìrú for instance; for example (e. g.); such as

例外 lìwài exception: ～法规 exception law. 毫无～ without (any) exception

例行 lìxíng ① routine: ～公事 routine; regular procedure; regular course of official duties ② mere formality: ～检查 routine inspection

例证 lìzhèng example; illustration

例子 lìzi example; case; instance

隶 lì 〈动〉 belong to; be under

隶书 lìshū *li* script; official script

隶属 lìshǔ be under the direct command (jurisdiction) of; be affiliated to; be subordinate to: ～关系 relationship of administrative subordination

力 lì 〈名〉 ① power; force; strength; ability: 财～ financial power ② force: 水～ hydraulic power ③ physical strength: 大～士 a man of great strength ④〈动〉make every effort; do all one can: 办事不～ not do one's best in one's work ⑤〈副〉energetically; strenuously: ～加驳斥 emphatically refute

力不从心 lìbùcóngxīn one's ability falling short of one's wish;

strength not equal to the will; unable to do as much as one would like to

力度 lìdù ①［乐］dynamics ② harsher measures：加大～ implement harsher measures（to do sth.）

力谏 lìjiàn try all one can to remonstrate

力克 lìkè overcome with effort

力量 lìliàng power; force; strength：～的对比 relation of forces; balance of forces; relative strength

力气 lìqi physical strength; effort

力求 lìqiú try one's utmost to; strive（to do，for）：～上进 strive for further progress

力所不及 lìsuǒbùjí beyond one's power（capacity）

力所能及 lìsuǒnéngjí in one's power; within one's reach（ability）; to the full extent of one's capability; to the best of one's ability

力图 lìtú strive（for，to do）; endeavour; vigorously seek to

力争 lìzhēng ① struggle for; do all one can to; work hard for：～主动 make every effort to gain the initiative ② have a strong argument（with）：据理～ put up strong arguments

力证 lìzhèng strong evidence; convincing proof

力作 lìzuò magnum opus; forceful work

历

lì ①〈动〉go through; undergo; pass; experience：经～了历史的考验 stand the test of history. ～尽千辛万苦 brave hardships; have gone through all kinds of hardships and difficulties ②〈形〉all previous（occasions，sessions，etc.）：～朝 in the past dynasties ③〈副〉all through; all over; one by one：～来认为 have always maintained that ④〈名〉calendar：阳～ solar calendar

历程 lìchéng process; course：胜利的～ pathway to victory

历次 lìcì all previous（sessions，contests，etc.）：我们在～比赛中都取得了好成绩。We did well in all previous contests.

历代 lìdài ① past dynasties ② for generations in the past; through the ages

历法 lìfǎ the recording of calendar time; calendar making; arrangement of the calendar; calendar

历届 lìjiè all previous（sessions，etc.）;（graduates）of all previous years

历尽 lìjìn have gone through a lot of

历来 lìlái always; all along：～如此。It has always been the case.

历历在目 lìlì-zàimù come clearly into view; leap up before the eyes

历年 lìnián over the years; for years in the past：～结余 accumulated surpluses ② calendary year

历时 lìshí last（a period of time）; take（a period of time）

历史 lìshǐ history：～包袱 burderns from the past. ～分期 historical periodization；periodization. ～剧 chronicle play. ～首创精神 creative initiative in the making of history. ～唯物主义 historical materialism. ～遗留的负债 leftover debts

历书 lìshū almanac

历数 lìshǔ count one by one；enumerate

沥 lì〈动，名〉drip；drop

沥青 lìqīng pitch；asphalt；tar

荔 lì

荔枝 lìzhī litchi

liǎ

俩 liǎ〈数〉① two：咱～ both of us；the two of us；we two ② several；some：她有～钱儿。She has some money.

lián

帘 lián〈名〉curtain

帘子 liánzi curtain；screen

廉 lián〈形〉① cheap：～价出售 sell at a low price ② clean-handed：～洁 be honest

廉耻 liánchǐ sense of shame (honour)：不知～ be shameless；have no sense of shame

廉价 liánjià cheap；low-priced；at a low price：～品 cheap goods. ～旅馆 budget hotel. ～处理 concessional disposal. ～劳动力 cheap labour

廉洁 liánjié clean-handed；clean；honest：～奉公 be honest in carrying out official duties；have integrity and public spirit. ～自律 be honest and disciplined

廉明 liánmíng integrity and awareness；clean-handed and clear headed；incorruptible and intelligent

廉政 liánzhèng institute clean government：～建设 build an honest government；keeping government employees honest

镰 lián〈名〉sickle：～刀 sickle；scythe

怜 lián〈动〉① pity，sympathize with：可～ have pity on；pity ② love tenderly

怜爱 lián'ài love tenderly；have tender affection for

怜悯 liánmǐn pity；compassionate；commiserate；take pity on；have compassion for

怜惜 liánxī feel pity for；feel tender and protective towards

怜香惜玉 liánxiāngxīyù show pity and tenderness to women

联 lián ①〈动〉unite；joint；connect：～合一致，共同奋斗 unite in the common struggle ②〈形〉joint：～合行动 joint action 〈名〉③ union；league：学生～合会 students' union ④ antithetical couplet：春～ Spring Festival couplet

联邦 liánbāng federation；union；

commonwealth

联播 liánbō a country-wide (national) radio hookup; broadcast over national radio network; simultaneous broadcast; chain broadcasting: 新闻～ news hookup

联产承包责任制 liánchǎn chéngbāo zérènzhì [农] production-related contract responsibility system; output-related responsibility system

联产到户 liánchǎn dàohù production-related household contract system

联产到人 liánchǎn dàorén production-related individual contract system

联产计酬 liánchǎn jìchóu calculating remuneration in relation to output: ～的生产责任制 system of responsibility for production in which payment is linked to output; system of production responsibility in agriculture in which remuneration is based on output quotas

联防 liánfáng citizen's patrol; citizen's watch; citizen's militia

联合 liánhé unite; join; ally; joint: ～抵押 joint mortgage. ～公司 integrated corporation. ～公报 joint communiqué. ～国 United Nations. ～诉讼 joint indictment

联户 liánhù joint households: ～林场 joint-household tree farm. ～选购 joint-household purchasing

联欢 liánhuān have a get-together: ～会 get-together; social party. ～节 festival

联结 liánjié join; connect; link; bind

联络 liánluò come into contact with; connection; liaison: ～处 liaison office

联袂 liánmèi go, come, etc. together

联盟 liánméng alliance; union; league

联名 liánmíng jointly signed; jointly

联赛 liánsài [体] league matches; tournament: 足球～ league football matches

联系 liánxì contact; connection; link with; combine with; get in touch with; contact: ～群众 link oneself with the masses; keep in touch with the masses

联想 liánxiǎng associate (connect) with; association (of ideas)

联销经营 liánxiāojīngyíng chain-store operations

联谊 liányì friendship ties: ～会 parties. ～活动 activities for developing friendship ties. ～晚会 evening get-together for developing friendship

联姻 liányīn (of two families) be related by marriage; form an alliance by marriage

联营 liányíng joint operation: ～户 joint management households

联运 liányùn through traffic; through service; combined transport; multimodal transport：～人 combined transport operator

连 lián 〈动〉① join; connect; link：～成一片 link up … into one contingous territory ② involve (in trouble); implicate：互相牵～ be implicative of each other ③〈名〉(of army) company 〈副〉④ in succession：～续 3 年 three successive years ⑤ even：我～想都没有想过。I didn't even give a thought. ⑥〈介〉including：这本书～邮费 200 元。This book is 200 yuan, postage included.

连本带利 liánběn-dàilì both principal and interest; both capital and interest

连播 liánbō chain broadcast：在节目表上有我喜爱的～节目。My favourite serial is on the programme.

连带 liándài ① be related to ② joint：～责任 joint and several liability

连贯 liánguàn ① link (up); connect; join：～性 coherence; consecution; connection ② consistent; coherent：文章写得很不～。This article is rather incoherent.

连环 liánhuán chain of rings：～画 serial pictures; picture-story book; serial pictorial story

连襟 liánjīn husbands of sisters

连累 liánlèi get sb. into trouble; involve; implicate; incriminate：～许多人 implicate a lot of people

连连 liánlián repeatedly; again and again

连忙 liánmáng hastily; hurriedly; promptly

连绵 liánmián unbroken; uninterrupted; continuous：～起伏的沙丘 the rolling sand dunes. 连日来阴雨～。There has been a spell of wet weather for the last few days.

连年 liánnián for years running; in successive or consecutive years; from year to year

连篇累牍 liánpiān-lěidú endless assortment; repeat at great length; keep on repeating; reiterate again and again; lengthy and tedious

连任 liánrèn renew one's term of office; be reappointed; be reappointed or reelected consecutively

连锁 liánsuǒ linkage; chain：～反应 chain reaction; response-chaining. ～商店 chain stores

连同 liántóng together with; along with

连续 liánxù successive; continuous; consecutive：～剧 serial play. ～片 serial movie. ～3 年 three consecutive years. ～生产线 transfer line

连用 liányòng use consecutively; use together

连载 liánzǎi serialize：～小说 serialized novel; serial story; installment of the story; serial

涟 lián 〈名〉ripples; riffle

涟漪 liányī riples; riffle

莲 lián 〈名〉lotus

莲花 liánhuā lotus flower; lotus

liǎn

脸 liǎn 〈名〉① face; countenance:撕破～ cast aside all considerations of face ② feelings; sensibilities

脸不变色心不跳 liǎn bù biànsè xīn bùtiào one's face not changing colour, his heart not beating any faster; without turning pale nor heart palpitating with fear

脸蛋儿 liǎndànr (usu. children's) cheeks; face

脸红 liǎnhóng blush; colour up:她因害羞而～。She blushed with shame.

脸颊 liǎnjiá cheeks; face

脸皮 liǎnpí cheek; face:～厚 be cheeky; have plenty of cheek

脸谱 liǎnpǔ types of facial make-up in operas; pattern of make-up:～化的作品 hackneyed literary creation

脸色 liǎnsè complexion; expression (on one's face):～刷白 ashen-faced. 他～一沉。He put on a grave face.; His face fell.

liàn

恋 liàn 〈动〉love; be attached to

恋爱 liàn'ài love:谈～ be in love (with); have a love affair (with)

恋歌 liàngē love song

恋旧 liànjiù yearn for one's native place; be filled with nostalgia

恋恋不舍 liànliànbùshě cling to; be reluctant to part with

恋情 liànqíng romantic love

恋人 liànrén sweetheart; loved one; girlfriend or boyfriend

练 liàn 〈动〉① train; drill; practise:操～ drill ②〈形〉practised; experienced:老～ experienced and assured

练兵 liànbīng drill (train) troops:～运动 training campaign

练(气)功 liàn(qì)gōng do exercises in gymnastics, *wushu*, acrobatics, etc.; practise one's skill; practise *qigong*; do breathing exercises

练球 liànqiú practise a ball game

练声 liànshēng vocalism:～曲 vocalise

练习 liànxí practise; exercise:做～ do exercises

练字 liànzì practise calligraphy

炼 liàn 〈动〉smelt; temper; refine:～铁 iron smelting. ～药 refining of the drug

炼钢 liàngāng make steel:～厂 steelworks; steel mill. ～炉 steel-making furnaces

炼焦 liànjiāo make coke; coke:～厂 coking plant; cokery. ～煤 coking coal

炼乳 liànrǔ condensed milk

炼油 liànyóu [石油]refine oil:～厂 (oil) refinery

链 liàn 〈名〉chain

链套 liàntào chain case

链条 liàntiáo ① chain ② [自行

车] roller chain; chain

liáng

梁 liáng 〈名〉①[屋的]beam:上～ set a roof beam in place ②[桥] bridge ③ ridge:山～ mountain ridge

梁上君子 liángshàng-jūnzǐ gentleman on the beam — burglar; thief; a gentleman in mid-air

凉 liáng 〈形〉① cool; cold:乘～ enjoy the cool air ② discouraged; disappointed:心～了半截 be disappointed

凉白开 liángbáikāi cold boiled water

凉拌 liángbàn (of food) cold and dressed with sauce

凉风 liángfēng refreshig (cool) breeze:～习习。A cool breeze is blowing.

凉快 liángkuai ① nice and cool; pleasantly cool ② cool oneself; cool off

凉气 liángqì cold air; chilly air

凉爽 liángshuǎng refreshing cool

凉台 liángtái veranda; balcony

凉亭 liángtíng roadside pavilion; kiosk; alcove; arbour

凉鞋 liángxié sandals

良 liáng ①〈形〉good; fine:～策 good strategy ②〈副〉very; really:用心～苦 have really given much thought to the matter

良材 liángcái ① good timber ② able person

良方 liángfāng ① effective prescription; good recipe ② good plan; sound strategy

良好 liánghǎo good; fine:～的社会风尚 create a society with high ethical standards; high social morals. ～的愿望 well-intentioned; good intention

良机 liángjī good (golden) opportunity

良久 liángjiǔ a good while; a long time

良师益友 liángshī-yìyǒu good teacher and helpful friend

良心 liángxīn conscience:～之痛苦 pangs (stings) of conscience; twitch of conscience

良性 liángxìng benign:～循环 benign cycle between; sound cycle; positive cycle

良药苦口 liángyào-kǔkǒu Good medicine tastes bitter.; Bitter pills have wholesome effect.; The remedy was tough, but it might be salutary.

良莠不分 liángyǒu-bùfēn indiscriminate intake of both the good and bad; the good and the bad are intermingled

良友 liángyǒu good friend

良知 liángzhī ① innate knowledge of the good; innate good consciousness ② [哲] intuitive knowledge

良种 liángzhǒng [植物] good (fine, better) strains of seed; fine seeds; fine breed

粮 liáng 〈名〉grain; food-grain; food:～荒 famines

粮仓 liángcāng barn; granary

粮草(秣) liángcǎo (mò) army

provisions; rations and forage; provisions and fodder

粮店 liángdiàn grain shop

粮票 liángpiào grain coupon

粮食 liángshi grain; food:～统购统销政策 policy of state monopoly for the purchase and marketing of grain. 健全～储备体系 amplify the system for stockpiling reserves of grain

粮油补贴 liángyóu bǔtiē grain and oil subsidy

粮站 liángzhàn grain distribution station; grain supply centre

量 liáng〈动〉measure:丈～土地 measure land
另见 liàng

量杯 liángbēi measuring glass; graduate

量具 liángjù measuring tool

liǎng

两 liǎng〈数〉① two:～栋楼房 two buildings ② some; a few: 有～下子 have some capabilities ③〈量〉*liǎng*, a unit of weight (= 50 grams) ④〈代〉both:～面 both sides

两败俱伤 liǎngbài-jùshāng both sides suffer (lose); end in defeat for both sides; both weakened by; Both sides would be losers in the fight

两半儿 liǎngbànr two halves; in half; in two

两边 liǎngbiān ① both sides; both directions; both places ② both parties; both sides

两重 liǎngchóng twofold; double; dual:～性 dual nature; duality

两抵 liǎngdǐ balance or cancel each other

两耳不闻窗外事 liǎng ěr bù wén chuāngwài shì not care what is going on outside one's window; hold aloft from the affairs of the world reality

两个文明 liǎng gè wénmíng two civilizations, i.e., material civilization and spiritual civilization of socialism

两公开一监督 liǎng gōngkāi yī jiāndū (办事制度公开,办事结果公开,加强群众监督) a system of "two opens and one supervision," referring to making public the work system and the result of work, as well as strengthening supervision by the masses of the people

两极分化 liǎngjí fēnhuà polarization

两可 liǎngkě both will do; either will do; could go either way

两面 liǎngmiàn two sides; both sides; both aspects:～派的伎俩 double-dealing tricks. ～讨好 try to please both sides; run with the hare and hunt with the hounds; try to keep the favour of both sides (in a dispute)

两难 liǎngnán in a dilemma; between the devil and the deep sea:进退～ be in a dilemma

两讫 liǎngqì the goods are delivered and the bill is cleared

两权分离 liǎngquán fēnlí [经]

separation of two rights, i. e., separation of the right of ownership and the right of management

两全 liǎngquán be satisfactory to both sides (parties); with due regard to both: ～其美 satisfy both parties (sides); be complete in both respects; satisfy rival claims; act in such a way to satisfy the two contending parties or resolve the contradiction confronting a person

两审终审制[法] liǎngshěn zhōngshěnzhì a system in which the second instance is the final instance

两手抓 liǎngshǒuzhuā strategic principle of "grasping two links at the same time," i. e., pursuing the process of reform and opening up and at the same time fighting crime; developing the economy and at the same time strengthening democracy and the legal system; and, achieving material process and at the same time fostering an advanced culture and ideology

两头在外 liǎngtóu zài wài [外贸] two ends abroad (meaning raw materials come from abroad and products are exported to other countries):要实现国际大循环,～,大进大出。We must realize the great international circulation, two ends abroad, to import and export on a large scale.

两厢情愿 liǎngxiāng-qíngyuàn mutal consent

两性 liǎngxìng both sexes:～情爱 sexual love

两袖清风 liǎngxiù-qīngfēng (of an official) remain uncorrupted; An honest official remains poor all the time.; an official free from corruption and bribery

两用 liǎngyòng dual-purpose:～人材 dual-purpose personnel; military-civilian man; double-function talents. ～帐户 two-way account

两院制 liǎngyuànzhì bicameral system; bicameralism; two-chamber system:～立法机构 bicameral (two-chamber) legislature

liàng

凉 liàng 〈动〉 cool; let sth. cool off:把粥～一～ let the porridge off. 老张吸着烟,把小田～在一边。Now Lao Zhang was enjoying his pipe, letting Little Tian cool his heels.

另见 liáng

谅 liàng 〈动〉 ① excuse; forgive; understand:体～ understand and forgive ② presume; suppose:～必是他。I think it must be him. ③〈副〉probably

谅必 liàngbì most likely; most probably:～如此。I think it must be so.

谅解 liàngjiě ① understanding; make allowance:达成～ reach an understandig ② entente

晾 liàng〈动〉① dry in the air; air:～干菜 dry vegetable in the air ② dry in the sun; sun:～被子 sun quilts

晾晒 liàngshài sun-cure; air; field

亮 liàng〈形〉① bright; light; shiny:敞～ light and spacious ② loud and clear:嗓子洪～ a rich resonant voice ③ open and clear; enlightened:他这一说，我心里～了。I find what he says most enlightening.〈动〉④ light; brighten; shine:天～了。Day is breaking. ⑤ show, reveal:～出真相 show one's true colour

亮底 liàngdǐ reveal the whole story; disclose one's plan, stand, views, etc.; put one's cards on the table

亮度 liàngdù brightness; brilliance

亮光 liàngguāng light

亮晶晶 liàngjīngjīng sparkling; twinkling; glittering:天上～的星 twinkling stars in the sky

亮堂 liàngtang ① light; bright ② (of voice) loud and clear ③ clear; enlightened

亮相 liàngxiàng ① strike a pose on the stage ② declare one's position; state one's views

亮证经营 liàngzhèng jīngyíng display certificate in doing business

靓 liàng〈方〉〈形〉pretty; beautiful

靓仔 liàngzǎi handsome young man

量 liàng〈名〉① quantity; amount; volume:热～ quantity of heat ② capacity:容～ capacity of container ③〈动〉meansure; estimate:估～ estimate; assess; appraise

量变 liàngbiàn［哲］quantitative change

量才录用 liàngcái-lùyòng give sb. employemnt commensurate with his abilities; employ people according to their talents; give sb. work suited to his abilities; assign jobs to people according to their abilities

量化 liànghuà quantification

量力 liànglì estimate one's strength; make an accurate estimate of one's own strength or ability; take one's ability into account:～而行 act according to one's capability; proceeding from actual capability

量入为出 liàngrù-wéichū plan one's expenditures in the light of one's income; base one's expenditure upon one's income; keep expenditures within the limits of income; live within one's means; Spending must be kept with the limits of income.

量体裁衣 liàngtǐ-cáiyī fit the dress to the figure; cut the garment according to the figure; suit one's action to actual circumstances; act according to actual circumstances

量刑 liàngxíng measurement of penalty; weighing of the penalty; measure punishment; sentencing:～标准 sentencing standards; criterion for imposing penalty. ～幅度 extent for measurement of punishment

liāo

撩 liāo〈动〉① raise; lift ② sprinkle (water):往地上～些水 sprinkle some water on the floor. ～帘子 raise the curtain
另见 liáo

撩动 liāodòng provoke; stir up

liáo

聊 liáo〈动〉① chat:午饭后咱们～～。Let's have a chat after lunch. ② depend; rely on:～以自慰 find relief oneself in ③〈副〉just; merely:～胜一筹 just a little better

聊表寸心 liáobiǎo-cùnxīn just to show my gratitude; It is a mere proof of my regard.

聊胜于无 liáoshèngyúwú A little is better than none.; Something is better than nothing.; A bit in the morning is better than nothing all day.

聊天 liáotiān have a gossip; gossip; chat (with); small talk

聊以解嘲 liáoyǐjiěcháo manage somehow to relieve embarrassment; say or do sth. in order to avoid mockery

聊以自慰 liáoyǐzìwèi just to console oneself; comfort oneself with the thought that…; just to console oneself

燎 liáo〈动〉(of fire) spread; burn; set ablaze

燎原 liáoyuán set a prairie ablaze:～烈火 blazing prairie fire

撩 liáo〈动〉① tease; tantalize ② stir up; provoke:～动肝火 excite one's wrath; provoke agitation
另见 liāo

撩拨 liáobō ① banter; tease ② provoke; incite

撩逗 liáodòu entice; provoke

嘹 liáo

嘹亮 liáoliàng clarion; round; resonant:～的歌声 round singing voice

僚 liáo official:～属 colleagues and subordinates; staff officers. ～佐 aide

缭 liáo〈动〉① twine; wind around; entangle ② stitch or sew with slanting stiches

缭乱 liáoluàn dazzled; in a confused state of:眼花～ be dazzled

缭绕 liáorào wind around; coil up; curl up; linger:～耳际 ring in one's ears. 歌声～。The song lingered in the air.

寥 liáo〈形〉① few; scanty; scarce:～～数语 with a few mild comments ② quiet; silent; deserted:寂～ silent and lonely; deserted and solitary

寥廓 liáokuò boundless; vast; immense

寥落 liáoluò sparse; scattered; few and far between

寥若晨星 liáoruò-chénxīng as few (scarce; rare; sparse) as the morning stars; very few

疗 liáo 〈动〉 cure; treat

疗程 liáochéng course of treatment; treatment periods

疗法 liáofǎ treatment; therapy: 针灸～ acupuncture therapy

疗效 liáoxiào curative effect: ～显著 marked treatment efficacy. ～食品 curative foods

疗养 liáoyǎng recuperate; receive convalescent treatment (for); convalesce: ～院 convalescent hospital; sanatorium

辽 liáo 〈形〉 distant; faraway

辽阔 liáokuò wide; extensive; vast: ～的土地 a vast expanse of land; vast territory

辽远 liáoyuǎn distant; faraway; remote: ～的边疆 faraway (distant) frontier regions

liǎo

潦 liǎo

潦草 liǎocǎo ① (of handwriting) hasty and careless; scratchy: 字迹～ careless handwriting ② [工作] sloppy; careless; perfunctory

潦倒 liǎodǎo live in misery; be down and out; be frustrated

了 liǎo 〈动〉 ① finish; complete; end: 未～之事 unfinished task ② understand; know; realize: ～解情况 be acquainted with the conditions

另见 lè

了不得 liǎobude ① terrific; extraordinary: 多得～ in terrific number ② awful; terrible: 真是～的大祸啊! What a terrible disaster!

了不起 liǎobuqǐ ① wonderful; amazing; extraordinary: ～的成就 wonderful achievement ② become swell-headed; be cocky; be conceited; be swollen with pride

了结 liǎojié finish; settle; put an end to: ～成本 settling up cost

了解 liǎojiě ① understand; know; comprehend; acquaint: ～国外市场动向 get acquainted with the trends of foreign markets ② find out; inquire into: ～全部事实 inquire into the whole matter

了却 liǎoquè settle; solve

了然 liǎorán understand; be clear

了如指掌 liǎorúzhǐzhǎng know … like the palm of one's own hand; know … like a book; have sth. at one's fingertips; know … like the back of one's hand; be perfectly clear of

了事 liǎoshì dispose of a matter; finish up sth.; get sth. over

liào

料 liào ①〈动〉 expect; predict;

anticipate：不出所～ as was expected〈名〉② material；stuff：草～ fodder；forage ③ stuff；makings：是个画家的～ have the makings of a painter
料到 liàodào foresee；expect
料酒 liàojiǔ cooking wine
料理 liàolǐ ① manage；handle；arrange ② look after；take care of：～家务 look after household affairs
料事如神 liàoshì-rúshén foretell like a prophet；foretell things accurately；foretell with miraculous accuracy；He has a prophetic eye.
料想 liàoxiǎng presume；expect；reckon
料子 liàozi ① material for making clothes ② woollen fabric ③ wood；timber ④ makings；material

撂 liào〈动〉put down；leave behind
撂荒 liàohuāng abandonment of arable land；desert land uncultivated
撂挑子 liàotiāozi refuse to work；throw up one's job；wash one's hands of the matter

廖 liào〈名〉a surname

镣 liào〈名〉fetters；shackles
镣铐 liàokào shackles；chains

瞭 liào
瞭望 liàowàng watch from a height or a distance；look into the distance from a height：～台［军］observation

liě

咧 liě〈动〉grin
咧嘴 liězuǐ grin：她对着我～大笑。She grinned broadly at me.

liè

列 liè〈动〉① line up；form line；put in a row：～队欢迎 line up to welcome sb. ② enter in a list；list：～入编制 include in the list of staff ③〈名〉line；row；rank：第 2～ the second row ④〈量〉一～火车 a train
列兵 lièbīng private
列车 lièchē train：～员 trainman or trainwoman；attendant on a train. ～长 train crew captain
列岛 lièdǎo chain of islands；archipelago
列举 lièjǔ enumerate；cite；list：～大量事实 cite numerous (many) facts
列入 lièrù include ：～计划 be included in the plan
列位 lièwèi all of you；gentlemen；ladies and gentlemen
列席 lièxí attend (a meeting) as a nonvoting delegate：～代表 delegate without the right to vote. ～作陪 sit at the same table with the guest of honour
列支 lièzhī list as an expenditure：排污费从生产成本中～。The pollutant-drainage fee paid by enterprises can be listed as an expenditure in the production

costs.

列传 lièzhuàn collected biographies; section on biographies in different dynastic histories

烈 liè 〈形〉① strong; violent; intense: ～性药 strong medicine ② stern; upright; staunch: 刚～ upright and unyielding 〈名〉③ martyr: ～士陵园 mausoleum to fallen heroes ④ achievements; exploits: 功～ contributions

烈度 lièdù earthquake intensity

烈火 lièhuǒ roaring fire; burning fire; raging flames: ～见真金。True gold stands the test of fire.; A man of true worth will come out of a severe test unchanged, untouched, intact, etc.

烈军属 lièjūnshǔ family members of a revolutionary martyrs and servicemen

烈日 lièrì burning (scorching, blazing) sun

烈性 lièxìng ① strong; spirited: ～汉子 a man of character. ～酒 strong liquor; spirits ② violent; strong: ～毒品 hard drug

烈焰 lièyàn raging flames; a roaring blaze

裂 liè 〈动〉break; split; crack: 撕～ tear apart

裂变 lièbiàn fission

裂缝 lièfèng crack; crevice; cleft; rip; rift

裂痕 lièhén crack; fissure; cleavages; rift

裂开 lièkāi crack open; split open

裂口 lièkǒu ① crack; split ② breach; gap; crack; split ③ vent (of a volcano)

裂纹 lièwén crack; [瓷器等的] crackle

劣 liè 〈形〉bad; inferior; poor: ～根性 bad characteristcs

劣等 lièděng bad; poor; low-grade; inferior: ～学生 dunce. ～货 goods of inferior quality

劣根性 liègēnxìng deep-rooted bad habits; an inherent weakness

劣迹 lièjì evil deeds; evildoings; notorious record; misdeed: 严重的～ flagrant misdeed

劣品 lièpǐn poor products

劣生学 lièshēngxué dysgenics

劣势 lièshì inferior (unfavourable, disadvantageous) position; inferiority: ～中的优势 superiority within inferiority

劣质 lièzhì of poor (bad) quality; inferior: ～产品 products of inferior quality

猎 liè 〈动〉hunt: ～狗 hunting dog; hound

猎场 lièchǎng hunting ground; hunting field

猎获 lièhuò capture or kill in hunting; bag

猎奇 lièqí hunt for (seek) novelty

猎枪 lièqiāng sporting gun; hunting rifle; fowling piece

猎取 lièqǔ ① hunt ② seek; hunt for: ～名利 hunt for fame and gain

猎装 lièzhuāng hunting dress

līn

拎 līn〈动〉lift; carry (in hand)
拎包 līnbāo handbag

lín

磷 lín〈名〉phosphorus
磷肥 línféi [农] phosphate fertilizer; phosphatic manure
鳞 lín〈名〉(of fish) scale:刮去鱼～ scrape the scales off a fish
鳞次栉比 líncìzhìbǐ row upon row (of houses); a continuous row of houses; arranged in rows
鳞伤 línshāng be covered with wounds:遍体～ be covered with bruises or injures; be a mass of bruises
林 lín〈名〉① woods; forest; grove:～中居民 woodlanders ② circles:部门～立 overlapping administrations ③ forestry
林场 línchǎng tree (forest) farm; forestry station (centre); lumber yard
林带 líndài forest belt:防风～ wind-prevention forest belt. 防沙～ sand-prevention forest belt
林立 línlì stand in great numbers; numerous; a forest of:～的烟囱 a forest of chimneys
林区 línqū afforested area; forest zone (region, district)
林权证 línquánzhèng certificate of forest rights, a document which certifies the ownership of a forest
林网 línwǎng forest network (a system of forests composed by crisscrossing and linking up many forest tracts and forest belts.)
林业 línyè forestry:～专业户 forestry specialty households (agricultural households that expend the majority of their labour and time in forestry work, and that derive their family incomes primarily from forestry)
林阴道 línyīndào boulevard; avenue
淋 lín〈动〉sprinkle; pour (on); drench:她被雨～得浑身湿透。She was drenched through with rain.
另见 lìn
淋巴 línbā [生理] lymph
淋漓 línlí dripping wet:大汗～ dripping sweat. ～尽致 vividly and incisively; most incisive; vivid; completely:～尽致地暴露 make a most telling exposure
淋湿 línshī get wet (from the rain)
淋浴 línyù shower bath; shower
琳 lín〈名〉beautiful jade
琳琅 línláng beautiful jade; gem:～满目 full of beautiful things that dazzle one's eyes; a feast for the eyes; a great variety of beautiful things; A multitude

of beautiful things dazzled the eyes.

临 lín 〈动〉① face; be close to; overlook: 面～两种抉择 be faced with two alternatives ② befall; arrive: 双喜～门。A double blessing has descended upon the house. ③ be going to; just before; on the point of: ～近深夜 towards midnight ④ copy: ～摹 counterdraw

临别 línbié at parting; just before parting: ～赠言 a piece of parting advice; parting words

临场教练员 línchǎng jiàoliànyuán bench coach

临场监督 línchǎng jiāndū be present at the scene to supervise

临床 línchuáng clinical: ～训练 clinical training

临画 línhuà paint from a copy

临机应变 línjī-yīngbiàn act as the occasion demands; act according to circumstances; adapt to changing circumstances

临近 línjìn draw near; approach; close to; near (to, by): 新年～了。New Year is drawing near.

临渴掘井 línkě-juéjǐng not digging a well until one's thirsty — start acting too late; begin to dig a well when feeling thirsty; do thing at the last minute and too late

临摹 línmó copy (a model of calligraphy or painting); counterdraw: ～字帖的笔法 imitate the strokes of model Chinese calligraphy

临时 línshí provisional; temporary: ～代办 [外] chargé d'affaires ad interim. ～工 temporary worker; odd-job man; casual labourers. ～契约 provisional contract. ～凑合 makeshifts; improvise. ～性外汇 foreign exchange of incidental use. ～执照 provisional certificate; temporary licence

临危不惧 línwēi-bùjù be undaunted in the face of perils; not shrink in the face of danger; be brave in a dangerous situation; betray no fear in the hour of danger

临行 línxíng before leaving; on the eve of departure

临阵磨枪 línzhèn-móqiāng sharpen one's spear only before going into battle; start to prepare only at the last moment

临终 línzhōng at the point of death; on one's deathbed: ～关怀 hospice care. ～遗嘱 last will and testment; deathbed will. ～遗言 dying declaration

邻 lín ①〈名〉neighbour: ～居 neighbour ②〈形〉neighbouring; adjacent: ～近年龄组之间 adjacent age groups

邻邦 línbāng neighbouring country

邻近 línjìn near; close to; adjacent to: ～地区 neighbourhood; vicinity

邻里 línlǐ neighbour: ～社区 neighbour community

lǐn

凛 lǐn〈形〉① cold ② strict; severe; stern ③ afraid; fearful

凛冽 lǐnliè biting cold (wind); piercingly cold: ～寒风。The (north) wind is bitingly cold.

凛凛 lǐnlǐn ① freezing; piercing; cold: 寒风～ a piercing wind ② awe-inspiring; stern: 威风～ with an awe-inspiring look (appearance); with great dignity; aweful air

凛然 lǐnrán awe-inspiring; full of dignity; dignified; stern: 大义～ righteous indignation; be all dignity. 正气～ show awe-inspiring righteousness

lìn

淋 lìn〈名〉filter; strain
另见 lín

淋病 lìnbìng [医] gonorrhoea

吝 lìn〈形〉stingy; mean: 尚希不～指教。We hope that you will not stint your criticism.

吝啬 lìnsè stingy; niggardly; miserly: ～鬼 niggard; miser; skinflint

吝惜 lìnxī stint; spare; grudge: 不～自己的力量 be spare (stint) no effort

赁 lìn〈动〉lease; rent; hire: 租～持股有限公司 Leasing Holdings Ltd.

líng

凌 líng〈动〉① insult; bully: 欺～ bully and humiliate ② soar; ascend; rise high: ～驾于唯物主义之上 rise above materialism ③ approach: ～晨 in the small hours; before dawn

凌迟 língchí (in imperial times) the punishment of dismemberment and the lingering death (for heinous crimes): ～处死 execute by the slow process

凌驾 língjià place oneself above; domineer over; override; lord it over: ～一切 lord it over everybody

凌空 língkōng rise (be high up) in the air; soar aloft; fly high; soar: ～盘旋的飞机 plane hovering over in the sky

凌厉 línglì quick and forceful; swift and fierce: ～攻势 overwhelming offensive; make a swift and fierce (powerful) attack

凌乱 língluàn in disorder; in a mess

凌辱 língrǔ insult; abuse; humiliate

凌汛 língxùn spring flood caused by melting river ice

凌云 língyún reach the clouds; soar to the skies

菱 líng〈名〉water caltrop

菱角 língjiǎo water caltrop (chestnut)

菱形 língxíng rhomb: 长～ rhombus

陵 líng〈名〉① hill；mound ② mausoleum；cemetery

陵墓 língmù mausoleum；tomb

陵寝 língqǐn imperial mausoleum；imperial tomb

陵园 língyuán cemetery；burial ground：烈士～ cemetery of revolutionary martyrs

绫 líng〈名〉damask silk；a thin silk fabric

绫裱 língbiǎo front mounting of thin silk

绫罗绸缎 líng-luó-chóu-duàn silks and brocades；silk and satin

零 líng〈数〉① zero；zero sign (0)；nought：一百～一号 No. 101 (number one-oh-one) ② odd；with a little extrta：年纪 80 有～ a little more than eighty years ③ zero；nought；nil：2 减 2 等于～。Two minus two leaves nought (zero). ④ zero：摄氏～上 5 度 5 degrees above zero centigrade ⑤〈形〉fractional ⑥〈动〉wither and fall：飘～ fade and fall

零部件 língbùjiàn components and parts；accessories and repairs

零存整取存款 língcún zhěngqǔ cúnkuǎn small savings being accumulated for later withdrawals；small deposits for lump withdrawal

零度 língdù zero degree

零工 línggōng ① odd jobs：打～ do odd jobs ② odd jobber；casual labourer；seasonal worker

零活儿 línghuór odd jobs

零件 língjiàn spare parts；spares

零料 língliào fragmentary material；odd piece；remnant；odd materials：～出售 remnant sale

零落 língluò ① be withered and fallen：草木～ bare trees and withered grass ② decline；decay ③ scattered；sporadic：～的枪声 scattered reports of gunfire；sporadic shooting

零卖 língmài ① sell retail；retail ② sell by the piece or in small quantities

零钱 língqián ① small change；change ② pocket money

零敲碎打 língqiāo-suìdǎ do sth. bit by bit (off and on)；adopt a piecemeal approach

零散 língsǎn scattered

零食 língshí between-meal nibbles；snacks：吃～ nibble (eat) between meals

零售 língshòu sell retail；retail：～价 retail price. ～商店 retail shop

零碎 língsuì fragmentary；scrappy；odd；piecemeal：～活儿 odd jobs

零头 língtóu ① the remaining sum beyond the round figure ② remnant (of cloth)

零星 língxīng odd；piecemeal；fragmentary：～土地 odd pieces of land. ～商品 miscellaneous commodities

零讯 língxùn scraps of news

零用 língyòng ① petty expenses；everyday expenses；small incidental expenses：～现金簿 petty cash book ② pocket money

零嘴 língzuǐ between-meal nibbles；snacks

玲 líng

玲珑 línglóng ① ingeniously and delicately wrought；exquisite：小巧～ small and exquisite ② smart；agile；clever and nimble：八面～ sail with every wind；manage to please everybody；good mixer；artful person

聆 líng〈动〉listen；hear

聆教 língjiào benefit by your advice；hear your instructions

聆听 língtīng listen (respectfully)

龄 líng〈名〉① age；years：同～ the same age ② length of time；duration：工～ length of the time employed；length of service；years of service

瓴 líng〈名〉water jar：高屋建～ pour water off a steep roof

铃 líng〈名〉bell：哑～ dumbbell

铃铛 língdang small bell

伶 líng〈名〉actor or actress；player

伶仃 língdīng left alone without help；single；solitary：孤苦～ alone and uncared for

伶俐 língli clever；smart；quick-witted；agile：口齿～ have a ready tongue；speak sensibly and well

翎 líng〈名〉plume；feather：～枝 feather；plume. 孔雀～ peacock plumes (feather)

灵 líng〈形〉① quick；smart；clever；sharp：嗅觉～ have a keen sense of smell ② effective；efficacious：～药 an effective remedy〈名〉③ spirit；soul；intelligence：～魂深处 in the recesses of one's mind；the innermost soul ④ fairy；sprite；elf：～怪 ghosts and spirits ⑤ remains of the deceased；bier：守～ keep vigil beside the bier；stand as guards at the bier

灵便 língbian ① nimble；agile ② easy to handle；handy

灵感 línggǎn inspiration；afflatus：～论 inspirationalism

灵魂 línghún soul；spirit：～的作用 actions of the soul

灵活 línghuó ① quick；agile ② flexible：～预算 flexible budget

灵机 língjī brain wave；sudden inspiration：～一动 have a sudden inspiration；hit upon an idea；get an idea；have a brain wave

灵柩 língjiù coffin containing a corpse；bier

灵快 língkuài nimble；agile

灵敏 língmǐn keen；sensitive；smart；agile；acute

灵巧 língqiǎo clever；smart；dexterous；deft；skilful；ingenious：一双～的手 a pair of clever hands

灵通 língtōng［对消息］well-informed；having quick access to information

灵童 língtóng［西藏佛教］soul boy：转世～的认定 confirmation of the reincarnated soul boy

灵犀 língxī tacit understanding or comprehension：～一点通 meeting of minds；empathize with

灵性 língxìng intelligence；sagacity

灵验 língyàn ① effective；efficacious；② accurate；come (turn) true

lǐng

领 lǐng 〈名〉① neck ② collar；neckband：竖～ stand-up collar ③ outline；main point：纲～ outline 〈动〉④ lead；usher；head：～错了路 head astray ⑤ take；receive；accept；draw：～工资 draw wages. ～奖 receive a prize (an award) ⑥ understand；comprehend；grasp：～悟地点头 nod understandingly ⑦〈量〉一～席 a mat

领班 lǐngbān ① head a work group ② gaffer；foreman

领唱 lǐngchàng ① lead a chorus ②leading singer (of a chorus)

领带 lǐngdài necktie；tie

领导 lǐngdǎo ① lead；exercise leadership：～班子 leading group ② leader；leadership：～艺术 leadership skill. ～骨干 leadership backbone. ～核心 leadership core

领队 lǐngduì ① lead a group ② [体] the leader of a group, sports team, etc.；team leader

领港 lǐnggǎng pilot a ship into or out of a harbour；pilot

领海 lǐnghǎi territorial waters；territorial sea：～管辖权 jurisdiction within territorial waters

领航 lǐngháng pilot；navigate：～图 pilotage chart. ～员 pilot；navigator

领会 lǐnghuì understand；grasp；comprehend；acquire an understanding of：～文件的精神 grasp the essence of the document. ～广度 span of apprehension

领教 lǐngjiào ① [用于接受人的教益或欣赏人的表演时]thanks；much obliged：你说得对，～！～！ Thanks！ You're quite right.；Thanks for your advice ② ask for sb.'s advice；seek sb.'s advice：我有个问题向您～。I wish to consult you on a question ③ have experience of：～够了 have had a plenty of experience of

领空 lǐngkōng territorial space；aerial domain；territorial air；territorial sky

领略 lǐnglüè enjoy the taste of；relish；appreciate：～粤菜风味 relish Guangdong dishes

领情 lǐngqíng feel grateful to sb.；appreciate the kindness

领取 lǐngqǔ take；receive；draw：～工资 draw one's pay. ～营业证 receive a business licence；receipt of business licence

领事 lǐngshì consul：～裁判权 consular jurisdiction；exterritorial jurisdiction；exterritoriality. ～馆 consulate

领受 lǐngshòu accept (kindness,

etc.); receive
领土 lǐngtǔ territory:～完整 territorial integrity
领头 lǐngtóu take the lead; lead; head:～定价 price leadership
领舞 lǐngwǔ ① lead a dancer ② leading dancer
领悟 lǐngwù grasp; realize; comprehend
领先 lǐngxiān take the lead; put… in the lead; lead:遥遥～ hold a safe lead. ～指标 leading indicator
领衔 lǐngxián head the list of signers (of a document); be the first on a name list:最近一部影片由她～主演。She has starred in a recent film.
领袖 lǐngxiù leader
领域 lǐngyù ① territory:～需要 territorial imperative ② domain; sphere; realm; field; sphere
领章 lǐngzhāng collar badge (insignia)
领子 lǐngzi collar

岭 lǐng〈名〉① mountain; ridge:崇山峻～ high mountain ridges ② mountain range

lìng

另 lìng〈形、副〉another; separately; on another occasion:～邮 by separate mail; post separately. ～议 discuss the matter on some other occasion. 在诗坛上～建旗鼓 hoist a new banner in the poetic circles
另案 lìng'àn separate case
另搞一套 lìnggǎo yītào go on one's own way; act in one's own; do what suits oneself
另起炉灶 lìngqǐ lúzào set up a separate kitchen; make a fresh start; make a new plan; start all over again
另行 lìngxíng separately; do separately:～处理 be dealt with separately. ～通知 be notified later
另眼相看 lìngyǎn xiāngkàn see… in a new light; regard sb. with special respect; view sb. in a new, more favourable light

令 lìng〈名〉① order; command; decree:法～ laws and decrees ② season:时～ season of the year〈形〉③ good; excellent:巧言～色 pleasing words and smooth manner ④ [尊称对方的亲属] your:～爱 your daughter ⑤〈动〉make; cause:～人垂涎 make one's mouth water. ～人鼓舞 inspiring; encouraging; heartening. ～人深思 provide food for thought; make one ponder. ～人神往的 enchanting; fascinating; captivating. ～人作呕 make one sick; revolting; nauseating. ～人惊心动魄 shake one to the core
令行禁止 lìngxíng-jìnzhǐ Every order is executed without fail.; If it is an order, it will be carried out.; strict enforcement of orders and prohibitions
令状 lìngzhuàng writ; warrant:～

副本 concurrent writ

令尊 lìngzūn your father

liū

溜 liū 〈动〉① slide; slip; glide: ～下山坡 slide down a slope ② sneak off; slip away: ～走 slink off ③〈形〉sleek; smooth: ～圆 very round

溜边 liūbiān keep to the edge (of a road, river, etc.)

溜冰 liūbīng skating: ～表演 ice show. ～场 (skating) rink

溜达 liūda take a stroll; saunter; go for a walk (stroll)

溜号 liūhào 〈方〉slink off; sneak away

溜须拍马 liūxū-pāimǎ fawn on; shamelessly flatter; toady to

溜之大吉 liūzhīdàjí take to one's heels; make good one's escape; sneak away

溜走 liūzǒu sneak off; steal away; slink off; slope off

liú

刘 Liú a surname

刘海儿 liúhǎir bang; fringe: 她留着～。She wears her hair in bangs.

浏 liú〈形〉① (of wind) swift ② (of water) clear

浏览 liúlǎn glance over; look over; run through; skim through; browse; scan; pass one's eyes over sth.

流 liú 〈动〉① flow: 江河～入海中。Rivers flow into the sea ② spread; circulate: ～传至今 have been passed down to the present ③ degenerate; change for the worse: ～于形式 turn out (be reduced) to be a mere formality 〈名〉④ stream of water; stream; current: 顺～而行 sail with the current ⑤ sth. resembling a stream of water; current: 寒～ cold current ⑥ grade; class; rate: 社会名～ well-known people

流弊 liúbì malpractice; abuse; corrupt practice

流产 liúchǎn ① abortion; miscarriage: 人工～ induced abortion ② miscarry; fail: 计划～了。The plan miscarried.

流畅 liúchàng fluent; flowing; smooth: ～的文体 fluid style; facile style

流程 liúchéng ① a distance travelled by a stream of water ② technological process ③ circuit

流传 liúchuán hand down; be made public; spread; circulate

流窜 liúcuàn flee hither and thither

流窜作案 liúcuàn-zuò'àn go from place to place committing crimes

流动 liúdòng ① flow ② mobile; circulating; floating: ～劳动力 mobile labour. ～资本 circulating capital. ～人口 floating population. ～服务 mobile service. ～售货 mobile vending

流毒 liúdú pernicious influence;

baneful influence; poison:~颇广 spread its poison widely; exert its poisonous influence widely

流芳百世 liúfāng-bǎishì leave a good name for a hundred generations; leave a reputation which will go down to posterity

流感 liúgǎn [医] influenza; flu

流浪 liúlàng roam about; lead a vagrant life

流离失所 liúlí-shīsuǒ become destitute and homeless; leave home and wander about; become displaced; lose one's home

流利 liúlì fluent; smooth; glib:讲~的法语 speak fluent French

流连忘返 liúlián-wàngfǎn enjoy oneself so much that one doesn't want to come back; enjoy oneself so much as to forget to go home; be so enchanted by the scenery as to forget to return

流量 liúliàng volume of flow; rate of flow; flow; discharge

流露 liúlù reveal; betray; show: ~真情 reveal one's true feelings

流落 liúluò roam about destitute; be stranded:~他乡 be stranded in a strange land

流氓 liúmáng hoodlum; rascal; rogue; hooligan: ~恶势力 hoodlums. ~集团 hooligan group. ~活动 hooligan activities. ~团伙 hoodlum gangs

流年 liúnián ① fleeting time ② (in fortune-telling) prediction of a person's luck in a given year

流派 liúpài sect; school; genre; current; shade:新康德主义~[哲学] the shades of neo-Kantianism. 决定~归属 determine the school to which one belongs

流散 liúsàn scatter; drift

流沙 liúshā shifting sands; drifting sands; quicksand

流失 liúshī run off; be washed away:水土~ soil erosion. ~的财政收入 revenue lost

流逝 liúshì pass; elapse:随着时间的~ with the passage of time

流水 liúshuǐ runnig water: ~不腐。Flowing water does not get stale.; Practice keeps one fit. ~帐 running account; day-to-day account. ~线 assembly line. ~作业 streamlined method of work; conveyer system; assembly line method

流淌 liútǎng (of liquid) flow

流通 liútōng circulate:~环节 circulation intermediaries. ~企业 circulation enterprises. ~市场 circulation market. ~手段 medium of circulation. ~领域 circulation domain. ~商品 circulation of commodities

流亡 liúwáng go into exile:~国外 live in exile abroad. ~政府 government-in-exile

流线型 liúxiànxíng streamlined: ~汽车 streamlined car

流向 liúxiàng ① the direction of a current ② the direction of the flow of personnel, commodities, etc.

流行 liúxíng ① prevail; be in vogue:～病 epidemic (disease) ② popular; pop:～歌曲 pop song. ～音乐 pop music. ～音乐会 pop concert

流血 liúxuè lose blood; shed blood; draw blood; bleed

流言 liúyán gossip; rumour:～飞语 rumours and slanders; stories and gossips; lie and slanders; gossips

流域 liúyù river basin; valley

流转税 liúzhuǎnshuì turnover tax system

琉 liú

琉璃 liúlí coloured glaze

硫 liú 〈名〉 sulphur

硫磺 liúhuáng [化] sulphur:～浴池 sulphurated water pools for bathing

硫酸 liúsuān [化] sulphuric acid

留 liú 〈动〉 ① remain; stay:～在家里 stay at home ② detain:拘～ hold in custody ③ reserve; save; keep:我答应给他～个房间。I promised to save a room for him. ④ grow; wear; let grow:～分头 with one's hair parted in the middle ⑤ accept; take:请～下这个小礼物作为纪念。Please accept this little gift as a souvenir. ⑥ leave:～言 leave word

留成 liúchéng preserve; retain; keep:～利润 retained profits. ～外汇 retain a portion of one's foreign exchange; retained foreign exchange earnings

留存 liúcún ① preserve; keep ② remain; be extant

留待 liúdài wait till later

留党察看 liúdǎng chákàn be placed on probation within the Party

留得青山在,不愁没柴烧 liúde qīngshān zài, bùchóu méi cháishāo As long as the green mountains are there one need not worry about firewood

留港时间 liúgǎng shíjiān turnaround time

留后手 liúhòushǒu leave room for manoeuvre

留话 liúhuà leave a message; leave word

留级 liújí fail to go up to the next grade (year); repeat the year's work; repeat courses; stay in the same class:～生 repeater; holdover

留恋 liúliàn ① be reluctant to part (from sb. or with sth.) can't bear to depart from; be unwilling to leave ② have a sentimental attachment for:～旧文化 be obsessed with ancient culture

留难 liúnàn make (raise) difficulties (for sb.); give sb. trouble:百般～ raise all manner of difficulties

留念 liúniàn keep (accept) as a souvenir (memento)

留情 liúqíng show mercy (to):手下～ hold one's hand; show mercy (to); be lenient

留任 liúrèn retain one's post; stay (remain) in office; hold over

留神 liúshén take care (of); on the alert; be careful (of); mind: 请～，不要摔倒。Mind you don't slip.

留守 liúshǒu ① act for the emperor during his absence from the capital ② stay behind to take care of things; stay behind for garrison or liaison duty

留宿 liúsù ① put up a guest for the night ②stay overnight; put up for the night

留心 liúxīn take care (of); pay attention (to); have an eye for

留学 liúxué study abroad; be (go) abroad for further study: ～生 student studying abroad; overseas Chinese students; returned student

留言 liúyán leave word; leave a message; leave a note: ～簿 visitors' book; comments notebook

留意 liúyì ① look out; be careful (of) ② pay attention to; notice: 过马路时要～。Look out when you are crossing the street.

留影 liúyǐng take a photo as a memento; have a picture taken as a souvenir

留有余地 liúyǒu-yúdì leave an appropriate margin for unforeseen circumstances; leave some leeway; allow for unforeseen circumstances; allow (leave) some leeway; make allowance for unexpected needs

留职停薪 liúzhí tíngxīn suspend sb.'s wages while retaining his job; leave without pay; retain job, stop salary

留置权 liúzhìquán right of lien; lien

留滞 liúzhì be detained; be held up

瘤 liú 〈名〉 tumour

liǔ

柳 liǔ 〈名〉 willow

柳编 liǔbiān wickerwork

柳条 liǔtiáo willow twig; wicker: ～筐 wicker basket

liù

六 liù 〈数〉 six

六边形 liùbiānxíng hexagon

六分仪 liùfēnyí sextant

六亲 liùqīn the six relations (father, mother, elder brothers, younger brothers, wife, children): ～不认 not to recognize one's closest relatives; refuse to acknowledge one's relations with one's kinsmen, even one's nearest kin; refuse to have any connection with one's relatives

六神无主 liùshén-wúzhǔ all six vital organs failing to function—out of one's wits; be struck all of a heap; distracted; in a trance; have a terrible upset (shock)

六一国际儿童节 Liù-Yī Guójì Értóngjié International Children's Day (June 1)

lóng

龙 lóng ①〈名〉dragon：～种 dragon's offspring ②〈形〉imperial：～恩 imperial grace

龙船 lóngchuán drangon boat

龙灯 lóngdēng dragon lantern

龙飞凤舞 lóngfēi-fèngwǔ like dragons flying and phoenixes dancing — lively and vigorous flourishes in calligraphy；flourish one's pen quickly and dexterously

龙凤呈祥 lóngfèng-chéngxiáng prosperity brought by the dragon and the phoenix；in extremely good fortune

龙卷风 lóngjuǎnfēng tornado

龙马精神 lóngmǎ jīngshén the spirit of a dragon horse (usu. said in praise of a vigorous old age)

龙套 lóngtào ① costume with dragon designs，worn by groups of soldiers or attendants in traditional opera ② actor playing a walk-on part in traditional opera；utility man；walk-on (part) in old-style opera：跑～ play a walk-on part；play a bit role

龙头 lóngtóu tap；faucet；cock

龙王 lóngwáng the Dragon King；the God of Rain in Chinese mythology

龙虾 lóngxiā lobster

龙眼 lóngyǎn longan

龙舟 lóngzhōu dragon boat：赛～ dragon-boat race

聋 lóng〈形〉deaf

聋哑 lóngyǎ deaf and dumb；deaf and mute：～人 deaf-mute

笼 lóng〈名〉① cage；coop：鸡～ chicken coop ② basket；container：竹～ bamboo basket ③ steamer：蒸～ food steamer

笼屉 lóngtì wooden or bamboo utensil for steaming food；food steamer

笼头 lóngtou headstall；halter

隆 lóng〈形〉① grand ② prosperous；flourishing；thriving：生意兴～。Business is brisk ③ intense；deep；profound

隆冬 lóngdōng the depth of winter；midwinter

隆起 lóngqǐ swell；bulge

隆重 lóngzhòng grand；ceremonious；solemn：～接待 grand reception；be treated to the red carpet. ～开幕 be ceremoniously inaugurated；open with great ceremony

lǒng

垄 lǒng〈名〉① ridge (in a field)：地无一～ have not a strip of land ② raised path between fields

垄断 lǒngduàn monopolize：～资本 monopoly capital. ～价格 monopoly prices. ～市场 corner (monopolize) the market

拢 lǒng〈动〉① approach；reach ② sum up；add up：把帐～一～

sum up the accounts ③ gather (hold) together：把孩子～在怀里 hold a child in one's arms

拢头发 lǒngtóufa comb hair

笼 lǒng〈动〉cover；envelop：烟雾～罩的油田 the smoke-shrouded oilfield
另见 lóng

笼络 lǒngluò win sb. over；be led by the nose；befriend sb. with an ulterior intention；draw sb. over：～人心 try to win people over by any means；cultivate popularity；win the hearts of the people

笼统 lǒngtǒng in an indiscriminating fashion；in general terms；lump … together as … vaguely；indiscriminatingly；generally：～的声明 sweeping statement. ～地说 generally speaking；general statement

笼罩 lǒngzhào cover；envelop；shroud：云雾～的山峰 peak shrouded in cloud and mist

lòng

弄 lòng〈名〉lane；alley；alleyway：里～ lanes and alleys；neighbourhood
另见 nòng

弄堂 lòngtáng lane；alley；alleyway

lóu

楼 lóu〈名〉① a storied building：教学～ teaching building ② storey；floor：三～ second floor［英国］；third floor［美国］③ superstructure；tower：城～ city-gate tower

楼层 lóucéng storey；floor

楼房 lóufáng building of two or more storeys

楼阁 lóugé pavilions：～式的木塔 tower-like wooden pagodas

楼盘"烂尾" lóupánlànwěi no definte date for the completion of a building's inspection and approval by the authorities concerned due to insufficient funds or substandard quality

楼堂馆所 lóutáng-guǎnsuǒ office buildings，large halls，hotels，and guest houses

楼上 lóushàng upstairs

楼梯 lóutī staircase；stairs

楼下 lóuxià downstairs

喽 lóu

喽罗 lóuluó ① rank-and-file of a band of outlaws ② lackey；flunkey；underling

lǒu

搂 lǒu〈动〉clasp in one's arms；embrace；hug：她把孩子～在怀里。She held a child in her arms.

搂抱 lǒubào embrace；hug；hold in one's arm；cuddle

篓 lǒu〈名〉basket：字纸～ wastepaper basket

lòu

漏 lòu〈动〉① leak; drip; escape:水从管子中～出。The water leaked from the pipe ② disclose; divulge; leak:注意，别～风! Not a word to anyone, mind! ③ bc missing; leave out:印刷工人把这一段～了一行。The printer has left out one line from this paragraph.

漏电 lòudiàn leak electricity

漏洞 lòudòng ① leak ② defect; hole; flaw; loophole:～百出 full of loopholes (contradictions); with gasping holes everywhere. 堵塞～ plug (stop) up a loophole

漏斗 lòudǒu funnel; filler

漏风 lòufēng leak out; be disclosed (divulged)

漏缝 lòufèng crack; leak

漏税 lòushuì evade payment of a tax; evade taxation; defraud the revenue; tax dodging

漏网 lòuwǎng escape from the net; (of criminal, enemy, etc.) escape unpunished:～之鱼 (as) fish escaping from the net

镂 lòu〈动〉carve; engrave

镂空 lòukōng ① hollow out ② perforation; openwork; fretwork

露 lòu〈动〉show; display; reveal
另见 lù

露丑 lòuchǒu make a fool of oneself in public

露脸 lòuliǎn become known (by doing sth.); be successful; shine

露马脚 lòumǎjiǎo reveal one's cloven hoof; let the cat out of the bag; give the game away; show one's hand; leave a great many holes

露面 lòumiàn appear in public; make public appearances

露馅儿 lòuxiànr let the cat out of the bag; give the game away; spill the beans

陋 lòu〈形〉① plain; ugly:丑～ ugly ② narrow; humble; mean:～室 a humble room ③ mean; low; vulgar; corrupt:鄙～ vulgar ④ (of knowledge) scanty; shallow:～识 scanty knowledge

陋规 lòuguī objectionable (evil) practices

陋俗 lòusú undesirable customs

陋习 lòuxí crusted habits; corrupt customs; bad customs

lú

庐 lú〈名〉hut; cottage

庐山真面目 lúshān zhēnmiànmù what Mt. Lushan really looks — the truth about a person or a matter; the real face of Mt. Lushan; the truth; one's true character (identity)

炉 lú ①〈名〉stove; furnace ②

〈量〉heat：一～钢 a heat of steel
炉火纯青 lúhuǒ-chúnqīng The stove fire is pure green — perfection in one's studies.；high degree of professional proficiency；make a masterly application of；reach (attain) perfection in (painting, acting, etc.)；in a masterful way
炉料 lúliào furnace charge；furnace burden
炉前工 lúqiángōng blast-furnace man；furnaceman
炉灶 lúzào kitchen range；cooking range；kitchen stove：重起～ make a fresh start；start afresh
炉渣 lúzhā slag；cinder
卢 Lú〈名〉a surname
卢比 lúbǐ ruppee
卢布 lúbù rouble
卢沟桥事变 Lúgōuqiáoshìbiàn Lugouqiao Incident (July 7, 1937)
芦 lú〈名〉reed：～苇荡 reed marshes

lǔ

卤 lǔ〈名〉① bittern ② gravy：打～面 noodles served with this gravy ③〈动〉stew in soy sauce：～肉 pot-stewed large cuts of meat
卤味 lǔwèi pot-stewed fowl, meat, etc.；served cold
虏 lǔ〈名〉① capitive；prisoner of war ② slave ③ enemy〈动〉④ capiture；take prisoner
虏获 lǔhuò capture (men and arms)
掳 lǔ〈动〉capture
掳掠 lǔlüě plunder；pillage；loot
鲁 lǔ〈形〉① dull；stupid ② rash；rough；rude：～莽的人 rash man；blundering hothead
鲁班门前弄斧（班门弄斧） lǔbān ménqián nòngfǔ (bānmén-nòngfǔ) take the adze from Lu Ban the Great Carpenter—overestimate oneself；teach one's grandmother how to suck eggs
鲁莽 lǔmǎng crude and rash；rash；reckless；heady；headlong：～驾驶 reckless driving. ～行事 act recklessly；take rash action

lù

鹿 lù〈名〉deer
鹿茸 lùróng pilose antler
鹿死谁手 lùsǐ-shuíshǒu At whose hand will the deer die.；who will win the prize or gain supremacy：～尚难预料。It's still hard to tell who will emerge victorious.
鹿砦 lùzhài［军］abatis
麓 lù〈名〉the foot of a hill or mountain
辘 lù
辘轳 lùlú hoisting tackle；jigger；windlass；winch：摇～取水 crank a winch to bring up wa-

ter from a well

辘辘 lùlù 〈象〉rumble：车轮的～声 the rumbling of cart wheels. 饥肠～ so hungry that one's stomach rumbles；one's stomach growling from hungers

路 lù 〈名〉① road；street；way；route；path ② journey；distance：～子越走越窄 travelling along a narrowing trail ③ way；means：财～ source of income ④ line；sequence；logic：思～ train of thought ⑤ route：10～公共汽车 No. 10 bus ⑥ kind；sort；grade：这～人 this kind of persons

路标 lùbiāo ① road sign ②［军］route sign (marking)

路不拾遗 lùbùshíyí No one picks up articles on the street — a peaceful and prosperous time.；No one picks up anything on the road and claims it as his own.

路程 lùchéng distance travelled；journey

路灯 lùdēng road (street) lamp

路段 lùduàn a section of a railway or highway

路费 lùfèi travelling expenses

路风 lùfēng work style of the railway workers；quality of the railway service

路过 lùguò pass (go by) on the way：他们～我的家。They passed my house on the way.

路基 lùjī roadbed；bed

路考 lùkǎo road test (a test to qualify the examinee for a driver's licence in which the examinee actually operates an automobile on a road)

路面 lùmiàn road surface；pavement

路牌 lùpái street nameplate

路人 lùrén passerby；stranger

路途 lùtú ① road；way ② way；journey

路线 lùxiàn ① route ② line：～斗争 line struggle

路椅 lùyǐ roadside bench

路遥知马力，日(事)久见人心 lùyáo zhī mǎlì，rì(shì)jiǔ jiàn rénxīn A long journey tests a horse's strength，a long acquaintance shows you a man's heart.；As distance tests a horse's strength，so time reveals a person's heart.；As a long road tests a horse's strength，so a long task proves a person's heart

路障 lùzhàng roadblock；barricade

路子 lùzi ① way；approach；means ② social connections；pull

路径 lùjìng route；way；path：～分析 path analysis

露 lù 〈名〉① dew：甘～ sweet dew ② fruit juice；beverage distilled from flowers，fruit，or leaves：果子～ fruit syrup ③〈动〉show；bare；lay bare；betray：暴～思想 bare one's thoughts

露出 lùchū show；reveal：～笑容 reveal a smile. ～真面目 show one's colours

露骨 lùgǔ barefaced；undisguised；

outright; outspoken:说话～ speak in undisguised terms. ～地宣扬 naked publicity

露水 lùshuǐ dew

露天 lùtiān in the open (air):～电影院 open-air cinema. ～交易会场 fair grounds. ～开采 opencast mining; surface (open-cut) mining

露头角 lùtóujiǎo (of a young person) begin to show talent or ability; cut (make) a figure; figure in:崭～ cut a fine figure

露营 lùyíng encamp; camp (out)

露珠 lùzhū dewdrop

戮 lù 〈动〉① kill; slay:杀～ slaughter ② unite; join:～力 unite; join hands

绿 lù

绿林 lùlín the greenwood—brigands; outlaws

录 lù ①〈名〉record; register:工商行名～ directory 〈动〉② record; write down; copy:实况～音 on-the-spot recording ③ employ; enroll; hire:～用 take sb. on the staff; employ

录取 lùqǔ enroll; admit:～分数 acceptance cut-off point. ～名额 number of enrollees. ～通知书 admission notice

录像 lùxiàng video tape recording:～带 videotape. ～盘 videodisc. ～机 TV video recorder; video tape recorder. ～片 video tape; videotape; video film

录音 lùyīn sound recording:～磁带 audio-tape. ～电话机 telegraphone. ～机 (tape) recorder. 放～ play back the recording. 实况～ live-recording

录影 lùyǐng record a scene video

录用 lùyòng employ; take sb. on the staff

录制 lùzhì make audio tapes or videotapes:～电视连续剧 tape television serial plays. ～流行歌曲 manufacture tapes of popular songs

禄 lù 〈名〉official salary in feudal China; emolument:～位 emolument and position

碌 lù 〈形〉① commonplace; mediorce:庸～ mediorce and unambitious ② busy

碌碌 lùlù ① mediorce; commonplace ② busy with miscellaneous work:～半生 toil half a lifetime

陆 lù 〈名〉land

陆地 lùdì dry land; land

陆军 lùjūn land force; army

陆路 lùlù land route:走～ go by land. ～交通 overland communication; land communication. ～运输 overland freight

陆相 lùxiàng [考] continental facies

陆续 lùxù in succession; one after another

陆运保险 lùyùn bǎoxiǎn land transportation insurance; land transit insurance

陆战队 lùzhànduì marine corps;

marines

lú

驴 lú〈名〉ass；donkey

驴车 lúchē donkey cart

驴唇不对马嘴 lúchún bù duì mǎzuǐ a doney's lips can not fit into a horse's mouth；be beside the point；irrelevant answer

驴打滚 lúdǎgǔn a form of usury in the old society，the borrower having to pay interest on interest；snowballing usury

lǚ

旅 lǚ ①〈动〉travel；tour；stay away from home：～居国外 stay abroad；expatriate oneself〈名〉②［军］brigade ③ army：军～之事 military affairs

旅伴 lǚbàn travelling companion；fellow traveller

旅程 lǚchéng journey；itinerary：～费用 expenses while in transit

旅费 lǚfèi travelling expenses：～补助 travel grant

旅馆 lǚguǎn inn；hotel

旅客 lǚkè traveller；passenger；［游客］tourist；［住旅馆的］hotel guest：～登记簿 hotel register. 入(出)境～ incoming (outgoing) traveller. 运送～ passenger services. ～组合游览 packed tours

旅途 lǚtú joruney；trip

旅行 lǚxíng travel；take a trip；tour：～社 travel service；tourist bureau. 乘飞机～ travel by plane. ～意外险 travel accident insurance. ～支票 traveller's checks

旅游 lǚyóu tour：～车 tour bus；touring car. ～事业 tourism. ～图 tour maps

屡 lǚ〈副〉repeatedly：～建奇勋 establish unusual merits repeatedly

屡次 lǚcì time and again；repeatedly：～三番 time and again；again and again；over and over；often；frequent

屡犯(累犯) lǚfàn (lěifàn) ① recidivism ② recidivist；repetitive offenders

屡见不鲜 lǚjiàn-bùxiǎn (of) frequent occurrence；(of) common sight：～的事 event of frequent (common) occurrence

屡教不改 lǚjiào-bùgǎi refuse to correct one's mistakes despite repeated warnings；do not reform after repeated education

捋 lǚ〈动〉stroke
另见 luō

捋胡子 lǚhúzi stroke one's beard

铝 lǚ〈名〉aluminium

铝制品 lǚzhìpǐn aluminium products

侣 lǚ〈名〉companion；associate：伴～ companion；partner

缕 lǚ ①〈名〉thread：千丝万～的联系 link to sb. or sth. in a hundred and one ways；a thousand and one links ②〈副〉in fine detail ③〈量〉strand; lock; wisp: 一～烟 a wisp of smoke from kitchen chimney

缕缕 lǚlǚ continuously: 山村炊烟～上升 Wisps of smoke rose from the mountain village chimneys.

缕析 lǚxī make a detailed analysis; undertake a detailed analysis

履 lǚ〈名〉① shoe: 布～ cloth shoes ② footstep: 步～维艰 walk with difficulty〈动〉③ walk (on); tread on: ～冰 walk on ice ④ fulfil; honour; carry out: ～行职务 discharge one's function

履带 lǚdài caterpillar tread; track

履历 lǚlì ① record; antecedents: 他的～不好。His record is against him ② personal autobiography: ～书 *curriculum vitae.*

履行 lǚxíng carry out; fulfil; perform; discharge: ～保证书 performance bond. ～合同 discharge (performance) of contract. ～诺言 fulfil (live up) one's promise; keep one's word. ～职责 discharge (do) one's duty. ～入党手续 go through the procedure of admission to the Party. ～诉讼手续 discharge of proceedings

履约 lǚyuē keep a promise, pledge, agreement, appointment, etc.

lǜ

率 lǜ〈名〉proportion; rate: 利～ rate of interest

虑 lǜ ①〈动〉consider; think over; ponder: 深谋远～的指挥员 judicious and farsighted commander ②〈名〉concern; worry; anxiety: 不足为～ give no cause for anxiety

滤 lǜ〈动〉filter; strain: 用沙子～水 filter the water through the sand. 过～嘴香烟 filter-tipped cigarette

律 lǜ ①〈名〉law; statute; rule: 刑～ criminal law discipline ②〈动〉keep under control; restrain; discipline: ～己 govern one's own conduct

律例 lǜlì laws and precedents; statutes

律师 lǜshī lawyer; attonery; counselor; barrister: ～与委托人的关系 lawyer-client relationship. 当～ practise law. 请～ engage a lawyer. ～代理权 power of attorney

律诗 lǜshī [古典文学] *lüshi*, a poem of eight lines, each containing five or seven characters, with a strict tonal pattern and rhyme scheme; regulated verse

绿 lǜ〈形〉green: ～灯 green light

绿茶 lǜchá green tea

绿肥 lǜféi [农] green manure

绿化 lǜhuà make (a place) green (by planting trees, etc.); green:～地带 greenbelt. ～费 afforestation fees

绿色长城 lǜsè chángchéng green Great Wall, the large-scale forest belt, being built to ward off wind and stop sand incursions, that extends from Xinjiang in the west to Heilongjiang in the east

luán

孪 luán 〈形〉twin

孪生 luánshēng twin:～子 twins

luǎn

卵 luǎn 〈名〉egg; ovum

卵巢 luǎncháo [生理]ovary

卵翼 luǎnyì cover with wings as in brooding; shield; protection; defence:～之下 under the wings of; be shielded by

luàn

乱 luàn ①〈名〉disorder; confusion; chaos; upheaval; riot; turmoil:叛～ armed rebellion; mutiny ②〈副〉blindly; wildly; at random; in disorder; in a confusion:～干 act recklessly ③〈形〉confused; disordered:～收费 arbitrary collection of fees; indiscriminate charges ④〈动〉confuse; mix up; jumble:以假～真 mix the spurious with the genuine

乱发(奖金) luànfā (jiǎngjīn) indiscriminate issuing bonuses

乱纷纷 luànfēnfēn disorderly; confused; chaotic

乱花 luànhuā waste; squander; dissipate:～钱 squander money

乱拉(资金) luànlā (zījīn) dishonest acquisition of and misuse of funds

乱伦(行为) luànlún (xíngwéi) incest behaviour

乱七八糟 luànqībāzāo topsy-turvy; in a terrible muddle; at sixes and sevens

乱上项目 luàn shàng xiàngmù undertaking unauthorized projects

乱世 luànshì (in) troubled (troublous) times; (in) turbulent days

乱说 luànshuō speak carelessly or foolishly; talk in a scatter-brained way; talk nonsense; make irresponsible remarks

乱摊成本 luàntān chéngběn unjustified additions to production costs; indiscriminate additions to production costs

乱摊派 luàntānpài ① unjustified financial levies ② imposition of production quotas:向农民～ imposition of production quotas for peasants

乱弹琴 luàntánqín act or talk like a fool; talk nonsense

乱套 luàntào create a mess; mess up; disrupt; fluster:他心里乱了套。He was flustered.

乱用 luànyòng ① waste;

squander; dissipate ② misuse; abuse:～讽刺 the abuse of satire

乱糟糟 luànzāozāo 〈形〉 ① chaotic; messy; cluttered ② in disorder; in confusion; in a mess:他们的房间总是～的。Their room is always in a mess.

乱子 luànzi ① disturbance; trouble:出～ lead to trouble; go wrong ② accident

lüè

掠 lüè 〈动〉 ① plunder; pillage; loot:～卖奴隶者 slave hunter ② move lightly (over); sweep past; brush past:闪电～过夜空。Lightning swept the night sky.

掠夺 lüèduó plunder; pillage; loot; rob:～婚 marriage by capture; kidnapping marriage

掠过 lüèguò ① sweep over; skim over:蜻蜓～水面。The dragonflies skimmed over the water ② [念头]flash through:她脑中～一个念头。An idea flashed through her mind.

掠取 lüèqǔ seize; grab; plunder

掠影 lüèyǐng glimpses (written):访美～ sketches of a trip to America

略 lüè ①〈形〉 brief; sketchy:～论 brief discussion ②〈副〉 somewhat; slightly:～有出入 vary slightly 〈名〉③ sketch; summary; brief account; outline:～史论 outline history ④ strategy; scheme; plan:方～ overall plan 〈动〉⑤ capture; seize:侵～ invade; commit aggression against ⑥ omit; delete; leave out

略表寸心 lüèbiǎo cùnxīn just to show my gratitude

略去 lüèqù leave out; omit; delete

略胜一筹 lüèshèng-yīchóu be a stroke (notch, cut) above; be slightly better (than); just a little better; slightly better

略图 lüètú sketch map; sketch; schematic diagram

略微 lüèwēi slightly; a little; somewhat

略为 lüèwéi slightly; a little; somewhat

略语 lüèyǔ abbreviation

lún

沦 lún 〈动〉 ① sink:沉～ sink into depravity ② be reduced to; fall; decline:一个独立国家～为半殖民地 degeneration of an independent country into a semi-colony

沦落 lúnluò fall low; be reduced to poverty:～风尘 be driven to prostitution; become a courtesan. ～街头 become destitute and drift about the street; become a tramp (beggar) in the street

沦丧 lúnsàng be lost; be ruined:道德～ decay of morals

沦亡 lúnwáng (of a country) be annexed (subjugated)

沦陷 lúnxiàn be occupied (by enemy troops):～区 enemy-occupied area

轮 lūn〈名〉① wheel:历史车～ the wheel of history ② wheel-like object; ring; disc:光～ halo ③ steamboat; streamer:江～ river streamer ④〈动〉take turns:～到他了。It is his turn. ⑤〈量〉一～红日 a red sun. 新的一～外交谈判 a new round of diplomatic talks

轮班 lúnbān by turns; in shifts; in relays; in rotation

轮船 lúnchuán steamer; steamship; steamboat

轮伐期 lúnfáqī timber rotation period

轮番提价 lúnfāntíjià price spiral

轮换 lúnhuàn change by turns; rotate

轮回 lúnhuí samsara; transmigration

轮奸 lúnjiā commit rape in succession

轮垦 lúnkěn［农］shifting cultivation

轮空 lúnkōng［体］bye:在第一轮比赛抽签～ draw a first-round bye

轮廓 lúnkuò outline; lineation; profile; contour:脸的～ outline (contour) of a face

轮流 lúnliú by turns; by rotation; alternately:～值班 take turns on duty; be on duty by turns. ～作东 be host by turns (in turn). ～坐庄 be bankers by turn; rule in turn

轮胎 lúntāi tyre

轮休 lúnxiū days off in rotation

轮训 lúnxùn training in (by) rotation

轮作(种) lúnzuò (zhòng)［农］crop rotation:～顺序 crop succession. ～制 rotation system

轮子 lúzi wheel

伦 lún〈名〉① human relationships; ethics:～常 human relationships ② logic; order:语无～次 speak incoherently ③ peer; match; the same kind

伦常名教 lúncháng-míngjiào human relationships and the ethical code; moral principles and ethical teachings

伦纪 lúnjì proper order of human relations

伦理 lúnlǐ ethics; moral principles; ethical codes and mores:～认同 ethical identification. ～学 ethics; moral philosophy. ～学家 moral philosopher. ～主义 moralism

lùn

论 lùn〈动〉① discuss; argue; discourse:～述 elaborate ② regard; consider; mention:相提并～ mention in the same breath ③ weigh; decide on:按质～价 fixing price according to quality〈名〉④ view; opinion; statement:～点 argument ⑤ dissertation; essay ⑥ theory:唯心～ idealism

论点 lùndiǎn point; argument; thesis

论调 lùndiào [贬义] tone; argument:这种～是站不住脚的。Such argument doesn't hold water.

论断 lùnduàn thesis; proposition; conclusion; inference; judgment:～方法 methods of reasoning

论功行赏 lùngōng-xíngshǎng reward one according to his merit; render to Caesar that which is Caesar's; dispense rewards or honours accordig to merit; award people according to their contributions; be entitled to benefits in line with one's achievements

论据 lùnjù grounds of argument; grounds; argument

论述 lùnshù discuss; deal with; discourse on; elaborate; elucidate; dissertate; exposition; explication

论坛 lùntán forum; tribune [常用于报刊的名字]; forum

论题 lùntí [逻] proposition; subject matter

论文 lùnwén treatise; thesis; paper; dissertation:毕业～ graduation thesis. 博士～ doctoral dissertation. ～集 collected papers on. 学术～ academic thesis

论战 lùnzhàn debate; polemics:就…进行公开～ be engaged in open polemics on…

论证 lùnzhèng ① expound and prove; theorize; substantiate; demonstrate; proof ② [逻] demonstration

论著 lùnzhù learned treatises; treatises; works:关于哲学的～ works on philosophy

论资排辈 lùnzī-páibèi go according to seniority

论罪 lùnzuì decide on the nature of the guilt:按贪污～ be found guilty of corruption

luō

捋 luō 〈动〉 tuck; roll
另见 lǚ

捋起袖子 luōqǐ xiùzi tuck up one's sleeves

啰 luō
另见 luó

啰唆 luōsuō ① verbose; long-windy; tedious; wordy:她说话太～。She is too wordy. ② overelaborate; troublesome:这事情真～。This is really troublesome.

luó

螺 luó 〈名〉 spiral shell

螺钿 luódiàn [工艺美术] mother-of-pearl inlay

螺钉 luódīng screw:木～ wood screw; screwnail

螺丝 luósī screw

螺旋 luóxuán ① spiral ② screw:～桨 (screw) propeller; [飞机的] airscrew:～式通货膨胀 spiral inflation

骡 luó 〈名〉 mule:～子 mule

罗 luó〈名〉① a net for catching birds:～网 trap; net ② screen; sieve; sifter〈动〉③ collect; gather together:收～资料 collect data ④ catch birds with a net:～雀 catch sparrows with net ⑤ display; spread out:～布 spread out; set out

罗锅儿 luóguōr ① hunchbacked; humpbacked ② hunchback; humpback

罗列 luóliè enumerate; list:～现象 list phenomena. ～事实 enumerate the facts

罗绮 luóqí damask

罗纱 luóshā silk gauze

罗网 luówǎng net; snare; trap:自投～ walk into a trap

罗织 luózhī frame up:～罪名 cook up charges; gather damaging imformation on sb.

罗致 luózhì enlist the services of; recruit:～人材 enlist the services of talents

逻 luó

逻辑 luójì logic:～学 logic. 合乎～ be logical

萝 luó trailing plants:藤～ Chinese wistaria

萝卜 luóbo turnip radish; radish

箩 luó〈名〉bamboo basket

锣 luó〈名〉gong

锣鼓 luógǔ gong and drum:～喧天 deafening sound of gongs and drums; a deafening sound of gongs and drums

luǒ

裸 luǒ〈形〉naked; nude; bare; exposed

裸露 luǒlù exposed; uncovered:～土地 naked land

裸体 luǒtǐ naked; nude

luò

落 luò〈动〉① fall; drop:坠～ drop down; sink into ② go down; set:潮水～了。The tide is low ③ lower:把帘子～下来 lower the blinds ④ decline; come down:衰～ go downhill; decline ⑤ fall behind; lag behind:～伍 fall behind the ranks; behind the times ⑥ leave behind; stay behind:～下痕迹 leave a trace behind
另见 là

落榜 luòbǎng fail in an entrance examination; fail as a candidate

落笔 luòbǐ put pen to paper; start to write or draw

落泊(魄) luòbó(pò) be down and out; be in dire straits

落差 luòchā ① drop in elevation (between two points in a stream) ② head drop (in hydroelectric power plants)

落成 luòchéng completion (of a building); be brought to completion:～典礼 inauguration ceremony

落第 luòdì fall in an imperial examination

落地 luòdì ① fall to the ground ②(of a baby) be born

落后 luòhòu ① fall (lag) behind ② backward：技术～ backward in technique

落户 luòhù settle down; take up one's abode; domicile oneself in (at) a place

落花有意，流水无情 luòhuā yǒuyì，liúshuǐ wúqíng Shedding petals, the waterside flower pines for love, while the heartless brook babbles on —unrequited love.; While the drooping flowers pine for love, the heartless brook babbles on.

落脚 luòjiǎo stay (for a time); stop over; put up

落空 luòkōng come to naught; become futile：计划～。The plan came to naught. 有～的危险。There is the danger that nothing may come of it.

落款 luòkuǎn write the names of the sender and recipient on a gift, letter or painting; inscribe (a gift, etc.)

落泪 luòlèi shed tears; weep

落难 luònàn become a refugee; be in reduced circumstances：～书生 an ill-fated scholar

落实 luòshí carry out to the letter; take concrete measures to ensure the fulfilment of; implement; fulfil：～政策 implement a policy

落水 luòshuǐ ① fall into water ② fall into evil ways

落汤鸡 luòtāngjī as bedraggled as a drenched chicken; like a drowned cat (rat); soaked through

落网 luòwǎng (of a criminal) be caught; be arrested; be brought to justice; be captured

落伍 luòwǔ fall behind the ranks; straggle; drop behind; drop out

落选 luòxuǎn fail in an election; not be elected; lose an election

落座 luòzuò take a seat (in restaurants, theatres, etc.)

骆 luò

骆驼 luòtuó camel

络 luò

络绎 luòyì in an endless stream; without interruption; continuously：～不绝 come and go in an endless stream; go to and fro in constant streams; a continuous stream; proceed and come in a steady stream

M m

mā

抹 mā 〈动〉 wipe；rub：～桌子 wipe a table clean
另见 mǒ

抹布 mābù rag

抹脸 māliǎn straighten one's face；put on a stern expression：抹不下脸 find it difficult to be strict with sb.

妈 mā 〈名〉 mother；mum；mummy：舅～（maternal）aunt（wife of mother's brother）

妈妈 māma mother；ma；mum；mummy

má

麻 má ①〈名〉general term for hemp，jute，flax，etc.：大～ hemp. 亚～ flax. 黄～ jute ②〈动〉numb；tingle：手发～ have tingle in one's hands ③〈形〉pockmarked；pitted；spotted：～脸 a pockmarked face

麻包 mábāo gunnybag；gunnysack；burlap sack；sack

麻痹 mábì ① paralysis；palsy：小儿～ infantile paralysis ② lull；lull the vigilance；blunt；immobilize；paralyze；benumb：～大意 lack of vigilance；slacken in vigilance；drop one's guard；lower one's guard and become careless；be off one's guard. ～人民的警惕性 blunt the vigilance of the people

麻布 mábù linen；gunny（cloth）

麻袋 mádài gunnybag；gunnysack；burlap sack

麻烦 máfan ① troublesome；cumbersome：对不起，～你了。Sorry to have troubled you so much ② trouble；bother：找～ look for trouble；ask for trouble；find fault with；carp at

麻酱 májiàng sesame paste

麻将 májiàng mah-jong(g)

麻利 máli quick and neat；deft；dexterous：干活～ be a quick and neat worker；be a dexterous worker；work dexterously

麻木 mámù numb；insensible：～不仁 apathetic；unfeeling

麻雀 máquè（house）sparrow

麻纱 máshā ① yarn of ramie，flax，etc ② cambric；haircords

麻线 máxiàn flaxen thread；linen thread

麻醉 mázuì ① anaesthesia；narcosis：～剂 anaesthetic；narcotic. ～品 narcotic；drugs. ～品管制 narcotic control ② anaesthetize；poison；dope：～精神 poison one's minds

mǎ

马 mǎ〈名〉horse:急促的～蹄声quick hoof beats

马鞍 mǎ'ān saddle:～形 saddle-shaped; shape of a saddle; U-shape. ～点 "saddle point"

马不停蹄 mǎbùtíngtí without a moment's respite; nonstop:他们～地赶到工地。They rushed nonstop to the worksite.

马车 mǎchē carriage; horse-drawn cart; cart

马大哈 mǎdàhā ① careless; forgetful ② careless person; scatterbrain

马到成功 mǎdào-chénggōng win success immediately upon one's arrival; carry out one's mission quickly; win instant success; gain an immediate success (victory)

马褂 mǎguà mandarin jacket (worn over a gown)

马后炮 mǎhòupào belated effort:放～ make a belated effort. ～的声明 a belated statement

马虎 mǎhu careless; casual; perfunctory; skimpy:～了事 be perfunctory in doing sth.; get sth. done in a slapdash (sloppy) manner; skimp; palter with sth.

马甲 mǎjiǎ sleeveless garment

马脚 mǎjiǎo sth. that gives the game away

马克思主义 mǎkèsīzhǔyì Marxism:～经典作家 author of Marxist classics

马口铁 mǎkǒutiě tinplate; galvanized iron

马拉松 mǎlāsōng marathon:～赛跑 marathon (race)

马路 mǎlù road; street; avenue:逛～ stroll around the streets; go window-shopping

马奶 mǎnǎi mare's milk

马屁 mǎpì flattery; soft soap; soft thing:～精 adulator; bootlicker

马前卒 mǎqiánzú pawn; foot soldier; cat's-paw

马上 mǎshàng at once; immediately; right away:我们～去看他吧。Let's go to see him right away.

马术 mǎshù horsemanship

马桶 mǎtǒng nightstool; stool; commode:抽水～ flush toilet

马戏 mǎxì circus:～团 circus (troupe)

马掌 mǎzhǎng horseshoes

马子 mǎzi ① nightstool; closestool; commode; chamber pot ② bandit; brigand

玛 mǎ

玛瑙 mǎnǎo agate

码 mǎ ①〈名〉a sign or thing indicating number; code:数～ numeral; number ②〈量〉[指一件事或一类的事]:两～事 two different things ③ yard (yd.)

码放 mǎfàng put or keep things in good order

码头 mǎtóu wharf; quay; dock; pier; jetty:～工人 docker; longshoreman. ～费 dockage. ～栈单 dock warrant. ～交货

ex dock

吗 mǎ
另见 má,ma

吗啡 mǎfēi morphine

蚂 mǎ

蚂蜂窝 mǎfēngwō wasp nest, a metaphor for fierce persons or units that one dare not provoke

蚂蚁啃骨头 mǎyǐ kěn gǔtou ants gnawing at a bone — a concentration of small machines on a big job; plod away at a big job bit by bit

mà

骂 mà 〈动〉① abuse; swear at: ～人 abusing people; curse; call sb. names ② chide; scold: ～几句 mouth a few phrases scolding sb.

骂街 màjiē shout abuses in the street; call people names in public; curse without naming names

骂骂咧咧 màmà-liēliē be foul-mouthed; fairly snarl; intersperse one's talk with curses

骂人 màrén abuse; swear at; call one names; give one a scolding; rail at: ～的话 abusive language; curse; a word of abuse

ma

嘛 ma 〈助动〉①［表示道理显而易见］:有意见就提～! Make a criticism (comment; suggestion) you want! ②［用在句子停顿处,唤起对下文的注意］:他～,就不用亲自去了。As for him, I don't think he has to go in person.

吗 ma 〈助动〉①［用在句末表示疑问］:明天他们来～? Will they come tomorrow? ②［用在句中停顿处,点出话题］:煤～,还是省着用吧。Coal, of course, must be saved in consumption.
另见 má,mǎ

mái

埋 mái 〈动〉bury; lay; cover: ～雷 lay mines
另见 mán

埋藏 máicáng lie (hide) in the earth; bury: ～的财物 hidden wealth

埋伏 máifu lie in wait for; ambush; hide: ～兵马 place soldiers in ambush

埋名 máimíng conceal one's identity; keep one's identity hidden; live incognito

埋没 máimò ① cover up; bury ② stifle; neglect: ～人才 stifle the talented; neglect talented people

埋设 máishè fit sth. underground

埋头 máitóu bury oneself in; be engrossed in: ～苦干 immerse oneself in hard work; be engrossed in hard work; bury oneself in work. ～业务 bury head in profession; immerse in vocational work; engross oneself in vocational work

埋葬 máizàng ① bury; inter:～风俗 burial custom ② wreck; wipe off

mǎi

买 mǎi 〈动〉buy; purchase

买得(不)起 mǎide (bu) qǐ can (not) afford (to buy):我～这件皮衣。I can't afford this fur coat.

买方 mǎifāng buying part; buyer:～市场 buyer's market

买好 mǎihǎo try to win sb. 's favour; ingratiate oneself with; play up to

买价 mǎijià buying price

买空卖空 mǎikōng-màikōng speculate on the stock market; fictitious bargain; buy on margin and sell short; cross trade

买路钱 mǎilùqián ① paper money thrown on the road during a funeral procession ② toll money (formerly asked for by highwaymen)

买卖 mǎimài buying and selling; deal; business; bargain; transaction:～合同 sales contract. ～公平 pay fairly for what you buy; be fair in buying and selling; fair dealings in business. ～股票 gambling on the stock exchange. 做～ do business

买期保值 mǎiqī bǎozhí hedge buying

买通 mǎitōng grease sb. 's hand; bribe; buy over; buy off

买帐 mǎizhàng acknowledge the superiority or seniority of; show respect for

买主 mǎizhǔ buyer; customer; purchaser:～意图 buyer's intention

mài

麦 mài 〈名〉wheat:荞～ buckwheat

麦秸 màijiē wheat straw

麦精 màijīng malt extract

麦克风 màikèfēng microphone; mike

麦浪 màilàng rippling wheat; billowing wheat fields

麦片 màipiàn oat meal

麦乳精 màirǔjīng extract of malt and milk; malted milk

麦收 màishōu wheat harvest

麦穗 màisuì ear of wheat; wheat ear

麦芽糖 màiyátáng malt sugar; maltose

麦子 màizi wheat

卖 mài 〈动〉① sell:买贱～贵 buying cheap and selling dear ② betray:～国协定 traitorous pact

卖出价 màichūjià selling rate

卖方 màifāng seller:～市场 seller's market

卖乖 màiguāi show off one's cleverness

卖关子 màiguānzi (stop a story at a climax to) keep the listeners in suspense; keep people guessing

卖国 màiguó betray one's country; sell out the country:～罪 crime of treason

卖价 màijià selling price

卖空 màikōng "short selling"; bear; short sale

卖力 màilì spare no effort; do one's best; exert one's utmost; with might and main; work overtime to do sth.

卖命 màimìng give one's life (unworthily) to; work oneself to death for sb.; work oneself to the bone for sb.; sweat blood

卖弄 màinòng parade; show off; make a show of:～手段 make a show of one's skill

卖人情 màirénqíng show favours for one's own ends; win gratitude by favours

卖身 màishēn ① sell oneself or a member of one's family:～契 indenture by which one sells oneself ② sell one's body; provide sexual services; prostitute

卖身投靠 màishēn-tóukào hire oneself out to…; barter away one's honour for sb.'s patronage

卖艺 màiyì make a living as a performer

卖淫 màiyín prostitution; harlotry:～嫖娼 prostitutes and patrons; prostitution. ～团伙 vice ring

卖主 màizhǔ seller; bargainor

卖座 màizuò draw large audiences; attract large numbers of customers; draw well:这部影片很～。The film draws well.

迈

mài ①〈动〉step; stride:～着矫健的步伐 walk firmly and vigorously ②〈形〉old; aged:年～ aged

迈步 màibù step forward; take a step

迈进 màijìn stride forward; advance in (with) big strides

脉

mài〈名〉① arteries and veins ② pulse:～搏摸不到了。The pulse is too weak to be felt.

脉搏 màibó pulse

脉冲 màichōng [物] pulse; impulse

脉管炎 màiguǎnyán [医] vasculitis

脉络 màiluò ① system of blood vessels ② thread (train) of thought; sequence of ideas; context:～分明[文章] present ideas clearly and logically. ～分析 contextual analysis

脉象 màixiàng types of pulse

mán

埋

mán

另见 mái

埋怨 mányuàn complain (of); blame; grumble (at, about); murmur at:她～我不当心。She blamed me for being careless.

蛮

mán ①〈名〉barbarians ②〈形〉rough; rude; fierce; unreasoning: 野～ uncivilized;

savage ③〈副〉very; quite; pretty:这部电影～好。This is quite a good film.

蛮不讲理 mánbùjiǎnglǐ be impervious to reason; persist in being unreasonable; wilful; obstinate

蛮干 mángàn do things rashly; act recklessly; be foolhardy:～到底 go on and on… regardless of consequences

蛮横 mánhèng rude and unreasonable; arbitrary; peremptory; imperious:～无理 be truculent (rude) and unreasonable; impervious to all reasons. 说话口气～ speak in an imperious tone

蛮劲 mánjìn sheer animal strength

瞒 mán〈动〉conceal sth. from; hide the truth from:实不相～ tell you the truth honestly

瞒哄 mánhǒng pull the wool over sb.'s eyes; hoodwink; deceive

瞒骗 mánpiàn cheat; dupe; bluff

瞒上欺下 mánshàng-qīxià hoodwink (deceive) those above and bully those below; conceal the true state of affairs from above and below

瞒税 mánshuì conceal facts to avoid proper taxation

鳗 mán〈名〉eel

鳗鲡 mánlí eel

馒 mán

馒头 mántou steamed bread; steamed bun

mǎn

满 mǎn〈形〉① full; filled; packed:～怀战斗的豪情 full of militant spirit ② contented; conceited; content:心～意足 to one's heart's content; satisfied ③ conceited; complacent:自～ self-conceited ④〈副〉completely; entirely; perfectly:～不是那么回事。That wasn't the way it was at all.〈动〉⑤ fill:她给每个人～上了酒。She filled everyone's cup. ⑥ expire; reach the limit:他明天就～5岁了。He will be five years old tomorrow.

满不在乎 mǎnbùzàihu not care a rush (rap, pin); not care in the least; be totally unconcerned; do not mind at all

满城风雨 mǎnchéng-fēngyǔ (make) a great commotion; raise a colossal uproar; become the talk of the town; (create) a stir (scandal, sensation):闹得～ create quite a sensation in society

满打满算 mǎndǎ-mǎnsuàn reckoning in every item of income or expenditure

满额 mǎn'é fulfil the quota:学校招生已～。The school has already fulfilled its enrolment quota.

满分 mǎnfēn full marks

满贯 mǎnguàn ① reach the limit ②［麻将、纸牌等］perfect score;［桥牌］slam:小～ little or small slam

满怀 mǎnhuái ① be full of; be filled with; be imbued with:～信心 be fully confident (of); with full confidence ② bosom: 撞了个～ bump right into sb.

满口 mǎnkǒu (speak) unreservedly or profusely; be full of

满面 mǎnmiàn all over the face: ～春风 beaming with joy (pleasure, satisfaction); radiant with happiness. ～笑容 be all smiles

满期 mǎnqī fall due; expire

满腔热忱 mǎnqiāng-rèchén feel warmth towards; in all earnestness; with zeal

满师 mǎnshī (of an apprentice) finish serving one's time; serve out one's apprenticeship:学徒 2 年～。The apprenticeship requires two years of service.

满堂灌 mǎntángguàn stuff to the gill, a teaching method in which facts are rigidly stuffed into students, not allowing them leeway to contemplate or digest, and not caring whether they can comprehend or grasp the facts.

满堂红 mǎntánghóng all-round victory (success; accomplishment); success in every field; red all over; triumph on all fronts

满天 mǎntiān all over the sky

满意 mǎnyì satisfied; pleased; content

满员 mǎnyuán ① filled to capacity (to reach the stipulated number of people, as applied to passengers on a train, persons in a military unit, etc.) ② all seats taken:戏院～了。The theatre is full.

满月 mǎnyuè ① full moon ② a baby's completion of its first month of life

满载 mǎnzài fully loaded; loaded to capacity:～而归 return home fully loaded; be much profited by one's trip

满足 mǎnzú satisfy; meet:～不同层次的需要 satisfying the needs of people from different social strata

满族 mǎnzú the Man (Manchu) nationality (mainly distributed over the provinces of Liaoning, Heilongjiang, Jilin and Hebei, Beijing and the Inner Mongolia Autonomous Region)

满座 mǎnzuò have a capacity audience; have a full house:场场～ have a capacity audience for every show

màn

漫 màn ①〈动〉brim over; overflow; flood:水～过膝。Water reached the knees.〈形〉② all over the places; everywhere:～山遍野 all over the mountains and wilderness ③ free; casual; unrestrained; random: ～步 stroll; ramble; roam; saunter

漫笔 mànbǐ informal essays; ramble; literary notes:文学～ literary ramble

漫步 mànbù stroll; ramble; roam:～街头 stroll along the street

漫不经心 mànbùjīngxīn pay no heed to; be careless about; wanting in care; be completely inattentive

漫长 màncháng very long; endless

漫画 mànhuà cartoon; caricature:～式的唯心主义 caricature of idealism

漫漫 mànmàn very long; boundless

漫评 mànpíng random remark

漫谈 màntán random talk (on); informal discussion (about):～古代中国文学 random talk on ancient Chinese literature. ～会 informal meeting; informal discussion

漫天 màntiān ① all over the sky ② boundless; limitless:～要价 ask an exorbitant price. ～大谎 monstrous lie

漫无止境 mànwúzhǐjìng know no bounds; be without limit

漫游 mànyóu wander; roam; go on a pleasure trip; excursion:社会学中的～ sociological excursions

慢 màn〈形〉① slow:缓～的溪流 a slow stream ② supercilious; rude:傲～ haughty; arrogant ③〈副〉slowly:～～说 speak slowly ④〈动〉slow down:放～汽车速度 slow down a motorcar

慢班 mànbān slow class; adjustment class; remove [英国公学]

慢车 mànchē slow train; way train:～道 slow traffic lane

慢镜头 mànjìngtóu [影视] slow motion:～影片 slow motion film

慢慢爬 mànman pá snail-like movement

慢跑 mànpǎo [体] jogging

慢腾腾 mànténgténg leisurely; unhurriedly; sluggishly:她做事～的。She does her work sluggishly.

慢性 mànxìng chronic:～病 chronic disease. ～失调 chronic disproportion. ～中毒 chronic poisoning

慢走 mànzǒu ① don't go yet; stay; wait a minute ② goodbye; take care

曼 màn〈形〉① graceful; soft and beautiful ② long-drawn-out

曼声 mànshēng (sing or recite in) lengthened sounds:～吟诵 recite in slow, measured tones

曼陀林 màntóulín [乐] mandolin

曼延 mànyán stretch; draw out (in length):森林～数百公里。The forests stretch for hundreds of kilometres.

谩 màn〈形〉disrespectful; rude

谩骂 mànmà abuse; revile; vituperate; fling abusive charges; rail at; vilify

蔓 màn

蔓延 mànyán ① spread; creep; ramble; sprawl:野草～。Weeds spread about ② infest:滋生～

breed and infest

幔 màn〈名〉curtain; screen: 帷～ heavy curtain; curtain hangings

máng

忙 máng ①〈形〉busy; bustling; fully occupied: ～得不可开交 terribly busy ②〈动〉hurry: ～了一阵 bustling about for a while. ～在点子上 make tireless efforts at key points

忙乎 mánghu be busy; bustle about

忙碌 mánglù be busy; bustling about; get (have) one's hands full: 为开会而～ be busy with meetings

忙乱 mángluàn be in a rush and a muddle; be in a bustle; tackle a job in a hasty and disorderly manner

忙人 mángrén busy person

忙于 mángyú be busy at (about, over, with); busy oneself with; be preoccupied with: ～工作 be up to one's ears in work

芒 máng〈名〉awn; beard

芒刺 mángcì brambles; thorn

茫 máng

茫茫 mángmáng ① boundless and indistinct; vast: ～的草原 boundless grassland ②［前途］bleak (prospects)

茫然 mángrán at a loss; in the dark; ignorant; blank; vacant: ～无知 be in the dark

茫无头绪 mángwútóuxù at a loss; lose track of the sequence of events; be confused without a clue; not know where to begin

盲 máng〈形〉blind: ～人 blind persons

盲肠 mángcháng caecum

盲从 mángcóng follow blindly

盲点 mángdiǎn blind spot; scotoma

盲动 mángdòng act blindly; act rashly

盲目 mángmù blind: ～崇拜 make a perfect fetish of; worship blindly. ～乐观 unfounded (unrealistic) optimism. ～竞争 unbridled competition. ～上项目 rashly launching new projects

盲区 mángqū blind area

盲人 mángrén blind person: ～哑人教育 education for the blind and deafmute. ～学校 school for the blind

盲文 mángwén ① braille ② braille publication

氓 máng 见"流氓"

mǎng

莽 mǎng〈形〉reckless; rude; rash

莽汉 mǎnghàn boorish fellow; boor

莽莽 mǎngmǎng ① (of plant growth) lush; rank ② (of fields, plains, etc.) vast; boundless

莽原 mǎngyuán wilderness overgrown with grass
莽撞 mǎngzhuàng saucy; imprudent; rash; reckless
蟒 mǎng〈名〉① huge serpent; boa ② former official costume of ministers decorated with gold-thread constrictor design
蟒袍 mǎngpáo robe embroidered with four-clawed dragons worn by high officials
蟒蛇 mǎngshé python; boa

māo

猫 māo〈名〉cat
猫睛石 māojīngshí[矿] cat's eye
猫头鹰 māotóuyīng owl

máo

毛 máo〈名〉① hair; wool; fur; feather: 鸡～ chicken feather ② mildew: 长～ become mildewed〈形〉③ crude; rough; semifinished: ～坯 semifinished product ④ gross: ～利润 gross profit ⑤ careless; rash; crude: ～手～脚 impetuous; rash ⑥ flurried; scared; frightened: 吓～了 be panic-stricken
毛笔 máobǐ writing brush; Chinese pen: ～画 brush drawing
毛病 máobìng ① illness; disease; ailment; sickness ② trouble; defect; something wrong: 出～ go wrong; be out of order
毛玻璃 máobōli frosted glass
毛豆 máodòu young soya bean
毛纺厂 máofǎngchǎng wool-spinning mill; woolen textile mill; woolen mill
毛骨悚然 máogǔ-sǒngrán ① (make) one's hair stand on end; make one's flesh creep; send cold shivers down one's spine; (make) one's blood run cold; ② hair-raising; horrible; horror-stricken; thrilling; creeping: 令人～的故事 thrilling story
毛烘烘 máohōnghōng hairy; furry
毛巾 máojīn towel
毛利 máolì gross profit; markup; gross margin
毛驴 máolǘ donkey
毛毛雨 máomaoyǔ fine rain; drizzle: 天在下～。It is drizzling.
毛皮 máopí fur; pelt
毛收入 máoshōurù gross income
毛遂自荐 máosuì-zìjiàn offer one's services as Mao Sui (of the Warring States Period) did—volunteer one's services
毛损 máosǔn gross loss
毛毯 máotǎn woolen blanket
毛细血管 máoxì-xuèguǎn blood capillary
毛线 máoxiàn knitting wool
毛衣 máoyī knitted garment; woolen sweater; [套衫] pullover; [开襟的] cardingan; [高领的] turtleneck: 结～ knit a sweater
毛躁 máozao short-tempered; irritable
毛织品 máozhīpǐn woolen fab-

rics; woolen textiles; woolens

毛重 máozhòng gross weight

锚 máo 〈名〉 anchor: 抛～ drop anchor; cast anchor. 起～ weigh anchor

锚泊 máobó lie at anchor; anchoring; anchorage

矛 máo 〈名〉 spear; lance; pike: 长～ pike; lance

矛盾 máodùn contradiction: ～百出 full of contradictions; rent by contradictions. ～上交 pass on the contradictions to one's superior. ～转化 transformation of contradiction. 有～ be at variance (with); be at odds (with)

矛头 máotóu spearhead: ～对准 direct its spearhead against. ～向上 point the spearhead upward

茅 máo 〈名〉 thatch

茅房 máofáng latrine; outhouse

茅塞顿开 máosè-dùnkāi become enlightened at once; be suddenly enlightened; suddenly see the light; come to an understanding all of a sudden

茅舍 máoshě thatched cottage; cottage

茅台酒 máotáijiǔ *Maotai* (a famous Chinese spirit)

茅屋 máowū thatched house (cottage); straw hut; hut

蟊 máo

蟊贼 máozéi public enemy of the people; person harmful to the country and people; pest

mǎo

铆 mǎo 〈名〉 riveting

铆钉 mǎodīng rivet

铆工 mǎogōng ① riveting ② riveter

mào

茂 mào 〈形〉 ① flourishing; luxuriant; lush; profuse ② fine; rich: 繁～的 rich

茂密 màomì thick; dense: ～的森林 dense forest; thickest wood

茂盛 màoshèng flourishing; luxuriant; exuberant: ～的农作物 exuberant crops

冒 mào 〈动〉① send out (up, forth); give off: 烟囱里～着黑烟。Black smoke rose from the chimneys ② brave; risk: ～险 run risks 〈副〉③ rashly; bodly: ～入会场 rashly enter the assembly hall ④ pretendedly; falsely: ～充内行 palm oneself off as an expert

冒充 màochōng pretend to be; simulate; pass sb. or sth. off as: 次品～正品 pass shoddy products off as ones of high quality. ～唯物主义 simulating materialism

冒犯 màofàn offend; affront; give offence

冒汗 màohàn perspire; sweat

冒尖儿 màojiānr become too conspicuous; stand out; become

prominent; outstanding: ～户 stand-out households. 她在班里算～的。She is topnotch in her class.

冒进 màojìn rash advance; premature advance; advance rashly

冒领 màolǐng falsely claim as one's own

冒昧 màomèi make bold; venture; take the liberty (of doing or to do): ～陈辞 venture an opinion; make bold to express one's views

冒名 màomíng assume another name; go under sb. else's name: ～顶替 replace sb. in his name

冒牌 màopái counterfeit of a well-known trademark; imitation brand; false; fake: ～货 counterfeit; imitation; fake; adulteration

冒失 màoshī pert; saucy; bold-faced: ～鬼 dare-devil; harum-scarum

冒天下之大不韪 mào tiānxià zhī dàbùwěi defy the universal will of the people; fly in the face of the will of the people; risk (disregard, regardless of) universal condemnation; face universal condemnation; despite universal condemnation; defy world opinion

冒险 màoxiǎn run the risk; run into danger; take a risk; run the hazard; be exposed to danger; stand the hazard of; incur danger; lay oneself open to danger: ～主义 adventurism

冒雨 màoyǔ braving the rain; in spite of the rain

帽

mào 〈名〉 hat; cap

帽徽 màohuī badge on a cap

帽檐 màoyán the brim of a hat

帽子 màozi ① hat; cap ② [政治上的]label: 扣～ pin (put) a label on (sb.). 摘～ remove the label

貌

mào 〈名〉 looks; appearance: 容～ looks; appearance

貌不惊人 màobùjīngrén be unprepossessing

貌合神离 màohé-shénglí one in appearance but each going his own way; apparently friendly but in fact not; apparently acquiescing while contrary-minded; seemingly in harmony but actually at variance

貌似 màosì seem to be; appear to be

貌似公正 màosìgōngzhèng pretend to play fair; be seemingly impartial

貌似强大 màosìqiángdà appear so powerful; look quite strong; powerful in apearance; be strong in appearance; seemingly powerful; outwardly strong

贸

mào 〈名〉 trade: 对外～易 foreign trade. 农～市场 agricultural trade market

贸促会 màocùhuì China Council for the Promotion of International Trade (CCPIT)

贸工农体制 màogōngnóng tǐzhì trade-industry-agriculture system

贸然 màorán without due (careful) consideration; rashly; hastily; thoughtlessly

贸易 màoyì trade: ～草约[协定书] trade protocol. ～差额 trade balance. ～赤字 trade deficits. ～额 trade volume. ～伙伴 trade partners. ～禁运 commercial embargo. ～逆差 trade deficit. ～顺差 trade surplus. ～货栈 commercial warehouse. ～协定 trade agreement. ～中心 trade centre. ～自由化 trade liberalization

méi

没 méi
另见 mò

没错儿 méicuòr ① I'm quite sure; you can rest assured ② can't go wrong

没法子 méi fǎzi can do nothing about it; can't help it; there is no way out

没关系(～什么) méi guānxi (～shénme) It's nothing.; It doesn't matter.; That's all right.; Never mind.

没精打采 méijīng-dǎcǎi listless; low-spirited; out of sorts; down-in-the-mouth; in the dumps

没救 méijiù incurable; incorrigible; beyond remedy or hope

没脸 méiliǎn feel ashamed; feel embarassed

没门儿 méiménr〈方〉① have no means of doing sth.; have no access to sth ② nothing doing; no go

没谱儿 méipǔr be unsure; have no idea

没趣 méiqù feel snubbed; feel put out: 自讨～ ask for a snub

没说的 méi shuōde ① really (totally) good, excellent: 她是个尖子学生,～。She is a top student, a really one ② without question; needless to say; It goes without saying: ～,这是我应该做的。It goes without saying that it's what I should do.

没挑儿 méitiāor faultless; perfect

没完 méiwán have not finished with sb. (in quarrelling)

没有 méiyǒu ① not have; there is not; be without: 教室里～人。There isn't anyone in the classroom. ～调查,～发言权。No investigation, no right to speak ② not so… as: 你～他高。You are not as tall as he ③ less than: 她来了还～2天就走了。She was here less than two days. ④[表示"已然""曾经"的否定]: 他们回来～? — 还～呢。They have come back yet? —No, not yet.

没辙 méizhé〈方〉be at the end of one's rope; can find no way out

没治 méizhì ① past remedy ② extremely good

没做亏心事,不怕鬼叫门 méi zuò kuīxīn shì, bùpà guǐ jiàomén Do nothing wrong, and no ghosts will knock at your door.

煤 méi〈名〉coal: 原～ raw coal. ～炭工业 coal industry

煤层 méicéng coal seam; coal bed
煤场 méichǎng coal yard
煤耗 méihào coal consumption
煤焦油 méijiāoyóu coal tar
煤矿 méikuàng coal mine; colliery
煤气 méiqì (coal) gas:~表 gas meter. ~厂 gasworks; gashouse. ~公司抄表人 gasman. ~罐 gas bottle. ~中毒 gas poisoning
煤炭 méitàn coal
煤田 méitián coalfied
煤烟 méiyān ① smoke from burning coal ② coal soot; soot
煤油 méiyóu kerosene; paraffin: 煤油炉 kerosene stove

媒 méi 〈名〉① matchmaker; go between: 做~人 act as a match-maker ② intermediary
媒介 méijiè medium; vehicle: 新闻~ news media
媒人 méirén matchmaker; gobetween

玫 méi
玫瑰 méigui rose: ~色 rose-coloured; rosy

枚 méi 〈名〉piece
枚举 méijǔ enumerate: 不胜~ defy enumeration

霉 méi 〈名,动〉mould; mildew: 地窖有~味。The cellar smelt of mildew.
霉变 méibiàn become mildewy; go mouldy
霉烂 méilàn go mouldy; become mildewed; got rotten

梅 méi 〈名〉plum
梅毒 méidú [医] syphilis: 患~ contract syphilis. ~患者 syphilitic. ~治疗 syphilotherapy
梅花 méihuā plum blossom; *mei* blossom
梅雨 méiyǔ plum rains; mould rains

眉 méi 〈名〉eyebrow; brow
眉笔 méibǐ eyebrow pencil
眉飞色舞 méifēi-sèwǔ beam with joy; smack one's lips; brighten up with joy; highly exultant
眉开眼笑 méikāi-yǎnxiào be radiant with smiles; be all smiles; look cheerful; beaming countenance; with a broad smile
眉来眼去 méilái-yǎnqù flirt with each other; make eyes at each other; exchange love glances with sb.; cast sheep's eyes at sb.
眉毛 méimáo eyebrow; brow
眉目 méimù ① features; looks: ~清秀 have delicate features ② logic; sequence of ideas; sign of a positive outcome; prospect of a solution: 这工作做得有~。The task is under way.
眉批 méipī notes and commentary at the top a page
眉清目秀 méiqīng-mùxiù have nice (delicate, beautiful) features; bright eyes and graceful eyebrows; with fine features; [指男] look handsome
眉题 méití [书刊] running title; running head; guide word
眉头一皱,计上心来 méitóu

yīzhòu, jì shàng xīn lái Knit the brows and you will hit upon a stratagem.; Knit the brows and a stratagem comes to mind.

měi

美 měi 〈形〉① beautiful; pretty: ～的花朵 beautiful flowers ② good; satisfactory; pleasing: 日子过得挺～ live quite happily; live a happy life

美不胜收 měibùshèngshōu too many nice things for the eyes to feast on; more beautiful things than one can take in; too beautiful to be absorbed all at once; be a feat for the eyes

美餐 měicān ① tasty food; table delicacies ②eat and drink one's fill; have an excellent dinner

美差 měichāi cushy job; pleasant task: 你去香港开会，这可是一趟～! What a pleasant assignment you've got going to Hong Kong for the conference!

美称 měichēng laudatory title; good name

美德 měidé virtue; moral excellence

美感 měigǎn sense of beauty; aesthetic perception (feeling)

美工 měigōng ① art designing ② art designer

美观 měiguān nice-looking; beautiful; artistic; pleasing to the eye: ～大方 artistic and simple; beautiful and dignified

美好 měihǎo good; fine; happy; bright; rosy: ～的前景 rosy prospects

美化 měihuà beautify; glorify; embellish; glamourize; prettify: ～环境 beautify the environment

美丽 měilì beautiful

美满 měimǎn happy; ideal: ～婚姻 happy marriage

美妙 měimiào splendid; wonderful; beautiful

美其名曰 měiqímíngyuē call… euphemistically; euphemistically describe … as; laud as intended for

美人计 měirénjì sex-trap; using a seductive woman as a bait

美容 měiróng ① improve one's looks ② cosmetology; beauty culture: ～化妆品 facial beautifiers (cosmetics). ～师 beauty specialist; beautician. ～院 beauty shop (parlour, salon)

美色 měisè woman's beauty; attractive woman: 不受～诱惑 be kept from lasciviousness

美食 měishí fine food; delicacy: ～家 gourmet; gastronome; gourmand

美术 měishù fine arts: ～馆 art gallery. ～学院 academy of fine arts. ～作品展览 exhibit of art works

美味 měiwèi tasty; delicious; palatable; delicious food; dainty delicacy

美学 měixué aesthetics

美育 měiyù art education; aesthetic education

美元 měiyuán American dollar; U. S. dollar; dollar: ～汇票

dollar bill of exchange
美展 měizhǎn art exhibition
美中不足 měizhōng-bùzú some blemishes in an apparently perfect thing; a flaw in something which might otherwise be perfect; a fly in the ointment
美洲狮 měizhōushī cougar; puma
每 měi 〈代〉① each; every: ～周 every week ② every time; whenever: ～当我们遇到困难时，他总来帮助我们。Whenever we met with difficulties, he came to help us.
每逢佳节倍思亲 měi féng jiājié bèi sī qīn On festive occasions more than ever one thinks of one's dear ones far away.
每隔 měigé at intervals of: ～一天 every other day; every second day. ～5年 every five years
每况愈下 měikuàngyùxià go from bad to worse; go down the drain; The situation grew steadily worse.; steadily deteriorate
每日行情表 měirì hángqíngbiǎo daily list of prices current

mèi

魅 mèi 〈名〉evil spirit; demon
魅力 mèilì charm; glamour; enchantment; fascination; spell
妹 mèi 〈名〉(younger) sister; sister
妹夫 mèifu younger sister's husband; brother-in-law
媚 mèi ①〈形〉enchanting; charming; fascinating: 妩～ charming; lovely ②〈动〉fawn on; flatter; toady: 谄～ flatter
媚骨 mèigǔ obsequiousness
媚态 mèitài ① obsequiousness ② feminine charms
媚外 mèiwài fawn on foreigners; curry favour with foreigners; toadying to foreigners; crawl before foreigners
媚眼 mèiyǎn seductive eyes

mēn

闷 mēn 〈形〉① stuffy; close: ～的房间 a stuffy room ② muffled; dull in sound: 说话的声音很～ speak in a muffled voice ③〈动〉cover tightly: 把火～灭 cover fire with ashes
另见 mèn
闷热 mēnrè hot and suffocating; sultry; stuffy; close: ～的天气 muggy (sultry) weather

mén

门 mén 〈名〉① door; entrance; gate: ～板 door plank ② valve; switch: 水～ water gate; sluice ③ way to do sth.; knack: 窍～ knack; key ④ family; (religion) sect; school (of thought): ～第 social status of a family. 佛～ Buddhism ⑤〈量〉3～功课 three subjects

(courses)

门把 ménbà door knob; door handle

门当户对 méndāng-hùduì be well-matched in social status (for marriage); (a marriage between) the families that are of equal social rank; (couples coming from) families of equal status

门房 ménfáng ① gate house; janitor's room; porter's lodge ② gatekeeper; doorman; janitor; porter

门户 ménhù ① door; gate:～开放政策 open door policy ② gate way; important passage gateway:上海是长江流域的～。Shanghai is the gateway to the Yangtze valley ③ sect; faction: ～之见 sectarian bias (mind); parochial prejudice; sectarianism

门禁 ménjìn police guard at an entrace; entrance guard:～森严 with the entrance carefully guarded

门槛 ménkǎn ① threshold ② secret; knack; trick:～精 play one's card well

门可罗雀 ménkěluóquè ① Birds can be caught by a net at the door — a deserted house.; Your can catch sparrows on the doorstep — visitors are few and far between.; have few customers

门框 ménkuàng doorframe

门脸儿 ménliǎnr ① the facade of a shop; shop front ② the vicinity of a city gate

门类 ménlèi kind; class; category

门帘 ménlián door curtain

门路 ménlù ① know-how; the ropes; knack:摸到一些～ have learned the ropes. 做生意的～ knack for business ② social connections; be made use of; pull:找～ solicit sb.'s patronage; try to get sth. done through pull

门面 ménmiàn ①［店面］shop front ② appearance:装～ keep up appearances

门牌 ménpái ① (house) number plate ② street number; house number

门票 ménpiào entrance ticket; admission ticket

门前三包 ménqián sānbāo three responsibilities in front of the gate (a responsibility system whereby each unit is responsible for environment sanitation in its own area and the area outside its gate. The "three responsibilities" are sanitation, landscaping and orderliness.)

门市 ménshì retail sales:～部 sales department; retail department; sales department. ～商品 goods sold over the counter

门庭 méntíng ① courtyard ② family status

门徒 méntú adherent; disciple; pupil; follower; apostle

门卫 ménwèi entrance guard

门诊 ménzhěn outpatient service: ～病人 outpatient. ～部 outpatient department

扪 mén〈动〉touch; feel

扪心自问 ménxīn-zìwèn examine one's own conscience and ask oneself; lay one hand on the heart and examine oneself; feel one's chest and ask oneself

mèn

闷 mèn 〈形〉① depressed; bored; in low spirits:烦～ worried; vexed ② tightly closed; sealed

另见 mēn

闷棍 mèngùn kicks in the pants; staggering blow (with a cudgel)

闷葫芦 mènhúlu riddle; puzzle; enigma

闷酒 mènjiǔ drinks taken alone to drown one's sorrows

闷雷 mènléi ① muffled thunder ② unpleasant surprise; shock

闷闷不乐 mènmèn-bùlè feel bored; be in a depressed mood; unhappy

焖 mèn〈动〉stew; braise:～饭 cook rice over a slow fire

men

们 men[用在代词或指人的名词后面,表示复数]:我～ we. 人～ people

mēng

蒙 mēng ①〈动〉cheat; deceive; dupe:别～我! Don't kid me!. 别瞎～,好好想想。Don't make a wild guess, think it over. ②〈形〉senseless; unconscious:给打～了 be knocked senseless

另见 méng,měng

蒙蒙亮 mēngmēngliàng first glimmer of dawn; daybreak; (at) dawn

蒙骗 mēngpiàn deceive; delude; hoodwink

méng

虻 méng〈名〉horsefly; gadfly:牛～ gadfly

氓 méng〈名〉the common people

另见 máng

蒙 méng〈动〉① cover:这些妇女～着面纱。These women are veiled ② receive; suffer; encounter:～冤 be unjustly accused. 承～指教,太感谢了。Thank you very much for your advice ③〈名〉ignorance:～昧无知 childish ignorance

另见 mēng,měng

蒙蔽 méngbì hoodwink; deceive; hide the truth from; pull the wool over sb.'s eyes

蒙汗药 ménghànyào knock drop; a narcotic believed to have been used by highwaymen, etc. to drug their victims

蒙混过关 ménghùn-guòguān get by under false pretences; slip by; steal away; gloss over one's faults; sneak away in the confusion

蒙昧 méngmèi ① savagery ② uncultured; barbaric; uncivilized: ～社会 uncultured society ③ ignorant; blind: ～无知 stupid and ignorant; unenlightened; childish ignorance

蒙上欺下 méngshàng-qīxià hoodwink superiors and subordinates alike

蒙受 méngshòu suffer; receive; sustain: ～重大损失 suffer heavy losses

蒙太奇 méngtàiqí [电影] montage

蒙在鼓里 méngzài gǔlǐ live in a drum; be completely ignorant (of); be kept in the dark

朦 méng

朦胧 ménglóng dim; obscure; hazy: ～的回忆 dim collection

朦胧诗 ménglóngshī hazy poetry; murky poetry (Poetic works with an obscure style which appeared in China's poetry circles in the late 1970s and early 1980s. Their characteristics are thematic ideas not obvious, poet's train of thought unclear, not easily understandable.)

萌 méng 〈动〉 sprout; bud; germinate

萌发 méngfā germinate; sprout; shoot: 芽在春天～。Buds sprout in the spring.

萌生 méngshēng come into being; arise

萌芽 méngyá bud; sprout; shoot; rudiment; seed; budding sprouts; buddings: 社会主义～ sprouts of socialism

盟 méng 〈名〉 ① alliance: 工农联～ the alliance of workers and peasants ② league

盟国 méngguó allied state; ally

盟军 méngjūn allied forces

盟约 méngyuē oath of alliance; treaty of alliance

盟主 méngzhǔ leader (chief) of an alliance

懵 měng 〈形〉 muddled

懵懵懂懂 měngměng-dǒngdǒng muddleheaded; muddled; ignorant

měng

蒙 měng 〈名〉 the Mongol nationality

另见 mēng, méng

蒙古 Měnggǔ Mongolia: ～人 Mongolian

蒙古包 měnggǔbāo yurt

猛 měng ①〈形〉fierce; violent; vigorous: ～攻 fierce assault ②〈副〉suddenly; abruptly: ～一转身 turn round abruptly

猛地 měngde suddenly; abruptly

猛跌 měngdiē [物价等] drop sharply; slump

猛将 měngjiàng valiant general

猛进 měngjìn ① push ahead vigorously; proceed in rapid strides ② make rapid progress：突飞～ advance by leaps and bounds
猛烈 měngliè violent; fierce; vigorous; heavy; drastic：～批评 devastating criticism; out-and-out critics of
猛然 měngrán suddenly; abruptly
猛兽 měngshòu beast of prey
猛省(醒) měngxǐng suddenly realize (wake up)
猛涨 měngzhǎng rise sharply; shoot up; be in spate：河水～。The river is in spate.

mèng

梦 mèng〈名〉dream
梦话 mènghuà ① talk in one's sleep ② foolish talk; nonsense
梦幻 mènghuàn illusion; vision; dream：～泡影 pipe dream; illusion
梦境 mèngjìng dreamland; dreamworld; dream
梦寐以求 mèngmèiyǐqiú long dream of; crave for; hanker after (for); long yearn for sth. day and night
梦想 mèngxiǎng ① dream of ② daydream; dream; reverie：～不到的 undreamed-of
梦呓 mèngyì somniloquence; sleep-talking; rave
孟 mèng〈形〉① first：～春 the first month of spring ② eldest
孟浪 mènglàng rash; impetuous; impulsive
孟子 mèngzǐ Mencius

mī

眯 mī〈动〉narrow (screw up) (one's eyes)
眯眼 mīyǎn screw up one's eyes：～看 squint at

mí

靡 mí〈形〉waste：奢～ wasteful; extravagant
另见 mǐ
靡费 mífèi spend extravagantly; waste
糜 mí〈名〉① thick porridge; gruel〈形〉② rotten; pasty ③ wasteful
糜费 mífèi spend extravagantly; waste; dissipation：～精力 dissipate energy
糜烂 mílàn corrupt; fast; dissipated; licentious; debauched; rotten to the core：过～的生活 lead a fast life
迷 mí〈动〉① lose one's way; be confused; get lost：～路 lose one's way ② indulge in; be enchanted with (by); be fascinated by：入了～ be enchanted; be fascinated ③〈名〉fan; enthusiast; votary：足球～ football fan (buff)
迷宫 mígōng labyrinth; maze
迷航 míháng[飞机、船只等] lose one's course; drift off course
迷糊 míhu confused; muddled;

indistinct; blurred:. 泪水～的眼睛 eyes blurred with tears

迷惑 míhuò confuse; perplex; puzzle; baffle; delude:～舆论 befuddle public opinion; throw dust in the eyes of the public. 感到～不解 feel puzzled (about)

迷恋 míliàn be infatuated with; be intoxicated with; indulge in; have a crush on; lose one's heart to:～一个女人 be infatuated with a woman

迷路 mílù lose one's way; go astray

迷漫 mímàn boundless and indistinct; vast and hazy

迷人 mírén charming; fetching; enchanting; fascinating:～的景色 charming scenery

迷失 míshī lose (one's way, etc.)

迷途 mítú wrong path:～知返 mend one's ways after realizing one's errors; become aware of one's errors and return from one's wrong path

迷惘 míwǎng be perplexed; be puzzled; at a loss

迷信 míxìn ① superstition ② have (place) blind faith in; make a fetish of; blindly worship

谜 mí〈名〉① riddle ② mystery; enigma:不解之～ unfathomable enigma

谜底 mídǐ solution (answer) to a riddle

谜团 mítuán doubts and suspicions

谜语 míyǔ riddle:猜～ guess a riddle. 出～ propose a riddle

弥 mí〈动〉① fill; overflow:～漫 fill the air ② cover; fill:～缝 plug up holes ③〈形〉full; whole:～年 a whole year ④〈副〉more:欲盖～彰 the more concealed, the more conspicuous

弥补 míbǔ make up for; compensate for:～损失 make up for a loss; make good a loss. ～赤字 cover the deficit

弥留 míliú be dying

弥漫 mímàn fill the air; spread all over the place; be enveloped in:～着烟雾 be suffused with smoke

弥撒 mísa Mass

弥天大谎 mítiān-dàhuǎng glaring falsehood; monstrous (thundering, outrageous, glaring) lie

弥天大罪 mítiān-dàzuì towering (monstrous, heinous) crime

mǐ

靡 mǐ
另见 mí

靡靡之音 mǐmǐzhīyīn demoralizing (decadent, voluptuous) music

米 mǐ ①〈名〉rice:白～ (polished) rice ②〈量〉metre

米醋 mǐcù rice vinegar

米袋子 mǐdàizi rice bag:"～"省长负责制 system of the provincial governor's responsibility for the "rice bag," which means that the grain supply within the province is the governor's responsibility

米饭 mǐfàn (cooked) rice

米粉 mǐfěn ① ground rice; rice flour ② rice-flour noodles

米酒 mǐjiǔ rice wine

米色 mǐsè cream-coloured; beige

米汤 mǐtāng ① water in which rice has been cooked ② thin rice or millet gruel; rice water

米蛀虫 mǐzhùchóng ① rice worm ② rice profiteer

mì

秘 mì ①〈形〉secret; confidential; mysterious: ～密资料 secret (classified) information ②〈动〉keep sth. secret ③〈名〉secretary

秘方 mìfāng secret prescription; nostrum

秘诀 mìjué secret; secret formula; key (to); trick

秘密 mìmì secret; confidential; private: ～谈判 secret talks; clandestine negotiation

秘史 mìshǐ secret history (as of a feudal dynasty); inside story

秘书 mìshū secretary: ～处 secretariat; secretarial office. ～长 secretary-general

蜜 mì〈名〉honey

蜜蜂 mìfēng (honey) bee

蜜饯 mìjiàn candied (preserved) fruit; sweetmeats

蜜月 mìyuè honeymoon: 度～ honeymoon

密 mì ①〈名〉secret: 保～ keep a secret ②〈形〉thick; dense; close: ～植 dense (close) planting ③ close; intimate: ～友 close friend ④ meticulous; careful: 周～ carefully considered

密度 mìdù density: 人口的～ population density

密封 mìfēng ① hermetical; airtight; airproof ② seal up: ～罐头 seal up a tin. ～投标 sealed bid

密集 mìjí concentrated; crowded together

密件 mìjiàn confidential paper (letter, document, etc.); classified document (material)

密令 mìlìng ① give a secret order or instructions ② secret order or instructions

密码 mìmǎ secret code; cipher

密谋 mìmóu plot; scheme; conspire

密切 mìqiè intimate; close: ～联系群众 maintain close ties with the masses; keep in constant touch with the masses; establish (forge) close links with the masses

密使 mìshǐ secret emissary; secret envoy

密室 mìshì room used for secret purposes: 策划于～ plot behind closed doors

密谈 mìtán have a secret (confidential, private) talk; talk behind closed doors

密探 mìtàn secret agent; spy

密纹唱片 mìwén chàngpiàn long-playing disc; micro-groove disc; maxisingle

密友 mìyǒu close (fast) friend; bosom friend

幂 mì ①〈名〉cloth cover ②〈数〉power

觅 mì 〈动〉look for; seek; hunt for

觅食 mìshí look for food

mián

眠 mián ①〈名〉sleep: 彻夜不～ lie awake all night ②〈动〉dormancy: 冬～ hibernate

棉 mián ①〈名〉cotton: ～布 cotton cloth; cotton ②〈形〉cotton-padded; wadded; quilted: ～大衣 cotton-padded overcoat

棉袄 mián'ǎo cotton-padded (quilted) jacket

棉被 miánbèi quilt with cotton wadding

棉布 miánbù cotton cloth; cotton

棉纺厂 miánfǎngchǎng cotton mill

棉铃虫 miánlíngchóng bollworm

棉毛裤 miánmáokù cotton-wool trousers; cotton trousers

棉毛衫 miánmáoshān cotton wool jersey; cotton jersey

棉纱 miánshā cotton yarn

棉絮 miánxù ① cotton fibre ② a cotton wadding (for a quilt)

棉织品 miánzhīpǐn cotton textiles; cotton fabrics; cotton goods

棉籽 miánzǐ cottonseed

绵 mián ①〈名〉silk floss 〈形〉② uninterrupted; continuous: 连～ uninterrupted; continuous; unbroken ③ soft; lithe

绵白糖 miánbáitáng fine white sugar

绵薄 miánbó (my) meagre strength; humble effort

绵亘 miángèn stretch continuously; extend: 这山～数百公里。The mountains stretch (extend) for several hundred kilometres.

绵绵 miánmián continuous; unbroken: 秋雨～。The autumn rain goes on and on.

绵延 miányán extend; stretch; continuous: ～不断的战争 continuous and unbroken warfare

绵羊 miányáng sheep

miǎn

腼 miǎn

腼腆 miǎndiǎn shy; coy; bashful: 她这个人有些～。She is a little shy.

缅 miǎn 〈形〉remote; far back; distant

缅怀 miǎnhuái recall; recollect; cherish the memory; think of: ～往事 recall past events with deep feeling; be reminiscent

免 miǎn 〈动〉① dismiss; remove; relieve: 被～职 be removed from office ② be free of; be exempted from: ～于处分 be exempted from punishment ③ avoid; escape; avert: 以～人手不够 avoid being short of hands

免不了 miǎnbuliǎo be unavoidable; be bound to be

免偿债务 miǎnchángzhàiwù forgive a debt; exemption of debt

免除 miǎnchú ① avoid; prevent ② exempt; remit; relieve:～某人纳税 exempt sb. from taxation. ～刑罚 exempt from criminal punishment

免得 miǎnde ① so as to avoid; so as not to:～引起误会 so as to avoid misunderstanding ② lest

免费 miǎnfèi free of charge; free; gratis:～检验 inspection free

免税 miǎnshuì be free of duty; be exempted from taxes; tax exemption; duty-free:～品 (duty-) free goods. ～单 bill of sufferance. ～期 generous tax holidays; tax holidays. ～投资 tax-free investment

免验放行 miǎnyàn fàngxíng pass without examination

免疫 miǎnyì be immune to (from) disease:～力 immunity from disease; immunized from disease

免予起诉 miǎnyú qǐsù exempt from prosecution:～决定书 decision to exempt from prosecution

免职 miǎnzhí dismiss (remove) sb. from office; relieve sb. of his post

免罪 miǎnzuì exempt from punishment

冕 miǎn〈名〉crown: 加～crowning

勉 miǎn〈动〉① endeavour; make effort; exert oneself:勤～work hard ② encourage; urge: 互～ encourage one another ③ force oneself to work hard; strive to do onerous work

勉励 miǎnlì encourage; urge:～某人做某事 encourage sb. to do sth.

勉强 miǎnqiǎng ① force sb. to do sth.:要是她不愿意去,就不要～她。Don't force her to go if she doesn't want to ② manage with an effort; do with difficulty:～餬口 eke out an existence ③ unconvincing; inadequate:他的理由相当～。The reason he gave is rather unconvincing. ④ barely enough:～的多数 a bare majority

勉为其难 miǎnwéiqínán exert oneself in spite of difficulties

miàn

面 miàn〈名〉① face:～上无光 lose face ② surface:路～ road surface ③ side; aspect:四～进攻 attack from all aspects ④ extent; scale; range:～上的工作 work on the area scale ⑤ wheat flour; flour:豆～ bean flour ⑥〈动〉face:～向群众 face the masses. 窗子～对着大街。The windows look out on the wide street. ⑦〈副〉personally; directly:～议 consult personally ⑧〈量〉一～锦旗 a silk banner

面包 miànbāo bread

面包车 miànbāochē minibus; "bread loaf" vehicle

面呈 miànchéng submit in person

面斥 miànchì give sb. a talking-to; reprove

面对 miànduì face; confront: ～现实 face reality; face the fact that…; be realistic

面额 miàn'é ① denomination ② forehead

面积 miànji area

面巾纸 miànjīnzhǐ face tissues

面料 miànliào material for making the outside (of a garment)

面临 miànlín be faced (confronted) with; be up against: ～重重困难 be confronted with numerous difficulties

面貌 miànmào ① face; features: ～端正的男子 a well-featured man ② look; appearance; aspect: 城市～ the appearance of a city

面膜 miànmó face-pack; mask

面目 miànmù ① face; countenance ② appearance; look; aspect: ～一新 take on a new look; assume a completely new appearance. ～全非 be changed beyond recognition

面庞 miànpáng contours of the face

面前 miànqián in (the) face of; in front of; before

面色 miànsè ① complexion: ～苍白 look pale ② facial expression; looks

面善 miànshàn ① look familiar; ② affable; amiable

面市 miànshì appear on the market

面试 miànshì examine by interview: 对考生要增加～。We should increase the use of the interview format in examining students.

面世 miànshì emerge: 一种新制的涂料将要～。A new experimental paint is about to come out.

面熟 miànshú look familiar

面谈 miàntán speak to sb. face to face; take up a matter with sb. personally

面相 miànxiang facial features; looks; appearance

面向 miànxiàng ① turn one's face to; face ② be geared to; be oriented to; cater to: ～广大读者 be suited to the needs of reading public. ～农村 be oriented towards rural areas; face in the direction of rural villages

面谢 miànxiè thank sb. in person

面议 miànyì negotiate face to face; take up a matter with sb. personally

面值 miànzhí face (nominal) value

面子 miànzi ① outside; outer part; face: 大衣的～ the outside of an overcoat ② face; honour; prestige: 爱～ be keen on face-saving; like to keep up appearance. 丢～ lose (one's) face. 给～ show due respect for sb.'s feeling; grant sb. favour; take care not to offend one's susceptibilities

miáo

苗 miáo〈名〉① seedling; sprout; shoot: 幼～ young sprout ② vaccine

苗床 miáochuáng seedbed; nursery bed; seedling bed

苗圃 miáopǔ nursery (of young plants); nursery garden

苗情 miáoqíng seedling condition

苗条 miáotiáo slender; *svelte*: 身材～ have a slender figure

苗头 miáotóu sign; indication (of some new development); symptom of a trend

苗子 miáozi ① seedlings; ② young successors

描 miáo〈动〉draw; trace; portray; depict: ～图样 copy (trace) a design

描画 miáohuà draw, portray; paint; describe; depict

描绘 miáohuì portray; depict; describe

描摹 miáomó depict; portray; delineate

描述 miáoshù describe; depict

描写 miáoxiě describe; depict; portray

瞄 miáo〈动〉aim at (a mark)

瞄准 miáozhǔn aim at; level at; take aim: ～靶心 aim at the bull's-eye

miǎo

秒 miǎo〈名〉second (=1/60 minute)

秒针 miǎozhēn second hand

渺 miǎo〈形〉① distant and indistinct: ～无声息 remote and noiseless ② expansive; vast: 烟波浩～ (of lake, etc.) vast and misty ③ tiny; insignificant: ～小的一撮 a handful of

渺茫 miǎománg vague; indistinct; blurred; uncertain: ～的前途 uncertain future

渺(藐)小 miǎoxiǎo tiny; negligible; insignificant; paltry

藐 miǎo ①〈动〉despise; ignore; slight: ～视敌人 despise the enemy ②〈形〉little; small; tiny: ～小 tiny

藐视 miǎoshì despise; disdain; hold in contempt; look down upon; defy: ～法庭罪 criminal contempt

miào

庙 miào〈名〉temple: ～宇 temple

庙会 miàohuì temple fair; fair: 逛～ go to the fair; stroll around the fairground

庙宇 miàoyǔ temple

庙主 miàozhǔ head priest of a temple

妙 miào〈形〉① fine; wonderful; extraordinary; excellent: ～论 extraordinary statements (arguments) ② clever; ingenious; subtle: ～用 subtle application

妙不可言 miàobùkěyán too wonderful for words; most amusing:多么～的推论! What a brilliant inference!

妙计 miàojì excellent plan; wise move; brilliant scheme (idea)

妙境 miàojìng fairyland; wonderland

妙龄 miàolíng youthfulness (of a girl)

妙趣横生 miàoqù-héngshēng full of wit and humour; (conversation) seasoned with humour; rich in wisecracks

妙手回春 miàoshǒu-huíchūn (of a doctor) effect a miraculous cure and bring the dying back to life

妙语 miàoyǔ happy expression; witticisms; witty (clever) remark:～连珠 endless witty remarks

miè

灭 miè〈动〉① (of a light or fire) put out; extinguish; go out:火～了。The fire has gone out ② do away with; wipe out; destroy:～敌人威风 destroy (crush, deflate) the arrogance of the enemy. 歼～敌人 wipe out the enemy ③ drown; inundate

灭顶 mièdǐng be drowned:～之灾 be buried beneath the waves; disaster of being drowned; be swamped

灭火 mièhuǒ ① put out a fire; extinguish a fire:～剂 fire-extinguishing chemical (agent) ② cut out an engine

灭绝 mièjué die out; be extinct:～人性的 savage; brutal; inhuman; cannibalistic

灭口 mièkǒu do away with a witness or accomplice

灭亡 mièwáng ① doom; extinction; ② perish; be ruined:自取～ invite self-destruction; draw ruin upon oneself

蔑 miè〈动〉① belittle; disdain; slight:轻～ disdain ② insult; smear

蔑视 mièshì defy; disdain; scorn; show contempt

篾 miè〈名〉thin bamboo strip

篾匠 mièjiàng a craftsman who makes articles from bamboo strips; bamboo-weaver

篾片 mièpiàn ① thin bamboo strip ② hanger-on; sycophant

mín

民 mín〈名〉① the people:～变 mass uprisings ② a member of a nationality:藏～ a Tibetan ③ a person of a certain occupation:牧～ herdsman ④〈形〉civil; popular; folk:～歌演唱家 folknik

民办 mínbàn public-run; civilian-run; community-run:～教师 community-sponsored teachers. ～集体 popular collectives

民兵 mínbīng militiaman or militiawoman;[集体] militia:～师 militia divisions

民不聊生 mínbùliáoshēng Life is made impossible for the people.; The people can hardly earn a living.; Life for the people is intolerable.

民法 mínfǎ civil law:～典 civil code. ～学 science of civil law. ～学家 civil jurist; civilian

民风 mínfēng folkways; local traits

民歌 míngē ballad; folk song

民工 míngōng ① civilian worker (builders); peasant workers (builders) ② migrant labourers:～潮 labour migration

民航 mínháng civil aviation:～飞机 civil airplane

民间 mínjiān ① popular; folk:～故事 folk story. ～说唱文学 folk ballads. ～艺术 folk art ② among the people:～贸易 non-government trade

民警 mínjǐng people's policeman or policewoman; people's police

民力 mínlì financial resources of the people

民品 mínpǐn civilian goods

民情 mínqíng ① condition of the people ② feelings of the people; public feeling

民权 mínquán civil rights; civil liberties; democratic rights

民生 mínshēng the people's livelihood:国计～ the national economy and the people's livelihood

民事 mínshì [法] civil:～案件 civil case. ～诉讼法 civil procedure

民俗 mínsú folk custom; folkways

民心 mínxīn popular feelings (sentiments); common aspiration of the people:得(失)～ win (lose) popular support

民选 mínxuǎn elected by the people

民谣 mínyáo folk song; ballad; folk rhyme

民意 mínyì public opinion; the will (volition) of the people:～测验 public opinion poll; opinion survey

民用 mínyòng for civil use; civil:～产品 production of goods for civilian use. ～工业 civilian industry

民政 mínzhèng civil administration

民众 mínzhòng the common people; masses

民主 mínzhǔ democracy:～党派 democratic parties. ～集中制 democratic centralism. ～人士 democratic personage

民族 mínzú nation; nationality:～大家庭 the big family of ethnic groups. ～独立 national independence. ～服装 national costume. ～隔阂 estrangement among ethnic groups. ～区域自治 autonomy of minority areas. ～性 nationalism; national make-up. ～学院 national minority institutes. 中华～ Chinese nation

mǐn

泯 mǐn 〈动〉 disappear; die out; vanish:良心未～ not be devoid

of conscience; still have some conscience

闽 Mǐn another name for 福建(Fújiàn)

闽剧 mǐnjù Fujian opera

悯 mǐn 〈动〉 pity: 怜～ pity; commiserate

敏 mǐn 〈形〉 quick; wise; nimble; agile: 有～锐的感觉 be acutely sensitive to

敏感 mǐngǎn sensitive; susceptible; subtle: ～问题 sensitive issue

敏捷 mǐnjié quick; prompt; nimble; agile: 才思～ have a quick mind. 文笔～ have a ready pen

敏锐 mǐnruì acute; sharp; keen: 目光～ have sharp eyes; be sharp-sighted. ～的洞察力 an acute insight

míng

冥 míng〈形〉 ① dark; obscure: ～夜 dark night ② deep; profound: ～思 be deep in thought ③ dull; stupid ④〈名〉the underworld; the nether world

冥思苦想 míngsī-kǔxiǎng cudgel (rack) one's brains; beat one's brains out; think long and hard

冥顽 míngwán thickheaded; stupid

瞑 míng

瞑目 míngmù close one's eyes in death; die content: 死不～ die discontent; die with regret

明 míng 〈形〉 ① brilliant; bright: ～月 a bright moon ② distinct; clear: ～显的优越性 a clear superiority ③ open; overt; visible: ～来暗往 make overt and covert contacts ④ sharp-eyed; clear-sighted: ～眼人 anyone with a discerning eye ⑤ next: ～年 next year ⑥〈名〉sight: 失～ lose one's sight ⑦〈动〉understand; know; comprehend: ～白真相 be aware of the facts

明白 míngbái ① understand; know; see: ～事理 know what's what ② clear; evident; plain; sensible: ～人 sensible persons ③ frank; explicit; unequivocal: 把真相讲～ explain the actual situation in explicit terms

明辨是非 míngbiàn-shìfēi distinguish clearly between right and wrong

明察秋毫 míngchá-qiūháo have eyes sharp enough to perceive an animal's autumn hair — be perceptive of the minutest detail; discover the minutest detail in everything; be able to penetrate deeply into all things

明澈 míngchè bright and limpid; transparent

明处 míngchù ① where there is light ② in the open; in public

明灯 míngdēng beacon: 指路～ beacon lighting up one's advance

明矾 míngfán alum

明快 míngkuài ①lucid and lively; sprightly ② straightforward;

forthright ③ bright

明朗 mínglǎng ① clear; bright: ～的天空 a clear sky ② obvious; clear-cut: 态度～ take a clear-cut attitude ③ frank; forthright: ～的性格 an open and forthright character

明理 mínglǐ ① sensible; reasonable ② an obvious truth or fact

明亮 míngliàng ① well-lit; bright ② bright; shining ③ become clear

明码 míngmǎ ① plain code ② with the price clearly marked: ～售货 put goods on sale with the prices clearly marked; sell at marked prices

明媚 míngmèi bright and beautiful; radiant and enchanting: ～的春光 a radiant and enchanting spring scene; The spring days are bright and charming.

明目张胆 míngmù-zhāngdǎn ① brazen; flagrant; outright: ～的侵略 flagrant aggression ② flagrantly; overtly; brazenly

明确 míngquè ① definite; explicit; clear: ～的产业政策 well-defined industrial policies ② be clear about; make clear (definite)

明日 míngrì ① tomorrow ② the near future

明示 míngshì explicitly instruct; clearly indicate

明文 míngwén proclaimed in writing; express provision: ～规定 regulate in definite terms; stipulate explicitly

明晰 míngxī clear; distinct; lucid: ～的文体 lucid style

明显 míngxiǎn clear; obvious; evident; marked; manifest: ～成效 marked result

明线 míngxiàn open-wire line; open wire

明星 míngxīng ① Venus ② a famous performer; star

明一套暗一套 míng yī tào àn yī tào act one way in the light and another in the dark

明哲保身 míngzhébǎoshēn be worldly wise and play safe; be cautious to save one's own skin

明争暗斗 míngzhēng-àndòu engage in overt and covert struggle; fight both in the open and in secret; both open strife and veiled rivalry

明证 míngzhèng clear evidence (proof); a case in point

明知 míngzhī know well; know for certain: ～故犯 commit an error deliberately; violate knowingly; commit an offence with the full knowledge of its implication; do sth. which one knows is wrong

明智 míngzhì wise; sagacious; sensible; judicious; reasonable: ～的妥协 a sensible compromise

明珠 míngzhū bright pearl; jewel

鸣

鸣 míng ①〈名〉the cry of birds, animals or insects: 鸟～ the chirp of a bird〈动〉② (of birds, animals, etc.) cry: 鸡～。The cock crows. ③ air; express; voice: 大～大放 air one's views freely. ～炮 21 响

致敬 fire a salute of 21 salvoes; fire a 21-gun salute

鸣不平 míngbùpíng make complaints against injustice; air grievance for; take up the cudgels for

鸣镝 míngdí whistling arrow (used in ancient times)

鸣锣开道 míngluó-kāidào beat (sound) gongs to clear the way for; pave the way for; clear the way for

鸣谢 míngxiè express one's thanks

鸣冤叫屈 míngyuān-jiàoqū make bitter complaints; call for the redress of a wrong; cry against injustice; air one's discontent; voice grievances

名 míng 〈名〉① name; appellation:书～ the title of a book ② fame; reputation:这支队的～声传开了。The fame of the team spread far and wide ③〈形〉famous; famous-brand products ④〈量〉300～代表 three hundred delegates

名不副实 míngbùfùshí more in name than in reality; unworthy of one's name; nominal

名不虚传 míngbùxūchuán have (enjoy) a well-deserved reputation; be true to one's fame; be equal to one's reputation; live up to one's reputation

名册 míngcè (name) list; roll; register; personnel roster

名垂青史 míngchuíqīngshǐ go down in history; be crowned with eternal glory; One's name will live in history.

名次 míngcì order in rank (in a name list); position in a name list; place (in a contest)

名存实亡 míngcún-shíwáng have a mere nominal existence; exist in name only; cease to exist except in name

名单 míngdān name list

名额 míng'é the number of people assigned or allowed; quota of people:招生～ number of sudents to be enrolled

名分 míngfèn status and rank in society; social ranks; social positions

名副其实 míngfùqíshí be true to one's name; be worthy of one's name; The name matches the reality.; be sth. in reality as well as in name

名贵 míngguì famous and precious; rare

名家 míngjiā famous expert; master

名利 mínglì fame and gain (profit); wealth and fame:～双收 gain both wealth and fame

名列前茅 mínglièqiánmáo come out in front; head the list; come out at the top of the list

名落孙山 míngluò-sūnshān fail (in) an examination

名目 míngmù item; denomination:～繁多 all sorts of items

名牌 míngpái famous brand:～货 famous-brand goods; name-brand product; name brand

名片 míngpiàn name card; visiting (calling) card

名气 míngqì reputation; fame; renown:～大的人 a man of great reputation

名人 míngrén prominent persons (figures, personages); man of renown; celebrity; luminary

名声 míngshēng reputation; repute; renown

名胜 míngshèng beauty spot; scenic spot; sights:～古迹 scenic spots and historical sites

名堂 míngtang ① result; achievement; outcome:搞不出～ can't produce any significant results ② reason; cause:她没有到场，一定有～。There must be some cause for her absence.

名望 míngwàng fame and prestige; reputation; renown:他～很高。He has (enjoys) a high reputation.

名言 míngyán well-known saying; celebrated dictum; famous remark

名义 míngyì name:以…名义 in the name of…. ～工资 nominal wages

名誉 míngyù ① name; honour; reputation:～扫地 be thoroughly discredited ② honorary:～会员 an honorary member

名优产品 míngyōu chǎnpǐn quality brand-name products

名正言顺 míngzhèng-yánshùn be fully (perfectly) justifiable; things called by their right names

名著(作) míngzhù(zuò) masterpiece; masterwork; classics; great book; famous work:～欣赏 appreciation of masterpieces

名字 míngzi ① name or given name ② name (of a thing)

铭 míng ①〈名〉inscription:～辞 inscriptions on bronzes ②〈动〉inscribe; engrave:～刻于心 engrave on the mind

铭感 mínggǎn be deeply grateful (to)

铭记 míngjì inscribe on one's memory; engrave on one's mind; always remember; be enshrined in the heart of

铭刻 míngkè inscribe; engrave on one's mind; always keep in mind

铭文 míngwén epigraphy; inscribed writing

mǐng

酩 mǐng

酩酊大醉 mǐngdǐng-dàzuì be completely drunk; be dead drunk

mìng

命 mìng〈名〉① life:生～的起源 the origin of life ② fate; lot; destiny:苦～ hard lot; ③ command; order:接受～令 take orders

命案 mìng'àn case involving the killing of a person; homicide case

命根子 mìnggēnzi one's very life; lifeline; life-spring; sth. meant everything to sb.

命令 mìnglìng order；command：执行～ carry out (execute) a command

命脉 mìngmài lifeline；lifeblood：经济～ economic lifelines

命名 mìngmíng give a name to；name；denominate；be designated by… as…

命题 mìngtí ① set a question ②［逻、数］proposition；thesis

命运 mìngyùn fate；lot；destiny：～寄托在… stake one's fate on

命中注定 mìngzhōng-zhùdìng predestined；decreed by fate；be fated to do sth.

命中 mìngzhòng hit it right；hit the mark：～率 percentage of hits；hitting accuracy

miù

谬 miù ①〈形〉wrong；erroneous ②〈名〉false；wrong

谬见 miùjiàn ① erroneous (wrong) view ② my humble opinion

谬论 miùlùn fallacy；absurd (false) theory；falsehood

谬误 miùwù error；mistake；falsehood；absurdity

mō

摸 mō〈动〉① feel；stroke；touch：棉花～上去很柔软。Cotton feels soft ② feel for；grope for；fumble：在箱子里～着几个螺丝钉 feel for a few screws in a tool box ③ try to feel at；feel out；sound out：先～～事情的原因 try to get at the reason

摸不着头脑 mōbuzháo tóunǎo feel at a loss；can't make head or tail of sth.：这件事我～。I can't make head or tail of it.

摸底 mōdǐ find out (know) the real situation；try to find out the essence of the matter：大家的思想他都～。He understands all the details in others' thinking.

摸老虎屁股 mō lǎohǔ pìgǔ touch the backside of a tiger；twist the tail of a tiger；kick the tiger in the rump；touch the tiger rump (a metaphor for having the courage to cross paths with those who are fierce，hard to deal with，and ideologically problematic.)

摸索 mōsuǒ ① feel (for)；fumble (for)；grope：～着走 grope one's way ② try to find out

摸透 mōtòu get to know sb. or sth. very well

mó

磨 mó〈动〉① rub；wear：袜子～破了。The socks are worn into holes ② grind；sharpen；whet：～刀 sharpen a knife ③ potter away；while away；dawdle away

另见 mò

磨蹭 móceng ① rub (lightly)；stroke (gently) ② move slowly；dawdle ③ pester；nag

磨床 móchuáng grinding machine; grinder

磨练 móliàn put oneself through the mill; temper oneself; steel oneself

磨灭 mómiè wear away; delete; obliterate:不可～的 indelible; ineffaceable; ineradicable

磨难 mónàn trial; tribulation; ordeal; hardship; suffering:历经～ have gone through all kinds of hardships

磨损 mósǔn wear and tear; attrition

磨洋工 móyánggōng potter away one's time; loaf on the job; dawdle along; slacking

蘑 mó

蘑菇 mógū mushroom: ～云 mushroom cloud

摩 mó

〈动〉① rub; stroke; scrape:抚～ stroke ② study; mull over:观～ watch and study

摩擦 mócā ① rub; grate ② friction; conflict

摩登 módēng modern; fashionable

摩肩接踵 mójiān-jiēzhǒng jostle one another on the way; be jam-packed with people

摩拳擦掌 móquán-cāzhǎng rub one's fists and wipe one's palms — be eager for a fight; roll up one's sleeves for battle

魔 mó

①〈名〉devil; demon; evil spirit:妖～ demon; evil spirit ②〈形〉magic; mystic:～力 magic power

魔方 mófāng magic cube (Rubik's cube)

魔鬼 móguǐ devil; demon

魔术 móshù magic; jugglery; conjuring; sleight of hand:～师 magician; prestidigitator

魔王 mówáng ① Satan ② tyrant; despot; fiend

魔掌 mózhǎng devil's clutches; evil hands

模 mó

①〈名〉model; standard; pattern:～范 model; pattern ②〈动〉imitate; copy:～仿动物的叫声 imitate the cries of animals

另见 mú

模范 mófàn model:～作用 set an example; exemplary role. 劳动～ model worker

模仿 mófǎng imitate; copy; pattern after; mock:～某人的动作 mock sb.'s actions

模糊 móhu not clear; indistinct; vague; blurred:～的印象 vague impression. ～语言 fuzzy language

模棱两可 mólíng-liǎngkě ambiguous; equivocal; dubious:抱～的态度 take an equivocal attitude

模拟 mónǐ simulate; imitate; mock; mimic

模特儿 mótèr model

模型 móxíng ① model; pattern ② mould; matrix

摹 mó

〈动〉imitate; copy

摹本 móběn copy; facsimile

摹仿 mófǎng imitate; copy; echo; parrot

摹拟 mónǐ imitate; simulate

膜 mó〈名〉① membrane:粘～ mucous membrane ② film; thin coating:塑料薄～ plastic film

膜拜 móbài worship: 顶礼～ prostrate oneself in worship; pay homage to

馍 mó〈名〉steamed bread; steamed bun

mǒ

抹 mǒ〈动〉① smear; apply; put on:把油～在机器零件上 smear oil on machine parts ② wipe; erase:～把脸 wipe one's face ③ cancel; cross out:～去录音 erase the recording from a tape

抹黑 mǒhēi discredit; defame; spoil the reputation (of); blacken one's name; bring shame on; throw mud at

抹杀(煞) mǒshā write off; obliterate; efface; deny:一笔～ deny completely; reject offhand; write off wholesale

mò

磨 mò ①〈名〉mill; mill stones:推～ use a handmill ②〈动〉grind; mill:～谷物 mill grain

磨坊 mòfáng mill

磨面 mòmiàn mill flour:～机 flour-milling machine

末 mò〈名〉① end; tip ② last stage; end:周～ weekend ③ minor details; nonessentials:本～倒置 put the nonessentials before the essentials ④ dust; powder:肉～儿 minced meat

末班车 mòbānchē ① last bus ② last chance or turn

末节 mòjié minor details; nonessentials

末流 mòliú ① the later and decadent stage of a school of thought, literature, etc ② inferior; low-grade

末路 mòlù dead end; blind alley:穷途～ go into a blind alley; be driven into an impasse

末年 mònián last (the latter) years of a dynasty or regin

末期 mòqī last stage; final phase

末日 mòrì ① end; doom ② Day of Judgment; Judgment Day

末梢 mòshāo tip; end

末尾 mòwěi end

末叶 mòyè last years (at the close, in the late) of a century: 19 世纪～ in the late 19th century

沫 mò〈名〉foam; froth

沫子 mòzi foam; froth; scum:肥皂～ soapsuds; lather. 啤酒～ froth on beer

茉 mò

茉莉 mòlì jasmine:～花茶 jasmine tea

抹 mò〈动〉plaster; daub:～墙 plaster a wall

抹不开 mòbukāi ① feel embarrassed; be put out ② be unable

to act impartially for fear of offending sb.; be afraid of impairing personal relations

秣 mò〈名〉fodder: 粮～ grain and fodder; rations and forage

秣马厉兵 mòmǎlìbīng feed the horses and sharpen the weapons — prepare for battle; keep the army ready for combat; make the army combat-ready

莫 mò ①〈代〉no one; none; nothing: ～过于 nothing is more… than ②〈副〉no; not: 请～见怪。Please don't take it to heart.

莫测高深 mòcè-gāoshēn too profound to be understood; unfathomable; enigmatic

莫大 mòdà utmost; greatest: ～的讽刺 an irony of the first magnitude

莫非 mòfēi could it be (that); could it be possible (that)

莫过于 mòguòyú nothing is more … than; nothing is better than

莫名其妙 mòmíngqímiào ① puzzling; baffling; unintelligible; enigmatic ② be at a loss to understand the mystery; be unable to make head or tail of sth.; be baffled

莫逆 mònì intimate; very friendly: ～之交 sworn friends; bosom friends; friends with complete mutual understanding

莫如 mòrú would be better …; might as well: 求人～求己。It would be better to depend on ourselves than ask for help from others.

莫须有 mòxūyǒu fabulous; unwarranted; groundless; fabricated; unfounded: ～的罪名 groundless (phoney, false) charge

莫衷一是 mòzhōngyīshì unable to agree (decide) which is right; no unanimous conclusion can be drawn

漠 mò ①〈名〉desert: 沙～ desert ②〈形〉indifferent: 冷～ cold and indifferent

漠不关心 mòbùguānxīn be indifferent to; be unconcerned; care nothing about; pay no attention at all

漠漠 mòmò ① dense; thick ② vast and desolate: ～荒原 vast expanse of wasteland

漠然 mòrán coldly; with indifference; in an indifferent manner: ～置之 show no concern (for); pay no heed (to)

漠视 mòshì show indifference to; ignore; neglect

寞 mò〈形〉solitary; lonely: 落～ lonely; desolate

陌 mò〈名〉footpath (running east and west) between fields: 阡～纵横。The paths criss-crossed in the fields.

陌路 mòlù stranger: 视同～ regard sb. as a stranger

陌生 mòshēng strange; unfamiliar; inexperienced: ～面孔 an unfamiliar (strange) face

墨 mò ①〈名〉ink; ink stick:～迹未干 before the ink is dry ②〈形〉black; dark:～绿 dark green

墨宝 mòbǎo ① treasured scrolls of calligraphy or painting ② your beautiful handwriting

墨黑 mòhēi pitch-black; pitch-dark

墨迹 mòjì ① handwriting or painting of sb ② ink mark:～未干 before the ink is dry; The ink was scarcely dry.; The ink was hardly dry before.

墨家 mòjiā Mohist School (a school of thought in the Spring and Autumn and Warring States Periods, 770—221 B. C.); Mohist:～学说 Mohism

墨镜 mòjìng sunglasses

墨守成规 mòshǒu-chéngguī cling (stick) to established practices; get into a groove (rut); stick to accustomed rules

墨水 mòshuǐ ink

墨汁 mòzhī prepared Chinese ink

墨渍 mòzì ink blot; ink spot

默 mò ①〈形〉silent; tacit:～认 recognize tacitly ②〈动〉write from memory:～生词 write the new words from memory

默哀 mò'āi stand in silent tribute to:在死者遗像前～3分钟 observe three minutes' silence in front of the portrait of the deceased

默不作声 mòbùzuòshēng keep silence; hold one's tongue

默读 mòdú read to oneself; read silently

默记 mòjì learn by heart; keep in memory

默默 mòmò quietly; silently:～无闻 be not known to the public; remain obscure

默念 mòniàn ① read silently ② think back; recollect; recall

默契 mòqì ① tacit understanding (agreement) ② secret agreement:双方早有～。The two parties reached a secret agreement long before.

默然 mòrán silent; speechless

默认 mòrèn approve tacitly:～合伙 implied partnership

默想 mòxiǎng think deeply; ponder over; reflect on

默写 mòxiě write from memory

默许 mòxǔ tacitly consent to; acquiesce in

脉 mò〈副〉affectionately:温情～～ full of tender affection
另见 mài

脉脉 mòmò affectionately; lovingly:他～地注视着伏案苦读的女儿。He stared at his daughter studying at the table with loving eyes.

没 mò〈动〉① submerge; sink:淹～ be drowned; submerge ② rise beyond; overflow:雪深～膝。The snow was knee-deep ③ disappear; hide
另见 méi

没落 mòluò decline; be on the wane

没收 mòshōu confiscate; expropriate:～走私货物 seize smuggled goods. ～财产 confiscation of property

móu

谋 móu ①〈名〉plan; scheme; strategy: 有勇有～ brave and astute〈动〉② plan; plot; work for: 搞阴～ plan a conspiracy ③ consult: 不～而合 agreement without prior consultation; happen to coincide with

谋反 móufǎn conspire against the state; plot a rebellion

谋害 móuhài seek to kill sb. (seek sb.'s life); plot to murder

谋略 móulüè astuteness and resourcefulness; strategy

谋求 móuqiú seek; be after; strive for: ～与人和解 seek reconciliation with sb.

谋取 móuqǔ try to gain; seek

谋杀 móushā ① attempt sb.'s life; murder ② [法] premeditated murder; deliberate murder

谋生 móushēng earn one's living; make a livelihood: ～手段 means of livelihood; means of making a living

谋士 móushì counsellor; braintrust; adviser

谋事 móushì ① seek for job; look for work ② plan matters

谋事在人,成事在天 móushì zài rén, chéngshì zài tiān Man proposes, God disposes.

牟 móu〈动〉try to get; seek

牟利 móulì make (seek) profit

牟取 móuqǔ try to get (gain); seek; obtain: ～暴利 seek fat (big, exorbitant) profits; make high profits; making of exorbitant profits

眸 móu〈名〉pupil (of the eye); eye

mǒu

某 mǒu〈代〉certain; some

某处 mǒuchù at a certain place; somewhere

某某 mǒumǒu so-and-so: ～同志 Comrade so-and-so

某人 mǒurén a certain person; some person; someone: 张～ a certain person called Zhang

mú

模 mú〈名〉mould
另见 mó

模板 múbǎn ① shuttering; formwork ② pattern plate

模具 mújù mould; matrix; pattern; die

模样 múyàng ① look; appearance; shape: 他长的什么～? What did he look like? ② about; around: 2 小时～ about two hours

模子 múzi mould

mǔ

亩 mǔ〈名〉a unit of area (=0.

0667 hectares)

亩产量 mǔchǎnliàng per-*mu* yield; yield per *mu*

亩均 mǔjūn average per *mu*

牡 mǔ〈形〉male

牡丹 mǔdān (tree) peony

母 mǔ ①〈名〉mother:家～ my mother ②〈形〉female:～虎 tigress

母爱 mǔ'ài maternal love; mother love

母公司 mǔgōngsī parent company (firm)

母机 mǔjī ① machine tool ② mother aircraft

母鸡 mǔjī hen

母舰 mǔjiàn mother ship

母亲 mǔqīn mother

母权 mǔquán mother right; matriarchal right:～社会 matriarchate

母乳 mǔrǔ breast milk; mother's milk

母系 mǔxì ① maternal side (line):～亲属 maternal relatives ② matriarchal:～社会 matriarchal society

母校 mǔxiào mother school; Alma Mater; one's old school

母性 mǔxìng maternity motherhood: ～本能 maternal (mother) instinct

母语 mǔyǔ ① mother tongue ② parent language; linguistic parent

拇 mǔ

拇指 mǔzhǐ thumb

mù

墓 mù〈名〉grave; tomb

墓碑 mùbēi tombstone; gravestone; grave monument

墓地 mùdì graveyard; cemetery; burial ground

墓穴 mùxuè grave; tomb; vault; open grave

墓志铭 mùzhìmíng inscription on the memorial tablet within a tomb; epitaph

暮 mù ①〈名〉dusk; evening:薄～ dusk ②〈形〉late; towards the end:～春 late spring

暮年 mùnián old age; evening of one's life; (in) one's declining years

暮气 mùqì lifelessness; lethargy: ～沉沉 lifeless; lethargic

暮色 mùsè dusk; twilight; gloaming

幕 mù〈名〉① curtain; screen: 落～。The curtain falls ② act: 第3～ the thrid act; Act Ⅲ

幕后 mùhòu behind the scenes; behind the curtain:～操纵 pull the strings (wires); behind the scenes. ～交易 backstage deal. ～人物 wire-puller; the man who directs behind the scenes

幕僚 mùliáo aides and staff; assistant to a ranking official or general in old China

募 mù〈动〉① enlist; recruit:～兵 enlist soldiers ② raise; collect; gather～款 collect contri-

butions; raise funds (money)
募集 mùjí collect; gather; raise: ～资金 collect funds
募捐 mùjuān collect donations; solicit contributions
慕 mù 〈动〉 admire; yearn for; adore: 爱～ adore; love
慕名而来 mùmíng'érlái come to see a person on account of his established reputation; come to sb. because one admires his fame
木 mù 〈名〉 ① tree ② wood; timber: ～材加工业 wood processing industry 〈形〉③ wooden: ～弹枪 wooden projectiles ④ numb; wooden: 呆若～鸡 dumb as a wooden chicken
木板 mùbǎn board; plank
木板画 mùbǎnhuà wood engraving; woodcut
木材 mùcái wood; timber
木工 mùgōng ① woodwork ② carpenter
木简 mùjiǎn [考]inscribed wooden slip
木匠 mùjiàng carpenter
木结构 mùjiégòu [建] timber structure; wood construction
木刻 mùkè woodcut
木料 mùliào timber; lumber
木马 mùmǎ ① rocking horse: ～计 stratagem of the Trojan horse ② [体] vaulting horse
木乃伊 mùnǎiyī mummy
木偶 mù'ǒu ① wooden idol ② puppet; marionette: ～戏 puppet show (play). ～片 marionette film
木器 mùqì wooden furniture (articles)
木琴 mùqín [乐] xylophone
木梳 mùshū wooden comb
木炭 mùtàn charcoal
木星 mùxīng Jupiter
木已成舟 mùyǐchéngzhōu What's done is done.; Things past cannot be recalled.; It is a fait accompli.
木俑 mùyǒng [考]wooden figurine (used as a burial object)
木鱼 mùyú wooden fish
沐 mù 〈动〉 wash one's hair
沐浴 mùyù take a bath; bath; be bathed in
目 mù 〈名〉 ① eye: 亲眼～睹 see with one's own eyes ② item: 细～ inventory item ③ list; catalogue: 书～ book list
目标 mùbiāo ① aim; goal ② objective; target: ～管理 goal management; management by objective. ～价格 target price
目不识丁 mùbùshídīng not know A from B; be unlettered; be totally illiterate
目不暇接 mùbùxiájiē the eye cannot take it all in; have too many things for the eye to see; have too much to watch
目不转睛 mùbùzhuǎnjīng look fixedly; fix one's eyes on; stare at; gaze intently
目测 mùcè range estimation
目瞪口呆 mùdèng-kǒudāi dumbfounded; stunned; be struck dumb; agape: 惊骇得～ be agape with terror

目的 mùdì purpose; aim; end; goal; objective: ～地 destination. ～地交货 free on board destination

目睹 mùdǔ see with one's own eyes; witness: 亲眼～ see with one's own eyes; see oneself

目光 mùguāng eye; view; sight: ～短浅 short-sighted. ～锐利 sharp-sighted; perspicacious. ～远大 far-sighted; long-sighted

目击 mùjī witness: ～者的报告 eyewitnesser

目空一切 mùkōng-yìqiè look down on everyone; be supercilious; be proud of oneself

目录 mùlù table of contents; contents; catalogue; list

目前 mùqián at present; at the moment

目送 mùsòng follow sb. with one's eyes; watch sb. go; gaze after

目无法纪 mùwúfǎjì defy (flout, disregard) law and discipline

目眩 mùxuàn dizzy; dazzled

目中无人 mùzhōng-wúrén have no respect for anyone; be overweening; be supercilious; consider nobody worth his notice

睦

mù 〈形〉 peaceful; harmonious

睦邻 mùlín good-neighbourliness: ～友好关系 good neighbourly and friendly relations. ～政策 good-neighbour policy

牧

mù 〈动〉 graze; herd; tend: ～马 herd horses

牧草 mùcǎo forage plants; forage grass; pasture; herbage

牧场 mùchǎng livestock farm; pasture land; pasture; grazing land

牧歌 mùgē ① pastoral song; pastoral ② [乐]madrigal

牧工商联合企业 mùgōngshāng liánhé qǐyè stock-raising-processing-marketing allied enterprise

牧区 mùqū pastoral area; pasture region

牧犬 mùquǎn shepherd dog; sheep dog

牧师 mùshī [宗]pastor; priest; clergyman

牧童 mùtóng [放牛的]cowherd; cowboy; [牧羊的]shepherd

牧畜 mùxù livestock farming; cattle breeding

牧业 mùyè stockbreeding; animal husbandry; stock raising: ～基地 livestock breeding areas. ～生产 pastoral production

穆

mù ①〈形〉reverent; solemn: 肃～ solemn ②〈名〉(Mù) a surname

穆民 mùmín believers in Islam

穆斯林 mùsīlín Moslem; Muslim

N n

ná

拿 ná〈动〉① take; hold:～一本书 take a book ② capture; seize; catch:～下要塞 capture a fort. 这个贼被当场～住。The thief was caught in the act ③ deliberately make things difficult for sb.:这件事你～不住人。Don't think that you can make things difficult by not doing the job.〈介〉④［引进所凭借的工具、材料、方法等］:～大帽子吓唬人 intimidate people by pinning political labels on people ⑤［引进所处置的对象］:他们～她当孩子看。They treat her as a child.

拿办 nábàn arrest and deal with according to law; bring to justice

拿大头 nádàtóu ①take the lion's share ② take sb. for a sucker; cheat sb. out of his money; fleece sb.

拿获 náhuò catch; arrest

拿手 náshǒu strong point; adept; expert; be good at; excel in (at):～好戏 one's own masterpiece; what one most excels in; one's own speciality. 她烧菜～。She is good at cooking.

拿着鸡毛当令箭 názhe jīmáo dànglìngjiàn take a chicken feather for a warrant to issue orders—treat one's superior's casual remarks as an order and make a big fuss about it

拿主意 názhǔyi decide; make up one's mind; come to (make) a decision

nǎ

哪 nǎ〈代〉① which; what:你们中间～一位是张先生? Which one of you is Mr. Zhang? ② any:他～一天来都可以。He may come any day ③［表示反问］:～会有这种事? How can there be things as such?

哪儿 nǎr ① where:你上～去啦? Where have you gone? ② wherever; anywhere ③［用于反问句,表示否定］:我～记得住。How could I remember all those words?

哪个 nǎge ① which; which one:～公司 which firm? ② who:～? Who is it?

哪里 nǎli ①［疑问副词］where:我～知道他在什么地方。How can I know where he is? ②［连接副词］where; wherever:我要到～去就到～去。I can go wherever I will. ③［用于反问,表示否定］:我～知道她费了那么大的劲。Little did I know what a great effort she'd made.

哪能 nǎnéng how can:她~这样不讲理? How can she be so unreasonable?

哪怕 nǎpà even if; even; even though:~下雪我也得去。I'll have to go even it snows.

哪些 nǎxiē which; who; what:~问题 what questions. 你要~书? Which books do you want?

哪样 nǎyàng ① what kind (of); which ② any kind of

哪知 nǎzhī who would have thought

nà

捺 nà ①〈动〉press down; restrain:~着性子 keep (control) one's temper ②〈名〉right-falling stroke (in Chinese characters)

呐 nà

呐喊 nàhǎn shout loudly; cry out; yell; raise a hullabaloo

纳 nà〈动〉① receive; admit:~新 take in the fresh ② accept; take in:~忠言 accept advice ③ pay:交~公粮 pay taxes in grain ④ sew in close stitches:~鞋底 stitch soles (of cloth shoes)

纳贡 nàgòng tribute

纳贿 nàhuì ① take a bribe ② offer a bribe

纳凉 nàliáng enjoy the cool (air)

纳闷儿 nàmènr be puzzled; be baffled; be perplexed

纳入 nàrù come under; bring sth. into (within):~轨道 bring sth. within the orbit of (sth. else); bring sth. into line with; be placed in line with

纳税 nàshuì pay taxes; pay duty:~对象 object of taxation. ~凭证 tax payment receipt. ~人 taxpayer. ~收据 duty receipt. ~义务 duty to pay taxes; obligation to pay tax

纳西族 Nàxīzú Naxi nationality, living in Yunnan Province

那 nà ①〈代〉that:~是谁? Who is that? ②〈副〉then, in that case:如果你喜欢,~就买吧! If you like it, take it, then.

那(一)个 nà(yī)gè that:你认识~女孩吗? Do you know that girl? ② [那东西、那事情]that:她为了~在生气。She is angry at that ③〈口〉[用在动词、形容词之前,表示夸张]:瞧她干得~欢哪! See how she's throwing herself into her work! ④〈口〉[代替不便直说的话]:我说他的所做所为太~了。I say his behaviour is somewhat — you know what I mean.

那里 nàli that place; there:他刚从~回来。He's just come from there.

那么 nàme ① like that; in that way:你们不该~做。You shouldn't have behaved like that ② about; or so ③ then, in that case:听说他不在家,~我们不去了。He is said to be not at home. In that case, we shall not go there.

那时 nàshí at that ime; then:从

～起 from that time on; since that time; since then
那些 nàxiē those
那样 nàyàng like that; so; such: 他不是你所想象的～的人。He is not such a man as you think.

nǎi

乃 nǎi ①〈动〉be; be really; be indeed: 失败～成功之母。Failure is the mother of success ②〈副,连〉so; then ③〈副〉only: 惟虚心～能使人进步。You can make progress only if you are modest.
乃至 nǎizhì and even: 他精通英语、法语、俄语～葡萄牙语。He has a good command of English, French, Russian and even Portuguese.
奶 nǎi〈名〉① breast ② milk: ～茶 milk tea ③〈动〉give (a child) the breast; breast-feed: ～孩子 breast-feed a baby
奶粉 nǎifěn milk powder; powdered milk
奶酪 nǎilào cheese
奶奶 nǎinai (paternal) grandmother; grandma
奶牛 nǎiniú milk (milch) cow; milker; [总称]dairy cattle
奶瓶 nǎipíng feeding bottle; nursing bottle; (baby's) bottle
奶油 nǎiyóu cream: ～茶 buttered tea. ～蛋糕 cream cake
奶罩 nǎizhào brassiere; bra
奶嘴 nǎizuǐ nipple (of a feeding bottle)

nài

奈 nài〈副〉how; however; to one's regret
奈何 nàihé ① how; to no avail: 无可～ be utterly helpless; absolutely helpless ② do sth. to a person: 你～不了她。You can do nothing to her.
耐 nài〈动〉be able to bear; endure; stand: ～穿～用 stand wear and tear
耐穿 nàichuān wear well; be durable: 一双～的鞋 a pair of durable shoes
耐烦 nàifán have patience; be patient: 不～ impatient
耐寒 nàihán cold-resistant
耐旱 nàihàn drought-enduring
耐火 nàihuǒ fireproof; refractory
耐火砖 nàihuǒzhuān refractory brick; firebrick
耐久 nàijiǔ durable; lasting
耐劳 nàiláo stand (be able to endure) hard work
耐力 nàilì endurance; staying power; stamina
耐磨 nàimó (of metals) wear-resisting; wearproof
耐热 nàirè heat-resisting; heat-proof
耐人寻味 nàirénxúnwèi provide (afford) much food for thought: 影片中～的重头角色 a meaty role in the film
耐心 nàixīn patient; patience: ～说服 patient persuation. ～的批评教育 painstaking criticism

and education

耐性 nàixìng patience; endurance

耐用 nàiyòng durable: ～物品 durable goods; durables. 经久～ stand wear and tear

nán

南 nán 〈名〉 south 〈形〉 southern: 华～ south China

南半球 nánbànqiú the Southern Hemisphere

南北对话 nán-běi duìhuà North-South dialogue (亦称"南北会议 North-South conferences," the international economic conferences in which developing nations and industralized nations conduct dialogues.)

南边 nánbiān ① south; the southern side ② the southern part of the country, esp. the area south of the Changjiang (Yangtze) River; the South

南方 nánfāng ① south ② the southern part of the country, esp. the area south of the Changjiang (Yangtze) River; the South

南瓜 nánguā pumpkin; cushaw

南极 nánjí South Pole: ～洲 Antarctic Continent; Antarctica

南南对话 nánnán duìhuà South-South dialogue (conferences convened by developing nations to coordinate among themselves their respective stands.)

南腔北调 nánqiāng-běidiào (speak with) a mixed accent; mixed accent of north and south

南水北调 nánshuǐ-běidiào trasfer Southern water to the North (to divert water from the Yangtze River to the water-lacking areas in the North)

南辕北辙 nányuán-běizhé go south by driving the chariot north — act in a way that defeats one's purpose; go south by driving the chariot northward — act in direct contravention; have nothing in common; move in the opposite direction

南针 nánzhēn ① compass ② a guide to action

喃 nán

喃喃 nánnán murmur; mutter: ～不休 make endless speeches

男 nán 〈名〉 ① man; male: ～耕女织。Men till the land and women weave cloth. ② son; boy: 生有2～2女 have two sons and two daughters

男厕所 náncèsuǒ ① men's lavatory (toilet, room) ② (used to indicate a lavatory) Gentlemen; Men; Gents

男盗女娼 nándào-nǚchāng behave like thieves and prostitutes (whores); men as robbers and women as prostitutes; be out-and-out scoundrels

男女老少 nán-nǚ lǎo-shào men and women, young and old

男女同酬 nán-nǚ tóngchóu equal pay for men and women

男配角 nánpèijué supporting actor

男朋友 nánpéngyǒu ① male

friend ②［恋爱中的］boyfriend

男生 nánshēng man student; boy student;［中小学］schoolboy

男声 nánshēng male voice

男性 nánxìng male sex

男主角（～主人公） nánzhǔjué（～zhǔréngōng）hero; male protagonist

男装 nánzhuāng menswear; men's clothing

难 nán〈形〉① difficult; hard: 很～爬的一座山 a hill hard to climb ② bad; unpleasant: ～看的脸色 hard looks〈动〉③ can not bear to part ④ put sb. into a difficult position: 这回把她～住了。This puts her in a difficult position.

另见 nàn

难熬 nán'áo hard to bear

难保 nánbǎo ① there is no guarantee; one cannot say for sure; it's hard to say ② difficult to preserve, protect, defend, etc.

难缠 nánchán (of a person) unreasonable and hard to deal with

难产 nánchǎn ①［医］difficult delivery (labour); dystocia ② difficult to be fulfilled; hard to materialize

难处 nánchǔ hard to get along (on) with

难处 nánchu difficulty; trouble

难倒 nándǎo daunt; baffle; beat

难道 nándào Is it possible that …?; Could it be true that …?; Shouldn't it be …?

难得 nándé ① hard to come by; not easy (for one) to get; rare: ～的机会 rare chance ② seldom; hardly ever

难点 nándiǎn difficult point; difficulty; hard nut to crack

难度 nándù degree of difficulty; difficulty

难怪 nánguài ① (it is) no wonder (that)… ② excusable

难关 nánguān difficulty; crisis: 渡过～ tide over a crisis (difficulty). 技术～ technical barrier

难过 nánguò ① have a hard time; hard to get by: 日子～ lead a hard life ② uneasy; uncomfortable; not feel well

难解难分 nánjiěnánfēn ① be locked together (in a struggle) ② be inextricably involved (in a dispute) ③ cannot bear to part

难堪 nánkān ① hard (for one) to bear; intolerable; unbearable: 令人～ unbearable; trying ② awkward; embarrassed

难看 nánkàn ① ugly; unattractive ② disgraceful; shameful ③［脸色］pale; pallid: 脸色～ look pallid; look displeased

难免 nánmiǎn hard to avoid; unavoidable

难能可贵 nánnéng-kěguì difficult of attainment, hence worthy of esteem; deserving praise for one's excellent performance or behaviour; estimable; commendable

难色 nánsè reluctant or embarrassed expression

难舍难分 nánshě-nánfēn find it difficult to tear apart; be loath to part from each other

难受 nánshòu ① feel unwell; feel ill ② feel sorry; feel unhappy; feel bad: 我为她感到～。I feel sorry for her.

难说 nánshuō it's hard to say; you never can tell

难题 nántí difficult (thorny, knotty) problem; baffling problem; a hard nut to crack: 科学的～ difficulties of a science

难听 nántīng ① unpleasant to the ear; rough ② uncivil; coarse; bad; offensive: 说～的话 use bad language ③ scandalous: 这件事情说出去多～。The matter will create a scandal once it gets out.

难忘 nánwàng unforgettable; memorable

难为情 nánwéiqíng feel shy (abashed); be embarrassed

难闻 nánwén smell bad; smell nasty: ～的气味 bad smell; unpleasant smell

难以 nányǐ difficult to: ～启齿 too embarrassed to say it; hard to speak out. ～逆料 difficult to conjecture; hard to forecast (predict)

难于 nányú hard to; difficult to

nàn

难 nàn ①〈名〉disaster; misfortune; calamity: 大～临头 be faced with imminent disaster ②〈动〉blame; accuse: 非～ reproach; blame; bring charges against 另见 nán

难船救助人员 nànchuán jiùzhù rényuán salvor

难民 nànmín refugee

难友 nànyǒu fellow sufferer

náng

囊 náng〈名〉bag; sack; purse: 胶～ capsule

囊空如洗 nángkōng-rúxǐ be penniless; with empty pockets; be broke to the wide (world); not have a penny to bless oneself with

囊括 nángkuò embrace; include; make a clean sweep of all; sweep all: ～全部金牌 make a clean sweep of all gold medals

囊中物 nángzhōngwù things in one's bags; be easily got at; sth. certain of attainment

náo

挠 náo〈动〉① scratch: ～痒痒 scratch an itch ② hinder: 阻～ obstruct ③ yield; flinch: 不屈不～ unswerving; unbending; unyielding; indomitable

挠钩 náogōu long-handled hook

挠头 náotóu ① scratch one's head ② difficult to tackle

nǎo

恼 nǎo〈形〉① angry; irritated:

～恨 resent ② worried; annoyed

恼火 nǎohuǒ be annoyed (vexed); lose patience; enrage; be irritated:令人～的 annoying; vexing; provoking; irritating

恼怒 nǎonù angry; irritated

恼人 nǎorén irritating; annoying

恼羞成怒 nǎoxiū-chéngnù be ashamed into anger; fly into a rage from (with) shame; become angry and red-faced; exasperate

脑 nǎo 〈名〉brain

脑袋 nǎodai ① head ② brains; mind

脑电图 nǎodiàntú［医］electroencephalogram

脑海 nǎohǎi mind; brain:～里翻腾着母亲的话。The words spoken to me by my mother were tossing around in my mind.

脑际 nǎojì mind; memory

脑浆 nǎojiāng brains

脑筋 nǎojīn ① brains:～好(坏) have good (poor) brains; have a good (bad) memory. 动～ use one's brains ② ideas:旧～ outdated ideas; old-fashioned ideas

脑力 nǎolì mental faculties; brains:～劳动 mental work; intellectual work. ～劳动者 mental worker; brain worker

脑满肠肥 nǎomǎn-chángféi heavy-jowled and potbellied (said of the idle rich)

脑体倒挂 nǎotǐ-dàoguà Income of mental labour is much lower than that of manual labour.

脑炎 nǎoyán cerebritis; encephalitis

脑汁 nǎozhī brains

脑子 nǎozi ① brain ② brains; mind; head

瑙 nǎo 见"玛瑙"(mǎnǎo)

nào

闹 nào ①〈形〉noisy:这屋里太～。This room is too noisy. 〈动〉② make a loud noise; stir up trouble:～事 create disturbances ③ give rent (to one's anger, resentment, etc.):～意气 pick quarrels; sulk ④ suffer from:～水灾 suffer from flood ⑤ make; do; undertake:～革命 make revolution

闹病 nàobìng be ill; fall sick

闹不清 nàobuqīng cannot tell; be unclear about

闹待遇 nào dàiyù fuss over remuneration

闹翻 nàofān fall out with sb.

闹鬼 nàoguǐ ① be haunted ② play tricks behind sb.'s back

闹哄哄 nàohōnghōng noisy; boisterous; clamorous

闹乱子 nào luànzi make a disturbance; cause trouble

闹脾气 nào píqi vent one's spleen; lose one's temper; be in a tantrum

闹情绪 nào qíngxù be disgruntled; be dissatisfied; fall into a mood

闹市 nàoshì busy street; busy shopping centre; downtown

area

闹事 nàoshì make trouble; stir up trouble; create (raise) a disturbance

闹笑话 nào xiàohuà make a fool of oneself; make a stupid mistake

闹心 nàoxīn ① be vexed; be annoyed ② feel sick; feel queasy

闹新房 nào xīnfáng give sb. a shivaree

闹意见 nào yìjian be on bad terms because of a difference of opinion; be divided in opinion and engage in bickerings

闹钟 nàozhōng alarm clock

ne

呢 ne 〈助〉①[用在疑问句的末尾,表示疑问的语气]:他们都去,我们～? They are all going. What about us? ② [用在陈述句的末尾,表示确认事实]:稻子长得才好～。The rice is coming along fine ③ [用在陈述句的末尾,表示动作或情况正在继续]:天下着雪～。It is snowing now. ④ [用在句中表示停顿]:他爸爸～,也就回到乡下了。As for his father, he went back to his village afterwards.

另见 ní

něi

馁 něi 〈动〉be dispirited; be disheartened:气～ lose heart; become down-hearted; be disheartened

nèi

内 nèi ①〈形〉inside; inner; internal; interior:～地 the interior areas ②〈名〉one's wife or her relatives:～人 my wife

内部 nèibù inside; interior:人民～矛盾 contradictions among the people. ～董事 inside director. ～政策 a policy for internal observance

内地 nèidì inland; interior:～工业 industry in the interior

内定 nèidìng decided at the higher level but not officially announced

内耳 nèi'ěr internal ear; inner ear

内分泌 nèifēnmì endocrine; internal secretion

内服 nèifú taken by the mouth; oral

内阁 nèigé cabinet:～改组 cabinet reshuffle; cabinet reorganization. ～会议 cabinet meeting (council). ～总理 prime minister; primary member of the cabinet

内海 nèihǎi inland sea; continental sea

内涵 nèihán connotation; intension:～扩大再生产 intensive expanded reproduction

内行 nèiháng ① be adept in; be expert in; be in one's line ② adept; expert; professional; one who knows how

内耗 nèihào ① energy consumed by a machine without getting any work done ② losses suffered in internal strife

内讧 nèihòng internal strife (conflict, dissension); internecine struggle; fabricated strife

内奸 nèijiān secret enemy agent within one's ranks; a hidden traitor

内疚 nèijiū guilty conscience; prickings of conscience; compunction:奇怪的是他做了这种事却毫无～之心。It is strange that he did such a thing without the slightest compunction.

内聚力 nèijùlì cohesive force; cohesion

内科 nèikē internal medicine (department):～医生 physician

内陆 nèilù inland; interior; hinterland

内陆运输 nèilù yùnshū inland transportation

内乱 nèiluàn internal troubles; civil strife

内贸 nèimào domestic commerce

内幕 nèimù inside story; lowdown (on)

内勤 nèiqín ① internal or office work ② office staff

内情 nèiqíng inside knowledge; inside story; true picture (of a unit)

内容 nèiróng content; substance: ～丰富 be rich in content

内伤 nèishāng ① internal injury ② disorder of internal organs caused by improper diet, fatigue, emotional strains, sexual excess, etc.

内外 nèiwài ① inside and outside; at home and abroad:～交困 be in dire straits at home and abroad; beset by (with) troubles at home and abroad; beset with difficulties both at home and abroad ② around; about: 一个月～ in about a month

内务 nèiwù ① internal affairs ② daily routine tasks to keep the barracks, etc. clean and tidy

内线 nèixiàn ① planted agent ② interior lines ③ inside (telephone) connections

内向 nèixiàng [心] introversion: ～性格者 introvert

内销 nèixiāo sell on the domestic market; for the home market; market products inside China; domestic sales: ～商品 commodities for the home market

内心 nèixīn ① heart; innermost being ② [数]incentre (of a triangle)

内衣 nèiyī underwear; underclothes

内因 nèiyīn [哲] internal cause: ～论 theory of the internal origin

内应 nèiyìng person operating from within in coordination with outside forces; a planted agent; a plant

内在 nèizài internal; intrinsic; immanent:～因素 internal (immanent) factor

内债 nèizhài internal debt; domestic debt

内政 nèizhèng internal (home, domestic) affairs:互不干涉～ noninterference in each other's internal affairs

内资企业 nèizī qǐyè Chinese-funded enterprises

nèn

嫩 nèn 〈形〉① tender; delicate; young: 脸皮～ shy; bashful ② light: ～绿 tender green ③ inexperienced; unskilled: 她还是～得很。She is still too immature.

嫩芽 nènyá tender shoot; young bud; new bud: 抽～ bud

néng

能 néng ①〈助动〉can: 你～开车吗? Can you drive a car? ②〈形〉able; capable: ～人 man of large calibre; able person; man of ability ③〈名〉ability; capability; skill: 工作～力 working ability

能动 néngdòng active; dynamic: ～性 activity; dynamic role; role of conscious activity. 人的～作用 man's dynamic role; man's initiative

能干 nénggàn able; capable; competent

能够 nénggòu can; be able to; be capable of

能官能民 néngguān néngmín be able to be both an official and a citizen; both serve as official and remain one of the common people

能耗 nénghào energy consumption

能力 nénglì ability; capability: ～测验 tests of ability. ～强 be very capable

能量 néngliàng ① energy: ～转化 conversion of energy ② capabilities

能耐 néngnài ability; skill

能人 néngrén able person

能上能下 néngshàng-néngxià be able to work at both higher and lower levels; be able to go up or down; be ready to accept a higher or lower post

能说会道 néngshuō-huìdào have a glib tongue; smart talker

能手 néngshǒu expert; a good hand at; dab; proficient; a crack hand at: 网球～ a dab at tennis

能源 néngyuán energy source; energy: ～结构 energy resource structure

能者 néngzhě able man: ～多劳。An able man is always busy.; Able people should do more work. ～为师 Let those who know teach.

ní

霓 ní 〈名〉 secondary rainbow

霓虹灯 níhóngdēng neon lamp; neon light; neon: ～广告 neon sign

尼 ní 〈名〉(Buddhist) nun

尼姑 nígū (Buddhist) nun

尼龙 nílóng nylon: ～伞 nylon umbrellas

泥 ní 〈名〉① mud; clay; earth:

～石流 mudflow; mud-rock-flow ② any paste-like, mashed vegetable or fruit:土豆～ mashed potato
另见 nì

泥浆 níjiāng slurry; mud

泥坑níkēng mud pit; morass; mire; quagmire:陷入…的～ fall (sink) into the mire (morass) of…

泥泞 nínìng muddy; miry; slushy; sloppy:雨后道路～。The road was muddy after the rain.

泥菩萨过江,自身难保 nípúsà guò jiāng,zìshēn nánbǎo like a clay idol fording a river — hardly able to save oneself (let alone anyone else); can't save himself any more than a clay idol can save itself while crossing a river; idols of clay which can hardly survive when crossing a river

泥沙 níshā silt:～俱下鱼龙混杂 Mud and sand are carried along — there is a mingling of good and bad.; Water flows down with sand and mud together.

泥土 nítǔ ① earth; soil ② clay

泥瓦匠 níwǎjiàng mason; plasterer; bricklayer

泥俑 níyǒng clay figures buried with the dead; funerary clay figures; earthen figurines

泥沼 nízhǎo mire; swamp; morass; slough

呢 ní 〈名〉 woollen cloth
另见 ne

呢绒 níróng woollen cloth; wool fabric

nǐ

拟 nǐ 〈动〉 ① draw up; draft:～定议定书 draft a protocol ② intend; plan:～于下周前往上海 plan to go to Shanghai next week ③ imitate:～古 imitate the ancients

拟订 nǐdìng draw up; map out; work out:～计划 work out a plan

拟稿 nǐgǎo prepare (make) a draft; draft

拟议 nǐyì ① proposal; recommendation ② draw up; draft

你 nǐ 〈代〉 ① [第二人称单数和复数] you:～喜欢吗? Do you like it? ～方 your side; you ② [泛指任何人] you; anyone; one:碰上这么一个人,～有什么办法? What can you do with a person like that?. ～追我赶的局面 be seethed with emulation; heated emulation

你死我活 nǐsǐ-wǒhuó life-and-death:～的斗争 life-and-death struggle; mortal struggle. ～竞争 cut-throat competition

nì

溺 nì 〈动〉 ① drown ② indulge oneself in; addict oneself to:～于感情 sentimentalism

溺爱 nì'ài love blindly; pamper; be excessively fond of; dote on:

～孩子 dote on one's child; lavish care on one's child

溺死 nìsǐ be drowned; drown; drowning

溺婴罪 nìyīngzuì infanticide by drowning

溺职 nìzhí neglect one's duty; dereliction

逆 nì ①〈形〉counter; contrary: ～风 contrary (adverse) wind ②〈动〉go against; disobey; defy: ～历史潮流而动 go against the tide (trend) of history ③〈名〉traitor; betrayer

逆差 nìchā［商］unfavourable balance; adverse balance; deficit: ～国家 deficit country. 国际收支～ adverse (unfavourable) balance of international payments. 贸易～ unfavourable trade balance; trade deficit

逆耳 nì'ěr offend the ear; be unpleasant to the ear; grate upon the ear: ～之言 words that offend the ear

逆风 nìfēng ① go against the wind ② contrary wind; head wind

逆光 nìguāng backlighting

逆境 nìjìng adverse (untoward) circumstances; adversity: 在～中奋斗 struggle in adversity

逆来顺受 nìlái-shùnshòu meekly submit to oppression, maltreatment; resign oneself to adversity; meekly accept humiliations

逆利率 nìlìlǜ negative interest rate

逆料 nìliào see beforehand; foresee; anticipate: 尚难～。It's hard to say.; There is no telling.

逆流 nìliú adverse (back) current; countercurrent

逆水 nìshuǐ against the current: ～行舟 sail against the current

逆行 nìxíng ① (of vehicles) go in a direction not allowed by traffic regulations; go in the wrong direction ② retrograde motion

逆转 nìzhuàn become worse; reverse

逆子 nìzǐ unfilial son; impious son

匿 nì〈动〉hide; conceal: 隐～ go into hiding; hide

匿藏 nìcáng conceal; hide; go into hiding

匿迹 nìjì go into hiding; stay in concealment

匿名 nìmíng anonymous: ～的文学 anonymous literature. ～(控告)信 anonymous letter of accusation. ～者 anonymity

腻 nì〈形〉① oily; greasy: 汤太～了。The soup is too oily. ② meticulous: 细～的描写 a minute description ③〈动〉be bored; be tired of

腻烦 nìfan ① be sick of; be tired of; be fed up; be disgusted at ② hate; loath

泥 nì〈动〉cover or daub with plaster, putty, etc.: ～墙 cover the crevices in a wall with mud or plaster

另见 ní

niān

拈 niān 〈动〉pick up (with one's fingers)

拈阄 niānjiū draw lots (cuts)

拈花惹草 niānhuā-rěcǎo lust after flowers and grasses — chase after loose women; dally with women

拈轻怕重 niānqīng-pàzhòng prefer the light to the heavy — pick easy jobs and shirk hard ones; prefer light work to the heavy

nián

粘 nián 同"黏"
另见 zhān

黏 nián 〈形〉sticky; glutinous: ～～糊糊的小伙子 a dilly-dally fellow

黏附 niánfù adhere: ～力 adhesion

黏合 niánhé ① [化]bind; adhere: ～剂 adhesive; binder ② adhesion

黏性 niánxìng stickiness; viscosity: ～工资 sticky wages

年 nián 〈名〉① year: 明～ next year ② age; era: ～高望重 aged and celebrated ③ New Year (Spring Festival): 拜～ pay a New Year call ④ harvest: 丰～ a bumper year; rich harvest ⑤ 〈形〉yearly; annual: ～度计划 annual plan

年表 niánbiǎo chronological tables; annals; chronology

年成 niáncheng harvest: 好～ good (bumper) harvest. 不好～ lean year

年初 niánchū the beginning of the year

年代 niándài years; age; era: 90～ (in) the nineties (1990s)

年底 niándǐ the end of the year

年度 niándù year: 会计～ fiscal year; financial year. ～结算 annual closing. ～亏损 annual loss. ～预算 annual budget

年富力强 niánfù-lìqiáng in the full vigour of manhood; in the prime of life

年根 niángēn the end of the year

年关 niánguān the end of the year (formerly time for settling accounts)

年号 niánhào the title of an emperor's reign

年华 niánhuá years; time: ～虚度 spend vainly the best of one's days; have wasted the best years of one's life

年画 niánhuà New Year pictures

年会 niánhuì annual meeting (conference, session); yearly meeting

年货 niánhuò goods for use during the Spring Festival; special purchases for the Spring Festival

年级 niánjí year; [中小学的] form; grade: ～导师 year tutor

年纪 niánjì age

年假 niánjià ① New Year holidays ② winter vacation

年鉴 niánjiàn yearbook; almanac;

annals

年景 niánjǐng ① the year's harvest ② holiday atmosphere of the Spring Festival

年均 niánjūn annual average

年利率 niánlìlǜ annual interest rate

年历 niánlì single-page calendar：～工资 wages based on seniority and education

年龄 niánlíng age：达到法定～ come of age．～性别结构 age-sex structure

年轮 niánlún annual ring；growth ring

年谱 niánpǔ chronological biography；year-by-year account of one's life

年轻 niánqīng young

年息 niánxī annual interest；interest per annum

年限 niánxiàn fixed number of years

年薪 niánxīn annual salary；yearly pay

年夜 niányè the eve of the lunar New Year

年终 niánzhōng (at) the end of a year；year-end：～奖金 year-end bonus．～结帐 year-end settlement of account

niǎn

碾 niǎn ①〈名〉roller：～子 roller〈动〉② grind or husk (with a roller)：把小麦～成面粉 grind down the wheat into flour ③ crush：～得粉碎 be crushed to powder (pieces)

碾米 niǎnmǐ husk rice：～机 rice mill

碾子 niǎnzi roller

捻 niǎn ①〈动〉twist with the fingers：～佛珠 fingering prayer beads ②〈名〉sth. made by twisting：灯～儿 lampwick

撵 niǎn〈动〉drive out；oust：～下台 oust from a leading position

niàn

念 niàn〈动〉① think of；miss：我非常想～你们。I miss you very much ② attend school；study：她～过中学。She has been to middle school ③ read aloud：～得清楚些 read more distinctly ④〈名〉thought；idea：万～俱灰。All ambitions are blasted.

念白 niànbái［剧］spoken part of a Chinese opera；recitation

念叨 niàndao be always talking about；talk about again and again in anticipation or collection；harp on

念佛 niànfó chant the name of Buddha；pray to Buddha；the recitation of Buddha's name；tell one's beads

念经 niànjīng chant scriptures (sutras)

念头 niàntou thought；idea；intention

niáng

娘 niáng 〈名〉 mamma; ma; mother

娘家 niángjiā a woman's premarital home; [法] original house

娘亲 niángqīn relatives of the maternal side

娘子军 niángzǐjūn detachment of women

niàng

酿 niàng 〈动〉 ① make (wine); brew (beer) ② lead to; result in:～祸 lead to disaster ③〈名〉 wine:佳～ good wine

酿成 niàngchéng lead to; give rise to; breed:危机业已～。The crisis has already been brought on.

酿酒 niàngjiǔ make wine; [啤酒] brew beer:～厂 winery; brewery

酿造 niàngzào make (wine, etc); brew (beer):～食品 fermentating food

niǎo

袅 niǎo 〈形〉slander and delicate

袅袅 niǎoniǎo ① roll up; curl up:炊烟～。Smoke is curling upward from kitchen chimneys ② linger (about, on):余音～。The melody is still lingering about ③ wave gently; sway:晨风中垂柳～。The drooping willows are waving gently in the morning breeze.

鸟 niǎo 〈名〉 bird:～虫书 bird and insect calligraphy

鸟尽弓藏 niǎojìn-gōngcáng cast aside the bow once the birds are all killed—cast sb. aside when he has served his purpose

鸟瞰 niǎokàn (get a) bird's-eye view:从山顶～全城 get a bird's-eye view of the city from the hilltop

鸟枪 niǎoqiāng ① fowling piece ② air gun

niào

尿 niào ①〈名〉urine ②〈动〉pass water; urinate

尿布 niàobù nappy; diaper:替孩子换～ diaper (change) a baby

尿床 niàochuáng wet the bed

niē

捏 niē 〈动〉 ① hold between the fingers; pinch; nip:～住一枚别针 hold a pin with one's fingers ② knead with the fingers; mould:～泥人儿 mould clay figures ③ make up; fabricate:～造罪名 frame charges

捏一把汗 niēyībǎhàn break into a sweat with fear (fright); sweat with anxiety (fear)

捏造 niēzào make up; cook up; concoct; invent; fabricate:～事

实 make up (invent) a story; fabricate facts. ～谣言 fabricate a rumour

niè

涅 niè ①〈名〉alunite ②〈动〉dye sth. black

涅槃 nièpán [佛] nirvana

蹑 niè ①〈动〉lighten one's step; walk on tiptoe ② follow

蹑手蹑脚 nièshǒu-nièjiǎo walk gingerly; walk on tiptoe

蹑足潜踪 nièzúqiánzōng walk stealthily

孽 niè〈名〉evil; sin: 作～ commit a sin; do evil

孽子 nièzǐ ① unfilial son; unworthy descendant ② son of a concubine

níng

宁 níng〈形〉peaceful; tranquil; quiet; calm

另见 nìng

宁静 níngjìng peaceful; quiet; tranquil: ～的夜空 peaceful night sky

柠 níng

柠檬 níngméng lemon: ～水 lemonade

拧 níng〈动〉① wring; twist; squeeze: ～干毛巾 twist a wet towel ② pinch; tweak: 在孩子脸颊上～一下 give the child a pinch on the cheek

另见 nǐng

拧断 níngduàn twist off; wring off

拧干 nínggān wring (dry); squeeze dry

狞 níng〈形〉ferocious; hideous; fierce; grim

狞笑 níngxiào smile hideously and hypocritically; grim smile (laugh)

凝 níng〈动〉① coagulate; congeal; curdle: ～结在商品中的社会必要劳动时间 the socially necessary labour time congealed in commodities ② fix: ～视天空 gaze into the sky

凝固 nínggù solidify

凝结 níngjié congeal; condense; curdle; coagulate

凝聚 níngjù condensation; coagulation; cohesion: ～力 cohesive forces; cohesion

凝神 níngshén with concentrated (fixed) attention; attentively: ～细听 listen attentively (to); be all ears

凝视 níngshì stare at; gaze at; peer at; gaze fixedly

凝思 níngsī be buried in thought; meditate on; muse on

凝想 níngxiǎng be lost in thought; meditate

凝重 níngzhòng ① dignified; imposing ② (of sound or voice) deep and forceful ③ deep; dense; thick

nǐng

拧 nǐng〈动〉① turn; twist; screw:～紧螺丝 tighten up a screw ② differ; be at cross-purpose:两人越说越～。The more they talked, the more they disagree. ③〈形〉mistaken; wrong:全给弄～了。All is wrong.
另见 níng

nìng

宁 nìng〈助〉(would) rather; (had) better prefer:～可站着死,不愿跪着生 better to die standing than to live on one's knees
另见 níng

宁可 nìngkě would rather; had better:天下雪我～留在家里。I would rather stay at home if it snows.

宁死不屈 nìngsǐ-bùqū (would) rather die than surrender; prefer death to humiliation

宁为玉碎,不为瓦全 nìng wèi yù suì,bù wèi wǎ quán rather be a shattered vessel of jade than an unbroken piece of pottery — better to die in glory than live in dishonour; rather be a jade broken than a tile intact; rather die for a noble cause than continue to live a shameful life

宁愿 nìngyuàn would rather; had better; prefer:我～做这事而不愿做那事。I prefer to do this rather than that.

宁"左"勿右 nìngzuǒ-wùyòu it is better to be much to the "Left" than too much to the Right

niú

牛 niú〈名〉ox;[雌性] cow;[雄性] bull

牛痘 niúdòu ① cowpox ② smallpox pustule:种～ vaccinate

牛黄 niúhuáng [中药] bezoar

牛马生活 niúmǎ shēnghuó live like beasts of burden; a subhuman standard of life; a dog's life; live worse than beasts of burden

牛排 niúpái beefsteak

牛脾气 niúpíqi stubbornness; obstinacy; bullheadedness

牛气 niúqi arrogant; overbearing

牛头不对马嘴 niútóu bù duì mǎzuǐ horses' jaws don't match cows' heads; contradict each other; irrelevant; incongruous with

牛蛙 niúwā bullfrog

牛仔裤 niúzǎikù jeans; cowboy pants:一条～ a pair of jeans

niǔ

忸 niǔ

忸怩 niǔní shy; timid; bashful:～不安 feel (be) embarrassed; feel abashed ～作态 behave coyly; be affectedly shy; behave in an affected way

扭 niǔ〈动〉① turn round：～过头去 turn one's head away ② twist；wrench：把铁丝～断 twist and break a wire ③ sprain：他把肩部～伤了。He gave a wrench to his shoulder. ④ seize：～获 seize；catch；arrest

扭摆 niǔbǎi (of one's body) sway

扭打 niǔdǎ grapple (with)；scuffle (with)

扭动 niǔdòng sway；writhe

扭亏增盈 niǔkuī-zēngyíng turn from deficits to profits；reduce losses and increase profits；make up deficits and increase surpluses

扭伤 niǔshāng sprain；wrick；wrench：～手腕 sprain one's wrist

扭送公安机关 niǔsòng gōng'ān jīguān seize and deliver to the public security organ

扭转 niǔzhuǎng turn；turn back；reverse：～局势 reverse the trend；save a critical situation；turn the tide. ～亏损 eliminate losses. ～乾坤 bring about a radical change in the situation；reverse the course of events

钮 niǔ〈名〉button

钮扣 niǔkòu button：钉～ sew on a button. 扣上衣服的～ button up one's coat

纽 niǔ〈名〉① knob；handle ② bond；tie

纽带 niǔdài bond；tie；link：结成兄弟友谊的～ forge ties of fraternal friendship

nóng

农 nóng〈名〉① agriculture；farming：～业适度规模 farming on an optimum scale ② peasant；farmer：～民工 peasant worker

农产品 nóngchǎnpǐn agricultural products；farm produce：～征购 purchase quotas of farm produce

农场 nóngchǎng (agricultural) farm：～交货 ex plantation

农村 nóngcūn rural area；countryside：～城市化 urbanize the countryside. ～村民委员会 rural villagers' committees. ～集市贸易 country market trade. ～社会化服务体系 rural community-run service system

农贷 nóngdài agricultural loan

农副产品 nóng-fù chǎnpǐn agricultural and sideline products；subsidiary agricultural products

农工商联合企业 nóng-gōng-shāng liánhé qǐyè agricultural-industrial-commercial combines

农户 nónghù peasant household

农机 nóngjī agricultural machinery：～户 agricultural machinery households

农家肥 nóngjiāféi farmyard manure

农具 nóngjù farm tools；agricultural implements

农科示范户 nóngkē shìfànhù agricultural science model households (advanced agricultural households that promote applied agricultural science and technology)

农垦 nóngkěn agricultural reclamation：～企业 state-owned land-reclamation enterprises

农口 nóngkǒu agricultural agencies (an overall term for organizations responsible for work in the field of agriculture)

农贸市场 nóngmào shìchǎng farmers' market；farm produce market

农民 nóngmín ① peasant ② peasantry

农牧区 nóngmùqū agricultural and pastoral areas

农时 nóngshí farming season：不违～ not miss the farming season

农田 nóngtián farmland：～水利化 bring most of the farmland under irrigation

农闲 nóngxián slack farming season

农药 nóngyào farm chemical；insecticide；pesticide

农业 nóngyè agriculture；farming：～保险制度 agricultural insurance system. ～工程 agricultural engineering. ～区划 agricultural districting. ～合作化 cooperative transformation of agriculture. ～生产责任制 agricultural production responsibility system. ～信用合作社 agricultural credit cooperatives

农艺师 nóngyìshī agronomist；masters of agricultural skills

农用工业 nóngyòng gōngyè agroindustry

农转非 nóng zhuǎn fēi turning to nonagricultural trades from agriculture；change from rural to nonrural；transfer from farming to nonfarming

浓 nóng 〈形〉 ① thick；dense：一头～密的头发 a thick head of hair ② (of degree or extent) strong；great：兴趣很～ take a great interest in sth.

浓度 nóngdù density；thickness；concentration；［酒等的］strength

浓厚 nónghòu ① thick；dense；～的烟雾 thick smog ② intense；strong：～的民族色彩 strong national colour. ～的生活气息 savouring of life ③ great；keen：～的兴趣 great interest (in)

浓烈 nóngliè strong；thick；heavy

浓眉 nóngméi thick (bushy) eyebrows：生得～大眼 have heavy features

浓密 nóngmì dense；thick：～的森林 a dense forest

浓缩 nóngsuō concentrate；enrich

浓郁 nóngyù strong；rich：～的时代气息 rich in the topics of the current epoch；plumbing the depths of the present epoch

浓重 nóngzhòng dense；thick；strong

浓妆 nóngzhuāng heavy makeup and gaudy dress

脓 nóng 〈名〉 pus；matter

脓包 nóngbāo ① pustule ② good-for-nothing；worthless fellow

脓疮 nóngchuāng fester; ulcers; running sore
脓肿 nóngzhǒng abscess

nòng

弄 nòng 〈动〉 ① do; make; handle; manage; get sb. or sth. into a specified condition: 把问题～糊涂 obscure the question; befog the issue. 你在这儿～什么? What are you up to here? ② get; fetch: 你去～点水来。Go and get some water ③ play with; meddle with: 小孩爱～水。Children like to play with water.
另见 lòng
弄错 nòngcuò be mistaken; make a mistake; misuderstand
弄好 nònghǎo get sth. right; put … in order; do well; be through (with); finish
弄坏 nònghuài spoil (ruin) sth.; make a mess of; put out of order: 把事情～ make a mess of things
弄假成真 nòngjiǎ-chéngzhēn What was make-believe has become reality.; Pretence may become reality.; say in fun what is fulfilled in earnest; fulfil what was promised as a joke
弄僵 nòngjiāng land sth. in an impasse; bring to a deadlock
弄巧成拙 nòngqiǎo-chēngzhuō try to be clever only to end up with a blunder; try to be clever but end in being a fool (but turn out the contrary)
弄清 nòngqīng clarify; make clear; figure out: ～事实 make sure of fact. ～是非 clarify what is right from what is wrong; clarify right and wrong; distinguish right from wrong; thrash out the rights and wrongs
弄权 nòngquán manipulate power for personal ends
弄死 nòngsǐ put to death; kill
弄虚作假 nòngxū-zuòjiǎ resort to deceit; resort to deception; practise fraud; employ trickery; use fraudulent means. ～者 falsifier
弄糟 nòngzāo spoil; muddle; make a mess of: 你把事情～了。You have spoiled the whole thing.; You have made a mess of the job.

nú

奴 nú 〈名〉 slave; bondservant
奴才 núcai flunkey; lackey; benchman: ～相 servility; servile behaviour. ～哲学 lackey's philosophy; slavish philosophy
奴化 núhuà enslave: ～教育 enslaving education; slave education. ～政策 policy of enslavement
奴隶 núlì slave; bondman; bond servant; vassal: ～主贵族 slave-owning nobility. ～主义 slavishness
奴仆 núpǔ servant; menial; serf
奴颜婢膝 núyán-bìxī servile flat-

tery; slavish; sycophancy; servility;obsequiously beg to …; subservient to; sedulously fawn upon; abjectly do a thing to curry favour with; adulation

奴役 núyì enslave; bond service; servitude: ～制 enslavement system; bondage

nǔ

弩 nǔ 〈名〉 crossbow

努 nǔ 〈动〉 exert (effort); put forth (strength):～力学习马克思主义 make great effort in studying Marxism

努力 nǔlì exert oneself; make efforts; strive; endeavour: ～攀登科学高峰 strive to scale the heights of science

nù

怒 nù 〈形〉 ① angry; furious:～目而视 look at with angry eyes; glare at ② raging; violent; wild:狂风～号。A violent wind is howling.

怒不可遏 nùbùkě'è boil with indignation; be beside oneself with rage

怒潮 nùcháo raging tide

怒发冲冠 nùfà-chōngguān become so angry that one's hair lifted (raised) his cap; His hair bristled up with anger.; bristle with anger

怒吼 nùhǒu roar; howl; bellow: 风在～。Wind is howling.

怒火 nùhuǒ anger; fury: ～中烧 burn with anger

怒气 nùqì anger; rage; wrath: ～冲冲 in a rage; in a huff. ～冲天 be in a towering rage; give way to unbridled fury; boil over

怒色 nùsè angry look; scowl: 面有～ look angry

怒视 nùshì glare at; glower at; scowl at

怒涛 nùtāo angry waves; raging billows

怒形于色 nùxíngyúsè be black in the face; be betrayed into anger; look angry

怒族 Nùzú the Nu nationality (living in Yunnan Province)

nǚ

女 nǚ 〈名〉 ① woman; female: ～兵 enlisted women ② daughter; girl: 子～ sons and daughters

女厕所 nǚcèsuǒ ① women's lavatory (toilet); ladies' room ② (used as a sign for a public toilet) Ladies; Women

女车 nǚchē woman's bicycle; lady's bicycle

女犯人 nǚfànrén offendress

女高音 nǚgāoyīn soprano

女皇 nǚhuáng empress

女将 nǚjiàng female "general" (metaphor for a woman of exceptional talent and ability): 排球～ female volleyball kingpin

女眷 nǚjuàn the womenfolk of a family

女朋友 nǚpéngyǒu ① female friend ② [恋爱中的]girl friend

女色 nǚsè woman's charm：好～ be fond of women

女生 nǚshēng woman student；[中小学] schoolgirl

女声 nǚshēng [乐] female voice

女士 nǚshì lady；madam

女王 nǚwáng queen

女性 nǚxìng female sex；woman

女婿 nǚxù son-in-law

女演员 nǚyǎnyuán actress

女职员 nǚzhíyuán office girl

女中音 nǚzhōngyīn mezzo-soprano

nuǎn

暖 nuǎn ①〈形〉warm；genial：一股～流 a warm flow ②〈动〉warm up：房子里～和起来了。The room is warming up.

暖房 nuǎnfáng greenhouse；hothouse

暖壶 nuǎnhú ① thermos flask；thermos bottle ② a teapot or waterpot with a cosy ③ a metal or earthen hot-water bottle

暖和 nuǎnhuo warm；mild；genial

暖流 nuǎnliú ① warm current ② warm feeling

暖气 nuǎnqì central heating：～装置 central heating system；heating installation

暖气片 nuǎnqìpiàn heating radiator；radiator

暖色 nuǎnsè warm colour

暖洋洋 nuǎnyángyáng warm

nüè

疟 nüè

疟疾 nüèji malaria fever；malaria；ague：恶性～ pernicious malaria

虐 nüè〈形〉cruel；tyrannical

虐待 nüèdài abuse；ill-treat；maltreat：～儿童 abusing children；cruelty to children. ～老人 maltreatment of the aged

虐政 nüèzhèng harsh (tyrannical) government；misrule；misgovernment；tyranny

nuó

挪 nuó〈动〉move；shift：～动 move；shift

挪动 nuódong move；shift

挪用 nuóyòng ① divert (funds) ② embezzle；peculate；misappropriate；unauthorized use of：～公款 embezzle (misappropriate) public funds；defalcate；embezzlement of public funds. ～公款者 peculator

nuò

懦 nuò〈形〉weak；timid；cowardly

懦夫 nuòfū coward；milksop

懦弱 nuòruò weak；cowardly：～

无能 be weak and useless：～性 spinelessness

糯 nuò

糯米 nuòmǐ glutinous rice：～粉 glutinous rice flour

诺 nuò ①〈动〉promise：承～ promise to undertake ②〈叹〉yes

诺贝尔奖金 Nuòbèi'ěr jiǎngjīn Nobel Prize：～获得者 Nobelist；Nobel-man；Nobel Laureate

诺亚方舟 Nuòyàfāngzhōu Noah Ark

诺言 nuòyán promise：（不）守～ keep（break）one's promise；keep（break）one's word. 履行～ carry out one's promise

O o

ō

喔 ō 〈叹〉oh：～，原来你也这么想！Oh，so you feel the same way！

喔唷 ōyō 〈叹〉[表示惊讶、痛苦] oh：～这么大的梨！Oh，what a big pear！～，好痛！Ouch，it hurts！

ó

哦 ó 〈叹〉[表示将信将疑]what：～，他们已经完工了吗？What！Have they finished their work already？
另见 é；ò

哦嗬 óhē oho：～，你们来了！Oho，so you've come！

ò

哦 ò 〈叹〉[表示领会]oh：～，我知道了。Oh，I see.
另见 ó

ōu

讴 ōu 〈动〉sing

讴歌 ōugē 〈动〉① sing the praises of；eulogize；laud ② folk song

鸥 ōu 〈名〉gull：海～ sea gull

欧 ōu 〈名〉Europe

欧化 ōuhuà Europeanize；Occidentalize

欧佩克 Ōupèikè [石油输出国组织] OPEC （Organization of Petroleum Exporting Countries）：～成员国 a member nation of OPEC

欧印语系 Ōu-Yìnyǔxì Indo-European family

欧元 Ōuyuán [1999年1月1日起，欧洲实行的统一货币] euro

欧洲安全和合作会议 Ōuzhōu ānquán hé hézuò huìyì[简称"欧安会"] Conference on Security and Cooperation in Europe；European Security and Cooperation Conference

欧洲共同体市场 Ōuzhōu gòngtóngtǐ shìchǎng European Common Market （ECM）；Euromarket

欧洲经济共同体 Ōuzhōu jīngjì gòngtóngtǐ European Economic Community （EEC）

欧洲议会 Ōuzhōu yìhuì European Parliament

殴 ōu 〈动〉beat；hit：斗～（of two people）fight；brawl

殴打 ōudǎ beat；beat up；hit：互相～ exchange blows；come to

blows. ～罪 battery

殴斗 ōudòu have a fist fight; have fisticuffs

ǒu

藕 ǒu 〈名〉 lotus root

藕断丝连 ǒuduàn-sīlián A section of arrowroot is separated, but the clinging fibre remains; (of lovers) separated but still in each other's thought.; One's love, like a lotus root, linked by fibres though divided.

藕粉 ǒufěn lotus root starch

偶 ǒu 〈名〉① idol; image: 玩～ toy figure; doll ② even (number); in pairs ③ spouse; mate: 佳～ good spouse ④〈形〉casual; accidental; fortuitous: ～然的东西 something accidental

偶尔 ǒu'ěr occasionally; casually

偶犯 ǒufàn ① casual felon; accidental felon ② casual offender; nonhabitual offender

偶合 ǒuhé coincidence

偶然 ǒurán chance; accidental; fortuitous: ～论(说) fortuitism; casualism; accidentalism. 绝非～ be by no means fortuitous

偶像 ǒuxiàng idol; image: ～崇拜 idolatry; idol worship

偶因 ǒuyīn occasional cause: ～论 occasionalism

呕 ǒu 〈动〉 vomit; throw up

呕出 ǒuchū vomit out; throw up; reject

呕吐 ǒutù vomit; throw up; be sick

呕心沥血 ǒuxīn-lìxuè spend one's life energy; make painstaking efforts; strain one's heart and mind: ～的艺术 the most contrived of arts

òu

沤 òu 〈动〉soak; steep

沤肥 òuféi make compost by waterlogging; wet compost; waterlogged compost

沤田 òutián soggy fields

怄 òu 〈动〉① irritate; annoy ② be annoyed; be irritated

怄气 òuqì be difficult (annoyed) and sulky: 怄了一肚子气 have a bellyful of repressed grievances. 他动不动就跟我～。He's frequently difficult (at odds) with me.

P p

pā

啪 pā〈象〉bang

啪嚓 pāchā〈象〉a sudden loud noise as made by sth. falling to the ground and breaking apart: ～一声镜子掉在地上碎了。The mirror dropped with a crash.

啪嗒 pādā〈象〉clatter; patter: 打字机～～地响着。The typewriter was clattering away.

趴 pā〈动〉① lie on one's stomach; lie prone: 经过抢修,～窝的两辆汽车又开动起来了。After a rush-repair job, the two grounded automobiles got started again ② bend over: ～在桌子上 bend over a desk

趴伏 pāfú lie on one's stomach; lie prone

趴架 pājià (of houses) collapse; topple down

pá

扒 pá〈动〉① scratch; rake up (together): 把枯树叶～在一起 rake together the dead leaves ② pick; pilfer: ～口袋 pick sb.'s pocket ③ stew; braise: ～羊肉 stewed mutton
另见 bā

扒窃 páqiè pick and steal; frisk: ～犯 pickpockets

扒手 páshǒu pickpocket; pickpurse: 谨防～。Beware of pickpockets.

耙 pá ①〈名〉rake; harrow: 木～ wooden rake ②〈动〉rake: 把炉灰～出来 rake out a fire

耙地 pádì hoeing

耙平 pápíng rake (the soil) smooth; make smooth with a rake

耙子 pázi rake

爬 pá〈动〉① crawl; creep: 跟在人家后面～行 crawl behind others ② climb: ～满青藤的小屋 the log cabin overgrown with creepers. ～山 climb a mountain

爬格子 págézi crawl over squared or lined paper—write (esp. in order to make a living)

爬行 páxíng crawl; creep: ～动物 reptile. ～思想 idea of moving at a snail's pace

爬泳 páyǒng [体] crawl

爬在别人头上 pá zài biérén tóu shàng tread on people's necks; lord it over others; sit on the backs of others

pà

帕 pà〈名〉handkerchief: 头～

kerchief; turban

怕 pà ①〈动〉fear; dread; be afraid of:～丑 be afraid of disgracing ②〈副〉I suppose; perhaps:会议～要延期了。I'm afraid the meeting will be postponed.

怕得要命 pà de yàomìng fear intensely; mortally fear; be frightened out of one's wits; go in mortal fear of; be frightened to death

怕老婆 pà lǎopo be henpecked

怕人 pàrén ① frightening; horrible; terrible:那情形可真～。What a terrible scene! ② timid; shy:～的鸟 shy bird

怕生 pàshēng [指小孩] be shy in the presence of strangers; be shy with strangers

怕是 pàshì I guess; I suppose; perhaps; maybe

怕事 pàshì be afraid of getting into trouble (involved):胆小～ timid and overcautious; coward

怕羞 pàxiū shy; bashful; sheepish; coy:～得说不出话来 be coy of speech

pāi

拍 pāi〈动〉① beat; tap lightly; pat; clap:～掉苍蝇 flap the flies away ②[照相]take (a photo) ③[电报]send (a telegram) ④ flatter; fawn on:能吹会～ be good at boasting and toadying〈名〉⑤ bat; racket ⑥ (of music) beat; time:～子记号 time signature

拍板 pāibǎn ① "beat the clappers"; call the shots (a metaphor for decision-making by the person-in-charge) ② beat time with clappers:你唱，我～。You sing, I will beat time with the clappers.

拍打 pāida pat; slap

拍击 pāijī (of waves) beat; run against

拍马屁 pāi mǎpì curry favour with; lick sb.'s boots; suck up to; fawn on; make up to

拍卖 pāimài auction; sale by auction:～某物 sell sth. by (at) auction. ～价格 auction price

拍摄 pāishè [照片]take (a photo, picture); [电影]shoot (a film); film:把一部小说～成电影 film a novel

拍手 pāishǒu clap one's hands:～称快 clap one's hands with satisfaction; gleefully hailing; clap and cheer. ～叫好 applaud

拍照 pāizhào take a photo; [请人拍]have one's photo taken:不准～ No Camera

拍子 pāizi ① bat; racket ② [乐] time; beat:打～ beat time

pái

排 pái〈动〉① line up; arrange in order:～在公共汽车站上的人们 people lining up at the bus stop ② drain; discharge:～险 eliminating a hazard ③ rehearse:～练戏中的角色 rehearse a part in a play〈名〉④

row; line: 坐在前～座位 sit in the front row ⑤［军］platoon ⑥ raft: 木～ timber raft ⑦〈量〉row: 一～建筑物 a row of buildings

排版 páibǎn［印］compose; set type

排比 páibǐ parallelism; parallel form (construction)

排场 páichǎng display of splendour; show of extravagance; ostentation and extravagance; grand style: 讲～ go in for pomp

排斥 páichì exclude; repel; get rid of; reject; preclude: ～异己 exclude ousiders (dissidents); discriminate against those who hold different views; renounce persons who do not agree with sb.

排除 páichú remove; exclude; get rid of; rule out: ～异己［见"排斥异己"］. ～障碍 remove an obstacle

排队 páiduì form a line; line up; queue up

排放 páifàng release: ～废气 release waste gas

排灌 páiguàn drainage and irrigation: ～站 drainage and irrigation station

排挤 páijǐ crowd out; squeeze out: 互相～ each trying to squeeze out the other

排解 páijiě ① mediate; reconcile

排涝 páilào drain waterlogged fields

排练(演) páiliàn(yǎn) rehearse: ～节目 have a rehearsal

排列 páiliè put in order, rank; arrange: ～成行 arrange in a line (row)

排气 páiqì exhaust

排山倒海 páishān-dǎohǎi great in momentum and irresistible: 以～之势 with the irresistible force of an avalanche; with the force of a landslide; with the momentum of an avalanche

排头兵 páitóubīng soldier at the head of the line (a metaphor for an advanced individual in a unit or group who is worthy of being emulated by others)

排外 páiwài exclusive; antiforeign: ～主义 exclusionism; antiforeignism; xenophobia

排泄 páixiè drain; excrete: ～糟粕 discard waste matter

排序榜 páixùbǎng［工业、企业］industrial rankings

排演 páiyǎn rehearse

排印 páiyìn set (up) type and print; print

排忧解难 páiyōu-jiěnàn relieve worries and overcome difficulties

排字 páizì typesetting; composing: ～工人 typesetter; compositor

徘 pái

徘徊 páihuái ① pace up and down; linger; wander about: 在马路上～ wander up and down the road ② hesitate: ～歧路 hesitate at the crossroads ③ fluctuate; fluctuation: 农轻重工业长期～不前。Agriculture, light and heavy industries suffered from fluctuations for a long period of time.

牌 pái 〈名〉① tablet; plate; board; placard: 车～ number plate (on a vehicle) ② trademark; brand: 名～货 famous-brand goods ③ playing cards

牌号 páihào ① the name of a shop; shop sign ② trademark

牌价 páijià ① market price; market quotation; quoted price ② list price

牌局 páijú game at dominoes, mahjong, or cards; gambling game

牌位 páiwèi memorial tablets

牌照 páizhào license plate (tag): ～税 license tax; fee of permit. ～持有人 holder of license

牌子 páizi ① trademark; brand: ～老 old brand; well-known brand ② sign; sign post; plate

pǎi

迫 pǎi
另见 pò

迫击炮 pǎijīpào mortar: ～弹 mortar shell

pài

派 pài ①〈动〉send; dispatch; appoint: ～重兵进驻 send large numbers of troops to be stationed in …〈名〉② faction; sect; clique; school: ～性 factionalism. 各种不同学～ different schools of thought ③ style; manner; air: 大～头 have great style ④〈量〉两～意见 two different views

派别 pàibié faction; sect; group; school; persuasion: ～纠纷 factional disputes (squabbles)

派出机构 pàichū jīgòu detached office; agency

派出所 pàichūsuǒ police post; police substation; (local) police station

派饭 pàifàn arranged meals (meals in peasant's homes arranged for cadres sent to work in rural areas for short periods)

派购 pàigòu purchase by state quotas; assigned purchasing; purchase by assigned quotas

派活 pàihuó assign work

派款 pàikuǎn collection of compulsory contributions

派遣 pàiqiǎn send (sb. on a mission); dispatch

派生 pàishēng derive (from): ～词 derivative

派头 pàitóu style; air; manner: 她～真不小! She certainly puts on quite a show!

派系 pàixì factions

派驻 pàizhù dispatch to a post: 联合国～贝鲁特的观察员有 50 人。The United Nations has dispatched and stationed fifty observers at Beirut.

pān

攀 pān 〈动〉① climb; clamber; scale ② seek connections in

high places：高～ make friends or claim ties of kinship with someone of a higher social position

攀比 pānbǐ compare with the higher；vie：～产值 compete with one another in the pursuit of superficial output values

攀登 pāndēng climb；clamber；scale；escalate：～科技新高峰 scale new heights in science and technology

攀附 pānfù ①（of a plant）climb（a support）② seek connections with

攀高 pāngāo ① climb to a higher point ② make friends or claim ties of kinship with someone of a higher social position

攀亲 pāngqīn claim kinship；profess to be sb. else's relation

攀谈 pāntán chitchat；have a free and easy talk；chat with：与朋友～ have a chat with a friend

攀缘 pānyuán ① climb；clamber ② climb the social ladder through pull

攀折 pānzhé break off（twigs，etc.）；pick；pluck：请勿～花木 Please don't pick the flowers.；Please don't break off the branches.

pán

蹒 pán

蹒跚 pánshān walk haltingly；limp；hobble；stagger

盘 pán

①〈名〉plate；dish；tray：茶～儿 tea tray〈动〉② coil；roll；wind：蛇～绕在树枝上。The snake coiled itself round the branch ③ examine；check：～问 cross-examine ④ take inventory：～货 take stock ⑤〈量〉两～菜 two dishes. 一～棋 a game of chess

盘剥 pánbō lend money at usury；exploit by means of usury；practise usury

盘查 pánchá interrogate and examine；question；examine thoroughly

盘存 páncún take inventory

盘道 pándào winding mountain paths；bends

盘点（货） pándiǎn（huò）make（take）an inventory of；take stock：～存货 take stock

盘费（缠） pánfèi（chán）travelling expenses

盘根错节 pángēn-cuòjié with twisted（coiled）roots and gnarled branches；too complicated to cope with；deep-rooted；interlocked and impregnable

盘桓 pánhuán ① stay；linger ② winding；coiling ③ wind round and round；spiral up or down

盘踞 pánjù illegally（forcibly）occupy；entrench；infest

盘库 pánkù make an inventory of goods in a warehouse

盘绕 pánrào twine；coil；spiral；wreathe

盘算 pánsuàn calculate；plan；premeditate；figure；weigh：～好 premeditate everything. 心

中～一件事 weigh a matter in one's mind

盘条 pántiáo wire rod

盘问 pánwèn crossexamine; bring sb. to book (for sth.); interrogate: 详细地～某人 cross-examine sb. in detail

盘旋 pánxuán twist; circle; spiral: ～而上 spiral up

盘帐 pánzhàng audit accounts; check accounts

磐 pán monolith; bedrock

磐石 pánshí huge rock: 坚如～ as firm (solid) as a rock; rock-firm

pàn

判 pàn 〈动〉① judge; decide: ～卷子 mark examination papers ② sentence; condemn: ～5年徒刑 be sentenced to five years' imprisonment ③ discriminate; distinguish: ～别好坏 discriminate good from bad

判案 pàn'àn decide the case

判处 pànchǔ sentence; condemn; impose a sentence; sentence to …: ～死刑 sentence sb. to death

判定 pàndìng judge; decide; determine

判读 pàndú machine reading

判断 pànduàn judge; decide; determine; ascertain: ～市场机会 assess market opportunities. ～曲直 pronounce a judicial decision or sentence

判决 pànjué decide (by judgement); judge; sentence: ～书 written judgement. ～某人有(无)罪 pronounce sb. (not) guilty

判例 pànlì legal precedent; judicial precedent; precedent; example (instance) of judgement

判令 pànlìng order

判明 pànmíng distinguish; discriminate: ～是非 discriminate between right and wrong

判刑 pànxíng pass sentence on sb.; punish; sentence

判罪 pànzuì convict (of): ～的确证 proof of conviction. 判盗窃罪 convict (sb.) of theft

畔 pàn 〈名〉side; bank (of a lake, river, etc.): 湖～ the shore of a lake

叛 pàn 〈动〉rebel; betray: ～变革命 turn against the revolution; turn traitor to the revolution

叛变 pànbiàn ① turn traitor; betray; defect ② mutiny (against): ～者 mutineer

叛国 pànguó betray one's country; turn traitor to one's country: ～罪 (crime of) treason; high treason

叛乱 pànluàn rebellion; insurrection; rise in rebellion

叛卖 pànmài betray; sell: ～行为 betrayal

叛逆 pànnì rebel

叛徒 pàntú traitor; turncoat; renegade

盼 pàn 〈动〉hope; long for; look

forward to：～家信 look forward to hearing from one's family

盼头 pàntou good prospects；hope：事情有了～。Things are looking up.

盼望 pànwàng hope；expect；long for：～重见光明 long to see the light of day

pāng

滂 pāng

滂湃 pāngpài (of water) roaring and rushing：～的急流 rushing torrent

滂沱 pāngtuó pouring；torrential：大雨～。It rained in torrents.；The rain poured down in torrents.

páng

旁 páng

①〈名〉side：站在路～ stand by the side of the road 〈形〉② other；else：～人 other people ③ lateral radical of a Chinese character

旁白 pángbái aside (in a play)

旁边 pángbiān side：～有一棵树。There is a tree nearby.

旁观 pángguān stand by；look on；observe from the sideline：袖手～ stand by with folded arms. ～者清。An onlooker sees clearly.；A bystander is always clear-minded.

旁敲侧击 pángqiāo-cèjī make oblique thrust；beat about the bush；attack by innuendo；make veiled attack

旁若无人 pángruòwúrén act as if no one was nearby；have no regard for others；unwarranted assumption of airs；look self-assured (supercilious)

旁听 pángtīng ① attend a class in the capacity of an auditor；audit a class：～生 guest student；auditor ② be a visitor at a meeting：～席 visitors' seats；public gallery

旁系 pángxì collateral line；lateral branch：～亲属 collateral relative；collateral

旁征博引 pángzhēng-bóyǐn quote copiously to support one's thesis；be well documented

旁证 pángzhèng circumstantial evidence；collateral evidence；side witness

磅 páng

另见 bàng

磅礴 pángbó ① boundless；grand；majestic：气势～的泰山 the majestic Taishan Mountain ② fill；spread all over：热情～ be filled with immense zeal

螃 páng

螃蟹 pángxiè crab

膀 páng

膀胱 pángguāng bladder

彷 páng

彷徨 pánghuáng ① walk back and forth；wander (about) ② uncertainty；indecision；hesitation；hesitate：～不定 be unable to make up one's mind

庞 páng〈形〉① huge ② innumerable and disordered

庞大 pángdà huge; colossal; massive; enormous:～的赤字 huge deficits

庞然大物 pángrán-dàwù huge monster (creature) colossus; formidable giant

庞杂 pángzá numerous and jumbled; unwieldy and complex; jumbled:内容～。The contents are in a jumble.

pàng

胖 pàng〈形〉fat; stout; plump:长～了。Put on weight.

胖乎乎 pànghūhū plump; chubby; pudgy:婴儿～的脸 chubby face of a baby

胖子 pàngzi fat person; fatty; stout

pāo

抛 pāo〈动〉① throw; cast; toss; fling:～救生圈 throw a life buoy ② leave behind; cast aside; abandon:被～在后面 be left far behind

抛出 pāochū ① cast; expel; eject ② put forward; come up with; dish up; rush out with:～伪装 fling off the disguise

抛光 pāoguāng polishing; buffing

抛离 pāolí abandon; leave behind

抛锚 pāomáo ① cast anchor ② [车]break down; stall:汽车～了。The car broke down.

抛弃 pāoqì cast aside; throw away; abandon; discard; desert:～得一干二净 throw overboard; throw to the winds

抛售 pāoshòu sell (goods, etc.) in large quantities:～物资 sell large quantities of goods

抛头露面 pāotóu-lùmiàn show one's face in public; show oneself up much in public; appear in public

抛砖引玉 pāozhuān-yǐnyù cast away a brick and attract a jade stone; offer one's (humble) opinions to elicit others' valuable ones

páo

炮 páo
另见 pào

炮制 páozhì dish up; cook up; concoct:如法～ follow suit; do what sb. else has done; act after the same fashion

袍 páo〈名〉gown; robe

咆 páo

咆哮 páoxiāo rage and roar; roar; howl; thunder; bark:～如雷 be in a thundering rage; roar with anger (rage)

刨 páo〈动〉① dig; excavate:～地 dig the ground ② deduct; exclude; minus:20天～去10天，只剩下10天了。Twenty minus ten — there are only ten days to go now.

刨根究(问)底 páogēn-jiū(wèn)dǐ inquire into the root of the matter; get to the root (bottom) of the matter

pǎo

跑 pǎo 〈动〉① run:～得很快 run very fast ② run away; flee:一个犯人～了。A prisoner has escaped ③ walk:～了10公里 have walked ten kilometres ④ run about doing sth.; run errands:～买卖 be a travelling salesman

跑步 pǎobù ① run; march at the double ② jogging (a form of physical exercise)

跑单帮 pǎodānbāng make business trips on one's account; travel around trading on one's own:～的 self-employed travelling trader

跑刀 pǎodāo race skates

跑道 pǎodào ① track ② [机场的]runway

跑电 pǎodiàn leakage of electricity

跑了和尚跑不了庙 pǎole héshàng pǎobùliǎo miào A monk may run away but he can't take his monastery with him.; The monk may run away, but the temple remains (but the temple can't run with him.)

跑龙套 pǎo lóngtào ① be a utility man; carry a spear in the supporting role; play a walk-on part:～的小配角 supernumerary ② be a handyman

跑马灯 pǎomǎdēng slowly revolving lantern

跑题 pǎotí digress from the subject; stray from the point

跑腿儿 pǎotuǐr run errands; do legwork

跑鞋 pǎoxié running shoes; track shoes

pào

泡 pào 〈名〉① bubble; foam:戳破肥皂～ prick a bubble ② blister:手上起了～ raise (get) blisters one one's palm ③〈动〉soak; steep:用开水～茶 steep the tea in boiling water

泡病号 pào bìnghào shun work on pretence of illness

泡菜 pàocài pickled vegetables; pickles

泡茶 pàochá make (brew) tea

泡饭 pàofàn ① soak cooked rice in soup or water ② cooked rice reheated in boiling water; gruel from recooked rice

泡沫 pàomò foam; froth; suds; bubble:～经济 bubble economy. ～塑料 foam plastics; styrofoam. ～灭火器 styrofoam fire extinguisher

泡影 pàoyǐng visionary hope; bubble; illusion:化为～ end up in smoke; melt into thin air; come to nothing; vanish like soup bubbles

疱 pào 〈名〉blister; bleb

炮 pào 〈名〉① gun; cannon; ar-

tillery piece：充当～灰 serve as cannon fodder ② firecrackers ③［象棋］cannon
另见 páo

炮兵 pàobīng artillery；［个人］artilleryman

炮弹 pàodàn cannon ball；shell

炮火 pàohuǒ artillery fire；gunfire

炮击 pàojī shell；bombard：～司令部 bombard the headquarters

炮舰 pàojiàn gunboat：～政策 gunboat policy

炮声 pàoshēng report of a gun；gunshot：～隆隆 roar of guns；roll of cannon

炮眼 pàoyǎn ① porthole；embrasure ② blasthole；dynamite hole；borehole

炮战 pàozhàn artillery action (duel)

炮仗 pàozhang firecracker；cracker；squib：放～ fire off crackers

pēi

呸 pēi〈叹〉bah；pah；pooh：～！胡说八道！Bah！That's nonsense！

胚 pēi

胚胎 pēitāi embryo：～的特殊社会科学 embryonic special social sciences

胚芽 pēiyá germ

péi

培 péi〈动〉① bank up (with earth)：～土 earth up ② cultivate；train；foster：～养优良品种 cultivate fine strains of seed

培训 péixùn cultivate；train：～班 training class；clinic. ～结业后成绩考核 post test. 写作～班 a writing clinic

培养 péiyǎng ① foster；train；rear；bring up；nurture；cultivate：～对音乐的兴趣 cultivate a taste for music ②［生］culture：～细菌 culture bacteria

培育 péiyù cultivate；breed；bring up：～人才 cultivate men of ability. ～市场体系 foster (cultivate) a market system

培植 péizhí cultivate；foster：～亲信 foster one's cohorts

赔 péi〈动〉① compensate (for)；pay for：因为…向某人～偿 compensate sb. for ② stand a loss：～钱 lose money in business；run at a loss

赔本 péiběn lose one's capital；make a loss；lose；sustain losses in business；run a business at a loss：～生意 losing business；bad bargain

赔不是 péi bùshi apologize

赔偿 péicháng compensate (for)；make amends (for)；make up (for)：～名誉 indemnity for defamation (libel). ～人 compensator. ～损失 compensation for losses

赔款 péikuǎn ① pay an indemnity；pay reparations ② indemnity；reparation：战争～ war reparations

赔礼 péilǐ apologize (to)：～道歉

make (offer) an (formal) apology(to sb.)

赔了夫人又折兵 péile fūrén yòu zhébīng lose one's wife as well as one's soldiers — pay a double penalty; throw the helve after the hatchet; suffer a double loss

赔帐 péizhàng pay for the loss of cash or goods entrusted to one

赔罪 péizuì make an apology; beg sb.'s parden; apologize (to)

陪 péi 〈动〉keep sb. company; accompany:～客人到火车站 accompany a visitor to the railway station

陪伴 péibàn accompany; keep sb. company; attend:～某人回家 accompany sb. home

陪衬 péichèn ① set off; contrast with:绿叶～红花。The green leaves set off the red flowers ② set off; foil:作～ serve as a foil

陪床 péichuáng be by someone's bedside (to visit a family member, relative, friend, or colleague in the hospital to keep him company and to take care of him)

陪房 péifang a maidservant that follows the bride to her husband's house as her personal maid

陪客 péike a guest invited to a dinner party to help entertain the guest of honour

陪审 péishěn take part in adjudication; act (serve) as an assessor in a law case:～团 jury. ～员 jurors; juryman

陪同 péitóng accompany:～前往参观 accompany sb. on a visit

陪葬 péizàng be buried with the dead:～品 funeral objects. ～墓 attendant tomb; subordinate tomb

pèi

配 pèi 〈动〉① join in marriage:婚～ marriage ② mate (animals):～猪 mate pigs ③ mix; compound:～方 make up a prescription; fomula ④ match:颜色不～。The colours don't match. ⑤ deserve; be qualified; be worthy of:她～做一名教师。She is qualified to be a teacher. ⑥ distribute; allocate; according to plan:～售 ration ⑦〈名〉spouse; mate:～偶选择 mate selection

配备 pèibèi ①［装备等］fit (with); equip (with):～着现代机器 be equipped with modern machines ②[人]assign; appoint

配餐 pèicān special diet meals

配电 pèidiàn［电］distribution (of power supply):～网 electric distribution networks

配额 pèi'é quota:出口～ export quota

配股 pèigǔ［股票］rationed shares

配合 pèihé coordinate; cooperate with; be in keeping with

配给 pèijǐ be rationed:～制 ration system

配件 pèijiàn ① fittings; accessories; parts ② replacement

配角儿 pèijuér minor role; supporting actor or actress

配料 pèiliào ① mix ingredients according to a recipe; get materials ready (for the manufacture of sth.) in the right proportion ② [冶金]burden

配套 pèitào form a complete set: ～成龙 serialize the process of production. 社会保障体系的～改革 supporting reform of the social security system. ～工程 parts and accessories for imported equipment; auxiliary project. ～的行政法律体系 a complete set of administrative law system

配音 pèiyīn [影视] dub: 给外国电影～ dub foreign films

配乐 pèiyuè dub in background music: ～广播 broadcast with background music

配置 pèizhì deploy; dispose (troops, etc.); allocate: 合理地～和使用教育资源 judiciously allocating and using resources for education

沛 pèi 〈形〉abundant; copious: 精力充～ be full of energy; be full of vim and vigour

佩 pèi 〈动〉① wear (at the waist, etc.): ～刀 wear a sword ② admire: ～服 express admiration for

佩带 pèidài wear; bear: ～校徽 wear a school badge

佩服 pèifú admire: ～得五体投地 admire sb. from the bottom of one's heart

pēn

喷 pēn 〈动〉① spout; spurt; gush: 血从伤口～出 blood spurted from the wound ② spray; sprinkle: 给植物～一种杀虫剂 spray an insecticide upon plants

喷灌 pēnguàn spray irrigation: ～设备 sprinkling devices

喷壶 pēnhú watering can; sprinkler

喷漆 pēnqī spray-paint

喷气式 pēnqìshì jet-propelled: ～飞机 jet plane; jet. ～客机 jet airliner

喷泉 pēnquán fountain

喷射 pēnshè spray; spurt; jet

喷嚏 pēntì sneeze: 打～ sneeze

喷头 pēntóu ① shower nozzle ② sprinkler head

喷雾 pēnwù spray; atomization: ～器 sprayer; atomizer

喷嘴 pēnzuǐ spray nozzle; spray head

pén

盆 pén 〈名〉basin; tub pot: 脸～ washbasin

盆地 péndì basin

盆花 pénhuā potted flower

盆景 pénjǐng potted landscape; miniature trees and rockery; tray landscape; miniature gardening

盆栽 pénzāi ① grown

(cultivated) in a pot ② potted flowers or miniature trees

pèn

喷 pèn

喷香 pènxiāng fragrant; delicious:饭菜～。The dishes smell delicious.

pēng

烹 pēng 〈动〉cook; boil

烹饪 pēngrèn cooking:～法 cookery; cuisine

烹调 pēngtiáo ① cook (dishes) ② cooking; cuisine

怦 pēng 〈象〉pit-a-pat:她的心～～直跳。Her heart went pit-a-pat.; Her heart was beating fast.

砰 pēng〈象〉bang; thump:～的一声门关上了。The door banged shut.

抨 pēng 〈动〉attach; impeach

抨击 pēngjī [用语言文字] attack; flay censure; lash out at

澎 pēng 〈动〉splash; spatter

澎湃 pēngpài [波浪等] rising high (tide); be in an upsurge; surging: 心潮～ have one's mind in a turmoil; feel an upsurge of emotion

péng

膨 péng

膨大 péngdà expand; inflate

膨化食品 pénghuà shípǐn inflated food

膨体纱 péngtǐshā [纺] bulk yarn

膨胀 péngzhàng expand; inflate; swell:通货～ inlfation of currency; inflation

蓬 péng〈形〉fluffy; dishevelled

蓬荜生辉 péngbì-shēnghuī Friends grace sb.'s houses with their presence.; My humble house is honoured by your presence (with your visit).

蓬勃 péngbó vigorous; prosperous; thriving; full of vitality: ～发展 develop vigorously; go full steam; advance briskly; grow apace; surge vigorously forward

蓬松 péngsōng puffy; fluffy:～的头发 fluffy hair

蓬头垢面 péngtóu-gòumiàn with dishevelled hair and a dirty face; (with) an unkempt appearance

篷 péng 〈名〉covering or awning on a car, boat, ect.: 车～ awning on a car

篷布 péngbù paulin; tarpaulin

篷车 péngchē covered truck; [铁路上的] box wagon; boxcar

篷子 péngzi awning (for protection from the sun, rain, wind, etc.)

朋 péng〈名〉friend：宾～满座。There was a houseful of guests.；Visitors filled all the seats.

朋党 péngdǎng faction；rival；equal

朋友 péngyǒu friend：够～ be a true friend. 男（女）～ boy (girl) friend

彭 Péng〈名〉a surname

棚 péng〈名〉① shed；shack；awning：车～ bicycle shed (park) ② awning

棚户 pénghù slum inhabitants；shack-dwellers：～区 slums；gutter

鹏 péng

鹏程万里 péngchéng-wànlǐ A roc can reach a destination of a myriad miles away at one jump — (said of those who) have a bright future；brilliant prospects

pěng

捧 pěng〈动〉① hold or carry in both hands：～着一个碗 hold a bowl in both hands ② boost；extol；exalt：大～自己 lavish praise on oneself

捧场 pěngchǎng ① lavish praise on；sing the praise；flatter；exalt ② [演员等]be a member of a claque；root (for)

捧腹大笑 pěngfù-dàxiào roar (scream) with laughter；burst out laughing；split one's sides with laughter

pèng

碰 pèng〈动〉① touch；knock；bump：把墨水瓶～翻了 knok the ink-bottle over ② meet (with)；run into：在街上～到一个熟人 bump (run) into an acquaintance in the street ③ try one's luck (chance)：～运气 try one's luck

碰杯 pèngbēi clink glasses (with)

碰壁 pèngbì run up against a stone wall；run into a brick (blank) wall；run one's head against a wall；meet with a rebuff (refusal)

碰钉子 pèng dīngzi receive serious rebuff；meet with a rebuff；run into (run up against) snags；get the cheese；get snubbed

碰见 pèngjiàn meet unexpectedly；run into

碰巧 pèngqiǎo happen；coincidently；by chance：她～也在那里。She happened to be there too.

碰头 pèngtóu meet and discuss；put (our, your or their) heads together：～会 (have) a brief meeting

碰硬 pèngyìng confront firmly：敢于～ dare to confront firmly

碰运气 pèng yùnqì try one's luck；take a chance

pī

砒 pī 〈名〉arsenic

砒霜 pīshuāng arsenic

批 pī 〈动〉① write instructions or comments on (a report or document, etc.): ～文件 write instructions on documents ② criticize; repudiate: ～判修正主义纲领 repudiate the revisionist programme ③〈名〉batch: 新到的一～货 a new lot of goods

批驳 pībó refute; criticize; rebut

批调 pīdiào approved transfer (the transfer of materials from one unit to another after it has been approved by the department in charge.)

批发 pīfā wholesale: ～价 at wholesale price. ～商 wholesaler

批改 pīgǎi correct; go over: ～学生作业 correct students' papers

批量 pīliàng batch size: ～生产 batch production

批零差价 pīlíngchājià differences between wholesale and retail prices

批判 pīpàn criticize; repudiate; criticism: ～现实主义 critical realism

批评 pīpíng criticize; criticism: ～与自我～ criticism and self-criticism

批示 pīshì ① write instructions on (a report, etc.) ② written instructions; official comments

批语 pīyǔ comments; remarks

批阅 pīyuè read over (official papers, composition, etc.); read and amend or comment on a piece of writing

批注 pīzhù annotate; notes; remarks; annotations; comments

批转 pīzhuǎn write comments and transmit (a superior writing comments or instructions on a document or notification submitted by a subordinate, and then transmitting it to appropriate quarters)

批准 pīzhǔn approve; sanction; confirm; ratify: ～公约 approve a convention. ～书 instruments of ratification

纰 pī

纰漏 pīlòu careless mistake; small error; slip: 出～ commit a mistake; make a slip

披 pī 〈动〉drape over one's shoulders: 把棉大衣～在肩上 drape a padded overcoat over one's shoulders

披肝沥胆 pīgān-lìdǎn lay bare one's mind; speak without reserve; disembosom oneself

披挂 pīguà ① put on a suit of armour ② a suit of armour

披肩 pījiān cape

披荆斩棘 pījīng-zhǎnjí open a way by breaking through bramble and thistle; clear away obstacles in one's way; break through brambles and thorns; blaze one's way through all difficulties: ～的人 trailblazer

披露 pīlù ① announce; publish

② disclose; reveal

披星戴月 pīxīng-dàiyuè not knock off work till the moon rises; work under the moon and stars; travel (work) night and day

霹 pī

霹雳 pīlì thunderbolt:晴天～ a bolt from the blue. ～舞 break dancing

劈 pī 〈动〉chop; cleave; split:～木柴 chop wood

劈开 pīkāi chop (up); cleave

劈头 pītóu ① right in the face; straight on the head:～一拳 hit sb. on the head ② at the very start:～第一个大问题 the first and foremost question

劈头盖脸 pītóu-gàiliǎn right in the face:大雨～地浇了下来。The rain came pelting (kept pouring) down.

pí

琵 pí

琵琶 pípá *pipa*, a plucked string instrument with a fretted fingerboard; Chinese lute

枇 pí 〈名〉loquat

毗 pí

毗连 pílián adjoin; be adjacent to:我们的房子与公园相～。Our house adjoins the park.

啤 pí

啤酒 píjiǔ beer:～厂 brewery. 生～ draught beer. 黑～ dark beer

脾 pí 〈名〉spleen

脾气 píqì temper; disposition; temperament:～好(坏) have a good (bad) temper. 发～ lose one's temper; show temper; go (fly) into a tantrum; flare up

皮 pí 〈名〉① skin:擦破一块～ scrape a bit of skin off ② leather; hide:～革加工场 tannery ③ fur:～袄 fur-lined jacket ④ cover; wrapper:塑料～的 plastic-coated 〈形〉⑤ become soft and soggy; no longer crisp:花生～了。The peanuts aren't crisp any more. ⑥ naughty:这男孩真～! What a naughty boy! ⑦ case-hardened; thick-skinned; impervious (to criticism):她老挨批评，都～了。She is always in for criticism so she no longer cares.

皮包 píbāo leather bag, briefcase:～公司 fundless company engaged in a speculation; paper company

皮包骨头 píbāogǔtóu be all skin and bone; be little more than bone; skinny:瘦得～ be reduced to a skeleton

皮带 pídài ① leather belt ② [机] (driving) belt:三角～ triangle belt

皮肤 pífū skin

皮革 pígé leather; hide

皮筋儿 píjīnr rubber band

皮夹子 píjiāzi wallet; notecase;

pocketbook

皮毛 pímáo ① fur ② superficial knowledge; smattering:她对法语只懂得一点～。She has only a smattering of French.

皮棉 pímián ginned cotton

皮实 píshi ① sturdy ② durable

皮箱 píxiāng (leather) trunk; (leather) suitcase

皮鞋 píxié leather shoes; leathers:～油 shoe polish. 擦～ polish shoes; shine shoes

皮衣 píyī ① fur clothing ② leather clothing

皮影戏 píyǐngxì leather-silhouette show; shadow play

皮重 pízhòng tare

疲 pí〈形〉tired; weary:～劳沮丧 reduce to a tired and demoralized state

疲惫 píbèi ① tired out; exhausted ② tire sb. out

疲乏 pífá worn out; fatigued

疲倦 píjuàn tired and sleepy

疲劳 píláo tired; exhausted; fatigued:～过度 be overtired

疲软 píruǎn ① fatigued and weak ②［经］weaken; slump

疲软市场 píruǎn shìchǎng weak market

疲塌 píta slack; sluggish; languid:工作～ be (get) slack at (in) one's work

疲于 píyú be tired with:～奔命 be kept constantly on the run; exhaust oneself running around; having to run around all the time wears sb. out; be weighed down with work

pǐ

痞 pǐ

痞子 pǐzi ruffian; scoundrel; riffraff:地～ local ruffian

匹 pǐ ①〈名〉bolt:2～布 two bolts of cloth ②〈动〉be equal to; be a match for; match

匹敌 pǐdí be well matched; be equal in force; match; rival:在游泳方面无人能同她～。Nobody can rival her in swimming.

匹夫 pǐfū ① ordinary man ② ignorant person; fool:～之勇 reckless courage; mere physical courage; foolhardiness

匹料 pǐliào bolt materials

匹配 pǐpèi marry; mate

癖 pǐ〈名〉weakness for; addiction:嗜酒成～ be addicted to drinking

癖好 pǐhào special (favourite) hobby; partiality (for); fondness for; weakness (for):他有下棋的～。He has a partiality for chess.

癖性 pǐxìng natural inclination; propensity; proclivity

劈 pǐ〈动〉split; divide:把绳子～成 2 股 split the rope into two strands

另见 pī

pì

屁 pì〈名〉wind (from bowels);

fart

屁股 pìgu ① buttocks; backside; bottom: 她打孩子的～。She smacked the child's bottom ② [动物等的]rump; hindquarters ③ [物体等的]end; butt: 香烟～ cigarette end

屁滚尿流 pìgǔn-niàoliú wet one's pants in terror: 吓得～ be frightened out of one's wits

屁话 pìhuà nonsense; rubbish; rot; shit

媲 pì

媲美 pìměi be on a par with; compare favourably with; rival: 我认为她的才能不能与你相～。I don't think her ability is on a par with yours.

辟 pì

〈动〉① open up; open ② refute; repudiate ③〈形〉penetrating: 精～ incisive; profound

辟谣 pìyáo refute a rumour; deny a rumour

譬 pì

〈名〉example; analogy

譬如 pìrú for example; for instance

譬喻 pìyù metaphor; simile; comparison

僻 pì

〈形〉① out-of-the-way; remote: 偏～的山区 the remote mountain areas ②［字］rare (word)

僻静 pìjìng quiet and out-of-the way; secluded; lonely: ～的地方 secluded spot

piān

篇 piān

〈名〉① a piece of writing: 不朽的诗～ an immortal poem ② sheet (of paper, etc.): 歌～儿 song sheet ③〈量〉一～文章 a piece of writing; an article

篇幅 piānfú ① length (of an article) ② space: 限于～ due to limited space. 用了不少～叙述 devote a lot of space to describing

篇目 piānmù table of contents; contents; list of articles

篇章 piānzhāng ① piece of writing; literary piece; writings ② sections and chapters

偏 piān

〈形〉① inclined to one side; slanting; skew: 方向略～ in a slight slanting direction ② one-sided; partial: 不～不倚 impartial; unbiased ③〈动〉move to one side; slant; lean: 带有～见的报道 slanted reports ④〈副〉deliberately; contrary to what is expected; simply: 她～不听。She simply wouldn't listen.

偏爱 piān'ài be partial to; favour

偏差 piānchā deviation; error: 纠正工作上的～ correct errors in one's work

偏方 piānfāng folk and empirical prescription; local folk prescription

偏废 piānfèi overemphasize one thing to the neglect of the other; attach undue importance to one thing to the neglect of the other; do one thing and neglect another:两者不可～。Neither should be overemphasized at the expense of the other.

偏好 piānhào have a special fondness for sth.; have a partiality for sth.

偏激 piānjī go to extremes; extreme; radical:～措施 extreme measures

偏见 piānjiàn prejudice; bias; partial opinion

偏科 piānkē lopsided concentration (i. e.; the phenomenon of students concentrating in one or a few courses, and neglecting others):现在中小学是不允许～的。Lopsided concentration is not permitted in elementary and secondary schools now.

偏离 piānlí deviate; diverge

偏旁 piānpáng [汉字] radicals

偏僻 piānpì out-of-the-way; remote; secluded

偏偏 piānpiān ① deliberately; stubbornly; simply; just:他～不肯同我们一起走。He simply refused to come with us ② coincidence:为什么你不叫别人而～叫她去? Why did you ask her to go, of all people?

偏袒 piāntǎn take sides with; be partial to; show partiality for (to):不～任何一方是对的。It is right to show no partiality to either side.

偏题 piāntí catchy exam questions

偏听偏信 piāntīng-piānxìn be partial to; believe in one-sided stories

偏向 piānxiàng ① erroneous tendency; deviation ② be partial to; give unprincipled support or protection to

偏远 piānyuǎn remote; faraway

偏重 piānzhòng lay special (particular) stress on:～数量,不重质量是不对的。It is wrong to unduly emphasize quantity to the neglect of quality.

翩 piān

翩翩 piānpiān ① (move, dance, etc.) trippingly; lightly:～起舞 dance trippingly (gracefully) ② elegant; graceful; smart; stylish:风度～的年轻人 young man with a graceful bearing; a suave young man

pián

便 pián

另见 biàn

便宜 piányi ① cheap:～货 bargain. 买得～ buy (sth.) cheap; buy at a (good) bargain ② small gains (advantages):贪小～ be covetous of small gains; greedy for small advantages

piàn

片 piàn

〈名〉① thin piece; slice:面包～ slices of bread ② part of a place; subdivision of an area：分～包干 divide up the work and assign a part to each individual (or group) ③〈形〉incomplete; partial; fragmentary：～面观点 lopsided views 〈量〉④ [用于成片的东西]一～安眠药 a sleeping tablet ⑤ [用于地面和水面等]：一～汪洋 a vast sheet of water ⑥ [用于景色、气象、语言]：一～欢腾 a scene of great rejoicing

片断(段) piànduàn fragment; part; passage; section

片(儿)警 piàn(r)jǐng policemen in charge of certain neighbourhoods or communities

片刻 piànkè a moment; a little while

片面 piànmiàn one-sided; lopsided; unilateral：～观点 lopsided view; one-sided view. ～之词 account given by one party only

骗 piàn 〈动〉① deceive; fool：～某人去做某事 deceive sb. into doing sth ② cheat; swindle：哄～某人相信…：Cheat sb. into the belief that… ② demagogic; deceitful; deceptive; fraudulent：～的勾当 fraudulent practice

骗局 piànjú fraud; swindle; hoax; trickery; trap; jugglery; con game (job)：政治～ a political swindle

骗取 piànqǔ gain (get) sth. by cheating; cajole; defraud：～钱财 cheat sb. out of money (property). ～信任 worm one's way into sb.'s confidence; win sb.'s confidence by false pretences

骗人 piànrén ① deceive people; pull the wool over people's eyes

骗税 piànshuì tax fraud

骗子 piànzi deceiver; swindler; cheat; juggler; charlatan：政治～ political swindler

piāo

漂 piāo 〈动〉drift; float：使木材顺流～浮而下 float timber down a stream
另见 piǎo, piào

漂泊 piāobó lead a wandering life; have no fixed abode; wander (from place to place); rove; roam; drift：～异乡 lead a wandering life (drift aimlessly) in a strange land

漂浮 piāofú ① float ② (of style of work) superficial; showy

漂流 piāoliú drift about：随波～ drift with the tide

漂移 piāoyí drift

剽 piāo ①〈动〉rob ②〈形〉nimble; swift

剽悍 piāohàn agile and brave; quick and fierce

剽窃 piāoqiè plagiarize; lift：～行为 plagiarism

飘 piāo 〈动〉float (in the air); fly; flutter：～扬在广场上的红旗 red flags floating above the square

飘带 piāodài streamer; ribbon

飘荡 piāodàng drift; flutter; wave

飘零 piāolíng ① fading and falling; whirling and scattering ② wandering; adrift; homeless
飘落 piāoluò drift and fall slowly; descend slowly and lightly
飘飘然 piāopiāorán be carried away with one's own importance; walk on air; be light-headed; be (feel) self-satisfied: 心中～ feel quite self-satisfied
飘扬 piāoyáng fly (in the wind); flutter; wave: 迎风～ fly in the wind
飘摇 piāoyáo ① drift about (swing) in the wind ② [局势等] tottering; precarious; unstable: 风雨～ precarious situation; tottering
飘逸 piāoyì possessing natural grace; elegant

piáo

瓢 piáo 〈名〉 gourd ladle
瓢泼大雨 piáopō-dàyǔ torrential rain; downpour
嫖 piáo 〈动〉 go whoring; visit prostitutes

piǎo

漂 piǎo 〈动〉① bleach ② rinse: 一种有～白作用的肥皂 a soap that rinses easily
另见 piāo, piào
漂白 piǎobái bleach; decolourize: ～粉 bleaching powder
瞟 piǎo 〈动〉 glance sideways at: ～了一眼 cast a sidelong glance at; dart a glance at; look askance at

piào

票 piào 〈名〉① ticket: 电影～ movie ticket ② ballot: 投～ cast a vote (ballot); vote. ～数相等 equality of votes ③ bank note; bill
票额 piào'é sum stated on a check or bill
票房 piàofáng [车站等] ticket office; booking office; [戏院等] box office: ～价值 box-office value; box-office income. 这部剧已经没有～价值了。The play has lost its box-value appeal.
票根 piàogēn stub; counterfoil; stubs of a checkbook
票价 piàojià price of a ticket; admission fee
票据 piàojù note; bill: ～交换所 clearing house. ～结算 clearing. ～全额 amount of the instrument
票面价值 piàomiàn jiàzhí face value; par value; nominal value
票友 piàoyǒu amateur performer (of Beijing opera, etc.)
漂 piào
另见 piāo, piǎo
漂亮 piàoliang ① handsome; good-looking; pretty; beautiful: ～的花园 a pretty garden ② brilliant; smart; fine: ～话 fine words; high-sounding (honeyed) words

piē

撇 piē 〈动〉① cast aside; throw overboard; neglect; leave behind: ～下不管 desert; abandon ② skim off: ～油 skim off the grease
另见 piě

撇开 piēkāi leave (put) aside; bypass

瞥 piē 〈动〉shoot; glance at; dart a look at: 一～ (get) a glimpse of sth.

piě

撇 piě ①〈动〉throw; hurl; flint; cast ②〈名〉left falling stroke (in Chinese characters)
另见 piē

撇嘴 piězuǐ twitch one's mouth; make a wry mouth; curl one's lip

pīn

拼(拚) pīn 〈动〉① put together; piece together: 把零头碎布～拢 piece together odds and ends of cloth ② go all out in work; be ready to risk one's life (in fighting, work, etc.): 跟敌人～ fight the enemy to the finish

拼搏 pīnbó go all out in work; combat (fight) (with, against); fight with all one's might: ～精神 combatant spirit; the spirit of fighting with all one's might

拼凑 pīncòu ① piece together; patch up: 把一件东西～到另一件东西上 piece one thing to another ② put together; assemble; line up; rig up; whip up; pull together; scrape up (together): ～一笔款子 scrape up a sum; make out a sum

拼法 pīnfǎ spelling: 这个词有两种～。This word has two spellings.

拼接 pīnjiē piece together; join together

拼命 pīnmìng ① risk one's life; fight tooth and nail; put up a desperate fight: ～精神 death-defying spirit ② with might and main; at full split; desperately: ～工作 work with might and main

拼盘 pīnpán assorted cold dish; made dish

拼死 pīnsǐ desperately; frantically; at the risk of one's life: ～拼活地干 work with all one's might

拼音 pīnyīn phoneticize; spell: ～文字 alphabetic writing. ～字母 phonetic alphabet; phonetic letters

拼装 pīnzhuāng assemble from odd parts

pín

频 pín ①〈形〉frequent: 这儿春雨很～。Rains are frequent

here in spring ②〈副〉frequently; repeatedly:～～点头 nod repeatedly ③〈名〉frequency

频传 pínchuán (of good news, etc.) keep pouring in

频道 píndào [电视](frequency) channel

频繁 pínfán frequently; often:与…接触～ have frequent contacts with…

频率 pínlǜ [物] frequency

频频 pínpín again and again; repeatedly

贫 pín 〈形〉① poor; impoverished:～困落后 be impoverished and backward ② inadequate; deficient:～油国 oil-poor country

贫乏 pínfá poor; short; meagre; scanty; lacking:矿产～的地区 district poor in minerals. 知识～ be lacking in knowledge

贫富悬殊 pínfù-xuánshū gaps between the rich and poor; divisions between the rich and poor

贫瘠 pínjí [土地] poor; infertile; barren:～的土壤 poor (barren, lean) soil

贫苦 pínkǔ poor; poverty-stricken:生活～ be badly off

贫困 pínkùn poverty; privation: 遭受～ suffer privations

贫民 pínmín poor people; the poor:～窟 slum (area); gutter

贫嘴 pínzuǐ garrulous; loquacious

pǐn

品 pǐn 〈名〉① goods; article:工业～ industrial goods. 农产～ farm (agricultural) produce ② grade; class; rank:上～ top grade ③ character:人～ moral quality; character ④〈动〉have a taste of; taste sth. with discrimination:～酒的人 wine taster

品尝 pǐncháng have a taste of; savour (the flavour of)

品德 pǐndé moral character:～鉴定书 character sketch

品格 pǐngé ① character; personality:人的～ moral tone of a person ② quality and style (of literary or artistic works)

品貌 pǐnmào ① looks; appearance ② character and looks; personality and appearance

品评 pǐnpíng judge; appraise; comment on

品头论足 pǐntóu-lùnzú ① find fault with; be overcritical ② make frivolous remarks about sb.'s appearance

品行 pǐnxíng conduct:～端正(恶劣) have good (bad) conduct

品学兼优 pǐnxué-jiānyōu good both in character and scholarship; excellent in character and learning:～的学生 a student of good character and fine scholarship

品质 pǐnzhì quality; character:～优良 of the best quality. ～证明书 quality certificate

品种 pǐnzhǒng ① variety; strain: 货物～齐全 have a good assortment of goods. 花色～ variety of colours and designs; varieties and styles ② breed; strain;variety:小麦的优良～ improved strain of wheat

pìn

聘 pìn 〈动〉 engage; employ; invite:～某人为教授 engage sb. as a professor

聘金 pìnjīn betrothal money for the bride's family

聘礼 pìnlǐ betrothal gifts (presents)

聘请 pìnqǐng invite; engage; employ; hire:～律师 brief a barrister

聘任 pìnrèn appoint; engage:～制 system of appointment

聘书 pìnshū letter of appointment; letter of employment; contract of employment; engagement (appointment) contract

聘用 pìnyòng appoint and employ:～制 system of employment by appointment

pīng

乒 pīng

乒乓 pīngpāng table tennis; ping-pong:打～ play ping-pong

乒乓球 pīngpāngqiú ping-pong ball:～拍 table tennis bat

píng

瓶 píng 〈名〉bottle; jar; flask; vase:花～ flower vase

瓶装 píngzhuāng bottled:～牛奶 bottled milk

屏 píng 〈名〉screen:画～ painted screen
另见 bǐng

屏蔽 píngbì ① screen; shield ② protective screen ③ screen:～电缆 screened cable

屏风 píngfēng screen

屏幕 píngmù screen on a television or monitor

屏障 píngzhàng protective screen; defence; barrier:天然～ natural barrier (defence)

平 píng 〈形〉① flat; level; smooth:～地 flat land ② equal; on the same level:～起～坐 on an equal footing ③ air; equal; impartial:～分天下 divide the world equally between two parties ④ quiet; calm; peaceful:风～浪静的海洋 a calm sea ⑤ average; common:～均利润 average profit〈动〉⑥ level; even:～整土地 level the fields ⑦ calm; pacify:气～了 feel pacified

平安 píng'ān safe (and sound); fine; well:～到达 arrive safe and sound. ～险[海运] free of particular average

平辈 píngbèi of the same generation

平常 píngcháng ① ordinary; common; usual ② generally; as a rule:她～不大出门。She seldom goes out as a rule.

平淡 píngdàn flat; insipid; commonplace：～无奇 nothing out of the ordinary

平等 píngděng equality：～互利 equality and mutual benefit. ～和睦相处 live together in equality and harmony. ～权利 equal rights

平地 píngdì ① level the land (ground)；rake the soil smooth ② level ground；flat ground

平凡 píngfán common；commonplace；ordinary

平反 píngfǎn redress (a mishandled case)；rehabilitate：～冤假错案 redress individual injustices. 宣布给某人～ announce sb.'s reha bilitation

平方米 píngfāngmǐ square metre

平房 píngfáng ① single-storey house；one-storey house ② a house with a flat plastered roof

平分 píngfēn ① divide equally：～秋色（of two parties）have equal shares（of honour，power，glory，etc.）；share equally；split even；go fifty-fifty ② [体] deuce

平和 pínghé gentle；mild；moderate；placid

平衡 pínghéng balance；equilibrium：～价格 equilibrium price. ～生产 balanced production. ～木 [体] balance beam

平缓 pínghuǎn ①（of the terrain，flow of water，etc.）gentle；smooth ② mild；placid；gentle

平价 píngjià fair（state）price；par；parity：～商店 fair-price（cut-price，reduced-price）shop

平静 píngjìng calm；quiet；tranquil

平局 píngjú draw；tie：扳成～ [体]level the score；play even. 比赛以～结束。The match ended in a draw.

平均 píngjūn ① average；mean：～劳动时间 average labour time. ～数 mean；average. ～寿命 average life span ② equally；share and share alike：～分摊 share out equally

平叛 píngpàn suppress rebellion

平面 píngmiàn plane

平民 píngmín common people；civilians；populace；commoners：～文学 literature of the common people. ～主义 populism

平平 píngpíng average；mediocre；indifferent

平铺直叙 píngpū-zhíxù speak or write in a dull，flat way；flat，directive narrative；tell in a simple，straightforward way

平起平坐 píngqǐ-píngzuò sit as equals at the same table；be on an equal footing

平生 píngshēng in one's life；all one's life

平时 píngshí ① at ordinary times；in normal times ② in peacetime

平摊费用 píngtān fèiyòng go Dutch：昨晚在饭店吃饭后她要同我～。She wanted to go Dutch with me at the restaurant last night.

平坦 píngtǎn flat；level；even；smooth：一条宽阔～的公路 a broad smooth highway

平添 píngtiān add or give as an effect or a result

平稳 píngwěn smooth; calm; stable: 物价～。The prices are stable. 香港的～过渡 smooth transfer of power in Hong Kong

平息 píngxī ① calm down; quiet; subside: 海上风浪～了。The sea calmed down ② put down; suppress: ～叛乱 put down a rebellion

平心而论 píngxīn'érlùn be honest; in all fairness; objectively speaking

平心静气 píngxīn-jìngqì keep calm; calmly; dispassionately; composedly

平信 píngxìn ① ordinary mail ② surface mail

平行 píngxíng ① of equal rank; on an equal footing: ～单位 units at the same level ② parallel: ～线 parallel lines

平易近人 píngyìjìnrén modest and unassuming; easy of approach; approachable; easy to get along with; folksy

平抑 píngyì suppress: ～价格 control (stabilize) prices

平庸 píngyōng mediocre; commonplace: 才能～的人 man of limited ability; of mediocre calibre

平装 píngzhuāng paperback; paperbound: ～本 paperbound edition; paperback

评 píng 〈动〉① comment; review; criticize: 书～ book review ② appraise; evaluate: ～历史人物 appraise historical characters ③ judge; adjudge: ～判 pass judgement

评比 píngbǐ compare and appraise; compare and evaluate; appraise through comparison

评定 píngdìng evaluate; assess; adjudge; rate: 被～为优秀作品 be rated as works of excellence. ～职称 conferring of academic titles

评分 píngfēn give a mark; mark; grade; marking: 给试卷～ mark (grade) papers

评级 píngjí grade; rate; rank evaluation

评价 píngjià appraise; size up; assess; evaluate: 你对那本书～如何? How do you evaluate that book?

评奖 píngjiǎng grant (decide on) awards through discussion; bonuses issued on the basis of a general voicing

评剧 píngjù *pingju*, a local opera of north and northeast China

评理 pínglǐ ① decide which side is right ② reason things out

评论 pínglùn ① comment on; discuss; make (give) comment on: ～是非 discuss right and wrong ② commentary; comment; review: ～家 critic writer; critic, reviewer

评判 píngpàn pass judgement (on); decide: ～员 [运动等的] judge; [音乐比赛等的] adjudicator

评审 píngshěn appraise and select: ～国家重大发明奖 judge and determine the national awards for important inventions

评弹 píngtán storytelling and ballad singing in Suzhou dialect

评薪 píngxīn salary evaluation; discuss and determine wage-grade

评选 píngxuǎn choose through discussion; elect through appraisal:～先进工作者 evaluate and elect advanced workers

评议 píngyì deliberate (on); discuss; appraise:～会 appraisal meeting

评语 píngyǔ comment; remark:品德～[对学生的] remarks on the conduct of a pupil. 作简短的～ make short remarks

评阅 píngyuè read and appraise; grade; mark:～试卷 grade papers

评注 píngzhù ① make comments and annotations ② notes and commentary

评传 píngzhuàn critical biography

坪 píng〈名〉level ground:草～ lawn

苹 píng

苹果 píngguǒ apple

萍 píng〈名〉duckweed

萍水相逢 píngshuǐ-xiāngféng (of strangers) meet by chance like patches of drifting duckweed; a chance acquaintance; chance encounter

凭 píng〈动〉① rely on; be based on:～持三寸之舌 depend on one's eloquence ② lean against; lean on:～栏远眺 lean on a railing and gaze into the distance ③ proof; evidence:真～实据 ironclad evidence ④ no matter (what, how, etc.):～他们怎么劝说,她也不听。No matter how hard they tried to persuade her, she wouldn't listen.

凭单 píngdān bill; certificate; indenture:～支票 voucher check

凭借 píngjiè rely on; depend on; by dint of; by virtue of; by means of:～经验办事 do sth. by virtue of experience

凭据 píngjù proof; evidence

凭空 píngkōng groundless; unfounded:～捏造 sheer fabrication; groundless allegation

凭证 píngzhèng certificate; proof; voucher; receipt

pō

泊 pō〈名〉lake; pool
另见 bó

坡 pō〈名〉slope

坡度 pōdù slope; gradient

颇 pō〈副〉rather; fairly; quite; pretty; considerably

泼 pō ①〈动〉pour out; spill; splash:～水在地板上 splash water over the floor ②〈形〉rude and unreasonable

泼妇 pōfù shrew; scold; vixen; harridan:～骂街 like the abuses hurled by a harridan

泼辣 pōlà ① shrewish ② [文风] pungent; forceful:～的文风 a

strong literary style ③［工作］bold and vigorous：办事～ be bold and vigorous in one's work
泼冷水 pō lěngshuǐ pour cold water on；dampen the enthusiasm；discourage
泼墨 pōmò ［美］splash-ink，a technique of Chinese ink-painting

pó

婆 pó〈名〉① old woman ② husband's mother；mother-in-law
婆家 pójia husband's family
婆婆 pópó ① husband's mother；mother-in-law ② grandmother
婆婆妈妈 pópo-māmā ① shilly-shallying about like an old woman；womanishly fussy：～的话 a womanish talk ② emotionally fragil

pò

破 pò〈形〉① damaged；torn；broken；worn-out：～房子 a tumble-down（dilapidated）house ② poor；bad：谁看那部～电影！Who wants to see that poor film！〈动〉③ break；cleave；split：这男孩把茶壶打～了。The boy broke the teapot. ④ do away with；abolish；get rid of：～旧立新 destroy the old and establish the new ⑤ defeat：大～敌军 deal a crushing blow at the enemy ⑥ lay bare；find out the truth about：～译 crack a code；decode
破案 pò'àn solve a case；clear up a case；crack a criminal case：～率 detection rate
破败 pòbài ruined；dilapidated；tumbledown
破财 pòcái suffer unexpected personal financial losses；lose money
破产 pòchǎn ① go bankrupt；become insolvent；become impoverished：～法 bankruptcy law；insolvent law ② be wrecked；fall through；ruin；collapse；come to naught：他的计划～了。His plan was thwarted.
破除 pòchú do away with；get rid of；give up：～迷信 do away with superstitions；break down fetishes and superstitions；destroy the myths
破费 pòfèi spend money；go to some expense：让你～请客 impose on your hospitality
破釜沉舟 pòfǔ-chénzhōu burn one's boats；cross（pass）the Rubicon
破格 pògé break a rule；make an exception：～提升 break a rule to promote sb.
破罐破摔 pòguàn-pòshuāi throwing around a broken jar（a metaphor for the negative resigned attitude of people who have erred. They feel that they will always carry a black mark，so they have no incentive to correct their errors，and simply

allow themselves to fall further behind or continue to slide down the erroneous path.)

破坏 pòhuài destroy; undermine; disrupt; spoil:~名誉 spoil sb.'s reputation; defame. ~治安 disrupt public order. ~社会秩序 undermine social order

破获 pòhuò ferret out; uncover:~一起刑事案件 crack a criminal case

破戒 pòjiè ① break a religious precept ② break one's vow of abstinence

破镜重圆 pòjìng-chóngyuán reunion of husband and wife after a rupture or separation

破旧 pòjiù old and shabby; worn-out; dilapidated

破口大骂 pòkǒu-dàmà give vent to a torrent of abuse; let loose a stream of savage invective; let loose of a torrent of abuse

破烂 pòlàn ragged; shabby; tattered; worn-out:~的衣服 worn-out clothes

破例 pòlì make an exception; break a rule

破裂 pòliè break; split; rupture:谈判~了。The negotiations broke down.

破落 pòluò decline (in wealth and position); fall into reduced circumstances:~户 impoverished family

破灭 pòmiè (of hopes, illusion) vanish; be shattered:他们的希望~了。Their hope was shattered.

破碎 pòsuì ① tattered; broken ② smash (break) sth. to pieces; crush

破天荒 pòtiānhuāng unheard-of; unprecedented; for the first time

破土 pòtǔ ① break ground (in starting a building project, etc.) ② start spring ploughing ③ (of a seedling) break through the soil

破绽 pòzhàn weak point; defect; flaw:论点中有~ flaw in an argument

迫

迫 pò〈动〉① force; compel; press:~使敌人投降 force the enemy to surrender (into surrendering) ② go near; approach:~近 get close to ③〈形〉urgent; pressing:~切的需要 urgent needs

另见 pǎi

迫不得已 pòbùdéyǐ can't help (but do); have no alternative (but to do):~做某事 do sth. against one's will

迫不及待 pòbùjídài too impatient to wait; impatiently; hurriedly; hurry-skurry; urgently; in haste

迫害 pòhài persecute:残酷的~ relentless persecution

迫降 pòjiàng [航空]forced landing

迫近 pòjìn draw near; approach:考试~。The examination is drawing near.

迫切 pòqiè urgent; pressing; imminent; imperious:~陈词 state one's views with a keen sense of urgency

迫使 pòshǐ force; compel; oblige: 下雪～我呆在家里。The snow compelled me to stay indoors.

迫降 pòxiáng forced surrender

迫在眉睫 pòzàiméijié extremely urgent; imminent: 大规模战争～。A large-scale war is imminent.

魄 pò 〈名〉① soul: 他的绘画没有气～。His paintings lack soul ② spirit; vigour: 体～ physique

魄力 pòlì daring and resolution; boldness; be bold and resolute; courage: 工作有～ be bold and resolute in one's work

pōu

剖 pōu 〈动〉① rip (cut) open; dissect: 解～麻雀 dissect a sparrow ② analyse: ～析 anatomy

剖白 pōubái explain oneself; vindicate oneself

剖面 pōumiàn section

剖析 pōuxī analyse; dissect: ～事理 analyse the whys and wherefores

pū

扑 pū 〈动〉pounce on; throw oneself on: 一心～在工作上 devote oneself heart and soul to one's work ② rush at; attack: ～蝴蝶 catch butterflies ③ flap; flutter: ～翅飞行的鹰 an eagle flapping its wings

扑哧 pūchī titter; snigger: ～一声，瓶子打开了。The bottle opened with a fizz.

扑击 pūjī ① pounce on; fall on; set on ② lap against; beat against

扑救 pūjiù ① put out a fire to save life and property ② (in volleyball, football, etc.) diving save

扑克 pūkè ① playing cards ② poker

扑空 pūkōng fail to meet sb. one intends to meet; fail to get or achieve what one wants; come away empty-handed

扑灭 pūmiè wipe (stamp) out; put out; extinguish: ～森林大火 extinguish a forest fire

扑朔迷离 pūshuò-mílí confusing; puzzling: ～的现象 fuzzy situation

仆 pū 〈动〉fall forward: 前～后继 one stepping into the breach as another falls

另见 pú

铺 pū 〈动〉① spread; extend: 把桌布～在桌子上 spread a tablecloth on the table ② pave; lay: ～设铁路支线 lay the siding

另见 pù

铺床 pūchuáng make (do) the bed

铺陈 pūchén narrate in detail; describe at great length

铺盖 pūgai bedding; bedclothes

铺平 pūpíng ① smooth out; spread sth. out smoothly ② make the ground, etc. level or even; level

铺设 pūshè lay; build: ～输油管 lay an oil pipeline

铺摊子 pū tānzi rashly putting up establishments

铺张 pūzhāng extravagant: ～浪费 extravagance and waste; conspicuous consumption

pú

菩 pú

菩萨 púsà ①［宗］Bodhisattva ②［佛，神］Buddha; Buddhist idol ③［心肠慈善的人］a term applied to a kindhearted person

菩提树 pútíshù pipal; bo tree; bodhi tree

葡 pú

葡萄 pútáo grape: ～酒 grape wine; wine

葡萄糖 pútaotáng glucose; grape sugar; dextrose

蒲 pú〈名〉① reed mace; cattail; club grass ②（Pú）a surname

蒲公英 púgōngyīng dandelion

蒲节 píjié the Dragon Boat Festival (the 5th day of the 5th lunar month)

蒲扇 púshàn cattail leaf fan

蒲式耳 púshì'ěr bushel (＝8 gallons)

匍 pú

匍匐 púfú crawl; creep; grovel: ～哀求 beg piteously; implore heartrendingly. ～前进 advance on all fours; creep forward (on elbows)

仆 pú〈名〉servant
另见 pū

仆从 púcóng henchman; follower; hangers-on; satellites: ～国 vassal (satellite, client) state

仆人 púrén (domestic) servant

pǔ

普 pǔ〈形〉general; universal: ～遍裁军 universal disarmament

普遍 pǔbiàn general; universal: ～发行的影片 movies on general release. 有～意义 hold good universally; of universal significance

普查 pǔchá general survey: ～人口 census

普及 pǔjí ① popularize disseminate; spread: ～科学知识 spread scientific knowledge ② universal; popular: ～中等教育 make secondary education universal

普教 pǔjiào common education; universal education

普天同庆 pǔtiān-tóngqìng The whole world joins in the jubilation.; universal rejoicing (joy)

普通 pǔtōng common; ordinary: ～话 common speech of the Chinese language; standard spoken Chinese: ～股 common stock. ～教育水平 general educational development. ～支票 open check

普选 pǔxuǎn general election

谱 pǔ〈名〉① table; chart: 家～

family tree; genealogy ② manual; guide: 棋～ chess manual ③ music score; music ④〈动〉compose; set to music: 为诗～曲 set a poem to music

谱牒 pǔdié genealogical tree; family tree; genealogy

谱分析 pǔfēnxì spectral analysis

谱系 pǔxì ancestry; genealogy; pedigree: ～树 family tree

谱写 pǔxiě compose (music)

谱子 pǔzi music score; music

朴 pǔ〈形〉simple; plain; modest; homely: ～素的语言 plain language

朴实 pǔshí ① modest; plain: ～无华 simple and unadorned; unsophisticated ② sincere and honest: ～的工作作风 a down-to-earth style of work

朴素 pǔsù simple; plain; austere: ～大方 plain and decent; unaffected and modest. 生活～ live (lead) a simple life

浦 pǔ〈名〉① riverside; river mouth ② (Pǔ) a surname

pù

铺 pù〈名〉① shop; store ② plank bed
另见 pū

铺面 pùmiàn shop front

铺位 pùwèi [车、船的] berth: 上(下)～ upper (lower) berth

瀑 pù〈名〉waterfall

瀑布 pùbù waterfall; [大的] cataract

曝 pù〈动〉expose to the sun; sun
另见 bào

曝光 pùguāng ①[摄] exposure ② be made public

曝露 pùlù exposed to the open air

Q q

qī

期 qī〈名〉① a period of time; stage; phase:中国革命的所有各个时～ all stages of the Chinese revolution ② scheduled (designated) time:限～ set a time limit ③〈量〉issue; number, terms:最近一～的《中国社会科学》the current issue of *Social Science in China* ④〈动〉expect:不～而遇 meet unexpectedly; meet by chance

期待 qīdài expect; hope; wait for; anticipate; look forward to (doing):～加薪 anticipation of an increase in salary

期货 qīhuò futures; forward:～市场 forward (futures) market

期间 qījiān period; time; duration; course:战争～ during the war

期刊 qīkān periodical

期满 qīmǎn expire:合同下月～。The contract will expire next month. ～释放 release upon the completion of one's terms

期票 qīpiào promissory note; term bill

期望 qīwàng ① hope; expect; wish; place high hopes on; look forward to (doing):～和平 wish for peace ② hope; expectation:不负～ live up to the expectations (of)

期限 qīxiàn deadline; due time; term of time; time limit:超过～ exceed the time limit

欺 qī〈动〉① deceive; swindle; cheat:～骗不明真相的人 mislead those who are not aware of the true facts ② bully:～人太甚 bully others too much

欺负 qīfu bully; treat sb. high-handedly; bluff; play the bully:～好人 bully a good man

欺凌 qīlíng bully and humiliate

欺瞒 qīmán hoodwink; dupe; pull the wool over sb.'s eyes

欺骗 qīpiàn deceive; cheat; hoodwink; cajole; dupe; swindle:～蒙混 throw dust (dirt; mud) in (into) the eyes of sb.; pull the wool over sb.'s eyes; dupe and hoodwink sb.

欺人太甚 qīréntàishèn bully others too much; go to extreme lengths; go too far:这未免～。That's going too far (in bullying others).

欺人之谈 qīrénzhītán (sheer) humbug (deception); deceitful talk

欺软怕硬 qīruǎn-pàyìng bully the faint-hearted but fear the stout-hearted; bully the weak and fear the strong; cringe before the strong and bully the weak; browbeat the weak but fear the strong

欺善怕恶 qīshàn-pà'è bully the good people and be scared of the evil ones

欺生 qīshēng ① bully or cheat strangers ② (of horses, mules, etc.) be ungovernable by strangers

欺侮 qīwǔ bully; browbeat; humiliate:你们～他? Do you let him down?

欺压 qīyā bully and oppress; ride roughshod over

欺诈 qīzhà cheat; deceive; swindle; fraud:～行为 fraudulent conduct. ～罪 crime of false pretenses

栖

qī 〈动〉① roost; perch:鸟儿～在树上。Birds roost on the trees. ② dwell; stay; rest

栖身 qīshēn stay; dwell; rest:无处～ have no place to stay

栖息 qīxī [鸟] perch; roost

漆

qī 〈名,动〉paint; lacquer; varnish

漆包线 qībāoxiàn enamel-insulated wire

漆黑 qīhēi pitch-dark:～一团 ① be totally dark without a glimmer of light; be in the dark; be in a complete mess:把…描绘得～一团 paint a dark picture of … ② be completely ignorant of; be in a fog; utterly hopeless

漆画 qīhuà lacquer painting

漆匠 qījiàng painter; lacquerer

漆器 qīqì lacquerware:～工艺 lacquerware manufacturing

七

qī 〈数〉seven

七绝 qījué a four-line poem with seven characters to a line and a strict tonal pattern and rhyme scheme

七零八落 qīlíng-bāluò in disorder; in confusion; at sixes and sevens; in ruins; scattered about here and there:被打得～ be battered into confusion

七律 qīlǜ an eight-line poem with seven characters to a line and a strict tonal pattern and rhyme scheme

七拼八凑 qīpīn-bācòu knock together; rig up; a patchwork without pattern or design; piece together:～搞来几个钱 scrape together a little sum

七上八下 qīshàng-bāxià in anxiety and nervousness; in a terrible fidget; with misgivings; in a mental flurry of indecision:他心里～。His heart misgave him.

七手八脚 qīshǒu-bājiǎo in disorderly haste; in a bustle; helter-skelter; too many cooks

沏

qī 〈动〉infuse:～茶 infuse tea; make tea

妻

qī 〈名〉wife

"妻管严" qīguǎnyán [指家庭生活中] under petticoat government; The wife's control is stern.; The husband is henpecked.

妻离子散 qīlí-zǐsàn break up families; separated from wife and children; have a broken home with one's wife and children drifting apart; with one's family broken up

妻子 qīzi wife

凄 qī 〈形〉① cold; chilly ② sad; miserable: 过着～凉的日子 life becoming more and more miserable ③ bleak and desolate

凄惨 qīcǎn wretched; sad; miserable; tragic

凄凉 qīliáng lonesome; dreary; desolate; gloomy; miserable: 晚景～ miserable in old age

蹊 qī

蹊跷 qīqiāo queer; odd; fishy

qí

齐 qí 〈形〉① neat; tidy; even, in good order: 把桌子摆～ arrange the tables in an orderly way ② simultaneous: ～声欢呼 cheer in unison ③ complete; all ready; all present: 客人都来～了。The guests are all present. ④〈动〉reach the height of: 河水～岸。The river is flush with its banks.

齐备 qíbèi complete; all ready

齐唱 qíchàng sing in unison

齐名 qímíng enjoy equal popularity; be equally famous

齐全 qíquán complete; all in readiness: 货物品种～ have a large assortment of goods; have a satisfactory variety of goods

齐声 qíshēng in chorus; in unison

齐头并进 qítóu-bìngjìn advance shoulder to shoulder; do two or more things at the same time; do many things at once

齐心 qíxīn be of one mind: ～协力 work as one man; with one heart; make concerted efforts; pull together

其 qí 〈代〉① his; her; its; their: ～母 his mother. 物尽～用 make the best use of everything ② he, she, it, they: 任～自流。Let things run their own course. ③ that; such: 确有～事 That is certainly a fact.

其次 qícì next; secondly: 我最喜欢这个，～是那个。I like this best and that next.

其实 qíshí in fact; in reality; actually; as a matter of fact: ～不然。Actually, that's not the case.

其势汹汹 qíshìxiōngxiōng look threatening (formidable); bluster; put up quite a show

其他 qítā other; else: 还有～事情吗? Is there anything else?

其余 qíyú all the other (persons or things); the rest; the remainder

其中 qízhōng of or among (them, which, whom); in (which, it, etc.): 乐在～ find pleasure in it

旗 qí 〈名〉 flag; banner: 国～ national flag

旗杆 qígān flagpole; flag post

旗鼓相当 qígǔ-xiāngdāng be well-matched in strength; be equal in match or contest of strength; be a match for; be keen rivalry; be equal in power; be on the same level

旗号 qíhào［多用于贬义］flag; banner:打着…～ flaunt the banner of; under the signboard of; under the pretext of

旗开得胜 qíkāi-déshèng win victory the moment one raises one's standard; win speedy success; win victory as soon as one's banner is displayed; succeed at the first try; achieve immediate success

旗袍 qípáo a close-fitting woman's dress with high neck and slit skirt; a sheath with a slit skirt; cheongsam

旗手 qíshǒu standard-bearer

旗帜 qízhì ① flag; banner ② stand:～鲜明 have (take) a clearcut stand; show one's unequivocal stand

棋 qí〈名〉chess or any board game:下一盘～ play a game of chess; have a game of chess. ～王 chess master

棋逢对手 qíféng-duìshǒu a chess player meets his match; be equally matched (in a game of chess); diamond cut diamond; be well-matched in a contest; meet a powerful opponent

棋盘 qípán chessboard; checkerboard

棋谱 qípǔ chess manual

棋手 qíshǒu chess player

棋子 qízǐ piece (in a board game); chessman

歧 qí ①〈名〉branch; fork ②〈形〉divergent; different:～异 divergence

歧路 qílù branch road; forked road; crossroad

歧视 qíshì discriminate against:反对种族～ protest against racial discrimination

歧途 qítú ① branch road ② off the right road; wrong path:误入～ stray into a wrong path; go astray; be led astray

歧义 qíyì different meanings; ambiguity

奇 qí〈形〉① strange; odd; queer:～事 strange things; unusual phenomenon ② unexpected:出～制胜 win victory through unexpected moves ③〈动〉surprised at; wonder:大为惊～ be filled with amazement

奇才 qícái prodigy; remarkable (unusual) talent

奇耻大辱 qíchǐ-dàrǔ unprecedented shame and humiliation; galling shame and humiliation; crying shame and crowning humiliation

奇怪 qíguài strange; queer; odd; curious; surprising

奇观 qíguān remarkable (marvellous) spectacle; wonderful (impressive) sight; wonder:蔚为～ present a remarkable spectacle

奇货可居 qíhuò-kějū hoard as a rare commodity; corner the market; goods kept back to raise the price; rare commodity worth hoarding to corner the market

奇迹 qíjì miracle; wonder:创造～

perform miracles; work (do) wonders

奇妙 qímiào marvellous; intriguing; wonderful

奇缺 qíquē critical shortage of

奇人 qírén ① eccentric person; eccentric ② person of unusual ability

奇谈 qítán strange talk; absurd argument:海外～ strange tales from overseas. ～怪论 strange tale; ridiculous argument; absurd argument; fantastic stories and theories; nonsensical and preposterous argument

奇特 qítè peculiar; queer; singular

奇闻 qíwén strange story; sth. unheard-of; fantastic story

奇形怪状 qíxíng-guàizhuàng grosteque in shape or appearance; weirdly-shaped

奇异 qíyì ① queer; strange; odd; bizarre:奇花异草 unique flowers and grasses ② amazing; curious:用～的眼光看人 look at sb. with curious eyes

奇遇 qíyù ① happy encounter; fortuitous meeting ② adventure

奇缘 qíyuán relationship entered into unexpectedly; romance

崎 qí

崎岖 qíqū rugged; rough; uneven:曲折～的山路 tortuous mountain trails

骑 qí〈动〉ride (an animal or bicycle); sit on the back of:～车 go by bicycle

骑兵 qíbīng cavalry; cavalryman

骑虎难下 qíhǔ-nánxià ride a tiger and find it hard to get off; have (hold) a wolf by the ears; be unable to extricate oneself from a difficulty; be in an awkward predicament

骑墙 qíqiáng sit on the fence:～派 fence-sitter; sitter on the fence

骑手 qíshǒu horseman

骑术 qíshù horsemanship

畦 qí〈名〉rectangular pieces of land in a field; separated by ridges usually for growing vegetables

祈 qí〈动〉① pray:～雨 reciting prayers for timely rainfall ② beg; entreat; implore

祈祷 qídǎo pray; give prayers; tell one's beads; say one's prayers

祈求 qíqiú entreat; pray for:～和平 pray for peace

祈愿大法会 qíyuàn dàfǎhuì grand prayer convention

qǐ

启 qǐ〈动〉① open:幕～。The curtain rises. ② initiate; start ③ state; inform:敬～者 I beg to state; I wish to inform you. ④ enlighten:就某事对某人作～发 enlighten sb. on sth.

启程 qǐchéng set out; leave (for); start (for):～赴上海 leave for Shanghai

启齿 qǐchǐ open one's mouth; start to talk about sth.
启迪 qǐdí enlighten; inspire
启动 qǐdòng start (a machine, etc.); switch on
启发 qǐfā enlighten; arouse; edify: ～式(教学) heuristic method (of teaching); method of enlightenment
启封 qǐfēng ① unseal; break (remove) the seal ② open an envelope or wrapper
启航 qǐháng set sail; weigh anchor
启蒙 qǐméng enlighten: ～老师 the first teacher (in one's life or in a certain field of study); abecedarian: ～读物 elementary readings. ～思想家 philosophe
启事 qǐshì notice; announcement
启示 qǐshì enlightening guidance; enlightenment; revelation; message; illuminating remarks
启用 qǐyòng start using (an official seal, etc.)
启运国 qǐyùnguó country of departure

企 qǐ 〈动〉 hope; expect; look forward to
企盼 qǐpàn hope for; look forward to; long for
企求 qǐqiú seek for; hanker after; desire to gain
企图 qǐtú try; attempt; design; seek; contrive
企业 qǐyè enterprise; business; venture; establishment: ～管理 business management. ～家 entrepreneur. 合资～ joint venture. ～背景 business background. ～倒闭 business failure. ～集团 business conglomerate; enterprise groupings. 加强～文化建设 increase the cultural activities in enterprises. ～税 taxes on enterprises. ～素质 quality of an enterprise

乞 qǐ 〈动〉 beg; entreat: ～食 beg one's bread
乞哀告怜 qǐ'āi-gàolián piteously beg help; throw oneself on sb.'s mercy; beg for mercy
乞怜 qǐlián beg for mercy: 摇尾～ abjectly beg for mercy
乞灵 qǐlíng seek help from; reliance on; resort to; by raising the spectre to: ～于诡辩 resort to sophistry
乞求 qǐqiú beg for; entreat; supplicate; go begging; fall on one's knees; throw oneself at the feet of: ～某人帮个忙 entreat a favour of sb.
乞讨 qǐtǎo beg; go begging

起 qǐ〈动〉 ① stand up; get up: 早晨5点～床 get up at five in the morning ② remove; extract; pull: 把照片～下来 take down a photo ③ grow; rise: ～风了。The wind is rising. ④ draft: ～草一项决定 draft a decision ⑤ appear; raise: 她背上～痱子了。Heat rash rises on her back. ⑥ set up; build: ～一堵墙 build a wall ⑦ begin; start: 从明天～ starting from tomorrow 〈量〉 ⑧ 3～罪案 three criminal cases ⑨ batch; group: 分两～出发 set out in two groups (batches) ⑩[用在动词后,表示向上]:把桌子抬～来 lift (up) the table ⑪[用在动词后,表示力量够得上或够不上]:经得～考验 can stand the test

起草 qǐcǎo draft; draw up:～委员会 drafting committee

起步 qǐbù start; move

起程 qǐchéng start on a journey; leave (for)

起初 qǐchū originally; at first; at the outset

起点 qǐdiǎn starting point

起飞 qǐfēi take (lift) off:班机下午 3 时～。The airliner will take off at 3 p. m.. 经济～ economic take-off

起伏 qǐfú rise and fall; undulating; heaving; rolling; fluctuating; ups and downs:～的山脉 undulating mountain ranges

起哄 qǐhòng gather together to create a disturbance; kick up a fuss about

起家 qǐjiā grow and thrive; build up a fortune; make one's fortune; begin an undertaking:白手～ start from scratch; start empty-handed; build up from nothing

起劲 qǐjìn energetically; vigorously; enthusiastically:我们谈得很～。We talked very enthusiastically.

起居 qǐjū daily life:～室 sitting room; living room

起来 qǐlái ① stand up; sit up; rise to one's feet:你～吃药吧。Sit up and take your medicine. ② get up; get out of bed ③ rise; arise; revolt ④[用在动词或形容词后] up; upwards:他能坐～了吗? Can he sit up? ⑤ become; start to:她胖～了。She's getting fat. ⑥[表示完成或达到目的]:锁～ lock up ⑦ when one comes to:看～要下雪。It looks like snow.

起立 qǐlì stand up; rise to one's feet

起码 qǐmǎ ① at least ② elementary; minimum:～常识 elementary (rudimentary) common knowledge. ～的公平 a modicum of fairness

起色 qǐsè a change for the better; improvement; pickup:他的生意有～。His trade is picking up.

起身 qǐshēn ① get up; get out of bed ② leave; set out; get off

起始 qǐshǐ ① originate; stem from ② at first; in the beginning

起诉 qǐsù bring an action against sb.; prosecute an action; take legal action; sue:～人 accuser; suitor; indicter. ～书 bill of prosecution; statement of charges. ～之日 date of filing the suit

起先 qǐxiān at first; in the beginning

起行 qǐxíng leave; set out; start on a journey

起义 qǐyì rise in revolt; launch uprisings; stage an uprising; uprising; insurrection

起因 qǐyīn cause; origin:事故的

～ cause of an accident

起用 qǐyòng ① reinstate (an official who has retired or been dismissed) ② call sb. to office; appoint sb. to an important position

起源 qǐyuán ① originate in; stem from; come from：知识～于劳动 knowledge originates from labour ② origin; beginning：生命的～ the origin of living things

起运 qǐyùn start shipment：～地点 starting place for shipping; place of shipping

起…作用 qǐ zuòyòng play a part (role); become operative：规律在～。The laws operate.

杞 qǐ

杞人忧天 qǐrén-yōutiān The man of Qi worries in case the sky should fall — unnecessary worry.; entertain groundless fears

岂 qǐ [表示反问]：～不是…? Does it not…?

岂但 qǐdàn not only

岂非 qǐfēi Wouldn't it be…; Isn't that …：～笑话? Isn't that ridiculous?

岂敢 qǐgǎn 〈套〉 You flatter me; I don't deserve such praise or honour.; I don't deserve your compliment.

岂有此理 qǐyǒucǐlǐ How could such a thing be possible?; This is arrant nonsense indeed!; What nonsense!; How unreasonable!; This is sheer effrontery!

qì

泣 qì 〈动〉 sob; weep：～诉 accuse in tears; sob out

弃 qì 〈动〉 throw away; abandon; discard：～恶从善 shun evil and do good

弃暗投明 qì'àn-tóumíng forsake darkness for light — leave the reactionary side and cross over to the side of progress

弃权 qìquán ① abstain from voting ② [体]waive the right (to play); default

弃世 qìshì pass away; die

弃邪归正 qìxié-guīzhèng mend one's ways; correct one's conduct; alter (change) from bad to good

弃置 qìzhì lay aside; abandon; discard：～不用 be discarded

契 qì 〈名〉 contract; agreement; deed

契合 qìhé tally with; agree with：～法 method of agreement

契机 qìjī moment; juncture; turning point; favourable opportunities whenever they present themselves

契据 qìjù contract; deed：信托～ deed of trust

契约 qìyuē contract; indenture：～生效 execution of contract. ～有效期间 duration of contract. 与某人订立～ make a contract with sb.

砌 qì〈动〉 build by laying bricks

or stones：～围墙 build an enclosed wall

器 qì〈名〉 tool；instrument；utensil：乐～ musical instrument

器材 qìcái material；equipment；equipment and parts

器官 qìguān physical organ：发音～ organ of speech

器件 qìjiàn parts of an apparatus

器具 qìjù appliance；utensil；instrument：家用～ household utensils (wares)

器皿 qìmǐn household utensils；vessels；[可用以构成复合词] ware：厨房～ kitchenware

器械 qìxiè appliance；instrument；apparatus：医疗～ medical appliances

器乐 qìyuè [乐]instrumental music：～重奏曲 instrumental ensemble. ～家 instrumentalists

器重 qìzhòng think highly of；have a high opinion of；regard highly：老师很～她。The teacher had a very high opinion of her.

气 qì〈名〉① air：新鲜空～ fresh air ② gas：点燃煤～灶 light the gas ③ breath：上～不接下～ gasp for breath ④ odour；smell：香～ sweet smell ⑤ airs；style；manner：官～ bureaucratic airs ⑥ *qi* [古代哲学] primordial breath，energy〈动〉⑦ get angry；be enraged：～得直哆嗦 tremble with rage ⑧ enrage；make angry：故意～某人 deliberately try to annoy sb.

气泵 qìbèng air pump

气垫 qìdiàn air cushion：～船 hovercraft；cushioncraft

气度 qìdù ① bearing；manner；② tolerance；magnanimity

气短 qìduǎn ① short of breath；panting ② discouraged；disheartened

气氛 qìfēn atmosphere：～效应 atmosphere effect. 节日～ festival atmosphere

气愤 qìfèn angry；indignant；furious：对…感到～ be indignant at …. 令人～的 irritating；exasperating

气概 qìgài lofty quality；mettle；spirit：英雄～ heroic spirit (mettle)

气缸 qìgāng air cylinder；cylinder

气功 qìgōng breathing exercises；*qigong*：练～ take breathing exercises. ～疗法 treatment method based on a system of *qi*；breathing therapy

气管炎 qìguǎnyán ① tracheitis ② "bronchitis"；under petticoat government (A play on pun. "～" is an ailment，it puns with "妻管严" the wife's control is stern，" hence the term is a jocular way of saying that the husband is henpecked.)：现在盛行一种"～"。Presently，a type of "bronchitis" henpecking is prevalent.

气贯长虹 qìguàn-chánghóng imbued with a spirit as lofty as the rainbow spanning the sky；full of noble aspiration and daring

气候 qìhòu ① climate; weather: ～宜人 pleasant weather ② climate; situation: 政治～ political climate

气话 qìhuà words said in a fit of rage

气急败坏 qìjí-bàihuài be fuming with rage; get (so) exasperated; utterly discomfited; yell (be) in exasperation

气节 qìjié unyielding integrity; moral courage; integrity: 民族～ national integrity

气量 qìliàng tolerance; mind: ～大 large-minded; magnanimous. ～小 narrow-minded

气流 qìliú ① air current; airflow; airstream ② breath

气馁 qìněi become downcast (down-hearted, dejected, discouraged); lose heart

气派 qìpài manner; style; airs: 学者～ scholarly manner

气魄 qìpò boldness of vision; courage; daring; breath of spirit

气色 qìsè complexion; colour: ～好 have a high (rosy) complexion; look well

气势 qìshì momentum; imposing manner: ～磅礴 of great momentum; great and momentous; powerful. ～汹汹 in a threatening manner; an aggressive posture; fierce; overbearing; ferociously; violently

气味 qìwèi ① smell; odour; scent; flavour: ～相投 be congenial to; have the same likes and dislikes; birds of a feather ② smack; taste

气息 qìxī ① breath; odour: ～奄奄 breathing one's last; at one's last gasp; at the point of death ② flavour; smell; scent: 强烈的生活～ a rich flavour of life

气象 qìxiàng ① meteorological phenomenon; weather: ～台 weather station ② atmosphere; appearance; scene: ～万千 magnificent; spectacular

气焰 qìyàn arrogance; bluster; overbearing pride: ～嚣张 be swollen with arrogance

气质 qìzhì ① disposition; temperament ② makings; qualities: 军人的～ qualities of a soldier

气壮山河 qìzhuàng-shānhé with a heroic spirit that conquers the mountains and rivers; full of power and grandeur; sublime and heoric

讫

讫 qì〈动〉① complete; settle: 收～ received in full ② end

汽

汽 qì〈名〉steam; vapour

汽车 qìchē motor vehicle; automobile; car: ～保险 motor vehicle insurance. ～公司 vehicle corporation. ～制造厂 automobile factory. ～执照 car license

汽船 qìchuán steamship; steamer

汽化器 qìhuàqì ① carburettor ② vaporizer

汽水 qìshuǐ soda water; soft drink

汽油 qìyóu petrol; gasoline; gas

迄

迄 qì〈介〉till; up to

迄今 qìjīn till now; up to the present; so far; hitherto: ～为止 to this day; to date

qiā

掐 qiā 〈动〉 ① press hard; squeeze ② pinch; nip

掐断 qiāduàn cut off; nip off: ～电源 disconnect the mains

掐丝 qiāsī [工艺]filigree; wire inlay

掐腰 qiāyāo (of a dress) have a waistline

qiǎ

卡 qiǎ ① 〈动〉 get stuck; wedge: 钥匙～在锁里了。The key has stuck in the lock. 〈名〉 ② clip; fastener: 发～ hairpin ③ checkpost: 边～ border checkpost
另见 kǎ

卡具 qiǎjù clamping apparatus; fixture

卡壳 qiǎké ① (of cartridge or shell case) jam ② get stuck; be held up; have a temporary stoppage

qià

洽 qià 〈动〉 ① be in harmony (with): 融～ be in harmony; be on good terms ② consult; arrange: ～购 arrange a purchase

洽商 qiàshāng negotiate with; consult with: ～解决 solve through negotiations. ～服务 services for trade talks

洽谈 qiàtán talk over with; consult with: ～贸易 hold trade talks (with)

恰 qià ①〈形〉 proper; appropriate: ～如其分的批评 appropriate criticism ②〈副〉just; exactly

恰当 qiàdàng proper; suitable; fitting; appropriate: ～的例子 appropriate example; a case in point

恰好 qiàhǎo just right; exactly right; as luck would have it: 当时她～在场。It happened that she was on the spot.

恰恰 qiàqià just; exactly; precisely: ～相反 just the opposite

恰巧 qiàqiǎo by chance; as chance would have it; happen: ～我在家。I happened to be at home.

恰如其分 qiàrúqífèn just right; apt; appropriate; well-measured: 作出～的评价 make an appropriate appraisal of sth.

恰似 qiàsì just like

qiān

谦 qiān 〈形〉 modest: ～逊 modesty

谦卑 qiānbēi humble; modest

谦恭 qiāngōng modest and courteous; courteous and polite

谦让 qiānràng modestly decline: 请不要～。Please don't decline

out of modesty.

谦虚 qiānxū modest; self-effacing:～谨慎 modest and prudent

谦逊 qiānxùn modest; unassuming; unobtrusive

牵 qiān 〈动〉① pull; drag; lead along:～着鼻子走 lead by the nose ② involve:～连很多人 involve great numbers of people

牵扯 qiānchě involve; drag in:～某人利益 involve the interests of sb.

牵动 qiāndòng influence; affect:～全局 affect the whole situation

牵挂 qiānguà worry about; be anxious (concerned) about:没有～ have nothing to care for; be carefree

牵累 qiānlěi ① be tied down by:受家务～ be tied down by chores ② implicate; involve

牵连 qiānlián implicate;entangle; involve (in trouble); drag into trouble, become involved in; have connections with:～犯 implicated offender; one whose acts related to a crime

牵强 qiānqiáng far-fetched:～附会 make a far-fetched comparison; draw a forced analogy; strain (stretch, wrest) the sense (meaning)

牵涉 qiānshè involve; concern; drag in:～面广 involve many persons (areas)

牵头 qiāntóu pull people together (lit. "to lead in heads"):由厂长～。The factory director will pull people together.

牵线 qiānxiàn ① control from behind the scenes; pull (the) wires (strings):～搭桥 pull strings and build bridges; bring sb. into contact with sb. ② act as go-between:～人 wire-puller; go-between

牵一发而动全身 qiān yī fà ér dòng quánshēn A single change may affect the whole picture; pull one hair and the whole body is affected.; A slight move in one part may affect the situation as a whole.

牵引 qiānyǐn ① tow; draw ② traction:～器 tractor

牵制 qiānzhì pin down; contain; restrain; tie up:[军]～敌人 pin down the enemy. 受人～ be held in check

签 qiān ①〈动〉sign:在支票上～字 sign (one's name to) a cheque 〈名〉② tag; label; sticker:标～ sticker; label ③ lot:抽～ draw lots

签到 qiāndào sign for one's presence (attendance); sign in:～簿 attendance book

签订 qiāndìng sign; conclude:～合同 sign (conclude, enter) a contract

签发 qiānfā sign and issue (a document, certificate, etc.)

签名 qiānmíng sign one's name:～盖章 sign and affix one's seal. ～使契据生效 execute a deed

签收 qiānshōu sign after receiving sth.

签证 qiānzhèng visa:～机关 visa-granting office. 出(入)境～ exit (entry) visa. 过境～ transit visa

签字 qiānzì sign one's name; sign:～国 signatory state. ～批准法案使其成为法律 sign a legislative bill into law. ～仪式 signing ceremony

铅 qiān 〈名〉 lead

铅笔 qiānbǐ pencil: ～画 pencil drawing; pencil sketch

铅封 qiānfēng lead sealing

铅球 qiānqiú [体] shot:推～ shot put. ～运动员 shot-putter

铅印 qiānyìn letterpress printing; stereotype

铅中毒 qiānzhòngdú lead poisoning; saturnism

铅字 qiānzì type; letter

千 qiān 〈数〉 thousand

千变万化 qiānbiàn-wànhuà ever-changing; the myriads of changes; vicissitude; kaleidoscopic:形势是～的。The situation is ever changing.

千疮百孔 qiānchuāng-bǎikǒng riddled with a thousand gaping wounds; heavily damaged; suffer disaster: ～的烂摊子 a hopeless mess

千锤百炼 qiānchuí-bǎiliàn ① thoroughly steeled and tempered; well-experienced; has gone through fire and water ② (of literary works) polished and refined over and again; be polished meticulously

千方百计 qiānfāng-bǎijì in a thousand and one ways; in every possible way; by every possible means; by hook or by crook; resort to every trick:要～完成任务 have to fulfil the task in every possible way

千古 qiāngǔ through the ages; for all time; eternal:～遗恨 eternal regret. ～传诵 have been read through all ages

千斤顶 qiānjīndǐng hoisting jack; jack

千钧一发 qiānjūn-yīfà at a critical moment; hanging by a thread; a hundred weight hanging by a hair:她在～的时候赶到。She arrived at the critical moment.

千克 qiānkè kilogram (kg.)

千里送鹅毛,礼轻情意重 qiānlǐ sòng émáo, lǐ qīng qíngyì zhòng To send the feather of a swan one thousand *li*: the gift in itself may be insignificant, but the good-will is deep.; The gift itself may be light as a goose feather, but sent from afar, it conveys deep feeling.

千篇一律 qiānpiān-yīlǜ following a set pattern; stereotyped; repeating each other; monotonous

千秋万代 qiānqiū-wàndài throughout the ages; from generation to generation; thousands of generations:社会主义的～大计 the everlasting and great cause of socialism

千丝万缕 qiānsīwànlǚ a thousand and one links; be tied to sb. in many ways:～的经济联系 be bound together by every economic thread

千头万绪 qiāntóu-wànxù a host of miscellaneous problems; a multitude of things; a thousand things to attend to

千瓦 qiānwǎ kilowatt (kw.):～小时 kilowatt-hour (kwh.)

千辛万苦 qiānxīn-wànkǔ (go through) trials of all kinds; (endure) untold hardships

千载难逢 qiānzǎi-nánféng once in a blue moon; very rare:不要错过这样一个～的机会。Don't miss such a golden opportunity.

千载一时 qiānzǎi-yīshí once in a thousand years; an extremely rare opportunity; an opportunity only once in a thousand years; a golden opportunity

迁 qiān〈动〉① move; remove:～居农村 move to the countryside ② change:事过境～。The matter is all over, and the situation has changed.

迁户口 qiānhùkǒu report to the local authorities for change of domicile

迁就 qiānjiù appease; accommodate (adapt) oneself to; give in to; yield to:～眼前的事变 adapt oneself to the events of the day

迁居 qiānjū move house; change one's residence

迁怒 qiānnù vent one's anger on sb. who's not to blame; take it out on sb.

迁徙 qiānxǐ move; change one's residence:～自由 freedom to change one's residence; freedom of residence (movement)

迁移 qiānyí move; remove; migrate

阡 qiān

阡陌 qiānmò criss-cross paths in the fields

qián

潜 qián ①〈动〉go under (the water); dive:～水采珠 dive for pearls ②〈形〉hidden; secret; latent:～能 latent energy

潜藏 qiáncáng hide; lurk; go into hiding

潜伏 qiánfú ① hide; conceal; lie low (dormant):～期[医] incubation period

潜科学 qiánkēxué latent (potential) science

潜力 qiánlì latent force (capacity); potential; potentiality:挖掘～ tap potentialities

潜入 qiánrù ① enter secretly; sneak in ② dive into:～水中 dive into the water; submerge

潜台词 qiántáicí unspoken words in a play left to the understanding of the audience or reader

潜逃 qiántáo sneak away; abscond:携款～ abscond with the money; make away with the money

潜心 qiánxīn with great concentration

潜移默化 qiányí-mòhuà be unconsciously influenced; subconsciously affect; change imperceptibly; influence character by environment

潜在 qiánzài latent; potential: ～市场 potential market

前 qián① 〈形〉previous; preceding: ～几年 preceding years ② 〈名〉front: 建筑物的～面: the front of a building ③〈介〉before; in front of: 午饭～ before lunch. 在房屋～面有个水塘。There is a pond in front of the house. ④〈副〉ahead; forward: 勇往直～ go bravely forward

前辈 qiánbèi elders; senior; predecessor; progenitor; older generation

前车之鉴 qiánchēzhījiàn warning taken from the overturned cart in front; a lesson from the failure of one's predecessor; take warning from others' mistakes

前程 qiánchéng prospect; future: ～远大 have bright prospects

前锋 qiánfēng ①［军］vanguard ②［体］forward

前赴后继 qiánfù-hòujì advance wave upon wave; indomitably stepping into the breach as others fall; with fresh forces always stepping forward as others fell

前功尽弃 qiángōng-jìnqì All previous efforts are wasted. All labour is lost.; All that has been achieved has come to nothing.

前后 qiánhòu ① before and behind: ～夹攻 attack both from the front and in the rear ② about; around: 春节～ around the Spring Festival ③ from start to finish; from beginning to end; altogether: 他写书～花了 5 年时间。From start to finish it took him five years to write his book. ～矛盾 be inconsistent

前进 qiánjìn go forward; advance: ～道路上 on the road of advance

前景 qiánjǐng ①［图画等的］foreground ② prospect; future; vista: 开辟广阔～ open up vast vistas. ～调查 anticipation survey

前科 qiánkē criminal record; pedigree: ～档案 conduct sheet. ～犯 criminal with previous conviction; pedigree-man

前例 qiánlì precedent: 史无～的 unprecedented

前列 qiánliè forefront; front rank (row): 站在斗争的～ stand in the forefront of the struggle

前面 qiánmian ① in front; at the head; ② above; preceding

前怕狼,后怕虎 qiá npà láng,hòu pà hǔ fear the wolves in front and the tiger behind; be full of misgivings; have too many fears

前驱 qiánqū forerunner; vanguard; precursor; pioneer

前人 qiánrén forefathers; predecessors

前任 qiánrèn predecessor: ～总统 ex-president

前提 qiántí ① premise ② prerequisite; presupposition

前途 qiántú future; prospect: ～

光明。The prospects are bright for the future.

前往 qiánwǎng go to; leave for; proceed to

前卫 qiánwèi ①[军] advance guard ②[体] halfback

前夕(夜) qiánxī(yè) (on the) eve (of):春节～ on the eve of the Spring Festival

前线 qiánxiàn frontline; front

前言 qiányán preface; foreword; introduction

前沿 qiányán frontier; forward position:～科学 front line sciences

前因后果 qiányīn-hòuguǒ cause and effect; antecedents and consequences; the beginning and end of the matter; the sequence of events

前兆 qiánzhào forewarning; omen

前奏 qiánzòu prelude:～曲 [乐] prelude; preludio

乾 qián

乾坤 qiánkūn the universe; heaven and earth:扭转～ reverse the course of events; bring about a radical change in the existing state of affairs; reverse the trend

掮 qián 〈动〉 carry on one's shoulder

掮客 qiánkè broker:～佣金 commission; brokerage

虔 qián 〈形〉 pious; sincere

虔诚 qiánchéng pious; devoted; devout:～的基督徒 a devout Christian

黔 qián 〈形〉 black

黔驴技穷 qiánlǘ-jìqióng at one's wits' end; at the end of one's rope; on one's last legs

钱 qián 〈名〉 money:零～ small (pocket) money

钱包 qiánbāo wallet; purse

钱币 qiánbì coin:～收藏 coin collecting. ～收藏(学)家 numismatist

钱币鉴定人 qiánbì jiàndìngrén shroff

钱柜 qiánguì money-locker; money-box; till

钱庄 qiánzhuāng money houses; money shop

钳 qián ①〈名〉pincers; pliers:一把～子 a pair of pincers ②〈动〉grip (with pincers); clamp:用钳子把烧红的铁～住 grip a piece of red-hot iron with a pair of tongs

钳工 qiángōng ① benchwork ② fitter

钳口结舌 qiánkǒu-jiéshé keep one's mouth shut

钳形 qiánxíng pincerlike:～攻势 pincer movement

钳制 qiánzhì [军] contain; pin down:～兵力 containing forces ② muzzle; gap:～言论自由 muzzle freedom of speech

qiǎn

浅 qiǎn 〈形〉 ① shallow:～溪 a shallow stream ② simple;

easy：这篇课文很～。This lesson is very easy. ③ superficial：～薄的知识 superficial knowledge ④ (of colour) light：～绿 thin green

浅薄 qiǎnbó superficial；shallow：～涉猎[艺术等的] dilettantism

浅见 qiǎnjiàn〈谦〉(in) my humble opinion

浅陋 qiǎnlòu superficial；meagre；poor：学识～ be poor in learning

浅显 qiǎnxiǎn plain；easy to read and understand

浅易 qiǎnyì simple and easy；easy：～读物 easy readings

遣 qiǎn〈动〉① send；send out；dispatch：派～ dispatch ② expel；dispel：消～ diversion；pastime

遣返 qiǎnfǎn repatriate：被～回国者 repatriate

遣散 qiǎnsàn send away；disband；dismiss：～费 severance pay；separation pay

遣送 qiǎnsòng send back；repatriate：～出境 deport. ～回国 repatriate

谴 qiǎn

谴责 qiǎnzé blame；denounce；censure；repudiate；condemn：～小说 novel of condemnation. 良心受到～ be conscience-smitten

qiàn

歉 qiàn ①〈形〉poor harvest；crop failure ②〈名〉apology：道～ make an apoplogy

歉疚 qiànjiù having a guilty conscience

歉年 qiànnián lean year

歉收 qiànshōu poor harvest；crop failure

歉意 qiànyì apology；regret：表示～ offer an apology；apologize (for)；express one's regret (for). 谨致～ please accept my apologies

倩 qiàn〈形〉handsome，pretty：～影 a well-proportioned form；a beautiful figure

堑 qiàn〈名〉moat；cham：天～ natural chasm. ～战 trench warfare

欠 qiàn〈动〉① owe (a debt，etc.)：～某人 100 元 owe sb. 100 yuan ② lacking；short of：说话～考虑 speak without due consideration ③ raise slightly (a part of the body)：～身坐起 raise oneself to a half sitting position

欠产 qiànchǎn shortfall in output；production shortfall

欠单 qiàndān accommodation note (kite，paper)

欠付工资 qiàn fù gōngzī back pay；back salary

欠佳 qiànjiā not good enough；not up to the mark：身体～ not feel well；be under the weather

欠款 qiànkuǎn money that is owing；arrears；balance due；debt：～金额 amount in arrear

欠缺 qiànquē be short of; be deficient in; be lacking in:～经验 be short of experience
欠税 qiànshuì owing taxes
欠条 qiàntiáo bill signed in acknowledgement of debt; IOU (I owe you)
欠妥 qiàntuǒ not proper
欠债(帐) qiànzhài (zhàng) ① owe sb. a debt; run into debt ② debt due; outstanding accounts; bills due

嵌 qiàn〈动〉embed; inlay:～花的地面 a mosaic pavement

纤 qiàn〈名〉a rope for towing a boat:拉～ track (a boat)
纤夫 qiànfū boat tracker

qiāng

枪 qiāng〈名〉① spear:红缨～ red-tasseled spear ② gun; rifle; pistol:～架 rifle rack
枪毙 qiāngbì execute by shooting; shoot
枪打出头鸟 qiāng dǎ chūtóu niǎo shoot the bird which takes the lead; The outstanding usually bear the brunt of attack.
枪决 qiāngjué shoot:执行～ shoot sb. (dead); execute
枪林弹雨 qiānglín-dànyǔ hails of bullets; storm of shots and shells; scene of heavy fighting; intensive fighting in the battle field
枪杀 qiāngshā shoot dead; kill by shooting
枪伤 qiāngshāng bullet wound
枪声 qiāngshēng shot; crack
枪支 qiāngzhī firearms:～管理规定 gun control regulations
枪子儿 qiāngzǐr ① cartridge ② bullet; shot

呛 qiāng〈动〉choke:吃饭吃～了 choke over one's food
另见 qiàng

腔 qiāng〈名〉① cavity:胸～ thoracic cavity ② tune; pitch:高～ high pitched tune ③ accent:学生～ schoolboy talk
腔调 qiāngdiào ① tune:京剧的～ tunes of Beijing opera ② accent; intonation:他谈话带有南方～。He speaks with a southern accent.

qiáng

墙 qiáng〈名〉wall
墙报 qiángbào wall newspaper
墙倒众人推 qiáng dǎo zhòngrén tuī When a wall is about to collapse, everybody gives it a push — everybody hits a man who is down.; Everyone gives a shove to a falling wall.
墙脚 qiángjiǎo ① foot of a wall ② foundation; cornerstone:挖～ undermine the foundation (of)

强 qiáng〈形〉① strong; powerful:～敌 formidable enemy ② better:他们的生活一年比一年～。Their life is getting better each year. ③ slightly more than; plus:四分之一～ slightly more than one fourth ④〈副〉by force:～取 take by force 另见 qiǎng

强暴 qiángbào ① violent; outrageous; brutal ② brute force; violence:不畏～ defy brute force

强大 qiángdà big and powerful; powerful; formidable

强盗 qiángdào robber; bandit:～行为 robbery

强调 qiángdiào lay stress on; stress; emphasize:～指出 point out emphatically

强悍 qiánghàn fierce; intrepid; doughty

强横 qiánghèng rude and unreasonable; tyrannical; surly; arrogant

强化 qiánghuà intensify; strengthen:～训练 intensive training. ～职能 reinforce one's function

强加 qiángjiā impose; force

强奸 qiángjiān rape; violate:～犯 raper; rapist. ～妇女 indecent assault on a woman. ～罪 offence of rape

强劲 qiángjìng powerful; forceful

强烈 qiángliè strong; intense; vehement:～的感情 vehement passions

强令 qiánglìng arbitrarily give orders

强权 qiángquán power; might:～政治 power politics

强人 qiángrén strongman

强盛 qiángshèng powerful and prosperous; powerful

强手 qiángshǒu strong hand:超过名将～ outdo the super stars

强硬 qiángyìng strong; tough; uncompromising; unyielding; formidable:～的谈判者 formidable negotiator

强制 qiángzhì compel; enforce:～机关 institutions of law enforcement. ～措施 coercive measure. ～劳动教养 forced labour education. ～执行[法] compulsory execution

强壮 qiángzhuàng strong; sturdy; robust

qiǎng

抢 qiǎng〈动〉① loot; rob:～钱财 rob a man of his money ② snatch; grab; seize:把信～过去 snatch away the letter ③ vie for; scramble for:～球 scramble for the ball ④ rush:～收 rush in the harvest; rush-harvest

抢夺 qiǎngduó rob; seize; wrest; snatch; forcibly seize

抢购 qiǎnggòu rush to buy; make a panic purchase of:～物资 panic buying of goods

抢劫 qiǎngjié rob; loot; sack:～财物 rob sb. of his valuables

抢救 qiǎngjiù ① rush to save; rescue ② give (the patient) an emergency treatment

抢手 qiǎngshǒu in big demand; popular :～货 goods in big demand; hot consumer goods; shopping-rush goods; "grabbed" items

抢戏 qiǎngxì scene-steal

抢先 qiǎngxiān compete to be the

first (to do sth.)

抢险 qiǎngxiǎn rush to deal with an emergency; take immediate measures against (the flood, etc.)

抢修 qiǎngxiū rush to repair; rush-repair; do emergent (rush) repairs (on): ～房屋 make urgent repair on houses

抢种 qiǎngzhòng rush-plant: ～晚稻 rush-plant the late rice

强 qiǎng 〈动〉 make an effort; compel; strive: ～作镇静 try hard to keep one's composure
另见 qiáng

强辩 qiǎngbiàn argue sophistically; defend oneself by sophistry; lame defence

强词夺理 qiǎngcí-duólǐ resort to sophistry; reason fallaciously; sophisticate; use lame arguments and perverted logic

强记 qiǎngjì learn by rote; cram

强加 qiǎngjiā force (on); impose (upon): ～于人 force sth. on others; impose opinions on others

强迫 qiǎngpò compel; force; impel; coerce (into): ～某人做某事 make sb. do sth. by force; coerce sb. into doing sth.

强求 qiǎngqiú insist on; forcibly demand: ～一律 follow a single pattern

强人所难 qiǎngrén-suǒnán constrain sb. to do sth. that are beyond his power; make sb. do what is beyond his power or against his will

强作笑容 qiǎngzuò-xiàoróng force a smiling face; force a smile

襁 qiǎng

襁褓 qiǎngbǎo swadding clothes: ～中 in one's infancy

qiàng

呛 qiàng 〈动〉 irritate (respiratory organs): 辣椒味～鼻子 the smell of red pepper irritates the nose
另见 qiāng

跄 qiàng

跄踉 qiàngliàng stagger

qiāo

敲 qiāo 〈动〉 ① knock; beat; strike: 有人～门。Someone is knocking. ② extort; over charge: 给～去 100 元 be stung for 100 yuan

敲骨吸髓 qiāogǔ-xīsuí suck the life-blood; break the bones and suck the marrow

敲门 qiāomén knock at the door: ～砖 a brick picked up to knock on the door and thrown away when it has served one's purpose — a stepping-stone to success; use… as a door-knocker for

敲诈 qiāozhà racketeer; extort; blackmail: ～勒索 extort by blackmail

敲竹杠 qiāozhúgàng overcharge sb. or extort money from him by taking advantage of his weakness or ignorance; soak; fleece:向某人～ fleece a man of his money

悄 qiāo

悄悄 qiāoqiāo quietly; stealthily; softly:～地说话 talk in undertones

锹 qiāo 〈名〉 shovel; spade

橇 qiāo 〈名〉 sled; sledge; sleigh

跷 qiāo 〈动〉 ① lift up (a leg); hold up (a finger):～起大姆指 hold up one's thumb; thumbs up ② on tiptoe

qiáo

乔 qiáo

乔迁 qiáoqiān move to a better (new) place

乔装打扮 qiáozhuāng-dǎbàn disguise oneself (as); doll oneself up; deck oneself

桥 qiáo 〈名〉 bridge

桥洞 qiáodòng bridge opening; arch of a bridge

桥梁 qiáoliáng bridge:起～作用 serve as a link

桥牌 qiáopái bridge: ～大师 grand master. 打～ play bridge

桥头 qiáotóu either end of a bridge; bridgehead: ～堡 bridgehead

翘 qiáo 〈动〉 raise (one's head): ～首 raise one's head ② become warped:木板～了。The board has warped.

另见 qiào

憔 qiáo

憔悴 qiáocuì haggard; emaciated; withered; be fading away: 面容～ look emaciated

侨 qiáo ①〈动〉living abroad ②〈名〉a person living abroad:华～ overseas Chinese

侨胞 qiáobāo countrymen (nationals) residing abroad; overseas Chinese

侨汇 qiáohuì overseas remittance; remittance by Chinese nationals residing abroad

侨居 qiáojū live abroad: ～国 country of residence

侨眷 qiáojuàn relatives of nationals living abroad; relatives of overseas Chinese

侨联 qiáolián Returned Overseas Chinese Federation

侨民 qiáomín nationals residing abroad:外国～ foreign nationals

侨委 qiáowěi Overseas Chinese Affairs Committee

侨务 qiáowù affairs concerning nationals living abroad

侨乡 qiáoxiāng Overseas Chinese hometowns

侨资 qiáozī overseas Chinese funds:～企业 overseas Chinese ventures

樵 qiáo〈名〉 firewood

樵夫 qiáofū woodman

瞧 qiáo 〈动〉 see; look

瞧不起 qiáobuqǐ look down upon; despise; hold … in contempt

瞧不上眼 qiáobushàngyǎn turn up one's nose at; belittle

瞧得起 qiáodeqǐ have a high opinion of; hold sb. in esteem

瞧见 qiáojiàn see; catch sight of

qiǎo

巧 qiǎo 〈形〉① skilful; clever; ingenious: ～手 clever with one's hands ② cunning; artful: ～言 cunning words; deceitful talk ③〈副〉accidentally; by chance; as it happens: 来得～ arrive at a most opportune moment

巧辩 qiǎobiàn argue skilfully or plausibly

巧夺天工 qiǎoduó-tiāngōng superb craftsmanship; wonderful workmanship; Art beats nature.; a marvellous creation excelling nature

巧(媳)妇难为无米之炊 qiǎo(xí)fù nánwéi wú mǐ zhī chuī Even a clever housewife can't cook a meal without rice.; You can't make something out of nothing.; If you have no hand you can't make a fist.; One can't make bricks without straw.

巧干 qiǎogàn work ingeniously; do sth. in a clever way

巧合 qiǎohé ① coincidence; fortuity; coincide (with): 真是～! What a happy coincidence!

巧克力 qiǎokèlì chocolate

巧立名目 qiǎolì-míngmù invent various names of items; devise a variety of titles; concoct various pretexts; rack one's brains for ingenious devices

巧妙 qiǎomiào skilful; deft; clever; smart: ～的表演 deft performance

巧取豪夺 qiǎoqǔ-háoduó obtain by force or deception; get by hook or by crook; rob by force or by trick

巧遇 qiǎoyù encounter by chance

qiào

窍 qiào 〈名〉①aperture ② key to sth.: 他对音乐一～不通。He is utterly ignorant of music.

窍门 qiàomén knack; know-how; key (to a problem); secret to success: 找～ try to find out the knack (key) (of doing things)

壳 qiào 〈名〉 hard surface; shell: 贝～ sea shell
另见 ké

翘 qiào〈动〉stick up; hold up; lift up; tilt: 不要把椅子～起来。Don't tilt the chair.
另见 qiáo

翘尾巴 qiào wěiba beome cocky; wag one's tail in the air; stuck-up

撬 qiào〈动〉prize; pry: ～石头 pry (lift) up a stone

撬杠 qiàogàng pinch bar; crowbar; pry

峭 qiào 〈形〉① high and steep;

precipitous：～壁 cliff；precipice ② severe；rigid；stern

峭立 qiàolì rise steeply

俏 qiào 〈形〉 pretty；smart；cute；chic：打扮得真～ be smartly dressed；wear the cute dress

俏话 qiàohuà ① sarcastic remark ② witty remark；hit

俏丽 qiàolì handsome；pretty

俏皮 qiàopí ① pretty；good-looking；smart ② humorous；witty

qiē

切 qiē 〈动〉 cut；chop；slice：～下一块肉 slice off a piece of meat

切除 qiēchú ① cut off；sever；remove ② [医] excision；resection：～肿瘤 remove a tumour

切磋 qiēcuō study and learn by mutual discussion；compare notes：～琢磨 learn from each other by exchanging views

切断 qiēduàn cut off；sever：～电源 cut off the power supply

切割 qiēgē cut metal (by lathes，etc.)

切削 qiēxiāo cut；cutting：机械～ machine cutting

qié

茄 qié 〈名〉 eggplant
另见 jiā

茄汁 qiézhī tomato sauce

茄子 qiézhi eggplant；aubergine

qiě

且 qiě 〈副〉 ① for the time being；just：～等一下 just wait a little while ② for a long time：她～来不了呢。She's a long time coming. ③ not to mention；let alone：～不说你，连她最好的朋友的话，她都不听。She would not listen even to her best friend，not to mention you. ④〈连〉both… and…：这种马既高～大。This breed of horses is both tall and heavily grown.

且慢 qiěmàn just wait；wait a minute；not leave so soon；not go or do so soon

且信且疑 qiěxìn-qiěyí half believing and half doubting

qiè

怯 qiè 〈形〉 timid；nervous；cowardly

怯步 qièbù draw back (in fear)；hang back

怯场 qièchǎng (have) stage fright

怯懦 qiènuò timid；timorous；nervous

怯弱 qièruò timid and weak-willed；cowardly

怯阵 qièzhèn ① feel nervous when going into battle；be battle-shy

妾 qiè〈名〉 concubine

锲 qiè〈动〉engrave; carve

锲而不舍 qiè'érbùshě keep on carving; work with perseverance; unflaggingly

挈 qiè〈动〉① take along:～眷 take one's family along ② raise; lift; take up:提纲～领 bring up the chief points; keep up the key points

切 qiè〈动〉① correspond to; be close to:译文不～。The translation does not correspond to the original. ② be sure to:～勿迟延 be sure not to delay ③〈形〉eager; anxious:回家心～ be anxious to return home

切齿 qièchǐ grind (gnash) one's teeth:～痛恨 have a deep hatred for; hate extremely; gnash the teeth in bitter hatred

切合 qièhé fit in with; suit:～实际 suit the actual conditions; in the light of realities

切记 qièjì be sure to remember; always bear in mind; never forget

切忌 qièjì must guard against; avoid by all means

切盼 qièpàn eagerly look forward to; wait impatiently for

切身 qièshēn of immediate concern to oneself; of personal concern:～利益 one's vital interests. ～体会 intimate experience of; first-hand experience; personal understanding

切实 qièshí ① practical; feasible:～有效的经济发展 down-to-earth and effective economic development ② strictly; conscientiously; in all seriousness:～抓好基础教育 make great genuine efforts to improve basic education

切中要害 qièzhòng-yàohài hit the nail on the head; hit the mark; strike home

窃 qiè ①〈动〉steal:为某人偷～某物 steal sb. sth. ②〈副〉secretly; surreptitiously

窃据 qièjù usurp:～要津 craftily seizing key posts

窃密 qièmì steal secret information; steal secrets

窃窃私语 qièqiè-sīyǔ talk in whispers; whisper

窃取 qièqǔ steal; grab; usurp:～某人权力 usurp sb.'s authority. ～情报 steal intelligence

窃听 qiètīng overhear; eavesdrop; bug:～器 tapping (bugging) device; bug; listening device

窃贼 qièzéi thief; pilferer

qīn

亲 qīn〈名〉① parent:双～ parents ② relative:近～ close relative ③ marriage; match:成～ get (be) married〈形〉④ related by blood; next of skin:～兄弟 blood brother ⑤ intimate; close; dear:～如一家 as dear to each other as members of one family ⑥〈副〉in person; personally ⑦〈动〉kiss:～孩子的脸 kiss the child on the cheek

另见 qìng
亲爱 qīn'ài dear; beloved
亲笔 qīnbǐ (in) one's own handwriting: ～签名 one's own signature; autograph. ～信 a personal, hand-written message; an autograph letter
亲近 qīnjìn be close to; be on intimate terms with
亲口 qīnkǒu (tell sb.) personally (in person): 这是他～告诉我的。He told me this himself.
亲临 qīnlín come or go to a place personally
亲密 qīnmì very intimate; close
亲昵 qīnnì very intimate; affectionate
亲戚 qīnqi relative
亲切 qīnqiè kind; cordial; sincere: ～关怀 show kind concern for; loving care; kind attention: ～交谈 have a cordial talk with sb.
亲热 qīnrè warm; affectionate; cordial
亲人 qīnrén ① one's family members; kinsfolk; spouse ② (beloved) ones
亲善 qīnshàn close and friendly; goodwill (between countries)
亲身 qīnshēn in person; personally; first-hand: ～经历 personal experience
亲生 qīnshēng (parents or children) of one's own: ～子女 one's own children
亲手 qīnshǒu with one's own hands; personally; oneself
亲属 qīnshǔ relatives; relations
亲吻 qīnwěn kiss
亲信 qīnxìn one's own man; trusted follower (supporter, associate); righthand man
亲眼 qīnyǎn with one's own eyes: ～目睹 see with one's own eyes
亲自 qīnzì in person; personally; oneself: ～动手 do the job oneself; act personally

钦 qīn ①〈动〉admire; respect: ～敬之忱 have great admiration and respect for ②〈副〉by the emperor himself: ～赐 granted by an emperor
钦差 qīnchāi imperial envoy
钦佩 qīnpèi admire; esteem; respect: 表示～ express admiration for. 令人～的 admirable; praiseworthy

侵 qīn〈动〉invade, intrude; encroach upon; infringe; violate: ～略军队 invading forces
侵犯 qīnfàn ① encroach upon; infringe; violate: ～财产罪 crime of property violation. ～人权 infringe upon human rights ② invade; intrude into: ～领土 violate a country's territorial integrity
侵害 qīnhài encroach on; make inroads on
侵略 qīnlüè aggression; invasion: ～战争 war of aggression. ～军 invading army
侵扰 qīnrǎo invade and harass: ～边境 harass a country's frontiers; make border raids
侵入 qīnrù invade; intrude into; make incursions into
侵蚀 qīnshí corrode; weather: 受

风雨～ weathered by wind and rain

侵吞 qīntūn ① misappropriate; swallow up:～公款 embezzle public funds ② annex:～别国领土 annex another country's territory

侵袭 qīnxí invade and attack; make a sneak attack on; make inroads upon (into); [大风等] hit:这座城市受到了风暴的～。The city was hit by a storm.

侵占 qīnzhàn invade and occupy; occupy by force; seize:～公有土地 seize public land

qín

勤 qín ①〈形〉hardworking; diligent; industrious; assiduous:～～恳恳地为人民服务 be diligent and conscientious in serving the people ②〈副〉frequently; regularly:她来得～。She comes very often. ③〈名〉attendance:考～ check on work attendance

勤奋 qínfèn diligent; hardworking; assiduous:工作～ work hard

勤工俭学 qíngōng-jiǎnxué study on a work-study basis; work-study programme; part-work and part-study

勤俭 qínjiǎn industrious and frugal:～建国 build a country through hard work (diligence, industriousness) and thrift. ～节约 be industrious and practise economy. ～持家 manage a household industriously and thriftily; be industrious and thrift in managing households

勤恳 qínkěn diligent and conscientious; earnestly and conscientiously:做事勤勤恳恳 be diligent and conscientious in one's work

勤快 qínquài〈口〉hardworking; diligent

勤劳 qínláo diligent; hardworking; industrious:中国人民是～勇敢的人民。The Chinese people are industrious and valiant people.

勤勉 qínmiǎn diligent; studious; assiduous:～好学 diligent and eager to learn

勤王 qíwáng ① come to the rescue of the king:发兵～ send troops to save the throne ② do one's best to serve the throne

勤务 qínwù service; duty:～员 orderly; servant

勤学 qínxué study hard:～苦练 study and train hard

勤杂工 qínzágōng odd-jobman; handyman; odd-jobber

勤政廉政 qínzhèng-liánzhèng keep (government employees) honest and industrious

芹 qín

芹菜 qíncài celery

秦 qín

秦腔 qínqiāng Shaanxi opera, popular in the northwestern provinces

禽 qín〈名〉birds:家～ (domestic) fowls; poultry

禽兽 qínshòu birds and beasts:～行为 bestial acts

擒 qín 〈动〉 catch; capture; seize:生～ capture alive

擒拿 qínná arrest; capture; catch

擒贼先擒王 qín zéi xiān qín wáng To catch bandits, first catch the ringleader.; Capture the ringleader in order to capture all his followers.

噙 qín〈动〉 hold in the mouth or the eyes:～着眼泪 eyes brimming with tears; eyes filled with tears

琴 qín 〈名〉① *qin*, a seven-stringed plucked instrument in some ways similar to the zither ② a general name for certain musical instrument:口～ harmonica

琴拨 qínbō plectrum

琴书 qínshū [曲艺] *qin shu* (story-telling in song and monologue with musical accompaniment)

琴弦 qínxián string (of a musical instrument)

qǐn

寝 qǐn ①〈动〉 sleep; get into bed:独～ sleep alone〈名〉② bedroom:就～ go to bed; retire to rest ③ coffin chamber:陵～ mausoleum

qìn

沁 qìn〈动〉 seep; ooze; exude:她额上～出了汗珠。Her forehead was oozing sweat.

沁人心脾 qìnrén-xīnpí gladden people's hearts; mentally refreshing; gratifying

qīng

青 qīng〈形〉① green; blue:～椒 green pepper (chilli) ② black:～布 black cloth ③ young:～工 young workers

青出于蓝而胜于蓝 qīng chūyú lán ér shèngyú lán Indigo blue is extracted from the indigo plant but is bluer than the plant it comes from.; The younger generation outdoes the older generation.; The pupil often surpasses his teacher (master).

青春 qīngchūn youth; youthfulness:～的活力 youthful vigour. ～期 puberty

青翠 qīngcuì verdant; fresh and green:～欲滴 be green and luxuriant

青黄不接 qīnghuáng-bùjiē Green and yellow have not joined — a new crop has not yet come.; When the crop is still in the blade, the old stock is nearly consumed.; food shortage between two harvests; a temporary shortage; a time to tide over:科学家～ a serious shortage of scientists

青睐 qīnglài favour; good graces

青梅竹马 qīngméi-zhúmǎ green plums and a bamboo horse—a girl and a boy playing innocently together; a man and a woman who had an innocent affection for each other in childhood

青年 qīngnián young people; the youth: 在～时期 in one's youth. ～节 Youth Day

青少年 qīngshàonián teenagers; teensters; youngsters

青史 qīngshǐ annals of history

青饲料 qīngsìliào green fodder (feed)

青天 qīngtiān ① blue sky: ～霹雳 a bolt from the blue ② upright official

青铜 qīngtóng bronze: ～器 bronze vessels (articles). ～器时代 the Bronze Age

青云直上 qīngyún-zhíshàng rapid advancement in one's career

青贮 qīngzhù [农] ensiling: ～饲料 silage; preserved green fodder

清

清 qīng〈形〉① clean; clear; pure; unmixed: ～水 clear water ② distinct; clarified: 说不～ hard to explain ③ quiet: 享～福 live in quiet comfort ④〈动〉clean up; settle: ～组织 clean up the organization. 帐～了吗? Has the account been cleared up?

清白 qīngbái clean; pure; stainless; unsullied: 历史～ be of unsullied antecedents; have a clean personal record

清仓 qīngcāng make an inventory of warehouse (the stock in the storehouse): ～查库 take inventory of warehouse stock. ～拍卖 clearance

清册 qīngcè detailed list; list

清查 qīngchá ① investigate; check: ～帐目 audit the accounts. ～物资 take stock of property ② clear out; comb out; ferret out; uncover: ～反革命分子 uncover counter-revolutionaries

清茶 qīngchá ① green tea ② tea served without refreshments

清产核资 qīngchǎn-hézī reappraise the stocks and assets of enterprises; take inventory of property and make an accounting of funds

清偿 qīngcháng pay (clear) off: ～债务 pay (clear) off debts

清澈 qīngchè crystal; limpid; lucid: ～的河水 the limpid water of the river

清除 qīngchú do away with; clear away; get rid of; eliminate; sweep away; weed out: ～出党 clear sb. out of the Party. ～垃圾 clear (do) away with the rubbish

清楚 qīngchu ① clear; distinct; explicit ② be clear about: 搞～ clear up; clarify

清单 qīngdān ① bill ② detailed list; list; detailed account: 存货～ inventory

清淡 qīngdàn ① plain; light; not greasy: ～的食物 light food ② dull; slack: 生意～。Business is

slack.
清点 qīngdiǎn check; sort and count; make an inventory:~货物 take stock. ~人数 check the number of people
清风 qīngfēng cool breeze:~徐来。The cool breeze blows gently.
清官 qīngguān honest and upright official:~难断家务事。Even an honest official finds it hard to settle a family quarrel.
清规戒律 qīngguī-jièlǜ taboos and prohibitions (commandments); restrictions and fetters; rigorous regulations
清洁 qīngjié clean
清净 qīngjìng peace and quiet
清静 qīngjìng quiet
清理 qīnglǐ ① clean up; put in order; check up; sort out:~在建项目 checking up on the projects under construction. ~帐目 check up the accounts ②[企业破产] liquidate
清廉 qīnglián free from corruption; honest and upright
清凉 qīngliáng cool and refreshing:~饮料 cold drink
清贫 qīngpín poor; badly off
清爽 qīngshuǎng ① cool and fresh; brisk; refreshing ② easy; relieved; relaxed; feeling good and fit:心里~了一些 feel relieved (relaxed)
清算 qīngsuàn ① clear (accounts); audit; square:~帐户 clearing account ② settle accounts (with); expose and criticize
清汤 qīngtāng clear soup; light soup
清晰 qīngxī clear; distinct:~度 visibility; [电视] clarity
清洗 qīngxǐ ① wash; clean ② purge; comb out; weed out; eliminate
清闲 qīngxián quiet and leisure; at leisure; idle:过~生活 lead a leisurely life
清香 qīngxiāng fresh fragrance; sweet scent:~扑鼻。A sweet scent assails the nostrils.
清醒 qīngxǐng ① sober; clear-headed; sane:~的估计 a clear-headed appraisal; a sober estimate ② come to; regain consciousness:病人已经~过来了。The patient has come to.
清秀 qīngxiù delicate-looking; delicate and pretty; handsome; comely:面貌~ of fine; delicate features
清样 qīngyàng [印]final proof; press proof:~校对人 press reader
清一色 qīngyīsè all of the same colour; uniform; of one colour:~地穿着西装 be all dressed alike in Western suits
清早 qīngzǎo early in the morning; early morning
清真 qīngzhēn ① simple and unadorned; plain ② Islamic; Muslim

蜻 qīng

蜻蜓 qīngtíng dragonfly:~点水 touch superficially; skim over one's work

倾 qīng ① incline; lean; slope: 向前～ lean forward ② pour out; empty: ～盆 pour down in torrents. ③ collapse: 大厦将～ a great mansion on the point of collapse

倾巢 qīngcháo (of the enemy or bandits) turn out in full force (strength)

倾城 qīngchéng the whole city or town

倾倒 qīngdǎo ① topple and fall; topple over ② greatly admire: 为之～ be infatuated with sth.

倾倒 qīngdào 〈动〉 pour out; empty: ～垃圾 dump rubbish

倾覆 qīngfù overturn; topple; capsize

倾家荡产 qīngjiā-dàngchǎn lose a family fortune; be reduced to abject poverty; go bankrupt or broke

倾慕 qīngmù have a strong admiration for; adore

倾盆大雨 qīngpén-dàyǔ heavy downpour; rain cats and dogs; pouring (torrential) rain: 遇到一场～ be caught in a torrential rain

倾诉(吐) qīngsù (tǔ) pour out (one's heart, troubles, etc.); unbosom oneself

倾谈 qīngtán have a good, heart-to-heart talk; get into intimate conversation with

倾听 qīngtīng listen attentively to; lean an attentive ear to; incline the ear to listen: ～群众的意见 listen attentively to the views of the masses

倾向 qīngxiàng ① inclination; tendency; trend: ～性 tendentiousness ② tend to; be inclined to; prefer: 我～第一种方案。I prefer the first plan.

倾销 qīngxiāo dumping; unload: ～商品 dump commodities. ～市场 market for dumping goods

倾斜 qīngxié tilt; incline; slant; tip: ～度 gradient. 向北～ have a tip to the north

倾泻 qīngxiè pour; come down in torrents

倾卸 qīngxiè tip; dump; empty; pour out

倾心 qīngxīn ① admire; fall in love with: 一见～ (fall in) love at first sight ② cordial: ～交谈 have a heart-to-heart talk

倾轧 qīngyà engage in factional strife; jostle against each other

倾注 qīngzhù pour into; concentrate sth. on; devote to: 把全部精力～在工作上 devote all one's energies to a job

轻 qīng 〈形〉 ① light: ～工业 light industry ② small in number (degree): 病很～. The illness is not serious. ③ easy; light: 工作很～。It is an easy job. 〈副〉④ softly; gently: ～拿～放 handle gently ⑤ rashly: ～信 readily believe ⑥ belittle; make light of; despise: ～敌 take the enemy lightly; underestimate enemy strength

轻便 qīngbiàn light; handy; portable: ～铁路 light railway. ～工具箱 handy tool-box

轻薄 qīngbó given to philandering；frivolous

轻而易举 qīng'éryìjǔ easy to handle (do)

轻纺工业 qīngfǎng gōngyè light and textile industries

轻浮 qīngfú light；frivolous；flighty：举止～ be frivolous in one's manner

轻工业 qīnggōngyè light industry：～市场 market for manufactured goods turned out by light industries

轻举妄动 qīngjǔ-wàngdòng take a reckless action；act rashly：不可～ make no move without careful thought

轻快 qīngkuài ① brisk；spry ② lighthearted；lively

轻慢 qīngmàn treat sb. without proper respect；slight

轻描淡写 qīngmiáo-dànxiě touch on the matter lightly；mild comments；make light of；mention casually

轻蔑 qīngmiè contemptuous；scornful：～的眼光 a disdainful look

轻巧 qīngqiǎo ① light and handy ② dexterous；deft ③ simple；easy

轻取 qīngqǔ win an easy victory (in a game)；beat easily；win hands down

轻生 qīngshēng commit suicide

轻视 qīngshì look down upon；despise；belittle；take lightly；underestimate

轻率 qīngshuài rash；hasty；imprudent；indiscreet：～的态度 reckless attitude

轻松 qīngsōng light；easy；relaxed：～愉快 cheerful and relaxed

轻佻 qīngtiāo skittish；flirtatious；frivolous；giddy

轻微 qīngwēi light；slight；trifling；to a small extent

轻信 qīngxìn readily place trust in；be credulous：不要～谣言。Give no credence to rumours. ～口供 readily believe confessions

轻易 qīngyì ① easily ② lightly；rashly

轻音乐 qīngyīnyuè light music

轻盈 qīngyíng ① slim and graceful；lithe；lissom ② lighthearted；relaxed

轻重 qīngzhòng ① weight：两个～不一样。The two boxes do not weigh the same. ② degree of seriousness；relative importance；propriety：他说话不知～。He doesn't know the proper way to talk.

轻重缓急 qīngzhòng-huǎnjí order of importance and urgency；order of priority；relative importance and urgency

轻装 qīngzhuāng with light packs；light：～旅行 light travel. ～上阵 go into battle lightly-outfitted

氢 qīng 〈名〉 hydrogen

氢弹 qīngdàn hydrogen bomb；H-bomb

qíng

情 qíng 〈名〉 ① feeling；affection; sentiment:温～ tender sentiment② love; passion:谈～说爱 talk love; be courting ③ favour; kindness:求～ plead with sb.; ask for a favour ④ circumstances; situation:病～ patient's condition

情报 qíngbào information; intelligence:～检索 information retrieval. 搜集～ collect intelligence

情不自禁 qíngbùzìjìn can't help (doing sth.); can't refrain from

情操 qíngcāo sentiment; moral integrity; noble mind

情调 qíngdiào sentiment; emotional appeal; tone; [艺术的] feeling:异乡的～ tone of a strange land

情分 qíngfèn mutual affection:夫妻～ marital affection (relationship)

情夫 qíngfū an illicit lover of a married woman; lover

情妇 qíngfù mistress

情感 qínggǎn emotion; feeling; sentiment:～价值 sentimental value. 伤害某人～ hurt sb.'s feelings. 易动～ apt to be emotional

情节 qíngjié ① circumstances; particulars; details; case:～严重的 cases of gross violation. 弄虚作假～严重者 those who have engaged in glaring fraud ② (of story, play, etc.) plot:小说中～复杂的章节 the plotty episodes of a novel

情景 qíngjǐng scene; sight; circumstances:难忘的～ unforgettable scence

情况 qíngkuàng situation; condition; state of affairs:～在好转。Things are getting better. 根据具体～ in accordance with specific conditions

情理 qínglǐ reason; sense:合乎～ be reasonable

情侣 qínglǚ lovers; sweethearts:快乐的～ the happy lovers

情面 qíngmiàn sentimental considerations; sensibilities; feelings:留～ spare sb.'s feelings. 不留～ have no consideration for sb.'s feelings

情趣 qíngqù ① temperament and interest; disposition and taste ② good taste; interest; appeal:～高雅 be in good taste

情人 qíngrén sweetheart; [指男] lover:～节 (Saint) Valentine('s) Day (2月14日). ～眼里出西施。Beauty is in the eye of the gazer (beholder).; Every lover sees a thousand graces in the beloved object.; Love is blind.; Lover sees no fault.

情书 qíngshū love letter

情思 qíngsī ① tender regards; affection; goodwill ② state of mind; mood

情态 qíngtài spirit; mood:～动词 modal verb

情同手足 qíngtóngshǒuzú treating sb. like one's own brother; be affectionate to each other like brothers

情投意合 qíngtóu-yìhé find each other congenial; be in perfect harmony (with); suit each other perfectly; hit it off well; see eye to eye in everything; find so much in common with one another

情绪 qíngxù ① mood; feeling; emotion ② depression; the sulks: 闹～ be in a fit of depression; be in the sulks; be in low spirits

情谊 qíngyì feelings; sentiments; affection

情意 qíngyì ① good will; kindness; favour ② affection: ～绵绵 be very much enamoured

情由 qíngyóu the hows and whys: 不问～ without asking about the circumstances or causes

情有可原 qíngyǒukěyuán pardonable; excusable

情欲 qíngyù sexual passion; lust

情愿 qíngyuàn ① be willing to ② would rather; prefer: 我～留在家里。I would rather stay at home. 一厢～ wishful thinking

情知 qíngzhī know perfectly well (what is going on); know for certain; be fully aware

情致 qíngzhì interest; appeal

晴 qíng 〈形〉 fine; clear

晴空 qíngkōng clear sky: ～万里 clear open sky

晴朗 qínglǎng fine; clear: 天气～。It is a fine day.

晴天 qíngtiān fine day; fine weather: ～霹雳 a bolt from the blue

晴雨表 qíngyǔbiǎo barometer

擎 qíng 〈动〉 lift up; hold up; prop up

qǐng

请 qǐng〈动〉 ① ask; request: ～她进来 ask her in ② invite; engage: ～医生 send for a doctor ③ please: ～坐 sit down, please

请安 qǐng'ān pay respect to sb.; wish sb. good health

请便 qǐngbiàn Do as you please (wish); please yourself

请功 qǐnggōng ask the higher level to record sb.'s meritorious deeds

请假 qǐngjià ask for leave: ～2天 ask for two days' leave. 请病假回家 go home on sick leave

请柬 qǐngjiǎn invitation card

请教 qǐngjiào ask for sb.'s advice; consult

请客 qǐngkè invite sb. to dinner; stand treat; entertain; treat sb. to (an ice-cream, a theatre, etc.): ～送礼 invite guests and give them presents. 这次由我～。This is my treat.; It's on me this time.

请求 qǐngqiú ask; reguest: 向某人提出一个～ make sb. a request

请示 qǐngshì ask for instructions; make a request for instructions

请帖 qǐngtiē invitation card; invitation

请问 qǐngwèn ① excuse me; please: ～邮局在哪里? Excuse me, but could you tell me where the post office is? ② We should like to ask…; It may be asked…

请愿 qǐngyuàn present a petition; petition:～书 petition

请罪 qǐngzuì ① admit one's error and ask for punishment ② confess one's fault; apologize

顷 qǐng *qing*, a unit of area (=6.6667 hectares)〈副〉just:～接来信。I have just received your letter.

顷刻 qǐngkè in a moment; instantly

qìng

亲 qìng
另见 qīn

亲家 qìngjia parents of one's son-in-law or daughter-in-law; relatives by marriage

庆 qìng ①〈动〉celebrate; congratulate:～祝胜利 celebrate a victory ②〈名〉occasion for celebration:国～ National Day

庆典 qìngdiǎn celebration:大～ grand celebration

庆功会 qìnggōnghuì celebration meeting for achievements gained; meritorious service celebration meeting

庆贺 qìnghè congratulate (on); celebrate:～某人生日 congratulate sb. on his birthday

庆幸 qìngxìng rejoice (at):值得～的事 a matter for rejoicing

庆祝 qìngzhù celebrate:～国庆 celebrate National Day

罄 qìng〈动〉use up; exhaust:告～ run out; be all used up

罄竹难书 qìngzhú-nánshū (of crimes, etc.) too numerous to record (mention)

qióng

穹 qióng〈名〉① dome; vault ② the sky

穹苍 qióngcāng the vault of heaven; the sky; the heavens

穷 qióng〈形〉① poor; poverty-stricken; needy:～学者 needy scholar ② exhausted; pushed to limit ③〈名〉end; limit:无～无尽 inexhaustible; endless ④〈副〉extremely; exceedingly; thoroughly:～究 make a thorough inquiry. ～奢极侈 extremely extravagant and luxurious

穷兵黩武 qióngbīng-dúwǔ prosecute war adventures; wage sanguinary wars; love wars and military exploits

穷尽 qióngjìn limit; end

穷寇 qióngkòu hard-pressed enemy; tottering foe

穷困 qióngkùn poverty-stricken; destitute; in straitened circumstances

穷年累月 qióngnián-lěiyuè year after year; from year to year

穷人 qióngrén poor people; the poor

穷奢极侈 qióngshē-jíchǐ indulge in luxury and extravagance; (live a life of) wanton extravagance; be lapped (swathed) in luxury; live in extreme luxury;

live on the fat of the land

穷途末路 qióngtú-mòlù be at the end of one's rope (tether); in a sorry plight; dead end; at one's last gasp

穷乡僻壤 qióngxiāng-pìrǎng remote and backward place in the countryside

穷凶极恶 qióngxiōng-jí'è extremely vicious; utterly evil; devilish; diabolical; utterly atrocious

qiū

秋 qiū〈名〉① autumn; fall:~风 autumn wind ② year:千~万代 for thousands of years ③ a time of period:多事之~ an eventful period

秋波 qiūbō bright eyes of a beautiful woman:送~ (of a woman) make eyes; ogle

秋毫 qiūháo autumn hair; sth. so small as to be almost indiscernible:~无犯 discipline which forbids the slightest violation of the people's interests; without the slightest violation of the people's interests. 明察~ be so sharp-sighted as to be able to detect the smallest flaws

秋季 qiūjì autumn

秋千 qiūqiān swing (a seat for swinging):打~ have a swing. 荡~ play on the swing; have a swing

秋收 qiūshōu ① autumn harvest ② autumn crops

丘 qiū〈名〉 hillock; knoll; mound:沙~ a sand dune

丘陵 qiūlíng hills:~地带 hilly region

蚯 qiū

蚯蚓 qiūyǐn earthworm

qiú

酋 qiú

酋长 qiúzhǎng ① tribal chief ②[尊称] sheikh; emir:~国 sheikhdom; emirate

求 qiú〈动〉① beg; entreat; request:有~于人 have to look to others for help ② seek; try; strive for:~进步 strive for further progress ③ demand:供不应~。Supply falls short of demand.

求爱 qiú'ài court; woo; pay court to

求偿权 qiúchángquán right of claim

求过于供 qiúguòyúgòng Demand outstrips (exceeds) supply.

求和 qiúhé ① sue for peace ②[球赛]try to draw a match

求婚 qiúhūn make an offer of marriage; make a proposal (marriage); propose:你向她~了吗? Have you proposed to her?

求见 qiújiàn request an interview

求教 qiújiào ask for advice:登门~ call on sb. for counsel; come to seek advice

求救 qiújiù ask for immediate rescue when in distress; cry for help; seek help

求亲 qiúqīn seek a marriage alliance

求情 qiúqíng plead; intercede; ask for a favour: 向某人～ plead with sb.

求全 qiúquán ① ask for perfection; demand perfection: ～责备 nitpicking ② try to round sth. off: 委曲～ stoop to compromise; suffer wrong for the sake of general interest

求饶 qiúráo beg for mercy

求胜 qiúshèng strive for victory: ～心切 be anxious to gain victory

求实精神 qiúshí jīngshén matter-of-fact attitude

求同存异 qiútóng-cúnyì seek common ground while reserving differences; seek common ground among us, while keeping our differences

求学 qiúxué ① go to school ② pursue one's studies

求证 qiúzhèng seek to prove; seek evidence or verification

求之不得 qiúzhībùdé just what one wished for; most (exceedingly) welcome

求知 qiúzhī seek knowledge

求职 qiúzhí seek a job; job wanted

求助 qiúzhù ① ask for help ② have recourse to; resort to: ～于武力 resort to force

球 qiú 〈名〉 ① ball: 传～ pass the ball ② sphere; the globe; the earth: 全～战略 global strategy

球场 qiúchǎng [篮球、排球、网球等] court; [足球、棒球等] field

球迷 qiúmí (ball game) fan

球拍 qiúpāi [网球羽毛球等的] racket; [乒乓球的] bat

球赛 qiúsài ball game; match

球市 qiúshì football market

球坛 qiútán ball-playing circles

球鞋 qiúxié gym shoes; sneakers; tennis shoes

球星 qiúxīng ballplayer star

球艺 qiúyì ball game skills

裘 qiú〈名〉 fur coat

囚 qiú ①〈动〉 put in prison; imprison: 被～ be thrown into prison ②〈名〉prisoner: 死～ a convict sentenced to death

囚车 qiúchē patrol wagon; prison van; black maria

囚犯 qiúfàn prisoner; convict: ～监狱 convict prison

囚禁 qiújìn put in prison; imprison; enjail; captivity

囚室 qiúshì prison cell

囚徒 qiútú prisoner; convict

泅 qiú 〈名〉 swim

泅渡 qiúdù swim across: 武装～ swim (across) fully armed

qū

趋 qū〈名〉 ① hasten; run fast; hurry along ② tend to become; tend towards: ～于稳定 tend towards stability

趋附 qūfù ingratiate oneself with; curry favour with

趋势 qūshì tendency; trend: ～分

析 trend analysis. 有恶化的～be tending to deteriorate

趋向 qūxiàng ① tendency; trend ② incline to; tend to: ～好转 tend to improve

趋炎附势 qūyán-fùshì curry favour with the powerful; fawn upon the rich and powerful persons; sycophantic; serve the time: ～的人 timeserver

祛 qū〈动〉remove; dispel: ～暑 drive away summer heat

祛除 qūchú get rid of; dispel; drive out: ～疑虑 dispel one's misgivings

区 qū〈名〉① district; area; region: ～域性经济合作 regional economic cooperation ② an administrative division: 自治～ autonomous region ③〈动〉classify; subdivide; distinguish

区别 qūbié distinguish; discriminate: ～不同情况 distinguish among differing cases. ～对待 deal with different cases in different ways

区分 qūfēn differentiate; distinguish

区划 qūhuà division into regions (districts)

区间 qūjiān a sectioned-off route of a train or bus: ～车 shuttle train or bus

区区 qūqū trifling; trivial; petty: ～小事 a trifling matter

区域 qūyù region; district; area; zone: ～经济 regional economy. ～自治 regional autonomy

驱 qū〈动〉① drive (a horse, car, etc.) ② send away; expel; disperse: ～散乌云 disperse dark clouds

驱车 qūchē drive a vehicle: ～前往 drive (in a vehicle) to a place

驱除 qūchú wipe out; get rid of; expel

驱动 qūdòng drive: ～齿轮 driving gear

驱赶 qūgǎn ① drive (a cart, etc.) ② drive away; brush away

驱寒 qūhán dispel cold; warm oneself up

驱散 qūsàn disperse; dispel; break up

驱使 qūshǐ ① make sb. do sth.; order about ② prompt; spur on; urge; be driven by: 为好奇心所～ be prompted by curiosity

驱逐 qūzhú send away; expel; oust: ～出境 deportation

躯 qū〈名〉the human body

躯干 qūgàn trunk

躯体 qūtǐ body; frame

蛆 qū〈名〉maggot

曲 qū〈形〉① bent; crooked; tortuous: 弯～的小道 a tortuous path ② wrong; unjustifiable: ～直不分 Right and wrong are not discriminated; make no distinction between right and wrong ③〈名〉bend (of a river, etc.)
另见 qǔ

曲别针 qūbiézhēn paper clip

曲解 qūjiě distort；twist；misinterpret：～事实 distort a fact

曲线 qūxiàn［数］curve

曲意逢迎 qūyì-féngyíng fawn on sb. by all means；do everything to please sb.

曲折 qūzhé ① tortuous；winding：长期～的斗争 protracted tortuous struggle ② twists and turns；complications：故事情节是～的。The story has a complicated plot.

屈 qū〈动〉① bend；bow；crook：～臂 crook one's arm ② yield to；submit；subdue：～从 submit oneself to ③ be in the wrong：理～ have a weak case ④〈名〉wrong；injustice：叫～ complain about an injustice

屈从 qūcóng submit oneself to；yield to；knuckle down (under)；knock under；truckle to

屈服 qūfú subdue；submit；yield；knuckle under

屈就 qūjiù condescend to take a post offered

屈辱 qūrǔ shame；disgrace；mortification；humiliation：～求和 sue for peace on the most humiliating terms

屈膝 qūxī ① bend one's knees ② bow (before，to)；yield (to)：～投降 fall on one's knees in capitulation；bend (bow，submit，give in) and surrender to；throw oneself at the feet of；fall on one's kness in surrender

屈指可数 qūzhǐ-kěshǔ can be counted on one's fingers；not many；only a few；very few

屈尊 qūzūn condescend

qú

渠 qú〈名〉ditch；canal

渠道 qúdào ① irrigation ditch ② medium of communication；channel：外交～ diplomatic channels

qǔ

取 qǔ〈动〉① take；get；fetch：去～行李 go to fetch one's luggage. ～款 draw money (from one's account) ② seek；aim at：～乐 seek pleasure ③ adopt；choose：给孩子～名儿 choose a name for a child；give a name to a child

取保候审 qǔbǎo-hòushěn obtain a guarantor and await trial out of custody

取材 qǔcái draw materials：这本小说～于现实生活。This novel has drawn its materials from real life.

取长补短 qǔcháng-bǔduǎn overcome one's weak points by learning from others' strong points；learn from each other and swap experience；learn from others' strong points to offset one's weakness

取代 qǔdài replace；supplant；supercede；substitute for：用煤气～煤作燃料 replace coal by (with) gas

取道 qǔdào by way of; via:～香港回国 come back to China by way of Hong Kong

取得 qǔdé get; obtain; gain; achieve:～经验 gain experience. ～财产权 acquisition of property right. ～进展 make progress. ～好成绩 chalk up good results. ～一致意见 reach complete identity of views. ～群众支持 enlist popular support

取缔 qǔdì ban; prohibit; stop; forbid; clamp down (on); outlaw; suppress:～投机倒把 ban speculation and profiteering

取而代之 qǔ'érdàizhī take sb.'s place; replace; succeed

取经 qǔjīng obtain sacred texts (The term originally referred to Buddhist going to India to seek sacred Buddhist texts. Now it is a metaphor for absorbing experiences from advanced persons, units, or regions.); learn sb.'s experience

取决 qǔjué be decided by; depend on

取巧 qǔqiǎo resort to trickery to serve oneself

取舍 qǔshě make one's choice; accept or reject

取向 qǔxiàng orientation

取消 qǔxiāo cancel; abolish; call off; nullify; negate; discard; annul:～报价 withdraw an offer. ～订单 cancellation of order. ～合约 rescind a contract. ～资格 disqualify;［会员资格］deprive sb. of his membership

取笑 qǔxiào make fun of; ridicule

取信于民 qǔxìnyúmín win the people's confidence; attain the people's trust

取样 qǔyàng sample; sampling: ～检验 take a sample for a test

取悦 qǔyuè try to please

取证 qǔzhèng collect evidence

娶

qǔ〈动〉marry (a woman); take (sb.) to wife

娶亲 qǔqīn (of a man) get married

龋

qǔ

龋齿 qǔchǐ ①［医］dental caries ② decayed tooth

曲

qǔ〈名〉① song; tune; melody:高歌一～ lustily sing a song. 小～ ditty ② music (of a song):作～ compose music

另见 qū

曲调 qǔdiào［乐］melody (of a song); tune (of a song)

曲高和寡 qǔgāo-hèguǎ Songs of a highbrow type will find very few people to join in the chorus.; too highbrow to suit the taste of the public; too profound to be popular

曲艺 qǔyì *quyi* (Chinese folk art forms, including ballad singing, story-telling, comic dialogues, clapper talks, and cross-talks, etc.); *quyi* balladry:～团 troupe of ballad singers

qù

趣 qù〈名〉① interest; delight: 自讨没～ ask for snub ② bent; inclination; purport: 志～ aspirations and interests ③〈形〉interesting; amusing: ～事 an interesting episode

趣话 qùhuà funny remarks; joke

趣味 qùwèi interest; taste: ～盎然 be full of interest. 低级～ vulgar taste

趣闻轶事 qùwén-yìshì priceless anecdote

去 qù ①〈动〉go; leave for; depart: 她～多久了? How long has she been away? ② remove; get rid of: ～皮 remove the skin; peel ③〈形〉past; last: ～冬 last winter ④[用在动词前,表示要做某事]: 你～问一问。Please go and ask. ⑤[用在动宾结构后面,表示去做某事]: 他游泳～了。He's gone to swim.

去处 qùchù ① place to go; whereabouts ② place; site

去粗取精 qùcū-qǔjīng rid the coarse and obtain the refined; discard the dross and select the essential

去路 qùlù the way to advance; outlet

去世 qùshì die; pass away

去伪存真 qùwěi-cúnzhēn eliminate the false and retain the true; rid the fake and retain the genuine

去向 qùxiàng the direction in which sb. or sth. has gone; whereabouts: 不知～ be nowhere to be found

去职 qùzhí give up one's position; no longer hold the post

觑 qù〈动〉① look; gaze: 偷偷地～了他一眼 steal a glance at him ② narrow (one's eyes); squint

quān

圈 quān〈名〉① circle; ring: 画～ draw a circle ② group: 她不是～里人。She doesn't belong to the inner circle. 〈动〉③ encircle, enclose: 用篱笆把菜园～起来 enclose the vegetabe garden with a fence ④ mark with a circle: 把那个错字～了。Mark the wrong word with a circle.

圈定 quāndìng draw a circle around sth. to show approval or selection

圈套 quāntào noose; trap; toils: 落入～ fall into a trap; be taken in the toils

圈阅 quānyuè make a circle round one's name listed on a document after reading it

圈子 quānzi ① circle; ring: [巡回]round: 说话绕～ speak in a roundabout way ② circle; community; coterie: 走出家庭小～ come out of the narrow family circle

quán

拳 quán〈名〉① fist ② boxing

拳打脚踢 quándǎ-jiǎotī beat up; cuff and kick; boxing and kicking

拳击 quánjī boxing

拳术 quánshù Chinese boxing

拳头 quántóu fist:～产品"fist" commodities (Commodities in large quantities have a stable market. Their quality and specifications meet the requirements of the market, and their supply source is in equilibrium. These commodities compete well on the market.); quality product; competitive product

蜷 quán〈动〉curl up; huddle up

蜷伏 quánfú〈动〉lie with the knees drawn up; huddle up

蜷曲 quánqū coil; curl; twist

蜷缩 quánsuō curl up; roll up

颧 quán〈名〉cheekbone

颧骨 quángǔ cheekbone

鬈 quán〈形〉wavy; curly:～发 curly hair

鬈曲 quánqū curl; crimp; crinkle

权 quán〈名〉① right:选举～ the right to vote ② power; authority:～力机关 organs of power ③ advantageous position:主动～ initiative ④〈动〉weigh:～其轻重 weigh up one thing against another ⑤〈副〉tentatively; for the time being: ～充 act temporarily

权柄 quánbǐng power; authority:掌握～ be in power

权衡 quánhéng judge and weigh; weigh; balance:～得失 weigh gains and losses. ～利弊 weigh the pros and cons; weigh the advantages and disadvantages

权力 quánlì power; authority:～下放 delegate power to the lower levels. ～与义务 rights and obligation

权利 quánlì right:劳动的～ the right to work. 政治～ political rights. ～能力[法] capacity for rights

权且 quánqiě tentatively; for the time being

权势 quánshì power and influence; influence

权术 quánshù political trickery; shifts in politics:玩弄～ play politics

权威 quánwēi authority:～人士 authoritative person

权限 quánxiàn limits of authority; jurisdiction; competence; within the rights (power) of jurisdiction; purview:～之外(内) outside (within) one's purview. 超过～ overstep one's authority

权宜 quányí expedient:～之计 makeshift device; expedient measure; matter of expediency; stop-gap measure

权益 quányì rights and interests

全 quán〈形〉① complete:手稿已不～。The manuscript is no longer complete. ② all; whole; entire; total; full:～称

full name ③〈副〉completely; fully; entirely: ～怪你。It's entirely your fault. ④〈动〉make perfect; keep intact: 两～其美 satisfy both sides

全包工程(**全承包工作**) quánbāo gōngchéng(quánchéngbāo gōngzuò) turn-key job

全部 quánbù complete; whole; all; total: ～成本 complete cost. ～损失 actual total loss

全才 quáncái a versatile person; all-rounder

全场 quánchǎng ① the whole audience; all those present ② full-court; all-court: ～紧逼[篮球] full-court press

全程 quánchéng whole journey; whole course: ～运输 through transit (carriage)

全额保险 quán'é bǎoxiǎn full insurance

全额利润分成 quán'é lìrùn fēnchéng sharing the entire (total) profit

全方位 quánfāngwèi in all fields; in all directions: ～对外开放 open to the outside world in all directions. ～外交 omnibearing diplomacy

全集 quánjí collected (complete) works

全景 quánjǐng full view; whole scene: ～山水 panoramic landscape. ～照相机 panoramic camera

全局 quánjú overall situation; situation as a whole: 事关～。The matter concerns the situation as a whole.

全劳动力 quánláodònglì fully able-bodied worker

全力 quánlì in full power; all-out; sparing no effort; with might and main: ～以赴 do one's utmost; go all out. 竭尽～ exert all one's strength; strain every nerve

全貌 quánmào complete picture; full view

全面 quánmiàn overall; all-round; comprehensive: ～紧缩 overall austerity

全民 quánmín the whole people; the entire people: ～健身计划 body-building plan for all Chinese people. ～所有制 ownership by the whole people

全能 quánnéng [体] all round: ～运动 all-round athletic event

全盘 quánpán overall; wholesale; total: ～否定 totally repudiate

全勤 quánqín perfect work attendance

全权 quánquán full (plenary) powers: ～代表 plenipotentiary. ～大使 ambassador plenipotentiary

全然 quánrán completely; entirely

全身 quánshēn the whole body; all over (the body)

全神贯注 quánshén-guànzhù be absorbed in; be preoccupied with; be all attention: ～地倾听某人说话 hang on (upon) sb.'s lips

全盛 quánshèng flourishing; in full bloom; in the heyday; at its height (most prosperous); best years

全速 quánsù full (maximum, top) speed

全套 quántào complete set: ～设备 complete set of equipment

全体 quántǐ all; entire; whole: ～大会 general meeting; plenary session

全天候 quántiānhòu all-weather: ～飞机 all-weather aircraft

全托 quántuō put one's child in a boarding nursery; total child-care: ～托儿所 a boarding nursery

全文 quánwén full text

全武行 quánwǔháng ① full-scale battle scenes (in traditional opera) ② gang fight; free-for-all

全息电影 quánxī diànyǐng holographic movie

全线 quánxiàn ① all fronts; the entire length ② the whole line (of a railway or highway)

全心全意 quánxīn-quányì with one's whole heart; wholeheartedly; heart and soul

全新 quánxīn completely new; brand-new

全优工程 quányōu gōngchéng all-round excellent projects; projects meeting all the quality standards

全员 quányuán full number of persons: ～劳动生产率 overall labour productivity; all-personnel labour productivity

痊 quán〈动〉recover from an illness; [伤口等] heal

痊愈 quányù recover (from an illness); recover one's health; fully recovered: 望早日～。I wish you a speedy recovery.

泉 quán〈名〉spring; fountain: 温～ hot spring

泉水 quánshuǐ spring water; spring

泉源 quányuán ① springhead ② source of (wisdom, strength, etc.)

诠 quán

诠释 quánshì annotation; explanatory notes: ～学 textualism

诠注 quánzhù note or comment; notes and commentary

quǎn

犬 quǎn〈名〉dog: 警～ police dog

犬牙交错 quǎnyá-jiāocuò jigsaw-like; zigzag: 形成～的局面 form a jagged, interlocking pattern

quàn

券 quàn〈名〉certificate; ticket; bill; note: 入场～ admission ticket. 债～ bond

劝 quàn〈动〉① advise; try to persuade; urge: ～某人做某事 advise sb. to do sth. ② encourage: ～学 encourage learning

劝导 quàndǎo persuade; advise; induce; talk sb. round; exhort

劝告 quàngào urge; exhort; warn

劝架 quànjià try to reconcile parties to a quarrel

劝解 quànjiě ① make peace between; mediate ② help sb. get over his worries; pacify; try to make sb. stop worrying

劝戒 quànjiè admonish; expostulate

劝说 quànshuō persuade; advise

劝退 quàntuì persuade someone to resign (① The Chinese Communist Party or the Chinese Communist Youth League persuades members who are not up to standards to voluntarily withdraw from the organization. ② A work unit persuades members who do not meet the requirements to voluntarily resign and leave.)

劝慰 quànwèi conciliate; console; soothe

劝阻 quànzǔ dissuade sb. from; advise sb. against; advise sb. not to

quē

缺 quē ①〈动〉be short of; want; lack:～人手 be short of hands ②〈形〉incomplete; missing; imperfect:完美无～ flawless; perfect ③〈名〉post; vacancy:补～ fill a vacancy

缺编 quēbiān understaffed

缺德 quēdé virtueless; mean; wicked; villainous; vile:～行为 vile practice. 做～事 do sth. mean

缺点 quēdiǎn weak point; shortcoming; defect

缺额 quē'é vacancy

缺乏 quēfá be short of; lack; be wanting in:～经验 be short of (lack) experience. ～资源 be deficient in resources

缺憾 quēhàn regrettable imperfection; regret

缺货 quēhuò be out of stock; be in short supply

缺斤少两 quējīn-shǎoliǎng short on the catty and the ounce

缺课 quēkè miss school; be absent from school:因病～ miss some classes on account of illness

缺门 quēmén gap (in a branch of learning, etc.):填补～ fill a gap. ～技术 a technological gap

缺口 quēkǒu breach; gap:打开～ make a breach

缺勤 quēqín be absent from duty

缺少 quēshǎo lack; want; be short of; be in need of; be in want of:～人手 be in need of hands; be short-handed

缺席 quēxí ① be absent (from school, office, etc.) ② [法] default:～判决 judgement by default

缺陷 quēxiàn defect; drawback; flaw; deficiency:生理～ physical defect

qué

瘸 qué〈动〉be lame; limp:一步一～ walk with a limp

瘸子 quézi lame person; cripple

què

却 què〈动〉① step back:退～ retreat; go back ② refuse; decline:～之不恭。It is disrespectful to decline. ③ repulse; drive back:～敌 repulse the enemy ④〈副,连〉yet; but; while:我很同情他,～又不知说什么好。I was full of sympathy of him, yet I didn't know what to say.

却步 quèbù step back (in fear or disgust); hang back; recede:望而～ step back at the sight of (sth. disgusting or dangerous)

雀 què〈名〉sparrow

雀斑 quèbān freckle; fleck; heatspot

雀跃 quèyuè jump (leap) for joy

鹊 què〈名〉magpie

确 què〈形〉① true; authentic; reliable:～证 ironclad proof ② exact; precise; accurate:精～的描述 an exact description ③ firmly:～信 firmly believe

确保 quèbǎo ensure; guarantee:～粮食丰收 ensure a bumper harvest of grains. ～质量 guarantee quality

确定 quèdìng determine; decide; fix:～方案 decide on plan

确立 quèlì establish

确切 quèqiè exact; precise; definite:～的日期 an exact date. ～地说 to be exact

确认 quèrèn acknowledge; affirm; confirm

确实 quèshí ① true; reliable; actual:～的成效 tangible results ② really; indeed

确信 quèxìn firmly believe; be sure; be convinced of

确诊 quèzhěn make a definite diagnosis; diagnose

确证 quèzhèng ① prove conclusively or positively

确凿 quèzuò reliable; irrefutable; ironclad:～的证据 conclusive evidence; tangible proofs

qún

裙 qún〈名〉skirt:绸～ silk skirt

裙带 qúndài connected through one's female relatives:～关系 nepotism; petticoat influence;

群 qún ①〈名〉crowd; mass; group:成～ in crowds; in flocks ②〈量〉[牛、猪等] herd; [马、羊等] flock; [狗等] pack; [鱼] shoal; [昆虫] swarm:一～孩子 a group of children. 一～牛 a herd of cattle. 一～蜜蜂 a swarm of bees

群策群力 qúncè-qúnlì pool the wisdom and efforts of everyone; let's pool our ideas and make concerted efforts; by collective wisdom and efforts

群岛 qúndǎo archipelago

群芳 qúnfāng ① beautiful and fragrant flowers; all kinds of flowers:～竞艳 flowers vying with each other in beauty ② a group of beauties or artists：艳压～ the queen of beauties

群居 qúnjū living in groups；gregarious；social：～动物 social animal

群龙无首 qúnlóng-wúshǒu a host of dragons without a head — a group without a leader

群情 qúnqíng public sentiment；feelings of the masses

群体 qúntǐ group；integral entity：～产量 productivity of the group (the integral entity). ～建筑 modular building. 英雄～ heroic group

群英会 qúnyīnghuì a gathering of heroes

群众 qúnzhòng mass：～管制 public surveillance；mass control. ～团体 mass organizations. ～性治安保卫组织 mass security defence organization

R r

rán

然 rán ①〈形〉right; correct:大谬不～ absurd; entirely wrong. 不以为～ not approve; object to ②〈代〉so; like that: 不尽～ not exactly so ③〈连〉but; yet; however:此事虽小，～亦不可忽视。This is a minor point, but it must not be overlooked. ④[副词或形容词后缀]:飘飘～ complacent; smug

然而 rán'ér but; however; nevertheless

然后 ránhòu then; afterwards; after that

燃 rán〈动〉① burn:纸张易～。Paper burns easily. ② kindle; light; ignite:～起革命的烈火 spark off the flame of revolution

燃放 ránfàng set off (fireworks, etc.)

燃料 ránliào fuel

燃眉之急 ránméizhījí a matter of great urgency; a burning necessity

燃起 ránqǐ spark off (ignite, set off, fan); kindle, set ablaze

燃烧 ránshāo ① burn ②[化] combustion: ～弹 incendiary bomb

rǎn

染 rǎn〈动〉① dye:～布 dye a piece of cloth ② catch (a disease):～上了流感 have caught in the flu ③ acquire (a bad habit, etc.); soil; contaminate:～上恶习 acquire a bad habit; be stained with vice (bad habits)

染病 rǎnbìng catch (contract) an illness; be infected with a disease

染发 rǎnfà dye the hair

染料 rǎnliào dyestuff; dye:活性～ reactive dye

染上 rǎnshàng ① acquire ② catch; contract; be infected with:～疾病 catch an illness

染指 rǎnzhǐ lay a finger on; take an illegal share of sth.; have a finger in the pie; encroach on; interfere in; dip (put, stick) one's finger in:妄图～别国资源 attempt to encroach on the resources of other countries

冉 rǎn〈形〉slowly

冉冉 rǎnrǎn slowly; gradually

rāng

嚷 rāng

嚷嚷 rāngrang ① shout; yell;

clamour; make an uproar: 吵吵～ raise a hue and cry; make a noise ② disclose (a secret) freely; make widely known

ráng

瓤 ráng〈名〉pulp; flesh; pith: 西瓜～ the flesh (pulp) of a water melon

rǎng

壤 rǎng〈名〉① soil: 一种多腐殖质的土～ a soil rich in humus ② earth: 有霄～之别。There is a world of difference. ③ area: 接～ have a common border

ràng

让 ràng〈动〉① give in; give way; yield; give ground; give up: 寸步不～ refuse to yield an inch. 请～一～。Please step aside. ② offer; invite: 把客人～进来 invite guests into the inner room ③ let; allow; make: ～事实说话。Let the facts speak for themselves. ④ let sb. have sth. at a fair price: 我可以按半价把这部车～给你。I can let you have this car at half its price.

让步 ràngbù concede (to); yield (to); make a concession; give in; make compromises (in); give way (to): ～政策 policy of making concessions

让渡 ràngdù alienate: ～土地 alienate lands

让价 ràngjià concessional rate

让开 ràngkāi get out of the way; step aside; make way

让利放权 rànglì-fàngquán transferring part of profits to lower organization or enterprises and instituting decentralization

让利消售 rànglì-xiāoshòu sell at discount

让路 rànglù make way (for); give way (to); give sb. the right of way: 给重点工程～ make way for the main projects

让位 ràngwèi ① resign sovereign authority; abdicate ② yield to; change into

让与 ràngyǔ transfer; yield; alien; concede: ～所有权 yield possession

让座 ràngzuò make room (for); offer one's seat to sb.: ～给老年人 offer one's seat to an old man

ráo

饶 ráo ①〈形〉rich; abundant; plentiful: ～有风趣 full of wit and humour〈动〉② forgive; have mercy on; let sb. off: 求～ beg for mercy ③ give sth. extra: 给你～上一个。Let you have one more.

饶命 ráomìng spare sb.'s life; [对敌人] give quarter

饶舌 ráoshé ① wag one's tongue; chatter ② too talkative; garrulous

饶恕 ráoshù pardon; forgive; excuse

rǎo

扰 rǎo〈动〉disturb; harass; trouble; perturb:纷～ tumult

扰动 rǎodòng be in turmoil; be turbulent

扰乱 rǎoluàn disturb; disrupt; harass:～治安 disturb public order. ～货币金融罪 offence of disrupting the money and banking. ～经济秩序 disrupt the economic order. ～视线 interfere with sb.'s view

rào

绕 rào〈动〉① wind; coil; wrap:～线 wind thread ② move; circle; revolve:～场一周 march around the arena ③ go round; make a detour:～过暗礁 bypass (steer clear of) hidden reefs

绕道 ràodào make a detour; go by a roundabout way (route)

绕嘴 ràozuǐ be difficult to articulate

绕弯儿 ràowānr go for a stroll (walk)

绕行 ràoxíng ① make a detour; bypass ② move round; circle

rě

惹 rě〈动〉① ask for; invite; stir up; cause:～是生非 provoke a mischief ② tease; offend:我～不起她。I did nothing to provoke her. ③ cause; attract:～人讨厌 make a nuisance of oneself

惹火烧身 rěhuǒ-shāoshēn bring trouble upon oneself; burn one's own fingers

惹祸 rěhuò incur (court) disaster; stir up trouble; incur mischief

惹人讨厌 rěrén-tǎoyàn ① make oneself disgusting ② boring; annoying; disgusting

惹事 rěshì give rise to trouble; cause trouble; stir up trouble

惹是生非 rěshì-shēngfēi provoke a dispute; stir up (create) trouble

rè

热 rè〈形〉① hot; warm:～水 hot water ② enthusiastic; ardent; warmhearted:～烈欢迎 a warm welcome ③ eager; envious:眼～ feel envious at the sight of sth.〈名〉④ heat:传～ conduct heat ⑤ fad; craze:英语～ make a fad of English language ⑥ temperature; fever:发～ have a fever ⑦〈动〉heat up; warm:把汤～～ heat up the soup

热爱 rè'ài ardently love; cherish deep love (affection) for; devoted love for

热潮 rècháo upsurge:掀起…的～ unfold a vigorous campaign for

热忱 rèchén enthusiasm and devotion; zeal; ardour

热诚 rèchéng warm and sincere; cordial

热带 rèdài torrid zone; the tropics

热点 rèdiǎn hot spot; favourite subject; key point:研究中国历史的～ favourite subject in the study of Chinese history

热度 rèdù ① heat; degree of heat ② fever; temperature:量～ take sb.'s temperature

热狗 règǒu hot dog

热核反应堆 rèhéfǎnyìngduī thermonuclear reactor

热火朝天 rèhuǒ-cháotiān seething with enthusiasm; burning with ardour; bustling with activity; in full swing; stirring with activity; flaming:工地上～。The worksite was stirring with activity. 生产～。Production is in full swing.

热泪盈眶 rèlèi-yíngkuàng One's eyes swim with tears.; One's eyes run over with tears.; One's eyes brim over (with) warm tears.; eyes glistening with tears

热恋 rèliàn be passionately in love (with); be head over heels in love

热量 rèliàng [物] quantity of heat

热烈 rèliè warm; enthusiastic; ardent:～祝贺 warm congratulations. ～欢送 give sb. a warm send-off

热门 rèmén popular; in great demand; hot:～货 goods which sell well; goods in great demand; popular ware; hot item. ～股票 glamor stock; "blue chip" stock

热闹 rènao ①〈形〉busy; bustling with noise, excitement and activity:～的街头情景 an animated street scene ②〈名〉fun:凑～ join in the fun ③〈动〉liven up:～一番 have a jolly time. 晚会很～。It was a very lively evening party.

热能 rènéng [物] heat (thermal) energy

热切 rèqiè earnest; fervent

热气腾腾 rèqì-téngténg ① steaming hot ② invigorating atmosphere; bubbling with life; seething with vitality (enthusiasm, activity); astir with emotion

热情 rèqíng enthusiasm; zeal; warmth:～洋溢 be very enthusiastic. 待人～ have a warm heart; be warmhearted

热身赛 rèshēnsài warm-up competition; warm-up

热线 rèxiàn ① hot line ② [物] heat ray

热销 rèxiāo selling hot:～货 hot-sale commodities

热心 rèxīn warmhearted; ardent; enthusiastic:～肠 warmheartedness. ～公益 public-spirited. ～科学 eager to promote science

热血 rèxuè warm blood:～沸腾 burn with righteous indignation

热中(衷) rèzhōng(zhōng) ① be crazy for; hanker after; crave:～名利 hanker after fame and gain ② be keen on; be wild about; have a bug about

rén

人 rén〈名〉① human being; man; person; people: ~来~往。People are hurrying to and fro. ② adult: 长大成~ have become a grown-up ③ a person engaged in a particular activity: 军~ soldier ④ (other) people: 助~为乐 take pleasure in helping people ⑤ personality; character: 为~公正 upright in character ⑥ manpower; hand: ~力资源 resources of manpower ⑦〈代〉each, everbody: ~手一册。Everyone has a copy.

人才 réncái talented people; talent; person of ability; qualified (trained) personnel: ~储备 personnel reserve. ~合理分流 rational flow of personnel. ~济济 a host of talented people. ~市场 personnel-recruiting market; labour exchange. ~学 study of human ability

人次 réncì person-time

人道 réndào ① humanity; human sympathy ② humane; human: ~主义 humanitarianism. 不~ inhuman

人定胜天 rénd ìng-shèngtiān Man can overpower (conquer) nature.; Man's will, not heaven, decides.

人犯 rénfàn offender

人贩子 rénfànzi trader in human beings

人防工程 rénfáng-gōngchéng civil air defense construction

人浮于事 rénfúyúshì be overstaffed

人格 réngé personality; character: ~化 personify. ~主义 personalism. 有高尚~的人 man of a noble character

人工 réngōng ① artificial; man-made: ~流产 induced abortion. ~智能 artificial intelligence ② man-day; manpower ③ work done by hand; manual work

人际关系 rénjìguānxì interpersonal relationship

人家 rénjiā ① household: 5户~ five households ② family

人家 rénjia ① [指别人]others; other people: ~都这么说。That's what everybody says. ② [指某个人或者某些人]he; she; they: 把信给~送去。Take the letter to him (her, them). ③[指说话本人]: 把~吓了一大跳。You gave me quite a fright.

人间 rénjiān man's world; (in the) world; (on) earth: 创造~奇迹 create a miracle on earth

人尽其才 rénjìnqícái give full scope to the talents; Let everybody display his or her talents.

人均 rénjūn per capita

人均生活费收入 rénjūn shēnghuófèi shōurù per-capita income used for living expenses

人口 rénkǒu population: ~登记站 census registration station. ~高峰 pouplation peak. ~普查 census

人类 rénlèi mankind; human beings; humanity: ～学 anthropology

人力 rénlì ① manpower; labour power: ～资源 human (manpower) resources; ② human effort

人们 rénmen people; men; the public

人面兽心 rénmiàn-shòuxīn a fiend (beast) in human shape

人民 rénmín people: ～法院 people's court. ～检察院 people's procuratorate. ～陪审员 people's assessor. 重视～来信来访 pay close attention to the letters and visits received from persons reporting illegal activities

人名地址录 rénmíng dìzhǐ lù directory

人品 rénpǐn ① moral quality; character: ～很好 a person of excellent character ② looks; bearing

人情 rénqíng ① human feelings; sentimental considerations; sympathy: ～味 milk of human kindness; human touch ② favour: 做～ do sb. a favour; do sb. a good turn ③ gift; present: 送～ send gifts

人权 rénquán human rights

人群 rénqún crowd; throng; multitude

人山人海 rénshān-rénhǎi huge crowds of people; a sea of heads

人身 rénshēn person; body: ～攻击 offences against the person; personal attack (abuse); personalities. ～权利 rights of the person. ～侮辱行为 act that subjects one's person to indignity

人参 rénshēn ginseng

人生 rénshēng life: ～观 philosophy of life; one's outlook on life; view of life

人士 rénshì personage; figure: 知名～ well-known figures

人事 rénshì ① human affairs ② matters concerning personnel: ～处 personnel office (department). ～调动 transfer of personnel ③ ways of the world: 不懂～ unacquainted with the ways of the world

人手 rénshǒu manpower; hand: ～不足 be short of hands

人梯 réntī human ladder: 甘当～ be willing to be a human ladder (stepping stone) for others

人为 rénwéi artificial; man-made: ～的困难 man-made difficulties

人文科学 rénwén kēxué humanities

人物 rénwù ① personage; figure: ～素描[速写] character sketch ② [剧] character: 典型～ typical character. ～塑造 characterization

人心 rénxīn feelings of the people; popular feelings: ～所向 reflect popular feelings; be the common aspiration of the people. 不得～ unpopular. 大快～ to the great satisfaction of the people

人行横道 rénxíng héngdào pedestrian crossing; crosswalk; zebra crossing

人性 rénxìng human nature; humanity

人性 rénxing human feelings; reason:不通～ unreasonable; unfeeling

人选 rénxuǎn person selected; candidate:适当～ suitable person

人烟 rényān signs (indications) of human habitation:～稀少 sparsely populated

人影儿 rényǐngr ① the shadow of a human figure ② the trace of a person's presence; figure

人欲横流 rényùhéngliú unbridled indulgence of human desires and passions; universal decadence

人员 rényuán personnel; staff:～往来增多。Visits back and forth by individuals have increased.

人缘儿 rényuánr relations with people; popularity

人云亦云 rényún-yìyún repeat the words of others; repeat like a parrot

人造 rénzào artificial; man-made; synthetic:～卫星 man-made satellite. ～革 synthetic leather; leatheret(te)

人证 rénzhèng [法] testimony of a witness; personal witness

人之常情 rénzhīchángqíng the way of the world; human nature in general; what's common and natural; natural and normal practice in human relationship

人质 rénzhì hostage

人种 rénzhǒng race

仁 rén〈名〉① benevolence; humanity:～政 policy of benevolence; benevolent government ② kernel:核桃～ walnut kernel ③〈形〉sensitive:麻木不～ insensitive; apathetic

仁爱 rén'ài kindheartedness; philanthropism

仁慈 réncí kind; merciful; benevolent

仁学 rénxué theory of *ren* (benevolence); doctrine of *ren* (benevolence); study on the concept of benevolence

仁义道德 rényì-dàodé humanity, justice and virtue; virtue and morality; kindness and magnanimity

仁者见仁,智者见智 rénzhě jiàn rén, zhìzhě jiàn zhì each according to his lights; Different people have different views (opinions).

仁政 rénzhèng policy of benevolence; benevolent government:施～ apply a policy of benevolence

仁至义尽 rénzhì-yìjìn has done everything which one may be called upon to do; exercise great restraint and do one's very best; the extreme patience (tolerance) and magnanimity; exert one's utmost effort

rěn

忍 rěn〈动〉① tolerate; bear;

endure; put up with:～不住 unable to bear ② be so hard-hearted enough to; have the heart to:于心不～ not have the heart to

忍不住 rěnbuzhù be unable to bear; can't help (doing):～放声大笑 can't help bursting into laughter

忍耐 rěnnài exercise patience; bear; stand; endure; restrain oneself

忍气吞声 rěnqì-tūnshēng submit to humiliation; eat humble pie; swallow an insult; endure humiliation in silence

忍让 rěnràng exercise forbearance; forbear; show oneself forbearing and conciliatory

忍辱负重 rěnrǔ-fùzhòng swallow humiliation and bear a heavy load; submit to humiliation for the sake of an important mission that one feels obliged to fulfil

忍受 rěnshòu bear; stand; endure; put up with:～艰难困苦 endure hardships. 我不能～他的侮辱。I can't put up with his insult.

忍痛 rěntòng ① endure pain ② very reluctantly:～牺牲 give up sth. very reluctantly

忍无可忍 rěnwúkěrěn driven beyond the limits of forbearance (endurance); have reached the end of one's forbearance; beyond (past) all bearing; not to be endured any longer; come to the end of one's patience

忍心 rěnxīn have the heart to; be so hard-hearted enough to:不～拒绝 don't have the heart to refuse

忍住 rěnzhù bear; endure

rèn

认 rèn〈动〉① know; recognize; know; make out:～出某人 identify a person ② adopt; enter into a certain relationship with:～闺女 adopt sb. as a daughter. ～师傅 apprentice oneself to sb. ③ recognize; admit; own:公～ be generally acknowledged

认出 rènchū recognize; make out; identify

认错 rèncuò admit (own) one's mistakes; acknowledge one's error

认定 rèndìng ① firmly believe; maintain; hold ② affirm; confirm:～有(无)罪 find guilty (not guilty). 转世灵童的～ confirmation of the reincarnated soul boys of the great living Buddhas

认购 rèngòu offer to buy; subscribe for (bonds, etc.):～公债 subscribe for bonds

认股 rèngǔ subscription for shares

认可 rènkě approve; agree; okay:得到领导的～ be approved by the leadership

认领 rènlǐng claim (a lost article, etc.)

认命 rènmìng accept fate; resign oneself (be resigned) to fate

认清 rènqīng have a clear understanding of; recognize; gain clearer insight on; see clearly: ～性质 have a clear understanding of the character

认识 rènshi ① know; understand; be aware of; realize; be acquainted with; get (come) to know: ～问题的严重性不够 underestimate the gravity of the problems ② knowledge; cognition: ～论 theory of knowledge; epistemology

认输 rènshū admit (acknowledge) one's defeat; give up; throw up the sponge; throw in the towel: 她不肯～。She refused to acknowledge herself (to be) defeated.

认为 rènwéi consider; regard as; hold; maintain; think: 你～怎样? What do you think of it?

认帐 rènzhàng ① acknowledge a debt ② own to having done sth.; admit one has said or done: 他自己做的事,怎么不～? How can he refuse to admit what he has done?

认真 rènzhēn seriously; earnestly; conscientiously: ～学习 study conscientiously

认字 rènzì learn or know how to read

认罪 rènzuì plead guilty; acknowledge one's guilt; avow one's guilt; confess: ～态度 attitude towards admission of guilt

任 rèn〈动〉① appoint: 新～市长 the newly-appointed mayor of the city ② assume a post; take up a job: 她～教多年了。She has been a teacher for many years. ③ official post; office: 上～ assume office. 离～ leave office ④ let, allow: ～其自流 Let things run their course. ⑤〈连〉no matter (how, what, etc.): ～她怎么说,也别信她。Don't trust her, no matter what she says. ⑥〈量〉[用于任职的次数]: 做过两～总理 have been twice the prime minister

任便 rènbiàn as you like; as you see fit

任何 rènhé any; whichever; whatever: ～时候 (at) any time

任劳任怨 rènláo-rènyuàn work hard regardless of unfair criticism or unjustifiable complaints; work hard without complaint; work hard and not be upset by criticism; willingly bear the burden of office

任免 rènmiǎn appoint and remove (dismiss): ～事项 appointments and removals

任命 rènmìng appoint; nominate: ～市长 appoint sb. mayor

任凭 rènpíng ① at one's discretion; at one's convenience: ～感情支配 blindly obey the mood of the moment; give way to the mood of the moment ② no matter (how, what, etc.) ③ in spite of: ～你怎么说,事实总是事实。Whatever you say, facts are facts.

任期 rènqī term (tenure) of office: ～已满。One's term of office has run out.

任情 rènqíng to one's heart's content; as much as one likes; do as one pleases

任人摆布 rènrén-bǎibù be at the mercy of; under sb.'s thumb; allow oneself to be ordered about

任人唯亲 rènrén-wéiqīn appoint people by favouritism; practise nepotism

任人唯贤 rènrén-wéixián appoint people on (by) their merits

任务 rènwù assignment; task; job: ～观点 get-it-over-and-done-with attitude; perfunctory attitude. 赶～ hurry through one's job

任性 rènxìng wilful; self-willed; capricious

任意 rènyì at one's own will; wantonly; wilfully; arbitrarily: ～法规 permission legislation. 对外接待中～提高标准 spend money freely in playing host to foreign guests in disregard of set standards

任用 rènyòng assign sb. to a post; appoint

任职 rènzhí hold a post; be in office

任重道远 rènzhòng-dàoyuǎn take a heavy burden and embark on a long road; shoulder a heavy responsibility through thick and thin; embark on a long road with formidable tasks lying ahead; task is both arduous and of long duration

妊 rèn〈形〉pregnant

妊妇 rènfù pregnant woman; expectant mother

妊娠 rènshēn pregnancy

刃 rèn〈名〉① the edge of a knife, sword, etc.; blade: 刀～ knife blade ② knife; sword: 利～ sharp sword ③〈动〉kill (with a sword or knife): 手～ stab sb. to death

刃具 rènjù cutting tool (instrument); cutter

韧 rèn〈形〉tough; tenacious: ～性 tougness; tenacity

韧带 rèndài ligament

韧劲 rènjìn indomitableness; dauntlessness; tenacity

rēng

扔 rēng〈动〉① throw; cast; toss: ～球 throw a ball ② cast aside; throw away

扔掉 rēngdiào throw away; cast away

扔下 rēngxià leave behind; put aside; abandon

仍 réng ①〈动〉remain: 一～其旧 remain the same ②〈副〉still; yet: ～有效用 be still effective

仍旧 réngjiù remain the same; still; yet; as before; as ever: 有些问题～没有解决。Some problems remain to be solved.

仍然 réngrán still; yet

rì

日 rì〈名〉① sun: ～落 sunset ②

daytime; day:～～夜夜 day and night. ～托 day-care ③ time:春～ spring time ④〈副〉daily; with each passing day; every day:产量～增 output is going up every day

日班 rìbān day shift:做～ be (work) on the day shift

日薄西山 rìbó-xīshān decline like the setting sun; (like) the sun setting beyond the western hills; on the wane; in one's later days

日常 rìcháng day-to-day; everyday; daily

日场 rìchǎng day show; daytime performance; matinée

日程 rìchéng schedule; programme:议事～ order of the day; agenda. 提到～上来 put on the agenda

日光 rìguāng sunshine; sunlight; sun:～浴 sunbath

日积月累 rìjī-yuèlěi accumulate through long years; accumulate over along period

日记 rìjì diary:记～ keep a diary. ～帐 daybook; journal account; journal

日历 rìlì calendar:～年度 calendar year

日暮途穷 rìmù-túqióng come to a dead end; be at (come to) the end of one's rope; on one's last legs; approach the end of one's days

日内 rìnèi in a few days:～会有好消息。There will be good news in a few days.

日前 rìqián the other day; a few days ago

日全食 rìquánshí total solar eclipse

日食 rìshí eclipse of the sun; solar eclipse

日新月异 rìxīn-yuèyì change with each passing day; make advances everyday; change rapidly; ever-improving; fast-changing; increasingly developed:文化生活～。The cultural life is constantly enriched.

日夜 rìyè day and night; round the clock:～服务 round-the-clock servide; 24-hour service. ～商店 day-and-night (service) shop

日以继夜 rìyǐ-jìyè night and day; day in and day out

日益 rìyì day by day; increasingly; more and more:～尖锐 increasingly acute. ～壮大 grow stronger day by day

日用 rìyòng of (for) daily use:～必需品 daily necessities. ～工业品 manufactured goods for daily use; articles of daily use

日杂商店 rìzá shāngdiàn sundries store

日照 rìzhào sunshine

日子 rìzi ① day; date:定个结婚的～ set a date for the wedding ② life; time:勤俭过～ lead an industrious and frugal life

róng

荣 róng ①〈动〉grow luxuriantly; flourish:春～冬枯 grow in spring and wither in winter ②

〈形〉flourishing; luxuriant: 我们欣欣向～的祖国 our flourishing motherland ③〈名〉glory; honour

荣归 rónguī return in glory

荣华富贵 rónghuá-fùguì glory, splendour, wealth and rank; high position and great wealth

荣获 rónghuò have the honour to win: ～冠军 win the championship. ～英雄称号 be awarded the honourable title of hero

荣枯 róngkū vicissitude: ～盛衰 transmutations of fortune; the swing of the pendulum

荣任 róngrèn be honoured with a post

荣辱 róngrǔ honour and disgrace: 人生的～盛衰 prosperities and adversities of this life. ～与共 share weal and woe

荣幸 róngxìng be highly honoured; have the honour: 感到十分～ feel highly honoured

荣誉 róngyù glory; honour: ～感 sense of honour. ～学位 honourary degree

戎 róng〈名〉army; military affairs: ～马生涯 army life

茸 róng ①〈形〉fine and soft; downy: 绿草～～ a carpet of green grass ②〈名〉young pilose antler

绒 róng〈名〉① fine hair; wool; down: 鸭～ eiderdown ② cloth with a soft nap or pile: 丝～ velvet ③ fine floss for embroidery

绒布 róngbù cotton flannel; flannelette

绒毛 róngmáo ① fine hair; down; villus ② pile; nap

绒线 róngxiàn woollen yarn; knitting wool: ～衫 knitted woollen garment; woollen sweater; [套衫] pullover; [高领的] turtleneck; [开襟的] cardingan

绒绣 róngxiù woollen cross-stitch work; woollen needlepoint tapestry

容 róng〈动〉① hold; contain: 能～500 人 can hold five hundred people ② let; allow; permit: 不～歪曲 brook no distortion ③ tolerate ④〈名〉looks; appearance: 市～ the look of a city

容光焕发 róngguāng-huànfā one's face glowing with health; a radiant look on one's face

容积 róngjī volume: ～吨 measurement ton

容量 róngliàng capacity

容留 róngliú give shelter to; take sb. in; keep

容貌 róngmào looks; appearance; features: ～秀丽 have nice features; look pretty

容纳 róngnà have a capacity of; accommodate; hold: 这礼堂能～1000 人。This auditorium can accommodate 1000 people.

容人 róngrén regard people with kindly tolerance; tolerant towards others; magnanimous; broad-minded

容忍 róngrěn tolerate; put up with: ～原则 principle of tolerance

容身 róngshēn take shelter

容许 róngxǔ allow; permit: 任何人也不～违犯法律。Nobody is allowed to violate the law.

容颜 róngyán appearance; looks

容易 róngyì ① easy; ready: ～控制的局面 a situation easy to handle ② likely; easily; prone; apt: ～发生事故 be prone to accidents

溶 róng〈动〉dissolve; melt: 盐～于水。Salt dissolves in water.

溶合 rónghé fusion: ～语言 fusional language

溶化(解) rónghuà (jiě) dissolve; melt

溶剂 róngjì [化] solvent

溶液 róngyè solution: ～栽培法 hydroponics

熔 róng〈动〉fuse; melt; smelt

熔点 róngdiǎn melting point

熔化 rónghuà melt; fuse: 玻璃在高温下～。Glass melts at a high temperature.

熔炉 rónglú smelting furnace; furnace: ～理论 smelting pot theory

熔铸 róngzhù smelting; casting

融 róng〈动〉① melt; thaw: 雪已～了。The snow has thawed. ② blend; fuse; be in harmony: 水乳交～ blend as well as milk and water

融合 rónghé mix together; melt together; fuse; merge; blend

融会贯通 rónghuì-guàntōng achieve mastery through a comprehensive study of the subject; gain thorough understanding through comprehensive study of the subject; have a thorough and profound grasp of

融化(解) rónghuà (jiě) thaw; melt: 点火～冻土 make a fire to thaw (out) the frozen earth

融洽 róngqià harmonious; on friendly terms; very friendly: 我们谈得十分～。We had a very friendly talk.

融通业务 róngtōng yèwù accommodation line

融通资金 róngtōng zījīn financing; floatation of loans

rǒng

冗 rǒng〈形〉① superfluous; redundant ② full of trivial details

冗长 rǒngcháng lengthy; cumbersome; prolix: ～的引证 lengthy quotation

冗词 rǒngcí superfluous words (in a piece of writing)

冗官 rǒngguān unnecessary local officials

冗员 rǒngyuán redundant personnel; supernumeraries

冗赘 rǒngzhuì diffuse; verbose

róu

柔 róu〈形〉① soft; supple; meek; tender: ～枝 supple twigs ② gentle; mild; yielding: ～中有刚 firm but gentle

柔肠 róucháng soft heart

柔道 róudào [体] judo

柔和 róuhé soft; mild; meek; gentle; mellow: ～光线 soft light. ～色彩 soft (mellow) colour

柔滑 róuhuá soft and smooth; satiny; creamy

柔嫩 róunèn tender; delicate; lithe: 使某人的肌肉～灵活 make sb.'s muscles lithe

柔情 róuqíng tender feelings; heart-throbs; tenderness

柔软 róuruǎn soft; tender; supple: ～体操 callisthenics

柔弱 róuruò weak; tender; delicate: 体质～ have a delicate constitution

柔顺 róushùn meek; compliant: 非常～ as meek as a lamb

揉 róu〈动〉rub; knead: ～成一团 crumple sth. into a ball

揉搓 róucuo rub; knead

蹂 róu

蹂躏 róulìn trample (on); ravage; make havoc; devastate; crush under one's feet: 遭到～ suffer devastation, oppression, etc.

ròu

肉 ròu〈名〉① flesh; meat: 瘦～ lean meat. 猪～ pork ② meat; pulp (of fruit): 桂圆～ longan pulp

肉搏 ròubó bayonet fighting; hand-to-hand fight (combat)

肉畜 ròuchù livestock raised for meat

肉感 ròugǎn sex appeal; sexiness

肉鸡 ròujī table hen; broiler

肉麻 ròumá nauseating; disgusting; sickening; revolting; make one's flesh creep: ～吹捧 use words of praise that give one the creeps; praise fulsomely

肉末 ròumò minced meat; ground meat

肉色 ròusè yellowish pink

肉松 ròusōng dried meat floss

肉体 ròutǐ the human body; body; flesh: ～感官 physical sense organs

肉刑 ròuxíng physical punishment; corporal punishment

肉眼 ròuyǎn naked eye: ～看不清 not visible to the naked eye

肉欲 ròuyù carnal desire (appetite); sensual appetite; carnality: ～的迷恋 carnal infatuation

rú

如 rú〈动〉① in compliance with; according to: ～命 in compliance with your instructions ② like; as if: ～临大敌 as if faced with a formidable enemy ③ be as good as: 我不～她。I'm not as good as she is.; I can't compare with her. ④〈连〉as; in accordance with; if: ～有困难,找我好了。In case of difficulty, just call on me.

如出一辙 rúchūyīzhé be exactly the same; run in the same groove; follow the same pattern (track); be cut from the same cloth as; be so alike; be no different from

如此 rúcǐ such; so; thus; in this way:～而已。That is what it all adds up to.; That's all.

如法炮制 rúfǎ-páozhì follow the prescribed rule; take a leaf out of another's book; follow the same formula; follow suit; be modelled on; do as someone else has done

如故 rúgù ① the same as before ② like old friends:一见～ feel like old friends at the first meeting; hit it off well right from the start

如果 rúguǒ if; in case (of); in the event of

如何 rúhé how; what:词典工作进展～? How are you getting along with the dictionary work?

如火如荼 rúhuǒ-rútú like a raging fire; seething with enthusiasm; flaring (up) like fire set to dry tinder; in full swing:工作正～地进行着。The work was in full swing.

如饥似渴 rújī-sìkě with great eagerness; voraciously; eagerly; avidly; fervently:～地学习 study assiduously; learn with great eagerness

如今 rújīn now; at present; nowadays:～情况不同了。Nowadays things have changed.

如期 rúqī as scheduled; at the appointed time; on time:货物已～运到。The goods arrived on schedule.

如实 rúshí strictly according to the facts:～反映情况 reflect things as they really are

如释重负 rúshìzhòngfù as if relieved of a heavy burden (load); as if a heavy burden were lifted

如数 rúshù ① exactly the number or amount ② in full; fully:～偿还 repay in full

如同 rútóng like; as

如下 rúxià as follows:发表～声明 make the following statement

如意 rúyì after one's heart; comply with one's wish; as one wishes:～算盘 wishful thinking; smug calculations

如鱼得水 rúyúdéshuǐ (feel) just like a fish in water; be in congenial company or do congenial work

如愿以偿 rúyuàn-yǐcháng obtain what is desired; achieve (get) what one wishes; have one's wish fulfilled

如坐针毡 rúzuòzhēnzhān feel as if sitting on a bed of nails; sit on thorns; be on pins and needles; be on tenterhooks; as if sitting on a spiked rug; in an extremely uncomfortable position

儒

儒 rú〈名〉Confucianism; Confucianist ② scholar; learned man:腐～ pedantic scholar

儒家 rújiā Confucianists; Confucian school

儒雅 rúyǎ scholarly and refined

儒宗 rúzōng descendants of Confucius

蠕 rú〈动〉crawl；wriggle：～动 wriggle

孺 rú〈名〉child：妇～ women and children

rǔ

乳 rǔ〈名〉① milk ② breast

乳癌 rǔ'ái breast cancer

乳房 rǔfáng ① breast；mamma ② udder

乳胶 rǔjiāo emulsion：～漆 emulsion paint；latex

乳酪 rǔlào cheese

乳牛 rǔniú milch cow；dairy cattle；milker：出奶多(少)的～ a good (bad) milker

乳臭未干 rǔxiù-wèigān be wet behind the ears；be young and inexperienced like a sucking child；be at an age when one smells still of one's mother's milk

乳罩 rǔzhào brassiere；bra

乳制品 rǔzhìpǐn dairy (milk) products

辱 rǔ ①〈名〉shame；dishonour；disgrace ②〈动〉bring disgrace to；put to shame；insult

辱骂 rǔmà abuse；vilify；revile；call sb. names；rail at：百般～ shout all sorts of abuse；call (sb.) all kinds of names

辱没 rǔmò bring disgrace to；be unworthy of

rù

入 rù〈动〉① enter：列～议程 put on the agenda ② join；be admitted into：～党 join the Party ③ agree with；conform to：～时 fashionable ④〈名〉income：～不敷出。The income falls short of the expenditure.

入场 rùchǎng entrance；admissions；enter the stadium (theatre, etc.)：～券 admission ticket. ～式 march-in

入超 rùchāo unfavourable balance of trade；adverse trade balance；trade deficit；import surplus (excess)

入股 rùgǔ buy a share；become a shareholder

入籍 rùjí naturalization

入境 rùjìng enter a country：～签证 entry visa. ～申报单 customs declaration made at the time of entry. ～许可证 entry permit

入殓 rùliàn put a corpse in a coffin；encoffin

入门 rùmén ① cross the threshold ② learn the rudiments of a subject；ABC (of a subject)；elementary course

入迷 rùmí be fascinated with (by)；have a bug about sth.

入魔 rùmó be spellbound；be infatuated

入侵 rùqīn invade；intrude

入神 rùshén ① be entranced；be enthralled ② superb；marvellous

入时 rùshí in vogue; in fashion; fashionable:衣着～ be fashionably dressed

入手 rùshǒu begin with; start with:从调查研究～ start with the investigation

入睡 rùshuì go to sleep; fall asleep

入伍 rùwǔ enter the army; join up

入席 rùxí take one's seat (at a banquet, ceremony, etc.)

入选 rùxuǎn be selected; be chosen

入学 rùxué ① enter a school:～考试 entrance examination;[大学的] matriculation ② start school:～年龄 school age

入帐 rùzhàng enter an item in an account

褥 rù〈名〉cotton-padded mattress:被～ bedclothes; bedding

褥套 rùtào bedding sack; mattress cover

ruǎn

软 ruǎn〈形〉① soft; flexible; supple; pliable ② gentle; mild; soft:～语 soft words ③ weak; feeble:～骨头 a weak-kneed fellow ④ poor in quality, ability, etc.:工夫～ inadequate skill ⑤ easily moved or influenced:手～ be soft-hearted in handling matters

软包装 ruǎnbāozhuāng foods sold in soft packages

软贷款 ruǎndàikuǎn soft loan (loan with low interest)

软雕塑 ruǎndiāosù soft sculpture (indoor non-plane handicraft ornamentation in majesty made of cotton, hemp, woollens.)

软化 ruǎnhuà ① soften ② win over by soft tactics ③ bate (leather)

软环境 ruǎnhuánjìng soft environment (the social conditions including organization system, law, policy, working efficiency, etc.):大力改善外商投资的～ devoting major efforts to improve the soft environments for foreign investments

软技术 ruǎnjìshù soft technology (the organizational management of science, technology, and economics, including methods of management and policies on technology)

软件 ruǎnjiàn [计] software

软禁 ruǎnjìn put (place) sb. under house arrest

软科学 ruǎnkēxué soft science

软绵绵 ruǎnmiānmiān ① soft; sentimental ② weak:他病好了,但身体仍然～的。He's recovered but still weak.

软任务 ruǎn rènwù soft task (tasks that are not taken seriously; they are not considered urgent or necessary to be accomplished on time):有人把教育工作当作～。Some people consider education to be a soft task.

软弱 ruǎnruò weak; flabby; feeble:～无能 be weak and incompetent

软商品 ruǎn shāngpǐn soft commodities (products of the service enterprises)
软席 ruǎnxí [火车上的] soft (cushioned) seat:～卧铺 soft berth
软饮料 ruǎn yǐnliào soft drinks
软硬兼施 ruǎnyìng-jiānshī resort to both hard and soft tactics; combine harsh and mild measures; couple threat with blandishment; both tough and soft tactics
软指标 ruǎn zhǐbiāo soft targets (targets that do not stipulate completion deadlines and stiff requirements)
软着陆 ruǎnzhuólù soft landing: 经济～ economic soft landing

ruǐ

蕊 ruǐ〈名〉stamen or pistil: 花～ pistil; stamen

ruì

锐 ruì〈形〉sharp; keen; acute; piercing
锐利 ruìlì sharp; keen; acute: 目光～ sharp-sighted
锐气 ruìqì drive; dashing spirit: 青年人的～ dashing spirit of young people
锐意 ruìyì firm; resolute; determined; be bent on: ～革新 be bent (keen) on reform

瑞 ruì〈形〉good; auspicious
瑞雪 ruìxuě auspicious (seasonable, timely) snow: ～兆丰年。Auspicious (timely) snow promises good harvest.

rùn

闰 rùn
闰年 rùnnián leap (intercalary) year
闰月 rùnyuè leap (intercalary) month

润 rùn ①〈动〉moisten; lubricate: ～喉 moisten one's throat ②〈形〉smooth; sleek ③〈名〉profit: 分～ share in the benefit
润滑 rùnhuá lubricate: ～油 lubricating oil
润色 rùnsè [文章等] add a few touches to (a piece of writing, etc.); polish; touch up
润泽 rùnzé ① moist; smooth; sleek ② moisten; lubricate: 用油～轮轴 oil an axle

ruò

若 ruò ①〈连〉if: 她～能来，我们一定热烈欢迎。If she could come, we would give her a warm welcome. ②〈介〉like
若非 ruòfēi ① if it were not for … ② but for: ～你们帮助，她也许不会成功。But for your help, she would not have succeeded.
若干 ruògān ① a few; some; several: ～分项改革方案 sub-plans for this reform ② how many;

how much

若即若离 ruòjí-ruòlí be within reach yet beyond touch; keep sb. at arm's length

若是 ruòshì if; in case; supposing

若无其事 ruòwúqíshì as if nothing had happened

若要人不知,除非己莫为 ruò yào rén bù zhī, chúfēi jǐ mò wéi If you don't want others to know about it, don't do it.; The only way to keep people from knowing something is not to do it.

弱 ruò〈形〉① weak; feeble: 由～变强 go from weakness to strength ② inferior: 他的能力并不比别人～。He's no less capable than the others.

弱点 ruòdiǎn weak point; weakness

弱肉强食 ruòròu-qiángshí The weak will stand an easy prey to the strong.; The weak serves as a prey to the strong.; the law of the jungle

弱小 ruòxiǎo small and weak: ～民族 small and weak nations

弱智 ruòzhì retarded: ～儿童 retarded children. ～教育 education for the retarded

S s

sā

撒 sā〈动〉① set loose; let go; cast:～网 cast a net ② let oneself go; throw off all restraint: ～酒疯 be roaring drunk
另见 sǎ

撒欢儿 sāhuānr gambol; frisk

撒谎 sāhuǎng tell lies; lie: ～者 liar. 当面～ tell a barefaced lie

撒娇 sājiāo act like a spoiled child

撒气 sāqì ① (of a ball, tyre, etc.) leak ② vent one's anger or ill temper:别拿我～。Don't take it out on me.

撒手 sāshǒu ① let go; leave hold of ② give up; abandon:～不管 refuse to take any further part in; wash one's hands of

撒网 sāwǎng ① cast a net; pay out a net ② invite relatives and friends to weddings, funerals, etc. with the intention of collecting presents

撒野 sāyě act wildly; behave rudely

sǎ

洒 sǎ〈动〉sprinkle; spray; spill:把汤～了 spill the soup

洒泪 sǎlèi shed tears

洒落 sǎluò ① drip; trickle down

洒水 sǎshuǐ sprinkle (with water); water: ～车 watering car; sprinkler

洒脱 sǎtuō unrestrained; free and easy:举止～ have an easy and unaffected manner

撒 sǎ〈动〉① scatter; spread; sow:～种 sow seeds ② drop; spill:～了一地的盐 spill the salt all over the floor
另见 sā

撒播 sǎbō spread; broadcast; disseminate: 均匀～ uniform broadcasting

sà

飒 sà

飒飒 sàsà [风] sough; rustle

飒爽 sàshuǎng of martial bearing; valiant; bright and brave

sāi

塞 sāi ①〈动〉fill in; cram; stuff; squeeze in:管子～住了。The pipe is clogged up. ②〈名〉stopper; cork; plug: 瓶～ a bottle cork
另见 sài

塞住 sāizhù stop up; block up; clog up:～漏洞 stop up the leak

塞子 sāizi stopper; plug; spigot; cork

腮 sāi〈名〉cheek

sài

塞 sài〈名〉a place of strategic importance; fortress:边～ frontier fortress

另见 sāi

塞外 sàiwài beyond the Great Wall:～风光 northern-frontier scene

塞翁失马,安知非福 sàiwēng shī mǎ,ān zhī fēi fú When the old man on the frontier lost his mare, who could have guessed it was a blessing in disguise —— a loss may turn out to be a gain.; A loss sometimes spells a gain.

赛 sài ①〈名〉match; contest; competition:田径～ track and field events ②〈动〉match; compete; contest; surpass:我要和他～跑。I will match him in a race.

赛场 sàichǎng competition arena

赛车 sàichē ①［体］motorcycle race ② racing bicycle

赛马 sàimǎ horse race

赛跑 sàipǎo race; running:与某人～ run a race with sb.

赛球 sàiqiú play a football match, etc.; play ball game

赛事 sàishì arrangements for competition:上海赛区的～结束了。Arrangements for the competition in the Shanghai district have concluded.

sān

三 sān〈数〉① three ② more than two; several:～思 think twice (about doing sth.); think again and again

三八妇女节 Sān-Bā Fùnǚjié International Working Women's Day

三包(包修,包换,包赔) sānbāo (bāoxiū, bāohuàn, bāopéi) three guarantees (for repair, replacement or compensation of faulty products)

三北地区 sānběi dìqū the three north areas:三北防风林 planting shelter forests in northeast China, north China and northwest China

三部曲 sānbùqǔ trilogy

三不管 sānbùguǎn come within nobody's jurisdiction; be nobody's business

三段论法 sānduànlùnfǎ［逻］syllogism

"三废"治理 sānfèi zhìlǐ disposal of waste gas, water and industrial residue; pollution control

三合板 sānhébǎn three-ply board; plywood

三角 sānjiǎo triangle:～洲 delta

三教九流 sānjiào-jiǔliú ① various religious sects and academic schools ② all professions and persuasions; people of all sorts

三明治 sānmíngzhì sandwich
三来一补 sānláiyìbǔ three "imported s" and one "compensatory," i. e., processing according to foreign specimen, processing imported materials, assembling imported parts and conducting compensatory trade
三类物资 sānlèi wùzī three categories of supplies
三联单 sānliándān triplicate form
三十六行,行行出状元 sānshíliù háng, hánghángchūzhuàngyuan Every trade has its master.
三十六计,走为上计 sānshíliù jì, zǒu wéi shàngjì of the thirty-six strategems, the best is running away—the best thing to do now is to quit; Decamping is the best of the thirty-six stratagems.; Of all stratagems, to go away is the best.
三思而行 sānsī' érxíng Think twice before taking any action.; Look before you leap.
三天打鱼,两天晒网 sān tiān dǎyú liǎng tiān shàiwǎng spend three days fishing and two days drying nets; blow hot and cold; play fast and loose; by fits and starts
三通 sāntōng [机] triplet; tee joint; tee
三心二意 sānxīn-èryì half-hearted; in (of) two minds (about sth.); shilly-shally
三言两语 sānyán-liǎngyǔ in one or two words; in a few words
三资企业 sānzī qǐyè enterprises run with Chinese-foreign joint ventures, cooperative enterprises and enterprises owned exclusively by foreign capital; three kinds of foreign-funded enterprises; three investments enterprises
三字经 sānzìjīng *san zi jing*, an old-time children's primer

sǎn

散 sǎn ①〈形〉come loose; fall apart:背包～了。The blanket roll has come loose. ②〈名〉medicinal powder
散兵 sǎnbīng skirmisher:～游勇 stragglers and disbanded soldiers; deserters
散光 sǎnguāng astigmatism
散记 sǎnjì narrative essay
散架 sǎnjià fall apart; fall to pieces
散乱 sǎnluàn in disorder
散漫 sǎnmàn undisciplined; careless and sloppy; loose; unorganized
散手 sǎnshǒu [体] karate
散文 sǎnwén prose:～诗 prose poem
散装 sǎnzhuāng loose; (in) bulk; unpacked:～货物 bulk cargo. ～饼干 loose biscuits. ～奶粉 loose powdered milk

伞 sǎn〈名〉umbrella;[女用阳伞]parasol ② parachute
伞兵 sǎnbīng parachute; paratrooper:～部队 parachute troops; paratroops

sàn

散 sàn〈动〉① break up; disperse; scatter: 风起云~。Clouds were scattered by the wind. 会议~了没有? Is the meeting over now? ② distribute; spread; disseminate: ~布一种说法 spread a notion ③ let out; dispel: ~~烟。Let the smoke out.
另见 sǎn

散布 sànbù spread; scatter; diffuse; disseminate: ~流言蜚语 spread slanderous rumours

散步 sànbù take a walk; go for a walk; go for a stroll

散场 sànchǎng [剧场等] empty after the show (performance): 电影已~。The (film) show is over.

散发 sànfā ① distribute; issue: ~传单 give out hand bills ② send out; diffuse; emit: ~阵阵清香 send out wafts of delicate fragrance

散伙 sànhuǒ break up partnership; dissolve; disband

散落 sànluò ① fall scattered ② be scattered ③ scatter and disappear

散热 sànrè ① dissipate heat ② radiate heat

散摊子 sàntānzi dissolve; disband; break up

散心 sànxīn drive away one's cares; relieve boredom; amuse oneself (by, with); divert oneself (by): 他们下象棋~。They diverted themselves by playing chess.

sāng

丧 sāng〈名〉funeral; mourning
另见 sàng

丧服 sāngfú mourning apparel

丧礼 sānglǐ burial service; funeral; obsequies

丧事 sāngshì funeral arrangements

丧葬 sāngzàng burial; funeral: ~费 funeral expenses: ~仪式和风俗 death rites and customs

丧钟 sāngzhōng funeral bell; death-bell; knell: 敲响~ sound the death-bell (of)

桑 sāng〈名〉mulberry: ~树 mulberry (tree)

桑巴 sāngbā samba (a Brazilian dance)

桑蚕 sāngcán silkworm

桑那浴 sāngnàyù sauna bath

桑葚 sāngshèn mulberry

桑梓 sāngzǐ one's native place

sǎng

嗓 sǎng〈名〉① throat ② voice

嗓门 sǎngmén ① glottis ② voice: 提高~ raise one's voice

嗓音 sǎngyīn voice: 他~洪亮。He has a sonorous voice.

嗓子 sǎngzi ① throat; larynx ② voice: ~好 have a good voice

sàng

丧 sàng〈动〉① lose：～失理智 lose one's reason ② forfeit
另见 sāng

丧胆 sàngdǎn lose courage; be terror-stricken; tremble with fear; panic-stricken：闻风～ be panic-stricken at the news (of)

丧魂落魄 sànghún-luòpò be driven to distraction; be scared out of one's wits; be barttered out of one's senses

丧尽天良 sàngjìn-tiānliáng heartless; conscienceless

丧命 sàngmìng meet one's death; lose one's life; be killed; get killed in an accident

丧气 sàngqì lose heart; be filled with despair; be in low spirits：垂头～ downcast; disheartened. 令人～的 disheartening; discouraging

丧权辱国 sàngquán-rǔguó humiliate the nation and forfeit its sovereignty; national betrayal and humiliation; surrender a country's sovereign rights under humiliating terms

丧生 sàngshēng meet one's death; lose on'e life; get killed

丧失 sàngshī ① lose：～信心 lose confidence ② be deprived of; forfeit：～健康 forfeit one's health. ～名誉 infamy

丧心病狂 sàngxīn-bìngkuáng frenzied; preposterous and unscrupulous

sāo

臊 sāo〈形〉stinking

臊气 sāoqì foul smell; stink

搔 sāo〈动〉scratch：～痒 scratch where it itches

搔首踟蹰 sāoshǒuchíchú scratch one's head in great perplexity

骚 sāo〈动〉disturb; upset

骚动 sāodòng agitation; riot; commotion; tumult：引起～ give rise to a commotion

骚乱 sāoluàn turbulence; unrest; riot

骚扰 sāorǎo disturb; perturb; harass; molest

缫 sāo〈名〉reel：～丝 silk reeling; filature

sǎo

扫 sǎo〈动〉① sweep; clear away：～雪 sweep away the snow ② pass quickly along or over：～了一眼 sweep one's eye

扫除 sǎochú wipe out; clear away：～文盲 eliminate (wipe out) illiteracy

扫荡 sǎodàng mop up; sweep：～残敌 mop up the remnant enemy troops

扫地 sǎodì ① sweep the ground or floor ② be dragged in the dust; lose entirely：名誉～ be thoroughly discredited

"扫黄" sǎohuáng campaign against pornography (pornographic publications)

扫描 sǎomiáo scanning

扫墓 sǎomù sweep a grave; pay respects to a dead person at his tomb; sweep the grave mounds of; visit grave

扫清 sǎoqīng clear away; get rid of

扫尾 sǎowěi wind up: ～工作 rounding-off work

扫兴 sǎoxìng have one's spirits dampened; dampen one's spirits; throw a wet blanket over; wet-blanket: 大雨使人～。The heavy rain wet-blanketed the sight-seers.

嫂 sǎo〈名〉elder brother's wife; sister-in-law

sào

臊 sào〈形〉bashful; shy: ～得脸通红 blush scarlet

扫 sào
另见 sǎo

扫帚 sàozhou broom

sè

涩 sè〈形〉① puckery; astringent: 这柿子～不～? Are these persimmons puckery? ② hard-going; unsmooth

涩味 sèwèi astringent; acerbity: 有～ taste acerbic; be harsh to the taste

塞 sè〈动〉fill in; stuff: 堵～ block (stop) up

塞责 sèzé not do one's job conscientiously: 敷衍～ perform one's duty in a perfunctory manner

色 sè〈名〉① colour: 原～ primary colour ② look; expression countenance: 满面喜～ beaming with joy ③ description; kind: 各～人等 all kinds of people

色彩 sècǎi colour; tint; hue; shade: 带有一些资本主义的～ have some capitalist colouration. 感情～ emotional colouring

色调 sèdiào tone; shade of colour; hue

色厉内荏 sèlì-nèirěn fierce of visage but faint of heart; outwardly strong but inwardly weak; appear to be tough outwardly and timid inwardly

色情 sèqíng sexy; obscene; pornographic: ～电影 sexy movie; blue film. ～文学 pornography

色素 sèsù pigment

色泽 sèzé colour and lustre: ～鲜明 brightly coloured and lustrous

sēn

森 sēn〈形〉① full of trees; thick with trees ② dark; gloomy: 阴～～ grim; gloomy

森林 sēnlín forest: ～保护 forest

conservation. ～保护员 forest ranger. ～资源 forest reserves

森严 sēnyán strict; severe; austere: 戒备～ be heavily guarded. 等级～ form a strict hierarchy

sēng

僧 sēng〈名〉(Buddhist) monk

僧侣 sēnglǚ ① monks and priests ② clergy

僧徒 sēngtú Buddhist monks

shā

沙 shā〈名〉① sand ②〈形〉(of voice) hoarse; husky

沙场 shāchǎng battlefield

沙尘 shāchén dust and sand in the air

沙发 shāfā sofa; settee

沙锅 shāguō earthenware pot

沙皇 shāhuáng tsar

沙里淘金 shālǐ-táojīn get small returns for great effort

沙龙 shālóng *salon*; saloon

沙漠 shāmò desert; sands

沙滩 shātān sandy beach; sands

沙文主义 shāwénzhǔyì chauvinism

沙哑 shāyǎ hoarse; husky; raucous

沙眼 shāyǎn trachoma

沙洲 shāzhōu shoal; sandbank

沙子 shāzi ① sand; grit ② small grains; pellets

鲨 shā〈名〉shark: ～鱼 shark

砂 shā〈名〉sand; grit

砂布 shābù emery cloth

砂砾 shālì gravel

砂糖 shātáng granulated sugar

砂纸 shāzhǐ sandpaper: 玻璃～ glass paper

纱 shā〈名〉①(cotton) yarn; thread: ～厂 cotton mill ② gauze; sheer: 铁～ wire gauze

纱布 shābù gauze: ～绷带 gauze bandage

纱窗 shāchuāng gauze window; window screen

纱锭 shādìng spindle

杀 shā〈动〉① kill; slay; slaughter: ～人不眨眼 slaughter people without blinking ② fight; go into battle: ～出重围 fight one's way out of a double line of besieges ③ reduce; weaken: 风势稍～。The wind abated.

杀虫剂 shāchóngjì insecticide; pesticide

杀敌 shādí fight the enemy; engage in battle

杀风景 shāfēngjǐng cast a chill over sb.; spoil the fun; be a wet blanket: 这真是～! It's really a wet blanket!

杀害 shāhài murder; kill; slaughter

杀鸡取卵 shājī-qǔluǎn kill the hen to get all its eggs; kill the goose that lays the golden eggs

杀价 shājià force down prices; slash prices

杀菌 shājūn destroy harmful microorganisms; disinfect; sterilize

杀气 shāqì ① murderous look ② vent one's ill feeling

杀青 shāqīng ① [烟草] kill out ② finalize a manuscript

杀人 shārén kill a man; commit homicide: ～犯 murderer. ～罪 crime of killing another person

杀伤 shāshāng inflict casualties on

杀身成仁 shāshēn-chéngrén die for the sake of a just cause

杀手 shāshǒu killer

杀一儆百 shāyī-jǐngbǎi punish the offender as a warning to others; execute one man to warn a hundred; punish one as an example to others

刹 shā〈动〉put on the brakes; stop; halt: ～住歪风 check an unhealthy tendency
另见 chà

刹车 shāchē ① put on the brakes; brake a car; brake: 对中央严令禁止的事要立即～。We must immediately put a stop to things the Central Government has prohibited. ② turn off a machine

煞 shā〈动〉① stop; halt; check; bring to a close: ～住脚 stop short ② tighten: 把车上的东西～紧 firmly fasten a load on a vehicle

煞尾 shāwěi ① end; conclusion ② bring to a close; wind up

煞住 shāzhù stop; bring to a halt; check: ～歪风 check an unhealthy trend; check bad tendency

shǎ

傻 shǎ〈形〉foolish; stupid; muddleheaded; silly: 装～ pretend not to know

傻瓜 shǎguā fool; blockhead; simpleton

傻里傻气 shǎlǐ-shǎqì clumsy and stupid

傻笑 shǎxiào laugh foolishly; giggle; smirk

傻眼 shǎyǎn be stunned; be dumbfounded

傻子 shǎzi fool; blockhead; simpleton

shà

霎 shà〈名〉instant; moment; a very short time

霎时间 shàshíjiān in an instant; in a twinkle; in a split second; in a jiffy

厦 shà〈名〉a tall building; mansion: 高楼大～ tall buildings and large mansions

煞 shà〈名〉evil spirit; goblin 〈副〉very; extremely
另见 shā

煞费苦心 shàfèi-kǔxīn cudgel (rack) one's brains; take great pains; painstakingly; laboriously

煞有介事 shàyǒujièshì make a great fuss about sth. of little consequence; be ludicrously pompous; pretend to be serious; in all apparent seriousness; in pretentious earnest: ～地说 say sth. in pretentious earnest

啥 shà〈代,方〉what: 有～说～ say what one has to say

shāi

筛 shāi〈动〉① sieve; screen; sift: ～粮食 sieve grain ②〈名〉sieve; sifter; screen

shài

晒 shài〈动〉①（of the sun）shine upon; be weather-beaten: ～黑了 be deeply tanned by the sun ② dry in the sun: ～被子 air the quilt

晒黑 shàihēi sunburnt; suntanned: ～的脸 sun-tanned face

晒台 shàitái flat roof; terrace

晒图 shàitú make a blueprint; blue print: ～纸 blueprint paper

shān

扇 shān〈动〉fan: ～炉子 fan a stove

另见 shàn

扇动 shāndòng fan; flap: ～翅膀 flap the wings

煽 shān〈动〉① fan ② incite; fan up; instigate: ～阴风 fan up an evil wind

煽动 shāndòng fan; stir up; incite; instigate; inflame; egg on: ～情绪 fan emotions; inflame feeling against. ～群众闹事 stir up trouble among the masses

煽风点火 shānfēng-diǎnhuǒ inflame and agitate people; fan the flames; stir up trouble

煽惑 shānhuò agitate; incite; inflame with delusions: ～人心 agitate people by demagogy. ～他人犯罪 incite sb. to commit a crime

山 shān〈名〉mountain; hill

山坳 shān'ào depression in a mountain range; col

山崩 shānbēng landslide; avalanche

山川 shānchuān mountains and rivers—land; landscape

山地 shāndì ① mountainous region; hilly area; hilly country ② hillside field

山歌 shāngē folk song (sung in the fields during or after work); mountain songs: ～交响乐 symphony on a mountain song

山河 shānhé ① mountains and rivers ② land of one's country

山洪 shānhóng mountain torrents: ～暴发 outburst of mountain torrents

山货 shānhuò ① mountain products ② household utensils made of wood, bamboo, clay, etc.

山岭 shānlǐng mountain ridge

山脉 shānmài mountain range

山盟海誓 shānméng-hǎishì (made) a solemn pledge of love; (make) a vow of eternal love

山民 shānmín mountain people; hillmen

山坡 shānpō hillside; mountain slope; hillslope

山青水秀 shānqīng-shuǐxiù green hills and clear waters — picturesque scenery

山穷水尽 shānqióng-shuǐjìn be at the end of one's rope (tether, resources); in desperate straits; come to an end

山水 shānshuǐ natural scenery with hills and streams: ～画 landscape painting

山乡 shānxiāng mountain village; mountain area

山雨欲来风满楼 shānyǔ yù lái fēngmǎnlóu The wind sweeping through the tower heralds a rising storm in the mountains.; The turbulent wind precedes the mountain storm.; The rising wind forebodes the coming storm.

山寨 shānzhài mountain fastness; fortified mountain village

山珍海味 shānzhēn-hǎiwèi rare delicacies of every kind; dainties of every kind; the choicest delicates of sea and land

山庄 shānzhuāng ① mountain villa ② mountain village

舢 shān

舢板 shānbǎn sampan

珊 shān

珊瑚 shānhú coral: ～岛 coral island

衫 shān〈名〉unlined upper garment: 汗～ undershirt

删 shān〈动〉cancel; leave out; delete; cross out: ～去细节 cut out the details

删除 shānchú cancel; delete; cross out; strike out

删繁就简 shānfán-jiùjiǎn simplify sth. by leaving out the superfluous; simplify complicated materials

删改 shāngǎi delete and change; revise (draft, etc.)

删节 shānjié abridge; shorten: ～本 abridged edition

姗 shān

姗姗来迟 shānshān-láichí be slow in coming; be late; arrive late

shǎn

闪 shǎn〈动〉① flash; sparkle; shine: 一～而过 streak past ② twist; strain; sprain: ～了腰 sprain one's back ③ dodge; get out of the way: 往边上～一～ dodge swiftly to one side ④ lightning: 打～ flashes of lightning

闪电 shǎndiàn lightning: ～战 lightning war; blitzkrieg; blitz

闪动 shǎndòng flash; twinkle; flicker

闪躲 shǎnduǒ dodge; evade

闪光 shǎnguāng flash of light;

sparkle; gleam

闪开 shǎnkāi get out of the way; jump aside; dodge

闪念 shǎnniàn idea which flashes through one's mind

闪射 shǎnshè glitter; shine; radiate

闪身 shǎnshēn ① dodge ② move sideways

闪失 shǎnshī mishap; accident

闪烁 shǎnshuò ① flicker; glint; twinkle ② dodge about; evade; vague: ～其词 speak evasively; hedge

闪现 shǎnxiàn flash before one

闪耀 shǎnyào shine; glitter; glare; glisten; sparkle

shàn

擅 shàn〈动〉① arrogate to oneself; claim arbitrarily: ～权 usurp power ② be skillful in; be good at: 不～辞令 lack facility in polite or tactful speech ③〈副〉do sth. on one's own authority; arbitrarily: ～作主张 make a decision without authorization

擅长 shàncháng be good at; be skilled in (at); be versed in: ～绘画 be good at painting

擅离职守 shànlí-zhíshǒu be absent without official leave; leave one's post without permission

擅自 shànzì do sth. without authorization; arbitrarily: ～决定 decide arbitrarily; make arbitrary decisions

善 shàn ①〈名〉good: 改恶从～ give up evil and return to good〈形〉② good; satisfactory: ～策 the best policy ③ friendly; kind: 友～ be friendly ④ familiar: 面～ look familiar〈动〉⑤ make a success of; perfect ⑥ be good at; be expert in: 不～经营 be not good at management ⑦〈副〉properly: ～为说辞 put in a good word for sb.

善本 shànběn authentic version; reliable text; good edition

善变 shànbiàn be apt to change; be changeable

善待 shàndài treat sb. well

善恶 shàn'è good and evil; right and wrong

善后 shànhòu deal with problems arising from an accident, etc.; properly handle the remaining problems; deal with the aftermath (of an accident, etc.): ～措施 rehabilitation measures

善举 shànjǔ philanthropic act or project

善良 shànliáng good and honest; kindhearted; virtuous: ～的人民 good and honest people

善始善终 shànshǐ-shànzhōng start well and end well; do well from beginning to end; have a good ending as well as a good beginning

善事 shànshì charitable deeds; good deeds

善忘 shànwàng be forgetful; have a short memory

善心 shànxīn mercy; kindness; benevolence

善意 shànyì ① goodwill; good faith;kindness ② well-intentioned: ～的劝告 well-intentioned advice

善有善报,恶有恶报 shàn yǒu shànbào, è yǒu è bào Good will be rewarded with good, and evil with evil.

善于 shànyú be good at; be adept at; know how; be skilful in (at):他～辩论。He is convincing in debate.

善终 shànzhōng ① die a natural death; die in one's bed ② end well

膳 shàn〈名〉meals; mess; board:～食费 board expenses

膳食 shànshí meals; food

膳宿 shànsù board and lodging

鳝 shàn〈名〉(yellow) eel; finless eel

缮 shàn〈动〉① repair; mend:房屋修～ house repairing ② copy; write out:～清 make a fair copy

禅 shàn

禅让 shànràng abdicate and hand over the crown to another person; abdicate the throne (in favour of another person)

扇 shàn〈名〉① fan:电～ electric fan ② leaf:门～ door leaf 另见 shān

扇贝 shànbèi scallop; fan shell

扇形 shànxíng ① fan-shaped ②[数] sector

扇坠 shànzhuì fan pendants

扇子 shànzi fan

赡 shàn ①〈动〉support; provide for:～养父母 support one's parents ②〈形〉abundant; plentiful

赡养 shànyǎng support; maintain:～父母的义务 duty to support parents. ～费 alimony; cost of support

讪 shàn ①〈动〉mock; ridicule ②〈形〉awkward; embarrased:～～地走开 walk away looking embarrased

讪笑 shànxiào deride; ridicule; mock

shāng

商 shāng ①〈动〉consult; discuss:我有要事和你相～。I have important matters to discuss with you.〈名〉② commerce; trade; business:经～ engage in trade ③ businessman; merchant; dealer:皮货～ fur dealer ④ quotient:智～ intelligence quotient

商标 shāngbiāo trademark; brand; brand name:注册～ registered trademark. ～权 trademark right

商场 shāngchǎng market; bazaar; emporium

商船 shāngchuán mercantile marine; merchant ship (vessel); merchantman

商店 shāngdiàn shop; store

商调 shāngdiào transfer of personnel through consultation; negotiate the transfer of personnel

商定 shāngdìng decide through consultation; agree (on, upon); come to an agreement (about)

商贩 shāngfàn pedlar; small retailer

商行 shāngháng commercial house; commercial firm; firm

商会 shānghuì chamber of commerce

商界 shāngjiè commercial circles; business circles

商量 shāngliang consult; discuss; talk over

商品 shāngpǐn goods; commodity; merchandise:～化 commercialize. ～粮 commodity grain. ～经济 commodity economy. 小～ small commodities. ～住宅 commercial residential buildings

商情 shāngqíng market conditions:～预测 business forecasting

商榷 shāngquè discuss; deliberate:值得～be open to question

商人 shāngrén businessman; trader; merchant

商社 shāngshè company

商谈 shāngtán exchange views; confer; discuss; negotiate

商讨 shāngtǎo discuss; deliberate over

商务 shāngwù business affairs; commercial affairs:～参赞 commercial counsellor. ～代表 commercial agent; trade representative

商业 shāngyè commerce; trade; business:～比赛 commercial match. ～代理制度 commercial agencies. ～道德 commercial morality. ～发票 commercial invoice. ～区 business quarter. ～萧条 commercial depression. ～中心 commercial centre

商议 shāngyì confer; discuss

商战 shāngzhàn commercial war; trade war

商酌 shāngzhuó have consultations with

伤

伤 shāng ①〈名〉wound; injury: 刀～ a knife wound〈动〉② injure; harm; hurt:在一场车祸中～了一只手臂 injure an arm in a car accident ③ be distressed:哀～ sorrowful; sad ④ hinder; be detrimental:～身体 be harmful to one's health

伤悲 shāngbēi sad; sorrowful

伤风 shāngfēng have a cold; catch cold

伤风败俗 shāngfēng-bàisú offend public decency; pervert the manners and customs; corrupt public morals:不干～的事 abstain from immoralities

伤感 shānggǎn feel sick at heart; sentimental:～故事 sob story

伤害 shānghài injure; hurt; harm:～某人的感情 offend (wound) one's susceptibilities. ～罪 battery; (crime of) injury

伤痕 shānghén bruise; scar; seam; wound:～文学 trauma literature; "scar" literature

伤口 shāngkǒu wound; cut:洗～

bathe a wound

伤脑筋 shāngnǎojīn troublesome; bothersome; annoying: 这事使她大～。It was a big headache for her.

伤人 shāngrén ① hurt sb.'s feelings ② inflict injuries ③ injure the health

伤神 shāngshén overtax one's nerves

伤势 shāngshì condition of an injury (wound): ～很重 be seriously wounded

伤痛 shāngtòng ① grieved; distressed ② the pain of an injury or wound

伤亡 shāngwáng injuries and deaths; casualties: ～惨重 suffer heavy casualties

伤心 shāngxīn sad; grieved; broken-hearted; sorrowful

伤员 shāngyuán wounded personnel; the wounded; [个人] invalid

shǎng

赏 shǎng ①〈名〉reward; award: 领～ receive a reward ②〈动〉enjoy; admire appreciate: ～花 admire the beauty of flowers

赏赐 shǎngcì grant (bestow) a reward; award

赏罚 shǎngfá rewards and punishments: ～严明 be strict and fair in meting out rewards and punishments

赏光 shǎngguāng asking sb. to come to a party, meeting, etc.

赏金 shǎngjīn money reward

赏脸 shǎngliǎn honour me with your presence

赏玩 shǎngwán admire the beauty of sth.; delight in; enjoy; fondle

赏心悦目 shǎngxīn-yuèmù find the scenery pleasing to both the eye and the mind

赏识 shǎngshí recognize the worth of; appreciate

晌 shǎng

晌午 shǎngwu (at) midday; (at) noon: ～饭 lunch; midday meal

shàng

尚 shàng ①〈副〉still; yet; as yet: ～待进一步讨论 pending further discussion ②〈动〉esteem; value: ～武 set great store by martial qualities; respect for military spirit

尚且 shàngqiě even: 这种事我们大人～做不来,何况小孩子。Even we grown-ups can't do it, let alone children.

尚未 shàngwèi not yet: ～解决 remain to be settled

上 shàng〈形〉① upper; upward; up: 往～看 look up ② higher; superior; better: ～级机关 higher authorities ③ first (part); previous; preceding: ～半夜 the first half of the night 〈动〉④ go up; get on: ～山 go uphill; go up a hill ⑤ go to; leave for: 他～图书馆去。He's going to the library. ⑥ serve;

supply：～水 fill sth. with water⑦ set；fix；wind：我给钟～弦。I wound my clock. ⑧ submit；present；send in ⑨ be engaged (in work，study，etc.) at a fixed time：～大学 be in college ⑩ apply；paint；smear：～药膏 apply ointment ⑪ up to；as many as：～万 as many as ten thousand

上班 shàngbān ① go to work；be on duty ② go on shift：～时间 work hours；office hours

上策 shàngcè the best plan；the best way out；the best thing to do

上层 shàngcéng upper stratum：～建筑 superstructure. ～管理人员 major executives

上场 shàngchǎng ①［剧］appear on the stage；enter ② enter the court (field)；join in a contest

上乘 shàngchéng first-class：～之作 first-class work

上床 shàngchuáng go to bed；get into bed

上当 shàngdàng be fooled；be taken in；be duped；play into someone's hands：她～了。She has been taken in.

上等 shàngděng first-class；first-rate：～货 first-class goods；firsts

上调 shàngdiào transfer up (transfer from one work unit to a higher work unit)

上访 shàngfǎng (of popular masses) complain to the higher authorities about an injustice and request fair settlement；meet with the higher authorities；apply for an audience with the higher authorities to appeal for help

上古 shànggǔ ancient times：～史 ancient history

上光 shàngguāng ① glazing；polishing ② ferrotyping

上环 shànghuán［计生］installing an I. U. D.

上级 shàngjí higher authorities；higher-ups；higher level；one's superior：～和下级之间 between those in higher and those in lower positions of responsibility

上交 shàngjiāo hand in (over) to sb. above oneself；pass on to the higher authorities

上缴 shàngjiǎo turn over (hand in) to higher authorities：～利润 turn over profits to the state

上街 shàngjiē ① go to the street；go shopping ② take to the streets；go on to the streets

上进 shàngjìn make progress；go forward；advance：力求～ do one's best to make progress

上课 shàngkè ① attend class：八点钟～。Class is at eight. ②［教师］give a lesson (to a class)：明天不～。There will be no lessons tomorrow.

上来 shànglái ① begin；get started ② come up ③ come up to a place or state regarded as higher or above ④［作为动词的补足语］up (here)：把箱子抬～ bring the trunk up ⑤［用在动词后，表示成功］：这个问题他答

得～吗？Can he answer this question?⑥［表示程度的增加］：天色黑～了。It is getting dask.

上流 shàngliú ① upper reaches (of a river) ② upper classes：～社会 upper-class society

上路 shànglù set out on a journey；start off

上面 shàngmian ① above；over；on top of；on the surface of ② above-mentioned；aforesaid；foregoing ③ higher authorities；higher-ups ④ aspect；respect；regard ⑤ the elder generation of one's family；the elders

上去 shàngqù ① go up ② rise to a place or state regarded as higher or above

上升 shàngshēng go up；rise；ascend

上市 shàngshì ① appear on the market ② go on the market；be in season：～的证券 listed securities

上司 shàngsi superior；boss

上诉 shàngsù［法］appeal (to a higher court)：～案 appealed case. ～状 appeal petition

上税 shàngshuì pay taxes (duties)

上算 shàngsuàn profitable；more economical；worthwhile；paying：买这种东西不～。It doesn't pay to buy such a thing.

上台 shàngtái ① appear on the stage ② come to power

上下 shàng-xià ① high and low；old and young；② up and down；from top to bottom ③ relative superiority or inferiority ④ about；around

上下文 shàng-xiàwén［语］context

上限 shàngxiàn upper limit；ceiling

上行下效 shàngxíng-xiàxiào Those in subordinate positions will follow the example set by their superiors.；If a leader sets a bad example, it will be followed by his subordinates.；The inferiors imitate the superiors.

上学 shàngxué go to school；attend school

上旬 shàngxún the first ten days of a month

上演 shàngyǎn be put on the stage；be performed；be staged

上衣 shàngyī upper outer garment；jacket

上瘾 shàngyǐn be addicted (to sth.)；get into the habit (of doing sth.)

上映 shàngyìng show (a film)；screen：～期 play-date

上游 shàngyóu ① upper reaches (of a river) ② advanced position

上涨 shàngzhǎng go up；rise：物价在～。Prices are going up.

上帐 shàngzhàng make an entry in an account book

shāo

烧 shāo〈动〉① burn：～掉废纸 burn up the waste paper ② cook；do；boil；heat；bake：～

水 heat up some water ③ stew; roast; fry: ～鸡 roast chicken ④〈名〉(run a) fever: 病人～得很厉害。The patient has a high temperature.

烧菜 shāocài ① boil vegetables ② cook (food): 她很会～。She is good at cooking.

烧饭 shāofàn ① cook (boil) rice ② cook a meal; prepare meals

烧毁 shāohuǐ burn out; burn

烧火 shāohuǒ make a fire; light a fire

烧鸡 shāojī roast chicken

烧酒 shāojiǔ spirit usu. distilled from sorghum or maize; colourless spirit

烧烤 shāokǎo barbecue

烧垦 shāokěn [农]shifting cultivation

烧伤 shāoshāng get burnt: 小心别～。Be careful not to get burnt.

烧香 shāoxiāng burn joss sticks (before an idol)

烧灼 shāozhuó burn; scorch; singe

捎 shāo〈动〉take along sth. to or for sb.; bring to sb.: ～来点苹果 bring sb. some apples

捎带 shāodài incidentally; in passing: ～提一下 mention (sth.) in passing

捎信 shāoxìn send word; take a message to sb.

稍 shāo〈副〉a little; a bit; somewhat: ～微认真学习 make a cursory study of

稍稍 shāoshāo a little; a bit; slightly; a trifle

稍微 shāowēi a trifle; somewhat; slightly

稍纵即逝 shāozòng-jíshì transient; fleeting

sháo

勺 sháo〈名〉spoon; ladle; scoop

勺子 sháozi spoon; [长柄的] ladle; dipper; scoop

芍 sháo

芍药 sháoyào Chinese herbaceous peony

shǎo

少 shǎo ①〈形〉little; less; few: ～而精 fewer but better〈动〉② be short of; want; lack: 缺医～药 be short of doctor and medicine ③ lose; be missing: ～两个字 There's two words missing. ④ quit; stop: ～废话 stop talking rubbish

另见 shào

少不了 shǎobuliǎo ① can't do without; can't dispense with; (sth.) be indispensible ② be bound to; be unavoidable: 空气对生命是～的。Air is indipensible to life.

少见 shǎojiàn ① (a form of greeting) I haven't seen you for a long time; I have seen very little of you these days—I'm very glad to see you again ② seldom seen; infrequent; rare

少量 shǎoliàng a small quantity of;a little; a few

少陪 shǎopéi (an apology for taking leave of sb.) if you'll excuse me; I'm afraid I must be going now

少顷 shǎoqǐng after a short while; after a few moments; presently

少数 shǎoshù ① a small number of; a few ② minority:～服从多数。The minority must obey the majority. ～民族 minority nationalities

少许 shǎoxǔ a little; a few; a modicum

少有 shǎoyǒu rare; few and far between

少走弯路 shǎozǒu-wānlù save twists and turns; avoid detours

shào

哨 shào〈名〉① sentry post:观察～ observation post ② whistle:吹～ blow a whistle

哨兵 shàobīng sentinel; guard

哨所 shàosuǒ sentry post

少 shào〈形〉young

另见 shǎo

少妇 shàofù young married woman

少年 shàonián teenager; youngster;lad:～宫 children's palace. ～犯管教 the reform and education of juvenile offenders (deliquents)

少女 shàonǚ young girl; lass

少先队 shàoxiānduì Young Pioneers:～员 Young Pioneer

少壮派 shàozhuàngpài the up-and-coming

shē

奢 shē〈形〉① luxurious:穷～极欲 (indulge in) luxury and extravagance ② excessive:～望 extravagant hopes; wild wishes

奢侈 shēchǐ luxurious; extravagant; prodigal:～品 articles of luxury; luxuries. 过～生活 live in luxury. ～主义 poshism

奢华 shēhuá luxurious; sumptuos; extravagant:陈设～ be luxuriously furnished

奢求 shēqiú extravagant claims; excessive demands; unreasonable demands

畲 Shē

畲族 Shēzú She nationality (distributed over Fujian, Zhejiang, Jiangxi and Guangdong)

赊 shē〈动〉buy or sell on credit

赊购 shēgòu buy on credit; buy on tally

赊欠 shēqiàn give or get credit

赊销 shēxiāo sell on credit; credit sales

赊帐 shēzhàng ① a system of buying or selling on credit; the credit system ② outstanding bills or accounts ③ have outstanding bills or accounts

shé

折 shé〈动〉① break；snap：扁担～了。The shoulder pole broke. ② lose money (in business)
另见 zhē，zhé

折本 shéběn lose money (in business)；lose：～生意 losing business；bad bargain

蛇 shé〈名〉snake；serpent：～形 snakelike；S-shaped

蛇蝎 shéxiē snakes and scorpions—vicious people

蛇行 shéxíng crawl (creep) along

舌 shé〈名〉tongue

舌敝唇焦 shébì-chúnjiāo talk till one is completely exhausted；talk oneself hoarse

舌头 shétou ① tongue ② an enemy soldier captured for the purpose of extracting information

舌战 shézhàn have a verbal battle with；argue heatedly with

shě

舍 shě〈动〉give up；abandon；forsake：～己为人 sacrifice oneself for others
另见 shè

舍本逐末 shěběn-zhúmò pay attention to trifles but neglect the essentials；put the cart before the horse；grasp the shadow instead of the essence

舍不得 shěbude hate to part with or use；grudge；be unwilling to give or part with：～乱花一分钱 hate to waste a single cent

舍得 shěde be willing to part with；not grudge

舍己为人 shějǐ-wèirén ① sacrifice one's own interests for the sake of others ② self-sacrificing；unselfish

舍命 shěmìng risk one's life；sacrifice oneself

舍弃 shěqì give up；abandon；forsake

舍身 shěshēn sacrifice oneself：～报国 die for one's country

舍生取义 shěshēng-qǔyì lay down one's life for justice

舍死忘生 shěsǐ-wàngshēng pay no attention to one's own safety；risk one's life

shè

涉 shè〈动〉① wade；ford：～水过河 wade across a river ② involve ③ undergo；go through：～险 go through dangers

涉及 shèjí concern；involve；relate to：这些问题都～到政治。All these questions relate to politics.

涉猎 shèliè read cursorily；do desultory reading；dabble in；dip into：～艺术 dabble in art

涉世 shèshì gain life experience

涉讼 shèsòng be involved in a lawsuit：～人 person involved in lawsuit

涉外 shèwài involving (concerning) foreign affairs (elements) or foreign nationals：～单位

foreign affairs unit. ～合同 contracts involving foreign interests

涉嫌 shèxián be suspected of being involved; be a suspect

涉险 shèxiǎn go through dangers

涉想 shèxiǎng be lost in thought; indulge in fanciful thinking

涉足 shèzú set foot (in):～仕途 start an official career; join the civil service

社 shè〈名〉① society; organized body; community:～会保障体制 social security system ② commune:～办企业 commune-managed enterprises

社会 shèshuì society:～丑恶现象 social evils. ～地位 social position (status). ～力量办学 running of schools by non-governmental sectors

社会保障制度 shèhuì bǎozhàng zhìdù social security system

社会风俗小说 shèhuì fēngsú xiǎoshuō novel of manners

社会科学 shèhuìkēxué social sciences

社会商品零售总额 shèhuì shāngpǐn língshòu zǒng'é total volume of retail commodity sales

社会统筹基金 shèhuì tǒngchóu jījīn pooled funds

社会学 shèhuìxué sociology

社会治安综合治理 shèhuì zhì'ān zōnghé zhìlǐ improve all facets of public security

社会主义 shèhuìzhǔyì socialism: ～法制 socialist legal system

社稷 shèjì the country; the state

社交 shèjiāo social intercourse; social contact; social activities: 举行～晚会 have a sociable evening

社论 shèlùn editorial; leading article

社区 shèqū community:～联谊中心 intercommunity social centre. 加强～文化建设 increase the cultural activities in communities

社团 shètuán mass organizations

设 shè〈动〉① set up; arrange; establish; found: ～立新机构 set up a new organization ② workout:～计 plot ③〈连〉if; in case:～有困难,当助一臂之力。You can count on me to help in case of difficulty.

设备 shèbèi equipment; installation; facilities; accommodations:～利用率 capacity utilization rate

设法 shèfǎ think of a way; try; manage; do what one can; contrive:他～靠微薄的收入过活。He contrived to live on a small income.

设计 shèjì〈动,名〉design; plan: ～师 designer

设立 shèlì set up; establish; found

设身处地 shèshēn-chǔdì put oneself in sb. else's place; place oneself in others' position

设施 shèshī installation; facilities

设想 shèxiǎng ① conceive; imagine; envisage:计划中～的指标 the targets envisaged in the programme ② tentative idea; assumption ③ take into account

(consideration); have consideration:为人民的利益～ take the interests of the people into account

设宴 shèyàn give a dinner party; give a banquet:～欢迎 give a welcome dinner party to sb. ～招待 give a dinner in honour of sb.

设置 shèzhì ① set up; place; put up:课程～ courses offered in a school or college ② install:～扩音器 install a megaphone

赦 shè〈动〉 pardon; remit:大～ general pardon

赦免 shèmiǎn pardon; remit (a punishment); amnesty; grace; absolve; excuse:～无罪 absolution from all one's sin

赦罪 shèzuì absolve sb. from guilt; pardon sb.; absolution; remit a sin

摄 shè〈动〉 ① absorb; assimilate:～取营养 absorb nourishment ② take (a photo); shoot (a film)

摄取 shèqǔ ① absorb ② take (a photo); shoot (a film)

摄食 shèshí (of animals) feed

摄像机 shèxiàngjī pickup camera:电视～ television camera

摄影 shèyǐng take a photo:～留念 have a souvenir photograph taken; post for a souvenir photograph. ～师 photographer

摄制 shèzhì [影视] produce:～组 production unit

慑 shè〈动〉 fear; be awed

慑服 shèfú ① submit in fear; succumb ② cow sb. into submission

舍 shè ①〈名〉 house; shed; hut:校～ school buildings ②〈代〉〈谦〉my:～弟 my younger brother

另见 shě

舍间 shèjiān my house; my place

射 shè〈动〉 ① shoot; fire:～箭 shoot an arrow ② send out (light, heat, etc.):～出强光 project powerful beams of light ③ discharge in a jet:喷～ spurt; spout ④ allude to sb. or sth.:有意影～ make pointed allusions to

射程 shèchéng range (of fire)

射击 shèjī ① shoot; fire ② [体] shooting:～技术 marksmanship. ～运动员 shooter; marksman or markswoman

射箭 shèjiàn ① shoot an arrow ② [体]archery:～运动员 archer

射门 shèmén shoot (at the goal)

射频 shèpín radio frequency

射中 shèzhòng hit the mark; hit

shēn

深 shēn〈形〉 ① deep:～耕 deep ploughing ② difficult; profound:这本书太～了。The book is too difficult. ③ thoroughgoing; penetrating:功夫～ have put in a great deal of effort ④ close; intimate:交情～ be on intimate terms ⑤ dark:

～红 deep red ⑥ late：工作至～夜 work late into the night ⑦〈副〉greatly；deeply；very：～～感到 be keenly aware of

深奥 shēn'ào profound；abstruse recondite：～的哲理 an abstruse philosophy；a profound truth

深沉 shēnchén ① deep；dark：暮色～。The dusk is deepening. ② dull (sound，voice，etc.)；deep：～的音调 dull sound；deep notes

深处 shēnchù depths；recesses：在内心～ in the innermost recesses of the heart

深度 shēndù ① degree of depth；depth ② profundity；depth；thoroughness ③ advanced stage of development

深海 shēnhǎi deep sea

深厚 shēnhòu ① deep；profound：～感情 deep feelings ② solid；strong

深化 shēnhuà deepen：～经济改革 deepen economic reforms

深究 shēnjiū go into (a matter) seriously；get to the bottom of (a matter)

深刻 shēnkè deep；profound；penetrating；deepgoing：留下～印象 make a deep impression (on sb.)

深谋远虑 shēnmóu-yuǎnlǜ think carefully and plan deeply；be thoughtful and farsighted；foresight：～的指挥员 a judicious and farsighted commander

深浅 shēnqiǎn ① depth：河的～ the depth of a river ② [文字] degree of difficulty ③ shade (of colour) ④ proper limits (for speech or action)；sense of propriety：说话没～ speak carelessly and bluntly

深切 shēnqiè deep；profound；heartfelt：～同情 feel deep sympathy for sb. ～悼念 mourn with deep grief

深情 shēnqíng deep feeling (love)：～厚谊 deep feelings of friendship

深入 shēnrù go deep (into)：～浅出 profound but easily understood. ～人心 go deep into the hearts of the people；strike root in the hearts of the people. ～开展爱国主义教育 conduct intensive education in patriotism

深深 shēnshēn deeply；keenly；profoundly

深思 shēnsī think deeply about；be absorbed (engrossed) in thought；deliberate：～熟虑 full deliberation；careful consideration

深邃 shēnsuì ① deep ② profound；abstruse；recondite

深透 shēntòu deep and thorough

深恶痛绝 shēnwù-tòngjué hate bitterly；detest；abhor

深信 shēnxìn firmly believe；be fully convinced：～不疑 believe beyond all doubt

深夜 shēnyè late at night；at late hours；late into the night；at dead of night；in the small hours of the morning

深渊 shēnyuān abyss：苦难的～ abyss of misery

深远 shēnyuǎn far-reaching；pro-

found：～的意义 profound significance. ～的影响 far-reaching influence

深造 shēnzào pursue advanced studies; take up advanced studies or further training：出国～ go abroad for further studies

深挚 shēnzhì deep and sincere

深重 shēnzhòng very grave; extremely serious

申 shēn〈动〉state; express; explain：重～前令 reiterate the previous order

申报 shēnbào ① report (to a higher body) ② declare sth. (to the customs)：～单 declaration form. ～纳税 make tax declaration

申辩 shēnbiàn defend oneself; justify oneself; argue

申明 shēnmíng declare; state; set forth; avow：～理由 state (set forth) one's reasons

申请 shēnqǐng apply (for, to)：～书 (written) application. ～注册 application for registration. ～离婚 petition for a divorce

申述 shēnshù state (explain) in detail; expound：～来意 explain the purpose of one's visit

申诉 shēnsù ① appeal (to higher authorities) ② petition [法]; complain; declaration：～人 petitioner; declarant

申冤 shēnyuān ① redress an injustice ② appeal for redress of a wrong

呻 shēn

呻吟 shēnyín groan; moan：无病～ moan and groan without being ill; make a fuss about nothing

伸 shēn〈动〉stretch; extend; spread：～懒腰 stretch oneself

伸开 shēnkāi stretch out

伸手 shēnshǒu ① stretch out one's hand; reach out：～去拿报纸 reach (out) for the newspaper ② ask for help, etc.：～派 those who hold out their hands (for favours); self-seeker

伸缩 shēnsuō ① stretch out and draw back; expand and contract ② flexible; elastic; adjustable：～条款 escalator clauses

伸展 shēnzhǎn spread; stretch; extend：～计划 outreach programme

伸张 shēnzhāng uphold; promote; enhance：～正义 uphold justice

绅 shēn〈名〉gentry

绅耆 shēnqí gentry and elders

绅商 shēnshāng gentry-merchants

绅士 shēnshì gentleman; gentry

身 shēn〈名〉① body：转～ turn round ② life：以～殉职 die a martyr at one's post ③ one's moral character and conduct：修～ cultivate one's mind ④〈副〉personally; oneself：～体力行 set an example by personally taking part

身败名裂 shēnbài-míngliè bring disgrace upon oneself and ruin one's reputation; end up in

shame and ruin; be utterly ruined; be thoroughly discredited

身边 shēnbiān ① at (by) one's side ② (have sth.) on one; with one

身材 shēncái figure; stature; build: ～苗条 have a slender (slim) figure. ～魁梧 be powerfully built; strongly-built

身段 shēnduàn ① (woman's) figure; shape: 她～优美。She's got a shape. ② (dancer's) posture

身分 shēnfen ① position; status; capacity; identity: ～不明。Identity is unclear. ～证 identity card; ID card. 以私人～ in a private capacity. ② dignity: 有失～ be beneath one's dignity

身高 shēngāo height (of a person)

身价 shēnjià social status: 抬高～ raise one's social status

身教 shēnjiào teach others by one's own example: ～重于言教。Example (practice) is better than precept.

身躯 shēnqū body; stature

身上 shēnshang ① on one's body ② on; about: 我～没有零钱。I have no change on me.

身世 shēnshì one's life experience; one's lot

身手 shēnshǒu skill; talent

身体 shēntǐ ① body: ～上的伤害 infliction of body ② health: ～好(坏) be in good (bad) health

身体力行 shēntǐ-lìxíng earnestly practise what one advocates; practise what one preaches

身心 shēnxīn body and mind: ～健康 sound in body and mind; physical and mental health. ～愉快 be in good spirits; be in a cheerful mood

身子 shēnzi ① body ② pregnancy

shén

神 shén〈名〉① god; deity; divinity ② mind; spirit: 凝～ focus one's attention ③ expression; look: ～情庄重地 look gravely at ④〈形〉supernatural; divine; magical: ～效 miraculous effect

神采 shéncǎi look; expression: ～奕奕 with a radiant look; in fine fettle; be radiant with health and vigour

神出鬼没 shénchū-guǐmò disappear as suddenly as one appears; move about mysteriously; come and go like a shadow

神汉 shénhàn sorcerer

神乎其神 shénhū-qíshén miraculous; wonderful; unimaginable: 他们把原子弹看得～。They looked upon the atom bomb as something miraculous.

神化 shénhuà deify

神话 shénhuà fairy tale; myth; mythology

神魂 shénhún state of mind; mind: ～不定 be deeply perturbed; be on tenterhook

神交 shénjiāo ① friends with mutual understanding and admiration ② friendship grown out of mutual admiration without the

friends ever having met
神经 shénjīng nerve：～病 neuropathy；mental disorder. ～紧张 be nervous
神秘 shénmì mysterious；mystic：～化 make a mystery of. ～莫测 mysterious and hard to guess；enigmatically strange
神妙 shénmiào wonderful；marvellous；mystic
神奇 shénqí magical；miraculous；supernatural：～的效果 magical effect
神气 shénqì ① air；manner：～活现 give oneself airs；be very cocky；be as proud as a peacock ② vigorous；energetic；spirited：她看起来很～。She looks quite impressive. ③ arrogant；cocky：～十足 very arrogant
神情 shénqíng look；expression
神色 shénsè countenance；look：～慌张 look confused (flustered). ～自若 be unperturbed；look composed (unruffled)
神圣 shénshèng sacred：～不可侵犯 sacred and inviolable
神似 shénsì be alike in spirit；be an excellent likeness
神速 shénsù marvellously quick；with amazing speed
神态 shéntài expression；manner；bearing；mien：～悠闲 look perfectly relaxed
神通广大 shéntōng-guǎngdà be infinitely (very) resourceful；have remarkable ability
神往 shénwǎng be carried away；be rapt
神威 shénwēi martial prowess
神仙 shénxiān supernatural being；celestial being；immortal
神学 shénxué theology
神韵 shényùn romantic charm (in literature and art)；artistic appeal：油画画面呈现的～ texture of an oil painting
神志 shénzhì senses；consciousness；mind：～清醒 be fully conscious；be sober-minded；in full control of one's senses

甚 shén

另见 shèn
甚么 shénme 见"什么"

什 shén

什么 shénme ①[表示疑问、单用、问事物]这是～？What is this? ②[用在名词前面，问人或事物]她说～？What did she say? ③[虚指，表示不肯定的事物]好像出了～事？It seems something is amiss. ④[用在"也"或"都"前面，表示所指范围之内没有例外]她～也没说。She didn't say anything. ⑤[两个"什么"前后照应，表示由前者决定后者]有～就说～。Just say what's on your mind. ⑥[表示惊讶或不满]～！没有钱？What! No money?

shěn

审 shěn

① 〈形〉careful：～察 careful observation 〈动〉② examine；go over：～稿 go over a manuscript or draft ③ try；interrogate：～案 try a case

审查 shěnchá ① examine；investigate；check：～进口项目 evaluating imported projects ② review

审订 shěndìng examine and revise：～教材 revise teaching material

审定 shěndìng examine and approve

审改 shěngǎi examine and revise (a manuscript)；revise

审核 shěnhé examine and verify；check：～预算 examine and approve budget

审计 shěnjì audit；fiscal investigation：～员 auditor

审校 shěnjiào ① check and revise ② reviser

审理 shěnlǐ try；hear：～经济案件 try (hear) economic cases

审美 shěnměi aesthetic：～能力 aesthetic judgement. ～文化 aesthetic culture

审判 shěnpàn adjudicate；bring to trial；judge；try：～委员会 adjudication committee. ～员及人民陪审员合议庭 collegiate panel (bench) of judges and people's assessors

审批 shěnpī examine and approve；examine and give instructions

审评 shěnpíng examine and appraise

审慎 shěnshèn cautious；careful；circumspect；prudent：～考虑问题 consider a question carefully

审视 shěnshì scrutinize

审问 shěnwèn try；interrogate；question

审讯 shěnxùn try；interrogate；hearing

审议 shěnyì consider；deliberate；discuss

审阅 shěnyuè check；examine

婶

shěn〈名〉wife of father's younger brother；aunt

shèn

慎

shèn〈形〉careful；cautious：～重考虑 prudent (careful) consideration

慎重 shènzhòng careful；cautious；prudent；discreet：～处理 handle with great care

甚

shèn〈副〉① very：～佳 very good ② more than：她的病情，日～一日。Her condition got worse and worse.

另见 shén

甚而(至) shèn'ér(zhì) ① even：这一点对物理学～更适用。This applies even more to physics. ② go so far as to；go to the length of：他～说谎。He went so far as to tell lies.

甚嚣尘上 shènxiāochénshàng The dust and din of… fill the air.；arouse a public clamour；make a lot of noise；A great clamour has risen around.

肾

shèn〈名〉kidney

渗

shèn〈动〉ooze；seep：血～出来了。Blood oozed out.

渗出 shènchū leak out；ooze；

seep
渗漏 shènlòu leakage
渗入 shènrù permeate; seep into: ～地下 seep into the ground
渗透 shèntòu ① permeate; seep; soak ② infiltrate; penetrate: 经济～ economic infiltration

shēng

声 shēng〈名〉① sound; voice; noise: 脚步～ the sound of footsteps ② tone: 四～ the four tones of Chinese character ③ reputation: ～誉扫地 discredit ④〈动〉make a sound: 不～不响 not utter a word; keep quiet
声辩 shēngbiàn argue; justify oneself; explain away
声称 shēngchēng claim; assert; declare; profess; allege: ～被强奸(欺诈) allegation of rape (fraud)
声调 shēngdiào ① tune; tone; note: ～低沉 in a low and sad voice ② the note of Chinese character
声东击西 shēngdōng-jīxī make a feint in the east but attack in the west; pretend to attack the east while attacking the west; divert the attention of the enemy from a particular point
声名 shēngmíng reputation; fame: ～狼藉的 discredited; notorious; unsavoury
声明 shēngmíng declare; announce; state
声色 shēngsè voice and countenance: ～俱厉 (speak) in a severe tone and with a severe look on one's face; stern in voice and countenance; fulminate
声势 shēngshì momentum; impetuous force: ～浩大 spectacular; awe-inspiring; grand. 虚张～ make a show of strength; bluff and bluster
声嘶力竭 shēngsīlìjié shout oneself hoarse; shout at the top of one's voice
声讨 shēngtǎo denounce; condemn
声望 shēngwàng popularity; prestige: ～很高 enjoy great prestige
声响 shēngxiǎng sound; noise
声音 shēngyīn voice; sound
声誉 shēngyù reputation; fame; renown; prestige: ～卓著 enjoy a very high reputation
声援 shēngyuán express support for
声乐 shēngyuè vocal music
声张 shēngzhāng make known; make public; disclose

生 shēng〈动〉① give birth to (a child); bear: 她昨晚～了一个男孩。She gave birth to a boy last night. ② grow: ～根 take (strike) root ③ light (a fire) ④ get; have: ～冻疮 get chilblains〈形〉⑤ living: ～物 living things ⑥ green; unripe: ～苹果 a green apple ⑦ raw: ～肉 raw meat ⑧ crude; unprocessed; unrefined: ～铁 pig iron ⑨ strange; unfamiliar: ～词 new word〈名〉⑩ life; livelihood：～命哲学 philosophy of life. 谋～ earn one's livelihood ⑪ pupil；student

生搬硬套 shēngbān-yìngtào apply mechanically；copy mechanically in disregard of specific conditions；mimic rigidly

生变 shēngbiàn trouble arises

生病 shēngbìng fall ill；get sick

生财 shēngcái develop financial resources；make money

生产 shēngchǎn ① produce；production；manufacture：～经营 production management；operation. ～线 production line. ～责任制 system of responsibility in production ② give birth (to a child)

生成 shēngchéng ① come or bring into being；generate；produce ② be born with；be gifted with

生存 shēngcún live；exist：～竞争 struggle for existence

生动 shēngdòng lively；vivid：～活泼 vivid and vigorous；lively

生根 shēnggēn take root；strike root

生活 shēnghuó ① life：日常～ daily life. ～作风 life style；behaviour ② livelihood：～补助 living subsidies ③ live：他们～幸福。They live a happy life.

生机 shēngjī ① lease of life ② life；vitality

生计 shēngjì means of livelihood；livelihood

生理 shēnglǐ physiology：～缺陷 physiological defect (deficiency). ～需要 physiological requirements

生力军 shēnglìjūn ① fresh troops (combatants) ② new young members of an organization；new force；fresh activists

生路 shēnglù way out；way to survive

生米煮成熟饭 shēngmǐ zhǔchéng shúfàn The rice is already cooked — what is done can't be undone.；It is no use crying over spilt milk.

生命 shēngmìng life

生僻 shēngpì (of words，expressions，etc.) uncommon；rare

生平 shēngpíng all one's life

生气 shēngqì ① be angry (with，at)；be offended (with，for，at) ② life；vigour；vitality：～勃勃 full of vitality

生前 shēngqián before one's death；during (in) one's lifetime

生手 shēngshǒu sb. new to a job；new (green) hand；beginner；novice

生疏 shēngshū ① be unfamiliar (with) ② out of practice；rusty：我的德语有点～了。My German is a bit rusty.

生死 shēngsǐ life and death：～攸关 a matter of life and death

生态 shēngtài ecology：～爆炸 ecological explosion. ～环境 ecological environment. ～效益 ecological benefits

生物 shēngwù living things；living beings；organisms

生效 shēngxiào come (go) into force，become (take) effect

生涯 shēngyá career；profession：

政治～ political career

生意 shēngyì business; trade: ～兴隆(清淡)。Business is brisk (slack). 做～ do business. 拉～ canvass trade (for)

生硬 shēngyìng harsh; stiff; rigid: 态度～ be stiff (harsh) in manner

生育 shēngyù give birth to; bear: ～观念 ideas about producing offspring. 不能～ sterile. 以妇女为中心的～健康 women-centered reproductive health

生长 shēngzhǎng ① grow ② grow up; be brought up

生殖 shēngzhí reproduction: ～崇拜文化 culture based on genital worship. ～系统 reproductive system

甥

shēng 〈名〉 sister's son; nephew

甥女 shēngnǚ sister's daughter; niece

升

shēng 〈动〉 ① go up; rise; hoist: 太阳～起。The sun is rising. ② promote; raise: 被提～为大副 be promoted (to be or to the rank of) first mate 〈名〉 ③ litre: 2～啤酒 two litres of beer ④ *sheng*, a unit of dry measure for grain (=1 litre)

升班 shēngbān go up (one grade in school)

升调 shēngdiào ① rising tone ② be transferred to a higher post

升格 shēnggé promote; upgrade: 将外交关系～为大使级 upgrade diplomatic relations to ambassadorial level

升华 shēnghuá ① sublimation ② raising of things to a higher level; distillation; sublimation

升级 shēngjí ① move students up to higher grades; get one's promotion; be promoted (to a higher class) ② escalate

升降 shēngjiàng go up and down

升旗 shēngqí hoist a flag: ～典礼 flag raising ceremony; ceremony of raising (hoisting) the flag

升学 shēngxué go to a school of a higher grade; enter a higher school; be admitted (promoted) to a higher school: ～率 proportion of students entering schools of a higher grade. ～考试 promotion examination

升值 shēngzhí ① revalue ② appreciate

牲

shēng

牲畜 shēngchù domestic animal; [总称] livestock

牲口 shēngkou draught animal

shéng

绳

shéng ①〈名〉rope; cord; string: ～子 rope; cord; string ②〈动〉restrict; restrain: 要～之以法 must be dealt with according to law

shěng

省

shěng ①〈名〉province: ～委 provincial Party committee〈动〉

② save；economize：能～就～ economize wherever possible ③ leave out；omit：～一道工序 eliminate one step from the process

另见 xǐng

省吃俭用 shěngchī-jiǎnyòng live frugally；practise austerity

省会(城) shěnghuì (chéng) provincial capital

省力 shěnglì ① save effort (labour)；labour-saving ② simple；easy

省略 shěnglüè omit；leave out：这段可以～。This paragraph can be left out.

省钱 shěngqián save money；be economical

省时 shěngshí save time；time-saving

省事 shěngshì save trouble；simplify matters

省心 shěngxīn save worry

省长 shěngzhǎng governor (of a province)

shèng

盛 shèng〈形〉① great；grand；magnificent：～举 a grand occasion (event) ② prosperous；flourishing：繁荣昌～的景象 a flourishing and invigorating scene ③ vigorous；energetic：火势很～。The fire is raging. ④ popular；common：～传 be widely known ⑤ abundant；plentiful：～意 great kindness ⑥〈副〉deeply；greatly：～赞 praise profusely；acclaim

另见 chéng

盛产 shèngchǎn abound in；teem with；be rich in：这河～鱼蟹。The river teems with fish and crabs.

盛大 shèngdà grand；spectacular；magnificent：～欢迎 a rousing welcome

盛典 shèngdiǎn grand ceremony

盛会 shènghuì grand meeting；distinguished (impressive) gathering；great occasion；gala

盛极一时 shèngjíyīshí be in fashion (vogue) for a time；prevail for a time

盛开 shèngkāi [花] be in full bloom

盛况 shèngkuàng grand occasion；spectacular event；pomp：～空前 exceptionally grand occasion

盛名 shèngmíng great fame；great (high) reputation：～之下，其实难副。Fail to live up to a high reputation.；One's fame is greater than one deserves.；It is hard to live up to a great reputation.

盛怒 shèngnù be very angry；be in a rage

盛气凌人 shèngqì-língrén arrogant；overbearing；domineering

盛情 shèngqíng great kindness；boundless (warm) hospitality：～难却。Your great kindness makes me impossible to decline.；It would be ungracious not to accept your invitation.

盛夏 shèngxià (at) the height of summer；midsummer

盛行 shèngxíng be in vogue (fashion); prevail

盛宴 shèngyàn grand banquet; gorgeous dinner

盛誉 shèngyù high reputation; great fame

盛赞 shèngzàn highly praise; speak of sb. in glowing terms

盛装 shèngzhuāng splendid dress (attire); one's Sunday best; rich dress:她穿着～赴会。She went to the party in her Sunday best. ～打扮 be rigged out in one's best

剩 shèng ①〈形〉remnant; surplus:～货 surplus goods ②〈动〉remain; be left (over)

剩下 shèngxià remain; be left (over)

剩余 shèngyú remainder; surplus:～价值[经] surplus value. ～购买力 discretionary purchasing power

胜 shèng ①〈名〉victory; success; triumph:得～ win (victory)〈动〉② win; beat; defeat:战～自然 conquer nature ③ be superior to; surpass:聊～于无 better than nothing ④〈形〉superb; wonderful; lovely

胜败 shèngbài victory or defeat; success or failure; win or lose:～乃兵家常事。Defeats or victories are ordinary things to a general.

胜地 shèngdì scenic spot; resort:避暑～ summer resort

胜迹 shèngjì famous historical site; famous relic

胜景 shèngjǐng beautiful scenery; fine scenes

胜利 shènglì victory; triumph

胜任 shèngrèn be competent; be qualified; be equal to; be up to:～工作 be fully equal to one's work

胜诉 shèngsù win a case; carry the cause; recover:～人 winner of a lawsuit. ～债权人 judgement creditor

圣 shèng ①〈名〉saint; sage ②〈形〉sacred; holy

圣诞 shèngdàn the birthday of Jesus Christ:～节 Christmas Day. ～老人 Santa Claus

圣地 shèngdì ①[宗] the Holy Land ② sacred place

圣经 shèngjīng the Bible

圣人 shèngrén saint; sage

圣旨 shèngzhǐ imperial edict

shī

湿 shī〈形〉wet; damp; moist; humid:～衣服 wet clothes

湿壁画 shībìhuà fresco painting

湿度 shīdù humidity

湿淋淋 shīlínlín dripping (soaking) wet; drenched

湿润 shīrùn moist

湿透 shītòu wet through; dripping wet:浑身～ be wet through

湿租赁(约) shīzūlìn (yuē) wet leasing

诗 shī〈名〉poem; poetry; verse:～朗诵 recitation of poems; poetry readings

诗词歌赋 shīcí-gēfù verses，ditties;odes and songs (the four forms of poetry)
诗赋 shīfù *shi fu* (poetry and descriptive prose)；poetry and essay；prose-poems
诗歌 shīgē poems and songs；poetry
诗节 shījié stanza
诗经 shījīng *The Book of Songs*
诗句 shījù verse；line
诗剧 shījù drama in verse；poetic drama
诗情画意 shīqíng-huàyì implications of poetic and picturesque sentiments；poetic and artistic conception；idyllic
诗人 shīrén poet：女～ poetess
诗兴 shīxìng poetic inspiration (mood)：～大发 full of poetry
诗意 shīyì poetic flavour(quality);poetic：富有～ very poetic
诗韵 shīyùn ① rhyme (in poetry) ② rhyming dictionary

师

shī〈名〉① teacher；master；tutor：尊～ respect teaches ②［军］division：～部 division headquarters ③ army；troops：正义之～ an army fighting for a just cause
师范 shīfàn teacher-training；pedagogical：～教育 normal (teacher) education. ～专科学校 normal training college. ～大学 teachers university；nomal university
师傅 shīfu master worker；master
师生 shīshēng teacher and student
师徒 shītú apprentice and master
师长 shīzhǎng ①［尊称］teacher ② commander of a division
师资 shīzī qualified teachers；teachers；teaching personnel：～训练班 teachers training class

狮

shī〈名〉lion
狮子 shīzi lion：～舞 lion dance

失

shī〈动〉① lose：～去平衡 lose one's balance ② miss；let slip：坐～良机 lose a good chance ③ fail to achieve one's end：大～所望 be greatly disappointed ④ deviate from the normal：～色 turn pale ⑤ break (a promise)；go back on (one's word)：～信于人 break faith with others ⑥〈名〉mistake；defect：唯恐有～ fear that there may be some mischap
失败 shībài ① failure；defeat：～是成功之母。Failure is the mother of success. ② fail；be defeated
失策 shīcè ① miscalculate；misjudge ② unadvisable；unwise；inexpedient
失常 shīcháng abnormal；odd：精神～ be mentally abnormal；be distraught
失宠 shīchǒng fall into disfavour；be out of favour；lose favour：～于某人 be out of favour with sb.
失传 shīchuán fail to be handed down from past generations；be lost：～的艺术 a lost art
失措 shīcuò lose one's head；be at a loss as to what to do：仓皇～ unable to stay collected；scared

out of one's wits

失当 shīdàng inappropriate; improper: 处理～ be not properly handled

失和 shīhé fail to keep on good terms; become estranged

失火 shīhuǒ catch fire; be on fire

失节 shījié ① forfeit one's integrity; be disloyal ② lose one's chastity

失控 shīkòng out of control; runaway: ～的通货膨胀 runaway inflation

失口 shīkǒu slip of the tongue

失礼 shīlǐ breach of proprieties; impoliteness; discourtesy

失利 shīlì suffer a setback (defeat); lose ground

失恋 shīliàn disappointed in a love affair; suffer from unrequited love

失落 shīluò lose; drop: ～感 sense of loss

失眠 shīmián (suffer from) insomnia; have a sleepless night

失明 shīmíng lose one's sight; become (go) blind: 双目～ beome blind in both eyes

失散 shīsàn ① be scattered and lost; ② be separated from and lose touch with each other

失声 shīshēng ① ejaculate (involuntarily); burst out ② lose one's voice

失实 shīshí inconsistent with the facts; untrue; false; unfounded: 报道～。The report proved untrue.

失事 shīshì ① (meet with an) accident ② wreck

失手 shīshǒu have a slip of the hand; drop accidentally; lose hold (of): 她～打破了一只碗。She lost hold of a bowl and broke it.

失算 shīsuàn miscalculate; make a wrong move

失调 shītiáo imbalance; dislocation; unbalanced: 供求～ imbalance in supply and demand. 雨水～ abnormal rain

失物 shīwù lost thing; lost article: ～招领[揭示语] Found

失误 shīwù error; mistake; [打球、下棋等] fault

失效 shīxiào ① losing effect; null and void; be no longer effective; be invalid ② [药]lose efficacy

失信 shīxìn break one's word (promise); go back on one's word; bad faith; breach of faith: ～于人 break faith with others

失学 shīxué be unable to go to school; have to discontinue one's studies; be deprived of education

失言 shīyán make an indiscreet remark; a slip of the tongue (lip); say sth. indiscreet; make a gaffe

失业 shīyè be unemployed; lose one's job; be out of work: ～保险基金 unemployment insurance funds. ～率 unemployment rate. ～者 the unemployed

失意 shīyì be frustrated (in an attempt, etc.); be disappointed;

be unlucky

失约 shīyuē fail to keep an appointment

失真 shīzhēn ① (of voice, images, etc.) lack fidelity; not be true to the original ② distortion: 新闻～ false reports of news

失之东隅,收之桑榆 shī zhī dōngyù, shōu zhī sāngyú lose at sunrise and gain at sunset — make up on the roundabouts what you lose on the swings; lose in the morning and gain in the evening; lose at the start and win at the finish; lose in hake but gain in herring

失职 shīzhí breach of duty; neglect of duty; delinquency; official misconduct: ～罪 offence of misconduct in office

失主 shīzhǔ owner of a lost article

失踪 shīzōng ① missing; disappear ② [法] absence

失足 shīzú ① lose (slip, miss) one's footing ② take a wrong (false) step in life: ～青年 juvenile delinquents. 一～成千古恨。A single slip can cause a lasting sorrow.; One false step brings everlasting grief.

施

shī 〈动〉 ① carry out; execute: 无所～其技 no chance (for sb.) to play his tricks ② give; bestow; hand out; grant: ～恩 bestow favour ③ exert; exercise: ～压力 exert pressure ④ use; apply: ～肥 apply manure (fertilizer); fertilize

施工 shīgōng engage in construction; be under construction: ～单位 unit in charge of construction. ～人员 constructors; builders

施加 shījiā exert; exercise; bring to bear on: ～压力 exert pressure on sb.; apply pressures. ～影响 exercise one's influence over

施舍 shīshě give alms; give in charity; dole out

施行 shīxíng carry out; put in force; carry (go) into effect; implement; enforce: ～细则 rules for implementation. 公布～ come into force upon promulgation

施展 shīzhǎn give full (free) play (to); put to good use; display: ～才华 give full play to one's talent; display one's ability

施政 shīzhèng administration: ～方针 administrative policies

尸

shī 〈名〉 dead body; corpse; remains

尸骨 shīgǔ bones of the dead; skeleton

尸体 shītǐ dead body; corpse

尸位素餐 shīwèisùcān get pay without doing any work; occupy a position without doing any work; feed at the public trough; sinecure

虱

shī 〈名〉 louse

虱子 shīzi louse

shí

实

shí 〈形〉 ① solid: ～心球 a

solid ball ② true; real; honest: 情况属～ It's true.〈名〉③ fact; reality: 失～ inconsistent with the facts ④ seed; fruit: 结出果～ bear fruit

实报实销 shíbào-shíxiāo be reimbursed for what one spends (one's actual expenses); pay for all spending

实词 shící [语] notional word

实地 shídì on the spot: ～调查 on-the-spot investigation; first-hand investigation of conditions; field investigation

实干 shígàn do solid work: ～家 man of action; workhorse. ～精神 workhorse spirit; spirit of getting on with the job

实话 shíhuà truth: 说～ tell the truth

实惠 shíhuì material benefit; real benefit

实绩 shíjì actual achievements

实际 shíjì real; actual; practical: ～工资 real wages. ～偿还能力 actual capacity to repay

实价 shíjià net price; actual price

实践 shíjiàn practice: ～是检验真理的唯一标准。Practice is the sole criterion for testing truth.

实况 shíkuàng ① actual happenings ② live: ～转播 [广播] live (radio) broadcast; [电视] live telecast. ～播讲员 [体] play-by-announcer

实据 shíjù substantial evidence; substantial proof

实力 shílì strength; power: ～派 power group. ～政策 strong-arm policy

实例 shílì living example; example

实情 shíqíng fact; true state of affairs

实权 shíquán (real) power; authority

实施 shíshī put into practice; carry out; enforce: ～条例 enforcement regulations. 付诸～ put into effect; carry out

实事求是 shíshì-qiúshì seek truth from facts; get down to facts: ～的批评 criticism based on facts

实体 shítǐ ① substantial body; substance ② [法] entity: 经济～ economic entity

实物 shíwù ① object: ～教学 object lesson ② material object; in kind: ～税 tax paid in kind

实习 shíxí practice; probation; fieldwork; field trip: 去工厂～ go on a field trip to a factory. 进行～教学 do practice teaching

实现 shíxiàn realize; bring about; achieve; materialize: 他的梦想～了。His dream has come true.

实效 shíxiào actual effect; substantial (practical) results

实行 shíxíng carry out; practise; follow; put into practice (effect); implement: ～教育改革 carry out reforms in education

实验 shíyàn test; experiment: ～室 laboratory; lab. 做～ make a test; do an experiment

实业 shíyè industry; industry and commerce: ～家 industrialist

实用 shíyòng practical；pragmatic；functional：～主义 pragmatism

实在 shízài ① real；true ② really；indeed；in fact；as a matter of fact：她～不懂什么。As a matter of fact she knows nothing.

实质 shízhì essence；substance

实足 shízú full；solid：～年龄 calendar age；exact gage. ～100 公斤 a full hundred kg.

识 shí ①〈动〉know：～时务 know the trend of the times ②〈名〉knowledge：常～ general knowledge

识别 shíbié distinguish；discriminate；discern：～真伪 distinguish truth from falsehood

识大体 shídàtǐ have the overall interest at heart；take the interest of the whole into consideration

识货 shíhuò be able to tell good from bad；appreciate the true；worth of sb. or sth. 's quality；know what's what：～的购买者 discriminating buyer

识破 shípò see through；penetrate；uncover：～花招 see through a trick

识时务者为俊杰 shí shíwùzhě wéijùnjié He is wise who understands the times.；Whosoever understands the times is a great man.；Those who suit their actions to the times are wise.；Time-servers are clever.

识相 shíxiàng sensible；tactful：不～ be insensible

识字 shízì can read；be literate：～班 literacy class

十 shí〈数〉ten

十恶不赦 shí'è-bùshè guilty beyond forgiveness；unpardonable crime；guilty of unpardonable evil；unpardonably wicked：～的罪恶 heinous crime

十进币制 shíjìnbìzhì decimal currency system

十分 shífēn ① very；very much；quite ② entirely；completely；perfectly

十拿九稳 shíná-jiǔwěn be quite certain of；as good as assured；quite sure (of)；practically certain (of)；(the chances are) ten to one：他～会成功。Ten to one he will succeed.

十年树木，百年树人 shínián shùmù，bǎinián shùrén It takes ten years to grow a tree and a century to bring up a generation of good men — a long-term plan.；It takes ten years to grow trees，but a hundred to rear people.

十全十美 shíquán-shíměi flawless and perfect；perfect；impeccable

十之八九 shízhībājiǔ ten to one；most likely：～她会同意。Most likely she will agree.

十字架 shízìjià cross

十字路口 shízì-lùkǒu (at the) crossroads

十足 shízú ① hundred per cent；out-and-out；sheer；to the hilt；downright：～劲头 be full of pep；be all energy ②［金、银］pure

石 shí〈名〉stone; rock
石碑 shíbēi stone tablet; stele
石沉大海 shíchén-dàhǎi Like a stone dropped (sunk) into the sea—disappear for ever; disappear like a pebble thrown into the sea; make no response
石雕 shídiāo stone carving:～佛像 statue of Buddha
石膏 shígāo gypsum; [熟的] plaster stone:～雕像 gypsography. ～像 plaster figure (statue)
石灰 shíhuī lime:熟～ slaked lime. 生～ quick lime
石刻 shíkè ① carved stone ② stone sculpture; stone inscriptions
石窟 shíkū rock cave; grotto:～画 cave painting. ～造像 sculpture
石器 shíqì stone implement; stoneware:～时代 the Stone Age
石头 shítou stone; rock
石英 shíyīng quartz:～钟 quartz clock
石油 shíyóu petroleum; oil:～开采权 oil concession. ～化工产品 petrochemicals. ～输出国组织 Organization of Petroleum Exporting Countries (OPEC)

拾 shí ①〈动〉pick up; collect:～起某人的帽子 pick up sb.'s hat ②〈数〉ten
拾掇 shíduo ① put in order; tidy up ② repair; fix
拾荒 shíhuāng collect rags (scraps); scavenge:～者 scavenger
拾金不昧 shíjīnbùmèi not pocket the money one picks up; return money found
拾遗 shíyí ① appropriate lost property ② make good omissions:～补缺 pick up the neglected and supply the deficient; make good omissions and deficiencies

时 shí〈名〉① time; times; days:～代潮流 the trend of the times ② 按～上班 get to work on time ③ hour:报～ announce the hour ④ season:四～ the four seasons ⑤ opportunity; chance:失～ miss the chance; lose the opportunity ⑥ tense:现在～ present tense ⑦〈形〉current; present:～事 current affairs ⑧〈副〉often; occasionally:～有出现 occur now and then
时差 shíchā ① time diference:适应～ adjust to time zone ② [天] equation of time
时代 shídài age; period; epoch; times:～潮流 current (trend) of the times; tendency of the day
时光 shíguāng ① time ② times; years; days
时过境迁 shíguò-jìngqiān change with the passage of time; Circumstances alter cases.; Times have changed.
时候 shíhou (the duration of) time; (a point in) time; moment
时机 shíjī opportunity; chance;

occasion：等待～ wait one's time (chance, opportunity)

时价 shíjià currnet price; market prices

时间 shíjiān time

时局 shíjú current political situation

时令 shílìng ① season ② seasonal disease

时髦 shímáo fashionable; stylish; in vogue：～哲学 philosophical fashion; fashionable philosophy. 赶～ follow the fashion

时期 shíqī period; stage：～生育状况 period fertility

时尚 shíshàng fashion; fad

时势 shíshì current situation; the way things are going：～造英雄。The times produce their heroes.

时事 shíshì current events (affairs); current news：～评述 comment on current affairs

时限 shíxiàn time limit

时效 shíxiào [法] prescription; limitation

时针 shízhēn ① hands of a clock or watch ② hour hand (of a clock or watch)

时装 shízhuāng fashionable clothes：～表演 fashion show. ～店 fashion shop. ～设计师 fashion designer

食

shí ①〈动〉eat：不劳动者，不得～。He who does not work, shall not eat either.〈名〉② food：主～ staple food ③ feed：鸡～ chicken feed

食道 shídào esophagus; gullet：～癌 cancer of the esophagus

食疗 shíliáo food therapy

食品 shípǐn food; foodstuff; provisions：～商店 provision store; food store

食堂 shítáng dining room; mess hall; canteen：吃～ have one's meals in the mess

食言 shíyán break one's word (promise); go back on one's word; swallow one's word

食用 shíyòng ① used for food ② edible

食欲 shíyù appetile：～不振 have a poor appetite. 促进～ stimulate the appetite; be appetizing

食指 shízhǐ forefinger; index finger

蚀

shí〈动〉① lose：亏～ lose (money) in business ② erode：酸腐～金属。Acid erodes metal. ③〈名〉[日、月]eclipse：日～ solar eclipse

蚀本 shíběn lose one's capital; lose：～出售 sell sth. at a loss. ～生意 a business running at a loss; a losing business

shǐ

史

shǐ〈名〉history：古代～ ancient history

史册 shǐcè annals; history：载入～ go down in the annals of; go down in history

史馆 shǐguǎn historiographers' office in ancient China

史话 shǐhuà stories about historical events

史料 shǐliào historical materials

(data)

史前 shǐqián prehistoric：～人 preman. ～珍贵遗物 precious relics of prehistoric times

史诗 shǐshī epic；heroic poem

史实 shǐshí historical fact

史无前例 shǐwú-qiánlì unprecedented；without precedent in history；unheard of

史学 shǐxué historical studies；historiography；historical science；science of history：～家 historian；historiographer. ～流派 schools in historiography

使 shǐ〈动〉① tell sb. to do sth.；send：～人去打听消息 send sb. to make inquiries ② use；employ；apply：～用词典 use a dictionary ③ make；cause；enable：～人痛心 make people grieve ④〈名〉messenger；envoy：特～ special envoy ⑤〈连〉if；supposing：纵～ even if；even though

使不得 shǐbude ① can't be used ② won't do：他们这样搞下去恐怕～。It probably won't do if they go on like that.

使出 shǐchū exert；use：～全副本领 use all one's resources

使得 shǐde ① can be used ② will do；feasible ③ make；cause

使馆 shǐguǎn embassy

使节 shǐjié diplomatic envoy；envoy

使劲 shǐjìn make efforts；exert all one's strength；strain (at)

使命 shǐmìng mission

使用 shǐyòng ① use；employ：～价值 use value ② with；by means of

使者 shǐzhě messenger；emissary；envoy

驶 shǐ〈动〉① drive；sail：～入港口 sail into the harbour ② speed：疾～而过 speed by；fly past

矢 shǐ ①〈名〉arrow：～如雨下 shower of arrows ②〈动〉swear；vow：～志不移 vow to adhere to one's chosen course

矢口否认 shǐkǒufǒurèn flatly deny

始 shǐ〈动〉begin；start：认识从实践开～。Knowledge begins with practice.

始末 shǐmò beginning and end；the whole story

始业 shǐyè the beginning of the school year：秋季～。The school year begins in autumn.

始终 shǐzhōng from beginning to end；from start to finish；throughout；all along；all the way：～不渝 steadfast；unswerving. ～如一 consistent；constant

始祖 shǐzǔ first ancestor

shì

室 shì〈名〉room

室内 shìnèi indoor：～音乐会 chamber concert. ～游泳池 indoor swimming pool. ～装修 interior decoration

室外 shìwài outdoor：～活动 outdoor activities

市 shì〈名〉① market：～场波动 market fluctuations. ～场调节 regulation through the market. 上～ be on the market ② city；municipality：～中心 downtown；city centre ③ pertaining to the Chinese system of weights and measures：～尺 *chi*，a unit of length（＝1/3 metre）

市场 shìchǎng market：～不规范 Market still needs to be standardized. ～经济 market economy. ～繁荣 brisk market. 增强～观念 increase one's awareness concerning the market

市集 shìjí ① small town ② fair

市价 shìjià market prices；market value

市郊 shìjiāo suburbs；outskirts：在北京～ in the suburbs（on the outskirts）of Beijing

市井 shìjǐng market-place；town：～之言 subject of general conversation；town talk

市侩 shìkuài philistine；sordid merchant：～哲学 philistine philosophy

市面 shìmiàn market（conditions）；business：～繁荣（萧条）。The market is brisk（slack）.

市民 shìmín residents of a city；townspeople；townsfolk

市区 shìqū urban district；city proper

市容 shìróng appearance of a city：参观～ see the sights of the city；have a look around the city

市委 shìwěi municipal Party committee

市长 shìzhǎng mayor

市镇 shìzhèn（small）town；township

市政 shìzhèng municipal administration：～工程 municipal works（engineering）. ～建设 urban construction

柿 shì〈名〉persimmon

柿饼 shìbǐng dried persimmon

视 shì〈动〉① look at：凝～ look fixedly ② inspect；watch：巡～ go on an inspection tour ③ regard（as）：～如仇敌 look upon sb. as one's enemy

视察 shìchá inspect；visit；view：～工厂 inspect a factory

视而不见 shì'érbùjiàn ① look but fail to see ② shut one's eyes to；turn a blind eye to；ignore

视景 shìjǐng what comes into a driver's or a pilot's view as the vehicle or the craft proceeds

视觉 shìjué visual sense；sense of sight；vision

视力 shìlì eyesight；vision；sight：～好（差）have good（poor）eyesight

视若无睹 shìruòwúdǔ shut one's eyes to；take no notice of what one sees；ignore

视死如归 shìsǐrúguī meet one's death like a hero；face death calmly（with equanimity）；defy death

视听 shìtīng ① visible and audible parts of human life；seeing and hearing; what is seen and heard:混淆～ throw dust in people's eyes; confuse the public ② audio-visual:～教学 audio-visual teaching

视同儿戏 shìtóng'érxì treat (a serious matter) as child's play; regard sth. as laughing matter; trifle with

视线 shìxiàn visual line; line of vision; view:挡住～ obstruct the view

视野 shìyě visual field; field of vision

式 shì〈名〉① pattern; form:行为型～ behaviour pattern ② type; style:新～ new type ③ ceremony; ritual:闭幕～ closing ceremony ④ formula:分子～ molecular formula ⑤ mood; mode:陈述～ indicate mood

式样 shìyàng type; style; model; pattern:～美观 be beautiful in style; graceful-looking

试 shì〈动〉① try; test; experiment:～飞 test (trial) flight ② examine; test:口～ oral examination

试办 shìbàn run (an enterprise, etc.) as an experiment

试产 shìchǎn trial production

试车 shìchē trial run; test working

试穿 shìchuān try on (a coat, shoes, etc.); have a try-on

试点 shìdiǎn ① make experiments; launch a pilot project; experiment at selected points ② experimental unit:～班 experimental class. ～企业 enterprises under experiment; pilot enterprises

试读 shìdú study on a probationary basis

试购 shìgòu purchase on a trial basis; trial (sample) order

试管 shìguǎn test tube:～婴儿 test-tube baby

试航 shìháng trial run; test trip

试金石 shìjīnshí touchstone

试卷 shìjuàn examination paper; test paper:批改～ go over examination papers

试刊 shìkān trial publication

试论 shìlùn preliminary study of; tentative discussion on

试探 shìtàn probe; sound (feel) out; explore

试题 shìtí examination (test) questions:出～ set examination questions

试图 shìtú try; attempt; intend:～完成许多科研项目 attempt many scientific experiments

试析 shìxī tentative analysis

试销 shìxiāo trial sale:～商品 commodities for trial sale. ～零售店 trial-retailing stores

试行 shìxíng try out:～规则 tentative regulations. ～资产负债比例管理 managing the assets to liabilities ratio on a trial basis

试演 shìyǎn trial performance

试验 shìyàn test;try;experiment:～场 proving ground. ～田 experimental field

试样 shìyàng (test) sample

试映 shìyìng trial showing (of a

movie); preview

试用 shìyòng on probation; on trial:～本 trial edition. ～人员 probationer

试制 shìzhì trial-produce

拭 shì〈动〉wipe away; wipe

拭目以待 shìmùyǐdài look forward to the fulfilment of one's wish; wait and see; on the alert; watchful

拭去 shìqù wipe away; rub off

示 shì〈动〉show; notify; indicate; instruct:请出～票子。Show your ticket, please. 请～ ask for instructions

示范 shìfàn set an example; show (as an example); demonstrate:～表演 put on a demonstration. 科技～户 technological model household. ～教学 teach by demonstration. 起～作用 play an exemplary role

示威 shìwēi demonstrate:～游行 demonstration; parade

示意 shìyì sign; signal; hint:～她出去 motion to her to go out. ～图 sketch map. 以目～ give a hint with the eyes

示众 shìzhòng put before the public; publicly expose

士 shì〈名〉① scholar ② (commendable) person:勇～ brave fighter ③ non-commissioned officer:下～ corporal ④ a person trained in a centain field:护～ nurse

士兵 shìbīng rank-and-file soldiers; privates

士气 shìqì morale; fighting spirit:鼓舞～ boost morale. ～颓丧 flagging morale

仕 shì〈动〉be an official; fill an office:学而优则～。A good scholar will make an official.

仕女 shìnǚ [美] traditional Chinese painting of beautiful women

仕途 shìtú official career

恃 shì〈动〉rely on; depend on:有～无恐 be fearless because one has powerful backing

恃才傲物 shìcái-àowù be contemptuous of others on the strength of one's own ability; be conceited and contemptuous; overweening

恃强凌弱 shìqiáng-língruò bully the weak because one is backed by one's own strength; use one's strength to bully the weak

恃势凌人 shìshì-língrén trust to one's power and insult people

侍 shì〈动〉attend upon; wait upon, serve:～立 stand at sb.'s side in attendance

侍从 shìcóng attendants; retinue

侍候 shìhòu look after; serve; wait upon

侍女 shìnǚ maid; maidservant

世 shì〈名〉① life; lifetime:今～ this present life ② world; earth:举～闻名 well-known all over the world ③ generation:～～代代 generation after generation; from generation to

generation ④ age; era:当今之～at present; nowadays

世仇 shìchóu ① family feud ② vendetta

世传 shìchuán be handed down through generations:～秘方 secret recipe handed down through generations

世代 shìdài ① years; ages ② for generations; from generation to generation; generation after generation

世道 shìdào the manners and morals of the time

世风 shìfēng public morals

世故 shìgù the ways of the world; world wisdom:老于～的人 a worldly-wise man

世纪 shìjì century:～之交 at the turn of the century

世家 shìjiā old and well-known family; a family holding high positions for generations; aristocratic family

世交 shìjiāo friendship spanning two or more generations; old family friend

世界 shìjiè world:～观 world outlook. ～纪录 world record. ～贸易组织 World Trade Organization (WTO)

世面 shìmiàn world; life; society:见过～ have experienced life; have seen the world

世上无难事,只怕有心人 shìshàng wú nánshì, zhǐpà yǒu xīnrén Nothing in the world is difficult for one who sets his mind to it.

世事 shìshì affairs of the world; affairs of human life; mundane affairs

世俗 shìsú ① common customs ② worldly; secular; mundane

世态 shìtài the ways of the world:～炎凉 inconstancy of human relationships

世外桃源 shìwài-táoyuán a land of external peace far from the madding crowd; a place of taking refuge

世袭 shìxí hereditary:～制 the hereditary system

世系 shìxì genealogy; pedigree

事 shì〈名〉① affair; matter; thing; business:国家大～ affairs of state ② accident; trouble:交通～故 a traffic accident ③ job; work:找～ look for a job ④〈动〉be engaged in:无所～～ doing nothing

事半功倍 shìbàn-gōngbèi achieve (get) twice the result with half the effort; By doing half the work, one will get double the result

事倍功半 shìbèi-gōngbàn achieve (get) half the result with twice (double) the effort

事变 shìbiàn ① incident:七七～ the July 7 Incident of 1937 ② emergency; exigency:准备应付可能突发～ be prepared against all possible emergencies

事出有因 shìchū-yǒuyīn There is a reason for it.; There is good cause (reason) for…; There is no smoke without fire.

事典 shìdiǎn topical reference book:经济～ reference book on

economics

事端 shìduān disturbance; incident: 挑起～ provoke incidents. 制造～ create (make) disturbances

事故 shìgù accident; mishap; trouble: 飞机出了～。The plane met with an accident.

事过境迁 shìguò-jìngqiān When the matter (incident) is over, the circumstances will be different (change).; The events have passed and the times have changed

事后 shìhòu after the event; later on; afterwards: ～诸葛亮 be wise only after the event; hindsight

事迹 shìjì deed; achievement: 先进～ advanced deeds

事假 shìjià leave of absence (for personal affairs): 请一天～ ask for a day's leave of absence

事件 shìjiàn ① event; incident ② affair; matter: 重大～ affair of great importance

事例 shìlì case; example; instance

事前 shìqián in advance; beforehand; before the event: ～请示 ask for instructions in advance

事情 shìqing business; matter; affair; thing: ～真相 the facts of the case

事权 shìquán authority which controls the enterprises and undertakings power: 中央和地方～划分范围 division of power between the central and local governments

事实 shìshí fact: ～胜于雄辩。Facts speak louder than eloquence. 与～不符 not tally with the facts. ～俱在。The facts are all there.

事态 shìtài state of affairs; situation: ～严重。The situation is serious.

事务 shìwù ① general affairs ② routine; work; business: ～性商谈 negotiations on specific issues. ～员 general clerk; office clerk. ～性工作 routine work (duties)

事物 shìwù thing; object: ～都是一分为二的。Everything tends to divide into two.

事先 shìxiān in advance; beforehand

事项 shìxiàng item; matter

事业 shìyè enterprise; undertaking; cause: 公用～ public utilities. 教育～ educational undertaking. ～单位 undertakings; institutions. ～心 devotion to one's work; dedication; spirit of enterprise

事宜 shìyí (usu. used in official language) matters concerned; arrangements

事由 shìyóu ① the origin of an incident; particulars of a matter ② (used in official language) main content ③ job; work

事与愿违 shìyǔyuànwěi Things go contrary to (against) one's wishes.

事在人为 shìzàirénwéi All success hinges on human effort.; It all depends on human effort.; It's man who disposes.

事主 shìzhǔ the victim of a crime

誓 shì〈动〉swear; vow; take an oath; pledge: 发～ swear; take an oath. ～死捍卫 vow to defend with one's life

誓不罢休 shìbùbàxiū swear not to give up (stop, rest): 不达目的～。We'll never give up before we reach our goal.

誓不两立 shìbùliǎnglì swear not to coexist (with); be irreconcilable (to, with)

誓词(言) shìcí (yán) oath; pledge

誓师 shìshī a rally (meeting) to pledge resolution; oath-taking rally; take a mass pledge

誓死 shìsǐ swear to die; pledge one's life: ～不屈 swear to die rather than yield

誓约 shìyuē solemn promise; pledge

逝 shì〈动〉① pass: 时光易～。Time passes quickly. ② die; pass away: 病～ die of illness

逝世 shìshì die; pass away

势 shì〈名〉① power; force; influence: ～盛 at the height of one's power ② situation; state of affairs; circumstances: ～在必然 as a matter of course; inevitably ③ momentum; impetus: 以排山倒海之～ with the momentum of an avalanche (a landslide)

势必 shìbì ① be bound to; be sure; certainly will: ～对…产生影响 be bound to have an effect on ② definitely; inevitably

势不可当 shìbùkědāng irresistible

势不两立 shìbùliǎnglì mutually exclusive; irreconcilable; completely incompatible; diametrically opposed to

势均力敌 shìjūn-lìdí be evenly matched in strength; balance of forces (power); be in equilibrium: 双方～。The two sides match each other in strength.

势力 shìlì power; force; influence: ～范围 sphere of influence; orbit

势利 shìlì snobbish: ～小人 snob. ～眼 snobbish attitude; snobbery

势如破竹 shìrú-pòzhú (smash into enemy territory) "like splitting bamboo"— without difficulty; meet with no resistance; advance swiftly unhindered; develop apace

势头 shìtóu ① momentum; impetus ② tendency

势在必行 shìzàibìxíng be imperative (under such a circumstance): 改革～。The reform must be enforced.

是 shì ①〈形〉right; correct: 他说得～。what he said is right. ②〈代〉this; these; that; those: ～时 that time. 如～ like this ③〈动〉be: 她～一个学生。She is a student. ④〈副〉yes, right: 你准备好了吗? — ～, 准备好了。Are you ready? — Yes, I'm (ready).

是非 shìfēi ① right and wrong: ～

问题 a matter of right and wrong. ～曲直 truth and falsehood; merits and demerits. ～题[教] true-false item ② dispute; controversy:引起～ provoke a dispute

是否 shìfǒu whether (or not); if; whether:～符合实际 whether or not it corresponds to reality

是古非今 shìgǔ-fēijīn denounce the present and praise the past (antiquity); admire everything ancient and belittle present-day achievements

是可忍,孰不可忍 shì kěrěn, shú bù kěrěn If this can be tolerated, what cannot?; If this can be tolerated, what cannot be tolerated?; How can this be tolerated?

嗜 shì〈动〉have a liking for; be addicted to

嗜好 shìhào liking; hobby; [烟酒等]habit; addiction:没有吸烟的～ have no habit of smoking

嗜酒 shìjiǔ be addicted to drink; be crazy about wine

释 shì〈动〉① explain; elucidate:解～难题 explain a difficult problem ② dispel; clear up:～疑 remove doubts; dispel suspicion ③ let go; set free:～放战俘 release war prisoners

释放 shìfàng set (render) free; release:～囚犯 release a prisoner; discharge of prisoner

释手 shìshǒu loosen one's grip; let go

释义 shìyì explain the meaning (of a word, etc.)

适 shì〈形〉① fit; suitable; proper:～当的场面话 words suitable to the occasion ② comfortable; well:感到不～ not feel well ③ right; opportune:～当时机 opportune moment ④〈动〉follow; go; pursue:无所～从 not know what course to pursue; not know what to do

适当 shìdàng suitable; proper; fit; appropriate:给予～的处分。Proper punishment should be meted out to.

适度 shìdù moderate degree; appropriate measure:农业～规模经营 farming on an optimum scale. ～从紧和量入为出的财政方针 a moderately tight financial policy and keeping expenditures within the limits of income

适合 shìhé suit; fit

适可而止 shìkě'érzhǐ stop before going too far; know how far to go; Stop where you reach the limit.

适时 shìshí timely; opportune; at the right moment; in good time:～播种 sow in (good) time

适销 shìxiāo suitable to the market:～对路的商品 readily marketable goods; goods that have a ready market

适宜 shìyí fit; suitable; proper; appropriate:她不～做这工作。She is not fit for the job.

适意 shìyì comfortable; agreeable; enjoyable

适应 shìyìng adapt；fit；suit：～新情况 be in keeping with the new situation
适用 shìyòng ① apply；suit；hold good （for）：～范围 scope (sphere) of application ② serve (the purpose)；prove useful：东西虽不太好但很～。It isn't very good but it will serve.
适中 shìzhōng ①［价格等］reasonable；moderate ②［地点等］suitable；well-situated；convenient：地点～ be conveniently situated

似 shì
另见 sì
似的 shìde 雪～白 as white as snow

氏 shì〈名〉family name；surname
氏族 shìzú clan：～公社 clan commune；gentile community

饰 shì ①〈名〉decorations；ornaments：服～ clothes and ornaments〈动〉② adorn；dress up；polish：文过～非 cover up one's errors (mistakes)；gloss over one's fault ③ play the role of；act the part of
饰词 shìcí pretext；excuse
饰物 shìwù ① decorations；ornaments ② articles for personal adornment；jewelry

shōu

收 shōu〈动〉① receive；accept：～到一封信 receive a letter. 不～小帐 don't accept gratuities ② put away；take in：～工具 put the tools away ③ collect：～废品 collect scrap ④ bring to an end；stop：看你将如何～场？How are you going to wind up the whole affair? ⑤ harvest；gather in：～庄稼 harvest crops ⑥ close：伤～口了。The wound has healed.
收编 shōubiān incorporate into one's own forces
收兵 shōubīng withdraw (recall) troops；call of a battle：～休整 retire to rest and consolidate
收藏 shōucáng store up；collect：～古画 collect old paintings. ～家 collector (of books，antiques，etc.). 现代派绘画作品的～ a collection of moderns
收场 shōuchǎng ① ending；conclusion：圆满的～ a happy ending ② come to an end；wind up：会议草草～。The meeting wound up hastily (perfunctorily).
收成 shōuchéng harvest；crop：～好(坏) have a good (poor) harvest
收到 shōudào receive；get；achieve；obtain
收发 shōufā ① receive and dispatch：～室 dispatch office；office for incoming and outgoing mail ② dispatcher；mail clerk
收费 shōufèi ① collect fees ② charge：～电视 pay-TV
收复 shōufù recover；recapture
收工 shōugōng stop work for the day；knock off；pack up

收购 shōugòu purchase；buy：～农副产品 purchase farm produce and sideline products. ～价格 purchasing price

收回 shōuhuí ① take back；regain；call in；recall：～贷款 recall (recover) loans. ～投资 recoup capital outlay ② withdraw：～建议 withdraw a proposal

收活 shōuhuó take-in work；accept jobs

收获 shōuhuò ① harvest；gather in the crops：～量 harvest yield；yield ② gains；results；achievement：不下苦功，便无～。No pains，no gains.

收集 shōují collect；gather：～资料 collect data

收件人 shōujiànrén addressee；consignee

收缴 shōujiǎo take over；capture

收据(条) shōujù(tiáo) receipt：～簿 receipt book

收看 shōukàn watch；look in：～电视 watch television

收礼 shōulǐ accept gifts

收敛 shōuliǎn ① weak；disappear：他的笑脸突然～起来了。The smile suddenly vanished from his face. ② restrain oneself；show restraint

收留 shōuliú take sb. in；have sb. in one's care

收录 shōulù take down；record：～两用机 radio cassette recorder

收买 shōumǎi ① purchase；buy：～旧书 buy used books ② buy over；win sb. over by bribery：～人心 buy popular support；buy popularity

收盘 shōupán ［经］closing quotation (on the exchange，etc.)：～价格 closing price

收讫 shōuqì payment received；paid；received (in full)

收容 shōuróng ① take in；accommodate；house：～难民 take in refugees ② detain：～教养 shelter and rehabilitate. ～审查 detain sb. for questioning. ～所 detention centre

收入 shōurù ①income；earnings；revenue：～分配 income distribution. 财政～ state revenue ② take in；include

收拾 shōushi ① put in order；clean up ② get things ready；pack up one's things：～行李 pack one's luggage

收视率 shōushìlǜ audience rating

收缩 shōusuō ① contract；shrink ② concentrate one's forces；draw back ③ systole

收摊儿 shōutānr pack up the stall —wind up the day's business or the work on hand

收听 shōutīng listen (in) to；tune in：～新闻节目 tune in the news programme. ～新闻广播 listen to the news broadcast

收尾 shōuwěi ① ending (of an article，etc.) ② wind up：～工作 round-off work

收效 shōuxiào yield (attain) results；bear fruit；produce effect：～显著 yield (bear) notable results

收信人 shōuxìnrén addressee

收押 shōuyā detain；hold in custody

收养 shōuyǎng adopt (a child):～人 adopter; adoptive parents. ～孤儿 adopt an orphan

收益 shōuyì income; profit; gains:～递增 increasing returns

收帐 shōuzhàng ① charge to an account ② collect debts

收支 shōuzhī income and expenses; revenue and expenditure; receipts and payments:～平衡 balance between income and expenditure; balance of income and outlay; income and expenses are balanced. 使～相抵 make (both) ends meet

收治 shōuzhì receive and cure (a patient); accept and treat (a patient)

shǒu

守 shǒu〈动〉① defend; guard: ～卫在祖国的边防线上 keep guard on the frontiers of the motherland ② keep watch; look after:～着伤员 look after the wounded ③ observe; keep; abide by:～纪律 observe discipline

守备 shǒubèi be on guard (garrison) duty; perform garrison duty; garrison

守法 shǒufǎ be law-abiding; abide by the law:～的私人工商户 law-abiding private industrial and commercial units

守寡 shǒuguǎ live as a widow; live in widowhood; remain a widow

守恒定律 shǒuhéng-dìnglǜ [物] conservation law

守候 shǒuhòu ① wait for; expect ② keep watch

守护 shǒuhù guard; defend

守旧 shǒujiù be accustomed to old ways; stick to old ways; be conservative; adhere to past practices

守口如瓶 shǒukǒurúpíng keep one's mouth shut; tight-lipped; tight-mouthed; mouth as tight as a jar lid; as close as an oyster

守灵 shǒulíng keep vigil beside the coffin; stand vigil before the bier

守门 shǒumén [体] keep goal:～员 goalkeeper

守时 shǒushí be on time; be punctual

守势 shǒushì defensive:采取～ be on (take) the defensive

守卫 shǒuwèi guard; defend

守信 shǒuxìn keep one's word

守夜 shǒuyè keep watch at night; keep vigil

守则 shǒuzé rules; regulations:学生～ school regulations

守株待兔 shǒuzhū-dàitù stand by a tree stump waiting for a hare to dash itself against it; hope for gains without pains; await a windfall

首 shǒu〈名〉① head:昂～ hold one's head high ② leader; chief; head:～脑人物 leading figures ③ piece:一～诗 a piece of poetry ④ bring charges against sb.:出～ inform against sb. ⑤〈形〉first：～批 the first batch

首倡 shǒuchàng initiate；start：～者 initiator

首创 shǒuchuàng initiate；originate；pioneer：历史～精神 creative initiative in the making of history

首次 shǒucì for the first time；first：～公演 opening performance

首当其冲 shǒudāngqíchōng bear the brunt（of）；first to be affected

首恶 shǒu'è chief criminal；principal culprit

首犯 shǒufàn main （principal） culprit

首富 shǒufù the wealthiest family in the locality

首航 shǒuháng first （madien） flight；first open water；madien voyage

首肯 shǒukěn nod approval；nod assent；approve；consent

首领 shǒulǐng leader；head；[部落、匪徒等]chieftain；ringleader

首脑 shǒunǎo head（of government，etc.）：～会议 summit conference；conference of heads of state

首屈一指 shǒuqū-yīzhǐ come first on the list；first-rate；top-notch；second to none

首日封 shǒurìfēng first-day cover

首善之区 shóushànzhīqū the best of places（i. e.，the capital of a country）

首饰 shǒushì woman's valuable ornaments；jewelry：～盒 jewel case

首尾 shǒuwěi ① the head and the tail；the beginning and the end ② from beginning to end

首席 shǒuxí ① seat of honour ② chief：～代表 cheif representative（delegate）. ～法官 chief judge（justice）

首先 shǒuxiān first and foremost；in the first place；first of all；above all；first：她～发言。She was the first to speak.

首相 shǒuxiàng prime minister；premier

首演 shǒuyǎn first（opening）performance；premiere

首要 shǒuyào of（the）first importance：～分子 ringleader；major culprit. ～任务 priority in the task. ～问题 the first important question；a question of first importance

首长 shǒuzhǎng leading cadre；senior officer；chief；head

手

shǒu ①〈名〉hand：左～ left hand ②〈动〉have in one's hand；hold：人～一册。Everyone has a copy. ③〈形〉handy；convenient：～册 handbook ④〈副〉personally：～植 personally plant（a tree，etc.）

手臂 shǒubì ① arm ② a reliable helper

手册 shǒucè handbook；manual：英语语法～ a handbook of English grammar

手段 shǒuduàn means；device；medium；measure：流通～ medium of circulation. 不择～

by hook or by crook; unscrupulously. 支付～ means of payment

手法 shǒufǎ ① technique; skill ② trick; gimmick; game: ～拙劣 play a clumsy game

手感 shǒugǎn feel

手稿 shǒugǎo manuscript; hand writing

手工 shǒugōng ① handwork: ～费 payment for a piece of handwork. ～业合作社 handicraft cooperative ② by hand; manual: ～劳动 hand (manual) labour

手工艺 shǒugōngyì handicraft art: ～工人 craftsman; artisan. ～品 handicrafts

手机 shǒujī hand-held telephone (i. e., mobile telephone)

手迹 shǒujì sb.'s original handwriting or painting

手脚 shǒujiǎo movement of hands or feet; motion: ～利落 agile; nimble. 一定有人从中作～。Someone must have juggled things.

手紧 shǒujǐn ① closefisted; tightfisted ② be short of money; be hard up

手铐 shǒukào handcuffs

手忙脚乱 shǒumáng-jiǎoluàn in a frantic rush; in a flutter; in great confusion; in a muddle

手气 shǒuqì luck at gambling, card playing, etc.

手巧 shǒuqiǎo skilful with one's hands; nimblefingered; deft; dexterous

手球 shǒuqiú handball: 打～ play handball

手软 shǒuruǎn softhearted; be irresolute when firmness is needed

手生 shǒushēng lack practice and skill; be out of practice

手势 shǒushì sign; signal; gesture: 做～ make a gesture; gesticulate

手术 shǒushù operation: 动～ perform (undergo) an operation

手套 shǒutào gloves; [四指相连的或露指的] mittens: 皮～ leather gloves

手提包 shǒutíbāo handbag; bag

手头 shǒutóu ① right beside one; on hand; at hand: ～无现款 have no cash on hand ② financial condition: ～拮据 be hard up for money

手腕 shǒuwàn ① wrist ② craft; trick; skill; artifice; finesse: 外交～ diplomacy. 耍～ play tricks (on)

手无寸铁 shǒuwú-cùntiě barehanded; defenceless; unarmed

手舞足蹈 shǒuwǔ-zúdǎo dance with joy

手写体 shǒuxiětǐ handwritten form; script

手续 shǒuxù procedures; formalities: ～费 service charge. 办～ go through formalities

手艺 shǒuyì craft; craftsmanship; workmanship: ～人 craftsman

手印 shǒuyìn handprint

手语 shǒuyǔ hand language; sign language

手足 shǒuzú brothers; member: ～之情 brotherly affection

手足无措 shǒuzú-wúcuò in a flurried manner; at a loss what to do; helter-skelter; panic-stricken

shòu

瘦 shòu〈形〉thin; lean

瘦长 shòucháng tall (long) and thin; lanky

瘦弱 shòuruò thin and feeble; lean and weak; puny; emaciated

兽 shòu ①〈名〉animal; beast: 人面～心 a beast in human shape ②〈形〉beastly; bestial

兽类 shòulèi animals; beasts

兽行 shòuxíng beastliness; bestiality; [暴行]brutality

兽性 shòuxìng brutish nature; brutalism; bestiality

兽医 shòuyī veterinary surgeon; vet

兽欲 shòuyù bestial (animal) desire

寿 shòu〈名〉① longevity ② life; age: 长～ long life; longevity ③ birthday: 祝～ congratulate sb. on his birthday ④ for burial: ～材 coffin

寿比南山,福如东海 shòu bǐ nán shān, fú rú dōnghǎi May your age be as Mount Tai and your happiness as the Eastern Sea!

寿辰(诞) shòuchén (dàn) birthday (of an elderly person): 八十～ eightieth birthday

寿礼 shòulǐ birthday present

寿命 shòumìng life; life-span: ～长(短) long-(short-) lived. 平均～ average life expectancy; average life-span

寿终 shòuzhōng die old; die at a ripe age: ～正寝 die a natural death; die in one's bed

受 shòu〈动〉① receive; accept: ～致命伤 receive a mortal wound ② suffer; sustain; be subjected to: ～损失 suffer losses ③ endure; bear; stand: ～不了 cannot bear

受潮 shòucháo become damp; be affected with damp; get damped: 切勿～ Keep from moisture

受宠若惊 shòuchǒng-ruòjīng receive favour with awed excitement; be overwhelmed by a special favour; feel (be) overwhelmingly flattered

受挫 shòucuò suffer a setback; be foiled (frustrated); be baffled

受罚 shòufá be punished

受害 shòuhài be injured; suffer injury: ～不浅 suffer a lot. ～人 injured party; victim

受贿 shòuhuì accept a bribe; take bribes: ～人 receiver of bribes; bribee

受奖 shòujiǎng be rewarded

受尽 shòujìn suffer enough from; suffer all kinds of; have one's fill of

受惊 shòujīng get (be) frightened (at); be startled (at)

受苦 shòukǔ undergo hardships; suffer (hardships): ～受难 have a rough time; live in misery

受累 shòulěi be involved (in); be

incriminated

受累 shòulèi be put to much trouble; inconvenienced：对不起，让你～了。Sorry to have troubled you.

受礼 shòulǐ receive gifts

受理 shòulǐ accept and hear; hear; receive：～案件 accept and hear a case; take up a case

受凉 shòuliáng catch cold; have a chill

受命 shòumìng receive instructions

受难 shòunàn be in distress; suffer a calamity (disaster)

受骗 shòupiàn be deceived (cheated; fooled); be taken in

受气 shòuqì be irritated; be offended; suffer wrong

受权 shòuquán be authorized：～声明 be authorized to announce. ～宣布 announce upon authorization

受辱 shòurǔ be insulted; be disgraced

受伤 shòushāng get injured; be wounded

受审 shòushěn be tried; on trial：～人 person on trial

受托 shòutuō be entrusted (with a task); be commissioned

受刑 shòuxíng be tortured (with); be put to torture

受训 shòuxùn receive training

受益 shòuyì profit by; benefit (from, by); be benefited：～匪浅 be benefited a great deal (from). ～人 beneficiary

受用 shòuyòng benefit from, enjoy; profit by

受孕 shòuyùn become pregnant (with a child); conceive (a child); be impregnated

受灾 shòuzāi be hit by a natural calamity (adversity)：～地区 disaster area

受罪 shòuzuì endure (suffer) hardships, tortures, rough conditions, etc.; have a hard time

授

shóu〈动〉① teach; instruct：函～ teach by correspondence ② award; confer; give; vest：～权给某人 vest sb. with authority

授奖 shòujiǎng give a prize (reward); award a prize：～仪式 prize-awardig (giving) ceremony

授课 shòukè give lessons; teach; schooling

授命 shòumìng give orders：～组阁 authorize sb. to form a cabinet

授权 shòuquán authorize; empower

授勋 shòuxūn confer orders or medals on sb.

授意 shòuyì incite sb. to do sth.; get sb. to carry out one's plan; suggest：在…～之下 on the instructions of; take one's cue from

授予 shòuyǔ give; award; confer

售

shòu〈动〉① sell：零～ sell retail ② make (one's plan, trick, etc.) work; carry out (intrigues)：其计不～ one's plan was not adopted

售后服务 shòuhòu fúwù after-sales service

售货 shòuhuò sell goods：～机 vending machine. ～员 shop assistant；salesman or saleswoman；salesclerk

售价 shòujià (selling) price

售票 shòupiào sell tickets：～处[戏院等] ticket office；box office；[火车站等] booking office. ～员 ticket seller；ticket agent；[公共汽车等] conductor or conductress

售完 shòuwán be sold out：对不起，票子已～。Sorry，the tickets are sold out.

狩 shòu〈名〉hunting (esp. in winter)～猎 hunting

shū

梳 shū〈名，动〉comb

梳辫子 shūbiànzi braid the hair (originally，the term meant combing hair into braids. Later，it came to be used metaphorically to mean pulling together，arranging，and categorizing matters.)

梳洗 shūxǐ wash and dress：～用具 toilet articles

梳妆 shūzhuāng dress and make up；make one's toilet：～打扮 deck oneself out；dress smartly；be dressed up. ～台 dressing table；toilet table

疏 shū〈动〉① dredge (a river，etc.) ② neglect：～于防范 neglect to take precautions ③ scatter；disperse：～开队形 spread out in dispersed formation ④ thin；sparse：稀～的头发 sparse hair ⑤ (of family or social relations) distant ⑥ scanty：志大才～ have great ambition but little talent ⑦〈形〉not familiar with：人地生～ be unfamiliar with the place and the people

疏导 shūdǎo ① dredge ② remove obstructions：～交通 relieve traffic congestion

疏忽 shūhu carelessness；negligence；oversight：偶然的～ accidental oversight

疏浚 shūjùn dredge and deepen；dredge：～航道 dredge a channel

疏理 shūlǐ unclog and readjust：～商品的流通渠道 unclog and readjust channels for commodities

疏漏 shūlòu careless omission；omission through negligence；slip；oversight

疏落 shūluò sparse；thin；scattered：山上～的树木 sparse trees on a hill

疏散 shūsàn ①sparse；dispersed；scattered ② evacuate：～人口 evacuate inhabitants；evacuation

疏失 shūshī careless mistake；oversight；remissness

疏松 shūsōng ① loose ② loosen

疏通 shūtōng ① dredge；unclog；open channels：～渠道 unclog the channels ② mediate between two parties：经过～，争执解决了。The dispute was settled through mediation.

疏远 shūyuǎn become estranged; drift apart; keep (hold) at arm's length

蔬 shū〈名〉vegetables

蔬菜 shūcài vegetables; greens; greenstuff：～栽培 vegetable farming; vegetable growing

枢 shū〈名〉pivot; centre; hub

枢纽 shūniǔ pivot; key position; axis; hub：～工程 pivotal project; key project. 交通～ a hub of communications

叔 shū〈名〉① uncle ② husband's younger brother; brother-in-law

叔父 shūfù father's younger brother; uncle

叔母 shūmǔ wife of father's younger brother; aunt

输 shū〈动〉① transport; convey：～电 transmit electricity ② lose; be defeated; be beaten：～人一着 lose a move to someone

输出 shūchū ① export：～限额 export quota ②［电］output

输电 shūdiàn power transmission：～网 power transmission network. ～线路 transmission line

输入 shūrù ① import：～许可 import admission ②［电］input

输送 shūsòng send; convey; transport：～带 conveyer belt

输血 shūxuè［医］blood transfusion：～者 blood donor

输氧 shūyǎng［医］oxygen therapy

输液 shūyè［医］inject intravenously; drip：病人正在～。The patient is on a drip.

输油管 shūyóuguǎn petroleum pipeline; oil pipeline

殊 shū〈形〉① different：悬～ differ widely ② special; outstanding; remarkable：～礼 unusual ceremony ③〈副〉very much; really：～难相信。It is hard to believe.; very difficult to believe

殊不知 shūbùzhī hardly know (realize); little imagine

殊死 shūsǐ life-and-death; desperate：～的搏斗 a most courageous fight against

殊途同归 shūtú-tóngguī reach the same goal by different routes (ways); obtain the same results through not by the same method

舒 shū〈动〉① spread out; stretch; unfold ②〈形〉relaxed; easy; leisurely

舒畅 shūchàng happy; easy in mind; free from worry; relaxed：心情～ have ease of mind

舒服 shūfu ① have an easy time; have satisfaction; be comfortable; ②［身体好］be well：她今天觉得不大～。She is not feeling very well today.; She is not quite herself today.

舒缓 shūhuǎn ① slow and unhurried; leisurely ② relaxed; mild ③ (of a slope) gentle; gradual

舒适 shūshì comfortable；snug；cozy；pleasant：～的生活 a comfortable life

舒心 shūxīn comfortable；happy

舒展 shūzhǎn ① stretch（one's legs，etc.）② spread out；unfold；extend

抒 shū〈动〉express；convey；give expression to

抒发 shūfā express；give expression to；voice：～情感 express one's feelings

抒情 shūqíng ① express（convey）one's emotion ② lyric：～小说 lyrical novel. ～诗 lyric poetry；lyrics. ～诗人 lyric poet；lyricist

书 shū ①〈动〉write：大～特～ write volumes about〈名〉② book：教师用～ a teacher's book ③ letter：家～ a letter from home ④ script：楷～ regular script ⑤ document：国～ letter of credence；credentials

书包 shūbāo schoolbag；satchel；bookbag

书报 shūbào books and newspapers：～检查法 censorship system

书橱 shūchú bookcase

书呆子 shūdāizi pedant：［爱读书的］bookworm

书店 shūdiàn bookstore；bookshop

书法 shūfǎ calligraphy；chirography；penmanship：～家 calligrapher. 练习～ practise penmanship；have drills in calligraphy

书房 shūfáng study；library

书稿 shūgǎo manuscript

书画 shūhuà calligraphy and painting：～同源 calligraphy and painting of common origin. ～展览会 painting and calligraphy exhibition

书籍 shūjí books；works；literature

书脊 shūjǐ spine of a book

书记 shūjì ① secretary：～处 secretariat. 总～ general secretary ②［法］clerk

书库 shūkù（stack）room

书眉 shūméi the top of a page；top margin：～标题 running head（line，title）

书面 shūmiàn in written form；written：～报告 written report. ～声明 written statement

书名 shūmíng title（of a book）：～页 title page

书目 shūmù booklist；title catalogue：参考～ bibliography

书评 shūpíng book review：～家 reviewer

书签 shūqiān bookmark

书生 shūshēng ① scholar ② pedant：～气 bookishness；pedantry. ～之见 pedantic view

书摊 shūtān bookstall；bookstand

书香门第 shūxiāng-méngdì an intellectual background；families of education；a scholarly family；a family of scholar(s)

书信 shūxìn letter；written message

书证 shūzhèng［法］documentary evidence

书志学 shūzhìxué bibliology

书桌 shūzhuō desk; writing desk

shú

熟 shú 〈形〉① ripe: 这些葡萄～了。The grapes are ripe. ② cooked: ～肉 cooked meat ③ processed: ～铜 wrought copper ④ skilled; skilful (at, in); experienced: ～练工人 skilled worker ⑤ familiar; acquainted: ～悉的声音 a familiar voice

熟谙 shú'ān be familiar with; be good at

熟地 shúdì cultivated land

熟记 shújì learn by heart; memorize

熟练 shúliàn skilled; adept (in); experienced; proficient (in): ～工人 skilled (experienced) worker

熟能生巧 shúnéng-shēngqiǎo Skill comes from practice.; Practice makes perfect.

熟人 shúrén (old) acquaintance; friend

熟食 shúshí cooked food; [出售的] delicatessen: ～店 delicatessen

熟视无睹 shúshì-wúdǔ pay no attention to a familiar sight; ignore; be indifferent to; turn a blind eye to; close one's eyes to; take no notice of

熟识 shúshi know well; be familiar with; be acquainted with

熟悉 shúxī have an intimate knowledge; know well; be familiar with; acquaint oneself with; familiarize: ～内幕 be familiar with the inside story. ～情况 be familiar with the situation

熟习 shúxí be skilled at; have the knack of; be practised in: ～业务 be well versed in one's field of work

熟字 shúzì words already learned; familiar word

赎 shú 〈动〉① redeem; ransom: ～抵押品 redeem a mortgage ② expiate; atone for (a crime): ～罪 expiate sin (a crime)

赎金 shújīn ransom money

赎买 shúmǎi redeem; buy out; purchase

赎罪 shúzuì atone for one's crime; make amends for one's crime; satisfaction for a crime: 将功～ make amends for one's crimes by good deeds

shǔ

数 shǔ 〈动〉① count: 从一～到五 count from one to five ② enumerate; reckon; regarded as: 历～其罪 enumerate the crimes sb. has committed
另见 shù, shuò

数得着 shǔdezháo be reckoned (regarded) as outstanding; be counted among the best

数典忘祖 shǔdiǎnwàngzǔ give all the historical facts except those about one's own ancestors; forget one's own origins

数来宝 shǔláibǎo [曲艺] rhythmic storytelling to clapper accompaniment

数落 shǔluo scold; blame: 把某人～一顿 give sb. a good scolding (ticking-off)

数一数二 shǔyī-shǔ'èr one of the best; be among the very best

数珠念佛 shǔzhū-niànfó count (tell, say) one's beads

暑 shǔ〈名〉hot weather; heat

暑假 shǔjià summer vacation; summer holidays

暑期 shǔqī summer vacation time: ～训练班 summer course

暑气 shǔqì summer heat

署 shǔ ①〈名〉government office; office: 专员公～ prefectural commissioner's office〈动〉② arrange: 部～ make arrangements for ③ handle by proxy; act as deputy

署名 shǔmíng put one's signature to; sign: ～文章 a signed article

曙 shǔ〈名〉daybreak; dawn

曙光 shǔguāng the first light of morning; dawn; daybreak: 胜利的～ the dawn of victory

蜀 shǔ〈名〉another name for Sichuan Province

蜀道之难,难于上青天 shǔdào zhī nán, nányú shàng qīngtiān Walking on the narrow paths of Sichuan is as difficult as climbing up to heaven.

蜀锦 shǔjǐn Sichuan brocade

鼠 shǔ〈名〉mouse; rat

鼠标器 shǔbiāoqì [计] Genius mouse; mouse

鼠窜 shǔcuàn scamper off like a rat; scurry away

鼠目寸光 shǔmù-cùnguāng A mouse can see only an inch; short-sighted; unable to see beyond one's nose

属 shǔ〈名〉① category: 金～ metals ② genus: 亚～ subgenus ③〈动〉belong to: ～于人民范围 come within the category of the people ④〈形〉subordinate to: 所～单位 subordinate units

属地 shǔdì dependency

属国 shǔguó dependent state

属相 shǔxiàng any of the twelve animals, representing the twelve Earthly Branches, used to symbolize the year in which a person is born

属于 shǔyú belong to; pertain to; be part of; come into the category: ～唯心主义世界观 be part and parcel of the idealist world outlook

shù

树 shù ①〈名〉tree: 玫瑰～ a rose tree〈动〉② cultivate; plant: 十年～木,百年～人。It takes ten years to grow trees, but a hundred years to rear people. ③ set up; establish; uphold: ～立良好的体育道德 foster fine sports ethics

树碑立传 shùbēi-lìzhuàn build up sb.'s prestige by an overdose of praise; glorify sb. by singing the praises of his life; try to give sb. a niche in the temple of fame

树丛 shùcōng thicket; grove; shrubbery:矮～ bush; coppice

树倒猢狲散 shù dǎo húsūn sàn Once the tree falls, the monkeys on it will flee (disperse) helter-skelter.; When an influential person falls from power, his hangers-on disperse.; Rats leave a sinking ship.

树敌 shùdí make an enemy of sb.; set others against oneself: ～过多 antagonize too many people; make too many enemies

树立 shùlì set up; erect; establish: ～榜样 set an example (to, for sb.)

树林 shùlín woods; grove

树皮画 shùpíhuà bark painting

树欲静而风不止 shù yù jìng ér fēng bù zhǐ The tree desires stillness but the wind will not cease.; The trees may prefer clam but the wind will not subside.

漱 shù 〈动〉 rinse out; gargle

漱口 shùkǒu rinse one's mouth (out); gargle

庶 shù 〈形〉 numerous; multitudinous: 富～ rich and populous

庶民(人) shùmín(rén) the common people; commoner; the multitude

数 shù 〈名〉 ① number; figure: 偶～ an even number ② mathematics ③〈形〉 a few; some; several: ～人 several people 另见 shǔ, shuò

数词 shùcí [语] numeral: 基～ cardinal number

数额 shù'é amount; number

数据 shùjù data

数量 shùliàng quantity; amount

数码 shùmǎ ① numeral ② number; amount

数目 shùmù number; amount

数学 shùxué mathematics; maths: ～家 mathematician

数值 shùzhí numerical value

数字 shùzì ① [表示数量] amount; quantity ②[数目的符号] digital; numeral; figure: ～程控交换机 digital programme-controlled switchboards. ～式激光视盘 digital video disc (DVD). ～通信网络 digital telecommunication network. ～影音光碟 digital video disc (DVD)

数罪并罚 shùzuìbìngfá combined punishment for more than one crime; concurrent punishment for several crimes

数罪并合 shùzuìbìnghé merger of offenses; joinder of offences

术 shù 〈名〉 ① art; technique; skill: 医～ the art of healing; doctor's skill ② method; tactics: 战～ tactics

术语 shùyǔ technical terms; terminology; jargon: ～学 terminology

述 shù 〈动〉 tell; state; relate: 略～经过 relate briefly how it happened

述评 shùpíng ① commentary ② comment(on); review: 时事～ comment on current affairs

述职 shùzhí report on one's work

束 shù〈动〉① bind; tie: ～紧腰带 tighten one's belt ② restrain; control: 无拘无～ without any restraint ③〈名〉bundle; sheaf; bunch: 一～鲜花 a bunch of flowers

束缚 shùfù tie; bind up; fetter: ～生产力 fetter the productive forces. ～手脚 bind sb. hand and foot; tie sb.'s hands; manacle; handcuff; shackle

束手 shùshǒu have one's hands tied; be helpless: ～待毙 wait helplessly for death; resign oneself to extinction. ～无策 be at one's wits' end; be at a loss what to do; feel quite helpless. ～束脚 undue caution; timid and hesitant; overcautious

束之高阁 shùzhīgāogé put (lay) on the shelf; shelve; pigeonhole

恕 shù〈动〉① forgive; excuse; pardon: 他得到宽～了。He is forgiven. ② excuse me; beg your pardon: ～不奉陪 excuse me (for not keeping your company)

恕罪 shùzuì pardon an offence; forgive a sin (mistake); forgivingness

竖 shù ①〈形〉upright; vertical; perpendicular: ～线 vertical line ②〈动〉erect; set upright; stand: ～旗杆 erect a flagstaff ③〈名〉[笔划]vertical stroke

竖立 shùlì errect; set upright; stand: 坟前～着一块墓碑。In front of the tomb stood a gravestone.

竖起 shùqǐ erect; raise; hold up: ～大拇指 hold up an approving thumb. ～耳朵 pick up one's ears

shuā

刷 shuā ①〈动,名〉brush: 鞋～ shoe brush. ～鞋 brush shoes 〈动〉② paste up; daub: ～墙 whitewash a wall ③ eliminate: 她在第2轮比赛中就被～下来了。She was eliminated in the very second round.
另见 shuà

刷洗 shuāxǐ wash (with a brush); scrub: ～地板 scrub the floor

刷新 shuāxīn ① refurbish; renovate: ～政事 introduce political reforms ② break: ～纪录 break a record

刷牙 shuāyá brush (clean) one's teeth

刷子 shuāzi scrub; brush

shuǎ

耍 shuǎ〈动〉① play; amuse oneself: 孩子们在花园内玩～。The kids are playing in the garden. ② play with; flourish: ～

刀 flourish a sword ③ play (tricks)：～两面派手法 resort to two-faced tactics

耍花招 shuǎ huāzhāo display showy movements; play tricks; perform sleight of hand; manoeuvre

耍赖 shuǎlài play the rascal; act (behave) shamelessly

耍流氓 shuǎ liúmáng take liberties with women; act indecently; behave like a hoodlum

耍弄 shuǎnòng ① play with：～刀枪 play (with) swords and spears ② make fun of; make a fool of; deceive：～手段 use strategy

耍脾气 shuǎ píqì get into a huff

耍威风 shuǎ wēifēng make a show of authority; throw one's weight about; be overbearing

耍无赖 shuǎ wúlài be perverse; act shamelessly

耍心眼儿 shuǎ xīnyǎnr be calculating; exercise one's wits for personal gain

shuà

刷 shuà

另见 shuā

刷白 shuàbái pale; white：他吓得脸色～。He turned pale with fright.; His face paled with fear.

shuāi

衰 shuāi〈动〉wane; grow weak; decline：兴～ rise and fall

衰败 shuāibài decline; fall into decay; wane; be at a low ebb

衰减 shuāijiǎn extinction

衰竭 shuāijié exhaustion; prostration

衰老 shuāilǎo (be) infirm with age; (grow) decrepit; senile; senescent：我可能是有点～了。I may be senescent.

衰落 shuāiluò be on the wane; decline; go down hill; falling; deteriorate：日趋～ be on the wane (decline)

衰退 shuāituì ① fail; decline：她的视力在～。Her eyesight is failing. 记忆力～ be losing one's memory ② recession; slump：经济～ economic recession

衰亡 shuāiwáng wither away; become feeble and die; die out; decline and fall (demise)

摔 shuāi〈动〉① fall; tumble; lose one's balance：从自行车上～下来 tumble off a bicycle ② crash; plunge：飞机～下来了。The plane plunged to the ground. ③ throw; fling; cast：把帽子一～ throw one's cap

摔打 shuāidǎ ① beat; knock ② rough it; temper oneself

摔跟头 shuāigēntou ① tumble; trip and fall ② trip up; make a blunder; come (get) a cropper

摔跤 shuāijiāo ① tumble; trip and fall ② come (get) a cropper ③［体］wrestling：～运动员 wrestler

shuǎi

甩 shuǎi〈动〉① move backward andforward; swing: ～胳膊 swing one's arms ② throw; fling; toss: ～手榴弹 throw hand grenades ③ leave sb. behind; throw off; desert: 他把好了三年的对象给～了。He deserted his girlfriend he had dated for three years.

甩掉 shuǎidiào throw away; cast off: ～包袱 cast off a burden

甩卖 shuǎimài off a clearance sale; sale at a reduced price; markdown sale; reduction sale

甩手 shuǎishǒu ① swing one's arms ② refuse to do; wash one's hands of

shuài

率 shuài ①〈动〉lead; command; head: ～师 command troops 〈形〉② rash; hasty: 草～ cursory; careless ③ frank; candid; straightforward: 坦～的回答 a frank reply

率领 shuàilǐng lead; head: ～代表团出国 head a delegation to go abroad

率先 shuàixiān be the first to do sth.; take the lead (in doing sth.)

率直 shuàizhí forthright; openhearted; unreserved; straightforward

帅 shuài ①〈名〉commander-in-chief: 元～ marshal ②〈形〉beautiful; graceful; smart: 字写得很～ write a beautiful hand

帅气 shuàiqì dashing

shuān

闩 shuān〈动,名〉bolt; latch: 把门～好 bolt the door

栓 shuān〈名〉bolt; plug: 消防～ fireplug ② stopper; cork

拴 shuān〈动〉tie; fasten; tether: 把马～在树上 tether a horse to a tree

shuàn

涮 shuàn〈动〉① rinse ② boil slightly

涮羊肉 shuànyángròu instantly-boiled mutton; dip-boiled mutton slices

shuāng

霜 shuāng ①〈名〉frost ②〈形〉white; hoar: ～鬓 hoary temples

霜冻 shuāngdòng frost

霜害 shuānghài frosty injury; frost-bite

霜叶 shuāngyè red (maple) leaves

孀 shuāng widow

孀居 shuāngjū be a widow; live in widowhood

双 shuāng〈形〉① two; twin;

both; dual: ～重打击 twin blows② double; twofold: ～人房间 double room ③ pair; couple: 一～鞋 a pair of shoes

双百方针 shuāngbǎifāngzhēn "Double Hundred" policy (guiding principle), i. e., let a hundred flowers blossom, and a hundred schools of thought contend

双边 shuāngbiān bilateral: ～条约 bilateral treaty. ～关系 bilateral relations. ～贸易 bilateral trade; two-way trade

双层 shuāngcéng double-deck: ～桥 double-decked bridge; double-decker

双重 shuāngchóng double; dual; twofold: ～国籍 dual nationality. ～人格 dual personality. ～征税 doube taxation

双打 shuāngdǎ [体] doubles: 混合～ mixed doubles

双方 shuāngfāng two parties; both sides: ～当事人 both litigants; both parties

双杠 shuānggàng [体] parallel bars

双关 shuāngguān having a double meaning: ～语 equivoque; pun

双管齐下 shuāngguǎn-qíxià paint a picture with two brushes at the same time — work along both lines; do both things at one and the same time; do both things simultaneously

双轨 shuāngguǐ double-track: ～铁路 double-track railway. 物价～制 double-track pricing system

双簧 shuānghuáng [曲艺] a two-man act, with one speaking or singing while hiding behind the other who does the acting

双簧管 shuānghuángguǎn oboe

双料 shuāngliào double material (a metaphor for the high quality of a product and also a metaphor for a person with two special skills): ～大学生 a college student with double quality

双面 shuāngmiàn two-sided; double-edged: ～刀片 double-edged razor blade. ～式上衣 reversible coat

双亲 shuāngqīn (both) parents; father and mother

双全 shuāngquán complete in both respects; possess both complementary qualities: 智勇～ possessing both wisdom and courage; endowed with both wisdom and courage. 文武～ be adept with both the pen and the sword

双生 shuāngshēng twin: ～子 twins. ～兄弟(姐妹) twin brothers (sisters)

双薪 shuāngxīn double pay

双拥运动 shuāngyōng yùndòng double support movement, i. e., support the army and give preferential treatment to their dependents, (of the army) support the government and cherish the people

双语 shuāngyǔ bilingualism: ～词典 bilingual dictionary

双月刊 shuāngyuèkān bimonthly

双职工 shuāngzhígōng worker-couple; man and wife both employed; working couple; two-job employees: ～家庭 two-job family

双周刊 shuāngzhōukān biweekly; fortnightly

shuǎng

爽 shuǎng〈形〉① clear; bright; crisp: 空气清～。The air is crisp. ② straightforward; frank; openhearted: 豪～ forthright ③〈动〉feel well: 身体不～ not feel well

爽口 shuǎngkǒu pleasant to the taste; tasty and refreshing: 这道菜很～。This dish tastes very refreshing.

爽快 shuǎngkuài ① comfortable; refreshed: 心理很～ be quite at ease ② straightforward; frank: 说话～ speak frankly. 办事～ work readily and briskly

爽朗 shuǎnglǎng ① crisp; serene: 天空异常～。The sky is crystal clear. ② hearty; open-minded: ～的笑声 hearty laughter; ringing laughter. ～的性格 a frank and open personality

爽约 shuǎngyuē break one's engagements

爽直 shuǎngzhí frank; straightforward; candid

shuí

谁 shuí〈代〉① who: 她是～? Who is she? ② anybody, anyone; somebody; someone: ～都不甘落后。Nobody wanted to lag behind.

谁笑到最后,谁笑得最好 shuí xiàodàozuì hòu, shuí xiàode zuì hǎo He who laughs last, laughs best.

shuǐ

水 shuǐ〈名〉① water: 淡～ fresh water ② a general term for rivers, lakes, seas, etc.: 汉～ the Hanshui River ③〈形〉aquatic; marine: ～生植物 an aquatic plant

水坝 shuǐbà dam

水表 shuǐbiǎo water meter

水彩 shuǐcǎi watercolour: ～画 watercolour (painting)

水产 shuǐchǎn aquatic (marine) product

水到渠成 shuǐdào-qúchéng when the water comes, a channel is formed—when conditions are ripe, success is achieved

水道 shuǐdào ① waterway; water route ② water course

水电 shuǐdiàn water and electricity: ～费 charges for water and electricity. ～站 hydropower station

水分 shuǐfèn ①moisture②"moisture content"; exaggeration: 报告有～。The report is exaggerated.

水沟 shuǐgōu ditch; [下水道] drain; gutter

水果 shuǐguǒ fruit

水壶 shuǐhú ① water bottle ②

［烧水用的］kettle ③［浇水用的］watering can

水火不相容 shuǐhuǒ bù xiāngróng be incompatible as fire and water; diametrically contrary; exclude each other like fire and water; opposed to each other like fire and water; absolutely irreconcilable; mutually exclusive

水货 shuǐhuò ①［冒牌货］fake; imitation; counterfeit ② smuggled goods

水利 shuǐlì water conservancy: ～电力综合工程 project for irrigation and power generation. ～工程 water conservancy project. ～化 build water conservancy works on an extensive scale; bring all farmland under irrigation

水力 shuǐlì waterpower; hydraulic power; hydropower: ～发电站 hydropower station. ～资源 waterpower resources

水路 shuǐlù waterway; water route: 从～去 go by water

水陆交通线 shuǐlù jiāotōngxiàn land and water communication lines

水落石出 shuǐluò-shíchū When the water subsides the rocks emerge — the truth is out.; Everything is thrashed out.; come to light: 辩个～ argue a matter out; When facts are known, doubts will clear up.

水墨画 shuǐmòhuà［美］ink and wash painting; wash painting: 中国～ Chinese ink and wash

水暖 shuǐnuǎn ① hot water central heating system ② water supply and heating

水球 shuǐqiú［体］water polo

水泥 shuǐní cement: ～标号 cement grade. ～厂 cement plant

水平 shuǐpíng level; standard: ～流动 horizontal mobility. 文化～ cultural level; standard of education

水乳交融 shuǐrǔ-jiāoróng be hand in glove with sb.; be in perfect harmony

水上 shuǐshàng water; overwater; water borne; aquatic: ～芭蕾 water ballet. ～公园 lakeside park. ～技艺表演 aquacade; aquashow. ～警察队 marine police. ～运动 aquatic sports

水深火热 shuǐshēn-huǒrè be plunged … into dire suffering; deep water and scorching fire — an abyss of suffering; in extreme (great) misery

水手 shuǐshǒu seaman; sailor;［总称］crew

水土 shuǐtǔ ① water and soil: ～流失 water losses and soil erosion ② climate: ～不服 not accustomed to the climate; not acclimatized

水位 shuǐwèi water level

水文 shuǐwén hydrology

水污染 shuǐwūrǎn water pollution; water contamination

水泄不通 shuǐxiè-bùtōng be watertight; very crowded; packed with people; be so jammed as to be impassable

水性 shuǐxìng skill (ability) in swimming

水域 shuǐyù waters; water area; a body of water

水灾 shuǐzāi flood; inundation

水栽法 shuǐzāifǎ [农] hydroponics

水涨船高 shuǐzhǎng-chuángāo When the river rises the boat goes up — things improve when the general situation improves

水中捞月 shuǐzhōng-lāoyuè catch the moon in the water; fish for the moon's reflection; a fruitless attempt; plough the sands; fish in the air; make vain efforts

水准 shuǐzhǔn level; standard

水渍险 shuǐzìxiǎn with particular average (W.P.A.)

水族 Shuǐzú ① Shui nationality; Shuis (living mainly in Guizhou Province) ② aquatic animals: ～馆 aquarium

shuì

税 shuì〈名〉tax; duty: 对…征税 levy a tax on

税额 shuì'é amount of tax to be paid

税款 shuìkuǎn tax payment; taxation: ～专用 earmarking of taxes

税率 shuìlǜ tax rate; rate of taxation; tariff rate

税目 shuìmù tax items; taxable item

税收 shuìshōu tax revenue; taxation: ～政策 tax policy

税务 shuìwù taxation: ～稽查员 inspector of taxes. ～员 tax collector. ～局 tax bureau

税则 shuìzé tax regulations (rules)

税政 shuìzhèng tax administration

税制 shuìzhì tax system; taxation

税种 shuìzhǒng items of taxation; categories of taxes

睡 shuì〈动,名〉sleep: 好好～一觉 have a good sleep. ～得好 sleep well

睡梦 shuìmèng sleep; slumber

睡眠 shuìmián sleep

睡衣 shuìyī night clothes; pajamas

睡意 shuìyì sleepiness; drowsiness: 有～ be drowsy

睡着 shuìzháo get asleep; fall asleep

shǔn

吮 shǔn〈动〉suck

吮吸 shǔnxī suck: ～人民血汗的寄生虫 a parasite who lived on the people's sweat and blood

shùn

瞬 shùn〈动,名〉wink

瞬时 shùnshí instantaneous: ～速度 [物] instantaneous velocity

瞬息 shùnxī in a wink; in an instant; twinkling: ～间 in the twinkling of an eye. ～万变的局势 the fast-changing situation

顺 shùn〈介〉① in the same direction as; with:～流而下 go (float) downstream ② along; in the direction of:～着小道上山 go up the mountain along the path ③〈形〉agreeable; suitable:不～她的意 not fall in with her wishes〈动〉④ arrange; put in order:把船头～过来。Set the boat orderly ⑤ obey; yield to; act in submission to:～从某人的旨意 submit to sb.'s behest ⑥ act at one's convenience:～手关门 close the door after you

顺便 shùnbiàn ① at one's convenience; in passing:～访问 call in passing. 这一点现在～提一下。I mention this point now in passing. ② by the way; incidentally:～说一句 by the way; incidentally

顺差 shùnchā [外贸] favourable balance (of trade); surplus

顺畅 shùnchàng smooth and easy; unhindered

顺次 shùncì in order; in succession

顺从 shùncóng submit to; be obedient; yield to:～行为 submissive behaviours

顺风 shùnfēng following wind; tailwind; favourable (fair) wind:～转舵 tack with the wind; trim one's sails; chop around with the wind:一路～! Have a good journey!; a pleasant journery; bon voyage

顺乎人心 shùnhūrénxīn fulfil the common aspirations of the people

顺口 shùnkǒu ① speak casually; say without thinking:～答应 agree without thinking ② read smoothly; easy to read; smooth:～溜 jingle; doggerel

顺利 shùnlì smoothly; successfully:会议进行得很～。The meeting went off without a hitch.

顺路 shùnlù ① on one's way (to); in passing:～买些东西 do some shopping on the way ② direct route

顺手 shùnshǒu ① without difficulty; smoothly:事情办得相当～。It was done without a hitch. ② conveniently; without any trouble:出去时请～关门。Please, close the door when you go out. ③ do sth. as a natural sequence or simultaneously:我们扫完院子,～把房间也扫了一扫。After sweeping the courtyard, we might as well clean the rooms.

顺手牵羊 shùnshǒu-qiānyáng lead away a goat in passing — pick up something on the sly; walk off with something; lead away the sheep offhand; spirit … away

顺水 shùnshuǐ with the current; downstream:～人情 do sb. a favour without causing the slightest trouble to oneself. ～推舟 sail with the current; take advantage of the favourable trend

顺我者存,逆我者亡 shùnwǒzhě cún,nìwǒzhě wáng Those who

are with us will thrive and prosper, those who are against us will come to their doom.; Those who submit will prosper, those who resist shall perish.

顺序 shùnxù order; sequence: 按字母～排列 be arranged in alphabetical order

顺眼 shùnyǎn pleasing to the eye: 看不～ be offensive to the eye

顺应 shùnyìng comply with; conform to

shuō

说 shuō〈动〉① say; speak; talk: 直～出来。Say it out. ② explain: ～明真相 explain the true situation ③ blame; criticize; scold: ～了她一顿 give her a scold ④〈名〉theory; doctrine; teaching: 著书立～ write books to expound a theory

说白 shuōbái recitation

说不过去 shuō bu guòqù can't be justified; be unreasonable

说不上 shuōbushàng ① can't say; be hard to tell: 她是否在家还～。It's hard to tell whether she is at home or not. ② not worth mentioning: 他们所举的理由都是～的。None of the reasons they gave were worth mentioning.

说曹操,曹操到 shuō cáocāo, cáocāo dào Talk (speak) of the devil, and he is sure to appear (come).

说唱 shuōchàng a genre of popular entertainment consisting mainly of talking and singing, e. g., comic dialogue, *dagu* (大鼓), etc.: ～艺术 art of speech and song. 民间～文学 folk ballads

说出 shuōchū take the words out of sb.'s mouth: ～话来滴水不漏。However much you may say, nothing ever leaks out.

说穿 shuōchuān ① disclose; reveal ② to put it bluntly; to tell the plain truth; the simple fact is that…

说大话 shuōdàhuà talk big; brag; boast

说到 shuōdào speak of; talk about: ～做到 put words into deeds; do what one says; carry out one's pledge; match one's deeds to one's words; live up to one's words

说法 shuōfǎ ① formulation; statement; argument; assertion; view: 这种～是不正确的。This argument is unsound. ② way of saying; way of putting things; wording: 换一个～ put it in another way

说风凉话 shuō fēngliánghuà make irresponsible and carping comments

说服 shuōfú persuade; convince; talk sb. over: 用～教育的方法 by the method of persuasion and education

说话 shuōhuà speak; talk; say: ～算数 mean what one says. 孩子还不会～。The child can't talk yet.

说话听声,锣鼓听音 shuōhuà tīng shēng,luógǔ tīng yīn The words are the mirror of one's mind.; The words are the criterion of the man.

说谎 shuōhuǎng tell a lie; lie

说教 shuōjiào deliver a sermon; sermonize; moralize; preach

说空话 shuōkōnghuà use empty (fine) words

说来话长 shuōlái-huàcháng It is a long story.

说理 shuōlǐ reason things out; be reasonable; appeal to reason; argue:咱们找她～去。Let's go and have it out with her.

说漏嘴 shuōlòuzuǐ slip of the tongue; Conversation was getting out of hand.

说明 shuōmíng ① explain; illustrate; show; give an account of; make (sth.) clear:～理由 give reasons ② demonstrate; indicate:～书 (a booklet of) directions; technical manual; (of a play or film) synopsis

说情 shuōqíng plead for mercy for sb.; say a good word for sb.; intercede for sb.:为另一个人(为某事)向某人～ intercede with sb. for another person (for sth.)

说书 shuōshū tell stories:～艺术 narrative art

说闲话 shuōxiánhuà make critical or sarcastic remarks on the sidelines; make idle talk; talk behind sb.'s back

说一不二 shuōyī-bù'èr say one and it never become two; mean what one says; stand by one's word

shuò

烁 shuò〈形〉bright; shining:闪～ glimmer; twinkle

朔 shuò〈名〉① the first day of the lunar month ② new moon ③ north:～风 north wind

朔望月 shuòwàngyuè lunar month

硕 shuò〈形〉great; large

硕大无朋 shuòdàwúpéng exceptionally large; gigantic

硕果 shuòguǒ great achievements; rich fruits

硕士 shuòshì Master:～学位 Master's degree

数 shuò〈副〉frequently; repeatedly

另见 shǔ,shù

数见不鲜 shuòjiànbùxiān common occurrence; nothing new; It is often seen.

sī

斯 sī ①〈代〉this:～时 at this moment ②〈副〉then; thus

斯文 sīwén refined; gentle; graceful:～扫地 be a disgrace to the educated class. 举止～ refined in manner

厮 sī〈名〉① male servant ② fellow; guy:那～ that guy ③〈副〉with each other; together;

mutually：～混 play (fool) around together

厮打 sīdǎ come to blows；scuffle

撕 sī〈动〉rip；tear：把某物～成碎片 tear sth. to pieces (shreds，bits)

撕毁 sīhuǐ tear up；tear to pieces (shreds)：～协定 tear up an agreement

撕开 sīkāi tear open：把信～ tear open a letter

撕破脸 sīpòliǎn put aside all considerations of face；not spare sb.'s sensibilities

撕下 sīxià tear off；tear down：～假面具 tear off the mask；unmask

嘶 sī〈动〉① neigh：人喊马～ men shouting and horses neighing ② become hoarse：声～力竭 shout oneself hoarse

嘶叫 sījiào ① shout；yell；scream ② (of horses) neigh；whinny；(of donkeys) bray

嘶哑 sīyǎ hoarse

思 sī〈动〉① think；deliberate；consider：前～后想 think over again and again ② long for；think of：～亲 think of one's parents with affection ③〈名〉thought；thinking；idea：学会～考 learn to think

思辩 sībiàn [哲] speculation：～表述 speculative exposition

思潮 sīcháo ① trend of thought；ideological trend；trend；intellectual trend：文艺～ literary trends ② thoughts：～澎湃 thoughts surging in one's mind

思考 sīkǎo think deeply；ponder over；consider；reflect：～问题 reflect upon a problem. 哲学的～ philosophical thinking

思量 sīliang turn sth. over in one's mind；ponder (over)；consider

思路 sīlù train of thought；thinking：打断～ interrupt one's train of thought

思虑 sīlǜ contemplate；consider carefully；deliberate

思慕 sīmù think of sb. with respect；admire

思念 sīniàn think of；long for；be anxious about；miss：～母亲 miss one's mother

思索 sīsuǒ think over；ponder；reflect upon：反复～这个问题 turn the problem over and over in one's mind

思维 sīwéi [哲] thinking；thought；reasoning

思乡 sīxiāng be homesick

思想 sīxiǎng thought；idea；thinking；ideology：～包袱 something weighing on one's mind. ～见面 have a frank exchange of ideas；candid exchange of ideas. ～家 thinker. ～内容 ideological content. ～开小差 be absent-minded. 解开了～疙瘩 dispel a mental knot. 有～准备 be mentally prepared (for，to do)

思绪 sīxù ① train of thought；thinking ② feeling

私 sī〈形〉① private；personal：～事 private affairs ② selfish：

～利 selfish interest ③ secret：～话 confidential talk ④ illegal；illicit：～卖 sell products illicitly

私奔 sībēn elopement：～婚姻 Gretna (Green) marriage. ～者 eloper

私藏武器 sīcáng wǔqì unlawful possession of weapons

私产 sīchǎn private (personal) property

私仇 sīchóu personal enmity (grudge)：报～ satisfy a personal grudge

私邸 sīdǐ private residence (of a high-ranking offical)

私底下 sīdǐxia in private；in secret

私法 sīfǎ private law

私访 sīfǎng (of officials) go incognito among the people to make investigations

私愤 sīfèn personal spite：泄～ vent personal spite

私货 sīhuò smuggled goods；contraband goods

私交 sījiāo personal friendship

私利 sīlì private intrests；personal gain：图～pursue private ends

私立 sīlì privately run；private：～学校 private school

私了(私下和解) sīliǎo(sīxià héjiě) [法] compounding

私囊 sīnáng private purse：饱～ line one's pockets；feather one's nest

私情 sīqíng personal relationships：不徇～ not swayed by personal considerations

私人 sīrén ① private；personal：～企业 private enterprise ② one's own man：任用～ fill a post with one's own man

私生活 sīshēnghuó private life

私生子 sīshēngzǐ illegitimate child；child born out of wedlock；bastard

私塾 sīshú old-style private school

私通 sītōng ① have secret communication with (the enemy) ② have illicit relationship with；adultery

私相授受 sīxiāngshòushòu make an illicit transfer；make an underhand transaction；illegally pass things between individuals

私心 sīxīn selfish motives；selfishness：～杂念 selfish ideas and personal considerations

私刑 sīxíng illegal punishment meted out by a kangaroo court；extralegal punishment

私营 sīyíng privately owned；private：～工商业 privately-owned industrial and commercial enterprise

私有 sīyǒu privately owned；private：～权 private property. ～制 private ownership

私欲 sīyù selfish desire；lust

私自 sīzì ① in secret；privately；without permission ② [非法的] illegally：～拆开邮件 open mail of one's own accord. ～出售公产 illegally sell public property

司

sī ①〈动〉manage；administer；take charge of：各～其事 Each attends to his own duties.

②〈名〉department (under a ministry):外交部礼宾～ the Protocol Department of the Ministry of Foreign Affairs

司法 sīfǎ administration of justice:～程序 judicial process. ～独立 judicial independence. ～工作人员 judicial personnel. ～机关 judicial organs; judiciary. ～鉴定 expert testimony (evidence)

司机 sījī driver; chauffeur

司空见惯 sīkōng-jiànguàn common sight (occurrence); it is quite common for

司令 sīlìng commander: ～部 headquarters. ～员 commander

司马昭之心,路人皆知 sīmǎzhāo zhīxīn, lùrén jié zhī Sima Zhao's ill intent is known to all—the villain's design is obvious.; Sima Zhao's trick is obvious to every man in the street.; all too evident; obvious to everybody

司售人员 sīshòu rényuán drivers and ticket conductors

司务长 sīwùzhǎng quartermaster; supply chief

司仪 sīyí master of ceremonies

丝 sī〈名〉① silk:生～ raw silk ② wire; threadlike thing:蛛网～ the threads of a spider web ③ a tiny bit; trace:一～不差 not a bit of difference

丝绸 sīchóu silk:～之路 the Silk Road

丝毫 sīháo a bit; a jot; an iota: ～也不 not a bit; not a jot

丝网印刷 sīwǎng yìnshuā screen printing

丝织品 sīzhīpǐn ① silk fabrics; silks ② silk knit goods

丝织业 sīzhīyè silk weaving industry

丝竹画 sīzhúhuà painting on bamboo splints

sǐ

死 sǐ ①〈动〉die; pass away:病～ die of illness〈形〉② dead:～人 a dead person ③ fixed; rigid:～规矩 a rigid rule ④ implacable; deadly:～敌 sworn (mortal) enemy ⑤〈副〉extremely; to death:高兴得要～ be extremely happy

死板 sǐbǎn rigid; stiff; inflexible; mechanical:办事～ work in a mechanical way

死别 sǐbié be parted by death; part forever

死不瞑目 sǐbù-míngmù turn in one's grave; die with some injustice unredressed; die without closing one's eyes (with grudge unsatisfied)

死沉沉 sǐchénchén ① heavy as lead; extremely heavy ② silent as the grave; still as death ③ glum; sullen; gloomy:脸色～的 look glum; put on a sullen countenance

死党 sǐdǎng sworn followers

死得其所 sǐdéqísuǒ die a worthy death

死等 sǐděng wait indefinitely:他们不能在这里～,应该派人去打听一下,看出了什么事。They can't wait here indefinitely. They should send someone to find out what's happened.

死敌 sǐdí deadly enemy; mortal enemy; implacable foe

死对头 sǐduìtou deadly enemy; irreconcilable opponent

死工夫 sǐgōngfu hard persevering work; sheer hard work: 你想通过考试,不下～是不行的。You won't pass the exam unless you put in some real hard work.

死胡同 sǐhútòng dead end; blind alley

死缓 sǐhuǎn death sentence (penalty) with reprieve

死灰复燃 sǐhuī-fùrán dying embers glowing again—resurgence; come to life again; rise again from the ashes; dying embers flaring up again

死机 sǐjī [计算机] crash (of computer); a crashed computer

死记 sǐjì memorize mechanically; learn by rote; learn without comprehension

死角 sǐjiǎo ① dead angle; dead space ② a spot as yet untouched by a trend, political movement, etc.

死教材 sǐjiàocái fixed teaching material

死老虎 sǐlǎohǔ a dead tiger—a man who has lost his power and influence

死里逃生 sǐlǐ-táoshēng escape by the skin of one's teeth; have a narrow escape; barely escape with one's life; escape with one's neck

死路 sǐlù road to ruin (destruction); dead end; impasse: ～一条。There is no way out.

死马当做活马医 sǐmǎ dàngzuò huómǎ yī doctor a dead horse as if it were still alive—make every possible effort; not give up for lost

死难 sǐnàn die in an accident or a political incident (esp. for a revolutionary cause): ～烈士 martyr

死皮赖脸 sǐpí-làiliǎn thick-skinned and hard to shake off; brazen and unreasonable

死气沉沉 sǐqì-chénchén lifeless; spiritless; stagnant

死囚 sǐqiú a convict sentenced to death; a convict awaiting execution

死去活来 sǐqù-huólái be half alive (dead); be mad with grief; be in deep pain: 哭得～ weep one's heart out

死伤 sǐshāng the dead and the wounded; casualties

死神 sǐshén Death (personified)

死生有命,富贵在天 sǐshēng yǒu mìng, fùguì zài tiān life and death are a matter of Destiny; wealth and honour depend on Heaven

死尸 sǐshī corpse; dead body

死亡 sǐwáng death; doom: ～率 death rate; mortality. ～证明书 certificate of death

死无葬身之地 sǐ wú zàngshēn zhīdì die without a place for

burial—come to a bad end

死心 sǐxīn give up the idea; drop the idea forever; have no more illusions about sth.

死心塌地 sǐxīn-tādì be dead set (on); be hell-bent on; dance obediently

死心眼儿 sǐxīnyǎnr stubborn; as obstinate as a mule

死刑 sǐxíng death penalty (sentence); capital punishment: ～缓期执行 death penalty with a suspension of execution. 判处～ sentence sb. to death

死因 sǐyīn cause of death: ～调查 death inquiry

死有余辜 sǐyǒu-yúgū One's crime deserves more than death.; Even death would not expiate all one's crimes.; Even death would be too good for him.

死于非命 sǐyú fēimìng die an unnatural (violent) death; die in one's boots

死者 sǐzhě the dead; the deceased

死症 sǐzhèng incurable disease

死罪 sǐzuì capital crime (offence)

sì

肆 sì ①〈形〉wanton; unbridled: ～意侮谩 unbridled insults and vilification ②〈名〉shop; store: 茶楼酒～ teahouses and wineshops ③〈数〉four

肆虐 sìnüè indulge in wanton massacre or persecution; wreak havoc

肆无忌惮 sìwújìdàn brazen; unscrupulous; unbridled; without any scruples

肆意 sìyì wantonly; recklessly wilfully: ～攻击 make wanton attacks on sb.. ～挥霍公款 freely (recklessly) squander public money

寺 sì〈名〉temple: 清真～ mosque

寺院 sìyuàn temple; monastery

寺主 sìzhǔ abbot

四 sì〈数〉four

四边形 sìbiānxíng quadrilateral

四部 sìbù the four bibliographic categories—the four traditional divisions of a Chinese library

四不像 sìbùxiàng a hodge-podge of something that resembles nothing; neither fish nor fowl; nondescript ②［动物］mi-lu; David's deer

四重唱 sìchóngchàng (vocal) quartet

四处 sìchù all round; on all sides; everywhere: ～奔走 run (go) hither and thither

四方 sìfāng ① the four directions (north, south, east, west); all sides; all quarters: ～响应。Response came from every quarter. ② square; cubic: 一个～的盒子 a square box

四分五裂 sìfēn-wǔliè fall apart; split up; disintegrate; be rent by disunity; be split

四个现代化 sìgè xiàndàihuà the Four Modernizations (i. e. of industry, agriculture, defence, and science and technology)

四顾 sìgù look around (about):

～无人 look around and find no one in sight

四海 sìhǎi the four seas; the whole country; the whole world:～为家 make one's home wherever one is. ～之内皆兄弟 within the four seas all men are brothers

四合院儿 sìhéyuànr *siheyuanr*, a compound with houses around a square courtyard; quadrangle

四郊 sìjiāo suburbs; outskirts

四邻 sìlín one's near neighbours

四面八方 sìmiàn-bāfāng in all directions; far and near; everywhere; all around

四面楚歌 sìmiàn-chǔgē be besieged on all sides; be utterly isolated; land oneself in a tight place (spot); be driven to the wall; under fire from all quarters; be in dire straits; completely isolated; be assailed on all sides

四平八稳 sìpíngbāwěn ① (act) in a methodical and well-balanced way; very steady; on an even keel:做事～ handle affairs on an even keel ② be overcautious

"四人帮" Sìrénbāng the Gang of Four

四舍五入 sìshě-wǔrù round up or down; round off

四时 sìshí the four seasons:～鲜果 fresh fruits of every season

四体 sìtǐ the four limbs (of man); arms and legs

四通八达 sìtōng-bādá lead to all directions; accessible from all directions; with great facilities of communication; rediate in every direction:公路～。Highways radiate in every direction.

四乡 sìxiāng the countryside around a town

四项基本原则 sìxiàng jīběn yuánzé Four Cardinal Principles, i. e., keeping to the socialist road and adhering to the people's democratic dictatorship, to leadership by the Communist Party of China and to Marxism-Leninism and Mao Zedong Thought

四肢 sìzhī the four limbs; arms and legs

四周 sìzhōu all around; on all sides

四座 sìzuò all the people present:语惊～ words that startle all present

似 sì ①〈形〉like; similar:内容相～ be similar in content ②〈动〉seem; appear:～乎不起什么作用 don't seem to function 另见 shì

似曾相识 sìcéngxiāngshí seem to have met before

似乎 sìhū as if; it seems:她～在说谎。It seems that she was lying.

似是而非 sìshì'érfēi appear what it is really not; apparently true, but really wrong; not such as it seems; specious:～的推理 specious reasoning

似水流年 sìshuǐliúnián time passes swiftly like flowing water; youth slips away like flowing water

俟 sì〈动〉wait：～机进攻 wait for the right moment to attack

伺 sì〈动〉① watch：～机 watch for a chance ② wait for；abide：～机再起 wait for an opportunity to stage a comeback

伺机 sìjī wait (for) one's chance；abide one's time：～而动 wait for the opportune moment to go into action

伺隙 sìxì wait for a chance；watch for an opportunity

饲 sì〈动〉raise；rear；breed；feed：～养家畜 breed cattle

饲料 sìliào fodder；feed：～作物 feed crop

饲养 sìyǎng raise；rear；breed；tend：～场 breeding farm；feed lot；[养猪的] pig farm. ～家禽 rear poultry

驷 sì〈名〉① a team of four horses ② horse

驷马 sìmǎ a team of four horses

嗣 sì ①〈动〉succeed；inherit：～位 succeed to the throne ②〈名〉heir；descendant：无～ heirless；without issue

嗣后 sìhòu subsequently；afterwards；hereafter；later on

sōng

松 sōng ①〈名〉pine：～柏长青 as evergreen as the fir and pine ②〈形〉loose；slack；lax：土质很～。The soil is loose. ③〈动〉loosen；relax；slacken：～开螺丝 loosen screws

松绑 sōngbǎng have one untied；free a person (or an organization) from unnecessary restrictions：为企业～ unfetter enterprises

松弛 sōngchí loose；slack；lax limp；flabby：纪律～ be loose in discipline

松动 sōngdòng ① become less crowded；have more space ② become flexible：口气～ take a flexible tone；become flexible

松劲 sōngjìn relax one's efforts；slack (off)：～情绪 slack mood

松快 sōngkuai ① be less crowded：搬走了一些桌子和椅子，屋里～多了。With desks and chairs moved out, there's much more space in the room. ② feel relieved：吃了药以后身上～多了。I feel much better after taking the medicine. ③relax：干了几天活，～～吧。After several days' work, let's relax a bit.

松散 sōngsǎn ① shaky；loose：文章结构～。The article is loosely organized. ② inattentive

松树 sōngshù pine tree；pine

松松垮垮 sōngsōng-kuǎkuǎ ① not solid or firm；unsteady ② slack；sluggish

松懈 sōngxiè slack；relax；weaken：工作～ be slack in one's work

松心 sōngxīn feel relieved；have ease of mind；feel carefree and

happy
松脂 sōngzhī rosin; pine resin
嵩 sōng ①〈名〉a high mountain ②〈形〉high; lofty

sǒng

悚 sǒng〈形〉terrified; afraid
悚然 sǒngrán terrified; horrified: 毛骨～ with one's hair standing on end; horror-stricken
竦 sǒng〈形〉① respectful ② terrified; horrified
怂 sǒng
怂恿 sǒngyǒng ① urge; prompt; encourage; egg sb. on (to do sth.) ② abet; instigate
耸 sǒng〈动〉① tower; rise: 高～在平原上 tower over the plain ② frighten; shock; alarm: 危言～听 exaggerate things just to frighten people
耸动 sǒngdòng ① shrug (one's shoulders) ② create a sensation
耸立 sǒnglì tower aloft; rise straight up
耸人听闻 sǒngréntīngwén deliberately exaggerate so as to create a sensation; sensational; thrilling: ～的新闻报道 a sensational news report
耸入云霄 sǒngrùyúnxiāo tower to the skies: ～的高山 a high mountain towering to the skies

sòng

宋 sòng ① a feudal state in the Zhou Dynasty (c. 11th century—256 B.C.), covering the present-day Shangqiu) area in Henan Province ② the Song Dynasty (420—479), one of the Southern Dynasties ③ the Song Dynasty (960—1279) ④ a surname
宋词 sòngcí poetry of the Song Dynasty
送 sòng〈动〉① deliver; send; carry: ～个信 send a message ② see off: 到火车站～人 see sb. off at the station ③ give; present: ～他一支钢笔 give him a pen
送别 sòngbié see (send) sb. off; wish sb. bon voyage
送殡 sòngbìn attend a funeral; take part in a funeral procession
送达 sòngdá [法] service: ～传票 service of summons. ～人 person serving (a document). ～证 service certificate
送股 sònggǔ [股票] gift shares
送货 sònghuò send (deliver) goods: ～上门 deliver goods to the customer's house; send goods to customer's doorstep; provide people with door-to-door service
送客 sòngkè see a guest to the door; see a visitor (guest) out
送礼 sònglǐ give sb. a present; present a gift (to) sb.

送命 sòngmìng lose one's life; get killed

送人情 sòngrénqíng ① do favours at no great cost to oneself ② make a gift of sth.

送上门 sòngshàngmén deliver to the doorstep (fig)

送死 sòngsǐ court death

送温暖工程 sòng wēnnuǎn gōngchéng "warmth extending-project" (i. e., gifts or welfare donations of food, money, etc. to the needy)

送信 sòngxìn ① send a letter to sb. ② send word; give sb. a message

送行 sòngxíng ① see sb. off; send sb. off; wish sb. bon voyage ② [饯行] give a send-off party

送养人 sòngyǎngrén donors for adoption (people who give up their own natural-born children for others to raise as their own children in accordance with legal procedures)

送葬 sòngzàng take part in a funeral procession; attend a funeral; have a funeral ceremony

送终 sòngzhōng attend upon a dying parent or other senior member of one's family: 养老～ provide for (support) one's parents and attend upon them when they are dying.

诵 sòng〈动〉① read aloud; chant ② recite

诵读 sòngdú read aloud; recite; chant: ～诗篇 recite poems

讼 sòng〈动〉① bring a case to court: 诉～ lawsuit ② dispute; argue

讼案 sòng'àn lawsuit

讼词 sòngcí legal cases: 包揽～ engage in pettifoggery

讼事 sòngshì lawsuit; litigation

颂 sòng ①〈动〉praise; laud; extol: ～古非今 eulogize the past at the expense of the present; extol the past and negate the present ②〈名〉song; eulogy; ode:《黄河～》Ode to the Yellow River

颂词 sòngcí complimentary address; panegyric; eulogy: 向某人致～ pronounce a eulogy on sb.

颂歌 sònggē song of praise; ode

颂扬 sòngyáng praise; extol; eulogize; sing the praise of; laud: ～备至 extol (laud) sb. to the skies

颂谀 sòngyú flatter (with overpraise); praise to the skies; fawn upon

sōu

搜 sōu〈动〉search; seek; ransack: ～山 search the hills

搜捕 sōubǔ track down (search) and arrest

搜查 sōuchá search: ～证 search warrant

搜肠刮肚 sōucháng-guādù rack one's brains

搜刮 sōuguā extort; fleece; plunder：～民脂民膏 fleecing people

搜集 sōují gather；collect：～资料 collect data

搜罗 sōuluó collect；gather；recruit：～人才 recruit talented persons

搜身 sōushēn frisk；make a body search

搜索 sōusuǒ search for；seek for：～枯肠 ransack（rack）one's brains；think hard

搜寻 sōuxún search for；look for；seek

嗖 sōu〈象〉whiz：汽车～的一声从她身边开过。The car whizzed by her.

馊 sōu sour；spoiled：～主意 rotten（lousy）idea. 牛奶～了。The milk has turned sour.

馊点子 sōudiǎnzi stupid suggestion；lousy idea：谁出的这个～？Who made this stupid suggestion？

艘 sōu〈量〉（for boats or ships）：一～油船 one tanker

sǒu

叟 sǒu〈名〉an old man：邻～ the old man who lives next door

薮 sǒu〈名〉① a shallow lake overgrown with wild plants ② a gathering place of fish or beasts；den；haunt

sòu

嗽 sòu〈动〉cough：干～ a dry cough

sū

苏 sū ①〈动〉return to life；come to；revive：死而复～ come back to life ②〈名〉Soviet

苏打 sūdá soda：～饼干 soda biscuit（cracker）

苏区 sūqū Chinese Soviet Areas（established during the Second Revolutionary Civil War Period，1927-1937）

苏醒 sūxǐng come to；regain consciousness；revive

酥 sū ①〈形〉crisp；short：～糖 crunchy candy ②〈名〉shortbread；crisp biscuit：杏仁～ almond shortbread

酥脆 sūcuì crisp：～的饼干 crisp（short）biscuit

酥胸 sūxiōng soft and white breasts（of a woman）

酥油 sūyóu butter：～茶 buttered tea

sú

俗 sú ①〈名〉custom；convention：社会风～ social customs〈形〉② vulgar：～不可耐 unbearably vulgar ③ worldly；mundane；secular：凡夫～子所关心的事 secular concerns

俗话 súhuà common saying; proverb:～说 as the saying goes

俗民 súmín folk:～生活研究 folk life research

俗气 súqì ① vulgarity; philistinism ② vulgar; in poor taste

俗曲 súqǔ folk ballads:中国～演唱文学 Chinese oral and performing literature

俗人 súrén ① layman ② vulgar person; philistine

俗套 sútào convention; set practices:不落～ break with set practices

俗文学 súwénxué popular literature:～资料 vernacular literary works

俗务 súwù everyday matters; routine business:～缠身 be tied up with routine business

俗语 súyǔ common saying; folk adage; vernacular

俗众 súzhòng profane crowd

sù

宿 sù ①〈动〉put up for (lodge for) the night; stay over night:提供某人膳～ board and lodge sb.〈形〉② long-standing; old:～志 long-cherished ambition ③ veteran:～将 veteran general

宿娼 sùchāng frequent prostitutes; fornication

宿仇 sùchóu long-standing enmity

宿敌 sùdí old enemy

宿疾 sùjī old disease (trouble)

宿酒 sùjiǔ hangover:～未醒 still having a hangover

宿命论 sùmìnglùn [哲] fatalism; predestination; determinism:～者 fatalist

宿营 sùyíng take up quarters; encamp

宿缘 sùyuán predestined relationship

宿怨 sùyuàn old scores (grudge); hereditary feud

宿愿 sùyuàn long-cherished wish (desire)

宿债 sùzhài long-standing debt; old debt

塑 sù〈动〉mould (with clay); model:～像 mould a statue

塑胶 sùjiāo plastic cement:～跑道 plastic cement race track

塑料 sùliào plastics:～薄膜 plastic film. ～炸弹 plastic bomb

塑像 sùxiàng ① mould a statue ② statue; graven image; sculpture

塑造 sùzào ① mould; model:～人像 mould a statue. ～艺术 modelling ② portray; create images:～英雄形象 create heroic images

诉 sù〈动〉① tell; inform; relate:告～我住在哪儿。Tell me where you live. ② accuse; complain:倾～ pour out (one's troubles; feelins, etc.) ③ appeal to; resort to:～诸武力 resort to force

诉败 sùbài lose a case

诉辩 sùbiàn pleading

诉苦 sùkǔ complain of one's sufferings; pour out one's

grievances

诉讼 sùsòng lawsuit; suit; litigation; action: ～参与人 participant in proceedings. ～活动 procedural activities. ～权利 procedural rights. ～文件 procedural document. 对某人提出～ bring an action against sb.; take legal proceedings against sb.

诉讼法 sùsòngfǎ procedural law

诉因 sùyīn cause of action; cause

诉冤 sùyuān[法] inform

诉诸 sùzhū resort to; have recourse to; appeal to: ～法律 have recourse to law; recource to proceedings. ～武力 resort (appeal) to arms; have recourse to force

诉状 sùzhuàng written accusation; indictment; plaint; petition

素 sù〈形〉① white: ～绢 white silk ② plain; simple: ～色 plain colour ③ native: ～情 one's disposition〈名〉④ vegetable: 两荤一～ two meat dishes and one vegetable dish ⑤ basic element: 毒～ poison ⑥〈副〉usually; always: 我和她～不相识。I don't know her at all.

素不相识 sùbùxiāngshí have never met; not be acquainted with each other

素材 sùcái (source) material: 搜集小说～ gathering material for a novel

素菜 sùcài vegetable dish

素常 sùcháng usually; habitually; ordinarily

素来 sùlái always; all along: 他们～守法。They always abide by the law.

素昧平生 sùmèipíngshēng have never met before; be a complete stranger to; know nothing about sb.: 我与她～。I have never made her acquaintance.; I don't know her at all.

素描 sùmiáo ① sketch; drawing ② literary sketch

素食 sùshí ① vegetarian foods (diet) ② be a vegetarian

素雅 sùyǎ simple but elegant; unadorned (quiet) and in good taste

素养 sùyǎng accomplishment; attainment; refinement: 音乐～ musical refinement

素愿 sùyuàn long-cherished desire (wish, aspiration)

素质 sùzhì quality; natural ability; timber: 那个青年人～好。That young man has good timber in him.

愫 sù〈名〉sincerity; sincere feeling

速 sù ①〈形〉quick; fast; rapid; speedy: 迅～完成的工作 fast work ②〈名〉speed; velocity: 加快～度 put on speed ③〈动〉speed up: 心跳加～。The heart speeds up.

速成 sùchéng speeded-up educational programme: ～班 crash course; streamlined course. ～识字法 accelerated literary method

速冻 sùdòng quick-freeze: ～饺子

quick-frozen dumplings

速度 sùdù speed; velocity; pace; [乐]tempo:工业化的～ the pace of industrialization. ～滑冰 speed skating

速记 sùjì ① take down in shorthand ② shorthand; stenography:～记者 shorthand reporter. ～员 stenographer

速决 sùjué quick decision:速战～ fight a quick battle for a quick decision

速率 sùlǜ speed; rate; velocity

速溶 sùróng quick-dissolving; instant

速效 sùxiào quick-acting; quick results; speedy effect

速写 sùxiě ① sketch ② literary sketch

粟

sù〈名〉millet

粟米 sùmǐ maize; Indian corn; corn

夙

sù〈形〉① early in the morning:～兴夜寐 rise early in the morning and sleep well at night ② long-standing; old:～世冤家 a bitter enemy

夙夜 sùyè morning and night

夙愿 sùyuàn long-cherished desire

肃

sù〈形〉① respectful ② solemn; serious:表情严～ look serious ③〈动〉wipe out; eliminate:～清…的思想影响 liquidate the ideological influence of

肃静 sùjìng solemn silence

肃立 sùlì stand solemnly; stand at attention:～默哀 stand in silent mourning

肃穆 sùmù ① solemn and quiet; solemn and respectful:纪念会气氛～。The commemoration meeting was permeated with a solemn atmosphere. ② respectful and congenial

肃清 sùqīng wipe out; clean up; weed out; eradicate; clear out; eliminate; mop up:～遗毒 wipe out pernicious influence

肃然起敬 sùrán-qǐjìng be filled with deep respect for sb.

肃杀 sùshā (of autumn or winter) stern; harsh:秋气～。The breath of autumn is harsh and raw.

肃政 sùzhèng rectify administration

簌

sù

簌簌 sùsù ①〈象〉rustle:风吹树叶～。The leaves are rustling in the wind. ② (tears) streaming down

suān

酸

suān ①〈名〉acid:～雨 acid rain ②〈形〉sour; sharp; tart:～梨 sour pear〈动〉③ feel grieved; distressed:心～ feel sad; be sick at heart ④ ache; tingle:腰～背痛 have a pain in the back

酸楚 suānchǔ grieved; distressed; miserable

酸溜溜 suānliūliū ① tart; sour ② pain; ache; tingle:周身～ have a vague feeling of pain all over ③ sad; mournful

酸梅汤 suānméitāng sweet-sour plum juice

酸牛奶 suānniúnǎi yoghurt; sour milk

酸软 suānruǎn aching and limp 四肢～ one's limbs all aching and limp

酸甜苦辣 suān-tián-kǔ-là sour, sweet, bitter, hot—joys and sorrows of life

酸痛 suāntòng dull pain; ache: 浑身～ have aches all over

酸味 suānwèi tart flavour; sour

酸辛 suānxīn misery; bitterness: 倾诉～ pour out one's bitterness

酸心 suānxīn ① be grieved; feel sad: 这出戏看了叫人～。It was heart-rending to see the play. ② suffer from heartburn

酸雨 suānyǔ acid rain

suàn

蒜 suàn〈名〉garlic: 一辫～ a braid of garlic

蒜黄 suànhuáng blanched garlic leaves

蒜苗 suànmiáo garlic bolt (sprout)

蒜头 suàntóu bulb (head) of garlic

算 suàn〈动〉① count; compute calculate; reckon: ～剥削帐 calculate the extent of exploitation ② consider; regard as; count as: 他可以～一个舞蹈家。He can be counted as a dancer. ③ include; count: 不要把他～在内。Count him out. ④ plan; calculate: 我打～下个月到上海去。I'm planning to going to Shanghai next month. ⑤〈副〉at long last; in the end; finally: 问题～解决了。The problem is finally solved.

算卦 suànguà tell sb.'s fortune or divine by using the Eight Trigrams

算计 suànji ① reckon; calculate ② plot; scheme: 暗中～别人 secretly scheme against others

算旧帐 suàn jiùzhàng settle an old account; settle an old score

算命 suànmìng fortune-telling: ～先生 fortune-teller

算盘 suànpán abacus; swanpan; suanpan: 打～ use (work) an abacus

算术 suànshù arithmetic

算数 suànshù count; stand; hold good (true): 我们说话是～的。We mean what we say.

算帐 suànzhàng ① reckon up a bill; do accounts; balance the books; state an account ② settle accounts with sb.; get even with sb.

suī

虽 suī〈连〉though; although; while; even if: ～死不足以蔽其辜。Even death could not expiate his crime.

虽然 suīrán though; although

虽死犹生 suīsǐyóushēng live on in spirit

suí

随 suí〈动〉① follow; go along with: ～军家属 the families who have followed the army ② adapt to; comply with: ～顺 yield and comply ③ let (sb. do as he likes): ～他们的便。They may do so, if they please. ④ along with (some other action): 请你～手把门带上。Please close the door as you go out.

随笔 suíbǐ informal essays; casual literary notes; jottings: ～作家 essayist

随便 suíbiàn ① casual; informal; random: ～说了几句 make some casual remarks ② careless; slipshod: 工作～ be slipshod in work ③ do as one likes: ～你吧。Do as you like. ④ any: ～什么时候 at any time

随波逐流 suíbō-zhúliú serve the time; drift with the stream (tide; current); be swayed by fashion

随从 suícóng ① accompany (one's superior); attend ② retinue; suite; entourage; retainer

随大溜 suídàliù drift (swim) with the stream; follow (conform to) the trend; do as others do

随带 suídài going along with; have sth. taken along with one: 她～行李三件。She took along with her three pieces of luggage.

随地 suídì anywhere; everywhere: 不要～乱扔东西。Don't litter.

随风倒 suífēngdǎo bend with the wind—be easily swayed (by whichever side has more power or influence)

随风转舵 suífēng-zhuǎnduò trim one's sails

随感 suígǎn random thoughts: 《旅美～》*Random Thoughts on Travels in the United States*

随行就市 suíháng-jiùshì (of prices) fluctuate in line with market conditions

随和 suíhe amiable; obliging; sociable; accommodating

随机 suíjī random; stochastic: ～抽样 random (stochastic) sampling

随机应变 suíjī-yìngbiàn be able to change (act) according to circumstances; adjust to changing circumstances; change to suit occasions; adapt oneself to changing conditions

随即 suíjí immediately; at once; presently

随军 suíjūn go along with an army

随口 suíkǒu ① speak thoughtlessly (casually) ② without hesitation; readily: ～用法语回答 answer in French without hesitation

随人俯仰 suírénfǔyǎng follow sb. servilely; live under the thumb of others; submit to others' whim and will; submit to (stand at) one's beck and call; be at one's mercy; find oneself at the mercy of others

随身 suíshēn (carry) on one's

person; (take) with one: ～听 Walkman. ～行李 personal luggage

随声附和 suíshēng-fùhè echo what others say; parrot the opinions of others; agree to what other people say

随时 suíshí at any time; as the occasion demands; at a moment's notice; at all times

随手 suíshǒu conveniently: ～关门。Shut the door after you.

随俗 suísú comply with convention; follow the customs; do as everybody else does

随同 suítóng accompany; be in company with

随想曲 suíxiǎngqǔ [乐] capriccio

随心所欲 suíxīn-suǒyù get (have) one's own way; do as one likes (pleases); follow one's bent; wilfully; arbitrarily

随行人员 suíxíng rényuán suite; party; entourage

随意 suíyì at will; as one pleases; at one's pleasure

随遇而安 suíyù'ér'ān adapt oneself to circumstances; reconcile oneself to one's situation: ～的喜剧演员 happy-go-lucky comedian

随员 suíyuán ① entourage; suite; party ② [外] attaché

随葬品 suízàngpǐn burial accessories; funeral objects; burial objects

随着 suízhe along with; in pace with; in the wake of: ～时间的过去 with the lapse of time

绥 suí ①〈形〉 peaceful ②〈动〉 pacify

绥靖 suíjìng appease; pacify: ～政策 policy of appeasement (pacification)

suǐ

髓 suǐ〈名〉 ① marrow ② pith

髓腔 suǐqiāng medullary cavity

suì

碎 suì〈形〉 ① broken; fragmentary: 瓷器～片 broken bits of china ② garrulous; gabby: 嘴太～ be a regular chatterbox; talk too much ③〈动〉 break to pieces; smash: 玻璃杯打～了。The glass is smashed to pieces.

碎步 suìbù quick short steps

碎片 suìpiàn fragment; chip

碎尸万段 suìshī-wànduàn tear the body to thousands of pieces (said when swearing to destroy sb.)

碎石 suìshí broken stones; crushed stones: ～机 stone crusher. ～路 macadam road; broken stone road

遂 suì〈动〉 ① fulfil; satisfy: ～愿 have one's wish fulfilled; meet one's wishes ② succeed: 她自杀未～。She did not succeed in committing suicide. ③〈副〉then; thereupon

遂心 suìxīn after one's own heart; to one's liking: ～如意 be perfectly satisfied

遂意 suìyì attain one's heart's desire; be perfectly satisfied; to one's liking

遂愿 suìyuàn meet one's wishes; have one's wish fulfilled; fulfilment of one's wish

隧 suì

隧道 suìdào tunnel; underground passage

岁 suì〈名〉year

岁出科目 suìchū-kēmù account title for annual expenditures

岁除 suìchú New Year's Eve

岁寒三友 suìhánsānyǒu the three plant friends who thrive in cold weather—the pine, the bamboo, and the plum

岁入 suìrù account title for annual receipts

岁收 suìshōu annual income (in a state budget); revenue

岁月不饶人 suìyuè bù ráorén Time and tide wait for no man (one).

岁月蹉跎 suìyuè-cuōtuó The years roll by — spend one's life in fruitless efforts.; Let time slip by without accomplishing anything.; The years drift by.

岁月峥嵘 suìyuè-zhēngróng the most uncommon years and months of one's life

穗 suì〈名〉① ear of grain; spike: 麦～ the ear of wheat ② fringe; tassel

祟 suì〈名〉evil spirit; ghost: 作～ act like an evil spirit; haunt and plague; exercise an evil influence on

燧 suì〈名〉① flint ② beacon fire

sūn

孙 sūn〈名〉① grandchild ② generations below that of grandchild: 曾～ great-grandson

孙女 sūnnǚ granddaughter

孙子 sūnzi grandson

孙子兵法 Sūnzǐ bīngfǎ *The Art of War* by Sunzi

sǔn

损 sǔn〈动〉① decrease; lose: 增～ increase and decrease ② harm; injure: ～害人民的利益 impair (at the expense of) the interests of the people ③〈名〉loss; damage: ～害… do damage to…

损兵折将 sǔnbīng-zhéjiàng suffer heavy casualties

损公肥私 sǔngōng-féisī damage the public and fatten the private; benefit oneself at the expense of public interests; gain private interests at public expense

损害 sǔnhài hurt; impair; damage; infringe on; trespass upon; encroach upon; injury; harm: ～独立和主权 infringe on the independence and sovereignty. ～结果[法] harm-

ful consequences
损耗 sǔnhào ① loss; wear and tear:～率 proportion of goods damaged. ～费 cost of wear and tear ② wastage; wasting
损坏 sǔnhuài spoil; damage
损毁 sǔnhuǐ [法] damage
损人利己 sǔnrén-lìjǐ injure others for the sake of one's own advantage; profit at the expense of others (at other's expense); injure others in order to benefit oneself; gain at others' expense; seek satisfaction for oneself at the cost of others; benefit oneself at the cost (expense) of others; enrich oneself at the expense of others
损失 sǔnshī loss; damage:受到重大～ suffer heavy losses
损益 sǔnyì profit and loss; gains and losses:～计算书 profit-and-loss statement

笋 sǔn〈名〉bamboo shoot
笋干 sǔngān dried bamboo shoots
笋鸡 sǔnjī young chicken; broiler

隼 sǔn falcon

榫 sǔn tenon

suō

蓑 suō
蓑衣 suōyī straw or palm-bark rain cape; mat (reed) cape; rain cape

梭 suō〈名〉shuttle:穿～外交 shuttle diplomacy
梭标 suōbiāo spear:～队 spear corps
梭子 suōzi ① shuttle ② clip:打了一～子弹 fire a whole clip of ammunition

唆 suō〈动〉abet; instigate
唆使 suōshǐ abet; instigate; set on; put up to:～某人捣乱 put sb. up to do (doing) mischief

缩 suō〈动〉① shrink; contract:冷得～成一团 shrink with cold ② withdraw; drawback; recoil:吓得退～ recoil in terror
缩编 suōbiān cut down on staff member; cut army's strength
缩短 suōduǎn shorten; cut down; reduce:～距离 reduce the distance
缩减 suōjiǎn cut (down); reduce; diminish:～开支 cut down one's expenses
缩手 suōshǒu ① withdraw one's hand ② draw back; shrink (from):～缩脚 be overcautious
缩水 suōsuǐ [布匹] shrink:～率 shrinkage
缩微 suōwēi microcopy
缩小 suōxiǎo reduce; diminish; narrow:～高低工资的差距 bridging the irrational gaps in wages
缩写 suōxiě ① abbreviate ② abridge:～本 abridged edition
缩衣节食 suōyī-jiéshí economize on food and clothing
缩印 suōyìn reduced reprint:～本 compact edition; edition in reduced format
缩影 suōyǐng epitome; miniature;

microcosm：历史的～ a microcosm of history

suǒ

索 suǒ ①〈名〉large rope：船～ ship's rigging〈动〉② search：探～ search after ③ ask (for)；demand；exact：～取巨额赔偿费 extort huge amounts of indemnities

索道 suǒdào cableway；ropeway：高架～ telpher line；telpher

索价 suǒjià asking price

索赔 suǒpéi claim indemnity；demand compensation：～期限 deadline for demanding compensation. ～证件 document for claims；claims document

索取 suǒqǔ ask for；demand；claim

索然 suǒrán dull；insipid；tedious：～无味 dry；tedious

索性 suǒxìng just；simply；flatly：～否定说… simply deny that…

索引 suǒyǐn index：《中国社会科学》标题～ a subject index to *Social Sciences in China*

琐 suǒ〈形〉trivial；trifling；petty

琐事 suǒshì trifles；trivial matters；trivialities

琐碎 suǒsuì trifling；petty

琐闻 suǒwén bits of news

锁 suǒ ①〈名〉lock：挂～ padlock ②〈动〉lock up：～门 lock a door. ～住了滚滚黄沙的绿色林带 the green forest belt that hems in the moving sands

锁骨 suǒgǔ clavicle；collarbone

锁匠 suǒjiàng locksmith

锁链 suǒliàn ① chain ② shackles；fetters

锁钥 suǒyào ① key ② strategic gateway

所 suǒ〈名〉① place：住～ dwelling place ② [用做机关或其他办事地方的名称]institute；office：经济研究～ an institute of economics ③〈量〉[用于房屋等]：3～学校 three schools〈助〉④ [跟"为""或""被"合用，表示被动]：为人～笑 be laughed at ⑤[跟动词连用，代表接受动作的事物的词]：各尽～能 from each according to his ability ⑥[跟动词连用，动词后再用接受动作的事物的词]：他们～提的意见 the opinions they put forward

所长 suǒcháng one's strong point；one's forte：各有～。Each has his or her strong point.

所答非所问 suǒdá fēi suǒwèn not give a direct answer to a question；not answer to the point；give an irrelevant answer

所得 suǒdé ① what one gets ② earnings；income：～税申报表 income tax return

所属 suǒshǔ ① what is subordinate to one or under one's command ② what one belongs to or is affiliated with

所谓 suǒwèi what is called；so-called

所向披靡 suǒxiàng-pīmǐ sweep all before one；be ever-victorious; mowing down all resistance;(of troops) carry all before one

所向无前 suǒxiàngwúqián carry all before one; be irresistible

所以 suǒyǐ ① [表示因果关系]as a result; so; therefore:天太冷，～我不去了。It's too cold, so I'm not going. ② [用于固定词组中作宾语,表示实在的情由或适宜的举动]:忘乎～ forget oneself

所以然 suǒyǐrán the reason why; the whys and wherefores:知其然而不知其～ know it is so, but don't know why it is so

所有 suǒyǒu possess; own:～权 proprietary rights; title; ownership. ～制 system of ownership; ownership. ～人 owner; possessor

所在 suǒzài place; spot; location:～地 location; seat; locality; site

所长 suǒzhǎng director; head of an institute

T t

tā

它 tā〈代〉it

它们 tāmen they；them：～的 their；theirs. ～自己 themselves

塌 tā〈动〉① fall down；collapse：墙～了。The wall has fallen. ② fall in；cave in：～方 cave in ③ sink；droop：～鼻梁 a flat nose ④ calm down：～下心去 settle down to (work，etc.)

塌方 tāfāng ① cave in；collapse ② landslide

塌台 tātái fall from power；collapse

塌陷 tāxiàn fall in；cave in

踏 tā

另见 tà

踏实 tāshi steadfast；dependable；in a down-to-earth way：工作～ be steadfast in one's work；work in a down-to-earth way ② feel at ease：睡得～ have a sound sleep

踏踏实实 tātā-shishi in a thoroughgoing manner；on a firm footing：～地改革 reform in a thoroughgoing manner

他 tā〈代〉① he；him ② other；another

他处 tāchù in some other place；elsewhere

他方当事人 tāfāng dāngshìrén adverse party

他律(性) tālǜ(xìng) heteronomy

他们 tāmen they or them (referring to people)

他人 tārén another person；other people；others：～取向 other-orientation. ～支配的性格 other-directed personalities

他日 tārì some day；some other day；another time

他杀 tāshā homicide；killing by sb.

他物权 tāwùquán over the property of another；right over things of another

他乡 tāxiāng a place away from home；a strange land；an alien land

她 tā〈代〉she；her

她们 tāmen they；them：～的 their；theirs. ～自己 themselves

tǎ

塔 tǎ〈名〉① pagoda ② tower：水～ water tower

塔吊 tǎdiào tower crane

塔楼 tǎlóu turret；tower-like building

塔台 tǎtái ［航空］control tower

tà

拓 tà〈动〉make rubbings from inscriptions; picture, etc. on stone tablets or bronze vessels 另见 tuò

拓本 tàběn copy (book) of rubbings

拓片 tàpiàn rubbings from a tablet

榻 tà〈名〉couch: 竹～ bamboo couch. 同～ share a bed; sleep in the same bed

榻榻米 tàtàmì tatami; floor mats

挞 tà〈动〉flog; whip: 鞭～ castigate; lash

踏 tà〈动〉step (on); stamp; tread: 顶寒风～冰雪 tramp over frozen snow in icy winds 另见 tā

踏板 tàbǎn ① step; tread: 卡车的～ the step of a truck ② pedal; treadle (of a sewing machine, etc.)

踏步 tàbù mark time: ～不前 make no headway

踏勘 tàkān make an on-the-spot survey

踏破铁鞋无觅处,得来全不费工夫 tàpò tiěxié wú mìchù, délái quán bùfèi gōngfu You can wear out iron shoes in fruitless searching, and yet by a lucky chance you may find the lost thing without even looking for it.; Find sth. accidently after tracking miles in vain for it.

踏青 tàqīng have (go for) an outing in spring

tāi

胎 tāi〈名〉① foetus; embryo: 怀～ become or be pregnant ② birth: 头～ first born; first baby ③ padding; wadding; stuffing: 棉花～ the cotton padding of a quilt, etc.

胎儿 tāi'ér foetus; embryo

胎教 tāijiào antenatal instruction (i. e. influencing the development of the foetus by maternal impressions)

胎盘 tāipán placenta

胎生 tāishēng viviparity

tái

台 tái〈名〉[戏台] stage; [讲台、月台等] platform; [看台] stand: 讲～ rostrum ② table; desk ③ broadcasting station: 电视～ television broadcasting station ④ a special telephone service: 长途～ trunk call service

台本 táiběn acting copy; acting script; script; acting version; playscript with stage directions

台秤 táichèng platform-scale

台词 táicí (actor's) lines

台灯 táidēng desk lamp; table lamp

台风 táifēng [气]typhoon

台阶 táijiē flight of stairs; steps

台历 táilì desk calendar

台面 táimiàn ① on the table; aboveboard;in public ② winnings and losses (in gambling)

台球 táiqiú ① billiards ② billiard ball ③ table tennis; ping-pong

台柱子 táizhùzi backbone; pillar; mainstay

抬 tái〈动〉① lift up; raise ② carry (between persons):~担架 carry a stretcher

抬杠 táigàng argue for the sake of arguing; squabble (with); bicker (with); wrangle

抬高 táigāo raise; advance; boost:~身价 boost one's prestige; raise one's status

抬价 táijià raise prices; boost prices; force up prices; force up commodity price; at high price

抬轿子 táijiàozi carry a sedan chair (metaphor for flattering and currying favour with sb.)

抬举 táijǔ praise or promote sb. to show favour:不识~ not know how to appreciate sb.'s favour (kindness)

抬头 táitóu ① lift up one's head ② rise; gain ground ③ name of the buyer or payee:~支票 order check

tài

泰 tài〈形〉① calm; peaceful:国~民安。The country is prosperous and the people live in peace. ② extreme; most

泰斗 tàidǒu a leading authority; luminary; mogul:电影界~ a movie mogul

泰然 tàirán calm; composed:~自若 with great composure; be self-possessed. 处之~ take things calmly; take it easy

泰山 tàishān Mount Tai:~盖顶 with the force of an avalanche. ~压顶 bear down on one with the weight of Mount Tai

太 tài ①〈形〉highest; greater; remotest:~空 outer space〈副〉② too; excessively; over:~霸道 too truculent and tyrannical ③ extremely:~感谢你了。Thanks a lot. ④ very; quite:不~好 not very well

太公钓鱼,愿者上钩 Tàigōng diào yú, yuànzhě shànggōu like the fish rising to Jiang Tai Gong's hookless and baitless line — a willing victim letting himself be caught; a willing victim to sb.'s wiles

太古 tàigǔ remote ages (antiquity); grand antiquity; time immemorial

太后 tàihòu mother of an emperor; empress dowager; queen mother

太极拳 tàijíquán *taijiquan* (a kind of traditional Chinese shadow boxing); *tai chi chuan*; hexagram boxing; physical exercises:打~ do *taijiquan*

太监 tàijiān eunuch

太空 tàikōng outer space:~服 space suit

太平 tàipíng peaceful; quiet; pacific:~无事。Everything is all

right. ; All is in peace.

太平间 tàipíngjiān mortuary

太平门 tàipíngmén exit (of a building, etc.)

太平洋 tàipíngyáng the Pacific Ocean

太上皇 tàishànghuáng supreme ruler; overlord; supersovereign

太岁头上动土 tàisuì tóushàng dòngtǔ scratch the Buddha's head; beard the lion in his den; provoke sb. far superior in power or strength

太太 tàitai ① Mrs.; madame: 张～ Mrs. Zhang ② the mistress of a household; madam; lady ③ [多带人称代词]wife ④ (paternal) great-grandmother or great-grandfather

太阳 tàiyáng sun: ～能 solar energy. ～眼镜 sunglasses. ～灶 solar stove

太子 tàizǐ crown prince

汰

tài〈动〉eliminate; discard

态

tài〈名〉① appearance; condition; form: 观念形～ ideological forms ② manner; attitude: ～度生硬 rigid in attitude ③ voice: 被动语～ passive voice

态度 tàidù (对人的) manner; behaviour: ～生硬 be stiff in manner ② attitude; approach: 劳动～ attitude towards labour

态势 tàishì situation; state; posture: 敌军～ how things stand with the enemy

tān

坍

tān〈动〉tumble; fall; collapse: 墙～了。The wall collapsed.

坍塌 tāntā collapse; cave in; fall down

坍台 tāntái ① (of enterprises, etc.) collapse; fold ② fall into disgrace; lose face

贪

tān ①〈形〉corrupt ②〈动〉have an insatiable desire for; covet

贪杯 tānbēi be excessively fond of drinking; love a drop too much

贪财 tāncái be greedy for money; have an itching palm

贪得无厌 tāndéwúyàn be insatiable of profits; flay a flint; be grasping; Greed knows no bounds

贪多必失 tānduō-bìshī Grasp all, lose all.; All Covet, all lose.

贪多嚼不烂 tān duō jiáo bù làn bite off more than one can chew

贪官污吏 tānguān wūlì corrupt (venal) officials

贪婪 tānlán greedy; avaricious; rapacious: ～的目光 greedy eyes

贪恋 tānliàn can't bear (be reluctant) to part with; be greedy for; cling to: ～舒适生活 cling to an easy life

贪便宜 tān piányì anxious to get things on the cheap

贪求 tānqiú seek; hanker after; covet

贪生怕死 tānshēng-pàsǐ niggardly(cravenly) cling to life instead of braving death; be afraid to risk one's neck; care for nothing but saving one's skin

贪图 tāntú seek; hanker after; be avid for; desire for: ～安逸 desire for an easy and comfortable life; love of pleasure and a comfortable life; seek ease and comfort. ～小利 be greedy for small gains

贪污 tānwū corruption; graft: ～盗窃 graft and embezzlement. ～犯 person guilty of corruption. ～分子 grafter. ～腐化 graft and corruption; corruption and degeneration. ～公共财物 corruption involving articles of public property

贪小便宜 tān xiǎopiányì covet little advantages; covetous of small gains; greedy for small advantages

贪小失大 tānxiǎo-shīdà penny wise and pound foolish; covet a little and lose a lot

贪心 tānxīn ① greedy; insatiable; voracious ② greed; avarice; rapacity

贪赃 tānzāng practise graft; take bribes: ～枉法 take bribes and bend the law; pervert the law (justice) for a bribe; bend the law for personal gains

贪占行为 tānzhàn xíngwéi grabby behaviour

瘫 tān〈名〉paralysis: 吓～ be paralysed with fright

瘫痪 tānhuàn ① be paralysed; break down; be at a standstill: 交通运输陷于～。Transportation was paralysed. ② paralysis; palsy

瘫软 tánruǎn (of arms, legs, etc.) become weak and limp

瘫子 tānzi paralytic

摊 tān〈动〉① spread out: 把豆子～开 spread the beans out ② fry batter in a thin layer: ～煎饼 make pancakes ③ take a share in; apportion ④ vendor's stand, booth; stall: 水果～ a fruit stand

摊贩 tānfàn street vendor (pedlar); pitcher: ～业税 tax on stalls

摊牌 tānpái lay one's cards on the table; show one's hand; have a showdown

摊派 tānpài apportion; allot: ～粮款 demand grain and money from

摊税 tānshuì toll

摊子 tānzi ① stall; booth; stand ② setup: 不要～铺得太大。Don't do it on too large a scale.

tán

痰 tán〈名〉phlegm; sputum

痰盂 tányú spittoon; cuspidor

谈 tán ①〈动〉talk; chat; discuss: 他们在～些什么? What are they talking about? ②〈名〉what is said or talked about: 奇～ strange talk; fantastic tale

谈不上 tánbushàng out of the

question; far from being

谈到 tándào speak of; talk about; mention; refer to

谈得来 tándelái get along well

谈锋 tánfēng eloquence; volubility:～甚健 talk volubly; be a good talker; have the gift of the gab

谈虎色变 tánhǔ-sèbiàn turn pale at the mention of a tiger; pale even at the mere mention of something terrible

谈话 tánhuà talk; conversation:书面～ written statement

谈恋爱 tánliàn'ài be in love; have a love affair; sweethearting

谈论 tánlùn discuss; talk about:～国事 discuss state affairs

谈判 tánpàn talks; negotiations:举行～ hold talks (with)

谈情说爱 tánqíng-shuō'ài talk love; be courting; be concerned with love and romance

谈天 tántiān have a chat (with):～说地 talks about everything; chat idly

谈吐 tántǔ style of conversation

谈笑风生 tánxiàofēngshēng talk cheerfully and humorously; talk with great animation; brim with wit and humour

谈笑自若 tánxiào-zìruò go on talking and laughing with gusto and composure; talk and laugh naturally

谈心 tánxīn heart-to-heart talk:促膝～ have a heart-to-heart talk (with)

坛 tán〈名〉① altar ② platform; rostrum; forum:讲～ speaker's platform ③ world; circles:诗～ the poetic world (circles) ④ earthen jar:酒～ wine jug

昙 tán〈名〉 densely covered clouds

昙花一现 tánhuā-yīxiàn a flash in the pan; a transient success; be very ephemeral; vanish as soon as it appears:～的人物 a transient figure; passer-by on the stage of history

檀 tán

檀香 tánxiāng sandalwood:～扇 sandlwood fan

潭 tán〈名〉① deep pool; pond ② pit; depression

弹 tán〈动〉① shoot; send forth:～石子 shoot pebbes with a catapult ② flip; flick:～灰尘 flick the dust off ③ leap; spring:球～回打在他身上。The ball sprang back and hit him. ④ play:～钢琴 play the piano ⑤ accuse; impeach:～劾 impeach

另见 dàn

弹拨乐 tánbōyuè string music (played by plucking):～器 plucked instruments

弹词 táncí storytelling (in various southern dialects) to the accompaniment of stringed instruments; fiddle ballads

弹冠相庆 tánguānxiāngqìng be jubilant over one's new appointments and honours; congratulate each other on the prospect of getting good appointments

弹劾 tánhé impeach (a public official)

弹簧 tánhuáng spring：～秤 spring balance. ～锁 spring lock

弹力 tánlì ① elastic force；spring ② stretch：～衫 stretch shirts

弹射 tánshè ① launch (as with a catapult)；catapult；shoot off；eject：～器 ejector；catapult ② pick faults and criticize；censure

弹跳 tántiào bounce；spring：～力好 have a lot of spring

弹性 tánxìng ① elasticity；resilience ② elastic；flexible：～工作时间制度 elastic work schedule system

弹压 tányā suppress by force；quell

弹指可待 tánzhǐ-kědài during the snapping of the fingers；can be accomplished in a very brief space of time；in a twinkling

弹奏 tánzòu play (a stringed musical instrument)

tǎn

毯 tǎn〈名〉[地毯] carpet；rug；[床毯] blanket

忐 tǎn

忐忑 tǎntè uneasy；agitated；perturbed mentally；disturbed：～不安 be fidgety；feel uneasy；ill at ease

袒 tǎn〈动〉① leave (the upper part of the body) uncovered ② shield；shelter：偏～ be partial to

袒护 tǎnhù be partial to；show favour to；side with；give unprincipled protection to；shield

袒露 tǎnlù expose；bare：袒胸露臂 expose one's neck and shoulders

坦 tǎn〈形〉① flat；even；level：平～的原野 even country ② candid；open ③ calm；composed：～然自若 in a state of peaceful repose；with great composure

坦白 tǎnbái ① frank；candid；open-hearted：～对你说 to be frank with you ② confess；make a clean breast of；come clean：～从宽 leniency to those who confess their crimes. ～承认(罪行) confess and acknowledge (one's crimes)

坦诚 tǎnchéng frank and sincere

坦荡 tǎndàng ① (of a road，etc.) broad and level ② magnanimous；bighearted：胸怀～ have largeness of mind；be open-hearted and aboveboard

坦然 tǎnrán calm；unperturbed；having no misgivings

坦率 tǎnshuài frank；straightforward；open-minded：～地交换意见 have a frank exchange of views. 为人～ be frank and open

坦途 tǎntú level road；highway

坦挚 tǎnzhì frank and sincere；frank and open

case ② the art of war：～晦之计 the stratagem of concealment ③〈动〉conceal；hide

韬晦 tāohuì conceal one's true features or intentions；lie low

韬略 tāolüè military strategy

táo

逃 táo〈动〉① run away；flee；escape：～荒 escape (flee from) the famine ② avoid；evade；dodge；shirk：～避对…的责任 shirk one's duty towards…. ～税 evade a tax；avoidance of tax

逃避 táobì evade；dodge；avoid：～困难 avoid difficulties. ～现实 try to escape reality

逃兵 táobīng deserter

逃窜 táocuàn run away；flee in disorder

逃遁 táodùn flee；escape；evade

逃犯 táofàn runaway criminal；escaped prisoner (convict)；fugitive from justice

逃汇 táohuì evasion of foreign exchange control；evade foreign exchange

逃婚 táohūn escape unwanted marriage

逃命 táomìng run for one's life

逃难 táonàn flee from a disaster；seek refuge from (war, etc.)：～者 refugee

逃匿 táonì escape and hide；go into hiding

逃跑 táopǎo run away；flee；escape；take flight：～主义 flightism

逃票 táopiào evade paying a bus ticket

逃生 táoshēng flee for one's life

逃税 táoshuì evade (dodge) a tax

逃脱 táotuō succeed in escaping；make good one's escape；get clear of：～责任 succeed in evading responsibility

逃亡 táowáng run away from home；become a fugitive：～的重罪犯人 fugitive felon

逃学 táoxué play truant；play hookey；cut classes (school)；truant

逃之夭夭 táozhīyāoyāo make good one's escape；show a clean pair of heels；slip out；sneak away；make one's getaway；decamp

逃走 táozǒu run away；flee；take flight；take to one's heels

桃 táo〈名〉peach

桃花 táohuā peach blossom

桃李 táolǐ ① peaches and plums ② one's pupils or disciples：～满天下 have (with) pupils everywhere；have (with) students all over the country (world)

桃仁 táorén walnut meat

桃色 táosè ① peach ② illicit love：～新闻 news of illicit love

桃源生活 táoyuán shēnghuó lead an idyllic life

淘 táo〈动〉① wash in a pan or basket：～米 wash rice ② dredge；clean out：～井 dredge a well

淘金 táojīn［矿］panning；gold washing；pan for gold：～者

fortune hunter

淘井 táojǐng dredge a well

淘气 táoqì naughty; mischievous; prankish: ～鬼 mischief. 爱～ be fond of mischief; like to play pranks (on)

淘汰 táotài ① die out; be obsolete ② eliminate (through selection); phase out; knock out: ～落后产品 eliminating of outmoded products. ～赛 elimination series. 在第 2 轮比赛中被～ be knocked out in the second round

陶 táo ①〈名〉pottery; earthenware: ～范 pottery mould〈动〉② make pottery ③ cultivate; educate; train: 熏～ exert a gradual influence on; intellectual training ④〈形〉happy; contented

陶瓷 táocí pottery and porcelain; ceramics: ～器 pottery and procelain articles

陶工 táogōng potter's craft

陶器 táoqì pottery; earthenware; crockery: ～纹样 pottery design motifs

陶土 táotǔ potter's clay; pottery clay; kaolin

陶冶 táoyě ① make pottery and smelt metal ② cultivate; form; mould: ～品性 form the character; mould a person's character

陶俑 táoyǒng terracotta figurine; pottery figurine

陶醉 táozuì be intoxicated (with success, etc.); revel in: 自我～ be intoxicated with self-satisfaction

tǎo

讨 tǎo〈动〉① send troops to suppress: ～平叛乱 put down a rebellion ② condemn; denounce ③ ask for; demand; beg for: ～回公道 seeking legal redress for (an accident) ④ incur; invite: ～欢心 win the favour of ⑤ marry (a woman): ～老婆 take a wife ⑥ discuss: ～论下一步干什么 discuss what to do next

讨伐 tǎofá send a punitive expedition (against)

讨饭 tǎofàn go begging; be a beggar

讨好 tǎohǎo ① flatter; curry favour with; fawn on; toady to; ingratiate oneself with; ② [多用于否定] get good result: 吃力不～的工作 It is a thankless job.

讨还 tǎohuán get (claim) sth. back: ～血债 make sb. pay his blood debt

讨价 tǎojià ask a price; name a price: ～还价 bargain; haggle (about); chaffer (about); huckster over

讨教 tǎojiào ask for sb.'s advice; consult

讨论 tǎolùn talk over; discuss: ～会 discussion; [学术性的]symposium; seminar

讨便宜 tǎo piányì seek undue advantage; look for a bargain

讨巧 tǎoqiǎo get the best for oneself at the least expense; act artfully to get what one wants; choose the easy way out

讨饶 tǎoráo ask for forgiveness; beg for mercy

讨嫌 tǎoxián disagreeable; annoying

讨厌 tǎoyàn ① disgusting; boring; repugnant: ～的天气 abominable weather ② troublesome; bothersome; nasty: ～的病 a nasty illness ③ hate; dislike; loathe: 工人～他。The workers dislike him.

讨债 tǎozhài demand the payment of a debt or loan

讨帐 tǎozhàng demand the payment of a debt; dun

tào

套 tào〈名〉① cover; sheath; case: 椅～ slipcover for a chair ② that which covers (other garments, etc.): ～袖 oversleeve ③ knot; noose; loop: 拴个～ tie a knot ④ set; suit; suite: 一～茶具 a tea set. 两～政策 two sets of polices〈动〉⑤ tie; put a ring round: ～马 lasso a horse ⑥ copy; model on: 到处～用 be arbitrarily applied everywhere ⑦ coax a secret out of sb.; draw out: 想法儿～她的话。Let's try to draw the secret out of her. ⑧ try to win (sb.'s friendship): ～近乎 cotton up to; become close to sb.

套车 tàochē harness an animal to a cart

套服 tàofú coordinated outfit; suit

套购 tàogòu illegally buy up; arbitrage; buy in speculation; fraudulently purchase: ～证券 stock arbitrage

套话 tàohuà empty conventional talk

套汇 tàohuì speculative arbitrage; illegal procurement of foreign exchange; arbitrage of exchange

套间 tàojiān ① inner room opening off another ② apartment; flat

套交情 tàojiāoqing try to get in good with sb.

套利 tàolì interest arbitrage; straddle

套路 tàolù a series of skills and tricks in *wushu*

套色 tàosè [印]chromatography; colour process: ～木刻 coloured woodcut

套用 tàoyòng apply mechanically; use indiscriminately

套语 tàoyǔ polite formula; civilities

套种 tàozhòng intercropping

tè

特 tè ①〈形〉special; particular; peculiar; exceptional: ～别注意 pay special attention to. ～快专递 express mail service (EMS) ②〈副〉for a special purpose; specially: ～为此而来 come specially for this purpose ③〈名〉secret agent; spy: ～工人员 secret service agents

特别 tèbié special；particular；peculiar：～存款 special deposits
特产 tèchǎn special product；speciality
特长 tècháng strong point；speciality；forte：她有什么～？What is she skilled in？
特大 tèdà especially (exceptionally) big；the most
特等 tèděng special grade；top grade：～舱 stateroom. ～劳模 special-class model workers
特地 tèdì for a special purpose；specially
特点 tèdiǎn (special) feature；trait；characteristic
特定 tèdìng ①specially appointed ② specific；particular；given：在～的条件下 under given conditions
特惠关税制 tèhuìguānshuìzhì preferential tariff system
特辑 tèjí special issue (of a magazine，etc.)
特集 tèjí anthology
特级 tèjí special-grade；superfine：～教师 special-grade (class) teacher
特技 tèjì ① stunt；trick：～镜头 trick ② special effects
特价 tèjià special offer；bargain price：～出售 sell at a bargain price
特刊 tèkān special (issue)
特例 tèlì special case
特派 tèpài specially appointed：～代表 special representative. ～记者 special correspondent
特区 tèqū special economic zone：～文化 culture in the special economic zones
特权 tèquán privilege；prerogative：～阶层 privileged stratum. ～思想 special privilege mentality
特色 tèsè (distinctive，unique) feature；speciality；characteristic：有中国～的社会主义 socialism with Chinese characteristics. 有民族～ with distinctive national features
特赦 tèshè special pardon；[对特定范围罪犯的赦免] special amnesty：～令 special amnesty decree
特设 tèshè ad hoc
特殊 tèshū special；particular；peculiar；extraordinary：～风味食品 foods of special flavour；specialty foods. ～化 become privileged；become special. ～性 particularity；peculiarity；speciality
特写 tèxiě ① special article；feature (article) ② [影视] close-up：～镜头 close-up (shot)
特性 tèxìng characteristic；specific property
特许 tèxǔ special permission：～权 chartered right. ～出口商品 goods exported under special license. ～证 special permit
特邀 tèyāo specially invite：～代表 specially invited representative；special representative；representative by special invitation. ～教授 visiting professor
特异功能 tèyìgōngnéng exceptional function
特约 tèyuē ① specially engage ②

special：～稿 special contribution. ～记者 special correspondent. ～监察员 invited supervisor. ～经销处 special sales agency. ～商店 appointed store. ～演员 guest actors

特征 tèzhēng feature；characteristic；distinction

特种 tèzhǒng special type；particular kind：～工艺 special arts and crafts

téng

疼 téng ①〈名〉ache；pain；sore：头～ have a headache ②〈动〉love dearly；be fond of
另见 tòng

疼爱 téng'ài love dearly；dote on；be fond of：～小孙子 dote one's little grandson

疼痛 téngtòng ache；pain：手臂～ have pains in the arm

誊 téng〈动〉copy out：～稿 fair copy

誊清 téngqīng make a fair copy of；copy out

誊写 téngxiě copy out

藤 téng ① rattan；cane：～椅 rattan (cane) chair ② vine：生在一根～上的两个瓜 two melons growing on the same vine

腾 téng〈动〉① jump；gallop；prance：～身而过 jump over sth. ② go up；rise：升～ ascend ③ make room；vacate：～出房子 make clean rooms available for；vacate one's rooms

腾出 téngchū make way；empty；clear：～资金 save and divert funds to；transfer funds to

腾达 téngdá ① rise；soar ② make rapid advances in one's career；rise to power and position

腾飞 téngfēi take off；soar：要使中华民族～不改革是不行的。Reforms are absolutely necessary if we are to have our nation soar.

腾空 téngkōng rise to the sky；soar

腾挪 téngnuó ① transfer (funds, etc.) to other use ② move sth. to make room

腾跃 téngyuè ① prance；bounce ② (of prices) go up；rise

tī

梯 tī〈名〉ladder

梯队 tīduì echelon：第一(二，三)～ the first (second, third) echelon

梯田 tītián terraced fields

梯形 tīxíng ① trapezoid；trapezium ② ladder-shaped

剔 tī〈动〉① pick：～骨头 pick a bone ② reject：挑～ find fault with；pick holes in

剔出 tīchū pick out；sort out；reject

剔除 tīchú get rid of；reject；discard

踢 tī〈动〉kick；play：～开绊脚石 kick away a stumbling

block. ～足球 play football. ～进一球 kick a goal

踢开 tīkāi kick aside; spurn away

踢皮球 tīpíqiú ① kick a ball ② pass the buck to; kick the ball: 官僚主义就是喜欢～。Bureaucrats just love to kick the ball around.

体 tī

另见 tǐ

体己 tīji ①confidential; intimate: ～话 things one says only to one's intimates ② private savings

tí

啼 tí〈动〉① cry; weep aloud: ～哭 wail; cry ② crow; caw: 鸡～。Cocks crow.

啼饥号寒 tíjīháohán lament (cry out) in cold and hunger

啼笑皆非 tíxiàojiéfēi be at a loss whether to laugh or cry; not know whether to laugh or cry

题 tí〈名〉① subject; title topic: 讨论的～目 a subject for discussion ② problem; question: 考～ examination questions ③〈动〉inscribe: 把自己写的一本书～赠给一个朋友 inscribe one's book to a friend

题跋 tíbá annotation on a picture or its mounting

题材 tícái subject matter; theme: ～范围 range of subjects

题词 tící ①inscription; dedication ② write an inscription; write a few words of encouragement, appreciation or commemoration ③ foreword

题解 tíjiě ① explanatory notes on the title or background of a book ② key to exercises or problems

题名 tímíng write one's name (on, in); autograph

题目 tímù ① subject; title; topic ② problem; question: 考试～ examination questions

题诗 tíshī poem inscribed on a painting or its mounting; write poem on occasion

题旨 tízhǐ ① the meaning of the title of an article ② the theme of a literary work

题字 tízì inscribe; autograph

提 tí〈动〉① carry (in one's hand): ～着篮子 carry a basket ② raise; lift; promote: 把一桶水从地上～起来 lift a pail of water from the ground ③ bring up; put forward; raise: ～出要求 raise the requirements ④ mention; refer to: 旧事重～ bring up the matter again ⑤ extract; draw out: ～取积累 accumulation fund drawn by

提案 tí'àn proposal; motion

提拔 tíbá promote; raise; advance

提倡 tíchàng promote; encourage; advocate: ～晚婚 advocate late marriage. ～国货 encourage native products

提成 tíchéng deduct a percentage from a sum of money: ～工资制 deduction wage system

提出 tíchū set forth; put forward;bring up; lodge; bring up; advance; pose; raise:～抗议 lodge a protest. ～离婚申请 file a petition for divorce. ～上诉 lodge an appeal; entry of appeal. 对某人～诉讼 take (start) legal proceedings against sb.

提词 tící [剧] prompt: ～员 prompter

提单 tídān bill of lading (B/L)

提干 tígàn ① make sb. a cadre ② promote a cadre to a higher position

提纲 tígāng outline:～挈领 bring out the essentials; concentrate on the main points; bring up the chief points

提高 tígāo heighten; raise; enhance; improve; upgrade:～产品质量 improve (upgrade) the quality of products. ～企业效益 improve the performance of enterprises. ～资金使用效率 make a better use of capital

提供 tígòng provide; supply; offer; furnish: ～贷款 offer a loan. ～食品 provide sb. with food

提货 tíhuò pick up goods; take delivery of goods:～单 bill of lading (B/L)

提价 tíjià raise the price

提交 tíjiāo submit (a draft resolution, a problem, etc.):把计划～委员会讨论 submit the plan to the committee for discussion

提款 tíkuǎn draw money; withdraw deposit:从银行～ withdraw money from the bank

提炼 tíliàn extract and purify; abstract; refine

提名 tímíng nominate; propose:被～为…候选人 be nominated as a candidate for …

提起 tíqǐ ① lift up; raise:～公诉 initiate a public prosecution ② speak of; talk of

提前 tíqián ① move up (a date); advance:会议的日期已从星期四～到星期二。The date of meeting has been advanced from Thursday to Tuesday. ② ahead of time; in advance:～完成 fulfil ahead of time

提请 tíqǐng submit sth. to:～大会批准 submit to the congress for approval. ～批准逮捕书 application for approval of arrest

提取 tíqǔ ① draw (money):～企业基金 draw (retain) … as enterprise fund ② pick up (one's luggage, etc.) ③ extract; abstract:从油页岩～石油 extract oil from shale

提神 tíshén refresh oneself:他喝杯咖啡提～。He refreshed himself with a cup of coffee.

提审 tíshěn bring up and adjudicate (a case); bring a criminal before the court (bar); bring (sb. in custody) to trial

提升 tíshēng ① [向高处] hoist ② promote; advance:～某人为… promote sb. to be …

提示 tíshì give necessary information to; point out; prompt; brief on:开会前他向人们～了讨论的内容。Before the meeting, he briefed them on what to discuss.

提问 tíwèn ask a question; put questions to; quiz:向某人纷纷～ fire questions at sb.

提心吊胆 tíxīn-diàodǎn have one's heart in one's mouth; be kept in suspense; be always on tenterhooks; be in fear of; be breathless with fear

提醒 tíxǐng remind (of); warn; bring to mind; call attention:请～她明天开会。Please remind her of tomorrow's meeting.

提要 tíyào summary; synopsis; abstract; epitome

提议 tíyì ① propose; suggest; move:我～休会。I move the meeting be adjourned. ② proposal; suggestion; motion

提早 tízǎo be earlier than planned or expected; in advance:～出发 start earlier than planned

蹄 tí〈名〉① hoof:马有四个～儿。A horse has four hoofs. ② trotter:猪～pig's trotters

tǐ

体 tǐ〈名〉① body; part of the body:肌肉发达的身～ a muscular body ② (state of a) substance:液～ liquid ③ form; style:新～诗 new-style poems ④ system:国～ state system ⑤〈动〉personally do or experience sth.:身～力行 earnestly practise what one advocates
另见 tī

体裁 tǐcái style or forms of literature; *genre*

体操 tǐcāo physical exercises; gymnastics:～表演 gymnastic exhibition

体察 tǐchá experience and observe; observe and learn by experience:深入～情况 be ready to look into matters

体罚 tǐfá physical (corporal, bodily) punishment

体格 tǐgé constitution; physique; build:～健全 in the best physical condition. ～检查 physical examination; medical checkup

体会 tǐhuì know (learn) from experience; understand; realize; experience; understanding:深有～ have an intimate knowledge of sth.

体积 tǐjī volume (of a container); bulk

体力 tǐlì physical strength:～劳动 manual (physical) labour. ～劳动者 manual workers

体例 tǐlì stylistic rules and layout; style

体谅 tǐliàng show understanding and sympathy for; make allowances for

体面 tǐmiàn dignity; honour; face:有失～ lose (one's) face

体能 tǐnéng (physical) stamina

体态 tǐtài figure; posture; carriage:～轻盈 have a graceful figure

体贴 tǐtiē thoughtful; considerate; give every care to:～入微 show every consideration for; look after with meticulous (every) care

体统 tǐtǒng decency; decorum; propriety:不成～ most improper. 有失～ be disgraceful

体外受精 tǐwài shòujīng external fertilization

体温计 tǐwēnjì (clinical) thermometer

体无完肤 tǐwúwánfū ① have cuts and bruises all over the body; be covered with cuts and bruises; be beaten black and blue ② be refuted down to the last point; be thoroughly refuted; smash … to smithereens; be refuted to the hilt

体系 tǐxì system; setup

体现 tǐxiàn embody; incarnate; reflect; manifest; find expression in; bespeak; give expression to:他的一言一行～了党性。His every word and deed bespoke Party spirit.

体形 tǐxíng form (of a man); figure

体型 tǐxíng type of build; body type; form:～匀称的 well-proportioned form

体恤 tǐxù understand and sympathize with; show solicitude for

体验 tǐyàn learn through practice or one's personal experience:～生活 observe and learn from real life

体育 tǐyù physical culture:～队伍的管理 management of sports teams. ～锻炼 physical training. ～馆 gymnasium; gym. ～记者 sports writer. ～教师 physical education teacher. ～用品 sports goods. ～运动 physical culture and sports. ～学校 athletic schools. ～学院 physical education institute

体质 tǐzhì (physical) constitution; physique:增强人民～ improve the people's physique

体制 tǐzhì system (of organization); structure:国家～ state system

体重 tǐzhòng weight:～增加(减轻) put on (lose) weight; make (lose) flesh. 量～ try one's weight; weigh oneself

tì

剃 tì〈动〉shave:～掉胡须 shave (off) one's beard

剃刀 tìdāo razor

剃头 tìtóu have one's hair shaved; have one's hair cut; have a haircut

剃须膏 tìxūgāo shaving cream

涕 tì〈名〉① tears:痛哭流～ shed bitter tears ② snivel

涕零 tìlíng shed tears

涕泣 tìqì weep

替 tì ①〈动〉take the place of; replace; substitute for:用甲代～乙 substitute A for B; substitute B by A; substitute B with A ②〈介〉for; on behalf of:你倒会～自己打算。You certainly know how to look out for yourself.

替班 tìbān take sb. else's place (in a work shift)

替补 tìbǔ alternate：～队员［体］substitute；option；sub；replacement

替代 tìdài take the place of；replace；substitute for

替工 tìgōng substitute (worker)：做～ work as a substitute

替换 tìhuàn replace；substitute for；displace；take the place of

替身 tìshēn ［影视］stand-in；pinch hitter；substitute

替罪羊 tìzuìyáng scapegoat

惕 tì〈形〉cautious；watchful：警～ be on the alert；watch out；be vigilant

嚏 tì〈动〉sneeze：喷～ sneeze

tiān

添 tiān〈动〉add；increase：～衣服 put on more clothes

添补 tiānbu ① replenish；add ② interpolated by

添加 tiānjiā increase；add：～剂［化］additive

添油加醋 tiānyóu-jiācù add colour and emphasis to；play up

添枝加叶 tiānzhī-jiāyè embellish the truth (facts)；embroider

天 tiān〈名〉① sky；heaven：～不变，道亦不变。Heaven changes not，like the Way changes not. ② day：忙了一～ have had a busy day ③ overhead：～桥 overline bridge ④ a period of time in a day：～不早啦。It's getting late. ⑤ weather：下雨～ wet weather ⑥ nature：～灾 act of Nature (God)；natural calamity (disaster)

天才 tiāncái genius；talent；gift：～纵横的诗人 a poet of universe genius

天长地久 tiāncháng-dìjiǔ enduring as the universe；everlasting and unchanging

天赐良机 tiāncì-liángjī heaven-provided opportunity；heaven-sent chance

天敌 tiāndí natural enemy

天翻地覆 tiānfān-dìfù ① turning everything upside down ② causing tremendous changes ③ earthshaking

天赋 tiānfù ① gift；talent；endowment ② inborn；innate：有～的儿童 gifted child. ～人权 innate rights of man

天公地道 tiāngōng-dìdào absolutely fair

天花乱坠 tiānhuā-luànzhuì elaborate in high-flown phraseology；talk about it in superlative terms；in extravagant terms；extravagantly laud；laud sth. to the skies；praise … in superlative terms；give an extravagant account of；make a wild boast about

天机 tiānjī ① nature's mystery；something inexplicable ② God's design；secret

天经地义 tiānjīng-dìyì nature's law and earth's way；stand to reason；very reasonable indeed；universal accepted principle；by nature；unalterable principles—right and proper；perfectly justified

天籁 tiānlài sounds of nature-(i. e. the sound of the wind or flowing waters, the call of birds, etc.)

天理 tiānlǐ ① heavenly principles—feudal ethics as propounded by the Song Confucianists ② (divine) justice

天良 tiānliáng conscience：丧尽～ have no conscience

天伦 tiānlún the natural bonds and ethical relationships between members of a family

天罗地网 tiānluó-dìwǎng tight encirclement；dragnet：布下～ spread a dragnet

天命 tiānmìng God's will；the mandate of heaven；destiny；fate

天年 tiānnián ① a natural span of life；one's allotted span ② the year's harvest ③ times；age；era

天平 tiānpíng balance；scales

天气预报 tiānqì yùbào weather forecast

天堑 tiānqiàn natural moat：～变通途 build a new road to replace the natural obstacle that barred the way

天桥 tiānqiáo overbridge；[铁路的] platform bridge；[十字路口的] overpass；flyover

天穹 tiānqióng the vault of heaven

天然 tiānrán natural：～财富 natural resources (wealth)

天壤之别 tiānrǎngzhībiě as far apart as heaven and earth；a world of difference；poles apart

天色 tiānsè colour of the sky；time of the day as shown by the colour of the sky；weather

天生 tiānshēng born；inborn；innate；inherent

天堂 tiāntáng paradise；heaven：人间～ heaven on earth；earthly paradise

天体 tiāntǐ celestial body

天网恢恢 tiānwǎng-huīhuī Justice has long arms：～，疏而不漏。Heaven's vengeance is slow but sure.

天文 tiānwén astronomy：～数字 astronomical figure；enormous figure

天下 tiānxià land under heaven；world：～无难事，只怕有心人。Nothing in the world is difficult for one who sets his mind to it.；Nothing is diffucult to a man who wills.

天下大治 tiānxià-dàzhì great order throughout the land；a well ordered world

天下太平 tiānxià-tàipíng peace reigns under heaven；the world (the country) is at peace

天下乌鸦一般黑 tiānxià wūyā yībān hēi All crows under the sun are black—evil people are bad all over the world；Crows are black the world over

天险 tiānxiǎn natural barrier

天线 tiānxiàn [无] aerial；antenna

天性 tiānxìng natural disposition；nature：～善良 good-natured

天涯 tiānyá the end of the world；the remotest corner of the earth

天衣无缝 tiānyīwúfèng seamless heavenly robe—flawless

天意 tiānyì God's will; the will of Heaven

天有不测风云 tiān yǒu bù cè fēngyún Something unexpected may happen any time.; a bolt from the blue; A storm may arise from a clear sky.

天灾 tiānzāi natural disaster (calamity)

天真 tiānzhēn innocent; naive:～烂漫 simple and unaffected

天职 tiānzhí bounden duty; vocation

天主教 tiānzhǔjiào Catholicism:～徒 Catholic

天资 tiānzī natural gift (endowments); genuis; talent:～聪颖的 gifted; talented

天子 tiānzǐ son of Heaven (supreme ruler); emperor

天字第一号 tiānzì dì-yī hào a thing of the greatest importance; a work of the highest order; the world's number one

tián

恬 tián〈形〉① tranquil; calm; quiet ② carefree

恬不知耻 tiánbùzhīchǐ be lost to shame; have no sense of shame; be past shame; be shameless

恬淡 tiándàn indifferent to fame or gain

恬静 tiánjìng quiet; calm; peaceful:～的生活 sedate life

恬然 tiánrán unperturbed; quietly; calmly; nonchalantly:处之～ take things calmly

填 tián〈动〉① fill; stuff:用泥土～洞 fill a hole with mud ② fill in; write:～表 fill (in) a form

填补 tiánbǔ fill:～缺额 fill a vacancy. ～空白 fill in the gaps. ～理论空白 fill in theoretical gaps

填充 tiánchōng ① fill up; stuff ② fill in the blanks

填平 tiánpíng level up; even up; fill up:～鸿沟 close the gap; fill in the gap

填写 tiánxiě fill in; fill out; fill up:～申请单 fill out an application form

填鸭 tiányā force-fed duck; stuffed duck:～式教学法 the spoon-feeding (lit. "stuffing ducks") method of teaching; cramming method of teaching. ～式教育 spoon-fed education

田 tián〈名〉field; farmland:种～状元 number one in farming

田产 tiánchǎn landed property

田地 tiándì field; farmland; land

田赋 tiánfù land tax

田间 tiánjiān field; farm:～管理 farm management. ～作业 field work

田径 tiánjìng [体]track and field:～赛 track and field meet. ～运动 track and field; athletics. ～运动员 athlete

田契 tiánqì land deeds

田赛 tiánsài [体] field events; field sports:～项目 field event

田野 tiányě field; open country
田园 tiányuán fields and gardens; rural areas; countryside: ～风光 rural scenery. ～交响曲 pastoral symphony. ～诗 pastoral poems; idyl (1). ～诗人 pastoral poet; idylist

甜 tián〈形〉sweet: ～酒 sweet wine
甜点 tiándiǎn sweet snacks; sweets
甜蜜 tiánmì sweet; happy: ～的微笑 a sweet smile
甜食 tiánshí sweetmeats; sweet food: 爱吃～ have a sweet tooth
甜睡 tiánshuì sleep soundly; be fast asleep
甜头 tiántóu ① sweet taste; pleasant flavour ② good; benefit (as an inducement): 尝到～ draw benefit from it
甜言蜜语 tiányán-mìyǔ sweet words and honeyed phrases; honey-mouthed; honeyed; fine-sounding words; smooth-tongued; glib talk

tiǎn

舔 tiǎn〈动〉lick; lap: ～嘴唇 moisten one's lips with the tongue

tiāo

挑 tiāo〈动〉① tote with a carrying pole; shoulder: ～一担柴 carry two bundles of firewood on a shoulder pole ② choose; select; pick: 不能～精拣肥 can't choose and pick ③ nitpick: ～毛病 find fault with
另见 tiǎo
挑大梁 tiāo dàliáng shoulder a big beam (i. e., take responsibility for an important task)
挑肥拣瘦 tiāoféi-jiǎnshòu pick and choose sth. to one's own advantage; choose whichever is to one's personal advantage; be fastidious (about): 她对工作～。She was fastidious about her work.
挑拣 tiāojiǎn pick and choose
挑食 tiāoshí be very choosy about what one eats
挑剔 tiāotì find fault with; carp at; nitpick; be hypercritical
挑选 tiāoxuǎn choose; select; pick

tiáo

条 tiáo〈名〉① twig: 柳～儿 willow twigs ② strip; slip: 布～儿 a strip of cloth ③ article; item. 逐～ item by item ④ order: 有～不紊 in perfect order; orderly
条幅 tiáofú vertically-hung scroll; scroll
条件 tiáojiàn ① condition; terms; factor: 利用有利的～ make use of the favourable factor ② requirement; prerequisite: 提出～ list the prerequisites; put forward the requirements

条块分割 tiáokuài fēngē barriers between higher and lower levels or between different departments and regions; cut up the links among departments and regions

条款 tiáokuǎn clause; article; provision; item

条理 tiáolǐ proper arrangement or presentation; orderliness; method:～清楚的论文 present a lucid discourse

条例 tiáolì regulations; rules; ordinance

条目 tiáomù ① clauses and subclauses ② entry (in a dictionary)

条条块块 tiáotiáo-kuàikuài ① the vertical strips and the squares ② departments and regions:～管理 manage economy along the vertical lines of division between the central ministries or along the horizontal lines of division between localities

条条框框 tiáotiáo-kuàngkuàng restrictions and fetters; stereotypes; conventions; rules and regulations:打破～ break down conventions

条文 tiáowén article; clause; provision:～范例 standard clause

条纹 tiáowén stripe; streak:～布 striped cloth; stripe

条形码 tiáoxíngmǎ bar code; (U. S.) Universal Product Code (UPC)

条约 tiáoyuē treaty; pact; convention

调

tiáo〈动〉① mix; adjust:～色 mix colours ② mediate:在双方之间～和 mediate between the two parties ③ regulate:～剂供求 rgulate supply and demand ④ tease; provoke

调幅 tiáofú amplitude modultion (AM)

调和 tiáohé ① reconcile; mediate:从中～ mediate ② be in harmony (with); be in harmonious proportion:这两种颜色很～。These two colours blend well. ③ compromise; make concessions:没有～的余地。There is no room for compromise.

调剂 tiáojì ① adjust; regulate:～劳动力 redistribute labour power ② enliven:～生活 enliven one's life

调价 tiáojià readjust (modify) prices

调节 tiáojié regulate; adjust:～市场 regulate the market. ～税 regulatory business tax. 合理～个人收入 sound regulation of personal income

调解 tiáojiě mediate; reconcile; make peace:～争执 reconcile disputes. ～委员会 mediation committee

调理 tiáolǐ ① nurse (recruit) one's health; recuperate:～病人 recuperate a patient ② look after; take care of

调皮 tiáopí ① naughty; mischievous:～捣蛋 mischievous ② tricky; artful

调频 tiáopín frequency modula-

tion (FM)
调情 tiáoqíng flirt (with)
调色 tiáoshǎi mix colours
调试 tiáoshì debugging
调停 tiáotíng mediate; conciliate; reconcile: 对争端进行～ mediate a dispute. 居间～ mediate between two parties
调味 tiáowèi season; sauce; flavour: ～品 condiment; seasoning; flavouring
调戏 tiáoxì take liberties with (a woman); assail (a woman) with obscenities
调笑 tiáoxiào make fun of; tease; poke fun at
调谐 tiáoxié ① harmonious ② tune
调养 tiáoyǎng take good care of oneself (after an illness); be nursed back to health
调音 tiáoyīn tune
调整 tiáozhěng adjust; readjust; regulate; restructure: ～价格 readjust prices. ～产品方向 reorienting production

迢 tiáo 〈形〉far; remote
迢迢 tiáotiáo far away; far off; remote: 千里～ from a thousand *li* away; from afar; over a great distance

笤 tiáo ～帚: broom

tiǎo

挑 tiǎo 〈动〉① push sth. up with a pole or stick; lift up; raise: ～帘子 raise the curtain ② pick; poke: ～刺 pick out a splinter ③ instigate; provoke; incite: ～起武斗 provoke conflicts in which force is used
另见 tiāo
挑拨 tiǎobō sow discord; incite; instigate: ～离间 incite one against the other; play off against one another; foment (sow) dissension
挑动 tiǎodòng provoke; incite; instigate; stir up: ～内战 provoke civil war
挑起 tiǎoqǐ provoke; stir up; instigate
挑唆 tiǎosuō abet; incite; set on
挑衅 tiǎoxùn provoke an incident; defiance; provocation: 武装～ armed provocation
挑战 tiǎozhàn throw down the gauntlet; give a challenge: 接受～ accept a challenge; take up the gauntlet. 向某人～ challenge sb. to a contest

tiào

眺 tiào 〈动〉look into the distance from a high place: 远～ look far into the distance
眺望 tiàowàng look far from a high place; overlook; survey: ～周围的景色 survey the surrounding landscape

跳 tiào 〈动〉① jump; leap; bounce; spring: ～进汽车 jump in the car ② beat; move up and down; throb: 心～正常 one's heartbeat is normal ③ skip (over); make omissions:～过了4页 skip over four pages

跳班 tiàobān advanced standing

跳板 tiàobǎn ① gangplank; gangboard ② springboard; diving board

跳槽 tiàocáo job-hopping

跳高 tiàogāo[体] high jump:～运动员 high jumper

跳级 tiàojí[教]advanced placement; skip a grade; skip:～生 accelerated students

跳栏 tiàolán[体] hurdle race:～运动员 hurdler

跳棋 tiàoqí Chinese checkers (draughts)

跳伞 tiàosǎn ① bale out; parachute ②[体] parachute jumping:～运动员 parachuter

跳绳 tiàoshéng rope skipping

跳水 tiàoshuǐ[体] diving:～运动员 diver

跳台 tiàotái diving platform; diving tower

跳舞 tiàowǔ dance:～厅 dancing saloon; ballroom. ～音乐 dance music

跳远 tiàoyuǎn [体] long jump; broad jump

跳跃 tiàoyuè jump; leap; bound

跳蚤 tiàozao flea:～市场 flea market (fair)

tiē

贴 tiē〈动〉① paste; stick; glue:在信封上～邮票 stick a stamp on an envelop ② keep close to:紧～在父亲身上 nestle closely to one's father ③〈名〉subsidies; allowance:房～ housing allowance

贴标签 tiēbiāoqiān[社会学]labelling

贴补 tiēbǔ ① give financial help to; subsidize:～家用 help out with the family expenses ② subsidies; allowance:物价～ price subsidies; dearness allowance

贴花 tiēhuā applied (floral decoration); applique; applied design

贴金 tiējīn ① cover with gold leaf (gold foil); gild ② touch up; prettify

贴近 tiējìn press close to; nestle up against; be close to:史学应～现实生活。 Historical science should draw close to real life.

贴面舞 tiēmiànwǔ cheek-to-cheek dancing

贴谱 tiēpǔ proper; appropriate; sound; relevant

贴切 tiēqiè appropriate; pertinent; pretty; apt:措词～ be aptly worded; well-put

贴身 tiēshēn ① next to the skin:～衣服 underclothes; underclothing ② constantly accompanying

贴水 tiēshuǐ ① pay an agio ② agio

贴息 tiēxī ① pay interest in the form of a deduction when selling a bill of exchange, etc.:～贷款 subsidized loans ② interest so deducted; discount

贴现 tiēxiàn discount:期票～ discount on a promissory note; time discount. ～率 6%的债券 bonds callable at a premium of six per cent

贴心 tiēxīn close; intimate: ～朋友 bosom friend. ～人 close friend. ～话 words spoken in confidence

tiě

铁 tiě〈名〉① iron: 铸～ cast iron ② arms; weapon: 手无寸～ bare-handed; unarmed〈形〉③ hard or strong as iron: ～拳 iron fist ④ indisputable; unalterable: ～的事实 hard (iron-clad) facts

铁板 tiěbǎn iron plate; sheet iron: ～一块 a monolithic block; of one cut

铁饼 tiěbǐng ①[体] discus throw ② discus: ～运动员 discus thrower

铁窗 tiěchuāng prison bars; prison: ～滋味 life in prison

铁道 tiědào railway; railroad: 地下～ underground; subway; tube; metro

铁饭碗 tiěfànwǎn iron rice bowl—a stable, lifelong job regardless of performance; a permanent income they would never lose whether they work hard or not

铁公鸡 tiěgōngjī iron cock (from which no feathers can be plucked)—a stingy person; miser

铁画 tiěhuà iron picture

铁匠 tiějiang blacksmith; ironsmith

铁交椅 tiějiāoyǐ iron armchair (a metaphor for the system of lifelong cadre leadership)

铁矿 tiěkuàng ① iron ore ② iron mine

铁路 tiělù railway; railroad; rail: ～复线 alternate railway lines. ～联运 railroad through transport. ～运输 railway transportation

铁面无私 tiěmiàn-wúsī be completely impartial (to); be inflexibly just; be just and stern (to sb.); impersonal; impartial and incorruptible

铁幕 tiěmù iron curtain

铁皮 tiěpí iron sheet; [马口铁] tinplate; tin

铁器 tiěqì ironware: ～时代 the Iron Age

铁石心肠 tiěshí-xīncháng be marble-hearted; be hard-hearted; have a heart of stone

铁丝 tiěsī iron wire: ～网 wire netting; (barbed) wire entanglement

铁索 tiěsuǒ iron chain; cable

铁腕 tiěwàn iron hand: ～人物 iron-handed person; strong man

铁证 tiězhèng irrefutable (hard) evidence: ～如山 irrefutable and conclusive evidence

帖 tiě〈名〉a book containing models for learners to copy: 字～ calligraphy models

帖子 tiězi memorandum

tīng

厅 tīng〈名〉① hall:餐～ dining hall;restaurant ② office:办公～ general office ③ a government department at a provincial level:教育～ the Education Department

听 tīng〈动〉① hear; listen to:去～音乐会 go to hear a concert ② obey; heed:～从指挥 obey orders ③ let; allow:～任摆布 allow oneself to be ordered about ④〈名〉tin; can:～头 can; tin

听便 tīngbiàn as one pleases; please oneself

听从 tīngcóng obey; heed; comply with:～吩咐 be at sb.'s beck and call; do one's bidding. ～劝告 accept sb.'s advice

听而不闻 tīng'érbùwén hear but pay no attention; turn a deaf ear to

听候 tīnghòu ① wait for; await:～分配 wait for one's assignment (to work) ② pending:～另行指示 pending further instructions. ～拘押 impending apprehension

听话 tīnghuà ① obedient; tractable:～的孩子 tractable child ② pay heed to the words of

听讲 tīngjiǎng listen to a lecture; attend a lecture

听觉 tīngjué (sense of) hearing

听课 tīngkè ① attend a lecture ② [参观访问的] visit a class

听力 tīnglì ① hearing ② [听力课]aural comprehension

听命 tīngmìng take orders from; be at sb.'s command; be under the thumb of

听其言而观其行 tīng qí yán ér guān qí xíng listen to what a person says and watch what he does; judge people by their deeds, not just by their words; hear their words and judge them by their deeds; hear what a man says and see how he acts

听其自然 tīngqízìrán let things take their natural course

听取 tīngqǔ listen to:～群众意见 solicit opinions from the masses. ～双方当事人的律师陈述 hear counsels on both sides. ～证词 hear witnesses

听任 tīngrèn allow; let (sb. do as he pleases):～摆布 be at sb.'s disposal; be at the mercy of sb.

听讼 tīngsòng audience; preside at lawsuit

听天由命 tīngtiān-yóumìng resign to one's fate; meet one's fate with resignation; submit to the will of God; abide by the will of Heaven and fate

听信 tīngxìn believe:～谣言 believe rumour

听诊 tīngzhěn [医] auscultation:～器 stethoscope

听之任之 tīngzhīrènzhī ① let sb. have his own way ② leave things as they are; let matters drift

听众 tīngzhòng audience; listeners

听装 tīngzhuāng tinned; canned: ～饼干 tinned biscuits

tíng

亭 tíng〈名〉① pavilion: 八角～ octagonal pavilion ② bower; arbour ③ stall; kiosk: 书～ bookstall

亭台楼阁 tíngtái-lóugé pavilions, terraces and towers

亭亭 tíngtíng upright; erect: ～玉立 (of a woman) slim and graceful; stand gracefuly erect

停 tíng〈动〉① stop; cease; halt; suspend: 雪～了。The snow has stopped. ② stay; stop over: 我去英国途中,在巴黎～了三天。On my way to England, I stopped over in Paris for three days. ③ (of cars) be parked; (of ships) lie at anchor: 车～在大门口。The car parked at the gateway.

停办 tíngbàn close down

停泊 tíngbó anchor; berth: 船～在3号码头。The ship is berthed at No. 3 wharf.

停产 tíngchǎn stop (halt) production

停车 tíngchē ① stop ② park; place: ～场 parking lot. 此处不准～! No Parking!

停当 tíngdang ready; settled

停电 tíngdiàn ① cut off the power supply ② power cut; power failure

停工 tínggōng stop work; shut down; suspend production: ～待料 stop work for lack of material. ～期 downtime

停航 tíngháng ① suspend shipping service ② suspend air service

停火 tínghuǒ cease fire: ～协定 ceasefire agreement

停机 tíngjī [影视] wrap

停建 tíngjiàn stop construction

停刊 tíngkān stop publication

停靠 tíngkào (of a train) stop; (of a ship) berth

停课 tíngkè suspend classes

停留 tíngliú ① stop; stay; remain ② stopover; brief stop: 在北京作短暂～ have a brief stopover in Beijing

停水 tíngshuǐ cut off the water (supply)

停学 tíngxué ① stop going to school ② suspend sb. from school

停业 tíngyè stop doing business; close down; termination of business; wind up business: 修理内部,暂时～ closed temporarily for repairs

停战 tíngzhàn cease hostilities: ～协定 armistice agreement

停职 tíngzhí suspend sb. from one's duties: ～反省 be temporarily relieved of one's post for self-examination. ～停薪 suspend sb. from duties and stop his salary

停止 tíngzhǐ halt; cease; stop; suspend; call off: ～生效 cease to have effect

停滞 tíngzhì be at a standstill; remain stagnant; stagnate; bog down

廷 tíng〈名〉the court of a feudal ruler; the seat of a monarchical government：宫～ royal or imperial court

廷臣 tíngchén courtier

廷议 tíngyì court conference; imperial council

庭 tíng〈名〉① courtyard; front yard ② law court：法～ court house; court of judicature (justice)

庭审 tíngshěn court hearing

庭外调解 tíngwài tiáojiě mediation out of court

庭园 tíngyuán flower garden; grounds

庭长 tíngzhǎng president of a law court; presiding judge

tǐng

挺 tǐng ①〈形〉straight; stiff; erect：～直的体态 an erect bearing 〈动〉② stick out; straighten：～直脊背 straighten one's back ③ stand; endure; hold out：你能～得住吗？Can you hold out? ④〈副〉very; quite; rather：～好 very good

挺拔 tǐngbá ① tall and upright; upright ②［书法］vigorous; forceful：～的树木 upright tree

挺进 tǐngjìn ［军］(of troops) boldly drive on; press onward

挺举 tǐngjǔ［体］clean and jerk

挺身 tǐngshēn draw oneself up; straighten one's back：～而出 step forward boldly (bravely); come out bodly; come forward courageously

挺实 tǐngshi strong; sturdy

铤 tǐng〈副〉(run) quickly

铤而走险 tǐng'érzǒuxiǎn risk danger in desperation; make a desperate effort; make a reckless move

艇 tǐng〈名〉a light boat：汽～ steamboat

tōng

通 tōng〈动〉① open up or clear out by poking or jabbing：～炉子 poke up the fire ② open：路～了。The road is now open. ③ lead to; go to：直～广州 go straight to Guangzhou ④ connect; communicate：3个房间是～的。The three rooms are connected. ⑤ tell; notify：～个电话 give sb. a ring; call (phone up) sb. ⑥ know; understand：她～3种语言。She knows three languages ⑦〈名〉expert; authority：中国～ an old China hand〈形〉⑧ coherent; logical：文理不～ ungrammatical and incoherent (writing) ⑨ common; general：～称 a general term

通报 tōngbào ① circulate a notice (of commendation); ② circular (on the situation) ③ journal; bulletin ④ brief：相互～某事 brief each other on sth.

通病 tōngbìng common failing
通常 tōngcháng ① general; usual; normal ② generally; usually; ordinarily; as a rule
通畅 tōngchàng ① unobstructed ② easy and smooth; fluent:文字～ make smooth reading
通车 tōngchē ① (of a railway or highway) be open to traffic ② have transport service
通称 tōngchēng ① be commonly called (known as) ② common name; general term
通敌 tōngdí have illicit relations with enemy; collaborate with the enemy
通电 tōngdiàn ① circular telegram ② [电] set up an electric circuit; electrify
通牒 tōngdié diplomatic note:最后～ ultimatum
通风 tōngfēng ① ventilate:～装置 ventilation installation; draft ② [气流] draft:～报信 give secret information
通告 tōnggào give public notice; public notice; announcement
通观全局 tōngguān quānjú take a comprehensive view of the situation as a whole
通过 tōngguò ① pass through; get past; traverse:船～海峡。The ship passed the channel. ② [议案等] pass; adopt:提案已～。The motion was adopted. ③ by means (way) of; through:～协商 through consultation
通航 tōngháng open to navigation or air traffic
通红 tōnghóng very red; red through and through
通婚 tōnghūn be related by marriage; intermarry
通货 tōnghuò currency; current money:～膨胀 inflation. 硬～ hard currency. ～收缩 deflation
通缉 tōngjī order the arrest of a criminal at large. 被警察局～ be wanted by the police. ～令 wanted order. ～在案 wanted for arrest
通奸 tōngjiān commit adultery (with); illicit intercourse; criminal conversation
通考 tōngkǎo comprehensive examination
通栏标题 tōnglán biāotí banner (streamer) headline; banner
通览 tōnglǎn take an overall view of (a situation, etc.)
通例 tōnglì general rule; usual practice
通力合作 tōnglì hézuò make concerted efforts; act in concert (with)
通令 tōnglìng (issue a) circular order:～嘉奖 issue an order of commendation
通论 tōnglùn general theory (survey); introduction:《哲学～》*An Introduction to Philosophy*
通谋 tōngmóu conspire
通盘 tōngpán all-round; overall; comprehensive:～计划 overall planning
通票 tōngpiào through ticket
通气 tōngqì ① ventilate ② be in touch with each other; keep each other informed

通情达理 tōngqíng-dálǐ show good sense; use reason in; be reasonable: ～地处理每一个问题 use reason in tackling every problem

通融 tōngróng ① make an exception in favour of sb. ② accommodate sb. with (a loan): ～票据 accommodation paper

通商 tōngshāng (of nations) have trade relations (with); trade: ～口岸 treaty (trading) port; ports open to foreign trade

通史 tōngshǐ general (comprehensive) history

通顺 tōngshùn (of writing) clear and coherent; smooth; well-written: 句子～。The sentence reads smoothly.

通俗 tōngsú popular: ～读物 books for popular consumption. ～文学 popular literature. ～音乐 popular music. ～艺术 pop art; Pop

通晓 tōngxiǎo be well versed in; be at home in; have a good command of: ～法语 have a good command of French

通信 tōngxìn correspond (with); communicate (with): 你还与通她～吗? Have you been corresponding with her?. ～自由 freedom of correspondence

通行 tōngxíng ① pass through: ～证 pass; permit ② current; general

通讯 tōngxùn ① communication: ～卫星 communications satellite; comsat ② news dispatch; correspondence: ～社 news agency. ～员 correspondent

通用 tōngyòng in general use; current: ～货币 current money; currency. ～月票 intra-city monthly ticket; a monthly ticket for all urban and suburban lines. ～语种 commonly used languages

通邮 tōngyōu accessible by postal communication

通则 tōngzé general rules; regulations

通知 tōngzhī ① notify; give notice: ～上诉 give notice of appeal ② notice: ～书 notice. ～登记簿 advice book

tóng

童 tóng 〈名〉 child

童工 tónggōng child labour; child labourer

童话 tónghuà children's stories; fairy tales: ～剧 pantomime

童婚 tónghūn child betrothal (marriage); infant marriage

童年 tóngnián childhood

童声 tóngshēng child's voice

童心 tóngxīn innocent mind of a child; childlike mind; childlike heart

童谣 tóngyáo children's folk rhymes; nursery rhymes

童装 tóngzhuāng children's wear

童子 tóngzǐ boy; lad

瞳 tóng〈名〉pupil (of the eye)

瞳孔 tóngkǒng pupil: 放大～ have one's pupils dilated

同 tóng〈形〉① same; alike; similar:他们在～一个车间干活。They work in the same workshop. ② the same as before:～上 ditto ③ together; in common:～甘苦,共患难 share weal and woe ④〈介〉with:我～他一起去。I'll go with him. ⑤〈连〉and:他们～我在一起。They are together with me.

同伴 tóngbàn companion; pal

同胞 tóngbāo ① born of the same parents:～孪生子女 identical twin. ～兄弟(姐妹) full brothers (sisters) ② fellow countryman; compatriot

同辈 tóngbèi of the same generation

同病相怜 tóngbìng-xiānglián Those who have the same complaint (illness) sympathize with each other.; People similarly afflicted feel pity for one another.; Fellow sufferers sympathize with one anotehr.; Misery loves company.

同步 tóngbù coordinated; synchronized:～富裕 everyone becomes prosperous simultaneously. ～建设 synchronized construction. ～卫星 synchronous satellite. ～增长 grow in step (pace, phase) with

同窗 tóngchuāng ① study in the same school ② schoolmate

同仇敌忾 tóngchóu-díkài nurse hatred for the common enemy

同床异梦 tóngchuáng-yìmèng share the same bed but dream different dreams — be strange bedfellows; try hard to keep up an appearance of unity

同党 tóngdǎng ① belong to the same political faction or party ② fellow member of a political faction or party

同道 tóngdào ① people cherishing the same ideals and following the same path; people having a common goal ② people of the same trade or occupation

同等 tóngděng equal; on an equal basis (footing); of the same rank, status or class:～效力 equal effect. ～约束力 equally binding. ～学历 have the same educational level

同甘共苦 tónggān-gòngkǔ share joys and sorrows (with)

同工同酬 tónggōng-tóngchóu equal pay for equal work

同归于尽 tóngguīyújìn perish together (with)

同行 tóngháng ① of the same trade or occupation ② person of the same trade or occupation

同化 tónghuà ① assimilate (ethnic groups) ② assimilation

同居 tóngjū ① live together; ② cohabit:非法～ illegal cohabitation

同僚 tóngliáo colleague; fellow official

同龄 tónglíng of the same age or about the same age

同龄人 tónglíngrén contemporary

同流合污 tóngliú-héwū wallow in the mire with sb.; collude with sb. in evil doings; consort with evil doers

同路 tónglù go the same way：～人 fellow traveller

同盟 tóngméng alliance；league：结成～ form a league

同谋 tóngmóu ① conspire（with）② confederate；accomplice：～杀人罪 offence of homicide by conspiracy

同前 tóngqián ditto；idem

同情 tóngqíng sympathize（with）；have sympathy（with，for）：表示～ sympathize with sb.

同声传译 tóngshēngchuányì simultaneous interpretation

同时 tóngshí at the same time；simultaneously：～兼两份工作 take a second job；moonlight

同事 tóngshì ① work together ② colleague；associate；fellow worker

同位素 tóngwèisù isotope

同乡 tóngxiāng fellow townsman；fellow villager：～会 regional associations according to native place；provincial organizations

同心 tóngxīn with one heart：～同德 work with one heart and one mind；work together as one. ～协力 work with one heart；pull together

同性 tóngxìng ① of the same sex：～恋 homosexuality. ～恋者 homophile ② of the same nature

同样 tóngyàng ① same；similar；identical ② in the same way；likewise

同意 tóngyì agree（with，to）；consent：我～他的意见。I agree with him.

同一性 tóngyīxìng identity

同舟共济 tóngzhōu-gòngjì cross a river in the same boat — people in the same boat help each other；in times of trouble or crisis pull together；stick together through thick and thin；share with sb. in trouble

同轴 tóngzhóu coaxial：～电缆 coaxial cable

同宗 tóngzōng of the same clan；have common ancestry

铜 tóng〈名〉copper；［黄铜］brass；［青铜］bronze：～奔马 bronze galloping horse

铜版 tóngbǎn copperplate：～画 copperplate etching；copperplate

铜管乐器 tóngguǎn yuèqì brass wind-instruments；brass wind

铜镜 tóngjìng bronze mirror

铜牌 tóngpái copper medal

铜器 tóngqì copperware：～铭文 inscriptions on bronzes. ～时代 the Bronze Age；the Copper Age

铜钱 tóngqián copper cash；copper coins

铜像 tóngxiàng bronze statue

tǒng

筒 tǒng〈名〉① a section of thick bamboo：竹～ bamboo tube ② tube-shaped object：～裤 tube trousers

桶 tǒng〈名〉［有手提环的］bucket; pail; [有底有盖的] cask; barrel; tank; [盆] tub: 水～ water bucket. 汽油～ petrol drum. 一～牛奶 a pail of milk

捅 tǒng〈动〉① poke; stab: ～炉子 give the fire a poke ② disclose; give way: ～破了谎言 give the lie to the claim

捅娄子 tǒnglóuzi make a blunder; get into trouble; make a mess of sth.

捅马蜂窝 tǒng mǎfēngwō stir up a hornets' nest; bring a hornets' nest about one's ears

统 tǒng ①〈名〉interconnected system: 系～ system ②〈动〉unite; gather into one: ～一对外 unite against the foreign enemy ③〈副〉all; together: 这些东西～～归你们使用。You have all these things at your disposal.

统编 tǒngbiān centralized compilation: ～教材 centralized writing and compilation of teaching materials

统舱 tǒngcāng steerage: 乘～ travel steerage

统称 tǒngchēng be generally called

统筹 tǒngchóu plan as a whole: ～兼顾 overall planning with due consideration for all concerned. ～全局 take the whole situation into account. 失业保险基金应该～管理。Unemployment insurance funds should be managed under unified arrangements. ～医疗 centralized medical care (a form of mutual-aid medical care, and also a kind of medical insurance)

统存统贷 tǒngcún-tǒngdài centralized savings and loans (a system of credit based on centralized savings and loans)

统购统销 tǒnggòu tǒngxiāo centralized purchase and marketing; state monopoly for the purchase and marketing of

统计 tǒngjì ① sum up; count: ～出席人数 count up the number of people present (at a meeting, etc.) ② statistics: 据不完全～ according to incomplete statistics

统考 tǒngkǎo unified examination: 全国～ unified nationwide exam

统配煤 tǒngpèiméi coal under the unified ration system: ～矿 coal mine under the unified allocation system

统配物资 tǒngpèi wùzī materials earmarked for unified distribution

统收统支 tǒngshōu tǒngzhī unified state control over income and expenditure; centralized income and expenditure

统帅 tǒngshuài ① commander-in-chief; marshal ② command; lead

统辖 tǒngxiá have under one's command; exercise control over; govern

统一 tǒngyī unify; unite: ～的多民族国家 unified multi-ethnic country. ～战线 united front. ～思想(行动) unity of thinking

(action)

统制 tǒngzhì keep under control; control

统治 tǒngzhì rule; dominate:～阶级 ruling (governing, dominant) class

tòng

痛 tòng ①〈动〉pain; ache:肚子～ stomach pains ②〈形〉painful; aching; sore:惨～的教训 painful lessons ③〈名〉sadness; grief ④〈副〉bitterly; severely; deeply:～骂 severely scold; scathingly denounce

痛陈 tòngchén state or present in strong terms

痛斥 tòngchì strongly (sharply) denounce; severely reproach

痛楚 tòngchǔ pain; anguish; suffering

痛处 tòngchù sore spot; tender spot; sore:触及～ touch sb.'s sore spot; touch sb. on the raw

痛打 tòngdǎ give a sound beating; trounce; thrash:～落水狗 relentlessly beat the dog in the water

痛定思痛 tòngdìng-sītòng recall (relieve) a painful (bitter) experience

痛改前非 tònggǎi-qiánfēi reform with a keen sense of error; sincerely mend one's ways; earnestly reform one's misdeeds

痛恨 tònghèn hate bitterly; extremely detest:令人～的 detestable; hateful

痛悔 tònghuǐ bitterly repent; deeply regret; be filled with remorse

痛击 tòngjī deal a severe blow; deliver a telling blow

痛哭 tòngkū weep bitterly; wail:～失声 be choked with tears. ～流涕 cry and shed bitter tears; lament bitterly

痛苦 tòngkǔ pain; suffering; distress:精神上的～ mental agony

痛快 tòngkuài ① very happy; joyful; delighted:玩个～ have a wonderful time ② forthright; straightforward; simple and direct:说话～ speak simply and direct. 她～地答应了。She readily agreed. ③ to one's great satisfaction; to one's heart's content:唱个～ sing to one's heart's content

痛切 tòngqiè with intense sorrow; most sorrowfully:～陈词 make an earnest plea. ～反省 examine oneself seriously

痛恶 tòngwù bitterly detest; abhor; hate

痛惜 tòngxī be deeply sorry for; deeply regret; deplore

痛心 tòngxīn distressed; pained; grieved:～疾首 hate with very strong feeling

痛痒 tòngyǎng ① well-being; sufferings; difficulties:关心人民群众的～ show concern for the well-being of the masses ② consequence; importance:无关～ a matter of no consequence

痛责 tòngzé severely rebuke; castigate

tōu

偷 tōu ①〈动〉steal；pilfer：为某人～窃某物 steal sb. sth. ②〈副〉stealthily；furtively；on the sly：～跑 run away covertly

偷安 tōu'ān seek temporary ease and comfort

偷盗 tōudào steal；pilfer

偷渡 tōudù slip out of a blockade in a water area；run a blockade

偷工减料 tōugōng jiǎnliào do shoddy work and use inferior material；cheat in work and cut down material

偷鸡不着蚀把米 tōujī bùzháo shí bǎ mǐ try to steal a chicken only to end up losing the rice；go for wool and come back shorn

偷看 tōukàn cast a furtive (sidelong) glance at；steal a glance；peep

偷空 tōukòng ① snatch a moment：～休息 snatch a rest ② at one's leisure

偷懒 tōulǎn be lazy；loaf (on the job)

偷梁换柱 tōuliáng-huànzhù steal the beams and pillars and replace them with rotten timber—perpetrate a fraud；try by underhand means to；resort to fraudulence

偷情 tōuqíng carry on a clandestine love affair；have a love affair stealthily

偷生 tōushēng cling niggardly to life；draw (linger) out an ignoble existence：～怕死 live on in humiliation and fear death

偷税 tōushuì evade (dodge) a tax

偷天换日 tōutiān-huànrì steal the sky and put up a sham sun — perpetrate a gigantic fraud；distort the truth by despicable means；substitute the fake for the genuine

偷听 tōutīng overhear；eavesdrop；[用窃听器] bug：谨防～。Walls have ears.

偷闲 tōuxián snatch a rest：忙里～ snatch a moment from one's busy life；enjoy occasional leisure in a busy life

偷运 tōuyùn smuggle：～入(出)境 smuggle sth. into (out of) a country

偷越国境 tōu yuè guójìng illegally cross the national border

tóu

头 tóu〈名〉① head：从～到脚 from head to foot ② hair or hair style：梳～ comb the hair ③ beginning or end：提个～儿 give sb. a lead ④ top；end：山～ hilltop ⑤ chief；head：他们的～儿是谁？Who is the head of their section？〈形〉⑥ first：～等大事 an event of paramount importance ⑦ leading：带～羊 leading sheep

头版 tóubǎn front page (of a newspaper)

头寸 tóucùn [商]① cash ② money supply；money market：～宽松(支绌) easy (tight) monetary position

头等 tóuděng first-class; first-rate; first: ～重要 of (the) first importance

头更 tóugēng first watch; evening watch

头功 tóugōng greatest service; highest merit

头号 tóuhào ① number one; size one: ～敌人 enemy number one ② first-rate; best: ～大米 top-grade rice

头面人物 tóumiàn rénwù prominent figure; top people; bigwig; leading light: 外交界～ leading lights in diplomatic circles

头目 tóumù chieftain; ringleader; head of a gang

头脑 tóunǎo brain; head; mind: ～公司 brain trust. ～冷静 cool-headed; sober-minded. 有经济～ be economically-minded

头儿 tóur head; chief; leader; boss

头痛 tóutòng headache: ～医头，脚痛医脚 treat the head when the head aches, treat the foot when the foot hurts — treat symptoms but not the disease; take palliative (stop-gap) measures for one's illness. 令人～的 troublesome; annoying

头头是道 tóutóushìdào well-grounded and reasoned; clear and convincing: 说得～ speak in a convincing way

头衔 tóuxián title

头像 tóuxiàng head (sculpture or portrait)

头绪 tóuxù main threads (of a complicated affairs): ～纷繁 have too many things to attend to. 有了～ be in good working order

头重脚轻 tóuzhòng-jiǎoqīng feel one's head heavy and one's feet light; be top-heavy; heavy-headed

投 tóu 〈动〉① throw; cast; fling; hurl: ～手榴弹 throw a hand grenade ② go to; enter; join: ～到…方面去 go over to the side of… ③ put in; drop: 把信～进信箱 drop a letter into the letter-box ④ deliver; send: ～书 send a letter ⑤ fit in with; agree with: ～合口味 pander to the taste (palate) of

投案 tóu'àn give oneself up (surrender oneself) to the police: ～自首 come to the police to confess one's guilt; voluntarily surrender

投保 tóubǎo subscribe to insurance; insure; cover; take out (an insurance) policy: ～单位 insured unit. ～人 applicant; policy holder

投奔 tóubèn go to sb. for shelter

投标 tóubiāo tender (for); bid (for); make a tender (for); submit a tender; enter a bid

投产 tóuchǎn go (put) into production; go into operation

投诚 tóuchéng come over to; surrender (to): 向人民～ surrender to the people

投敌 tóudí go over to the enemy; defect (to): ～叛变 defect to the enemy and turn traitor

投递 tóudì deliver：～员 mail carrier；postman or postwoman

投(放)毒(物) tóu(fàng)dú(wù) spread poison

投放 tóufàng ① put into；throw in ② put (goods) on (the market)：春节前将有大批商品～市场。A large quantity of commodities will be put on the market before the Spring Festival.

投稿 tóugǎo contribute (to)

投机 tóujī ① speculation；profiteering：～倒把 engage in profiteering and speculation. ～取巧 gain advantage by trickery；indulge in manoeuvres ② agreeable；congenial：谈得～。The conversation became more and more friendly.

投考 tóukǎo enter oneself (sign up) for an examination：～大学 enter oneself for a matriculation

投靠 tóukào go and seek refuge with sb.；go to sb. for help；fall back on；throw oneself into the lap of；put oneself under the wing of

投票 tóupiào cast a vote；vote (for or against)：～表决 decide by ballot. 无记名～ secret ballot

投其所好 tóuqísuǒhào hit on what one likes；cater to sb.'s liking

投契期 tóuqìqī［咨询场合］period of getting to know you

投入 tóurù ① throw into；put into：～生产 be put into production ② inject money into；invest：把资金～农业 inject money into agriculture

投身 tóushēn throw oneself into；join (in)：～革命 join in the revolution

投宿 tóusù put up for the night；stay overnight (at an inn)

投诉 tóusù ① write to state or request；complain ② customers' complaints：～电话 hot line for customers' complaints. ～人 complainant. ～信 letter of complaint

投降 tóuxiáng surrender；capitulate：～主义 capitulationism

投映 tóuyìng projection：～电视接收机 projection television (TV) receiver

投资 tóuzī invest；investment：～结构 investment pattern. ～项目资本金制度 capital funds system for investment projects. ～主体法人责任制 system of responsibility for the legal person-main investor

tòu

透 tòu〈动〉① pass through；penetrate；soak (seep) through：阳光～过迷雾。The rays of the sun penetrated the mists. ② reveal；disclose：～露计划 divulge one's plans to ③〈副〉thoroughly；fully：熟～ be quite ripe

透彻 tòuchè penetrating；thorough：～分析 incisive analysis. ～认识 have a thorough understanding of sth.

透顶 tòudǐng downright；in the

extreme; out and out: 腐败～ rotten to the core

透风 tòufēng ① let in air; ventilate ② reveal a secret

透骨 tòugǔ ① (of cold air) chill one to the bone; be piercing: 冷得～ be chilled to the bone ② deep; profound; penetrating

透亮 tòuliàng ①bright; transparent ② perfectly clear

透露 tòulù reveal; disclose; divulge: ～风声 disclose information

透明 tòumíng transparent; diaphanous

透明度 tòumíngdù openness: 增加新闻报道的～ increase the openness of news coverage

透明水彩画(法) tòumíng shuǐcǎi huà (fǎ) aquarelle: ～画家 aquarellist

透气 tòuqì ① let air in; gather breath ② airy; well-ventilated: 房间不太～。The room is not well ventilated.

透视 tòushì ①［医］fluoroscopy ② perspective: ～布景 perspective scenery. ～图 perspective drawing

透支 tòuzhī ① overdraw; make an overdraft; overdraft: ～帐户 overdrawing account ② draw one's salary in advance; deficit: ～薪金 anticipate one's pay

tū

突 tū ①〈动〉dash forward; thrust; rush; charge: ～入敌阵 charge into the enemy positions ②〈形〉sudden; abrupt: ～然离去 an abrupt departure

突出 tūchū ① protrude; stick out ② put to the fore; give prominence to; stress: ～政治 give prominence to politics ③ outstanding; prominent: ～的贡献 outstanding contributions

突飞猛进 tūfēi-měngjìn advance (progress) by leaps and bounds; make big (giant) strides

突击 tūjī ① sudden attack; shock; assault: ～队 shock troops. ～任务 shock work; rush job. 新长征～手 a shock worker of the new Long March ② do a rush job: 为期四天的～课程 a four-day intensive course

突破 tūpò ① break through; pierce: ～防线 break through a defence line ② surmount; break: ～难关 break the neck of a job. ～口 breakthrough point

突然 tūrán ① sudden; abrupt; unexpected ② suddenly; abruptly; unexpectedly

突围 tūwéi break through an encirclement; fight one's way out

凸 tū〈形〉protruding; convex; salient; raised: ～花纺织品 raised textiles

凸凹法 tūāofǎ［美］convex-concave method

凸版 tūbǎn［印］relief printing plate: ～印刷 relief printing

凸出 tūchū bulgy; projective; prominent: ～的下颏 prominent

chin
凸透镜 tūtòujìng convex lens
秃 tū〈形〉① bald; bare:～山 bare hills ② blunt; without a point:铅笔～了。The pencil is blunt. ③ incomplete; unsatisfactory
秃笔 tūbǐ poor writing ability; low skill at composition
秃顶 tūdǐng ① bald ② bald head
秃发病 tūfàbìng alopecia

tú

屠 tú〈动〉① slaughter or butcher (animals for food) ② massacre; kill; slaughter
屠城 túchéng massacre the inhabitants of a captured city
屠刀 túdāo butcher's knife; chopper
屠夫 túfū butcher
屠杀 túshā slaughter; massacre
屠宰 túzǎi slaughter:～场 slaughterhouse; shambles. ～税 tax per head on slaughtered animals
图 tú〈名〉① picture; chart; drawing; map:制～ make a drawing (chart) ② plan; scheme; attempt:～谋 plot ③〈动〉seek; pursue:贪～享受 seek pleasure
图案 tú'àn design; pattern; figure:装饰～ decorative pattern
图报 túbào seek ways to return sb.'s kindness
图表 túbiǎo chart; diagram; graph
图画 túhuà picture; drawing; painting:～文字 pictograph characters; pictography; picture writing. ～纸 drawing paper
图解 tújiě ① graph; diagram ② [数]graphic solution ③ illustration
图例 túlì legend (of a map, etc.); key
图谋 túmóu scheme (for); seek; plot:～不轨 plot treason. ～私利 seek personal interests
图片 túpiàn photo; picture:～展览 picture show
图谱 túpǔ collection of illustrative plates; atlas
图穷匕见 túqióng-bǐxiàn When the map was unrolled, the dagger was revealed — the real intention is revealed in the end.; When the map was spread out, a stiletto was exposed — an attempt frustrated by its exposure.
图书 túshū books:～馆 library. ～编目 library cataloguing
图腾 túténg totem:～崇拜 totemism
图文并茂 túwén-bìngmào (of a book, magazine, etc.) both pictures and texts are excellent
图文传真 túwén chuánzhēn fax
图像 túxiàng picture; image
图形 túxíng graph; figure
图样 túyàng design; pattern
图章 túzhāng seal; stamp:在合同上加盖～ affix a seal to the contract
图纸 túzhǐ blueprint

涂 tú〈动〉① smear; spread on; apply:给伤口～上膏药 apply a plaster to a wound ② blot out:～掉几个字 cross out a few words ③ scribble; scrawl:在墙上到处乱～ scrawl all over the wall

涂层 túcéng coat; coating

涂改 túgǎi alter:～作废 invalid if altered

涂料 túliào paint; coating; daub

涂抹 túmǒ ① smear; daub ② scribble; scrabble

涂去 túqù blot out; cross out

涂炭 tútàn mud and ashes—utter misery; great affliction; misery and suffering

涂鸦 túyā poor handwriting; scrawl; chicken tracks

涂脂抹粉 túzhī-mǒfěn embellish; prettify; whitewash; apply powder and paint; make presentable; deck up; paint in glowing colours:为自己～ try to prettify oneself

途 tú〈名〉way; road:～中 on the way

途经 tújīng by way of; via:～南京前往上海 go to Shanghai by way of Nanjing

途径 tújìng way; channel:外交～ diplomatic channels

荼 tú〈名〉① a bitter edible plant ② the white flower of reeds, etc.

荼毒 túdú afflict with great suffering; torment

徒 tú〈名〉① apprentice:学木工的艺～ an apprentice carpenter ② follower; disciple:门～ pupil〈副〉③ on foot:～步回家 go home on foot ④ merely; only:～具形式 be merely formal

徒步 túbù on foot

徒弟 túdì ① apprentice ② follower; disciple

徒劳 túláo in vain; futile effort; fruitless labour; without result:～无益 come to naught; in vain; of no avail; end in smoke; to no purpose. ～往返 make a futile trip

徒然 túrán in vain; without avail

徒手 túshǒu bare-handed; unarmed:～搏斗 fight bare-handed

徒刑 túxíng imprisonment; (prison) sentence; gaol sentence:被判处5年～ be sentenced to five years' imprisonment (for)

徒有其名 túyǒuqímíng ① nominal; titular ② unworthy of one's name

tǔ

土 tǔ〈名〉① earth; soil; clay:沃～ good soil ② land; ground:领～ territory〈形〉③ native; local:～产 local products ④ old-fashioned; outmoded; unrefined; unenlightened:～里～气 boorish; rustic; uncouth

土崩瓦解 tǔbēng-wǎjiě collapse like a house of cards; crumble and perish; be disintegrated; disintegrate; crumble; fall apart

土产 tǔchǎn ① produced in a locality ② local (native) product

土地 tǔdì land; soil; ground: ～肥力下降 exhaustion of soil. ～改革 land reform. ～入股 pooling of land as shares. ～证 land certificates; title deed

土法 tǔfǎ indigenous method; local method: ～上马 get on the job with indigenous method

土方 tǔfāng ① earthwork ② folk prescription (recipe)

土木 tǔmù building; construction: ～工程 civil engineering. 大兴～ go in for large-scale construction

土特产品 tǔtèchǎnpǐn local and special products

土语 tǔyǔ local, colloquial expressions; local dialect

土葬 tǔzàng burial in the ground

土政策 tǔzhèngcè indigenous policy (regulations made by certain local areas and units)

吐 tǔ〈动〉① spit: ～舌头 put out one's tongue ② tell; pour: ～怨气 vent one's grievances
另见 tù

吐故纳新 tǔgù-nàxīn exhale the old and inhale the new; get rid of the stale and take in the fresh

吐露 tǔlù tell; reveal; unbosom: ～心事 unbosom oneself. ～一切详情 make a clean breast of

吐气 tǔqì ① breathe out; exhale ② ease one's mind; feel elated and exultant ③ aspirated

吐弃 tǔqì spurn; reject; cast aside

吐诉 tǔsù come out with what's on one's mind; pour out (one's heart, etc.)

吐字 tǔzì (of an actor in traditional opera) enunciate

tù

吐 tù〈动〉throw up; reject; vomit: ～血 vomit (spit) blood
另见 tǔ

吐血 tùxiě spitting blood; haematemesis

吐泻 tùxiè vomiting and diarrhoea

吐赃 tùzāng disgorge ill-gotten gains

兔 tù〈名〉rabbit; hare: ～毛 rabbit wool

兔死狗烹 tùsǐ-gǒupēng The hounds are killed for food once all the hares are bagged — trusted aides are eliminated when they have outlived their usefulness.; When the hares die, the dogs are killed and boiled — their services are required only in time of need.; slay the lackeys when they have outlived their usefulness

兔死狐悲，物伤其类 tùsǐ-húbēi, wùshāngqílèi The fox mourns over the death of the hare.; Like mourns over the death of like.

兔子不吃窝边草 tùzi bù chī wōbiāncǎo Rabbits don't eat the grass by their burrows.; A rabbit dosen't nibble the grass near its hole — a villain doesn't harm his next-door neighbours.

tuān

湍 tuān ①〈形〉(of a current) rapid; torrential ②〈名〉rapids; rushing waters

湍急 tuānjí (of a current) torrential; rapid

tuán

团 tuán〈形〉① round; circular: ～城 Round City ② sth. shaped like a ball: 汤～ boiled rice dumpling ③〈动〉unite; conglomerate: ～结一致 unite as one (as one man)〈名〉④ group; society; organization: 剧～ drama troupe ⑤ regime ⑥ the League: 入～ join the League

团伙 tuánhuǒ gang; gansters; band; clique

团结 tuánjié unite; rally: ～奋斗 work hard with a united spirit. ～就是力量。Unity (Union) is strength.

团聚 tuánjù gather together; reunite

团体 tuántǐ body; group; organization: ～赛 team competition. ～票 group ticket. ～签证 group visa. ～取向 organization orientation

团员 tuányuán ① member of a delegation (troupe, etc.) ② member of the Communist Youth League of China; League member

团圆 tuányuán reunion: ～饭 family reunion dinner

团长 tuánzhǎng ① commander of a regiment ② head (leader, chairman) of a delegation (troupe, etc.)

团支部 tuánzhībù League Branch

团子 tuánzi dumpling

tuī

推 tuī〈动〉① push; shove ② plane: 用刨子～光 plane a table smooth ③ infer; deduce: 从效果～知动机 infer a motive from an effect ④ push away; shirk; shift: 把责任～给别人 shift the responsibility onto others ⑤ put off; postpone: ～迟战争的爆发 put off the outbreak of a new war ⑥ elect; choose: 被～选到领导岗位 be elected to a leading post

推波助澜 tuībō-zhùlán add fuel to the fire; make a stormy sea stormier; increase troubles; fan the fire; instigate; help intensify the billows and waves

推测 tuīcè infer; guess; surmise; conjecture: ～学 art of conjecture

推陈出新 tuīchén-chūxīn weed through the old to let the new grow; weed through the old to create the new; the new emerging out of the old; weeding through the old to bring forth the new

推迟 tuīchí put off; postpone; delay:~一个月 be postponed for a month

推崇 tuīchóng have a profound respect for; hold in esteem:~备至 regard with the greatest respect; admire very much

推出 tuīchū introduce; put out; present

推倒 tuīdǎo ① push over; overturn ② repudiate; cancel; reverse

推动 tuīdòng push ahead; spur; promote:~工作 push the work ahead. ~力 motive force

推断 tuīduàn infer; deduce

推翻 tuīfān ① overthrow; upset; throw out of; overturn ② repudiate; cancel:~协议 repudiate an agreement. ~自己原来的证词 disaffirm one's former testimony

推广 tuīguǎng spread; popularize; expand:~经验 publicize experience. ~新式农具 popularize new types of farm tools. ~费用 promotion expenses

推荐 tuījiàn recommend:~文学作品 recommended literary works

推进 tuījìn ① push on; carry forward; give impetus to; advance:~政府机构改革 press ahead with the reform of government organs ② [军]move forward; push; drive

推举 tuījǔ ① elect; choose ② [体](clean and) press

推理 tuīlǐ inference; reasoning:~小说 whodun(n)it

推论 tuīlùn inference; deduction; corollary; analogism:~法则 rule of inference

推敲 tuīqiāo consider carefully; weigh; deliberate:~文字 weigh one's words

推却 tuīquè refuse; decline

推让 tuīràng decline (a position, favour, etc. out of modesty)

推算 tuīsuàn calculate; reckon

推土机 tuītǔjī bulldozer

推托 tuītuō ① plead; make (find) an excuse:他~头疼回家了。He made the excuse of a headache and returned home.; He returned home in excuse of a headache. ② in excuse of; on the pretext of

推委(诿) tuīwěi (wěi) shift responsibility onto others; shuffle (off); prevaricate; assign a false cause; evade by excuse:~职责 shuffle off a duty (upon sb.)

推想 tuīxiǎng reckon; guess; imagine

推销 tuīxiāo promote sales (of); peddle:~商品 promote the sale of goods. ~员 salesman. ~术 salesmanship

推卸 tuīxiè shirk; shift; shuffle off:~责任 shirk responsibility

推心置腹 tuīxīn-zhìfù bare one's heart (to); repose full confidence in sb.; take sb. into one's confidence; confide in sb.:他们彼此~。Their hearts were bared to each other.

推行 tuīxíng press on (forward) with; pursue; promote; put into operation; push (force) through; push; carry through; practise

推选 tuīxuǎn elect; choose

推延 tuīyán put off; postpone

推演 tuīyǎn derive; deduce

推移 tuīyí ① (of time) pass; elapse: 随着时间的～ as time goes on ② evolve; develop

tuí

颓 tuí〈形〉① ruined; fallen; dilapidated: ～垣断壁 crumbling walls and dilapidated houses ② decadent; declining: 衰～ on the decline

颓废 tuífèi decadent: ～潦倒的庸人 degenerate philistines. ～派 the decadent school; the decadents

颓靡 tuímí decadence; crestfallen; downcast; dejected

颓丧 tuísàng depressed; despondent; downcast

颓势 tuíshì declining trend: 军事上的～ military incompetency of the time. 挽回～ turn the tide in one's favour

颓唐 tuítáng dejected; dispirited

tuǐ

腿 tuǐ〈名〉leg; [大腿] thigh; [小腿] shank

tuì

蜕 tuì〈动〉① slough off ② exuviate

蜕变 tuìbiàn transform; change qualitatively; transmute

蜕化 tuìhuà ① [蛇、蝉等动物] slough off; exuviate ② degenerate: ～变质分子 degenerate elements

退 tuì〈动〉① fall back; move back; retreat: 迫使敌人(向某地)～去 force the enemy to retreat (on a place) ② cause to move back; withdraw; remove: ～敌 repulse the enemy ③ quit; withdraw from: ～出历史舞台 step down from the stage of history ④ recede; decline; ebb: 潮水～了。The tide receded. ⑤ return; give back; refund: ～货 return merchandise ⑥ cancel; break off: ～婚 break off an engagement ⑦ retire: ～休 retire

退避 tuìbì keep out of the way: ～三舍 keep a good distance from sb. (to avoid a conflict)

退步 tuìbù ① fall (lag) behind; retrogress: 学习成绩～ fall behind in one's studies ② leeway; room for manoeuvre: 留个～ leave some leeway; leave some room for manoeuvre

退场 tuìchǎng ① (of atheletes) withdraw from the arena (as after the opening ceremony); march off the arena ② (of an audience) leave the theatre (as when a play ends)

退出 tuìchū leave; withdraw from; secede; quit: ～比赛 withraw from a competition. ～

会场 walk out of a meeting. ～条约 withdraw from a treaty

退党 tuìdǎng withdraw from (resign, quit) a political party

退稿 tuìgǎo reject a literary contribution:～通知 rejection slip

退股 tuìgǔ withdraw shares; withdrawal

退化 tuìhuà ① degenerate; deteriorate; retrograde ② degeneration

退还 tuìhuán give back; send back; return: ～公物 return public property

退换 tuìhuàn exchange (replace) a purchase

退回 tuìhuí ① send back; return; reject: 原稿已～。The manuscript has been sent back. ② retrace one's steps; turn back

退货 tuìhuò cancel the orders

退居 tuìjū retreat:～二、三线 retreat to the second and third lines (of work)

退路 tuìlù ① route of retreat ② leeway:留一个～ leave some leeway

退赔 tuìpéi return and compensate; make restitution or pay compensation

退票 tuìpiào ① dishonour a cheque ② refund a ticket:他要求～。He asked to have his ticket refunded.

退让 tuìràng make a concession (to); yield (to); give in:在原则问题上决不～ never yield in matters of principle

退烧 tuìshāo ① bring down (allay) a fever ② (of a person's temperature) come down

退税 tuìshuì tax refund

退庭 tuìtíng withdraw from the court

退位 tuìwèi give up the throne; abdicate; abdication

退伍 tuìwǔ leave the army; retire or be discharged from active military service; muster out; be demobilized:～军人 demobilized soldier

退席 tuìxí [表示抗议]walk out

退休 tuìxiū retire:～工人 retired worker. ～年龄 retiring age. ～金 retirement pay; pension

退学 tuìxué leave school; discontinue one's schooling; flunking out;[因学业不及格被迫离开学校] order to quit school

退隐 tuìyǐn retire from public life; go into retirement:～生活 retired life

退赃 tuìzāng give up ill-gotten gains; returning spoils

退职 tuìzhí resign or be discharged from office; quit working:～费 severance pay

褪 tuì〈动〉① take off (clothes); shed (feathers) ② (of colour) fade:阳光使窗帘～了色。Sunlight has faded the window curtains.

tūn

吞 tūn〈动〉① swallow; gulp down:～下某物 swallow sth. (down) ② embezzle; take possession of：独～ take exclusive possession of

吞并 tūnbìng annex；gobble up；devour；swallow

吞灭 tūnmiè conquer and annex (a country)

吞没 tūnmò ① devour；swallow up ② embezzle；misappropriate：～公款 embezzle public money

吞食 tūnshí swallow；devour

吞吐 tūntǔ take in and send out in large quantities；handle：～量 handling capacity (of a harbour)

吞吞吐吐 tūntūn-tǔtǔ hesitate in speech；hem and haw；mince words；shilly-shally：说话别～。Don't mince matters.

吞占 tūnzhàn ① embezzle；misappropriate ② invade and occupy；seize

tún

屯 tún〈动〉① store up；collect：～粮 store up gain ② station (troops)：～兵 station troops

屯兵 túnbīng station troops

屯垦 túnkěn station troops to open up wasteland

屯田 túntián have garrison troops or peasants open up wasteland and grow food grain

囤 tún〈动〉store up；hoard；corner：～货 store goods

囤积 túnjī hoard for speculation；corner：～居奇 hoarding and cornering；corner the market

臀 tún〈名〉bottom；hips；buttocks；[兽类的]quarters；rump

臀部 túnbù buttocks

臀尖 túnjiān pork rump

tuō

脱 tuō〈动〉① (of hair, skin) shed；come (peel) off：头发～光了 lose all one's hair ② take off；remove；cast off：～帽 remove one's hat ③ escape from，get out of：～险 make a breathtaking escape from ④ miss (out)；drop：这一行里～了 2 个字。Two characters are missing in this line.

脱班 tuōbān be late；[车、船等] be behind time：火车～20 分钟。The train is twenty minutes late.

脱产 tuōchǎn be released from production or regular work (to take on other duties or for study)；divorce oneself from production：～学习(训练) off-the-job study (training)

脱稿 tuōgǎo complete a manuscript

脱钩 tuōgōu unhook：可以允许他们同农业～，专门从事林业生产。They may be unhooked from agriculture to concentrate on forestry production.

脱轨 tuōguǐ be derailed

脱节 tuōjié come apart；be disjointed；be out of line with

脱口而出 tuōkǒu'érchū say sth. unwittingly；speak offhand；

blurt out; escape (from) one's lips; let slip

脱离 tuōlí lose touch with; be divorced from: ～群众 be divorced from the masses. ～实际 lose touch with reality

脱盲 tuōmáng cast off illiteracy

脱贫 tuōpín shake off poverty: ～致富 shake off poverty and get rich (build up a fortune)

脱期 tuōqī fail to come out on time

脱身 tuōshēn get away; get free; extricate oneself

脱手 tuōshǒu ① slip out of the hand; let go ② be sold; sell

脱售(销) tuōshòu (xiāo) be in short supply; be out of stock; sold out

脱水 tuōshuǐ ① deprivation (loss) of body fluids; dehydration ② dewatering

脱胎换骨 tuōtāi-huàngǔ be reborn; cast off one's old self; thoroughly remould oneself

脱逃 tuōtáo run away; escape; flee

脱险 tuōxiǎn be out of danger

脱氧核糖核酸 tuōyǎng hétáng hésuān deoxyribonucleic acid (DNA)

脱衣舞 tuōyīwǔ striptease

脱颖而出 tuōyǐng'érchū the point of an awl sticking out through a bag—talent revealing itself

脱脂 tuōzhǐ de-fat; skim: ～奶粉 skimmed milk powder; de-fatted milk powder

拖 tuō〈动〉① pull; drag; draw: 这台机车～了一长列货车。The locomotive pulled a long line of freight cars. ② delay; drag on: 不要再～了。Don't delay any more.

拖后腿 tuōhòutuǐ hold sb. back

拖拉 tuōlā ① tug; drag ② dilatory; slow; sluggish: 办事～ be dilatory in doing things. ～作风 dilatory style of work; officialism

拖累 tuōlěi ① involve; implicate ② encumber: 受家务～ be tied down by household chores. 为债务所～ be encumbered with debts

拖泥带水 tuōní-dàishuǐ ① [做事] messy; sloppy; slovenly; untidy ② [说话或写文章] verbose; wordy; tedious: 说话～ talk at tedious length

拖欠 tuōqiàn be in arrears: ～房租 be in arrears with the rent; be behind in the rent. 企业间～债务 defaults between enterprises

拖人下水 tuōrén-xiàshuǐ drag (get) sb. into hot water; pull others in; drag others down; get sb. to share responsibility for; drag people into the abyss

拖沓 tuōtà dilatory; sluggish; laggard

拖延 tuōyán put off; delay; stall (for): ～时间 stall for time

托 tuō〈动〉① hold in the palm; support with the hand or palm: ～着盘子 hold a tray on one's palm ② ask; beg; entrust: ～人订票 ask sb. to book a ticket for one ③ plead; give as a pretext：～病 plead illness ④ rely upon；owe to：～庇 rely upon one's elder or influential person for protection；seek the protection of

托庇 tuōbì rely upon one's elder or an influential person for protection

托病 tuōbìng plead illness

托词 tuōcí ① pretext；excuse；subterfuge：～谢绝 deline on some pretext ② find a pretext；make an excuse

托福 tuōfú ①（usu. responding to greetings）thanks to you ② rely upon；owe to

托付 tuōfù entrust；commit sth. to sb.'s care

托故 tuōgù give（find）a pretext；make an excuse

托管 tuōguǎn trusteeship：～金 trust money

托拉斯 tuōlāsī［经］trust

托名 tuōmíng do sth. in sb.'s name

"托儿" tuōr〈方〉［受雇于他人，从旁诱人受骗上当，从事不正当商业行为的人］a pedlar's silent partner or side-kick hired to cheat customers

托人情 tuōrénqíng gain one's end through pull；seek the good offices of sb.；ask a favour through the good offices of sb.

托收 tuōshōu collection：～汇票 bill of collection；draft for collection. ～现款 collection of cash

托幼（教育） tuōyòu（jiàoyù）nursery education

托运 tuōyùn consign for shipment；check：～行李 check one's luggage. ～人 consignor；shipper

tuó

鸵 tuó

鸵鸟 tuóniǎo ostrich：～政策 ostrich policy

驼 tuó〈名〉camel

驼背 tuóbèi ① humpback；hunchback ② humpbacked；hunchbacked

驼绒 tuóróng camel hair cloth；camel's hair

驼色 tuósè the colour of camel's hair；right tan

驮 tuó〈动〉carry（on the back）

驮畜 tuóchù pack animal

tuǒ

椭 tuǒ

椭率 tuǒlǜ ellipticity

椭圆 tuǒyuán［数］ellipse：～形 oval

妥 tuǒ〈形〉① proper；appropriate：～否望复。Please reply whether you consider the above views sound. ②［多用在动词后］ready；settled：款已备～。The money is ready.

妥善 tuǒshàn proper；well-arranged：～安排 make appropriate arrangements

妥协 tuǒxié come to terms

(with); compromise (with sb. on sth.):～条款 compromise clause

tuò

拓 tuò 〈动〉open up; reclaim
另见 tà

拓荒 tuòhuāng reclaim wasteland; open up virgin soil:～者 pathbreaker; pioneer

拓宽 tuòkuān widen:～销售门路 expand marketing channels

拓扑学 tuòpūxué topology

拓展 tuòzhǎn expand; spread; extend; develop

唾 tuò ①〈名〉saliva; spittle ②〈动〉spit

唾骂 tuòmà spit on and curse; revile:万人～ be cursed by all the people

唾弃 tuòqì be cast aside; spurn

唾手可得 tuòshǒu-kědé can be obtained with a wet finger; be very easy to get; be extremely easy to obtain

唾余 tuòyú word of little importance; remarks(opinions) of little importance

W w

wā

挖 wā〈动〉dig; excavate:～隧道 excavate a tunnel

挖补 wābǔ mend by replacing a damaged part

挖掉 wādiào dig up; eradicate; dig out; root out; uproot

挖掘 wājué ① dig out; excavate:～古墓遗址 excavate an ancient burial site ② tap:～潜力 tap the potential; bring out latent power; tapping of reserves

挖空心思 wākōng-xīnsī rack one's brains

挖苦 wākǔ speak sarcastically or ironically; mock at; satirize:～话 satirical (ironical) remarks; verbal thrusts

挖潜改造资金 wāqián gǎizào zījīn funds to tap the potential of existing enterprises and finance their technical transformation

挖墙脚 wāqiángjiǎo undermine (dig at) the foundation (lit. "to dig at the foot of the wall"); cut the ground from under sb. 's feet; undermine

挖肉补疮 wāròu-bǔchuāng cut out a piece of one's flesh to cure a boil — to resort to a remedy worse than the ailment; sacrifice sth. as a makeshift to tide over a difficulty; rob one's belly to cover one's back

挖用库存 wāyòngkùcún borrowing from past reserves

洼 wā ①〈形〉hollow; low-lying:水～ a waterlogged depression ②〈名〉low-lying

洼地 wādì low-lying land; depression

蛙 wā〈名〉frog

蛙人 wārén frogman

蛙泳 wāyǒng [体] breaststroke

wá

娃 wá〈名〉① baby; child ② newborn animal:猪～ piglet

娃娃 wáwa baby:胖～ chubby baby

娃娃鱼 wáwayú giant salamander

wǎ

瓦 wǎ〈名〉① tile:无楞～ plain tile ② [电] watt ③〈形〉earthen:～罐 earthen jar
另见 wà

瓦房 wǎfáng tile-roofed building; tiled house

瓦匠 wǎjiàng bricklayer; tiler

瓦解 wǎjiě collapse; disintegrate, fall apart; undermine; demoralize; crumble:敌军全线～。The

whole enemy front crumbled.
瓦蓝 wǎlán azure; sky blue
瓦砾 wǎlì rubble; debris
瓦器 wǎqì earthenware; clayware
瓦斯 wǎsī gas: ～爆炸 gas explosion
瓦特 wǎtè watt
瓦纹 wǎwén [青铜器] tile pattern

wà

袜 wà〈名〉socks; stockings
袜带 wàdài suspenders; garters
袜子 wàzi [总称] hosiery; [短的] socks; [长的] stockings
瓦 wà〈动〉cover (a roof) with tiles; tile
另见 wǎ
瓦刀 wàdāo trowel; cleaver

wāi

歪 wāi〈形〉① crooked; inclined; askew; slant: 把画儿挂～了 hang a picture askew ② evil: ～风邪雨 ill winds and evil rains
歪道 wāidào ① evil ways; depraved life; vice: 走～ lead a depraved life; abandon oneself to evil ways ② evil ideas; devil's advice
歪风 wāifēng evil (ill) wind; sinister wind; "crooked wind"; corrupt (bad) tendencies: ～邪气 perverse trends; bad tendencies; unhealthy tendencies
歪理 wāilǐ false reasoning
歪曲 wāiqū ① crooked; wry: ～的统计资料 skewed statistical data ② distort; twist; wrest; misrepresent … as …: ～事实 distort facts

wài

外 wài〈形〉① outside; outward; outer: ～层空间 outer space ② foreign; external: ～国侨民 foreign nationals ③ other: ～省 other provinces ④ (relatives) of one's mother, sisters or daughters: ～孙 daughter's son; grandson ⑤ remotely related: ～人 a stranger; an outsider ⑥ unofficial: ～传 unofficial biography ⑦〈副〉beyond; in addition; besides: 此～ besides; into the bargain
外币兑换 wàibì duìhuàn foreign currency exchange
外表 wàibiǎo (outward) appearance; look; exterior: 根据～来判断 judge by appearances
外宾 wàibīn foreign guest (visitor)
外埠 wàibù outport; other places
外层空间 wàicéng kōngjiān outer space
外钞 wàichāo foreign bank note
外地 wàidì parts of the country other than where one is
外电 wàidiàn dispatches from foreign news agencies
外调 wàidiào ① transfer to other places: ～物资 transfer materials to other localities ② make

an investigation trip to other places(for some information)

外分泌 wàifēnmì exocrine; external secretion

外公 wàigōng (maternal) grandfather

外购 wàigòu external purchase

外观 wàiguān appearance; exterior

外国 wàiguó foreign country:～独资企业 solely foreign-funded enterprises. ～问题研究 foreign study

外行 wàiháng layman; outsider; be out of one's line; be not in one's line

外号 wàihào nickname

外患 wàihuàn foreign aggression

外汇 wàihuì foreign exchange:～兑换率 rate of (foreign) exchange. ～储备 foreign exchange reserve. ～管理 exchange control. ～行情 exchange quotations. ～收入 foreign exchange earnings

外汇分成 wàihuì fēnchéng share the foreign currency earnings; retention of a share of the foreign currency earned

外活 wàihuó ① orders taken by factories or craftsmen ② work taken in by housewives

外籍 wàijí foreign nationality:～华人 Chinese of foreign nationality. ～教师 foreign teacher

外交 wàijiāo diplomacy; foreign affairs:～家 diplomat. ～使节 diplomatic envoy. ～特权 diplomatic privilege

外界 wàijiè outside (external) world; outside:～人士 those on the outside

外景 wàijǐng scene shot on location; outdoor scene; exterior:拍摄～ shoot a scene on location; film the exterior

外科 wàikē ①surgical department ② surgery:～医生 surgeon

外快 wàikuài extra income; perquisite

外来 wàilái ① come from outside ② outside; external; foreign:～语 word of foreign origin; exotic word; loanword

外流 wàiliú outflow:人才～ brain drain; outflow of talented people

外貌 wàimào appearance; looks; exterior

外贸 wàimào foreign (external) trade:～企业 foreign trade enterprises

外婆 wàipó (maternal) grandmother

外强中干 wàiqiáng-zhōnggān outward appearance of strength but inner weakness; outwardly strong but inwardly weak

外侨 wàiqiáo foreign national; foreign residents; alien:～汇款 immigrants' remittance

外勤 wàiqín ① work done outside the office or in the field; outwork ② field personnel; outworker:他是干～工作的。He is an outworker.

外商 wàishāng foreign businessman; foreign tradesman; foreign merchant:～投资企业 foreign-funded enterprises

外生殖器 wàishēngzhíqì exernal genital organs
外事 wàishì foreign affairs：～口 foreign affairs departments. ～服务单位 service unit for foreigners
外侮 wàiwǔ foreign aggression；external aggression
外线 wàixiàn ①［军］exterior lines ②［电话］outside（telephone）connections
外向 wàixiàng［心］extroversion：～型性格者 extrovert
外向型 wàixiàngxíng［经］export-oriented； foreign-oriented：～经济（企业）export-oriented economy（enterprise）
外销 wàixiāo ① for sale abroad；for export；for sale in other parts of the country：～产品 products for export；products for sale in other areas ② export sales；export trade
外心 wàixīn ① unfaithful intentions（of husband or wife）② circumcentre
外形 wàixíng external form；appearance
外衣 wàiyī ① outer garment；coat ② cloak；garb：披着…～ under the cloak of…；in the garb of…
外因 wàiyīn［哲］external cause：～论 theory of the external origin
外用 wàiyòng external use（application）：～药 external remedy. ～药水 lotion
外运 wàiyùn ship out
外援 wàiyuán foreign aid；outside help
外债 wàizhài foreign debt；external debt
外传 wàizhuàn unofficial life history；unauthorized biography
外资 wàizī foreign capital：～经济 foreign-funded enterprises. ～投向 orientation in foreign investment
外族 wàizú ① people not of the same clan ② foreigner；alien ③ other nationalities

wān

豌 wān

豌豆 wāndòu pea：～黄 pea flour cake

剜 wān

〈动〉cut out；scoop out；gouge out

蜿 wān

蜿蜒 wānyán〈动〉①（of snakes，etc.）wriggle：～而上山脊 wriggle up to a ridge ② zigzag；wind；meander：沿着～的河岸散步 stroll along the meandered bank

弯 wān

① 〈形〉curved；tortuous；crooked：一～新月 a crescent moon ②〈动〉flex；bend：～弓 bend a bow ③〈名〉curve；bend：道路上的急转～ a sharp curve in the road
弯度 wāndù curvature
弯路 wānlù ① tortuous way ② roundabout route；detour：走～ make detours；take a roundabout route

弯曲 wānqū winding; meandering; curved; bent: 弯弯曲曲的河流 meandering river

湾 wān 〈名〉① a bend in a stream: 河～ river bend ② gulf; bay; [小的] inlet: 渤海～ Bohai Bay

wán

完 wán ①〈形〉whole; intact: ～好 in good condition; intact 〈动〉② finish; conclude; complete: 这个工作将在什么时候～成? When will the work be completed? ③ run out; use up: 信纸用～了。The writing pad is used up. ④ pay: ～税 pay taxes

完备 wánbèi perfect; complete; adequate: 订出～的规章制度 lay down adequate rules and regulations

完毕 wánbì finish; complete; end

完璧归赵 wánbì-guīzhào return the jade intact to the State of Zhao — return something to its owner in good condition

完成 wánchéng complete; fulfil; accomplish; discharge: ～生产指标 hit the production target

完稿 wángǎo finish a piece of writing; complete the manuscript

完工 wángōng complete a project; finish doing sth.; get through

完好 wánhǎo intact; in good condition: ～无缺 intact

完婚 wánhūn (of a man) marry; get married

完满 wánmǎn successful; satisfactory: ～结束 come to a successful close

完美 wánměi consummate; perfect: ～无缺 leave nothing to be desired; perfect in every way; flawless; consummate

完全 wánquán completely; perfectly; entirely; fully: ～竞争 perfect competition

完人 wánrén perfect man

完善 wánshàn improve; perfect: ～人民代表大会制度 improve the system of people's congress

完事 wánshì finish; get through; come to an end: 你～了没有? Have you finished (the job)?

完税 wánshuì pay taxes

完整 wánzhěng complete; intact; whole: ～的哲学 integral philosophy

玩 wán 〈动〉① play; have fun; amuse oneself: ～火者必自焚。Whoever plays with fire gets burnt. ② engage in some kinds of sports or recreational activities: ～篮球 play basketball ③ employ; resort: ～手段 play tricks ④ treat lightly; trifle with: ～法 trifle with the law

玩忽 wánhū trifle with; neglect: ～职守 neglect (dereliction) of duty

玩火 wánhuǒ play with fire

玩具 wánjù toy; plaything

玩弄 wánnòng ① play with; juggle with: ～词句 juggle with words ② coquet with; dally with; play fast and loose with;

flirt with：～女性 dally with women③ employ；resort to

玩偶 wán'ǒu doll；toy figure；plaything：～剧 toy theatre

玩儿命 wánrmìng play with one's life；risk one's life needlessly

玩儿票 wánrpiào play a role in Beijing opera as an amateur

玩儿去 wánrqù get away；clear off

玩赏 wánshǎng enjoy；take pleasure (delight) in；appreciate：～风景 admire the scenery

玩世不恭 wánshì-bùgōng be cynical；live in defiance of conventions；take a cynical attitude towards life；treat all things indecorously

玩耍 wánshuǎ ① play；sport ② enjoy oneself；amuse oneself

玩味 wánwèi chew the cud (of)；ruminate (over)；ponder

玩物 wánwù plaything；toy：～丧志 sap one's spirit by seeking pleasure；riding a hobby saps one's will to make progress；excessive attention to trivia saps the will

玩笑 wánxiào jest；joke；fun：开～ play a joke (prank) on；make jests

玩意儿 wányìr ① plaything；toy ② thing；gadget：这里有一个开罐头的～。Here is a new gadget for opening tins.

顽

顽 wán〈形〉① thick-headed；insensate：～石 hard stone；insensate stone ② naughty；mischievous ③ stubborn；obstinate：～敌 stubborn enemy

顽敌 wándí stubborn enemy；inveterate foe

顽固 wángù stubborn；obstinate：～不化 incorrigibly obstinate. ～分子 die-hard elements；diehards

顽疾 wánjí chronic and stubborn disease；persistent ailment

顽抗 wánkàng stubbornly resist；recalcitrate

顽劣 wánliè stubborn and stupid；stubborn and obstreperous

顽皮 wánpí naughty；mischievous

顽强 wánqiáng tenacious；persistent；staunch；unswerving；determined；indomitable：～的精神 indomitable spirit

顽症 wánzhèng chronic disease；persistent ailment

丸

丸 wán〈名〉① ball；pellet ② [胶囊] capsule

丸药 wányào pill (of Chinese medicine)；bolus

丸子 wánzi ① round mass of food；ball ② pill；bolus

纨

纨 wán〈名〉fine silk fabrics

纨绔子弟 wánkù-zǐdì rich men's sons；profligate son of the rich；a good-for-nothing young man from a wealthy family；dandy

烷

烷 wán[化] alkane

wǎn

宛

宛 wǎn〈形〉winding；tortuous

宛然 wǎnrán as if；as though

宛如 wǎnrú just like；as if：我想起这件事～昨天发生似的。I

remember it as if it happened yesterday.

莞 wǎn

莞尔 wǎn'ěr smile

惋 wǎn〈动〉sigh

惋惜 wǎnxī feel sorry for sb. or about sth.; sympathize with: 我为她感到～。I feel sorry for her.

碗 wǎn〈名〉bowl: 摆～筷 put out bowls and chopsticks for a meal; lay the table

碗橱 wǎnchú cupboard

婉 wǎn〈形〉① gentle; gracious; tactful: ～转批评某人的缺点 tactfully criticize sb.'s error ② beautiful; elegant; gracious: ～丽 lovely

婉辞 wǎncí ① graciously decline; politely refuse ② gentle words; euphemism

婉丽 wǎnlì beautiful; lovely

婉谢 wǎnxiè decline with thanks

婉言 wǎnyán gentle words; polite terms: ～拒绝 politely refuse; refuse with much regret

婉转 wǎnzhuǎn ① tactfully; gently: 措词～ put it in tactful terms ② sweet and agreeable; melodious: 歌喉～ sweet singing (voice)

挽 wǎn〈动〉① pull; draw: ～弓 draw a bow ② roll up: ～起袖子 roll up one's sleeves ③ mourn (lament) over sb.'s death: 敬～ with deep condolences from sb.

挽词 wǎncí memorial speech

挽回 wǎnhuí retrieve; redeem; save: ～面子 save face. ～名誉 redeem one's honour. 不可～回的 irrecoverable; irretrievable

挽救 wǎnjiù save; rescue: ～失足青年 try to save those young people who have done wrong

挽联 wǎnlián elegiac couplet

挽留 wǎnliú urge sb. to stay; ask sb. to remain; persuade sb. to stay

晚 wǎn ①〈名〉evening; night: 在～上 in the evening〈形〉② far on in time; late: 睡得～ go to bed late ③ junior; younger: ～辈 the younger generation; one's juniors

晚安 wǎn'ān good night

晚班 wǎnbān night shift: 做～ be (work) on the night shift

晚报 wǎnbào evening paper

晚场 wǎnchǎng evening show; evening performance

晚春 wǎnchūn late spring; late in the spring

晚点 wǎndiǎn late; past due; delay: 飞机～1 小时。The plane is delayed one hour.

晚饭 wǎnfàn supper; [正餐] dinner

晚会 wǎnhuì evening party

晚婚 wǎnhūn late marriage: ～晚育 late marriage and late childbirth

晚间 wǎnjiān (in the) evening; (at) night: ～新闻 evening news

晚节 wǎnjié moral integrity in one's later years: 保持～ hold fast to one's integrity in one's later years; uphold moral integrity as one grows old

晚景 wǎnjǐng ① evening scene ② circumstances in one's later years:～凄凉 miserable in one's later years

晚年 wǎnnián (in) one's old age; (in) one's later (declining, remaining) years

晚期 wǎnqī later period; late stage:～作品 sb.'s later works

晚秋 wǎnqiū late autumn:～作物 late-autumn crops

晚熟 wǎnshú late-maturing:～品种 late variety

晚霞 wǎnxiá evening (sunset) glow; sunset clouds

晚育 wǎnyù late childbirth

wàn

万 wàn〈数〉① ten thousand:～里边疆文化长廊 Cultural Corridor along Our Ten Thousand Li Borders ② a very great number; myriad; many:～物 all things on earth; all nature ③〈副〉extremely; by all means; absolutely:～难推辞 extremely difficult to say "no"

万般 wànbān ① all the different kinds ② utterly; extremely:～无奈 have no choice (alternative) but (to do)

万变不离其宗 wànbiàn bùlí qízōng change ten thousand times without departing from the original aim or stand; remain essentially the same despite all apparent changes; No matter how many changes he has made, he has not departed from his line.; In none of his changes has he departed from his stand.

万恶 wàn'è abosolutely vicious; diabolical:～之源 source (root) of all evil

万方 wànfāng ① all places ② extremely; incomparably

万分 wànfēn very much; extremely; deeply:～抱歉 be extremely sorry

万古 wàngǔ through the ages; forever; eternally:～长青 remain evergreen; remain fresh forever; last forever

万贯 wànguàn ten thousand strings of cash—great wealth

万花筒 wànhuātǒng kaleidoscope:～式的包装 kaleidoscopic packing

万机 wànjī myriad of state affairs

万家灯火 wànjiā-dēnghuǒ a myriad twinkling lights (of a city)

万籁俱寂 wànlài-jùjì All sounds are still.; All is quiet.; Silence reigns supreme.

万里长城 wànlǐ-chángchéng the Great Wall

万能 wànnéng ① all-powerful; omnipotent ② all-purpose; multi-purpose; universal:～机床 multi-purpose lathe

万年 wànnián ten thousand years; all ages; eternity; forever:遗臭～ be cursed forever by posterity; remain infamous in history

万千 wànqiān multifarious; myriad

万全 wànquán perfectly sound; surefire; completely safe: ～之策 a surefire plan; an absolutely safe measure

万世 wànshì generation after generation; all ages

万事 wànshì all things; everything: ～大吉。Everything goes off without a hitch.; All is well and propitious; have a plain sailing ahead. ～具备，只欠东风。Everything is ready except the east wind.; All is ready except what is crucial.

万水千山 wànshuǐ-qiānshān ten thousand torrents and a thousand crags—the trials of a long and arduous journey

万死不辞 wànsǐbùcí willing to risk any danger (to fulfil a task)

万万 wànwàn ① hundred million ② [用于否定] absolutely; (not)… on any account; wholly: ～不可放弃。Don't give it up on any account.

万无一失 wànwúyīshī without fail under any circumstances; no risk at all; absolutely safe

万物 wànwù all things; everything: ～的本体 the essence of all things

万象 wànxiàng all manifestations of nature; every phenomenon on earth

万幸 wànxìng very lucky (fortunate); by sheer luck

万一 wànyī ① in case; in case of; in the event of; by any chance; by any possibility: ～他忘记，请你提醒他一下。In case he forgets, please remind him about it. ② eventuality; contingency: 以防～ be prepared for any contingency

万丈深渊 wànzhàng-shēnyuān bottomless chasm; abyss

万众一心 wànzhòng-yīxīn with one heart and one mind; be united as one man; be of one mind

万紫千红 wànzǐ-qiānhóng a profusion (riot, blaze) of colour: 百花盛开，～。All kinds of flowers are blooming in a profusion of colour.

腕 wàn 〈名〉wrist

腕儿 wànr influential "wrist"; star

腕力 wànlì wrist strength

wāng

汪 wāng (of liquid) collect; accumulate

汪汪 wāngwāng ① swimming with tears; tearful: 眼泪～地诉说 complain with tearful eyes ② bowwow

汪洋 wāngyáng (of a body of water) vast; boundless (ocean)

wáng

亡 wáng〈动〉① flee; run away; escape: 逃～ flee; live in exile

② lose；be gone；③ die；fall；perish：阵～ fall in battle ④ conquer；subdue；subjugate：～党～国 destroy a party and subjugate a nation

亡故 wánggù die；pass away

亡国 wángguó ① lose one's country ② fall of a nation；ruin of a country

亡国奴 wángguónú slave without a country；a conquered people

亡灵 wánglíng soul of a deceased person；ghost；spectre

亡命 wángmìng seek refuge；flee；go into exile：～之徒 desperado；fugitive

亡羊补牢 wángyáng-bǔláo lock the stable door after the horse was stolen；mend the fold after a sheep is lost；The sheep has gone astray and its pen must be mended：～，犹未为晚。It is not too late to mend the fold even after some of the sheep have been lost.

王 wáng〈名〉king；monarch：国～ king

王朝 wángcháo ① dynasty ② royal court；imperial court

王储 wángchǔ crown prince

王道 wángdào the Way of the King；the Kingly Way；benevolent government

王宫 wánggōng (royal，imperial) palace

王国 wángguó ① kingdom ② realm；domain

王后 wánghòu queen；queen consort

王牌 wángpái trump card

王室 wángshì ① royal family (household，house)：～铭文 royal inscription ② imperial court

王位 wángwèi throne；regal office；regality：～继承权 royal succession

王政 wángzhèng monarchial rule；regal government；Kingly Rule

王子 wángzǐ prince

王族 wángzú persons of royal lineage；imperial kinsmen；royal clan；royal blood

wǎng

枉 wǎng ①〈形〉crooked；erroneous：矫～ straighten sth. crooked；right a wrong〈动〉② distort；twist；pervert ③ treat unjustly；wrong：～死 be wronged and driven to death ④〈副〉to no avail；in vain：～费工夫 work without avail

枉断 wǎngduàn settle a case by perverting the law

枉法 wǎngfǎ pervert (stretch，bend) the law：～裁判 orders and judgments that misuse the law. 贪赃～ bend the law for personal gains

枉费 wǎngfèi try in vain；waste：～心机 make futile efforts；rack one's brains in vain；scheme without avail

枉然 wǎngrán to no purpose；in vain

枉死 wǎngsǐ die unduly

惘 wǎng〈动〉feel disappointed；

feel frustrated

惘然 wǎngrán disappointed; frustrated

网 wǎng〈名〉① net: 乒乓球～ a table-tennis net ② network: 公路～ highway network ③〈动〉catch with a net; net

网袋(兜) wǎngdài(dōu) net bag; string bag

网点 wǎngdiǎn network: 饮食～ food and drink network: 商业～ commercial network

网罗 wǎngluó ① net for catching birds or fish ② enlist; recruit: ～人才 enlist talented people

往 wǎng ①〈动〉go (to): 来～于北京天津之间 travel to and fro between Beijing and Tianjin ②〈形〉past; previous: ～事 past events; the past ③〈副〉in the direction of; towards: ～西走 go in a westward direction 另见 wàng

往常 wǎngcháng ① used to: 她～回家很晚。She used to return home very late. ② (as) usual: 像～一样 as usual

往返 wǎngfǎn move to and fro; go there and back; make a round trip: ～需要 5 小时。It takes five hours to go there and back. ～贸易 countertrade

往返票 wǎngfǎnpiào return ticket; round-trip ticket

往复 wǎngfù ① move back and forth; reciprocate ② contact; dealings; intercourse

往后 wǎnghòu from now on; later on; in the future

往还 wǎnghuán intercourse; contact

往来 wǎnglái ① come and go: ～帐户 running account; current account; book account. ② contact; intercourse; dealings: 友好～ friendly intercourse

往年 wǎngnián (in) former years

往日 wǎngrì (in) former days; (in) the past

往事 wǎngshì past events; the past

往往 wǎngwǎng often; more often than not; frequently

wàng

妄 wàng〈形〉① rash; presumptuous: ～称 be so presumptuous to call oneself ② preposterous; absurd: 狂～ preposterous and arrogant

妄称 wàngchēng declare falsely or presumptuously

妄动 wàngdòng rash action; ill-considered action: 轻举～ take rash action

妄念 wàngniàn improper thought; wild fancy; false thought

妄图 wàngtú make a futile attempt; vainly attempt; try in vain: ～否认事实 vainly attempt to deny the facts

妄想 wàngxiǎng ① idle fancy; fantasy ② vainly hope; have an illusion about; indulge in vain hopes; give play to the fancy (imagination); give rein to the fancy (imagination)

妄言 wàngyán ① nonsense ② make improper remarks

妄自菲薄 wàngzì-fěibó make a humble estimate of one's abilities; unduly debase oneself; underestimate one's capabilities

妄自尊大 wàngzì-zūndà have too high an opinion of oneself; be overweening; be self-important; be given to swaggering; arrogant; be self-conceited; overbearing; haughty; aggrandize oneself

忘 wàng〈动〉① forget; dismiss from one's mind: 我～记告诉他这件事。I forgot to tell him about it. ② neglect; overlook: 走的时候别～了锁门。Don't neglect locking the door when you leave.

忘本 wàngběn forget one's origin; forget one's bitter past; forget one's roots

忘掉 wàngdiào forget; let slip from one's mind

忘恩负义 wàng'ēn-fùyì devoid of gratitude; sin one's mercies; ungrateful

忘乎所以 wànghū-suǒyǐ lose one's head; be carried away (by sth.); get swelled-headed: 心血来潮,～ lose one's head in a moment of excitement; forget oneself in a moment of excitement

忘怀 wànghuái forget; dismiss from one's mind

忘记 wàngjì ① forget ② overlook; neglect

忘年之交 wàngniánzhījiāo (become) good friends in spite of great difference in age

忘情 wàngqíng ① (usu. used in the negative) be unruffled by emotion; be unmoved; be indifferent ② let oneself go

忘我 wàngwǒ ① forget oneself ② selfless: ～精神 selfless spirit

忘形 wàngxíng be beside oneself (with glee, etc.): 得意～ be beside oneself with joy; be very pleased with oneself; get dizzy with success

忘性 wàngxìng forgetfulness: ～大 have a poor memory

望 wàng〈动〉① look over; gaze into the distance: 登高～远 climb high and gaze far ② visit; call on: 拜～ call to pay one's respects; call on ③ expect; hope: ～你今天下午来。You will be expected this afternoon. ④〈名〉reputation; prestige: 德高～重 enjoy high prestige and command great respect

望尘莫及 wàngchénmòjí so far behind that one can only see the dust of the rider ahead; too far behind to catch up; too inferior to bear comparison

望而生畏 wàng'érshēngwèi be terrified at the sight of sb. or sth.

望风 wàngfēng be on the lookout (watch); keep watch: ～而逃 flee pell-mell (helter-skelter) at the mere sight of the oncoming force

望乡台 wàngxiāngtái ① a terrace from which one can see one's home in the distance ② a terrace in hell from which the dead can see their homes

望眼欲穿 wàngyǎnyùchuān look forward with impatient expectancy; gaze anxiously till one's eyes are overrestrained

望洋兴叹 wàngyáng-xīngtàn feel helpless in face of a task beyond one's capability; bemoan one's inadequacy in the face of a great task

望子成龙 wàngzǐ-chénglóng hope that one's child will have a bright future; have great ambitions for one's child; hold high hopes for one's child

望族 wàngzú prominent family; distinguished family; prominent line

旺 wàng〈形〉prosperous; flourishing; busy: 购销两～。Both purchasing and marketing are brisk.

旺季 wàngjì busy season; peak period

旺盛 wàngshèng ① vigorous; exuberant: 士气～ have high morale. ～的生命力 exuberant vitality

旺销 wàngxiāo brisk sale

旺月 wàngyuè busy month

wēi

威 wēi ①〈名〉power; might; impressive strength: 军～ the might of an army; military prowess ②〈副〉by force

威逼 wēibī threaten by force; coerce; intimidate: ～利诱 threaten and cajole; coerce and bribe; alternate intimidation and bribery; combine threats with inducements; resort to both mild and severe (stern) measures

威风 wēifēng power and prestige; dignity; prestige: ～凛凛 awful air; awe-inspiring appearance; majestic-looking. ～扫地 sweep every bit of one's prestige into the dust; have lost one's prestige; be completely discredited. 逞～ make a display of one's power; flaunt one's power

威吓 wēihè threaten; menace; intimidate; bully

威力 wēilì power; might; force: ～无比 be extremely powerful

威名 wēimíng fame based on great strength or military exploits; mighty name; mighty reputation

威慑 wēishè deter: ～力量 deterrent (force, power)

威士忌 wēishìjì whisky

威望 wēiwàng prestige: 享有崇高～ enjoy high prestige. 有～的 prestigious

威武 wēiwǔ ① dignified; imposing ② might; power; force: ～不能屈,富贵不能淫 not to be subdued (overpowered) by force or corrupted by riches and honour

威胁 wēixié threaten; menace; intimidate

威信 wēixìn prestige; popular

trust：有～的 prestigious

威严 wēiyán ① dignified；majestic；stately；awe-inspiring ② dignity；prestige

威仪 wēiyí impressive and dignified manner

煨 wēi〈动〉① cook over a slow fire；simmer；stew：～鸡 stew chicken ② roast in fresh cinders

煨牛肉 wēiniúròu stewed beef

偎 wēi〈动〉snuggle up to；nestle up to；lean close to

偎抱 wēibào hug；cuddle

偎依 wēiyī snuggle up to；nestle up to；lean close to

微 wēi〈形〉① minute；tiny；slight：相差甚～。The difference is slight. ② profound；abstruse：精～ subtle ③〈动〉decline：衰～ be on the decline

微波 wēibō［电子］microwave：～通讯技术 microwave communication technology

微波炉 wēibōlú microwave oven

微薄 wēibó meagre；scanty；small：～的收入 small income

微不足道 wēibùzúdào not worth mentioning；minute；insignificant；trifling：～的人物 insignificant figure

微处理机 wēichǔlǐjī microprocessor

微词 wēicí veiled words of censure；veiled criticism

微电子技术 wēidiànzǐjìshù microelectronic technology

微雕 wēidiāo microscopic carvings

微观 wēiguān microcosmic：～经济学 microeconomics. ～世界 microcosm；microcosmos

微乎其微 wēihūqíwēi hardly noticeable；very little；extremely small；next to nothing

微机 wēijī microcomputer

微妙 wēimiào subtle；delicate：～的关系 subtle relations

微弱 wēiruò weak；slim；feeble；faint：～的光线 a faint light

微小 wēixiǎo small；little

微型 wēixíng miniature；mini-：～计算机 microcomputer. ～汽车 minicar；baby car. ～小说 short short story

微言 wēiyán words of subtle understanding

逶 wēi

逶迤 wēiyí winding；meandering；serpentine：～的小溪 meandering streamlet

巍 wēi〈形〉lofty；towering

巍然 wēirán lofty；towering；majestic：～屹立 stand (rise) majestically (like a mountain)；stand imposingly；tower

巍巍 wēiwēi lofty；towering：～泰山 the towering Mount Tai

危 wēi ①〈名〉peril；danger：居安思～ think of danger in times of peace〈形〉② dangerous；perilous；critical：～局 a dangerous (critical) situation ③ dying：病～ be critically ill；be dying ④〈动〉endanger；jeopardize：～害国家安全 jeopadizing national security

危房 wēifáng buildings that are ready to collapse; unsafe buildings

危害 wēihài harm; endanger; impair; undermine:～社会 endanger society

危机 wēijī crisis: ～重重 be bogged down in crises. ～四伏 be environed by perils; be threatened by growing crises; beset with crises; crisis-ridden

危及 wēijí endanger; imperil; jeopardize:～生命 endanger one's life

危急 wēijí critical; in imminent danger; in a desperate situation:～情况。The situation was desperate.

危难 wēinàn danger and disaster; calamity

危如累卵 wēirúlěiluǎn in a precarious situation; hazardous as eggs piled up; as precarious as a pile of eggs

危亡 wēiwáng in peril; at stake

危险 wēixiǎn danger; peril:～!切勿靠近! Danger! Keep away!. 冒生命～ at the risk of one's life. ～由货主自负 owner's risk of damage

危言耸听 wēiyán-sǒngtīng say frightening things just to raise an alarm; exaggerate things just to scare people; make sensational statements; make an inflammatory statement

危在旦夕 wēizàidànxī in imminent danger; on the verge of death or destruction; at the last gasp; Danger may come any time (day).

wéi

为 wéi〈动〉① do; act:～非作歹 do evil (mischief) ② act as; serve as:以此～凭。This will serve as a proof. ③ become:一分～二。One divides into two. ④ mean; be:一公斤～二市斤。One kilogramme is equivalent to two *jin* ⑤〈介〉by:～人民所唾弃 be cast aside by the people

为富不仁 wéifù-bùrén be rich and cruel; the heartless rich; unscrupulous rich

为害 wéihài cause harm; cause damage

为患 wéihuàn bring trouble

为民兴利 wéimín-xìnglì work for the welfare of the people

为难 wéinán ① be embarrassed; feel awkward; be in a dilemma:这会让你～。It would put you in an awkward position. ② embarrass sb.; make things difficult for sb.

为期 wéiqī (be completed) by a definite date:课程～2个月。The course of study covers two months.

为人 wéirén conduct oneself (in a certain way); behave:～正派 conduct oneself decently; be a man of decency

为人处世 wéirén-chǔshì the way one conducts oneself in society; one's attitude towards life

为人师表 wéirén-shībiǎo be worthy of the name of teacher; be a paragon of virtue and learning

为首 wéishǒu headed by; with sb. as the leader

为数 wéishù number; amount to

为所欲为 wéisuǒyùwéi do whatever one likes; do as one pleases

为伍 wéiwǔ associate with

为限 wéixiàn within the limit of; not exceed; not more than:有效期以一周～ be good for one week only

为止 wéizhǐ up to; till:到现在～ up to now; so far. 到本年底～ till the end of this year

为主 wéizhǔ give first place to; give priority to

圩 wéi 〈名〉 dyke; embankment:筑～ build dykes

圩田 wéitián ① low-lying paddy fields surrounded with dykes ② polder

违 wéi 〈动〉① break; violate; go against:～反诺言 break a promise ② leave; part; be separated:久～了。I haven't seen you for ages.

违背 wéibèi disobey; violate; go against; break:～民心 go against the will of the people

违法 wéifǎ break (violate) the law; be illegal:～乱纪 violate the law and discipline; break laws and violate discipline. ～情况 illegalities

违反 wéifǎn break; violate; infringe; conflict with; run counter to; go against:～合同 breach of contract

违禁 wéijìn violate a ban:～贸易 illicit trade. ～品 contraband (goods)

违抗 wéikàng disobey (orders, etc.); act in defiance of; be contrary to; defy (one's superior, etc.)

违例 wéilì breach of rules; violation

违令 wéilìng disobey orders

违心 wéixīn against one's will; contrary to one's convictions:做～事 act against one's conscience

违约 wéiyuē ① break a contract; violate a treaty ② break one's promise; fail to keep an engagement; break off an appointment

违章 wéizhāng break rules and regulations; unlawful; illicit:～建筑 houses, etc. erected without official permission. ～行驶 drive against traffic regulations

围 wéi ①〈动〉enclose; surround; encircle:用篱笆～住院子 enclose a yard with a fence ②〈副〉around; all round:四～都是山。There are mountains all around.

围捕 wéibǔ surround and seize; round up

围城打援 wéichéng-dǎyuán besiege the enemy in order to strike at his reinforcements; besiege a city to annihilate the enemy relief force

围攻 wéigōng ① besiege; lay

siege to; beset; launch converging attack on; beleaguer ② jointly attack sb.:遭到～come under attack from all sides; become a target of attacks

围观 wéiguān (of a crowd of people) watch; look on

围剿 wéijiǎo encircle and suppress

围困 wéikùn pin down; hem in

围猎 wéiliè round up and hunt

围拢 wéilǒng crowd around; gather round

围棋 wéiqí Go; *weiqi*

围绕 wéirào ① move; round; around:地球～太阳转。The earth moves round the sun. ② centre on; revolve around:学者主要～三个问题进行讨论。The scholars primarily focused their discussions on three questions.

桅 wéi 〈名〉① range light ② barn lantern

桅灯 wéidēng mast head light

惟 wéi ①〈副〉only; alone; solely:～你是问。You will be held personally responsible. ②〈连〉她工作努力,～注意身体不够。She works hard, but she doesn't care for her health

惟独 wéidú only; alone

惟恐 wéikǒng for fear that; lest:～落后 for fear that one should lag behind

惟利是图 wéilì-shìtú be bent solely on profit; be intent on nothing but profit; put profit-making first; try to turn everything to one's own advantage; pursue profit as one's only aim; engage in unscrupulous profiteering; profit-seeking; work exclusively for profit; care solely for profit; be greedy for profit

惟妙惟肖 wéimiào-wéixiào remarkably true to life; absolutely alike; be the very image of; fit to a hair

惟我独尊 wéiwǒ-dúzūn overweening; extremely conceited

惟一 wéiyī only; sole:～继承人 the sole heir

唯 wéi〈副〉only; alone:～一出路 the only way out
另见 wěi

唯恐 wéikǒng 见"惟恐"

唯恐天下不乱 wéikǒng tiānxià bù luàn desire to see the world plunged into chaos; desire (be anxious) to stir up trouble

唯利是图 wéilì-shìtú 见"惟利是图"

唯美主义 wéiměizhǔyì aestheticism; estheticism

唯名论 wéimínglùn [哲]nominalism; terminology

唯命是从 wéimìng-shìcóng always do as told; be absolutely obedient; be all submission; do sb.'s bidding; accept sb.'s instructions without a murmur

唯物辩证法 wéiwù biànzhèngfǎ materialist dialectics

唯物史观 wéiwùshǐguān materialistic concept of history

唯物主义 wéiwùzhǔyì materialism

唯心主义 wéixīnzhǔyì idealism

帷 wéi〈名〉bed-curtain
帷幕 wéimù heavy curtain
帷幄 wéiwò army tent
维 wéi〈动〉① tie up; hold together; link ② keep; maintain; preserve: ～持边界现状 maintain the status quo of the border ③〈名〉thinking; thought
维持 wéichí keep; preserve; maintain; support: ～秩序 keep order. ～原判 affirm the original judgment
维持和平部队 wéichí hépíng bùduì peace-keeping force
维护 wéihù uphold; defend; safeguard: ～国家主权 safeguard state sovereignty. ～费 sums of maintenance
维生素 wéishēngsù vitamin
维吾尔族 Wéiwú'ěrzú Uygur (Uighur) nationality (living in the Xinjiang Uygur Autonomous Region)
维新 wéixīn reform; reformism; modernization: ～变法 the Reform Movement of 1898
维修 wéixiū keep in repair; service; maintain: ～机器 maintain machinery. ～打字机 service a typewriter

wěi

伪 wěi〈形〉① false; sham; fake; bogus: ～币 a false coin ② puppet; illegal: ～政权 puppet regime
伪本 wěiběn spurious edition
伪币 wěibì ① counterfeit money; forged bank note ② bank note issued by a puppet government
伪钞 wěichāo counterfeit (forged) bank note
伪君子 wěijūnzǐ hypocrite
伪科学 wěikēxué pseudoscience
伪劣商品 wěiliè shāngpǐn fake and poor commodities
伪善 wěishàn hypocrisy: ～的姿态 hypocritical gesture
伪造 wěizào falsify; forge; counterfeit: ～公文 forge official document. ～国家货币 counterfeit national currency. ～帐目 falsify accounts. ～证据 falsify evidence
伪证 wěizhèng false evidence or testimony
伪装 wěizhuāng ① feign; pretend: ～亲善 put on an outward show of kindness ② disguise; mask: ～应当剥去。The mask must be stripped off. ③［军］camouflage
苇 wěi〈名〉reed
苇箔 wěibó reed matting
苇席 wěixí reed mat
苇箱 wěixiāng reed matting
伟 wěi〈形〉great; mighty
伟岸 wěi'àn tall and sturdy; stalwart; husky; strapping
伟大 wěidà great; mighty: ～的胜利 a signal victory
伟绩 wěijì brilliant achievements; great feats
伟人 wěirén great man: ～史观 great man theory of history
伟业 wěiyè great cause

纬 wěi 〈名〉① weft；woof ② latitude：北～40度 forty degrees north latitude

纬度 wěidù latitude

纬书 wěishū apocryphal texts

纬线 wěixiàn ①［纺］weft；woof ②［地］parallel

唯 wěi

另见 wéi

唯唯诺诺 wěiwěi-nuònuò be all submission；be a yes-man；be obsequious；be obedient and docile

委 wěi〈动〉① entrust；appoint：把权力～托给某人 entrust power to sb. ② throw away；discard：～之于地 cast sth. upon the ground ③ lay；shift：～过于人 lay the blame on others〈形〉④ indirect；roundabout：～婉 mild and roundabout；tactful ⑤ dispirited；listless：～顿 weary；tired；exhausted ⑥〈副〉really；actually：～系实情。This is the true story.

委顿 wěidùn tired；exhausted；weary

委(萎)靡不振 wěi (wěi) míbùzhèn in low spirits；dejected and apathetic；feel (look) blue；become dispirited

委派 wěipài appoint；designate；delegate

委曲 wěiqū ① feel wronged；nurse a grievance ② put sb. to great inconvenience

委曲求全 wěiqū-qiúquán compromise out of consideration for the general interest；stoop to compromise；suffer wrong for the sake of general interest；make concessions to achieve one's purpose；be quite accommodating and care for overall interests

委任 wěirèn appoint：～书 letter of appointment

委琐 wěisuǒ ① petty；trifling ② of wretched appearance

委托 wěituō entrust；trust；consign；commission：这件事就～你了。I leave this matter in your hands. ～机构 associated agency

委婉 wěiwǎn mild and roundabout；tactful

委员 wěiyuán committee member：～会 committee；commission；council

尾 wěi〈名〉① tail ② end：排～(a person) standing at the end of a line ③ remaining part；remnant：扫～工程 the final phase of a project

尾巴 wěiba tail：～工程 "tail" constructions

尾灯 wěidēng tail light；tail lamp

尾气 wěiqì tail gas

尾声 wěishēng ① epilogue；finale ② end：会议已接近～。The meeting is coming to an end.

尾随 wěisuí follow (at sb.'s heels)；tag along after；tail behind

尾追 wěizhuī pursue closely；follow at sb.'s heel；shadow；hot on the trail of

娓 wěi

娓娓 wěiwěi (talk) tirelessly: ～而谈 talk volubly. ～动听 speak with an absorbing interest

萎 wěi 〈动〉wither; wilt; fade

萎靡 wěimí dejected; dispirited

萎缩 wěisuō ① (of a market, economy, etc.) shrink; decline; sag ② wither; shrivel

猥 wěi〈形〉① numerous; multifarious ② base; obscene; indcent

猥贱 wěijiàn humble; lowly

猥琐 wěisuǒ ① vulgar; mean ② of wretched appearance

猥亵 wěixiè ① lewd; filthy; obscene: ～的语言 lewd language ② act indecently (towards a woman): ～幼童 carnal abuse. ～行为 act of indecency; indencent conduct

wèi

为 wèi〈介〉① for: ～民兴利 work for the welfare of the people ② for the sake of; in order to

另见 wéi

为此 wèicǐ on this account; to this end; for this reason; in this connection: 他～而生气。He was angry on this account.

为国 wèiguó for the country: ～效劳 render one's services to the country. ～争光 win honour for the country

为何 wèihé why; for what reason

为虎作伥 wèihǔ-zuòchāng play the jackal to the tiger; assist the evildoer; act as the paws of the tiger; serve as the enemy's jackal; act as guide to a tiger; help a villain do evil

为了 wèile for; for the sake of; in order to

为民请命 wèimínqǐngmìng plead for the people

为人作嫁 wèirénzuòjià work for others with no benefit to oneself; render sb. a service; toil just for the benefit of others; act on others' behalf

未 wèi〈副〉① have not; did not: ～成年 haven't grown up ② not: ～知可否 not know whether sth. can be done

未必 wèibì may not; not necessarily: 他～知道。He doesn't necessarily know.

未便 wèibiàn not be in a position to; find it hard to: ～立即答复 find it difficult to give an immediate reply

未卜先知 wèibǔ-xiānzhī have foresight; foresee

未尝 wèicháng have not; did not: ～不可试一试 might just as well have a try

未成年 wèichéngnián under age; not yet of age: ～人 juveniles; minors

未定 wèidìng uncertain; undecided; not yet fixed: ～边界 undefined boundary

未婚 wèihūn unmarried; single: ～夫 fiancé. ～妻 fiancée

未竟 wèijìng unfulfilled; unaccomplished

未决 wèijué undecided; unsettled; outstanding; pending: 胜负～。The outcome is not yet decided. ～犯 culprit

未可 wèikě cannot: ～乐观 nothing to be optimistic about; have no cause for optimism

未来 wèilái ① coming; approaching; next; future ② future; tomorrow

未了 wèiliǎo unfinished; unfulfilled: ～情缘 unrequited love affairs. ～事宜 unfinished business

未免 wèimiǎn a bit too; rather: ～太过分了 go a bit too far

未能 wèinéng cannot: ～得逞 be frustrated in. ～取得预期的结果 fail to achieve the expected result

未遂 wèisuì abortive; unaccomplished: ～犯［法］unaccomplished offender. ～的政变。The coup d'état aborted.; abortive coup d'état. 自杀～［法］attempted suicide

未完 wèiwán unfinished: ～基建工程 construction in process

未详 wèixiáng unknown: 病因～。What brought on the illness is not clear.

未雨绸缪 wèiyǔchóumóu provide for a rainy day; take precautions; provide against the future; take preventive measures

未知数 wèizhīshù ①［数］unknown number ② unknown; uncertain

味

wèi〈名〉① taste; relish; flavour: 甜～ a sweet taste ② smell; odour: 臭～ a foul smell ③ interest: 语言无～ insipid language

味道 wèidao taste; flavour

味精 wèijīng gourmet powder

味觉 wèijué sense of taste; taste

味同嚼蜡 wèitóngjiáolà It is like chewing wax — insipid.; be as dry as dust; It tastes no better than tallow.

畏

wèi〈动〉① fear; be afraid of; dread: 不～强暴 defy brute force ② awe; respect: 后生可～。Youth are to be regarded with respect.

畏避(缩) wèibì (suō) shrink (flinch) (from); recoil (from)

畏惧 wèijù be afraid of; fear; dread; be frightened: 令人～的 dreadful; terrible; awful

畏怯 wèiqiè timid; chickenhearted; cowardly

畏首畏尾 wèishǒu-wèiwěi be full of misgivings; be filled with misgivings and fear; be overcautious

畏途 wèitú dangerous road: 视为～ regard it as a dangerous road to take; be afraid to undertake it

畏罪 wèizuì be afraid of punishment for one's crime: ～潜逃 abscond to avoid punishment. ～自杀 commit suicide to escape punishment

喂

wèi ①〈动〉feed: ～小鸡 feed

the chickens ②〈叹〉hello; hey: ～,你去哪儿? Hey, where are you going?
喂奶 wèinǎi breast-feed; nurse; suckle:给婴儿～ give suck to a baby; suckle a baby
喂养 wèiyǎng feed; keep; raise: ～家禽 keep fowls

胃 wèi〈名〉stomach:～痛 stomachache
胃癌 wèi'ái stomach cancer; gastric cancer
胃病 wèibìng stomach trouble; gastric disease
胃出血 wèichūxuè gastric bleeding; gastric hemorrhage; gastrorrhagia
胃镜 wèijìng gastroscope: ～检查 gastrocopy; stomachoscopy
胃口 wèikǒu ① appetite: ～(不)好 have a good (poor) appetite. ② liking:合某人的～ to one's liking; to one's taste
胃溃疡 wèikuìyáng gastric ulcer
胃下垂 wèixiàchuí ptosis of the stomach; gastroptosis
胃液 wèiyè gastric juice

谓 wèi〈动〉① say; tell:可～ it may be said that … ② call; name: 所～ so-called ③〈名〉sense; meaning: 无～的话 senseless talk
谓语 wèiyǔ [语] predicate

位 wèi〈名〉① place; location:座～ seat ② position:名～ fame and position ③ throne: 即～ come to the throne
位次 wèicì ① precedence; seating arrangement ②rank
位于 wèiyú be situated; be located; lie:朝鲜～中国的东面。Korea lies to the east of China.
位置 wèizhi ① seat; place ② position; post

尉 wèi〈名〉① officer ② (Wèi) a surname
尉官 wèiguān military officer above the rank of warrant officer and below that of major; junior officer

慰 wèi〈动〉① console; comfort; soothe: ～勉 comfort and encourage ② get (be) relieved:得知你康复,甚～。I'm relieved to learn that you have recovered from your illness.
慰藉 wèijiè comfort; console
慰劳 wèiláo bring gifts to, or send one's best wishes to, in recognition of services rendered; visit and extend solicitude; give sb. much of a welcome
慰问 wèiwèn express sympathy and solicitude for; extend one's regards to; convey greetings to; salute: ～信 letter of sympathy (consolation); consolatory letter
慰唁 wèiyàn condole with sb.

蔚 wèi〈形〉luxuriant; grand
蔚蓝 wèilán deep blue; azure: ～的天空 azure sky
蔚然成风 wèirán-chéngfēng have become a common practice; have grown into a general

trend; become the order of the day; become prevalent

卫 wèi〈动〉defend; guard; protect: 保家～国 protect our homes and defend our country

卫兵 wèibīng guard; bodyguard

卫队 wèiduì squad of guards; escorts

卫冕 wèimiǎn defend one's championship; defend one's title

卫生 wèishēng health; sanitation; hygiene: ～检疫 health quarantine. ～院 health clinic. ～设备 sanitory equipment. ～食品 wholesome food. ～防疫站 sanitation and antiepidemic station

卫生间 wèishēngjiān toilet (room)

卫生巾 wèishēngjīn feminine napkin

卫士 wèishì bodyguard

卫戍 wèishù garrison: ～部队 garrison force

卫星 wèixīng ① satellite: 通讯～ communications satellite ② artificial (man-made) satellite; sputnik: ～城 satellite town

卫星天线 wèixīng tiānxiàn satellite antenna

魏 wèi〈名〉① one of the Warring States into which China was divided during the Eastern Zhou period (770—256 B.C.), occupying what is now northern Henan, eastern Shaanxi, southwestern Shanxi, and southern Hebei ② one of the Three Kingdoms into which China was divided during the period (220—280), occupying the present-day provinces in the Yellow River valley and what is now northern Hubei, Anhui, Jiangsu and central Liaoning ③ one of the Northern Dynasties, better known as the Northern Wei ④ (Wèi) a surname

wēn

温 wēn〈形〉① warm; lukewarm; tepid: ～水 lukewarm water ② mild; gentle: ～暖的气候 a mild climate ③〈名〉temperature (of the body): 量体～ take one's temperature〈动〉④ warm (up): 牛奶正在炉子上～热。The milk is warming up on the stove. ⑤ review; revise: ～习功课 review one's lessons

温饱 wēnbǎo have enough to eat and wear; live a life of reasonable comfort; enough food and clothing; warm and well-fed

温差 wēnchā difference in temperature; range of temperature

温床 wēnchuáng ①[农]hotbed ② breeding ground; hotbed: 官僚主义的～ breeding ground (hotbed) of bureaucracy

温存 wēncún ① gentle; kind ② attentive: ～体贴 attentive and considerate

温带 wēndài temperate zone

温度 wēndù temperature

温故而知新 wēngù ér zhīxīn gain new insights through restudying old material; reviewing the past helps to understand the present;learn the new by restudying the old; review what you have learned and know what is new.; learning about new things by reviewing old things

温和 wēnhé ① temperate; moderate; mild:～的天气 a moderate climate. ～派 moderates ② gentle; mild; facile:性情～ have a gentle disposition

温课 wēnkè review one's lessons:～迎考 review one's lessons for the examination

温暖 wēnnuǎn ① warm; mild ② warmth; geniality:送～工程 "warmth-extending project" (i. e., gifts or welfare donations of food, money, etc. to the needy)

温情 wēnqíng tender feeling; tender-heartedness:～脉脉 full of tender feeling

温柔 wēnróu tender; sweet; softness

温室 wēnshì hothouse; greenhouse:～生产 hothouse production. ～效应 greenhouse effect

温顺 wēnshùn docile; gentle; meek

温文尔雅 wēnwén'ěryǎ refined and cultivated

温习 wēnxí review; revise

瘟 wēn〈名〉acute communicable diseases

瘟神 wēnshén god of plague

瘟疫 wēnyì pestilence; plagues

wén

文 wén〈名〉① character; script; writing:金～ inscriptions on ancient bronze objects ② language:法～ the French language ③ literary composition; writing:～如其人。The writing mirrors the writer. ④ literary language:半～半白 half literary and half vernacular ⑤ culture:～物 cultural relics〈形〉⑥ civil; civilian:～武官员 civil and military officers (officials) ⑦ refined; gentle:举止～雅 refined in manner ⑧〈动〉cover up; paint over:～过饰非 cover up one's errors (mistakes); whitewash faults; gloss over one's mistakes (wrongs)

文本 wénběn text; version

文笔 wénbǐ style of writing; literary style:～流利 write in an easy and fluent style; easy and smooth style of writing

文不对题 wén bù duìtí be off the mark; miss the point; be wide of the mark

文采 wéncǎi ① literary talent (grace); elegance of writing; stylistic elegance ② rich and bright colours

文辞 wéncí diction; language:～优美 exquisite diction; The essay is written in an elegant style.

文从字顺 wéncóng-zìshùn readable and fluent

文牍 wéndú official documents

and correspondence：～主义 officialism；red tape

文房四宝 wénfáng-sìbǎo the "four precious articles of the writing table" (i. e., writing brush; ink stick; ink slab and paper); the "scholar's four jewels"

文风 wénfēng style of writing

文稿 wéngǎo manuscript; draft

文告 wéngào statement; message; proclamation; announcement

文工团 wéngōngtuán cultural troupe; art troupe

文豪 wénháo literary giant; great writer

文化 wénhuà ① culture; civilization：～扶贫工程 project of aiding the poor areas in developing culture. ～管理体制改革 reform of the system for managing cultural undertakings ② education; schooling：～程度 educational level

文化人 wénhuàrén a cultural professional; a cultural entrepreneur

文集 wénjí collected works; anthology

文件 wénjiàn documents; papers; instruments

文教 wénjiào culture and education

文具 wénjù writing materials; stationery：～店 stationery store; stationer's

文科 wénkē liberal arts：～教育 liberal education. ～硕士 Master of Arts (MA). ～院校 colleges of arts

文库 wénkù library

文盲 wénmáng ① illiteracy：扫除～ wipe out illiteracy ② illiterate (person)

文明 wénmíng ① civilization：物质(精神)～ material (spiritual) civilization ② civilized; civil：～村 civilized village. ～经商 civilized conduct of business. 建设～幸福的家庭 refine family life and make it more enjoyable

文凭 wénpíng diploma;［中小学的］certificate

文人 wénrén man of letters; scholar

文山会海 wénshān-huìhǎi mountain of documents and sea of meetings

文史 wénshǐ literature and history：～馆 Research Institute of Culture and History. ～资料 historical accounts of past events

文书 wénshū ① official dispatch (papers); document ② clerk

文思 wénsī the train of thought in writing：～敏捷 have a ready pen

文坛 wéntán literary circles (world); the world of letters

文韬武略 wéntāo-wǔlüè civil and military skills

文体 wéntǐ ① style (of writing); literary form ② recreation and sports：～活动 recreation and sports activities

文武双全 wénwǔ shuāngquán be well versed in both polite letters and martial arts; adept with both pen and sword

文物 wénwù cultural objects; cultural (historical) relics: ～保护 protection of cultural relics. 出土～ unearthed cultural relics

文献 wénxiàn literature; document: 科技～ literature of science and technology

文选 wénxuǎn selected works; selections

文学 wénxué literature: ～家 man of letters; literary man. ～沙龙 literary salon. ～院 college of liberal arts. ～语言 literary language; standard speech. ～作品 literary works

文雅 wényǎ elegant; refined; cultured: 举止～ be refined in manner

文言 wényán classical Chinese: ～文 writings in classical Chinese

文艺 wényì ① literature and art: ～界 literary and art circles. ～批评 literary and art criticism ② theatrical performance: ～调演 transfer and performance of the performing arts. ～会演 theatrical festival; joint performance. ～晚会 soiree

文娱 wényú cultural recreation: ～活动 (cultural and) recreational activities

文责 wénzé author's responsibility: ～自负。The author takes sole responsibility for his views.

文摘 wénzhāi digest; abstract: 报刊～ a press digest

文章 wénzhāng ① article; essay: 做～ write an essay ② literary works; writings ③ implication; hint: 他的话里有～。There is a hint in his remark.

文职 wénzhí civilian post: ～人员 nonmilitary personnel

文质彬彬 wénzhì-bīnbīn be so gentle and refined in manner; suave; urbane

文治武功 wénzhì-wǔgōng cultural and military achievements

文字 wénzì ① characters; writing; script: ～清通 lucid writing ② written language: 有～可考的历史 recorded history

蚊

wén〈名〉mosquito

蚊虫 wénchóng mosquito

蚊香 wénxiāng mosquito-repellent incense; anti-mosquito coil

蚊帐 wénzhàng mosquito net

纹

wén〈名〉vein; grain; lines; wrinkles: 眼角周围的皱～ wrinkles round one's eyes

纹理 wénlǐ vein; grain: ～细的木材 wood of fine grain

纹路 wénlù lines; grain

纹片 wénpiàn [瓷器] crackle in a ceramic glaze

纹饰 wénshì [青铜器] decoration; design; pattern; mark; motive (motif); ornamentation

纹丝不动 wénsī-bùdòng absolutely still

纹银 wényín fine silver

闻

wén〈动〉① hear: ～讯 hear the news ② smell: 我肯定～到了煤气味。I am sure I smell gas. ③〈形〉well-known; famous: ～人 well-known figure;

celebrity 〈名〉④ news; information; story: 要～ important news ⑤ reputation: 秽～ ill reputed (referrig to sexual behaviour); reputation for immorality

闻风而动 wénfēng'érdòng respond to a call at once; go into action without delay; act without delay upon hearing sth.

闻风丧胆 wénfēng-sàngdǎn become terror-stricken (panic-stricken) on hearing the news; become terrified at the news

闻过则喜 wénguòzéxǐ be pleased to have one's errors pointed out; be glad when told of one's own errors

闻名 wénmíng famous; well-known; renowned; noted: ～中外 be well-known at home and abroad

闻所未闻 wénsuǒwèiwén have never even heard of it; unheard-of; hear what one has never heard before; It has never been heard of before

闻讯 wénxùn hear the news

wěn

紊 wěn〈形〉disorderly; confused

紊乱 wěnluàn disorder; chaos; confusion: 秩序～ in a state of chaos

稳 wěn〈形〉① firm; stable; steady: ～的步伐 a steady pace ② certain; sure: 这事你拿得～吗? Are you quite sure of it?

稳步 wěnbù with firm (steady) steps; steadily: ～前进 forge ahead (advance) steadily

稳产 wěnchǎn stable yields

稳当 wěndāng reliable; safe; secure: ～的措施 reliable measures

稳定 wěndìng ① stable; steady; firm ② stabilize: ～物价 stabilize commodity prices

稳固 wěngù steady; firm; stable; solid: ～的基础 solid foundation

稳健 wěnjiàn steady; sane: ～的政策 sane policy. 办事～ go about things steadily

稳妥 wěntuǒ safe; reliable; sound: ～投资 sound investment

稳扎稳打 wěnzhā-wěndǎ wage a steady and sure struggle; go ahead steadily and strike sure blows

稳中有降 wěnzhōngyǒujiàng be stable with a slight decline

稳重 wěnzhòng (of speech, manner) calm and steady; staid; sedate

刎 wěn〈动〉cut one's throat

刎颈之交 wěnjǐngzhījiāo sworn friends (brothers)

吻 wěn ①〈动〉kiss〈名〉② lips ③ an animal's mouth

吻合 wěnhé dovetail (accord) with; coincide (tally, agree) with: 你的数字同我的～。Your figures tally with mine.

wèn

问 wèn〈动〉① ask; inquire:～(某人)一个问题 ask (sb.) a question ② inquire after; ask after:她信里～起你。She asks after you in her letter. ③ interrogate; cross-examine:询～目击者有关事故的情况 interrogate a witness about the accident ④ hold responsible:出了事唯你是～。You'll be held responsible if anything goes wrong.

问安 wèn'ān pay one's respects; wish sb. good health

问案 wèn'àn hear (try) a case

问答 wèndá questions and answers.

问好 wènhǎo send one's regards (respects) to; say hello to; extend greetings to:请代我向你的父母～。Please give my regards to your parents.

问候 wènhòu extend greetings to; give one's regards to:谨致～[信尾用语] with best regards

问话 wènhuà ask about; inquire

问卷 wènjuàn questionnaire:～设计 questionnaire design

问事处 wènshìchù information desk (office)

问世 wènshì be published; come out; appear

问题 wèntí ① question; problem; issue:～教学 specific-problem oriented teaching. ～小说 problem novel. ～戏剧 problem play. ② trouble; mishap:她又出～了。She has gone into trouble again.

问心无愧 wènxīn-wúkuì have a clear conscience; feel no qualms about self-examination

问心有愧 wènxīn-yǒukuì feel a twinge of conscience; feel guilty; have sth. on one's conscience

问讯 wènxùn inquire; ask:～处 inquiry office; information desk

问罪 wènzuì denounce publicly (for); condemn

wēng

翁 wēng〈名〉① old man:渔～ an old fisherman ② father:尊～ your father ③ husband's or wife's father; father-in-law:～姑 a woman's parents-in-law

翁婿 wēngxù father-in-law and son-in-law

嗡 wēng

嗡嗡 wēngwēng hum; buzz; drone:～叫的苍蝇 buzzing flies

wèng

瓮 wèng〈名〉earthen jar; urn

瓮城 wèngchéng barbican

瓮棺 wèngguān funeral urn

瓮声瓮气 wèngshēng-wèngqì in a low, muffled voice

瓮中捉鳖 wèngzhōng-zhuōbiē catch a turtle in a jar; make a sure catch; go after an easy prey

wō

涡 wō〈名〉whirpool; eddy (of water)

涡流 wōliú circular movement of a fluid; whirling fluid

涡轮 wōlún turbine

窝 wō〈名〉① nest: 鸟～ bird's nest ② lair; den: 贼～ thieves' den ③ hole; pit: 心～ the pit of the stomach〈动〉④ shelter; harbour (stolen goods): ～藏犯罪分子 harbour criminal elements ⑤ check; hold in: ～着一肚子火 be simmering with rage ⑥ bend: 别把画片～了。Be careful not to bend the picture. ⑦〈量〉brood; litter: 一～小鸡 a brood of chickens

窝藏 wōcáng give shelter to; harbour: ～赃物 conceal booty

窝工 wōgōng enforced idleness due to poor organization of work; work holdup: ～费用 expense of idleness

窝火 wōhuǒ be filled with anger

窝囊 wōnāng ① feel vexed; be annoyed (perturbed) ② hopelessly stupid; good-for-nothing

窝(窝)头 wō(wō)tóu steamed corn bread

窝赃罪 wōzāngzuì offence of harbouring the stolen goods and contrabands

窝主 wōzhǔ a person who harbour criminals, loot or contranbands

莴 wō

莴苣 wōjù lettuce

莴笋 wōsǔn asparagus lettuce

蜗 wō

蜗居 wōjū humble abode

蜗牛 wōniú snail

wǒ

我 wǒ〈代〉① I ② we: ～方 our side

我方帐户 wǒfāngzhànghù our account

我见 wǒjiàn my opinion

我们 wǒmen we or us

我群 wǒqún we-group

我行我素 wǒxíng-wǒsù persist in one's old ways (no matter what others may say); go one's own way; stick to one's old way of doing things

我族中心主义 wǒzú-zhōngxīnzhǔyì ethno-centrism

wò

沃 wò ①〈名〉fertile; rich ②〈动〉irrigate

沃土 wòtǔ rich soil; fertile soil

斡 wò

斡旋 wòxuán ① mediate ②［法］good offices: ～于双方之间 mediate between the two parties

卧 wò ①〈动〉lie: 俯～ lie face downwards ②〈形〉for sleeping in: ～铺 sleeping berth

卧病 wòbìng be confined to bed; be ill in bed; lie ill; be laid up

卧车 wòchē ① sleeping car; sleeper ② sedan; car
卧床 wòchuáng ① (of the old or the sick) lie in bed; be confined to bed ② bed
卧倒 wòdǎo drop to the ground; take a prone (lying-down) position
卧底 wòdǐ be a planted agent
卧轨 wòguǐ lay oneself on the railway tracks (either to commit suicide or as a form of protest)
卧具 wòjù bedding; bedclothes
卧铺 wòpù [车、船的] berth:订～票 book a berth
卧薪尝胆 wòxīn-chángdǎn sleep on the brushwood and taste the gall — to nurse vengeance; endure hardships to accomplish some ambition; put up with an insult in order to take revenge
卧姿 wòzī prone position

握 wò ①〈动〉hold; grasp:～有真理 possess truth ②〈名〉handful
握别 wòbié shake hands at parting; bid farewell to; part (with, from)
握手 wòshǒu shake hands (with)
握手言欢 wòshǒu-yánhuān hold hands and chat cheerfully (esp. in making up a quarrel)

龌 wò
龌龊 wòchuò dirty; foul; filthy: 卑鄙～ base; mean; sordid

wū

污 wū ①〈名〉dirt; filth:旧社会遗留下来的～毒 the filth and poison left over from the old society〈形〉② dirty; filthy:～泥 mire; mud; sludge ③ corrupt:贪官～吏 corrupt officials ④ defile
污点 wūdiǎn stain; spot; smirch; [不光彩的事情]blemish:洗去～ wash off (out) stains
污垢 wūgòu dirt; filth
污秽 wūhuì dirty; filthy; foul:～的语言 foul language
污迹 wūjì splodge; smudge; smear; splotch
污蔑 wūmiè slander; vilify; calumniate
污泥浊水 wūní-zhuóshuǐ sludge and filth; mire
污染 wūrǎn [空气、水等] pollute; contaminate:～水 water contamination. 噪音～ noise pollution
污辱 wūrǔ insult; disgrace
污水 wūshuǐ foul water; sewage:～处理 sewage disposal; sewage treatment. ～净化 sewage purification
污浊 wūzhuó (of air, water, etc.) dirty; muddy; foul; filthy

巫 wū〈名〉wizard; witch:男～ wizard
巫技(术) wūjì(shù) witchcraft; sorcery
巫婆 wūpó witch; sorceress
巫师 wūshī magician; spiritist
巫医 wūyī witch doctor; shamans; shamanistic healer

诬 wū〈动〉accuse sb. wrongly;

accuse falsely

诬告 wūgào frame an accusation; trump up a charge against; accuse sb. wrongly of a crime; bring a false charge against sb.; accuse falsely: ～陷害罪 offence of prosecuting false charges. ～罪 crime of false charge

诬赖 wūlài falsely incriminate

诬蔑 wūmiè slander; vilify; malign sb. as being; heap abuse on; calumniate; slanderously accuse; defile: ～某人说谎 stigmatize sb. as a liar

诬陷 wūxiàn frame sb. (up); frame a case against sb.; falsely accuse and frame

乌 wū ①〈名〉crow: 天下～鸦一般黑。All crows under the sun are black. ②〈形〉black; dark: ～云 black (dark) clouds

乌合之众 wūhézhīzhòng a horde of rough, lawless persons; a disorderly band; mob; rabble; a motley crowd; ragtag; casual crowd

乌黑 wūhēi pitch-black; jet-black

乌龙茶 wūlóngchá oolong (tea)

乌梅 wūméi smoked plum; dark plum

乌七八糟 wūqībāzāo ① be in horrible mess; in great disorder ② dirty; filthy; obscene

乌纱帽 wūshāmào ① black gauze hat; hat made of black gauze ② the headgear of an official; official post: 丢了～ be dismissed from office

乌托邦 wūtuōbāng Utopia (utopian): ～思想 utopianism. ～文学 utopian literature

乌烟瘴气 wūyān-zhāngqì foul (pestilential) atmosphere; vicious practices; befoul the atmosphere: 搞得～ foul up

乌有 wūyǒu naught; nothing: 化为～ come to nothing

乌云 wūyún black clouds; dark clouds

乌孜别克族 Wūzībiékèzú Uzbek nationality (living in the Xinjiang Uygur Autonomous Region)

呜 wū 〈象〉hoot; toot; zoom

呜呼 wūhū ① alack; alas; ② die: 一命～ breathe one's last

呜呼哀哉 wūhū'āizāi ① alas; Alas, it is sad indeed!; Oh! what's a pity! ② dead and gone; be already dead ③ give up the ghost; lament the cause as lost

呜咽 wūyè sob: ～地诉苦 sob out one's grievances

钨 wū〈名〉tungsten; wolfram

钨钢 wūgāng tungsten steel

钨丝 wūsī tungsten filament

屋 wú 〈名〉① house; building ② room

屋顶 wūdǐng house top; roof

屋脊 wūjǐ ridge (of a roof)

屋漏又逢连阴雨 wūlòu yòu féng liányīnyǔ The roof leaks and the rain pours down day and night without end.; Misfortunes never come singly.; When it rains it pours.

屋檐 wūyán eaves

wú

无 wú ①〈名〉nil; nothing: 从～到有 grow out of nothing ②〈动〉not have; there is not: 身～分文 not have a single penny left on ③〈副〉not: ～便多谈 need not go into details ④〈连〉regardless of; no matter what, whether, etc.: ～冬～夏 regardless of winter or summer ⑤〈介〉without: ～根之树 a tree without roots

无比 wúbǐ incomparable; matchless; unparalleled: ～幸福 boundless happiness

无笔画 wúbǐhuà brushless paintings

无边无际 wúbiān-wújì boundless; vast; limitless; immense: ～的大草原 a vast expanse of prairie

无补 wúbǔ of no avail; of no help

无不 wúbù all without exception; invariably: ～拍手称快。All without exception clapped and cheered.

无产阶级 wúchǎnjiējí proletariat: ～国际主义 proletarian internationalism

无偿 wúcháng gratis; gratuitous; free: ～援助 aid given gratis. ～出口 unrequited export

无常 wúcháng ① variable; changeable ② demon regarded as the messenger of death ③ die

无耻 wúchǐ shameless; impudent; brazen: ～之尤 brazen (shameless) in the extreme. ～之徒 a shameless person

无从 wúcóng have no way (of doing sth.); not be in a position (to do sth.)

无党派人士 wúdǎngpàirénshì nonpartisan person-age (figures)

无敌 wúdí invincible; unmatched; matchless: ～于天下 unmatched anywhere in the world; invincible

无的放矢 wúdì-fàngshǐ shoot at random; aimless shooting; shoot without a target

无地自容 wúdì-zìróng can find no place to hide oneself for shame; feel too ashamed to show one's face; look for a hole to crawl into

无动于衷 wúdòngyúzhōng aloof and indifferent; remain indifferent and apathetic; unmoved (untouched, unconcerned)

无端 wúduān for no reason

无恶不作 wú'è-bùzuò commit all manner of crimes; stop at no evil; commit all sorts of atrocities; do every imaginable evil; Evil doings know no limits.

无法 wúfǎ unable; incapable: ～应付 unable to cope with; be at one's wits' end. ～形容 be beyond description

无法无天 wúfǎ-wútiān stop at nothing in breaking the law; defy laws human and divine; run wild; trample law underfoot without batting an eyelid;

One's madness knows no bounds.

无妨 wúfáng may (might) as well; there is no harm:～试一试 might as well have a try

无非 wúfēi nothing but; no more than; only; simply:～是老一套。It's nothing but the same old stuff.

无辜 wúgū ① innocent ② innocent person:～的牺牲者 innocent victim

无故 wúgù without cause (reason):～缺席 be absent without reason

无怪 wúguài (it is) no wonder that…; not to be wondered at

无关 wúguān have nothing to do with:～紧要 of no importance; of little significance

无国籍人 wúguójírén stateless person

无害 wúhài harmless

无核区 wúhéqū nuclear-free zone

无话不谈 wúhuàbùtán keep no secrets from each other; tell each other everything

无稽 wújī unfounded; absurd; groundless:～之谈 unfounded (fantastic) talk; sheer nonsense; groundless statement; fabrication

无机化合物 wújī huàhéwù inorganic compound

无机盐 wújīyán inorganic salts

无济于事 wújìyúshì to no effect; of no avail; useless; won't help matters

无计可施 wújì-kěshī at one's wits' end

无记名 wújìmíng ① secret:～投票 secret ballot ② bearer:～股票 unregistered shares; bearer shares; stock to bearer

无价之宝 wújiàzhībǎo priceless treasure

无精打采 wújīng-dǎcǎi listless; depressed; in low spirits; out of sorts

无拘束 wújūshù unrestrained; free; unconstrained

无可非议 wúkě-fēiyì above (beyond) reproach (criticism); blameless; unimpeachable:他的行为是～的。His behaviour is above reproach.

无可奉告 wúkě-fènggào No comment.; have no comment to make

无可厚非 wúkě-hòufēi give no cause for much criticism

无可讳言 wúkě-huìyán there is no hiding the fact; beyond question; undeniable:～的事实 indisputable fact

无可救药 wúkě-jiùyào incorrigible; incurable

无可奈何 wúkě-nàihé ① have no alternative but (to do); can't help but (do); be reluctant to; it can't be helped ② helplessly; unwillingly; against one's will

无可置疑 wúkě-zhìyí indubitable; beyond doubt; unquestionable; above suspicion (doubt)

无孔不入 wúkǒng-bùrù poke into every nook and corner; get in by every opening; have a finger in every pie; worm one's way into every crevice; lose no way; (of persons) seize every opportunity;(of odours, ideas, etc.) be all pervasive

无愧 wúkuì be worthy of; have a clear conscience:～于先进工作者的称号 be worthy of the name of an advanced worker

无赖 wúlài ① scoundrel; rascal; rogue:耍～ play the rascal ② scoundrelly; rascally

无理 wúlǐ unreasonable;unjustifiable:～取闹 make trouble deliberately (wilfully); unreasonable quarrelling

无礼 wúlǐ impolite; ill-mannered; rude; saucy; impudent

无力 wúlì ① lack strength; feel weak; ② powerless; incapable; unable

无利可图 wúlì-kětú unprofitable; profitless

无利息 wúlìxī ex interest

无量 wúliàng measureless; immeasurable; boundless

无聊 wúliáo ① dull; flat; bored: 过～生活 lead a dull life ② silly; senseless: 说～话 make senseless remarks

无论 wúlùn no matter how (what, who, etc.); regardless of; in any case:～如何 anyhow; in any case; anyway; at any rate; whatever happens; at all events; under any circumstances; come what may; at any cost; in one way or another

无米之炊 wúmǐzhīchuī make bricks without straw

无名 wúmíng ① nameless; anonymous ② unknown; obscure:～英雄 unknown (unsung) hero; unknown soldier

无明火 wúmínghuǒ flames of anger

无奈 wúnài ① can't help but (do); have no choice but (to do):我～只好呆在家里。I had no choice but to stay at home. ② but (unfortunately):她本应帮我的忙,～当时缺少资金。She would have helped me but that she was short of money at the time.

无能 wúnéng inability; incompetence:～为力 can't help; be powerless; helpless

无期贷款 wúqī dàikuǎn perpetual loan

无期徒刑 wúqī túxíng life imprisonment

无情 wúqíng merciless; ruthless; heartless

无穷 wúqióng infinite; boundless; endless; inexhaustbile: ～大 [数] infinity

无人 wúrén ① nobody; no one:～能做此事。Nobody can do that. ② unmanned; [飞机]pilotless: ～驾驶飞机 pilotless aircraft ③ self-service:～售货商店 self-service store. ～售票 use of ticket vending machines

无人问津 wúrénwènjīn nobody troubles to ask; nobody is interested

无上 wúshàng highest; greatest; supreme:～光荣 highest honour

无神论 wúshénlùn atheism:～者 atheist

无声 wúshēng silent; noiseless: ～片 silent film

无时无刻 wúshí-wúkè all the time; incessantly; constantly

无事 wúshì ① free; not occupied ② out of job: ～生非 create (make) trouble out of nothing; make much ado about nothing

无事不登三宝殿 wúshì bù dēng sānbǎodiàn No one comes to the Hall of the Trinity without a reason.; Would not go to sb.'s place except business, for help, etc.

无视 wúshì ignore; pay no heed to; disregard; defy: ～国家的法律 defy the laws of the country

无数 wúshù ① innumerable; numberless; countless ② not know for certain; be uncertain; not sure: 对这件事我心中～。I am not sure about it.

无私 wúsī selfless; disinterested: ～的援助 disinterested aid

无损 wúsǔn ① cannot harm; be harmless; will not lessen ② intact; whole; in good condition

无所不为 wúsuǒbùwéi stop at nothing; do all manner of evil

无所事事 wúshuǒshìshì be at a loose end; have nothing to do; idle about; fool around; idle away one's time

无所适从 wúsuǒshìcóng be at a loss which way to follow; not know how to behave; not know where to turn to

无所谓 wúsuǒwèi ① no such thing as: 这是提意见，～批评。This is only advice, there is no such thing as criticism. ② indifferent; casual: 抱～的态度 take an indifferent attitude

无条件 wútiáojiàn ①unconditional: ～投降 unconditional surrender ② not qualified

无妄之灾 wúwàngzhīzāi unexpected calamity; undeserved ill turn

无微不至 wúwēibùzhì considerate right down to the most trivial detail; lavish every care on; in every possible way; meticulously: 关心老母～ take every care of one's old mother

无味 wúwèi ① tasteless; savourless; unpalatable ② dull; uninstersting; insipid

无谓 wúwèi meaningless; pointless; senseless: 不作～的争论 prevent a pointless argument

无畏 wúwèi fearless; dauntless

无隙可乘 wúxì-kěchéng no crack to get in by; no loophole to exploit; no weakness to take advantage of; no chink in one's armour

无暇 wúxiá have no time (to spare); be too busy (to do sth.): ～他顾 be too busy to attend to other things

无限 wúxiàn boundless; infinite; unlimited; immeasurable: ～公司 unlimited company

无线电报 wúxiàn diànbào wireless telegram; radiotelegram

无线电话 wúxiàn diànhuà radiotelephone; radiophone

无线电遥控 wúxiàndiàn yáokòng

wireless remote control

无效 wúxiào null and void; of no avail; invalid: ～合同 invalid contract. 过期～ invalid after the specified date

无懈可击 wúxiè kějī with no chink in one's armour; unassailable; invulnerable

无心 wúxīn ① be not in the mood for; be in no mood for; have no mind (to do sth.); not feel like: 他～跳舞。He was in no mood for dancing. ② inadvertently; unintentionally; unwittingly: 她说这话是～的。She didn't say it intentionally.

无形 wúxíng invisible: ～进(出)口 invisible imports (exports). ～资产 intangible assets

无休止 wúxiūzhǐ ceaseless; endless

无涯 wúyá boundless; limitless

无业 wúyè ① be out of work; be unemployed ② have no property

无以为生 wúyǐwéishēng have no means of livelihood; have no means of support

无益 wúyì unprofitable; useless; no good

无异 wúyì not different from; the same (as); tantamount (to): 他的答复～于拒绝。His answer is tantamount to a refusal.

无意 wúyì ① be not inclined (to do sth.); have no intention of: ～参加 be not inclined to join ② unintentionally; inadvertently; by chance; accidentally: 对这件事她～中露了一句。She dropped a remark about it inadvertently.

无用 wúyòng useless; (of) no use: 说也～。It is (of) no use talking.

无垠 wúyín boundless; vast

无原则 wúyuánzé unprincipled: ～纠纷 unprincipled disputes

无缘无故 wúyuán-wúgù without cause (rhyme) or reason; for no reason at all

无知 wúzhī ignorant; senseless: 出于～ out of ignorance

无止境 wúzhǐjìng know no end; have no limits

无中生有 wúzhōng-shēngyǒu come out of thin air; purely fictitious; cooked up; sheer fabrication; manufacture out of thin air; fabricate rumours out of thin air; create sth. out of nothing

无足轻重 wúzúqīngzhòng of little importance; insignificant; trivial

无罪 wúzuì not guilty; innocent: 宣告某人～ declare sb. (to be) not guilty. ～的人 innocent people

芜

wú 〈形〉① overgrown with weeds: 荒～ lie waste ② mixed and disorderly: ～杂 miscellaneous ③〈名〉grassland

梧

wú

梧桐 wútóng Chinese parasol: 法国～ plane (tree)

吾

wú〈代〉I or we

吾辈 wúbèi we

毋 wú 〈副〉not; no:～中奸计。Don't fall into the treacherous plot.

毋宁 wúníng rather … (than); (not so much…)as:她与其说是个作家,～说是个记者。She is not so much a writer as a reporter.

毋庸 wúyōng need not:～赘述 need not go into details; no need to repeat it

wǔ

武 wǔ〈形〉① military:～将 military commanders ② connected with martial arts:～林 the circle of *wushu* ③ valiant

武打 wǔdǎ [剧]acrobatic fighting in Chinese opera or film; stage fighting

武断 wǔduàn arbitrary decision; subjective verdict (assertion): ～专横 act arbitrarily

武工 wǔgōng skill in acrobatics in Chinese opera

武功 wǔgōng military accomplishments (achievements)

武官 wǔguān ① military officer ② [外] military attaché

武警 wǔjǐng armed police

武力 wǔlì ① force:用～占领 occupy by force ② military force; armed forces:～镇压 armed suppression

武林 wǔlín martial arts circles

武器 wǔqì arms; weapons:～装备 weaponry

武士 wǔshì ① warrior; man of prowess:～兵马俑 terra cotta figurines of warriors and horses ② palace guards in ancient times

武士道 wǔshìdào *bushido*

武术 wǔshù *wushu*; martial arts; art of personal attack and defence

武侠片 wǔxiápiàn swordsman film

武侠小说 wǔxiá xiǎoshuō martial fiction (novel); *wushu* novel (fiction); novel of swordsman; *gongfu* novel (fiction)

武装 wǔzhuāng ① armed:～部队 armed forces. ～起义 armed uprising ② military equipment; arms

武装干涉 wǔzhuāng gānshè armed intervention

五 wǔ 〈数〉five:～倍 fivefold

五彩 wǔcǎi multicoloured:～缤纷 a riot of colour; colourful

五个一工程 Wǔ gè yī gōngchéng Five-One Project, i. e., every year each region should produce at least a fine movie, a TV play (documentary), a book, a drama and a theoretical essay chosen by public evaluation

五更 wǔgēng the fifth watch — just before dawn

五谷 wǔgǔ ① five cereals (rice, two kinds of millet, wheat and beans) ② food crops:～不分 not to know pulse from corn; know nothing about farm work

五官 wǔguān ① five sense organs (ears, eyes, lips, nose and tongue) ② facial features:～端正 have regular features; be well-featured

五光十色 wǔguāng-shísè ① multicoloured; bright with many colours ② of great variety; multifarious; variegated; of all kinds

五湖四海 wǔhú-sìhǎi (from) all corners of the country; all corners of the land

五花八门 wǔhuā-bāmén all sorts of; multifarious; variegated; kaleidoscopic

五讲四美三热爱 wǔjiǎng sìměi sānrè'ài a nationwide campaign for the "five traditional standards," "four beautifications" and "three loves" (The five traditional standards are: civility, courtesy, sanitation, orderliness, and morality. Four beautifications are: beautiful soul, speech, behaviour, and environment. The three loves are: love of motherland, socialism, and the Communist Party)

五角大楼 Wǔjiǎodàlóu the Pentagon

五金 wǔjīn five metals; hardware:～厂 hardware factory

五年计划 wǔnián jìhuà five-year plan

五体投地 wǔtǐ-tóudì prostrate oneself before sb. in admiration; admire sb. in the extreme; worship sb.; on all fours before

五线谱 wǔxiànpǔ [乐]staff; stave

五颜六色 wǔyán-liùsè of various colours; varicoloured; colourful

五言诗 wǔyánshī a poem with five characters to a line

五子棋 wǔzǐqí gobang

妩

wǔ〈形〉lovely; charming

妩媚 wǔmèi〈形〉lovely; graceful; charming:～动人 lovely and touching; charming and moving

捂

wǔ〈动〉① cover (up); hide:～鼻子 cover one's nose with one's hand ② keep; hold

捂盖子 wǔgàizi put on a lid (a metaphor for covering the truth and not letting others know of it); conceal

午

wǔ〈名〉noon; midday

午餐 wǔcān lunch; midday meal

午觉 wǔjiào afternoon nap; noontime snooze

午门 wǔmén palace gate

午前 wǔqián (in the) forenoon; (in the)morning

午休 wǔxiū midday rest; noon break

午宴 wǔyàn luncheon

午夜 wǔyè (at) midnight

舞

wǔ〈动〉① dance:跳一个～ have a dance ② flourish; brandish:挥～ wield; wave

舞伴 wǔbàn dancing partner

舞弊 wǔbì ① engage in fraudulent practices ② embezzlement; corruption

舞场(厅) wǔchǎng(tīng) dance hall; ballroom

舞蹈 wǔdǎo dance:～家 dancer

舞会 wǔhuì dancing party; dance;

ball：举行～ hold (give) a dance
舞剧 wǔjù dance drama；ballet
舞迷 wǔmí dance fiend
舞弄 wǔnòng flourish；brandish
舞谱 wǔpǔ dance notation
舞曲 wǔqǔ dance (music)
舞台 wǔtái stage：～技术 stagecraft. ～监督 stage director (manager). ～效果 stage effects. ～音乐 theatrical music
舞文弄墨 wǔwén-nòngmò indulge in rhetorical flourishes；engage in phrase mongering；play on word
舞姿 wǔzī a dancer's posture and movements

侮 wǔ〈动〉insult；disdain；bully：不可～ not to be bullied
侮骂 wǔmà abuse；call sb. names；hurl insults
侮慢 wǔmàn treat disrespectfully；slight
侮蔑 wǔmiè treat with contempt；disdain；scorn
侮辱 wǔrǔ insult；humiliate：～妇女 humiliate women. ～人格 insult human dignity

wù

勿 wù〈副〉(used in prohibitions，admonitions，etc.) do not；never：请～入内。No Admittance.

误 wù ①〈名〉error；mistake：讹～ error in a text〈动〉② mistake；misunderstand：～解某人的意思 mistake sb. 's meaning ③ miss：～了火车 miss a train ④ harm：～人子弟 lead young people astray；harm the younger generation ⑤〈副〉by mistake；by accident
误差 wùchā error
误点 wùdiǎn late；overdue；behind schedule：火车～半小时。The train is half of an hour late.
误付 wùfù payment by mistake of fact
误工 wùgōng ① delay one's work ② loss of working time
误会 wùhuì ① misunderstand；mistake：～某人意图 misunderstand sb. 's intentions ② misunderstanding；misapprehension：引起～ give rise to misunderstanding
误解 wùjiě misunderstand；misread；misapprehend
误判 wùpàn erroneous judgement；miscarriage of justice
误期 wùqī be behind the appointed time
误人 wùrén mislead sb.；lead sb. astray：～不浅 do people great harm
误入歧途 wùrù-qítú take the wrong road by mistake；go astray；be misled
误杀 wùshā commit manslaughter；second degree murder；homicide by misadventure；death by misadventure；homicide death by misadventure
误伤 wùshāng accidentally injure；accidental injury
误事 wùshì ① cause delay in

work or business; spoil sth. by delay; hold things up ② bungle matters
误译 wùyì mistranslate; [口头] misinterpret
误诊 wùzhěn make a wrong diagnosis
恶 wù〈动〉loathe; hate; dislike: 好～ likes and dislikes
悟 wù〈动〉realize; awaken; enlighten: ～出其中的道理 realize why it should be so
悟解 wùjiě sudden enlightenment
悟境 wùjìng the realm of enlightenment; awakened state
悟性 wùxìng power of understanding; comprehension; intelligence: ～好(差) be quick (dull) of understanding (apprehen-
sion)
悟真 wùzhēn understand the truth
晤 wù〈动〉meet; interview; see
晤面 wùmiàn meet; see
晤谈 wùtán meet and talk; have a talk (with); interview
务 wù ①〈名〉affair; business; work: 财～ financial affair; devote one's efforts to. ～农 be a farmer; go in for agriculture ②〈动〉be engaged in ③〈助动〉must: 你～必去看她。Be sure to go and see her.
务必 wùbì must; be sure to: ～遵守纪律 must observe discipline
务请 wùqǐng please be sure to: ～按时出席。Please be sure to be present on time.
务实 wùshí deal with concrete matters; discuss concrete question relating to work
务使 wùshǐ make sure; ensure: ～本规则得以切实执行 ensure that these rules are faithfully carried out
务虚 wùxū discuss matters from the angles of politics and principles; deal with abstract matters: ～会 a meeting on theoretical matters
雾 wù〈名〉fog; mist: 浓～ dense fog
雾霭 wù'ǎi fog; mist; vapour
雾化 wùhuà atomize
雾茫茫 wùmángmáng misty; foggy
雾气 wùqì fog; mist
物 wù〈名〉① thing; matter; object; article: 实～ material object ② the outside wold; other people: 待人接～ one's conduct in social intercourse ③ substance; content: 言之无～ talk or writing devoid of substance
物产 wùchǎn products; produce: ～丰富 rich in all kinds of products
物化劳动 wùhuàláodòng materialized labour
物极必反 wùjíbìfǎn A thing turns into its opposite if pushed too far.; Things will develop in the opposite direction, when they reach the limit.; Once a certain limit is reached, a change in the opposite direction is inevitable
物价 wùjià price: ～波动 price

fluctuation. ～检查 price monitoring. ～指数 price index

物尽其用 wùjìnqíyòng make the best use of everything; turn material resources to good account; let all things serve their proper purpose

物理 wùlǐ physics:～化学鉴定 determination (authentication) through physical and chemical tests

物力 wùlì material resources

物美价廉 wùměi-jiàlián high quality and inexpensive

物品 wùpǐn article; things; goods:贵重～ valuables

物色 wùsè look for; seek out; choose; select:～人才 look for qualified personnel (talented people). ～新秀 talent-spot

物神 wùshén fetish: 崇拜～ fetishism

物体 wùtǐ object; body:～文字 object writing

物象 wùxiàng objective phenomena; phenomenal image

物业不动产 wùyè bùdòngchǎn real estate

物业管理 wùyè guǎnlǐ estate management

物以类聚 wùyǐlèijù Things of one kind come together.; Birds of a feather flock together.; Like attracts like.

物议 wùyì people's criticism; public criticism (censure):招致～ incur public censure

物证 wùzhèng material evidence

物质 wùzhì ① matter; substance ② material:～生活 material life. ～文明 material civilization. ～世界 material (physical) world; material universe. ～资源 material resources

物种 wùzhǒng species:～起源 origin of species

物资 wùzī goods and materials; matériel:～管理 materials management. ～交流 interflow of commodities. 军用～ military matériel

X x

xī

熹 xī〈名〉break of day

熹微 xīwēi (of morning sunlight) dim; faint; feeble; pale: 晨光～ the dim light of dawn; The light is faint at dawn.

嘻 xī

嘻嘻哈哈 xīxī-hāhā laughing and joking; giggling; tittering with joy

嘻笑 xīxiào laugh merrily

昔 bī〈名〉former times; the past: 今～对比 contrast the past with the present

昔日 xīrì (in) former days (times)

惜 xī〈动〉① value highly; cherish: 珍～时间 set a high value on one's time ② grudge; stint; spare: 不～工本 spare no expense ③ feel sorry for sb.; have pity on: 怜～弱者 take pity on the weak

惜别 xībié be reluctant to part; hate to see sb. go

惜力 xīlì be sparing of one's energy; not do one's best

熙 xī〈形〉① sunny; bright ② merry

熙熙攘攘 xīxī-rǎngrǎng with people bustling about; bustling with activity (life); be a beehive of activity

析 xī〈动〉① divide; separate: 离～ disperse; separate from one another ② dissect; analyse: 剖～ dissect; analyse

析义 xīyì analyse the meaning (of a word, etc.)

淅 xī〈动〉wash rice

淅沥 xīlì (of rain) patter

嬉 xī〈动〉play; sport: 小羊～戏在田野上。Lambs sport in the field.

嬉闹 xīnào laugh and frolic

嬉皮士 xīpíshì hippie

嬉皮笑脸 xīpí-xiàoliǎn smiling cheekily

嬉戏 xīxì play; sport

嬉笑 xīxiào be laughing and playing

晰 xī〈形〉clear; distinct: 一张清～的照片 a clear photograph

蜥 xī

蜥蜴 xīyì lizard

西 xī ①〈名,形〉west ②〈形〉Western; Occidental: ～方文化研究者 Occidentalists

西半球 xībànqiú the Western Hemisphere

西北 xīběi ① northwest ② northwest China; the Northwest (including Shaanxi, Gansu, Qing-

hai，Ningxia，and Xinjiang)
西北风 xīběifēng northwest wind；northwesterly wind
西伯利亚 Xībólìyà Siberia
西餐 xīcān Western-style food；Western cuisine：～馆 Western-style restaurant
西方 xīfāng ① the west ② the West；the Occident：～国家 the Western countries
西瓜 xīguā watermelon
西红柿 xīhóngshì tomato
西葫芦 xīhúlu pumpkin；summer squash
西化 xīhuà Westernize：全盘～ wholesale Westernization
西欧 Xī'ōu Western Europe
西皮 xīpí *xipi*，one of the two chief types of music in traditional Chinese opera；*xipi* melodies
西晒 xīshài (of a room) have a western exposure (hot on summer afternoons)
西天 xītiān ① Western Heaven (ancient Chinese Buddhists' name for India) ② [佛] Western Paradise
西学 xīxué Western learning
西洋 Xīyáng the West；the Western world
西洋景 xīyángjǐng ① peep show ② hanky-panky；trickery
西洋参 xīyángshēn [药] American ginseng
西药 xīyào Western medicine
西医 xīyī ① doctors trained in Western medicine ② Western medicine
西乐 xīyuè Western music
西藏自治区 Xīzàngzìzhìqū the Tibet Autonomous Region
西装(服) xīzhuāng(fú) Western-style clothes；Western suits：～料 suitings

牺 xī 〈名〉 sacrificial animal
牺牲 xīshēng ① sacrifice oneself；lay down one's life；die a martyr's death；sacrifice：英勇～ die a heroic death ② do sth. at the expense of；give up：～个人利益 sacrifice one's personal interests

锡 xī 〈名〉 tin
锡箔 xībó tinfoil (joss) paper
锡婚 xīhūn [结婚 10 周年纪念] tin wedding
锡匠 xījiàng tinsmith
锡矿 xīkuàng tin ore
锡纸 xīzhǐ silver paper；tinfoil

吸 xī〈动〉① inhale；breathe in：～入新鲜空气 inhale fresh air ② absorb；suck：～收知识 suck knowledge into one's mind ③ attract；draw to oneself：磁石～铁。A magnet attracts iron.
吸尘器 xīchénqì dust collector；vacuum cleaner
吸顶灯 xīdǐngdēng lamp with its shade affixed to the ceiling
吸毒 xīdú take drugs；drug addiction：～者 drug addict
吸附 xīfù adsorb：～作用 adsorption
吸力 xīlì attraction；suction：地心～ force of gravity；gravitation
吸盘 xīpán sucking disc (of certain animals)；sucker

吸取 xīqǔ draw; absorb; assimilate:～教训 draw a lesson (from). ～先进技术 assimilate (utilize) the advanced technology

吸热 xīrè absorption of heat

吸食 xīshí suck; take in (liquid foods, narcotic drugs, etc.)

吸收 xīshōu ① absorb; soak up; take in:～外国资金 take in foreign funds. ～外来文化 draw on foreign culture. ～存款 take deposits. ～某人为会员 enrol sb. as a member (of) ② assimilate

吸收作用 xīshōu zuòyòng absorption

吸吮 xīshǔn absorb; suck:～柠檬汁 suck the juice from a lemon

吸血鬼 xīxuèguǐ bloodsucker; vampire

吸引 xīyǐn attract; draw:～投资者 attract investors. 阴极射线被阳电荷所～。Cathode rays are attracted by a positive charge.

溪 xī〈名〉small stream; brook

溪涧 xījiàn mountain stream

溪流 xīliú brook; rivulet

奚 xī〈代〉why; how

奚落 xīluò taunt; scoff at; ridicule; make fun of; make gibes about

希 xī ①〈动〉hope:敬～读者指正。It is hoped that the readers will kindly point out my errors. ②〈形〉rare; uncommon; scarce

希罕 xīhan ① rare; uncommon ② care about; cherish:我不～她的钱。I don't care about her money.

希冀 xījì hope for; wish for; aspire after

希奇 xīqí strange; rare; curious:～古怪 queer; odd

希求 xīqiú ① hope for; wish for ② what one hopes or wishes for

希世 xīshì rare on earth

希图 xītú harbour the intention of:～牟取暴利 go after quick profits

希望 xīwàng hope; wish; expect:把～变成现实 turn hopes into reality. ～的家庭规模 desired family size. 他的～落空了。His hopes vanished.

希望工程 xīwàng gōngchéng Hope Project (the project is designed to help students in poverty-stricken and remote areas who are economically forced to drop out, to resume their studies by giving subsidies which are donations contributed by people from all walks of life)

稀 xī〈形〉① rare; scarce; uncommon:～有金属 scare metals ② sparse; scattered:～少的人口 sparse population ③ thin; watery:～疏的头发 thin hair

稀薄 xībó thin; rare:～的空气 thin air

稀客 xīkè rare visitor

稀里糊涂 xīlihútu muddleheaded

稀缺 xīquē scarce; rare

稀少 xīshǎo very few; thin; sparse:～的人口 sparse (thin)

population
稀释 xīshì dilution
稀疏 xīshū thinly scattered; thin; sparse
稀松 xīsōng ① sloppy; lax ② unimportant; trivial ③ loose; porous
稀有 xīyǒu rare; uncommon; unusual:～金属 rare metal

悉 xī ①〈动〉know; learn:得～ learn about; hear of ②〈副〉full; entirely
悉力 xīlì go all out; spare no effort
悉数 xīshǔ enumerate in full detail:不可～ can't be enumerated; defy enumeration; too many to enumerate
悉数 xīshù all; every single one: ～付清 pay in full
悉心 xīxīn devote all one's attention; with one's whole heart; take the utmost care:～研究 devote oneself to the study of sth.; study absorbedly

蟋 xī
蟋蟀 xīshuài cricket

息 xī〈动〉① cease; stop:～怒 cease to be angry ② breath:屏～ hold one's breath ③ news:信～ message〈名〉④ rest:休～ take a rest ⑤ interest:借款付～5 厘 pay 5 per cent interest on a loan
息工 xīgōng cease work; leave off work; knock off
息票 xīpiào interest coupon
息事宁人 xīshìníngrén let the matter rest so as to annoy nobody; gloss things over to stay on good terms; a policy of comproise to let everybody have peace
息息相关 xīxī-xiāngguān be closely linked (with each other); be closely bound up
息影 xīyǐng retire into private life
息战 xīzhàn cease fire; stop fighting

熄 xī〈动〉put out; extinguish:～灯 put out the light
熄火 xīhuǒ ① (of fuel, a stove, etc.) stop burning; die out ② (of an engine, etc.) stop working; go dead ③ stop (fuel) from burning; stop (an engine, etc.)
熄灭 xīmiè die out; go out; put out; extinguish; quench

夕 xī〈名〉① (at) sunset ② evening; night
夕阳 xīyáng setting sun:～西下。The sun is setting.
夕照 xīzhào evening glow

膝 xī〈名〉knee:～骨 kneecap
膝关节 xīguānjié knee joint
膝下 xīxià ① at one's knees [通常指有无子女] ② [给父母或祖父母写信时用语]:父亲大人～ Dear Father

犀 xī〈名〉rhinoceros
犀利 xīlì incisive; sharp:文笔～ wield a trenchant pen
犀牛 xīniú rhinoceros

xí

席 xí〈名〉① mat：草～ straw mat② 贵宾～ seats for distinguished guests ③ banquet; feast：流水～ dinner served separately as the guests arrive in succession

席间 xíjiān at or during the feast

席卷 xíjuǎn ① take all：～而去 take away everything ② sweep across (over); engulf：～全国 sweep across the country

席梦思 xímèngsī Simmons (a transliteration); innerspring mattress

席位 xíwèi seat; place：在委员会中有一～ have a seat on the commission

袭 xí〈动〉① make a surprise attack on; raid：空～ make an air aid ② follow the pattern of：承～ follow (a tradition, etc.); adopt

袭击 xíjī attack by surprise; surprise assault on; raid; hit：受到台风的～ be hit by a typhoon

袭扰 xírǎo harassing attack

袭用 xíyòng adopt sth. that has been used in the past

媳 xí〈名〉daughter-in-law

媳妇 xífù ① son's wife; daughter-in-law ② wife of a relative of the younger generation

习 xí〈动〉① practise; exercise：实～ practise; do field work ② study; learn：见～ learn on the job; be on probation ③ be accustomed to; be used to：不～水性 be not good at swimming ④〈名〉usual practice：固～ deep-rooted habit; inveterate habit

习惯 xíguàn ① habit; custom：旧～ outmoded customs ② be accustomed to; be used to (doing)：～于农村生活 be accustomed to country life

习气 xíqì bad habit (practice)

习俗 xísú custom; common practice; convention

习题 xítí exercises (in school work)：做～ do one's exercises

习习 xíxí (of a wind) blow gently

习性 xíxìng habits and characteristics

习以为常 xíyǐwéicháng be used (accustomed) to (doing)

习语 xíyǔ idiom

习字 xízì practise penmanship：～帖 copybook; calligraphy model

习作 xízuò ① do exercises in composition ② an exercise in composition (drawing, etc.)

檄 xí〈名〉① (a literary genre) a war proclamation setting forth the purpose of the expedition and enumerating the crimes of the enemy ②〈动〉send such a war proclamation to sb., or denounce sb. in it

檄书(文) xíshū(wén) war proclamation

xǐ

徙 xǐ〈动〉move from one place

to another

徙居 xǐjū move house

喜 xǐ ①〈形〉happy; delighted; glad:～降瑞雪。There was a welcome fall of seasonable snow.〈名〉② happy event (esp. wedding); occasion for celebration ③ pregancy:有～了。Be expecting a baby. ④〈动〉like; be fond of:～在心头 joy in one's heart

喜爱 xǐ'ài like; love; be fond of; be keen on

喜报 xǐbào report of success; a bulletin of glad tidings

喜出望外 xǐchū-wàngwài be happy beyond expectations; be overjoyed at the unexpectedly good news; be pleasantly surprised

喜房 xǐfáng ① bridal chamber ② private room temporarily given over to the delivery of a baby

喜欢 xǐhuān ① like; be fond of; love; be keen on:讨人～的 lovable; lovely ② filled with joy; elated; happy

喜酒 xǐjiǔ wine drunk at a wedding feast; wedding feast:吃～ attend sb.'s wedding feast

喜剧 xǐjù comedy:～演员 comedian

喜怒无常 xǐnù-wúcháng subject to changing moods; moody:～的人 man of moods

喜气洋洋 xǐqì-yángyáng be elated with joy; full of joy; be rejoicing (over); be jubilant over

喜庆 xǐqìng ① celebrate:～丰收 celebrate the bumper harvest ② jubilant; festival:～日 festival (day)

喜人 xǐrén gratifying; encouraging; satisfactory:形势～。The situation is gratifying.

喜事 xǐshì ① happy event; joyous occasion (event) ② wedding

喜闻乐见 xǐwén-lèjiàn love (be pleased) to see and hear; be enjoyed by; love:为人民～的艺术形式 artistic form loved by the people

喜新厌旧 xǐxīn-yànjiù love the new and loathe the old—be fickle in affection; be fond of the new and tire of the old

喜形于色 xǐxíngyúsè light up with pleasure; be radiant with joy; be visibly pleased

喜讯 xǐxùn good (happy) news; glad tidings

喜悦 xǐyuè ① joy; gladness; gratification ② happy; joyous; delightful:～的心情 joyful feeling

喜滋滋 xǐzīzī filled with joy; elated; feeling pleased

洗 xǐ〈动〉① wash; clean:～去污点 wash off (out) stains ② develop:冲～胶卷 develop a film ③ redress; right:～冤 right a wrong ④ slaughter; massacre:血～ slaughter sanguinarily

洗尘 xǐchén give a dinner of welcome (to a visitor from afar); give a dinner in honour of a visitor from afar

洗涤 xǐdí wash; clean:～旧社会

留下来的一切污泥浊水 wash away all the sludge and filth left over from the old society

洗耳恭听 xǐ'ěrgōngtīng listen with reverent attention; be all ears; prick up one's ears

洗发剂 xǐfàjì shampoo

洗劫 xǐjié sack; plunder; loot:～一空 plunder everything that could be found

洗礼 xǐlǐ ①[宗] baptism ② severe test

洗脑 xǐnǎo brainwashing; menticide

洗染店 xǐrǎndiàn cleaners and dyers; laundering and dyeing shop

洗手间 xǐshǒujiān toilet; lavatory; washroom; rest room

洗刷 xǐshuā ① wash and brush; scrub ② wash off; clear oneself of (opprobrium, stigma, guilt, etc.)

洗头膏 xǐtóugāo shampoo paste

洗碗机 xǐwǎnjī dishwasher

洗心 xǐxīn washing (cleansing) the mind:～革面 turn over a new leaf; reform oneself thoroughly

洗雪 xǐxuě wipe out (a disgrace); redress (a wrong)

洗衣 xǐyī wash clothes:～机 washing machine; washer. ～粉 detergent; washing powder

xì

系 xì〈名〉① system; series:根～ root system ② department; faculty:经济～ the department of economics〈动〉③ tie; bind; fasten:～马 tether a horse ④ be:纯～试验性质 be purely experimental in character ⑤ relate to; bear on:成败～于此举 stand or fall by this ⑤ feel anxious; be concerned

另见 jì

系词 xìcí ① link verb; copulative verb ② copula

系列 xìliè series:～片[影视] serial; serialized movie. 化妆品～ cosmetic series

系列化 xìlièhuà serialize; come out in serial form

系谱 xìpǔ genealogy; pedigree:～调查法 genealogical survey method

系数 xìshù [数] coefficient

系统 xìtǒng system:～工程 systems engineering. ～化食品 seriated foods. 文教～ organizations affiliated with culture and education

系图 xìtú family tree

戏 xì ①〈名〉play; show:看～去 go to the play (theatre)〈动〉② play; sport:～水 play with water ③ make fun of; joke:～言 say sth. for fun

戏班 xìbān theatrical troupe (company)

戏词 xìcí actor's part (lines)

戏单 xìdān playbill

戏德 xìdé actors' ethics (i. e. one's attitude towards playacting and fellow actors)

戏法 xìfǎ jugglery; trick; conjuring; magic:变～ perform tricks; juggle; conjure

戏剧 xìjù play; theatre; drama:

～家 dramtist. ～表演 dramatic performance

戏迷 xìmí theatre fan

戏目 xìmù theatrical programme

戏弄 xìnòng make fun of; play tricks on; kid; tease

戏曲 xìqǔ traditional opera; drama; operatic theatre; song-drama

戏台 xìtái stage

戏谑 xìxuè banter; crack jokes: ～关系 joking relationship

戏言 xìyán joking remarks; pleasantries

戏院 xìyuàn theatre: ～的顾客 clientele of theatre

戏照 xìzhào photo of a person in stage costume

戏装 xìzhuāng stage constume; theatrical constume

细 xì 〈形〉① thin; slender: ～线 thin thread ② fine; delicate: ～菜 fine vegetables ③ meticulous; detailed: ～目 detailed catalogue ④ minute; trifling: ～致的描写 a minute description

细胞 xìbāo cell

细活 xìhuó job requiring fine workmanship or meticulous care; skilled work

细节 xìjié details; particulars

细菌 xìjūn germ; bacterium: ～武器 germ weapon

细目 xìmù ① detailed catalogue ② specific item; detail

细腻 xìnì ① fine and smooth; delicate ② exquisite; minute: ～的表演 exquisite performance

细巧 xìqiǎo delicate; dainty; exquisite: ～的做工 exquisite workmanship

细软 xìruǎn jewellery; expensive clothing and other valuables

细石器 xìshíqì microlith: ～文化 microlithic culture

细水长流 xìshuǐ-chángliú ① economize to avoid running short ② keep on doing sth. bit by bit; plan on a long-term basis; go about sth. little by little without a letup

细微 xìwēi fine slight; subtle: ～的差别 subtle distinction

细想 xìxiǎng think over; consider

细小 xìxiǎo small; tiny: ～的事情 small matters; trifles

细心 xìxīn careful; attentive; meticulous: ～阅读 read carefully; peruse

细语 xìyǔ speak softly; whisper

细则 xìzé detailed rules and regulation; specific provisions

细帐 xìzhàng itemized account

细致 xìzhì ① fine; delicate: ～地刻划画 portray with superb delicacy ② careful; meticulous; minute

隙 xì〈名〉crack; crevice; chink: 墙～ a crack in the wall ② opportunity; chance: 无～可乘 no crack to get in by; loophole to take advantage of

xiā

呷 xiā 〈动〉sip: 把玻璃杯内饮料～干 sip the glass dry

瞎 xiā ①〈形〉blind: (人)变～ go

blind ②〈副〉groundlessly; foolish; to no purpose: ～讲 speak groundlessly
瞎扯 xiāchě talk rubbish; talk irresponsibly
瞎吹 xiāchuī boast in the most fantastic of terms
瞎干 xiāgàn act foolishly; go it blind
瞎话 xiāhuà untruth; lie
瞎聊 xiāliáo chat at random about anything under the sun; chat idly
瞎忙 xiāmáng make a fuss about nothing
瞎蒙 xiāmēng make a wild guess
瞎闹 xiānào ① act senselessly; mess about ② be mischievous; fool around
瞎说 xiāshuō ① talk nonsense (rubbish) ② tell lies; lie
瞎指挥 xiāzhǐhuī issue confused orders; give arbitrary and impracticable directions; give uninformed direction
瞎字儿不识 xiāzìr bùshí cannot read a single word; be completely illiterate

虾 xiā〈名〉shrimp: 对～ prawn. 龙～ lobster
虾兵蟹将 xiābīng-xièjiàng shrimp soldiers and crab generals—numerous underlings (ineffective troops)
虾酱 xiājiàng shrimp paste
虾米 xiāmi dried, shelled shrimps
虾皮 xiāpí dried small shrimps
虾仁 xiārén shelled fresh shrimps; shrimp meat

xiá

狎 xiá〈动〉be too close with (usu. a woman); be improperly familiar with
狎昵 xiánì be improperly familiar with

侠 xiá
侠客 xiákè a person adept in martial arts and given to chivalrous conduct (in old times); chivalrous swordsman; knight-errant
侠义 xiáyì chivalrous: ～行为 knight-errantry

峡 xiá〈名〉gorge: 长江三～工程 Three Gorges Project on the Yangtze River
峡谷 xiágǔ gorge; canyon

狭 xiá〈形〉narrow: ～小的朋友圈子 a narrow circle of friends
狭隘 xiá'ài narrow: ～观点 narrow view; parochial point of view. ～性 narrow-(petty-) mindedness; narrowness. 心地～ be narrow-minded
狭路相逢 xiálù-xiāngféng (of adversaries) meet face to face (run into each other) on a narrow path—come into unavoidable confrontation; collide with; be squeezed into ever-shrinking domain
狭小 xiáxiǎo narrow and small; narrow
狭义 xiáyì (in a) narrow sense: ～认识论 epistemology in its narrow sense

狭窄 xiázhǎi ①narrow；cramped：～的楼梯 narrow staircase ② narrow and limited：气量～ narrow-minded；intolerant

暇 xiá〈名〉free (spare) time；leisure：无～ have no time；be too busy

暇时 xiáshí (at one's) leisure

匣 xiá〈名〉small box；casket

匣钵 xiábō［瓷器］saggar

辖 xiá ①〈动〉have jurisdiction over；govern；administer：直～市 centrally administered municipality ②〈名〉linchpin；axlepin

辖区 xiáqū area under one's jurisdiction

辖制 xiázhì control

霞 xiá〈名〉morning or evening glow；rosy clouds

霞光 xiáguāng rays of morning or evening sunlight；rosy rays of sunlight：～四射。Bright rays shine out in all directions.

遐 xiá〈形〉① distant；far ② lasting；long：～龄 advanced age

遐迩 xiá'ěr far and near：闻名～ be well-known far and near；one's reputation spread far and wide

遐想 xiáxiǎng be lost in wild and fanciful thoughts；reverie；daydream

瑕 xiá〈名〉flaw；defect：～疵 blemish；flaw

瑕不掩瑜 xiábùyǎnyú one flaw cannot mar the jade—small defects cannot obscure great virtues

黠 xiá crafty；cunning

xià

下 xià ①〈副〉down；below；under：海平面～ below sea level〈形〉② lower；inferior：～等 lower grade；inferior ③ next；latter：～次 next time〈动〉④ descend；get off：从山上～到平地 descend from a hill ⑤ (of rain；snow，etc.) fall：～雪了。It's snowing. ⑥ issue；deliver；send：～命令 issue orders ⑦ form (an idea，opinion：～决心 make up one's mind ⑧ go to：～车间 go to the workshop ⑨ exit；leave：从右边门儿～ exit from the right door ⑩ put in；cast：～作料 put in condiments ⑪ finish work：～班 knock off；go off duty ⑫ take away；dismantle：从船上卸～货物 unload a ship ⑬ use；apply：～功夫研究 devote time and effort to the study ⑭ give birth to；lay：～蛋 lay eggs

下巴 xiàba ① the lower jaw ② chin

下班 xiàbān come or go off work；leave (work)；knock off；check off：他们 5 点钟～。They checked off at five o'clock.

下半辈子 xiàbànbèizi the latter half of one's life；the rest of

one's life
下半场 xiàbànchǎng second half (of a game)
下半旗 xiàbànqí fly a flag at half-mast
下辈子 xiàbèizi the next life
下本钱 xiàběnqián put in time, money and effort; make an investment
下不为例 xiàbùwéilì not to be taken as a precedent; not to be repeated
下策 xiàcè bad plan; unwise decision; worst (ill-advised) policy
下层 xiàcéng ① lower levels ② lower strata: ～社会 the lower strata of society
下场 xiàchǎng ① [演员等]go off stage; exit ② leaving the playing field ③ fate; end: 不会有好～ will come to no good end
下车 xiàchē get off; alight
下沉 xiàchén subside; sink; submerge
下船 xiàchuán go ashore; disembark
下达 xiàdá make known to lower levels: 任务已经～。The task has been assigned.
下跌 xiàdiē (of price, etc.) go down; drop; fall
下毒手 xià dúshǒu strike a vicious blow; lay murderous hands on sb.; deal a deadly blow
下放 xiàfàng transfer to a lower level: 权力～ transfer power to a lower level
下风 xiàfēng ① leeward ② disadvantageous position: 处在～ be at a disadvantage
下岗 xiàgǎng lay off (on basic pay): ～人员 lay-off personnel
下工 xiàgōng stop work; knock off
下工夫 xiàgōngfu put in time and energy; make painstaking effort; concentrate one's efforts
下海 xiàhǎi ① go to sea: ～去游泳 go swimming in the sea ② (of fishermen) go fishing on the sea ③ "plunge into the sea"—to go into business; engage in trade
下回 xiàhuí next time
下级 xiàjí ① lower level: ～服从上级。The lower level is subordinate to the higher level. ～人民法院 lower people's court ② lower; subordinate: ～干部 junior cadre
下家 xiàjiā ① (in mahjong, card games, or in wine games) the player whose turn comes next ② buying party in a commercial activity
下贱 xiàjiàn base; mean; low; degrading
下降 xiàjiàng come down; descend; fall; drop; decline: 生产成本～。Production costs come down.
下脚货 xiàjiǎohuò unsalable leftover goods of inferior quality
下届 xiàjiè the next session of a regular meeting; next (graduating class, etc.)
下课 xiàkè get out of class; finish class: 现在～。The class is dismissed.
下令 xiàlìng issue an order; order

下流 xiàliú mean; base; foul; obscene; coarse: ～话 foul (improper) language; obscenities

下落 xiàluò ① fall; drop ② whereabouts: ～不明。The whereabouts is (are) unknown.

下马 xiàmǎ ① get down from a horse; dismount ② discontinue (abandon) (a project)

下马威 xiàmǎwēi severity shown by an official on assuming office; prompt reprisals; instant severity: 给她个～ deal her a head-on blow at the first encounter

下聘 xiàpìn (of the bridegroom-to-be's family) send betrothal gifts and money over to the bride

下坡路 xiàpōlù downhill path: 走～ be on the decline

下棋 xiàqí play (at) chess

下情 xiàqíng ① conditions at the lower levels; feelings or wishes of the masses or one's subordinates ② the situation I am in; my feelings or wishes

下去 xiàqu [用作动词的补语] ① [表示动作由高处到低处或由近处向远处去] down (there): 跳～ jump down ② go on (doing sth.); continue: 坚持～ stick it out ③ [用在形容词后，表示程度继续增加] develop; grow: 他一天天地瘦～。He's getting thinner every day.

下身 xiàshēn ① the lower part of the body ② private parts; genitals ③ trousers

下手 xiàshǒu put one's hand to; start doing sth.; set about; set to

下属 xiàshǔ subordinate

下水 xiàshuǐ ① go into the water; (of a ship) enter the water; be launched: ～典礼 launching ceremony ② downriver: ～船 downriver boat

下水道 xiàshuǐdào sewer: ～体系 sewage systems

下榻 xiàtà stay (at a place during a trip)

下台 xiàtái ① step down from the stage or platform ② fall out of power; leave office ③ get out of an awkward position: 下不了台 unable to find a way out of an awkward situation

下限 xiàxiàn lower limit

下乡知识青年 xiàxiāng zhīshi qīngnián educated urban youth working in the countryside

下旬 xiàxún the last ten-day period of a month

下野 xiàyě (of a ruler) retire from the political arena; be forced to relinquish power

下意识 xiàyìshí subconsciousness

下议院 xiàyìyuàn lower house; lower chamber; the House of Commons; chamber of deputies

下游 xiàyóu ① lower reaches (of a river) ② backward position: 甘居～ resign oneself to lagging behind

下注 xiàzhù lay down a stake (in gambling)

吓

xià 〈动〉 frighten; terrify; scare; intimidate: 把鸟～走 frighten the birds away

吓倒 xiàdǎo daunt; intimidate; terrified by; cowed by
吓唬 xiàhu frighten; scare; browbeat
吓了一跳 xiàle yītiào get a scare; be scared (startled; frightened):你把我~。You gave me a scare (fright).
吓人 xiàrén ① give one a fright; browbeat others; overawe (intimidate) people; ② terrifying
吓死 xiàsǐ be scared to death

夏 xià〈名〉summer:~季剧院 summer theatre
夏播(种) xiàbō(zhòng) summer sowing
夏历 xiàlì the traditional Chinese calendar; the lunar calendar
夏粮 xiàliáng summer grain crops
夏令 xiàlìng summer season; summer:~商品 commodities of summer use. ~营 summer camp
夏时制 xiàshízhì the practice of adopting daylight-saving time in summer
夏收 xiàshōu summer harvest
夏娃 Xiàwá Eve (the first woman according to the Bible)
夏装 xiàzhuāng summer clothing; summer wear

厦 xià
厦门 xiàmén Xiamen (Amoy)

xiān

仙 xiān〈名〉celestial being; immortal:~化现象 phenomenon of becoming immortal
仙丹 xiāndān elixir of life
仙风道骨 xiānfēng-dàogǔ the demeanour of a transcendent being
仙后座 Xiānhòuzuò Cassiopeia
仙境 xiānjìng fairyland; wonderland; paradise
仙女 xiānnǚ fairy maiden; female celestial; fairy
仙女座 Xiānnǚzuò Andromeda
仙人 xiānrén celestial being; immortal
仙人掌 xiānrénzhǎng cactus
仙逝 xiānshì pass away
仙游 xiānyóu travel to fairyland—die

先 xiān ①〈形〉earlier; before; first; in advance:~做学生,然后再做先生。Be a pupil before you become a teacher.〈名〉② elder generation; ancestor:祖~ forefather; ancestor ③ the deceased; late:~母 my late mother
先辈 xiānbèi elder generation; predecessors
先导 xiāndǎo ① precursor; forerunner; guide ② herald
先睹为快 xiāndǔ-wéikuài regard it as a great pleasure to be among the first to see it; be all eagerness to read sth.
先发制人 xiānfā-zhìrén get the upper hand by taking the initiative; gain the initiative by striking first; gain mastery over one's opponent by striking first; strike first to forestall the enemy:采取~的手段 take pre-

emptive measures

先锋 xiānfēng vanguard; van: ～派[文]avant-garde. ～主义 avant-gardism. 打～ fight in the van. 起～作用 play a vanguard role

先河 xiānhé the beginning of sth.

先后 xiānhòu ① early or late; in order of priority: 按到达～登记 be registered in order of arrival ② one after another; in succession: ～出国 go abroad one after another

先见之明 xiānjiànzhīmíng foresight; prevision; prescience; prophetic vision

先进 xiānjìn advanced: ～集体 advanced group. ～设备 sophisticated equipment. ～工作者 advanced worker

先礼后兵 xiānlǐ-hòubīng take strong measures only after courteous ones fail; try peaceful means before resorting to force

先例 xiānlì precedent: 开～ set a precedent

先烈 xiānliè martyr

先遣 xiānqiǎn sent in advance

先驱 xiānqū forerunner; pioneer; precursor

先人之见 xiānrùzhījiàn preconceived ideas; preconception; prejudice

先声夺人 xiānshēng-duórén demoralize one's opponent by a show of strength; overawe people by displaying one's strength

先手 xiānshǒu offensive position (in chess)

先天 xiāntiān inborn; innate; congenital: ～病 congenital disease

先天不足 xiāntiān bùzú congenital deficiency; inborn weakness

先天下之忧而忧,后天下之乐而乐 xiān tiānxià zhī yōu ér yōu, hòu tiānxià zhī lè ér lè be concerned about affairs of state before others, enjoy comfort after others; the first to show concern and the last to enjoy himself

先天性缺陷 xiāntiānxìng quēxiàn birth defects

先天性心脏病 xiāntiānxìng xīnzàngbìng congenital heart disease

先下手为强 xiān xiàshǒu wéi qiáng The early bird gets the worm.; Whoever strikes the first blow has the advantage.; To take the initiative is to gain the upper hand.; He who strikes first gains the advantage.

先小人后君子 xiān xiǎorén hòu jūnzǐ let's allow impoliteness to precede courtesy (said when discussing the terms of a deal)

先行者 xiānxíngzhě forerunner

先验 xiānyàn [哲] a priori; prior: ～的思维规律 a priori law of thought. ～论 apriorism; transcendentalism

先斩后奏 xiānzhǎn-hòuzòu take decisive action without asking for approval and only report it later as a fait accompli; act first and report afterwards

先兆 xiānzhào omen

先哲 xiānzhé great thinker of the past;sage

先知先觉 xiānzhī-xiānjué person of foresight; having foresight; the foresighted

先祖 xiānzǔ ① my late grandfather ② my forefathers

鲜 xiān〈形〉① fresh:～肉 frest meat ② bright:～花满园。The garden is bright with flowers. ③ delicious; tasty; delicate:～美的食物 delicious food; delicacy ④〈名〉aquatic foods:海～ seafood

鲜红 xiānhóng bright red

鲜活商品 xiānhuó shāngpǐn fresh goods

鲜灵 xiānlíng ① fresh ② shining bright

鲜美 xiānměi ① (of cooked food, fruit, etc.) delicious; tasty ② (of flowers, grass, etc.) fresh and pleasing

鲜明 xiānmíng ① bright; vivid ② clear; clear-cut; sharp; distinct: 主题～ have distinct theme

鲜嫩 xiānnèn fresh and tender

鲜味 xiānwèi delicate flavour

鲜艳 xiānyàn fresh; vivid; colourful; bright (gaily)-coloured: ～夺目 dazzlingly beautiful

掀 xiān〈动〉raise; lift (a cover, etc.)

掀动 xiāndòng lift; start; set in motion

掀开 xiānkāi open; lift; draw

掀起 xiānqǐ ① raise; lift ② start; unfold; set off (a movement, etc.); stir up:～…高潮 start an upsurge of…

纤 xiān〈形〉① fine; delicate; minute ② fibre:化～ chemical fibre

纤尘不染 xiānchénbùrǎn ① without a speck of dust ② untainted with evil thoughts or bad habits

纤巧 xiānqiǎo delicate; subtle

纤弱 xiānruò slim and fragile; delicate:体质～ have a delicate constitution

纤维 xiānwéi fibre; staple:～板 fibreboard; particle board

纤细 xiānxì very thin; fine; slender; tenuous

xián

弦 xián〈名〉string (of musical instrument, etc.); bowstring; string:～乐四重奏 string quartet

弦外之音 xiánwàizhīyīn overtones; implication

弦乐 xiányuè string music:～部分[乐队] string section

弦乐器 xiányuèqì stringed wind instruments

舷 xián〈名〉the side of a ship; board:干～ freeboard

舷窗 xiánchuāng porthole

舷梯 xiántī ① gangway ladder; accommodation ladder ② (boarding) ramp

闲 xián〈形〉① not busy; idle:把吃～饭的人变为生产工人 turn

idle bread eaters into productive workers ② unoccupied; not in use: ～房 unoccupied room or house ③〈名〉leisure; spare time: 消～ pass time idly; kill time

闲不住 xiánbuzhù refuse to stay idle; always keep oneself busy

闲扯 xiánchě chat; engage in chitchat

闲工夫 xiángōngfu spare time; leisure

闲逛 xiánguàng stroll; idle about; loiter; loaf; saunter

闲话 xiánhuà ① idle chat; digression ② gossip; complaint: 对她的服务质量，顾客们～很多。The customers were full of complaints about her service.

闲聊 xiánliáo chat; chitchat: 与某人～ have a chitchat with sb.

闲气 xiánqì anger about trifles

闲钱 xiánqián spare money (cash)

闲情逸致 xiánqíng-yìzhì a leisurely and carefree mood; cultivated pleasures of a leisurely life; leisure and mood for enjoyments

闲人 xiánrén ① unoccupied person; idler ② outsider; stranger: ～免进。No admittance except on business.

闲散 xiánsǎn idle; disengaged; unoccupied: ～劳动力 idle labour. ～人员 idle personnel. ～资金 idle funds

闲事 xiánshì a matter that does not concern one; other people's business: ～休管。Mind your own business.

闲适 xiánshì leisurely and comfortable: ～音乐 laid-back music

闲书 xiánshū light reading

闲暇 xiánxiá spare time; leisure

闲言碎语 xiányán-suìyǔ gossip

闲杂 xiánzá without fixed duties

闲职 xiánzhí sinecure; nonsubstantive appointment

闲置 xiánzhì leave unused; let sth. lie idle; set aside

娴

xián〈形〉① refined; elegant ② adept; practised; proficient: ～熟 adept; skilled

娴静 xiánjìng gentle and refined (elegant)

娴雅 xiányǎ refined; elegant; graceful

咸

xián〈形〉① salt; salty: ～鱼 salt fish ② salted; pickled: ～菜 salted (pickled) vegetables; pickles

咸淡 xiándàn degree of saltiness

咸肉 xiánròu salt meat; bacon

咸水 xiánshuǐ salt water: ～湖 salt lake

贤

xián〈形〉① virtuous; worthy; able: 前～ people of virtue of the older generation ② an able and virtuous person; sage: 让～ relinquish one's post in favour of sb. better qualified

贤达 xiándá prominent personage

贤惠(淑) xiánhuì (shū) (of a woman) virtuous; capable

贤良 xiánliáng able and virtuous

贤明 xiánmíng wise and able;

sage; sagacious; judicious

贤内助 xiánnèizhù ①(said of another person's wife) a good wife ② my better half; my good wife

贤人 xiánrén virtuous person; wise man; sage; worthies

贤哲 xiánzhé a good and wise man

涎 xián 〈名〉saliva: 流～ slobber; slaver; drool

涎皮赖脸 xiápí-làiliǎn shameless and loathsome; cheeky; brazen

衔 xián 〈动〉① hold in the mouth: ～着烟斗 have a pipe between one's teeth ② nurse; bear; harbour ③〈名〉title; rank: 军～ military rank

衔恨 xiánhèn bear a grudge (against); nurse a hatred (against); harbour resentment

衔接 xiánjiē link (up); join; connection

衔冤 xiányuān suffer bitterly from an injustice; nurse a bitter sense of wrong: ～去世 die uncleared of a false charge

嫌 xián ①〈动〉dislike; mind; loathe: 不～麻烦 not want to take the trouble; not mind the bother〈名〉② suspicion: 避～ avoid suspicion ③ ill will; enmity

嫌弃 xiánqì dislike and avoid; cold-shoulder

嫌恶 xiánwù distest; loathe; disgust

嫌疑 xiányí suspicion: ～犯 suspect

xiǎn

显 xiǎn ①〈动〉display; show; manifest: ～示英雄气概 show heroism〈形〉② clear; apparent; evident: 明～的错误 an evident mistake ③ influential: ～要 powerful and influential

显出 xiǎnchū show; reveal

显达 xiǎndá illustrious and influential

显得 xiǎnde seem; appear; look: ～心事重重 look pensive

显而易见 xiǎn'éryìjiàn apparently; evidently; obviously; clearly

显赫 xiǎnhè illustrious; of great celebrity; celebrated: ～的名声 great renown. ～一时 celebrated for a time; once almighty

显露 xiǎnlù ① appear; become visible; manifest (oneself) ② reveal: ～身分 reveal one's identity

显明 xiǎnmíng clear; obvious; distinct; marked: ～的特点 marked (distinct) characteristics

显然 xiǎnrán obviously; evidently; clearly

显身手 xiǎnshēnshǒu display one's talent or skill

显示 xiǎnshì show; display; demonstrate; manifest: ～威力 make a show of force

显微镜 xiǎnwēijìng microscope

显微外科 xiǎnwēi wàikē microsurgery

显微阅读机 xiǎnwēi yuèdújī microfilm viewer (reader)

显现 xiǎnxiàn appear; show; reveal itself; come into sight

显像管 xiǎnxiàngguǎn [电子] picture tube; kinescope

显形 xiǎnxíng show one's (true) colours; reveal one's (true) features; come into one's own

显眼 xiǎnyǎn ① attract attention; catch the eye ② conspicuous; glaring; showy: 她的衣服太～了。Her dress is too showy.

显要 xiǎnyào ① influential and powerful ② influential figure; important personage; dignitary; VIP

显意识 xiǎnyìshí consciousness: ～的"自我" conscious "self"

显影 xiǎnyǐng develop

显著 xiǎnzhù significant; notable; striking; remarkable; marked; illustrious: ～成就 make remarkable success (achievements)

险 xiǎn〈名〉① a place difficult of access; narrow pass: 天～ natural barrier ② danger; peril; risk: 不顾一切危～ defy dangers〈形〉③ dangerous; critical ④ vicious; venomous: 阴～ sinister ⑤〈副〉by a hair's breadth; by inches: ～遭不幸 come within an ace of death

险隘 xiǎn'ài stragetic (narrow) pass; defile

险别 xiǎnbié categories of insurance

险地 xiǎndì ① strategical vantage point ② perilous situation; dangerous circumstances

险恶 xiǎn'è ① dangerous; perilous; ominous; critical: ～的海岸 a forbidding coast ② sinister; treacherous; insidious: ～的用心 sinister intentions

险工 xiǎngōng dangerous construction i. e., construction projects prone to danger, such as railways through precipitous mountain areas

险境 xiǎnjìng dangerous situation

险峻 xiǎnjùn precipitous; dangerously steep; scarry

险情 xiǎnqíng dangerous case (situation, circumstance, omen)

险球 xiǎnqiú (mostly football) a near miss (goal)

险胜 xiǎnshèng[体]win by a narrow margin; edge out; win by a neck; narrow victory: ～某人[赛跑] beat a person on the post

险象环生 xiǎnxiànghuánshēng dangers lurking on all sides; beset (surrounded) by perils

险要 xiǎnyào strategically located and difficult of access

险症 xiǎnzhèng dangerous illness; crucial symptoms

险阻 xiǎnzǔ (of roads) dangerous and difficult; barriers: 艰难～ all difficulties and hazards

xiàn

宪 xiàn〈名〉constitution

宪兵 xiànbīng [总称] military police; military policeman; gendarme: ～队 military police corps; gendarmerie

宪法 xiànfǎ constitution:～的起草者 architects of the Constitution

宪章 xiànzhāng charter:联合国～ United Nations Charter

宪政 xiànzhèng constitutional government; constitutionalism

羡 xiàn〈动〉admire; envy

羡慕 xiànmù admire; envy:我～他的好运气。I envy his good luck.

献 xiàn〈动〉① offer; present; dedicate; donate:～花 present bouquests (flowers); floral tribute ② show; put on; display:～殷勤 pay one's addresses; show sb. excessive attentions

献宝 xiànbǎo ① present a treasure ② offer a piece of advice (one's valuable experience)

献策 xiàncè make a suggestion; offer advice

献丑 xiànchǒu (speaking of one's own performance) show oneself up; show one's incompetence (inadequacy)

献词 xiàncí congratulatory message; message:新年～ New Year message

献给 xiàngěi dedicate (to):谨以本书～…[印在扉页] Dedicated to…

献花圈 xiànhuāquān lay a wreath

献计 xiànjì offer advice; make suggestions

献礼 xiànlǐ present a gift

献媚 xiànmèi fawn upon; toady; butter up to; make up to; try to ingratiate oneself with

献身 xiànshēn devote (dedicate, commmit) oneself (to); give one's life for:～精神 dedication

献血 xiànxuè donate blood

县 xiàn〈名〉county:～(处)级以上领导干部 leading cadres at the county level and (or) above (including department chiefs)

县城 xiànchéng county town; county seat

县委 xiànwěi county Party committee

县长 xiànzhǎng head of a county; magistrate

县志 xiànzhì general records of a county; county annals

现 xiàn ①〈副〉now:～在一切都准备好了。Everything is ready now.〈形〉② present; current; existing:～成的社会制度 the present social system ③ on hand:～钱 ready money ④〈动〉show; appear:他脸上渐～出了笑容。Gradually, a smile appeared on his face.

现场 xiànchǎng ① scene (of an accident or crime):保护～ keep the scene intact ② site; (on the) spot:～办公 on-site handling of matters. ～会议 on-the-spot meeting. ～交货 delivery on spot

现成 xiànchéng ① ready-made; ready:～饭 food ready for the table. ～衣服 ready-made clothes ② unearned gain

现存 xiàncún extant; in stock

现代 xiàndài ① modern times, the contemporary age ② present-day; modern; contemporary:～化建设 modernization drive. ～企业制度 modern enterprise system. ～戏 modern drama

现汇 xiànhuì spot exchange

现货 xiànhuò goods on hand; spots; spot goods; prompt goods:～交易 spot transaction. ～市场 spot market; cash market

现金 xiànjīn ready money; cash: ～交易 cash transaction. ～结算 cash settlement. ～帐 cash account ② cash reserve in a bank

现款 xiànkuǎn ready money; cash:付～ pay in cash

现任 xiànrèn ① now hold the office of:他～公司经理。At present he holds the position of company manager. ② currently in office; incumbent:该公司～董事长 the present incumbent of the presidential chair of the corporation

现身说法 xiànshēn shuōfǎ make a personal example as an effective means of convincing others; advise sb. (explain sth.) by using one's own experience as an example; warn people by taking oneself as an example

现实 xiànshí ① reality; actuality:脱离～ be divorced from reality ② real; actual; practical: ～意义 practical significance. ～主义 realism

现象 xiànxiàng appearance (of things); phenomenon

现行 xiànxíng ① currently in effect; in force; in operation ② (of a criminal) active

现眼 xiànyǎn make a spectacle (fool) of oneself; lose face

现役 xiànyì in active service; on service:～军人 servicemen; a member of the armed forces in active service. 服～ be on service

现有 xiànyǒu now available; on hand; existing

现原形 xiànyuánxíng reveal one's true features; drop (throw off; lift, remove, shed off) the mask; get unmasked

现状 xiànzhuàng current situation; present state of affairs; *status quo*:维持～ maintain the *status quo*. 安于～ be content with the present state of affairs

馅

xiàn 〈名〉filling; stuffing:饺子～ stuffing for dumplings

限

xiàn ①〈动〉limit; restrict:～于狭窄的范围内 be restricted within narrow limits ②〈名〉bounds; limit:以年底为～ set the end of the year as the deadline

限定 xiàndìng set (prescribe) a limit to; limit; restrict:～报价 limited offer

限度 xiàndù limit; limitation:超过～ go beyond the limit

限额 xiàn'é quota; norm; limit: ～以上建设项目 above-norm construction projects

限价 xiànjià price limit; price ceiling

限期 xiànqī ① set a time limit:~整顿 consolidation with a specified time ② time limit; deadline:~完成 be completed within the time limit

限于 xiànyú be limited; confined to:~篇幅 due to the limit of space; as space is limited. ~时间 owing to the limit of time

限制 xiànzhì limit; confine; restrict:~信用证 limited letter of credit. 年龄性别不受~。No restrictions are put on age or sex.

陷 xiàn〈动〉① sink; get stuck; be bogged down in:地基下~了2寸。The foundations have sunk two inches. ~于孤立 find oneself isolated ② (of a city) fall; be occupied ③ make false charges against sb.:捏造案情诬~他人 frame a case against sb.

陷害 xiànhài frame up; make false accusation against:~好人 frame up an innocent person

陷阱 xiànjǐng pitfall; trap; pit

陷落 xiànluò ① sink in; cave in; subside ② (of territory) fall into enemy hands

陷入 xiànrù ① be caught in; land oneself in; fall into:~困境 land oneself in a predicament; get into hot water. ~圈套 be caught in a trap ② be absorbed in; be immersed (deep) in:~沉思 be immersed in meditation; be lost in thought

陷于 xiànyú fall into (an unfavourable position)

线 xiàn〈名〉① thread:一团(卷)~ a reel of thread ② line:电话~路 telephone line

线材 xiàncái wire rod

线路 xiànlù ①［电］circuit ② route; line

线路图 xiànlùtú circuit diagram

线描 xiànmiáo［中国画］lines

线索 xiànsuǒ clue; thread:破案的~ clues for solving a case

线条 xiàntiáo line:~画 line drawing. ~艺术 linear art

线性 xiànxìng［数］linear:~成本 linear cost

线装 xiànzhuāng thread-binding:~本 thread-bound edition. ~书 thread-bound Chinese book

xiāng

镶 xiāng〈动〉inlay; fit; set; mount:~宝石 set gems

镶嵌 xiāngqiàn inlay; set

镶牙 xiāngyá insert (put in) a false tooth; insert an artificial tooth; have a tooth filled

相 xiāng〈副〉① each other; one another; mutually:~互支持 support each other ②［表示一方对另一方的动作］:以礼~待 treat sb. with due respect

相爱 xiāng'ài be in love with each other

相安 xiāng'ān live in peace with each other:~无事 live harmoniously in peace; live together peacefully

相比 xiāngbǐ compare with; match

相差 xiāngchà differ：两者～不远。There is not much difference (hardly any difference) between the two.

相称 xiāngchèn ① suit with (to); match; be commensurate to：颜色～。The colours match well. ② be worthy of：他这种工作作风与党员的称号很不～。His work style is not worthy of a Party member.

相持 xiāngchí be locked in a stalemate：战争处于～阶段。The war was at a stalemate.

相处 xiāngchǔ get along with：～得好 get along well with each other; be on good terms with each other

相传 xiāngchuán ① hand down or pass on from one to another ② according to legend; tradition has it that…

相当 xiāngdāng ① be equal to; match; correspond to：旗鼓～ be matched in skill and strength; be well matched ② quite; fairly; considerably：～成功 be quite successful ③ suitable; fit; proper：～的人选 suitable candidate

相得益彰 xiāngdéyìzhāng each shining more brilliantly in the other's company; bring out the best in each other; complement each other

相等 xiāngděng be equal (to); be tantamount to

相抵 xiāngdǐ offset; balance; counterbalance：收支～。The expenses balance the receipts.

相对 xiāngduì ① face to face (with); opposite to：～而坐 sit face to face ② relative：～论 theory of relativity

相反 xiāngfǎn contrary; opposite：～相成 be both opposite and complementary to each other; be opposed to and complementing each other; oppose each other and yet also complement each other. 与愿望～ contrary to one's expectations

相仿 xiāngfǎng similar; more or less the same：年龄～ be about the same age

相逢 xiāngféng meet (by chance); come across

相符 xiāngfǔ correspond to (with); conform to; tally with; agree with

相辅相成 xiāngfǔ-xiāngchéng be complementary to each other; supplement each other

相干 xiānggān be concerned with：这事与你不～。This has nothing to do with you.

相告 xiānggào inform (tell) you

相隔 xiānggé be apart; be at a distance of; be separated by：～多年 after an interval of many years

相关 xiāngguān be interrelated; be related to (with); be bound up with

相好 xiānghǎo ① be on intimate terms; be on familiar terms ② intimate friend ③ have an affair with；［男］lover；［女］mistress

相互 xiānghù mutual；reciprocal：～问好 exchange greetings. ～影响 influence each other；interact. ～订货 cross order. ～沟通 intercommunication

相会 xiānghuì meet

相继 xiāngjì one after another；in succession：～发表意见 air one's views one after another

相见恨晚 xiāngjiàn-hènwǎn regret not having met earlier

相距 xiāngjù be separated by（a distance of ...）；be ... apart；be ... away from

相连 xiānglián be linked together；be joined

相配 xiāngpèi be well-matched；be a good match

相扑 xiāngpū sumo（wrestling）

相亲相爱 xiāngqīn-xiāng'ài be friendly or on intimate terms

相濡以沫 xiāngrúyǐmò give mutual help and relief in time of distress

相劝 xiāngquàn persuade；offer advice

相商 xiāngshāng consult with

相识 xiāngshí ① be acquainted with：与某人素不～ be not acquainted with sb.；have never met ② acquaintance

相思 xiāngsī yearning between lovers；a sad longing love cherished by either or both sides：单～ unrequited love. ～病 lovesickness

相似 xiāngsì resemble；be similar；be alike

相提并论 xiāngtí-bìnglùn mention in the same breath；put on a par with

相通 xiāngtōng communicate with each other；be interlinked

相投 xiāngtóu agree with each other：兴趣～ find each other congenial

相托 xiāngtuō entrust sb. with sth.；commit to sb.'s care；ask sb. to do sth.

相象 xiāngxiàng resemble；be similar；be alike

相向 xiāngxiàng ① in opposite directions ② face to face；facing each other

相信 xiāngxìn believe（in）；have faith in；be convinced of：～群众 trust the masses；have faith in the masses

相形见绌 xiāngxíng-jiànchù be inferior by comparison；compare unfavourably with；appear deficient in comparison with；seem pallid by comparison；be pale before

相沿成习 xiāngyán-chéngxí become common practice through long usage

相依 xiāngyī be interdependent；depend on each other：～为命 depend on each other for survival；share one's life together

相宜 xiāngyí suitable；fitting；appropriate

相应 xiāngyìng corresponding；appropriate：采取～的措施 take corresponding measures

相映 xiāngyìng set each other off：～成趣 form a delightful

(pleasing) contrast; gain by contrast

相中 xiāngzhòng take a fancy to; settle on

箱 xiāng〈名〉box; case; chest; trunk:大木～ wooden trunk

箱笼细软 xiānglǒng-xìruǎn cases, baskets and bundles

箱子 xiāngzi case; box; chest; trunk

厢 xiāng〈名〉① of one-storeyed house wing:～房 wing-room; side-room ② railway carriage or compartment; (theatre) box ③ side:一～情愿 one-sided wish

香 xiāng〈形〉① sweet-smelling; fragrant; scented:～花与毒草 fragrant flowers and poisonous weeds ② (of food) delicious; appetizing:这饭真～。This food is really appetizing. ③〈副〉(of sleep) soundly ④〈名〉incense; josstick:蚊～ mosquito coil incense

香案 xiāng'àn long altar on which incense burners are placed; incense burner table

香波 xiāngbō shampoo

香槟酒 xiāngbīngjiǔ champagne

香草 xiāngcǎo vanilla:～冰淇淋 vanilla ice cream

香肠 xiāngcháng sausage

香椿 xiāngchūn [植]Chinese toon

香菇 xiānggū dried mushroom

香瓜 xiāngguā muskmelon

香蕉 xiāngjiāo banana

香精 xiāngjīng essence:食用～ flavouring essence

香料 xiāngliào ① perfume ② spice

香客 xiāngkè pilgrim

香炉 xiānglú incense burner

香喷喷 xiāngpēnpēn ① sweet-smelling ② savoury; appetizing

香片 xiāngpiàn scented tea

香水 xiāngshuǐ perfume; scent

香烟 xiāngyān ① cigarette:～盒 cigarette case ② incense smoke

香皂 xiāngzào toilet soap; perfumed soap

香泽 xiāngzé ① perfumed hair cream or oil ② fragrance (esp. of a lady)

香脂 xiāngzhī ① balm; balsam ② face cream

乡 xiāng〈名〉① country; village; countryside; rural area ② native place; home village:回～ return to one's native place ③ township:～长 township head

乡愁 xiāngchóu homesickness

乡村 xiāngcūn ① village ② rural area; countryside:～人口 rural population

乡规民约 xiāngguī-mínyuē folk regulations

乡间 xiāngjiān in the village; in the country

乡里 xiānglǐ ① home village or town ② fellow villagers or townsmen

乡民 xiāngmín villagers; country people

乡亲 xiāngqīn persons from the same village or town; fellow-villager; folks

乡思 xiāngsī homesickness; nostalgia

乡俗 xiāngsú local customs; village customs

乡土 xiāngtǔ ① native soil; home village: ~观念 localism; provincialism. ~文学 native soil literature; pastoral stories ② of one's native land; local: ~风味 local flavour

乡下 xiāngxià (in the) country (contryside); village: ~人 country folk(s)

乡音 xiāngyīn ① dialectal speech ② native accent

乡约 xiāngyuē local rules and regulations valid for all the inhabitants of a township

乡镇 xiāngzhèn small town; township: ~企业 township and village enterprises

襄 xiāng 〈动〉assist; help: 共~义举。Let everybody help to promote this worthy undertaking.

襄理 xiānglǐ assistant manager

xiáng

详 xiáng ①〈形〉detailed; minute: ~细的报告 a detailed report ②〈名〉details; particulars: ~细叙述 go into details ③〈动〉know clearly: 不~ be unknown

详尽 xiángjìn ① thorough; exhaustive; detailed: ~的研究 exhaustive studies ② to the smallest detail; in every detail; thoroughly

详略 xiánglüè details and omissions

详情 xiángqíng detailed information; details; particulars: ~后报 details to follow

详实 xiángshí full and accurate

详细 xiángxì detailed; minute: ~背书 endorsement in full. ~请问办事处 please apply to the office for particulars

祥 xiáng〈形〉auspicious; lucky; propitious: 不~ inauspicious; ominous

祥和 xiánghé ① happy and auspicious ② kind; benign

祥瑞 xiángruì auspicious sign

祥云 xiángyún auspicious clouds

翔 xiáng 〈动〉circle in the air; fly about; hover: 翱~ hover; soar

翔实 xiángshí full and accurate; detailed and accurate

降 xiáng〈动〉① surrender; capitulate: 乞~ beg to surrender ② subdue; tame; subjugate
另见 jiàng

降敌 xiángdí surrender to the enemy

降伏 xiángfú subdue; subjugate; tame

降服 xiángfú surrender; yield

降龙伏虎 xiánglóng-fúhǔ subdue the dragon and tame the tiger—overcome powerful adversaries

降顺 xiángshùn yield and pledge allegiance to

xiǎng

享 xiǎng 〈动〉enjoy：～有威望 enjoy prestige

享福 xiǎngfú live in happiness；enjoy a happy life

享乐 xiǎnglè indulge in creature comforts；seek pleasure：～主义 hedonism

享年 xiǎngnián died at the age of

享受 xiǎngshòu ① enjoy：～公费医疗 enjoy free medical care；enjoy public health services ② enjoyment；treat

享用 xiǎngyòng enjoy the use of；enjoy

享有 xiǎngyǒu enjoy (rights, prestige, etc.)

享誉 xiǎngyù enjoy good fame

想 xiǎng〈动〉① think：他～得深看得远。He thinks out problems in a deep and far-sighted way. ② suppose；consider；reckon：我～今天她不会来。I don't think she'll be coming today. ③ would like to；want to：我～试试。I'd like to have a try. ④ miss：我多么～你呀！I miss you terribly！

想必 xiǎngbì most likely；presumably

想不到 xiǎngbudào ① didn't expect；fail to give attention to ② unexpected；unthought-of：～的事 something unthought-of

想不开 xiǎngbukāi stick to things too hard；take a matter to heart

想不通 xiǎngbutōng can't see the logic；can't see why；be upset；can't think round to it

想当然 xiǎngdāngrán assume sth. as a matter of course；take sth. for granted：我～地认为她一定会来的。I took it for granted that she would certainly come.

想到 xiǎngdào think (of)；call to mind；occur to sb.：她～一个新主意。A new idea occurred to her.

想得开 xiǎngdekāi not take a matter to heart；take things philosophically；try to look on the bright side of things

想法 xiǎngfǎ opinion；idea：把你的～说出来 speak your mind out

想方设法 xiǎngfāng-shèfǎ do everything possible；try every means；leave no stone unturned

想念 xiǎngniàn long to see again；miss

想起 xiǎngqǐ remember；think of；call to mind；recall

想入非非 xiǎngrùfēifēi allow one's fancy to run wild；indulge in wishful thinking；indulge in fantasy；daydream

想通 xiǎngtōng straighten out one's thinking；get one's thinking straight；become convinced：你～没有？Are you convinced yet？

想象 xiǎngxiàng ① imagine；fancy ② imagination：～力 imagination

响 xiǎng ①〈名〉sound；noise：枪～ gun shot ②〈形〉loud；noisy ③〈动〉make a sound；ring：电

话铃～了。The telephone rang.

响板 xiǎngbǎn [板类乐器]castanets

响彻 xiǎngchè resound through:～云霄的凯歌 a song of triumph which resounds through the skies

响当当 xiǎngdāngdāng ①(of the sound made by a bell, a gong, etc.) loud and resounding ②(of a person) of resounding fame; outstanding; worthy

响动 xiǎngdòng sound of sth. astir

响亮 xiǎngliàng loud; ringing; resounding; sonorous:说话声音～ have a loud voice

响应 xiǎngyìng respond (to); answer:～号召 respond to a call

饷 xiǎng〈动〉① entertain (with food and drink) ② pay (for soldiers, policemen, etc.)

xiàng

项 xiàng〈名〉① nape (of the neck) ② item:出口～目 an export item ③[数] term

项背 xiàngbèi a person's back

项链 xiàngliàn necklace

项目 xiàngmù ① item:～经理负责制 manager responsibility system of a key project under construction ②[体] event

项庄舞剑,意在沛公 Xiàng Zhuāng wǔ jiàn, yì zài Pèi Gōng Xiang Zhuang performed the sword dance as a cover for his attempt on Liu Bang's life—act with a hidden motive.; have an ulterior object (motive, objective) in view (mind)

巷 xiàng〈名〉alley; lane
另见 hàng

巷口 xiàngkǒu entrance to a lane

巷议 xiàngyì street gossip

巷战 xiàngzhàn street fighting

相 xiàng〈名〉① appearance; looks:扮～ the appearance of an actor or actress in constume and makeup ② bearing; posture ③ photo:摄～ take photo
另见 xiāng

相册 xiàngcè photo album

相机 xiàngjī ① wait (watch) for an opportunity:～行事 act according to circumstances; act as the occasion demands ② camera

相角 xiàngjiǎo photo corners

相貌 xiàngmào facial features; looks; appearance:～端正 have regular features

相片 xiàngpiān photograph; photo; picture

相声 xiàngshēng comic dialogue; cross talk:说～ perform a comic dialogue (talk)

相术 xiàngshù fortune-telling by studying facial features; physiognomy

向 xiàng ①〈名〉direction:人心所～ the direction of popular sentiment〈动〉② face; turn towards:这间房子～西。This room faces west. ③ side with; take sb.'s part; be partial to:～工业倾斜的政策 a policy in favour of industry ④〈介〉towards;to; for:～上级汇报工作 report to one's superior on one's work

向背 xiàngbèi support or oppose

向导 xiàngdǎo guide:当～ act as guide

向来 xiànglái all along; always:我～不抽烟。I have never smoked.

向前 xiàngqián forward; ahead; forth; onward:～看 look forward

向钱看 xiàng qián kàn put money above all; money-grubbing

向上爬 xiàngshàng pá be intent on personal advancement; climb up social ladder; office seeker; climb to the upper echelon of society

向往 xiàngwǎng desire eagerly; yearn (for); look forward to:～美好的未来 look forward to a rosy future

向心力 xiàngxīnlì centripetal force

向阳 xiàngyáng ① exposed to the sun; sunny ② face the sun; face south; with a sunny (usu. southern) exposure

向隅而泣 xiàngyú'érqì grieve out in the cold; be left to grieve in the cold; weep all alone in a corner

向…作证 xiàng…zuòzhèng bear the record

象

xiàng〈名〉① elephant ② shape; form; appearance; image:倒～ inverted image

象棋 xiàngqí (Chinese) chess; *xiangqi*:～大师 grand master. 下～ play (at) chess

象形文字 xiàngxíng wénzì pictographic characters; pictographs

象牙 xiàngyá ivory:～雕刻 ivory carving

象征 xiàngzhēng ① symbol; emblem; token ② symbolize; represent:～主义绘画 symbolist painting

象征性 xiàngzhēngxìng symbolic; emblematic; token

橡

xiàng〈名〉① rubber tree ② oak

橡胶 xiàngjiāo rubber:～厂 rubber plant

橡皮 xiàngpí ① rubber ② eraser; rubber:～图章 rubber-stamp

像

xiàng〈动〉① resemble:这姐妹俩长得很～。The two sisters are very much alike. 这孩子～他母亲。The child takes after its mother. ② look as if; seem:～要下雪了。It looks like snow.〈名〉③ picture; portrait:铜～ bronze statue ④ image ⑤ likeness (of sb.):给某人画～ take sb.'s likeness

像话 xiànghuà [多用于否定或反问]reasonable; proper:真不～! It's simply outrageous!

像模像样 xiàngmó-xiàngyàng up to the mark; presentable; decent

像样 xiàngyàng up to the mark; decent; presentable; sound:不～ unpresentable; indecent

像章 xiàngzhāng badge (with sb.'s likeness on it)

xiāo

枭 xiāo〈名〉① owl ② brave; valiant:～将 a brave general ③ smuggler:毒～ drugpusher

消 xiāo〈动〉① disappear; vanish:～失不见 vanish from sight ② remove; eliminate; cancel:～除分歧 remove (eliminate) differences ③ pass the time in a leisurely way; while away:～夏 pass the summer in a leisurely way

消沉 xiāochén downhearted; downcast; low-spirited; depressed; dejected:意志～ demoralized; despondent

消愁 xiāochóu dispel or allay worries

消除 xiāochú remove; eliminate; iron out; dispel; clear up:～误会 clear up misunderstandings. ～顾虑 dispel misgivings

消毒 xiāodú disinfect; sterilize:～牛奶 sterilized milk

消防 xiāofáng fire control:～队 fire brigade. ～人员 fire fighters. ～车 fire engine

消费 xiāofèi consume:～基金 funds for consumption. ～品 consumer goods. ～方式 pattern of consumption. ～水平 standards of consumption. ～税 consumption tax. ～者 consumer

消耗 xiāohào deplete; use up; expend:～精力 consume one's energy

消化 xiāohuà digest:～不良 dyspepsia; indigestion. ～价格调整的影响 offset the effect of the price rises. ～所学的东西 digest what sb. has learnt

消极 xiāojí ① negative:～因素 negative factor ② passive; inactive:～等待和观望的态度 a passive wait-and-see attitude

消灭 xiāomiè ① eliminate; wipe out; abolish; annihilate:～赤字 eliminate the budget deficit ② die out; pass away

消磨 xiāomó ① wear down; sap:～精力 sap one's energy ② while away; idle away; kill:～岁月 kill time; while away the time; fill up the time; pass the time

消遣 xiāoqiǎn ① divert oneself (by); amuse oneself (by, with) ② pastime; diversion:下棋～ divert oneself by playing chess

消散 xiāosàn scatter and disappear; clear up; dissipate:雾～了。The mist has lifted.

消失 xiāoshī disappear; vanish; dissolve; die away:～在人群中 be lost in a crowd

消逝 xiāoshì fade away; elapse:随着时间的～ with the lapse of time

消瘦 xiāoshòu grow (become) thin; become emaciated

消受 xiāoshòu ① (usu. used in the negative) enjoy (having sth.) ② endure, bear, or stand (hardship, ill treatment, etc.)

消亡 xiāowáng wither away; die

out:自行～ perish of itself

消息 xiāoxi news; information:～灵通人士 well-informed circles; informed sources

消夏 xiāoxià spend a summer holiday

消闲 xiāoxián fill one's spare time; while away the time

消炎 xiāoyán reduce inflammation:～药 antiphlogistic

消灾 xiāozāi rid calamities

宵 xiāo〈名〉night:通～ the whole night; all night

宵禁 xiāojìn curfew:实行(解除)～ impose (lift) a curfew

宵夜 xiāoyè food (refreshments) taken late at night; midnight snack

逍 xiāo

逍遥 xiāoyáo free and unfettered; carefree; be at (one's) ease:～法外 be at large; go scot-free; escape from law; be on the loose. ～派 the unfettered faction. ～自在 carefree; easygoing

削 xiāo〈动〉① pare; peel with a knife:～苹果 pare an apple ② sharpen:～铅笔 sharpen a pencil ③ cut

另见 xuē

削球 xiāoqiú [乒乓球] cut; chop

骁 xiāo〈形〉valiant; brave; spirited

骁将 xiāojiàng valiant general

骁勇 xiāoyǒng valiant; brave:～善战 brave and battlewise

霄 xiāo〈名〉① clouds:高入云～ towering into the clouds ② sky; heaven:九重～ the highest heavens (believed to be of nine strata in ancient times)

霄壤 xiāorǎng heaven and earth:有～之别 be as far apart as heaven and earth

硝 xiāo ①〈名〉nitre; saltpetre ②〈动〉taw (animal skin):～皮 taw an animal skin into leather

销 xiāo〈动〉① cancel; write off; annul:注～一笔坏帐 write off a bad debt ② sell; market:购～ buy and sell ③ spend:开～ expenditure

销案 xiāo'àn close a case

销户口 xiāo hùkǒu cancel one's residence registration

销毁 xiāohuǐ destroy by melting or burning; melt down:～罪证 destroy incriminating evidence

销魂 xiāohún be overwhelmed with sorrow or joy; feel transported

销假 xiāojià report back after leave of absence

销量 xiāoliàng the quantity (of goods) sold; sales made

销路 xiāolù sale; market:～(不)好 have a good (bad) sale; be in great (little) demand

销声匿迹 xiāoshēng-nìjì make no public appearances; cease to make public appearances; withdraw from the scene; lie low

销售 xiāoshòu sell:～柜台计算机系统 computerized point-of-sales systems. ～量 sales volume

销赃 xiāozāng disposal of stolen goods

销帐 xiāozhàng cancel (remove) from an account; cross off an account

嚣 xiāo〈动〉clamour; hubbub: 叫～ clamour; raise a hue and cry

嚣张 xiāozhāng arrogant; insolent; aggressive; rampant: ～一时 be rampant for a time; be very noisy for a time; run wild (rampant) for a while. 气焰～ be swollen with arrogance

潇 xiāo〈形〉(of water) deep and clear

潇洒 xiāosǎ natural and unrestrained; smart; elegant and unconventional

潇潇 xiāoxiāo (of rain or wind) whistling and pattering (dripping); dizzly: 风雨～。The wind was whistling and the rain dripping.

萧 xiāo〈形〉desolate; dreary

萧墙 xiāoqiáng screen wall facing the gate of a Chinese house: ～之祸 trouble arising at home; trouble from within; internal strife

萧瑟 xiāosè ① bleak; dreary; desolate ② sough; sigh; rustle in the air: 秋风～。The autumn wind is soughing.

萧索 xiāosuǒ ① bleak and dreary; dull and desolate ② (of a person's mood) melancholy; depressed

萧条 xiāotiáo ① bleak; dreary; desolate ② dull; stagnant; depressed; slack; depression; slump: ～的市场 dull market. 经济～ economic depression; slump

箫 xiāo〈名〉*xiao*, a vertical bamboo flute: 洞～ *dongxiao*, a vertical bamboo flute

箫管 xiāoguǎn flute

xiáo

淆 xiáo〈动〉mix; confuse; mingle: 混～ confuse; obscure; mix up

淆惑 xiáohuò bewilder

xiǎo

晓 xiǎo ①〈名〉dawn; daybreak: 拂～ before dawn〈动〉② know: 知～ know; understand ③ let sb. know; notify: ～以利害 warn sb. of consequences

晓得 xiǎode know: 天～! Heaven knows!

晓示 xiǎoshì tell explicitly; let sb. know; notify

晓以利害 xiǎoyǐ-lìhài warn sb. of the possible consequences; impress on sb. the gains and losses involved

小 xiǎo〈形〉① small; little; minor: ～改革 minor reform ② young; junior: 他比我～2 岁。

He is two years junior to me. ③〈副〉for a short time：～住 stay for a few days

小百货 xiǎobǎihuò sundries；small articles of a daily use

小班 xiǎobān ① the bottom class in a kindergarten ② reception class

小报 xiǎobào insignificant paper；tabloid

小报告 xiǎobàogào telltaling：打～ practice telltaling

小辈 xiǎobèi younger member of a family；junior

小本经营 xiǎoběn jīngyíng ① do business in a small way ② business with a small capital

小便 xiǎobiàn ① urine：验～ urine test ② pass（make）water；urinate；piss

小辫子 xiǎobiànzi small queue（metaphor for a handle by which one can be taken to task）；vulnerable point；handle：抓住～不放 make things hard for sb.；get a handle on sb.

小标题 xiǎobiāotí subheading；subhead

小菜儿 xiǎocàir something extremely easy to do or manage

小册子 xiǎocèzi booklet；pamphlet

小产 xiǎochǎn（have a）miscarriage；abortion

小炒 xiǎochǎo small stir-fried dish

小吃 xiǎochī ① snack；refreshments：～店 snack shop（bar）；buffet：风味～ snack with a local flavour ② cold dish；made dish

小丑 xiǎochǒu ① clown；buffon；fool ② mean person；wretch：～跳梁 a wretch making trouble

小聪明 xiǎocōngming cleverness in trivial matters；petty trick

小道理 xiǎodàolǐ minor principle

小道消息 xiǎodào xiāoxi grapevine（news）；hearsay：听～说… hear on the grapevine that …

小调 xiǎodiào ① ditty ②［乐］minor

小动作 xiǎodòngzuò little trick；petty and mean action；petty manoeuvre：搞～ resort to little tricks

小额 xiǎo'é small amount：～储蓄 small savings deposit

小额活期存款 xiǎo'é huóqī cúnkuǎn petty cash deposit

小恩小惠 xiǎo'ēn-xiǎohuì petty（little；small）favours；a little bit of economic bait；do sb. small favours；economic baits（sops）

小儿科 xiǎo'érkē ① paediatrics department ② paediatrics：～医生 paediatrician ③ "kids stuff"（metaphor for professions disdained by people or matters not worthy of note）：有人说职业班是～。Some say that the vocational class is "kids stuff."

小贩 xiǎofàn pedlar；hawker；vendor

小费 xiǎofèi tip；gratuity

小个子 xiǎogèzi short person；

small fellow

小工 xiǎogōng (unskilled) labourer

小广播 xiǎoguǎngbō spreading hearsay (rumours); petty broadcast; gossip; circulating grapevine news; tell tales: 不要当～。Don't spread hearsay.

小鬼 xiǎoguǐ ① little devil; demon servant in Hell ② child; imp (a term of endearment used in addressing a child)

小户 xiǎohù ① a poor, humble family; a family of limited means and without powerful connections ② a small family

小伙子 xiǎohuǒzi youngster; lad; young fellow

小集体 xiǎojítǐ small collectives

小集团 xiǎojítuán faction; clique: ～主义 small groupism; cliquism

小家庭 xiǎojiātíng nuclear family

小将 xiǎojiàng ① young general ② young militant; young pathbreaker

小轿车 xiǎojiàochē sedan; car

小节 xiǎojié integrity in personal life; small matter; trifle: ～无害论 the view that small matters can do no harm. 不拘～ not bother about small matters; not be punctilious

小结 xiǎojié ① brief sum-up (summary) ② summarize briefly: ～前阶段的工作 summarize briefly the work done in the previous stage

小姐 xiǎojiě ① young lady ② [姓名前] Miss

小金库 xiǎojīnkù private gold storage (metaphor for funds or materials that certain enterprises and business units retain privately for their own use, in violation of fiscal regulations)

小看 xiǎokàn slight; look down upon; belittle

小康 xiǎokāng well-to-do; moderately well-off: ～水平 comfortably well-off standard. ～之家 moderately well-off family

小考 xiǎokǎo mid-term examination; quiz

小殓 xiǎoliàn dressing the corpse in burial clothes

小两口 xiǎoliǎngkǒu a young (married) couple

小量 xiǎoliàng a small amount or quantity

小买卖 xiǎomǎimai small business

小卖部 xiǎomàibù ① a small shop attached to a factory; theatre, etc. ② snack counter; buffet; retail department; retail section

小门小户 xiǎomén-xiǎohù poor humble families; families of limited means and without powerful connections

"小秘(蜜)" xiǎomì "little miss"; girl "secretary"

小名 xiǎomíng pet name for a child; childhood name

小年夜 xiǎoniányè ① the night before the lunar New Year's Eve ② the 23rd or 24th day of the 12th month of the lunar year

小妞儿 xiǎoniūr young girl

小农经济 xiǎonóngjīngjì small-scale peasant economy; small-scale farming by individual owners

小便宜 xiǎopiányì petty advantage; small gain:贪～ go after petty advantages

小票儿 xiǎopiàor bank notes of small denominations

小品 xiǎopǐn a short, simple piece of literary or artistic creation; essay; sketch; short act

小评论 xiǎopínglùn short comment

小气 xiǎoqì ① narrow-minded; small-minded ② stingy; mean; miserly; niggardly

小钱 xiǎoqián ① copper coin; copper ② a small amount of money ③ a small amount of money given as a bribe

小钱柜 xiǎoqiánguì private money cupboard

小巧玲珑 xiǎoqiǎo-línglóng small and exquisite (delicate); dainty

小圈子 xiǎoquānzi small circle

小人 xiǎorén ① a person of low position ② mean person; shabby villain:～得志 a villain holding sway

小人书 xiǎorénshū picture-story book

小人物 xiǎorénwù unimportant person; a nobody

小日用品 xiǎorìyòngpǐn small retail items

小商品 xiǎoshāngpǐn small commodities; small items

小商小贩 xiǎoshāng xiǎofàn small trade people and pedlars

小生产 xiǎoshēngchǎn small-scale production:～者 small producer

小时候 xiǎoshíhou in one's childhood; when one was young

小市民 xiǎoshìmín town-dweller of the lower middle class; urban petty bourgeois; plebeian; philistine

小试锋芒 xiǎoshì-fēngmáng display only a small part of one's talent or capability

小事 xiǎoshì petty thing; small matter; trifle:～聪明,大事糊涂 penny wise and pound foolish

小数 xiǎoshù [数] decimal:～点 decimal point

小水电 xiǎoshuǐdiàn small hydropower stations

小说 xiǎoshuō novel; fiction:～家 novelist; writer of fiction. ～素材 fictional material; material for novel

小算盘 xiǎosuànpán selfish calculation; penny-pinching:～打得精 be very calculating

小题大做 xiǎotí-dàzuò make a fuss over a trifling matter; make a mountain out of a molehill; make much ado about nothing; storm in a teacup

小天地 xiǎotiāndì small world (metaphor for the relatively small sphere of activity of some people)

小偷 xiǎotōu pilferer; (petty) thief; pickpocket:～小摸 pilfering

小我 xiǎowǒ the individual; the self

小巫见大巫 xiǎowū jiàn dàwū like a small sorcerer in the presence of a great one—feel dwarfed; pale into insignificance by comparison

小五金 xiǎowǔjīn metal fittings (e. g. nails, wires, hinges, bolts, locks, etc.); hardware

小写 xiǎoxiě ① the ordinary form of a Chinese numeral ② a small letter; minuscule

小心 xiǎoxīn be careful; be cautious; take care: ～轻放 handle with care

小心眼儿 xiǎoxīnyǎnr narrow-minded; petty

小型 xiǎoxíng small-sized; small-scale; miniature; baby: ～汽车 baby car; minibus

小学 xiǎoxué primary (elementary) school

小业主 xiǎoyèzhǔ small proprietor; small owners

小夜曲 xiǎoyèqǔ serenade

小意思 xiǎoyìsi small token of kindly feelings; mere trifle

小帐 xiǎozhàng tip; gratuity

小住 xiǎozhù stay for a few days

小传 xiǎozhuàn brief biography

小篆 xiǎozhuàn small seal

小字辈 xiǎozìbèi younger generation

小卒 xiǎozú ① an instrument; a private ② [国际象棋] pawn

小作坊 xiǎozuōfang individual workshop

xiào

校 xiào 〈名〉① school: 夜～ night (evening) school ② field officer
另见 jiào

校办工厂 xiàobàn gōngchǎng school-run workshop

校车 xiàochē school bus

校董事会 xiàodǒngshìhuì school board

校风 xiàofēng school spirit

校服 xiàofú school uniform

校规 xiàoguī school regulations

校徽 xiàohuī school badge: 戴～ wear a school badge

校刊 xiàokān school magazine; college journal

校庆 xiàoqìng school anniversary; anniversary of the founding of a school or college

校外辅导员 xiàowài fúdǎoyuán after-school activities counsellors

校务委员会 xiàowù wěiyuánhuì school council

校友 xiàoyǒu alumnus; alumna

校园 xiàoyuán campus; [中小学的] school yard: ～歌曲 school songs

校长 xiàozhǎng [大学的] president; chancellor; [中小学的] principal; headmaster or headmistress

校址 xiàozhǐ location of a school

哮 xiào ①〈名〉heavy breathing; wheeze ②〈动〉roar; thunder: 咆～如雷 roar with rage

效 xiào ①〈名〉effect; result; function:动机和～果的统一 the unity of motive and effect 〈动〉② imitate:～法长辈 imitate the example of one's elders ③ devote oneself to; render a service:替某人～劳 render sb. a service

效法 xiàofǎ model oneself on; follow the example of; imitate

效仿 xiàofǎng imitate; follow the example of

效果 xiàoguǒ effect; result:取得良好的～ achieve good results

效劳 xiàoláo do a service (to); serve; work for; work in the service:为国～ serve one's country

效力 xiàolì ① do a service (to); render a service to; serve ② effect; efficacy:这药很有～。The medicine is efficacious.

效率 xiàolǜ efficiency:～工程师 efficiency engineer

效命 xiàomìng go all out to serve sb. regardless of the consequences

效能 xiàonéng efflicacy; usefulness

效验 xiàoyàn desired result (effect); efficacy

效益 xiàoyì (beneficial) result; effectiveness:～工资 wages based on benefits. 提高经济～ improve economic performance

效用 xiàoyòng usefulness; effectiveness

效尤 xiàoyóu knowingly follow the example of a wrongdoer:以儆～ warn others against following a bad example

效忠 xiàozhōng pledge loyalty to; devote oneself heart and soul to; be loyal (to):～祖国 be loyal to one's country

孝 xiào〈名〉① filial piety ② mourning:穿～ wear mourning; be in mourning

孝道 xiàodào filial duty

孝服 xiàofú mourning (dress)

孝敬 xiàojìng show filial respect for; present gifts (to one's elders or superiors)

孝顺 xiàoshùn show filial obedience; filial piety

孝心 xiàoxīn filial sentiments; filial devotion

孝子 xiàozǐ filial (dutiful) son

孝子贤孙 xiàozǐ-xiánsūn worthy progeny; a fine son

肖 xiào〈动〉be like; be similar to:毕～ bear a striking resemblance to

肖像 xiàoxiàng portrait; portraiture:～画 portrait-painting

笑 xiào〈动〉① smile; laugh; grin:狂～ laugh wildly ② laugh at; ridicule:嘲～某人 hold sb. up to ridicule

笑柄 xiàobǐng laughingstock; butt; joke

笑话 xiàohuà joke; jest:～百出 make many ridiculous mistakes. 讲～ crack (cut, make) a joke. 闹～ make a fool of oneself

笑剧 xiàojù farce; opera bouffe

笑里藏刀 xiàolǐ-cángdāo hide a

dagger in a smile—with murderous intent behind one's smile; cover the dagger with a smile; daggers hidden behind smiles

笑料 xiàoliào something funny or laughable; laughingstock; joke

笑骂 xiàomà ① deride and upbraid; taunt ② scold in jest (jokingly)

笑纳 xiàonà kindly accept (this small gift of mine)

笑容 xiàoróng smiling expression; smile:～满面 be all smiles. ～可掬 be radiant with smiles

笑声 xiàoshēng laughter

笑窝 xiàowō dimple

笑嘻嘻 xiàoxīxī grinning from ear to ear; smiling broadly

笑逐颜开 xiàozhúyánkāi be wreathed in smiles; be radiant with joy; beam with smiles

啸 xiào ① (of humans) make a whistling sound ② (of certain birds and animals) give a long, loud cry:虎～ tigers roaring (growling) ③ (of the wind, the sea, etc.) howl; roar:风～ the wind howling ④ (of bullets, airplanes, etc.) whistle; whizz:飞机尖～着飞过顶空。A plane whizzed overhead.

xiē

楔 xiē〈名〉wedge:用～把某物劈开 force sth. apart with a wedge

楔形文字 xiēxíng wénzì cuneiform writing (characters)

楔子 xiēzi ① wedge:在……中打进～ drive a wedge into ② peg; bamboo peg ③ prologue in some modern novels

些 xiē〈量〉some; a little; a few:买～东西 do some shopping

些微 xiēwēi slightly; a little; a bit; a trifle

些许 xiēxǔ a few; a little:～小事 just some small matters

歇 xiē〈动〉have (take) a rest; rest:～口气 take a breather; stop for a breather

歇班 xiēbān stop work; knock off

歇工 xiēgōng off duty

歇后语 xiēhòuyǔ a two-part allegorical saying, of which the first part, always stated, is descriptive, while the second part, sometimes unstated, carries the message

歇脚 xiējiǎo rest the feet—stop on the way for a rest

歇斯底里 xiēsīdǐlǐ hysteria

歇息 xiēxī ① have a rest ② go to bed

歇业 xiēyè close a business; close down

xié

鞋 xié〈名〉shoe

鞋带 xiédài shoelace; shoestring:系～ tie shoelaces

鞋底 xiédǐ sole (of a shoe)

鞋垫 xiédiàn shoe-pad; insole

鞋匠 xiéjiàng shoemaker; cobbler

鞋刷 xiéshuā shoe brush
鞋楦 xiéxuàn a last for shaping a shoe; shoe tree
鞋样 xiéyàng shoe pattern; outline of sole
鞋油 xiéyóu shoe polish; shoe cream

挟 xié〈动〉① hold under one's arm ② coerce: 裹～ force; force to take part
挟持 xiéchí ① seize sb. on both sides by the arm ② hold sb. under duress
挟嫌 xiéxián nurse a grudge (against); harbour malice (against):～报复 retaliate against sb. on account of a previous grudge
挟制 xiézhì coerce (bully) sb. into doing one's bidding; force sb. into submission by taking advantage of his weakness

谐 xié〈形〉① in harmony; in tune; in accord ② humorous: 诙～ humorous; jocular ③〈动〉settle (a matter); come to an agreement: 事～之后，即可动身。We shall set out immediately once the matter is settled.
谐和 xiéhé harmonious; concordant
谐趣 xiéqù pleasantry
谐调 xiétiáo harmony
谐谑 xiéxuè humorous ridicule; banter
谐音 xiéyīn ① homonymic; euphony ② [乐] partials

携 xié〈动〉① carry; take with: ～眷 bring one's wife and children along ② lead sb. by the hand: 提～ lead a child by the hand
携带 xiédài carry about; take along (with one): ～方便 be easy to carry about. 随身～的物品 things carried on one's person
携手 xiéshǒu hand in hand: ～前进 advance (go forward) hand in hand

偕 xié〈副〉be together with; be in the company of
偕老 xiélǎo (husband and wife) grow old together: 白头～ remain a devoted couple to the end of their lives; live to a ripe old age in conjugal bliss
偕同 xiétóng accompanied by; together with; along with
偕行 xiéxíng travel together (with)

邪 xié〈形〉evil; vicious; heretical: 辟～ exorcise evil spirit
邪恶 xié'è evil; wicked; perverse: ～的念头 wicked idea; evil thought
邪乎 xiéhu ① extraordinary; abnormal; terrible ② fantastic; incredible
邪见 xiéjiàn wrong theories
邪教 xiéjiào heterodox sects
邪路 xiélù evil ways; foul road: 走上～ take to evil ways
邪门儿 xiéménr ① strange; odd; abnormal ② crooked ways; underhand means; dishonest practices (methods)

邪门歪道 xiémén-wāidào crooked ways (means); dishonest practices

邪念 xiéniàn evil thought; wicked idea

邪气 xiéqì perverse trend; evil (noxious) influence; unhealthy trend

邪说 xiéshuō heresy; heretical ideas; fallacy

邪行 xiéxing evil deeds; wrong actions

邪欲 xiéyù concupiscence

斜 xié〈形〉slanting; oblique; inclined: 倾～地形[军] oblique compartment

斜角 xiéjiǎo [数] oblique angle

斜路 xiélù wrong path: 走～ go astray

斜面 xiémiàn ①[数] inclined plane ②[机] oblique plane

斜坡 xiépō slope; incline

斜视 xiéshì cast sidelong glances; look sideways; look askance

斜体字 xiétǐzì italics

斜纹 xiéwén [纺] twill (weave): ～法兰绒 twilled flannel. ～布 drill; twill

斜线 xiéxiàn oblique line: ～符号 slant

斜眼 xiéyǎn ① strabismus ② wall-eye; cross-eye

斜阳 xiéyáng the setting sun

协 xié ①〈形〉join; common: 调～ be in perfect harmony ②〈副〉jointly: ～办 do sth. jointly ③〈动〉assist: ～办 assist sb. to do sth.

协定 xiédìng agreement; accord: 贸易～ trade agreement. ～关税 agreed tariff; fixed tariff duties

协方差 xiéfāngchā covariance

协和 xiéhé coordinate; harmonize

协会 xiéhuì association; society

协理 xiélǐ ① assist in the management (of an enterprise, etc.) ② assistant manager (in a bank, business enterprise, etc.)

协力 xiélì unite efforts; join a common effort: ～进攻 launch a joint assult on

协商 xiéshāng consult (with); confer (with); talk things over: ～解决 solve (resolve) by consultations

协调 xiétiáo coordinate; harmonize: ～观点 harmonize viewpoints

协同 xiétóng cooperate with; work in coordination with: ～办理 handle the matter in coordination with. ～式管理 cordinative management

协议 xiéyì agreement: 口头～ verbal agreement. 就某事达成～ reach an agreement on sth.

协约 xiéyuē agreement; convention: ～国 the Entente countries; the Allies

协助 xiézhù assist; help; give assistance; provide help

协奏曲 xiézòuqǔ concerto

协作 xiézuò cooperation; coordination: 经济～区 economically coordinated regions

胁 xié ①〈名〉the upper part of the side of a human body ②

〈动〉coerce；force：裹～ force to take part；coerce (sb. into doing sth.)

胁持 xiéchí hold sb. under duress；abduct

胁从 xiécóng be an accomplice under duress；submit under duress：～分子 accomplice under duress；unwilling (reluctant) followers

胁迫 xiépò coerce；compel

xiě

写 xiě〈动〉① write with a pen，etc.：默～ write from memory ② compose：～诗 compose a poem ③ depict；describe：～景 describe the scenery

写本 xiěběn hand-copied book

写法 xiěfǎ ① style of writing；literary style ② style of handwriting；penmanship

写稿 xiěgǎo write an article (for a magazine，etc.)：为儿童刊物～ contribute to children's magazines

写生 xiěshēng paint from life；draw (paint，sketch) from nature；make life sketches：静物～ still life (painting)．人物～ portrait from life

写实 xiěshí write or paint realistically；realistic：～小说 realistic novel．～主义 realism

写意 xiěyì write or paint according to one's impressions：～画 freehand drawing

写照 xiězhào (succinct) portrayal；portraiture；description

写真 xiězhēn draw a portrait；portray a person；mirror；portrait

写字楼 xiězìlóu office building

写作 xiězuò writing：～讲习班 writing clinic

血 xiě〈名〉blood：一滴～ a drop of blood

另见 xuè

xiè

亵 xiè ①〈动〉treat with irreverence；be disrespectful：猥～ act indecently towards a woman ②〈形〉obscene；profane：～渎的语言 profane (obscene) language

亵渎 xièdú blaspheme；desecrate；pollute；defile：～神明 blaspheme the gods

泻 xiè〈动〉① flow quickly；pour out；rush down：倾～ come down in torrents ② have loose bowels：吐～ vomit and have diarrhoea

泻肚 xièdù have loose bowels；have diarrhoea

泻药 xièyào purgative；laxative；cathartic

泄 xiè〈动〉① discharge；release：～洪 release floodwater ② let out；reveal；divulge；leak：这消息已～漏出去了。The news has leaked out. ③ give vent to；vent：～私愤 vent personal spite

泄底 xièdǐ reveal or expose what

gy

形体 xíngtǐ ① shape (of a person's body); physique; body ② form and structure

形同虚设 xíngtóng xūshè perform practically no function

形象 xíngxiàng image; figure:～树立 image-building. ～思维 thinking in (terms of) images

形形色色 xíngxíng-sèsè of all shades; of all descriptions; of all stripes; of various forms; of all kinds; of every kind; all brands of; of every hue

形影不离 xíngyǐng-bùlí (of two people) be inseparable; on very close terms; keep close to each other all the time; be always in company with each other:我们俩～。We buddy-buddied together.

形制 xíngzhì [考古] shapes

形状 xíngzhuàng shape; appearance; form

形"左"实右 xíngzuǒ shíyòu "Left" in form but Right in essence

刑 xíng〈名〉① punishment:从～ accessary punishment ② torture; corporal punishment:动～ subject sb. to torture

刑不当罪 xíngbùdàngzuì unsuitable punishment for the crime

刑场 xíngchǎng execution ground

刑典 xíngdiǎn criminal law

刑罚 xíngfá penalty; punishment; criminal punishment:～处罚 criminal penalities. ～学 penology

刑法 xíngfǎ criminal law; penal law

刑警 xíngjǐng criminal police

刑具 xíngjù instruments of torture; implements of punishment

刑律 xínglǜ criminal law:触犯～ violate the criminal law

刑满释放 xíngmǎn shìfàng be released after serving the full term of a sentence; be released after serving a sentence:～证 certificate of completion of sentence and release

刑期 xíngqī term of punishment (imprisonment); prison term; term of the sentence

刑事 xíngshì criminal:～犯 criminal (offender). ～处分 criminal sanction. ～辩护律师 criminal lawyer. ～调查 criminal investigation. ～法庭 criminal court. ～诉讼法 criminal procedure law. ～责任 crimical responsibility

刑讯 xíngxùn inquisition by torture:～逼供 use torture to coerce a statement

型 xíng〈名〉① type; pattern:成～ take shape ② mould:铸～ a casting mould

型钢 xínggāng section steel; shape

型号 xínghào size and type; type; model

行 xíng〈动〉① walk; go; run; sail:环～ go in a ring. ～船 sail a boat ② travel:欧洲之～ a trip to Europe ③ do; carry out; perform:～善 do good. 履

～职责 perform one's duty ④ be current; prevail; circulate: 风～一时 be popular for a time ⑤〈名〉behaviour; conduct: 好品～ good conduct ⑥〈形〉competent; capable: 他在这方面不～。He's not good at these things. ⑦ temporary: ～都 temporary capital

另见 háng

行板 xíngbǎn andante

行不通 xíngbutōng prove impractical; won't do (work); get (one) nowhere; can not be put into effect; be infeasible

行车 xíngchē drive a vehicle: ～速度 driving speed. ～执照 driver's license

行程 xíngchéng route or distance of travel; journey

行成于思 xíngchéngyúsī A deed is accomplished through taking thought.; Success depends on forethought.

行刺 xíngcì assassinate

行得通 xíngdetōng will do (work); be feasible

行动 xíngdòng ① move (about): ～不便 have difficulty getting about ② take action; act: ～起来 go into action ③ action; deed: 集体～ collective action

行方便 xíng fāngbian make things convenient for sb.

行宫 xínggōng imperial palace for short stays away from the capital; temporary dwelling place of an emperor when away from the capital

行贿 xínghuì bribe; offer (give, hand out) bribes to; resort to bribery

行将 xíngjiāng about to; on the verge of: ～灭亡的时候 on the verge of extinction

行劫 xíngjié commit robbery; rob: 拦路～ hold sb. up

行径 xíngjìng act; action; move; conduct: 可耻的～ shameful act

行军 xíngjūn (of troops) march

行乐 xínglè make merry; indulge in pleasures

行李 xíngli luggage; baggage

行礼 xínglǐ [军礼] (make a) salute; [鞠躬] (make a) bow

行骗 xíngpiàn practise fraud; swindle; cheat

行期 xíngqī date of departure

行乞 xíngqǐ beg one's bread; go begging

行窃 xíngqiè steal; thieve

行人 xíngrén pedestrian: ～要走人行道。Pedestrians, keep to the sidewalk.

行商 xíngshāng itinerant merchant

行使 xíngshǐ perform; exercise: ～宪法规定的权利 exercise one's constitutional rights. ～管辖 exercise jurisdiction over

行驶 xíngshǐ (of a vehicle, ship) run; drive; sail; travel; go: 向西～ be going west

行事 xíngshì ① act; do; handle matters: 见机～ act according to circumstances ② conduct; behaviour

行书 xíngshū [书法] cursive handwriting; running hand; cursive script

行为 xíngwéi behaviour; conduct;action:～范例 behaviour pattern. 不法～ illegal act

行销 xíngxiāo be on sale; sell:～国内外 be on sale at home and abroad

行刑 xíngxíng carry out a death sentence; execute

行凶 xíngxiōng do violence (to sb.); commit physical assault; perpetrate:～案 case of assault. ～者 perpetrator

行医 xíngyī practise medicine (usu. on one's own)

行政 xíngzhèng administrative; executive:～处分 administrative sanction. ～人员 administrative personnel. ～部门 administrative department. ～法 administrative law. ～拘留 administrative detention. ～隶属关系 administrative webs of affiliation. ～手段 administrative measures

行装 xíngzhuāng outfit for a journey; travel kit; luggage:整理～ pack (up) one's things

行踪 xíngzōng whereabouts; track; sojourn:～不定 be of uncertain whereabouts; be on a trip of no fixed destination

xǐng

醒 xǐng〈动〉① wake (up); awake:惊～ wake up with a start ② regain consciousness; come to:她～过来了。She's come to. ③ be clear in mind:保持头脑清～ keep a cool head

醒酒 xǐngjiǔ dispel the effects of alcohol; sober up

醒目 xǐngmù striking (to the eye); catch the eye; attractive looking:～的广告 eye-catching advertisement

醒世 xǐngshì rouse (awaken) the world

醒悟 xǐngwù come to see the truth, one's error, etc.; come to realize the truth; wake up to reality

省 xǐng〈动〉① visit (usu. one's parents or elders):归～ go home to pay respects to one's parents ② examine oneself critically:反～ make a self-examination ③ become conscious of; come to realize; be aware:不～人事 lose consciousness

另见 shěng

省察 xǐngchá examine oneself critically; examine one's thoughts and conduct; scrutinize oneself

省亲 xǐngqīn return to visit one's parents or elders

省视 xǐngshì ① return to visit; visit; call upon ② examine carefully; inspect

省悟 xǐngwù 见"醒悟"

xìng

兴 xìng〈名〉interest; mood or desire to do sth.:余～ lingering interest

另见 xīng

兴冲冲 xìngchōngchōng joyfully;

merrily; gleefully

兴高采烈 xìnggāocǎiliè in (high) spirits; in great delight; with a cheerful heart; jubilant; rejoice over; go into raptures

兴会 xìnghuì a sudden flash of inspiration; inspired apprehension; brain wave

兴趣 xìngqù interest; taste; inspired interest (gusto):感～ be interested (in). 对音乐有～ have an interest in music

兴头儿上 xìngtóurshang at the height of one's enthusiasm

兴味 xìngwèi interest; zest:～索然 flat and insipid; extremely uninteresting; have lost all interest in sth.; bored stiff. ～盎然 with keen (genuine) interest

兴致 xìngzhì mood to enjoy; interest:～勃勃 be of good cheer; be in spirits; (act) with great gusto

幸

幸 xìng ①〈名〉happiness; good fortune:～说 happiness theory ②〈动〉congratulate oneself; rejoice ③〈副〉by luck; fortunately:～未成灾。Fortunately it didn't cause a disaster.

幸臣 xìngchén favourite ministers of the sovereign; a favourite at court

幸福 xìngfú happiness; well-being:祝你～。I wish you happiness. ～的晚年 a happy life in one's remaining years

幸会 xìnghuì (a rather formal greeting) very pleased to meet you

幸亏 xìngkuī ① fortunately; luckily:～在我动身前雪停了。Fortunately the snow stopped before I started. ② thanks to:～他好意相助,我们提前完了工。Thanks to his kind help, we finished our work early.

幸免 xìngmiǎn have a narrow escape:～于难 have a narrow escape from death; escape death by sheer luck

幸事 xìngshì a piece of good fortune; a stroke of luck; blessing

幸运 xìngyùn ① lucky; fortunate ② good luck

幸灾乐祸 xìngzāi-lèhuò take pleasure in others' misfortune; gloat over others' misfortune; derive pleasure from others' misfortune

悻

悻 xìng

悻悻 xìngxìng resentful; angry:～而去 leave in a huff; go away angrily

杏

杏 xìng〈名〉apricot

杏脯 xìngfǔ sun-dried sweetened apricot; preserved sweetened apricot

杏花 xìnghuā apricot flower

杏黄 xìnghuáng apricot yellow; apricot

杏仁 xìngrén almond; apricot kernel

性

性 xìng〈名〉① nature; character; disposition:人～ human nature ② sex:～的本能 the sex distinct ③ gender:阳～ the masculine gender

性爱 xìng'ài sexual love

性别 xìngbié sexual distinction; sex;sexuality:～比例 sex ratio
性病 xìngbìng venereal disease; social disease; sexual diseases
性犯罪 xìngfànzuì sexual crime; sexual offence
性感 xìnggǎn sex appeal; sexy; sexuality: ～文学 sexy literature
性格 xìnggé nature; character; temperament; personality; disposition:～开朗 have a cheerful disposition. ～特写 character sketch. ～演员 character actor
性关系 xìngguānxì [法] carnal knowledge ; sexual intercourse
性急 xìngjí hasty; rash; impatient; short-tempered
性交 xìngjiāo have sex; sexual intercourse (commerce; act; relations)
性教育 xìngjiàoyù sex education
性禁忌 xìngjìnjì sex taboo
性命 xìngmìng life: ～攸关 (a matter) of life and death
性能 xìngnéng property: [机器等的]fuction; performance: ～试验 function (performance) test
性情 xìngqíng temper; temperament; disposition:～温柔 have a gentle disposition
性骚扰 xìngsāorǎo sexual harassment
性卫生 xìngwèishēng sex (social) hygiene
性文学 xìngwénxué literature on sexual love
性行为 xìngxíngwéi sexual behaviour; sex act
性欲 xìngyù sexual desire (passion, appetite)
性质 xìngzhì quality; nature; property:问题的～ nature of a problem
性状 xìngzhuàng properties:土壤的理化～ the physicochemical properties of soil

姓 xìng 〈名〉surname; family name:贵～ your surname
姓名 xìngmíng surname and personal name; full name
姓氏 xìngshì surnames: ～频率 frequency of surnames
姓系 xìngxì family line
姓族 xìngzú gens

xiōng

兄 xiōng 〈名〉elder brother:胞～ full (blood) elder brothers
兄弟 xiōngdì ① brothers ② fraternal; brotherly: ～民族 fraternal nationalities; fraternal ethnic groups. ～单位 fraternal units
兄长 xiōngzhǎng ① a respectful form of address for an elder brother ② a respectful form of address for a male friend

匈 xiōng〈旧〉breast
匈奴 xiōngnú Xiongnu or the Huns, an ancient nationality in China

凶 xiōng〈形〉① fierce; ferocious; fiendish:他这个人样子真～。He looks really fierce. ② ominous; inauspicious:～兆 ill omen; evil boding ③ terrible;

fearful:病势很～ terribly ill

凶暴 xiōngbào fierce and brutal; atrocious

凶残 xiōngcán savage and cruel

凶多吉少 xiōngduō-jíshǎo bode ill rather than well; be not a good omen:她长期住医院,终归～。After all, her long hospitalization is not a good omen.

凶恶 xiōng'è fierce; ferocious; fiendish; vicious

凶犯 xiōngfàn one who has committed homicide or mayhem; murderer

凶悍 xiōnghàn fierce and tough

凶狠 xiōnghěn fierce and malicious; ruthless; merciless

凶猛 xiōngměng fierce; violent; ferocious:来势～ with a terrifying force

凶年 xiōngnián year of famine; lean year; bad year

凶器 xiōngqì tool or weapon used to perpetrate a criminal act; lethal weapon

凶气 xiōngqì fierce manner; ferocious expression

凶杀 xiōngshā homicide; murder

凶手 xiōngshǒu murderer

凶险 xiōngxiǎn in a dangerous state; critical

凶相毕露 xiōngxiàng-bìlù look thoroughly ferocious; unleash all one's ferocity; reveal atrocious features; bare one's fangs; show one's teeth (ferocity)

凶宅 xiōngzhái haunted house; unlucky abode

凶兆 xiōngzhào illl omen; boding of evil

汹 xiōng

汹汹 xiōngxiōng ① (of seas, waves) roaring; turbulent ② violent; truculent:气势～ blustering and truculent ③ tumultuous; agitated:议论～ argue vociferously

汹涌 xiōngyǒng surge; run high; rage:～澎湃 rise in tempestuous waves; surge forward; torrential; sweeping and surging; rise in a surging tide; roll irresistibly onward; turbulent

胸 xiōng〈名〉① chest; breast; bosom:护～ chest protector ② heart; mind

胸靶 xiōngbǎ chest silhouette (used as a target in shooting practice)

胸部 xiōngbù thorax; chest:～手术 thoracic operation

胸怀 xiōnghuái ① mind; heart:～祖国 keep our country in mind; have our motherland at heart ② keep in mind; cherish:～大志 cherish high aspirations. ～坦白 largeness of mind; openhearted

胸襟 xiōngjīn (breadth of) mind:诗人的～ poet's mental capacity

胸口 xiōngkǒu the pit of the stomach; chest

胸膛 xiōngtáng chest:挺起～ throw out one's chest

胸围 xiōngwéi chest measurement; [女的] bust

胸无点墨 xiōngwúdiǎnmò ignorant; possess little learning; be unlettered; practically illiterate

胸像 xiōngxiàng bust

胸有成竹 xiōngyǒu-chéngzhú have (keep) a card up one's sleeve; have a well-thought-out plan (strategem); have a ready plan in mind

胸中无数 xiōngzhōng-wúshù have no idea as to how things stand; feel unsure of sth.

胸中有数 xiōngzhōng-yǒushù have a head for figures; have a good idea of how things stand; know well the true state of affairs

xióng

雄 xióng〈形〉① male: 雌～ male and female ② strong; powerful; mighty: 资力～厚的银行 a strong bank

雄辩 xióngbiàn eloquence: ～的口才 alchemies of eloquence. 事实胜于～。Facts speak louder than words.

雄才大略 xióngcái-dàlüè (of a man) great talent and bold vision; great wisdom coupled with bold strategy; rare gifts and bold strategy

雄风 xióngfēng ① strong wind ② awe-inspiring bearing; stately appearance

雄厚 xiónghòu ① strong; powerful; solid: ～的理论基础 solid theoretical basis ② rich; abundant: ～的资金 abundant funds

雄浑 xiónghún vigorous and firm; forceful vigour; forceful: ～的文学风格 virile literary style

雄健 xióngjiàn vigorous; robust; powerful: ～的笔力 virile style

雄赳赳 xióngjiūjiū valiantly; gallantly: ～气昂昂 be valiant and high-spirited

雄师 xióngshī powerful army; mighty army

雄伟 xióngwěi grand; magnificent; imposing; sublime: 一个伟大革命者的～胆略 the soaring and bold vision of a great revolutionary

雄心 xióngxīn lofty (great) ambition; high aspiration: ～壮志 lofty ambitions and high aims (great ideals); set one's sights high; great and lofty aspirations

雄壮 xióngzhuàng full of power and grandeur; power in strength and impetus; majestic; magnificent; powerful: ～的队伍 powerful contingents

雄主 xióngzhǔ king of great talent and bold vision; mighty emperor

熊 xióng 〈名〉 bear

熊包 xióngbāo good-for-nothing; coward

熊猫 xióngmāo panda: 大～ giant panda. 小～ lesser panda

熊瞎子 xióngxiāzi bear

熊熊 xióngxióng blazing; raging: ～的烈火 blazing fire; raging flames; fierce conflagration

xiū

羞 xiū ①〈形〉bashful; shy: ～怯

的微笑 a shy smile ②〈名〉shame;disgrace:因～惭而脸红 flush with shame ③〈动〉feel ashamed:～与为伍 consider it beneath one to associate with sb.

羞惭 xiūcǎn be ashamed; be abashed:为……感到～ feel ashamed of…

羞耻 xiūchǐ shame:不知～ have no sense of shame; be shameless

羞答答 xiūdādā shy; timid; sheepish; coy; bashful

羞感文明 xiūgǎn-wénmíng shame culture

羞愧 xiūkuì abashed; ashamed:～难言 be ashamed beyond words

羞恼 xiūnǎo be angry and ashamed

羞怯 xiūqiè timid; shy; shamefaced; sheepish

羞辱 xiūrǔ disgrace; shame; humiliation

羞恶 xiūwù feeling of shame and dislike

修 xiū〈动〉① repair; mend; overhaul:～表 repair a watch ② build; construct:～铁路 build a railway ③ revise:～订词典 revise a dictionary ④ compile; study:～历史 study history ⑤ trim; prune:～指甲 trim one's fingernails

修补 xiūbǔ repair; mend; patch (up); revamp:～衣服 patch clothes

修长 xiūcháng tall and thin; slender

修辞 xiūcí rhetoric:～学 rhetoric

修道院 xiūdàoyuàn monastery or convent

修订 xiūdìng revise:～报价 change in offer. ～本 revised edition. ～条约 revise a treaty

修复 xiūfù ① repair; restore; renovate ② repair (of destroyed cells or tissues)

修改 xiūgǎi alter; modify; revise; correct:～合同条款 modify the terms of a contract. ～权 power of amendment

修函 xiūhán write a letter

修好 xiūhǎo foster cordial relations between states; seek a rapprochement with

修旧利废 xiūjiù-lìfèi repair the old equipment and make use of waste material; repair and utilize old or discarded things

修理 xiūlǐ repair; mend; patch; fix:～机器 repair a machine

修面 xiūmiàn shave; have a shave

修配 xiūpèi make repairs and supply replacements

修缮 xiūshàn (of buildings) repair; revamp; renovate; refurbish:～老房子 refurbish an old house

修身 xiūshēn cultivate one's moral character; cultivating character; self-cultivation of character; moral culture

修饰 xiūshì ① embellish; decorate; adorn:用彩色电灯把大楼～起来 adorn a building with multi-coloured lamps ② polish (a piece of writing) ③ qualify; modify:～语[语] modifier

修养 xiūyǎng ① accomplishment;

training; culture:文化～很高的人 man of considerable culture. 有艺术～ be artistically accomplished ② self-cultivation

修业 xiūyè study at school:～年限 length of schooling. ～期满 finish one's school training. ～证书 certificate of showing courses attended

修正 xiūzhèng correct; revise; amend:～案 amendment

修筑 xiūzhù build; construct; put up

休 xiū〈动〉① stop; cease:～战 cease fire; truce ② rest:停下工作～息一下 rest (up) from one's work

休怪 xiūguài don't blame

休会 xiūhuì adjourn:无限期～ adjourn indefinitely

休假 xiūjià have a holiday or vacation; be on leave:～2 周 have two weeks' holiday

休克 xiūkè ① shock:处于～状态 be in a state of shock ② go into shock

休眠火山 xiūmián huǒshān dormant volcano

休戚 xiūqī joys and sorrows:～相关 be of close concern to each other; be bound together in a common cause; mutually affected; share joys and sorrows; be linked together in common joys and sorrows; share good and bad luck

休戚与共 xiūqī-yǔgòng share the same fate; throw in one's lot with; stand together through thick and thin; bound together in a comon cause

休憩 xiūqì have (take) a rest; rest

休息 xiūxi take a rest; have a day off; rest:～日 rest day; off day. ～室 rest room;[剧场] lobby; lounge

休闲 xiūxián lie fallow

休想 xiūxiǎng don't cherish any illusion that; it is impossible for sb. (to do); there is no chance for sb. (to do):她～抵赖。It is impossible for her to deny it.

休学 xiūxué suspend one's schooling without losing one's status as a student; be suspended from school

休养 xiūyǎng recruit oneself; recuperate:～生息 recuperate and multiply; recuperate and build up strength. ～所 rest home; sanitorium

休业 xiūyè suspention of business

休战 xiūzhàn truce; cease-fire; armistice

休整 xiūzhěng [军]rest and reorganize; rest and consolidation

休止 xiūzhǐ stop; cease; suspend:无～地 without end; ceaselessly

xiǔ

朽 xiǔ〈形〉① rotten; decayed:枯～ withered and rotten ② senile:老～ old and useless

朽坏 xiǔhuài decayed; rotten

朽木 xiǔmù rotten wood:～不可雕。One can't carve on rotten wood.; There is no hope for a good-for-nothing.

xiù

袖 xiù ①〈名〉sleeve：拂～ give a flick of one's sleeve ②〈动〉tuck inside the sleeve；put into the sleeve

袖标 xiùbiāo armband or badge worn on the sleeve for identification

袖手旁观 xiùshǒu-pángguān look on (stand by) with folded arms；look on unconcerned

袖章 xiùzhāng armband；sleeve badge

袖珍 xiùzhēn pocket：～合订本 pocket-size，single-volume edition. ～词典 pocket dictionary. ～照相机 vest-pocket camera

秀 xiù〈形〉① elegant；handsome；beautiful；delicate：清～ pretty and elegant ② excellent：优～ excellent；outstanding ③〈动〉(of grain crops) put ears and flowers

秀才 xiùcai ① a holder of a low degree in the imperial examination system ② scholar；intellectual

秀丽 xiùlì beautiful；pretty；fine：他书法～。He writes a beautiful hand.

秀气 xiùqì ① delicate；fine ② urbane；refined

秀色可餐 xiùsè-kěcān be a feast to the eye (usu. said of a very attractive woman，sometimes of beautiful scenery)

锈 xiù〈名，动〉rust；become rusty：生～ get rusty

锈蚀 xiùshí corrosion

绣 xiù〈动〉embroider

绣工 xiùgōng ① embroidery worker ② embroidery；embroidery work

绣花 xiùhuā do embroidery；embroider：～枕头 embroidered pillow. ～被面 embroidered quilt cover

绣画 xiùhuà embroidered pictures

绣球 xiùqiú ball made of rolled coloured silk

绣像 xiùxiàng ① tapestry portrait；embroidered portrait ② exquisitely drawn portrait

臭 xiù〈名〉smell；odour
另见 chòu

臭味相投 xiùwèi-xiāngtóu have common tastes；be two of a kind；be of the same kidney；like drawn to like；Birds of a feather flock together.

臭腺 xiùxiàn scent gland (a gland which secretes an odoriferous substance)

嗅 xiù〈动〉smell；scent

嗅觉 xiùjué (sense of) smell；smelling；scent；nose：良好的～ a fine sense of smell

xū

圩 xū〈名〉country fair：赶～ go to a fair

吁 xū ①〈动〉sigh ②〈叹〉(expressing surprise or amazement) why; oh

吁吁 xuxu 〈象〉:气喘～ puff hard; pant

需 xū ①〈动〉need; want; require:这机器～要修理。This machine needs repairing. ②〈名〉necessaries; needs; necessities:社会公众～要 social public needs

需求 xūqiú requirement; demand

需要 xūyào need; demand; requirement:满足消费者的～ meet the requirements of the consumers

须 xū〈助动〉must; have to:我们必～服从命令。We must obey orders. ②〈名〉beard:假～ false beard

须发 xūfà beard and hair

须眉 xūméi beard and eyebrows—a man

须要 xūyào must; have to

须臾 xūyú moment; instant

须知 xūzhī the musts; notice; guide; tip:游览～ tourist guide; tip for tourists; information for tourists. 旅客～ notice to travellers

虚 xū〈形〉① void; empty; vacant:～字 empty words ② false; unreal:～假的多数 false majority ③ timid:心里有点～ feel rather diffident ④ humble; modest:～心使人进步。Modesty helps one to go forward. ⑤ weak:～弱本质 feeble nature

虚报 xūbào (give a) false report:～帐目 cook accounts

虚词 xūcí〔语〕form word; function word; expletive

虚度 xūdù spend time in vain; waste; idle away; fritter away:～光阴 fritter away one's time. ～青春 trifle away one's youth

虚构 xūgòu make up; fabricate; novelize:～的情节 fabricated (made-up) story. ～的人物 fictious (imaginary) character

虚幻 xūhuàn unreal; illusory

虚假 xūjiǎ unreal; false; sham:～的声势 sham preponderance. ～证明 false testimony

虚价 xūjià nominal price

虚惊 xūjīng false alarm:受了一场～ be the victim of a false alarm

虚夸 xūkuā boastful; exaggerative:～之言 boastful words

虚名 xūmíng undeserved(inflated) reputation; reputation without the facts to support it; idle fame; vain titles:徒有～ have only idle fame

虚拟 xūnǐ ① fabricated; invented; fictitious ② subjunctive; suppositional:～语气〔语〕subjunctive mood

虚情假意 xūqíng-jiǎyì hypocritical show of friendship; false display of affection

虚荣 xūróng vainglory; vanity:～心 vanity

虚弱 xūruò ① in poor health; debilitated; weak:体质～ have a weak constitution ② feeble; weak:～无能 weak and powerless

虚设 xūshè set up (exist) nominally:～的公司 bubble company

虚实 xūshí ① false or true—the actual situation (as of the opposing side) ② theoretical and practical

虚数 xūshù［数］imaginary number

虚脱 xūtuō［医］prostration; collapse

虚伪 xūwěi false; sham; hypocritical:～的友好态度 hypocritical friendship

虚无 xūwú nothingness; nihility:～缥渺 utterly visionary; with no reality whatever; vague with nothing in it. ～主义 nihilism

虚线 xūxiàn ① dotted line ②［数］imaginary line

虚心 xūxīn open-minded; modest and unassuming; modest; humble:～学习 learn with an open mind (from)

虚掩 xūyǎn (of a door or window) be left unlocked or unlatched

虚张声势 xūzhāng-shēngshì make a display; bluff; make a false show of strength; put up a bold front; make (raise) a big fanfare

虚字 xūzì empty word; function word; form word

墟 xū〈名〉ruins:成为废～ lie in ruins

嘘 xū〈动〉① breathe out slowly:～气 exhale slowly ② utter a sigh ③ (of cooking fire, steam, etc.) come into contact with sth.; scald; burn:把馒头在火上～一～。Put the steamed bread over the fire for a while. ④〈叹〉sh; hush:～!轻一点,他们刚睡下。Hush! They have just gone to bed. ⑤〈方〉hiss; boo

xú

徐 xú〈副〉① slowly; gently ② by and by

徐步 xúbù walk slowly

徐徐 xúxú slowly:五星红旗～升起。The Five-Starred Red Flag slowly went up the pole.

xǔ

许 xǔ〈动〉① praise:赞～ commend ② allow; permit:请允～我说几句话。Permit me to say a few words. ③〈副〉perhaps; maybe; about:也～他需要我们的帮助。Perhaps he is in need of our help.

许多 xǔduō many; much; a lot of

许久 xǔjiǔ (for) a long time:～以前 for ages; a long time ago

许可 xǔkě allow; permit:～证 license; permit; warrant

许诺 xǔnuò promise; make a promise; consent

许配 xǔpèi betroth one's daughter

许愿 xǔyuàn ① promise sb. a reward (for some service) ② make a vow (to a god)

诩 xǔ〈动〉brag; boast

栩 xǔ

栩栩如生 xǔxǔ-rúshēng lifelike; true to life:这幅像画得～。The portrait speaks.

xù

畜 xù〈动〉raise (domestic animals); rear

另见 chù

畜产 xùchǎn livestock products

畜力 xùlì animal traction

畜牧 xùmù raise livestock or poultry: ～业 livestock breeding; animal husbandry. ～场 livestock farm

蓄 xù〈动〉① store (up); save up:～水保墒 store water and retain soil moisture ② keep; grow:～须 grow a beard ③ entertain (ideas)

蓄电池 xùdiànchí storage battery; accumulator

蓄洪 xùhóng store floodwater:～工程 flood storage project. ～区 flood storage areas

蓄积 xùjī save up; store up:～粮食 store up grain

蓄谋 xùmóu premeditate

蓄水 xùshuǐ retain (store) water

蓄养 xùyǎng build up; accumulate

蓄意 xùyì premeditated; deliberate:～挑衅 provoke premeditatedly; premeditated provocation

酗 xù

酗酒 xùjiǔ ① excessive drinking; intemperance: ～闹事 make trouble after getting drunk ② alcoholism; be mad with wine

叙 xù〈动〉① relate; narrate:～述一个实验的过程 narrate the process of an experiment ② talk; chat:～家常 chitchat ③ appraise; assess: ～功 assess service and give credit for it ④〈名〉foreword; preface

叙别 xùbié have a farewell talk (with); say good-bye (to)

叙旧 xùjiù talk about old times

叙事 xùshì narrate; relate; recount:～诗 epic (poem); heroic poem

叙述 xùshù relate; recount; tell; narrate:～学 narratology

叙说 xùshuō tell; narrate (in speech)

恤 xù〈动〉① pity; sympathize:怜～ have compassion on ② give relief; compensate

恤金 xùjīn pension

旭 xù

旭日 xùrì rising sun:～初升。The sun is just up.

序 xù〈名〉① order; sequence:按字母次～排列 be arranged in alphabetical order ② foreword; preface:在本书的～言中 in the preface to this book

序跋 xùbá preface and postscript

序目 xùmù preface and table of contents

序幕 xùmù prelude; prologue:战役的～ prelude to a battle

序曲 xùqǔ [乐] overture

序数 xùshù ordinal (number)

序言 xùyán preface:[特指非作者自己写的] foreword; prelude; preamble

絮 xù〈名〉(cotton) wadding; (willow) catkin; wad with cotton

絮叨 xùdao garrulous; wordy; prattle on; babble; grumble

絮棉 xùmián cotton for wadding; padding (wadding) cotton

絮语 xùyǔ ① prattle on ② endless chatter

婿 xù〈名〉① son-in-law ② husband:姐～ elder sister's husband

绪 xù〈名〉thread; order in sequence

绪论 xùlùn introduction

绪言 xùyán introductory remarks; introduction

续 xù〈动〉① continue; extend; join:继～做某事 continue doing (to do) sth. ② supply more; add:炉子该～煤了。The fire needs more coal。③〈形〉supplementary

续编 xùbiān supplementary volume; continuation (of a book); sequel

续订 xùdìng renew one's subscription (to a newspaper,etc)

续航力 xùhánglì endurance; flying range (of an airplane); cruising radius (of a ship)

续集 xùjí continuation (of a book); sequel

续假 xùjià extend one's leave; have one's leave extended:～一个星期 have one's leave extened for another week

续建 xùjiàn resume construction

续借 xùjiè renew (a library book)

续弦 xùxián ① remarry after the death of one's wife ② a second wife (after the death of one's first wife)

续约 xùyuē ① renew a treaty or contract ② a renewed treaty or contract; a supplementary contract

续展 xùzhǎn extend exhibit period

xuān

宣 xuān〈动〉① declare; announce; proclaim:～战 proclaim war ② propagate; publicize:～传和落实政策 progagate and carry out the policies

宣笔 xuānbǐ *Xuan* writing-brush, a high-quality writing-brush made in Xuancheng in Anhui Province

宣布 xuānbù declare; proclaim; announce:～共和国成立 proclaim (the country) a republic. ～无效 declare sth. invalid

宣称 xuānchēng allege; assert; profess

宣传 xuānchuán conduct propaganda; propagate; give publicity to; publicize; disseminate; give currency to; talk profusely about; talk a great deal about: ～工具 means of propaganda; mass media

宣读 xuāndú read out (in public): ～选举结果 read out the result of the voting

宣告 xuāngào declare; proclaim; announce; pronounce: ～无效 declare sth. null and void. ～无罪 pronounce sb. not guilty; announcement of not guilty. ～判决 pronounce a judgment

宣讲 xuānjiǎng ① explain and publicise (a policy, decree, etc.) ② preach (a religious doctrine)

宣教 xuānjiào progaganda and education

宣判 xuānpàn pass a sentence; pronounce a judgment (on); adjudge; sentence: ～徒刑 3 年 pronounce a sentence of three years on sb.

宣誓 xuānshì take an oath; make a pledge; swear (an oath): ～就职 be sworn in; take the oath of office

宣泄 xuānxiè ① get sth. off one's chest; unbosom oneself ② lead off (liquids); drain

宣言 xuānyán declaration; manifesto; proclamation

宣扬 xuānyáng give publicity to; advocate; propagate; advertise: ～好人好事 give publicity to good people and their good deeds. 大肆～ make a great noise about; ballyhoo

宣战 xuānzhàn declare(proclaim) war (on)

宣纸 xuānzhǐ rice paper; *Xuan* paper

宣旨 xuānzhǐ proclaim an imperial edict

喧

xuān〈形〉noisy

喧宾夺主 xuānbīn-duózhǔ The person (or matter) of greater importance is relegated to the background.; The secondary replaces the primary.; The sauce is better than the fish.; The person who plays second fiddle steals the limelight.

喧哗 xuānhuá make a noise; clamour; brawl: 禁止～。Make no noise.

喧闹 xuānnào noise and excitement; brawl; uproar; bustle

喧嚷 xuānrǎng clamour; din; hubbub; row

喧扰 xuānrǎo tumult; noise and disturbance

喧天 xuāntiān fill the air with noises; be terribly noisy

喧嚣一时 xuānxiāo-yīshí bluster for a time; stir up a commotion; raise a hue and cry for a while; very noisy for a time; sth. creates quite a stir

轩

xuān〈形〉lofty; high

轩昂 xuān'áng dignified; imposing

轩敞 xuānchǎng spacious and bright

轩然大波 xuānrán-dàbō (create) a big stir; (create) a great disturbance

xuán

旋

xuán〈动〉① revolve; turn; circle: 回～ circle round ② be back; return: ～里 return home 另见 xuàn

旋律 xuánlǜ [乐] melody

旋涡 xuánwō whirlpool; vortex; [小的]eddy; [大的]maelstrom: ～画派 vorticism

旋转 xuánzhuǎn revolve; spin; rotate; gyrate: ～球[体] spinning ball. ～舞台 trick scene

旋转乾坤 xuánzhuǎn-qiánkūn effect a drastic change in nature or the established order of a country; be earthshaking

漩 xuán〈名〉whirlpool; eddy; vortex

玄 xuán〈形〉① black; dark: ～狐 a black fox ② profound; abstruse ③ unreliable; incredible: 这话太～了。That's a pretty tall story.

玄表 xuánbiǎo signs in the dark beyond (i.e., the heaven)

玄乎 xuánhu fantastic; incredible

玄机 xuánjī secret key

玄览 xuánlǎn mystic vision

玄理 xuánlǐ mysticism

玄妙 xuánmiào abstruse; mysterious

玄孙 xuánsūn great-great grandson

玄武岩 xuánwǔyán basalt

玄象 xuánxiàng mysterious signs

玄虚 xuánxū deceitful; trick; mystery: 故弄～ deliberately mystify sth.; purposely turn simple things into mysteries; deliberately juggle with false ideas to hide the truth

玄学 xuánxué ① metaphysics: ～派诗歌 metaphysical poetry ② learning of the mystery

悬 xuán〈动〉① hang (up); suspend: ～灯结彩 hang up lamps and drape festoons ② keeping thinking about: ～念 be concerned about (sb. who is elsewhere) ③〈形〉pending; unresolved: ～而未决的问题 outstanding issue; unsettled question ④〈副〉far apart: ～隔 be separated by a great distance

悬案 xuán'àn ① pending case; unsettled law case ② unsettled question; outstanding issue; question at issue

悬而未决 xuán'érwèijué ① be in suspense; be (hang) in the scale(s); ② outstanding; pending; remaining; not yet decided

悬浮 xuánfú suspension

悬挂 xuánguà hang; fly

悬河 xuánhé ① hanging river—a river (a section of it) high above the surrounding countryside ② cataract; waterfall ③ a copious, rapid flow of words

悬乎 xuánhu dangerous; unsafe

悬空 xuánkōng ① dangle in the air ② be divorced from practice

悬梁 xuánliáng hang oneself from a beam

悬念 xuánniàn ① be concerned about (sb. who is elsewhere) ② suspense (felt as a story, play, etc. builds to a climax)

悬赏缉拿 xuánshǎng-jīná offer a reward for the capture of sb.; set a price on a person's head

悬殊 xuánshū great difference (between); (a) wide disparity (between); wide gap (between)：贫富～ a wide gap between the rich and the poor

悬腕 xuánwàn suspend the wrist (i.e. hold both wrist and elbow above the table when writing large characters, thus allowing the brush to operate over a greater ambit)

悬崖 xuányá overhanging cliff; precipice：～勒马 rein in (one's horse) on (at) the brink of the precipice; pull back before it is too late; stop riding into imminent disaster; desist from doing sth. before it is too late

悬帐 xuánzhàng［簿记］suspense account

xuǎn

癣 xuǎn〈名〉tinea; ringworm

选 xuǎn〈动〉① choose; select：从这些书中挑～2本 choose two from (among, out of) these books ② elect：被～到新的领导岗位 be elected to a new leading post

选拔 xuǎnbá screening; select; choose：～赛［体］tryouts; trials. ～运动员 select (draft) athletes

选本(集) xuǎnběn (jí) selected works; anthology; selections

选编 xuǎnbiān ① select and compile ② (usu. used in book titles) a collection of selected materials

选材 xuǎncái ① select a suitable person ② select suitable materials

选调 xuǎndiào recruit：～各地优秀运动员集中训练 recruit top-notch athletes from all over the country for intensified training

选读 xuǎndú ① pick out (pieces or passages) to read; read excerpts ② selected readings

选购 xuǎngòu pick out and buy; choose and buy：～商品 selective purchase; commodites purchased by choice. 欢迎～。You are welcome to make choice.

选辑 xuǎnjí compile; edit

选举 xuǎnjǔ elect; vote for：～权 right to vote; right to elect. ～法 electoral law. 差额～ competitive election. 等额～ non-competitive election

选民 xuǎnmín voter; elector;［集体］electorate：～榜 list of eligible voters. ～登记 registration of voters. ～证 voter's card

选派 xuǎnpài select; detail

选票 xuǎnpiào voting paper; vote; ballot

选区 xuǎnqū electoral district

选曲 xuǎnqǔ selected songs

选手 xuǎnshǒu［体］(selected) contestant; athlete;［球类的］player：优秀～ ace athlete. 种子～ seeded player; seed

选送 xuǎnsòng select and recommend sb. (for a position or for admission to a school, etc.)

选题 xuǎntí ① select a title, subject or topic (for writing or research) ② the title, subject or topic selected

选修 xuǎnxiū take… as an elective

course：～法语 take French as an elective course. ～课 elective (optional) (course)

选样 xuǎnyàng sampling

选择 xuǎnzé ① make a choice; choose; select; opt; pick (out)：～题测验 forced-choice test ② alternative：除……外别无～ have no alternative but (to do)…

选种 xuǎnzhǒng［农］seed selection：～育种 select and cultivate

选中 xuǎnzhòng pick on; decide on; settle on

xuàn

旋 xuàn〈动〉① whirl：树叶在风中回～。The leaves whirled in the wind. ② turn sth. on a lathe; lathe：～工 lathe operator; turner

旋床 xuànchuáng［机］(turning) lathe

旋风 xuànfēng whirlwind; cyclone

渲 xuàn

渲染 xuànrǎn ①［图画］apply colours to (a painting); colour ② play up; exaggerate; dwell excessively on：～战争恐怖 play up (dwell excessively on) the horrors of war

炫 xuàn〈动〉① dazzle; glare ② make a show (of); display：自～其能 show off one's ability

炫目 xuànmù glaring; dazzling; blinding：光彩～ blindingly bright

炫弄 xuànnòng show off; display; parade：～技巧 show off one's skill

炫耀 xuànyào ① make a display (of); cut a dash (figure); flaunt; parade：～学问 parade one's learning ② glaring

眩 xuàn〈形〉① dizzy; giddy：头晕目～ feel dizzy ② bewildered; dazzled：～于名利 dazzled by the prospect of fame and wealth

眩晕 xuànyùn ① dizziness ② vertigo

绚 xuàn〈形〉gorgeous

绚烂 xuànlàn gorgeous; resplendent; florid

绚丽 xuànlì splendid; magnificent; gorgeous：～多彩 bright and colourful

xuē

靴 xuē〈名〉boots：～子 boots

削 xuē〈动〉peel; cut; pare
另见 xiāo

削发 xuēfà cut off the hair (as a sign of renouncing the worldly life and entering the monkhood or nunhood); take the tonsure

削价 xuējià reduce (cut) prices; lower the price：～出售 sell at a reduced price

削减 xuējiǎn cut down; reduce; slash; whittle down：～预算 slash the budget

削弱 xuēruò weaken; impair;

cripple; curtail:～……基础 undermine the foundation of

削职 xuēzhí remove from office

削足适履 xuēzú-shìlǚ trim the toes to fit the shoes; cut (whittle down) the toes to fit the shoes; act in defiance of reality

xué

学 xué〈动〉① study; learn:～法律 study law ② imitate:～鸡叫 mimic the crowing of a cock 〈名〉③ learning; knowledge:西～ Western learning ④ school; college:中～ middle schools

学报 xuébào (learned, academic) journal;[学术团体的]transactions

学步邯郸 xuébù-hándān imitate others slavishly and lose one's own originality

学部 xuébù ① the Board of Education in the Qing Dynasty ② departments of the Chinese Academy of Sciences

学潮 xuécháo student strike (unrest); campus upheaval

学到手 xuédàoshǒu really master; have a real grasp of:把英语～ master the English language

学而优则仕 xué'éryōuzéshì Good scholar will make an official.; He who excels in learning can be official.

学阀 xuéfá scholar-lord; scholar-tyrant

学非所用 xuéfēisuǒyòng One does not do what one has learned.

学费 xuéfèi school fee; charging tuition and fees; tuition (fee): 付～ pay school fee

学分 xuéfēn (academic) credit:～豁免制 credit exemption. ～制 credit system

学风 xuéfēng style of study:～严谨 be rigorous in one's studies

学府 xuéfǔ institution of higher learning; seat of learning

学贯古今 xuéguàn-gǔjīn be well versed in both ancient and modern learning

学海 xuéhǎi ① like streams flowing ceaselessly until they reach the sea—persevering in one's studies until one reaches the goal ② sea of learning—a learned scholar

学坏 xuéhuài ① follow bad examples ②[通常与"了"连用] be corrupted by bad examples

学会 xuéhuì ① master; learn ② (learned) society; institute

学籍 xuéjí one's status as a student:保留～ retain one's name on the school roll. 开除～ be dismissed from school

学究 xuéjiū pedant

学刊 xuékān (academic) journal

学科 xuékē branch of learning; course (of study); subject; discipline:～带头人 leaders in their chosen fields of learning

学理 xuélǐ scientific principle or law; academic theory

学历 xuélì record of formal schooling; educational background; academic career

学力 xuélì academic attainments;

educational level; knowledge: 具有同等～ have the same educational level (as school graduates)

学龄 xuélíng school age: ～儿童 school-age children; schoolable children

学名 xuémíng ① formal name ② scientific name

学年 xuénián school year; academic year: ～考试 year-end examination

学派 xuépài school (of thought)

学时 xuéshí class hour; period

学识 xuéshí learning; knowledge; scholarly attainments; acquirements: ～渊博 of great learning; learned; erudite

学士 xuéshì ① scholar ② [学位] bachelor: 文～ Bachelor of Arts (B. A.). 理～ Bachelor of Science (B. S.). ～学位 bachelor's degree; bachelorship

学术 xuéshù learning; science: ～交流 academic exchange. ～界 academic circles (world). ～论文 treatise; dissertation; research (scientific, academic) paper. ～论坛 academic forum. ～思想 academic thought; learned thought

学说 xuéshuō theory; doctrine; teachings

学徒 xuétú trainee; apprentice: 当～ serve one's apprenticeship

学位 xuéwèi (academic) degree

学问 xuéwèn knowledge; learning; scholarship: ～家 scholars. 做～ engage in scholarship; do research

学无止境 xuéwúzhǐjìng There is no limit to knowledge.; Knowledge knows no limit (bounds).

学业 xuéyè one's studies; school work

学艺 xuéyì ① learn a craft or trade ② knowledge and skills

学员 xuéyuán student; [训练班] trainee

学院 xuéyuàn college; institute; academy: ～哲学 school philosophy. 外国语言～ the institute of foreign languages

学者 xuézhě scholar; learned man; man of learning: ～名流 scholar elite

学制 xuézhì ① educational system ② length (period) of schooling

学子 xuézǐ student

噱

xué 〈方〉 laugh: 发～ make one laugh

噱头 xuétóu ① words or act meant to amuse or to excite laughter: 卖弄～ play to the gallery ② tricks meant to deceive: 不要摆～! None of your tricks! ③ amusing; funny; comical

穴

xué 〈名〉 ① opening; cave; hole: ～居人 cave dwellers ② den; lair: 匪～ bandits' lair. 虎～ tiger's den ③ [针灸] acupuncture point

穴播 xuébō [农] bunch planting

穴居 xuéjū live in caves; cave dwelling; pit dwelling: ～的初民 primitive spelean people. ～

时代 cave period
穴位 xuéwèi acupuncture point; acupoint

xuě

雪 xuě ①〈名〉snow ②〈动〉clear oneself (of); rehabilitate: 洗～ wipe out a disgrace; clear sb. of a false charge
雪白 xuěbái snow-white; snowy: ～的头发 snowy hair
雪崩 xuěbēng snowslide; avalanche
雪耻 xuěchǐ avenge an insult; wipe out a humiliation (disgrace)
雪糕 xuěgāo ice cream
雪恨 xuěhèn avenge: 报仇～ take revenge; avenge oneself (on)
雪亮 xuěliàng bright as snow; shiny: ～的眼睛 sharp-sighted
雪片 xuěpiàn snowflake (usu. fig.)
雪冤 xuěyuān be cleared of a false charge; get exonerated (from an accusation)
雪中送炭 xuězhōng-sòngtàn send charcoal in snowy weather—provide timely help; offer fuel in snowy weather; send a present of firewood in cold weather; timely assistance

xuè

血 xuè〈名〉① blood: 呕～ spit blood ② related by blood: ～亲 blood relation
另见 xiě
血案 xuè'àn murder (case)
血沉 xuèchén erythrocyte sedimentation rate (ESR)
血仇 xuèchóu blood feud
血防工作 xuèfáng gōngzuò schistosomiasis prevention
血管 xuèguǎn blood vessel
血海深仇 xuèhǎi-shēnchóu huge debt of blood; intense and deep-seated hatred
血汗 xuèhàn sweat and blood: ～钱 wages earned by hard toil; hard-earned money
血口喷人 xuèkǒu-pēnrén make slanderous charges against sb.; venomously slander; malicious words to injure sb.
血库 xuèkù blood bank
血泪 xuèlèi tears of blood: ～史 history written in blood and tears
血淋淋 xuèlīnlīn dripping with blood; bloody
血气 xuèqì ① blood and vital spirits; sap; vigour: ～方刚 be in one's hot youth; be full of vigour (sap) ② courage and uprightness; uprightness and staunchness of character: 有～的青年 a young man of strong will and moral integrity
血亲 xuèqīn blood relation; consanguineous relative: ～婚姻 consanguineous marriage
血肉 xuèròu flesh and blood: ～关系 blood kinship. ～相连 flesh and blood relationship; be closely linked as flesh and blood; as close as flesh and

blood

血色 xuèsè redness of the face; colour

血书 xuèshū letter (expressing one's determination, last wish, etc.) written in one's own blood

血栓 xuèshuān thrombus

血糖 xuètáng blood sugar

血统 xuètǒng blood relationship; blood lineage; extraction; descent: ～工人 workers of working class origin

血吸虫 xuèxīchóng blood fluke: ～病 schistosomiasis; snail fever

血小板 xuèxiǎobǎn [生理] (blood) platelet

血腥 xuèxīng bloody; sanguinary; bloodstained: ～统治 bloodstained (sanguinary) rule. ～镇压 bloody suppression

血型 xuèxíng [生理] blood type; blood group

血压 xuèyā [生理] blood pressure: 高～ high blood pressure; hypertension. 低～ low blood pressure; hypotension

血缘 xuèyuán ties of blood; blood relationship; kinship

血友病 xuèyǒubìng [医] haemophilia

血债 xuèzhài blood debt: ～累累 heavy blood debts

血战 xuèzhàn bloody (sanguinary) battle: 同敌人～到底 fight the enemy to the bitter end

血渍 xuèzì bloodstain

血族 xuèzú cognates: ～关系 ties of lineage

谑 xuè 〈动〉crack a joke; banter; tease

xūn

勋 xūn 〈名〉exploit; meritorious service; brilliant feats; merit: 奇～ distinguished service

勋臣 xūnchén meritorious ministers

勋绩 xūnjì meritorious service; brilliant feats

勋爵 xūnjué lord

勋戚 xūnqī distinguished imperial relatives; favoured relatives of the emperor

勋章 xūnzhāng medal; decoration

熏 xūn 〈动〉① smoke; fumigate: ～火腿 smoked hem ② cultivate; influence

熏炉 xūnlú incense burner

熏染 xūnrǎn exert a gradual, corrupting influence on

熏肉 xūnròu smoked meat

熏陶 xūntáo exert a gradual, uplifting influence on; nurture; edify (exert) influence on

熏制 xūnzhì smoke; fumigate (sth. with jasmine, etc.)

xún

询 xún 〈动〉 ask; inquire: 查～ inquire about; make inquiries

询问 xúnwèn ask (about); inquire (about, after): ～某人的健康 inquire after sb.'s health ② question; interrogate:～被告人 interrogate the defendant

循 xún〈动〉follow; abide by; carry on as before:因～ follow; carry on as before

循规蹈矩 xúnguī-dǎojǔ follow the custom (rules, orders, law) docilely; observe due decorum; stick to convention; conform to convention; toe the line

循环 xúnhuán circulation; circle; cycle:～变化 cyclical change. ～赛[体]round robin series; (play) round robin

循例 xúnlì in accordance with the usual practice

循名责实 xúnmíng-zéshí expect the reality to correspond to the name; require the reality to correspond to the name

循序 xúnxù in proper order or sequence; in succession:～渐进 follow in order and advance step by step; go on step by step; make steady progress; proceed systematically

循循善诱 xúnxún-shànyòu be good at giving systematic guidance; teach with skill and patience

旬 xún〈名〉① a period of ten days:下～ the last ten days of a month ②[用于老年人的年龄] a peiod of ten years:八～老母 80-year-old mother

旬刊 xúnkān a publication appearing once every ten days

旬日 xúnrì ten days

巡 xún〈动〉patrol; make an inspection tour:出～ go out on an inspection tour

巡边员 xúnbiānyuán linesman

巡查 xúnchá make one's rounds; make an inspection (of)

巡航 xúnháng cruise:～导弹 cruise missile

巡回 xúnhuí make a circuit of; go the rounds:～演出队 mobile troupe. ～医疗 mobile medical service; medical tour

巡警 xúnjǐng patrolling policeman; patrolman

巡逻 xúnluó (go on) patrol:～队 patrol party

巡视 xúnshì make an inspection tour; go one's rounds; inspect

巡洋舰 xúnyángjiàn cruiser

巡夜 xúnyè go on night patrol; keep night watch

巡诊 xúnzhěn (of a doctor) make one's rounds; go on one's rounds

寻 xún〈动〉look for; search (after, for); seek:～欢作乐 seek pleasure. 搜～ search for; seek (for)
另见 xín

寻常 xúncháng common; ordinary; usual:异乎～的 extraordinary

寻短见 xún duǎnjiàn commit suicide; take one's own life

寻根 xúngēn seek origin (root):～究底… go to the bottom of things; get at the roots of things. ～文学 literature seeking origins (roots)

寻呼 xúnhū paging:～机 pager; beeper

寻开心 xún kāixīn make fun of; poke fun at; joke

寻觅 xúnmì seek; look for

寻求 xúnqiú ① look for; try to find out ② explore; seek: ～真理 seek truth

寻思 xúnsi think to oneself; think

寻死 xúnsǐ ① try to commit suicide; attempt suicide ② commit suicide

寻衅 xúnxìn seek (pick) a quarrel; provoke: ～滋事 stir up fights and cause trouble

寻找 xúnzhǎo look for; search (after, for); seek (for)

xùn

训 xùn〈动〉① teach; lecture; train: ～人 give sb. a dressing down. 整～ train and consolidate (troops) ② reprove; admonish; rebuke

训斥 xùnchì reprove; rebuke; reprimand

训词 xùncí instructions

训导 xùndǎo instruct and guide

训诂 xùngǔ explanations of words in ancient books; commentary work on classics; exegesis: ～学 exegetics

训话 xùnhuà give an admonitory talk to subordinates

训诫 xùnjiè ① admonish; advise ② rebuke; reprimand ③ admonishing

训练 xùnliàn train; drill

训练班 xùnliànbān training course; training class

训令 xùnlìng written instructions from superiors

训示 xùnshì instructions or orders (to subordinates or younger members of one's family)

训育 xùnyù school education concerned with development of character; discipline

训政 xùnzhèng give instruction on administration; political tutelage

讯 xùn〈名〉① news; message: 电～ dispatch ② ask; interrogate; question

讯号 xùnhào radio signal; signal

讯问 xùnwèn interrogate; inquire; question: ～证人 question a witness

讯息交换 xùnxī jiāohuàn communication switching

迅 xùn〈形〉rapid; fast; swift: ～速生效 produce speedy results

迅即 xùnjí at once; without delay

迅急 xùnjí very fast; rapidly; at high speed

迅雷不及掩耳 xùnléi bùjí yǎn'ěr a sudden peal of thunder leaves no time for covering the ears; as sudden as lightning; with the suddenness of a thunderbolt; with lightning speed; (of actions) lightning flash before precautions can be taken

迅猛 xùnměng swift and violent; rapid and vigorous; rapid

迅速 xùnsù fast; rapid; swift: ～发展的行业 growth industry. ～康复 speedy recovery

驯 xùn ①〈形〉tame and docile: ～象 a tame elephant ②〈动〉

揠苗助长 yàmiáo-zhùzhǎng help (try to make) the shoots grow by pulling them up; pull the shoots upward in a stupid effort to make them grow; spoil the show by ludicrous enthusiasm

亚 yà〈形〉inferior; second; minor

亚当 Yàdāng Adam (the first man according to the Bible)

亚军 yàjūn[体]runner-up; second (place):获得～ get a second

亚麻 yàmá flax: ～布 linen (cloth)

亚热带 yàrèdài subtropics

亚运会 Yàyùnhuì the Asian Games

轧 yà〈动〉① gin:～棉厂 a cotton ginning factory ② roll; run over:～钢轨 roll steel rails ③ husk; hull ④ oust; jostle; push out:倾～ jostle against each other; engage in internal strife

另见 gá,zhá

轧板机 yàbǎnjī mangle

轧花 yàhuā cotton ginning:～机 cotton gin; gin

轧伤 yàshāng be run over and injured (by a car)

轧碎 yàsuì crush (to pieces); roll asunder

讶 yà be surprised; be astonished; wonder

yān

淹 yān 〈动〉flood; inundate; submerge

淹埋 yānmái (of mud, sand, etc.) flow or blow over and cover completely

淹没 yānmò flood; inundate; submerge:大雨～了低地。Heavy rainfalls flooded the lowlands.

淹死 yānsǐ be drowned

阉 yān〈动〉castrate:～马 castrating a horse

阉割 yāngē ① castrate; spay ② deprive a theory, etc. of its essence; emasculate; tamper with

阉人 yānrén ① a castrated person ② eunuch

腌 yān〈动〉preserve in salt; cure; corn; pickle: ～牛肉 corned beef. ～鱼 salted fish

腌菜 yāncài pickled vegetables; pickles

腌渍 yānzì preserve in brine, vinegar, etc.; pickle

烟 yān〈名〉① smoke:一团～ a cloud of smoke ② tobacco; cigarette; cigar:抽支～ have a cigarette ③ opium:～土 crude opium

烟波 yānbō mist-covered waters

烟草 yāncǎo tobacco

烟尘 yānchén ① smoke and dust ② battle; war

烟囱 yāncōng chimney; funnel:～林立 a forest of chimneys

烟斗 yāndǒu (tobacco) pipe

烟花爆竹 yānhuā bàozhú fireworks

烟火 yānhuǒ fireworks:放～ let

off fireworks
烟酒税 yānjiǔshuì wine and tobacco tax
烟煤 yānméi soft (bituminous) coal
烟幕 yanmù smoke screen：～弹 smoke shell (bomb)
烟幕弹 yānmùdàn ① smoke shell; smoke bomb ② smoke screen
烟土 yāntǔ crude opium
烟雾 yānwù smoke; mist; vapour; smog：～弥漫 full of smoke; smoky; misty
烟消云散 yānxiāo-yúnsàn vanish like mist and smoke; disappear into thin air; vanish completely; disappear in a flash
烟瘾 yānyǐn a craving for tabacoo：～大 be a heavy smoker

咽

yān〈名〉pharynx; throat
另见 yàn
咽喉 yānhóu ① throat：～痛 sore throat ② stragetic (vital) passage; key link
咽喉要地 yānhóu yàodì strategic (vital) passage; key junction (link)
咽头 yāntóu［生理］pharynx
咽炎 yānyán pharyngitis

胭

yān
胭脂 yānzhi rouge：～红 rouge red; carmine. 在两颊上擦～ rouge one's cheeks

湮

yān〈动〉① fall into oblivion; bury in oblivion ② clog up; stop
湮没 yānmò ① fall into oblivion; be forgotten; be neglected：～无闻 fall into obscruity; sink into oblivion ②［物］annihilation

yán

颜

yán〈名〉① countenance; face：容～ facial appearance; looks ② prestige; dignity; face：无～见人 not have the face to appear in public ③ colour：～色视觉 colour vision
颜料 yánliào ① dyestuff ② colour; paint：～盒 colour-box; paint-box
颜面 yánmiàn ① face ② prestige
颜色 yánsè ① colour：～交响曲 colour symphony ② facial expression; countenance

言

yán〈名〉① word; speech：进～ give a word of advice ② character; word：五～诗 a poem with five characters to a line ③〈动〉say; speak; talk：胡～ talk nonsense
言不由衷 yánbùyóuzhōng speak (talk) insincerely; say one thing but mean another
言传 yánchuán explain in words：只可意会，不可～ only to be sensed, not explained. ～身教 teach by personal example as well as verbal instruction; set an example to the others in whatever one says or does; teach by words and influence by deeds
言辞 yáncí one's words; what

one says：～反应 verbal response. ～恳切 be sincere in what one says

言多必失 yánduō-bìshī Much talk leads to faults.

言而无信 yán'érwúxìn break (go back on) one's word; fail to keep faith

言归于好 yánguīyúhǎo make it up with sb.; make up a quarrel (with); become reconciled (with)

言归正传 yánguīzhèngzhuàn to return to the subject; to come back to our story; return from the digression

言过其实 yánguòqíshí overstate; exaggerate

言和 yánhé make peace; become reconciled; bury the hatchet

言简意赅 yánjiǎn-yìgāi concise and comprehensive; brief (precise) and to the point; short but making sense; compendious

言教 yánjiào give verbal directions; teach by word of mouth: ～不如身教。Example is better than precept.

言论 yánlùn opinion on public affairs; speech; view: ～自由 freedom of speech

言情小说 yánqíng xiǎoshuō novel of sentiment

言谈 yántán the way one speaks or what he says: ～举止 manner of speech and behaviour; speech and deportment

言听计从 yántīng-jìcóng act upon whatever sb. says; always follow sb.'s advice

言外之意 yánwàizhīyì meaning beyond words; implication; idea not expressed in words; beyond the actual words

言行 yánxíng words and deeds; statements and actions; saying and doing: ～不符。One's words and deeds are at variance. ～一致。One's behaviour is consistent with one's words.; Deeds accord with words; be as good as one's words

言语 yányǔ words; speech: ～和文字 spoken and written language

言之有理 yánzhīyǒulǐ sound reasonable; It stands to reason.; hold water; sensibly said; said with solid judgment; well said; have (make) sense

言重 yánzhòng overstate; exaggerate

阎 yán

阎罗 yánluó [宗] Yama

阎王 yánwáng ① Yama; King of Hell ② an extremely cruel and violent person: ～债 borrow money at extremely high interest rate

阎王殿 yánwangdiàn the Palace of the King of Hell

炎 yán

①〈形〉hot; torrid: ～夏 hot summer ②〈名〉inflammation: 消～ diminish inflammation

炎黄子孙 yánhuáng zǐsūn descendants of Yan Di and Huang Di

炎热 yánrè scorching; burning

hot

炎夏 yánxià a torrid (scorching) summer

炎炎 yányán scorching; sweltering; blazing

炎症 yánzhèng inflammation

研

yán〈动〉① grind:～碎 grind into powder ② study; research:～修 do research work

研读 yándú study carefully

研究 yánjiū ① discuss; consider; deliberate:这些问题正在～。These matters are under review. ② study; research; investigation:～成果 study (research) findings; research results. ～员 research fellow. ～所 research institute

研讨会 yántǎohuì symposium; workshop; seminar; colloquium

研制 yánzhì research and manufacture; develop; prepare; manufacture

妍

yán〈形〉beautiful; pretty:争～ contend in beauty

盐

yán〈名〉salt

盐碱地 yánjiǎndì saline or alkaline land

盐井 yánjǐng salt well

盐汽水 yánqìshuǐ salt soda water

盐水 yánshuǐ salt solution; brine

盐田 yántián salt pan; salina

盐务(政) yánwù (zhèng) salt (revenue) administration

严

yán〈形〉① strict; severe; rigorous; stern:～厉的谴责 a stern rebuke ② tight:嘴～ be tight-mouthed

严办(惩) yánbàn (chěng) deal with severely; punish … with the utmost severity; severely punish

严斥 yánchì reprove severely; reprimand

严打 yándǎ severely crack down on criminal offenders

严冬 yándōng hard (severe) winter

严防 yánfáng take strict precautions against

严格 yángé strict; rigid; rigorous; stark:～结算纪律 strict enforcement of the rules for settling accounts. ～要求自己 make (set) strict demands on oneself

严谨 yánjǐn ① strict; rigid:～的治学态度 rigid scholarship; careful and exact attitude towards academic research. ② compact:文章结构～。The essay is well-knit.

严禁 yánjìn strictly forbid (prohibit):～吸烟。Smoking is strictly forbidden.

严峻 yánjùn stern; rigorous; severe:～考验 severe test; ordeal

严酷 yánkù ① harsh; bitter; grim:～的现实 harsh reality ② cruel; unrelenting

严厉 yánlì stern; severe; stringent:～打击投机倒把 severely crack down on speculation

严令 yánlìng give strict orders

严密 yánmì tight; thorough; close:～监视某人 keep close watch over sb.

严明 yánmíng strict and impartial:赏罚～ give rewards and punishments impartially

严实 yánshi ① tight; close:他那嘴可不～。He has a loose tongue. ② (hide) safely:游击队把粮食藏～了才转移。The guerrillas carefully hid their food grain before they moved on.

严守 yánshǒu strictly observe; rigidly adhere to:～中立 strictly observe neutrality. ～秘密 maintain strict secrecy

严肃 yánsù earnest; solemn; serious:～处理责任者。Those who are held responsible for the accidents must be deal with severely. ～的当代小说作家 serious contemporary novelist. ～文学 serious literature. ～音乐 classical music; heavy music

严刑 yánxíng cruel punishment; cruel torture:～峻法 severe law; draconian law

严阵以待 yánzhènyǐdài be prepared to meet the challenge; stand ready in battle array; remain in combat readiness

严正 yánzhèng serious and principled; solemn and just; stern:～立场 solemn and just stand

严重 yánzhòng serious; severe; grave:～不法行为 gross misbehaviour; aggravated misconduct. ～后果 grave consequences. ～亏损 heavy losses

岩 yán〈名〉① rock ② cliff

岩岸 yán'àn rocky coast

岩壁 yánbì crag; cliff

岩洞 yándòng grotto

岩画 yánhuà petroglyph; petrogram

岩浆 yánjiāng magma

岩溶地貌 yánróng dìmào karst features; karst topography

岩石 yánshí rock

延 yán〈动〉① prolong; extend; protract:条约～长 10 年。The treaty has been prolonged for another ten years. ② delay; postpone; put off:～期二个月 be postponed for two months ③ engage; invite:～医 send for a doctor

延长 yáncháng lengthen; extend; prolong; protract:把访问时间～了几天 extend one's visit for a few days

延迟 yánchí delay; defer; postpone

延宕 yándàng procrastinate; delay; keep putting off

延缓 yánhuǎn put off; postpone; retard:～工作进度 retard the progress of work

延揽 yánlǎn enlist the services of

延年益寿 yánnián-yìshòu (of tonics, etc.) promise longevity; calculate to prolong one's life; promote longevity; prolong one's life

延期 yánqī put off; delay; postpone:～审理 postponement of the hearing. ～释放 release after the sentence expires. 会议～举行。The meeting has been postponed. ～付款 delayed payments

延伸 yánshēn extend; stretch;

reach：～教育 extension education. 橡胶容易～。Rubber stretches easily.

延误 yánwù incur loss through delay; fail because of procrastination; delay：～费 cost of delay. ～时机 miss an opportunity because of a delay

延续 yánxù continue; go on; last：～租约 continuation of tenancies

延展 yánzhǎn extend; stretch

筵 yán〈名〉① (in ancient times) a bamboo mat on the floor for people to sit on ② feast; banquet：～席 feast; banquet

沿 yán ①〈介〉along：～河的树 trees along by the river ②〈名〉edge; border：这座城镇位于平原的边～。The town stands on the edge of a plain. ③〈动〉follow; adopt：相～成习。The traditional practice has gradually become a social custom.

沿岸 yán'àn along the bank; along the coast：长江～ along (the banks of) the Yangtze River

沿革 yángé successive changes in the past; evolution

沿海 yánhǎi along the coast：～航运权 cabotage right. ～开放县 counties in coastal areas with the adoption of the open policy. ～贸易 coasting trade

沿江 yánjiāng along the river (usu. the Yangtze River); riparian; riverine

沿街 yánjiē along the street：～叫卖 peddle in the streets

沿路 yánlù along the road; on the way

沿途 yántú throughout a journey; along the road

沿袭 yánxí carry on as before; follow (old) conventions; adopt by tradition

沿用 yányòng contunue to use

yǎn

演 yǎn〈动〉① play; act：剧场里在～什么戏？What's playing at the theatre? ② develop; evolve：愈～愈烈 grow in intensity ③ elaborate：推～ deduce ④ practise; drill：～算 make (perform) mathematical calculations

演变 yǎnbiàn evolution; development：社会的～ social evolution

演播 yǎnbō telecast (a play, performance, etc.)

演唱 yǎnchàng sing (in a performance); act a part in Beijing or local operas

演出 yǎnchū offer; perform; show; play; put on a show：～海报 playbill. 歌剧团的～ offerings of an opera company. ～新戏 offer a new play

演化 yǎnhuà evolution

演技 yǎnjì performing technique; acting

演讲 yǎnjiǎng ① give a lecture; make (deliver) a speech ② speech：～稿 notes of a speech

演练 yǎnliàn manoeuvres and training

演双簧 yǎnshuānghuáng a kind of duet or joint performance with one acting in front and another dictating behind; put on a puppet show

演习 yǎnxí exercise; drill; practice; [军] manoeuvres

演戏 yǎnxì ① put on (perform) a play; act in a play; play ② playact; pretend: 别再～了。Stop playacting.

演义 yǎnyì historical romance

演绎 yǎnyì deduction; deduce; derive: ～定理 deduction theorem

演员 yǎnyuán player; performer; personator; actor or actress: ～表 cast. ～替身 stunt man (girl)

演奏 yǎnzòu ① play (a musical instrument): 用钢琴～《国际歌》play *The Internationale* on the piano ② give an instrumental performance; play a musical instrument; musical performance

偃 yǎn

偃旗息鼓 yǎnqí-xīgǔ lower one's banners and muffle one's drums; roll up the flags and silence the drums; stop fighting

奄 yǎn ①〈动〉cover ②〈副〉all of a sudden

奄奄 yǎnyǎn (of breathing) feeble (or weak): ～一息 be at one's last gasp; be near one's end; on one's last

掩 yǎn〈动〉① hide; cover; shelter: 谎言～盖不了事实。Lies cannot cover up facts. ② close; shut: ～卷 close a book

掩蔽 yǎnbì cover; shelter; conceal

掩耳盗铃 yǎn'ěr-dàolíng stuff one's ears when stealing a bell—self-deception; run away from one's own shadow; bury one's head in the sand like an ostrich

掩盖 yǎngài cover up; hide; conceal; veil: ～事实真相 cover up the facts

掩护 yǎnhù shelter; screen; cover: ～撤退 cover the retreat

掩埋 yǎnmái bury

掩人耳目 yǎnrén'ěrmù deceive (hoodwink) the public

掩饰 yǎnshì whitewash; veil; cover up; conceal; gloss over: ～真实的意图 conceal one's true intentions

掩体 yǎntǐ blindage; bunker

掩映 yǎnyìng set off (one another): 桃红柳绿相互～。The pink peaches and green willows set each other off.

眼 yǎn〈名〉① eye: 亲～目睹 see with one's own (very) eyes ② small hole; opening: 针～ eye of a needle ③ key point: 节骨～儿 critical juncture; vital link

眼巴巴 yǎnbābā ① (expecting) eagerly; anxiously ② helplessly (watching sth. unpleasant happen)

眼馋 yǎnchán cast covetous eyes at sth.; eye sth. covetously

眼福 yǎnfú the good fortune of

seeing sth. rare or beautiful：～不浅 be lucky enough to enjoy the beauty of sth. 一饱～ feast one's eyes on sth.

眼光 yǎnguāng eye；sight；eyesight；insight；vision：～锐利 have sharp eyes. 历史的～ historical perspective

眼红 yǎnhóng ① be envious of；be green with envy ② furious

眼花 yǎnhuā ① be dazzled；feel giddy：令人～的 dazzling ② have dim eyesight

眼尖 yǎnjiān be sharp-eyed；have sharp eyes；have keen sight

眼界 yǎnjiè view；horizon；outlook；field of vision：～狭窄 narrow horizon. 大开～ greatly widen one's horizon

眼科 yǎnkē ophthalmic department：～医生 ophthalmologist；oculist；eye-doctor

眼快 yǎnkuài be sharp-eyed (sharp-sighted)；have sharp eyes；have keen sight

眼力 yǎnlì ① eyesight：～好(差) have good (poor) eyesight ② judgment：看人有～ be good at sizing people up

眼帘 yǎnlián eye：映入～ meet the eye；come into view

眼明手快 yǎnmíng-shǒukuài quick of eye and deft of hand；sharp-eyed and quick-handed；clearly discerning and swift-handed

眼前 yǎnqián ① before one's eyes ② at the moment；just now；at present：只顾～ only think of the present. ～暂时的利益 momentary interests of the day

眼色 yǎnsè hint given with the eyes；wink；meaningful glance：对某人使～ wink at sb. 看～行事 take one's cue from sb.

眼神 yǎnshén ① eyesight：～不济 have poor eyesight ② expression in one's eyes

眼生(熟) yǎnshēng(shú) look unfamiliar (familiar)

眼下 yǎnxià at the moment；at present；now

眼药 yǎnyào［药水］eyewash；eyewater；［药膏］eye ointment

眼中钉 yǎnzhōngdīng thorn in one's flesh (side)；eyesore

眼拙 yǎnzhuō my bad eyes；my bad memory

俨

yǎn〈形〉majestic；dignified；solemn

俨然 yǎnrán ① solemn；dignified：望之～ look dignified ② neatly arranged；in neat order ③ just like：～以大人物自居 assume the airs of sb.

俨如 yǎnrú just like；almost the same as：～白昼 as bright as day

衍

yǎn ①〈动〉elaborate；develop；unfold ②〈形〉(of words) redundant superfluous

衍变 yǎnbiàn evolve；develop

衍传 yǎnchuán propagate

衍生 yǎnshēng derive：～物 derivative

衍续 yǎnxù flourish and continue

衍义 yǎnyì derivative meanings

yàn

宴 yàn〈名〉banquet; dinner; feast

宴会 yànhuì dinner; banquet; feast

宴请 yànqǐng give a dinner (banquet) in honour of (sb.); feast; fête

宴席 yànxí banquet; feast

谚 yàn〈名〉proverb; saying:古～ old saying (proverb)

谚语 yànyǔ proverb; saying; saw; adage

艳 yàn〈形〉① gorgeous; bright-coloured:鲜～ bright-coloured; gaily-coloured ② amorous:～诗 love poem in a flowery style

艳福 yànfú man's good fortune in love affairs

艳丽 yànlì gorgeous; bright-coloured and beautiful; resplendent:打扮得非常～ be gorgeously dressed

艳诗 yànshī erotic poetry

艳阳天 yànyángtiān bright spring day; bright sunny skies

燕 yàn〈名〉swallow

燕菜 yàncài delicacies made from bird's nests

燕麦 yànmài oats:～片(粥) oatmeal

燕尾服 yànwěifú swallowtail; swallow-tailed coat; tail-coat; tails

燕窝 yànwō edible bird's nest

厌 yàn〈动〉① be tired of; be disgusted with; loathe:～恶某物 be disgusted with (by) sth. ② be satisfied with:贪得无～ be insatisably greedy

厌烦 yànfán be bored with; be fed up with; be sick of:令人～的 boring; annoying; bothersome

厌倦 yànjuàn be tired of; be weary of

厌世 yànshì be tired of life; be world-weary; pessimistic

厌恶 yànwù detest; be disgusted with; loathe; abominate:令人～的 nauseating; disgusting; repugnant

厌战 yànzhàn be weary of war; be war-weary

雁 yàn〈名〉wild goose

唁 yàn〈动〉offer condolences

唁电 yàndiàn telegram message of condolence

唁函 yànhán letter (message) of condolence

咽 yàn〈动〉swallow
另见 yān

咽气 yànqì breathe one's last; die

咽下 yànxià swallow (up)

砚 yàn〈名〉inkstone; inkslab:～台 inkslab; inkstone

焰 yàn〈名〉flame; blaze

焰火 yànhuǒ fireworks

赝 yàn〈形〉counterfeit; spurious; fake

赝品 yànpǐn art forgery

验 yàn〈动〉① examine；test：点～examine item by item ② prove effective；produce the expected result：屡试屡～ prove successful in every test

验方 yànfāng proved recipe

验关 yànguān customs examination (inspection)；examination of cargo

验光 yànguāng optometry

验明 yànmíng verify；identify：～正身 verify the identity；identify

验讫 yànqì checked；examined

验尸 yànshī coroner's inquest；postmortem inspection：～官 coroner

验收 yànshōu check and accept；check upon delivery；acceptance test

验算 yànsuàn［数］checking computations

验血 yànxuè blood test

验证 yànzhèng test and verify

yāng

央 yāng ①〈动〉entreat；beseech ②〈名〉centre

央告 yānggào beg；plead；ask earnestly；implore

央求 yāngqiú plead；beg；implore：～宽恕 beg for mercy

殃 yāng ①〈动〉cause to suffer disaster；bring disaster to：遭～ suffer disaster ②〈名〉calamity；misfortune；disaster

殃及 yāngjí bring disaster to

秧 yāng〈名〉① sprout；seedling：拔～ pull up seedlings (for transplanting) ② sapling：花～ flower sapling ③ young；fry：鱼～ fingerling；young fish

秧歌 yānggē *yangko* (dance)：扭～ do the *yangko*；dance *yangko*

秧苗 yāngmiáo rice shoot；rice seedling

yáng

羊 yáng〈名〉sheep：母～ ewe. 公～ ram. 山～ goat. 替罪～ scapegoat

羊肠小道 yángcháng-xiǎodào winding foothpath；tortuous trail；narrow winding path

羊羔 yánggāo lamb

羊角锤 yángjiǎochuí claw hammer

羊毛 yángmáo wool：～衫 woolen sweater；［开襟的］cardingan. ～袜 woollen socks

羊绒衫 yángróngshān cashmere sweater

羊肉 yángròu mutton

羊肉串 yángròuchuàn mutton cubes roasted on a skewer；shish kebab (kabob)；shashlik

洋 yáng〈形〉① grand；abundant：～～ numerous；copious ② foreign：～里～气 foreign flavour ③ modern：～办法 modern methods ④〈名〉ocean：重～ the seas and oceans

洋白菜 yángbáicài cabbage

洋布 yángbù foreign-made cloths

洋财 yángcái unexpected big fortune; windfall money

洋车 yángchē rickshaw

洋葱 yángcōng onion

洋鬼子 yángguǐzi foreign devil (a term used in preliberation China for foreign invaders)

洋行 yángháng foreign (trading) firms; foreign business houses

洋灰 yánghuī cement

洋教条 yángjiàotiáo foreign dogmas

洋框框 yángkuàngkuàng restrictive foreign conventions

洋奴 yángnú slave of a foreign master; flunkey of imperialism; worshipper of everything foreign

洋嗓子 yángsǎngzi voice trained in the Western style of singing

洋为中用 yángwéizhōngyòng make foreign things serve China

洋务 yángwù Western affairs; foreign matters: ～派 Westernization group. ～运动 Westernization Movement (initiated by comprador bureaucrats in the latter half of the 19th century in order to preserve the feudal rule of the Qing government)

洋相 yángxiàng silly sight; awkward behaviour; show: 出～ make a show (an exhibition) of oneself

洋洋大观 yángyáng-dàguān great and impressive sight; spectacular (most majestic) sight; grandiose; imposing; spectacular; magnificent

洋洋得意 yángyáng-déyì be jubilant; revel in; gleefully

洋溢 yángyì brim with; be permeated with: ～着热烈的气氛 permeated with a warm atmosphere

洋装 yángzhuāng ① Western-style clothes ② Western-style binding

佯 yáng〈动〉pretend; feign: ～为不知 pretend not to know

佯攻 yánggōng feign (simulate) attack; make a feint

佯言 yángyán allege falsely; tell lies; lie; pretend

佯装 yángzhuāng pretend; feign; sham: ～同意 fein agreement

阳 yáng ①〈名〉the sun: 残～ the setting sun〈形〉② in relief: ～文 characters cut in relief; positive legend[中国绘画]③ overt; open ④ belonging to this world: ～间 this world ⑤ positive: ～电 positive electricity

阳春白雪 yángchūn-báixuě ① "The Spring Snow"—a highbrow song ② sth. selected among the best; highbrow art and literature

阳奉阴违 yángfèng-yīnwéi comply in public but oppose in private; overtly agree but covertly oppose; feign compliance while acting in opposition

阳刚 yánggāng masculine charm; masculinity: ～之气 vigorous and bold spirit

阳关道 yángguāndào broad highway; broad road; thoroughfare

阳间 yángjiān this world

阳历 yánglì ① solar calendar ② the Gregorian calendar

阳伞 yángsǎn sunshade；［女用的］parasol

阳台 yángtái balcony

阳性 yángxìng ①［医］positive：～反应 positive reaction ②［语］masculine gender

杨 yáng〈名〉poplar

杨柳 yángliǔ ① poplar and willow ② willow

杨梅 yángméi red bayberry

扬 yáng〈动〉① raise high；go up：～起灰尘 raise a dust ② fly；flutter：飘～ flutter；wave ③ make known；spread：宣～ propagate；play up；publicize ④ applaud；praise：赞～ speak highly of；praise

扬长避短 yángcháng-bìduǎn make best use of the advantages and bypass the disadvantages；develop the strong points and avoid the weak (points)；play up strengths and avoid weaknesses

扬长而去 yángcháng'érqù go away haughtily；stalk off；swagger off；stride off

扬帆 yángfān hoist the sails；set sail

扬眉吐气 yángméi-tǔqì hold one's head high；be highly exalted；feel proud and elated

扬名 yángmíng spread one's fame；become famous；make a name for oneslef：～天下 become famous throughout the country (world)

扬弃 yángqì［哲］sublate；sublation；discard；abolish；abolition

扬言 yángyán declare (that one is going to take action)；threaten；clamour：～要进行报复 threaten to retaliate

扬扬得意 yángyáng-déyì be proud and pleased with oneself；be very pleased with oneself；feel oneself highly flattered；self-complacent

扬子鳄 yángzǐ'è Chinese alligator

yǎng

痒 yǎng〈动〉itch；tickle：搔～ scratch where it itches

氧 yǎng〈名〉oxygen：～气 oxygen

氧吧 yǎngbā oxygen bar

氧化 yǎnghuà oxidize

氧化剂 yǎnghuàjì oxidizer；oxidant

氧气瓶 yǎngqìpíng oxygen cylinder

养 yǎng〈动〉① support；provide for：奉～ support and wait upon (one's parents or elders) ② give birth to：她～了个女儿。She gave birth to a girl. ③ raise；rear：～花 grow flowers ④ form；cultivate：～成教育 education in cultivation ⑤ rest；recuperate one's health；convalesce：～生之术 art of maintaining good health；art of preserve one's health ⑥ foster; adoptive:～父 foster-father ⑦ keep in good repair; maintain: ～路 maintain a road

养兵 yǎngbīng maintain an army

养病 yǎngbìng take rest and nourishment to regain one's health; recruit oneself after an illness; recuperate; convalesce:在家～ recuperate at home

养蚕 yǎngcán sericulture

养成 yǎngchéng form; cultivate; develop; contract (a bad habit):～仔细阅读的习惯 cultivate (form) the habit of reading carefully

养分 yǎngfèn nutrient

养蜂 yǎngfēng apiculture; beekeeping:～场 apiary; bee-yard

养虎遗患 yǎnghǔ-yíhuàn nourish a tiger to be a source of trouble in the future; rear a tiger is to court calamity; appease an enemy is to invite disaster

养护 yǎnghù ① maintain; conserve ② curing

养活 yǎnghuo support; feed:～全家 feed (support) a whole family

养精蓄锐 yǎngjīng-xùruì conserve strength and store (build) up energy; recuperate and build up energy

养老 yǎnglǎo ① provide for the aged; support one's parents (the aged) ② live out one's life in retirement; enjoy one's life in retirement:～金 old-age pension; annuity. 城镇基本～保险 basic old-age insurance in cities and towns

养料 yǎngliào nutrition; nutriment; nourishment:吸收～ draw nourishment from

养路 yǎnglù maintain a highway or railway:～费 highway maintenance tax

养神 yǎngshén rest to attain mental tranquility; repose:闭目～ sit in repose with one's eyes closed

养生之道 yǎngshēngzhīdào how to care for life (conserve one's vital powers); how to maintain good health

养鱼池 yǎngyúchí fishpond

养育 yǎngyù bring up; rear; foster:～子女 bring up children

养殖 yǎngzhí breed or cultivate (aquatics):～业 fish breeding and poultry raising; aquaculture

养猪场 yǎngzhūchǎng pig farm; piggery

养子 yǎngzǐ adopted son; adoptive son

养尊处优 yǎngzūn-chùyōu enjoy a high position and live in ease and comfort; revel in a high position and indulge in comfort; lead a comfortable life; live in clover

仰 yǎng〈动〉① face upward; lift up (one's head):俯～ (of the head) bend or lift ② esteem; respect:景～ admire and respect ③ depend on; rely on:～仗 look to sb. for backing (support); rely on; count on

仰角 yǎngjiǎo angle of elevation

仰面 yǎngmiàn face upward
仰慕 yǎngmù hold sb. in high esteem; look up to; admire
仰人鼻息 yǎngrénbíxī live at sb.'s mercy; curry to sb.'s every whim; be at sb.'s beck and call; depend on others and act slavishly
仰视 yǎngshì look up
仰望 yǎngwàng ① look up at:～星空 look up at the starlit sky ② respectfully seek guidance or help from; hope; look to sb.
仰卧 yǎngwò lie on one's back; lie supine
仰泳 yǎngyǒng backstroke
仰仗 yǎngzhàng rely on; look to sb. for backing (support)

yàng

样 yàng〈名〉① appearance; shape ② style; fashion:时～ the latest fashion ③ kind; type; sort:别～ other type ④ sample; pattern; model:货～ sample goods
样板 yàngbǎn ① sample plate; templet ② model; example; prototype:～田 demonstration fields
样本 yàngběn ① sample book (copy);[出版前的] advance copy ② sample; specimen:～调查 sample survey
样机 yàngjī prototype machine
样品 yàngpǐn sample (production); specimen:～免费赠送。Sample is sent gratis.
样式 yàngshì style; type:各种尺寸和～的帽子 hats in all sizes and styles
样张 yàngzhāng specimen page
样子 yàngzi ① appearance; shape ② manner; air ③ sample; model; pattern ④ tendency; likelihood

怏 yàng〈名〉
怏怏 yàngyàng sullen; disgruntled:～不乐 uphappy about sth.; look disgruntled and sad; morose

恙 yàng〈名〉illness; ailment; indisposition:无～ safe and sound; in good health

漾 yàng〈动〉brim over; overflow; ripple:荡～ undulate; ripple

yāo

要 yāo〈动〉① demand; ask (for):～求某人答复 demand an answer of (from) sb. ② coerce; force
另见 yào
要求 yāoqiú demand; ask (for); claim:～赔偿损失 claim compensation for the losses. ～报价 request for an offer
要挟 yāoxié coerce (into):～某人做某事 coerce sb. into doing sth.

腰 yāo〈名〉waist:伸～ straighten one's back; straighten oneself up
腰板儿 yāobǎnr ① back ②

physique; build
腰包 yāobāo purse; pocket:掏~ pay out of one's own pocket
腰缠万贯 yāochán-wànguàn be loaded; be very rich
腰杆子 yāogǎnzi ① back ② support; back:~不硬 bend down; droop. ~硬 have strong back
腰肌劳损 yāojī-láosǔn strain of lumbar muscles; psoatic strain
腰身(围) yāoshēn(wéi) waist; waistline; waist measurement: ~小 have a slender waist
腰痛 yāotòng pain in the small of one's back; lumbago
腰眼 yāoyǎn either side of the small of the back
腰椎 yāozhuī lumbar vertebra

夭
yāo〈动〉die young
夭亡 yāowáng die young
夭折 yāozhé ① die young; die early ② come to a premature (untimely) end:和平谈判中途~。The peace talks came to an untimely end.

吆
yāo
吆喝 yāohe ① shout; call; cry out ② cry one's wares:沿街~着生意 cry out for customers along the street ③ loudly urge on (an animal):牲口不听~。The animal wouldn't obey its driver.

妖
yāo〈名〉① monster; demon; evil spirit:~魔乱舞。Evil spirits of all kinds danced in riotous revelry. ② evil and fraudulent: ~术 witchcraft; sorcery ③ 〈形〉bewitching; enchanting; coquettish:打扮得~里~气 be seductively dressed
妖法 yāofǎ diabolism
妖风 yāofēng evil (ill) wind; evil (vicious, malicious) blast
妖怪 yāoguài bogey; bogle; goblin
妖精 yāojing ① evil spirit; demon ② seductress; siren
妖媚 yāomèi bewitching; enchanting; seductive
妖魔 yāomó demon; evil spirit; monster
妖孽 yāoniè ① person or event associated with evil or misfortune ② evildoer
妖娆 yāoráo enchanting; fascinating; bewitching
妖术 yāoshù sorcery; witchcraft; black art
妖言 yāoyán heresy; fallacy:~惑众 spread fallacies to deceive people
妖艳 yāoyàn petty and coquettish

邀
yāo〈动〉① invite; request: 特~ specially invite ② solicit; seek
邀功 yāogōng take credit for someone else's achievements
邀集 yāojí call together; invite to meet together
邀请 yāoqǐng invite:~国 inviting country; host country. ~赛 invitational tournament; invitation match. ~书 invitation

yáo

肴
yáo〈名〉meat and fish dish-

es:酒～ wine and delicacies

肴馔 yáozhuàn sumptuous courses at a meal; the courses at a banquet

窑 yáo〈名〉① kiln:石灰～ limekiln ② coal-pit:炭～ charcoal kiln ③ cave dwelling

窑变 yáobiàn kiln transmutation—the technique of making iridescent chinaware by the irregular application of glaze

窑洞 yáodòng cave dwelling; cave residence; cave

谣 yáo〈名〉① ballad; folk song:民～ folk song (rhyme) ② rumour:辟～ deny a rumour; refute slanders

谣传 yáochuán ① rumour; hearsay ② it is rumoured that…; rumour has it that…

谣言 yáoyán rumour; groundless allegation:～惑众。Wild rumours mislead the masses.

遥 yáo〈形〉far; distant; remote:～～ a long way off; far away

遥测 yáocè telemetering

遥感 yáogǎn[电子] remote sensing

遥控 yáokòng remote control

遥望 yáowàng get a distant view; look into the distance

遥相呼应 yáoxiāng-hūyìng echo each other at a distance

遥想 yáoxiǎng recall; recollect; reminisce

遥远 yáoyuǎn distant; remote:～的将来 in the remote (distant) future. 路途～ a long way to go

遥指 yáozhǐ point in the direction of

摇 yáo〈动〉shake; wave; rock; swing; sway:～旗 wave a flag. ～头 shake one's head

摇摆 yáobǎi sway; swing rock; wag; stagger; waver; vacillate:～不定 swing from side to side; be irresolute; vacillate. ～而行 stagger along. ～舞 rock and roll (rock'n'roll). 船身～。The ship rocked.

摇船 yáochuán row a boat

摇动 yáodòng ① wave; shake ② sway; rock

摇滚乐 yáogǔnyuè rock and roll music; big beat

摇撼 yáohàn give a violent shake to; shake to the root or foundation; rock

摇晃 yáohuàng shake; rock; sway

摇奖 yáojiǎng lottery

摇篮 yáolán cradle; matrix:～曲 cradlesong; nursery rhyme; lullaby. 文明的～ matrix of civilization

摇旗呐喊 yáoqí-nàhǎn wave the flags and shout slogans; drum up support; bang (beat) the drum for

摇钱树 yáoqiánshù ready source of income (money); milch cow; money-spinner

摇身一变 yáoshēnyībiàn assume an entirely different role in an instant; suddenly change one's identity; make an aboutface

摇头 yáotóu shake one's head

摇尾乞怜 yáowěi-qǐlián wag the tail and flatter (beg for pity); beg like a dog

摇摇欲坠 yáoyáo-yùzhuì tottering; crumbling; toppling: ～的政权 a tottering regime

摇曳 yáoyè flicker; sway

徭 yáo

徭役 yáoyì corvée

瑶 yáo precious jade; jasper

瑶族 Yáozú the Yao nationality or the Yaos, distributed over the Guangxi Zhuang Autonomous Region and other provinces

yǎo

窈 yǎo

窈窕 yǎotiǎo gentle and graceful: ～淑女 a gentle and graceful young woman; a quiet and modest maiden

杳 yǎo 〈动〉 remote; out of sight: ～无踪迹 disappear without a trace; vanish

杳然 yǎorán silently: ～无踪 left without a trace

杳如黄鹤 yǎorú-huánghè disappear without a trace

杳无音信 yǎowúyīnxìn have never been heard of since; no news whatever from sb. (for a long time); disappear for good and all

咬 yǎo 〈动〉① bite; snap at; gnaw: 她把线～断了。She bit the thread in two. ② (of a dog) bark: 鸡叫狗～。Cocks crow and dogs bark. ③ pronounce; articulate: ～字清楚 clear articulation ④ be nitpicking (on words)

咬定 yǎodìng speak assuredly; assert emphatically: 一口～ say with finality

咬耳朵 yǎo'ěrduo whisper (in sb.'s ear)

咬紧牙关 yǎojǐn yáguān clench one's teeth: ～克服困难 clench one's teeth and overcome the difficulty

咬文嚼字 yǎowén-jiáozì pay excessive attention to wording; be overfastidious in wording; juggle with words like a pedant; mince-words in speech or writing; chop logic: ～者 verbalist

咬牙 yǎoyá grind one's teeth (in sleep); grit one's teeth: ～切齿 gnash one's teeth (in hatred)

咬住 yǎozhù ① grip with one's teeth; bite into ② grip; take firm hold of: ～敌人 be close on the heels of the enemy

咬字儿 yǎozìr pronounce; articulate: 他～不清楚。His articulation is not clear.

舀 yǎo 〈动〉spoon (up, out); ladle (up, out); scoop up: ～汤 ladle out soup

舀子 yǎozi dipper; ladle; scoop

yào

药 yào 〈名〉① medicine; drug;

remedy：中草～ Chinese herbal medicine② certain chemicals：火～ gunpowder ③〈动〉kill with poision：～老鼠 poison rats

药补 yàobǔ build up one's health by taking tonic

药草 yàocǎo medicinal herbs

药厂 yàochǎng pharmaceutical factory (works)

药典 yàodiǎn pharmacopoeia

药店 yàodiàn chemist's shop; drugstore；［中药］traditional Chinese drugstore; herbal medicine shop

药方 yàofāng prescription：开～ write out a prescription; prescribe (the patient) a recipe

药房 yàofáng ① drugstore; chemist's shop; pharmacy ② hospital pharmacy; dispensary

药费 yàofèi charges for medicine

药膏 yàogāo ointment; salve

药剂 yàojì drug：～师 pharmacist; druggist

药酒 yàojiǔ medicinal liquor; medicated wine

药膳 yàoshàn medicated food; food cooked with medicinal herbs

药丸 yàowán pill；［大的］bolus

药物 yàowù medicines; drugs：～使用 drug use. ～实谱 illustrations of medicines. ～中毒 drug poisoning

药箱 yàoxiāng medical kit：急救～ first-aid kit

药效 yàoxiào efficacy of a drug (medicine)

药性 yàoxìng property of a medicine

药皂 yàozào medicated soap

要 yào ①〈形〉important; essential：～素 essential element; key element ②〈名〉important substance：纲～ outline〈动〉③ want; ask for; desire：谁没有票，问她～。Anyone without a ticket can ask her for one. ④ need; take：这活儿～不了这么多人。You don't need so many people for this job. ⑤ have to：路很滑，大家～小心。We have to be careful for the road. ⑥〈助动〉must; should：我们～相信群众。We must have faith in the masses. ⑦〈连〉if; suppose; in case：她～来不了呢. Suppose she can't come.

另见 yāo

要隘 yào'ài strategic pass

要案 yào'àn important case

要不得 yàobude intolerable; no good; objectionable; unacceptable：在公园里采花～。It is no good to pick flowers in the park.

要不是 yàobushi if it were not for; but for：～你帮助，她不能成功。But for your help she couldn't have succeeded.

要不要 yàobuyao whether or not to accept; whether or not there is need for; whether… is to be upheld or abandoned

要冲 yàochōng communications centre (hub)：军事～ strategic points

要道 yàodào thoroughfare; main route：交通～ important line of communications

要点 yàodiǎn ① main points; essentials; gist: 抓住～ grasp the main points ② key position; strategic strong point: 战略～ strategic point

要犯 yàofàn important criminal

要害 yàohài ①［身体上］vital part(s); vitals ② key (crucial) point; crux; vital issue: ～部门 key departments. 击中～ hit home; hit the nail on the head

要好 yàohǎo ① be on good terms (with) ② eager to improve oneself

要价 yàojià ask a price; charge: 漫天～ ask an exorbitant price; open one's mouth too wide

要件 yàojiàn ① important document ②［法］essentials; requirement

要津 yàojīn ① key place ② key post

要紧 yàojǐn ① important; essential ② be critical; be serious; matter: 不～。It doesn't matter. ［回答别人的感谢语］Never mind. ③ be in a hurry (to do): ～去上班 be in a hurry to go to work

要脸 yàoliǎn be keen on face-saving; care much about one's reputation

要领 yàolǐng main points; essentials; gist: 不得～ miss the main points; fail to get the gist

要么 yàome or; either … or …: ～他们来，～我去找他们。Either they come here, or I'll go to see them.

要面子 yàomiànzi be keen on face-saving; be anxious to keep up appearance

要命 yàomìng ① drive sb. to his death; kill ② confoundedly; extremely; awfully; terribly ③ a nuisance

要强 yàoqiáng be eager to excel in whatever one does

要人 yàorén very important person (VIP); important personage; big shot

要塞 yàosài fortress; fort; stronghold

要是 yàoshì if; in case; suppose: ～明天下雪，我就不同你去了。In case it snows tomorrow, I won't go with you.

要素 yàosù element; factor; essence: ～组合 factor mix

要闻 yàowén important news; front-page story

要员 yàoyuán important official

要约 yàoyuē［法］offer: ～人 party making the offer

要帐 yàozhàng demand payment of a debt

要职 yàozhí important post: 身居～ hold an important post

要旨 yàozhǐ gist; keynote; main idea

钥 yào

钥匙 yàoshi key

耀 yào

〈动〉① shine; illuminate; dazzle: 阳光照～。The sun shines brightly. ② boast of; laud; display: 光宗～祖 bring honour to one's ancestors. 炫～ make a display of; show off

耀武扬威 yàowǔ-yángwēi make a big show of one's strength; bluff and bluster; swashbuckling; sabre-rattling; brandish one's sword; swagger before others

耀眼 yàoyǎn dazzling; glaring

yē

椰 yē coconut tree (palm)

椰雕 yēdiāo coconut shell carving

椰蓉 yēróng shredded coconut stuffing

椰子 yēzi ① coconut tree; coco ② coconut

噎 yē〈动〉① choke: 留神别～着 be careful not to choke ② render sb. speechless with blunt or rude remarks

yé

爷 yé〈名〉father

爷们 yémen ① man or menfolk ② husband

爷们儿 yémenr a collective term for men of two or more generations

爷娘 yéniáng father and mother; parents

yě

冶 yě〈动〉smelt (metal)

冶金 yějīn metallurgy: ～工业 metallurgical industry

冶炼 yěliàn smelting: ～厂 smelting works; smeltery

冶铁 yětiě iron-smelting

冶铸 yězhù casting

野 yě〈名〉① open country; field; wilderness: 村～ villages and fields ② limit; bounds: 分～ dividing line ③ not in power: 下～ (of a ruler) retire from the political arena〈形〉④ wild; uncultivated; undomesticated: ～生植物 a wild plant ⑤ rough; rude: 动作太～ rough play ⑥ unrestrained; unruly: 撒～ behave rudely; act wildly

野菜 yěcài edible wild herbs

野餐 yěcān picnic

野鸡大学 yějīdàxué diploma mill

野蛮 yěmán ① uncivilized; wild; savage: ～状态 barbarism ② barbarous; brutal: ～装卸 barbarous loading and unloading

野人 yěrén ① an uncouth person; rustic ② savage; barbarian

野生 yěshēng wild: ～动物 wild animal. ～生物 wild-life

野史 yěshǐ unofficial histories

野外 yěwài open country; field: ～学习 field studies. ～作业 fieldwork

野心 yěxīn wild ambition: ～勃勃 be overweeningly ambitious; burn with ambition

野心家 yěxīnjiā careerist

野性 yěxìng wild nature; unruliness

野营 yěyíng camp: 出外～ go camping

野战 yězhàn fied operations: ～军 field army

也 yě〈副〉also; too; either; as well:她～要求去。She also asked to go.

也罢 yěbà ① well then; all right then:～,你既然不能多待一会儿,我就不留你了。Well then, I won't keep you since you can't stay any longer. ② whether … or …:天下雪～,不下雪～,今晚我一定要去。Whether it snows or not, I'll have to go tonight.

也好 yěhǎo it may not be a bad idea; may as well:说明一下～ better to give an explanation

也许 yěxǔ perhaps; maybe; probably

yè

夜 yè〈名〉night; evening:熬～ stay up late or all night

夜班 yèbān night shift; night duty:上～ work on the night shift. ～费 night-shift allowance

夜长梦多 yècháng-mèngduō There is many a slip between the cup and the lip.; When the night is long, dreams are many.; A long delay may give rise to many a hitch.; Delay may lead to adversity.

夜场 yèchǎng evening show

夜车 yèchē night train

夜大学 yèdàxué evening university

夜航 yèháng night flight or navigation

夜景 yèjǐng night scene (view)

夜阑人静 yèlánrénjìng in the dead of night; in the stillness of the night

夜郎自大 yèlángzìdà be blinded by one's presumptuous self-conceit; ludicrous conceit stemming from pure ignorance

夜盲 yèmáng nyctalopia; night blindness

夜幕 yèmù curtain of night; gathering darkness

夜曲 yèqǔ[乐]song of the night; night music; serenade; nocturne

夜入私宅罪 yèrùsīzháizuì burglary

夜望镜 yèwàngjìng snooperscope

夜宵 yèxiāo food (or refreshments) taken late at night; midnight snack

夜以继日 yèyǐjìrì round the rock; day and night

夜战 yèzhàn night operation (fighting)

夜总会 yèzǒnghuì nightclub

液 yè〈名〉liquid; fluid:补～ fluid infusion

液化 yèhuà liquefaction:～石油气 liquefied petroleum gas (LPG)

液晶 yèjīng liquid crystal

液体 yètǐ liquid:～燃料 liquid fuel

腋 yè〈名〉armpit:肘～ elbow and armpit

腋臭 yèchòu underarm odour

谒 yè〈动〉have an audience with; call on (one's superior or elder):拜～ pay a formal visit; pay one respects to

谒见 yèjiàn have an audience with; visit; pay a call on (a superior or senior person)

页 yè〈名〉page; leaf:扉～ title page

页岩油 yèyányóu shale oil

叶 yè〈名〉① leaf:新～ new leaves ② sth. resembling a leaf:肺～ a lobe of the lung ③ part of a historical century:初～ early years of (of a century) ④ leaf; page:茶～ tea-leaves; tea

叶公好龙 yègōng-hàolóng Lord Ye who claimed to be fond of dragons was scared out of his wits when a real one appeared; Lord Ye's love of dragons

叶绿素 yèlǜsù chlorophyll

叶落归根 yèluò-guīgēn Leaves fall to settle on their roots—end one's days on one's native soil.

业 yè〈名〉① line of business; trade:修理～ repairing trades ② profession; occupation; vocation:失～ be out of a job ③ property; estate:家～ family property ④ course of study:结～ complete a course; wind up one's studies

业大 yèdà sparetime university

业绩 yèjì outstanding achievement; feats; exemplary accomplishment

业师 yèshī one's (former) teacher

业务 yèwù vocational work; professional work; business:～部门 business agencies. ～班子 professional ranks. ～过失 professional negligence. ～尖子 top-notch professional person. ～专长 professional specialty

业余 yèyú sparetime; amateur:～爱好 amateur hobby; hobbies. ～教育 sparetime education. ～夜校 sparetime night school. ～演员 amateur actor or actress. ～作家 amateur author

业主 yèzhǔ owner (of an enterprise or estate); proprietor

曳 yè〈动〉haul; drag:拖～ drag and pull

曳光弹 yèguāngdàn tracer bullet or shell; tracer

曳力 yèlì drag force

yī

衣 yī〈名〉① clothes; clothing; dress:寒～ winter clothing ② coating:糖～ sugarcoating

衣钵 yībō mantle

衣冠 yīguān hat and clothes; dress

衣冠冢 yīguānzhǒng cenotaph

衣架 yījià ① coat hanger; clothes-rack ② clothes tree; clothes stand

衣锦还乡 yījǐn-huánxiāng return to one's hometown in silken robes—return home after making good

衣料 yīliào material for clothing; dress material cloth

衣食住行 yī-shí zhù xíng clothing, food, housing and transport; clothing, food, shelter, and means of travel

衣着 yīzhuó clothing; headgear and footwear: ～齐整 be decently dressed

铱 yī〈名〉iridium

铱金笔 yījīnbǐ iridium-point pen

依 yī〈动〉① depend on; count on: 相～ depend on each other ② comply (with); yield (to); listen to; agree: 劝她休息,她怎么也不～。She turned a deaf ear to my advice when I wanted her to take a breather. ③〈介〉according to: ～法惩办 punish according to law

依此类推 yīcǐ-lèituī The rest may be deduced by analogy; and so on and so forth.

依次 yīcì in proper order; successively: ～递补 fill vacancies in proper order

依从 yīcóng comply with; yield to; compliance: 认同性～ identitive compliance

依法 yīfǎ according to law; in accordance with law; by operation of law; in law: ～秉公处理 deal with… impartially according to law. ～裁决 adjudicate according to law. ～行政 perform one's duties according to law

依附 yīfù attach oneself to: ～关系 relations of dependence

依旧 yījiù as before; still

依据 yījù ① basis; ground; foundation: 提供科学～ provide scientific basis ② according to; on the basis of: ～上述意见 in accordance with the above views

依靠 yīkào ① depend on; rely on ② support; backing: 生活有～ have one's livelihood assured

依赖 yīlài be dependent on: ～思想 the dependent mentality

依恋 yīliàn be reluctant to leave; feel regret at parting from

依山傍水 yīshān-bàngshuǐ at the foot of a hill and beside a stream

依托 yītuō ① rely on; depend on ② support; prop; backing

依稀 yīxī vaguely; dimly

依依 yīyī be reluctant to part: ～不舍 be reluctant to part (from, with); unwilling to part from (with); cannot bear to leave; find it hard to part

依照 yīzhào according to; in accordance with; in the light of: ～情况而定 decide as circumstances require

一 yī ①〈数〉one: ～句话新闻 news in one sentence ②〈冠〉a (an)〈形〉③ same: 咱们是～家人。We are of the same family ④ whole; all; throughout: ～夏 the whole summer ⑤ concentrated; wholehearted: ～心～意 heart and soul; wholeheartedly ⑥ [表示动作是一次或短暂的]: 等～等 wait a bit ⑦ [用在动词或动量词前面,表示先做某个动作,下文说明动作的结果]: ～跳跳了过去 get over in one jump

一把手 yībǎshǒu first in command

一把抓 yībǎzhuā ① take everything into one's own hands ② try to tackle all problems at once regardless of their relative importance

一败涂地 yībài-túdì suffer an utter defeat; fail completely; be reuined completely

一般 yībān ① general; ordinary; common; usual: ～加工业 processing industries in general. ～商品 general goods ② as; just like

一板一眼 yībǎn-yīyǎn following a prescribed (set) pattern in speech or action; scrupulous and methodical

一辈子 yībèizi all one's life; throughout one's life; as long as one lives; a lifetime

一本正经 yīběn-zhèngjīng ① in sad (dead) earnest; in a matter-of-fact manner; in all seriousness ② serious; solemn; prim: 看起来～ look serious; look as if butter wouldn't melt in one's mouth

一笔勾销 yībǐ-gōuxiāo cancel once for all; write off (abolish) at one stroke; wipe out

一边倒 yībiāndǎo ① lean to one side; side with sb. without reservation ② predominate; enjoy overwhelming superiority

一步登天 yībù-dēngtiān reach the sky in a single bound—attain the highest level in one step; have a meteoric rise

一场空 yīchǎngkōng all in vain; futile

一唱一和 yīchàng-yīhè echo each other; chime in with; sing the same tune; sing in duet; sing in chorus with

一尘不染 yīchón bùrǎn not soiled by a speck of dust; spotless

一成不变 yīchéng-bùbiàn unchangeable; immutable; hard and fast

一筹莫展 yīchóu-mòzhǎn can find no way out; find oneself in the mire; be at one's wit's end; be at a loss; be absolutely helpless

一触即发 yīchù-jífā be triggered at any moment; ready to set off at a touch; imminent; touch-and-go; to an explosive point; be on the verge of breaking out

一锤定音 yīchuí-dìngyīn set the tune with one beat of the gong—give the final word

一 次能源 yīcì néngyuán primary energy

一次性 yīcìxìng one time only; only once; once for all: ～削价处理 one-time price cut (on damaged, substandard, or overstocked goods)

一代 yīdài ① a dynasty ② an era; the present age ③ all one's life; a lifetime; a generation

一旦 yīdàn ① in a single day; in a very short time ② once; as soon as; in case

一刀两断 yīdāo-liǎnduàn sever at one blow—make a clean break with; break with… once for all

一刀切 yīdāoqiē deal with different cases in one and the same way; cut with one knife; rigid uniformity

一定 yīdìng fixed; definite; regular; specified:～的生产指标 fixed production quotas. 在～程度上 to a certain extent; in a certain degree. 在～条件下 under given conditions

一度 yīdù once; at one time; for a time:～失业 be out of job for a time

一发千钧 yīfā-qiānjūn be a thread; in a very critical situation; in imminent danger (peril)

一帆风顺 yīfān-fēngshùn plain sailing:工作不会是～的。The work will not be all plain sailing.

一方面 yīfāngmiàn ① one side ② on the one hand:～…另一方面… on the one hand…, on the other hand…; for one thing… for another…

一风吹 yīfēngchuī disappear with one blow of the wind (metaphor for writing off at one stroke); dismiss all things as of no significance

一概 yīgài totally; entirely; without exception; one and all:～无效 be null and void without exception

一个中心,两个基本点(一个中心是经济建设,两个基本点是坚持四项基本原则、坚持改革开放) yī gè zhōngxīn liǎng gè jīběndiǎn (yī gè zhōngxīn shì jīngjì jiànshè, liǎng gè jīběndiǎn shì jiānchí sìxiàng jīběn yuánzé, jiānchí gǎigé kāifàng) one central task, two basic points (the central task is economic development; the two basic points are adherence to the Four Cardinal Principles and implementation of reform and the open policy)

一鼓作气 yīgǔzuòqì get sth. done in one effort; go ahead without letup

一贯 yīguàn consistent; persistent; all along; invariably

一锅端 yīguōduān take in one pot (① metaphor for rounding up all enemies or criminals in one fell swoop ② To let out one's views and opinions completely.)

一国两制 yīguó liǎngzhì one nation, two systems; the "one country, two systems" policy

一技之长 yījìzhīcháng have a professional skill to recommend oneself; have some professional skill; be skilful in one line; make oneself useful in some kind of work

一见如故 yījiàn-rúgù feel (be) like old friends at the first meeting; become fast friends at the first meeting

一见钟情 yījiàn-zhōngqíng fall in love at first sight

一箭双雕 yījiàn-shuāngdiāo kill two birds with one stone; achieve two things at one stroke; answer a double purpose

一经 yījīng as soon as; once:她的

书～出版一定会很受欢迎的。Once published, her book will surely be very popular.

一…就… yī…jiù… no sooner…than…; as soon as: 我的妻子一到家天就下雨了。No sooner had my wife reached home than it began to rain.

一举 yījǔ at one stroke; with one action; at a brush: ～消灭 annihilate …at one stroke

一举两得 yījǔ-liǎngdé gain two ends at one stroke; kill two birds with one stone

一举成名 yījǔ-chéngmíng become famous overnight; spring into fame

一句话 yījùhuà in a word; in short

一蹶不振 yījué-bùzhèn be unable to recover after the comedown; collapse after a setback

一孔之见 yīkǒngzhījiàn a peephole view; a limited (narrow) view; view through a peephole

一口 yīkǒu ① a mouthful; a bite ② with certainty; readily; flatly; categorically: ～答应 readily agree. ～咬定 say with finality

一口气 yīkǒuqì ① one breath: 深深地吸～ draw a deep breath ② in one breath; at a stretch: ～把工作做完 finish the work at a stretch (at one go)

一览 yīlǎn general survey; guidelook; bird's-eye view: ～表 table schedule. ～无余 take in everything at a glance

一揽子 yīlǎnzi package; wholesale: ～交易 a package deal

一劳永逸 yīláo-yǒngyì get sth. done once (and) for all; put things right once for all; be efficacious forever: ～的解决办法 solutions that hold good for all time

一连 yīlián in succession; on end; running: ～五年 for five years running

一路 yīlù ① all the way; all along: ～领先 lead all the way. ～平安! Have a good (pleasant) journey! ② of the same kind: ～货 one of a kind

一律 yīlǜ ① without exception; indiscriminately; all: 所有缴获必须～归公。All things captured must be turned in without exception. ② uniform; same; alike: 千篇～ stereotyped and monotonous

一落千丈 yīluò-qiānzhàng a drastic (sudden, disastrous, ruinous, calamitous) fail; a terrific (precipitate, great) drop

一马当先 yīmǎ-dāngxiān take the lead; lead the way: ～, 万马奔腾。One horse in the lead starts ten thousand galloping.

一毛不拔 yīmáo-bùbá very sparing in spending money; not willing to give a single cent; very stingy

一面 yīmiàn ① one side; one section; one aspect: 独当～ be solely responsible for one section; take charge of a branch of work ② one-sided: ～之词 one-sided statement ③ at the same time; while: ～教, ～学 learn and teach at the same time; learn while teaching

一面之交 yīmiànzhījiāo have a casual acquaintance (with); have met only once; have a once-met acquaintance

一鸣惊人 yīmíng-jīngrén amaze the world by one's successful maiden effort; surprise people with one's first success; make one's mark at a single shot

一模一样 yīmú-yīyàng exactly the same; completely identical; as like as two peas:他长得跟他父亲～。He is the image of his father.

一目了然 yīmù-liǎorán ① see clearly at a glance; understand fully at a glance; ② obvious; as clear as day

一年半载 yīnián-bànzǎi in a year or so; in about a year

一念之差 yīniànzhīchā make a wrong decision on the spur of the moment; a great mistake made in a moment of weakness

一瞥 yīpiē ① quick glance ② glimpse; brief survey

一气 yīqì ① at one go; without a break; at a stretch ② of the same gang; hand in glove ③ a spell; a fit

一钱不值 yīqián-bùzhí not worth a penny; not worth a hair

一窍不通 yīqiào-bùtōng have no knowledge of; know nothing about (a subject); out of one's element; be a complete ignoramus; be utterly ignorant of

一丘之貉 yīqiūzhīhè birds of a feather; be of a gang; be jackals of (from) the same lair; tigers from the same den

一如既往 yīrújìwǎng just as in the past; as always (before)

一扫而光 yīsǎo'érguāng make a clean sweep (of); clear off; sweep away

一生 yīshēng all one's life; throughout one's life; for life

一时 yīshí ① for the time being; for a while; temporarily:经济的～发展 temporary economic development ② for the moment; offhand:～的冲动 momentary impulse ③ [叠用,同"时而"]now…, now…:～冷,～热 now hot, now cold. 此～,彼～。Times have changed.; It's not what it was.

一视同仁 yīshì-tóngrén treat equally without discrimination; extend the same (equal) treatment to all; be treated the same

一事无成 yīshì-wúchéng accomplish (achieve) nothing; get nowhere; fail to achieve anything of consequence

一手 yīshǒu ① proficiency; skill:露～ show off one's skill ② single-handed; all by oneself:～包办 keep everything in one's own hands; take everything on oneself ③ on the one hand… and on the other hand:对文化事业要坚持～抓繁荣,～抓管理。We shall, on the one hand, encourage the development of cultural undertakings, and on the other hand tighten control

一丝不苟 yīsī-bùgǒu not be the least bit negligent; in a careful and thoroughgoing way; with meticulous care; be very scrupulous (meticulous)

一丝一毫 yīsī-yīháo a tiny bit (of); a trace; an iota (of):～也不变 not change by one iota

一塌糊涂 yītāhútú in a complete mess; in utter disorder; in an awful state

一体化 yītǐhuà integration

一条龙服务 yītiáolóng fúwù an integral coordinated service

一条心 yītiáoxīn be of one mind (with); be at one (with):和群众～ be at one with the masses

一统天下 yītǒng-tiānxià the whole empire under one ruler

一团和气 yītuán héqì keep on good terms with all people (at the expense of principle); have unprincipled amity; be always friendly with everybody on all occasions; an unprincipled peace

一团漆黑 yītuán-qīhēi pitch-dark—utterly hopeless; be completely in the dark; be entirely ignorant of

一团糟 yītuánzāo be in a complete (terrible) mess; make a mess of; utter chaos; hopelessly chaotic:把事情搞得～ make a mess of the job

一网打尽 yīwǎng-dǎjìn round up the whole gang; wipe out at a snap; capture (take) all with one haul of the dragnet; make a wholesale arrest of; make a clean sweep

一往无前 yīwǎngwúqián press forward with an indomitable spirit; advance indomitably:具有～精神的人 man of indomitable spirit

一味 yīwèi stubbornly; blindly: ～迁就 make one concession after another; make endless concessions. ～退让 constant retreat

一文不值 yīwénbùzhí not worth a cent; entirely worthless

一窝蜂 yīwōfēng like a swarm of bees

一无可取 yīwú-kěqǔ worthless; good for nothing

一无是处 yīwú-shìchù can never get anything right; without a single merit; wrong all over; have no merit to speak of

一无所长 yīwú-suǒcháng have no special ability (skill); be Jack of all trades

一无所有 yīwú-suǒyǒu be penniless (destitute); have nothing to call one's own; not own anything in the world; not have a thing to one's name

一无所知 yīwú-suǒzhī have no knowledge of; be ignorant of; know nothing about

一五一十 yīwǔ-yīshí (relate, narrate) systematically in full detail; (go) into the ins and outs (of sth.)

一席话 yīxíhuà what one says during a conversation

一系列 yīxìliè a series of

一下子 yīxiàzi ① all of a sudden;

all at once：灯～全亮了。The lamps lit up all at once. ② at one stroke; at a stretch; in (at) one go：～把工作做完 finish the work in one go ③ once：再试～ try once again

一线 yīxiàn a gleam; a ray of：～生机 a last hope of recovery. ～希望 a ray of hope

一显身手 yīxiǎnshēnshǒu display one's skill

一相(厢)情愿 yīxiāng(xiāng)-qíngyuàn one's own wishful thinking; Only one party is willing.; unilateral willingness

一向 yīxiàng consistently; all the while; always; all along：他们～努力工作。They are always hardworking.

一心 yīxīn wholeheartedly; heart and soul; of one mind：～为公 be heart and soul devoted to public interests; devote oneself wholeheartedly to public interests. ～一德 be of one heart and one mind. ～一意 be bent on; heart and soul

一宿 yīxiǔ one night

一言不发 yīyán-bùfā not say a word; keep one's mouth shut; remain silent

一言难尽 yīyán-nánjìn it's a long story (to tell); it is hard to explain in a few words; be difficult to put in a nutshell

一言为定 yīyán-wéidìng It's a deal.; That's settled then.

一言以蔽之 yī yán yǐ bì zhī (to put it) in a nutshell; in a word; to sum it up; in short; briefly; summarily：～，我们要有准备。In a nutshell, we must be prepared.

一眼看穿 yīyǎn-kànchuān see through sth. at a glance

一衣带水 yīyī-dàishuǐ a strip of water：～的邻邦 close neighbouring countries (separated only by a strip of water; with only a strip of water in between)

一意孤行 yīyì-gūxíng persist in wilfully and arbitrarily; act in disregard of the opinion of others; be bent on having one's own way; wilfully cling to one's own course

一语道破 yīyǔ-dàopò lay bare the truth with one remark; hit the nail on the head

一元化 yīyuánhuà centralized; unified：～领导 unified leadership

一元论 yīyuánlùn ［哲］ monism

一朝 yīzhāo ① in one day ② once

一针见血 yīzhēn-jiànxuè say straight to the point; hit the nail on the head; go right to the heart of the matter; penetratingly; incisively：说了一句～的话 make a pointed remark

一阵 yīzhèn a fit (of coughing, etc.); a spell (of cold weather); a burst (of applause, etc.); a gust (of wind)：～阵笑声 peals of laughter

一知半解 yīzhī-bànjiě have scanty knowledge; know sth. superficially; have a smattering knowledge (about); have a half-baked knowledge; have an imperfect understanding of sth.

一直 yīzhí ① straight：沿着这条街～走下去。Go straight down the street. ② all the way；continuously；all along；always

一纸空文 yīzhǐ-kōngwén empty words on a sheet of paper；a mere scrap of paper；a bit of waste paper

一致 yīzhì showing no difference；unanimous；identical；consistent：～通过 be adopted（carried）unanimously. 看法～ have identical views

一专多能 yīzhuān-duōnéng become expert in one field while at the same time possessing all-round knowledge and ability；expert in one thing and good at many；one specialty and multiple abilities

一字不提 yīzì bùtí not breathe a single word about…

一总 yīzǒng ① altogether；all told；in all ② all

医 yī ①〈动〉cure；treat：把她的病～好 cure her of her illness 〈名〉② doctor ③ medical science；medicine：行～ practise medicine

医道 yīdào art of healing；medical knowledge；physician's skill

医德 yīdé medical ethics

医科 yīkē medical courses in general；medicine：～大学 medical university

医疗 yīliáo ① medical treatment：～保险基金 medical benefits fund. ～保险制度 health insurance system. ～卫生机构 medical and public health departments. 公费～ free medical service；public health service ② treat；cure

医生 yīshēng doctor；mediciner；medical man

医师 yīshī （qualified） doctor；surgeon；physician

医士 yīshì medical assistant；practitioner with secondary medical education

医术 yīshù medical art；medical skill

医务 yīwù medical service：～室（所）medical clinic（office）

医学 yīxué medical science；medicine：～科学院 academy of medical science

医学院 yīxuéyuàn medical college

医药费 yīyàofèi medical expenses （charges）

医院 yīyuàn hospital：被送进～ be taken（sent）to hospital

医治 yīzhì cure；treat；heal：给某人～流行性感冒 treat sb. for influenza

医嘱 yīzhǔ doctor's advice（orders）

伊 yī〈代〉he or she

伊甸园 Yīdiànyuán the Garden of Eden；paradise

伊斯兰教 Yīsīlánjiào Islamism；Islam：～国家 Islamic countries

yí

宜 yí ①〈形〉appropriate；suitable；fitting：适～该场合的言词 words suitable to the occasion ②〈动〉should; ought to: 不～操之过急。You shout not act in haste.

宜人 yírén delightful; pleasant:景物～ attractive scenery

宜于 yíyú be suitable for

颐

yí〈动〉keep fit; take care of oneself

颐和园 yíhéyuán the Summer Palace (in Beijing)

颐养 yíyǎng keep fit; take good care of oneself

夷

yí ①〈形〉safe; smooth:化险为～ turn danger into safety ②〈动〉raze:～为平地 make the land level; raze (houses) to the ground

痍

yí〈名〉wound; trauma:满目疮～ be covered all over with wounds and scars

姨

yí〈名〉① one's mother's sister; aunt ② one's wife's sister; sister-in-law

姨表 yíbiǎo maternal cousin

姨夫 yífu the husband of one's maternal aunt; uncle

姨母 yímǔ maternal aunt; aunt

遗

yí〈动〉① lose ② omit; slip: 巨细无～ slip over nothing whether big or small ③ abandon; desert:～弃丈夫 desert one's husband ④ leave behind; bequeath; hand down:～留给我们的精神 spiritual legacy handed down to us by ⑤〈名〉something lost:路不拾～。No one pockets anything found on the road.

遗笔 yíbǐ writings left behind by the deceased

遗产 yíchǎn legacy; inheritance; heritage:～税 inheritance tax; succession duty; legacy tax. 文化～ cultural heritage

遗臭万年 yíchòu-wànnián leave behind an ill name forever; be cursed forever by posterity; leave a bad name forever; remain forever infamous; go down in history as a byword of infamy; everlasting shame

遗传 yíchuán heredity; inheritance:～工程 genetic engineering. ～学 genetics

遗毒 yídú pernicious influence; evil legacy

遗风 yífēng customs which have been handed down

遗稿 yígǎo a manuscript left unpublished by the author at his death; a posthumous manuscript

遗孤 yígū orphan

遗骨 yígǔ remains (of the dead)

遗憾 yíhàn pity; regret:对某事表示～ express regret over sth. 令人～的 regrettable; woeful

遗恨 yíhèn eternal regret

遗祸 yíhuò leave a legacy of trouble

遗迹 yíjì historical remains; traces; vestiges; sites

遗教 yíjiào teachings of the deceased

遗留 yíliú leave over (behind); hand down:历史上～下来的问题 problems left over from his-

tory
遗漏 yílòu omit; drop; leave out
遗弃 yíqì abandon; desert; forsake; cast off: ～妻儿 forsake one's wife and children
遗容 yíróng ① the looks of the deceased ② a portrait of the deceased
遗失 yíshī lose; drop: ～货物 missing goods. ～声明 lost property notice
遗事 yíshì ① incidents of past ages ② deeds of those now dead
遗书 yíshū ① a letter or note left by one immediately before death ② posthumous works
遗孀 yíshuāng widow
遗体 yítǐ remains (of the dead): 向～告别 pay one's last respects to the remains
遗物 yíwù things left behind by the deceased
遗像 yíxiàng portrait of the deceased
遗训 yíxùn teachings of the deceased
遗言 yíyán words of the deceased; dying words; one's last words
遗址 yízhǐ site; remains; ruins
遗志 yízhì unfulfilled wish; behest
遗嘱 yízhǔ testament; will: 立～ make a will
遗著 yízhù posthumous works (of an author)
遗族 yízú bereaved family

仪 yí〈名〉① appearance: 威～ impressive and dignified manner ② ceremony; courtesy; etiquette: 司～ master of ceremonies ③ gift; present: 赙～ a gift to a bereaved family ④ apparatus; instrument: 子午～ meridian instrument
仪表 yíbiǎo ① appearance; bearing; looks: ～堂堂 look dignified; look impressive and dignified. ～之美 personal beauty ② meter: ～厂 instrument and meter plant
仪器 yíqì apparatus; instrument
仪容 yíróng looks; appearance
仪式 yíshì ceremony; rites; exercises: 毕业～ commencement exercises
仪仗 yízhàng flags, weapons, etc. carried by a guard of honour: ～队 guard of honour
仪制 yízhì ritual system

移 yí〈动〉① move; remove; shift: ～山倒海 remove mountains and drain seas ② change; alter
移动电话 yídòng diànhuà mobile phone; cellular telephone
移风易俗 yífēng-yìsú change existing (prevailing) habits and customs; transformation of customs and habits; transform established traditions and practices
移交 yíjiāo turn over; hand over; transfer: 把工作～给某人 hand over one's job to sb. 完成～手续 complete the hand-over
移居 yíjū ① move house; remove one's residence ② migrate: ～别国 migrate to another country

移民 yímín ① migrate;[移出] emigrate;[移入] immigrate ② migrant;[移出者] emigrant;[移入者] immigrant
移民点 yímíndiǎn settlement
移送 yísòng transfer
移植 yízhí ① transplant:～外国法律 transplant foreign laws ② graft:～新皮肤 graft new skin (onto)

疑 yí〈动〉doubt; suspect; not believe:怀～某人 doubt sb.
疑案 yí'àn doubtful case; mystery:～小说 mystery novel
疑点 yídiǎn doubtful (questionable) point; problematic points
疑惑 yíhuò feel puzzled; be completely bewildered; feel uncertain; not be convinced:～不决 be hesitating and unable to decide
疑虑 yílǜ misgivings; doubts:～重重 be full of misgivings
疑难 yínàn difficult to solve; knotty:～问题 knotty problem
疑念 yíniàn suspicions; doubts
疑团 yítuán doubts and suspicions
疑问 yíwèn question; query; doubt
疑心 yíxīn suspicion; doubt; suspect:～太重 be too ready to suspect; become suspicious
疑义 yíyì doubt; question:毫无～ beyond (all) doubt; no doubt
疑云 yíyún misgivings or suspicions clouding one's mind

怡 yí〈形〉happy; cheerful; joyful
怡乐 yílè cheerful; happy
怡然 yírán contend; happy:～自得 happy and contended (pleased with oneself)

贻 yí〈动〉① make a gift of sth.; present ② leave behind; leave over:～患 sow seeds of disaster
贻害 yíhài leave a legacy of trouble; do harm (to); cause trouble (to):～无穷 leave endless troubles behind; entail untold troubles
贻患 yíhuàn leave a legacy of trouble
贻误 yíwù affect adversely; bungle; mislead:～终身 bring evil upon one's whole life
贻笑大方 yíxiàodàfāng make a laughing stock of oneself; incur the ridicule of experts; expose oneself to ridicule
贻训 yíxùn teachings of the deceased

彝 yí〈名〉wine vessel:～器 sacrificial vessel
彝族 Yízú Yi nationality (distributed over Yunnan, Sichuan and Guizhou provinces)

yǐ

椅 yǐ〈名〉chair:安乐～ easy chair
椅套 yǐtào slipcover for a chair

倚 yǐ〈动〉① lean on (against); rest against (on):～墙 lean against the wall ② rely on; depend on:～剑雄才 heroic genuis rely on the sword ③

〈形〉partial；biased：不偏不～ impartial；unbiased

倚靠 yǐkào rest (lean) on or against

倚老卖老 yǐlǎo-màilǎo unduly presumptions because of one's seniority or old age；get self-conceited because of seniority

倚势欺人 yǐshì-qīrén take an advantage of one's position to bully people；abuse one's power to bully others

倚仗 yǐzhàng rely on；count on：～权力 rely on one's power

倚重 yǐzhòng trust in sb.；rely on sb.'s service：受上级～ be relied on (upon) by one's superior

蚁

yǐ〈名〉ant

蚁巢 yǐcháo ant nest

蚁丘 yǐqiū ant hill

乙

yǐ〈形〉second

乙醇 yǐchún ethyl alcohol；ethanol；alcohol

乙等 yǐděng second rate；grade B

乙炔 yǐquē acetylene；ethyne

乙烷 yǐwán ethane

乙烯 yǐxī ethylene

乙型肝炎 yǐxíng gānyán hepatitis B

已

yǐ ①〈动〉stop；cease；end：争论不～ argue endlessly〈副〉② already：问题～解决。The problem has already been solved.

已拨款项 yǐbō kuǎnxiàng allotment issued

已产子女数 yǐchǎn zǐnǚshù [计生] parity

已到汇票 yǐdào huìpiào arrival draft

已故 yǐgù deceased；late

已婚人口 yǐhūn rénkǒu married persons

已经 yǐjīng already

已久 yǐjiǔ long ago：那事情发生～。That happened long ago.

已决犯 yǐjuéfàn convicted person；sentenced offender

已然 yǐrán be already so；have already become a fact

已实现利润 yǐ shíxiàn lìrùn realized profit

已收入金额 yǐ shōurù jīn'é amount received

已往 yǐwǎng in the past；before

已知数 yǐzhīshu [数] known number

已注册资本 yǐ zhùcè zīběn registered capital

以

yǐ ①〈动〉use；take：～毒攻毒 use poison as an antidote to poison〈介〉② by means of；by；with：～不变应万变 meet changes with constancy ③ because of：不～人废言 not reject a saying because the speaker is a person of no significance ④ according to：～销定产 basing production on sales prospects；producing according to sales ⑤ in order to；so as to：～儆效尤 in order to warn against bad examples

以备万一 yǐbèi-wànyī provide against any contingency (accidents, emergencies, eventualities)；be (prepared) ready for any contingency

以便 yǐbiàn in order to; so as to; in order that; so that:我们用电子计算机～节省时间。We use the computer in order to save time.

以产顶进 yǐchǎn dǐngjìn [经] substitution of the products manufactured by... for similar imported products

以产定销 yǐchǎn dìngxiāo basing sales on production

以次 yǐcì ① in proper order ② the following

以次冲好 yǐcì-chōnghǎo ① sell seconds at best quality prices ② shoddy:～的货物 shoddy goods

以德报怨 yǐdé-bàoyuàn return good for evil; repay injury with kindness

以毒攻毒 yǐdú-gōngdú fight poison with poison; use poison as an antidote for poison

以防万一 yǐfáng-wànyì be prepared for all contingencies; be ready for any eventuality:也许不会下雨,不过还是带把伞,～。It may not rain, but you'd better take an umbrella just in case.

以工代赈 yǐgōng-dàizhèn expand job opportunities in place of granting relief

以古非今 yǐgǔ-fēijīn negate the present with the ancient

以后 yǐhòu after; afterwards; later; hereafter

以及 yǐjí as well as; along with; and

以己度人 yǐjǐ-dùrén measure others after oneself; judge people by oneself

以假乱真 yǐjiǎ-luànzhēn confuse the genuine with the fake

以理服人 yǐlǐ-fúrén persuade through reasoning; convince people by reasoning (sound argument)

以力服人 yǐlì-fúrén force people to submit; dominate others by force

以邻为壑 yǐlíng-wéihè use the neighbour's field as an outlet for his overflow; shift one's troubles onto others; dump rubbish in the neighbour's yard

以貌取人 yǐmào-qǔrén judge (of) a man by his looks

以免 yǐmiǎn in order to avoid; so as not to

以偏概全 yǐpiān-gàiquán take a part for the whole

以其人之道,还治其人之身 yǐ qírén zhī dào, huán zhì qírén zhī shēn Deal with a man as he deals with you.; Pay him in his own coin.; Do unto them what they do unto us;

以前 yǐqián before; formerly; previously

以权谋私 yǐquán-móusī abuse power for personal gains; seek private gains through power

以上 yǐshàng ① more than; over; above ② the above; the foregoing; the above-mentioned

以身殉职 yǐshēn-xùnzhí die at one's post

以身作则 yǐshēn-zuòzé make

oneself an example for others; set an example with one's own conduct

以事实为根据,以法律为准绳 yǐ shìshí wéi gēnjù, yǐ fǎlǜ wéi zhǔnshéng take facts as the basis and the law as the criterion

以势压人 yǐshì-yārén overwhelm people with one's power; overawe others by the use of one's position (power)

以税代利 yǐshuì dàilì payment of tax in place of the handing of profit; substituting tax for profit

以退为进 yǐtuì-wéijìn retreat in order to advance; make concessions in order to gain advantages

以外 yǐwài beyond; outside; other than

以往 yǐwǎng before; formerly; in the past

以下 yǐxià ① below; under ② the following; hereafter

以小人之心,度君子之腹 yǐ xiǎorén zhī xīn, duó jūnzǐ zhī fù measure the stature of great men by the yardstick of small men; like a dwarf plumbing the heart of a giant with his midget sounding rod; measure the mind of an upright man by the yardstick of a knave

以虚带实 yǐxū-dàishí lead practice with ideology (metaphor for using correct ideology to lead people's practical activities)

以牙还牙 yǐyá-huányá tooth for tooth; tit for tat

以怨报德 yǐyuàn-bàodé return evil for good

以至 yǐzhì ① to such an extent to …; so… that… ② up to; down to

以致 yǐzhì(so) that; with the result that; as a result; consequently

以资 yǐzī as a means of:～鼓励 as an encouragement

yì

意 yì〈名〉① meaning; sense; idea:达～ express one's ideas ② intention; wish; desire:歹～ evil intention ③ hint; trace; suggestion:春～盎然。Spring is very much in the air. ④〈动〉expect; anticipate:不～ unexpectedly

意会 yìhuì understood by insight; sense:只可～,不可言传 can be fully understood but not in tangible terms

意见 yìjiàn ① idea; opinion; view:交换～ exchange ideas ② objection; different opinion (view):我对这种办法很有～。I strongly object to this method. ③ complaint:大家对他很有～。People have a lot of complaints about him.

意境 yìjìng artistic conception; realm of thought; realm of art:～高旷 full of poetic imagination

意料 yìliào expect; anticipate:～之外 beyond expectation; contrary to expectation

意念 yìniàn thought; idea

意气 yìqì ① will and spirit; spirit:～风发 elated and inspired with a lofty idea; daring and vigorus; high-spirited and vigorous ② personal feelings:～用事 be carried (swayed) away by personal feelings ③ temperament:～相投 be congenial (with); agree very well (with)

意趣 yìqù interest and charm:山水诗的～ picturesqueness of landscape poetry

意识 yìshì consciousness; mind:～到 be conscious of; be aware of. ～流 stream of consciousness. ～之外 outside the mind

意识形态 yìshìxíngtài ideology:～冲突 ideological contradiction

意思 yìsi ① meaning; idea:我没听清楚你的～。I didn't catch your meaning. ② wish; desire; opinion:照自己的～办 act up to one's opinions ③ hint; suggestion; trace:天有点下雪的～。It looks like snow. ④ fun; interest:滑冰很有～。Skating is good fun.

意图 yìtú intention; purpose; design:～伦理 ethic of intention

意外 yìwài ① unthought-of; unexpected; unforeseen ② accident:～保险 accident insurance. ～损失 windfall loss. 以免发生～ so as to avoid accidents

意味 yìwèi ① sense; significance:～深长 full of meaning; significant; profound ② interest:带有文学～ with a literary flavour

意向 yìxiàng intention; intent:～书 letter of intent; statement of intention

意象 yìxiàng image; imagery:～小说 imagery fiction

意兴 yìxìng mood to do sth.; interest; enthusiasm:～索然 have not the least interest

意义 yìyì sense; significance; meaning

意译 yìyì free(liberal)translation

意在言外 yìzài-yánwài There is something beyond the words.

意志 yìzhì will; volition; moral will:～薄弱 weakness of the will. 出于自己的～ of one's own volition

意中人 yìzhōngrén person of one's heart; the person one is in love with

臆

yì ①〈名〉chest; bosom ②〈副〉subjectively

臆测 yìcè conjecture; make certain assumptions; guess

臆断 yìduàn form a subjective judgment; assume

臆说 yìshuō hypothesis; supposition; assumption

臆造 yìzào invent; make up; concoct; fabricate:～的字眼 artificial verbal constructions

亦

yì〈副〉also; too

亦步亦趋 yìbù-yìqū If someone else takes one step, they follow with the same step.; ape someone at every step; follow in one's steps; perform to someone's baton; imitate sb.'s every move

亦工亦农 yìgōng-yìnóng engaged in industry and agriculture; be worker and peasant

奕 yì〈形〉grand

奕奕 yìyì energetic; vigorous; radiating health and vitality: 神采～ look hale and hearty; brim with energy and vitality; in buoyant spirits; in fine fettle

裔 yì〈名〉descendant; posterity: 华～美国人 an American of Chinese descent

益 yì ①〈名〉benefit; advantage; good: 受～ receive benefit ②〈形〉beneficial; helpful: 有～于健康的 beneficial to the health ③〈动〉increase ④〈副〉increasingly; all the more: 日～尖锐 become increasingly acute

益处 yìchù advantage; benefit; use; good

益友 yìyǒu helpful friend; friend and mentor

溢 yì ①〈动〉brim over; overflow: 洋～ be filled with; brim with ②〈形〉excessive; undue

溢出 yìchū overflow; spill over

溢价 yìjià at a premium

溢于言表 yìyúyánbiǎo shown in facial expressions; (feeling) shows between the lines

溢美 yìměi excessive praise; fulsome praise; undeserved praise

缢 yì〈动〉hang: 自～ hang oneself

谊 yì〈名〉friendship: 世～ friendship spanning two or more generations

抑 yì〈动〉① restrain; repress; curb: ～制不住眼泪 can hardly restrain tears ② keep down: 遏～ suppress; keep down

抑扬顿挫 yìyáng-dùncuò modulation in tone; cadence

抑郁 yìyù depressed; gloomy; despondent: ～不平 feel disgruntled

抑制 yìzhì restrain; check; control; inhibit: ～价格上涨 inhibit price hikes. ～政府官员贪污腐败 restrain government officials from embezzlement and corruption

易 yì〈形〉① easy: 简～ simple and easy ② amiable; gentle: 平～ amiable; unassuming〈动〉③ change; alter: ～手 change hands ④ exchange: 以物～物 barter

易货贸易 yìhuòmàoyì barter (trade)

易拉罐 yìlāguàn easy-open tin

易燃 yìrán inflammable; combustible: ～物 combustibles

易如反掌 yìrúfǎnzhǎng be simple and easy; as easy as turning one's hand; can be easily accomplished

易手 yìshǒu change hands

易于 yìyú be easy to

义 yì〈名〉① justice; righteousness: 社会正～ social justice ② human relationship or feelings:

情～ ties of friendship, comradeship, etc. ③ meaning; significance: 歧～ different meanings〈形〉④ equitable; just: ～战 just war ⑤ adopted; adoptive: ～母 adoptive mother

义不容辞 yìbùróngcí be duty-bound; have an unshirkable duty; act from a strong sense of duty; bounden duty; inescapable duty; an obligation one cannot escape

义愤 yìfèn just (moral) indignation; righteous anger: ～填膺 be filled with righteous indignation

义和团运动 yìhétuán yùndòng Yihetuan Movement (an anti-imperialist armed struggle in 1900, known to the West as the Boxers); Boxer Uprising

义举 yìjǔ magnanimous act undertaken for the public good; an undertaking in public interests

义理 yìlǐ righteousness and principle; moral principle

义卖 yìmài sale of goods for charity; charity bazaar

义气 yìqì personal loyalty; faithfulness to friends: 讲～ be loyal to one's friends

义塾 yìshú private school charging no tuition

义务 yìwù ① duty; obligation: 尽～ do one's duty ② unpaid; voluntary; compulsory: ～教育 compulsory education. ～劳动 voluntary labour; work without pay

义演 yìyǎn benefit performance (play, show); benefit: ～音乐会 benefit concert

义养 yìyǎng adoption

义勇军进行曲 Yìyǒngjūn jìnxíng qǔ March of the Volunteers (the national anthem of the People's Republic of China)

义诊 yìzhěn see patients on a volunteer basis

义正词严 yìzhèngcíyán speak sternly out of a sense of justice; speak in just and severe terms; speak with the force of justice

驿 yì〈名〉post

驿道 yìdào post road

绎 yì ①〈动〉unravel silk; sort out ②〈形〉continuous; unceasing

议 yì ①〈名〉opinion; view: 商～ exchange views on ②〈动〉talk over; discuss; negotiate: ～而不决 discuss sth. without reaching a decision

议案 yì'àn proposal; motion; bill: ～未通过。The bill did not get through.

议程 yìchéng agenda: 列入～ place on (include in) the agenda. ～项目 item on the agenda

议定书 yìdìngshū protocol

议和 yìhé negotiate peace; bury the hatchet

议会 yìhuì legislative assembly; [英国等的] parliament; [美国的] congress; [日本等的] diet; chamber; house

议价 yìjià ① negotiate a price ② negotiated price: ～粮 grain with negotiated price

议题 yìtí topic for discussion; subject under discussion

议销 yìxiāo nogotiated sale

议员 yìyuán member of a legislative assembly;［英国等的］Member of Parliament (MP);［美国的］Congressman or Congresswoman

议院 yìyuàn legislative assembly; parliament; congress

议长 yìzhǎng speaker; president

议政 yìzhèng discuss affairs of government

轶

yì〈动〉① be lost ② excel

轶事 yìshì anecdote (esp. about a famous person); historiette; ana

屹

yì〈形〉towering (like a peak)

屹立 yìlì stand lofty and firm like a mountain; stand erect; tower above

屹然 yìrán towering; majestic; imposing:～不动 stand firmly

诣

yì ①〈动〉call on (sb. one respects); visit (a place where sb. is) ②〈名〉(academic, artistic etc.) attainments:科学上的造～ scientific attainments

逸

yì ①〈形〉easy; leisurely:安～ easy and comfortable ②〈动〉escape; run away: 逃～ run away; escape

逸事 yìshì anecdote; story

逸致 yìzhì carefree mood

翌

yì〈形〉immediately following in time; next:～年 next year

肄

yì〈动〉study

肄业 yìyè study in school or at college; be at school; study:大学～二年 be in university for two years

毅

yì〈形〉firm; resolute; determined:刚～ resolute and steadfast

毅力 yìlì will power; resoluteness; stamina; strong will

毅然 yìrán resolutely; firmly; determinedly; with fortitude

疫

yì〈名〉epidemic; disease; pestilence:畜～ epidemic disease of domestic animals

疫病 yìbìng［流行病］epidemic;［瘟疫、鼠疫等］plague; pestilence

疫苗 yìmiáo vaccine

疫情 yìqíng epidemic situation

亿

yì〈数〉a hundred million

亿万 yìwàn hundreds of millions (of)

忆

yì〈动〉call (bring) to one's mind; recall; remember:～旧社会的苦 recall one's sufferings in the old society

忆旧 yìjiù recollect the past; recall the bygone days with nostalgia

忆念 yìniàn cherish the memory of; think of: ～战友 think of one's old comrades-in-arms

艺

yì〈名〉① skill; crafts-manship: 武～ skill in *wushu* ② art:文～ literature and art

艺龄 yìlíng length of sb.'s stage career

艺名 yìmíng stage name

艺人 yìrén ①professional player; actor; artist ② craftsman; handicraftsman; artisan

艺术 yìshù art:～表演团体 performing art troupes. ～感染力 artistic appeal; artistically compelling. ～学院 conservatory; art college. 富有～魅力的作品 works which have a great artistic appeal

艺坛 yìtán art circles

艺徒 yìtú apprentice:当～ serve as an apprentice

艺苑 yìyuàn realm of art and literature; art and literary circles

呓 yì〈动〉talk in one's sleep

呓语 yìyǔ ① talk in one's sleep ② ravings; ranting; nonsensical talk; delirium

役 yì〈名〉① labour; service ② military service:服兵～ perform military service ③ use a servant ④ servant ⑤ campaign; battle

役畜 yìchù draught animal; beast of burden

译 yì〈动〉translate; interpret:～成德语 translate into German. 编～ translate and edit

译本 yìběn translation; version; garb:法～ French version. 《哈姆莱特》的中～ *Hamlet* in Chinese garb

译丛 yìcōng translated theses:哲学～ translated theses on philosophy

译电 yìdiàn ① encode or encipher a telegram ② decode or decipher a telegram

译名 yìmíng translated term or name

译审 yìshěn ① translation and revision ② [职称]senior translator:副～ associate senior translator

译文 yìwén translation; version; rendering

译员 yìyuán interpreter

译者 yìzhě translator

译制 yìzhì dub; translate and make:～电视连续剧 translate and make over a television serial drama. ～片 dubbed film

译著 yìzhù translations

翼 yì〈名〉① the wing of a bird, aeroplane, etc.:飞机机～ the wings of an aeroplane ② flank:侧～攻击 a flank attack

翼翼 yìyì carefully; cautiously:小心～ with utmost care

异 yì〈形〉① different; differential:～词 dissenting words ② unusual; strange; foreign:～常现象 abnormal phenomena. ～民族 alien nation ③ another; other:～地扶贫 poverty alleviation by other areas

异邦 yìbāng foreign country

异常 yìcháng ① unusual; abnormal:～心理学 abnormal psychology ② extremely:～困难 extremely difficult

异词 yìcí dissenting words

异端 yìduān heterodoxy; heresy:

视为～ regard as heresy

异国 yìguó foreign country (land)

异化 yìhuà [哲] alienation; estrangement

异己 yìjǐ alien; dissident: 排除～ get rid of dissidents

异教 yìjiào heathenism; paganism: ～徒 pagan; heretic

异口同声 yìkǒu-tóngshēng speak with one voice; in (with) one voice; in unison

异曲同工 yìqǔ-tónggōng Different tunes rendered with equal skill—different in approach but equally satisfactory in result; the same result achieved by different methods

异说 yìshuō ① dissenting views; different views ② absurd remarks

异体字 yìtǐzì a variant form of a Chinese character

异味 yìwèi ① rare delicacy ② peculiar smell

异物 yìwù ① foreign matter; a foreign body ② a dead person; ghost: 化为～ give up the ghost; die ③a rare object

异乡 yìxiāng foreign land; strange land

异想天开 yìxiǎng-tiānkāi indulge in wildest fantasy; give free rein to one's fantasy; stretch of the imagination

异心 yìxīn disloyalty; infidelity

异性 yìxìng ① the opposite sex ② different in properties (nature)

异议 yìyì objection; dissidence; disagreement: 表示(提出)～ make (raise) an objection (to)

异族 yìzú alien races; different nation or race

yīn

音 yīn〈名〉① sound: 鼻～ nasal sound ② tone; accent ③ news; tidings: 佳～ welcome news. 乡～ local accent

音标 yīnbiāo phonetic symbol (sign)

音波 yīnbō sound wave

音符 yīnfú [乐] note

音阶 yīnjié [乐] scale

音节 yīnjié syllable

音量 yīnliàng volume (of sound)

音频 yīnpín audio frequency

音色 yīnsè tone colour; timbre

音箱 yīnxiāng speaker

音响 yīnxiǎng sound; acoustics; audio: ～设备 stereo system; hi-fi (acoustic, sound) equipment. ～效果 sound effects. ～组合 hi-fi components. 高保真～爱好者 audiophile

音像 yīnxiàng phonotape and videotape: ～产品 audio-video product. ～出版业 audio-visual publishing industry. ～公司 recording and video company. ～市场 tape market. ～书店 audio-visual shop

音信 yīnxìn news; tidings: ～全无。No news whatever has come from sb.

音乐 yīnyuè music: ～会 concert. ～人 musical producer. ～学院 conservatory of music

音质 yīnzhì ① tone quality ② acoustic fidelity

因 yīn ①〈动〉follow; carry on as before: ～循守旧 follow the beaten track; get stuck in the grooves ②〈名〉cause; reason: 成～ cause of formation; contributing factor〈介〉③ according to; in accordance with; in the light of: ～人而异。It differs from man to man. ④ because of; as a result of: ～公牺牲 die while on duty

因材施教 yīncái-shījiào educate a student according to his natural ability; teaching students in accordance with their aptitude; teaching according to individual talent

因地制宜 yīndì-zhìyí suit measures to local conditions; act in the light of local conditions; take such measures as are suitable to local conditions; adopt measures in the light of the realities of specific regions

因工负伤 yīngōng fùshāng work-related injury

因果 yīnguǒ cause and effect: ～关系 causality. ～律 law of causation

因祸得福 yīnhuò-défú Luck grows out of adversity.; Good comes out of misfortune.

因陋就简 yīnlòu-jiùjiǎn adapt oneself to the available conditions; make do with whatever is available; make do with the meagre means at hand

因势利导 yīnshì-lìdǎo guide sth. along its course of development; guide sth. in the light of its general trend; adroitly guide action according to circumstances

因素 yīnsù factor; element

因袭 yīnxí adopt by tradition; follow (old customs, rules, etc.); inherit

因小失大 yīnxiǎo-shīdà try to save a little only to lose a lot; lose a great deal by trying to save a little; suffer a big loss for a little gain; penny wise; pound foolish

因噎废食 yīnyē-fèishí give up eating for fear of choking; throw away the apple because of the core

因缘 yīnyuán ①[佛]principal and subsidiary cause; pratitya; causation ② predestined relationship

茵 yīn〈名〉mattress: 绿草～～ green and lush

姻 yīn〈名〉① marriage: 联～ be related by marriage; be connected by marriage ② relation by marriage

姻亲 yīnqīn relation by marriage; affinal; affine; in-laws: ～关系 affinity

姻缘 yīnyuán the happy fate which brings lovers together; marriage: 美满～ conjugal felicity; happy marriage

殷 yīn〈形〉① rich; abundant: ～实家庭 well-off family ② eager; ardent: ～～盼望 eagerly expect ③ hospitable

殷富 yīnfù wealthy; well-off

殷切 yīnqiè earnest; ardent; eager: ～期望 ardent expectation

殷勤 yīnqín eagerly attentive; solicitous; cordial: ～招待 offer cordial hospitality. 对某人献～ pay one's attentions to sb.; do everything to please sb.

殷实 yīnshí well-off; substantial

殷墟 yīnxū [历] the Yin ruins

阴 yīn〈名〉① (in Chinese philosophy, medicine, etc.) *yin*, the feminine or negative principle in nature: ～阳五行理论 *yin-yang* and five elements theory ② the moon: ～历 lunar calendar ③ shade: 树～ tree shade ④ back: 碑～ the back face of a tablet ⑤ private parts (esp. of the female)〈形〉⑥ cloudy; overcast: 天～了。The sky is overcast ⑦ hidden; covert; concealed: ～一套, 阳一套 wear one face in public and another in private ⑧ negative: ～电 negative electricity

阴暗 yīn'àn dark; gloomy: ～面 dark side; seamy side; negative aspect

阴风 yīnfēng evil wind

阴干 yīngān be placed in the shade to dry; dry in the shade

阴魂 yīnhún spirit; soul; ghost

阴间 yīnjiān netherworld; lower world

阴刻 yīnkè intaglio

阴凉 yīnliáng ① shady and cool ② a cool place; shade

阴谋 yīnmóu intrigue; plot; conspiracy; scheme: ～诡计 schemes and intrigues; conspiracies and plots

阴私 yīnsī shameful secret

阴天 yīntiān overcast sky; cloudy day

阴险 yīnxiǎn sinister; insidious; treacherous; vicious; malicious

阴笑 yīnxiào sinister smile

阴性 yīnxìng ①[医] negative ②[语] feminine gender: ～反应 negative reaction

阴阳 yīnyáng *yin* versus *yang* (negative principle versus positive principle); *yin yang*

阴影 yīnyǐng shadow

荫 yīn〈名〉shade: 绿～ shade of a tree
另见 yìn

荫蔽 yīnbì ① conceal; cover: ～集结 concentrate under cover ② be shaded; be hidden by foliage

yín

淫 yín〈形〉① excessive; over: ～雨 excessive rain ② lewd; undisciplined; wanton; licentious: ～妇 a wanton woman ③ obscene; pornographic ～画 pornographic (obscene) picture

淫荡 yíndàng loose in morals; lewd; lascivious; wanton; debauched: ～的引诱 libidinous temptations

淫秽(猥) yínhuì (wěi) obscene; bawdy; lewd: ～的出版物 ob-

scene publications
淫乱 yínluàn (sexually) promiscuous; licentious
淫书 yínshū obscene (pornographic) book; erotica
淫威 yínwēi abuse of authority (power); despotic power
淫雨 yínyǔ excessive rains
寅 yín 〈名〉 the third of the twelve Earthy Branches
寅吃卯粮 yínchīmǎoliáng eat next year's food; draw one's pay in advance
夤 yín ① 〈动〉hold sb. in respectful awe ② 〈形〉deep
吟 yín 〈动〉chant; recite: ～诗 recite poems; hum verse
吟咏 yínyǒng recite with a cadence; express or narrate in poetic form; chant: ～作诗 chant and write poems
吟游诗人 yínyóu shīrén bard
吟志 yínzhì sing one's heart's intent
银 yín〈名〉① silver ② concerning currency or money: ～币 silver coin
银白 yínbái silvery white
银本位 yínběnwèi silver standard
银锭 yíndìng silver ingot; sycee silver; sycee
银发 yínfà silver (silvery) hair: 满头～ silver-haired
银根 yíngēn money; money market: ～紧 tight money
银行 yínháng bank: ～承兑 banker's acceptance. ～存折 bankbook; passbook. ～担保 bank guarantee. ～团 syndicate; consortium. ～转帐 bank account transferences
银号 yínhào banking houses; money shops
银婚 yínhūn [结婚 25 周年纪念] silver wedding
银楼 yínlóu silverware shop; jeweller's shop
银幕 yínmù projection screen; screen: 宽～电影 wide screen film
银牌 yínpái silver medal; silver
银票 yínpiào (in former times) silver draft (a form of paper money)
银样蜡枪头 yínyàng làqiāngtóu pewter spearhead that shines like silver—an impressive looking but useless person; paper tiger
银圆 yínyuán silve dollar
银子 yínzi silver; money
霪 yín〈名〉 excessive rains

yǐn

饮 yǐn 〈动〉drink: 畅～ drink one's fill
另见 yìn
饮弹 yǐndàn be hit by a bullet
饮恨 yǐnhèn nurse a grievance
饮料 yǐnliào drink; beverage: 清凉～ cool drinks
饮食 yǐnshí food and drink; diet: ～服务行业 food, beverage trade
饮水思源 yǐnshuǐ-sīyuán When you drink water, think of its

source.；Think of the fountain when drinking the water.

饮鸩止渴 yǐnzhèn-zhǐkě drink poison to quench one's thirst; seek temporary relief regardless of the consequences

引 yǐn〈动〉① lead; guide:～导消费 guide consumption ② draw; pull; attract; lure:～而不发 draw the bow without shooting. ～入圈套 lure into a trap ③ cause; make; bring about:～出麻烦 cause troubles ④ cite; quote:～经据典 quote authoritative works

引爆 yǐnbào ignite; detonate

引产 yǐnchǎn induced labour

引导 yǐndǎo guide; lead

引渡 yǐndù [法] extradite

引火烧身 yǐnhuǒ-shāoshēn draw fire against oneself (① metaphor for asking for trouble and inviting destruction ② metaphor for leading cadres voluntarily exposing one's own problems to the masses to seek criticism and help.)

引见 yǐnjiàn present (a person) to another; introduce

引进 yǐnjìn ① introduce from elsewhere; import:～技术和设备的鉴定 appraise imported technology and equipment ② recommend

引咎 yǐnjiù take the blame; hold oneself responsible for a serious mistake:～辞职 take the blame to oneself and resign

引狼入室 yǐnláng-rùshì let a wolf into the house; invite a dangerous foe or wicked person in; throw the door open for a dangerous foe

引力 yǐnlì [物] gravitation; attraction

引起 yǐnqǐ cause; bring about; give rise to; evoke:～公愤 arouse (incur) public indignation

引人入胜 yǐnrén-rùshèng interesting and absorbing; fascinating; absorbing; enchanting; attractive; tempting; alluring

引人注目 yǐnrén-zhùmù attract sb.'s attention; attract the gaze of people; catch sb.'s eye; come to the front

引入歧途 yǐnrù-qítú lead sb. astray

引申 yǐnshēn extend (the meaning of a word, etc.):～义 extended meaning

引水 yǐnshuǐ ① draw water; lead water:～灌田 draw water into the fields ② pilot a ship into harbour; pilotage:～员 pilot

引退 yǐntuì retire from office; resign

引文 yǐnwén quoted passage; quotation

引言 yǐnyán introduction; preface; foreword

引以为戒 yǐnyǐwéijiè take warning from sth.; draw lessons from sth.

引用 yǐnyòng quote; cite

引诱 yǐnyòu lure; tempt; seduce; enticement:以金钱～某人 lure sb. with money

引证 yǐnzhèng cite as evidence;

quote as proof

引智工程 yǐnzhìgōngchéng project of introducing foreign expertise to China

引种 yǐnzhǒng introduce a fine variety

引子 yǐnzi ① an actor's opening words (either spoken or sung) ② introductory music ③ introductory remarks; introduction ④ an added ingredient (to enhance the efficacy of medicines)

隐 yǐn ①〈动〉hide; conceal: 对某人～瞒某事 conceal sth. from sb. ②〈形〉hidden; latent

隐蔽 yǐnbì conceal; cover (up); take cover: ～的阵地 concealed position. ～税 hidden tax

隐藏 yǐncáng hide; conceal; go into hiding; remain under; cover: ～的敌人 hidden enemy

隐恶扬善 yǐn'è-yángshàn conceal what is evil and publicize what is good

隐患 yǐnhuàn hidden trouble; hidden danger (peril): 消除～ remove a hidden peril

隐讳 yǐnhuì avoid mentioning; cover up

隐晦 yǐnhuì obscure; veiled: 写得很～ be couched in ambiguous terms

隐疾 yǐnjí unmentionable disease

隐居 yǐnjū live in seclusion; be a hermit

隐瞒 yǐnmán hold back; hide; conceal; [说假话] story (about): ～事实 hide the facts; withhold the truth. 她～年龄。She storied about her age.

隐匿 yǐnnì hide; conceal; veil: ～罪证 conceal criminal evidence

隐情 yǐnqíng facts one wishes to hide

隐忍 yǐnrěn forbear (from speaking); bear patiently: ～含垢 show utmost patience and forbearance towards insults

隐射 yǐnshè insinuate; hint

隐士 yǐnshì hermit; recluse

隐私 yǐnsī one's secrets; private matters one wants to hide: ～权 rights of privacy; privacy

隐形眼镜 yǐnxíngyǎnjìng contact lens

隐隐 yǐnyǐn indistinct; faint: ～作痛 feel a dull pain

隐语 yǐnyǔ enigmatic language

隐喻 yǐnyù metaphor

隐约 yǐnyuē dim; vague; indistinct: ～其词 use vague (ambiguous) language; speak in equivocal terms

瘾 yǐn〈名〉① addiction; habitual craving: 烟～ a craving for tobacco. 犯烟～ have an urge to smoke ② strong interest (in a sport or pastime): 有球～ have a passion for ball games

瘾君子 yǐnjūnzǐ pipe smoker

yìn

荫 yìn ①〈形〉shady; chilly and damp ②〈动〉shelter; bring under protection; patronage
另见 yīn

荫庇 yìnbì 〈旧〉protection by one's elders or ancestors;

protégés

荫凉 yìnliáng shady and cool

印 yìn〈名〉① seal；stamp：官～ an official seal ② print；mark：脚～ footprint；footmark ③〈动〉print：编～ compile and print

印本 yìnběn printed edition：～书 printed book

印发 yìnfā print and distribute

印花 yìnhuā ① printing：～绸 printed silk ② stamp：～税 stamp duty (tax). ～税票 revenue (fiscal) stamp

印记学 yìnjìxué sigillography

印款 yìnkuǎn seal and signature

印染 yìnrǎn printing and dyeing：～厂 printing and dyeing mill

印刷 yìnshuā printing：～厂 printing house；press. ～品 printed matter. ～术 art of printing；printing technique

印象 yìnxiàng impression：我对上海～很好。I have a good impression of Shanghai.

印象派(主义) yìnxiàngpài (zhǔyì) impressionism：～蒙太奇 impressionistic montage

印章 yìnzhāng seal；stamp；signet

印证 yìnzhèng corroborate；verify；testify；confirm；support

饮 yìn〈动〉give (animals) water to drink；water

饮场 yìnchǎng[旧]drink water to moisten one's throat

饮马 yìnmǎ water a horse

yīng

应 yīng〈动〉① answer；respond：～声开门 answer the door ② agree (to do sth.)；promise；accept：～战 accept a challenge (battle) ③〈助动〉should；must；ought to：本～ should have been so anyway

应当 yīngdāng should；ought to

应得 yīngdé well-deserved；due：～的惩罚 well-deserved (due) punishment

应该 yīnggāi should；ought to

应计(的) yīngjì(de) accrued：～利息 accrued interest. ～资产 accrued assets

应届毕业生 yīngjiè bìyèshēng this year's graduates；graduating students or pupils

应名儿 yīngmíngr ① hold a title but have no real power or responsibility ② only in name；nominally

应声 yīngshēng answer；respond

应收(的) yīngshōu(de) receivable：～帐款 accounts receivable；debt receivable

应税货物 yīngshuì huòwù dutiable goods

应有 yīngyǒu deserved；due；proper：做出～的贡献 make a due contribution

应有尽有 yīngyǒu-jìnyǒu have everything that one could wish for；have everything that one expects to find；have all that is necessary

应允 yīngyǔn consent；agree；assent：欣然～ willingly consent

鹰 yīng〈名〉eagle；hawk；falcon

鹰派 yīngpài War Hawks；hawks

鹰犬 yīngquǎn ① falcons and hounds ② hired thugs；lackeys

英 yīng〈名〉① flower：蒲公～ dandelion ② hero；outstanding person ③〈形〉heroic；talented；outstanding

英镑 yīngbàng pound sterling；pound

英才 yīngcái talented person；genius：～教育 elite education；meritocracy

英尺 yīngchǐ foot (a measure)

英吨 yīngdūn long ton；gross ton

英俊 yīngjùn good-looking；handsome；smart：相貌～ have a smart appearance；look handsome ② eminently talented；brilliant

英里 yīnglǐ mile

英灵 yīnglíng spirit of the brave departed

英名 yīngmíng illustrious (celebrated) name

英明 yīngmíng wise；sagacious

英亩 yīngmǔ acre

英年 yīngnián youthful years；youth

英雄 yīngxióng hero：～气概 heroic spirit；gallant mettle

英雄所见略同 yīngxióng suǒjiàn lüètóng Heroes have similar views.；Great minds think alike.；Great minds run the same channel.

英雄无用武之地 yīngxióng wú yòngwǔ zhī dì hero with no place to display his prowess；hero with no scope for displaying his heroism；no scope for one's energies

英勇 yīngyǒng brave；heroic；valiant；gallant：～牺牲 die a hero's death；heroic sacrifice

英制 yīngzhì the English system

英姿 yīngzī heroic manner (bearing)

婴 yīng〈名〉baby；infant

婴儿(孩) yīng'ér(hái) baby；infant：～死亡率 infant mortality (death) rate

罂 yīng〈名〉a small-mouthed jar

缨 yīng〈名〉① tassel ② sth. shaped like a tassel ③ ribbon

樱 yīng〈名〉cherry

樱花 yīnghuā cherry-blossom；[日本的] flowering cherry

樱桃 yīngtáo cherry：～树 cherry tree；cherry

鹦 yīng

鹦鹉 yīngwǔ parrot：～学舌 repeat the words of others like a parrot；parrot

yíng

赢 yíng〈动〉① win；defeat：这场比赛谁～了？Who won the game？② reap profits

赢得 yíngdé win；gain：～时间 gain time

赢利 yínglì gain；profit

赢余 yíngyú surplus；profit；gain

荧 yíng〈形〉① glimmering ② dizzy

荧光 yíngguāng fluorescent light; fluorescence: ～灯 fluorescent lamp. ～屏 fluorescent screen

荧荧 yíngyíng gleaming; twinkling

莹 yíng ①〈名〉jade-like stone ②〈形〉lustrous and transparent

莹莹 yíngyíng glistening; sparkling: 泪水～ eyes glistening with tears

营 yíng〈名〉① camp: 拔～ strike camp ② battalion: 加强～ reinforced battalion ③〈动〉pursue; seek: ～利 seek profits; make money

营地 yīngdì campsite; camping ground

营房 yíngfáng barracks; quarters

营火 yínghuǒ campfire: ～晚会 campfire party

营救 yíngjiù rescue; succour: 去～某人 go to sb.'s rescue. ～公司 wrecking company

营垒 yínglěi ① barracks and the enclosing walls ② camp

营利 yínglì seek profits

营生 yíngshēng earn a living; make a living

营私 yíngsī seek private gain; feather one's nest: ～舞弊 engage in malpractices for selfish ends; practise embezzlement

营养 yíngyǎng nutrition; nourishment: ～不良 malnutrition. ～品 nutriment

营业 yíngyè do business: ～额 business volume; turnover. ～时间 business hours. ～税 business tax; sales tax; transaction tax. ～收入 operating income. ～主任 sales manager

萦 yíng〈动〉entangle; twine

萦怀 yínghuái occupy (linger in) one's mind

萦回(绕) yínghuí(rào) linger; hover

蝇 yíng〈名〉fly

蝇头 yíngtóu small as the head of a fly; tiny; petty: ～微(小)利 small (petty) profits. ～小楷 very small (hand-written) characters; regular small-character script

盈 yíng〈动〉① be full of; be filled with: 充～ be plentiful; be full of ② have a surplus of

盈亏 yíngkuī ① wax and wane (of the moon) ② profit and loss: ～包干制 system whereby enterprises are responsible for their own profits and losses

盈利 yínglì profit; gain: ～税 business profit tax. 获得～10万元 gain a profit of 100,000 yuan

盈盈 yíngyíng ① clear; lucid ② delicate; dainty ③ brimming over ④ graceful; lissom

盈余 yíngyú surplus; profit; gain: ～帐户 surplus account

迎 yíng〈动〉① meet; receive; welcome: ～春接福 welcome spring and have blessing ② be directed; face: ～风 face the wind; (of a flag) flutter in the breeze

迎宾 yíngbīn receive visitors

迎合 yínghé cater to sth. or sb.; fawn on; pander to: ～对方心理 go along with the other side. ～顾客需要 cater to the needs of customers

迎候 yínghòu await the arrival of

迎接 yíngjiē welcome; meet; greet

迎面 yíngmiàn head-on; in one's face

迎亲 yíngqīn (of the bridegroom) send a party to meet the bride at the bride's home and escort her to the bridegroom's home for the wedding

迎刃而解 yíngrèn'érjiě be readily solved

迎头 yíngtóu head-on; directly

迎新 yíngxīn ① see the New Year in ② welcome new arrivals (comers): ～会 party to welcome the newcomers

迎战 yíngzhàn ① meet (an enemy) head-on ② take on; encounter: 甲队将～乙队。Team A will take on Team B.

yǐng

影 yǐng〈名〉① shadow; reflection; image: 倒～ inverted image or reflection in water ② photograph; picture: 留～ take a photo or have a picture taken as a souvenir ③ film; movie: ～迷 film (movie) fan; hipped on movies

影碟 yǐngdié videodisc; videodisk

影壁 yǐngbì ① screen wall (facing the gate inside or outside a traditional Chinese courtyard) ② a wall with carved murals

影集 yǐngjí photograph (photo, picture) album

影剧业 yǐngjùyè show business

影片 yǐngpiàn film; movie

影评 yǐngpíng film review

影迷 yǐngmí film (movie) fan

影射 yǐngshè insinuate; hint obliquely at; innuendo: ～攻击 attack by innuendo. ～史学 oblique historical studies

影视 yǐngshì cinema and television; film and television; screen and video: ～节目 movie and television programme. ～配音 sound-dubbing for movies and television

影响 yǐngxiǎng ① influence; effect; impression: 造成极坏～ create a very bad impression (on) ② have an effect (impact) on; affect; influence: 吸烟～健康。Smoking affects health.

影像 yǐngxiàng [摄] image; portrait; video: ～艺术 art of photo-taking

影星 yǐngxīng movie star

影音光碟(～～视唱盘) yǐngyīn guāngdié(～～ shìchàng pán) video compact disc (VCD); Video CD

影印 yǐngyìn photo-offset process: ～件 photocopy

影院 yǐngyuàn cinema: 多功能商业～ cinema complex; cineplex. 家庭～ home theatre

影展 yǐngzhǎn①photo exhibition; exhibit of photographic creations ② cinema exhibit

影子 yǐngzi shadow:～价格 shadow price. ～内阁 shadow cabinet. ～戏 shadow play; galanty show

颖 yǐng ①〈名〉glume; grain; husk ②〈形〉intelligent; clever: 聪～ clever; intellegent

颖慧 yǐnghuì (of a teenager) clever; intelligent; bright

颖悟 yǐngwù (of a teen-ager) clever; bright

yìng

应 yìng〈动〉① answer; respond: 一呼百～ Hundreds respond to a single call. ② comply with; grant; promise: ～广大读者的需要 meet the needs of the broad reading public ③ suit; respond to: ～景 do sth. for the occasion ④ accept; receive: ～战 accept a challenge (battle) ⑤ deal with; cope with: ～付裕如 cope with successfully

另见 yīng

应变 yìngbiàn meet an emergency: 随机～ adjust to changing circumstances; act according to circumstances

应酬 yìngchou ① treat courtesy; engage in social activities ② dinner party: 今天晚上我有个～。I've been invited to dinner this evening.

应答 yìngdá answer; reply; respond: ～者 respondent; respondee

应付 yìngfù ① cope with; deal with; handle: 难于～ be difficult to deal with ② do in a perfunctory manner; temporize: ～了事 do sth. perfunctorily

应急 yìngjí meet an exigency (emergency): ～措施 emergency measure; stopgap measure. ～计划 crash project. ～准备 contingent reserve

应接不暇 yìngjiē-bùxiá be too busy to attend to all comers or things

应考 yìngkǎo take (sit for) an examination

应聘 yìngpìn accept an offer of employment

应声虫 yìngshēngchóng echo; yesman

应时 yìngshí seasonable; in season: ～瓜果 fruits of the season

应市 yìngshì accommodate the market: ～商品 commodities that meet market demands

应验 yìngyàn come true; come to pass; be confirmed: 她说的话～了。What she said has now come to pass.

应邀 yìngyāo at the invitation (of); on invitation: ～出席大会 attend the meeting on invitation

应用 yìngyòng ① apply; use ② applied; practical: ～经济学 applied economics. ～研究 applied research. ～科学 applied sciences

应战 yìngzhàn ① meet an enemy

attack ② accept (take up) a challenge

应召女郎 yìngzhào nǚláng call girl

应征 yìngzhēng ① respond to a call for conscription and be enlisted (recruited):～服役 be called to active duty in the army ② respond to a call for contributions (to a publication)

硬 yìng〈形〉① hard; tough; stiff:～席 hard seats ② strong; firm:强～措施 strong measures ③〈动〉manage to do sth. with difficulty:～撑着干 force oneself to work hard

硬搬 yìngbān uncritical transplantation or copying from; import … mechanically

硬笔 yìngbǐ hard-tipped writing instruments:中国～书法悠久。"Hard pen" calligraphy has a long history in China.

硬币 yìngbì hard cash; specie; coin

硬顶 yìngdǐng ① resist stubbornly ② contradict rudely

硬度 yìngdù hardness

硬功夫 yìnggōngfū mastery (i.e., having profound attainment and great proficiency and skill); masterly skill

硬货 yìnghuò hard goods

硬件 yìngjiàn [计] hardware

硬木 yìngmù hardwood: ～家具 hardwood furniture

硬拼 yìngpīn fight (struggle) recklessly

硬任务 yìng rènwù firm tasks

硬是 yìngshì ① actually (accomplish sth. extremely difficult) ② just; simply

硬说 yìngshuō stubbornly insist; obstinately assert; allege

硬通货 yìngtōnghuò hard currency

硬卧 yìngwò hard sleeper (berth)

硬性 yìngxìng hard; stiff; rigid; inflexible: ～规定 inflexible rule; rigid regulation

硬仗 yìngzhàng ① hard-fought battle:打～ fight a hard battle ② tough contest; formidable task

硬指标 yìng zhǐbiāo firm objectives (stipulated goals that must be realized in strict accordance with the requirements)

硬纸板 yìng zhǐbǎn hardboard; cardboard

映 yìng〈动〉reflect; shine; mirror:朝霞～在湖面上。The glory of the morning is mirrored in the lake.

映衬 yìngchèn set off; serve as a foil

映射 yìngshè cast light upon; shine upon

映象 yìngxiàng image; photograph

yōng

庸 yōng〈形〉① commonplace:～言 commonplace words ② inferior; second-rate ③ vulgar:～俗风气 vulgar practices ④〈动〉need [多用于否定]无～ need not

庸才 yōngcái person of meagre ability; mediocrities; wretched scribblers

庸碌 yōnglù mediocre:～无能 mediocre and incompetent (unambitious)

庸人 yōngrén mediocre person; mediocrity; philistine:～自扰 worry about troubles of one's own imagining; make a fuss about nothing

庸俗 yōngsú vulgar; philistine; low

庸医 yōngyī quack doctor; quack

臃 yōng

臃肿 yōngzhǒng ① too fat to move; fat and clumsy:穿得太～ be cumbersomely dressed ② overstaffed:机构～ overstaffed organizations

雍 yōng〈形〉harmonious

雍容 yōngróng natural, graceful and poised:～华贵 both dignified and graceful; elegant and poised; distingué

拥 yōng〈动〉① hold in one's arm; hug:把孩子～在怀里 hug the child ② gather round:簇～ cluster round ③ crowd; swarm; throng:蜂～ swarm; flock ④ support; endorse; uphold:～护共和 support for a republic ⑤ have; possess; own:～有地产 possess landed property

拥抱 yōngbào embrace; hug

拥戴 yōngdài support (sb. as leader)

拥护 yōnghù support; uphold; endorse

拥挤 yōngjǐ crowd; pack; push and squeeze:交通～ traffic jam

拥军优属 yōngjūn-yōushǔ support the army and give preferential treatment to families of servicemen and martyrs

拥塞 yōngsè jam; congest; block up:交通～的街道 streets congested with traffic

拥有 yōngyǒu possess; have; own

拥政爱民 yōngzhèng-àimín support the government and cherish the people

佣 yōng ①〈动〉hire (a labourer):雇～ hire; employ ②〈名〉servant:女～ maid; woman servant
另见 yòng

yǒng

永 yǒng〈副〉permanently; perpetually; eternally; always; ever; forever:～不自满 never get conceited

永别 yǒngbié part forever

永垂不朽 yǒngchuí-bùxiǔ be immortal; go down to posterity; eternal glory to sb.; live forever in the hearts of

永磁 yǒngcí permanent magnetism

永冻层 yǒngdòngcéng permafrost horizon

永恒 yǒnghéng eternal; perpetual; everlasting:～的真理 eternal truth

永久 yǒngjiǔ eternal; everlasting; permanent:～所有权 perpetu-

ity. ～租赁 perpetual lease
永诀 yǒngjué part forever; be separated by death
永世 yǒngshì forever
永逝 yǒngshì pass away; be gone forever
永远 yǒngyuǎn always; forever; ever

咏 yǒng〈动〉① chant; intone ② express or narrate in poetic form
咏唱 yǒngchàng sing; chant

泳 yǒng〈动〉swim
泳道 yǒngdào lane (in a swimming race)

甬 yǒng
甬道 yǒngdào ① passage; passageway; ② corridor; paved path leading to a main hall or a tomb

涌 yǒng〈动〉① gush; surge: 清澈的水～进了灌溉渠道。Clear water gushed into the irrigation channel. ② rise; emerge: 风啸浪～。The wind howls and the waves rise.
涌进 yǒngjìn pour into
涌现 yǒngxiàn come to the fore; come forward; emerge: 大批积极分子～出来。Activists come forward in great numbers.

踊 yǒng
踊跃 yǒngyuè ① leap up; jump up ② actively; enthusiastically: ～响应号召 respond to a call enthusiastically

俑 yǒng〈名〉wooden or clay (earthen) human figures buried with the dead in ancient times; figurine: 兵马～ wooden or clay figures of warriors and horses buried with the dead

勇 yǒng〈形〉brave; bold; courageous: ～猛果敢 dashing courage
勇敢 yǒnggǎn brave; bold; courageous
勇猛 yǒngměng bold and powerful; vigorous and valiant; intrepid: ～无比 be unrivalled in bravery
勇气 yǒngqì nerve; courage; valour: 鼓起～ take courage (to do sth.)
勇士 yǒngshì brave man; hero
勇往直前 yǒngwǎng-zhíqián advance courageously (bravely)
勇于 yǒngyú have the courage (to do); be bold (to do): ～挑重担 be bold to take on heavy responsibilities. 在理论和实践中～探索 bold exploration in theory and practice

yòng

用 yòng〈动〉① use; employ; apply: ～脑筋 use one's brains ② spend: 零～ spend money in small sums ③ [多用于否定] need (not): 不～开灯。There is no need to turn on the light. ④ eat; drink: 请～茶 Won't you have some tea, please. ⑤〈介〉by means of; with: ～快车运送 by express

用兵 yòngbīng plan or direct the movements of military forces; use military forces; resort to arms: ～如神 deploy troops with great skill

用不了 yòngbuliǎo ① have more than is needed ② less than

用材林 yòngcáilín timber forest: 经济～ economic forests

用场 yòngchǎng use

用处 yòngchù ① advantage ② use; good: 这有什么～? What good is it?

用得着 yòngdezháo ① find sth. useful; need ② there is no need to…; it is necessary to…

用度 yòngdù expenditure; outlay; expenses

用法 yòngfǎ ① way to use; use; directions (for use): ～说明 directions ② usage: 现代英语～ modern English usage

用费 yòngfèi cost; expense: ～细帐 inclusive list of expenses

用非所学 yòngfēisuǒxué be engaged in an occupation not related to one's training

用功 yònggōng hardworking; diligent; studious: ～学习 be diligent at one's lessons

用工 yònggōng recruit and use (workers): ～制度 system of recruitment

用户 yònghù user; consumer

用具 yòngjù utensil; apparatus; appliance: 厨房～ kitchen utensils

用品 yòngpǐn article for use;: 日常～ articles for daily use

用人 yòngrén (of a person for a job) select; choose; make use of personnel: ～单位 employing units

用人 yòngren servant: 女～ maidservant

用武 yòngwǔ use force; display one's abilities or talents

用心 yòngxīn ① be diligent; carefully; attentively: ～听讲 listen attentively to a lecture ② intention; motive: ～良苦 cudgel one's brains. 别有～ have ulterior motives

用刑 yòngxíng put sb. to torture; torture

用意 yòngyì intention; purpose: 你的～何在? What are you up to?

用于 yòngyú use as: ～生活费的收入 income that can be used as living expenses; income used for living expenses

用语 yòngyǔ ① wording: 合同～务求精确。The wording of a contract should be exact. ② term; phraseology: 商业～ commercial phraseology

佣 yòng
另见 yōng

佣金 yòngjīn commission; middle man's fee; brokerage

yōu

忧 yōu ①〈动〉worry (about); be anxious (about): ～国～民 be concerned about one's country and one's people ②〈名〉sorrow; anxiety: 分～ share sb.'s sorrows, worries, etc.

忧愁 yōuchóu sad; worried; depressed

忧愤 yōufèn worried and indignant

忧患 yōuhuàn distress; misery: ～余生 survive countless distresses and worries

忧虑 yōulǜ worry about; be concerned about: 对前途感到～ worry about the future

忧伤 yōushāng sad; distressed; grieved; in deep sorrow

忧心忡忡 yōuxīn-chōngchōng heavy-hearted; uneasy; in dismay; laden with grief

忧郁 yōuyù melancholy; dejected

优 yōu 〈形〉① excellent; fine; superior; outstanding: ～良传统 excellent (fine) tradition ② preferential: ～惠办法 preferential measures

优待 yōudài ① give preferential (favoured) treatment: ～军属 give preferential treatment to soldiers' families ② on favourable terms: ～券 complimentary ticket; privilege ticket; courtesy card

优等 yōuděng first-rate; top; superior; excellent: ～生 grade A student; top student. ～证券 gilt-edged securities

优点 yōudiǎn strong point; merit; advantage

优抚 yōufǔ give special care to disabled servicemen, and to family members of revolutionary martyrs and servicemen: 烈属～金 allowance to the family members of revolutionary martyrs

优厚 yōuhòu liberal; favourable: 待遇～ excellent pay and conditions

优化 yōuhuà make superior; optimize: ～方案 perfect the plan. ～劳动组合 optimizing realignment of the work force

优惠 yōuhuì preferential; privilege; favourable: ～待遇 preferential treatment. ～价 preferential prices. ～贷款 loans on favourable terms; concessional loan. ～权 preferential rights. ～条件 soft terms

优教 yōujiào first-rate education

优良 yōuliáng excellent; good; fine: ～传统 excellent tradition. ～成绩 get good marks

优伶 yōulíng drama actors or actress

优美 yōuměi fine; exquisite; graceful: ～动人 exquisite and moving

优柔 yōuróu ① leisurely; unhurried ② gentle; amiable ③weak in character; hesitant

优柔寡断 yōuróu-guǎduàn irresolute; indecisive

优生 yōushēng give a good birth: ～优育 get a good birth and good care. ～学 eugenics

优胜 yōushèng winning; champion: ～杯决赛 cup tie. ～者 champion; winner

优胜劣汰 yōushèng-liètài survival of the fittest; select the superior and eliminate the inferior; the victory of the strong over the weak

优势 yōushì superiority; preponderance; dominant position; predominance; advantage: 经济～ economic supremacy. 竞争～ competitive superiority

优先 yōuxiān priority; precedence; preference: ～股 preferred stock (share). ～考虑 give priority to sth.

优秀 yōuxiù excellent; outstanding; model: ～教师 model teacher. ～作品 higher quality works; works of excellence

优选法 yōuxuǎnfǎ optimum seeking method; optimization

优雅 yōuyǎ fine; elegant; graceful; cultivated: 他弹的竖琴～动听。He played the harp beautifully.

优异 yōuyì outstanding; excellent; remarkable: ～儿童 gifted child. ～成绩 excellent results

优育 yōuyù good upbringing (of children)

优越 yōuyuè superior; advantageous; favourable: ～感 superiority complex

优质 yōuzhì high-quality; quality; high-grade: ～产品 high-quality products. ～名牌 high-quality brand name. ～优价 high quality and high price

幽

yōu〈形〉① deep and remote; secluded; dim: ～林 a secluded wood ② secret; hidden: ～居 live in seclusion ③ tranquil, quiet; serene: 清～ (of a land) quiet and beautiful ④ of the nether world: ～灵 ghost; spectre ⑤〈动〉imprison: ～禁 put under house arrest; imprison; confine

幽暗 yōu'àn dim; dark; obscure

幽会 yōuhuì (of lovers) meet; tryst with: 情人～处 a lover's tryst

幽魂 yōuhún ghost; spectre; spirit

幽静 yōujìng tranquil; quiet; secluded

幽灵 yōulíng ghost; spectre; spirit

幽美 yōuměi serene beauty

幽默 yōumò humour: 她的话富于～感。Her talk is full of humour.

幽思 yōusī ① ponder; muse; meditate ② deep contemplation; melancholy brooding

幽怨 yōuyuàn hidden bitterness (of a young woman thwarted in love)

悠

yōu〈形〉① remote in time ② leisurely

悠长 yōucháng long; long-drawn-out

悠久 yōujiǔ long; age-old; long-standing; time-honoured: ～的文化传统 time-honoured cultural tradition

悠然 yōurán carefree and leisurely

悠闲 yōuxián leirurely and carefree; easy-going

悠扬 yōuyáng (of music) melodious; rising and falling

悠悠 yōuyōu ① long; long-drawn-out ② leisurely ③ unhurried

悠远 yōuyuǎn ① a long time ago;

long ago; distant ② far off (away); remote; distant

yóu

游 yóu〈动〉① swim:～过一条河 swim across (over) a river ② travel; tour; visit:周～ travel round; journey round ③〈形〉roving; itinerant:～民 vagrant ④〈名〉reach:下～ the lower reaches of a river

游伴 yóubàn travel companion; fellow traveller

游船 yóuchuān pleasure-boat; yacht

游荡 yóudàng loaf about; loiter:～诗人 goliard

游动 yóudòng ① move about; go from place to place ② mobile; moving; roving

游魂 yóuhún wandering ghost

游击 yóujī guerrilla:～战 guerrilla warfare. 打～ wage guerrilla warfare; fight as a guerrilla

游记 yóujì travels; travel notes:～电影 travelogue

游街 yóujiē parade sb. through the streets

游客(人) yóukè (rén) visitor; tourist; sightseer

游览 yóulǎn see the sights (of); visit; be on a tour:～车 tourist coach; touring car; tourer. ～市容 see the sights of (go round) the city

游猎 yóuliè go on a hunting trip

游民 yóumín vagrant; vagabond

游牧 yóumù nomadic herding, i. e., roving with the livestock in search of pasture; rove around as a nomad; nomadism

游山玩水 yóushān-wánshuǐ travel from one beauty spot to another; visit various scenic spots

游手好闲 yóushǒu-hàoxián live in idleness; idle about; loaf

游说 yóushuì canvass; go about selling an idea; go canvassing; lobbying

游玩 yóuwán ① amuse oneself; play; sport ② visit; do (a place); go sightseeing; stroll about:～杭州两天 do Hangzhou for two days

游戏 yóuxì ① play; sport; amuse oneself ② game:做～ play games. ～机 recreational machines

游侠 yóuxiá (in former times) roving brave; knight-errant

游行 yóuxíng parade; demonstration; march:举行～示威 hold a demonstration

游兴 yóuxìng interest in going on an excursion or sight-seeing

游移 yóuyí waver; hesitate; falter; vacillate:～不定 falter in determination

游弋 yóuyì ply; cruise

游泳 yóuyǒng swim:～比赛 swimming contest. ～衣 swimming suit

游园会 yóuyuánhuì garden party

游资 yóuzī idle fund (capital, money)

尤 yóu ①〈形〉outstanding:择～ pick out the best ②〈副〉particularly; especially:～甚 especially bad ③〈名〉fault; wrongdoing：罪～ offence；fault ④〈动〉have a grudge againt：怨天～人 blame god and man

尤其 yóuqí especially；particularly

犹 yóu ①〈副〉still；yet：言～在耳。The words are still ringing in one's ears. ②〈介〉just as；like：虽死～生 live on in spirit

犹大 Yóudà Judas

犹如 yóurú as if；like；just；(as …) as：～白昼 as bright as day；as if in the daylight

犹太 yóutài Jew：～教 Judaism

犹豫 yóuyù waver；hesitate；falter：～不决 waver；be in two minds；be unable to make up one's mind

由 yóu ①〈名〉reason；cause：没有理～ have no reason for〈介〉② due to；because of：咎～自取 have only oneself to blame ③ from；by；to：～浅入深 from the shallower to the deeper ④〈动〉follow；obey：～她去吧。Let her do as she pleases.

由表及里 yóubiǎo-jílǐ proceed from the outside to the inside；proceed from the surface to what lies behind；proceed from outward appearance to inner essence

由不得 yóubude ① not be up to sb. to decide；be beyond the control of ② cannot help

由此及彼 yóucǐ-jíbǐ proceed from the one to the other；proceed from one point to another

由点到面 yóudiǎn-dàomiàn develop from isolated points into (to) a whole area

由近及远 yóujìn-jíyuǎn from the near to the distant

由来 yóulái origin；root；cause：～已久 long-standing；time-honoured：～已久的风俗 time-honoured custom

由于 yóuyú thanks to；due to；owing to；because of；on account of

由衷 yóuzhōng sincere；cordial；heartfelt：～的感谢 heartfelt thanks. ～之言 words spoken from the bottom of one's heart；sincere words

由…主办(持) yóu…zhǔbàn(chí) under the auspices of

由…转交 yóu…zhuǎnjiāo care of (c/o)

油 yóu ①〈名〉oil；fat；grease：豆～ soya-bean oil〈动〉② ［用桐油或油漆涂抹］apply tung oil or paint：～漆窗户 paint the windows ③ be stained with oil or grease：衣服～了。The coat has got oil stains on it. ④〈形〉oily；glib；slippery；greasy：～头滑脑 oily sharper

油饼 yóubǐng ① oilcake (as animal feed or fertilizer) ② deep-fried dough cake

油彩 yóucǎi grease paint

油船 yóuchuán tanker

油管 yóuguǎn ① oil pipe ② oil tube

油耗 yóuhào oil consumption

油滑 yóuhuá slippery；foxy

油画 yóuhuà oil paintig：画～ paint in oils

there is a way.

有种 yǒuzhǒng have guts; be plucky; be gritty

有追索权 yǒuzhuīsuǒquán with recourse

有罪 yǒuzuì be found guilty (of)

友 yǒu〈名〉friend:女朋～ girl friend

友爱 yǒu'ài friendly affection; fraternal love

友邦 yǒubāng friendly nation

友好 yǒuhǎo ① friendly:～访问 friendly visit ② (close) freinds

友邻 yǒulín friendly neighbours; good neighbours

友情 yǒuqíng friendly sentiments; friendship

友善 yǒushàn amicable

友谊 yǒuyì friendship:～赛 friendly match

莠 yǒu ①〈名〉green bristlegrass ②〈形〉bad; vicious; undesirable

黝 yǒu

黝黑 yǒuhēi swarthy; dark

yòu

诱 yòu〈动〉① guide; lead:～发 cause to happen; induce ② tempt; seduce; lure:～敌深入 lure the enemy in deep

诱导 yòudǎo induce; guide; lead:～证人回答的讯问 leading question

诱饵 yòu'ěr bait; decoy; lure

诱供 yòugòng induce a person to make a confession; inducement leading to confession

诱购 yògòu purchase by luring

诱拐 yòuguǎi abduct

诱惑 yòuhuò ① tempt; seduce; lure:受金钱的～ fall into the temptation of money ② fascinate; attract

诱奸 yòujiān seduce; debauch; betray

诱骗 yòupiàn cajole; trap; trick; inveigle; induce:～某人做某事 inveigle sb. into doing sth. (into sth.)

诱人 yòurén alluring; fascinating; captivating; enchanting

诱使 yòushǐ trick into; inveigle into; lure into

诱降 yòuxiáng lure into surrender

诱因 yòuyīn inducement

右 yòu〈形,名〉right

右派 yòupài Right wing:～分子 the Rightist

右倾 yòuqīng Right deviation:～机会主义 Right-deviationist opportunism

右翼 yòuyì ① right wing; right flank ② the Right

佑 yòu help; protect; bless

又 yòu〈副〉① again ② also

又打又拉 yòudǎ yòulā using the stick and the carrot, either alternately or simultaneously; strike and stroke one's opponent alternately

又名 yòumíng also called; alias; also known as

又想当婊子,又想立牌坊 yòu xiǎng dāng biǎozi, yòu xiǎnglì

páifāng Someone wants to be a prostitute, yet she insists on having a monument erected to her chastity.

又要马儿跑得快、又要马儿不吃草 yòu yàomǎr pǎodé kuài, yòu yào mǎr bù zhī cǎo You can't make a horse work without feeding it.

又…又… yòu…yòu… both… and …:又惊又喜 have mixed feelings of joy and surprise

幼 yòu ①〈形〉young; under age:妇～ women and children ②〈名〉children; the young

幼儿 yòu'ér child; infant:～园 kindergarten; nursery school. ～保育员 child-care worker; nurse. ～教育 preschool education

幼苗 yòumiáo seedling; sapling

幼年 yòunián childhood; infancy

幼小 yòuxiǎo young and small; immature

幼稚 yòuzhì infant; naive; immature; childish; infantile:～者的蒙昧 childish ignorance

幼子 yòuzǐ the youngest son

柚 yòu〈名〉pomelo; grapefruit

柚子 yòuzi pomelo

釉 yòu〈名〉glaze

釉里红 yòulǐhóng[瓷器] red within the glaze; under glaze red

釉面砖 yòumiànzhuān [建] glazed tile

yū

淤 yū〈动,名〉silt:放～ warp

淤积 yūjī deposit; silt up

淤泥 yūní silt; sludge; ooze

淤塞 yūsè be blocked up with silt; silt up

淤血 yūxuè extravasated blood

迂 yū〈形〉① sticking to outworn rules and ideas; pedantic:～论 pedantic talk ② roundabout; circuitous; winding:～回前进 roundabout ways of advance

迂腐 yūfǔ pedantry:～的见解 pedantic idea

迂回 yūhuí ① roundabout; circuitous; devious:～曲折 ups and downs; tortuous; circuitous ② [军] outflank:～战术 outflanking tactics

yú

于 yú〈介〉① in; at:生～1936年 be born in 1936. 长～ be good at ② to; be easy to ③ for:求助～人 ask people for help ④ from; out of:苦～ suffer from. 出～无知 out of sheer ignorance

于今 yújīn ① up to the present; up to now; since ② nowadays; today; now:她离别祖国～20载。It is twenty years since she left her motherland.

于是 yúshì thereupon; hence; consequently; as a result

娱 yú ①〈动〉give pleasure to; amuse;entertain:聊以自～ amuse oneself by (with) ②〈名〉amusement; pleasure; entertainment:文～ cultural recreation; entertainment

娱乐 yúlè amusement; entertainment:～场所 public place of entertainment. ～税 entertainment tax

愚 yú ①〈形〉foolish; stupid; silly:～蠢的问题 a silly question ②〈动〉make a fool of; fool:～弄某人 make a fool of sb.

愚笨 yúbèn foolish; dull; slow-witted

愚蠢 yúchǔn foolish; stupid; silly; blockhead; clumsy

愚钝 yúdùn dull-witted; slow-witted

愚民 yúmín ① ignorant people ② try to keep the people in ignorance; try to prevent the people from knowing the truth

愚人 yúrén fool; simpleton:～节 All (April) Fool's Day[西方风俗,每年的 4 月 1 日]

愚昧 yúmèi ignorant; benighted

愚弄 yúnòng deceive; hoodwink; make a fool of; fool; dupe

愚忠 yúzhōng blind devotion (to a master, ruler, etc.)

余 yú〈形〉① surplus; spare; remaining:结～ cash surplus ② odd; over; more than:40～年 forty odd years ③〈介〉after; beyond:工作之～ after working hours

余波 yúbō the swell after a storm—repercussions

余党 yúdǎng remnants of an overthrown clique (gang); remaining confederates

余地 yúdì leeway; margin; latitude; room:留有～ leave some leeway (margin) (for)

余毒 yúdú (remaining) pernicious influence; residual poison

余额 yú'é ① remaining sum; [收付差额] balance ② vacancies yet to be filled

余悸 yújì lingering fear:心有～ have a lingering fear

余力 yúlì surplus energy or strength

余粮 yúliáng surplus grain:～户 households with grain to spare

余年 yúnián one's remaining years

余孽 yúniè leftover evil; remaining evil element:封建～ dregs of feudalism

余缺调剂 yúquē tiáojì bring (channel) surplus goods to needy areas; balance surplus with deficiency

余热 yúrè "residual heat" (metaphor for continuing to work after one's retirement):发挥～ making some contributions in one's remaining years; contribute "residual heat" to

余生 yúshēng ① the remainder of one's life; one's remaining years ② survival (after a disaster)

余味 yúwèi agreeable aftertaste:～无穷 leave a lasting aftertaste; have a lingering interest

余暇 yúxiá time to spare; leisure
余兴 yúxìng entertainment after a meeting or a dinner party
余震 yúzhèn aftershock
渝 yú〈动〉(of one's attitude or feeling) change:始终不～ consistent; unswerving; steady; all the way
愉 yú〈形〉pleased; cheerful
愉快 yúkuài happy; pleasant; joyful; cheerful:令人～的 pleasant; delightful; cheerful; gratifying
愉悦 yúyuè joyful; cheerful; delighted
逾 yú〈动〉exceed; go beyond; overstep:过～ beyond the limit; excessive
逾期 yúqī exceed the time limit; be overdue; expire:～票据 overdue bill. ～作废 invalidate on expiry
逾越 yúyuè exceed; overstep; go beyond:～权限 exceed one's powers. 不可～的 impassable; insurmountable
舆 yú ①〈名〉carriage; chariot ②〈形〉public
舆论 yúlùn public opinion:～工具 mass media. ～监督 supervision by the mass media. ～界 the media; press circles
谀 yú〈动〉flatter; fawn on:阿～ flatter; curry favour with
谀辞 yúcí flattering words; flattery
鱼 yú〈名〉fish
鱼白 yúbái ① fish sperm; milt ② the whitish colour of a fish's belly—grey dawn
鱼翅 yúchì shark's fin
鱼虫 yúchóng water flea (used as fish feed)
鱼饵 yú'ěr (fish) bait
鱼竿 yúgān fishing rod
鱼钩 yúgōu fishhook
鱼贯而入 yúguàn'érrù enter in file; file in
鱼具 yújù fishing tackle (gear)
鱼雷 yúléi [军] torpedo
鱼鳞 yúlín fish scale; scale
鱼米之乡 yúmǐzhīxiāng region teeming with fish and rice; land of fish and rice; district where fish and rice are abundant
鱼目混珠 yúmù-hùnzhū pass fish eyes for pearls; palm off the bad as the good; pass off the sham as the genuine
鱼肉 yúròu ① fish and meat ② fish ③ oppress; fleece; bleed:～农民 fleece (outrage) the peasants
鱼水情 yúshuǐqíng relationship between fish and water—close relationship
鱼网 yúwǎng fishing net; fishnet
鱼尾纹 yúwěiwén crow's feet
鱼香肉丝 yúxiāng-ròusī fish-flavoured shredded pork
鱼腥草 yúxīngcǎo cordate houttuynia
鱼汛 yúxùn fishing season
鱼鹰 yúyīng ① sea eagle; fish hawk; osprey ② cormorant
鱼子酱 yúzǐjiàng caviare
渔 yú〈名,形〉fishing:～船 fish-

ing boat ② see sth. one does not have the right to claim
渔把式 yúbǎshi master fisherman
渔场 yúchǎng fishing ground; fishery
渔港 yúgǎng fishing port (harbour)
渔工商联合企业 yú-gōng-shāng liánhé qǐyè fishery-processing-sale joint enterprise
渔具 yújù fishing gear (tackle)
渔利 yúlì ① profit at the expense of others; reap unfair gain:从中～ take advantage of a situation to benefit oneself; cash in on other people's efforts ② easy gains; spoils:坐收～ profit from others' conflict
渔轮 yúlún fishing steamer
渔民 yúmín fisherman
渔汛 yúxùn fishing season
渔业 yúyè fishery:～资源保护区 fishery conservation zone

yǔ

宇 yǔ〈名〉world; space; universe
宇航 yǔháng space navigation:～飞船 spaceship; spacecraft. ～工业 astronautics industry. ～员 astronaut; cosmonaut; spaceman
宇宙 yǔzhòu universe; cosmos:～观 world outlook. ～空间 outer space; cosmic space
宇宙飞行 yǔzhòu fēixíng space travel:～员 astronaut; cosmonaut; spaceman
宇宙火箭 yǔzhòu huǒjiàn space rocket
宇宙空间 yǔzhòu kōngjiān cosmic space; outer space

语 yǔ〈名〉① language; speech; words:词～ words and expressions ② proverb; saying; idiom; set phrase:俗～ common saying ③〈动〉speak; say:低～ speak in a low voice
语病 yǔbìng faulty wording or formulation; unhappy choice of words
语调 yǔdiào intonation
语法 yǔfǎ grammar:～错误 grammatical mistakes
语汇 yǔhuì vocabulary
语境 yǔjìng context
语录 yǔlù recorded utterance; quotation
语气 yǔqì ① tone; manner (mode) of speaking:～友好 a friendly tone ②［语］mood:祈使～ imperative mood
语态 yǔtài［语］voice:被动～ passive voice
语体 yǔtǐ type of writing; style:口语～ colloquial style; colloquialism
语文 yǔwén ① language:～教师 language master ② Chinese language ③ language and literature
语无伦次 yǔwúlúncì be totally disorganized in one's speech; express oneself in a rambling way; speak incoherently
语系 yǔxì［语］language family; family of language
语言 yǔyán language:～训练

speech training. ～学 linguistics;philology

语义 yǔyì semantic meaning

语音 yǔyīn ① speech sounds ② pronunciation:～学 phonetics

语源学 yǔyuánxué etymology:～家 etymologist

语重心长 yǔzhòngxīncháng sincere words and earnest wishes; in all earnestness; meaningfully:～的劝告 meaningful advice

雨 yǔ 〈名〉rain

雨刮 yǔguā windscreen (windshield) wiper (of a car)

雨过天晴 yǔguò-tiānqíng The sun shines again after the rain.; After rain comes fair weather.; The sky clears up after the rain.

雨后春笋 yǔhòu-chūnsǔn spring up like bamboo shoots after a spring rain; mushroom up

雨花石 yǔhuāshí *yuhua* pebbles (colourful fine-grained pebbles found in the Yuhuatai area at Nanjing)

雨季 yǔjì rainy season

雨具 yǔjù rain gear

雨量 yǔliàng rainfall;precipitation

雨伞 yǔsǎn umbrella

雨衣 yǔyī raincoat; waterproof

雨鞋 yǔxié galoshes; rubber boots; rubbers

与 yǔ ①〈动〉give; offer:～人方便 give help to others; make thing easy for others ②〈连〉and:重工业～轻工业 heavy industry and light industry ③〈介〉to; with:～困难作斗争 grapple with difficulties

另见 yù

与…订约 yǔ…dìngyuē enter into an engagement with; make an engagement with

与其 yǔqí rather than; better than; would (had) rather … than:～你去,不如他去。Rather than having you go, it'd be better if he went. 我～等公共汽车还不如步行。I would rather go on foot than wait for the bus.

与人为善 yǔrén-wéishàn aim at helping others:～的批评 criticism aimed at helping those criticized

与日俱增 yǔrì-jùzēng grow with each passing day; be on the increase day by day; multiply daily

与世长辞 yǔshì-chángcí depart from the world for ever; pass away

与世无争 yǔshì-wúzhēng stand aloof from worldly strife

与众不同 yǔzhòng-bùtóng out of the ordinary; different from the common run

羽 yǔ〈名〉feather; plume

羽化 yǔhuà ① sprout wings—become an immortal ② (used by Taoists) pass away; die

羽毛 yǔmáo feather; plume:～丰满 become full-fledged. ～未丰的 unfledged

羽毛球 yǔmáoqiú ① badminton ② shuttlecock

羽绒 yǔróng duck down; down:～服 down garment; down-filled clothing

羽坛 yǔtán badminton circles; the badminton world

羽翼 yǔyì ① wing:～丰满的文学类型 full-fledged literary genre ② assistant

予 yǔ〈动〉give; offer; grant:赐～ grant; bestow. ～人口实 give people a handle

予人口实 yǔrén-kǒushí give people a handle

予以 yǔyǐ give; grant:～表扬 give praise to; commend

yù

誉 yù〈名〉fame; reputation:盛～ great fame; high reputation

育 yù〈动〉① give birth to; bear:生儿～女 give birth to children ② grow; raise; breed:抚～ nurture; foster ③ educate:美～ art education; aesthetic education

育才 yùcái cultivate (educate) people of ability

育龄 yùlíng child-bearing age; reproductive age:～妇女 women in their reproductive years

育苗(秧) yùmiáo (yāng) grow (cultivate) seedlings

育婴堂 yùyīngtáng orphanage;〈旧〉foundling hospital

育种 yùzhǒng [农] breeding:作物～ crop breeding

玉 yù ①〈名〉jade:金～ gold and jade ②〈形〉(of a person, esp. a woman) fair; beautiful:亭亭～立 fair; slender and graceful

玉帛 yùbó jade and silk

玉雕 yùdiāo jade carving; jade sculpture

玉兰片 yùlánpiàn dried slices of tender bamboo shoots

玉立 yùlì ① slim and graceful ② steadfast to principles

玉女 yùnǚ the Jade Maiden

玉器 yùqì jade article; jadeware; jade object:～工厂 jade workshop

玉容 yùróng beautiful face (usu. of a woman); good looks

玉石 yùshí jade:～俱焚 destruction of good and bad alike; destruction of all people good and bad alike

玉碎 yùsuì be like a broken piece of jade—die in glory

玉体 yùtǐ ① your person; your health ② jade-like frame—the naked body of a beautiful woman

玉兔 yùtù the Jade Hare—the moon

玉玺 yùxǐ imperial jade seal

玉液 yùyè jade-like wine; good wine

玉照 yùzhào your photograph

芋 yù〈名〉taro:洋～ potato

芋头 yùtou ① taro ② sweet potato

吁 yù〈动〉appeal; plead:呼～ appeal; call on

吁请 yùqǐng implore; plead; petition

域 yù land within certain boundaries; territory; region:外～

foreign lands

郁 yù〈形〉① strongly fragrant：馥～ strong fragrance ② luxuriant；exuberant：苍～ verdant and luxuriant ③ depressed；gloomy

郁愤 yùfèn worried and indignant

郁积 yùjī pent-up：～的不满 smouldering discontent

郁结 yùjié pent up

郁闷 yùmèn gloomy；depressed；unhappy

郁抑 yùyì depressed；despondent；gloomy

郁郁 yùyù ① exuberant；luxuriant ②melancholy；depressed ③ strongly fragrant

与 yù〈动〉participate in；have a hand in
另见 yǔ

与会 yùhuì participate in a conference

寓 yù ①〈动〉live；reside：寄～ live away from home ②〈名〉residence：公～ block of flats；apartment house

寓居 yùjū make one's home in (a place other than one's native place)

寓所 yùsuǒ residence；dwelling place；abode

寓言 yùyán fable；parable；allegory

寓意 yùyì implied meaning；moral；import；message：～深刻 be pregnant with meaning. 有～的影片 the message cinema

寓于 yùyú be contained in；reside in

遇 yù〈动〉① meet；encounter：遭～ meet with sth. undesired；encounter ② treat；entertain：优～ treat sb. with special consideration ③〈名〉chance；opportunity：机～ favourable circumstance

遇刺 yùcì be attacked by an assassin

遇到 yùdào meet (with)；encounter；come across；run into：～反抗 run up against the resistance of. 在街上～一个朋友 come across a friend in the street

遇害 yùhài be murdered；be killed

遇救 yùjiù be rescued；be saved

遇难 yùnàn die in an accident；be killed (murdered)

遇险 yùxiǎn meet with an accident；meet with a mishap；be in distress；be in danger

遇雨 yùyǔ be caught in the rain

浴 yù〈动〉bathe

浴场 yùchǎng outdoor bathing place

浴池 yùchí ① common bathing pool (in a public bathhouse) ② public bathhouse；public baths

浴缸 yùgāng bathtub；bath

浴室 yùshì bathroom；bath；(public) bathhouse

浴血 yùxuè bathed in blood：～奋战 fight a bloody battle；fight valiantly

裕 yù〈形〉plentiful；abundant：富～ prosperous；well-to-do；

well-off
裕如 yùrú with ease; effortlessly: 应付～ handle with ease
欲 yù ①〈名〉desire; wish; longing: 物～ material desire〈动〉② want; intend; wish: 畅所～言 speak one's mind freely ③ be about to; on the point of: 摇摇～坠 tottering on one's last legs
欲罢不能 yùbàbùnéng cannot help carrying on
欲盖弥彰 yùgàimízhāng The more one tries to cover up, the more he is exposed.; Attempts to gloss things over can only make them more conspicuous.; The more concealed, the more conspicuous.
欲火 yùhuǒ the fire of lust; lewd desire
欲念 yùniàn desire; wish; lust
欲求 yùqiú desire; wish; lust
欲速则不达 yùsù zé bùdá Haste does not bring success.; More haste, less speed. Haste makes waste.
欲望 yùwàng desire (wish); lust
愈 yù〈动〉① recover (from); heal; become well: 病～ recover from an illness ② be better (than); exceed ③〈副〉the more … the more …～多～好。The more, the better. ～来～不得人心 be increasingly unpopular
愈合 yùhé [伤口]heal up
愈加 yùjiā all the more; even more; more than ever; further
喻 yù〈动〉① explain; tell; inform: ～之以理 try to make sb. see reason; reason with sb. ② understand; know: 家～户晓 make known to every household ③〈名〉analogy: 暗～ a concealed analogy; metaphor
谕 yù〈动〉(of superiors or elders) instruct; tell
谕令 yùlìng order
谕旨 yùzhǐ imperial edict
御 yù〈动〉① drive (a carriage, horse, etc.): 驾～ drive (a cart, horse, etc.) ② resist; withstand: 抗～ resist and defend ③〈形〉imperial: ～花园 imperial garden. ～前演说 speech from the throne to
御赐 yùcì bestowed by the emperor
御敌 yùdí resist the enemy
御花园 yùhuāyuán imperial garden
御览 yùlǎn ① for the emperor's inspection ② books for the emperor's inspection
御膳房 yùshànfáng imperial kitchen
御医 yùyī imperial physician; court physician
御用 yùyòng ① for the use of an emperor ② served as a tool; in the pay of; hired; controlled: ～报刊 hired (controlled; subsidized) press. ～文人 a scribe in the pay of; hack writer
御苑 yùyuàn imperial garden or park
御制 yùzhì made by the emperor or by imperial order

狱 yù〈名〉① prison; jail: 入～ be sent to jail; be put in prison; be imprisoned ② lawsuit; case: 断～ hear and pass judgment on a case. 文字～ literary inquisition (in ancient time)

狱警 yùjǐng prison guard; jailer

狱室 yùshì prison; jail

豫 yù〈形〉pleased: 面有不～之色 look far from pleased

预 yù〈副〉beforehand; in advance

预报 yùbào forecast: 天气～ weather forecast

预备 yùbèi ① get ready; prepare ② preparatory; preliminary; probationary: ～党员 probationary Party member. ～工作委员会 preliminary working committee

预测 yùcè ① forecast; calculate: ～风险 forecasting risk ② pretest

预产期 yùchǎnqī expected date of childbirth

预订 yùdìng order; [书报等]subscribe (for); [座位等] reserve; book: ～报纸 subscribe to a newspaper. ～去北京的车票 book a ticket to Beijing

预定 yùdìng ① fix in advance; predetermine ② planned; scheduled; fixed: 船按照～时间开往欧洲。The ship sailed for Europe as scheduled. ③ 同"预订"

预防 yùfáng take precautions against; guard against; prevent: ～措施 precautionary measures; preventive measures

预付 yùfù payment in advance; advance: ～定金 advance money

预感 yùgǎn presentiment; premonition: 不祥的～ an ominous presentiment

预告 yùgào inform beforehand; announce in advance; give an advance notice; herald: 新书～ notice on forthcoming books

预购 yùgòu purchase in advance: ～合同 forward purchasing contracts

预计 yùjì calculate in advance; estimate

预见 yùjiàn ① see beforehand; foresee; predict ② prevision; foresight

预警 yùjǐng early warning

预谋 yùmóu plan in advance (beforehand); premeditate: ～的行动 premeditated action

预期 yùqī anticipate; expect: ～寿命 life expectancy

预赛 yùsài [体] preliminary trial; preliminary (contest); trial match; trial

预审 yùshěn preparatory examination

预示 yùshì foreshow; predict; presage; portend; augur; betoken

预收贷款 yùshōu dàikuǎn advances on sales

预售 yùshòu open to booking; advance sale: ～车票 tickets open to booking

预算 yùsuàn budget: ～结余 budget surplus. ～外资金的管理

management of extrabudgetary funds. ～总收入 total budgetary revenue

预先 yùxiān in advance; beforehand

预言 yùyán foretell; predict; prophesy

预演 yùyǎn preview

预映 yùyìng［影视］prerelease; prerelease screenings:～片 prerelease movies

预约 yùyuē ① make (have) an appointment (with):～就诊 have an appointment with a doctor ②［书刊等］subscribe (for)

预兆 yùzhào omen; foretoken; sign; harbinger;［凶兆］foreboding

预支 yùzhī draw in advance:～工资 draw one's pay in advance

预制 yùzhì prefabricate:～构件 prefabricated components

预祝 yùzhù congratulate beforehand; wish

妪 yù〈名〉old woman

yuān

渊 yuān ①〈形〉deep; profound ②〈名〉abyss; deep pool:深～ abyss

渊博 yuānbó broad and profound; erudite; learned:～的知识 extensive and profound knowledge

渊薮 yuānsǒu a gathering place of fish or beasts; haunt; den

渊源 yuānyuán trace to the source; source; origin

冤 yuān〈名〉① wrong; injustice:含～ suffer a wrong; be the victim of a false or unjust charge ② enmity; feeling of bitterness

冤案 yuān'àn unjust case

冤仇 yuānchóu rancour; enmity

冤大头 yuāndàtóu person deceived on account of his generosity; person who spends money wastefully and foolishly; squanderer

冤家 yuānjiā foe; enemy; adversary

冤情 yuānqíng facts of an injustice

冤屈 yuānqū ① injustice ② treat unjustly; wrong:受～ suffer an injustice; suffer wrong; be wronged

冤枉 yuānwàng ① do (one) an injustice; do (one) wrong; be wrongly disciplined; wrong:～好人 wrong an innocent man ② not worthwhile; unworthy:花～钱 spend one's money unworthily (on)

冤狱 yuānyù unjust verdict; false charge; miscarriage of injustice:平反～ reverse an unjust verdict

鸳 yuān

鸳鸯 yuānyáng ① mandarin duck ② (affectionate) couple

yuán

元 yuán〈形〉① first; primary;

initial：～月 the first month; the first lunar month ② chief; principal：～首 head of state ③ basic; fundamental：～素 element ④〈名〉[中国货币名] *yuan*, equal to 10 *jiao* or 100 *fen*

元宝 yuánbǎo shoe-shaped gold ingot

元旦 Yuándàn New Year's Day

元件 yuánjiàn component; element; cell

元老 yuánlǎo senior statesman; founding member (of a political organization, etc.)

元年 yuánnián the first year of an era or of the reign of an emperor

元配 yuánpèi first wife

元气 yuánqì sap (of life); vigour; primal energy; vitality：～旺盛 full of vigour (vitality). 伤～ sap one's strength; exhaust one's vitality

元首 yuánshǒu head of state

元帅 yuánshuài marshal

元宵 yuánxiāo ① the night of the 15th of the 1st lunar month ② sweet dumplings made of glutinous rice flour (for the Lantern Festival)

元凶 yuánxiōng prime culprit

元勋 yuánxūn a man of great merit; hero of great distinction; founding father

元月 yuányuè ① January ② the first month of the lunar year; the first moon

园

yuán〈名〉① an area of land for growing vegetables, flowers, trees etc.; garden：花～ flower garden; garden ② a place for public recreation：公～ park

园地 yuándì ① garden plot ② field; scope

园丁 yuándīng gardener

园林 yuánlín ① landscape gardens ② park：～绿化事业 gardening and afforestation

园陵 yuánlíng tombs surrounded by a park; cemetery

园艺 yuányì gardening; horticulture

猿

yuān〈名〉ape

猿人 yuánrén ape-man; preman：北京～ Peking man

原

yuán〈形〉① original; primitive; primary; former：～来面目 original features ② crude; raw; unprocessed：～粮 unprocessed food grain ③〈动〉pardon; excuse：请～谅，打扰你(们)了。Excuse me for interrupting you.; Excuse my interruption. ④〈名〉plain：准平～ quassi-plain

原班人马 yuánbānrénmǎ old cast

原版 yuánbǎn original edition (of a book, etc.)：～片 film in the original

原本 yuánběn ① master copy; the original manuscript ② a copy of the first edition ③ the original from which a translation is made

原材料 yuáncáiliào raw and processed materials; raw and semi-finished materials

原封 yuánfēng intact；untouched：～不动 keep sth. in its totality；be left (kept) intact；remain unchanged

原稿 yuángǎo (original) manuscript

原告 yuángào [民法] plaintiff；complainant [刑法] accuser；prosecutor

原籍 yuánjí native place (home)；ancestral home；domicile of origin：她～是北京。She is a native of Beijing.

原价 yuánjià original price

原件 yuánjiàn ① original manuscript (of a document)；master copy ② the original (from which a replica is made)

原来 yuánlái ① original；former ② originally；formerly；at first ③ as a matter of fact；as it turns out；actually

原来如此 yuánláirúcǐ so it is；so that's how matters stand on

原理 yuánlǐ principle；theory；axiom；tenet

原粮 yuánliáng unprocessed food grains

原谅 yuánliàng pardon；excuse；forgive：～某人的卤莽 forgive sb. for being rude

原料 yuánliào raw material

原貌 yuánmào original appearance (of things)

原任 yuánrèn ① formerly held the post of ② predecessor

原声带 yuánshēngdài original sound tape

原始 yuánshǐ ① primitive；primeval：～公社生产方式 primitive communal mode of production ② original：～产品 primary products. ～资料 first-hand information；source material

原糖 yuántáng raw sugar

原委 yuánwěi the whole story；all the details；ins and outs：知道问题的～ know the ins and outs of a problem

原文 yuánwén original (text)

原物 yuánwù the original thing

原形 yuánxíng true features；original shape (form)：～毕露 show one's (true) colours；reveal one's real nature；show sb. in his true colours

原型 yuánxíng [机] prototype

原野 yuányě open country；champaign

原因 yuányīn reason；cause；account：由于这个～ for this reason；on this account

原油 yuányóu crude (oil)

原原本本 yuányuán-běnběn from beginning to end；in detail：～的事实 the whole truth

原则 yuánzé principle：坚持～立场 persist in a principled stand

原址 yuánzhǐ former address

原主 yuánzhǔ former owner；[失物等的] rightful owner

原著(作) yuánzhù (zuò) original (work)

原装进口 yuánzhuāng jìnkǒu imported with original packaging

原子 yuánzǐ atom：～反应堆 atomic reactor. ～能 atomic energy

原子弹 yuánzǐdàn atom bomb; atomic bomb; A-bomb

原作 yuánzuò original work; original

源 yuán 〈名〉① river head or source:水～ the source of a river ② cause; source; origin:渊～ trace to the source

源泉 yuánquán source; wellspring; mainspring; springs:一切文学艺术的～ source of all literature and art. 集体财富的～ the springs of collective wealth

源头 yuántóu source; wellhead; fountainhead

源源 yuányuán continuously; steadily; in a steady stream:～而来 come in a steady stream; keep pouring in

源于生活,高于生活 yuányú shēnghuó,gāoyú shēnghuó draw from life, but on the higher plane

员 yuán 〈名〉① a person engaged in a field of activity:保管～ storeman; storekeeper ② member:共青团～ Youth League member ③ personnel:技术人～ technical personnel

员工 yuángōng staff; personnel

圆 yuán ①〈形〉round; circular; spherical:浑～ perfectly round 〈名〉② circle:内接～ inscribed circle ③ a coin of fixed value:铜～ copper coin ④〈动〉justify:自～其说 justify oneself; make one's statement consistent; make out a good case

圆场 yuánchǎng mediate; help to effect a compromise

圆房 yuánfáng (in former times of a foster daughter-in-law and her husband) consummate the union on reaching adulthood

圆规 yuánguī compasses

圆滑 yuánhuá smooth and evasive; slick and sly; tactful; diplomatic:说话～ speak in a tactful way

圆谎 yuánhuǎng patch up a lie

圆寂 yuánjì (of Buddhist monks or nuns) pass away; die

圆括号 yuánkuòhào parentheses

圆满 yuánmǎn satisfactory; successful:～成功 be crowned with complete success. ～结束 come to a successful conclusion; round off

圆润 yuánrùn mellow and full

圆熟 yuánshú proficient; skilful

圆通 yuántōng accommodating; flexible; tactful

圆舞曲 yuánwǔqǔ [乐] waltz

圆桌 yuánzhuō round table:～会议 round-table conference

援 yuán〈动〉① draw or pull by hand:攀～ climb up through pull ② help; support; rescue; aid:支～ give support to ③ cite; quote:～例 quote (cite) a precedent

援兵 yuánbīng relief troops; reinforcements

援救 yuánjiù rescue; save

援军 yuánjūn reinforcements; relief troops

援款 yuánkuǎn aid fund

援外 yuánwài foreign aid：～物资 materials in aid of a country
援引 yuányǐn quote；cite：～经典 quote from (cite) the classics
援助 yuánzhù help；support；aid：～捐款 assistance contribution. 经济～ economic aid (support)

缘 yuán〈名〉① reason；cause：无～无故 for no reason at all ② edge；brink；fringe：在森林的边～ on the fringes of a forest ③ predestined relationship；lot that brings people together：姻～ the happy fate which brings lovers together
缘分 yuánfèn lot or luck by which people are brought together；predestined relationship (lot)；fate
缘故 yuángù reason；cause
缘木求鱼 yuánmù-qiúyú like climbing a tree to catch fish；get blood from a stone；do the impossible；do things by the wrong method
缘起 yuánqǐ origin；genesis
缘由 yuányóu cause；reason

yuǎn

远 yuǎn ①〈形〉far；distant；remote：～离家乡 far from home ②〈动〉keep away：敬而～之 keep sb. at a respectful distance
远程 yuǎnchéng long-range；long-distance：～导弹 long-range missile
远大 yuǎndà ① far-reaching；long-range：目光～ be farsighted ② high；lofty：～理想 lofty ideals
远渡 yuǎndù travel across a vast expanse of water
远方 yuǎnfāng a distant place
远古 yuǎngǔ remote antiquity
远航 yuǎnháng take a long (sea) voyage；sail to a distant place
远见 yuǎnjiàn foresight；farsightedness：～卓识 foresight and sagacity；with farsightedness and insight
远郊 yuǎnjiāo the outer suburbs；the remoter outskirts of a city
远景 yuǎnjǐng ① prospect；distant view ② long-term；long-range：～规划 long-term plan (programme)；long-range plan
远虑 yuánlǜ foresight；long view
远期 yuǎnqī a specified future date；forward：～合同 forward contract. ～汇票 usance bill. ～外汇 forward (foreign) exchange
远亲 yuǎnqīn distant relative；remote kinsfolk：～不如近邻。A near neighbour is nearer (better) than a distant relative.
远涉 yuǎnshè make a long，arduous journey (esp. across the sea)
远视 yuǎnshì long-sighted；farsighted：～眼镜 spectacles for long sight
远水救不了近火 yuǎnshuǐ jiùbùliǎo jìnhuǒ Distant water cannot quench (put out) a nearby fire.；Slow remedy cannot meet an urgency.

远眺 yuǎntiào look far into the distance(from a high place)
远销 yuǎnxiāo sell goods to distant places
远行 yuǎnxíng go on a long journey
远洋 yuǎnyáng ocean:～货轮 oceangoing freighter. ～运输 ocean carriage
远因 yuǎnyīn remote cause
远征 yuǎnzhēng expedition:～军 expeditionary army
远足 yuǎnzú excursion;(walking) tour; hike

yuàn

院 yuàn〈名〉① court; courtyard; yard:前～ front courtyard ② a name used for some government offices and public places:博物～ museum ③ institute; college:社会科学～ academy of social sciences
院落 yuànluò courtyard; yard; compound
院士 yuànshì academician
院体画 yuàntǐhuà[中国绘画]imperial-court decorative painting
院外活动 yuànwài huódòng[美国]lobbying:～集团成员 lobbyer; lobbyist
院外调解 yuànwài tiáojiě[法]conciliation out of court
院校 yuànxiào educational institutions:大专～ universities and technical institutes
院长 yuànzhǎng director (of a hospital, museum, institute, etc.); president (of a university, court, etc.)

愿 yuàn〈动〉① wish; desire:初～ one's original wish ② be ready; be willing:～意坦白 want to come clean ③〈名〉promise:许～ promise sb. a reward; make promises
愿望 yuànwàng wish; desire; expectation; aspiration:满足某人的～ satisfy sb.'s wish
愿意 yuànyì ① be willing; be ready (to do):我们～同他们合作。We are willing to cooperate with them. ② want; wish; would like

怨 yuàn ①〈名〉grudge; discontent; resentment:含～ bear a grudge or grievance ②〈动〉blame; complain:这件事～他。He is to blame for this.
怨不得 yuànbude ① cannot blame ② no wonder; so that's why
怨敌 yuàndí foe; enemy
怨恨 yuànhèn ① have (bear) a grudge against sb.; harbour hatred for sb.; hate ② resentment; grudge; enmity
怨气 yuànqì complaint; resentment; grievance:一肚子～ be full of discontent (grievances). 吐～ vent one's grievances
怨声载道 yuànshēng-zǎidào Voices of discontent are heard everywhere.; Cries of discontent rise all round.
怨天尤人 yuàntiān-yōurén grumble against Heaven and lay the blame upon other people;

blame everything and everyone but oneself; complain about everything

怨言 yuànyán (words of) complaint; grumble: 毫无～ without a word of complaint

yuē

曰 yuē〈动〉① say; speak ② call; name: 美其名～ give sth. the fine-sounding name of

约 yuē〈动〉① make an appointment (with sb.); arrange: 他们～定一个地方交流经验。They appointed a place to exchange experience. ② ask or invite in advance: 他经常～她出去。He often asked her out. ③ restrict; bind: 制～ restrict; condition ④〈名〉pact; agreement; appointment: 相～ reach agreement; make an appointment ⑤〈形〉simple; brief: ～言之 in a word; in brief ⑥〈副〉about; around: ～40人 about forty people

约定 yuēdìng appoint; fix; arrange; agree on (upon): ～的期限届满 expiration of the agreed term. ～俗成 established by usage; accepted through common practice; accepted practice

约法三章 yuēfǎ-sānzhāng three-point covenant

约会 yuēhuì appointment; engagement; [男女间的] date; tryst: 与某人～ make a date with sb.

约计 yuējì come roughly to; add up to about; count roughly

约见 yuējiàn make an appointment to meet

约期 yuēqī set a date; fix the time

约请 yuēqǐng ask; invite

约束 yuēshù keep within bounds; keep a control over; restrain; bind: ～力 binding force (effect). ～购买力 committed purchasing power

约谈 yuētán interview

约因 yuēyīn [法] consideration

yuè

悦 yuè〈形〉happy; pleased; pleasant: 和颜～色 a genial look

悦耳 yuè'ěr pleasant to the ear; sweet-sounding; sweet: ～的歌声 sweet song. ～的音乐 melodious music

悦服 yuèfú heartily admire

悦目 yuèmù pleasant to the eye; good (nice)-looking: 赏心～ be pleasant to look at

阅 yuè〈动〉① read; go over; look over: 批～ read and appraise (sb.'s writing, etc.) ② review; inspect: 检～ review (troops, etc.)

阅兵 yuèbīng review troops: ～式 military review; parade

阅读 yuèdú read: ～材料 reading material

阅卷 yuèjuàn look over the examination papers; read exams

阅览 yuèlǎn read：～室 reading room. ～证 reader's card

阅历 yuèlì ① see, hear or do for oneself ② experience：～浅 inexperienced; have little experience. 有～ have seen much of the world

越 yuè〈动〉① get over; jump over; go across：翻山～岭 cross over mountain after mountain ② overstep; exceed：～出某些政策界限 overstep certain demarcation lines of policy ③〈副〉the more… the more：～战～强 have grown ever stronger in one's fight

越冬 yuèdōng live through (survive) the winter

越发 yuèfā all the more：～高兴 be pleased all the more

越轨 yuèguǐ go beyond the bounds; transgress：～行为 transgression

越过 yuèguò cross; surmount; negotiate

越级 yuèjí bypass the immediate leadership：～报告 bypass the immediate leadership and report directly to higher levels

越境 yuèjìng illegally cross the border：～犯罪 cross-border crime

越剧 yuèjù *yueju* (Shaoxing) opera

越权 yuèquán overstep (go beyond) one's authority (commission)

越位 yuèwèi [足球] offside

越野 yuèyě cross-country：～赛跑 cross-country race

越狱 yuèyù escape from prison; break prison; go over the wall; gaol break; jailbreak：～犯 prison breaker; escapee

越俎代庖 yuèzǔ-dàipáo exceed one's functions and meddle in others' affairs; take another's job into one's own hands

跃 yuè〈动〉jump; leap：雀～ jump for joy

跃进 yuèjìn leap forward：～阶段 leap forward stage

跃然 yuèrán appear vividly

跃跃欲试 yuèyuè-yùshì be eager for a try; itch to have a go; itch for

岳 yuè〈名〉① high mountain：山～ lofty mountains ② wife's parents

岳父 yuèfù father-in-law

岳母 yuèmǔ mother-in-law

月 yuè〈名〉① the moon：皎～ bright moon ② month：淡～ slack month

月报 yuèbào ① monthly magazine; monthly ② monthly report

月初 yuèchū the beginning of the month

月俸 yuèfèng monthly pay

月工 yuègōng a labourer hired by the month

月光 yuèguāng moonlight; moonbeam：～奏鸣曲 moonlight sonata

月经 yuèjīng menses; menstruation：～不调 abnormal menstruation

月历 yuèlì monthly calendar
月亮(球) yuèliang(qiú) the moon
月票 yuèpiào monthly ticket (for a commuter); commutation ticket; season (ticket):出示～ show one's season
月食 yuèshí [天] eclipse of the moon
月台 yuètái railway platform:～票 platform ticket
月息 yuèxī interest per mensem; monthly interest
月薪 yuèxīn monthly pay
月晕 yuèyùn lunar halo
月子 yuèzi ① month of confinement after giving birth to a child ② time of childbirth; confinement

乐 yuè〈名〉music:国～ traditional Chinese music
另见 lè
乐池 yuèchí orchestra pit; orchestra
乐段 yuèduàn period
乐队 yuèduì band; [管弦乐] orchestra:～指挥 bandmaster; conductor. 铜管～ brass band. 交响～ symphony (orchestra). 军～ military band. 弦～ string orchestra
乐句 yuèjù [乐] phrase
乐谱 yuèpǔ (musical) notation; (music) score; music:～架 music stand
乐器 yuèqì (musical) instrument: 打击～ percussion instrument. 管～ wind instrument. 弦～ stringed instrument
乐曲 yuèqǔ (musical) composition; composition; music
乐坛 yuètán music circles
乐团 yuètuán philharmonic orchestra (society)
乐章 yuèzhāng movement

钥 yuè〈名〉key

yūn

晕 yūn ①〈形〉dizzy; giddy:使人发～的高度 a dizzy height ②〈动〉faint
另见 yùn
晕倒 yūndǎo fall senseless; faint; fall in a faint; pass out
晕厥 yūnjué syncope; faint
晕头转向 yūntóu-zhuànxiàng confused and disoriented; get confused; lose one's bearings: 这个问题把我搞得～。The problem has got me confused.

yún

云 yún ①〈名〉cloud:低～ low cloud ②〈动〉say; speak:人～亦～ repeat word for word what others say
云彩 yúncǎi〈口〉cloud
云端 yúnduān high in the clouds
云集 yúnjí crowd together; converge; gather; swarm:万商～。The place is swarming with merchants.
云梯 yúntī scaling ladder
云消雾散 yúnxiāo-wùsàn The clouds melt and the mists disperse.; vanish (melt) into thin air

云烟 yúnyān cloud and mist; mist

云涌 yúnyǒng like surging clouds—in large numbers; in force

耘 yún〈动〉weed:耕～ plough and weed

耘锄 yúnzhú hoe

匀 yún ①〈形〉uniform; even:均～的节拍 an even tempo〈动〉② even up; divide evenly ③ share (with); spare:我可以～给他一些。I can spare him some.

匀称 yúnchèng well-proportioned; well-balanced; symmetrical:～的身材 well-proportioned figure

匀净 yúnjìng even (colour); uniform

匀整 yúnzhěng neat and well spaced; even and orderly

yǔn

允 yǔn ①〈动〉permit; allow; grant:概～ generously permit ②〈形〉just; fair:中～ fair; just; impartial

允诺 yǔnnuò promise; consent; assent:～订立一个临时协议 consent to a temporary agreement

允许 yǔnxǔ permit; allow; consent:～讨论的问题 open question

允准 yǔnzhǔn approve; permit; allow

陨 yǔn〈名〉fall from the sky or outer space

陨落 yǔnluò (of a meteorite, etc.) fall from the sky or outer space

陨石 yǔnshí aerolite; stony meteorite

陨铁 yǔntiě [考] meteoric iron

陨星 yǔnxīng meteorite

yùn

晕 yùn ①〈形〉dizzy; giddy:眩～ feel dizzy ②〈名〉halo:日～ solar halo

另见 yūn

晕场 yùnchǎng have stage fright; feel nervous and dizzy at an examination

晕车 yùnchē carsickness:常～ be liable to carsickness

晕船 yùnchuán seasickness:常～的人 a bad sailor

晕机 yùnjī airsickness

晕针 yùnzhēn have a fainting spell during acupuncture treatment

愠 yùn〈形〉angry; irritated

愠色 yùnsè irritated (angry) look

熨 yùn〈动〉iron; press:湿衣服容易～平。Damp clothes iron easily.

熨斗 yùndǒu iron:电～ electric iron

韵 yùn〈名〉① rhyme:词～ rhyme of *ci* poems ② charm:风～(of women) graceful bearing; charm

韵律 yùnlǜ ① metre (in verse) ② rules of rhyming; rhyme scheme:～体操 eurhythmics

韵目 yùnmù phonetic rhymes
韵诗 yùnshī rhyme verse
韵味 yùnwèi lingering charm; lasting appeal
韵文 yùnwén literary composition in rhyme; verse

蕴 yùn〈动〉accumulate; contain; hold in store
蕴藏 yùncáng hold (keep) in store; contain:～一种极大的积极性 have a potentially inexhaustible enthusiasm for
蕴涵 yùnhán implication
蕴蓄 yùnxù lie hidden and undeveloped; be latent

运 yùn〈动〉① carry; transport; convey:集～(of goods, etc.) gather together and transport ② use; utilize; wield:～用国家机器 wield state machinery ③〈名〉fortune; luck:财～ luck in making money
运筹帷幄 yùnchóu-wéiwò contrive strategic plans in the headquarters; plan (devise) strategies in a command tent
运筹学 yùnchóuxué operations research; operational research
运到收费 yùndào shōufèi freight to collect
运动 yùndòng ① motion:～规律 law of motion ② movement; campaign; drive:整风～ rectification campaign ③ athletics; sports; exercise:～会 athletic meeting (games); sports meet
运费 yùnfèi transport (freight) charges; transportation expenses; freight:～单 freight note
运河 yùnhé canal:大～ Grand Canal. ～通行费 canal tolls
运货单 yùnhuòdān waybill
运力 yùnlì transport capacity
运气 yùnqì luck; fortune:碰～ try one's luck
运输 yùnshū transport; conveyance; transportation:～工具 conveyance; transportation; means of transport. ～公司 transport company. ～量 freight volume
运送 yùnsòng transport; convey; send:～保险 transit insurance
运行 yùnxíng ① move; revolve; be in motion:在轨道上～ move in orbit. ② operate:机制～ the operation of mechanism
运营 yùnyíng (of buses, ships, etc.) operate; run; ply
运用 yùnyòng use; apply; exercise; utilize; handle:～自如 grasp and skilfully apply; handle sth. skilfully
运载 yùnzǎi carry:～工具 means of delivery. ～火箭 carrier rockets
运转 yùnzhuǎn [星体] turn round; revolve ② operate:～成本 cost of operation. 机器～正常。The machine operates smoothly.

酝 yùn
酝酿 yùnniàng ① brew; ferment:～着很大的不安 create great unrest ② make preparations for; deliberate on; have an informal discussion of:～候选人名单 have an informal discussion of the list of candidates

孕 yùn〈动〉be pregnant; be conceived:受～ become pregnant

孕妇 yùnfù pregnant woman; expectant mother

孕期 yùnqī pregnancy

孕育 yùnyù be pregnant with; carry within itself; breed; engender; contain:～着一些社会主义萌芽 seeds of socialism were engendered in…

Z z

zā

扎 zā ①〈动〉bind; tie; fasten: 包～ fasten a parcel ②〈名〉[文件等] sheaf (of papers): 一～手稿 a sheaf of manuscripts
另见 zhā

扎彩 zācǎi decorate with festoons; hang up festoons; festoon: 教室里挂灯～。The classroom was decorated with lanterns and festoons.

zá

砸 zá〈动〉① pound; crash; tamp: 被～得粉碎 be crashed to pieces ② smash; break: 把门～开 smash the door open

砸碎 zásuì break into pieces; smash; crash

杂 zá〈形〉① mixed; sundry: ～税 sundry tax ② miscellaneous; sundry: ～事 miscellaneous affairs ③〈动〉mix; blend; mingle: 夹～ be mingled with

杂费 záfèi ① incidental expenses; incidentals ② miscellaneous expenses; sundry fees

杂感 zágǎn random thoughts; miscellaneous impressions: ～漫谈式散文 digressive essay

杂烩 záhuì ① mixed stew; hotchpotch; hodgepodge ② mixture; miscellany

杂货 záhuò general cargo; groceries; sundry goods: ～店 grocery; variety store. ～零售商 general dealer

杂记 zájì ① jottings; random notes; notes ② miscellanies (as a type of literature); [文体] miscellanea: ～作家 miscellanists

杂技 zájì acrobatics: ～团 acrobatic troupe. ～艺术节 acrobatic art festival

杂家 zájiā miscellaneous writers; miscellaneous scholars; miscellaneous school

杂交 zájiāo hybridize; crossbreed; cross: ～育种 crossbreeding

杂居 zájū (of two or more nationalities) live together

杂粮 záliáng food grains other than rice and wheat; coarse grain (cereals)

杂乱 záluàn mixed and disorderly; in a jumble; in a muddle: ～无章 disorderly and unsystematic; disorganized; in a mess

杂念 zániàn distracting thoughts: 私心～ selfish ideas and personal considerations

杂色 zásè varicoloured; variegated

杂史 záshǐ heterodox histories; miscellaneous histories

杂耍 záshuǎ juggle; variety show; vaudeville: ～演员 juggler

杂说 záshuō miscellaneous remarks

杂谈 zátán miscellaneous comments on

杂文 záwén miscellaneous essays (writings); essay: ～作家 miscellaneous writer

杂务 záwù odd jobs; miscellaneous business

杂物 záwù odds and ends; sundries

杂项开支 záxiàng kāizhī sundry overhead

杂言诗 záyánshī poems with no fixed number of characters to each line

杂音 záyīn noise; [心脏] murmur; [无] interference

杂院儿 záyuànr a compound occupied by many households

杂志 zázhì magazine; periodical; journal

杂质 zázhì impurity; [化]foreign substance

杂族共居 zázú gòngjū medley of races

zāi

灾 zāi〈名〉① disaster; calamity: 闹～ suffer from natural disaster ② misfortune; mishap; adversity: 消～ remove (impending) ill fortune

灾变 zāibiàn catastrophy; upheavals

灾害 zāihài calamity; disaster: 自然～ natural disaster (calamity). ～保险 casualty insurance

灾荒 zāihuāng bad harvest; crop failure; famine

灾民 zāimín victims of a natural disaster; afflicted people

灾难 zāinàn calamity; disaster; misfortune; catastrophe: ～深重的 calamity-trodden; calamity-ridden; woe-stricken

灾年 zāinián famine (lean) year

灾情 zāiqíng the condition of a disaster

灾区 zāiqū disaster area; afflicted (affected) area

灾星 zāixīng the star of calamity—sb. or sth. that brings disaster

灾异 zāiyì calamities and abnormalities

栽 zāi〈动〉① plant; grow: ～树 plant trees ② fall; tumble ③ impose sth. on sb.: ～上罪名 trump up a charge against sb.

栽跟头 zāigēntou ① tumble; fall ② come to grief; come a cropper

栽培 zāipéi ① plant; grow; cultivate ② bring up; train: ～青年 bring up young people

栽赃 zāizāng shift the blame on (sb.); plant stolen (banned) goods on (sb.): ～诬害 frame a case against (sb.); plant the crime on (sb.)

栽种 zāizhòng plant; grow

zǎi

宰 zǎi〈动〉① kill; butcher; slaughter:～猪 butcher pigs ② govern; rule; dominate:主～ dominate; dictate

宰割 zǎigē oppress and exploit; carve; trample underfoot:任人～ allow oneself to be trampled upon; submit oneself to the tender mercies of

宰杀 zǎishā kill; slaughter; butcher

宰相 zǎixiàng prime minister (in feudal China); chancellor:～肚里能撑船。A prime minister's mind should be broad enough for poling a boat in—broad-minded.

载 zǎi ①〈名〉year:五～ five years ②〈动〉write down; record; carry; make a note of:～入史册 go down in history; be recorded in the history. 据报～ according to press reports 另见 zài

zài

再 zài〈副〉again; over again; once more:一～ time and again; repeatedly. ～思 think again; reconsider; rethink

再版 zàibǎn ① second edition; ② reprint; second impression

再出口 zàichūkǒu reexport

再度 zàidù once more; a second time; once again

再犯 zàifàn repeat an offence; recidivism

再分配 zàifēnpèi redistribution

再会 zàihuì goodbye; see you again

再婚 zàihūn remarriage; second marriage; digamy

再加工 zàijiāgōng further processing; reprocessing

再接再厉 zàijiē-zàilì make persistent efforts; make repeated efforts; continue to exert oneself; redouble one's efforts

再进口 zàijìnkǒu reimport

再就业 zàijiùyè reemploy

再拘留(捕) zàijūliú(bǔ) rearrest

再控告 zàikònggào recharge

再三 zàisān over and over again; time and again; again and again; repeatedly

再审 zàishěn reopening of a case; retrial; new trial

再生产 zàishēngchǎn [经] reproduction

再说 zàishuō ① put sth. off till some time later:等一等～。Put it off for a while. ② what is more; moreover; besides:这本字典很有用,～价钱也不很贵。The dictionary is very useful, and, what is more, not very expensive.

再投资 zàitóuzī reinvest; plough back

再现 zàixiàn (of a past event) reappear; be reproduced:在银幕上～ be reproduced on the screen

再循环 zàixúnhuán recycling

再造 zàizào give sb. a new lease of life

再则 zàizé moreover; furthermore; besides

载 zài〈动〉① carry; load; be loaded with: ～货 carry cargo ② be everywhere on the road: 怨声～道。Complaints are heard all over.

另见 zǎi

载歌载舞 zàigē-zàiwǔ singing and dancing joyously

载人(的) zàirén(de) manned: ～航天飞行 manned space flight. ～轨道研究站 manned orbital development station (MODS)

载体 zàitǐ carrier

载运 zàiyùn convey (by vehicles; ships, etc.); carry; transport

载重 zàizhòng carrying capacity; load: ～汽车 truck; lorry. ～吨位 deadweight tonnage. ～量 deadweight capacity

在 zài〈动〉① exist; being; live: 这问题还存～。The problem still exists. ② lie in; depend on: 事情的成败～他自己的努力。The success or failure of the matter depends on his own efforts. ③ remain: ～职 occupy a post ④〈介〉at; in; on [表示时间、处所、范围等]: ～会上发言 speak at a meeting. ～理论上 in theory ⑤〈副〉[表示动作正在进行]: 我的儿子～做功课。My son is doing homework.

在案 zài'àn be on the (police) record: 记录～ put on record

在编人员 zàibiān rényuán those on the regular payroll; permanent staff

在册 zàicè [教] on-roll: ～人数 number on roll

在产地 zàichǎndì at source

在场 zàichǎng be on the spot (scene); be present

在朝 zàicháo hold office at court: ～党 the ruling party; the governing party

在党 zàidǎng be a member of a political party (esp. the Chinese Communist Party)

在工厂交货 zài gōngchǎng jiāohuò at factory

在行 zàiháng be expert at sth.; be at home in; be skilled in; be in one's element

在乎 zàihu [多用于否定或疑问] care (about); mind: 我不～她说的话。I don't care what she says.

在教 zàijiào ① believe in a religion ② believe in Islam; be a Muslim

在劫难逃 zàijié-nántáo There is no escape from one's fate.; What is destined cannot be avoided.

在世 zàishì be living; live

在受审 zàishòushěn be on trial

在所难免 zàisuǒnánmiǎn be unavoidable; impossible to be avoided; can hardly be avoided

在逃 zàitáo be at large; fugitive; on the run: ～犯 criminal at large; escaped criminal

在途中 zàitúzhōng in transit; en route

在望 zàiwàng be visible; be in

sight; be in view

在位 zàiwèi be under the reign; be on the throne; reign:～君主 reigning sovereign

在握 zàiwò be in one's power; be under one's control; be in one's hands

在押 zàiyā be behind bars; be in custody; be in prison; be under detention:～犯 criminals in custody; prisoner on remand

在野 zàiyě in the opposition; out of office; not be in office:～党 party out of office, party not in office; out-party

在于 zàiyú ① lie (in); rest with: 平等就～… the equality consists in the fact that… ② be determined by; depend on

在职 zàizhí in service; on the job; at work:～干部 cadres at their posts (at work). ～训练 on-the-job training; in-service training. ～科技人员 working scientists

在作案时(～～～现场) zài zuò àn shí (～～～ xiànchǎng) in flagrant delict

在座 zàizuò be present (at a meeting, banquet, etc.)

zán

咱 zán〈代〉①[指谈话的双方] we ② I

咱们 zánmen we; us:～商量一下。Let's talk it over.

zǎn

攒 zǎn〈动〉accumulate; save; heap up:好不容易～几个钱 scrape up a little sum

攒钱 zǎnqián save up money

zàn

暂 zàn〈副〉temporarily; for the time being; of short duration

暂保单 zànbǎodān cover note

暂定 zàndìng provisional; tentative:～方案 tentative programme. ～一年 be tentatively fixed at a year

暂缓 zànhuǎn put off; defer; postpone:会议～举行。The meeting is postponed.

暂记帐 zànjìzhàng suspense account

暂且 zànqiě for the moment; for the time being

暂缺 zànquē (of a post) be left vacant for the time being

暂时 zànshí temporary; provisional:～代行职务 be in charge of office pro tempore. ～借款 temporary loans

暂停 zàntíng ① suspend:～营业 Business temporarily suspended. ～支付 suspend payment ②[体]time-out:要求～ ask for time-out

暂行 zànxíng temporary; provisional:～办法 interim procedures. ～条例 provisional regulations

暂住户口 zànzhù hùkǒu provisional residence registration

赞 zàn〈动〉① praise; commend: 盛～ speak highly of; praise ② favour; support: ～理 assist sb. with a task

赞不绝口 zànbùjuékǒu be profuse in praise; chant the praise (of); praise profusely; be full of praise

赞成 zànchéng favour; support; endorse; agree with; approve of: ～的请举手。Those in favour please raise their hands. ～票 affirmative vote

赞歌 zàngē ① song of praise; paean ② sing the praises of

赞美 zànměi eulogize; extol; praise

赞赏 zànshǎng appreciate; admire: 值得～ deserve (merit) one's admiration

赞叹 zàntàn gasp in admiration; highly praise; admire

赞同 zàntóng agree with; endorse; approve of

赞许 zànxǔ praise; commend; speak favourably of

赞扬 zànyáng speak highly of; speak in favour; eulogize; glorify; praise; extol: 受到高度～ win high praise

赞语 zànyǔ words of praise; praise

赞誉 zànyù praise; acclaim; commend

赞助 zànzhù sponsor; support (financially); donate money; give assistance to: 修复长城受到很多单位的～。The renovation of the Great Wall has received financial support from many units.

zāng

赃 zāng〈名〉① booty; stolen goods; spoil; loot: 分～ divide the spoils; share the booty ② bribes: 贪～ take bribes

赃官 zāngguān corrupt official; grafter

赃款 zāngkuǎn money stolen, embezzled or received in bribes; illicit money; illegally acquired money; funds received as bribes

赃物 zāngwù articles received as bribes; stolen goods; spoils; loot; ill-gotten goods; booty: ～窝藏人 holder of stolen goods

脏 zāng〈形〉① dirty; foul; filthy; sordid: ～衣服 dirty clothes ② base; despicable
另见 zàng

脏话 zānghuà obscene (dirty, foul) language; obscenities

脏乱 zāngluàn (of a place) dirty and messy

脏钱 zāngqián ill-gotten money

zàng

葬 zàng〈动〉bury: 陪～ be buried with the dead

葬礼 zànglǐ burial (funeral) rites; funeral service; funeral: 参加～ attend a funeral

葬身 zàngshēn be buried:～鱼腹 be(get) drowned; be swept to a watery grave
葬送 zàngsòng bring to ruin; bury; ruin; spell an end to:～前途 ruin one's future

藏 zàng〈名〉storing place; depository:矿～ mineral deposits
藏传佛教 Zàngchuán fójiào Tibetan Buddhism
藏历 zànglì Tibetan calendar:～新年 Tibetan New Year Festival
藏医 zàngyī Tibetan medicine
藏学 zàngxué Tibetology
藏族 Zàngzú the Tibetan (Zang) nationality (distributed over the Tibetan Autonomous Region, Qinghai, Gansu, Sichuan and Yunnan)

脏 zàng〈名〉internal organs of the body; viscera:五～六腑 the vital organs of the human body 另见 zāng

zāo

糟 zāo ①〈动〉be pickled with grains or in wine ②〈形〉rotten; not strong; terrible:很～糕的演出 a terrible performance ③〈名〉distillers' grains:酒～ distillers' grains
糟改 zāogǎi satirize; tease; make fun of
糟糕 zāogāo what a bad luck; too bad; how terrible:真～! What a bad luck!
糟糠 zāokāng distillers' grains, husks, chaff, etc.—foodstuffs for the poor
糟粕 zāopò dregs; scum; draff; dross; slag; refuse:弃其～ discarding the dross
糟蹋 zāota ① spoil; waste; ruin:～身体 spoil one's health ② insult; violate:～妇女 violate a woman

遭 zāo ①〈动〉encounter or meet with (disaster, misfortune, etc.):～难 meet with misfortune ②〈量〉time; round:好几～了 several times. 绕跑道跑了 2～ run around the track twice
遭到 zāodào meet with; suffer; come across; encounter; sustain:～失败 suffer a set-back; sustain a defeat
遭劫 zāojié meet with catastrophe
遭难 zāonàn meet with misfortune; suffer disaster
遭受 zāoshòu suffer; sustain; be subjected to:～损失 sustain losses
遭殃 zāoyāng suffer; be victimized
遭遇 zāoyù ① meet with; encounter; suffer:不幸～ unfortunate lot ② lot; fate:他们有着共同的～。They have shared the same experiences.
遭罪 zāozuì endure hardships, tortures, rough conditions, etc.; have a hard time

záo

凿 záo ①〈名，动〉chisel：～子 chisel②〈动〉open；dig；sink：～井 dig (sink，open) a well. 开～ cut (a canal，tunnel，etc.)

zǎo

枣 zǎo〈名〉(Chinese) date；jujube：酸～ wild jujube
枣泥 zǎoní date paste
枣树 zǎoshù jujube tree
早 zǎo ①〈名〉(early) morning ②〈形，副〉early：绝～ extremely early ③〈副〉long ago；for a long time：我～知道了。I have known that long ago.
早安 zǎo'ān good morning
早班 zǎobān morning shift：做～ be (work) on the morning shift
早操 zǎocāo morning exercises：做～ do morning exercises
早茶 zǎochá morning tea
早产 zǎochǎn premature birth (delivery，labour)
早场 zǎochǎng morning show
早婚 zǎohūn marrying too early；early marriage
早年 zǎonián at an early age；in one's early years
早期 zǎoqī early stage (phase)：～教育 preschool education
早日 zǎorì ① at an early date；soon ② as early as possible
早市 zǎoshì ① morning market ② morning business
早熟 zǎoshú ① early-ripening；early：蚕豆～了。The broad bean ripen early. ② precocity：～的孩子 precocious child
早衰 zǎoshuāi ［医］early ageing；premature senility
早晚 zǎowǎn ① morning and evening：～服务部 before-and-after-hours shop ② sooner or later
早先 zǎoxiān previously；before；in the past
早育 zǎoyù early child-bearing
早知 zǎozhī precognition
澡 zǎo〈名〉bath：洗～ have (take) a bath；bathe
澡堂 zǎotáng public baths；bathhouse
蚤 zǎo〈名〉flea：跳～市场 flea market (fair)

zào

灶 zào〈名〉kitchen range；cooking stove：炉～ kitchen range；cooking range
灶火 zàohuo ① kitchen range；cooking stove ② kitchen
灶间 zàojiān kitchen
灶坑 zàokēng stove pit
灶头 zàotou kitchen range；cooking stove
燥 zào〈形〉dry：干～ dry；arid
燥热 zàorè hot and dry
噪 zào〈动〉① (of a bird，insect，etc.) chirp：蝉～ the chirping of cicadas ② clamour：鼓～

make an uproar
噪音 zàoyīn noise：～污染 noise pollution
躁 zào〈形〉rash；impetuous：性子急～ quick-tempered
躁动 zàodòng move restlessly
造 zào〈动〉① make；manufacture；build：制～鞋子 make shoes ② invent；cook up：虚～ cook up；fabricate. ～假帐 cook accounts ③ cultivate；train；educate：～就 bring up；train
造币厂 zàobìchǎng mint
造表 zàobiǎo draw up a form (list)；tabulate
造册 zàocè compile a register；prepare detailed reports
造成 zàochéng cause；bring about；create：～巨大损失 cause heavy losses
造船 zàochuán shipbuilding：～厂 shipyard；dockyard；docks. ～工业 shipbuilding industry
造访 zàofǎng pay a visit (call)；call on
造福 zàofú benefit；bring benefit to：～千秋万代 benefit future generations. ～人类 bring benefit to mankind
造化 zàohuà ① good fortune (luck) ② [宗]creation
造价 zàojià cost of construction
造就 zàojiù ① bring up；cultivate；train：～人材 bring up men of talent；bring forward talented people ② attainments；achievements
造林 zàolín afforestation
造孽 zàoniè do evil
造物 zàowù the divine force that created the universe；Nature
造型 zàoxíng model；mould：～优美 unique (graceful) in shape. ～艺术 plastic (graphic) arts
造谣 zàoyáo start a rumour；cook up a story；fabricate rumours：～生事 start a rumour to make trouble；stir up trouble by rumourmongering
造诣 zàoyì attainments；achievements：学术上的～ academic attainments
造纸厂 zàozhǐchǎng paper mill
皂 zào ①〈名〉soap：香～ perfumed (toilet) soap ②〈形〉black
皂白 zàobái ① black and white ② right and wrong：～不分 make no distinction between right and wrong
皂隶 zàolì runner or bailiff in a feudal *yamen*
皂片 zàopiàn soap flakes

zé

责 zé ①〈名〉duty；responsibility，obligation：～权利 responsibility，power and benefits〈动〉② blame；scold；reproach：苛～ reproach severely ③ require；demand：严以～己 be strict with oneself ④ question closely；call sb. account：～问 bring (call) sb. to account
责备 zébèi blame；reproach；rebuke；reprove：～的眼光 a look

of reproach

责成 zéchéng enjoin (sb. to do sth.); charge (sb. with a task); instruct (sb. to fulfil a task):～某人起草一个计划 make sb. responsible for the drafting of a plan; enjoin sb. to draft a plan

责罚 zéfá punish

责怪 zéguài blame; fix the responsibility on:～某人粗心大意 blame sb. for his carelessness

责令 zélìng order

责骂 zémà scold; rebuke; dress down; reproach

责难 zénàn blame; accuse; censure

责任 zérèn responsibility; obligation; duty:～内阁 responsible cabinet. ～事故 accidents due to negligence. ～田 responsibility fields (plots). ～心 sense of duty. 追究～ ascertain where the responsibility lies

责问 zéwèn call (bring) sb. to account:厂长～他们为何不来开会。The director of the factory called them to account for their absence from the meeting.

责无旁贷 zéwúpángdài be in duty bound (to do); be duty-bound; be one's unshirkable responsibility

则 zé〈名〉① rule; regulation:细～ detailed rules and regulations ② example; stand; norm; criterion:以身作～ set an example by one's own conduct ③〈量〉item:新闻一～ an item of news〈连〉④[表示因果、条件等]:欲速～不达。More haste, less speed ⑤[表示对比、转折、让步]:漂亮～漂亮,只是不耐穿。It's pretty but not endurable.

则例 zélì precedents

泽 zé〈名〉① pond; pool:湖～ lakes and marshes ② lustre (of metals, pearls, etc.):光～ gloss; lustre ③〈动〉damp; moisten:润～ moisten; lubricate

择 zé〈动〉choose; select:别～ distinguish and choose
另见 zhái

择偶 zé'ǒu mate selection:～标准 mating criterion

择日 zérì fix a date:～起程 fix a departure date

择善 zéshàn selecting what is good

择校生 zéxiàoshēng students who choose their junior or senior middle schools beyond the area they live in

择要 zéyào give an outline:～说明计划内容 give an outline of the plan

择优 zéyōu select the best:～录取 enroll those who are outstanding; enroll the best. ～录用 accept by selection pertaining to employment; select for employment on the basis of one's qualification; recruit workers on a selective basis

zéi

贼 zéi〈名〉① thief：～巢 robbers'den ② traitor；enemy：卖国～ traitor (to one's country) ③〈形〉crooked；evil：～眼 furtive glance

贼船 zéichuán pirate ship：上～ board the pirate ship—join a reactionary faction

贼喊捉贼 zéihǎn-zhuōzéi thief crying "stop thief"；robber acting like a cop；thief crying for the thief

贼头贼脑 zéitóu-zéinǎo behaving stealthily like a thief；stealthy；furtive；sneaky

贼心 zéixīn evil design (intention)；wicked heart：～不死 does not give up one's gangster designs

贼赃 zéizāng stolen goods；booty；spoils

zěn

怎 zěn〈副〉how；why：～么得了！What a terrible thing it would be!

怎么 zěnme how；why；what：～办？What to do?；What is to be done?.（你）～啦？What's the matter (with you)?

怎么着 zěnmezhe ① what to do；what ② no matter what；whatever ③ [用在句子的开头，表示惊讶] what：～，他不去了？What? He's not going?

怎样 zěnyàng how；what：骑车去～？What about going by bike?. 广州天气～？What is the weather like in Guangzhou?

zēng

曾 zēng〈名〉relationship between great-grand children and great-grand parents
另见 céng

曾孙 zēngsūn great-grandson

曾孙女 zēngsūnnǚ great-granddaughter

曾祖 zēngzǔ (paternal) great-grandfather

憎 zēng〈动〉hate；detest：面目可～ repulsive in appearance

憎恨 zēnghèn hate；detest；abhor

憎恶 zēngwù loathe；abominate；abhor；be disgusted at (with)

增 zēng〈动〉increase；grow；add：递～ increase by degrees；increase progressively

增白剂 zēngbáijì brightening agent；brightener

增补 zēngbǔ supplement；augment：～本 enlarged edition

增产 zēngchǎn increase production：～节约 increase production and practise economy

增订 zēngdìng revise and enlarge：～版 enlarged edition

增高 zēnggāo ① get higher；rise；increase ② make higher；heighten；raise；increase

增光 zēngguāng add to the prestige of；win honour for；add

lustre to; do credit to:为国～ win honour for one's motherland

增辉 zēnghuī add lustre to; do credit to

增加 zēngjiā increase; raise; augment; boost:～积累 increase accumulation. ～效益 improve performance

增进 zēngjìn enhance; promote; increase; advance; further:～友谊 improve (promote) friendship

增刊 zēngkān supplementary issue; supplement

增强 zēngqiáng strengthen; reinforce; enhance:～体质 improve physical fitness. ～信心 enhance one's confidence

增色 zēngsè add colour to; add beauty to

增收节支 zēngshōu jiézhī increase revenue and reduce expenditures

增援 zēngyuán reinforce:～要塞 reinforced fortress

增长 zēngzhǎng increase; grow; rise:～率 rate of increase. ～才干 enchance abilities and talents

增值 zēngzhí added value; rise (increase) in value; appreciation:～税 value-added tax

zèng

赠 zèng〈动〉offer (present) as a gift; donate:馈～ present (a gift); give as a present

赠礼 zènglǐ ① present sb. with a gift ② gift; present

赠品 zèngpǐn gift;[做广告用的] giveaway

赠送 zèngsòng give; present; donate:～花篮 present a basket of flowers. ～仪式 presentation ceremony

赠言 zèngyán words of advice or encouragement given to a friend at parting; parting words:临别～ give a piece of parting advice; parting words of advice or encouragement

赠予 zèngyǔ present to; donate to

赠阅 zèngyuè be given free (by the publisher):～本 giftbook; presentation (complimentary) copy

zhā

渣 zhā〈名〉① dregs; residue; sediment:豆～ bean dregs ② broken bits; crumbs:面包～ (bread) crumbs

渣滓 zhāzǐ ① dregs; grounds; leavings ② riffraff; scum; refuse:社会～ dregs of society; riffraff

扎 zhā〈动〉① prick; run or stick (a needle, etc.):手指给一根刺～痛了 get one's fingers pricked by a thorn ② get into; plunge into:～进书堆里 bury oneself in books ③ set up; pitch:～营 encamp; pitch a tent

另见 zā

扎根 zhāgēn take (strike) root; settle down:～农村 take roots

in a rural area; base one's work in a rural area
扎实 zhāshi ① strong; sturdy; tough ② solid; down-to-earth: 扎扎实实地 in a down-to-earth manner (way); in a well-grounded way
扎手 zhāshǒu ① prick the hand ② difficult to handle; thorny
扎眼 zhāyǎn ① dazzling; offending to the eye; loud; garish ② offensively conspicuous
扎营 zhāyíng pitch a camp; camp
扎针 zhāzhēn [中医]have (give) an acupuncture treatment

zhá

闸 zhá〈名〉① sluice: 分洪～ flood-diversion sluice ② brake: 车～ brake (of a car, bicycle, etc.) ③〈动〉dam up (water)
闸盒 zháhé fuse box
闸门 zhámén sluice gate; lock gate: ～价格 sluice-gate price
铡 zhá ①〈动〉cut with a hay cutter ②〈名〉hand hay cutter; fodder chopper
铡草机 zhácǎojī chaff-cutter; hay cutter
铡刀 zhádāo hand hay cutter; fodder chopper
炸 zhá〈动〉fry in deep oil
另见 zhà
炸酱 zhájiàng fried bean sauce (usu. with minced meat)
炸土豆条 zhá tǔdòutiáo chips; French fries
炸鱼 zháyú fried fish
札 zhá〈名〉letter; note: 简～ brief letter
札记 zhájì reading notes; notes
轧 zhá〈动〉roll (steel): 精～ finish rolling
另见 gá; yà
轧钢 zhágāng steel rolling: ～厂 steel rolling mill

zhǎ

眨 zhǎ〈动〉bat (the eyes); wink; blink
眨眼 zhǎyǎn wink; blink; twinkle: 一～的工夫 in a twinkling of an eye

zhà

栅 zhà〈名〉railings; barriers; palisade; bars; paling: 木～ palisade. 用～栏隔开 fence off
乍 zhà〈副〉① first; for the first time: ～一听 at first hearing ② suddenly; unexpectedly: ～变 change suddenly
乍冷乍热 zhàlěng-zhàrè now hot, now cold; sometimes hot and sometimes cold: 天气～。The temperature changes abruptly.
炸 zhà〈动〉① blast; explode; blow up; bomb: 爆～一颗原子弹 explode an atom bomb ② fly into a rage: 她一听就气～了。She flew into a towering rage

when she heard it.
另见 zhá

炸弹 zhàdàn bomb:爆破～ demolition bomb. 定时～ time bomb

炸毁 zhàhuǐ destroy with dynamite; blast to pieces; blow up:～桥梁 blow up a bridge

炸药 zhàyào dynamite; explosive (charges); TNT

诈 zhà〈动〉① deceive; dupe; cheat; swindle:～骗 swindle; fraud ② pretend; feign:～降 pretend to surrender

诈病 zhàbìng pretend (feign) to be ill; pretend illness

诈唬 zhàhu bluff; bluster

诈骗 zhàpiàn deceive; swindle; defraud:～犯 swindler. ～金钱罪 obtaining pecuniary advantage by deception

诈欺 zhàqī deceive; stellionate; deception:～取财罪 obtain money or goods by false pretence

诈取 zhàqǔ get by dishonest means; swindle:～财物(罪) obtaining (property) by deception

诈降 zhàxiáng pretend to surrender; feign surrender

榨 zhà〈动〉squeeze; press; extract:～葡萄 press grapes

榨菜 zhàcài hot pickled mustard tuber

榨取 zhàqǔ squeeze; exploit; drain … of:～剩余价值 squeeze out (extort) surplus value

榨油 zhàyóu extract oil:～机 oil press

zhāi

斋 zhāi〈名〉① vegetarian diet; fast; abstain from:吃～ abstain from eating meat, etc. ② a room or building:书～ study ③〈动〉give food (to a monk):施～ give food to monks or nuns

斋饭 zhāifàn food given to Buddhist monks as alms

斋戒 zhāijiè abstain from meat, wine, etc.; fast; purification; fasting:～期(日) fast day; fast

斋月 zhāiyuè [伊斯兰教] Ramadan; Ramazan

摘 zhāi〈动〉① pluck; pick; gather:～苹果 pluck apples ② select; extract

摘编 zhāibiān ① select and edit; make extracts ② extracts

摘抄 zhāichāo take passages; excerpt (from); extract (from)

摘除 zhāichú [医] excise; remove

摘记 zhāijì ① take (make) notes; note (jot) down ② excerpts; extracts

摘录 zhāilù ① make extracts; extract ② excerpts; extracts

摘要 zhāiyào ① make a summary; summarize ② summary; abstract; digest; brief; résumé:～簿 abstract book

摘译 zhāiyì ① translate selected passages ② translations of selected passages

摘引 zhāiyǐn quote

摘由 zhāiyóu key extracts (of a document)

zhái

宅 zhái〈名〉house; residence:家～family dwelling

宅第 zháidì residence; dwelling; mansion

宅基 zháijī the foundations of a house; the site of a house

宅门 zháimén ① gate of an old-style big house ② family living in an old-style big house

择 zhái〈动〉choose; select; pick 另见 zé

择菜 zháicài trim vegetables for cooking

择席 zháixí be unable to sleep well in a new place

zhǎi

窄 zhǎi〈形〉① narrow:～轨铁路 narrow-gauge railway ② narrow-minded; petty: 心～ narrow-minded

窄小 zhǎixiǎo narrow and small

zhài

寨 zhài〈名〉① stockade; mountain stronghold:山～ fortified mountain village. 边～ stockaded villages on the border area ② camp:营～ military camp

寨子 zhàizi stockaded village

债 zhài〈名〉debt:背～ be in debt

债户 zhàihù debtor

债款 zhàikuǎn debt; loan

债权 zhàiquán creditor's rights; obligatory right: ～国 debtor country. ～人 creditor; debtee; obligee; holder of debt claims

债券 zhàiquàn bond; debenture: ～持有人 bond holders. ～发行人 floaters. ～股利 bond dividends. ～收益 bond yield

债台高筑 zhàitáigāozhù be deep (heavily) in debt; be over head and ears in debt; be up to one's ears in debt; run heavily into debt; become debt ridden

债务 zhàiwù debt; liabilities:～人 debtor. ～纠纷 dispute over obligation. ～清偿 performance of debt

债主 zhàizhǔ creditor; obligee

zhān

占 zhān〈动〉practise divination 另见 zhàn

占卜 zhānbǔ practise divination; divine; augur:～的签 divinatory lots. ～师 augur; diviner

占卦 zhānguà divine by means of the Eight Diagrams

占星 zhānxīng divine by astrology; cast a horoscope

沾〈动〉① moisten; soak; wet: 草被露水～湿了。Grasses were moist with dew. ② touch on (upon) only slightly:烟酒不～ abstain from smoking and drinking ③ benefit from association with sb. or sth.: 均～ share equally

沾边 zhānbiān ① touch on a little ② be relevant：她讲的话与本题不～。What she said is irrelevant to the subject (is wide of the mark).

沾光 zhānguāng share (in) the benefit (from, of); gain some advantage from another：沾某人的光 share in sb.'s profit

沾花惹草 zhānhuā-rěcǎo be promiscuous in sex relations

沾染 zhānrǎn be tainted with; be infected (affected) with; contaminate; pollute：～官僚主义的恶习 contamination with the bad habits of bureaucratism

沾沾自喜 zhānzhān-zìxǐ hug oneself for (on); swell with pride; feel complacent; be pleased with oneself

粘 zhān〈动〉stick; paste; glue 另见 nián

粘合 zhānhé stick together; glue together

粘连 zhānlián adhesion

粘贴 zhāntiē paste; stick：～广告 paste bills

毡 zhān〈名〉felt：细～ fine felt

毡房 zhānfáng yurt

瞻 zhān〈动〉look up or forward

瞻前顾后 zhānqián-gùhòu look ahead and behind—be overcautious and indecisive; look before and behind; hesitate to take actions; take into account both past experience and the situation that may possibly arise in the future

瞻望 zhānwàng look forward; look far ahead：～未来 look to the future

瞻仰 zhānyǎng ① look up to ② look at with reverence; pay one's respects to：～遗容 pay one's respects to sb.'s remains

zhǎn

盏 zhǎn ①〈名〉small cup：酒～ small wine cup ②〈量〉2～灯 two lamps

斩 zhǎn〈动〉① chop; cut; hack：～断魔爪 chop off the octopus arms; cut the claws of ② cut off the head; behead; decapitate：～尽杀绝 kill to the last man; kill all

斩草除根 zhǎncǎo-chúgēn pull the grass up by its roots; root up; uproot evil; extirpate; pull up weeds by the root; destroy evil; leaving no chance of its revival

斩钉截铁 zhǎndīng-jiétiě resolute and decisive; determined; categorical without mincing words：～地否认 deny categorically

斩首 zhǎnshǒu behead; decapitate

崭 zhǎn〈形〉towering; steep：～然 rising steeply

崭露 zhǎnlù newly reveal：～头角 have just begun to show one's talent; cut a striking (splendid) figure; make oneself conspicuous

崭新 zhǎnxīn span-new; brand-new; completely new:～的制度 a brand-new system

展 zhǎn〈动〉① unfold; unfurl; open up; spread out:开～群众运动 unfold a mass movement ② put to good use; give free play to:大～宏图 carry out a great plan ③ extend; postpone; prolong:～期 extend a time limit ④ show; display:把地图在桌上～开 display a map on the table

展播 zhǎnbō preceptive broadcasting (television stations broadcasting programmes with representative value for people to watch and emulate.)

展翅 zhǎnchì spread the wings; get ready for flight:～高飞 soar to great heights

展出 zhǎnchū put on display; be on show (view); exhibit

展开 zhǎnkāi ① unfold; spread (out); unroll:～画卷 unroll a picture scroll. ② develop; carry out; launch:～斗争 launch a struggle

展览 zhǎnlǎn exhibit; show; display:～馆(室) exhibition hall (room). ～会 exhibition; show. ～品 exhibit

展卖 zhǎnmài selling at expositions; sales at exhibition

展品 zhǎnpǐn exhibit; item on display

展评 zhǎnpíng exhibit and evaluate (i. e., exhibit, test-market, and evaluate new commodities)

展期 zhǎnqī ① put off (to a later date); extend a time limit; postpone; defer:～合同 renew a contract. ～信用证 extended letter of credit ② duration of an exhibition

展示 zhǎnshì open up before one's eyes; reveal; show; lay bare

展望 zhǎnwàng ① look (forward) to:～未来 look (forward) to the future ② forecast; prospect:21 世纪～ prospects for the twenty-first century

展现 zhǎnxiàn emerge; present itself; develop; be unfolded:～眼前 be unfolded before sb.'s eyes

展销(会) zhǎnxiāo(huì) sales exhibition; trade fair:～会场 exhibition park

辗 zhǎn

辗转 zhǎnzhuǎn ① pass through many hands or places:～相告 pass from mouth to mouth; mill around between … and … ② turn over in bed; toss about (in bed); restless:～反侧 toss about in bed

zhàn

湛 zhàn〈形〉profound and deep:深～ profound and thorough

湛蓝 zhànlán (of the sky, the sea, a lake, etc.) azure blue; azure

蘸 zhàn〈动〉dip in (water, ink,

etc.)

蘸笔 zhànbǐ dip one's pen in (into) the ink

栈 zhàn〈名〉① warehouse; storehouse: 粮～ wholesale grain store; grain deposit ② inn; tavern: 客～ inn

栈道 zhàndào a plank roadway built along perpendicular rock-faces by means of wooden brackets fixed into the cliff

栈房 zhànfáng ① warehouse; storehouse ② inn; tavern

栈租 zhànzū storage charges

占 zhàn〈动〉① take; occupy; seize: 侵～ invade and occupy ② make (up); account for: ～三分之二 account for two-thirds

占地 zhàndì (of a garden, farm, etc.) cover an area of

占据 zhànjù occupy; hold; possess: ～地 territory in occupation

占理 zhànlǐ reasonable; sensible; right

占领 zhànlǐng take; occupy; capture: ～区 occupied area

占便宜 zhàn piányi ① profit at other people's expense; make small gains for; reap gain: 好～ be fond of small advantages ② have an advantage (over sb. in sth.)

占上风 zhàn shàngfēng get (gain) the upper hand of; predominate over; prevail over; come out on top

占先 zhànxiān take the lead; precede; take precedence; get ahead of

占线 zhànxiàn [电话] The line's engaged (busy).; line (number) engaged

占用 zhànyòng employ; occupy; use: ～公款 conversion of public money to one's own use. ～资金付费原则 principle of payment for the use of funds

占优势 zhàn yōushì have (hold) the upper hand; prevail; be in a dominant position

占有 zhànyǒu ① possess; own: ～权 right of possession. ～第一手资料 have first-hand data ② occupy; hold

站 zhàn〈动〉① stand: ～得高，看得远 stand on eminence and become farsighted ② stop; halt: 中途不～ make no stops along the way ③〈名〉station; stop: 检查～ inspection station; checkpoint

站不住脚 zhànbùzhùjiǎo ① unable to stand one's ground (on one's feet) ② untenable: 这个论点～。This argument is untenable (does not hold water, won't stand scrutiny).

站队 zhànduì stand in line; line up

站岗 zhàngǎng stand guard; stand sentry

站柜台 zhàn guìtái serve as a shop assistant; serve behind the counter

站票 zhànpiào ticket for standing room; standing ticket

站台 zhàntái platform

站台票 zhàntáipiào platform ticket

站在…立场 zhànzài … lìchǎng have the standpoint; identify oneself with the stand of

站住脚 zhànzhùjiǎo ① plant one's feet firmly on the ground; stand (hold) one's ground:我们～。We hold our ground. ② be tenable; hold water

战 zhàn①〈名〉war; battle:参～ enter a war; take part in war〈名,动〉② fight; struggle:～斗在一起 fight side by side ③ shiver; tremble:寒～ shiver (with cold or fear)

战败 zhànbài ① be defeated (beaten); suffer (sustain) a defeat ② defeat; beat:～国 defeated (vanquished) nation

战备 zhànbèi war preparedness; combat readiness:～训练 military training in preparation for the eventuality of war

战场 zhànchǎng battlefield; battleground; field of operations (action)

战地 zhàndì combat zone; battlefield:～记者 war correspondent

战斗 zhàndòu fight; struggle; combat:～力 fighting strength (capacity); combat effectiveness. ～英雄 combat hero

战犯 zhànfàn war criminal:～管理所 prison for war criminals

战俘 zhànfú prisoner of war (P. O. W.); war prisoner; captive:～集中营 prison camp

战功 zhàngōng outstanding military exploits; military honour; meritorious military service; battle achievements

战果 zhànguǒ results (success) of battle; combat success:扩大～ exploit the success (victory) of battle

战火 zhànhuǒ conflagration of war; flames of war

战绩 zhànjì combat gains; military exploits (success)

战利品 zhànlìpǐn war spoils (booty, trophies); prize of war; captured equipment

战栗 zhànlì tremble; shiver; shudder

战略 zhànlüè strategy:～家 strategist. ～目标 strategic objective. ～要地 important strategic point

战前 zhànqián prewar

战区 zhànqū war zone; theatre of operations

战胜 zhànshèng defeat; win the battle; win; surmount; overcome:～敌人 defeat the enemy. ～困难 overcome difficulties

战时 zhànshí in time of war; during the war; wartime:～编制 wartime establishment; war footing

战士 zhànshì ① soldier; combatant:～转业费 military severance pay ② fighter; warrior; champion

战事 zhànshì war; hostilities:～结束 conclusion of the war

战书 zhànshū letter of challenge

战术 zhànshù (military) tactics

战无不胜 zhànwúbùshèng invincible;ever-victorious (triumphant); all-conquering

战线 zhànxiàn battle line; battle front; front:在政治思想～上 on the political and ideological fronts

战役 zhànyì battle; campaign

战友 zhànyǒu comrade-in-arms

战战兢兢 zhànzhàn-jīngjīng ① tremble with fear; shake with terror; quake with consternation; be tremblingly wary ② with caution; gingerly

战争 zhànzhēng war; warfare; hostilities:～状态 state of war

颤 zhàn〈动〉tremble; shiver; shake:寒～ shiver (with cold or fear)

另见 chàn

颤栗 zhànlì shudder; tremble; shiver

绽 zhàn〈动〉split open:开～ come unsewn

绽放 zhànfàng (of flowers) burst forth; burst into bloom

zhāng

章 zhāng〈名〉① seal; stamp:私～ personal seal ② chapter:篇～ sections and chapters ③ rules; regulations:典～ decrees and regulations ④ badge; medal:领～ collar badge; collar insignia

章程 zhāngchéng ① rules; regulations ② (of corporation, school, etc.) statutes

章法 zhāngfǎ ① presentation of ideas in a piece of writing; art of composition ② orderly ways; methodicalness

章回小说 zhānghuí xiǎoshuō a type of traditional Chinese novel with each chapter headed by a couplet giving the gist of its content; novels divided into chapters; episodic novel

章节 zhāngjié chapters and sections

蟑 zhāng

蟑螂 zhāngláng cockroach; roach

樟 zhāng〈名〉camphor tree

樟木 zhāngmù camphorwood:～箱 camphorwood trunk (chest)

樟脑 zhāngnǎo camphor:～丸 camphor ball; mothball

张 zhāng〈动〉① open; stretch:～大眼睛 open one's eyes ② set out; display; arrange:大～筵席 lay on a feast ③ look:东～西望 gaze around ④ exaggerate; magnify:～大其事 publicize the matter widely ⑤〈量〉:2～桌子 two tables. 5～纸 five pieces of paper

张弛 zhāngchí tension and relaxation

张灯结彩 zhāngdēng-jiécǎi decorate with laterns and coloured streamers

张冠李戴 zhāngguān-lǐdài put Zhang's hat on Li's head—attribute sth. to the wrong person; mistake one person or thing for another; put the boot on the wrong leg; substitute one for the other; confuse one thing with another

张皇失措 zhānghuáng-shīcuò be scared out of one's wits (senses); be seized with (a) panic; be panicky; lose one's head; shake (shiver) in one's shoes

张口结舌 zhāngkǒu-jiéshé be agape and tongue-tied; be at a loss for words; gape in astonishment; stare with the mouth open; be stumped by

张狂 zhāngkuáng flippant and impudent; insolent

张力 zhānglì tension

张罗 zhāngluo ① make arrangements for; take care of; be busy (at): 为婚事～ make arrangements for wedding ② raise funds; get together (money, etc.); try to get sth. (money, etc.) for certain needs

张三李四 zhāngsān-lǐsì any Tom, Dick and Harry; any man-in-the-street; either one or the other

张贴 zhāngtiē put up; post up

张望 zhāngwàng ① look about (around) ② peep (through a crack, etc.)

张牙舞爪 zhāngyá-wǔzhǎo bare fangs and brandish claws—make threatening gestures; show (bare) one's teeth; bluff and bluster

张扬 zhāngyáng make public; make widely known; publicize

张嘴 zhāngzuǐ ① open one's mouth (to say sth.) ② ask for a loan or a favour

zhǎng

掌 zhǎng〈名〉① palm (of hand) ② the sole of certain animals' feet: 熊～ bear's paw 〈动〉③ strike with the palm of the hand: 拍～ clap one's hands. ～嘴 slap sb. on the face ④ be in charge of; control: ～握至高无上的权力 wield the absolute power

掌灯 zhǎngdēng ① hold a lamp in one's hand ② light an oil lamp

掌舵 zhǎngduò be at the helm; operate the rudder; helm; steer a boat

掌故 zhǎnggù anecdotes

掌管 zhǎngguǎn be in charge of; take charge of; manage: ～财务 be in charge of financial affairs

掌权 zhǎngquán wield power; hold power; be in power

掌上明珠 zhǎngshàng-míngzhū a pearl in the palm—a beloved daughter; the apple of one's eye; treasured like pearls

掌声 zhǎngshēng applause; clapping: ～雷动 burst into thunderous applause

掌握 zhǎngwò ① hold; take; have in hand: ～第一手材料 possess first-hand material ② grasp; master: ～法语 have a good command of French; master French ③ preside (at, over): ～会议 preside at (over) a meeting

掌灶 zhǎngzào be the chef

掌嘴 zhǎngzuǐ slap sb.'s face; box sb.'s ears

长 zhǎng ①〈形〉eldest; elder; senior:～子 eldest son. 比他年～ older than him ②〈名〉chief; head:处～ head of a department or office〈动〉③ develop; grow:成～ grow to maturity ④ increase; enhance:增～ increase; grow; rise

另见 cháng

长辈 zhǎngbèi elder member of a family; elder; senior

长膘 zhǎngbiāo (of a domestic animal) get fat; put on flesh; flesh out

长大 zhǎngdà grow up:～成人 grow to manhood; come of age

长个儿 zhǎnggèr grow taller

长官 zhǎngguān senior officer or official; commanding officer:～意志 will of one's superiors; commanding officer's will

长进 zhǎngjìn (make) progress (in):学习德语很有～ make much progress in German

长老 zhǎnglǎo ① elder ② elder of a Buddhist monastery

长毛 zhǎngmáo become mildewed; be covered with mildew

长势 zhǎngshì the way a crop is growing

长嗣继承制 zhǎngsì-jìchéngzhì primogeniture

长相 zhǎngxiàng features; appearance; looks

长兄(姐) zhǎngxiōng(jiě) eldest brother (sister)

涨 zhǎng〈动〉(of water, prices, etc.) go up; rise; (of prices, etc.) soar; rise sharply

另见 zhàng

涨潮 zhǎngcháo flood tide; rising tide; tide;这条船～时离去。The ship departed on the tide.

涨风 zhǎngfēng upward trend of market prices

涨价 zhǎngjià rise in prices; price hike; inflation of prices:变相～ raise the prices in a disguised form; disguised increases in the prices

涨落 zhǎngluò ① (of tide) ebb and flow ② (of prices, etc.) fluctuate

zhàng

障 zhàng ①〈名〉barrier; obstruction:热～ heat barrier ②〈动〉hinder; keep out

障碍 zhàng'ài barrier; obstruction; obstacle:扫除～ remove (clear away) obstacles

障蔽 zhàngbì shut out; block; obstruct

障眼法 zhàngyǎnfǎ cover-up; camouflage

丈 zhàng〈名〉① *zhang*, a unit of length (=3 ⅓ metres) ② [对老者的尊称]:岳～ father-in-law ③〈动〉measure:清～ make an exact measurement of land

丈夫 zhàngfu ① husband ② man:大～ true man

丈量 zhàngliáng measure (land)
丈母 zhàngmǔ wife's mother; mother-in-law
丈人 zhàngrén wife's father; father-in-law

杖 zhàng〈名〉① stick; cane:拐～ walking stick ② rod or staff used for a specific purpose:禅～ Buddhist monk's staff

仗 zhàng〈名〉① battle; war:败～ lost battle ② weapons; weaponry〈动〉③ rely on; depend on:仰～ look to sb. for backing; rely on ④ hold (a sword)
仗势欺人 zhàngshì-qīrén take advantage of one's or sb.'s power to bully people; abuse one's power and bully people; bully people by reliance on one's powerful connections or positions
仗义 zhàngyì uphold justice:～疏财 be generous and aiding needy people. ～勇为 help a lame dog over a stile; take bold action to uphold justice. ～执言 speak out to uphold justice; speak boldly in defence of justice

涨 zhàng〈动〉① swell after absorbing water; being soaked ② (of the head) be swelled by a rush of blood:气得～红了脸 redden with anger
另见 zhǎng

帐 zhàng〈名〉① curtain; screen:青纱～ the green curtain of tall crops ② account:查～ check accounts ③ debt:老～ long-standing debts
帐簿 zhàngbù account book; ledger
帐单 zhàngdān bill; check
帐号 zhànghào number of a bank account
帐户 zhànghù account:～号码 account number. 贸易清算～ commercial clearing account. ～名称 account title. 往来～ current account
帐面 zhàngmiàn on the books:～赤字 deficit on the books. ～价值 book value. ～利润 book profit
帐目 zhàngmù accounts:清理～ square accounts. ～不清。The accounts are not in order.
帐外 zhàngwài off-the-book; invisible:～资产 invisible assets; unlisted property; off-the-book property

胀 zhàng〈动〉①swell (up); be bloated ② expand, inflate:热使金属膨～ Heat expands metals
胀饱 zhàngbǎo be bloated with overeating

zhāo

着 zhāo〈名〉① a move in chess:失～ make an unwise move ② device; trick; means:她没～了。She's at the end of her tether.
另见 zháo,zhuó
着数 zhāoshù ① a move in chess ② a movement in *wushu* ③

trick; device

朝 zhāo〈名〉① early morning ② day:今～ today; the present. 一～ in one day
另见 cháo

朝不保夕 zhāobù-bǎoxī not know in the morning what may happen in the evening; in a critical condition; in imminent danger; in a precarious state:病人已～。The patient's condition is critical.

朝辉 zhāohuī morning sunlight

朝令夕改 zhāolìng-xīgǎi make frequent changes in policies; be inconstant (inconsistent) in policy

朝气 zhāoqì spirit of youth; vigour; vitality:～蓬勃 full of youthful spirit; vigorous

朝三暮四 zhāosān-mùsì play fast and loose; chop and change; shift and veer; keep changing one's mind; blow hot and cold

朝阳 zhāoyáng the rising sun; the morning sun

招 zhāo〈动〉① beckon; summon by gesture:她～手要我进去。She beckoned me in. ② recruit; enroll; enlist:～生 enroll students ③ cause; invite; incur:～祸 invite calamity; court disaster ④ confess; acknowledge:～供 make a confession of one's crimes; confess

招标 zhāobiāo invite tenders (bids); call for tenders:～制 competitive-bidding system

招兵买马 zhāobīng mǎimǎ hire men and buy horses; raise or enlarge an army; recruit followers

招待 zhāodài receive (guests); entertain; serve (customers):～会 reception. ～所 guesthouse

招工 zhāogōng recruit workers

招股 zhāogǔ float shares to raise capital:～说明书 prospectus

招呼 zhāohu ① call ② greet; hail:打～ greet ③ look after; attend to:～顾客 attend to customers. ～病人 look after a patient

招架 zhāojià ward off; withstand; parry:～不住 unable to withstand (resist, ward off, stand up to, parry, defend)

招考 zhāokǎo admit (students, etc.) by examination

招揽 zhāolǎn solicit (customers or business); canvass:～生意 canvass (seek) business orders; drum up trade

招领 zhāolǐng notice to owners to make claims; announce the finding of lost property:失物～ Found

招牌 zhāopái signboard; (shop) sign

招聘 zhāopìng invite applications for a job:～工程师 advertise for engineers

招惹 zhāorě invite; incur; court:～是非 bring trouble on oneself; provoke dispute; stir up trouble (misunderstanding, ill will)

招认 zhāorèn make a confession;

confess one's guilt; plead guilty;own up

招商 zhāoshāng invite outside investment; invite businessmen to open companies

招生 zhāoshēng enrol new students; recruit students

招收 zhāoshōu enroll; recruit; admit; take in

招手 zhāoshǒu wave; beckon:向某人~致意 wave to sb. in acknowledgment

招贴 zhāotiē poster; placard; bill:不准~! Post No Bills!

招摇 zhāoyáo act ostentatiously; show off; flaunt:~过市 swagger through the streets; swagger about. ~撞骗 swindle by false pretences; bluff and deceive; cheat and bluff; hoodwink… with

招展 zhāozhǎn flutter; wave: 工地上红旗~。Red flags fluttered over the construction site.

招致 zhāozhì ① recruit (personnel); take in ② bring; cause; invite; incur:~失败 cause defeat

招租 zhāozū (house) for rent: 此房~。House to let.

昭 zhāo〈形〉obvious; conspicuous; clear:~示 declare publicly

昭告 zhāogào declare to the public

昭然若揭 zhāorán-ruòjiē be as clear as daylight; as plain as the nose on one's face; abundantly clear; as clear as if it were exposed to view:他们的险恶用心~。Their evil motives are clearly exposed.

昭示 zhāoshì make clear to all; declare publicly

昭雪 zhāoxuě exonerate; rehabilitate; redress a wrong or an injustice; right:许多冤案得到~。Wrongs have been righted.

昭彰 zhāozhāng clear; evident; manifest:罪恶~ have committed flagrant crimes

昭著 zhāozhù obvious; evident; clear: 成绩~ have achieved great successes. 臭名~ notorious

zháo

着 zháo〈动〉① touch; come into contact with:上下不~边 touch neither top nor the bottom ② be affected by; feel:~凉 catch cold ③ burn:火~得很旺。The fire is burning briskly. ④ fall asleep:她躺下就~。She fell asleep as soon as she lay down. ⑤[用在动词之后,表示已经达到目的或有了结果]:睡~了。Be asleep.

着风 zháofēng be chilled by the wind

着慌 zháohuāng get alarmed; become flustered

着火 zháohuǒ catch (take) fire; be on fire; burn

着急 zháojí worry (about); feel (be) anxious (about, for):为某人安全而~ be anxious about sb.'s safety

着迷 zháomí become (be) fascinated; lose oneself (in); be

crazy about; be obsessed with: 他～于足球。He was fascinated with football.

着魔 zháomó be bewitched; be possessed

zhǎo

沼 zhǎo〈名〉natural pond: 泥～ quagmire; swamp

沼气 zhǎoqì marsh gas; methane; biogas

沼泽 zhǎozé marsh; bog; swamp

找 zhǎo〈动〉① look for; find; seek: ～到克服困难的各种方法 find ways and means to overcome difficulties ② call on; want to see: 明天再来～你。I'll call on you again tomorrow. ③ give change: 两不～。That's just right.

找补 zhǎobu make up a deficiency

找不开 zhǎobukāi have no small change for (money of a higher denomination)

找差距 zhǎo chājù find out where one has lagged behind

找茬儿 zhǎochár find fault; pick holes; pick a quarrel

找出 zhǎochū find out; discover: ～发展国民经济的规律 deduce the laws governing the development of the national economy. ～根源 go to the root of

找出路 zhǎo chūlù seek a way out

找对象 zhǎo duìxiàng look for a partner in marriage; look for a mate

找矿 zhǎokuàng look for mineral deposits; prospect (for)

找麻烦 zhǎo máfan ① look for trouble; ask for trouble ② cause sb. trouble

找齐 zhǎoqí ① make uniform; even up ② make up a deficiency

找钱 zhǎoqián give change

找事 zhǎoshì ① look (hunt) for a job ② pick a quarrel

找死 zhǎosǐ court death

找头 zhǎotou change: 你应该给我5角钱～。You should give me five *jiao* change.

爪 zhǎo〈名〉claw; talon

爪牙 zhǎoyá henchman; lackey; pawn; accomplice

zhào

肇 zhào〈动〉① begin; start: ～岁 start a new year ② cause (an accident, trouble, etc.)

肇事 zhàoshì cause trouble; create a disturbance; kick up a row: ～后逃跑的司机 hit-and-runner. ～者 troublemaker

肇讼 zhàosòng institute (cause) proceedings

罩 zhào ①〈动〉cover; wrap: 迷雾笼～山顶。The mountain top is wrapped in mist. ②〈名〉shade; cover; hood: 防尘～ dust cover

罩袍 zhàopáo dust-gown; dust-robe; overall

罩衫 zhàoshān overall; dustcoat

罩袖 zhàoxiù oversleeve

罩子 zhàozi cover; shade

兆 zhào ①〈名〉omen; portent: ～头 omen; portent ②〈数〉million ③ a million millions

兆周 zhàozhōu [无] megacycle

召 zhào〈动〉① call together; convene; summon: 宣～ summon to imperial court or capital ② court; invite: ～祸 invite disaster

召唤 zhàohuàn call (on); summon

召回 zhàohuí recall: ～大使 recall an ambassador

召集 zhàojí call (together); assemble; convene: ～会议 call a meeting. ～人 convener

召见 zhàojiàn ① give an audience to; call in (a subordinate) ② [外]summon (an envoy) to an interview

召开 zhàokāi convene; convoke: ～会议 convoke a conference

召之即来 zhàozhījílái come as soon as called; report for duty at a moment's call; be ready to assemble at the first call; be at sb.'s beck and call

诏 zhào ①〈动〉instruct ②〈名〉imperial edict

诏版铭文 zhàobǎn míngwén inscriptions of imperial edicts

诏告 zhàogào proclaim … as emperor

诏书 zhàoshū imperial edict (decree, proclamation)

诏旨 zhàozhǐ imperial rescript

照 zhào〈动〉① shine; illuminate: 落～ the glow of the setting sun ② mirror; reflect: ～镜子 look in the mirror ③ take a picture; make a film: ～相 take a picture; have a picture taken ④〈名〉license; permit: 车～ license (of a car, bicycle, etc.)〈介〉⑤ in the direction of; towards: ～这个方向走 go in this direction ⑥ according to; in the light of: ～他的说法 according to what he says

照搬 zhàobān indiscriminately imitate; copy: ～西方理论 transplantation of Western theory

照办 zhàobàn do one's bidding; do as one is told; act accordingly; act in accordance with; comply with

照本宣科 zhàoběn-xuānkē repeat (echo) what the book says

照常 zhàocháng as usual: ～营业 business as usual

照抄 zhàochāo ① copy word for word

照顾 zhàogù ① look after; attend: ～病人 attend the sick man ② take into consideration (account); consider: ～某人的实际困难 take sb.'s actual difficulties into account ③ give consideration to; have (show) consideration for; make allowance for: ～老年人 show consideration for old people ④ preferential treatment; consideration: 予以适当～ give appropriate preferential treatment. ～价格 preferential prices

照管 zhàoguǎn look after; take

care of; take charge of

照会 zhàohuì ①[外] note:提出~ deliver (present, address) a note to ② notify

照价付款 zhàojià fùkuǎn pay according to the arranged price

照料 zhàoliào look after; take care of; see after

照面儿 zhàomiànr ①[通常用于否定式]put in an appearance; show up; turn up:她始终不~。She never showed up. ② encounter; come across

照明 zhàomíng illumination; lighting

照实 zhàoshí according to the facts

照相 zhàoxiàng ① photograph; photo; picture:文学中的~现实主义 photographic realism in literature ② take a photo (picture); have a photo taken

照样 zhàoyàng ① after a pattern or model:~出售 sale by sample ② in the same old way; all the same; usual; as before:~要感谢你。Thank you all the same.

照应 zhàoyīng look after; take care of; give consideration to

照章 zhàozhāng act in accordance with the regulations:~纳税 deliver taxes as required

照直 zhàozhí ① (go) straight on ② straightforward; direct

照准 zhàozhǔn ①[通常用于官方文件] request granted ② aim at:~靶子射击 aim at the target and fire

zhē

遮 zhē〈动〉① hide from view; cover:用帘子把窗户~起来 cover the window with a curtain ② block; obstruct; impede:~道 block the way ③ conceal

遮蔽 zhēbì hide from view; screen; cover ② block; obstruct

遮丑 zhēchǒu gloss over one's blemishes; hide one's shame; cover up one's defect

遮挡 zhēdǎng ① shelter from; keep out ② a shelter; a cover

遮幅电影 zhēfú-diànyǐng covered-up movie

遮盖 zhēgài ① cover; shelter; overspread ② hide; cover up; conceal

遮羞 zhēxiū cover (hush) up a scandal; conceal one's disgrace:~布 fig leaf; mask

遮掩 zhēyǎn ① cover; cloak ② hide; conceal:~天下人的耳目 pull the wool over the eyes of the world's people

遮阳 zhēyáng sunshade

折 zhē〈动〉① turn over; roll over:~个跟头 turn a somersault ② pour water, etc. back and forth between two containers

另见 zhé, shé

折腾 zhēteng ① turn from side to side; toss about ② do sth. over and over again ③ cause physical or mental suffering

zhé

折 zhé〈动〉① break; snap:～断腿骨 break one's leg ② turn; bend; twist:百～不回 keep on fighting in spite of all setbacks ③ suffer the loss of; lose ④ fold:将信～起来 fold a letter ⑤ convert:～实单位 unit converted from commodity prices〈名〉⑥ discount:～扣价格 price at a discount ⑦ bankbook; deposit book
另见 shé,zhē

折半 zhébàn reduce (a price) by half; give 50% discount

折叠 zhédié fold:～伞 folding umbrella

折断 zhéduàn break (off); break asunder:～胳膊 break one's arm

折兑 zhéduì exchange (gold or silver) for money; convert

折服 zhéfú be fully convinced

折合 zhéhé convert into; be equivalent to:一英镑～人民币是多少? How much is a pound in terms of Renminbi?

折价 zhéjià convert into money; evaluate in terms of money

折旧 zhéjiù [经] depreciation:～率 rate of depreciation. ～费 depreciation fund (charges). ～年限 depreciable life

折扣 zhékòu discount; allowance; rebate:打～出售 sell at a discount

折磨 zhémo cause physical or mental suffering; affliction; torment; harassment:受疾病的～ suffer severely from a lingering illness

折算 zhésuàn convert:～率 conversion rate

折腰 zhéyāo bend one's back—bow in obeisance; cringe

折中(衷) zhézhōng (zhōng) compromise:～主义 eclecticism

折子戏 zhézixì highlights from operas; selected scenes from operas

哲 zhé ①〈形〉wise; sagacious:睿～ divinely wise; sagacious ②〈名〉wise man; sage:先～ a great thinker of the past; sage

哲理 zhélǐ philosophical theory (principle)

哲学 zhéxué philosophy:～家 philosopher

辙 zhé〈名〉① the track of a wheel; rut:涸～ dry rut ② rhyme (of a song; drama, etc.):合～ in rhyme

zhě

者 zhě ①[用在"工作"和"主义"后面,表示从事某项工作或信仰某个主义的人]-er; -or; -ist:编～ editor; compiler. 马克思主义～ Marxist ②[用在"二、三"等数词后面,指上下文所说的几件事]:二～必居其一 either one or the other

褶 zhě〈名〉pleat; fold; crease:百～裙 a pleated skirt

zhè

这 zhè ①〈代〉this：～边 this side；this way；here ②〈副〉now：我～就走。I'm leaving right now.

这次 zhècì this time；present；current

这就是说 zhèjiùshì shuō It is as much as saying.；that is to say

这么 zhème so；such；like this；this：大家都～说。So they say. ～多 this much

这么着 zhèmezhe like this；so

这样 zhèyàng ① so；thus；like this：～说来 if that is the case，… ② such；of this kind

这种 zhèzhǒng of this kind；such kind of；such

蔗 zhè〈名〉sugarcane：～糖 cane sugar

鹧 zhè ～鸪 partridge

zhe

着 zhe〈助动〉①[表示动作的持续]：她正吃～午饭呢。She is having her lunch. ②[表示状态的持续]：门开～。The door is open. ③[用在动词或表示程度的形容词后面，以加强命令或嘱咐的语气]：快～点儿。Be quick. ④[加在某些动词后面，使变成介词]：照～ by；according to；in

着呢 zhene [表示程度深]：天还早～。It's still quite early.

zhēn

斟 zhēn〈动〉① pour (tea or wine) ② consider

斟酌 zhēnzhuó consider；balance；consult；weigh；deliberate (over)：～办理 act as one sees fit；at one's discretion. ～字句 weigh one's words

甄 zhēn〈动〉discriminate；distinguish；examine：～用 select for appointment

甄拔 zhēnbá select：～人才 select talented people

甄别 zhēnbié ① examine and distinguish；discriminate ② the work of determining the nature of the case；reexamine a case；screen：～委员会 screening committee

真 zhēn ①〈形〉real；true；genuine：～知 real knowledge〈副〉② really；indeed；truly：他～不知道。He really doesn't know. ③ unmistakably；clearly

真才实学 zhēncái-shíxué real ability and learning；genuine talent；sturdy knowledge；solid learning：有～ be genuinely talented and learned

真传 zhēnchuán be handed down in a direct line from the master

真谛 zhēndì true essence (meaning)；core truths；absolute (ultimate) truth；inner sense

真话 zhēnhuà truth：说～ speak

the truth
真迹 zhēnjì genuine (authentic) work (of painting or calligraphy); true specimen
真金不怕火炼 zhēnjīn bùpà huǒ liàn Genuine (pure) gold can be tried in the fire.; A genuine article can stand any test.; Truth fears not the flames of slander and injustice.
真理 zhēnlǐ truth
真面目 zhēnmiànmù true colours (features):露出～ show one's true features
真皮 zhēnpí ① genuine leather ② derma
真凭实据 zhēnpíng-shíjù hard (positive) evidence; conclusive (indisputable) evidence
真切 zhēnqiè clear; vivid; distinct
真情 zhēnqíng ① the real situation; the facts; truth ② true sentiments (feelings):～毕露 make no disguise of one's feelings
真善美 zhēn-shàn-měi the true, the good and the beautiful
真实 zhēnshí authentic; true; real:新闻～性 veracity of news
真率 zhēnshuài straightforward; unaffected
真相 zhēnxiàng real facts; truth; true picture; actual state of affairs; real situation:～大白。The whole truth has come out. 弄清事情的～ clarify the truth of the matter
真心 zhēnxīn sincerity; wholeheartedness:～实意 genuinely (earnestly) and sincerely; with all one's heart; in good earnest. ～话 sincere words; words from the bottom of one's heart
真知灼见 zhēnzhī-zhuójiàn real knowledge and deep insight; incisive (penetrating) judgement
真挚 zhēnzhì sincere; earnest; cordial:～的友谊 sincere friendship
真主 zhēnzhǔ Allah

贞 zhēn ①〈形〉faithful; loyal:忠～ loyal and steadfast ②〈名〉(of women) chastity or virginity
贞操 zhēncāo ① chastity; virginity ② moral integrity; loyalty
贞节 zhēnjié virginity; chastity
贞洁 zhēnjié chaste; pure and undefiled

侦 zhēn〈动〉detect; scout:外出～察 be out scouting
侦查 zhēnchá detect; investigate:～一起谋杀案 investigate a murder case. ～活动 investigatory activity. ～员 (preliminary) investigator
侦察 zhēnchá scout; reconnoitre; spy (upon):～犯罪 investigate a crime. ～敌人的行动 spy upon the enemy's movements. ～实验 investigative experiment
侦缉 zhēnjī track down and arrest
侦破 zhēnpò investigate and uncover; detect; solve
侦探 zhēntàn ① do detective work ② spy; detective:～小说 detective story; crime fiction
侦听 zhēntīng intercept

侦讯 zhēnxùn investigate

箴 zhēn ①〈动〉advise；admonish：～言 admonition；maxim ②〈名〉a type of didactic literary composition in ancient times

针 zhēn〈名〉① needle：唱～ gramophone needle ② stitch：在衬衫上缝几～ put a few stitches in a shirt ③ hand：时～ hands of a clock or watch

针刺 zhēncì needling；acupuncture：～疗法 acupuncture treatment. ～麻醉 acupuncture anaesthesia

针对 zhēnduì ① be aimed at；be directed at (against) ② in accordance with：这个警告不是～他的。This warnig is not directed at him.

针锋相对 zhēnfēng-xiāngduì give tit for tat；stand in sharp opposition to；be diametrically opposed to：～的斗争 tit-for-tat struggle

针灸 zhēnjiǔ acupuncture and moxibustion：～铜人 bronze acupuncture statue

针线 zhēnxiàn ① needle and thread：～包 sewing kit. ～盒 housewives ② needlework

针织品 zhēnzhīpǐn knit goods；knitware

珍 zhēn ①〈名〉treasure：奇～ rare treasures ②〈形〉precious；valuable：～贵的话 precious words

珍爱 zhēn'ài love dearly；treasure

珍宝 zhēnbǎo treasure；jewellery

珍本 zhēnběn rare book；rare edition

珍藏 zhēncáng consider valuable and collect appropriately；treasure (up)；keep；collect：～历史文物 keep historical relics

珍贵 zhēnguì precious；valuable；rare

珍品 zhēnpǐn treasure；rare things；museum piece；gem：无价的艺术～ priceless art treasures

珍视 zhēnshì treasure；value；prize；cherish

珍闻 zhēnwén news titbits；fillers：世界～ world briefs

珍惜 zhēnxī take good care of；set a high value on；treasure；cherish；value：～时间 set a high value on one's time

珍重 zhēnzhòng ① highly value；esteem；set great store by；treasure ② take care of oneself：千万～。Please take good care of yourself.

zhěn

枕 zhěn〈名〉pillow："～边风" uxorial influence

枕巾 zhěnjīn a towel used to cover a pillow

枕木 zhěnmù sleeper；tie

枕头 zhěntou pillow

诊 zhěn〈动〉examine (a patient)；diagnose：出～ (of a doctor) visit a patient at home

诊病 zhěnbìng diagnose a disease

诊断 zhěnduàn diagnose：～书 medical certificate
诊金 zhěnjīn consultation fee；hospital fee
诊疗 zhěnliáo diagnose and treat；treat：～所 clinic
诊脉 zhěnmài feel the pulse
诊室 zhěnshì consulting room
诊治 zhěnzhì make a diagnosis and give treatment

zhèn

震 zhèn〈动〉① shock；shake；quake：～动世界 shock the world ② be alarmed；be shocked：～惊 be greatly alarmed by
震荡 zhèndàng shake；shock；vibrate；quake
震动 zhèndòng shake；quake；vibrate；shock：她的话对我～很大。Her remarks made a great impact on me.
震耳欲聋 zhèn'ěr-yùlóng deafening；ear-splitting
震骇 zhènhài be frightened (at)；be startled (at)
震撼 zhènhàn shake；vibrate；shock：～中外 shock the country and the whole world
震级 zhènjí magnitude (of an earthquake)
震惊 zhènjīng shock；astonish；amaze；alarm：令人～的 shocking；startling；appalling
震怒 zhènnù fly into a rage (passion)；be enraged；be furious
震中 zhènzhōng epicentre

振 zhèn〈动〉① shake；flap：～翅飞行的鹰 an eagle flapping its wings ② rise vigorously；brace up：士气大～。The morale was greatly boosted.
振臂 zhènbì raise one's arm
振动 zhèndòng［物］vibrate
振奋 zhènfèn ① rouse oneself；brace oneself up：～精神 heighten (activate) one's spirit ② inspire；spur on；stimulate：～人心的 inspiring；heartening
振兴 zhènxīng revive；revitalize；promote；develop vigorously：～中华 make China prosper；invigorate the Chinese nation
振振有辞 zhènzhèn-yǒucí say plausibly (presumptuously) and at great length；assert eloquently
振作 zhènzuò bestir oneself；hearten up；exert oneself；pull oneself together；brace oneself up：～精神 stir oneself up to exertion；rouse oneself；pluck up one's heart；brace (cheer) up

赈 zhèn〈动〉relieve；aid：放～ give famine or flood relief
赈济 zhènjì relieve；aid：～灾民 aid the victims of natural calamities
赈款 zhènkuǎn relief fund
赈灾 zhènzāi give relief to the victims (relieve the people) in stricken areas

镇 zhèn ①〈名〉township；town：乡～企业 township and village

enterprises〈动〉② guard; garrison:～守 guard (a strategically important place); garrison ③ press down; check; control:～痛 ease pain ④ cool with cold water:冰～啤酒 iced beer ⑤ suppress; subdue:武装～压起义 put down the uprising by armed force ⑥〈形〉calm; tranquil; at ease

镇尺 zhènchǐ paperweight (in the shape of a ruler)

镇定 zhèndìng calm; composed; collected:～自若 be perfectly calm and collected

镇静 zhènjìng calm; sedate; composed; unruffled:保持～ remain calm

镇静剂 zhènjìngjì sedative; tranquillizer

镇慑 zhènshè cow sb. into submission

镇守 zhènshǒu guard; defend; garrison:～边疆 defend the frontier

镇物 zhènwù "deterrent"; talisman:中国～文化 China's "deterrent" (talisman) culture

镇压 zhènyā ① suppress; repress; quell:～机器 machinery of suppression ② execute; put to death

镇纸 zhènzhǐ paperweight

阵 zhèn〈名〉① battle array (formation):疑～ battle array to mislead or deceive the enemy ② position; front:思想～地 ideological position ③ a period of time:病了一～儿 be ill for some time ④〈量〉一～掌声 a burst of applause. 一～雨 a spatter of rain. 一～咳嗽 a fit of coughing. 一～寒潮 a cold spell

阵地 zhèndì position; bastion:教育～ the bastion of education

阵脚 zhènjiǎo ① front line ② position; situation; circumstances

阵容 zhènróng ① battle array; fighting formation ② lineup:～坚强 have a strong lineup. 演员～整齐 a well-balanced cast

阵势 zhènshì ① disposition of combat forces (troops); battle formation:摆开～ deploy the ranks in battle array ② condition; circumstances; situation

阵痛 zhèntòng [医] labour pains; throes; twinge; twitch

阵亡 zhènwáng be killed in action (battle):～将士纪念碑 monument to the war dead. ～烈士名单 roll of honour

zhēng

正 zhēng
另见 zhèng

正月 zhēngyuè the first month of the lunar year; the first month

症 zhēng
另见 zhèng

症结 zhēngjié crux (of a problem); crucial reason:～所在 the crux of the problem; where the trouble lies

征 zhēng〈动〉① go on an expedition:出～ go on an expedition;

go out to battle ② recruit; draft:～兵 recruit troops ③ collect; levy:开～ begin to levy (taxes) ④ ask for; solicit:～稿 solicit contributions (to a journal, etc.) ⑤〈名〉portent:候～ sign

征兵 zhēngbīng draft; call-up; conscription:～制 conscription system

征尘 zhēngchén dust which settles on one during a journey

征调 zhēngdiào call up; requisition

征伐(讨) zhēngfá(tǎo) go on a punitive expedition; military campaign

征服 zhēngfú conquer; subdue; subjugate

征购 zhēnggòu purchase on a requisition basis; requisition by purchase; purchase by the state:～土地 purchase the land

征管 zhēngguǎn collection and management:消费税～ collection and management of consumption taxes

征候 zhēnghòu symptom; sign; syndrome

征婚广告 zhēnghūn guǎnggào matrimonial advertisement

征集 zhēngjí ① collect; gather ② recruit; draft; call up; summon:～新兵 call up recruits

征粮 zhēngliáng impose grain levies

征聘 zhēngpìn ① give public notice of vacancies to be filled; invite applications for jobs; advertise for (a secretary, teacher, etc.) ② want ad; wanted (for a job)

征求 zhēngqiú ask for; seek; solicit:～顾客意见 solicit opinions from customers

征收 zhēngshōu collect; levy; impose (a duty) on:～所得税 levy an income tax (on sb. or sth.)

征税 zhēngshuì levy taxes; tax collection

征途 zhēngtú the road to be travelled; journey

征文 zhēngwén solicit articles or essays

征询 zhēngxún seek the opinion; ask for opinion; consult

征用 zhēngyòng make a requisition; take over for use; requisition; expropriate:～土地 requisition land. ～权 eminent domain

征召 zhēngzhāo call up; enlist:～入伍 enlist in the army

征兆 zhēngzhào portent; omen; sign

争 zhēng〈动〉① contend; strive; vie:力～ strive by every means ② argue; dispute; struggle:～项目、～投资 fight over construction projects and the related investments

争霸 zhēngbà contend (struggle) for hegemony; scramble (strive) for supremacy

争辩 zhēngbiàn dispute (with); argue (with); debate; contend:无可～的 indisputable

争吵 zhēngchǎo quarrel (with); wrangle (with); squabble:～不

休 quarrel with each other endlessly

争持 zhēngchí refuse to give in; stick to one's guns

争端 zhēngduān contend; controversial issue; dispute; conflict

争夺 zhēngduó scramble for; contest; grab; seize; contend (for); fight (for); vie (with, for):～市场 seize (scramble for) markets

争分夺秒 zhēngfēn-duómiǎo fight for every minute; make every minute count; seize the minute, seize the second

争光 zhēngguāng win honour (for); be a credit to:为国～ win honour for one's country

争论 zhēnglùn controversy; contention; dispute; debate:～的焦点 bone of contention. 同某人～某事 dispute with (against) sb. on (about) sth.

争鸣 zhēngmíng contend

争气 zhēngqì strive (try) to gain (win) credit (for); try to make a good showing

争取 zhēngqǔ strive for; struggle for; fight for:～入党 strive to qualify for Party membership. ～时间 race against time; win time

争权夺利 zhēngquán-duólì scramble for power and profit; struggle for power and wealth; vie with one another in pursuit of personal power and gain

争胜 zhēngshèng compete for first place

争先 zhēngxiān try to be among the first; compete to be the first; rush to the fore:～恐后 vie with each other (in doing sth.)

争雄 zhēngxióng fight for supremacy

争议 zhēngyì controversy; dispute:有～的人物 controversial figure

争执 zhēngzhí quarrel; dispute; disagree:他们～不下。They stuck to their own stand.

挣 zhēng

另见 zhèng

挣扎 zhēngzhá struggle; put up a desperate fight:作垂死～ put up a last-ditch struggle

睁 zhēng〈动〉open (one's eyes)

睁眼瞎 zhēngyǎnxiā illiterate person; be completely illiterate; illiteracy

睁一只眼,闭一只眼 zhēng yī zhī yǎn,bì yī zhī yǎn turn a blind eye to sth.; pretend not to see; wink at

峥 zhēng

峥嵘 zhēngróng ①［山］lofty and steep; towering:山势～ steep and towering mountains ② outstanding; remarkable:～岁月 extraordinary times; eventful years

狰 zhēng

狰狞 zhēngníng savage; ferocious; hideous:～面目 ferocious (hideous, fiendish, diabolical, brutish) features

蒸 zhēng〈动〉① steam：清～ steam in clear soup ② vaporize；evaporate：热使水～发。Heat evaporates water.

蒸发 zhēngfā evaporate

蒸馏 zhēngliú distillation：～水 distilled water

蒸笼 zhēnglóng food steamer；steam box

蒸汽 zhēngqì steam：～机 steam-engine. ～浴 steam bath

蒸蒸日上 zhēngzhēng-rìshàng grow more and more prosperous；prosper (flourish) day by day；ever more flourishing；thrive with each passing day

zhěng

整 zhěng〈形〉① whole；intact；entire；complete：～个世界 all the world ② in good order；tidy：～洁的人 a tidy person〈动〉③ put in (good) order；rectify；consolidate：～党 consolidating the Party organization；Party rectification ④ repair；mend：修～ repair and maintain

整编 zhěngbiān [军] reorganize：～师 reorganized division

整党 zhěngdǎng consolidate the Party organization

整顿 zhěngdùn put in order；put right；reorganize；consolidate：～城乡社会治安 rectify social order in both urban and rural areas. ～经济秩序 straighten out the economic order. ～企业 put the enterprises in a better shape. ～流通秩序 improve the order of circulation

整风 zhěngfēng rectify the style of work；rectify incorrect styles of work

整改 zhěnggǎi rectify and reform concurrently

整个 zhěnggè whole；entire

整理 zhěnglǐ put in (good) order；straighten out；put right；arrange；sort out：～财政 regulate finance. ～加工[文字、写作] reedit and revise

整齐 zhěngqí ① orderly；tidy；trim：字写得清楚～ clear and neat handwriting ② regular；even：～划一 uniform；regular

整容 zhěngróng ① tidy up one's appearance；tidy oneself up ② perform face-lifting

整饰 zhěngshì renovate and decorate

整数 zhěngshù ①[数]whole number；integer ②[十、百、千等] round figure (number)

整肃 zhěngsù ① strict；rigid ② rectify；consolidate

整体 zhěngtǐ integral whole；whole；entirety：～观念 view the situation as a whole

整天 zhěngtiān the whole day；all day；all day long

整形 zhěngxíng [医] plastic：～手术 plastic operation

整修 zhěngxiū fix up；rebuild；renovate；refurbish：～老屋 refurbish an old house

整训 zhěngxùn train and consolidate

整整 zhěngzhěng whole; full

整装 zhěngzhuāng get one's things ready (for a journey, etc.):～待发 be ready to start. ～待命 be ready for orders

拯 zhěng〈动〉save; rescue

拯救 zhěngjiù save; rescue (from); deliver (from); retrieve (from)

zhèng

郑 zhèng

郑重 zhèngzhòng solemn; serious; earnest:～表示 state in all seriousness. ～声明 solemnly declare

正 zhèng〈形〉① upright; straight:把画摆～ put a picture straight ② situated in the middle; main:～门 front door (gate); main entrance ③ (of time) punctually; sharp:十时～ ten o'clock sharp ④ right:～面 the right side ⑤ upright; honest:～大光Z明 upright and open-minded ⑥ correct:端～ proper; correct ⑦ principle; chief; fundamental:～驾驶员 first pilot ⑧〈动〉correct; put right; amend:补～ supplement and correct ⑨〈副〉just; right:～如他所说的 just as he says
另见 zhēng

正本 zhèngběn ① original (of a document) ② reserved copy (of a library book)

正比 zhèngbǐ[数]direct proportion

正餐 zhèngcān ① regular meal served in a restaurant ② dinner

正常 zhèngcháng normal; regular:～化 normalize; put… on a proper basis; make sound. 运转～ operate normally

正大光明 zhèngdà-guāngmíng open and aboveboard; upright and pure (open)-minded

正当 zhèngdāng just as; just when:～他要离开时电话铃响了。He was about to leave when the phone rang.

正当 zhèngdàng right; appropriate; proper; legal; legitimate:～的宗教活动 legitimate religious activities. ～防卫[法] legitimate defence. ～收入 legitimate income

正道 zhèngdào ① the right way (course); the correct path:走～ follow the correct path ② the correct principle; the correct way

正点 zhèngdiǎn on time; on schedule; punctually:～运行 running on schedule

正法 zhèngfǎ execute (a criminal)

正反 zhèngfǎn positive and negative:～两方面的历史教训 positive and negative historical lessons

正告 zhènggào tell (warn)… in all seriousness; warn seriously (sternly)

正规 zhèngguī regular; normal:～教育 regular education. ～部队 regular troops

正轨 zhèngguǐ right track; right

path：纳入～ put on the right track(course)

正经 zhèngjing ① honest；decent；respectable：～人 a decent person ② proper；serious；earnest：～货 standard goods

正楷 zhèngkǎi ［汉字］regular script

正路(道) zhènglù(dào) the right way；the correct path：走～ follow the right way

正面 zhèngmiàn ① positive；affirmative：～教育 positive education. ～人物 positive character. ～经验 positive experience ② front；facade ③［布等］right side

正派 zhèngpài decent；upright；honest：～人 a man of moral integrity；a decent person. 作风～ be honest in one's ways

正品 zhèngpǐn standard goods；quality products；certified products

正气 zhèngqì ① integrity；uprightness；probity；honour ② healthy atmosphere (tendency)：～上升 Healthy (wholesome) wind prevails. 发扬～ encourage healthy tendency (trends)

正巧 zhèngqiǎo ① happen to：我们～也在那里。We happened to be there, too. ② just in time；in good time

正人君子 zhèngrén-jūnzǐ a man of honour (noble character)；gentleman

正式 zhèngshì formal；official；regular：～收据 formal receipt. ～学科 formal discipline

正视 zhèngshì face (look) squarely：～缺点 acknowledge one's shortcomings. ～现实 look reality in the face.

正题 zhèngtí subject；topic (of a talk or essay)：转入～ come to the subject

正统 zhèngtǒng legitimate；orthodox：～戏剧 legitimate drama

正眼 zhèngyǎn look straight

正业 zhèngyè regular (proper) occupation；decent job；proper duties：不务～ ignore one's proper occupation

正义 zhèngyì justice；righteous；just：～力量 righteous strength

正直 zhèngzhí just；upright；honest；fair-minded：为人～ be an honest man

正中下怀 zhèngzhòng-xiàhuái fit in exactly with one's wishes；be just what one wants (hopes for)；come up just to one's expectation

正宗 zhèngzōng ① orthodox school ② genuine；real；authentic：～粤菜 authentic Guangdong cuisine (dish)

正座 zhèngzuò central seats that directly face the stage；stalls

症 zhèng〈名〉disease；illness；disease：急～ acute disease
另见 zhēng

症候(状) zhènghòu (zhuàng) symptom

证 zhèng ①〈动〉prove；testify；demonstrate：查～ check and testify〈名〉② proof；evidence：

作～ give evidence; testify ③ certificate; card

证词 zhèngcí testimony

证婚 zhènghūn be the chief witness at a wedding ceremony: ～人 chief witness at a wedding ceremony

证件 zhèngjiàn certificate; document; papers: 出示～。Show your papers.

证据 zhèngjù proof; evidence; testimony: ～确凿(不足)[法] (not) proven. 搜集～ collect evidence

证明 zhèngmíng prove; certify; testify; bear out: ～书 certificate; identification paper

证券 zhèngquàn (negotiable) securities: ～交易所 stock exchange. ～公司 security company. ～市场 stock market

证人 zhèngrén witness: ～席 witness stand

证实 zhèngshí confirm; verify; testify

证书 zhèngshū certificate; credentials: 毕业～ graduation certificate; diploma. 结婚～ marriage certificate; marriage lines

证言 zhèngyán testimony

证章 zhèngzhāng badge

政

zhèng〈名〉① politics; political affairs: 参～ participate in government and political affairs ② administrative affairs of a certain department of the government; management: 地～ administrative affairs of the utilization and requisition of land

政变 zhèngbiàn coup d'état; coup: 发动～ stage a coup d'état

政策 zhèngcè policy: ～性亏损 losses permitted by policy. ～性银行 noncommercial banks; policy-related banks. ～学 policy science

政敌 zhèngdí political opponent

政法机关 zhèngfǎ jīguān judicial agencies

政风 zhèngfēng government style

政府 zhèngfǔ government; [总统制国家的] Administration: ～公债 government bonds. ～工作人员 government functionaries. ～机构改革 reform of government organs; reform of organizational setups in local governments

政工 zhènggōng political work

政纪 zhèngjì administrative discipline (regulations)

政局 zhèngjú political situation; political scene

政历 zhènglì political history

政令 zhènglìng policies and administrative decrees; government decrees: ～畅通 policies and administrative decrees can be fully implemented

政权 zhèngquán political power: ～机关 organs of state power

政企分开 zhèng-qǐ fēnkāi separate the functions of the government from those of the enterprise

政审 zhèngshěn political investigation

政体 zhèngtǐ political system; system (form) of government

政委 zhèngwěi (political) commissar

政务 zhèngwù government affairs (administration):～活动公开 open operation of political affairs; making public the admninistrative activities

政治 zhèngzhì politics:～犯 political offender. ～经济学 political economy. ～局 Political Bureau. ～面目 political background or affiliation. ～信仰 political conviction (belief). ～学 political science; politics. ～嗅觉 political sense of smell. 算～帐 keep political accounts; concern oneself with the political significance.

政治家 zhèngzhìjiā statesman:～风度 statesmanship

政治协商会议(政协) zhèngzhì xié shāng huìyì(zhèngxié) Chinese People's Political Consultative Conference (C. P. P. C. C.)

诤 zhèng〈动〉criticize sb.'s faults frankly; admonish; expostulate

诤言 zhèngyán forthright admonition

挣 zhèng〈动〉① struggle to get free; struggle to free oneself: 进行垂死～扎 be in one's death-bed struggle ② earn; make; gain:～钱 earn money

另见 zhēng

挣脱 zhèngtuō struggle to free oneself; throw off; shake off:～枷锁 throw off the shackles

zhī

汁 zhī〈名〉juice; extract; gravy: 肉～ meat juice; gravy

之 zhī〈代〉①[代替人或事物,仅限于做宾语]:取而代～ take it over; replace someone ②[用在定语和中心词之间,表示领属关系或一般的修饰关系]:普天～下 all under heaven ③[虚用,无所指]:久而久～ with the passage of time ④〈介〉of:钟鼓～声 the sound of drums and bells

之后 zhīhòu later; after; afterwards

之类 zhīlèi …and the like; …and so forth; …and so on

之流 zhīliú …and company; … of a feather; … and his like

之前 zhīqián before; prior to; ago

之外 zhīwài besides; in addition to:除…～ except

之中 zhīzhōng in; in the midst of; among

芝 zhī

芝麻 zhīma sesame:～酱 sesame paste. ～油 sesame oil

支 zhī〈动〉① prop up; put up: 把伞～开 put up an umbrella ② sustain; bear; support:～援边远地区 support the remote border regions ③ send away; dispatch:把她～开 put her off with excuses ④ pay or draw (money):预～ draw money in advance ⑤〈名〉branch:～线

branch line

支部 zhībù ① branch office; branch ② Party branch:～书记 secretary of the Party branch

支撑 zhīchēng prop up; support; sustain; bolster up

支持 zhīchí ① support; back up; stand by, uphold:～产业 supportive industries ② sustain; hold out; bear:～不住 can't hold out any longer

支出 zhīchū ① pay; expend ② expenditure; outlay:～成本 outlay cost

支付 zhīfù pay; defray; disburse:～房租 pay rent. ～单位 paying unit. ～能力 capacity to pay. ～日期 date of payment

支行 zhīháng subbranch (of a bank)

支节产业 zhījié chǎnyè link-supporting industries

支离破碎 zhīlí-pòsuì shattered to pieces; torn to pieces; broken up

支流 zhīliú ① affluent; tributary ② secondary aspects; nonessentials

支配 zhīpèi ① arrange; apportion; allocate; budget:～时间 budget one's time ② control; dominate:～权 right to dispose of; right to control; power of control over

支票 zhīpiào cheque; check:～簿 chequebook. ～汇款 remittance by check. 开～ write a cheque

支取 zhīqǔ draw (one's deposit, money, etc.):～存款 draw one's deposit

支使 zhīshi ① order about ② send away; put sb. off

支吾 zhīwu falter; equivocate; prevaricate:～其词 quibble; speak evasively; hum and haw. ～搪塞 evade the issue; hedge and dodge; falter

支援 zhīyuán support; aid; help:～农业 support agriculture

支柱 zhīzhù support; pillar; mainstay:～产业 pillar industries

枝

zhī 〈名〉 branch; twig; bough:侧～ lateral branch

枝节 zhījié ① branch and knots—minor matters; side issue; minor aspect ② complication:横生～ create unexpected complications; complicate an issue

肢

zhī 〈名〉 limb:下～ lower limbs; legs

肢解 zhījiě dismember

肢体 zhītǐ ① limbs ② limbs and trunk

只

zhī ①〈形〉one only; single:～字未写 not write a single word〈量〉②[用于某些成对物中的一个]一～鞋 one shoe ③[用于某些器具]一～皮箱 a leather trunk ④[用于船只]船～ vessels

另见 zhǐ

只身 zhīshēn alone; by oneself:～在外 be away from home all by oneself

只言片语 zhīyán-piànyǔ a word or two; just a few words

只字不提 zhīzì-bùtí not to breathe a word about; say nothing (about); not even mention a single word

织 zhī〈动〉weave; knit: 纺～ spin and weave. ～毛衣 knit a sweater

织补 zhībǔ darn; knit up

织布 zhībù weaving (cotton cloth); weaving: ～机 weaving looms

织锦 zhījǐn ① brocade; tapestry; silk polychrome: ～缎 tapestry satin ② silk-woven picture: 风景～ silk-woven landscape

织物 zhīwù fabric: 合成纤维～ synthetic fabrics

织绣 zhīxiù silks and embroidery; tapestry and embroidery

知 zhī〈动〉① know; realize; be aware of: 有自～之明 know oneself ② inform; notify: 通～ notify; inform ③〈名〉knowledge: 求～ seek knowledge

知底 zhīdǐ know the inside story; be in the know

知而不言,言而不尽 zhī'érbù yán, yán'érbùjìn Though they knew everything, they would not have spoken or, if they spoke, would not have told all they knew.

知法犯法 zhīfǎ fànfǎ knowingly break the law; violate laws knowingly

知己 zhījǐ ① intimate: ～知彼,百战百胜。One who knows his own strength and that of the enemy is invincible in battle. ② intimate (bosom) friend

知己知彼 zhījǐ-zhībǐ know the enemy and know yourself; know both sides; know others and know oneself; know both ourselves and our adversaries

知觉 zhījué ① consciousness: 失去～ lose consciousness. 恢复～ recover (regain) consciousness; come to (oneself) ② [心] perception

知名 zhīmíng well-known; noted; famous; renowned: ～人士 well-known personage; celebrity; celebrated people

知名度 zhīmíngdù popularity: ～很高 enjoy great popularity; be very popular

知难而进 zhīnán'érjìn advance in the face of difficulties

知青 zhīqīng educated youths

知情 zhīqíng know the facts of a case; be in the know; know the inside story; have inside information: ～人 person in the know; insider

知人善任 zhīrén-shànrèn know one's subordinates and put them where they can do the best work; discover able people and put them at suitable posts

知人知面不知心 zhīrén zhī miàn bù zhī xīn One can know a man's face, but not his heart.; It is impossible to judge a man's heart from his face.

知识 zhīshi knowledge; know-how: ～产权 intellectual property rights. ～就是力量。Knowledge is power. ～库 knowledge bank

知无不言，言无不尽 zhī wú bù yán, yán wú bù jìn Say all you know and say it without reserve.

知音 zhīyīn friend keenly appreciative of one's talents; understanding friend

知遇 zhīyù have found a patron or superior appreciative of one's ability

知足 zhīzú be content with one's life (lot)：～者常乐。He who is contented is always happy.

蜘 zhī

蜘蛛 zhīzhū spider

指 zhī

另见 zhǐ

指甲 zhījiǎ nail：～油 nail polish

脂 zhī

〈名〉① fat; grease; resin：采～ tap resin. 脱～ degrease; de-fat ② rouge

脂肪 zhīfáng fat：～肝 fatty liver

脂粉 zhīfěn cosmetics; rouge and powder

zhí

职 zhí

〈名〉① duty; job：本～工作 one's duty (job) ② position; post：称～ be competent for one's position

职别 zhíbié official rank; level of position

职称 zhíchēng professional or technical title; positional titles

职大 zhídà workers' colleges

职代会 zhídàihuì workers' (employees') representatives conference

职工 zhígōng workers and staff members; workers：～代表大会 congress of workers and staff. ～集体承包经营制 system of contractual operation by workers and staff as a collective

职能部门 zhínéng bùmén fuctional departments

职前培训 zhíqián péixùn preprofessional training

职权 zhíquán authority; powers (of office)：行使～ exercise one's authority. 超越～ go beyond (overstep) one's authority; exceed one's powers

职位 zhíwèi position; post：～空缺 job vacancy

职务 zhíwù duty; post; job：～工资 pay according to one's post; professional wages. ～津贴 duty allowance

职业 zhíyè occupation; trade; career; profession; vocation：～介绍所 employment agency. ～道德 professional ethics. ～培训 job training. ～资格证书制度 system for vocational certification. ～中学 vocational middle schools

职员 zhíyuán staff member; office worker; clerk

职责 zhízé duty; responsibility

直 zhí

〈形〉① straight：笔～ perfectly straight ② vertical; perpendicular：陡～的峭壁 a vertical cliff ③ straightforward：朴

～ honest and straightforward ④upright；just：憨～ honest and upright ⑤〈动〉straighten：挺～脊背 straighten one's back 〈副〉⑥ straight；directly：径～ directly；straight. ～飞巴黎 fly nonstop to Paris ⑦ continuously：她～按汽车喇叭。She kept honking the horn.

直笔 zhíbǐ a straight pen—unprejudiced writings

直播 zhíbō［电视］live telecast：电视～足球比赛 televise a football match；live telecast of a football match

直陈 zhíchén speak frankly；state outright

直达 zhídá［火车等］through；direct：～汇票 straight arrival bill. 到上海去的～火车 through train to Shanghai

直到(至) zhídào(zhì) ① till；until ② up to：他们～现在还未完工。They have not finished their work up to now.

直观 zhíguān audio-visual；intuitional：～教具 audio-visual aids. ～教学 intuitional instruction；object teaching

直接 zhíjiē direct；immediate：～产品 direct products. ～长途拨号［美国］direct distance dialing；［英国］subscriber trunk dialing. ～贸易 direct trade. ～责任人员 person directly responsible. ～原因 immediate cause

直截了当 zhíjiéliǎodàng say without mincing words；straightforward；outspoken；blunt；point-blank

直觉 zhíjué［心］intuition

直抒己见 zhíshū-jǐjiàn air (state) one's views frankly；be plain-spoken

直率 zhíshuài frank；candid；forthright；directness

直爽 zhíshuǎng forthright；frank；straightforward：性子～ be straightforward in character

直系 zhíxì lineal：～亲属 lineal dependent (relation，relative)

直辖 zhíxiá directly under the jurisdiction of：～市 municipality directly under the Central Government

直言 zhíyán speak frankly (bluntly)；tell straight out；state outright：～不讳 mince no words；without mincing words；call a spade a spade；frankly

直译 zhíyì literal translation

直喻 zhíyù imagery

直至 zhízhì ① until ② up to

植

zhí〈动〉① plant；grow：春～ plant in spring ② set up

植被 zhíbèi［植］vegetation；vegetation cover

植树 zhíshù plant trees：～节 National Tree-planting Day. ～造林 afforestation

植物 zhíwù plant；vegetable：～检疫证明书 plant quarantine certificate. ～社会学 phytosociology. ～学 botany. ～园 botanical garden

植物人 zhíwùrén vegetable (a human being)

殖

zhí〈动〉reproduce；breed；

multiply：兔子繁～很快。Rabbits breed quickly.

殖民 zhímín colonize：～国家 colonialist power. ～主义 colonialism

殖民地 zhímíndì colony；colonial possessions：～的保护地 colonial protectorates. ～国家 colonial country

侄 zhí〈名〉nephew

侄女 zhínǚ niece

侄子 zhízi nephew

执 zhí〈动〉① hold in hand：手～旗子 hold a banner ② stick to；persist in：固～错误 persist in one's mistakes ③ carry out；implement：～行政策 implement policies ④ execute：～行刑罚 execute a punishment

执笔 zhíbǐ ① hold a pen ② do the actual writing：这篇文章是由她的秘书～的。The actual writing of this article was done by her secretary.

执导 zhídǎo[影视] direct

执法 zhífǎ enforce the law；law enforcement；carry out the law；administration of law：～如山 enforce the law strictly. 加强～队伍的建设 improve the quality of law-enforcement personnel

执迷不悟 zhímí-bùwù refuse to come to one's senses；persist in error；adhere to one's foolish way without awakening；persist in one's wrong course；adhere obstinately to one's foolish ways

执拗 zhíniù stubborn；obstinate；self-willed；pigheaded

执行 zhíxíng carry out；execute；enforce；implement：～董事 executive director. ～机关 executing organ. ～判决 execute a judgment. ～委员会 executive council (committee). ～主席 presiding (executive) chairman

执刑 zhíxíng carry out the execution

执意 zhíyì insist on；persist in；be determined to；be bent on

执照 zhízhào license：申请～ apply for a license. ～税 fee of permit

执政 zhízhèng be in office (power)；hold the reins of government；govern：～党 party in office (in power)；the ruling party

执著 zhízhuó rigid；inflexible；punctilious

值 zhí ①〈名〉value：产～ output value〈动〉② be worth：这～多少钱？How much (What) is this worth？③ happen to；on the occasion：适～ just happen to be ④ deserve：～得注意 deserve (merit) attention ⑤ be on duty；take one's turn at sth.：轮～ work in shifts；take turns

值班 zhíbān be on duty：～工程师 shift engineer. ～工人 worker on duty

值不当 zhíbudàng not be worthwhile

值得 zhíde deserve；merit；be worthy of：～称赞 be worthy of

praise; deserve to be praised

值钱 zhíqián valuable; costly; of great worth

值勤 zhíqín be on duty

值日 zhírì be on duty for the day: ～生 student on duty

值夜 zhíyè be on night duty; be on the night shift

zhǐ

止 zhǐ ①〈动〉stop; halt: ～住伤口出血 stop a wound ②〈介〉to; till: 到目前为～ to date; up to now ③〈副〉only: 何～ not only

止步 zhǐbù stop; halt: 游人～ No Visitors

止付通知书 zhǐfù tōngzhīshū stop-payment notice

止境 zhǐjìng end; limit: 学无～。There is no limit to one's knowledge.

止痛 zhǐtòng relieve pain: ～药 pain-killer; anodyne

止血 zhǐxuè stop (stanch) bleeding: ～药 styptic; hemostatic

址 zhǐ〈名〉① site; location: 厂～ the site of a factory ② address: 住～ address

趾 zhǐ〈名〉① toe ② foot

趾高气扬 zhǐgāo-qìyáng ride the high horse; give oneself airs and swagger about; step high and look proud; proud as a peacock; get a swelled head; crow over; breed pride and arrogance

只 zhǐ〈副〉only; merely: 不～ not merely; not only

另见 zhī

只不过 zhǐbuguò only; merely; nothing but; but

只得 zhǐdé have no alternative but to; have no choice but (to do); be obliged to; have to

只顾 zhǐgù ① be concerned only about; only care for: 你们不能～自己的利益。You must not be concerned only about your own interests. ② be absorbed in: 她～看书,连饭都忘记吃了。She was so absorbed in reading that she even forgot her meal.

只管 zhǐguǎn ① by all means; not hesitate to: 有什么问题请～问。If you have any questions, please don't hesitate to ask. ② just; merely

只是 zhǐshì ① only; but; just; merely ② simply

只要 zhǐyào so (as) long as; provided: ～他们用功,就会有进步。So long as they study hard, they'll surely make progress.

纸 zhǐ〈名〉paper: ～上盈利 paper profit. 一张～ a sheet (piece) of paper

纸板 zhǐbǎn cardboard: ～箱 carton; cardboard box (case)

纸裱 zhǐbiǎo front mounting of paper

纸币 zhǐbì paper money; paper currency

纸浆 zhǐjiāng paper pulp; pulp: ～原材 pulpwood

纸老虎 zhǐlǎohǔ paper tiger

纸牌 zhǐpái playing cards

纸钱 zhǐqián paper made to resemble money and burned as an offering to the dead

纸上谈兵 zhǐshàng-tánbīng talk about stratagems on paper—empty talk; armchair strategy; make empty talks about warfare; fight on paper

纸型 zhǐxíng［印］paper matrix; paper mould

纸鸢 zhǐyuān kite：放～ fly a kite

纸醉金迷 zhǐzuì-jīnmí lead a voluptuous (dissipated) life; live in luxury; indulge in a wanton life

旨 zhǐ〈名〉purpose; intention; aim：意～ intention; wish

旨趣 zhǐqù objective; purport：～相同。Essential thoughts are alike.

指 zhǐ ①〈名〉finger：中～ middle finger〈动〉② point (at, to)：～向东方的路牌 a signpost pointing to the east ③ point out; indicate：～出某人的缺点 point out one's shortcomings ④ depend on; count on：～望某人会来 count on sb.'s coming (on sb. to come)

另见 zhī

指标 zhǐbiāo target; quota; indicator; norms：～落实 fix targets in relation to specific measures for their fulfilment. 完成～ fulfil the quota

指斥 zhǐchì reproach; reprove; reprimand

指出 zhǐchū point out; indicate; show

指导 zhǐdǎo guide; direct：～思想 guiding ideology. ～性计划 guidance plan

指点 zhǐdiǎn point out; show; instruct

指定 zhǐdìng name; appoint; nominate; assign：老师～的作业 homework assigned by the teacher. ～的承保风险 named peril. ～继承人 designated heir;［地产］remainder man

指挥 zhǐhuī command; conduct; direct：～棒 baton. ～乐队 conduct an orchestra

指教 zhǐjiào〈套〉give advice; advise：请～。Please give us your advice.

指控 zhǐkòng accuse; charge：～某人偷窃 accuse sb. of stealing; charge sb. with stealing

指令性 zhǐlìngxìng of a directive nature：～计划 mandatory plans

指鹿为马 zhǐlùwéimǎ call a stag a horse; talk black into white; deliberately misrepresent a fact; misname the thing by saying that…

指名 zhǐmíng point out sb.'s name; name：～攻击 assail … by name. ～批评 criticize sb. by name

指明 zhǐmíng show clearly; point out; demonstrate

指南 zhǐnán guide; manual; guidebook：～仪器 direction determinants. ～针 compass. 旅行～ guidebook

指派 zhǐpài appoint; designate; nominate; assign

指认 zhǐrèn［法］identify

指日可待 zhǐrì-kědài The day is not far off.; be just round the corner; be within sight:我们的成功～。Our success is within sight.

指桑骂槐 zhǐsāng-màhuái revile the locust while pointing to the mulberry—point at one but abuse another; make innuendoes; make veiled abuses; make oblique accusations

指使 zhǐshǐ incite; instigate:受某人～ act on sb.'s instigation; under sb.'s instigation

指示 zhǐshì ① show; indicate:～性计划 indicative planning ② directive; instructions

指手划脚 zhǐshǒu-huàjiǎo ① make gestures ② criticize this and condemn that; order people about

指数 zhǐshù index; index number:生活费～cost of living index. 物价～ price index

指望 zhǐwàng ① count on; look to; expect:我～你的帮助。I count on your help. ② hope; prospect

指纹(印) zhǐwén(yìn) fingerprint

指责 zhǐzé criticize; reproach; censure; accuse; find fault with:受舆论～ be subjected to the censure of public opinion. 无可～ above (beyond) reproach

指针 zhǐzhēn ① pointer; indicator ② guide

指正 zhǐzhèng ① point out mistakes so that they can be corrected ② make a comment or criticism

zhì

滞 zhì ①〈形〉stagnant; sluggish:迟～ slow-moving; sluggish ②〈动〉stagnate; be at a standstill

滞洪 zhìhóng flood detention

滞后 zhìhòu lag:～相关性 lagging correlation

滞缓 zhìhuǎn slow; tardy; sluggish

滞留 zhìliú be detained; be held up

滞纳金 zhìnàjīn fine for delaying payment; surcharge for overdue tax payment

滞销 zhìxiāo unsalable; unmarketable; shop-worn:～货 unsalable goods; slow-selling goods

滞胀 zhìzhàng [经] stagflation

治 zhì〈动〉① administer; govern; rule:法～ rule by law ② cure; treat; heal:救～ treat and cure. ～好创伤 heal the wounds of ③ harness (a river); control:～理河流 harness a river; bring a river under control ④ punish:惩～ punish; mete out punishment to ⑤ study; research:～史 make a study of history

治安 zhì'ān public security; public order:～管理工作人员 security administration personnel. ～机关 law enforcement office. 维持～ keep public order

治保 zhìbǎo public security:～工

作 public security work

治本 zhìběn provide fundamental solutions to the problems；take radical measures

治标 zhìbiāo provide temporary solutions to the problems；take stopgap measures

治病 zhìbìng cure an illness：～救人 cure the sickness to save the patient；help sb. mend his ways so as to save him

治国 zhìguó run a country；manage state affairs：～安邦 govern and bring peace to the nation. ～安民 run the country well and give the people peace and security

治理 zhìlǐ ① govern；rule；manage：～城乡社会治安 improve social order in both urban and rural areas ② harness（a river）；tame；bring under control

治疗 zhìliáo treat；cure：～错误 malpractice. 住院～ be hospitalized

治丧 zhìsāng manage a funeral：～委员会 funeral committee；committee for the obsequies of

治水 zhìshuǐ regulate rivers and watercourses

治外法权 zhìwài fǎquán extraterritoriality；exterritoriality；extrality

治学 zhìxué ① conduct（pursue）one's studies；conduct academic research；do scholarly research ② scholarship：～严谨 one's meticulous scholarship. ～严谨的学者 accurate scholar

治罪 zhìzuì punish sb.（for a crime）

志 zhì〈名〉① will；aspiration；ideal；ambition：大～ lofty aspiration；great ambition ② records；annals：县～ annals of a county；③ sign；mark：载重线标～ load-line mark ④〈动〉bear（keep）in mind：永～不忘 forever bear in mind

志哀 zhì'āi indicate mourning

志大才疏 zhìdà-cáishū great ambition but little talent

志气 zhìqì aspiration；ambition：～高 have high aspirations

志趣 zhìqù inclination；bent；aspiration：和某人～相合 be congenial to（with）sb.

志士 zhìshì ① person with lofty ideals：～仁人 people with lofty ideals；people who are actuated by high ideals ② patriot：爱国～ noble-minded patriot

志同道合 zhìtóng-dàohé cherish the same ideals and take（follow）the same path；have a common goal

志喜 zhìxǐ offer congratulations（as on sb.'s wedding day）

志向 zhìxiàng ideal；aspiration；ambition

志愿 zhìyuàn ① aspiration；wish；ideal：填写入党～书 fill out an application form for the Party membership ② do sth. of one's own free will；volunteer：～军 volunteers

志在必得 zhìzàibìdé be determined to win

峙 zhì〈动〉stand erect; tower: 对～ stand opposite to each other; confront each other

至 zhì ①〈介〉till; up to; to: 截～ by (a specified time); up to ②〈副〉most; best; extremely: ～交 best friend. 感人～深 extremely moving

至诚 zhìchéng ①[zhìchéng] complete sincerity ②[zhìcheng] sincere; straightforward

至此 zhìcǐ up to this point; at this stage

至多 zhìduō at (the) most

至高无上 zhìgāo-wúshàng highest; supreme; paramount; most lofty

至交 zhìjiāo most intimate friend; best friend

至今 zhìjīn up to now; to this day; up to the present; so far: 他～尚无消息。So far there is no news from him.

至理名言 zhìlǐ-míngyán famous (celebrated) dictum; golden saying; most true sayings; axiom

至亲 zhìqīn close relatives

至情 zhìqíng true feelings; real sentiments

至少 zhìshǎo at (the) least

至圣先师 zhìshèng-xiānshī the most holy sage

至死 zhìsǐ unto death; till death

至于 zhìyú as to; as for: ～那件事,她还未决定。As to that, she hasn't decided yet.

至尊 zhìzūn the most revered and respected—the emperor

窒 zhì〈动〉stop up; obstruct

窒息 zhìxī stifle; choke; suffocate; smother: 令人～的 stifling; choking; suffocative

桎 zhì〈名〉fetters

桎梏 zhìgù ① fetters and handcuffs; shackles ② restraint

致 zhì ①〈名〉manner or style that attracts attention or arouse interest: 笔～ style of writing, painting, etc. 〈动〉② give; send; present; deliver: 引～ give rise to; cause. ～电 send a telegram ③ devote (one's efforts, etc.): ～力 devote oneself to; exert oneself (to do); endeavour ④ incur; result in: 招～重大损失 incur a heavy loss ⑤〈形〉delicate; fine: 密～ fine and close

致哀 zhì'āi express one's condolences (to); pay one's respects to: 我们向革命烈士～。We paid our respects to the revolutionary martyrs.

致癌 zhì'ái cause (produce) cancer; be carcinogenic

致词(辞) zhìcí (cí) make a speech; address: 新年～ New Year message. 向大会～ address the meeting

致富 zhìfù become rich; make a fortune

致函 zhìhán write (a letter) to

致贺 zhìhè extend (offer) one's congratulations; congratulate

致敬 zhìjìng pay one's respects (to); greet; salute: ～电 message of greeting (salutations)

致命 zhìmìng fatal; mortal; deadly: ～的弱点 fatal weakness

致人残废罪 zhìrén cánfèizuì mayhem

致人伤残 zhìrén shāngcán cause a person's injury or disability

致人重伤(死亡) zhìrén zhòngshāng(sǐwáng) cause serious injury (death) to a person

致使 zhìshǐ make; cause; result in

致死 zhìsǐ cause death or die

致谢 zhìxiè extend one's thanks to; express one's thanks to (gratitude)

致意 zhìyì send one's (best) regards (wishes); give one's compliments: 请代我向你的家人～。Please give my regards to your family.

掷 zhì〈动〉throw; cast; fling: ～手榴弹 fling a grenade

掷标枪 zhìbiāoqiāng [体] javelin throw

掷还 zhìhuán please return (to the writer, etc.)

掷铅球 zhìqiānqiú [体] shotput

掷铁饼 zhìtiěbǐng [体] discus throw

帜 zhì〈名〉flag; banner: 旗～ flag; banner

挚 zhì〈形〉sincere; earnest; 恳～ earnest and sincere

挚爱 zhì'ài true love: 深情～ deep love

挚情 zhìqíng deep emotion; deep feeling

挚友 zhìyǒu intimate friend; bosom friend

置 zhì〈动〉① place; put: 安～ put sth. in a proper place; help sb. to settle down ② set up; establish; install: 装～ install; fix ③ buy: ～办 buy; purchase

置办 zhìbàn buy (durables); purchase

置产 zhìchǎn buy property (esp. an estate)

置买 zhìmǎi purchase; buy

置若罔闻 zhìruòwǎngwén turn a deaf ear to; pay no heed to; keep quiet on

置身 zhìshēn place oneself (in); stay: ～事外 keep (stay) aloof from the affair; keep out of the business; refuse to get involved in the matter

置之不理 zhìzhī-bùlǐ pay no attention (regard) to; turn a cold shoulder to; turn a deaf ear to; sit idly by; ignore

置之度外 zhìzhī-dùwài leave out of consideartion; put (sth.) entirely out of one's mind; ignore; not take into account

置之脑后 zhìzhī-nǎohòu banish (sth.) from one's mind; place … in the back of one's mind; cast (sth.) behind one's back; consign sth. to oblivion

制 zhì ①〈名〉system: 币～ currency (monetary) system〈动〉② make; produce; manufacture: ～茶业 tea-making ③ formulate; map out; form: ～定政策 formulate (work out) a policy ④ control; restrain; restrict:～止小孩胡闹 restrain a child from (doing) mischief

制币 zhìbì standard national currency

制裁 zhìcái punish; sanction;:～对象 object of sanctions. 受到法律～ be punished according to law

制成品 zhìchéngpǐn finished products; manufactured goods; manufactures

制订 zhìdìng map out; work out; draw up; formulate:～计划 work out a plan

制动 zhìdòng apply the brake; brake

制度 zhìdù system; institution:～化 systematize

制伏(服) zhìfú (fú) subdue; tame; bring under control; obtain control; gain the upper hand

制海权 zhìhǎiquán mastery of the sea; command of the sea

制空权 zhìkōngquán mastery (command) of the air; air control (supremacy)

制冷设备 zhìlěng shèbèi refrigeration facility

制品 zhìpǐn products; goods

制式 zhìshì standard model:～标准 specific standards. 电视～ standard television model

制售 zhìshòu production and sale:～假冒伪劣商品 production and sale of fake or poor quality commodities

制图 zhìtú ① map-making; charting:～学 cartography ② drafting; mapping; make charts (blueprints)

制药 zhìyào pharmacy:～厂 pharmaceutical works (factory)

制约 zhìyuē restrict; condition; restrain:～作用 restrictive function

制造 zhìzào ① make; produce; manufacture:～成本 manufacturing cost. ～假货币 counterfeiting bank notes. ～许可证 manufacturing license ② create:～纠纷 create trouble; sow dissension. ～舆论 create (prepare) public opinion

制止 zhìzhǐ stop; check; curb; prevent

秩 zhì〈书〉order:维持～序 keep order

智 zhì〈名〉wisdom; resourcefulness; intelligence:才～ ability and wisdom

智齿 zhìchǐ wisdom tooth

智慧 zhìhuì wisdom; wit; intelligence

智力 zhìlì mental faculties; mentality; intelligence; intellect:～工业 brain industry. ～开发 expand intellectual resources; develop intellectual ability. ～库 intelligence bank. ～投资 intellectual investment; investments in brains

智囊 zhìnáng brain truster:～班子 think tank; think factory

智能 zhìnéng intelligence; intellectual faculties; intellect; brain power:～测验 aptitude test. ～化产品 intelligent products

智穷力竭 zhìqióng-lìjié be at the end of one's tether (rope); be at one's wit's end

智商 zhìshāng intelligence quotient (IQ)

智育 zhìyù intellectual education

智者千虑，必有一失 zhìzhě qiānlǜ, bìyǒu yīshī No man is wise at all times.; (Even) Homer sometimes nods.

质 zhì〈名〉① nature; character; quality: 水～ water quality; 性～ nature ② substance; matter: 矿物～ mineral substance ③〈形〉simple; plain: ～朴 simple and unadorned; natural

质变 zhìbiàn [哲] qualitative change

质地 zhìdì ① quality (of a material); texture; grain; material: ～细密 of close texture; fine grained. ～好(坏) be of high (poor) quality ②[人的]disposition; character

质量 zhìliàng ① quality: ～管理 quality control. ～指标 quality index. ～月活动 quality month activities ②[物]mass

质量守恒 zhìliàng shǒuhéng conservation of mass

质问 zhìwèn call to account; interrogate; query: 提出～ bring sb. to account

质询 zhìxún address inquiries to: ask for explanations

质押 zhìyā pledge: ～品 collateral security

质疑 zhìyí call in question; raise a query

质子 zhìzǐ [物] proton

稚 zhì〈形〉young; childish

稚嫩 zhìnèn ① young and tender: ～的脸蛋儿 a delicate face ② immature: 她早期作品比较～。Her early works are relatively immature.

zhōng

中 zhōng〈名〉① centre; middle: 正当～ right in the middle ② between two extremes: ～年 middel-aged ③ medium; intermediate: ～号 medium size ④ China: ～英关系 relations between China and Britain ⑤〈介〉in; among: 在宇宙～ in the universe

中班 zhōngbān ① middle shift: 做～ be (work) on the middle shift ②[幼儿园等的]intermediate class

中不溜儿 zhōngbùliūr fair to middling; middling

中草药 zhōngcǎoyào Chinese herbal medicine

中产阶级 zhōngchǎnjiējí middle class

中长期计划 zhōngchángqī jìhuà mid-and-long-term plan

中成药 zhōngchéngyào prepared Chinese medicine

中程导弹 zhōngchéng dǎodàn intermediate missiles

中等 zhōngděng middle; middling; medium: ～城市 medium-sized cities. ～教育 secondary education. ～身材的人

man of medium height. ～专业人材 intermediate specialists

中断 zhōngduàn break off; suspend; discontinue; hold up: ～贸易 suspension of trade. ～谈判 break off the negotiations. 使交通～ hold up the traffic

中锋 zhōngfēng[足球、水球] centre forward;[篮球] centre

中共中央 zhōnggòng zhōngyāng Central Committee of the Communist Party of China (PRC)

中古 zhōnggǔ the middle ancient times; medieval times

中观 zhōngguān intermediate perspective (between microcosmic and macrocosmic pertaining to the intermediate or link of the matter in question): ～改革 reforms at the intermediate level. ～经济 medium economy

中号 zhōnghào medium size

中华民族 Zhōnghuá mínzú Chinese nation

中华人民共和国 Zhōnghuá rénmín gònghéguó the People's Republic of China (PRC)

中级 zhōngjí intermediate; middle-rank; secondary: ～人民法院 intermediate people's court

中纪委 zhōngjìwěi the Central Commission for Discipline Inspection of the Communist Party of China

中坚 zhōngjiān backbone; mainstay

中间 zhōngjiān ① middle; intermediate: ～商人 middleman. ～人物 middle character ② among; between

中看 zhōngkàn be pleasant to the eye

中流 zhōngliú midstream: ～砥柱 mainstay

中篇小说 zhōngpiān xiǎoshuō novelette

中期贷款 zhōngqī dàikuǎn medium-term loan

中秋节 Zhōngqiūjié the Mid-autumn Festival

中山装 zhōngshānzhuāng Chinese tunic suit

中世纪 zhōngshìjì Middle Ages

中师 zhōngshī secondary normal school: ～教育 secondary normal school education

中枢 zhōngshū centre: 神经～ nerve centre

中途 zhōngtú midway; halfway: ～下车 get off the bus (train, etc.) midway

中西医结合 zhōngxīyī jiéhé integrating Chinese and Western medicine

中心 zhōngxīn centre; heart; hub: ～思想 central idea. ～汇率 central rate. ～小学 core elementary school. 商业～ hub of commerce; business centre. 市～ centre of the city

中兴 zhōngxīng [国家] resurgence

中学 zhōngxué middle school; secondary school: ～生 middle school student (pupil). 初(高)级～ junior (senior) middle school

中旬 zhōngxún middle ten-day period of a month

中央 zhōngyāng ① central; middle ② central authorities：～财政赤字 deficit in the central budget. ～和地方的重要商品储备制度 systems for stockpiling reserves of major commodities at the central and local levels

中药 zhōngyào traditional Chinese medicine：～店 traditional Chinese drugstore

中医 zhōngyī ① doctor of traditional Chinese medicine；traditional Chinese doctor ② traditional Chinese medicine

中庸 zhōngyōng Middle Way；the Mean；golden mean：～之道 doctrine of the mean

中游 zhōngyóu ① middle reaches of a river ② the state of being middling：～思想 feel content with remaining mid-stream without making further advance；middling mentality

中止 zhōngzhǐ stop；pause；suspend：～营业 wind up its operations. ～犯 one who discontinues a crime

中州 Zhōngzhōu Central Region (old name for Henan Province, so called from its central location in the country)

中专(中等专业学校) zhōngzhuān (zhōngděng zhuānyè xuéxiào) special or technical secondary school；secondary specialized school；polytechnic school

中转 zhōngzhuǎn ［交］change trains：～站 transfer station. ～签字 sign a transfer

衷

zhōng〈名〉heart；mind：由～from the bottom of one's heart

衷情 zhōngqíng heartfelt emotion；inner feelings

衷心 zhōngxīn heart-felt；wholehearted；cordial：～感谢 express one's heart-felt thanks (to). 表示～祝贺 extend cordial greetings

忠

zhōng〈形〉loyal；faithful；devoted：尽～ serve the country faithfully

忠诚 zhōngchéng loyal，faithful；fidelity；truthful

忠告 zhōnggào ① advice；counsel；expostulation ② advise：接受～ take sb.'s advice

忠厚 zhōnghòu honest and tolerant；sincere and kindly；candid

忠良 zhōngliáng ① faithful and upright；honest and staunch ② a faithful and upright person

忠实 zhōngshí true；faithful；loyal；reliable：～翻译 close translation. ～于原文 true to the original

忠恕之道 zhōngshùzhīdào doctrine of loyalty and consideration to others

忠孝 zhōngxiào loyalty and filiality；loyalty and filial piety

忠心 zhōngxīn loyalty；faithfulness；devotion；fidelity：～耿耿 infinitely loyal；loyal and devoted；most faithful and true；faithfully and conscientiously. 赤胆～ utter devotion；ardent loyalty

忠言 zhōngyán candid opinion；truthful words：～逆耳。Good advice jars on the ear.；Sincere advice often offends the ear.; Faithful admonitions are unpleasant to hear.

忠义 zhōngyì loyal and dutiful; loyalty and justice

忠于 zhōngyú be true to; be loyal to; be devoted to:～职守 be devoted to one's duty

忠贞 zhōngzhēn loyalty:～不渝 unswerving in loyalty

钟 zhōng〈名〉① bell ② clock:自鸣～ striking clock ③ time as measured in hours and minutes:10点～ ten o'clock. 3分～ three minutes

钟爱 zhōng'ài love dearly; dote on (a child); make a pet of; show affection for

钟表 zhōngbiǎo clocks and watches; timepiece

钟鼎 zhōngdǐng bronze:～文 inscriptions on a bronze; inscriptions on bronze bells or tripods

钟情 zhōngqíng be deeply in love; fall in love (with):一见～ fall in love at first sight

钟乳石 zhōngrǔshí stalactite

终 zhōng〈名〉① end; finish; close:告～ come to an end ② death; end:善～ die a natural death ③〈形〉whole; entire:～岁 the whole year ④〈副〉eventually; in the end

终场 zhōngchǎng ① end of a performance or game ② final session in an examination

终点 zhōngdiǎn terminal (point):～站 terminal (station); terminus. ～线[体] finishing line

终端 zhōngduān terminal; terminus:～机 terminating machine; terminals

终极 zhōngjí ultimate; final:～原因 ultimate (final) cause. ～真理 final truth

终结 zhōngjié end; final stage; terminal:～案件 end a case. ～性教育 terminal education

终究 zhōngjiū after all; in the end; eventually

终身 zhōngshēn all one's life; lifelong; for life:～大事 the important affair of a final settlement in life—marriage; the main affair of one's life. ～教育 lifelong education. ～制 lifelong system

终审 zhōngshěn[法]trial of final instance; last instance:～判决 final judgement (sentence); last judgement

终生保险 zhōngshēng bǎoxiǎn insurance for life

终止 zhōngzhǐ ① end; stop ② terminate:～契约(条约) terminate a contract (pact). ～日期 closing date

zhǒng

种 zhǒng〈名〉① seed; strain; breed:麦～ wheat seeds ② race:白～ the white race ③ species:物～ species. 亚～ subspecies ④ kind; sort:四～书 four kinds of books

种蛋 zhǒngdàn breeding eggs

种类 zhǒnglèi kind; sort; variety:～繁多 a larg variety (of)

种畜 zhǒngxù breedig stock; stud animal

种种 zhǒngzhǒng various; a variety of; all kinds (sorts) of: 钢有～用处。Steel has a variety of uses.

种子 zhǒngzi seed; germ: ～田 lands allocated for seed growing. ～选手 seeded player; seed

种族 zhǒngzú race; ethnical group: ～偏见 ethnical prejudice. ～歧视 racial discrimination. ～文化考古学 ethnoarchaeology

肿 zhǒng〈动〉swell; be swollen

肿瘤 zhǒngliú tumour: 恶(良)性～ malignant (benign) tumour

肿胀 zhǒngzhàng ① swelling ② oedema and abdominal distension

zhòng

中 zhòng〈动〉① hit; fit exactly: 命～ hit the target ② suffer; affected by; be hit by: 腿上～了一枪 be shot in the leg

中标 zhòngbiāo win a bid (for a construction contract, etc.)

中彩 zhòngcǎi win a prize in a lottery

中的 zhòngdì hit the mark

中毒 zhòngdú poisoning; toxicosis: 食物～ food poisoning

中风 zhòngfēng [医] apoplexy; stroke: 她不幸～。Unfortunately she had a stroke.

中计 zhòngjì fall into a trap; be entrapped, be taken in: 中奸计 fall into the sinister traps of

中奖 zhòngjiǎng win a prize in a lottery; draw a prizewinning ticket in a lottery

中肯 zhòngkěn to the point; apropos; pertinent: 评论是～的。The comments are to the point.

中签 zhòngqiān be the lucky number (in drawing lots, etc.)

中伤 zhòngshāng malign; slander; calumniate; vilify: 造谣～ spread rumours to defame others

中暑 zhòngshǔ ① suffer sunstroke ② sunstroke; heatstroke

中选 zhòngxuǎn win selection; be elected; be chosen

中意 zhòngyì suit one's taste; strike one's fancy; be to one's liking (taste)

仲 zhòng〈形〉① (of the three months in season) second; mid: ～夏 mid-summer ② in the middle

仲裁 zhòngcái arbitrate: ～法庭 arbitral tribunal. ～书 (arbitration) award

仲春 zhòngchūn second month of spring; the middle of spring

种 zhòng〈动〉sow; plant; grow: 在斜坡上～茶树 plant tea on the slopes
另见 zhǒng

种地 zhòngdì till (cultivate) land; go in for farming

种痘 zhòngdòu be vaccinated

种瓜得瓜,种豆得豆 zhòngguā déguā, zhòngdòu dédòu reap what

one has sown; plant melons and you get melons, sow beans and you get beans; As a man sows, so does he reap.

种田 zhòngtián till the land; farm

种植 zhòngzhí grow; plant; cultivate: ～业 farm production; crop cultivation

众 zhòng ①〈形〉many; numerous ②〈名〉crowd; multitude: 民～ the masses of the people

众多 zhòngduō numerous; multitudinous; populous: 北京是个人口～的城市。Bejing is a populous city.

众寡悬殊 zhòngguǎ-xuánshū a great disparity in numerous strength

众口一词 zhòngkǒu-yīcí with one mouth (voice); in chorus; unanimously

众目睽睽 zhòngmù-kuíkuí under the watchful eyes of the people; in the public eye

众怒 zhòngnù public wrath

众叛亲离 zhòngpàn-qīnlí be opposed by the masses (people, public) and deserted by one's followers; be utterly isolated; with one's followers in revolt and one's close associates deserting

众矢之的 zhòngshǐzhīdì be under attack from all sides; be the target of attacks from all sides; be the target of public criticism (censure)

众说纷纭 zhòngshuō-fēnyún opinions vary

众所周知 zhòngsuǒzhōuzhī as (is) known to all; as everyone knows: 由于～的原因 owing to the reasons as known to all

众望 zhòngwàng people's expectations; popular confidence: ～所归 enjoy popular confidence; command public respect and support. 不孚～ fall short of people's expectations

众议院 zhòngyìyuàn [美国、澳大利亚、日本等国国会中的] House of Representatives; [意大利、墨西哥、智利等的] Chamber of Deputies; Lower Chamber; Lower House

重 zhòng ①〈名〉weight: 毛～ gross weight〈形〉② heavy: ～型轰炸机 a heavy bomber ③ serious; severe; grave: 深～ very heavy; extremely serious ④ important: ～要特点 important hallmark ⑤〈动〉attach importance to; appreciate; esteem: 看～ regard as important; attach importance to

另见 chóng

重办 zhòngbàn severely punish (a criminal)

重创 zhòngchuàng inflict heavy losses (casualties) on; maul (heavily)

重大 zhòngdà ①great; important; major; significant; vital: ～违约 fundamental breach. ～嫌疑分子 major suspect. ～问题 vital issues; important points at issue ② serious; heavy: ～火灾 serious conflagrations

重担 zhòngdàn heavy burden; burdensome task; heavy load;

heavy responsibility：挑～ shoulder heavy responsibilities (loads)

重点 zhòngdiǎn ① important (major, essential) point; emphasis ② major; key：～大学(中学) key university (middle school). ～建设项目 key project of construction. ～调查 investigation on a selected basis. ～扶持贫困地点 lay stress on helping poverty-stricken areas. ～企业 selected enterprises. 抓～ grasp the essential point; pay special attention to the essentials

重活 zhònghuó heavy work

重价 zhòngjià high price

重奖 zhòngjiǎng give ample rewards to

重利 zhònglì ① high (huge) profit ② high (rate of) interest; usury：～盘剥 lend money at usury

重男轻女 zhòngnán-qīngnǚ regard men as being superior to women; Males are better than females.

重任 zhòngrèn heavy responsibility; important task

重伤 zhòngshāng serious injury

重视 zhòngshì think highly of; attach importance to; pay great attention to; set store by; value：我们很～他的才能。We set great store by his ability.

重税 zhòngshuì heavy (oppressive) taxation

重托 zhòngtuō great trust

重望 zhòngwàng ① good reputation ② high hopes; great expectations

重心 zhòngxīn ① centre of gravity：工作～ centre of gravity of the work ② core; focus

重刑 zhòngxíng heavy penalty; severe punishment

重型 zhòngxíng heavy-duty; heavy：～卡车 heavy-duty truck

重要 zhòngyào important; significant; major：～商品储备制度 system for stockpiling reserves of major commodities

重用 zhòngyòng put (sb.) in an important (key) position (post)

重镇 zhòngzhèn place of strategic importance

重证据 zhòngzhèngjù place emphasis on evidence

重罪 zhòngzuì grave crime; heavy offence; felony

zhōu

州 zhōu〈名〉① an administrative division ② (autonomous) prefecture：自治～ autonomous prefecture

州学 zhōuxué ［史］institutions of learning in prefectures

洲 zhōu〈名〉① continent ② shelf; shoal：沙～ sand shoal

洲际 zhōujì intercontinental：～导弹 intercontinental missile

诌 zhōu〈动〉fabricate (tales, etc.); make up stories：胡～ make up wild stories; cook up

舟 zhōu〈名〉boat; ship:龙～ dragon boat

舟车 zhōuchē ① vessel and vehicle ② journey

舟楫 zhōují vessels; ships:～和灌溉 water transport and irrigation

周 zhōu ①〈名〉circle; periphery; circuit; circumference:绕场一～ make a circuit of the arena ② week:～末 weekend〈形〉③ whole; entire; all:众所～知 as is known to all ④ attentive; thoughtful:招待不～ not be attentive to guests ⑤〈介〉all round; round:团结在党中央的～围 unite around the Central Committee of the Party ⑥〈动〉relieve

周报 zhōubào［刊物］weekly

周长 zhōucháng perimeter; circumference

周到 zhōudào attentive and satisfactory; thoughtful; considerate:服务～ offer good service

周刊 zhōukān a weekly publication (e. g. a magazine, a supplement to a newspaper, etc.); weekly

周密 zhōumì careful; well-considered; thorough; well-conceived:～的计划 well-conceived (well thought-out) plan

周期 zhōuqī ① circle; cycle:～性通货膨胀 cyclical inflation ② period:～性 periodicity; cyclical character

周全 zhōuquán ① thorough; comprehensive ② help sb. attain his aim

周岁 zhōusuì ① one full year of life:满～ one's first birthday ② exact age

周旋 zhōuxuán ① contend with; struggle with (against); keep … on the run:与敌人～到底 fight the enemy to the bitter end ② mix with other people; have social intercourse with; socialize:～于上流社会 mix in high society

周游 zhōuyóu travel round (from place to place); tour:～世界 tour the world

周折 zhōuzhé twists and turns; setbacks:遭到许多～ encounter a lot of setbacks

周转 zhōuzhuǎn ① turnover:～税 turnover tax ② revolve; circulate:～资金 revolving (working, circulating) capital

粥 zhōu〈名〉gruel; porridge:小米～ millet gruel

zhóu

轴 zhóu〈名〉① axle; pivot; shaft:后～ rear axle ② axis:坐标～ coordinate axis ③ spool; rod:画～ roller for a scroll of Chinese painting

轴承 zhóuchéng［机］bearing:滚珠～ ball bearing

轴心 zhóuxīn axis; axle centre:～国 Axis powers; the Axis. ～时代 axial period

zhǒu

肘 zhǒu〈名〉elbow

肘子 zhǒuzi ① elbow ② upper part of a leg of pork

帚 zhǒu〈名〉broom：扫～ broom

zhòu

咒 zhòu ①〈名〉incantation；charm；spell：被符～镇住 under a spell ②〈动〉curse：诅～某人 lay (call down) a curse upon sb.

咒骂 zhòumà curse；revile；abuse；swear

咒语 zhòuyǔ incantation；spell：念～ chant incantations

咒诅 zhòuzǔ［宗］anathema

皱 zhòu〈动〉① wrinkle；crease：褶～ wrinkle (in the skin) ② knit：～眉头 knit one's brow；frown (at)

皱纹 zhòuwén wrinkles；lines；furrows：满脸～ have a face seamed with wrinkles (lines)

绉 zhòu〈名〉crape

绉纱 zhòushā crape

绉纸 zhòuzhǐ crinkled paper

昼 zhòu〈名〉daytime；day

昼夜 zhòuyè day and night；round the clock：奋战3～ fight for three days and nights

骤 zhòu ①〈形〉sudden；abrupt：枪声～起 sudden burst of gunfire ②〈动〉(of a horse) gallop；trot：驰～ gallop

骤然 zhòurán all of a sudden；suddenly

zhū

诸 zhū〈形〉all；various：～事如意。All goes as you wish.

诸多 zhūduō (used for abstract things) a good deal；a lot of

诸葛亮会 Zhūgéliànghuì Zhuge Liang meeting (a meeting of a group of people, each with a certain amount of expertise, experience, and skills, to discuss and solve difficult problems in production or work)；brain storming

诸公 zhūgōng (used in addressing a group of men) gentlemen

诸侯 zhūhóu dukes or princes under an emperor；principalities；noble lords：～爵称 the titles of feudal princes

诸君 zhūjūn (used in addressing a group of people) ladies and gentlemen；you

诸如 zhūrú such as：～此类 and so on and so forth；and such like；and the like；things like that

诸事 zhūshì everything；every matter

诸位 zhūwèi (used in addressing a group of people) ladies and gentlemen；you

诸子 zhūzǐ［史］pre-Qin masters；philosophers：～百家 Hundred Schools

猪 zhū〈名〉pig；hog
猪场 zhūchǎng pig farm；piggery
猪倌 zhūguān swineherd
猪圈 zhūjuàn pigpen；pigsty
猪排 zhūpái pork chop
猪鬃 zhūzōng (hog) bristles
朱 zhū
朱红 zhūhóng vermilion；bright red
朱门 zhūmén vermilion gates；red-lacquered door of a wealthy home
朱批 zhūpī comments or remarks written in red with a brush
朱颜 zhūyán ① beautiful face (of a woman) ② youthful colour
珠 zhū〈名〉① pearl：夜明～ a legendary luminous pearl ② bead；ball：一串～子 a string of beads
珠宝 zhūbǎo pearls and jewels；jewelry：～店 jeweller's (shop)
珠光宝气 zhūguāng bǎoqì resplendent with jewels；bedecked with jewels
珠穆朗玛峰 Zhūmùlǎngmǎfēng Mount Qomolangma
珠算 zhūsuàn calculation with an abacus
珠子 zhūzi ① pearl ② bead
株 zhū〈名〉① trunk of a tree；stem of a plant ② plant：病～ diseased or inflected plant
株连 zhūlián involve (others) in a criminal case；implicate；be found guilty by association：～几个友人的假供词 a false confession implicating several of one's friends
蛛 zhū〈名〉spider
蛛丝马迹 zhūsī-mǎjì thread of a spider and trail of a horse—traces，clues
蛛网 zhūwǎng cobweb；spider web：～理论 cobweb theorem
侏 zhū〈名〉dwarf
侏罗纪 Zhūluójì Jurassic Period
侏儒 zhūrú midget；pygmy；manikin；dwarf
诛 zhū〈动〉① put (a criminal) to death ② punish
诛戮 zhūlù kill；put to death

zhú

烛 zhú ①〈名〉candle：香～ joss sticks and candles ②〈动〉illuminate：火光～天。The blaze lit up the sky.
烛光 zhúguāng candlepower；candle
逐 zhú〈动〉① pursue；run after；chase：～水草放牧 driving the animals from pasture to pasture ② drive out；expel：下～客令 show sb. the door ③〈副〉one by one：～级上诉 file one's appeal level by level
逐步 zhúbù step by step；progressively
逐出 zhúchū drive out；expel；evict：～教会 excision；excommunication. ～会场 expel from the meeting hall
逐个 zhúgè one by one

逐渐 zhújiàn gradually; by degrees
逐年 zhúnián year by year; year after year
逐一 zhúyī one by one
逐字逐句 zhúzì-zhújù word for word; literally:～的翻译 word-for-word (verbal) translation

竹 zhú〈名〉bamboo:斑～ mottled bamboo
竹编 zhúbiān bamboo woven articles
竹雕 zhúdiāo bamboo carving
竹筏 zhúfá bamboo raft
竹简 zhújiǎn bamboo strips; bamboo slips
竹篮 zhúlán bamboo basket:～打水一场空 draw water with a bamboo basket—a useless effort
竹帘 zhúlián bamboo screen or curtain
竹林 zhúlín bamboo grove (thicket)
竹马 zhúmǎ ① bamboo stick used as a toy horse ② bamboo horse used in a folk dance
竹器 zhúqì article made of bamboo; bamboo ware
竹笋 zhúsǔn bamboo shoots
竹席 zhúxí bamboo mat

zhǔ

主 zhǔ〈名〉① host:宾～ guest and host ② master; owner; proprietor:厂～ factory owner; mill owner ③〈形〉chief; principal; main:～流方面 principal aspect〈动〉④ stand for; advocate:～和 advocate peace ⑤ take charge of; manage:～事 be in charge of the business
主办 zhǔbàn sponsor; hold; direct; host:～大型产品交易会 hold a large product fair. ～会计 accountant in charge
主笔 zhǔbǐ ① editor in chief ② chief commentator
主编 zhǔbiān editor-in-chief; chief editor; chief compiler
主宾 zhǔbīn guest of honour
主场优势 zhǔchǎng yōushì［体］home-court advantage
主持 zhǔchí ① preside over; chair:～会议 preside at (over) a meeting. ～广播节目 compere a radio programme. ～人 compere; host; hostess; anchorman; anchorwoman; moderator (of a TV news show) ② take charge of; manage; direct:～日常事务 take charge of routine matters ③ uphold; support:～正义 uphold justice
主次 zhǔcì primary and secondary
主打歌曲 zhǔdǎgēqǔ hit songs; hits
主导 zhǔdǎo leading; dominant:～作用 dominant (leading) role
主调音乐 zhǔdiào yīnyuè homophony
主动 zhǔdòng ① on one's own initiative; of one's own accord:～帮助某人 help sb. of one's own accord ② initiative:争取～ try to gain the initiative
主队 zhǔduì［体］host team; home team

主犯 zhǔfàn principal offender; principal

主峰 zhǔfēng the highest peak in a mountain range

主妇 zhǔfù housewife

主干 zhǔgàn ① trunk; stem:～家庭 a stem family ② main force; mainstay

主攻手 zhǔgōngshǒu [体] ace spiker

主顾 zhǔgù customer; client

主观 zhǔguān subjective:～能动性[哲] subjective initiative; conscious activity. ～愿望 subjective desire; wishful thinking

主管 zhǔguǎn in charge of; competent:～人员 persons in charge; supervisory staffs; head. ～机关 competent authorities; authorities in charge; responsible institution

主和 zhǔhé advocate peace; be for a peaceful settlement: ～派 peace party

主婚 zhǔhūn (usu. of the parents of the bride and the bridegroom) preside over a wedding ceremony

主机 zhǔjī ① main engine; main processor ② lead plane; leader

主见 zhǔjiàn one's own judgement; independent opinion of one's own; definite view; set view; ideas of one's own

主讲 zhǔjiǎng be the speaker; give a lecture

主角 zhǔjué leading role; lead:男(女)～ leading actor (actress, lady)

主考 zhǔkǎo ① be in charge of an examination ② chief examiner (in a school, etc.)

主力 zhǔlì [军] main forces:～兵团 main formations. ～队员[体] key (top) players of a team

主流 zhǔliú ① main stream; main current ② principal (essential, main) aspect; main trend:～和支流 principal and secondary aspects

主谋(者) zhǔmóu(zhě) chief instigator; principal conspirator

主权 zhǔquán sovereignty; sovereign rights:领土～ territorial sovereignty

主人 zhǔrén ① master:女～ hostess ② owner; possessor:楼房的～ the owner of the building ③ host:宴会的～ host at a dinner party

主人公(翁) zhǔréngōng(wēng) ① [小说等的]hero or heroine; leading character; protagonist ② master of one's own country

主任 zhǔrèn director; head; chief:～委员 chairman (of a committee). ～医师 physician in charge

主食 zhǔshí staple food; principal food

主使 zhǔshǐ instigate; incite; set on; abet

主题 zhǔtí subject; theme:～歌[影视] theme (song). ～小说 tendentious (thesis) novel. ～演讲 keynote speech (lecture)

主体 zhǔtǐ ① chief (main, principal) part; main body:以…为～ with … forming the main body;

with the main emphasis on; be based primarily on. ～工程 main part of a project ②［哲］subject:～和客体 subject and object

主席 zhǔxí chairman or chairwoman; chairperson:～团 presidium. ～台 rostrum

主心骨 zhǔxīngǔ backbone; pillar; mainstay:你们回来了,乡亲们更有～。Now, you're back, that'll put fresh heart into our folk.

主刑 zhǔxíng principal punishment

主凶 zhǔxiōng prime (chief) culprit (in a murder case); principal

主修 zhǔxiū specialize (in a subject); major:～化学 major in chemistry

主旋律 zhǔxuánlǜ central theme; theme; subject:我们时代的～ the central theme of our times

主演 zhǔyǎn play (act) the leading part (role)

主要 zhǔyào chief; main; principal; leading; major:～工业 major industries. ～合伙人 senior partner. ～市场 staple market

主义 zhǔyì doctrine; -ism:唯物～ materialism

主意 zhǔyi ① idea; plan; thought:出～ give counsel; offer advice ② decision; definite view:打定～ make up one's mind; make a decision

主宰 zhǔzǎi be master of; dictate; dominate; decide:～人类的命运 dictate the destiny of mankind

主张 zhǔzhāng ① advocate; stand for; maintain; hold; propose:～改革 stand for reform ② opinion; view; stand:各人有各人的～。So many men, so many opinions.

主旨 zhǔzhǐ purport; gist; substance:～演说 key speech

主治医生 zhǔzhì yīshēng physician or surgeon in charge; doctor in charge; attending doctor

煮 zhǔ〈动〉boil; cook

嘱 zhǔ〈动〉advise; enjoin; urge:叮～ repeatedly advise (on department)

嘱咐 zhǔfù exhort; tell; bid; enjoin:～某人遵守规则 enjoin sb. to obey the rules

嘱托 zhǔtuō entrust:～某人办件事 entrust sb. with a certain task

瞩 zhǔ〈动〉stare; gaze

瞩目 zhǔmù focus one's attention upon; fix one's eyes upon

瞩望 zhǔwàng ① look forward to ② look long and steadily upon; gaze at

zhù

贮 zhù〈动〉store (up); keep; reserve; save:～粮 store grain

贮藏 zhùcáng store (up); hoard (up):～货币 hoarding of money

贮存 zhùcún lay in; store; stock;

keep in storage：～白菜 lay in cabbages

贮运 zhùyùn storage and shipping

注 zhù〈动〉① pour：浇～混凝土 pour concrete ② concentrate；fix：贯～ concentrate on ③ register；record：给学生～册 register the students〈名〉④ notes：附～ notes appended to a book，etc. ⑤ stakes：赌～ stakes (in gambling)

注册 zhùcè register：～商标 registered trademark. ～入学 matriculate. ～资本 registered capital

注定 zhùdìng be doomed (destined) (to)：～要失败 be doomed to failure

注脚 zhùjiǎo footnote

注解(释) zhùjiě(shì) note；annotation；annotate

注明 zhùmíng give clear indication of

注目 zhùmù fix one's eyes on；look fixedly at；gaze at：引人～ attract people's attention；spectacular；attractive；eye-catching

注入 zhùrù ① pour into；empty into ② injection

注射 zhùshè inject：静脉～ intravenous injection

注塑 zhùsù mould plastics

注销 zhùxiāo cancel；cross out；write off：～登记 nullify one's registration. ～户口 cancel one's residence registration

注意 zhùyì pay attention to；take notice of；note；notice：～事项 points for attention

注音 zhùyīn phonetic notation：～汉字 Chinese characters with phonetic annotations

注重 zhùzhòng pay attention to；attach importance to；lay stress on；emphasize：～实效 emphasize practical results

柱 zhù〈名〉post；column；pillar：房～ pillars of a house

柱石 zhùshí pillar；cornerstone

蛀 zhù〈动〉(of moths，etc.) eat；bore through：给虫子～了 be moth-eaten

蛀虫 zhùchóng moth；borer：蛀衣服的～ a clothes moth

蛀牙 zhùyá decayed tooth

住 zhù〈动〉① live；stay；reside：～在同一幢房子里 live under the same roof ② stop；cease：不～的 ceaselessly；continuously

住处(～所,～宅) zhùchù(～suǒ，～zhái) dwelling；residence

住地 zhùdì dwelling (place)；lodging

住房 zhùfáng housing；lodgings：～改革 reform in housing. ～津贴 house allowance. ～问题 housing problem

住户 zhùhù ① household；resident ② tenant

住家 zhùjiā ① (of one's family) live；reside in ② household；resident

住口 zhùkǒu hold one's tongue；shut up；stop talking

住手 zhùshǒu stay one's hand；stop

住宿 zhùsù stay (at)；get accommodation; stop (at); put up (at):～学校 boarding school; residential institution. 在招待所～ stay at a hostel

住院 zhùyuàn be hospitalized; be in hospital:～病人 inpatient. ～医生 resident physician

住宅 zhùzhái (dwelling) house; residence:～区 residential quarters

住址 zhùzhǐ address; dwelling sites

住嘴 zhùzuǐ stop talking

驻

zhù〈动〉① stay; halt:～足 make a temporary stay ② be stationed:进～ enter and be stationed in; enter and garrison

驻办公使 zhùbàn gōngshǐ minister resident

驻防 zhùfáng be on garrison duty:～部队 garrison (troops)

驻军 zhùjūn stationary troops; garrison:～权 garrison rights

驻守 zhùshǒu garrison; defend

驻外公使馆 zhùwài gōngshǐguǎn resident legation abroad

驻在国 zhùzàiguó state to which a diplomatic envoy is accredited

驻扎 zhùzhā (of troops) be stationed; be quartered

驻足 zhùzú halt; stop; go no further

祝

zhù〈动〉extend or express good wishes; wish:祷～ pray and express one's wishes

祝词 zhùcí congratulatory speech (address); congratulations:致～ give a congratulatory address

祝福 zhùfú wish happiness to; blessing; benediction:得到母亲的～ receive one's mother's blessing

祝贺 zhùhè congratulate (on):～某人成功 congratulate sb. on his success

祝捷 zhùjié celebrate a victory:～大会 victory celebration (meeting)

祝酒 zhùjiǔ propose a toast; drink to; toast:答谢～ reply (respond) to a toast; toast back (to). 向某人～ give (propose) a toast to sb.; toast sb.. 致～辞 propose a toast

祝融 Zhùróng God of fire

祝寿 zhùshòu congratulate (an elderly person) on his or her birthday; birthday celebration:～大典 observance of birthday

祝愿 zhùyuàn wish:谨致良好的～[信末] with best wishes

著

zhù ①〈形〉notable; remarkable; outstanding:以勇敢～称 be remarkable for one's bravery 〈动〉② show; manifest; prove:颇～成效 prove rather effective ③ write:撰～ write; compose ④〈名〉work; book:名～ famous works

著称 zhùchēng noted (for); renowned (for); famous (for):苏州以风景优美～。Suzhou is noted for its scenic beauty.

著名 zhùmíng famous; noted; celebrated; well-known

著述 zhùshù ① write; compile ② book; work

著者 zhùzhě author; writer

著作 zhùzuò works; writings: ～权 copyright; right of author. ～权法 copyright law. ～界 profession of letters

助 zhù〈动〉help; aid; assist: ～人为乐 find joy in helping others

助产士 zhùchǎnshì [医] midwife

助教 zhùjiào assistant (of a college faculty); teaching assistant; assistant instructor

助理 zhùlǐ assistant: ～工程师 assistant engineer. ～研究员 assistant research fellow

助跑 zhùpǎo [体] approach; run-up

助人为乐 zhùrén-wéilè take pleasure in helping others; be ready to help others

助手 zhùshǒu assistant; helper; help

助听器 zhùtīngqì audiphone; hearing aid; deaf-aid

助威 zhùwēi cheer (for); boost the morale of: 为运动员～ cheer for the athletes

助兴 zhùxìng liven things up; aid to the fun: ～的轻音乐 mood music

助学金 zhùxuéjīn grant-in-aid; stipend; student subsidies

助一臂之力 zhù yī bì zhī lì lend (give) a helping hand; lend an arm (a hand)

助长 zhùzhǎng foment; encourage; help; inflate; abet: ～…的骄气 feed (increase) the arrogance of

筑 zhù〈动〉construct; build: ～铁路 build railways

铸 zhù〈动〉cast; found; make: 冷～ chill casting. 陶～ make pottery and smelt metal

铸币 zhùbì specie; coin

铸成大错 zhùchéng-dàcuò make a gross mistake; commit a blunder

铸工 zhùgōng ① foundry worker; founder ② foundry work

铸件 zhùjiàn casting; cast

铸铁 zhùtiě ① iron casting ② cast iron

铸造 zhùzào cast; found: ～厂 foundry. ～税 seigniorage

铸字 zhùzì [印] typefounding; typecasting: ～工人 typefounder

zhuā

抓 zhuā〈动〉① seize; catch; clutch; grab: 她紧紧～住孩子的手。She clutched her child's hand. ② scratch: ～痒痒 scratch an itch ③ arrest; catch: 她被～起来了。She was arrested. ④ pay special attention to; grasp: ～意识形态 grasp work in the field of ideology ⑤ be responsible for: ～创作的同志 comrades in charge of creative work

抓辫子 zhuā biànzi seize on sb.'s mistake as a handle against him; take advantage of sb.'s minor fault to gain his own purpose; capitalize on sb.'s mistake

抓差 zhuāchāi draft sb. for a particular task

抓典型 zhuā diǎnxíng grasp (seize on) typical examples (cases); keep hold of typical cases

抓赌 zhuādǔ (of police) break up a gambling party and arrest the participants

抓好 zhuāhǎo take a good grasp of; do a good job of

抓紧 zhuājǐn grasp firmly; take well in hand; take a firm grasp of:～时间 make the best use of one's time

抓阄儿 zhuājiūr draw lots

抓拍 zhuāpāi ① take a candid photograph (picture) ② a candid photograph (picture); candid

抓瞎 zhuāxiā find oneself at a loss; be in a rush and muddle; be thrown off balance

抓重点 zhuā zhòngdiǎn tackle the focal points; grasp the essential points

抓住 zhuāzhù ① seize hold of; seize:～机遇,深化改革 seizing the current opportunity to deepen the reform ② catch; capture; arrest

zhuān

专 zhuān〈形〉① concentrated or focussed on one thing:心不～ not concentrated (on any one thing) ② special:～机 special (chartered) plane ③ expert:又红又～ be both red and expert ④〈动〉monopolize:～权 monopolize power

专案 zhuān'àn (special) case:～组 special group for the examination of a case; group for handling a special case

专长 zhuāncháng special skill or knowledge; speciality; expertise:学有～ have specialized knowledge; be expert in a special field of study; have sound scholarship

专场 zhuānchǎng special performance

专程 zhuānchéng make a special trip to:～前往上海 make a special trip to Shanghai

专断 zhuānduàn act arbitrarily; make one's decision without consulting others

专攻 zhuāngōng specialize in; major in:～中国历史 make a specialty of Chinese history

专横跋扈 zhuānhéng-báhù despotic; dictatorial; bossy

专家 zhuānjiā specialist; expert:～小组会议 panel meeting

专刊 zhuānkān special issue; [报纸]special column

专科 zhuānkē special course:～学校 training school; junior (training) college

专控商品 zhuānkòng shāngpǐn controlled commodities

专款 zhuānkuǎn special fund:～专用 funds earmarked for a specific purpose

专栏作家 zhuānlán zuòjiā columnist

专利 zhuānlì patent:～权 patent

(right). ～法 patent law. ～使用费 patent royalty

专卖 zhuānmài monopoly; have a monopoly in: ～税 monopoly tax

专门 zhuānmén special; professional; specialized: ～人材 people with professional knowledge. ～贸易 special trade. ～人民法院 special people's court

专区 zhuānqū subprovincial administrative region; prefecture

专属 zhuānshǔ exclusive: ～经济区 exclusive economic zone. ～渔区 exclusive fishing zone

专题 zhuāntí special topic (subject): ～报告 report on a special topic. ～讨论会 seminar; symposium; workshop

专线 zhuānxiàn ① special telephone line ② special railway line

专心 zhuānxīn concentrate on; make a concentrated effort; be attentive; apply one's mind to; be intent on: ～致志 give all one's mind to; be absorbed in

专修 zhuānxiū specialize in; major in: ～科 special course. ～美国文学 specialize in American literature. ～学校 special training school

专业 zhuānyè ① speciality: ～对口 a job suited to one's special training ② specialized trade or profession: ～公司 specialized company (corporation). ～课 specialized course. ～知识 professional knowledge; expertise

专业承包 zhuānyè chéngbāo contracting jobs along specialized lines; contracting specialized undertakings

专业户 zhuānyèhù households engaging in some kind of specialized production; specialized households

专用 zhuānyòng for special purpose; for use by sb. in particular: ～存款 special deposit

专员 zhuānyuán ① assistant director; (administrative) commissioner ② prefectural commissioner ③ person specially assigned for a job

专政 zhuānzhèng dictatorship: ～工具 instruments of dictatorship. ～机关 organs of dictatorship

专职 zhuānzhí ① specific duty; sole duty ② full-time: ～教师 full-time teacher

专制 zhuānzhì ① autocratic; despotic; absolute: ～君主 absolute monarchy ② autocracy

专著 zhuānzhù monograph; treatise; special work (written)

砖 zhuān 〈名〉brick: 冰～ ice-cream brick

砖茶 zhuānchá brick tea

砖厂 zhuānchǎng brickfield; brickyard

砖画 zhuānhuà brick carvings

砖窑 zhuānyáo brickkiln

zhuǎn

转 zhuǎn 〈动〉① turn; shift; change: 中～ change trains ②

pass on; transfer; convey:承～ pass on or forward (a document to the next level)
另见 zhuàn

转败为胜 zhuǎnbài-wéishèng turn defeat into victory; turn the tide

转包合同 zhuǎnbāo hétóng subcontract:～人 subcontractor

转变 zhuǎnbiàn change (into); turn (into); transform (into): ～政府职能 altering the functions of the government

转播 zhuǎnbō relayed broadcasting; relay (a radio or TV broadcast):～站 relay station

转产 zhuǎnchǎn change the line of production; shift in production

转车 zhuǎnchē change trains or buses; transfer to another train or bus

转达 zhuǎndá pass on; convey:请向她～我的问候。Please give her my regards.

转发 zhuǎnfā transmit, i. e., to send documents, memorandums, etc. to concerned departments after they have been read and commented upon

转告 zhuǎngào pass on a message (to sb.)

转关系 zhuǎn guānxi transfer the registration of Party membership, etc. from one unit to another

转化 zhuǎnhuà transform (into); turn (into); change (into):向反面～ change into the reverse

转换 zhuǎnhuàn transform; change; alter:～国营企业经营机制 alter the way in which state enterprises operate

转机 zhuǎnjī a turn for the better; a favourable turn:她的病有了～。Her illness took a favourable turn.

转嫁 zhuǎnjià shift (sth.) on to (sb.); transfer:～负担到顾客头上 shifting losses upon customers. ～危机 crisis export

转交 zhuǎnjiāo ① pass on (to); send on (to); forward (to):请将此信～张同志。Please forward this letter to Comrade Zhang. ②［信封上用］care of (c/o):烦王同志～ c/o Comrade Wang

转口 zhuǎnkǒu transit:～货物 transit goods. ～贸易 entrepôt trade; carrying trade. ～税 transit duty

转亏为盈 zhuǎnkuī-wéiyíng show a turn from loss to profit; turn losses into gains

转批 zhuǎnpī accommodation sale

转让 zhuǎnràng ① make over:他把房子～给一个朋友。He made over his house to a friend. ② transfer; negotiation; assignment; change; alienate:～土地给别人 alienate lands to another

转入 zhuǎnrù pass to; shift to:～下页［记帐］carried forward (c. f.)

转世 zhuǎnshì［佛］reincarnate; transmigrate:～灵童的认定 confirmation of the reincarnated soul boys

转手 zhuǎnshǒu ① pass on ② sell what one has bought; change hands

转述 zhuǎnshù report; relate (tell) sth. as told by another; paraphrase; retell

转送 zhuǎnsòng ① transfer (to); pass on (to) ② make a present of another

转弯 zhuǎnwān make a turn; turn a corner:急～ take a sharp turn

转弯抹角 zhuǎnwān-mòjiǎo in a devious way; in a round-about way; obliquely; insinuatingly

转危为安 zhuǎnwēi-wéi'ān turn danger into safety; pull through a crisis; steer clear of danger to safety

转型 zhuǎnxíng transformation; conversion:社会～期 period of social transformation

转学 zhuǎnxué transfer from one school to another; transfer:～分 trasfer credit. ～生 transfer student

转眼 zhuǎnyǎn in the twinkling of an eye; in an instant

转业 zhuǎnyè ① change one's occupation (profession); switch to another type of enterprise; conversion from one kind of industry to another ② be transferred to civilian work:～军人 armymen transferred to civilian work

转移 zhuǎnyí ① shift; move; divert; turn:～国家资金 misuse state funds ② transform; change:～社会风气 change prevalent social customs

转运 zhuǎnyùn transfer; transport; convey:～站 transfer post. ～费 gateway charges

转载 zhuǎnzǎi reprint; reproduce

转帐 zhuǎnzhàng transfer accounts:～支付 payment by the transfer of accounts; transfer payment. ～支票 check only for account

转折 zhuǎnzhé ① a turn in the course of events:～点 turning point ② transition (of an essay)

转正 zhuǎnzhèng ① (of a probationary member) become a full member ② (of a temporary worker) become a regular worker:民办教师～ converting the status of community-sponsored teachers to that of regular teachers

转致 zhuǎnzhì[法] transmission

转租 zhuǎnzū sublease; sublet

zhuàn

传 zhuàn〈名〉① commentaries on classics:经～ Confucian classics and commentaries on them ② biography:评～ critical biography

另见 chuán

传记 zhuànjì biography:～文学 biographical literature. ～体小说 fictionalized biography

传略 zhuànlüè brief biography; biographical sketch

转 zhuàn〈动〉turn; rotate; revolve:空～ (of a wheel) turn

without moving forward
另见 zhuǎn

转炉 zhuànlú converter

转台 zhuàntái revolving stage

转转 zhuànzhuan take a short walk; go for a stroll

转悠 zhuànyou〈口〉① stroll; walk about; saunter ② move from side to side; turn

赚 zhuàn〈动〉make a profit; earn; gain

赚钱 zhuànqián earn (one's) money; make money; make a profit

撰 zhuàn〈动〉write (a book, an essay, etc.); compose: 为杂志~稿 write articles for a magazine

撰稿 zhuàngǎo contribute to newspapers, magazines, etc.: ~人 contributor

撰史 zhuànshǐ writing history

撰述(著) zhuànshù(zhù) write; compose

zhuāng

装 zhuāng ①〈名〉dress; clothing; outfit: 便~ plain clothes 〈动〉② dress up; make up; play the part of: ~扮成唯物主义者 posing as a materialist. 上~ dress and put on makeup (for a theatrical performance) ③ pretend; feign: ~成若无其事 look as though nothing has happened ④ contain; pack; hold: ~船口岸 loading port ⑤ equip; install: 安~暖气设备 install a heating apparatus

装扮 zhuāngbàn ① deck out; dress up; make up; attire ② disguise

装备 zhuāngbèi ① equip; fit out: ~精良 be well equipped ② equipment; outfit

装裱 zhuāngbiǎo mount (a picture, etc.)

装出 zhuāngchū assume a posture of; pose as; parade as; give the appearance of

装船地点 zhuāngchuán dìdiǎn shipping point

装订 zhuāngdìng binding: 硬面~ hardbound

装潢 zhuānghuáng ① mount (a picture, etc.); decorate; dress ② decoration; mounting; packaging

装货 zhuānghuò load (cargo): ~清单 loading list

装机容量 zhuāngjī róngliàng installed capacity of

装甲 zhuāngjiǎ ① plate armour ② armoured

装假 zhuāngjiǎ pretend, feign; make believe

装聋作哑 zhuānglóng-zuòyǎ play (pretend to be) deaf and dumb; feign deaf-mutism; pretend to be ignorant of sth.

装门面 zhuāngménmiàn keep up appearances; put up a front

装模作样 zhuāngmú-zuòyàng make a pretence; put on an act; be affected

装配 zhuāngpèi assemble; fit together: ~厂(车间) assembly

plant (shop). ～线 assembly line

装腔作势 zhuāngqiāng-zuòshì put on (strike) a pose (an attitude); make grand gestures

装饰 zhuāngshì adorn; decorate; embellish; deck:～艺术 art deco; Decorative Art. 室内～ interior decoration

装束 zhuāngshù dressing; attire: ～入时 be dressed in the latest fashion

装蒜 zhuāngsuàn pretend not to know; feign ignorance

装卸 zhuāngxiè ① load and unload:～工 loader;[码头上的] docker; stevedore. ～费 terminal charges ② assemble and disassemble

装修 zhuāngxiū ① fit up (a house, etc.):～门面 fit up the shop front; give a building a face-lift ② fittings; fixtures; fitments

装运 zhuāngyùn load and transport; ship: ～单据 shipping documents

装载 zhuāngzǎi load; carry:～量 loading capacity

装帧 zhuāngzhēn (of a book, magazine, etc.) binding and layout

装置 zhuāngzhì ① install; equip; fit ② installation; equipment; appliance:暖气～ heating installation

妆 zhuāng ①〈动〉apply makeup; make up:化～ put on makeup; make up ②〈名〉trousseau; dowry:嫁～ dowry; trousseau

妆扮 zhuāngbàn dress up; attire; deck out

妆奁 zhuānglián trousseau; dowry

妆饰 zhuāngshì dress up; deck out; adorn

庄 zhuāng〈名〉① village ② a place of business:钱～ old-style Chinese private bank

庄户 zhuānghù peasant household

庄稼人 zhuāngjiarén peasant; farmer

庄票 zhuāngpiào notes issued by money houses

庄严 zhuāngyán solemn; dignified; stately:～的声明 solemn statement

庄园 zhuāngyuán manor:～经济 manor economy

庄重 zhuāngzhòng grave; solemn; serious; sober:～而富于热情 dignified yet full of warm feeling. 面容～ look serious

桩 zhuāng〈名〉stake; stock; pile:打～ drive piles into the earth

zhuàng

撞 zhuàng〈动〉strike; knock; collide; bump (against, into): ～在树上 bump against a tree

撞车 zhuàngchē ① collision of cars (buses, etc.) ② "vehicular collision"; clash:有时电影、电视几家同时抢一个剧目,造成"～"现象。Several movie or television studios vie for the same programme, creating a clash in the process.

撞倒 zhuàngdǎo knock down：被自行车～ be knocked down by a bicycle

撞击 zhuàngjī strike; dash against; collide; ram

撞见 zhuàngjiàn ① meet or discover by chance; come across; knock (up) against; catch sb. in the act ② catch：他～自己的孩子在吸烟。He caught his child smoking a cigarette.

撞骗 zhuàngpiàn swindle

撞锁 zhuàngsuǒ ① spring lock ② find that sb. is not home

幢 zhuàng〈方〉：一～5层楼房 a five-storeyed building
另见 chuáng

壮 zhuàng〈形〉① strong; robust; sturdy：肥～ stout and strong ② grand; magnificent：豪～ grand and heroic ③〈动〉strengthen; make stronger

壮大 zhuàngdà grow; expand; strengthen：迅速～成长 rapidly grow and gain strength

壮胆 zhuàngdǎn boost sb.'s courage; embolden; put on a bold front; whistle in the dark (to keep up one's courage)

壮观 zhuàngguān grand (magnificent, splendid) sight; spectacle; grandeur

壮举 zhuàngjǔ heroic undertaking; magnificent feat

壮劳力 zhuàngláolì ① strong labour power ② an able-bodied adult (esp. for farming)

壮丽 zhuànglì majestic; grand; splendid; magnificent; glorious：～的凯歌 a magnificent (splendid) song of victory

壮烈 zhuàngliè brave; heroic：～牺牲 die heroically

壮年 zhuàngnián prime of life; middle age; in one's prime：在～ in the prime of life; in the flower of one's age (life)

壮士 zhuàngshì heroic man; hero：～暮年，雄心不已。The heart of the hero in his old age is as stout as ever.

壮志 zhuàngzhì lofty ideal (aspirations)：～凌云 cherish high aspirations; have soaring aspirations

状 zhuàng〈名〉① form; shape：性～ shape and properties ② state; condition：情～ state of affairs ③ written complaint; plaint：～子 written complaint; plaint ④ certificate：委任～ certificate of appointment

状况 zhuàngkuàng state; condition; position：健康～(不)好 be in (out of) condition

状态 zhuàngtài state of affairs; state; situation; condition：在混乱～中 in a chaotic state

状子 zhuàngzi written complaint; plaint; indictment

zhuī

锥 zhuī〈名〉① awl; ② cone：圆～ circular cone ③〈动〉bore or

drill with an awl

追 zhuī〈动〉① chase; pursue; follow:跟～ follow the tracks of ② trace:～查谣言的根源 trace a rumour to its source ③ seek; go after:～名逐利 seek fame and gain

追捕 zhuībǔ pursue and capture; pursue a criminal; pursue for arrest:～归案 pursue for arrest and bring to justice

追查 zhuīchá find out; investigate into; trace:～责任 find out where the responsibility lies

追悼 zhuīdào mourn over sb.'s death:～会 a memorial meeting in sb.'s honour; memorial service (meeting); hold a ceremony to pay last respects to

追肥 zhuīféi ［农］ topdressing with fertilizer

追根 zhuīgēn get to the root (bottom) of sth.

追回 zhuīhuí take back; recover: ～赃物 recover stolen property

追悔 zhuīhuǐ regret; repent:～莫及 too late to repent

追击 zhuījī pursue and attack; follow up

追加 zhuījiā supplement:～预算 supplement a budget. ～支出 added items of expenditure; additional expenditure

追缴 zhuījiǎo press for payment afterwards; recover: ～税款 pursue the tax payment

追究 zhuījiū find out; probe into; get to the roots of; investigate thoroughly:～刑事责任 investigate criminal responsibility. 概不～ No action will be taken against those who…

追名逐利 zhuīmíng-zhúlì seek (be after) fame and wealth

追求 zhuīqiú ① go after; seek; pursue:～名誉地位 be after fame and position. 盲目～指标 blindly push up the targets ② court; woo; chase

追认 zhuīrèn ① subsequently confirm or endorse; recognize retroactively ② confer or admit posthumously:被～为烈士 be posthumously confirmed as a martyr

追溯 zhuīsù ① date from; trace back to:～到更远 be traced back to still earlier times ② ［法］ retroactive: ～效力 retroactive effect; retroaction

追诉 zhuīsù［法］prosecute

追随 zhuīsuí follow; toe sb.'s line; hang on to sb.'s coattails:～者 followers

追问 zhuīwèn make an inquiry (about); cross-examine; question closely; investigate

追寻 zhuīxún pursue; search; haunt (track) down

追忆 zhuīyì recall; recollect; look back

追赃 zhuīzāng order the return of stolen money or goods

追逐 zhuīzhù ① pursue; chase; run (go) after ② quest; seek: ～高额利润 seek exorbitant profits

追踪 zhuīzōng follow track (trail) of; trace; track:～调查 follow-up investigation (field work).

～嫌疑犯 trail a suspect

zhuì

赘 zhuì ①〈形〉redundant; superfluous ②〈动〉marry into and live with one's bride's family: 入～ marry into and live with one's bride's family

赘词 zhuìcí superfluous words; redundancy

赘述 zhuìshù give unnecessary details; pleonasm: "很小的小孩"这种说法是～。"A little child" is a pleonasm.

赘婿 zhuìxù son-in-law married into his bride's family; son-in-law who lives in the home of his wife's parents

赘言 zhuìyán say more than is needed; unnecessary words

惴 zhuì

惴惴不安 zhuìzhuì-bù'ān be anxious and fearful; uneasy; perturbed

坠 zhuì〈动〉fall; drop: ～落 fall; drop

坠毁 zhuìhuǐ (of a plane) crash

坠楼 zhuìlóu ① fall off a building ② commit suicide by jumping off a building

zhūn

谆 zhūn

谆谆 zhūnzhūn earnest and tireless; patiently: ～教导 earnestly instruct; inculcate; earnstly enjoin. ～嘱咐 earnest advice; caution earnestly

zhǔn

准 zhǔn ①〈动〉allow; permit; grant; approve: ～一个月假 grant sb. a month's leave ②〈名〉standard; norm; criterion: 水～ level; standard ③〈形〉accurate; exact: ～确率高的打字员 an accurate typist ④〈副〉certainly; definitely: 我明天～去。I'll certainly be there tomorrow. ⑤〈前缀〉para-; quasi-: ～决战 quasi-decisive campaign

准备 zhǔnbèi ① prepare; get ready: ～两手 prepare for two eventualities. 作好思想～ be mentally prepared. 他不～做这件事。He doesn't intend to do it.

准得 zhǔnděi certainly; for sure

准话 zhǔnhuà definite message or answer

准确 zhǔnquè accurate; exact; precise; correct: ～说明 explain in exact terms

准绳 zhǔnshéng criterion; yardstick

准时 zhǔnshí on time; punctual; on schedule: ～到达 arrive on time

准则 zhǔnzé guiding principle; standard; norm; criterion; code: 行为～ code of conduct

zhuō

捉 zhuō〈动〉① catch; clutch; arrest:活～ capture sb. alive ② hold; grasp:～笔 hold a pen

捉襟见肘 zhuōjīn-jiànzhǒu expose one's elbow when drawing tight the lapel of one's jacket; have too many difficulties to cope with; be in a predicament

捉迷藏 zhuōmícáng (play) hide-and-seek

捉摸不定 zhuōmō-bùdìng difficult to ascertain; unpredictable; fickle; elusive:～的词句 ambiguous phrases

捉拿 zhuōná arrest; seize; round up:～逃犯 arrest an escaped prisoner. ～治罪 be arrested and punished

捉弄 zhuōnòng play a trick on; play pranks; make fun of; tease:～某人 play pranks on (upon) sb.

拙 zhuō ①〈形〉clumsy; stupid; awkward:愚～ stupid and awkward ②〈代〉my:～著 my writing

拙笨 zhuōbèn clumsy; dull; unskilful

拙见 zhuōjiàn〈谦〉my humble opinion

拙劣 zhuōliè clumsy; inferior:～手法 clumsy tactics

卓 zhuō〈形〉① tall and straight:～立 stand upright ② remarkable; outstanding; eminent

卓见 zhuōjiàn ① excellent opinion; remarkable insight; brilliant idea ②〈套〉your opinion:～以为如何? What do you think of it?

卓绝 zhuōjué matchless; unsurpassed; unparalleled; extreme:艰苦～ extremely hard and bitter; most arduous

卓然 zhuórán outstanding; splendid; remarkable

卓有成效 zhuōyǒu-chéngxiào fruitful; highly effective

卓越 zhuōyuè prominent; brilliant; remarkable; distinguished; superb; outstanding:～的外交才能 one's superb diplomatic talents

卓著 zhuōzhù remarkable; notable; outstanding; brilliant:～成效 distinguished (outstanding) results. 声誉～ enjoy a good reputation; be held in high repute

桌 zhuō〈名〉table:八仙～ old-fashioned square table for eight people

桌布 zhuōbù tablecloth

zhuó

浊 zhuó〈形〉① muddy; turbid; dirty:污～ (of water, air, etc.) dirty; muddy. ～水 turbid water ② voiced

浊物 zhuówù absurd creature; insensitive creature; ignoramus

浊音 zhuóyīn voiced sound

镯 zhuó〈名〉bracelet:玉～ jade

bracelet

着 zhuó〈动〉① wear (clothes); put on:穿～一件大衣 wear an overcoat ② touch; get in touch with:附～ stick to; adhere to ③ apply; use:～色 put colour on; colour
另见 zháo, zhe

着笔 zhuóbǐ set pen to paper; start writing or painting; begin to write or paint

着陆 zhuólù ① land; touch down:飞机安全～。The plane landed safely. ② landing:经济软～ economic soft landing

着落 zhuóluò ① whereabouts ② assured source

着墨 zhuómò apply ink to paper—write or paint

着实 zhuóshí ① indeed; really ② severely

着手 zhuóshǒu begin; start (out); set about:～一项工作 set about a task

着想 zhuóxiǎng consider (the interests of sb. or sth.); think about; have sth. in mind:替人民～ think in terms of the people

着眼 zhuóyǎn fix one's attention on; with… in mind:～于未来 fix one's attention on the future

着重 zhuózhòng lay stress (emphasis) on; stress; make a special effort to:现在我们～地说一说我国的对外关系。Now we shall go on specifically to discuss China's relations with foreign countries.

灼 zhuó ①〈动〉burn; scorch; singe:烧～ scorch; burn ②〈形〉bright; light; penetrating

灼急 zhuójí anxious; worried

灼见 zhuójiàn profound (penetrating) view:真知～ real knowledge and deep insight; profound insight; incisive judgement

灼热 zhuórè scorching hot

灼灼 zhuózhuó brilliant; shining:目光～ with keen, sparkling eyes

酌 zhuó〈动〉① pour out (wine); drink (wine); 对～ (of two people) have a drink together ② think over; consider; deliberate over:商～ discuss and consider

酌办 zhuóbàn act according to one's judgment; act at one's discretion; do as one thinks fit

酌处权 zhuóchùquán [法] discretionary power; discretion

酌量 zhuóliàng consider; weigh; deliberate:～办理 act at one's discretion

酌情 zhuóqíng give consideration according to the circumstances; take into consideration the circumstances; at one's discretion:～处理 deal with on the merits of each case; act according to circumstances

酌予 zhuóyǔ give sth. as one thinks fit; ～补助 give some financial assistance

茁 zhuó

茁实 zhuóshi healthy and strong; sturdy

茁壮 zhuózhuàng healthy and strong; strong; sturdy:～成长 grow up sturdily; grow and mature; steadily mature

琢 zhuó〈动〉① carve; sculpture ② refine:雕～ write in an ornate style
另见 zuó

琢磨 zhuómó ① polish (jade); carve ② improve (literary works); refine upon; turn sth. over in one's mind; polish:～诗句 refine upon (on) the verses

啄 zhuó〈形〉peck:～食谷子的母鸡 hens pecking grain

啄木鸟 zhuómùniǎo woodpecker

zī

咨 zī〈动〉take counsel; consult

咨文 zīwén report delivered by the head of a government on affairs of state; message; note:国情～[美国总统的]State of the Union Message

咨询 zīxún seek (take) advice from; hold counsel with; consult;～服务 advisory (consulting) service. ～机关 consultative (advisory) body. ～民意 consult the people for their opinion

资 zī〈名〉① money; capital; expense:集～ raise funds. 茶～ payment for tea (in a teahouse) ② endowment; gift; natural ability:天～ natural gift ③ qualifications:师～ persons qualified to teach〈动〉④ support; subsidize; give finance to:～贫 subsidize the poor ⑤ provide; supply:以～借鉴 use for reference

资本 zīběn capital:～积累 accumulation of capital. ～与债务比例 ratio of debt to capital

资产 zīchǎn ① property ② capital (fund) ③ assets:～保值增值 maintenance or addition of the value of assets. ～负债比例管理 asset-liability ratio management; managing the assets to liabilities

资产阶级 zīchǎn jiējí bourgeoisie:～自由化 bourgeois liberalization

资敌 zīdí aid an enemy

资格 zīgé ① have the right to; be qualified to; qualifications:有～当教师 be qualified as a teacher ② [能力] capacity; competence:以…的～ in the capacity of… ③ seniority

资金 zījīn funds; capital:～市场 capital market. ～周转 capital turnover; cash flow. 流动～ current funds. 企业相互之间～拖欠的问题 problems concerning defaults between enterprises

资力 zīlì financial strength:～雄厚 have a large capital

资历 zīlì qualifications and record of service; seniority; work record:凭～提升 promote by seniority

资料 zīliào ① means:生产～

means of production ② material;information; data:～读物 source books. ～室 reference room. 第一手～ firsthand data

资望 zīwàng seniority and prestige; reputation:～很高 enjoy a high reputation

资源 zīyuán resources:～勘探 prospecting of resources. ～条件较差的企业 enterprises with less fortunate natural conditions

资质 zīzhì (natural) endowment (gift); intelligence; temperament aptitude

资助 zīzhù aid financially; subsidize:～款 grant-aid

姿 zī〈名〉① looks; appearance:雄～ majestic appearance ② gesture; posture:立～ standing position

姿色 zīsè (of a woman) good looks; nice features:有几分～ be fairly good-looking

姿势 zīshì pose; posture; gesture:摆好～拍照 pose for a picture

姿态 zītài ① carriage; posture; gesture:～优美 have a graceful carriage ② pose; attitude:采取高～ take a magnanimous attitude (towards)

滋 zī ①〈动〉grow; multiply; breed:繁～ multiply profusely ②〈副〉more:为害～甚 cause greater havoc than ever

滋补 zībǔ nourishing; tonic:～食品 nourishing food. ～药 tonic

滋蔓 zīmàn grow vigorously; grow and spread

滋润 zīrùn ① moisten ② moist

滋生 zīshēng ① breed; multiply; propagate; flourish ② cause; create

滋事 zīshì make trouble; cause (make, raise) a disturbance

滋味 zīwèi taste; savour; flavour

滋养 zīyǎng nourish:～品 nourishing food; nutriment

滋长 zīzhǎng grow; develop; thrive:在一些领导机关容易～官僚主义。Bureaucracy thrives in some leading organs.

孜 zī

孜孜不倦 zīzī-bùjuàn industrious; diligent; hardworking; assiduous; indefatigable; take great pains over;她～地投入工作。She threw herself tirelessly into her work.

zǐ

紫 zǐ〈形〉purple; violet:绛～ dark reddish purple

紫菜 zǐcài [植] laver (Porphyra spp.)

紫禁城 zǐjìnchéng the Forbidden City (in Beijing)

紫罗兰 zǐluólán violet

紫砂 zǐshā[陶瓷] red ware; boccaro (buccaro) ware

紫檀 zǐtán red sandalwood

姊 zǐ〈名〉elder sister

姊妹 zǐmèi sisters:～城市 sister city. ～篇 companion piece (volume)

姊妹花 zǐmèihuā the two sisters
姊妹篇 zǐmèipiān companion volume (piece)

子 zǐ〈名〉① son; child: 爱～ beloved son. 独生～ only son ② seed: 结～儿 bear seed ③ person: 女～ woman; female ④ sth. small and hard: 铜～儿 copper coin. 棋～儿 piece (in a board game); chessman
子弹 zǐdàn bullet; shot
子弟 zǐdì sons and younger brothers; children; juniors: ～兵 the people's own army. 职工～ children of the workers and staff
子公司 zǐgōngsī subsidiary company (corporation); subsidiary
子宫 zǐgōng[生理]womb; uterus: ～环 intrauterine device (I. U. D.)
子女 zǐnǚ sons and daughters; children: ～抚养费用 child-care expense. ～赡养父母的责任 duty of child to support parents
子孙 zǐsūn children and grandchildren; descendants; posterity; offspring
子午线 zǐwǔxiàn [地] meridian (line)
子夜 zǐyè midnight
子猪 zǐzhū pigling

籽 zǐ〈名〉seed: 棉～ cotton seed

仔 zǐ (of domestic animals or fowls) young
仔细 zǐxì ① careful; attentive; meticulous: ～地工作 be careful with one's work ② look out; be careful

zì

字 zì〈名〉① word; character: 白～ wrong written or mispronounced character ② form of a written or printed character; style of hand writing: 粗体～ boldfaced word ③ pronunciation (of a word or character): 咬～清楚 pronounce every word clearly ④ name: 签～ sign one's name ⑤ calligraphy: 美术～ artistic calligraphy; art lettering ⑥ another name taken at the age of twenty: 孔子～仲尼 Conficius styled himself Zhongni (or Confucius, whose courtesy name Zhongni, …)
字辈 zìbèi one's branch of the clan
字典 zìdiǎn dictionary; lexicon: 查～ consult a dictionary
字典纸 zìdiǎnzhǐ India paper
字号 zìhào the name of a shop
字画 zìhuà calligraphy (scripts) and painting: ～古玩 calligraphy and antiques
字迹 zìjì handwriting; writing
字据 zìjù written (signed) pledge paper (e. g. receipt; contract; IOU etc.)
字里行间 zìlǐ-hángjiān between (in-between) the lines
字谜 zìmí riddle about a character or word
字面 zìmiàn literal; verbal: ～上的意思 literal meaning

字母 zìmǔ letter；alphabet：大写～ capital letter

字幕 zìmù［影视］captions；subtitles：～机［与电视机相连使用］closed caption decoder；telecaption. 有中文对白～的英语电影 an English film with Chinese subtitles

字体 zìtǐ ①［印］typeface ② script（in writing）③ style of calligraphy

字条儿 zìtiáor brief note；note

字帖 zìtiè model（Chinese）calligraphy

字样 zìyàng ① model of written characters ② printed or written word（which succinctly inform，instruct，warn，etc.）

字源学 zìyuánxué etymology

字斟句酌 zìzhēn-jùzhuó weigh every word

恣 zì〈动〉act with no restraint；be self-indulgent：放～ proud and undisciplined

恣情 zìqíng ① to one's heart's content；as much as one likes ② wanton；arbitrary；wilful

恣肆 zìsì ① unbridled；unrestrained；wilfully ②（of writing style）forceful and unrestrained；free and natural

恣意 zìyì unscrupulous；wilful；rackless；unbridled；at will：～妄为 behave unscrupulously. ～践踏 arrogantly（wifully）trample on

恣欲 zìyù libidinous orgies

自 zì ①〈代〉self；one's own；oneself：～制 self-command ②〈副〉certainly；of course：～当悔改 will willingly amend one's ways ③〈介〉from；since：～幼 since childhood

自爱 zì'ài ① take good care of one's health ② cherish one's good name；self-respect

自拔 zìbá free or extricate oneself（from pain or evildoing）

自白 zìbái ① confession；make a clean breast of：～书 confession ② explain or vindicate oneself

自报公议 zìbào-gōngyì self-assessment and public discussion

自暴自弃 zìbào-zìqì give oneself up as hopeless；abandon oneself to despair；give oneself up to vice

自卑 zìbēi feel oneself inferior；be self-abased：～感 inferiority complex；sense of inferiority

自备 zìbèi provide for oneself：～外汇 self-provided foreign exchange

自便 zìbiàn at one's convenience：听其～。Let him do as he pleases.

自惭形秽 zìcǎn-xínghuì feel ashamed of one's ungainly appearance；feel ashamed of one's lack of creative talent；feel（look）small

自产自销 zìchǎn-zìxiāo produce and market all by oneself（on one's own）；Producers market their own products.

自称 zìchēng ① claim to be；style oneself；call oneself；assert：～内行 call oneself an expert ② profess：～不知情 profess ignorance

自持 zìchí ① control oneself; restrain oneself; exercise self-restraint ② reserved; self-possessed

自吹自擂 zìchuī-zìlěi blow one's own trumpet; advertise oneself; brag about

自大 zìdà self-important; self-conceited; arrogant

自动 zìdòng ① automatic:～装配线 automatic assembly line ② of one's own accord; on one's own initiative; voluntarily:～交待 admit one's errors voluntarily

自发 zìfā spontaneous:～势力 spontaneous forces

自费 zìfèi at one's own expense:～公派留学 self-financed study abroad on the commission of the authorities concerned; self-sponored overseas study on public commission. ～留学 study abroad at one's own expense. ～生 self-funded students

自封 zìfēng ① confine oneself; isolate oneself ② proclaim (style) oneself; self-appoint

自负 zìfù ① think highly of oneself; be conceited:～不凡 have an extraordinarily high opinion of oneself ② be responsible for one's own action:～盈亏 be responsible (be accountable) for one's own profits or losses; assume a sole responsibility for one's profits or losses. ～盈亏的商店 financially independent stores

自高自大 zìgāo-zìdà self-important; arrogant; overbearing; disgustingly self-satisfied

自告奋勇 zìgào-fènyǒng volunteer to undertake a difficult task; offer to take the responsibility upon oneself; volunteer one's service for

自古以来 zìgǔyǐlái from time immemorial; from ancient times to the present

自顾不暇 zìgù-bùxiá be busy enough with one's own affairs; have not even any leisure for oneself; be unable even to fend for oneself

自豪 zìháo be proud of; pride oneself on:～感 sense of pride

自己 zìjǐ ① oneself:～揭穿～ expose oneself ② own; closely related to; one's own:～动手 use one's own hands. ～人 people on one's own side; one of us. ～说了算 consider one's own words as final

自给 zìjǐ self-supporting; self-sufficient:～自足 self-sufficient and self-contained

自家人 zìjiārén people on one's own side; one of us

自咎 zìjiù blame oneself; rebuke oneself

自居 zìjū consider oneself to be; pose as

自决 zìjué self-determination:～权 right to self-determination

自绝 zìjué alienate oneself

自觉 zìjué ① self-conscious; conscious; aware:人的～能动性

man's conscious dynamic role. ～遵守纪律 conscientiously observe discipline ② voluntary: ～自愿 of one's own accord; voluntarily

自夸 zìkuā boast (of, about); brag (of, about); crow (about, over); sing one's own praise

自来水 zìláishuǐ running water; piped water; tap water: ～厂 waterworks

自立 zìlì support oneself; depend on oneself; stand on one's own feet; earn one's own living

自力更生 zìlì-gēngshēng ① rely on one's own efforts ② regeneration through one's own efforts; self-reliance

自量 zìliàng estimate one's own ability or strength: 不知～ overrate one's abilities

自流 zìliú ① (of water) flow by itself: ～灌溉 irrigate by the force of gravity ② (of a thing) be left to take its own course: 听其～ let things drift along ③ (of a person) do as one pleases

自留地 zìliúdì small plot (of land) for personal use; family plot; private plot

自律制度 zìlǜ zhìdù self-disciplinary system

自满 zìmǎn self-satisfied; self-conceited; (self-) complacent; smug

自鸣得意 zìmíng-déyì sing one's own praises; crow over (one's success); plume oneself on (one's accomplishments); pride oneself; flatter oneself

自明 zìmíng self-evident; self-explanatory; obvious

自命不凡 zìmìng-bùfán pride oneself on being out of the ordinary; consider oneself an exceptional person; have a high opinion of oneself

自欺欺人 zìqī-qīrén deceive oneself as well as others; fool others as well as oneself

自谦 zìqiān be modest

自取灭亡 zìqǔ-mièwáng court one's own ruin (disaster); bring destruction on oneself; head for (ride to) disaster

自然 zìrán ① nature ② natural: ～保护区 nature reserve. ～灾害 natural calamity (disaster). ～人[法] natural person ③ naturally: 人们～要问为什么。One will naturally ask why.

自认晦气 zìrèn-huìqì admit defeat in (with) good grace; accept bad luck without complaint; be resigned to bad luck

自如 zìrú freely; smoothly; with facility

自杀 zìshā kill oneself; commit suicide

自上而下 zìshàng'érxià from above to below; from top to bottom

自食其果 zìshí-qíguǒ be made to pay for one's rabid evil doings; eat the bitter fruit of one's own doing; reap what one has sown; reap the result of one's own sowing; reap the harvest of one's misdeeds

自食其力 zìshí-qílì live by one's own work; earn one's own living; live on one's own labour

自恃 zìshì ① over confident and conceited ② be self-assured for having sth. or sb. to rely on; count on; capitalize on

自首 zìshǒu ① surrender oneself (to justice, police, etc.); give oneself up (to); voluntarily surrender oneself ② make a political recantation; surrender to the enemy

自诉 zìsù [法] private prosecution: ～案件 case of private prosecution: ～人 private prosecutor

自讨苦吃 zìtǎokǔchī ask (look) for trouble; seek out hardships

自讨没趣 zìtǎo-méiqù bring contempt upon oneself; ask for rebuff (a snub)

自卫 zìwèi ① defend oneself: ～能力 the capacity to defend oneself ② self-defence: ～行动 an act in self-defence

自我 zìwǒ self; oneself: ～吹嘘 boost oneself; boast smugly. ～标榜 glorify oneself; advertise oneself. 建立～防范机制 build a self-preventive mechanism

自习 zìxí study by oneself in scheduled time or free time; review one's lessons

自相矛盾 zìxiāng-máodùn self-contradictory

自销 zìxiāo (of a factory, etc.) sell goods through one's own channels

自新 zìxīn make a fresh start; turn over a new leaf: 悔过～ repent and start anew

自信 zìxìn self-confident: ～心 self-confidence

自行 zìxíng ① of one's own accord; of one's self: ～到来 come of itself ② by self: ～解决 settle (a problem) by oneself

自修 zìxiū ① (of students) have self-study; study by oneself: ～课 self-study hours ② study on one's own; teach oneself; study independently: ～德语 teach oneself German

自选商店 zìxuǎn shāngdiàn self-service stores

自学 zìxué study on one's own; teach oneself: ～成功的人 autodidact. ～考试 self-study qualification examination. ～课本 teach-yourself books

自寻烦恼 zìxún-fánnǎo bring vexation (trouble) on oneself; worry over for nothing; vex oneself; give oneself unnecessary trouble

自言自语 zìyán-zìyǔ speak (talk, say, murmur, mutter) to oneself

自以为是 zìyǐwéishì consider oneself (always) right (correct); regard oneself as infallible; presumptuously claim infallibility; be opinionated

自由 zìyóu freedom; liberty: ～化 liberalization. ～恋爱 freedom to choose one's spouse. ～市场 free market. ～通商口岸 open (free) port. ～外汇 convertible foreign exchange. 出版～ freedom of press

自圆其说 zìyuán-qíshuō make one's statement consistent; make out a good case (for oneself); justify oneself; make one's argument sound plausible

自愿 zìyuàn of one's own accord; voluntarily:～互利 voluntariness and mutual benefit

自在 zìzài ① comfortable; at ease ② unrestrained; free

自知之明 zìzhīzhīmíng wisdom to know oneself; self-knowledge (understanding)

自治 zìzhì self-government; autonomy; autonomous rule:～区(州) autonomous region (prefecture)

自重 zìzhòng ① conduct oneself with dignity; be self-possessed ② dead weight

自主 zìzhǔ act on one's own:～经营、自负盈亏、自我发展、自我约束[简称"四自"] operate and develop enterprises independently, impose their own restrictions and assume responsibility for their profits and losses (simplfied as "four aspects of autonomous operation")

自主权 zìzhǔquán right to make one's own decision; autonomy

自助餐 zìzhùcān buffet:～式的晚餐 buffet supper. ～厅 self-service cafeteria

自传 zìzhuàn autobiography

自足 zìzú self-satisfied; complacent; smug

自尊 zìzūn self-esteem; self-respect; (proper) pride:伤了她的～心 injure her self-esteem; wound her pride

自作聪明 zìzuò-cōngmíng think (consider, fancy) oneself clever; act on the strength of one's own imagined clever

自作主张 zìzuò-zhǔzhāng follow one's own bent; have one's own way of doing things; decide all by oneself

自作自受 zìzuò-zìshòu carry what one makes; hoist with one's own petard; take the consequences of one's own deeds; reap what one sows; suffer for one's own act (account)

渍 zì〈动〉① soak; ret; 浸～ soak; ret ② be soiled (with grease, etc.):墨水～ an ink stain

zōng

宗 zōng〈名〉① ancestor:祖～ ancestor ② clan:归～ (of an adopted child) return to one's own parents or clan ③ sect; faction; school:禅～ the Chan sect; Zen; Dhyana. 正～ orthodox school ④〈形〉principal aim; purpose:开～明义 make clear the purpose and main theme from the very beginning

宗法 zōngfǎ patriarchal clan system:～思想 patriarchal ideology

宗教 zōngjiào religion;:～活动场所 site of religious activities

宗庙 zōngmiào ancestral temple
宗派 zōngpài sect; faction; denomination: ～主义 sectarianism; factionalism
宗谱 zōngpǔ clan genealogy; genealogy; family genealogies
宗亲 zōngqīn members of the same clan; clansmen
宗室 zōngshì royal (ruling) house; royal family; dynastic family; imperial (royal) clan
宗旨 zōngzhǐ aim; purpose; object
宗主国 zōngzhǔguó suzerain; metropolitan state
宗族 zōngzú ① patriarchal clan; clan: 封建～统治 feudal clan rule ② clansman

棕 zōng〈名〉① palm ② palm fibre; coir
棕榈 zōnglǘ palm: ～叶写本 palm-leaf manuscripts of
棕色 zōngsè brown: ～人种 brown race

踪 zōng〈名〉trace; track; footprint; 追～ follow the tracks of; trace
踪迹 zōngjì trace; track

综 zōng〈动〉sum up; put together
综观 zōngguān make a comprehensive survey
综合 zōnghé comprehensive; all-round; multipurpose; synthetical: ～报导 summing-up report; composite (comprehensive) dispatch. ～经营 diverse economic undertakings. ～利用 multi-purpose utilization; comprehensive use (utilization). 社会治安～治理 improve all facets of public security
综计 zōngjì sum up; add up
综括 zōngkuò sum up
综览 zōnglǎn present an overview; general survey of
综述 zōngshù ① summarize; sum up ② roundup; summary report; synopsis

zǒng

总 zǒng ①〈动〉sum up; assemble: ～结经验 sum up experience ②〈形〉general; chief; main; central: ～动员 general mobilization ③〈形,名〉total; aggregate: ～额 total (amount) 〈副〉④ anyway; inevitable; after all: ～是要解决的 be settled sooner or later ⑤ always; consistently: 我晚上～在家。I always stay at home in the evening.
总罢工 zǒngbàgōng general strike
总编辑 zǒngbiānjí editor in chief
总裁 zǒngcái (of corporation, etc.) president; chairman
总产量 zǒngchǎnliàng total output
总产值 zǒngchǎnzhí total value of output; gross output value
总店(～行,～公司) zǒngdiàn (～háng, ～gōngsī) main office; head office
总动员 zǒngdòngyuán general mobilization
总督 zǒngdū governor-general;

governor
总而言之 zǒng'éryánzhī to put it in a nutshell; to sum up; in a word; in brief
总方针 zǒngfāngzhēn general principle (policy)
总干事 zǒnggànshì director-general
总纲 zǒnggāng general programme (principles)
总工程师 zǒnggōngchéngshī chief engineer
总工会 zǒnggōnghuì federation of trade unions: 中华全国～ All-China Federation of Trade Unions
总公司 zǒnggōngsī head office (of a corporation)
总共 zǒnggòng in all; altogether; in the aggregate
总和 zǒnghé sum total; sum; total
总汇 zǒnghuì ① (of streams) come or flow together ② confluence; concourse; aggregate
总机 zǒngjī[电话]telephone exchange; switchboard
总计 zǒngjì ① add up to; amount to; foot up; total: 参观者～2万人。The visitors totalled 20,000. ② grand total
总结 zǒngjié ① summarize; sum up ② summing-up; summary: ～报告 summing-up (summary) report
总经理 zǒngjīnglǐ general manager; president
总经销 zǒngjīngxiāo exclusive distribution: ～人 general sale agent
总揽 zǒnglǎn assume overall responsibility; take on everything
总理 zǒnglǐ premier; prime minister
总领事 zǒnglǐngshì [外] consul general: ～馆 consulate general
总论 zǒnglùn introduction (at the beginning of a book)
总评 zǒngpíng general comment; overall appraisal
总数 zǒngshù (sum) total; aggregate
总书记 zǒngshūjì general secretary; secretary-general
总司令 zǒngsīlìng commander in chief: ～部 general headquarters
总算 zǒngsuàn ① at (long) last; finally: 我～做完了。At last I am finished. ② considering everything; all things considered; on the whole: 会～开得很成功。On the whole the meeting was a success.
总体 zǒngtǐ overall; total: ～方案 master plan
总统 zǒngtǒng president
总务 zǒngwù general affairs; general service: ～科(处) general affairs section (department)
总则 zǒngzé general provisions (principles, rules)
总帐 zǒngzhàng general ledger
总之 zǒngzhī ① in a word; in short; in brief ② anyway; anyhow
总支 zǒngzhī general (Party or Youth League) branch
总值 zǒngzhí total value; gross value: 国民生产～ gross national product (GNP)

zòng

粽 zòng
粽子 zòngzi pyramid-shaped dumpling made of glutinous rice wrapped in bamboo or reed leaves

纵 zòng ①〈形〉from the front to the back; from north to south; vertical; longitudinal:～断面 vertical section〈动〉② indulge in:放～ let sb. have his own way; allow to run wild ③ set free; release; let go:～虎入室 allow a tiger into the house ④ jump; leap:～身一跳 vault up onto ⑤〈连〉even if (though)
纵队 zòngduì file; column
纵贯 zòngguàn pass through from north to south or from south to north
纵横 zònghéng ① lengthwise and sidewise; in length and breadth ② free; unrestrained:～家 political strategists; elocutionist. ～交错的 crisscross. ～驰骋 advance freely and quickly; manoeuvre freely; sweep through the length and breadth
纵火 zònghuǒ set (sth.) on fire; commit arson:～犯 arsonist
纵酒 zòngjiǔ drink to excess
纵览 zònglǎn look far and wide; scan
纵情 zòngqíng ① indulge (oneself) in; indulge one's affections:～地赏新猎奇 indulge a taste for the exotic ② to one's heart's content; as much as one likes ～歌唱 sing to one's heart's content
纵容 zòngróng connive at; indulge; pamper:～包庇 protect and connive at. ～孩子 indulge one's child
纵深 zòngshēn depth:向～发展 depth in development
纵谈 zòngtán talk freely; have a free talk (with sb., about sth.)
纵向 zòngxiàng longitudinal; vertical:～调查 longitudinal enquiry
纵欲 zòngyù indulge in sensual pleasure; sensual (carnal) indulgence

zǒu

走 zǒu〈动〉① walk; go; move:退～ move back; retreat ② run:奔～ run ③ leave; depart; go away:我该～了。It's time for me to leave. ④ visit:～亲戚 call on one's relatives ⑤ escape; leak:～漏风声。The secret leaked out. ⑥ depart from the original; out of tune:她唱歌常～调。She frequently went off-key.
走板 zóubǎn ① (of opera singing) be out of tune ② digress from the subject; stray from the point
走道 zǒudào ① path; walk; footpath ② sidewalk; pavement
走读生 zǒudúshēng day student; nonresident student

走钢丝 zǒu gāngsī wirewalking

走狗 zǒugǒu running dog; lackey; flunkey; stooge; servile follower

走过场 zǒu guòchǎng ① walk across the stage (a character in an opera entering the stage from one end, quickly going across, then exiting at the other end, without staying on the stage) ② do sth. as a mere formality; simply go through the motions; be reduced to mere formality: 运动~ make the movement a sham

走红 zǒuhóng have good luck; be in luck

走后门 zǒu hòumén go through the back door; get (go) in by the back door; get sth. done through pull; secure advantages through pull or influence; make back-door deals

走火 zǒuhuǒ ① (of firearms) go off by accident; discharge accidently ② overstate; exaggerate; go too far in what one says

走江湖 zǒu jiānghú wander from place to place and earn a living by juggling, fortune-telling, etc.; become a vagrant

走漏 zǒulòu leak (let) out; reveal; disclose; divulge: ~消息 divulge a secret

走马灯 zǒumǎdēng trotting horse lamp; a lantern adorned with a revolving circle of paper horses

走马看花 zǒumǎ-kànhuā look at the flowers while on horseback; give a hurried and cursory glance at things; take a brief look at

走南闯北 zǒunán-chuǎngběi journey north and south; travel widely

走俏 zǒuqiào ① become popular; ② be in great demand; sell well: 花布~。Calico sells well.

走入歧途 zǒurùqítú go astray; deviate from the right track (path); take the wrong track

走上…道路 zǒushàng…dàolù embark on a course; set out a road

走私 zǒusī smuggle: ~贩私 smuggling. ~货物 smuggled (uncustomed, contraband) goods. ~投机倒把集团 group that smuggles or speculates. ~者 contrabandists; smugglers

走投无路 zǒutóu-wúlù have no way out; be in an impasse; go down a dead (blind) alley; come to the end of one's tether; find oneself cornered: 被逼得~ be driven to the wall

走向 zǒuxiàng ① head for; move towards: ~胜利 advance towards victory ② orientation; trend; developmental direction: 价值~ the orientation of value. 南北~的山脉 mountain ranges trending north and south

走穴 zǒuxué [文艺] performing in self-organized travelling groups

走样 zǒuyàng be deformed

走运 zǒuyùn have a good luck; be in luck

走自己的道路 zǒu zìjǐ de dàolù blazing a path of one's own;

take one's own road

走嘴 zǒuzuǐ make a slip of the tongue; let slip an inadvertent remark

zòu

奏 zòu〈动〉① play (music):～乐 play music; strike up a tune ② gain; achieve; produce:～效 get the desired result ③ present a (written or verbal) memorial to the throne:～章 submit memorials to the throne

奏捷 zòujié win a battle; score a success

奏鸣曲 zòumíngqǔ sonata

奏效 zòuxiào produce results; prove effective; get the desired result

奏乐 zòuyuè play music; strike up a tune

奏折 zòuzhé memorial to the throne

揍 zòu〈动〉① hit; beat; strike: 他被人～了一顿。He was beaten up by sb.. ② break; smash:别把杯给～了。Don't smash the cup.

zū

租 zū〈动〉① hire; rent:向…～房子 rent a house from ② lease; let out:以较低的租金出～ lease at a lower rental ③〈名〉rent:地～ land rent

租船 zūchuán chartering:～费 charterage. ～合同(契约) charter party. ～人 charterer. ～市场 chartering market

租佃 zūdiàn land tenancy:～制 land-leasing system

租户 zūhù ① tenant (of a building or part of it); lessee ② hirer (of a thing)

租界 zūjiè foreign settlement; (foreign) concession

租借 zūjiè hire; rent; lease:～条件 lease terms. ～地条约 treaty of leased territory

租金 zūjīn rent; rental

租赁 zūlìn lease; rent; hire:～公司 leasing company. ～经营 be run under lease; leasing management; management on a lease basis. ～合同(契约) lease contract; contract of tenancy

租期 zūqī lease term

租用 zūyòng rent; hire; take on lease:～出租汽车 hire a taxi. ～房屋 rent a house

租约 zūyuē lease agreement; lease:～的延续 continuation of tenancies

zú

足 zú ①〈名〉foot; leg:立～ have a foothold somewhere ②〈形〉full; enough; sufficient:～以应付需要 be sufficient (adequate) to meet one's needs

足本小说 zúběn xiǎoshuō full-length novel

足秤 zúchèng full measure (by a steelyard)

足赤 zúchì pure gold:金无～,人

无完人。There are lees to every wine.

足够 zúgòu enough; ample; sufficient

足迹 zújì footprint; footmark; track

足球 zúqiú football[英国等国家]; soccer[美国]:～暴力 soccer violence. ～迷 football fiend

足坛 zútán the football world

足以 zúyǐ enough; sufficiently

足智多谋 zúzhì-duōmóu wise and full of strategems; resourceful

卒 zú〈名〉① soldier; private ② servant ③ pawn, one of the pieces in Chinese chess〈动〉④ finish; end ⑤ die:病～ die of illness ⑥〈副〉finally; at last

族 zú〈名〉① clan ② a death penalty in ancient China, imposed on an offender and his whole family, or even the families of his mother and wife ③ race; nationality ④ a class or group of things with common features

族亲 zúqīn clansmen; members of a clan

族长 zúzhǎng the head of a clan; clan elder

zǔ

诅 zǔ

诅咒 zǔzhòu curse; imprecate (upon); swear; wish sb. evil

祖 zǔ〈名〉① grandfather ② ancestor:远～ remote ancestor ③ founder or originator (of a school of thought, religious sect, etc.):佛教鼻～ the originator of Buddhism

祖传 zǔchuán be handed down from one's ancestors:～秘方 secret recipe handed down from one's ancestors

祖父 zǔfù (paternal) grandfather

祖国 zǔguó one's country; motherland; fatherland

祖籍 zǔjí one's ancestral home; original family home; land of one's ancestor

祖母 zǔmǔ (paternal) grandmother

祖师 zǔshī founder (of a school of learning); patriarch; progenitor

祖先(宗) zǔxiān(zōng) ancestry; ancestors; forefathers; forbears

祖祖辈辈 zǔzǔ-bèibèi from generation to generation; for generations

阻 zǔ〈动〉obstruct; hinder; block; impede:～止历史车轮前进 stem the advance of history

阻碍 zǔ'ài obstruct (from); hinder (from); block:～交通 block the traffic. ～生产力的发展 retard the growth of productive forces

阻挡 zǔdǎng block; stop; obstruct; resist; halt; hold back; dam:～时代潮流 halt the tide of our epoch

阻击 zǔjī intercept; block; check:～阵地 blocking position

阻截 zǔjié stop; obstruct; bar the

way
阻拦 zǔlán stop; obstruct; block; bar the way
阻力 zǔlì resistance; obstruction
阻挠 zǔnáo obstruct; hinder; hamper; thwart; stand in the way:～历史发展 check the course of historical development
阻塞 zǔsè obstruct; block; hold up; clog:交通～。The traffic is held up.
阻止 zǔzhǐ prevent (from); stop; hold back; check:大雨～了他们前来。The heavy rain prevented them (from) coming.

组 zǔ〈名〉① group:教研～ teaching and research group ② set; series:一～邮票 a set of stamps ③〈动〉organize; form:编～军队 organize an army
组成 zǔchéng make up; form; constitute; compose:～部分 component part; constituent; part and parcel (of)
组稿 zǔgǎo commission authors to write on given topics; solicit contributions
组歌 zǔgē suite of songs
组阁 zǔgé form a cabinet
组合 zǔhé ① combine; compose; make up; grouping:～机床 combined machine tool. ～音响设备 hi-fi ② association:～主义 associationism
组件 zǔjiàn subassembly
组建 zǔjiàn put together (a group); form
组距 zǔjù [社]class interval
组曲 zǔqǔ [器乐套曲] suite
组织 zǔzhī ① organize; form:～好农村剩余劳动力的合理有序流动。Surplus rural labour and its flow should be organized in a sound and orderly way. ② organization; setup:党的～关系 Party membership credentials. ～生活 regular activities of an organization ③[生理]tissue:～疗法 tissue therapy

zuān

钻 zuān〈动〉① drill; bore; auger:～孔 drill a hole; bore ② get into; dig into; go through:～进人堆里 plunge into the crowd ③ study assiduously:～上了英语 study hard at English
另见 zuàn
钻劲 zuānjìn zest in probing into sth.
钻空子 zuān kòngzi avail oneself of loopholes (in a law, a statute, a contract, etc.); exploit a loophole to one's own advantage; work on the weak side of sb.'s character:不留空子给人钻 leave no loopholes
钻牛角尖 zuān niújiǎojiān ① take unnecessary pains to study an insignificant problems; quibble over trivialities; split hairs ② get into a blind alley (a dead end)
钻探 zuāntàn drilling; probing:～机 drilling machine
钻研 zuānyán study intensively; dig into; delve into:～业务 dig

into one's job; perfect (improve) one's professional skill; go in for professional efficiency; perfect one's professional competence

钻营 zuānyíng curry favour with sb. in authority for personal gain; seek (secure) personal gain:～功名的人 social climber

zuàn

钻 zuàn〈名〉① drill; auger; borer:手提～ a portable drill ② diamond; jewel:优质～石 diamond of the first water ③〈动〉drill; bore:～木头 drill into the wood

另见 zuān

钻床(机) zuànchuáng(jī) drilling machine; driller

钻井 zuànjǐng well-drilling:～队 drilling team

钻石 zuànshí ① diamond:～婚[结婚 60 周年纪念] diamond wedding ② jewel (used in a watch)

钻塔 zuàntǎ boring tower

钻头 zuàntóu bit (of a drill)

zuǐ

嘴 zuǐ〈名〉① mouth:张～ open one's mouth (to say sth.) ② sth. shaped or functioning like a mouth:烟～儿 cigarette holder

嘴巴 zuǐba mouth:他～不饶人。He got a sharp tongue.; There was always a sharp edge to his tongue.

嘴笨 zuǐ bèn clumsy of speech; clumsy in speaking:我是个～的人。I'm a man clumsy of speech.

嘴馋 zuǐ chán fond of good food; gluttonous; greedy

嘴乖 zuǐ guāi (of children) clever and pleasant when speaking to elders

嘴紧 zuǐ jǐn tight-lipped; close-mouthed; secretive:～的人 clam

嘴快 zuǐ kuài have a loose tongue; loose-tongued:～心直 outspoken; frank; straightforward

嘴脸 zuǐliǎn look; features; countenance:丑恶的～ ugly features

嘴上没毛,办事不牢 zuǐshàng méi máo,bànshì bù láo Downy lips make thoughtless slips.; Young people cannot be trusted with important tasks because they lack experience

嘴松 zuǐ sōng have a loose tongue

嘴碎 zuǐ suì loquacious; talkative; garrulous; flippant

嘴甜 zuǐ tián ingratiating in speech; honeymouthed; honeylipped

嘴严 zuǐ yán tight-lipped; close-mouthed

嘴硬 zuǐ yìng stubborn and reluctant to admit mistakes or defeats

嘴直 zuǐ zhí outspoken; plainspoken

zuì

醉 zuì〈形〉① drunk; tipsy; intoxicated: 喝～了酒 be intoxicated from wine. 烂～ dead drunk ② (some kind of food) steeped or saturated in liquor: ～蟹 liquor-saturated crab

醉鬼 zuìguǐ drunkard; sot; inebriate

醉汉 zuìhàn drunkard; drunkman

醉酒 zuìjiǔ be intoxicated

醉生梦死 zuìshēng-mèngsǐ lead an aimless and often dissipated life; lead a befuddled (gay) life; live a life of dreams

醉态 zuìtài the state of being drunk; drunkenness

醉翁之意不在酒 zuìwēng zhī yì bù zài jiǔ The drinker's heart is not in cup—have ulterior motives.; The intention of the drunkard lies not in wine, but in other purposes.; Though one professes to be a drinker, he is really not interested in wine.

醉心 zuìxīn be infatuated with; be obsessed by; be keen about; be bent on: ～名利 be bent on seeking fame and gain

醉意 zuìyì sign or feeling of getting drunk: 带着～地宣称… somewhat intoxicatingly assert that…

最 zuì〈副〉[表示某种属性超过所有同类的人或事物] worst; most; best; last; -est: ～光荣的时刻 the most glorious moment. ～广泛的民主 the fullest democracy

最初 zuìchū initial; earliest; first: ～印象 first impressions

最大限价 zuìdà xiànjià ceiling price

最低 zuìdī lowest; minimum: ～价格 bottom (rock-bottom) prices; lowest prices: ～纲领 minimum programme. ～年龄 minimum age

最高 zuìgāo highest; supreme; tallest; maximum: ～人民法院 Supreme People's Court. ～人民检察院 Supreme People's Procuratorate. ～年产量 peak annual output

最高级 zuìgāojí ① highest; summit: ～会议 summit conference ② superlative degree

最好 zuìhǎo ① best: 历史是～的见证。History is the most telling witness. ② had better (do): 你～马上就干。You had better do it at once.

最后 zuìhòu last; final; ultimate: ～交货日期 end delivery date. ～通谍 [外] ultimatum

最惠国 zuìhuìguó most-favoured-nation: 给以～待遇 accord (a country) most-favoured-nation treatment

最佳 zuìjiā optimum; the best: ～电影 a smash hit

最近 zuìjìn ① in the near future; soon ② recently; lately; of late: ～的消息 recent news

最终 zuìzhōng ultimate; final: ～裁决 final ruling (verdict). ～

判决 final judgement (decision); conclusive sentence. ～依据 ultimate basis

罪 zuì〈名〉① crime; guilt; offence: 犯～ commit a crime ② fault; error: 归～ put the blame on ③ suffering; hardship: 受～ endure suffering; have a hard time

罪案 zuì'àn details of a criminal case; case

罪不容诛 zuìbùróngzhū deserve more than death for one's crimes; Even death cannot excuse one's offence.

罪大恶极 zuìdà-èjí be guilty of the most heinous (atrocious) crimes; commit the most serious (heinous) crimes

罪恶 zuì'è crime; evil; vice; villainy: ～的渊薮 seminary of vice and crime. ～滔天 be guilty of monstrous (towering) crimes. ～累累 be guilty of innumerable crimes; be crime-steeped. ～重大 monstrous crime

罪犯 zuìfàn criminal; offender; convict; convicted person, culprit: ～的供词 prisoner statement

罪该万死 zuìgāiwànsǐ be guilty of crimes for which even death can't atone

罪过 zuìguo ① fault; offence; sin ② thanks, but this is really more than I deserve

罪魁 zuìkuí principal offender; arch-criminal: ～祸首 arch-criminal; chief culprit (criminal)

罪名 zuìmíng accusation; charge

罪人 zuìrén guilty person; sinner: 成为千古～ be branded as a traitor through the ages

罪行 zuìxíng criminal act; crime; offence; guilt: ～累累 cumulation of crimes. ～细节 particulars of offence

罪有应得 zuìyǒuyīngdé deserve one's punishment

罪责难逃 zuìzé-nántáo can't shirk one's responsibility for the crimes

罪证 zuìzhèng evidence of a crime (guilt); proof of a crime; criminal evidence: ～确凿 proof of a crime beyond a shadow of a doubt; The evidence of these crimes is conclusive.

罪状 zuìzhuàng charge in an indictment; facts about a crime; criminal acts

zūn

尊 zūn ①〈动〉respect; revere; honour: ～重事实，讲道理 respect the facts and be reasonable ②〈形〉high; dignified; senior; of a senior generation: ～卑身份关系 relationship between a superior and an inferior ③〈代〉your: 令～ your father

尊称 zūnchēng ① address sb. respectfully ② a respectful form of address; honorific title

尊崇 zūnchóng revere; worship; honour; respect: ～孔教 honour Confucianism

尊贵 zūnguì distinguished; honourable; respectable

尊号 zūnhào respectful title conferred on an emperor or empress

尊敬 zūnjìng respect; honour; esteem; revere

尊师重教 zūnshī-zhòngjiào respect teachers and value education

尊严 zūnyán ① dignity; sanctity: 法律～ sanctity of the law ② dignified

尊重 zūnzhòng respect; honour; esteem; hold in esteem: 我们必须～他们的劳动。We must give due weight to their work.

遵 zūn〈动〉obey; abide by; observe; keep; follow: ～守信义 keep faith with

遵从 zūncóng follow; listen to; defer to; comply with: ～经济规律 adherence to economic laws

遵纪守法 zūnjì-shǒufǎ observe law and discipline; observe disciplines and obey laws

遵命 zūnmìng comply with your wish; obey your command (instruction); in compliance with the order: ～文学 literature written to order

遵守 zūnshǒu adhere to; keep; observe; abide (go) by; follow: ～法律 abide by the law. ～时间 be punctual

遵循 zūnxún act upon; be true to; abide by; comform to: ～马克思主义原则 in line with Marxist principle

遵照 zūnzhào act in deference to; comply with; do in accordance with; obey; conform to: ～上级指示 in accordance with instructions from above

zuō

作 zuō〈名〉workshop: 小器～ workshop producing or repairing hardwood or exquisite furniture

另见 zuò

作坊 zuōfáng workshop

zuó

琢 zuó

另见 zhuó

琢磨 zuómo ① carve and polish (jade) ② turn sth. over in one's mind; polish; refine; ponder: ～出个办法 figure out a way (to do sth.)

zuǒ

左 zuǒ ①〈名〉left; the left side; the left: 向～转 turn left〈形〉② queer; unorthodox: 她说～了。What she said is wrong. ③ different; opposite; contrary: 意见相～ hold different views ④ the left; progressive; revolutionary: ～翼文学思潮 Left-wing literary trend. 极～ ultra-Left

左不过 zuǒbuguò ① anyway;

anyhow; in any event ② only; merely; just

左顾右盼 zuǒgù-yòupàn look right and left; peep right and left at each step; look warily right and left

左邻右舍 zuǒlín-yòushè neighbouring families; next door neighbours

左派 zuǒpài ① the Left; the left wing ② Leftists

左撇子 zuǒpiězi left-handed person; left-hander; lefty

左倾 zuǒqīng ① left-leaning; progressive: 日益～ growing radicalization ② "Left" deviation: "～"机会主义 "Left" opportunism

左嗓子 zuǒsǎngzi ① sing out of key ② a person who sings out of key

左思右想 zuǒsī-yòuxiǎng turn sth. over in one's mind; rack one's brains; ponder on; keep thinking

左袒 zuǒtǎn take sides with; give improper protection to; screen (shield)

左翼 zuǒyì ①[军]left wing; left flank ② the left wing; the Left: ～文艺运动 Left-wing literary and art movement

左右 zuǒyòu ① right and left ② on both sides: ～逢源 win advantage from both sides; be blessed with good luck all along. ～为难 be in a dilemma; be in an awkward predicament (position); between two fires ③ about; around; in the vicinity of: 她每月收入在500元～。Her monthly income is about 500 *yuan* ④ influence; dominate: ～公司的命运 manage the destiny of a corporation ⑤ attendants; suite: ～手 right-hand man; one's valuable assistant

左证 zuǒzhèng evidence; proof

佐 zuǒ ①〈动〉assist: 辅～ assist a ruler in governing a country ②〈名〉assistant: 僚～ assistant in a government office

佐餐 zuǒcān go with rice or bread; be eaten together with rice or bread

佐理 zuǒlǐ assist sb. in management

佐证 zuǒzhèng proof; evidence

zuò

坐 zuò〈动〉① sit; take a seat: ～观世变 sit and watch how the wind blows ② travel by (a ship, train, plane, etc.): ～飞机 travel by plane ③ have its back towards: 房子～北朝南。The house faces south. ④ put (a pan, pot, etc.) on a fire: 在炉子上～一壶水 put the kettle of water on the fire

坐班 zuòbān have office hours; do desk work: 大学的教师一般是不～的。University teachers usually do not have stipulated office hours.

坐标 zuòbiāo [数] coordinate

坐不下 zuòbuxià (of a vehicle,

table, room, etc.) have not enough seats for (a certain number of people);cannot seat

坐不住 zuòbuzhù cannot sit still; be restless; fidget

坐禅 zuòchán [佛]sit in meditation

坐吃山空 zuòchī-shānkōng remain at home eating in idleness; sit at home eating away one's resources; consume without producing; use up one's resources without working

坐床 zuòchuáng[佛] ① enthrone ② seat

坐得下 zuòdexià (of a vehicle, table, room, etc.) have seats for (a certain number of people); seat

坐得住 zuòdezhù can sit still; can sit for long

坐垫 zuòdiàn cushion

坐井观天 zuòjǐng-guāntiān see the sky from the bottom of a well; view things from one's limited experience; have a narrow view

坐科 zuòkē undergo professional training at an old type opera school

坐蜡 zuòlà be in trouble; be on the spot

坐牢 zuòláo be imprisoned; be in prison (jail); put into prison; send to prison; goal

坐冷板凳 zuò lěngbǎndèng ① wait long for an appointment; get a cold shoulder ② hold a title with little or no duties

坐立不安 zuòlì-bù'ān be ill at ease; sit on thorns; be on tenterhooks; be on needles and pins

坐落 zuòluò be situated(located); stand: 房屋～在江边。The house stands by the river.

坐山观虎斗 zuò shān guān hǔ dòu sit on top of the mountain to watch the tigers fight; watch from a distance a fight between two tigers

坐商 zuòshāng tradesman; shopkeeper

坐失良机 zuòshī-liángjī let a golden opportunity slip

坐视 zuòshì look on with indifference; sit by and watch:～不救 sit idle by without lending a helping hand; look on with folded arms

坐收渔人之利 zuòshōu yúrén zhī lì reap the spoils of victory without lifting a finger; have victory (an advantage) fall into one's lap

坐享其成 zuòxiǎng-qíchéng sit idle and enjoy the fruits of others' labour; reap where one has not sown

坐以待毙 zuòyǐdàibì sit passively for one's end; await one's doom

坐月子 zuòyuèzi 〈口〉lying-in; confinement in childbirth

坐镇 zuòzhèn (of a commander) personally attend to garrison duty; assume personal command

坐庄 zuòzhuāng ① be in a resident buyer of a business firm ② be the banker or dealer (in a gambling game)

座 zuò〈名〉① seat; place:就～ take one's seat; be seated ② stand; base; pedestal:柱～ column base

座舱 zuòcāng ① passenger cabin (in an airliner) ② cockpit (of a fighter)

座次 zuòcì order (arrangement) of seats:排～ arrange the seats

座上客 zuòshàngkè guest of honour

座谈 zuòtán have a discussion meeting:～会 symposium; seminar; forum; discussion meeting; round-table discussion

座无虚席 zuòwúxūxí have a full house; All seats are occupied.

座右铭 zuòyòumíng motto; maxim; permanent reminders

做 zuò〈动〉① make; produce; manufacture:～衣服 make clothes ② write (a book, an essay, etc.):～文章 write an essay ③ do, engage in; act:～好本职工作 do a good job at one's post ④ be; become:先～学生,然后再～先生。Be a pupil before you beome a teacher. ⑤ form or establish a relationship:～朋友 make friends with ⑥ cook; prepare:～饭菜 prepare a meal

做爱 zuò'ài love-making

做伴 zuòbàn keep sb. company

做东 zuòdōng play the host; stand treat; host sb.

做法 zuòfǎ way of doing (making) things; method of work; act; conduct; practice:通常的～ usual practice

做梗 zuògěng create difficulties; obstruct; hinder

做工 zuògōng ① do manual work ② workmanship; tailoring:～考究的家具 furniture of fine workmanship ③ charge for the making of sth.

做功 zuògōng (of actor) performing technique; art of gesture; acting

做古 zuògǔ〈书〉pass away; die

做广告 zuò guǎnggào advertising; advertisement

做鬼脸 zuò guǐliǎn make a face at

做好人 zuò hǎorén try to be a good fellow; try to get along with everyone (often at the expense of principle)

做绝 zuòjué leave no room for manoeuvre

做礼拜 zuò lǐbài be at church; go to church

做媒 zuòméi match making; be a matchmaker; try to arrange matches for young people

做梦 zuòmèng ① dream; have a dream ② have a pipe dream; daydream:做美梦 cherish fond hopes. 白日～ daydream

做人 zuòrén ① conduct oneself in society; behave:～要做这样的人。We must be like that kind of man. ② be a decent person:重新～ turn over a new leaf. 做不起人 can never again hold up one's head

做生意 zuò shēngyì do business; carry on trade:～做好做活

handle one's business transactions flexible and successfully

做事 zuòshì ① do a deed; handle affairs; act: ～得手 work smoothly ② work; have a job

做手脚 zuò shǒujiǎo play a trick; tamper with sth.; mess about with

做寿 zuòshòu hold a birthday party; celebrate the birthday

做私活 zuò sīhuó do illicit private work

做戏 zuòxì ① act in a play ② playact; put on (up) a show

做演员 zuò yǎnyuán go on the stage; take to the stage

做一天和尚撞一天钟 zuò yītiān héshàng zhuàng yītiān zhōng go on tolling the bell as long as one is a monk—take a passive attitude towards one's work; So long as one remains a monk, one goes on tolling the bell.; do one's job perfunctorily; follow a routine

做贼心虚 zuòzéi-xīnxū have a guilty conscience; have sth. on one's conscience

做作 zuòzuò affected; artificial; pretentious: 矫揉～的举止 affected manners

作 zuò〈动〉① do; make: ～画 do a painting ② act as; be: 当～长条酒台用的边桌 a side-table that acts as a bar ③ pretend; affect: 故～怒容 pretend to be angry ④ regard as: 他把我当～亲儿子。He treats me as his own son. ⑤〈名〉work: 创～ creative work

另见 zuō, zuó

作案 zuò'àn commit a crime or an offence: ～现场 the scene of a crime

作罢 zuòbà give up; drop; relinquish: 这件事～算了。Let's drop the matter.

作保 zuòbǎo go bail for sb.; be sb.'s guarantor (sponsor)

作弊 zuòbì practise fraud; engage in malpractice; indulge in corrupt practice; [考试等] crib

作对 zuòduì oppose; set oneself against: 她没有理由和你～。She has no reason to set herself against you.

作恶 zuò'è do evil: ～多端 commit all sorts of wickness; do all kinds of evil; perpetuate numerous crimes

作废 zuòfèi become invalid; be nullified; be made null and void: 宣布～ declare null and void (invalid)

作风 zuòfēng style of work; style: ～正派 be honest and upright

作梗 zuògěng make (create, raise) difficulties; put obstacles in the way; hinder; obstruct; impede

作古 zuògǔ die; pass away

作怪 zuòguài make (create) trouble; do mischief; play trick

作家 zuòjiā writer; literary man; literator

作假 zuòjiǎ ① counterfeit; falsify ② cheat; play tricks ③ behave affectedly

作价 zuòjià fix a price for; making a price; evaluate

作茧自缚 zuòjiǎn-zìfù weave a cocoon and get imprisoned in it; be caught in one's own trap; fry in one's own grease; get enmeshed in a web of one's own spinning

作践 zuòjian 〈口〉① waste; spoil:～东西 spoil things ② insult; humiliate ③ run sth. down; disparage:故意～人 just to run sb. down

作乐 zuòlè enjoy oneself; make merry; amuse oneself

作脸 zuòliǎn win honour (glory) for; try to make a good showing

作料 zuòliao seasoning; flavouring; condiments

作乱 zuòluàn stage an armed rebellion

作美 zuòměi (usu. used in the negative) (of weather, etc.) help; cooperate; make things easy for sb.:天公不～。Heaven is not cooperative.

作难 zuònán ① feel embarrassed; feel awkward; find oneself in a predicament ② make things difficult for sb.

作孽 zuòniè commit a sin; do evil

作弄 zuònòng tease; make a fool of; play a trick on; poke fun at

作呕 zuò'ǒu feel sick; be disgusted (at, with); be overcome by nausea:令人～的 disgusting; nauseating; offensive

作陪 zuòpéi help entertain the guest of honour; be invited along with the chief guest

作品 zuòpǐn works (of literature and art); production

作曲 zuòqǔ write music; compose:～家 composer

作数 zuòshù be valid; count:那不可～。That doesn't count.

作祟 zuòsuì ① (of ghosts, spirits, etc.) haunt ② cause trouble; make mischief; exercise evil influence

作威作福 zuòwēi-zuòfú play (act) the tyrant; ride roughshod over; abuse one's power tyrannically; lord it over others

作为 zuòwéi ① conduct; deed; action:她的～是无可非议的。Her conduct was blameless. ② regard as; look on as:～靠山 look upon sb. as one's prop ③ accomplish; do sth. worthwhile:无所～ be in a state of inertia; attempt nothing and accomplish nothing ④ as:～一个科学家,他为真理而献身。As a scientist, he was dedicated to the truth.

作文 zuòwén ① write a composition ② composition

作息 zuòxī work and rest:～时间表 timetable

作业 zuòyè ① school assignment:家庭～ homework. 做～ do one's assignment ② work; task; production; operation:～组 production group

作用 zuòyòng ① act on; affect:～于社会 act on the society ② function; role:起重要～ play an important role ③ action; effect:副～ side effect ④ intention; motive:她这样说是有～的。She said that with an ulterior motive.

作战 zuòzhàn fight (with, against, for); battle (with); do battle; conduct operations: ～计划 plan of operations

作者 zuòzhě writer; author;[歌曲的]composer;[戏剧的]playwright

作证 zuòzhèng give evidence (witness); testify; bear witness

作主 zuòzhǔ ① take up the responsibility for making a decision; decide:当家～ be master of one's own affairs; be master in one's own house; run one's own house. 我作不了主。I'm not in a position to decide. 这要你～。It's up to you. ② support; back up

作准 zuòzhǔn count; be valid